INTELLECTUAL PROPERTY LAW

INTELLECTUAL PROPERTY LAW

Text, Cases, and Materials

FIRST EDITION

Tanya Aplin and Jennifer Davis

OXFORD
UNIVERSITY PRESS

OXFORD
UNIVERSITY PRESS

Great Clarendon Street, Oxford OX2 6DP

Oxford University Press is a department of the University of Oxford.
It furthers the University's objective of excellence in research, scholarship,
and education by publishing worldwide in

Oxford New York

Auckland Cape Town Dar es Salaam Hong Kong Karachi
Kuala Lumpur Madrid Melbourne Mexico City Nairobi
New Delhi Shanghai Taipei Toronto

With offices in

Argentina Austria Brazil Chile Czech Republic France Greece
Guatemala Hungary Italy Japan Poland Portugal Singapore
South Korea Switzerland Thailand Turkey Ukraine Vietnam

Oxford is a registered trade mark of Oxford University Press
in the UK and in certain other countries

Published in the United States
by Oxford University Press Inc., New York

© Tanya Aplin and Jennifer Davis 2009

The moral rights of the authors have been asserted

Crown copyright material is reproduced under Class Licence
Number C01P0000148 with the permission of OPSI
and the Queen's Printer for Scotland

Database right Oxford University Press (maker)

First published 2009

British Library Cataloguing-in-Publication Data

Aplin, Tanya Frances, 1972–
Intellectual property law : text, cases, and materials / Tanya Aplin and
Jennifer Davis.—1st ed.
p. cm.
ISBN 978–0–19–927157–3
1. Intellectual property—Great Britain.   2. Copyright—Great Britain.
I. Davis, Jennifer, 1964–   II. Title.
KD1269.A78 2009
346.4104"82—dc22   2009020067

Library of Congress Cataloging in Publication Data

Typeset by Newgen Imaging Systems Pvt Ltd., Chennai, India
Printed in Great Britain
on acid-free paper by
Ashford Colour Press, Gosport, Hampshire

ISBN 978–0–19–927157–3

1 3 5 7 9 10 8 6 4 2

PREFACE

Intellectual property encompasses broad areas of human endeavour, from the invention of a life-saving medicine, to the authorship of a best-selling novel, to the marketing of a world-famous footballer. Bringing the disparate subject matter which is defined as intellectual property into one volume has been a challenging task. For the most part we have taken a traditional approach by dedicating discrete chapters to the key areas of intellectual property—i.e. copyright, trade marks, patents, passing off, designs, and confidential information. In the case of patents, trade marks, and copyright, we have split these topics into two chapters so as to avoid the reader being overwhelmed by the amount of relevant material. However, the subject matter of intellectual property is not always so easily divided. Thus, we have dedicated separate chapters to the topics of character merchandising and information technology, since these cut across a variety of intellectual property rights.

Like any area of the law, intellectual property has its controversies. In our Introduction we have set out to identify the key thematic, contextual, and political debates which characterize this field. Throughout the rest of the book we have sought to encourage the reader to ask questions about the normative basis, policy implications, and internal coherence of intellectual property law. There is, of course, a wealth of interesting and thought-provoking literature on these themes, only a small proportion of which could be included in this book. For those readers who wish to engage further with these debates, we have identified a selection of further reading to supplement the passages that we have extracted from primary and secondary materials.

This book is predicated on the assumption that any examination of intellectual property law cannot be solely confined to a domestic context. There are a number of reasons for this. For example, since the 19th century, there have been an increasing number of international treaties concerned with intellectual property. Furthermore, in recent years there has been important harmonization of intellectual property rights across the European Community. It is also difficult to contain the subject matter of intellectual property within national boundaries, given the global nature of the marketplace and technological developments. Wherever appropriate, we have sought to place domestic intellectual property law in its international context. At times, where it may be particularly illuminating, we have offered a comparative perspective on developments in intellectual property law in the United Kingdom and other jurisdictions.

Numerous people have assisted us during the process of writing this book. In particular, we would like to thank the many anonymous reviewers who took the time to read and comment upon draft chapters. Their feedback was enormously helpful. The comments of Makeen F. Makeen and John Phillips on the copyright chapters were also invaluable, as were those from the undergraduate and postgraduate patent students, to whom draft chapters were circulated. Our publishers, OUP have been a constant source of support and motivation. We are extremely grateful to the editorial team, in particular to Eleanor Williams who saw this project through to fruition. We would also like to thank both Andrew Dyson and Connie Robertson for their efforts in helping us to obtain permissions. Finally, thanks must go to our family and friends (as well as to each other) for showing empathy, tolerance, and encouragement throughout the writing process.

We have sought to set out the law as at 1 March 2009.

Tanya Aplin and Jennifer Davis

ACKNOWLEDGEMENTS

N.B. Original footnotes and references have been omitted from all extracts.

Grateful acknowledgement is made to all the authors and publishers of copyright material which appears in this book, and in particular to the following for permission to reprint material from the sources indicated:

Extracts from Reports of Patent Cases (RPC) Intellectual Property Office are Crown copyright © and are reproduced with the permission of the Controller of HMSO and the Queen's Printer for Scotland. Other Crown copyright material is reproduced under Class Licence Number C2006010631 with the permission of the Controller of HMSO and the Queen's Printer for Scotland. Parliamentary copyright material is reproduced with the permission of the Controller of HMSO on behalf of Parliament.

Ashgate Publishing: extract from Peter Drahos: *A Philosophy of Intellectual Property* (Ashgate, 1996).

James Boyle and Duke University School of Law for J Boyle: 'The Second Enclosure Movement and the Construction of the Public Domain' in *Law and Contemporary Problems*, Vol 66:33 Winter/Spring 2003.

Buffalo Law Review via Copyright Clearance Center: extract from *Buffalo Law Review*:

R Gutowski: 'The Marriage of Intellectual Property and International Trade in the TRIPS Agreement: strange bedfellows or a match made in heaven?', 47 Buff L R 744 (1999)

Cambridge University Press and the authors: extracts from Huw Beverley-Smith: *The Commercial Appropriation of Personality* (CUP, 2002), Donald S Chisum: 'Common Law and Civil Law approaches to Patent Claim interpretation' in D Vaver and L Bently (eds.): *Intellectual Property in the New Millennium: Essays in honour of William R Cornish* (CUP, 2004), and Susan K Sell: *Private Power, Public Law: The Globalization of Intellectual Property Rights* (CUP, 2003), and extracts from Fritz Machlup and Edith Penrose: 'The Patent Controversy', 10 *Journal of Economic History* 1 (1950).

Earthscan: extract from P Drahos and J Braithwaite: *Information Feudalism: Who Owns the Knowledge Economy?* (Earthscan, 2002).

European Communities: extracts from *European Court Reports* (ECR) from http://eur-lex. europa.eu, © European Communities 2009, and extracts from COM series. Only European Community legislation printed in the paper edition of the Official Journal of the European Union is deemed authentic.

Fordham Intellectual Property, Media & Entertainment Law Journal: extract from Daniel J Gervais: 'The Internationalization of Intellectual Property: New Challenges from the Very Old and the Very New', 12 *Fordham Intellectual Property, Media & Entertainment Law Journal* 929 (2002).

Hart Publishing for extract from Tanya Aplin: *Copyright Law in the Digital Society: The Challenges of Multimedia* (Hart, 2005).

The Belknap Press of Harvard University Press for extracts from W M Landes and R A Posner: 'The Economic Theory of Property' in *The Economic Structure or Intellectual Property Law* (2003), copyright © 2003 by the President and Fellows of Harvard College.

Incorporated Council of Law Reporting: extracts from the *Law Reports: Appeal Cases* (AC), *Chancery Division* (Ch), *Queen's Bench Division* (QB), and *Weekly Law Reports* (WLR).

Intellectual Property Institute and the authors: extracts from *Intellectual Property Quarterly*: H Carty: 'Advertising, Publicity Rights and English Law', IPQ 237 (2004), I Stamatoudi: 'Moral Rights of Authors in England: The Missing Emphasis on the Role of Creators', IPQ 478 (1997) and J Griffiths: 'Copyright law after Ashdown—time to deal fairly with the public', IPQ 240 (2002).

Max Planck Institute for Intellectual Property, Competition and Tax: extract from R Hilty, A Kur and A Peukert: 'Statement of the Max Planck Institute for Intellectual Property, Competition and Tax Law on the Proposal for a Directive of the European Parliament and of the Council on Criminal Measures aimed at ensuring the enforcement of intellectual property rights', *International Review of Intellectual Property and Competition Law* (*IIC*) 970 (2006).

Oxford University Press for extracts from David T Keeling: *Intellectual Property Rights* (OUP, 2003), and J Davis: 'The Need to Leave Free for Others the Use and the Trade Mark Common', A Folliard- Monguiral: 'Distinctive Character Acquired Through Use: The Law and the Case Law', and J Sunroy and T Badger: 'Infringing "Use in the Course of Trade": Trade Mark Use and the Essential Function of a Trade Mark', in J Phillips and I Simon (eds.): *Trade Mark Use* (OUP, 2005).

Oxford University Press Journals and the authors: extracts from Judith McNamara and Lucy Cradduck: 'Can we protect how we do what we do? A consideration of business methods patents in Australia and Europe', *International Journal of Law and Information Technology* 96 (2008).

Ridinghouse and the author: extract from Michael Spence: 'Justifying Copyright' in D McClean and K Schubert: *Dear Images: Art, Copyright and Culture* (Ridinghouse, 2002)

Sweet & Maxwell Ltd for extracts from Graham Dutfield: Indigenous Peoples, Bioprospecting and the TRIPS Agreement' in P Drahos and M Blakeney: *IP In Biodiversity and Agriculture: Regulating the biosphere* (Sweet & Maxwell, 2001), and Thomas Hays: *Parallel Importation under European Union Law* (Sweet & Maxwell, 2004); extracts from *Law Quarterly Review*: H Carty: Dilution and Passing Off: Cause for Concern', 112 LQR 632 (1996); *Entertainment Law Review*: J Ginsburg: 'Moral Rights in the Common Law System', Ent LR 121 (1990), and G Harbottle: 'Criminal Remedies for Copyright and Performers' Rights Infringement under the Copyright and Patents Act 1988', Ent LR 12 (1994); and *European Intellectual Property Review*: T I Blanco White: 'Intellectual Property: a future for British concepts', EIPR 229 (1988), Kirstin Huniar: 'The enforcement directive—its effects on UK Law', EIPR 92 (2006), J Phillips and L Bently: 'Copyright Issues; The Mysteries of Section 18', EIPR 133 (1999), A Robertson and A Horton: 'Does the United Kingdom or the European Community Need and Unfair Competition Law?', EIPR 568 (1995), and A Wagner: 'Infringing Trade Marks: Function, Association and Confusion of Signs According to the E C Trade Marks Directive' 21(3) EIPR 127 (1999); and extracts from Case Reports: *Fleet Street Reports* (FSR), *European Copyright and Design Reports* (ECDR), *Entertainment and Media Law Reports* (EMLR), *European Patent Office Reports* (EPOR), and *European Trade Mark Reports* (ETMR.

Tottell Publishing: extract from C Howell: 'O2 v Hutchinson 3G comparative advertising: European Trade Mark law beyond compare?', 13 (5) *Communication Law* 155 (2008).

Wiley-Blackwell Publishing Ltd: extract from Edwin C Hettinger: 'Justifying Intellectual Property', 18 *Philosophy and Public Affairs* 31 (1989).

World Intellectual Property Organization: extract from 'Character Merchandising', WIPO document WO/INF/108 (1994). The secretariat of WIPO assumes no liability or responsibility with regard to the transformation of this data.

World Trade Organization: extract from 'TRIPS: A more detailed overview of the TRIPS agreement', published at http://www.wto.org/english/tratop_e/trips_e/intel2_e/htm.

The Yale Law Journal Company, Inc: extract from Jessica Litman: 'Breakfast with Batman; The Public Interest in the Advertising Age', 108 *Yale Law Journal* 1717 (1998–1999).

Zed Books and Penguin Books India: extract from Vandan Shiva: *Protect or Plunder? Understanding Intellectual Property Rights* (Zed Books, 2001).

Every effort has been made to trace and contact copyright holders prior to going to press but this has not been possible in every case. If notified, the publisher will undertake to rectify any errors or omissions at the earliest opportunity.

OUTLINE TABLE OF CONTENTS

CONTENTS

3 COPYRIGHT II: INFRINGEMENT AND EXCEPTIONS 112

7 CHARACTER MERCHANDISING AND PUBLICITY RIGHTS 339

8 BREACH OF CONFIDENCE 380

9 PATENTS I: JUSTIFICATIONS, REGISTRATION, AND VALIDITY — 442

10 PATENTS II: INFRINGEMENT AND ENTITLEMENT   585

13 INTELLECTUAL PROPERTY IN ACTION   776

TABLE OF CASES

Where cases are dealt with in detail the relevant page numbers are shown in **bold**.

TABLE OF STATUTES

Page references in **bold** indicate that the section is reproduced in the text.

TABLE OF EU LEGISLATION

Page references in **bold** indicate that the section is reproduced in the text.

1

AN INTRODUCTION TO INTELLECTUAL PROPERTY

Consider the following hypotheticals:

1. An airline company plainPlanes, which advertises services using the colour yellow is planning to expand into the mobile-phone market. Its plainPhones will also be advertised using the colour yellow. A mobile-phone company, called Yellow, has for many years advertised its own mobile-phone services using the colour and name 'Yellow'. Yellow is now objecting to plainPlanes' use of the colour yellow in relation to plainPhones. plainPlanes is now questioning whether anyone should have exclusive right to the use of a single colour, in this case yellow, in relation to their own goods.

2. A famous rock band, Mirage, is planning the cover for their latest album. They decide to photograph the band members, alongside a collection of items situated in the grounds of an expensive country hotel. The items include a Rolls Royce partially submerged in a swimming pool, a scooter, and a clock. During the official photography session, a freelance photographer surreptitiously takes photographs of the scene which he sells to a tabloid newspaper. Mirage seeks to restrain the newspaper from publishing photographs of the scene, claiming that the scene is an artistic work which has been unlawfully copied. The newspaper disputes that the collection of objects constitutes a work of art. Mirage also argues that the scene is confidential in nature, whereas the newspaper argues that it is in a public space and hence not confidential.

3. An online retail store, Nile.com, sells a range of media products, including books, DVDs, CDs, and electronic equipment. To speed up the purchasing process, it develops a system, called 'one-touch shopping'. Once a customer enters his personal and bank details, these are saved for future purchases which the customer can then complete by clicking on the 'one-touch' button. A rival online retail store, Swan.com, starts using the 'one-touch' process in its business. Nile.com objects that they invented the 'one-touch shopping' system and so no one else should be able to use it. Swan.com argues both that the one-touch system is a fairly obvious way of saving customer time and that, in any event, it should not be protected because its use is crucial for online businesses to compete.

4. The farmers of the Excot area in Ethiopia have been growing a particularly flavourful coffee bean over hundreds of years. The coffee is known worldwide as Excot coffee. A large US conglomerate called CoffeeCo isolates the DNA structure that is responsible for producing the unique flavour of the coffee bean and produces seeds incorporating this DNA. It has obtained exclusive rights to grow and sell the coffee bean in the US under the name, 'Excot coffee'. Farmers from Excot object to the fact that CoffeeCo will profit from their selective breeding of the bean over many years, and that they will be prevented from selling their coffee bean in the US in future. Others argue that CoffeeCo should not get a monopoly on the use of a geographical place name which is associated with the product.

Even without knowledge of intellectual property law you will undoubtedly have opinions as to the rights and wrongs in these hypotheticals. In fact, each of these is based on recent cases that have involved intellectual property rights (IPRs) and each highlights key issues that are central to the protection of intellectual property (IP) and which will be considered in the course of this book.

IP is often used as a collective noun for a number of individual rights, which include copyright, patents, trade marks, designs and confidential information. Individually, each of these may be referred to as an IPR. What unites them is that they are dealing with the regulation of intangible property or forms of intangible creation. Intellectual property as 'a discrete and separate area of the law'[1] did not emerge until the mid nineteenth century, although, as we shall see in subsequent chapters, some IPRs have a far longer history. In this introductory chapter, we will consider the philosophical and justificatory context in which IPRs have developed and the international and regional frameworks which have emerged for their protection. In addition, we will examine some of the important contemporary debates surrounding IPRs. In succeeding chapters, these topics will be re-examined in relation to each of the individual IPRs.

1.1   THE INTANGIBLE NATURE OF IP

A unifying feature of IPRs is that they are concerned with incorporeal or intangible creations. By contrast, the law of property is concerned with tangible or corporeal objects. In the following extract, Professor Drahos looks at some of the consequences for intellectual property law which derive from the fact that it is regulating the ownership and infringement of what he refers to as 'abstract objects'. He identifies two main consequences for intellectual property law. First, the courts must identify the abstract object which may be the subject of an intellectual property case. Secondly, there is a difficulty in drawing the boundary between two abstract objects where, in the context of an infringement action, the one is alleged to have overlapped with the other.

P. Drahos, *A Philosophy of Intellectual Property* (Dartmouth Publishing, England, 1996), pp. 153–6

The term 'abstract object' refers to a putative category of being. It is not a term of legal art. We saw in chapter 2 that intellectual property rights are classified legally as incorporeal rights. The objects to which these rights relate and over which relations between individual

---

[1] B. Sherman and L. Bently, *The Making of Modern Intellectual Property Law: The British experience, 1760–1911* (Cambridge: Cambridge University Press, 1999), p. 6.

actors are formed are abstract objects. However, the identity of the abstract object becomes known by the law through the physical object. At some point before property rights attach to the abstract object the various different regimes of different intellectual property law require some form of 'corporealization' of the abstract object. A given abstract object is not, however, just the ethereal mirror image of its concrete physical counterpart. The book or the invention is not, at least within the legal universe, to be exclusively identified with its abstract, intangible twin. If the abstract object is not identical with its concrete counterpart, what is it? An answer is that the abstract object is that core structure that is integral to the identity of the concrete object. This core structure forms the basis upon which an observer makes an identity judgement between two particular physical objects. It is the criterion by which 'sameness' of objects is assessed. Abstract objects are those core structures that are used by legal actors in the process of making a decision about whether disparate physical objects are the same or similar, or resemble each other.

As a rule, the law relating to infringement in the different areas of intellectual property recognises that infringement will occur in those cases where something less than the whole abstract object is taken. Naturally the law relating to infringement of a given intellectual property right varies from jurisdiction to jurisdiction. And even in the same jurisdiction, some domains of intellectual property are thought to offer less protection for abstract objects than others. But, despite this variation between different jurisdictions and separate fields of intellectual property, it is a basic proposition that intellectual property law protects abstract objects in the form of core structures rather than abstract objects that are identical with their material counterparts.

Judgements of identity and recognition lie at the heart of infringement issues in intellectual property. Whether a judge has to decide an issue of copyright, patent, design or trademark, the basic process involves a comparison of two physical objects or processes and deciding whether or not one is an impermissible imitation of the other. Judges see the answer to this question as being a matter of fact. But this conclusion of fact is underpinned by a complex dynamic of social, psychological and ideological factors. In order to make the decision, judges are necessarily involved in a process of abstraction in which they, as it were, create the abstract object that then forms the basis of their identity judgement. This process is deeply problematic because the abstractness of abstract objects is a matter of variation rather than being an all or nothing matter. Abstractness comes in degrees. Imagine, for example, stories based on the idea of the last three of something left in the world, whether these be nations, people or dinosaurs. The concrete expression of these stories is likely to be very different. Yet at a sufficient level of abstraction they might be thought to be equivalent. At the most abstract level it might be claimed these are stories which are a concretization of a three-point geometry in which it is assumed that there are no more than three points, no more than two points form a line and there is always a point not on a line. In these stories the lines and points are given an interpretation and definition such that, for example, the points and lines become respectively actors and possible alliances. The reduction of stories to geometric structures is probably a level of abstraction that no judge would choose. But some level must be chosen so that the identity judgement which has to be made in the case of an infringement matter can be made. Clearly, if judges choose high levels of abstractness for the core structures upon which they base their judgments of identity then the more likely it is that isomorphisms, equivalences of all kinds, will be 'seen' which in turn will lead to an increase in the findings of infringement.

So far the analysis of abstract objects reveals that they have two distinct roles: first, they form the object of relations in intellectual property; second, they form the basis for identity judgements in the context of infringement actions in intellectual property. The degree of discretion that judges have in the construction of abstract objects has two sources. The first we have already mentioned. There are many degrees of abstractness. The second stems from the fact that the conventional task of drawing boundaries in relation to abstract objects is far more difficult than in the case of physical objects. Real property has boundaries. Boundary is a conventional concept. Boundaries are socially, politically or militarily created, but because they relate to a real-world physical object the boundaries of physical property, once decided, can be maintained with some precision. The intangible abstract object of intellectual property rights cannot be marked with boundaries in the manner of physical objects. The result is that an abstract object can be used to group very different physical objects. Under copyright law, for example, a film can be said to reproduce or be a copy of a literary work, and a three-dimensional work can be a reproduction of a two-dimensional work. Very different physical objects, in other words, can be said to share the same identity in intellectual property law because they all imitate the same abstract object. Such judgements of identity are dependent upon the existence of a core structure that provides the conditions of identity for the relevant judgement. This core structure, we have suggested, is itself a matter of judicial composition. Constitutive judgements about core structures are judgements of convention. Once in place they determine the extensional reach of a given property right into the material world.

A well known example where this conventional judgement has proved difficult to make is in the field of copyright and computer software. It is a feature of computer programs that the functions of a program can be captured in detail by a program written in a different computer language. Protection for the literal expression of a program or a substantial part of it does not help to protect the functions of that program. A now famous judicial solution in the United States was to begin talking about protection for the structure and sequence of a program. This approach basically amounted to increasing the abstractness of the abstract object so that identity judgements concerning computer software could include their non-literal elements. The protection of computer software raises in a stark fashion a problem that had always been there in other parts of copyright and other regions of intellectual property. This is a problem of identifying and determining the boundaries of the core structures that form the basis of identity judgements in intellectual property.

Drahos highlights the difficulties of defining the abstract object which is the subject of IPRs for the purposes of legal transactions and infringement actions. He concludes that it may only be in the context of intellectual property litigation that the boundaries of abstract objects will be delineated. This is perhaps more true for some IPRs than others. For example, in the case of patents, there is the patent specification which attempts to describe and define the invention that is protected. Similarly, registered trade marks must be capable of graphical representation to be registered. We will explore in later chapters the extent to which patent specifications or trade mark registration can actually overcome the uncertainty as to the definition of abstract objects which Drahos raises.

1.2 JUSTIFICATIONS

IPRs grant to owners exclusive rights to do certain acts and prohibit others from doing these same acts. Such exclusive rights allow owners, for example, to charge higher prices for their intellectual products than they would otherwise be able to do and to restrict others from using them. Thus, the owner of a pharmaceutical patent will be able to charge more for the pharmaceutical than would otherwise be the case were it merely valued on its physical composition. To the extent that IPRs confer a monopoly, it has generally been thought necessary to justify this privilege. What follows is a general introduction to the justifications for IPRs. It is important to remember that some of these justifications are more apt for some IPRs than for others.

1.2.1 UNJUST ENRICHMENT

There is a significant amount of literature about the justifications for granting IPRs. The literature reveals a number of justificatory bases for intellectual property law of which the most important are the natural rights, utilitarian, and economic justifications. But before we address these, it is worthwhile looking at a fairly simple justification, which is frequently resorted to because of its rhetorical force. This is the argument from 'unjust enrichment', popularly described as 'reaping without sowing'. Michael Spence discusses this argument and its limitations in the following extract.

M. Spence, 'Justifying copyright' in McClean and Schubert (eds.), *Dear Images: Art, copyright and culture* (Manchester: Ridinghouse, 2002), pp. 389–403, at pp. 395–6

b. The Argument from Unjust Enrichment

The argument from unjust enrichment is that the unauthorised user of a work receives a benefit from its use and thereby 'reaps where she has not sown'. This behaviour of 'reaping without sowing' is assumed to be morally reprehensible. The phrase is biblical and assumes much of its rhetorical power from that resonance, although its equivalent biblical usage occurs in a New Testament parable in which the behaviour is neither condoned nor condemned. This principle, and the corresponding argument from unjust enrichment, are even more problematic than the argument from harm to the creator.

First, it is clear that the principle against reaping without sowing is not absolute. We all reap without sowing, and regard ourselves as justified in doing so, even without the consent, implicit or explicit, of those upon whose efforts we build. For example, the pioneer of a new style or technique in the visual arts might establish an artistic language and educate a public to understand it. The pioneer may wish to preserve the style or technique she develops for her own use, or for the use of those within her circle. But subsequent creators will imitate, adapt and expand that style or technique. Imitation—authorised and unauthorised—is a vital part of ongoing artistic discourse. To condemn all reaping without sowing would be to condemn all imitation and to stifle the development of artistic traditions. It would be to condemn us to live in a world of self-sufficiency mitigated only by agreement, a world in which few of us either could, or would want to, live.

Second, the principle against reaping without sowing is not an independent principle that can be used to justify entitlements to the exclusive use of a work. It is relevant, if at all, only once such an entitlement has been established. Given that the principle is not absolute, the question upon which its application depends is precisely when, if ever, it is wrong to reap without sowing. The answer implicit in the principle is that it is wrong to reap without sowing if someone else, and in particular the sower, has a stronger claim to that which is reaped. But this, of course, assumes that the sower does have a claim to that which is reaped and that its strength can be assessed. This assumption cannot be justified on the basis of the principle itself. In the copyright context, whether a particular unauthorised use constitutes an *unjust* enrichment depends upon whether, and how strongly a creator's claim to exclude others from its use can be justified. But that is exactly what the various justifications for copyright are seeking to determine. So the principle against reaping without sowing turns out to be one that can only apply once it has been determined on other grounds that a creator ought to be able to exclude others from the use of her work. It adds nothing to the substantive justification of the law of copyright.

Spence demonstrates that although the argument from unjust enrichment may be intuitively appealing, it is not particularly persuasive. This is because it does not assist us with determining when enrichment at another's expense is *unjust*. In other words, it does not establish why the creator has a stronger claim to his or her work than other persons. A stronger claim might be based on the fact that the creator has *laboured* to produce a work or because the work that has been produced is a *valuable contribution* to society. However, these reasons do not form part of the 'unjust enrichment' justification. Rather, they represent a natural-rights justification stemming from the work of John Locke.

1.2.2 NATURAL RIGHTS

It is important to note that John Locke's writing supports a theory of *property*, as opposed to *intellectual property*. Nonetheless, scholars have utilized Locke's theory of property to justify the existence of intellectual property, arguably because of its rhetorical force and because his arguments translate effectively. The following passage from Locke's writing has been relied upon by legal scholars to support property rights and, by extension, IPRs.

J. Locke, *The Second Treatise on Government*, 1690 (Indianapolis, IN: Hackett Publishing, 1980)

Chapter V: Of Property

25. God, who hath given the world to man in common, hath also given them reason to make use of it to the best advantage of life and convenience. The earth and all that is therein is given to man for the support and comfort of their being. And though all the fruits it naturally produces, and beasts it feeds, belong to mankind in common, as they are produced by the spontaneous hand of Nature, and nobody has originally a private dominion exclusive of the rest of mankind in any of them, as they are thus in their natural state, yet being given for the use of men, there must of necessity be a means to appropriate them some way or other before they can be of any use, or at all beneficial, to any particular men. The fruit or venison which nourishes the wild Indian, who knows no enclosure, and is still a tenant in common, must be his, and so his—i.e., a part of him, that another can no longer have any right to it before it can do him any good for the support of his life.

26. Though the earth and all inferior creatures be common to all men, yet every man has a 'property' in his own 'person'. This nobody has any right to but himself. The 'labour' of his body and the 'work' of his hands, we may say are properly his. Whatsoever, then, he removed out of the state that Nature has provided and left it in, he hath mixed his labour with it, and joined to it something that is his own, and thereby makes it his property. It being by him removed from the common state Nature hath placed it in, it hath by this labour something annexed to it that excludes the common right of other men. For this 'labour'

being the unquestionable property of the labourer, no man but he can have a right to what that is once joined to, at least where there is enough, and as good left in the common for others.

27. He that is nourished by the acorns he picked up under an oak, or the apples he gathered from the trees in the wood, has certainly appropriated them to himself. Nobody can deny but the nourishment is his. I ask, then, when did they begin to be his? When he digested? Or when he ate? Or when he boiled? Or when he brought them home? Or when he picked them up? And it is plain, if the first gathering made them not his, nothing else could. The labour put a distinction between them and common. That added something to them more than Nature, the common mother of all, had done, and so they became his private right. And will any one say he had no right to those acorns or apples he thus appropriated because he had not the consent of all mankind to make them his? Was it a robbery thus to assume to himself what belonged to all in common? If such a consent as that was necessary, man had starved, notwithstanding the plenty God had given him. We see in commons, which remain so by compact, that it is the taking any part of what is common, and removing it out of the state Nature leaves it in, which begins the property, without which the common is of no use. And the taking of this or that part does not depend on the express consent of all the commoners... The labour that was mine, removing them out of the common state they were in, hath fixed my property in them.

...

30. It will perhaps be objected to this, that if gathering the acorns or other fruits of the earth, etc., makes a right to them, then any one may engross as much as he will. To which I answer, Not so. The same law of Nature that does by this means give us property does also bound that property too. 'God has given us all things richly.' Is the voice of reason confirmed by inspiration? But how far has He given it us—'to enjoy'? As much as any one can make use of any advantage of life before it spoils, so much he may by his labour fix a property in. Whatever is beyond this is more than his share, and belongs to others...

31. ...As much land as a man tills, plants, improves, cultivates, and can use the product of, so much is his property. He by his labour does, as it were, enclose it from the common. Nor will it invalidate his right to say everybody else has an equal title to it, and therefore he cannot appropriate, he cannot enclose, without the consent of all his fellow-commoners all mankind. God, when He gave the world in common to all mankind, commanded man also to labour, and the penury of his condition required it of him. God and his reason commanded him to subdue the earth—i.e., improve it for the benefit of life and there in lay out something upon it that was his own, his labour. He that, in obedience to this command of God, subdued tilled, and sowed any part of it, thereby annexed to it something that was his property, which another had no title to, nor could without injury take from him.

32. Nor was this appropriation of any parcel of land, by improving it, any prejudice to any other man, since there was still enough and as good left, and more than the yet unprovided could use. So that, in effect, there was never the less left for others because of his enclosure for himself. For he that leaves as much as another can make use of does as good as take nothing at all. Nobody could think himself injured by the drinking of another man, though he took a good draught, who had a whole river of the same water left him to quench his thirst. And the case of land and water, where there is enough of both, is perfectly the same.

33. God gave the world to men in common, but since He gave it them for their benefit and the greatest conveniences of life they were capable to draw from it, it cannot be supposed He meant it should always remain common and uncultivated. He gave it to the use of the industrious and rational (and labour was to be his title to it); not to the fancy or covetousness of the quarrelsome and contentious. He that had as good left for his improvement as was already taken up needed not to complain, ought not to meddle with what was already improved by

> another's labour; if he did it is plain he desired the benefit of another's pains, which he had no right to, and not the ground which God had given him, in common with others to labour on, and whereof there was as good left as that already possessed, and more than he knew what to do with, or his industry could reach to.

Applying Locke's theory of property to intangible or intellectual property, it can be said that every person has property in their *intellectual labour*, so that whenever a person mixes their intellectual labour with something from the commons (of ideas, theories, or raw material), he thereby makes it his property. Property rights in intangible creations operate as a *reward* for the author's intellectual *labour*. Alternatively, they are a reward for the *contribution* that the intangible creation makes to society. In both cases, the argument is that a person's labour or contribution *should* be rewarded per se. In other words, it is a natural-rights justification. The argument is not that a reward is given in order to encourage labour or contributions to society. This type of reasoning is utilitarian in nature and, although Locke's theory of property could be used in this way, it has primarily been used to support a natural-rights justification of intellectual property.

Probably the most serious objection to Locke's theory of property (and thus to its usefulness for justifying intellectual property) concerns the role of labour. First, it is not clear that the total value of an intellectual creation is entirely attributable to the labour of an individual, given that intellectual creations may be considered as social products, i.e. influenced by a range of previous creators and works. Secondly, it is unclear why labour should entitle an individual to ownership over the whole work when a person's labour may only explain the added value within the intellectual creation and not its entire value. Finally, labour is an imprecise tool for designating the boundaries of intangible objects. For example, if an author takes a stock-in-trade plot of two lovers who, because of their different backgrounds, are prevented from being together and whose thwarted love reaches a tragic climax, and develops this into a detailed narrative, are we to conclude that every aspect of the story should be owned by the author?

Another objection to the Lockean theory of property is that alternative mechanisms could be used to reward creators instead of property rights. It might be possible, for example to rely on 'fees, awards, acknowledgment, gratitude, praise, security, power, status, and public financial support' to reward a creator of intangible works.[2]

1.2.3 THE UTILITARIAN JUSTIFICATION

Though Locke's work is generally used to support a natural-rights theory of IP, we have noted that his theory of property can also be used to support a utilitarian justification. However, it is Jeremy Bentham, rather than John Locke, who tends to be cited in support of utilitarianism. Bentham rejected the idea that laws derive from natural rights. Rather, he argued that laws were socially justified if they brought the greatest happiness, or benefit, to the greatest number of people. The utilitarian approach to law making, and in particular to intellectual property protection, has traditionally found favour in the US. Perhaps the most prominent example of the influence of utilitarian ideas on intellectual property law is

---

[2] E. C. Hettinger, 'Justifying intellectual property' (1989) 18 Philosophy & Public Affairs 31, 41.

to be found in the Copyright and Patents clause of the US Constitution itself, which gives Congress power to:

> promote the progress of science and useful arts, by securing for limited times to authors and inventors the exclusive right to their respective writings and discoveries.[3]

According to the US Supreme Court, this clause is:

> intended definitely to grant valuable, enforceable rights to authors, publishers, etc, without burdensome requirements to afford greater encouragement to the production of literary [or artistic] works of lasting benefit to the world.[4]

A general account of the way utilitarian ideas might justify IPRs is provided by Hettinger.

E. C. Hettinger, 'Justifying intellectual property' (1989) 18 Philosophy & Public Affairs 31, 47–51

The strongest and most widely appealed to justification for intellectual property is a utilitarian argument based on providing incentives. The constitutional justification for patents and copyrights—'to promote the progress of science and the useful arts'—is itself utilitarian. Given the shortcomings of the other arguments for intellectual property, the justifiability of copyrights, patents, and trade secrets depends, in the final analysis, on this utilitarian defense.

According to this argument, promoting the creation of valuable intellectual works requires that intellectual laborers be granted property rights in those works. Without the copyright, patent, and trade secret property protections, adequate incentives for the creation of a socially optimal output of intellectual products would not exist. If competitors could simply copy books, movies, and records, and take one another's inventions and business techniques, there would be no incentive to spend the vast amounts of time, energy, and money necessary to develop these products and techniques. It would be in each firm's self-interest to let others develop products, and then mimic the result. No one would engage in original development, and consequently no new writings, inventions, or business techniques would be developed. To avoid this disastrous result, the argument claims, we must continue to grant intellectual property rights.

Notice that this argument focuses on the users of intellectual products, rather than on the producers. Granting property rights to producers is here seen as necessary to ensure that enough intellectual products (and the countless other goods based on these products) are available to users. The grant of property rights to the producers is a mere means to this end.

This approach is paradoxical. It establishes a right to restrict the current availability and use of intellectual products for the purpose of increasing the production and thus future availability and use of new intellectual products. As economist Joan Robinson says of patents: 'A patent is a device to prevent the diffusion of new methods before the original investor has recovered profit adequate to induce the requisite investment. The justification of the patent system is that by slowing down the diffusion of technical progress it ensures that there will be more progress to diffuse... Since it is rooted in a contradiction, there can be no such thing as an ideally beneficial patent system, and it is bound to produce negative

---

[3] Art. 1, s. 8.   [4] *Washington Pub Co v Pearson* 59 S Ct 397, 400, para. 36.

results in particular instances, impeding progress unnecessarily even if its general effect is favourable on balance.' Although this strategy may work, it is to a certain extent self-defeating. If the justification for intellectual property is utilitarian in this sense, then the search for alternative incentives for the production of intellectual products takes on a good deal of importance. It would be better to employ equally powerful ways to stimulate the production and thus use of intellectual products which did not also restrict their use and availability.

Government support of intellectual work and public ownership of the result may be one such alternative. Governments already fund a great deal of basic research and development, and the results of this research often become public property. Unlike private property rights in the results of intellectual labor, government funding of this labor and public ownership of the result stimulate new inventions and writings without restricting their dissemination and use. Increased government funding of intellectual labor should thus be seriously considered.

This proposal need not involve government control over which research projects are to be pursued. Government funding of intellectual labor can be divorced from government control over what is funded. University research is an example. Most of this is supported by public funds, but government control over its content is minor and indirect. Agencies at different governmental levels could distribute funding for intellectual labor with only the most general guidance over content, leaving businesses, universities, and private individuals to decide which projects to pursue.

If the goal of private intellectual property institutions is to maximize the dissemination and use of information, to the extent that they do not achieve this result, these institutions should be modified. The question is not whether copyrights, patents, and trade secrets provide incentives for the production of original works of authorship, inventions, and innovative business techniques. Of course they do. Rather, we should ask the following questions: Do copyrights, patents, and trade secrets increase the availability and use of intellectual products more than they restrict this availability and use? If they do, we must then ask whether they increase the availability and use of intellectual products more than any alternative mechanism would. For example, could better overall results be achieved by shortening the length of copyright and patent grants, or by putting a time limit on trade secrets (and on the restrictions on future employment employers are allowed to demand of employees)? Would eliminating most types of trade secrets entirely and letting patents carry a heavier load produce improved results? Additionally, we must determine whether and to what extent public funding and ownership of intellectual products might be a more efficient means to these results.

We should not expect an across-the-board answer to these questions. For example, the production of movies is more dependent on copyright than is academic writing. Also, patent protection for individual inventors and small beginning firms makes more sense than patent protection for large corporations (which own the majority of patents). It has been argued that patents are not important incentives for the research and innovative activity of large corporations in competitive markets. The short-term advantage a company gets from developing a new product and being the first to put it on the market may be incentive enough.

That patents are conducive to a strong competitive economy is also open to question. Our patent system, originally designed to reward the individual inventor and thereby stimulate invention, may today be used as a device to monopolize industries. It has been suggested that in some cases 'the patent position of the big firms makes it almost impossible for new firms to enter the industry' and that patents are frequently bought up in order to suppress competition.

Trade secrets as well can stifle competition, rather than encourage it. If a company can rely on a secret advantage over a competitor, it has no need to develop new technologies to stay ahead. Greater disclosure of certain trade secrets—such as costs and profits of particular product lines—would actually increase competition, rather than decrease it, since with this knowledge firms would then concentrate on one another's most profitable products. Furthermore, as one critic notes, trade secret laws often prevent a former employee 'from doing work in just that field for which his training and experience have best prepared him. Indeed, the mobility of engineers and scientists is often severely limited by the reluctance of new firms to hire them for fear of exposing themselves to a lawsuit.' Since the movement of skilled workers between companies is a vital mechanism in the growth and spread of technology, in this important respect trade secrets actually slow the dissemination and use of innovative techniques.

These remarks suggest that the justifiability of our intellectual property institutions is not settled by the facile assertion that our system of patents, copyrights, and trade secrets provides necessary incentives for innovation and ensures maximally healthy competitive enterprise. This argument is not as easy to construct as one might at first think; substantial empirical evidence is needed. The above considerations suggest that evidence might not support this position.

In the above extract, Hettinger claims that the utilitarian argument is the 'strongest and most widely appealed to justification for intellectual property'. In considering this statement, it is important to remember that Hettinger's focus is on the US and that the constitutional justification which he relies upon is not mirrored in other jurisdictions, such as the UK. Thus, while the utilitarian justification tends to be more closely associated with common law rather than civil law jurisdictions, we should be wary of assuming that the utilitarian argument is the definitive basis for intellectual property law in the UK.

As Hettinger points out, the essence of the utilitarian justification is that IPRs provide the incentives needed for the creation of intangible works. However, his discussion raises three key difficulties with this rationale. First, there is an absence of empirical evidence that authors or inventors would not create in the absence of IPRs. Second, since IPRs restrict the use and dissemination of intangible creations, we should expect to see laws calibrated in a manner which provides an optimal amount of protection, i.e. only as much protection as is needed to stimulate creation. Finally, there may exist alternative ways of providing incentives to create which do not restrict the use and availability of works: an example of this is government funding of university research.

The case of computer software is useful in illustrating the above difficulties.[5] In the early to mid 1980s, courts and legislatures in countries such as the UK, US, and Australia came under pressure to clarify whether computer software was protected by copyright law. However, in countries such as the US, this lack of clarity did not apparently inhibit the growth of the software industry. Nonetheless, in various jurisdictions, copyright laws were amended explicitly to protect computer programs as literary works and, as such, they obtained protection for at least fifty years after the death of the author. Yet it may be queried whether software, which has a relatively short life cycle, really warrants such a lengthy term of protection. Further, the investment of software producers can be protected by means other than intellectual property law. In particular, the use of software can be regulated via contract, and the ease of entering into contracts with purchasers of software has been facilitated by so-called

---

[5] For further discussion see Ch. 12.

'shrink-wrap' licences and, in an online context, 'click-wrap' licences. In addition to these licences, technological protection measures can be used to restrict access to, and the use of, software.

1.2.4 LAW AND ECONOMICS

The law and economics approach also addresses the question of what incentives are needed to create IP and the optimal amount of protection which should be afforded to it, but does so from the perspective of what is best for the functioning of the market. In general, the law and economics approach looks to the allocative efficiency of a market where intellectual property is privately owned. Private ownership provides incentives for the production of intellectual goods for which there is a market. If intellectual property were not protected then the needs of the market would not be met. For many adherents of law and economics theory, a natural corollary is that intellectual property should have strong protection since the ability to 'free-ride' on another's intellectual property would undermine allocative efficiency. However, the more sophisticated advocates of the law and economics approach, such as William M. Landes and Richard A. Posner, recognize that strong IP protection can bring both costs and benefits. In the following extract they begin by comparing the benefits of property rights in intellectual property to the enclosure of common agricultural land, which gave exclusive ownership in the products of that land to the landowner. They suggest that the benefit of such property rights can be static, enabling the owner to exclude others from use of the property and to transfer that property to another, as well as dynamic.

W. M. Landes and R. A. Posner, *The Economic Structure of Intellectual Property Law* (Harvard University Press, 2003), pp. 13–14

The dynamic benefit of a property right is the incentive that possession of such a right imparts to invest in the creation or improvement of a resource in period 1 (for example, planting a crop), given that no one else can appropriate the resource in period 2 (harvest time). It enables people to reap where they have sown. Without that prospect the incentive to sow is diminished. To take an example from intellectual property, a firm is less likely to expend resources on developing a new product if competing firms that have not borne the expense of development can duplicate the product and produce it at the same marginal cost as the innovator; competition will drive price down to marginal cost and the sunk costs of invention will not be recouped. This prospect provides the traditional economic rationale for intellectual property rights, though it involves as we shall see a significant degree of oversimplification. The possibility that such rights might also confer static benefits, eliminating congestion externalities comparable to those of the common pasture with which we began, has been neglected because of the widely held belief that intellectual property, not being physical, cannot be worn out, crowded, or otherwise impaired by additional uses. It is a 'public good' in the economist's sense that consumption of it by one person does not reduce its consumption by another. More accurately, it has public good characteristics, for we shall show that in some circumstances propertizing intellectual property can prevent overuse or congestion in economically meaningful senses of these terms.

Landes and Posner then consider the costs involved in propertizing intellectual output. Among these costs, they identify: transaction costs (or the costs of transferring IPRs); rent seeking (the opportunity to charge monopoly prices); and the cost of protection, which they see as likely to be high in relation to intellectual property because of its nature as a public good. They continue at pp. 19–21:

> The public-good character of intellectual property is pronounced. In the case of farmland, whether cultivated or uncultivated, adding a user will…impose costs on the existing user(s). So the fact that a fence keeps additional users out need not impose a net cost on users as a group, and if not, the only cost of the property right will be the fence.
>
> …
>
> Often and not merely exceptionally, adding users will impose no costs on previous users of intellectual property. One farmer's using the idea of crop rotation does not prevent any other farmer from using the same idea. It is true that when more farmers use crop rotation, output will rise and prices will fall, hurting farmers already using crop rotation. But the price effects of the diffusion of the idea are purely pecuniary externalities because the losses to the farmers are completely offset by the gains to consumers; there is no reduction in the aggregate value of the society's economic resources. However, when the marginal cost of using a resource is zero, excluding someone (the marginal purchaser) from using it by charging a positive price for its use creates a deadweight loss, in addition to the out-of-pocket cost of enforcing exclusion by fences, security guards, police, lawyers and registries of title deeds, because the price deflects some users to substitute goods that have a positive marginal cost. This loss is rarely significant in the case of physical property because, as we said, it brings with it a benefit; it avoids crowding in the pasture and shopping-center cases, and worse when joint consumption is not possible. More broadly, it allocates scarce resources to their highest-valued uses. Two people cannot eat the same radish or wear the same pair of shoes at the same time. There must be a mechanism for allocation, and normally the most efficient is the price system. Hence, Plant's point that intellectual property rights create scarcity whereas property rights in physical goods manage scarcity.
>
> But the point is incomplete. Unless there is power to exclude, the incentive to create intellectual property in the first place may be impaired. Socially desirable investments (investments that yield social benefits in excess of their social costs) may be deterred if the creators of intellectual property cannot recoup their sunk costs. That is the *dynamic* benefit of property rights, and the result is the 'access versus incentives' tradeoff; charging a price for a public good reduces access to it (a social cost), making it artificially scarce (Plant's point), but increases the incentive to create it in the first place, which is a possibly offsetting social benefit.

The conclusion reached by Landes and Posner is that expansive IPRs are not necessarily always socially or economically optimal. The law and economics approach to intellectual property has been particularly influential over the past few decades, although not always with the caveats recognized by Landes and Posner.

1.2.5 CONCLUSION

The above discussion shows that each of the key justifications—natural rights, utilitarian and economic—for IPRs has contentious aspects. As such, you may feel that one justification is no more persuasive than any other. Moreover, as we shall see in later chapters, none of these justifications adequately explains the entire bundle of IPRs. We should also be wary of seeking a single justification for IPRs because if we look to history we see that the development of intellectual property was neither linear, teleological, nor inevitable, but historically contingent.[6] Thus, attempting to explain IPRs according to one particular justification, apart from anything else, oversimplifies the ways in which laws are generated. That being said, it is still useful to be aware of the key features and limitations of the justifications usually propounded for IPRs, not least because these arguments tend to be utilized, either separately or cumulatively, in the context of law reform.

1.3 INTERNATIONAL AND REGIONAL FRAMEWORK

1.3.1 THE GLOBAL CONTEXT

1.3.1.1 Introduction

We have noted that it was in the mid nineteenth century that a coherent intellectual property regime began to emerge. This coincided with, and arguably was in part a consequence of, a period of growth in international trade. Individual countries were concerned that the interests of their traders should be protected when they ventured into foreign markets. Thus, from the latter half of the nineteenth century onwards, we begin to see a series of international treaties dealing with various aspects of IP. Of these, the most important are the Berne Convention and the Paris Convention because they were the first multilateral treaties dealing with, in the case of the former, copyrights and, in the case of the latter, patents, trade marks and designs. Indeed, these conventions continue to have relevance to the present day and will be discussed in more detail in later chapters.[7] The most recent and arguably most comprehensive international treaty relating to IPRs is the Agreement on Trade Related Aspects of Intellectual Property Rights 1994 (TRIPS Agreement). The TRIPS Agreement, which was negotiated and is administered under the auspices of the World Trade Organization (WTO), sets minimum standards of protection for all the members of the organization. In the following extract Susan Sell places the TRIPS Agreement in a historical context, recognizing the importance of earlier international agreements relating to IP.

S. Sell, *Private Power, Public Law: The globalization of intellectual property rights* (Cambridge University Press, 2003), pp. 10–12

TRIPS in historical perspective

The TRIPS agreement introduces a new era in the evolution of IP rights by effectively globalizing IP protection. The history of IP protection can be divided into three broad phases: national, international and global. Until the end of the nineteenth century, IP protection covering patents and copyrights was strictly a national matter. States passed laws of their own design; the protection that these laws provided did not extend beyond national borders. The expansion of international commerce increasingly strained this national patchwork of IP protection, and, by the early 1800s, a number of European governments had negotiated a network of bilateral copyright agreements. In the early nineteenth century British authors and publishers complained of 'widespread piracy' of British books abroad. Reprinting books was perfectly legal in many other countries; in fact, the reprinting of texts by popular British

---

[6] See Sherman and Bently, *The Making of Modern Intellectual Property Law.*
[7] See Chs. 2 and 9.

authors such as Charles Dickens was a thriving industry in America. The British book trade recognised that this practice was reducing potential profits and eliminating major export markets for legitimate British editions. There was a growing demand for codification in an international treaty. States with copyright laws sought international regulation of the book trade to protect copyrighted works beyond their territorial borders.

Similarly, inventors who sought protection of their inventions within foreign countries raised concerns over patents. In the 1870s, the Austro-Hungarian Empire sought to host in Vienna international exhibitions of inventions. Foreigners were reluctant to participate because they feared their ideas would be stolen. German and American inventors were particularly concerned, as they were widely recognised to be among the most innovative. Therefore, in 1873 the empire adopted a temporary law providing protection for foreigners in order to encourage foreign inventors' participation in the international exhibitions; this protection was to last through the duration of the exhibition. A number of European countries already had domestic patent systems, and met in Vienna in 1873 to discuss prospects for an international agreement to protect patents. They convened several follow up Congresses in 1878 and 1880; the latter Congress adopted a draft convention which became the basis for the 1883 Paris Convention. As in the case of copyright, the overriding objective was to devise a system in which states would recognise and protect the rights of foreign artists and inventors within states own domestic borders.

States responded to the increasingly strained patchwork of national legislation by adopting two international IP conventions: the Paris Convention for the Protection of Industrial Property (covering patents, trademarks, and industrial designs) in 1883, and the Berne Convention of 1886 (for copyright). The underlying principles of these international agreements were non-discrimination, national treatment, and the right of priority. Non-discrimination provides that there should be no barriers for entry of the foreign author or inventor in a member state's national market. National treatment means that once an inventor or author has entered a member state's market that person should be treated no differently than nationals. The right of priority protects the rights holder from unauthorised use of the copyrighted or patented work. Under this system, states were free to pass legislation of their own design but were obligated to extend their legislative protection to foreigners of member states.

In the international era the territorial basis of IP rights was preserved, albeit extended beyond jurisdictional confines through the 'contractual device of treaty making'. Unlike the TRIPS agreement these conventions neither created new substantive law nor imposed new laws on member states; rather they reflected a consensus among member states that was legitimated by domestic laws already in place.

This system permitted wide variation in the scope and duration of protection. For example, many countries denied patent protection for pharmaceutical products in order to contain the cost of necessary medicines. This was perfectly acceptable under the terms of the Paris Convention. Indeed, before TRIPS, practices that US stakeholders decried as 'piracy' were often lawful economic activities under various national legal systems and existing international IP agreements. States had considerable autonomy to craft laws that reflected their levels of economic development and comparative advantages in either innovation or imitation. Thus, the 'old system' recognised inherent variations in the development levels of different countries.

Today, the Paris and Berne Conventions, together with a number of other IP conventions and agreements, are administered by the World Intellectual Property Organization

(WIPO), an agency of the United Nations.[8] WIPO itself dates back to 1967[9] and is located in Geneva. Apart from administering these treaties, WIPO plays a wider role in various aspects of intellectual property regulation, such as for example the arbitration of domain name disputes.[10]

1.3.1.2 TRIPS Agreement

In the 1980s and 1990s, developed countries became increasingly frustrated with WIPO. This was for two main reasons. First, numerous developing countries were now signatories to conventions administered by WIPO and attempts to revise those conventions inevitably gave rise to complex and highly politicized negotiations which a number of countries concluded could not be resolved within a specialist organization such as WIPO. Secondly, and importantly for countries who were net exporters of intellectual property, there were no real international enforcement mechanisms available if signatories did not comply with their convention obligations. The answer to both these problems for these latter countries was to seek to bring the international regulation of IP within the jurisdiction of the WTO. The TRIPS Agreement was a product of the Uruguay Round of Multilateral Trade Negotiations, which established the GATT (i.e. the WTO Agreement). The TRIPS Agreement forms part of the Agreement establishing the WTO and thus binds all WTO Members. The UK and EC have been WTO Members since 1 January 1995. A summary of the main features of the TRIPS Agreement is provided on the WTO website[11] and is extracted below:

> The areas of intellectual property that it covers are: copyright and related rights (i.e. the rights of performers, producers of sound recordings and broadcasting organizations); trademarks including service marks; geographical indications including appellations of origin; industrial designs; patents including the protection of new varieties of plants; the layout-designs of integrated circuits; and undisclosed information including trade secrets and test data.
>
> The three main features of the Agreement are:
>
> • Standards. In respect of each of the main areas of intellectual property covered by the TRIPS Agreement, the Agreement sets out the minimum standards of protection to be provided by each Member. Each of the main elements of protection is defined, namely the subject-matter to be protected, the rights to be conferred and permissible exceptions to those rights, and the minimum duration of protection. The Agreement sets these standards by requiring, first, that the substantive obligations of the main conventions of the WIPO, the Paris Convention for the Protection of Industrial Property (Paris Convention) and the Berne Convention for the Protection of Literary and Artistic Works (Berne Convention) in their most recent versions, must be complied with. With the exception of the provisions of the Berne Convention on moral rights, all the main substantive provisions of these conventions are incorporated by reference and thus become obligations under the TRIPS Agreement between TRIPS Member countries. The relevant provisions are to be found in Articles 2.1 and 9.1 of the TRIPS Agreement, which relate, respectively, to the Paris Convention and to the Berne Convention. Secondly, the TRIPS Agreement adds a substantial number of additional obligations

---

[8] See <http://www.wipo.int/>.

[9] Athough its predecessor, the United International Bureaux for the Protection of Intellectual Property, was established in 1893 to administer the Paris Convention and Berne Convention.

[10] See Ch. 12.   [11] <www.wto.org/english/tratop_e/trips_e/intel2_e.htm>.

on matters where the pre-existing conventions are silent or were seen as being inadequate. The TRIPS Agreement is thus sometimes referred to as a Berne and Paris-plus agreement.

- Enforcement. The second main set of provisions deals with domestic procedures and remedies for the enforcement of intellectual property rights. The Agreement lays down certain general principles applicable to all IPR enforcement procedures. In addition, it contains provisions on civil and administrative procedures and remedies, provisional measures, special requirements related to border measures and criminal procedures, which specify, in a certain amount of detail, the procedures and remedies that must be available so that right holders can effectively enforce their rights.

- Dispute settlement. The Agreement makes disputes between WTO Members about the respect of the TRIPS obligations subject to the WTO's dispute settlement procedures.

In addition the Agreement provides for certain basic principles, such as national and most-favoured-nation treatment, and some general rules to ensure that procedural difficulties in acquiring or maintaining IPRs do not nullify the substantive benefits that should flow from the Agreement. The obligations under the Agreement will apply equally to all Member countries, but developing countries will have a longer period to phase them in. Special transition arrangements operate in the situation where a developing country does not presently provide product patent protection in the area of pharmaceuticals.

The TRIPS Agreement is a minimum standards agreement, which allows Members to provide more extensive protection of intellectual property if they so wish. Members are left free to determine the appropriate method of implementing the provisions of the Agreement within their own legal system and practice.

It is clear from this description that the TRIPS provisions have an inevitable impact on each of the IPRs. The details of this impact will be looked at in the individual chapters concerning those rights.

Not surprisingly for such a far-reaching international agreement TRIPS has proved to be immensely controversial in a number of ways. For example, the high level of harmonization in relation to various IPRs, together with the coercive effect of the WTO Dispute Resolution Procedure, has created an enormous pressure on developing countries to raise their standards of intellectual property protection. Although they were given some leeway in the time frame for compliance (developing countries by 1999, and least developed countries by 2005), nonetheless, it has proved difficult and some would argue counterproductive for developing countries to meet these standards. Indeed much of the criticism of TRIPS has revolved around the relative disadvantages that it is supposed to create for developing countries. This is a view taken by Peter Drahos and John Braithwaite.

P. Drahos and J. Braithwaite, *Information Feudalism: Who owns the knowledge economy?* (London: Earthscan, 2002), pp. 10–13

Why sign TRIPS?

During the course of an interview in 1994 with a senior US trade negotiator he remarked to us that 'probably less than 50 people were responsible for TRIPS'. TRIPS is the most important agreement on intellectual property of the 20th century. More than one hundred signed it on behalf of their nations in the splendid Salle Royale of the Palais des Congres in Marrakesh on 15th April 1994.

TRIPS is one of 28 agreements that make up the Final Act of the Uruguay Round of MultiLateral Trade Negotiations, the negotiations that had begun in Punta del Este in 1986. Another of those agreements established the WTO, and it is the WTO that administers TRIPS. In the US, high technology multinationals greeted the signing of TRIPS with considerable satisfaction. TRIPS was the first stage in the global recognition of an investment morality that sees knowledge as a private, rather than public, good. The intellectual property standards contained in TRIPS, obligatory on all members of the WTO, would help them to enforce that morality around the world. In India, after the signing of TRIPS, hundreds of thousands of farmers gathered to protest the intrusion of patents on the seeds of their agricultural futures. The Indian generics industry warned of dramatic price increases in essential medicines that would follow from the obligation in TRIPS to grant 20-year patents on pharmaceutical products. In Africa, there was little discussion of TRIPS.

TRIPs is about more than patents. It sets minimum standards in copyright, trade marks, geographical indications, industrial designs and layout designs of integrated circuits. TRIPS effectively globalizes the set of intellectual property principles it contains, because most states of the world are members of, or are seeking membership of, the WTO. It also has a crucial harmonizing impact on intellectual property regulation because it sets, in some cases, quite detailed standards of intellectual property law. Every member, for example, has to have a copyright law that protects computer programs as a literary work, as well as a patent law that does not exclude micro-organisms and microbiological processes from patentability. The standards in TRIPS will profoundly affect the ownership of the 21st century's two great technologies—digital technology and biotechnology. Copyright, patents and protection for layout-designs are all used to protect digital technology, whereas patents and trade secrets are the principle means by which biotechnological knowledge is being enclosed. TRIPS also obliges states to provide effective enforcement procedures against the infringement of intellectual property rights.

One of the puzzles this book sets out to solve is why states should give up sovereignty over something as fundamental as the property laws that determine the ownership of information and the technologies that so profoundly affect the basic rights of their citizens. The puzzle deepens when it is realized that in immediate trade terms the globalization of intellectual property really only benefitted the US and to a lesser extent the European Community. No one disagrees that TRIPS has conferred massive benefits on the US economy, the world's biggest net intellectual property exporter or that it has strengthened the hand of those corporations with large intellectual property portfolios. It was the US and the European Community that between them had the world's dominant software, pharmaceutical, chemical and entertainment industries, as well as the world's most important trade marks. The rest of the developed countries and all developing countries were in the position of being importers with nothing really to gain by agreeing to terms of trade for intellectual property that would offer so much protection to the comparative advantage the US enjoyed in intellectual property-related goods.

...

One standard reply we received in our interviews when we put this puzzle to policy-makers was that 'TRIPS was part of a package in which we got agriculture'. The WTO Agreement on Agriculture, however, does not confer anything like the benefits on developing countries that TRIPS does on the US and the European Community. There is also another irony here. Increasingly, agricultural goods are the subject of intellectual property rights as patents are extended to seeds and plants. Agricultural counties will find that they have to pay more for the patented agricultural inputs that they purchase from the world's agro-chemical companies. In addition they will have to compete with the cost-advantages that biotechnology brings to US farmers (not to mention the subsidies that US and EU farmers continue to receive). By signing TRIPS, agricultural exporters have signed away at least some of their comparative advantage in agriculture.

Sometimes we were told that 'we will be eventual winners from intellectual property'. While it is good to be optimistic about one's distant destiny, it does explain why normally hard-nosed trade negotiators would take the highly dangerous route of agreeing to the globalization of property rules over knowledge that had brought their countries so few gains in the past. Of the 3.5 million patents in existence in the 1970s, the decade before the TRIPS negotiations, nationals of developing countries held about 1 percent. Developing countries such as South Korea, Singapore, Brazil and India, that were industrializing, were doing so in the absence of a globalized intellectual property regime.

More disturbing for developing countries is the development cost of an intellectual property regime. The basis of competition lies in the development of skills. The acquisition of skills by newcomers disturbs roles and hierarchies. After India built a national drug industry, it began exporting bulk drugs and formulations to places such as Canada. A developing country which had acquired skills threatened those at the top of the international hierarchy of pharmaceutical production—the US, Japan, Germany and the UK.

. . .

The answer to our question about why developing countries signed TRIPS has much to do with democracy—or rather, its failure . . . Put starkly, the intellectual property rights regime we have today largely represents the failure of democratic processes both nationally and internationally. A small number of US companies, which were established players in the knowledge game . . . captured the US trade-agenda-setting process and then, in partnership with European and Japanese multinationals, drafted intellectual property principles that became the blueprint for TRIPS . . . The resistance of developing countries was crushed through trade power . . .

One retort to this might be that corporations are entitled to lobby, and, in any case, developing countries agreed to TRIPS through a process of bargaining amongst sovereigns. It is indeed true that corporations are entitled to lobby. It is important that big business makes its views and policy preferences known to government since around the globe it represents hundreds of millions of jobs and investors. However, that lobbying in relation to property rights should take place under conditions of democratic bargaining. Democratic bargaining matters crucially to the definition of property rights because of the consequences of property rules for all individuals within a society. Property rights confer authority over resources. When authority is granted to the few over resources on which the many depend, the few gain power over the goals of the many. This has consequences for both political and economic freedom within a society.

The stakes are high in the case of intellectual property rights. Intellectual property rights are a source of authority and power over informational resources on which the many depend— information in the form of chemical formulae, the DNA in plants and animals, the algorithms that underpin digital technology and the knowledge in books and electronic databases. These resources matter to communities, regions and to the development of states.

Drahos and Braithwaite argue that adherence to TRIPS has come at a cost to developing and least developed countries. By way of contrast, Gutowski suggests that such a view is too simplistic. In particular, it fails to recognize that the TRIPS Agreement is based on economic rather than moral principles.

R. Gutowski, 'The marriage of intellectual property and international trade in the TRIPs agreement: Strange bedfellows or a match made in heaven' (1999) 47 Buff LR 754, 754–60

Indeed, outside the ballyhooed rhetoric of politicians and industry lobbyists, IP protection is generally recognized as an economic, not a moral issue. The fact that an ever-increasing percentage of international trade involves IP corroborates this observation. The WTO is thus the appropriate forum to address the international impacts of IP. At another time IP may have more properly been left to bilateral arrangements; however, today's truly global economy and the paramount importance of technology and information point to the strong link between trade and IP. Even concerns about ideological imperialism and insensitivity to cultural differences are less than compelling today given the global movement towards market economies and free trade. This shift is consistent with inclusion of IP in trade negotiations. The fact that most nations have actively selected this course makes it difficult to point a finger at the West for stamping out indigenous beliefs or alternate notions of property. Local governments are complicit. They have accepted the market paradigm, for better or worse, of which IP is an increasingly important component. Indeed, one author who contends that 'the culture and heritage of developing countries [are] on a collision course with the global consumer culture of the more powerful developed countries,' nonetheless urges that an IP regime can and should be used as a 'cultural shield' to protect native and indigenous culture. Sound development strategies must therefore recognize local and foreign IPRs. In this context IP concerns cannot and should not escape the auspices of the WTO, as the fortunes of the developing countries and the world trading system are closely intertwined.

Developing countries ultimately accepted the TRIPs Agreement in a bargained-for exchange which included concessions on agricultural export subsidies by the European Community, increased market access for tropical products, generous transitional arrangements, and protection against unilateral measures primarily by the United States and other powerful, Western industrialized nations. Certainly the dispute resolution procedures of the WTO make developing countries less vulnerable to bilateral confrontation with the United States and the European Community. Moreover, developing nations also realized that IP protection is increasingly important in order to attract multinational capital and investment. For certain large developing countries such as India and Brazil, it is likely that they recognized IP protection was in their own best interests in benefiting local inventors. Some analysts have found that in newly industrializing economies, recognition of IPRs correlates with the level of economic development. That is, once a country reaches a certain 'development threshold,' then protection of IPRs will generate economic activity sufficient for the political structure to favour innovation over imitation.

The result of increased global IP protection is a balance between gains and concessions. While the effect of protecting foreign IP will likely increase the short-term cost of knowledge-intensive goods to developing countries as importers, this loss is set against concessions on important exports, such as textiles and agriculture, from developing nations. Additionally developing countries will benefit from the advantages of a multilateral agreement over the likely stricter consequences of unilateral accords. At a minimum, for developing countries inclusion of IP protection into GATT was a lesser evil than assured pressure and likely sanctions from developed-world trading partners.

Ultimately, recognition and protection of IPRs is important not simply because Madonna or Nike or Microsoft has a 'right' to stop international piracy and copying of their intellectual property. More importantly, there are compelling arguments that IP protection will indeed benefit the developing world in the long-run—particularly in creating incentives for domestic and foreign researchers and entrepreneurs to invest resources in innovative technologies and solutions to problems indigenous to their countries.

The impact of IP on diverse fields ranging from scientific research to creative authorship to commercial development highlights its pervasive importance to industrial progress. Furthermore, protection of IP in developing nations will reduce the 'brain drain' of talented individuals who leave poor countries in order to make a better living elsewhere. Recognition of IPRs will make it possible for these professionals to profit from their creativity and inventiveness in their home country.

We must disabuse ourselves of the image that all technology comes from developed countries. Incremental innovation rather than media-hyped technological 'break-throughs' can be of immense value to a developing nation. Developing nations recognized this potential in signing on to TRIPs. IP protection is not a singular prescription for development, but it is one important aspect to a development plan. Although the origins of IPRs may hearken back to a brute egoist carving out exclusive proprietorship of ideas, utilized appropriately they can and often have transcended their raw foundation to advance economic development.

Gutowski characterizes the TRIPS Agreement as a balance of gains and concessions for both developed and developing countries. Others have seen the TRIPS Agreement as imbalanced, with its advantages accruing largely to the developed countries. Certainly it is the case that the developed countries of the North, most notably the US, the European Union, and Japan, have wielded the greatest influence in TRIPS negotiations in the past. However, it is possible to argue that, with the growing importance of countries such as India, China, and Brazil in the field of international trade, this situation will not necessarily hold in the future.

FURTHER READING

M. Blakeney, *Trade Related Aspects of Intellectual Property Rights: A concise guide to the TRIPs agreement* (London: Sweet & Maxwell, 1996).

C. M. Correa, *Trade Related Aspects of Intellectual Property Rights: A commentary on the TRIPS agreement* (Oxford: Oxford University Press, 2007).

1.3.2 THE EUROPEAN CONTEXT

Another influence on the shape of UK intellectual property law has been EC law. As a Member State of the European Community, the UK is bound by the EC Treaty (i.e. the Treaty of Rome) and succeeding legislation. The EC Treaty does not refer to intellectual property as such. Yet, over the past few decades (and coinciding with the increased importance of intellectual property to global economies), the European Community has become increasingly preoccupied with the protection of intellectual property and with its implications for the single European market and the promotion of undistorted competition between Member States. This preoccupation has manifested itself in three key areas: free movement of goods and the exhaustion doctrine; the harmonization of IPRs and the introduction of Community wide IPRs; and the relationship between IPRs and competition law. The common thread between these three areas is that they all, at some level, concern the relationship between the internal market and competition.

1.3.2.1 Free movement of goods and exhaustion of rights

One of the key goals of the EC Treaty is to attain a single market. Article 3 prohibits *inter alia* the quantitative restrictions on the import and export of goods, and all measures having equivalent effect. Furthermore it seeks to establish an internal market characterized by the abolition, as between Member States, of obstacles to the free movement of goods, services, persons and capital. More specifically, Articles 28 and 29 prohibit quantitative restrictions on the import and export of goods and all measures having an equivalent effect. Article 30 creates an exception to this prohibition, in that it does not preclude prohibitions or restrictions in relation to the protection of industrial and commercial property, which has been interpreted by the ECJ to include IPRs. However, Article 30 also states that such prohibitions or restrictions shall not constitute a means of arbitrary discrimination or a disguised restriction on trade between Member States. Such a problem might arise because IPRs are territorial in nature. As a result, an IPR owner in one Member State might seek to prevent the importation of goods embodying their IPR and legitimately placed on the market in other Member States. So, for example, Dior, which has a trade mark for Dior perfume in both France and the Netherlands may seek to prevent perfumes legitimately purchased under their trade mark in France from being imported and resold in the Netherlands. Obviously, if IPRs are used to control in this way the import or export of goods this could be seen as a means of arbitrary discrimination or a disguised restriction on trade between Member States.

The apparent contradiction within Article 30 between the aim of establishing free movement of goods and the protection of IPRs is one that the ECJ has sought to reconcile via the doctrine of exhaustion of rights. Put briefly, the exhaustion-of-rights doctrine is that where goods have been first placed on the market in one Member State by an IPR owner or with his consent the IPR owner cannot rely on his IPRs to oppose further dealings in those particular goods in that or other Member States. In more positive terms, Keeling has described the doctrine of exhaustion as meaning: 'simply that the lawful owner of specific products that have been placed on the market by, or with the consent of the right-owner may use, sell, or otherwise dispose of those products'.[12] The doctrine was first established in *Deutsche Grammophon v Metro*.

Deutsche Grammophon v Metro Case 78/70 (1971) CMLR 631

A subsidiary of Deutsche Grammophon had marketed sound recordings in France. These sound recordings were purchased by Metro who sought to import them into Germany. Deutsche Grammophon objected that this was an infringement of its distribution right under German copyright law and obtained an injunction from the German regional court (Landgericht), Hamburg, prohibiting Metro from selling or otherwise distributing the sound recordings. On appeal to the Main regional court (Oberlandesgericht), proceedings were stayed and questions referred to the ECJ. In delivering its preliminary ruling, the ECJ clarified the scope of Article 30 (then Article 36).

[11] Article 36 mentions among the prohibitions or restrictions on the free movement of goods permitted by it those that are justified for the protection of industrial and commercial

---

[12] D. T. Keeling, *Intellectual Property Rights in EU Law*, vol. 1 (Oxford University Press, 2003), p. 76.

property. If it be assumed that a right analogous to copyright can be covered by these provisions it follows, however, from this Article that although the Treaty does not affect the existence of the industrial property rights conferred by the national legislation of a member-State, the exercise of these rights may come within the prohibitions of the Treaty. Although Article 36 permits prohibitions or restrictions on the free movement of goods that are justified for the protection of industrial and commercial property, it only allows such restrictions on the freedom of trade to the extent that they are justified for the protection of the rights that form the specific object of this property.

[12] If a protection right analogous to copyright is used in order to prohibit in one member-State the marketing of goods that have been brought onto the market by the holder of the right or with his consent in the territory of another member-State solely because this marketing has not occurred in the domestic market, such a prohibition maintaining the isolation of the national markets conflicts with the essential aim of the Treaty, the integration of the national markets into one uniform market. This aim could not be achieved if by virtue of the various legal systems of the member-States private persons were able to divide the market and cause arbitrary discriminations or disguised restrictions in trade between the member-States.

[13] Accordingly, it would conflict with the provisions regarding the free movement of goods in the Common Market if a manufacturer of recordings exercised the exclusive right granted to him by the legislation of a member-State to market the protected articles in order to prohibit the marketing in that member-State of products that had been sold by him himself or with his consent in another member-State solely because this marketing had not occurred in the territory of the first member-State.

In *Deutsche Grammophon* the ECJ sought to justify the exhaustion of rights doctrine in the context of Article 30 (then Article 36) by drawing a distinction between the existence and exercise of the IPR. The doctrine was meant to impact only upon the exercise of the IPR and not its existence. The existence/exercise dichotomy held sway for much of the 1970s, however, it came to be seen as a vague and artificial distinction[13] and eventually gave way to the idea first canvassed in *Deutsche Grammophon* that the Article 30 exception is only relevant where it is being used to protect the specific subject matter of the IPR.

An early attempt to define the somewhat 'esoteric concept' of the 'specific subject matter' of the IPR,[14] at least in relation to patents and trade marks, occurred in *Centrafarm v Sterling Drug*.

Centrafarm v Sterling Drug Case 15/74 [1974] ECR 1147

A patented drug had been marketed under the trade mark 'Negram' by a subsidiary of the patent owner (Sterling Drug) in both Germany and the UK. Centrafarm purchased quantities of this drug placed on the market in the UK and sought to import it into the Netherlands and to sell it under the name 'Negram'. Sterling Drug brought proceedings in the Dutch court for both patent and trade mark infringement. The Hoge Raad referred a number of interrelated questions concerning free movement of goods to the ECJ. In its judgment, the ECJ first considered the relationship between the free movement of goods and patent protection.

---

[13] Keeling, *Intellectual Property Rights in EU Law*, pp. 54–5.   [14] Ibid., p. 61.

As regards question I (a)

4. This question requires the court to state whether, under the conditions postulated, the rules in the EEC Treaty concerning the free movement of goods prevent the patentee from ensuring that the product protected by the patent is not marketed by others.

5. As a result of the provisions in the Treaty relating to the free movement of goods and in particular of Article 30 [now Article 28], quantitative restrictions on imports and all measures having equivalent effect are prohibited between Member States.

6. By Article 36 [now Article 30] these provisions shall nevertheless not include prohibitions or restrictions on imports justified on grounds of the protection of industrial or commercial property.

7. Nevertheless, it is clear from this same Article, in particular its second sentence, as well as from the context, that whilst the Treaty does not affect the existence of rights recognized by the legislation of a Member State in matters of industrial and commercial property, yet the exercise of these rights may nevertheless, depending on the circumstances, be affected by the prohibitions in the Treaty.

8. Inasmuch as it provides an exception to one of the fundamental principles of the common market, Article 36 in fact only admits of derogations from the free movement of goods where such derogations are justified for the purpose of safeguarding rights which constitute the specific subject matter of this property.

9. In relation to patents, the specific subject matter of the industrial property is the guarantee that the patentee, to reward the creative effort of the inventor, has the exclusive right to use an invention with a view to manufacturing industrial products and putting them into circulation for the first time, either directly or by the grant of licences to third parties, as well as the right to oppose infringements.

10. An obstacle to the free movement of goods may arise out of the existence, within a national legislation concerning industrial and commercial property, of provisions laying down that a patentee's right is not exhausted when the product protected by the patent is marketed in another Member State, with the result that the patentee can prevent importation of the product into his own Member State when it has been marketed in another state.

11. Whereas an obstacle to the free movement of goods of this kind may be justified on the ground of protection of industrial property where such protection is invoked against a product coming from a Member State where it is not patentable and has been manufactured by third parties without the consent of the patentee and in cases where there exist patents, the original proprietors of which are legally and economically independent, a derogation from the principle of the free movement of goods is not, however, justified where the product has been put onto the market in a legal manner, by the patentee himself or with his consent, in the Member State from which it has been imported, in particular in the case of a proprietor of parallel patents.

12. In fact, if a patentee could prevent the import of protected products marketed by him or with his consent in another Member State, he would be able to partition off national markets and thereby restrict trade between Member States, in a situation where no such restriction was necessary to guarantee the essence of the exclusive rights flowing from the parallel patents.

13. The plaintiff in the main action claims, in this connection, that by reason of divergences between national legislations and practice, truly identical or parallel patents can hardly be said to exist.

14. It should be noted here that, in spite of the divergences which remain in the absence of any unification of national rules concerning industrial property, the identity of the protected

invention is clearly the essential element of the concept of parallel patents which it is for the courts to assess.

15. The question referred should therefore be answered to the effect that the exercise, by a patentee, of the right which he enjoys under the legislation of a Member State to prohibit the sale, in that state, of a product protected by the patent which has been marketed in another Member State by the patentee or with his consent is incompatible with the rules of the EEC Treaty concerning the free movement of goods within the common market.

In *Centrafarm*, the ECJ explained that Article 30 (previously Article 36) allowed derogations from the prohibitions set out in Articles 28 and 29 (previously Articles 30 and 31) where those derogations were necessary to protect the specific object (or subject matter) of the IPR. In other words, the exhaustion of rights doctrine was justified on the basis that it does not derogate from the specific subject matter of an IPR. We have seen, in the above passage, the definition of specific subject matter in relation to patents. While the ECJ has been willing also to define the specific subject matter of trade marks,[15] they have been less keen to do so in the context of copyright and related rights, along with design rights.[16]

The doctrine of exhaustion of rights has given rise to several issues. A key question has been in what circumstances does an IPR owner consent to goods being first marketed in a Member State?[17] It is important to note that where goods are placed on the market by related undertakings this will amount to consent. As stated by the ECJ in *IHT International Heiztechnik v Ideal Standard* Case C-9/93:[18]

[The principle of exhaustion of rights] applies where the owner of the trade mark in the importing State and the owner of the trade mark in the exporting State are the same or where, even if they are separate persons, they are economically linked. A number of situations are covered: products put into circulation by the same undertaking, by a licensee, by a parent company, by a subsidiary of the same group, or by an exclusive distributor.

Where goods are placed on the market as a result of a compulsory licence, the ECJ has held that this does not constitute consent. This is because a compulsory licence, 'deprives the patent proprietor of his right to determine freely the conditions under which he markets his products'.[19]

Another issue that has arisen is whether the exhaustion doctrine applies where goods are first marketed in Member States that have some peculiarity in their law which prevents the owner from obtaining a proper reward. An example of this is reflected in the following case.

Merck v Stephar Case 187/80 [1981] ECR 2063

Merck held patents in all Member States, except Luxembourg, Italy, Denmark and Germany, relating to the manufacture of a drug to treat hypertension. Merck marketed its drug in Italy and the defendant, Stephar, imported the drug from Italy into

---

15 See for example, *IHT International Heiztechnik v Ideal Standard* Case C-9/93 [1994] ECR I-2789.
16 Keeling, *Intellectual Property Rights in EU Law*, pp. 66–7.
17 A detailed analysis of the jurisprudence on this issue is available in ibid., pp. 82–95.
18 [1994] ECR I-2789, para. 34.   19 *Pharmon v Hoechst* Case 19/84 [1985] ECR 2281, 2298.

the Netherlands and resold it a lower price than that charged by Merck. Merck sought interim relief against Stephar and the Dutch court referred questions to the ECJ, which essentially asked whether the doctrine of exhaustion applied where a product had been first marketed in a Member State where no patent protection existed.

> [9] …The substance of a patent right lies essentially in according the inventor an exclusive right of first placing the product on the market.
>
> [10] That right (…of first placing a product on the market…) enables the inventor, by allowing him a monopoly in exploiting his product, to obtain the reward for his creative effort without, however, guaranteeing that he will obtain such a reward in all circumstances.
>
> [11] It is for the proprietor of the patent to decide, in the light of all the circumstances, under what conditions he will market his product, including the possibility of marketing it in a Member State where the law does not provide patent protection for the product in question. If he decides to do so he must then accept the consequences of his choice as regards the free movement of the product within the Common Market, which is a fundamental principle forming part of the legal and economic circumstances which must be taken into account by the proprietor of the patent in determining the manner in which his exclusive right will be exercised.

Keeling[20] has criticized the application of the exhaustion doctrine to a first sale of a patented product in a Member State, where no patent protection exists, on the basis that this will severely undermine the value of a patent in another Member State where patent protection does exist. This is because the patent owner will face competition from parallel imports which he has placed on the market in a country where there is no patent protection and which will invariably be priced more cheaply. Nevertheless, the principle established in *Merck v Stephar* was confirmed in the later ECJ ruling in *Merck v PrimeCrown Ltd*.[21] It is worthwhile noting (as the ECJ did in *Merck v PrimeCrown*), that pharmaceutical products are now patentable in all Member States, so the situation that occurred in the *Merck* cases will not arise again.

Finally, there has been the issue of whether international, as opposed to Community-wide exhaustion, is recognized. The type of exhaustion that was established in *Deutsche Grammophon* and which has been discussed so far is Community-wide exhaustion. According to this doctrine, first marketing of goods *in any Member State* by an IPR owner exhausts the right of distribution in those particular goods in the European Community. Thus, the IPR owner would be precluded from invoking the right to prevent importation of the goods into any other Member State. At this point, it is also worth noting that the Agreement on the European Economic Area of 17 March 1993[22] widened the principle of Community-wide exhaustion to include EFTA states Iceland, Liechtenstein and Norway. In contrast, a doctrine of international exhaustion occurs where first marketing of goods *outside the Community* by the IPR owner exhausts the right of distribution in those goods within the European Community.

The provisions of the EC Treaty do not preclude a doctrine of international exhaustion as part of the domestic law of Member States. Thus, it is left up to individual Member States as to whether they apply this doctrine or not. However, and very importantly, this is subject to

---

[20] Keeling, *Intellectual Property Rights in EU Law*, pp. 105–8.
[21] [1997] FSR 237.   [22] OJ L1, 3 Jan. 1994.

the Community legislature not having intervened to provide otherwise. It is not proposed to discuss all of the instances in which the Community legislature has so intervened.[23] Instead, this point will be illustrated through the example of trade marks. Article 7(1) of the Trade Marks Directive[24] states:

> The trade mark shall not entitle the proprietor to prohibit its use in relation to goods which have been put on the market in the Community under that trade mark by the proprietor or with his consent.

Article 7(1) has been interpreted by the ECJ in *Silhouette v Hartlauer*,[25] to mean that Member States are not permitted to apply a doctrine of international exhaustion in the area of trade marks. Thus, in the trade mark field, only Community-wide (or more accurately EEA-wide exhaustion) applies. Whether a doctrine of international exhaustion should be adopted is now a political, rather than legal, question.

FURTHER READING

D. T. Keeling, *Intellectual Property Rights in EU Law*, vol. 1 (Oxford: Hart, 2003).

C. Stothers, *Parallel Trade in Europe: Intellectual Property, Competition and Regulatory Law* (Oxford: Hart, 2007).

1.3.2.2 Harmonization and unitary rights

Harmonization of Member States' national laws on intellectual property is another means of addressing the conflict between free movement of goods and IPRs. For example, if a musical work is protected for life of the author plus 70 years in Germany and for life of the author plus 50 years in the UK, this would mean the musical work entered the public domain in the UK 20 years before it did so in Germany. In other words, copyright in the musical work would be enforceable in Germany for an additional 20 years and the right-sholder in Germany would be able to restrain the importation of copies of the musical work that had lawfully been put on the market in the UK at the expiration of the copyright period in the UK. This, in turn, would give rise to an impediment to the free movement of goods. Obviously, then, a way of removing this impediment would be to harmonize the term of copyright protection throughout the European Community. In fact, in the field of copyright and related rights, we have seen harmonization of the term of protection by virtue of the Term Directive.[26]

Thus, harmonization of intellectual property laws in the European Community, by ironing out discrepancies between Member States, helps minimize obstacles to the free

---

[23] See Keeling, *Intellectual Property Rights in EU Law*, pp. 130–46 for further details.

[24] First Council Directive 89/104/EEC of 21 Dec. 1988 to approximate the laws of the Member States relating to trade marks. The relationship between trade marks and exhaustion of rights will be considered at 6.5.

[25] Case C-355/96 [1998] ECR I-6.

[26] Directive 93/98/EEC, which was subsequently codified by Directive 2006/116/EC of 12 Dec. 2006 on the term of protection of copyright and certain related rights.

movement of goods. Unsurprisingly, therefore, the Community legislature has been active in the field of harmonization. Significant harmonization has occurred in the field of trade mark law (Trade Marks Directive[27]) and in the law relating to registered designs (Designs Directive[28]). In the field of copyright law, there have been several harmonizing directives most of which have focused on either particular subject matter (Software[29] and Database[30] Directives), particular rights (Cable and Satellite Directive,[31] Rental Rights Directive,[32] Resale Royalty Right Directive[33]), or particular issues (Term Directive[34]). The most far-reaching harmonization of copyright law to date has occurred through the Information Society Directive,[35] which harmonizes aspects of copyright and related rights, in particular in relation to the digital environment. In the field of patent law, however, harmonization has been limited to biotechnological inventions (Biotechnology Directive[36]). Finally, across the different regimes of IPRs, there has been harmonization of enforcement measures via the Enforcement Directive.[37] The details, and impact, of these directives will be discussed in more detail in later chapters.

While harmonization can reduce the discrepancies between national laws and thus minimize obstacles to free movement of goods, it cannot address the problems that flow from the territoriality of IPRs. For example, even if musical works are protected for the same amount of time, i.e. life of the author plus 70 years, the owner of copyright in a musical work, A, who puts copies on the market in the UK could still try and prohibit the importation of those copies into another Member State, such as France. Of course, as was discussed in the previous section, the doctrine of exhaustion of rights was developed to remove this type of obstacle to the free movement of goods. However, it is also possible to alleviate this sort of problem by creating unitary, Community-wide IPRs. In other words, to create IPRs which are valid and enforceable throughout the entire Community, as one single territory, as opposed to within each individual Member State, which is the extent of national IPRs. In the following extract, the difference between harmonization and unification of IPRs is explained.

---

[27] First Council Directive 89/104/EEC of 21 Dec. 1988 to approximate the laws of the Member States relating to trade marks.

[28] Directive 98/71/EC of the European Parliament and of the Council of 13 Oct. 1998 on the legal protection of designs.

[29] Directive 91/250/EEC on the legal protection of computer programs OJ L122, 17 May 1991, pp. 42–6.

[30] Directive 96/9/EC of the European Parliament and of the Council of 11 Mar. 1996 on the legal protection of databases OJ L77, 27 Mar. 1996, pp. 20–8.

[31] Directive 93/83/EEC of 27 Sept. 1993 on the coordination of certain rules concerning copyright and rights related to copyright applicable to satellite broadcasting and cable retransmission OJ L248, 6 Oct. 1993, pp. 15–21.

[32] Directive 92/100/EEC of 19 Nov. 1992 on rental and lending rights and on certain rights related to copyright in the field of intellectual property OJ L346, 27 Nov. 1992, pp. 61–6, codified in Directive 2006/115/EC of the European Parliament and of the Council of 12 Dec. 2006 on rental right and lending right and on certain rights related to copyright in the field of intellectual property.

[33] Directive 2001/84/EC of the European Parliament and of the Council of 27 Sept. 2001 on the resale right for the benefit of the author of an original work of art OJ L272, 13 Oct. 2001, p. 32.

[34] Directive 93/98/EEC, which was subsequently codified by Directive 2006/116/EC of 12 Dec. 2006 on the term of protection of copyright and certain related rights.

[35] Directive 2001/29/EC on the harmonization of certain aspects of copyright and related rights in the information society OJ L167, 22 Jun. 2001, pp. 10–19.

[36] Directive 98/44/EC of the European Parliament and of the Council of 6 Jul. 1998 on the legal protection of biotechnological inventions.

[37] Directive 2004/48/EC of the European Parliament and of the Council of 29 Apr. 2004 on the enforcement of intellectual property rights [2004] OJ L195/16.

H. Ullrich, 'Harmony and unity of European intellectual property protection' in Vaver and Bently (eds.), *Intellectual Property in the New Millennium* (Cambridge: Cambridge University Press, 2004), pp. 20–46, at pp. 27–8

Unification of intellectual property protection differs from harmonization not only as regards the legal status of the property titles granted—supranational instead of national— but foremost as regards the breadth and depth of the exercise of Community authority. Unification cannot be had at a 'minimum'. While there are interfaces with national law in general which naturally limit the scope of unification, the basic principle of Community intellectual property rights is their independence from national law. They are acquired, assigned, maintained, protected and invalidated as a matter of Community law only; their claim to unity rests on the basis that the Community will not only ensure their individuality, but also their substantive integrity throughout the Common Market. Therefore, the establishment of Community intellectual property implies the development of a self-contained system of protection that ultimately must be extended even to the remedies for infringement.

The EC has introduced two unitary rights: the Community trade mark (introduced by the Community Trade Mark Regulation[38]) and the Community design right (introduced by the Community Design Right Regulation[39]). Attempts have been made to introduce a Community patent, but they have proved unsuccessful. In later chapters of the book, the harmonizing directives and unitary rights will be discussed in detail. For the moment it suffices to note two things about the Community trade mark and Community design right.[40] First, these unitary rights are alternatives to, rather than replacements of, national trade marks and national design rights. Secondly, centralization of the granting procedure (i.e. registration) represents a key feature and benefit of these rights. It provides benefits to applicants, in terms of lower transaction costs for the acquisition and maintenance of IPRs within the Community.

1.3.2.3 Competition law and IPRs

As we have seen from our discussion in previous sections, Article 30 of the EC Treaty and the doctrine of Community-wide exhaustion address the way in which the territorial nature of IPRs can create barriers to trade within the internal market. Articles 81 and 82 of the EC Treaty, on the other hand, relate to a different aspect of IPRs, namely, the fact that owners of IPRs are granted a monopoly right (i.e. an exclusive right) to do certain acts. As such, these monopoly rights may be misused or abused in ways that restrict competition. Article 81 is concerned with anti-competitive agreements and Article 82 targets abuse of a dominant position.

Article 81 provides:

1. The following shall be prohibited as incompatible with the common market: all agreements between undertakings, decisions by associations of undertakings and concerted

---

38 Council Regulation (EC) 40/94 of 20 Dec. 1993 on the Community Trade Mark.
39 Council Regulation (EC) 6/2002 of 12 Dec. 2001 on Community designs.
40 See Ullrich 'Harmony and unity of European intellectual property protection', pp. 39–41.

practices which may affect trade between Member States and which have as their object or effect the prevention, restriction or distortion of competition within the common market, and in particular those which:

(a) directly or indirectly fix purchase or selling prices or any other trading conditions;

(b) limit or control production, markets, technical development, or investment;

(c) share markets or sources of supply;

(d) apply dissimilar conditions to equivalent transactions with other trading parties, thereby placing them at a competitive disadvantage;

(e) make the conclusion of contracts subject to acceptance by the other parties of supplementary obligations which, by their nature or according to commercial usage, have no connection with the subject of such contracts.

2. Any agreements or decisions prohibited pursuant to this Article shall be automatically void.

3. The provisions of paragraph 1 may, however, be declared inapplicable in the case of:

– any agreement or category of agreements between undertakings;

– any decision or category of decisions by associations of undertakings;

– any concerted practice or category of concerted practices;

which contributes to improving the production or distribution of goods or to promoting technical or economic progress, while allowing consumers a fair share of the resulting benefit, and which does not:

(a) impose on the undertakings concerned restrictions which are not indispensable to the attainment of these objectives;

(b) afford such undertakings the possibility of eliminating competition in respect of a substantial part of the products in question.

The purpose of Article 81 is to prevent collusion (through agreements, decisions, or concerted practices) between competitors, which would undermine the workings of a healthy market economy. Article 81(1) prohibits collusion of this nature and indicates the sorts of agreements, decisions or concerted practices that may have an anti-competitive effect, one such example being 'price-fixing'.[41] Article 81(2) declares agreements or decisions of this kind null and void.

Article 81(1) may apply to assignments or licences of IPRs. For example, it would forbid a patent licence from including a price-fixing or tie-in clause. An example of a tie-in clause would be where a patent licensor, in exchange for granting a licence to manufacture a patented good, required the licensee to purchase the components necessary for manufacturing that good from him.

Article 81(3), however, exempts certain agreements, decisions, or concerted practices which are beneficial to technical or economic progress, i.e. which are pro-competitive. In the field of intellectual property, this provision empowered the Commission to introduce the Technology Transfer Agreement Regulation No. 772/2004.[42] The Regulation creates a

---

[41] Art. 81(1)(a) EC Treaty.

[42] Commission Regulation (EC) 772/2004 of 27 Apr. 2004 on the application of Art. 81(3) of the Treaty to categories of technology transfer agreements.

'block' exemption for technology transfer agreements, which are defined in Article 1(b) as patent licensing agreements, know-how licensing agreements, software copyright licensing agreements and mixed patent, know-how, and software copyright licensing agreements. Article 81(1) is declared not to apply to technology transfer agreements between competing undertakings (on the relevant technology or product market) where the combined market share of the parties does not exceed 20 per cent of the relevant market.[43] The exemption also applies to non-competing undertakings where the combined market share of the parties does not exceed 30 per cent of the relevant market.[44] Agreements containing restrictions that are severely anti-competitive are excluded from the benefit of the block exemption, one such example being price-fixing.[45] Certain restrictions (as opposed to the whole agreement) are also excluded from the benefit of the block exemption. For example, a direct or indirect obligation on the licensee to assign or grant an exclusive licence to the licensor in respect of its own severable improvements to it or its own new applications of the licensed technology.[46] Finally, the Commission may withdraw the benefit of the exemption where it finds in any particular case that a technology transfer agreement nevertheless has effects which are incompatible with Article 81(3) of the EC Treaty.

Where the Technology Transfer Regulation does not apply (e.g. because there is a trade mark licensing agreement), persons would then fall back on general principles, as established by Council Regulation (EC) 1/2003 on the implementation of Articles 81 and 82 of the Treaty.[47] Article 1 of the Regulation makes clear that if agreements satisfy the requirements of Article 81(3) of the EC Treaty they will not be considered prohibited by Article 81(1) and this will be the case without the need for a prior decision to that effect by either the European Commission or a national competition authority. This does not, however, prevent the European Commission or national competition authority from acting on a complaint, or on its own initiative, to determine whether an infringement of Article 81 has occurred.

Whereas Article 81 is concerned with anti-competitive agreements, Article 82 targets situations where persons having exceptional market power abuse their dominance. Article 82 provides:

> Any abuse by one or more undertakings of a dominant position within the common market or in a substantial part of it shall be prohibited as incompatible with the common market insofar as it may affect trade between Member States:
>
> Such abuse may, in particular, consist in:
>
> (a) directly or indirectly imposing unfair purchase or selling prices or other unfair trading conditions;
>
> (b) limiting production, markets or technical development to the prejudice of consumers;
>
> (c) applying dissimilar conditions to equivalent transactions with other trading parties, thereby placing them at a competitive disadvantage;
>
> (d) making the conclusion of contracts subject to acceptance by the other parties of supplementary obligations which, by their nature or according to commercial usage, have no connection with the subject of such contracts.

---

[43] Art. 3(1) Technology Transfer Regulation.   [44] Ibid., Art. 3(2).   [45] Ibid., Art. 4(1)–(2).
[46] Ibid., Art. 5.   [47] [2003] OJ L1, p. 1.

As mentioned earlier, intellectual property law grants exclusive rights to owners and, as such, this may cause the IP owner to occupy a dominant position in the market. For example, as Keeling (2003) describes at p. 371:

> Suppose someone patents, throughout Europe, a pharmaceutical that is capable of curing AIDS. If no other pharmaceutical capable of curing AIDS exists, the proprietor of the patent will inevitably hold a dominant position. The relevant product market can only be defined as the market in pharmaceuticals for successfully treating AIDS, since no other product could be substituted for the patented pharmaceutical. The patentee would enjoy a legal monopoly on the relevant market throughout Europe and the entry barrier would be insuperable during the life of the patent (unless, of course, someone else developed a non-infringing drug also capable of curing AIDS).

However, the fact that an IP owner occupies a dominant position is not enough to infringe Article 82—there must be an *abuse* of that dominant position. As discussed by Keeling, this is somewhat problematic—how can it be said that the exercise of an IPR, which right is intended to confer a limited monopoly on an owner, constitutes an abuse?

D. T. Keeling, Intellectual Property Rights in EU Law, vol. 1 (Oxford: Oxford University Press, 2003), pp. 376–8

The idea that an undertaking may commit an unlawful abuse of its dominant position by exercising its intellectual property rights is problematical. The very essence of an intellectual property right is that the State grants a limited monopoly to someone for a specific purpose, e.g. to reward inventiveness, creativity, investment in research, or to help firms to protect their goodwill. The laws governing the grant of intellectual property rights generally involve a balancing exercise. Patent laws, for example, balance the need to reward and stimulate innovation against the need to grant public access to knowledge and to encourage competition in the production of goods. Similar considerations apply to design rights and to copyright. In all these cases the law, as an act of policy, places the intellectual property owner in a privileged position, partially exempting him from competition. It does so with the deliberate intention of allowing him to exploit his statutory monopoly and thereby obtain his just reward.

...

   It is legitimate, then, to ask whether competition law should be allowed to censure the exploitation of intellectual property rights when intellectual property law itself attempted to strike a balance between public and private interests.

...

   The point is that intellectual property rights are a fairly crude method of rewarding innovation and excellence in the market-place. They are granted on the basis of general criteria, no account being taken of the particular circumstances of each case. Intellectual property legislation cannot address all of the concerns that fall within the province of competition law. Above all, intellectual property legislation cannot examine whether effective competition in a particular market is being damaged as a result of the manner in which a dominant undertaking is exercising its intellectual property rights.

It follows that there is a legitimate role for Article 82 in relation to the exercise of intellectual property rights by dominant undertakings. The problem is to determine precisely what that role should be. Not surprisingly, the Court of Justice has generally taken a cautious approach. It has been reluctant to accept that mere exercise of an intellectual property right can constitute an abuse of dominant position, except in very specific circumstances.

As Keeling notes, there have been very few instances where the ECJ has held that exercise of an IPR infringes Article 82 of the EC Treaty. A famous example is the *Magill* decision[48] where the ECJ held that the refusal by certain broadcasting organizations to licence the reproduction of their advance weekly programme listings (which were protected as copyright works) was an abuse of dominant position. The ECJ stressed that ownership of an IPR will not always result in a dominant position. However, it did so on the facts of the case because the broadcasting organizations enjoyed a de facto monopoly over the data used to compile listings for television programmes and thus were in a position to prevent effective competition on the market in weekly television guides. The Court also emphasized that exercise of an IPR may, in exceptional circumstances, involve abusive conduct. Such exceptional circumstances existed in *Magill* because there was no actual or potential substitute for a weekly television guide and yet there was a specific, constant and regular demand on the part of consumers for such a guide. Thus, the refusal to licence the copyright work (i.e. the listings data), which was indispensable to Magill's business prevented the appearance of a new product on the market. Further, there was no objective justification for such a refusal and, finally, by their conduct, the broadcasting organizations had reserved to themselves the secondary market of weekly television guides by excluding all competition in that market by denying access to the basic listings data.

It is fair to say that the issue of when the exercise of IPRs will amount to an abuse of Article 82 remains an important question, which seems to be raised with greater frequency in the courts.[49] However, it must also be remembered that aside from the external controls of competition law represented by Articles 81 and 82 of the EC Treaty, there are internal mechanisms *within* the various intellectual property regimes that seek to lessen the anti-competitive impact that IPRs may have on the market, by virtue of granting exclusive rights. These mechanisms are sometimes judicially developed doctrines or legislative interventions, and some of these will be explored in greater detail in later chapters.[50]

FURTHER READING

S. Anderman (ed.), *The Interface between Intellectual Property and Competition Policy* (Cambridge: Cambridge University Press, 2006).

V. Korah, *Intellectual Property Rights and the EC Competition Rules* (Oxford: Hart, 2006).

---

[48] *Radio Telefís Eireann and Independent Television Publications Ltd (Intellectual Property Owners Inc intervening) v EC Commission (Magill TV Guide Ltd intervening)* Joined Cases C-241 & 242/91P [1995] 4 CMLR 718.

[49] *BHB Enterprises plc v Victor Chandler (International) Ltd* [2005] EWHC 1074, [2005] ECC 40; *Attheraces Ltd v British Horseracing Ltd* [2007] EWCA Civ 38, [2007] ECC 7; *Intel Corporation v Via Technologies Inc* [2003] EWCA Civ 1905, [2003] ECC 16; *Microsoft Corp v Commission of the European Communities* Case T-201/04 [2007] 5 CMLR 11.

[50] e.g. see the idea/expression dichotomy discussed in Ch. 3 and the 'must fit' and 'must match' exceptions discussed in Ch. 11.

1.4 TRENDS: THE PUBLIC DOMAIN AND TRADITIONAL KNOWLEDGE

1.4.1 THE PUBLIC DOMAIN

Earlier in this chapter we considered the main justifications for intellectual property protection. A common feature of these justifications is that each recognizes the need for the protection of what is often referred to as a 'public domain' (or less frequently, a 'commons') where intellectual property laws should not operate. Thus, the Lockean theory emphasizes the need to preserve an intellectual commons where 'enough and as good' is left for others to access once intellectual creations have been removed. The utilitarian justification also recognizes the need to limit IP protection. In this instance, this aim is achieved by limiting the period of protection which is given to intellectual property, so that when the relevant IP rights expire, the intellectual creations will return to a public domain and be available for others to use in their own creative endeavours. We shall see when we consider the individual IPRs later in this book that each sets limits to what will be legally protected. Thus, ideas do not receive copyright protection and discoveries are not protected by patents.

While there is wide recognition of the need to preserve a public domain, there is less agreement on how its boundaries should be mapped. For example, should the public domain encompass only intellectual production for which the period of protection has expired or which is not suitable subject matter for protection, such as ideas? Or should the public domain also contain intellectual products which may in principle fall within a protectable category of IP but for which, nonetheless, there may be a public interest in leaving them free? An example, from our hypotheticals, might be the colour yellow, which could in principle function as a badge of product origin but, given the limited number of colours available, might also be a mark of identity which many traders would wish to use.

The various ways one might constitute a public domain are examined by James Boyle.

J. Boyle, 'The second enclosure movement and the construction of the public domain' (Winter/Spring 2003) 66(33) Law and Contemporary Problems 58–62

By defense of the public domain, I do not mean mere usage of the word. Though 'public domain' was a term widely used to describe public lands in the United States, the intellectual property usage of the term comes to us from the French *domaine public* which made its way into American law in the late nineteenth century via the language of the Berne Convention. But at what point do we find a defense of the public domain, rather than merely a criticism of the costs of intellectual property?

Many starting points are defensible. In the United States, the work of Ralph Brown and Ben Kaplan is sometimes mentioned as initiating this way of looking at things. The Supreme Court itself can plausibly be given some credit. In a 1966 patent case, repeatedly citing the work of Jefferson, the court made it clear that the public domain has a constitutional dimension:

> The Congress in the exercise of the patent power may not overreach the restraints imposed by the stated constitutional purpose. Nor may it enlarge the patent monopoly without regard to the innovation, advancement or social benefit gained thereby. Moreover, Congress may not authorize the issuance of patents whose effects are to remove existent knowledge from the public domain, or to restrict free access to materials already available.

This is a remarkable statement. It goes beyond mere recitation of the Framer's attitude toward the dangers posed by monopoly, and makes an affirmative defense of the public domain. Notice how the limitations are stated as additive and not as mutually equivalent, or even as mere corollaries; the Court does not say that 'enlargement of the patent monopoly must promote innovation and *this limits* Congress's power to remove material from the public domain.' Instead, it postulates an existent public domain and makes it unconstitutional under the patent clause for Congress to privatize any portion of that domain. There are echoes here of 'the public trust doctrine' which restricts the state's ability to privatize public resources or waterways and turn them over to private parties. Notice also that the court gives the public domain both direct and indirect protection: Protection from measures which formally create patent rights over portions of the public domain, but also from those which also merely 'restrict free access to the materials already available'.

Thus, there are a number of possible places where one could say, 'the defense of the public domain begins here'. But, like most people, I attribute central importance to the writing of my friend and colleague David Lange, whose article *Recognizing the Public Domain* really initiated contemporary study of the subject. Lange's article was driven by indignation about, indeed eloquently sarcastic ridicule of, expansions of intellectual property protection in the 1960s and 1970s. Lange claims that one major cause of this expansion was that intellectual property rights are intangible, abstract, and thus, imprecise. He argues, in a way that would have been familiar to Macaulay or Jefferson, that we should cease the reckless expansion. But he also argues that 'recognition of new intellectual property interests should be offset today by equally deliberate recognition of individual rights in the public domain'.

Lange is not arguing:

> that intellectual property is undeserving of protection, but rather that such protection as it gets ought to reflect its unique susceptibility to conceptual imprecision and to infinite replication. These attributes seem to me to require the recognition of two fundamental principles. One is that intellectual property theory must always accept something akin to a 'no-man's land' at the boundaries; doubtful cases of infringement ought always to be resolved in favour of the defendant. The other is that no exclusive interest should ever have affirmative recognition unless its conceptual opposite is also recognized. Each right ought to be marked off clearly against the public domain.

But what does this *mean*? What is the nature of these 'individual rights in the public domain'? Who holds them? Indeed, what *is* the public domain? Does it consist only of works that are completely unprotected, say books whose copyright term has lapsed? Does it include *aspects* of works that are unprotectable, such as the ideas or the facts on which an argument is based, even if the expression of that argument is protected? What about limitations on exclusive rights, privileges of users, or affirmative defenses, are those part of the public domain too? Is the parody-able aspect of your novel in the public domain? What about the short quote on which a critical argument is mounted? Earlier in this article, I discussed the 'commons of the mind'. What is the relationship between the public domain—however defined—and the commons? If the public domain is so great, why? What does it do for us? What is its role? These questions can be reduced to two: (1) What is the public domain? (2) Why should we focus on it? In the following pages, I will argue that the answer to the first question depends on the answer to the second.

Work that followed Lange's article offered various answers to the questions posed. For example, Lindberg and Patterson's book *The Nature of Copyright* (L. R. Patterson and Stanley W Lindberg, *The Nature of Copyright: A Law of Users' Rights* (1991)) reverses the polarity from the normal depiction, and portrays copyright as a law of users' rights. The public domain is the figure and copyright the ground. The various privileges and defenses are not exceptions, they are at the heart of copyright, correctly understood. Copyright is, in fact, a system designed to feed the public domain providing temporary and narrowly limited rights, themselves subject to considerable restrictions even during their existence—all with the ultimate goal of promoting free access.

Jessica Litman's fine 1990 article, *The Public Domain*, portrays the public domain's primary function as allowing copyright law to continue to work notwithstanding the unrealistic, individualistic idea of creativity it depends on:

> The public domain rescues us from this dilemma. It permits us to continue to exhort originality without acknowledging that our claims to take originality seriously are mostly pretense. It furnishes a crucial device to an otherwise unworkable system by reserving the raw material of authorship to the commons, thus leaving that raw material available for other authors to use. The public domain thus permits the law of copyright to avoid a confrontation with the poverty of some of the assumptions on which it is based.

Litman's definition of the public domain is both clear and terse: '[A] commons that includes those aspects of copyrighted works which copyright does not protect.' Precisely because she sees the function of the public domain as allowing the kinds of additive and interstitial creation that the language of individual originality fails to capture, her *definition* of the public domain includes the recyclable, unprotected elements in existing copyrighted works as well as those works that are not protected at all. Form follows function.

Yochai Benkler takes a slightly different approach. He follows Litman in rejecting the traditional, absolutist conception of the public domain, a conception which included only those things which are totally unprotected by copyright:

> The particular weakness of the traditional defintion of the public domain is that it evokes an intuition about the baseline, while not in fact completely describing it. When one calls certain information 'in the public domain', one means that it is information whose use, absent special reasons to think otherwise, is permissible to anyone. When information is properly subject to copyright, the assumption (again absent specific factors to the contrary) is that its use is *not* similarly allowed to anyone but the owner and his or her licensees. The limited, term-of-art (public domain) does not include some important instances that, as a descriptive matter, are assumed generally to be permissible. For example, the traditional definition of public domain would treat short quotes for purposes of critical review as a fair use—hence as an affirmative defense—and not as a use in the public domain. It would be odd, however, to describe our system of copyright law as one in which users assume that they may not include a brief quotation in a critical review of its source. I venture that the opposite is true: such use generally is considered permissible, absent peculiar facts to the contary.

Benkler's alternative definition, however, does not include every privileged use—such as, for example, the fair use privilege that I am able to vindicate only after litigating an intensely complicated case that involves highly specific factual inquiries.

> The functional definition therefore would be: The public domain is a range of uses of information that any person is privileged to make absent individualized facts that make a particular use by a particular person unprivileged. Conversely, the enclosed domain is the range of uses of information as to which someone has an exclusive right, and that no other person may make absent individualized facts that indicated permission from the holder of the right or otherwise privilege the specific use under the stated facts. These definitions add to the legal rules additionally thought of as the public domain, the range of privileged uses that are 'easy cases'.

The key to Benkler's analysis is his focus on the public domain's role in information production and use by all of us in our roles as consumers, citizens and future creators. We need to focus on those works, and aspects of works, that the public can notably free without having to go through a highly individualized factual inquiry. 'Free' meaning what? Earlier in this essay

I asked what we mean when we speak of the freedom that the public domain will allow. Free trade in expression and innovation, as opposed to monopoly? Free access to expression and innovation, as opposed to access for pay? Or free access to innovation and expression, in the sense of not being subject to the right of another person to pick and choose who is given access, even if all have to pay some flat fee? Or is it common ownership or control that we seek, including the communal right to forbid certain kinds of uses of the shared resources? I *think* Benkler is arguing that the most important question here is whether lay people would know that a particular piece or aspect of information is free—in the sense of being *both* uncontrolled by anyone else and costless.

In this piece, Boyle identifies a number of different models of the public domain. We have noted earlier that others have described the public domain as a commons. However, as Boyle rightly points out, the public domain is not the same as a commons, although many commentators, such as Litman, quoted in the above extract, use the terms interchangeably. The crucial difference is that a commons, as it is generally understood, will incorporate intellectual resources which have been developed communally and which have a positive value. By contrast, the public domain is a repository for intellectual products which will become valuable only when they are mixed with the labour of others. Another key difference between the commons and the public domain is that while it is easy to see how intellectual produce taken from the public domain and mixed with the labour of others might be protected under existing intellectual property laws, it is less obvious how the communally produced intellectual resources of the commons fit within the present intellectual property regime.

1.4.2 TRADITIONAL KNOWLEDGE

In our hypotheticals, we described the coffee produced by the residents of the Excot area of Ethiopia. By isolating the DNA of the coffee, CoffeeCo has been able to obtain exclusive rights to the use of that DNA in coffee production. CoffeeCo would argue that the DNA was a natural resource in the public domain. By mixing its labour with the plant, that is by isolating its DNA, CoffeeCo would claim that it deserves to receive the benefit of intellectual property protection for its own coffee. However, the coffee producers of Excot would answer that the coffee was not always present in nature. Rather, it was the product of selective breeding by the community of Excot coffee growers over decades, possibly hundreds of years.

At present, there is urgent and wide-ranging debate as to whether and indeed how the interests of those who produce intellectual products communally and over time should be protected. The general term used to characterize the skills which lie behind the production of these resources (often biological or genetic) is 'traditional knowledge'. As we shall see from the extract below, it is developing countries, many of whom are rich in traditional knowledge, who are leading the call for the introduction of new forms of IPRs which would both protect traditional knowledge from exploitation by those who did not have a hand in producing it and allow those who are responsible for its production to protect it from appropriation. This debate has been given added urgency by the passage of the TRIPS agreement. As we have seen, TRIPS imposes a uniform regime of IPRs on all members of the WTO, but its critics suggest those rights do not acknowledge the claims of traditional knowledge. In 2000, WIPO established an Intergovernmental Committee on IP and Genetic Resources, Traditional Knowledge and Folklore in response to these concerns, which recently held its twelfth meeting. In the extract below, Daniel Gervais looks at traditional knowledge and the challenges it poses for our current intellectual property laws.

D. J. Gervais, 'The internationalization of intellectual property: New challenges from the very old and the very new' (2001–2) 12 Fordham Intellectual Property Media and Entertainment Law Journal 929, 955–65

i. The Importance of Traditional Knowledge

The expression 'traditional knowledge' is a shorter form of 'traditional knowledge, innovations and practices'. It includes a broad range of subject matters, for example traditional agricultural, biodiversity-related and medicinal knowledge and folklore. In the Model Provisions for National Laws on the Protection of Expressions of Folklore Against Illicit Exploitation and Other Prejudicial Actions, the WIPO and UNESCO define folklore as 'production consisting of characteristic elements of the traditional individuals reflecting the traditional artistic expectations of such a community...' The protection of traditional knowledge is progressively taking center stage in global discussions concerning intellectual property and trade.

There are several reasons for the issue's sudden move to the forefront. First, a large number of countries believe that up to now they have not derived great benefits from 'traditional' forms of intellectual property, yet find themselves rich with traditional knowledge, especially genetic resources and folklore. They would like to exploit these resources, and several major companies share this interest. The second reason is the growing political importance of aboriginal communities in several countries.

...

ii. The Nature of the Challenge

Why is traditional knowledge such a challenge for the intellectual property framework? Expressions of folklore and several other forms of traditional knowledge do not qualify for protection because they are too old and are, therefore, in the public domain. Providing exclusive rights of any kind for an unlimited period of time would seem to go against the principle that intellectual property can be awarded only for a limited period of time, thus ensuring the return of intellectual property to the public domain for others to use. That way, it promotes the constitutional objective of progress in science and the useful arts. In other cases, the author of the material is not identifiable and there is thus no 'rightsholder' in the usual sense of the term. In fact, the author or inventor is often a large and diffuse group of people and the same 'work' or invention may have several versions and incarnations. Textile patterns, musical rhythms and dances are good examples of this kind of material. Additionally, expressions of folklore are refined and evolve over time.

Apart from the above-mentioned reasons for excluding some forms of traditional knowledge, there is clearly a lot of traditional material that is unfit for protection as intellectual property in any form. Examples include spiritual beliefs, methods of governance, languages, human remains and biological and genetic resources in their natural state, i.e. without any knowledge concerning their medicinal use. With the exception of these types of material not proper subject matter for protection per se, however, most other forms of traditional knowledge *could* qualify for copyright or patent protection if they had been created or invented in the usual sense. In response, holders of traditional knowledge argue that the current intellectual property regime was designed by Western countries for Western countries. It is certainly true that the main intellectual property agreements, including the Berne Convention, the Paris Convention and the more recent TRIPS Agreement were negotiated among mostly industrialized countries.

After considering the difficulties of incorporating traditional knowledge within the subject matter protected by copyright and patents, Gervais continues:

Property rights, as they are understood in Western legal systems, often do not exist in indigenous and local communities that hold traditional knowledge. In fact, because of its exclusionary effect, they now tend to see the attempt to obtain property rights on derivatives of their traditional knowledge as 'piracy'. Regarding the pharmaceutical, seed and agrochemical industries, they coined the term 'biopiracy' to denote the extraction and utilization of traditional knowledge, associated biological and genetic resources, and the acquisition of intellectual property rights on inventions derived from such knowledge or resources without providing for benefit-sharing with the individuals or community that provided the knowledge or resources.

iii. Assessing the Criticism

Some of the criticism leveled at the current intellectual system concerning its exclusionary effect is fair, but may be dealt with by relatively minor changes to current practices. For example, for applications for patents concerning drugs or other products that are derived from traditional knowledge sources, prior art searches could include traditional knowledge sources to ensure that the invention is indeed novel and non-obvious as required by patent laws worldwide. That said, cases in which patents should not have been granted are examples of bad patents, not of a bad patent system. Clearly, in that respect a dialogue has to be established among holders of traditional knowledge, the private sector and governments. 'Greater awareness-raising may assist to dispel certain misconceptions concerning intellectual property and result in more technical, finely-calibrated and nuanced assessments of the traditional knowledge/intellectual property nexus.'

Arguments used to show that the current intellectual property system cannot protect traditional knowledge are not all convincing either. The fact that a community owns traditional knowledge does not in itself exclude all forms of intellectual property protection. The example of collective marks and geographical indications show that in certain cases, rights can be granted to 'representatives' of a group or a community. There are also real property law concepts that would most closely match the needs of the traditional knowledge community and could perhaps be applied to intellectual property. The best example is probably the concept of 'communal property'.

[**Gervais** then goes on to ask how nonetheless traditional knowledge can be protected. He concludes that there is a second question which needs answering, that is on what basis intellectual property, itself, should be protected, as a way to answering the first.]

The challenge of protecting traditional knowledge forces one to think about what intellectual property actually is. An 'intellectual property-like' system could be adopted but this would beg the question of *what it is*, if *not* intellectual property. In other words, *why is it not intellectual property?* If we look at the constitutional 'requirement' that intellectual property promote the progress of science and useful arts, why would certain forms of traditional knowledge not be protected by intellectual property? Put differently, in the absence of a statutory exception, should intellectual property be defined by the common characteristics of current forms of intellectual property, namely (a) identifiable authors or inventors, (b) an identifiable work or invention or other object, and (c) defined restricted acts in relation to the said object without the authorization of the rightsholders? Or are these historical accidents, as it were, of the nineteenth century world in which these forms of intellectual property emerged? And yet, even if that is the case, how can one protect amorphous objects or categories of objects and grant exclusive rights to an ill-defined (and ill-definable) community or group of people?

These are the questions coming from traditional knowledge holders.

Gervais concludes his discussion of traditional knowledge by asking whether our current conceptions of intellectual property, particularly in relation to who we identify as creators of IP and what we deem to be appropriate subject matter for IP protection, should be rethought. These assumptions are, as he says, an accident of history. Similar questions might be raised in relation to intellectual property and new forms of technology. The introduction of both the Internet and the digital technology on which it depends have raised a number of pressing problems for the present intellectual property regime. For example, the Internet facilitates collaborative creation between many unrelated individuals and the resulting works may not fit easily with the authorial paradigm which dates from the nineteenth century. The ability of a single, private individual to make and distribute multiple copies of a protected work, via the Internet, may again fit uneasily into a legal framework which was intended to be directed primarily against unlicensed commercial copying. These and other issues, which are raised by the new technology, will be examined later. Suffice to say, that while the present intellectual property regime has changed markedly since the nineteenth century, and indeed is changing now, it will inevitably incorporate legal rules which appear to contradict our present commonsense understanding of what is deserving of protection and to what extent.

FURTHER READING

M. Blakeney, 'The protection of traditional knowledge under intellectual property law' (2000) 22(6) EIPR, 251–61.

N. S. Gopalakrishnan, 'TRIPs and protection of traditional knowledge of genetic resources: New challenges to the patents system' (2005) 27(1) EIPR, 11–18.

E. Lee, 'The public's domain: The evolution of legal restraints on the government's power to control public access through secrecy or intellectual property' (2003–04) 55 Hastings LJ 91, 103.

COPYRIGHT I:

SUBSISTENCE, OWNERSHIP,
AND EXPLOITATION

2.1 INTRODUCTION

Copyright may be described as a set of exclusive rights in relation to, broadly speaking, cultural creations. As such, it underpins an array of cultural works, such as novels, poetry, educational texts, newspapers, photographs, drawings, paintings, sculpture, films, music, and plays. In our daily lives these are works that we regularly enjoy, consume, and use and they may be a source of entertainment, education, pleasure, or profit. The importance, therefore, of copyright law cannot be underestimated. Indeed, one needs only to mention Hollywood, Bollywood, and the US record industry, to be reminded of how much may be at stake when it comes to copyright-protected material. Copyright, thus, has a global significance, but its nature is territorial (i.e. the exclusive rights that it grants are limited to a particular territory, such as the UK). This has led to attempts at international and regional levels to ensure some basic uniformity of approach, through various conventions, which will be discussed below. The focus of this chapter will be on elucidating the principles of UK copyright law, but it should never be far from one's mind that this law sits within and is increasingly framed by international and European imperatives.

2.2 HISTORY

In order to better appreciate UK copyright law this section will attempt briefly to place it in historical context. The origin of copyright law is linked to one particularly important technological development—the printing press—and its later development has also been significantly shaped by technological change. In the 15th and 16th centuries, many European states were in the habit of granting printing privileges to printers. In England, printing privileges first appeared in 1518 and were granted via royal prerogative. Also in existence in the 16th century was a guild system for the printing of books, which was run by the Stationers' Company. The Stationers' Company derived its authority from a Royal Charter of 1557, which granted the guild a monopoly on the printing of books. The right to print a book was obtained by entering it in the company's register and only members of the company might own 'copies' of books. The guild was self-regulating and also had powers to enforce claims of infringement against unlicensed printers. In return for this monopoly, the Stationers' Company was expected to implement the Crown's censorship policies to prevent the publication of seditious and heretical books. The monopoly of the Stationers' Company over the book trade and its censorship role was cemented by the Licensing Act 1662. Thus, early copyright law was very much a mixture of trade regulation and censorship.

A crucial turning point, however, came in 1695 when the Licensing Act 1662 lapsed and with it the privileges and powers of the Stationers' Company. Attempts by the guild to persuade Parliament to restore the powers under the Act were unsuccessful, largely because of concerns about the damaging effects of monopolies. But renewed lobbying efforts on the part of the Stationers' Company led to the first copyright Act, The Statute of Anne 1710, which was entitled, 'An Act for the Encouragement of Learning, by vesting the Copies of Printed Books in the Authors or Purchasers of such Copies, during the Times therein mentioned'. Anyone, i.e. printer or author, was eligible for protection under the Act by enrolling their book in the register of the Stationers' Company. The Act gave authors and proprietors of 'copies' (or manuscripts) the right to print and reprint their works. This protection was for a term of 14 years, with the possibility of a renewal for a further 14 years if the author was still alive.

Much has been written about the Statute of Anne and its significance for copyright law. Some commentators argue that it was a way of securing the interests of printers and booksellers (albeit through using the rhetorical device of 'author'), while others have characterized it as a device for breaking the printing monopolies. Others suggest that the statute in fact brokered a deal between authors, booksellers, *and* the reading public. Certainly, it can be said that with the introduction of the Act, the roles of censorship and printing were decoupled.

The Statute of Anne was also a source of considerable controversy during its existence. Once the first copyrights under the Act began to expire and attempts to extend the term of protection failed, the London publishers argued that perpetual copyright existed at common law. The issue became whether or not the Statute of Anne was exhaustive of protection, or whether it merely supplemented a common law right to property that was perpetual. Legal disputes, as well as much public debate ensued and this became known as the 'Literary Property Debate'. The culmination of the debate was the case of *Donaldson v Becket* (1774), in which the House of Lords had to decide whether Donaldson (a Scottish bookseller) had infringed any (common law) rights that existed in the poem *The Seasons*. What exactly was decided in *Donaldson* has itself been the subject of some confusion, caused partly by the misreporting of some of the lords' opinions and partly by the fact that the common law judges gave their opinion to the House of Lords but the entirety of the House voted, it seems, contrary to the opinion of the judges. One view of *Donaldson* is that the House of Lords held that the Statute of Anne took away any common law rights that existed in published works. Another view is that the House in fact denied the existence of common law copyright. Whichever view is taken, it is fair to say that the decision at least quelled the Literary Property Debate.

The early 19th century saw the Statute of Anne replaced by the Copyright Act 1814. The Act extended copyright in literary works to 28 years after publication and, if the author was still alive at the end of this period, for the remainder of his life. This extension of term was relatively uncontroversial, in stark contrast to later proposals put forward by Thomas Noon Talfourd in 1837. Talfourd proposed a term of life of the author plus 60 years, which met with intense opposition from publishers, printers and radical politicians. Eventually, a compromise was reached and the Copyright Amendment Act 1842 provided for a term of either the life of the author plus 7 years or 42 years from the first publication (whichever was longer). This was the first time that term of protection had been calculated on a post-mortem basis.

What of creative works other than literary ones, such as plays, music, and art works? The 18th and 19th centuries saw other types of creations being protected on a subject-specific basis. For example, the Engravers' Act 1735, gave persons who invented and designed engravings and etchings, 'the sole right and liberty of printing and reprinting their work' for a term of 14 years from first publication. This was the first time copyright extended to matter other than literary works. The Models and Busts Act 1798 granted exclusive rights to persons who created new models or casts of humans or animal figures for a period of 14 years. The Dramatic Literary Property Act 1833 was the first time in which authors of dramatic manuscripts were granted rights of reproduction and public performance and this protection lasted for 28 years from the day of first publication. Paintings, drawings, and photographs did not attract copyright protection until the passing of the Fine Arts Copyright Act 1862. This Act gave authors of 'original' paintings, drawings, and photographs the sole and exclusive right of 'copying, engraving, reproducing, and multiplying' their work 'by any means and of any size'. This was the first occasion on which the requirement of 'originality' was introduced (a requirement discussed at length later).

Thus, by the end of the 19th century it is fair to say that copyright was a chaotic collection of subject-specific statutes. Attempts to codify this legislation (in 1837 and in 1857) failed. It was not until the beginning of the 20th century that codification successfully occurred in the form of the Copyright Act 1911. The 1911 Act conferred copyright protection on several works, including some that had previously been unprotected (works of architecture, sound recordings, and films). Protection was granted to unpublished *and* published works and, as such, common law copyright in unpublished works was abolished. The term of protection was for the life of the author plus 50 years and all formalities, in particular the requirement of registration with the Stationers' Company, were abolished. The 1911 Act was exported to numerous Commonwealth states. As such, it had an enormous influence in shaping the copyright laws of many common law countries.

Following a review of the 1911 Act by the Gregory Committee, the Copyright Act 1956 was introduced. Protection was extended to sound and television broadcasts, along with typographical arrangements of published editions. These new rights were grouped together with rights in relation to sound recordings and films and were classified as 'subject matter'. This was in contrast to 'works' (i.e. literary, dramatic, musical, and artistic works). The 1956 Act was later amended to provide protection for cable transmissions and software.

A review of the 1956 Act by the Whitford Committee resulted in the Copyright Designs and Patents Act 1988 ('CDPA'). Importantly, the CDPA removed the distinction between 'works' and 'subject matter' and classified all creations as 'works'. The protection given to copyright owners was extended significantly, to include distribution and rental rights, and authors were granted for the first time 'moral rights' in their works. Performers rights were also included in the CDPA, along with a new unregistered design right. The CDPA has been amended on numerous occasions since its enactment, largely to implement the plethora of EU directives concerning copyright law. The CDPA, as most recently amended, is the law currently governing copyright in the UK.

FURTHER READING

M. F. Makeen, *Copyright in a Global Information Society: The scope of copyright protection under international, US, UK and French law* (London: Kluwer, 2000), pp. 1–12, 23–4.

B. Sherman and L. Bently, *The Making of Modern Intellectual Property Law* (Cambridge: Cambridge University Press, 1999).

R. Deazley, *On the Origin of the Right to Copy: Charting the movement of copyright law in eighteenth-century Britain (1695–1775)* (Oxford: Hart, 2004).

L. R. Patterson, *Copyright in Historical Perspective* (Nashville, TN: Vanderbilt University Press, 1968).

AHRC Primary Sources on Copyright (1450–1900) <http://copyright-project.law.cam.ac.uk/htdocs/index.html>.

2.3 JUSTIFICATIONS

In Chapter 1, we explored the justifications for intellectual property law generally, including natural rights, utilitarian, and economic rationales. When it comes to copyright in particular, the economic and natural-rights justifications are frequently invoked. The applicability of these justifications to copyright is discussed in the following extract.

M. Spence, 'Justifying copyright' in D. McClean and K. Schubert,
Dear Images: Art, copyright and culture (Manchester: Ridinghouse, 2002), pp. 389–403

Economic Justifications for Copyright

The economic justifications for copyright focus on the need to provide incentives for the creation and dissemination of creative works. For economic theorists the intended beneficiary of the copyright system is the community as a whole, which demands the production of, and access to, as many creative works as possible. It is assumed that, in perfect conditions, the market will ensure the production of goods and those goods will be allocated to the party who values them the most. There will be incentive to produce goods because their selling price will allow a producer to recoup both the costs of production and the benefit of the goods to a purchaser. But creative works are said to be 'public goods' in that it is difficult to exclude non-purchasers from their enjoyment. Because of the difficulty of excluding non-purchasers, there will be no incentive to create and to disseminate works. They will be under-produced unless the law intervenes to cure this 'market failure'. Even assuming that the rights given to the copyright owner constitute some type of 'monopoly' and entail the dead-weight loss associated with all monopolies, the advantages of the copyright system in curing this market failure are said to outweigh those losses. Other potential methods of curing the relevant market failure, such as systems of state or private patronage, are seen as less desirable in that they involve the centralization of decisions about which types of works will be produced.

. . .

The problem with the economic justification of copyright is that: (i) there is much which copyright protects that would be produced and disseminated even without the incentive effects of the copyright regime, and (ii) it is difficult to structure copyright such that the monopoly losses associated with the regime are no greater than those required to ensure the production and dissemination of a given category of work, especially given the wide range of subject matter that copyright protects.

...

Deontological Justifications for Copyright

The economic arguments for copyright assume that the regime exists to serve a public purpose. But it may be that the regime exists, not to advance the common weal, but to give force to certain ethical obligations owed to creators.

...

The Argument from Desert

It is a claim frequently made that the creator of a work 'deserves' control over its use. There are two ways in which such a desert claim may be established. First, a creator might deserve control over the use of the work as a reward for her efforts in producing it. Second, a creator might deserve control over the use of the work as a reward for the contribution that it makes to her culture...Desert is an uncertain concept that has only recently become the subject of rigorous philosophical analysis. But, even assuming that the concept of desert can be clearly expounded, it proves a difficult basis for the justification of copyright. This is for three reasons.

First, there is no direct correlation between a creator's effort or contribution and the works which copyright might be expected to protect. If it is effort that is deserving of reward, then the question arises what the minimum threshold of effort might be for a work to be deserving of protection and whether works that required little effort should be protected. Copyright would be in danger of protecting only the perspiring, and not the inspired, creator. If it is contribution that is deserving of reward, then the question becomes what level of contribution is deserving.

...

Second, even if the creator of a work can establish her desert there may be good reasons for not recognizing her claim to control the use of the work. She may already have been rewarded in other ways...She may have been amply rewarded in the payment she receives and copyright protection might be more than she deserves.

...

Third, there is no reason why, even if the creator of the work deserves something as a reward for effort or contribution, it ought necessarily to be the control over the use of the work that copyright affords. We reward those who work hard to establish world peace and thereby contribute to our public life, with gratitude, praise and, perhaps, a Nobel prize. It is hard to see that the creator of an artistic wok expends more effort, or contributes more, than such people.

...

The Argument from Personhood

This argument is that a work is an embodiment of the personality of the creator. Control over the work is essential to secure the creator's control over her own personality...There are two principal difficulties with this approach.

First, it is questionable just how many works constitute, or are intended to constitute, an embodiment of the creator's personality.

...

Second, even assuming personality to mean something as discernible as self-presentation, it is unclear precisely how much control over her self-presentation a creator ought to be afforded...such control might be appropriate in contexts in which there is a threat that unauthorized use will change the meaning of the work in a way that does the creator harm. But that she ought to have control over her self-presentation to the extent of being able to prohibit the reproduction or publication of her work in a way which is perfectly faithful to its meaning though, perhaps, at a time or by someone not of her choosing, is far more questionable.

...

The Argument from Personal Autonomy

This attractive argument flows from the intuition that valuing personal autonomy must involve granting an individual at least some control over those things with which she is most closely associated: to allow her to carve out an area of individual dominion. If a creator can show a close association with a particular work, then respect for her personal autonomy may require that she be given at least some degree of control over its use.

...

First, none of the usual arguments from personal autonomy can establish a nexus between the creator and her work such that recognition of her right to control the work is essential to recognition of her personal autonomy.

...

Second, against the claim that control over a creator's work is essential to the protection of her personal autonomy, must be set the claim that the grant of such control is a limitation of the autonomy of those who would seek to use the work without her permission. It is therefore necessary to demonstrate that the impact on the creator's personal autonomy of refusing her control over the work would outweigh the impact on the world-be user's autonomy of granting the creator such control.

In your view, which is the most persuasive justification when it comes to copyright—is it economic or deontological (i.e. natural rights) and why? How important is it, do you think, for rationales to underpin a copyright system, i.e. what should be their role? Finally, which, if any, of the above justifications is likely to be favoured in the UK? Numerous commentators associate common law copyright systems, such as the UK, with economic or utilitarian justifications. Others, however, are less convinced that UK copyright law has a clear rationale. By way of contrast, commentators frequently cite civil law authors' rights systems, such as France, as having clear natural-rights foundations that are reflected in robust protection for authors. As you progress through this chapter, it will be important to bear in mind the various copyright justifications and ask whether any one of them adequately explains the principles of UK copyright law.

FURTHER READING

T. Aplin, *Copyright Law in the Digital Society* (Oxford: Hart, 2005), Ch. 2.

P. Geller, 'Must copyright be for ever caught between marketplace and authorship norms?' in Sherman and Strowel (eds.), *Of Authors and Origins* (Oxford: Clarendon, 1994), pp. 159–201.

2.4 SOURCES OF LAW

2.4.1 INTERNATIONAL

A collection of international conventions and treaties exist to regulate copyright law. As such, it is vital to understand the extent of the obligations imposed by these instruments and we consider the most important of them below.

2.4.1.1 Berne Convention on the Protection of Literary and Artistic Works 1886 ('Berne Convention')

The Berne Convention occupies an extremely important place in international copyright law since it was the first multilateral treaty on copyright law. Signed in 1886, membership of the Berne Union has grown from 10 to 164 countries.[1] As such, the Berne Convention has had a dominant influence on the development of copyright standards at an international, regional, and national level and this has been reinforced by the TRIPS Agreement 1994, which incorporates most of the Berne Convention obligations.

Since its inception, the Berne Convention has been revised on several occasions—in 1908 at the Berlin Revision Conference, in 1928 at the Rome Revision Conference, in 1948 at the Brussels Revision Conference, and in 1967 and 1971 at the Stockholm and Paris Revision Conferences, respectively.[2] In terms of membership, the UK, France, and Germany were three of the original signatories to the Convention. Other major countries did not join until much later—the US on 1 March 1989, Russia on 13 March 1995, and China on 15 October 1992.[3]

The ambit of the Berne Convention is succinctly summarized by Article 1, which states:

> The countries to which this Convention applies constitute a Union for the protection of the rights of authors in their literary and artistic works.

According to Article 3 of the Berne Convention protection applies to the following categories of persons:

- authors who are nationals of a Union country for their unpublished or published works
- authors who are not nationals of a Union country, but have their habitual residence in a Union country for their unpublished or published works
- authors who are *not* nationals of a Union country, but whose works are first published in a Union country or simultaneously published in a Union country and non-Union country.[4]

---

[1] As at 1 Sept. 2008.

[2] There are also the 1896 and 1914 protocols to the Berne Convention.

[3] For details of contracting parties see <http://www.wipo.int/treaties/en/ShowResults.jsp?lang=en&treaty_id=15>.

[4] Simultaneous publication is publication in a Union country within 30 days of first publication in a non-Union country.

In relation to cinematographic works, Article 4 states that protection shall apply, even if Article 3 is not fulfilled to:

- authors of cinematographic works the maker of which has his headquarters or habitual residence in a Union country
- authors of architectural works erected in a country of the Union or of other works incorporated in a building or other structure located in a Union country.

Two fundamental principles underpin the Berne Convention—that of national treatment and minimum rights. They are both contained in Article 5(1) of the Berne Convention, which states:

> Authors shall enjoy, in respect of works for which they are protected under this Convention, in countries of the Union other than the country of origin, the rights which their respective laws do now or may hereafter grant to their nationals, as well as the rights specially granted by this Convention.

The principle of national treatment may be explained as follows: Union country A is obliged to confer the same rights on an author from Union country B as it confers on nationals of Union country A. In other words, a country of the Berne Union cannot discriminate, when it comes to copyright protection, between its own nationals and authors from other countries of the Union. This means that UK authors can expect to go to France and receive the same copyright protection that is offered to French authors and vice versa.

There are four exceptions to the principle of national treatment. These relate to: the *droit de suite*, which is a right to receive a percentage of the sale price on original works of art and original manuscripts that are subsequently sold;[5] duration of protection;[6] works of applied art and industrial designs and models;[7] and the exception in Article 6 that was crafted to deal with the United States before it became a member of the Berne Union.

The principle of minimum rights requires Union country A to offer the rights specially granted by the Berne Convention to authors of all Union countries, except Union country A. In other words, the minimum standards of protection that are contained in the Berne Convention apply only to authors from *other* Berne countries and no Berne member is obliged to accord this protection to their own authors. That said, most Berne countries do offer the minimum rights to their own authors as well. For a Berne member to do otherwise would be to privilege foreign authors and create a sense of unfairness, as well as unpopularity.

The minimum rights that must be offered have steadily expanded since the Convention was signed in 1886. They include a collection of economic rights (which may be subject to certain permitted reservations, exceptions, or limitations), moral rights, and duration of protection. Of course, if Berne countries so wish they may offer protection in excess of these minimum standards. As and when the Berne Convention minimum rights are relevant to explaining UK copyright law, they will be discussed below.

FURTHER READING

L. Bently and B. Sherman, 'Great Britain and the signing of the Berne Convention in 1886' [2001] Journal of the Copyright Society of the USA 311.

---

[5] Art. 14*ter*(2).   [6] Art. 7(8).   [7] Art. 2(7).

S. Ricketson and J. Ginsburg, *International Copyright and Neighbouring Rights: The Berne Convention and beyond* (2nd edn., Oxford: Oxford University Press, 2005).

2.4.1.2 International Convention for the Protection of Performers, Producers of Phonograms and Broadcasting Organizations 1961 ('Rome Convention')

Technological developments post-World War I led to a new trio of interests that sought copyright protection. These were producers of phonograms (i.e. sound recordings), performers, and broadcasters. Sound recordings lacked any kind of international protection and were vulnerable to use without remuneration, particularly by broadcasters. Broadcasters had no rights in relation to the broadcasts that they made and for performers their live performances could be fixed and disseminated in a manner not previously possible. Thus it was at the Brussels Revision Conference 1948 that performers, sound recording producers, and broadcasters sought protection under the Berne Convention. This was unsuccessful, however, because these persons were not seen as 'authors of literary and artistic works' within the meaning of the Convention. Instead, a resolution was passed that the governments of the Union should study the way in which protection could be granted to these interests, without prejudice to the rights of authors. Negotiations subsequently occurred during the 1950s between three organizations: the International Federation of Musicians (representing performers), the International Federation of the Phonographic Industry (representing phonogram producers), and the European Broadcasting Union (representing broadcasting organizations in Europe). The International Federation of Actors and the International Federation of Variety Artists were also involved. Three international governmental organizations promoted and sustained the progress of the negotiations: the ILO, UNESCO, and WIPO (known then as the United International Bureaux for the Protection of IP (BIRPI)). The conference for the preparation of the Draft Convention was held at The Hague in 1960 and this was followed in 1961 by the Diplomatic Conference on the Protection of Performers, Producers of Phonograms and Broadcasting Organizations, in which a total of 41 states participated. The signatories to this Convention has now grown to 86,[8] of which the UK is one.

The protection under the Rome Convention in no way affects the protection of copyright in literary and artistic works.[9] The beneficiaries of protection are, unsurprisingly, performers, phonogram producers, and broadcasting organizations. The two basic principles of the Rome Convention are national treatment and the obligation of Contracting States to afford minimum rights.

The conditions for national treatment differ depending on whether it is being claimed for performers, phonogram producers, or broadcasting organizations. For performers, national treatment shall be granted if either: (i) the performance takes place in another Contracting State; (ii) the performance is incorporated in a phonogram which is protected by Article 5 of the Rome Convention; or (iii) the performance is carried by a broadcast which is protected by Article 6 of the Convention.[10] In the case of producers of phonograms, national treatment shall be granted by Contracting States if: (i) the producer of the phonogram is a national of another Contracting State; (ii) the first fixation of the sound was made in another Contracting State; or (iii) the phonogram was first published in another Contracting State.[11] Finally, each Contracting State shall grant national treatment to broadcasting

8 See <http://www.wipo.int/treaties/en/ShowResults.jsp?lang=en&treaty_id=17>.
9 Art. 1.   10 Art. 4.   11 Art. 5.

organizations if either of the following conditions is met: (i) the headquarters of the broadcasting organization is situated in another Contracting State; (ii) the broadcast was transmitted from a transmitter situated in another Contracting State.[12]

According to Article 7, performers are to be granted the possibility of preventing the broadcasting and communication to the public, without their consent, of their performance; the fixation without their consent of their unfixed performance; and the reproduction without their consent of a fixation of their performance if the original fixation itself was made without their consent or the reproduction is made for purposes different from those for which the performers gave their consent. It is important to note that once a performer has consented to the incorporation of his or her performance in a visual or audio-visual fixation, these rights do not apply.

Both producers of phonograms and broadcasting organizations have stronger rights, insofar as they are exclusive rights, as opposed to merely 'the possibility of preventing' certain acts. This latter formulation was included for performers' rights in order to allow Contracting States flexibility as to how they protected performers. This enabled, for example, the UK to continue to protect performers through the use of criminal sanctions only.

Producers of phonograms are granted the right to authorize or prohibit the direct or indirect reproduction of their phonograms.[13] Where a phonogram is published for commercial purposes, or a reproduction of such phonogram, is used directly for broadcasting or any communication to the public, then a single equitable remuneration is to be paid by the user to the performers, or the producers, or to both.[14]

Broadcasting organizations are granted the right to authorize or prohibit: (i) the rebroadcasting of their broadcasts; (ii) the fixation of their broadcasts; and (iii) the reproduction of fixations, made without their consent, of their broadcasts or of fixations of their broadcasts made in accordance with the stipulated exceptions in Article 15, if the reproduction is made for purposes different from those stated in Article 15. They are also granted the exclusive right to authorize or prohibit the communication to the public of their television broadcasts if such communication is made in places accessible to the public against payment of an entrance fee.[15]

The above rights must last for at least 20 years from the end of the year in which the fixation was made (in the case of phonograms or performances incorporated therein); or when the performance took place (for performances not incorporated in phonograms); or, in the case of broadcasts, when the broadcast took place. Notably, there are no obligations concerning moral rights.

2.4.1.3 Agreement on Trade Related Aspects of Intellectual Property Rights 1994 ('TRIPS Agreement')

As explained in Chapter 1,[16] the TRIPS Agreement forms part of the WTO Agreement and thus binds all WTO members, currently standing at 153. The UK has been a WTO member since 1 January 1995.

The TRIPS Agreement incorporates, *inter alia*, the key provisions of the Berne Convention. It does this via Article 9, which stipulates that Members shall comply with Arts. 1 through 21 of the Berne Convention (as revised in 1971). Importantly, however, there is no obligation to comply with Article 6*bis* of the Berne Convention, which deals with moral rights.

---

[12] Art. 6.   [13] Art. 10.   [14] Art. 12.   [15] Art. 13.   [16] See 1.3.1.2.

The TRIPS Agreement also contains a number of provisions that seek to clarify and also extend the minimum standards of copyright protection. For example, Article 9(2) of TRIPS emphasizes that 'Copyright protection shall extend to expressions and not to ideas, procedures, methods of operation or mathematical concepts as such' and Article 10(1) clarifies that computer programs shall be protected as literary works under the Berne Convention. An example of extending protection is Article 11, which provides that for at least computer programs and cinematographic works, Member States shall provide authors and their successors in title with the right of commercial rental to the public.

The TRIPS Agreement also provides for protection of performers, producers of phonograms (i.e. sound recordings), and broadcasters in Article 14. This protection mirrors that stated in the Rome Convention, except that the term of protection for performers and phonogram producers is increased to 50 years from the end of the calendar year in which the fixation was made or the performance took place.[17]

As discussed in Chapter 1,[18] an important feature of the TRIPS Agreement is that it makes disputes between WTO Members about compliance with TRIPS obligations subject to the dispute settlement procedures of the WTO. This has created both formal and informal pressure to implement TRIPS obligations. Given that TRIPS incorporates Berne Convention obligations (except for Article 6*bis*), it has provided an effective mechanism for (indirectly) enforcing the Berne Convention.

2.4.1.4 WIPO Copyright Treaty 1996 ('WCT')

Developments in technology during the 1980s and 1990s created various problems and uncertainties for copyright law. For example, it was unclear whether computer programs and electronic databases fell within the scope of the Berne Convention and whether the Convention minimum rights covered transmission of works via electronic networks, such as the Internet. There was also the more general problem of how to ensure effective enforcement of copyright in an increasingly global, networked society.

In 1991 and succeeding years, WIPO summoned Committees of Experts to consider these problems and to draft a possible protocol to the Berne Convention. Revision of the Berne Convention itself was not feasible, in light of the fact that amendments to the substantive provisions of Berne require unanimity of votes[19] and it was felt that such unanimity would be difficult to achieve given the diversity of opinions and the complexity of problems to be solved. Therefore, a more practical option was to establish a protocol to the Berne Convention.

The Diplomatic Conference on Certain Copyright and Neighbouring Rights Questions was held in Geneva from 2–20 December 1996. It was one of the largest diplomatic conferences on copyright law, with over 120 Berne countries being represented, together with a special delegation of the EC, and representatives of seven intergovernmental organizations, 76 non-governmental organizations and the International Bureau of WIPO. Two treaties sprang from this conference, one of which was the WIPO Copyright Treaty 1996 ('WCT'). The relationship of this Treaty to the Berne Convention is that it is a special agreement within the meaning of Article 20 of Berne, i.e. an agreement entered into by Berne Union countries.

The WCT contains clarifying provisions—for example, Article 4 which states that computer programs are protected as literary works within the meaning of Article 2 of the Berne Convention and Article 5, which says the same for databases. Article 2 emphasizes that

---

[17] Art. 14(5).   [18] See 1.3.1.2.   [19] See Art. 27(3) Berne Convention.

copyright protection extends to expressions and not to ideas, procedures, methods of operation, or mathematical concepts as such.

In terms of exclusive rights, Article 1(4) of the WCT states that Contracting Parties shall comply with Arts. 1–21 (Article 6*bis* inclusive) of Berne (Paris Act, 1971). The effect is to institute or confirm the regime of the Berne Convention in all countries which are Contracting Parties to the Treaty, whether they are members of the Berne Convention or not. The WCT also introduces two new economic rights not provided for in the Berne Convention—the right of distribution[20] and the right of rental—[21] and extends the right of communication to the public to include on-demand transmissions.[22]

By virtue of incorporating the Berne Convention obligations, the minimum term of protection is 50 years *post mortem auctoris* (*pma*). However, it is important to note that Article 9 of the WCT stipulates that Contracting Parties shall not apply Article 7(4) of the Berne Convention. This provision allows countries of the Union to determine the term of protection for photographic works and works of applied art (insofar as they are protected as artistic works), provided it is a minimum of 25 years from the making of the work. The effect of Article 9 of the WCT is that 50 years *pma* will now be applicable to photographic works and works of applied art.

In an attempt to combat widespread digital piracy of copyright works, Article 11 of the WCT imposes obligations to provide adequate legal protection and effective legal remedies against the circumvention of effective technological measures. To facilitate the exploitation of copyright works in a digital environment, Article 12 creates obligations in respect of rights management information that is applied to copyright works. The role and scope of these provisions is discussed further in Chapter 12.[23]

2.4.1.5 WIPO Performances and Phonograms Treaty 1996 ('WPPT')

Developments in digital technology also created pressures on the protection of related rights, in particular those applicable to performers, phonograms (i.e. sound recordings), and broadcasters. In order to amend the Rome Convention, which governs these related rights, it would have been necessary to bring together the three organizations responsible for the Convention and to balance the interests of the three groups. It was thought to be more practical to focus on a separate treaty and one that dealt with the rights of performers and phonogram producers (the rights of broadcasters to be dealt with later). Thus, the second treaty to emerge from the 1996 Diplomatic Conference was the WIPO Performances and Phonograms Treaty 1996 ('WPPT').

There is no provision in the WPPT imposing an obligation on Contracting States to comply with the Rome Convention, but nothing in the WPPT is taken to derogate from the existing obligations that Contracting Parties have to each other under the Rome Convention.[24]

The protection given to performers improves significantly on that available under the Rome Convention. This is because performers are given exclusive rights in relation to their performances[25] and also moral rights in respect of live aural performances or performances fixed in phonograms.[26] Producers of phonograms are given exclusive rights of authorizing the reproduction,[27] distribution,[28] and commercial rental[29] of their phonograms, as well as the making available of their phonograms via on-demand transmissions, such as

---

[20] Art. 6.   [21] Art. 7.   [22] Art. 8.   [23] See 12.6.5.   [24] Art. 1.
[25] See Arts. 6–10.   [26] Art. 5.   [27] Art. 11.   [28] Art. 12.   [29] Art. 13.

the Internet.[30] There is also a right to equitable remuneration for the use of phonograms published for commercial purposes for broadcasting or for any communication to the public, which can be claimed by the performer or producer or both.[31]

The term of protection for both performers and phonogram producers is 50 years measured, in the case of the former, from the end of the year in which the performance was fixed in a phonogram and, in terms of the latter, 50 years from the end of the year in which the phonogram was published or, failing publication within 50 years of fixation, 50 years from the end of the year in which the fixation was made.[32]

As with the WCT, there are obligations in the WPPT concerning adequate legal protection and effective legal remedies in respect of circumvention of technological measures and removal or altering rights management information.[33]

2.4.2 REGIONAL

Since 1991, the EC has, pursuant to Article 95 of the EC Treaty, issued numerous harmonizing directives in the field of copyright law with the object of promoting the smooth functioning of the internal market. As such, there has been a major intervention of the EC in the field of copyright and this has had a significant impact on UK copyright law.

The directives may be broadly classed into three types. The first type deals with specific subject matter. These are the Software Directive[34] and the Database Directive.[35] The second type are directives dealing with specific rights or specific issues, namely, the Rental Right Directive,[36] the Cable and Satellite Directive,[37] the Term Directive,[38] and the Droite de Suite Directive.[39] The final type is that focusing on broader harmonization across several copyright areas. Only one directive falls into this category, namely, the Information Society Directive.[40]

There is no need here to list the details of all seven directives concerning copyright law since, as and when the directives relate to UK copyright law, they will be discussed below. The main point to note is that the UK has had to implement a substantial amount of EC law in the copyright field and that it has not always done this in the most faithful or elegant fashion.

---

[30] Art. 14.   [31] Art. 15.   [32] Art. 17.   [33] Arts. 18–19.

[34] Directive 91/250/EEC on the legal protection of computer programs, OJ L122, 17 May 1991, pp. 42–6.

[35] Directive 96/9/EC of the European Parliament and of the Council of 11 Mar. 1996 on the legal protection of databases OJ L77, 27 Mar. 1996, pp. 20–8.

[36] Directive 92/100/EEC of 19 Nov. 1992 on rental and lending rights and on certain rights related to copyright in the field of intellectual property OJ L346, 27 Nov. 1992, pp. 61–6, codified in Directive 2006/115/EC of the European Parliament and of the Council of 12 Dec. 2006 on rental right and lending right and on certain rights related to copyright in the field of intellectual property.

[37] Directive 93/83/EEC of 27 Sept. 1993 on the coordination of certain rules concerning copyright and rights related to copyright applicable to satellite broadcasting and cable retransmission OJ L248, 6 Oct. 1993, pp. 15–21.

[38] Directive 93/98/EEC, which was subsequently codified by Directive 2006/116/EC of 12 Dec. 2006 on the term of protection of copyright and certain related rights.

[39] Directive 2001/84/EC of the European Parliament and of the Council of 27 Sept. 2001 on the resale right for the benefit of the author of an original work of art OJ L272, 13 Oct. 2001, p. 32.

[40] Directive 2001/29/EC on the harmonization of certain aspects of copyright and related rights in the information society OJ L167, 22 Jun. 2001, pp. 10–19.

2.4.3 NATIONAL

The history of copyright protection in the UK has been discussed already in s. 2.2 above. The statute that presently governs UK copyright law is the CDPA, as amended.

2.5 SUBSISTENCE OF COPYRIGHT

As we have seen copyright began life as a registered right. However, since the beginning of the 20th century it has been an unregistered right, meaning that protection arises automatically without having to satisfy any formalities, such as registration, deposit, or notice. The absence of formalities is mandated by the Berne Convention, specifically Article 5(2) which states that 'The enjoyment and the exercise of these rights shall not be subject to any formality.' This principle was introduced at the Berlin 1908 Revision Conference and the current wording of Article 5(2) was refined at the Stockholm and Paris Revision Conferences.

The absence of formalities makes it much easier and less expensive to acquire and maintain copyright protection than other forms of IPRs, such as trade marks and patents. But when it comes to enforcing copyright through infringement proceedings, owners may have to establish that they are entitled to copyright protection because the defendant puts this matter in issue. This is when it will become necessary to show that the requirements for subsistence of copyright have been satisfied.

In the UK, for copyright to subsist, it is necessary to show appropriate subject matter and qualification and, in the case of literary, dramatic, musical, and artistic works, originality and fixation. We turn now to consider these requirements.

2.5.1 SUBJECT MATTER

2.5.1.1 'Open' and 'closed' lists of subject matter

According to the Berne Convention, the principles of national treatment and minimum rights apply 'in respect of works for which [authors] are protected under this Convention'.[41] These are 'literary and artistic works' and Article 2(1) of the Berne Convention states that 'the expression "literary and artistic works" shall include every production in the literary, scientific and artistic domain, whatever may be the mode or form of its expression' and goes on to provide an extensive but non-exhaustive list of examples. Some of the more notable works listed are: books, lectures, dramatic works, musical compositions, cinematographic works, paintings, sculptures, photographic works, and works of applied art. It is clear that the works enumerated in Article 2(1) are to be protected by Members of the Berne Union, but there are no definitions of these works and also no stipulations about how this is to be achieved. This leaves open the possibility of different approaches to subject matter in the national laws of Union Members. One of the major differences is the 'open list' versus 'closed list' approach to subject matter, exemplified by France and the United Kingdom.

An 'open list' approach is one that broadly identifies the subject matter of protection and provides an illustrative list of such subject matter. For example in France, Article L 112–1 of the Intellectual Property Code 1992 refers to, 'the rights of authors in all works of the

---

[41] Art. 5(1) Berne Convention.

mind, whatever their kind, form of expression, merit or purpose'. Article L 112–2 then goes on to provide an illustrative list of 'works of the mind' that largely corresponds to Article 2(1) of Berne, but has some additional illustrations, namely, that of software and its preparatory design material and 'creations of the seasonal industries of dress and articles of fashion'. Notably, there are no statutory definitions of what can or cannot constitute protectable subject matter.

By contrast, the UK is a prime example of a 'closed list' system. This is where copyright protection is given to specifically stated categories of subject matter. Thus, the CDPA grants protection to eight—and *only* eight—categories of works. These are literary, dramatic, musical, and artistic works; films; sound recordings; broadcasts; and typographical arrangements of published editions.[42] As such, a person must bring his or her creation within one or more of these categories in order to obtain copyright—failure to do so will preclude protection. The scope of the eight categories is elaborated upon, in varying degrees, via statutory definitions. Some definitions are exhaustive in nature, such as that for 'artistic work',[43] whereas others are inclusive, such as that for 'dramatic work'.[44]

The next section will consider some of the more contentious categories of subject matter in the CDPA. In reading this section, it is worth bearing in mind the following questions: (1) what are the advantages and disadvantages of both the closed- and open-list approaches to subject matter and (2) at the end of the day, do the open-list and closed-list approaches to subject matter lead to fundamentally different results?

FURTHER READING

T. Aplin, 'Subject matter' in E. Derclaye (ed.), *Research Handbook on the Future of EU Copyright Law* (Cheltenham: Edward Elgar, 2008), pp. 94–135.

2.5.1.2 Literary work

Section 3 of the CDPA defines 'literary work' to mean:

> any work, other than a dramatic or musical work, which is written, spoken or sung, and accordingly includes—
>
> (a) a table or compilation other than a database,
>
> (b) a computer program,
>
> (c) preparatory design material for a computer program, and
>
> (d) a database.

Several things are apparent from this definition, the first being that literary works are mutually exclusive of dramatic and musical works. This means that in the case of a song, the copyright works will be split into two—the literary work (for the lyrics) and the musical work (for the music). The second point is that literary works include new technological works, namely software and databases. The history of these inclusions and the challenges they pose are dealt with elsewhere in this book.[45] The final point is that literary works are

---

[42] CDPA, s. 1(1).   [43] Ibid., s. 4.   [44] Ibid., s. 3.   [45] See Ch. 12.

works that are 'written, spoken or sung'. 'Writing' is defined in s. 179 to mean, 'any form of notation or code, whether by hand or otherwise and regardless of the method by which, or medium in or on which, it is recorded' and 'written' shall be construed accordingly. Thus, the fact that a work is stored in digital or electronic form will not preclude it from being a literary work. Nor will the fact that it is recorded in notation (such as shorthand) or code (such as source or object code used in computer programs). The definition of 'written' also highlights that aesthetic or qualitative criteria are irrelevant when it comes to identifying a literary work. This was a principle established in the early case law.

University of London Press v University Tutorial Press [1916] 2 Ch 601

The issue was whether mathematics examination papers were 'original literary works' within the meaning of s. 1(1) of Copyright Act 1911. On the question of whether they were 'literary works' Peterson J held as follows:

Peterson J, at p. 608:

The first question that is raised is, Are these examination papers subject of copyright? Section 1, sub-s. 1, of the Copyright Act of 1911 provides for copyright in 'every original literary dramatic musical and artistic work', subject to certain conditions which for this purpose are immaterial, and the question is, therefore, whether these examination papers are, within the meaning of this Act, original literary works. Although a literary work is not defined in the Act, s. 35 states what the phrase includes; the definition is not a completely comprehensive one, but the section is intended to show what, amongst other things, is included in the description 'literary work', and the words are ' "Literary work" includes maps, charts, plans, tables, and compilations.' It may be difficult to define 'literary work' as used in this Act, but it seems to be plain that it is not confined to 'literary work' in the sense in which that phrase is applied, for instance, to Meredith's novels and the writings of Robert Louis Stevenson. In speaking of such writings as literary works, one thinks of the quality, the style, and the literary finish which they exhibit. Under the Act of 1842, which protected 'books', many things which had no pretensions to literary style acquired copyright; for example, a list of registered bills of sale, a list of foxhounds and hunting days, and trade catalogues; and I see no ground for coming to the conclusion that the present Act was intended to curtail the rights of authors. In my view the words 'literary work' cover work which is expressed in print or writing, irrespective of the question whether the quality or style is high. The word 'literary' seems to be used in a sense somewhat similar to the use of the word 'literature' in political or electioneering literature and refers to written or printed matter. Papers set by examiners are, in my opinion, 'literary work' within the meaning of the present Act.

Does it make sense, as Peterson J does, to avoid aesthetic or qualitative judgments when it comes to identifying a literary work? Is this approach in keeping with the justifications for copyright?

When we think of literary works what may spring to mind are appreciable amounts of text, in the form of, say, a letter, set of instructions, poem, or a book. But what about very short forms of text, such as names, single words, or short phrases? Do these, and should these, qualify as 'literary works'? The Court of Appeal considered this issue in the following case.

Exxon v Exxon Insurance [1982] Ch 119

'Exxon' was an invented word developed as a result of considerable research and expenditure and used as the corporate name of several of the claimant companies. The defendant used Exxon in its corporate name and, as a result, the claimants sought injunctions against them, alleging both copyright infringement and passing off. At first instance, Graham J held that the claimants were entitled to an injunction to restrain passing off by the continued use of Exxon but refused the injunction to restrain an infringement of copyright, on the basis that Exxon was not an original literary work within the meaning of s. 2 of the Copyright Act 1956.

Graham J, at pp. 130–2:

As I have already stated, the question that I have to decide is, shortly stated, whether Exxon is an 'original literary work' within section 2? I do not think it is. 'What is it then?', one may ask. It is a word which, though invented and therefore original, has no meaning and suggests nothing in itself. To give it substance and meaning, it must be accompanied by other words or used in a particular context or juxtaposition. When used as part of any of the plaintiffs' corporate names, it clearly has a denominative characteristic as denoting the company in question. When used, as I assume it is, with the plaintiffs' goods, it would clearly have the effect of denoting origin or quality. It is in fact an invented word with no meaning, which is a typical subject for trade mark registration, and which no doubt, with adequate use, is capable also of becoming, if it has not already become, distinctive of the plaintiffs and their goods at common law. It is not in itself a title or distinguishing name and, as I have said, only takes on meaning or significance when actually used with other words, for example indicating that it is the name of a company, or in a particular juxtaposition as, for example, upon goods.

Nothing I have said above is intended to suggest that I consider that a word which is used as a title can, as a matter of law, never in any circumstances be the subject of copyright, and I would disagree with dicta in previous cases to the contrary effect. Such a word would, however, I think, have to have qualities or characteristics in itself, if such a thing is possible, which would justify its recognition as an original literary work rather than merely as an invented word. It may well turn out not to be possible in practice, but, as at present advised, I consider that the mere fact that a single word is invented and that research or labour was involved in its invention does not in itself, in my judgment, necessarily enable it to qualify as an original literary work within section 2 of the Act.

[Referring to the Lewis Carroll poem 'Jabberwocky' which features in his book *Through the Looking Glass*]…Assuming the poem had been recently written and was the subject of the Act of 1911 or 1956, it is I suppose just conceivable that the use in some literary context of either of the single words 'Jabberwock' or 'Jabberwocky' alone might also be held to be an infringement as being a substantial part of the whole poem. But could Lewis Carroll, if he had merely invented the word 'Jabberwock' and had never written the poem of which it is a part, have successfully contended that he had copyright in the word alone? In the absence of its registration as a trade mark, could he, by virtue of copyright, prevent a commercial company adopting it as part of such company's corporate name? I think not, the legal reason being that the word alone and by itself cannot properly be considered as a 'literary *work*', the subject of copyright under the Act. It becomes part of a 'literary work' within the Act when it is embodied in the poem, but it is the poem as a composition which is a work within the Act and not the word itself.

The claimants' appeal was dismissed.

In the Court of Appeal, Stephenson LJ gratefully adopted the above passages from the judgment of Graham J. He referred also to the observations of Davey LJ in *Hollinrake v Truswell*—[46] a case that raised the issue of whether copyright could subsist in a cardboard pattern sleeve featuring scales, figures, and descriptive words on it. Davey LJ stated that, 'a literary work is intended to afford either information and instruction, or pleasure, in the form of literary enjoyment'[47] and found that the sleeve chart did not satisfy this test. Stephenson LJ, after referring to the test in *Hollinrake v Truswell*, made the following comments:

Stephenson LJ, at p. 143:

The words do, however, appeal to me as stating the ordinary meaning of the words 'literary work'. I would have thought, unaided or unhampered by authority, that unless there is something in the context of the Act which forbids it, a literary work would be something which was intended to afford either information and instruction, or pleasure in the form of literary enjoyment, whatever those last six words may add to the word 'pleasure'. Mr Price has not convinced me that this word 'Exxon' was intended to do, or does do, either of those things; nor has he convinced me that it is not of the essence of a literary work that it should do one of those things. Nor has he convinced me that there is anything in the Act, or in what Peterson J said about the words in the earlier Act, or in any authority, or in principle, which compels me to give a different construction from Davey LJ's to the words 'literary work'. As I have already said, I agree with the way in which Graham J put the matter; I am not sure whether this can be said to be a 'work' at all, I am clearly of the opinion that it cannot be said to be a 'literary work'. I therefore agree with Graham J and I would dismiss this appeal.

...

Oliver LJ, at pp. 144–5:

I entirely agree. Section 2 of the Act of 1956 provides that copyright should subsist in every 'original literary work', and in essence Mr Price's submissions were very simple. First, he said that the name 'Exxon' is undoubtedly original; it had not been thought of before or, so far as is known, used before; it is an artificial word, which does not appear in any known language. It is, he said, literary; it is composed of letters and it is written, typed or printed. It is a 'work' because work or effort went into its invention, and its selection as a suitable name for the plaintiff group which had no meaning, offensive or otherwise, in any other language. But 'original literary work' as used in the statute is a composite expression, and for my part I do not think that the right way to apply a composite expression is, or at any rate is necessarily, to ascertain whether a particular subject matter falls within the meaning of each of the constituent parts, and then to say that the whole expression is merely the sum total of the constituent parts. In my judgment it is not necessary, in construing a statutory expression, to take leave of one's commonsense, and the result to which Mr Price sought to drive us is one which, to my mind, involves doing just that.

Stephenson LJ has already referred to the judgment of Davey LJ in *Hollinrake v Truswell* [1894] 3 Ch 420, 428, where he said: 'Now, a literary work is intended to afford either information and instruction, or pleasure, in the form of literary enjoyment.' Admittedly, that was said in relation to the preamble of the Act of 1842, which referred to affording 'encouragement to the production of literary works of lasting benefit to the world'. But it does seem

---

[46] [1894] 3 Ch 420.   [47] Ibid., at pp. 427–8.

to me, as it seems to Stephenson LJ, that what Davey LJ said was a fair summary of what the expression means in ordinary language. We have been referred to a number of cases in which copyright has been successfully claimed in, for instance, examination papers, football coupons and tables of ciphers; but all these—and I do not exclude the case of the telegraphic code in *DP Anderson & Co Ltd v Lieber Code Co* [1917] 2 KB 469—seem to me to fall fairly within Davey LJ's commonsense formulation. But that for which protection is sought in the instant case does not appear to me to have any of the qualities which commonsense would demand. It conveys no information; it provides no instruction; it gives no pleasure that I can conceive; it is simply an artificial combination of four letters of the alphabet which serves a purpose only when it is used in juxtaposition with other English words, to identify one or other of the companies in the plaintiffs' group. Whether, as might perhaps be the case if one followed up the suggestion made in the judgment of Graham J, the insertion of the extra 'x' was to avoid the risk of involving the Bishop of Exeter in proceedings for infringement every time he wrote to 'The Times' newspaper, I do not pause to inquire. I am clearly of the opinion that Graham J arrived at the correct conclusion when he held that this was not an 'original literary work' in which copyright subsists, and I agree that the appeal should be dismissed.

Do you agree with the test for 'literary work' adopted by the Court of Appeal in *Exxon*? If so, do you think the court correctly applied it to the facts of the case? Assume for a moment that the factual scenario involved an ordinary English word, rather than an invented one—would the application of the *Exxon* test lead to a different result? What about if the subject of protection was a short phrase or title of a song? In considering your responses it is important to identify what, if any, policy objectives exist for excluding words (invented or otherwise) or short phrases from copyright protection. It is also interesting to note that other jurisdictions have taken a different approach to the one taken in *Exxon*. For example, in France, Article L 112–4 of the Intellectual Property Code 1992 states that a title may be protected provided it is original.

FURTHER READING

Francis Day & Hunter Ltd v Twentieth Century Fox Corp Ltd [1940] AC 112.

J. Cullabine, 'Copyright in short phrases and single words' [1992] EIPR 205.

J. Klink, 'Titles in Europe: Trade names, copyright works or title marks' [2004] EIPR 291.

2.5.1.3 Musical work

Section 3(1) of the CDPA defines 'musical work' as:

a work consisting of music, exclusive of any words or action intended to be sung, spoken or performed with the music.

The above definition again highlights the mutual exclusivity between musical, literary, and dramatic works. Its usefulness is limited, however, because 'a work consisting of music' is left undefined. What, then, can we say constitutes music? Can John Cage's '4 minutes 33 seconds', a work in three parts in which the performer is required to remain absolutely silent at his instrument for exactly this length of time, qualify as music?[48] What about

---

[48] For a performance of this by David Tudor see <http://uk.youtube.com/watch?v=HypmW4Yd7SY>.

Steve Reich's 'Clapping Music for Two Performers'[49] in which two performers clap together rhythmically? Or music which comes from the 'industrial' genre?[50] Some guidance on the meaning of 'music' has fortunately been provided by the Court of Appeal decision in *Hyperion Records v Sawkins*.

Hyperion Records v Sawkins [2005] RPC 32, [2005] 1 WLR 3281

This was a case involving the music of 17th and 18th century baroque composer Michel-Ricard de Lalande. The claimant, Dr Lionel Sawkins, is a musicologist of high repute and the leading authority on the music of Lalande. In relation to some of Lalande's pieces (namely his grand motets) he produced modern performing editions—i.e. scores from which today's performers can play Lalande's music. In producing the modern performing editions, Dr Sawkins aimed to reproduce Lalande's music as faithfully as possible. He therefore consulted and drew upon manuscript and printed sources from the 17th and 18th centuries and transcribed music from the original scores into modern notation. In addition, to make the music playable Dr Sawkins made numerous corrections and additions to the notation, figured the bass line and recreated missing parts. Producing these editions required considerable expertise, as well as skill and effort—approximately 300 hours on each of the performing editions of the four pieces. The defendants recorded a performance of Lalande's music from the modern performing editions prepared by Dr Sawkins. The claimant alleged that he owned copyright in the editions as original musical works and that the defendants' actions had infringed his copyright. Dr Sawkins argued that he had expended considerable effort in producing the editions and they contained musical information in the form of conventional modern notation and directions to the performers. The defendant denied that the performing editions were original or musical. The originality point is dealt with later in this chapter. What is relevant here is the approach to whether the work was a 'musical work'. On this point, the defendants argued that the performing edition did not amount to a new and substantive musical work in itself—it simply reproduced Lalande's music. The court rejected this argument.

Mummery LJ:

42. On the approach advocated by the defendant most of the exertions of the claimant, such as researching the source materials, selecting the best versions to edit, transcribing them into modern notation, making them playable, or more easily playable, correcting errors, inserting missing material from other sources, the inclusion of the figured bass and determining such matters as layout of the scores on the page and inserting 'advisory' or courtesy indications, such as tempo and ornamentation, are irrelevant to the issue whether he created an original musical work. They were not part of the music. Thus the material shown on the marked up copies of the scores adduced in evidence by the claimant, in order to illustrate the nature and extent of the editorial interventions by him to the text bar by bar, might be academically sound and valuable, but was insufficient to attract musical copyright...

43. ...I do not accept the narrow approach advocated by the defendant as to the type and nature of the work required to attract musical copyright.

. . .

---

[49] For a performance of this work see <http://uk.youtube.com/watch?v=BhhIZscEE_g>.
[50] See for example, the music of the band 'Throbbing Gristle'.

53. In the absence of a special statutory definition of music, ordinary usage assists: as indicated in the dictionaries, the essence of music is combining sounds for listening to. Music is not the same as mere noise. The sound of music is intended to produce effects of some kind on the listener's emotions and intellect. The sounds may be produced by an organised performance on instruments played from a musical score, though that is not essential for the existence of the music or of copyright in it. Music must be distinguished from the fact and form of its fixation as a record of a musical composition. The score is the traditional and convenient form of fixation of the music and conforms to the requirement that a copyright work must be recorded in some material form. But the fixation in the written score or on a record is not in itself the music in which copyright subsists. There is no reason why, for example, a recording of a person's spontaneous singing, whistling or humming or of improvisations of sounds by a group of people with or without musical instruments should not be regarded as 'music' for copyright purposes.

...

55. In principle, there is no reason for regarding the actual notes of music as the *only* matter covered by musical copyright, any more than, in the case of a dramatic work, only the words to be spoken by the actors are covered by dramatic copyright. Added stage directions may affect the performance of the play on the stage or on the screen and have an impact on the performance seen by the audience. Stage directions are as much part of a dramatic work as plot, character and dialogue.

...

56. It is wrong in principle to single out the notes as uniquely significant for copyright purposes and to proceed to deny copyright to the other elements that make some contribution to the sound of the music when performed, such as performing indications, tempo and performance practice indicators, if they are the product of a person's effort, skill and time, bearing in mind, of course, the 'relatively modest' level ... of the threshold for a work to qualify for protection. The work of Dr Sawkins has sufficient aural and musical significance to attract copyright protection.

Is Mummery LJ's approach to determining what constitutes a 'musical work', for copyright purposes, a sensible one? Would it embrace a wide variety of musical creations and, if not, is this problematic?

2.5.1.4 Dramatic work

Section 3(1) of the CDPA defines 'dramatic work' as including a 'work of dance or mime'. This is an inclusive definition, but one that sheds little light on the scope of this particular category of subject matter. The main questions that have arisen about the scope of 'dramatic works' are whether they include television formats and also films. We turn first to consider the protection of television formats.

Green v Broadcasting Corporation of New Zealand [1989] RPC 700

The appellant (Green) was a well-known personality who was the author and presenter of a highly successful television show in England entitled 'Opportunity Knocks'. The show was essentially a talent contest and featured several characteristic catch phrases, the use of sponsors to introduce competitors and the use of a 'clapometer' to measure audience reaction to the performances of competitions. The respondent (Broadcasting

Corporation of New Zealand) broadcast a similar television show under the same title in New Zealand. As a result the appellant commenced proceedings, claiming damages for passing off and infringement of copyright. In respect of the copyright claim, the appellants argued that copyright subsisted in the scripts and dramatic format of the show. The action was dismissed by the New Zealand High Court and the appeal to the Court of Appeal was unsuccessful. The appellant then appealed on the copyright issue to the Privy Council.

Lord Bridge of Harwich (delivering the opinion of the Council), **at p. 702:**

[His Lordship began by agreeing with the Court of Appeal that what little evidence of scripts that existed pointed to no more than a general idea or concept for a talent contest and as such could not attract copyright. He then considered the alternative argument that copyright subsisted in the 'dramatic format' of the show.]

It is stretching the original use of the word 'format' a long way to use it metaphorically to describe the features of a television series such as a talent, quiz or game show which is presented in a particular way, with repeated but unconnected use of set phrases and with the aid of particular accessories. Alternative terms suggested in the course of argument were 'structure' or 'package'. This difficulty in finding an appropriate term to describe the nature of the 'work' in which the copyright subsists reflects the difficulty of the concept that a number of allegedly distinctive features of a television series can be isolated from the changing material presented in each separate performance (the acts of the performers in the talent show, the questions and answers in the quiz show etc.) and identified as an 'original dramatic work'. No case was cited to their Lordships in which copyright of the kind claimed had been established.

The protection which copyright gives creates a monopoly and 'there must be certainty in the subject matter of such monopoly in order to avoid injustice to the rest of the world': *Tate v Fulbrook* [1908] 1 KB 821, per Farwell J at page 832. The subject matter of the copyright claimed for the 'dramatic format' of 'Opportunity Knocks' is conspicuously lacking in certainty. Moreover, it seems to their Lordships that a dramatic work must have sufficient unity to be capable of performance and that the features claimed as constituting the 'format' of a television show, being unrelated to each other except as accessories to be used in the presentation of some other dramatic or musical performance, lack that essential characteristic.

For these reasons their Lordships will humbly advise Her Majesty that the appeal should be dismissed. The appellant must pay the respondent's costs of the appeal to the Board.

In recent years we have seen a plethora of new, highly successful television shows, such as 'Big Brother', 'The Weakest Link', 'Who Wants to be a Millionaire?', 'I'm a Celebrity Get Me Out of Here!', and 'The X Factor'. Do you think that *Green* precludes protection for these types of shows and, if so, does this seem unduly harsh on their creators?

The issue of whether films qualify as dramatic works was raised in the *Norowzian* litigation.

Norowzian v Arks Ltd (No 2) [2000] FSR 363

Mr Norowzian had created and produced a film, entitled 'Joy', which depicted a man, casually dressed, dancing to music in a quirky manner against a plain backdrop. The film was shot with a camera in a fixed position and the editing process heavily used the 'jump cutting' technique. This is a process whereby the editor excises pieces of film, joining together the remaining pieces. When shown, the film depicted a series of movements by the actor that appeared to be performed successively, but which in real life could not be so. The defendants produced an advertisement for Guinness, called 'Anticipation'.[51] This also used the 'jump cutting' technique and showed a man dancing around to music in a quirky manner, waiting for his pint of Guinness to settle.

Initially, Mr Norowzian sought to rely on his film copyright. Section 5B of the CDPA provides that 'film' means 'a recording on any medium from which a moving image may by any means be produced'. Mr Norowzian's film clearly fell within this definition and was protected by copyright as a 'film' work. It was on this basis that he initially sued the defendants in *Norowzian v Arks Ltd (No 1)* [1998] FSR 394. However, this claim was unsuccessful because Mr A. G. Steinfeld QC held that the scope of protection for films is limited to copying the actual images, i.e. the recording from which the moving image constituting the film has been produced, and the defendants had made their own film that had allegedly similar images. In relation to dramatic works, however, the scope of protection is not limited in this way and this is why the claimant sought to argue that his film also qualified for copyright protection as a 'dramatic work'. Before Rattee J this argument was rejected. He held that a film could record a dramatic work, but could not itself be a dramatic work. This was not a record of a dramatic work since, as a result of the 'jump cutting' technique, what was depicted in the claimant's film could not actually be performed. In obiter, he stated that even if 'Joy' was a dramatic work it was not infringed by 'Anticipation' because of the differences between the two films.

The claimant appealed. The Court of Appeal disagreed with Rattee J that a film per se could not be a dramatic work, but agreed that a substantial part of the claimant's dramatic work was not reproduced in the defendant's film.

Nourse LJ (Brooke LJ in agreement; **Buxton LJ** delivering a concurring judgment), **at pp. 366–7:**

Rattee J was of the opinion that a film per se cannot be a dramatic work within the meaning of the 1988 Act, though it can be a recording of such a work for the purpose of section 3(2); see page 77. His view was based partly on the different categorisations adopted by paragraphs (a) and (b) of section 1(1) and partly on the express exclusion of films from the definition of dramatic work in the Copyright Act 1956; see section 48(1) of that Act. Although we were not referred to transcripts of the arguments in the court below, my strong impression is that the judge's view was influenced by the submissions of counsel then representing the claimant, who do not appear to have argued that *Joy* was itself a dramatic work. At page 77 the judge records the submission of the claimant's leading counsel as being that 'Joy is clearly a work of dance and mime which has been recorded on film.'

...

In my judgment a film can be a dramatic work for the purposes of the 1988 Act. The definition of that expression being at large, it must be given its natural and ordinary meaning. We were referred to several dictionary and textbook definitions. My own, substantially a distilled synthesis of those which have gone before, would be this: a dramatic work is a work of action, with or without words or music, which is capable of being performed before an

---

[51] The advertisement may be viewed at < http://uk.youtube.com/watch?v=3MuEtGPXLPI>.

audience. A film will often, though not always, be a work of action and it is capable of being performed before an audience. It can therefore fall within the expression 'dramatic work' in section 1(1)(a) and I disagree with the judge's reasons for excluding it.

As to those reasons, no mutual exclusivity between paragraphs (a) and (b) is expressed, and the absence of the requirement of originality in paragraph (b) is sufficient ground for none to be implied. Moreover, it is unsafe to base any construction of the material provisions of the 1988 Act on those of the 1956 Act. Indeed, it might be said that Parliament's omission to repeat the exclusion of films from the definition of dramatic work points rather towards their inclusion. But whether that be right or wrong, the material provisions of the 1988 Act must be construed as they stand. Where a film is both a recording of a dramatic work and a dramatic work in itself they do not exclude an overlap. In other cases there will be no overlap. Sometimes a film will simply be a recording of something which is not a dramatic work. At other times it will not be a recording of a dramatic work but a dramatic work in itself.

Once it is established that a film can be a dramatic work for the purposes of the 1988 Act it is clear that *Joy*, being a work of action capable of being performed before an audience, is such a work. Clearly, it is an original work. Two further points must be mentioned in relation to the primary question. First, in support of his argument on the 1988 Act, Mr Arnold relied on certain European materials, in particular the Berne Copyright Convention (as revised and amended up to 1979). In my view it is unnecessary to have to resort to those materials as an aid to the construction of the 1988 Act. Secondly, Mr Arnold submitted, in the alternative, that *Joy* was a recording of a dramatic work. In agreeing with Rattee J that that submission must be rejected, I need do no more than read the following passage from his judgment at page 78:

> *Joy*, unlike some films, is not a recording of a dramatic work, because, as a result of the drastic editing process adopted by Mr Norowzian, it is not a recording of anything that was, or could be, performed or danced by anyone...It may well be, in the case of *Joy*, that the original unedited film of the actor's performance, what I believe are called 'the rushes', was a recording of a dramatic work, but Mr Norowzian's claim is not in respect of copyright in them or their subject matter. His claim is in respect of the finished film.

Joy, just like many cartoon films, is, without being a recording of one, a dramatic work in itself.

Does the Court of Appeal's decision in *Norowzian* distort the meaning of 'dramatic work'? Or does the case reflect a sensible interpretation to achieve a legitimate result, i.e. proper protection for cinematographic works? What sorts of complications could arise by being able to treat films as both 'film works' and 'dramatic works'? In considering this question it is worth asking whether there will be different authors, owners, and terms of protection depending on the classification of the subject matter?

FURTHER READING

I. Stamatoudi, '"Joy" for the claimant: Can a film also be protected as a dramatic work?' (2000) 1 IPQ 117.

R. Arnold, '*Joy*: A Reply' (2001) 1 IPQ 10.

P. Kamina, 'British film copyright and the incorrect implementation of the EC Copyright Directives' (1998) 9(3) Ent LR 109.

> U. Klement, 'Protecting television show formats under copyright law: New developments in common law and civil law countries' [2007] EIPR 52.

2.5.1.5 Artistic work

An artistic work, according to s. 4 of the CDPA means:

> (a) a graphic work, photograph, sculpture or collage, irrespective of artistic quality,
>
> (b) a work of architecture being a building or model for a building, or
>
> (c) a work of artistic craftsmanship.

A number of these subcategories—building, graphic work, photograph, and sculpture—are further defined in s. 4. Importantly, 'graphic work' is defined to include:

> (a) any painting, drawing, diagram, map, chart or plan, and
>
> (b) any engraving, etching, lithograph, woodcut or similar work.

Apparent from the definition of artistic work is that it covers a range of artistic creations, from the purely aesthetic to those of a more functional kind. The fact that s. 4(1)(a) specifically states that certain subcategories of artistic work are protected 'irrespective of artistic quality' highlights that courts should not engage in a subjective evaluation of the artistic merits of a work. This also facilitates the protection of works of a more functional or industrial nature. As such, this has, and still does, create tension between copyright protection of industrial or functional items and the protection available under designs law, a point which is explored in greater detail in Chapter 11.[52]

In interpreting the scope of the 'artistic works' category courts have, on occasions, been fairly conservative. An example of this conservatism is the following case, where the court considered whether facial make-up could be protected as a painting.

Merchandising Corporation of America Inc v Harpbond [1983] FSR 32

The case concerned the facial make-up of performer, Adam Ant (from 'Adam and the Ants'). He adopted a new style (his Prince Charming look) in the early 1980s, in which he wore make up that comprised two red stripes, with a light blue stripe in the middle, running diagonally from nose to jaw on one cheek, as well as a heart over the left eye-brow and a beauty spot near the left nostril. The claimants made photographs and sketches of him in his Prince Charming look. The defendants reproduced these images in a variety of ways—by reproducing one of the photographs, altering existing photographs to erase the old make-up and superimposing the new, and painting a portrait of Adam Ant in his new style based on one of the claimants' photographs. The claimants sought interim relief for, *inter alia*, copyright infringement. Walton J granted such relief in respect of reproduction of one of the photographs, but not for the altered photograph

---

[52] See 11.4.

or portrait. The claimants appealed, arguing that copyright existed in the facial make-up of Adam Ant. The Court of Appeal dismissed the appeal.

Lawton LJ (with whom Oliver LJ and Brightman LJ agreed), at p. 46:

Mr Wilson's bold submission at the beginning of his presentation of his clients' case was that the marks on Mr Goddard's face by way of facial make-up were painting. That caused me very considerable surprise, because, although there are various statutory provisions in the Act defining various words used in it, there is no statutory definition of a painting. 'Painting' is a word in the ordinary usage of the English language and it is a question of fact in any particular case whether that which is under discussion is or is not a painting. It seemed to me, right at the beginning of Mr Wilson's submissions (and I want to be restrained in my language), that it was fantastic to suggest that make-up on anyone's face could possibly be a painting.

Mr Swift, in his succinct and concise reply, pointed out what had occurred to me and I had mentioned to Mr Wilson in the course of argument, that a painting must be on a surface of some kind. The surface upon which the startling make-up was put was Mr Goddard's face and, if there were a painting, it must be the marks plus Mr Goddard's face. If the marks are taken off the face there cannot be a painting. A painting is not an idea: it is an object; and paint without a surface is not a painting. Make-up, as such, however idiosyncratic it may be as an idea, cannot possibly be a painting for the purposes of the Copyright Act 1956.

Do you think that the Court of Appeal's interpretation of 'painting', albeit in the Copyright Act 1956, is a sound one? Would it exclude other forms of body art, such as tattoos?

The following is another case in which the court was asked to test the boundaries of the 'artistic work' category.

Creation Records Ltd v News Group Newspapers Ltd [1997] EMLR 444

Noel Gallagher arranged an ensemble of objects for the purposes of a 'photo-shoot', the results of which were to be used for the front sleeve of the Oasis album, 'Be Here Now'. The defendant newspaper engaged a freelance photographer to take an unauthorized photograph of the scene, which it subsequently published and offered for sale. In an action for an interlocutory injunction restraining further publication of the photograph, Lloyd J considered whether copyright subsisted in the 'photo-shoot' scene as a dramatic or artistic work.

Lloyd J, at pp. 447–50:

Mr Gallagher exhibits to his affidavit a photograph which, he says, he envisaged as being used for the front sleeve of the album. This has the swimming pool in the foreground with the Rolls Royce seemingly emerging from the water towards the camera. The hotel is beyond and to the right. In the far distance is a wooded area with a partly clouded sky above. The five members of the group are posed round the pool, one on a scooter, one climbing out of the pool and others with or near other objects seemingly unrelated to each other. The various objects were ordered two days before from a warehouse in London; none of them was made for the purpose.

. . .

It is said, first, that the scene itself (the arrangement or composition of the members of the group, the various objects and the site) is a copyright work. I do not see how that can be so. Mr Merriman argued faintly that it was a dramatic work. Since the scene is inherently static, having no movement, story or action, I cannot accept this. Primarily, he argued that it was an artistic work, as a sculpture or collage within section 4(1)(a) of the Copyright, Designs and Patents Act 1988 or a work of artistic craftsmanship within section 4(1)(c) of that Act.

I do not regard this as seriously arguable. I do not see how the process of assembling these disparate objects together with the members of the group can be regarded as having anything in common with sculpture or with artistic craftsmanship. No element in the composition has been carved, modelled or made in any of the other ways in which sculpture is made (see *Breville (Europe) plc v Thorn EMI Domestic Appliances Ltd* [1995] FSR 77 at 94). Nor does it seem to me to be the subject or result of the exercise of any craftsmanship (see *George Hensher Ltd v Restawile Upholstery (Lancs) Ltd* [1976] AC 64, especially Lord Simon at 91).

I should also mention in this context the case of *Shelley Films Ltd v Rex Features Ltd* [1994] EMLR 134. In this case Mr Martin Mann QC, sitting as a deputy judge of this division, held it to be seriously arguable that a film set prepared for the film to be called 'Mary Shelley's Frankenstein' was a work of artistic craftsmanship so that an unauthorised photograph taken of an actor on the set was a breach of copyright in the set as well, for different reasons, as of other elements in the photograph. That seems to me quite different on the facts. I can readily accept that a film set does involve craftsmanship. It is not merely an assembly of 'objets trouvés'. I will need to come back to another aspect of that case later.

As for collage, a subject of copyright new to English law in the 1988 Act, the traditional understanding of that word is that it involves the use of glue or some other adhesive in the process of making a work of visual art, being derived from the French. Two Oxford Dictionary definitions were put before me. *The Oxford English Dictionary* (2nd edn, 1989) has this:

> An abstract form of art in which photographs, pieces of paper, newspaper cuttings, string etc are placed in juxtaposition and glued to the pictorial surface; such a work of art.

It then goes on to quote examples which include some loose uses of the word, for example, in relation to poems and music. *The Concise Oxford Dictionary* (9th edn) has a shorter version of these two definitions, but also as its third:

> A collection of unrelated things.

Mr Merriman submits that it is at least seriously arguable that the composition which Mr Gallagher put together as the subject of the photography is within the definition of collage in this sense, even though it did not involve the use of any adhesive. More generally, he submitted that this composition is the result of the exercise of artistic creativity and originality and that at a time when the creativity of visual artists is finding outlets in a great variety of novel forms the 1988 Act should not be construed so as to deny such novel works of art the possibility of copyright protection as artistic works within section 4. He asked forensically how it might be found that copyright subsisted in Carl Andre's bricks, in stone circles created by Richard Long, in Rachel Whiteread's house, in the living sculptures of Gilbert and George and in examples of installation art generally. I do not find it necessary or appropriate to answer that question. I would distinguish Mr Gallagher's composition from all of those examples as being put together solely to be the subject matter of a number of photographs and disassembled as soon as those were taken. This composition was intrinsically ephemeral, or indeed less than ephemeral, in the original sense of that word of living only for one day. This existed for a few hours on the ground. Its continued existence was to be in the form of a photographic image. Accordingly, it seems to me materially different from all the particular examples put to me in this context by Mr Merriman.

Even if it were otherwise, I would not accept that it is seriously arguable that this composition is a collage. In my view a collage does indeed involve as an essential element the sticking of two or more things together. It does not suffice to point to the collocation, whether or not with artistic intent, of such random, unrelated and unfixed elements as is seen in the photographs in question.

Accordingly, I am not prepared to regard the plaintiffs' case based on copyright in the subject matter of the shoot as sufficiently arguable to be the basis of an interlocutory injunction.

The claimants were successful in obtaining an injunction on the basis of breach of confidence (the scene was treated as confidential as regards photography).[53] Nevertheless, does their failure to establish copyright in the scene highlight an unduly narrow interpretation of artistic works? What impact would it have on the protection of works of modern art, such as those mentioned in the above extract? Finally, does this case reflect the limitations of a 'closed list' approach to subject matter?

The apparent restrictiveness of the *Harpbond* and *Creation Records* decisions may be contrasted with those involving protection of functional items. For example, in *Wham-O Manufacturing Co v Lincoln Industries*[54] the New Zealand Court of Appeal protected a wooden prototype of a Frisbee as a 'sculpture' and the moulds for manufacturing Frisbees as 'engravings'. While in *Hi Tech Autoparts Ltd v Towergate Two Ltd (No 2)*[55] Christopher Floyd QC held that metal plates for the manufacture of rubber car mats were protected as engravings. Another example is *Breville Europe plc v Thorn EMI Domestic Appliances Ltd*,[56] where Falconer J held that plaster casts of a sandwich maker were 'sculptures' within the meaning of s. 3 of Copyright Act 1956. Does it make sense for courts to interpret the 'artistic works' category generously when it comes to industrial or functional items, but less so in relation to other types of creations, such as facial make-up or arrangements of objects?

In a recent case, *Lucasfilm Ltd v Ainsworth*,[57] Mr Justice Mann, after considering several decisions (including *Wham-O* and *Breville Europe*), laid down guidelines to assist in identifying works of 'sculpture'. Of particular note are the following guidelines:

(vi) It is of the essence of a sculpture that it should have, as part of its purpose, a visual appeal in the sense that it might be enjoyed for that purpose alone, whether or not it might have another purpose as well. The purpose is that of the creator... He may fail, but that does not matter (no judgments are to be made about artistic merit). It is the underlying purpose that is important.

...

(vii) The fact that the object has some other use does not necessarily disqualify it from being a sculpture, but it still has to have the intrinsic quality of being intended to be enjoyed as a visual thing.[58]

One of the issues in *Lucasfilm* was whether the helmet and armour worn by the stormtrooper characters in the first *Star Wars* film were copyright sculptures. Mann J held that they were not because they lacked artistic purpose. Rather, their primary function was utilitarian, i.e. to be worn as items of costume and to identify and portray characters in a film.[59] Mann J commented obiter that the conclusions in *Wham-O* and *Breville* were probably incorrect, given that in those cases there was 'no intention that the object itself should

53 See Ch. 8, p. 401. 54 [1985] RPC 127. 55 [2002] FSR 16.
56 [1995] FSR 77. 57 [2008] ECDR 17. 58 Ibid., pp. 356–7. 59 Ibid., p. 358.

have visual appeal for its own sake, and every intention that it be purely functional'.[60] Does it make sense to determine whether subject matter is a 'sculpture' based on the intention or purpose of the creator? If not, what would be an appropriate way of defining 'sculpture' without straying into considerations of artistic or aesthetic merit?

Probably the most controversial aspect of the 'artistic works' category is the scope of the subcategory 'works of artistic craftsmanship'. The difficulty stems mainly from determining whether or not the work is one of *artistic* craftsmanship. In the following decision, the House of Lords formulated a variety of approaches to this assessment.

George Hensher Ltd v Restawile Upholstery (Lancs) Ltd [1976] AC 64

The appellants produced a prototype of a suite of furniture (comprising two chairs and a settee), known as the 'Bronx' suite. It subsequently offered the suite (and variations of it) for sale to the general public. The respondents manufactured a suite of furniture (known as the 'Amazon' suite), which the appellants alleged infringed copyright in their suite and prototypes of the suites as artistic works. Graham J held that the prototype of the 'Bronx' suite was a work of artistic craftsmanship within the meaning of s. 3(1)(c) of the Copyright Act 1956. An appeal by the respondents to the Court of Appeal was allowed. The appellants then appealed to the House of Lords. The respondents admitted that the prototype was a work of craftsmanship but not that it was of 'artistic craftsmanship'. Each of the law lords delivered a speech.

Lord Reid, at pp. 78–9:

But here two questions must be determined. What precisely is the meaning of 'artistic' in this context and who is to judge of its application to the article in question? There is a trend of authority with which I agree that a court ought not to be called on to make an aesthetic judgment. Judges have to be experts in the use of the English language but they are not experts in art or aesthetics. In such a matter my opinion is of no more value than that of anyone else. But I can and must say what in my view is the meaning of the word 'artistic'.

. . .

It is I think of importance that the maker or designer of a thing should have intended that it should have an artistic appeal but I would not regard that as either necessary or conclusive. If any substantial section of the public genuinely admires and values a thing for its appearance and gets pleasure or satisfaction, whether emotional or intellectual, from looking at it, I would accept that it is artistic although many others may think it meaningless or common or vulgar.

I think that it may be misleading to equate artistic craftsmanship with a work of art. 'Work of art' is generally associated more with the fine arts than with craftsmanship and may be setting too high a standard. During last century there was a movement to bring art to the people. I doubt whether the craftsmen who set out with that intention would have regarded all their products as works of art, but they were certainly works of artistic craftsmanship whether or not they were useful as well as having an artistic appeal.

. . .

In the present case I find no evidence at all that anyone regarded the appellants' furniture as artistic. The appellants' object was to produce something which would sell. It was, as

---

[60] Ibid., p. 357.

one witness said, 'a winner' and they succeeded in their object. No doubt many customers bought the furniture because they thought it looked nice as well as being comfortable. But looking nice appears to me to fall considerably short of having artistic appeal. I can find no evidence that anyone felt or thought that the furniture was artistic in the sense which I have tried to explain. I am therefore of opinion that this appeal should be dismissed.

Lord Morris, at pp. 81–2:

So I would say that the object under consideration must be judged as a thing in itself. Does it have the character or virtue of being artistic? In deciding as to this some persons may take something from their ideas as to what constitutes beauty or as to what satisfies their notions of taste or as to what yields pleasure or as to what makes an aesthetic appeal. If, however, there is a resort to these or other words which may themselves have their own satellites of meanings there must follow a return to the word 'artistic' which is apt without exposition to contain and convey its own meaning.

As to the second question, I consider that as in all situations where a decision is required upon a question of fact the court must pay heed to the evidence that is adduced. Though it is a matter of individual opinion whether a work is or is not artistic there are many people who have special capabilities and qualifications for forming an opinion and whose testimony will command respect. In practice a court will not have difficulty in weighing their evidence and in deciding whether it clearly points to some conclusion. In cases where the court is able to see the work which is in question that will not warrant a decision on the basis of a spot opinion formed by the court itself but it will be a valuable aid to an appreciation of the evidence.

In the present case the evidence fell short of establishing that the knock-up qualified to be characterised as a work of artistic craftsmanship.

I would dismiss the appeal.

Viscount Dilhorne, at p. 87:

I am conscious, as was the Court of Appeal, of the need to avoid judicial assessment of artistic merits or quality, but I do not think that any such assessment is involved in deciding whether a work is an artistic work.

This question of fact in relation to copyright is decided not by a jury but by a judge sitting alone. Evidence may be called with regard to it. Expert witnesses may testify. At the end of the day, it will be for the judge to decide whether it is established that the work is one of artistic craftsmanship. If that is not established, the claim to copyright on that ground will fail. I do not think that it suffices to show that some section of the public considers the work to be artistic, though that fact will be one for the judge to take into account, for the decision has to be made by the judge and cannot be delegated.

In this case there was no evidence before Graham J that the prototype as a whole or that part of it which has been called a plinth was a work of an artistic character.

...

I would therefore dismiss this appeal.

Lord Simon, at pp. 94–6:

Not only is artistic merit irrelevant as a matter of statutory construction, evaluation of artistic merit is not a task for which judges have any training or general aptitude. Words are the tools and subject matter of lawyers; but even in matters of literary copyright the court will not concern itself with literary merit: *Walter v Lane* [1900] AC 539. Since the tribunal will not attempt a personal aesthetic judgment (Stewart J in *Hay and Hay Construction Co Ltd v Sloan* (1957) 16 Fox Pat C 185, 190), it follows, again, that whether the subject matter is or is not a work of artistic craftsmanship is a matter of evidence; and the most cogent evidence is likely to be from those who are either themselves acknowledged artist-craftsmen or concerned with the training of artist-craftsmen—in other words, expert evidence.

...

Against this construction of the statutory phrase, the result of the instant appeal cannot be in doubt: there was no, or certainly no adequate, evidence that the prototype of the Bronx chair was a work of artistic craftsmanship.

...

I would therefore dismiss the appeal.

Lord Kilbrandon, at p. 97:

The conscious intention of the craftsman will be the primary test of whether his product is artistic or not; the fact that many of us like looking at a piece of honest work, especially in the traditional trades, is not enough to make it a work of art.

Whether a given object is a work of artistic craftsmanship can be posed as a question of fact, but only after the meaning of the word 'artistic' has been determined; what that meaning is, is a question of law, since it involves a decision of what Parliament meant by the word Parliament used. I do not believe that it is possible, as matter of law or of exegesis, to arrive at a comprehensive definitive interpretation of such a familiar English word, so as to be armed with a test which will enable one, by the application of it, at a glance, to exclude all that does not properly fall within the scope of the simple word itself. It is, indeed, seldom that a simple word can, by translation into some easier or more difficult phrase, be rendered the more capable of furnishing such a test. But it is quite plain, in my opinion, that you cannot get on without exercising, in any case in which this kind of dispute arises, the judicial function of holding whether the facts bring the object within the meaning of the statutory definition. You will get no assistance, until you have exercised that judicial function, by asking the opinion of an expert; if he says 'I regard that object as artistic', the next question which must be asked in order to make his last answer intelligible is 'What do you mean by artistic?' That question is incompetent, because the answer would be irrelevant. Since the word is a word of common speech, it requires, and permits of, no interpretation by experts. It is for the judge to determine whether the object falls within the scope of the common meaning of the word.

...

In the result I have failed, perhaps inevitably, to find a substitute formula which will replace the word 'artistic,' and be one which will serve to qualify as artistic or non-artistic any given piece of craftsmanship. I do not think it is necessary to do so. I would put it in this way, that in my opinion the common meaning of the word 'artistic' does not permit that word to be used as a description of the craftsmanship involved in the production of the prototype 'Bronx' chair, having regard to all the evidence of the circumstances surrounding its manufacture, and I have endeavoured to show the reason why that should be so.

Is it possible to discern a *ratio decidendi* from the above speeches of the House of Lords? Or do the law lords each propound different tests for determining whether something qualifies as a 'work of artistic craftsmanship'? If so, which in your view is the preferable test?

In *Merlet v Mothercare*,[61] one of the issues raised was whether a prototype of a rain-cape for children (the 'Raincosy') was a work of artistic craftsmanship. At first instance, Walton J, at pp. 126–7 took the following view of *Hensher*:

> At any rate in the first instance, it is not for the court to make a value judgment: the question is primarily the intention of the artist-craftsman. If his intention was to create a work of art and he has not manifestly failed in that intent, that is all that is required. It is not for the court to say that he has merely done the equivalent of flinging a paint pot in the face of the public. But, of course, he may have manifestly failed in his object, and his own *ipse dixit* cannot therefore be the sole, although it is the initial and predominant, test.
>
> There is one further reflection. Although there must always come a first time when an artist-craftsman seeks to create a work of art, and the court may well look with just suspicion upon the first claim of this nature, it will be much easier to recognise the claim if the crafts-man is already a recognised artist.
>
> Finally, I say nothing as to the evidence which should be properly admitted as to whether the artist has succeeded in his aim of creating a work of art. There was a diversity of views in the House as to what evidence (apart of course from the intentions of the presumed artist-craftsman) was properly admissible, and especially on this last point. I do not think it would be right, since it is not required for the purposes of this case, to express any opinion thereon.

Walton J concluded that the Raincosy was not a work of artistic craftsmanship because, in designing the cape, the claimant had in mind purely utilitarian considerations, namely complete protection from inclement weather.

Does Walton J's interpretation of the ratio in *Hensher v Restawhile* reflect your understanding of the case? In any event, do you agree with the approach that he adopts, judging whether something is a work of artistic craftsmanship according to the intention of the artist-craftsman? In *Lucasfilm Ltd v Ainsworth*[62] Mann J also focused on the intention with which subject matter is created. In rejecting the argument that the helmet worn by the stormtrooper characters was a work of artistic craftsmanship, he found that it was not the creators' purpose that the helmet should in any way have aesthetic appeal. The Australian High Court has taken a contrasting approach in *Burge v Swarbuck*,[63] where it held that the primary concern is 'the extent to which the particular work's artistic expression, in its form, is unconstrained by functional considerations'.[64] Which, if any, of these contrasting approaches is preferable in your view?

Another issue that has arisen in the context of works of artistic craftsmanship is the extent to which the elements of artistry and craftsmanship can derive from different persons, as opposed to from the same person. In the New Zealand decision *Bonz Group (Pty) Ltd v Cooke*[65] Tipping J stated that the author must be both a craftsman and an artist. The former is 'a person who makes something in a skilful way and takes justified pride in his workman-ship' whereas an artist 'is a person with creative ability who produces something which has aesthetic appeal'.[66] Tipping J went on to comment that '[i]f two or more people combine to design and make the ultimate product I cannot see why that ultimate product should not be regarded as a work of artistic craftsmanship'.[67] This approach was adopted by Evans-Lombe J in *Vermaat and Powell v Boncrest*.[68]

---

61 [1986] RPC 115. 62 [2008] ECDR 17. 63 [2007] FSR 27, paras. 63–5.
64 Ibid., para. 83. 65 [1994] NZLR 216. 66 Ibid., at p. 223.
67 Ibid. 68 [2001] FSR 5.

FURTHER READING

A. Barron, 'Copyright law and the claims of art' [2002] IPQ 368.

A. Christie, 'A proposal for simplifying United Kingdom copyright law' [2001] EIPR 26.

2.5.2 ORIGINALITY

A requirement of 'originality' is not expressly included in the Berne Convention. Rather, the *travaux préparatoires* for the Brussels Revision Conference indicates that the requirement of 'intellectual creation' is implicit in the concept of 'literary and artistic work'.[69] This view is arguably reinforced by the fact that Article 2(5) expressly refers to 'collections of literary or artistic works' being 'intellectual creations' by virtue of the 'selection and arrangement of their contents'. Professors Ricketson and Ginsburg argue that, 'while such a stipulation is necessary in the case of these kinds of borderline works, it hardly needs to be stated in relation to the "mainline" works covered by article 2(1)'.[70] There is, however, very little guidance on what constitutes 'intellectual creation' and, as a result, Union Members may (and do) differ in their approach to what minimum standard of originality is required.

In the UK, s. 1(1)(a) of the CDPA makes clear that literary, dramatic, musical, and artistic works must be 'original' in order for copyright to subsist. Aside from databases, for which 'originality' is defined as the 'author's own intellectual creation', the CDPA is otherwise silent on the meaning of this requirement. This has meant that, for the most part, the meaning of 'originality' has been judicially defined. One of the seminal cases in this area is *Walter v Lane*.

Walter v Lane [1900] AC 539

The Earl of Rosebery (who made no claim in the action) gave public speeches on five occasions. Reporters from *The Times* newspaper took down the speeches verbatim in shorthand and later transcribed them, adding punctuation, revisions, and corrections. The respondent published a book, which included Lord Rosebery's speeches taken substantially from the reports in *The Times*. The newspaper brought an action against the respondents for infringement of copyright under the Literary Copyright Act 1842. The issue that arose was whether or not the reporters of a speech could be considered 'authors'. If so, *The Times* would be entitled to copyright since the reporters were their employees and had assigned their rights to them. The Court of Appeal held that the reporters were not 'authors'. This was reversed in the House of Lords.

Lord Davey, at pp. 551–2:

In my opinion the reporter is the author of his own report. He it was who brought into existence in the form of a writing the piece of letterpress which the respondent has copied. I think also that he and he alone composed his report. The materials for his composition were his notes, which were his own property, aided to some extent by his memory and trained

---

[69] Ricketson and Ginsburg, *International Copyright and Neighbouring Rights: The Berne Convention and beyond* (2nd edn., Oxford: Oxford University Press, 2005), para. 8.03.

[70] Ibid.

judgement. Owing to the perfection which the art of shorthand writing has attained in recent years, memory and judgement bear a less important part in the composition of a report of a speech than was formerly the case. But the question whether the composer has copyright in his report does not seem to me to vary inversely with or to depend on his skill in stenography. Nor, as it appears to me, does the fact that the subject-matter of the report had been made public property, or that no originality or literary skill was demanded for the composition of the report, have anything to do with the matter. Again, it is said that the lucidity of diction and perfection of expression which characterise the eminent person named render an exact reproduction of his words a comparatively easy and almost mechanical task. But is it argued that the reporter of the hesitating or half-completed utterances of an inferior speaker might have copyright, though the reporter of Lord Rosebery may not? Or does the question of copyright in the report depend on the clearness of thought and speech of the orator? In my opinion the question must be decided on general considerations, and not on any grounds which are personal either to the orator or to the reporter. Copyright has nothing to do with the originality or literary merits of the author or composer. It may exist in the information given by a street directory: *Kelly v Morris*; or by a list of deeds of arrangement: *Cate v Devon and Exeter Constitutional Newspaper Co*; or in a list of advertisements: *Lamb v Evans*. I think those cases right, and the principle on which they proceed directly applicable to the present case. It was of course open to any other reporter to compose his own report of Lord Rosebery's speech, and to any other newspaper or book to publish that report; but it is a sound principle that a man shall not avail himself of another's skill, labour, and expense by copying the written product thereof.

Lord James, at pp. 553–5:

Whilst the Act supplies no definition of the word 'author', and whilst it may be difficult for any judicial authority to give a positive definition of that word, certain considerations controlling the meaning of it seem to be established. A mere copyist of written matter is not an 'author' within the Act, but a translator from one language to another would be so. A person to whom words are dictated for the purpose of being written down is not an 'author'. He is the mere agent or clerk of the person dictating, and requires to possess no art beyond that of knowing how to write. The person dictating takes a share in seeing that the person writing follows the dictation, and makes it his care to give time for the writing to be made. But an 'author' may come into existence without producing any original matter of his own. Many instances of the claim to authorship without the production of original matter have been given at the bar. The compilation of a street directory, the reports of proceedings in courts of law, and the tables of the times of running of certain railway trains have been held to bring the producers within the word 'author'; and yet in one sense no original matter can be found in such publications. Still there was a something apart from originality on the one hand and mere mechanical transcribing on the other which entitled those who gave these works to the world to be regarded as their authors.

Now, what is it that a reporter does? Is he a mere scribe? Does he produce original matter or does he produce the something I have mentioned which entitles him to be regarded as an 'author' within the Act? I think that from a general point of view a reporter's art represents more than mere transcribing or writing from dictation. To follow so as to take down the words of an ordinary speaker, and certainly of a rapid speaker, is an art requiring considerable training, and does not come within the knowledge of ordinary persons. Even amongst professional reporters many different degrees of skill exist. Some reporters can take down the words of a speaker however rapidly he speaks; others less practised or proficient cannot, as the term is, keep up with the rapid speaker. Apart from the dealing with the rapidity of speech, there are some reporters whose ears and thoughts and hands never fail them, and who therefore produce reports of complete accuracy. On the other hand, reporters less skilled may be so deficient in this quality of accuracy as to produce reports which certainly tend to perturb the speakers whom they have endeavoured to report. Thus there seems to be a degree of skill in one class of reporters over the other…

After taking such matters as these into consideration, I have, after some doubt, come to the conclusion that a reporter of a speech under the conditions existing in this case is the meritorious producer of the something necessary to constitute him an 'author' within the meaning of the Copyright Act of 1842 , and that therefore the judgement of the Court of Appeal should be reversed.

Lord Brampton, at p. 556:

The material facts which have led me to the opinion I am about to express are admitted, and may be very briefly stated. On the several occasions when the speeches were delivered, reporters for *The Times* and other newspapers attended by invitation to enable them to compose and write, for publication in their respective journals, descriptive articles of the occurrences, containing full and accurate reports of the speeches as they were delivered from the lips of the speaker. The reporters who represented *The Times*, with whom alone I have now to deal, were undoubtedly gentlemen of education, great ability, and long and varied experience in the duties of their vocation. They wrote the descriptive parts of their reports from personal observation, the speeches they took down in shorthand, word for word, transcribed them verbatim in longhand, carefully corrected and revised and punctuated them, so that when they appeared in the columns of *The Times* they might, as perfectly as printed words could do, convey to the readers all that was to be seen or heard upon those occasions. From these reports all that appeared in *The Times* was first published to the world. It is obvious that the preparation of them involved considerable intellectual skill and brain labour beyond the mere mechanical operation of writing.

[**Lord Halsbury** delivered a speech, in which he reversed the Court of Appeal's decision. **Lord Robertson** delivered a dissenting speech.]

Given that the Literary Copyright Act 1842 did not have an express requirement of 'originality' and that their Lordships were considering the meaning of 'author', how is it that this House of Lords decision remains relevant to 'originality' under existing copyright law? Subsequent cases have certainly treated the decision as authority on the meaning of 'originality'.

Express Newspapers plc v News (UK) Ltd [1990] 1 WLR 1320

This was a case of 'tit for tat' copying between two newspapers. The claimant newspaper had brought an action against the defendant newspaper, alleging that it had copied the report of their exclusive interview with a Mrs Bordes. They applied for and obtained summary judgment. The defendant issued a counterclaim, in which it alleged that it had copyright in an exclusive interview with a Miss Ogilvy in which some of her words were quoted verbatim and that the claimant newspaper had published substantial extracts from their article.

Sir Nicolas Browne-Wilkinson V-C (giving judgment for the defendant), at pp. 1325–6:

What then of the position of the quotations of the exact words used by Miss Ogilvy? The law as to copyright in verbatim reports of the spoken words of another was settled by the House of Lords in *Walter v Lane* [1900] AC 539…The question was, did the reporter of Lord Rosebery's words have any copyright in the report? The House of Lords held that he did. Lord Halsbury LC said, at p. 548:

> And though I think in these compositions there is literary merit and intellectual labour, yet the statute seems to me to require neither, nor originality either in thought or in language.

Lord Davey said, at p. 552:

> It was of course open to any other reporter to compose his own report of Lord Rosebery's speech, and to any other newspaper or book to publish that report; but it is a sound principle that a man shall not avail himself of another's skill, labour, and expense by copying the written product thereof.

As a result of that House of Lords decision it was established that the mere reporting of the words of another gives rise to a reporter's copyright so long as skill and judgement have been employed in the composition of that report.

The decision was made under the Copyright Act 1842 which contains no express requirement for the work in which copyright subsists to have been an original work. From the Copyright Act 1911 onwards there has been an express statutory requirement in relation to works of this kind that the work shall be an original work (see now section 1(1)(a) of the Act of 1988). In *Roberton v Lewis* [1976] RPC 169, 174 Cross J suggested *obiter* that the statutory requirement that the work should be an original work might mean that the decision in *Walter v Lane* was no longer good law. He was not referred to the decision of the High Court of Australia in *Sands & McDougall Proprietary Ltd v Robinson* (1917) 23 CLR 49, where the court considered the impact of the introduction into the Act of 1911 of the requirement for the work to be original, dealt with the matter very fully and reached the conclusion that *Walter v Lane* was still good law. They held that the word 'original' in the statute does not imply inventive originality; it is enough that the work is the production of something in a new form as a result of the skill, labour and judgement of the reporter. I prefer the view expressed by the High Court of Australia. It seems to me sound. The possibility of the continued existence of reporters' copyright is reflected in section 3(3) of the Act of 1988, which expressly refers to the possibility of the recorder of spoken words having a copyright in the record of those words as distinct from the work recorded.

Mr Burton also referred me to passages on the meaning of the word 'original' in the statutes in the speeches in *Interlego AG v Tyco Industries Inc* [1989] AC 217. It was, I think, suggested that that decision might have impliedly modified the law as laid down in *Walter v Lane* [1900] AC 539. But *Walter v Lane* was not referred to in argument, and the Privy Council were there considering quite a different point on originality which does not, in my judgement, touch on *Walter v Lane*. I therefore approach this case on the basis that *Walter v Lane* is undeniably still good law. On that footing, if skill, labour and judgement was put into the reporting of Miss Ogilvy's words in the 'Today' newspaper, copyright will subsist in the report of those words even though the words themselves are Miss Ogilvy's.

Sir Nicolas Browne-Wilkinson (as he then was) held, following *Walter v Lane*, that 'skill, labour and judgment' was the appropriate test for originality under UK copyright law. This test has been confirmed in a later House of Lords decision.

Ladbroke (Football) Ltd v William Hill (Football) Ltd [1964] 1 WLR 273

The respondents (William Hill) claimed copyright in their football betting coupons and alleged that the appellants (Ladbroke) had produced infringing coupons. The judge at first instance found against the respondents, but the Court of Appeal reversed this decision, finding that the respondents' coupons were entitled to copyright, and granted an injunction to restrain the appellants. On appeal to the House of Lords the appellants argued, *inter alia*, that the coupons were not original literary works under s. 2(1) of the Copyright Act 1956. They submitted that while a considerable amount of skill, judgment, and labour went into deciding what bets to include in the coupons, the expression of these bets in the coupon lacked skill, judgment, and labour since it only involved them writing down the bets.

Lord Reid, at pp. 277–8:

A wrong result can easily be reached if one begins by dissecting the plaintiffs' work and asking, could section A be the subject of copyright if it stood by itself, could section B be protected if it stood by itself, and so on. To my mind, it does not follow that, because the fragments taken separately would not be copyright, therefore the whole cannot be. Indeed, it has often been recognised that if sufficient skill and judgement have been exercised in devising the arrangements of the whole work, that can be an important or even decisive element in deciding whether the work as a whole is protected by copyright.

. . .

The appellants' main argument was based on quite a different ground. They deny that the respondents' coupon is an original compilation. There is no dispute about the meaning of the term 'original'. 'The word "original" does not in this connection mean that the work must be the expression of original or inventive thought. Copyright Acts are not concerned with the originality of ideas, but with the expression of thought, and, in the case of "literary work", with the expression of thought in print or writing. The originality which is required relates to the expression of the thought. But the Act does not require that the expression must be in an original or novel form, but that the work must not be copied from another work—that it should originate from the author.' *Per* Peterson J in *University of London Press Ltd v University Tutorial Press Ltd*. And it is not disputed that, as regards compilation, originality is a matter of degree depending on the amount of skill, judgement or labour that has been involved in making the compilation.

In the present case, if it is permissible to take into account all the skill, judgement and labour expended in producing the respondents' coupon, there can be no doubt that it is 'original'. But the appellants say that the coupon must be regarded as having been produced in two stages: first, the respondents had to decide what kind of business they would do—what kinds of bets they would offer to their clients—and then they had to write these out on paper. The appellants say that it is only the skill, judgement and labour involved in the latter stage that can be considered and that that part of their operation involved so little skill, judgement or labour that it cannot qualify as 'original'. In fact, the respondents did not proceed in that way. Their business was to devise a coupon which would appeal to the betting public, and its form and arrangement were not something dictated by previous decisions about the nature of the bets to be offered. The appellants likened the coupon to a trader's catalogue of his wares, and argued that in considering whether a catalogue is entitled to copyright you must disregard the trader's skill and work in deciding what wares he will stock for sale and only consider the skill and labour involved in the actual preparation of the catalogue. I do not think that that is a true analogy. And even in the case of a catalogue there may be a question whether the work, in deciding what to sell, and the work, in deciding how to sell it, are not so inter-connected as to be inseparable. Copyright in a catalogue in no way prevents honest competition—any other trader can decide to stock and sell any or all of the catalogued articles, and he can thereafter make a new catalogue of his own wares. What he must not do is simply to copy the other trader's catalogue.

Lord Devlin, at pp. 289–90:

The appellants argue that the skill, industry and experience admittedly employed by the respondents was not employed in the production of the coupon. It was employed, they say, in the selection of types of wager. These wagers were, so to speak, the articles which the respondents offered for sale to the public. Like other salesmen, the respondents had as a matter of business to decide what sort of wares they were going to offer. The making of that choice is a matter of business which, it is argued, is irrelevant for the purposes of copyright. So the skill and labour devoted to the work of selection must be exercised. What is left, that is, the skill and labour required to express in writing a business decision, is negligible; and so there is no originality. This is the short point taken by the appellants which found favour with Lloyd-Jacob J at the trial and with Diplock LJ dissenting in the Court of Appeal.

...

I do not think it necessary in this type of case that the work done should have as its sole, or even as its main, object the preparation of a document such as a list or catalogue or race card. It is sufficient that the preparation of the document is an object of the work done. If that be so, the work cannot be split up and parts allotted to the several objects. The value of the work as a whole must be assessed when the claim to originality is being considered. If, when the work of selection is being done, there is no intention of listing results, the matter might well be different. A line could then be drawn between the work of selecting and the work of recording a selection independently made. No such line can be drawn in the present case which is, to my mind, much stronger than the ordinary case in which goods are being catalogued. The whole object of the work done was the production of the coupon.

Lord Pearce, at pp. 292–3:

In deciding therefore whether a work in the nature of a compilation is original, it is wrong to start by considering individual parts of it apart from the whole, as the appellants in their argument sought to do. For many compilations have nothing original in their parts, yet the sum total of the compilation may be original.

...

So in each case it is a question of degree whether the labour or skill or ingenuity or expense involved in the compilation is sufficient to warrant a claim to originality in a compilation.

...

It emerges clearly that the arrangement and contents of the coupons are the central point of the business—what one witness called the heart of the business. The coupon must contain an assorted selection of bets that will attract a customer and induce him to fill up the coupon in preference to rival coupons. To this end, the plaintiffs have devoted much work and money and ingenuity. Out of the vast number of bets that can be offered, they select and devise those which, while being profitable to them, will fill the coupon with the greatest allure.

The appellants seek to say that this work is preliminary and has been directed to decisions as to what types of bets the plaintiffs shall pursue in the business; that such decisions are merely ideas and as such not the subject of copyright; and that the work of actually writing down those ideas in the coupon is too easy and negligible to justify any claim to originality.

An argument on those lines was unsuccessful in the cases of the *British Broadcasting Co v Wireless League Gazette Publishing Co* and *Football League Ltd v Littlewoods Pools Ltd.* There may be cases where such a dichotomy might be justified between some preliminary work and the actual transcription of a compilation, if the work was done with no ultimate intention of a compilation. But on the facts of the present case such an argument cannot succeed. The whole of the plaintiff's efforts from the beginning were devoted to arranging a coupon that would attract punters and be the basis of the plaintiffs' business. Types of bets were not considered *in vacuo* but only in relation to the part which they would play in the coupon.

In my opinion, the majority of the Court of Appeal rightly held that the plaintiffs had established copyright in the coupon.

[**Lord Hodson** and **Lord Evershed** delivered concurring speeches.]

Having considered the decisions in *Walter v Lane* and *Ladbroke*, how would you describe the originality test in UK copyright law? Can it be equated to the concept of novelty? When it comes to the originality of compilations particular issues seem to arise. On the facts of *Ladbroke* do you agree with the House of Lords that there was originality of expression?

Whether there is a universal test of originality, applicable to every type of work, was doubted by the Privy Council in *Interlego v Tyco*.

Interlego v Tyco [1989] AC 217

The appellants (Interlego) were the manufacturers of Lego and Duplo toy bricks for children. They previously had patent and registered design protection for the design of their bricks, which had expired. Design drawings from pre-1973 existed for both types of bricks. These pre-1973 drawings were later redrawn (the post-1972 drawings). The main features of the pre-1973 drawings were reproduced, the only changes being to the written information on the drawings, which had technical importance for manufacturing purposes. The respondents (Tyco), a US toy manufacturing company, decided to make and sell in Hong Kong toy bricks that were compatible with those of the appellants. They achieved this by studying the appellants' bricks and copying the principal features of the design. The appellants brought an action in the High Court of Hong Kong, alleging infringement of copyright in the design drawings. An injunction was granted at first instance. An appeal was partly allowed by the Court of Appeal, which held that copyright did not subsist in the pre-1973 drawings because the designs were capable of registration under the Registered Designs Act 1949, but that the post-1972 drawings were original artistic works that had been infringed. The appellants appealed on the issue of copyright in the pre-1973 drawings, while the respondents cross-appealed in relation to the post-1972 drawings.

Lord Oliver, delivering the Opinion of the Privy Council, held that the Court of Appeal were correct in denying copyright protection to the pre-1973 design drawings. He then turned to the cross-appeal.

Lord Oliver (delivering the opinion of the Privy Council), **at pp. 256–63:**

Thus the primary question on Tyco's appeal can be expressed in this way: can Lego, having enjoyed a monopoly for the full permitted period of patent and design protection in reliance upon drawings in which no copyright any longer subsists, continue their monopoly for yet a further, more extensive period by redrawing the same designs with a number of minor alterations and claiming a fresh copyright in the redrawn designs?

...

The significant thing about all these changes is that they involve no substantial alteration to the drawing as such. The outline of the object depicted is, in each case, virtually identical save for the minute differences occasioned by the abandonment of the flow-rib, the depicting of radii on the edges of the knobs and the abandonment of the radius on the outer diameter of the tubes. The significant changes, however important technically, are not indicated by any substantial alteration of the drawing as an artistic work. That remains basically the same and was admittedly copied from the 1968 drawing in the same way as if it had been actually traced...What is important about a drawing is what is visually significant and the redrawing of an existing drawing with a few minimal visual alterations does not make it an original *artistic* work, however much labour and skill may have gone into the process of reproduction or however important the technical significance of the verbal information that may be included in the same document by way of information or instruction.

...

Not altogether surprisingly there is no statutory definition of the word 'originality' but there is a classical statement of what is comprised in the concept of originality in the context of copyright in the judgement of Peterson J in *University of London Press Ltd v University Tutorial Press Ltd* [1916] 2 Ch 601, 608–9:

> The word 'original' does not in this connection mean that the work must be the expression of original or inventive thought. Copyright Acts are not concerned with the originality of ideas, but with the expression of thought, and, in the case of 'literary work,' with the expression of thought in print or writing. The originality which is required relates to the expression of the thought. But the Act does not require that the expression must be in an original or novel form, but that the work must not be copied from another work—that it should originate from the author.

That statement is, of course, not complete in itself because there may clearly be original work which makes use of material obtained by the author from pre-existing sources. Perhaps the most useful exegesis is to be found in three passages from the opinion of the Board delivered by Lord Atkinson in the Privy Council case of *Macmillan & Co Ltd v Cooper* (1924) 40 TLR 186, a case concerned with university textbooks consisting of abridgements of or excerpts from existing works with appropriate notes for students. Lord Atkinson observed, at p. 188:

> it is the product of the labour, skill, and capital of one man which must not be appropriated by another, not the elements, the raw material, if one may use the expression, upon which the labour and skill and capital of the first have been expended. To secure copyright for this product it is necessary that labour, skill and capital should be expended sufficiently to impart to the product some quality or character which the raw material did not possess, and which differentiates the product from the raw material.

...

Originality in the context of literary copyright has been said in several well known cases to depend upon the degree of skill, labour and judgement involved in preparing a compilation. *Macmillan & Co Ltd v Cooper*, 40 TLR 186 was such a case. So was *GA Cramp & Son*

Ltd v Frank Smythson Ltd [1944] AC 329. Similarly in the speeches of Lord Reid and Lord Hodson in *Ladbroke (Football) Ltd v William Hill (Football) Ltd* [1964] 1 WLR 273, 277 (Lord Reid) and at pp. 285 and 287 (Lord Hodson) it is stressed that the amount of skill, judgement or labour is likely to be decisive in the case of compilations. To apply that, however, as a universal test of originality in all copyright cases is not only unwarranted by the context in which the observations were made but palpably erroneous. Take the simplest case of artistic copyright, a painting or a photograph. It takes great skill, judgement and labour to produce a good copy by painting or to produce an enlarged photograph from a positive print, but no one would reasonably contend that the copy painting or enlargement was an 'original' artistic work in which the copier is entitled to claim copyright. Skill, labour or judgement merely in the process of copying cannot confer originality. In this connection some reliance was placed on a passage from the judgement of Whitford J in *LB (Plastics) Ltd v Swish Products Ltd* [1979] RPC 551, 568–9, where he expressed the opinion that a drawing of a three-dimensional prototype, not itself produced from the drawing and not being a work of artistic craftsmanship, would qualify as an original work. That may well be right, for there is no more reason for denying originality to the depiction of a three-dimensional prototype than there is for denying originality to the depiction in two-dimensional form of any other physical object. It by no means follows, however, that that which is an exact and literal reproduction in two-dimensional form of an existing two-dimensional work becomes an original work simply because the process of copying it involves the application of skill and labour. There must in addition be some element of material alteration or embellishment which suffices to make the totality of the work an original work. Of course, even a relatively small alteration or addition quantitatively may, if material, suffice to convert that which is substantially copied from an earlier work into an original work. Whether it does so or not is a question of degree having regard to the quality rather than the quantity of the addition. But copying, per se, however much skill or labour may be devoted to the process, cannot make an original work. A well executed tracing is the result of much labour and skill but remains what it is, a tracing. Moreover it must be borne in mind that the Copyright Act 1956 confers protection on an original work for a generous period. The prolongation of the period of statutory protection by periodic reproduction of the original work with minor alterations is an operation which requires to be scrutinised with some caution to ensure that that for which protection is claimed really is an original artistic work.

What is the ratio of *Interlego*? Is it that an exact copy of an existing artistic work will never satisfy the test of originality? Or is it more limited than this? *Walter v Lane*, where an exact report of a speech was protected, does not appear to have been cited to the Privy Council. Can *Interlego* be reconciled with *Walter v Lane*?

The originality requirement, as it relates to artistic works, has been the subject of further judicial comment, as well as academic debate. In the United States decision of *Bridgeman Art Library Ltd v Corel*[71] District Judge Kaplan commented obiter that, if the governing law was UK copyright law, photographic images of paintings could not qualify as original artistic works because of the *Interlego* decision. This gave rise to a debate in the UK about the originality requirement for artistic works, particularly for photographs. In the UK decision of *Antiquesportfolio.com plc v Rodney Fitch & Co Ltd*[72] an issue arose as to whether a photograph of a static three-dimensional object (such as a vase) could qualify as an original artistic work. Neuberger J was referred to the *Bridgeman* decision, however, he

[71] (1999) 36 F Supp 2d 191 (SDNY).   [72] [2001] FSR 23.

distinguished it on the basis that it involved a photograph of a two dimensional work. He stated at pp. 353–4:

> 36. In the case of photographs of a three-dimensional object, with which I am concerned in the present case, it can be said that the positioning of the object (unless it is a sphere), the angle at which it is taken, the lighting and the focus, and matters such as that, could all be matters of aesthetic or even commercial judgement, albeit in most cases at a very basic level.
>
> 37. Further, the instant photographs appear to have been taken with a view to exhibiting particular qualities, including the colour (in the case of some items), their features (e.g. the glaze in pottery) and, in the case of almost all the items, the details. It may well be that, in those circumstances, some degree of skill was involved in the lighting, angling and judging the positioning.

In the light of *Antiquesportfolio.com* and *Interlego* what do you think a UK court would decide if presented with the facts of *Bridgeman*?

FURTHER READING

K. Garnett, 'Copyright in photographs' [2000] EIPR 229.

R. Deazley, 'Photographing paintings in the public domain: A response to Garnett' [2001] EIPR 179.

The issue of whether a work can be original where there has been considerable skill, judgment and labour directed towards producing a faithful copy of pre-existing material has also arisen in the context of musical works.

***

Hyperion Records v Sawkins [2005] RPC 32, [2005] 1 WLR 3281

The facts of this case were described above at p. 60. The Court of Appeal upheld the decision at first instance that Dr Sawkins' modern performing editions of Lalande's grand motets were original musical works.

Mummery LJ:

Principles of copyright law

27. I now turn to consider the policy of copyright law, its governing principles and their application to the facts found by the judge.

A. Originality

28. The general policy of copyright is to prevent the unauthorised copying of certain material forms of expression (literary, dramatic, artistic and musical, for example) resulting from intellectual exertions of the human mind. The scope of protection available is subject to numerous qualifying conditions, restrictions, exceptions and defences, which are not relevant to this case.

29. The important point is that copyright can be used to prevent copying of a substantial part of the relevant form of expression, but it does not prevent use of the information,

thoughts or emotions expressed in the copyright work. It does not prevent another person from coincidentally creating a similar work by his own independent efforts. It is not an intellectual property monopoly in the same sense as a patent or a registered design. There is no infringement of copyright in the absence of a direct or indirect causal link between the copyright work and the alleged copy.

30. Thus, if the claim of the claimant to copyright in the performing editions were upheld, that would not prevent other musicologists, composers, performers or record companies from copying Lalande's music directly or indirectly or from making fresh performing editions of their own. All that the claimant can prevent them from doing, without his consent, is taking the short cut of copying his performing editions in order to save themselves the trouble that he went to in order to produce them.

31. The policy of copyright protection and its limited scope explain why the threshold requirement of an 'original' work has been interpreted as not imposing objective standards of novelty, usefulness, inventiveness, aesthetic merit, quality or value. A work may be complete rubbish and utterly worthless, but copyright protection may be available for it, just as it is for the great masterpieces of imaginative literature, art and music. A work need only be 'original' in the limited sense that the author originated it by his efforts rather than slavishly copying it from the work produced by the efforts of another person.

32. The first question is whether the performing editions are incapable of being regarded as 'original' works because Lalande composed the music and the claimant made his editions of that music with the intention that they should be as close as possible to the Lalande originals.

33. The essential elements of originality were expounded by the House of Lords over a century ago in *Walter v Lane* [1900] AC 539, a decision on the Copyright Act 1842 (5 & 6 Vict c 45). It remains good law: see *Express Newspapers plc v News (UK) Ltd* [1990] 1 WLR 1320, 1325–6.

...

36. In my judgment, on the application of *Walter v Lane* to this case, the effort, skill and time which the judge found the claimant spent in making the three performing editions were sufficient to satisfy the requirement that they should be 'original' works in the copyright sense. This is so even though (a) the claimant worked on the scores of existing musical works composed by another person (Lalande); (b) Lalande's works are out of copyright; and (c) the claimant had no intention of adding any new notes of music of his own.

Jacob LJ:

78. …But in the end, in my opinion it is essential to consider exactly what the claimant did to decide (both qualitatively and quantitatively) whether he created an original music work within the meaning of the Act. For, whilst it is trite that mere servile copying (for instance tracing or photocopying) does not amount to originality, there are clearly forms of 'copying' which do—the shorthand writer's copyright is a paradigm example which has stood since *Walter v Lane* [1900] AC 539.

79. In this connection I accept the opinion of the authors of *The Modern Law of Copyright*, 3rd edn, para. 3.52 that it is 'highly probable [that] *Walter v Lane* is still good law', notwithstanding the addition of the word 'original' to the Act in 1911. The reasoning in *Sands & McDougall Pty Ltd v Robinson* (1917) 23 CLR 49 (High Court of Australia) adopted in *Express Newspapers plc v News* (UK) Ltd [1990] 1 WLR 1320 (Sir Nicolas Browne-Wilkinson V-C) is right. The authors of *Copinger and Skone James on Copyright*, 15th edn (2005), vol. 1, para. 3–124 are of the same opinion (indeed do not qualify it with 'highly probable'). Indeed we were not presented with a full frontal attack upon *Walter v Lane*.

80. Both textbooks maintain that view despite what was said obiter in the *Interlego case* [1989] AC 217, 255–6, per Lord Oliver:

Take the simplest case of artistic copyright, a painting or a photograph. It takes great skill, judgement and labour to produce a good copy by painting or to produce an enlarged photograph from a positive print, but no one would reasonably contend that the copy painting or enlargement was an 'original' artistic work in which the copier is entitled to claim copyright. Skill, labour or judgement merely in the process of copying cannot confer originality.

81. The authors of *The Modern Law of Copyright* comment on this passage at para. 4.39. Although the comment is long it is worth setting it out:

However, whilst the remarks made in *Interlego* may be valid if confined to the subject matter then before the Privy Council, they are stated too widely. The Privy Council was there considering fairly simple technical drawings. This is a rather special subject matter. While the drawing of such a work is more laborious than it looks, it is a fact that any competent draftsman (perhaps, any conscientious amateur) who sets out to reproduce it exactly will almost certainly succeed in the end, because of the mathematical precision of the lines and measurements. This should be contrasted with, e.g. a painting by Vermeer, where it will be obvious that very few persons, if any, are capable of making an exact replica. Now, assume a number of persons do set out to copy such a painting, each according to his own personal skill. Most will only succeed in making something which all too obviously differs from the original—some of them embarrassingly so. They will get a copyright seeing that in each instance the end result does differ from the original yet it took a measure of skill and labour to produce. If, however, one of these renders the original with all the skill and precision of a Salvador Dali, is he to be denied a copyright where a mere dauber is not? The difference between the two cases (technical drawing and old master painting) is that in the latter there is room for individual interpretation even where faithful replication is sought to be attempted while in the former there is not. Further, a photographer who carefully took a photograph of an original painting might get a copyright and, if this is so, it is rather hard to see why a copy of the same degree of fidelity, if rendered by an artist of the calibre forementioned, would not be copyright. These considerations suggest that the proposition under discussion is suspect. It is therefore submitted that, for example, a picture restorer may get a copyright for the result of his efforts. Be that as it may, it is submitted that the *Interlego* proposition is anyway distinguishable where the replicator succeeds in preserving for posterity an original to which access is difficult.

82. The authors of *Copinger on Copyright*, para. 3–142, likewise take the view that the passage should be read as confined.

83. I agree with the textbooks. I do not think the comment as a generality is consistent with *Walter v Lane* [1900] AC 539. I think the true position is that one has to consider the extent to which the 'copyist' is a mere copyist—merely performing an easy mechanical function. The more that is so the less is his contribution likely to be taken as 'original'. Professor Jane C. Ginsburg ('The concept of authorship in comparative copyright law', 10 January 2003, Columbia Law School, Public Law Research Paper No. 03–51, http://ssrn.com/abstract=368481) puts it this way, at p. 21:

reproductions requiring great talent and technical skill may qualify as protectable works of authorship, even if they are *copies* of pre-existing works. This would be the case for photographic and other high quality replicas of works of art.

In the end the question is one of degree—how much skill, labour and judgement in the making of the copy is that of the creator of that copy? Both individual creative input and sweat of brow may be involved and will be factors in the overall evaluation.

...

85. Therefore, as it seems to me, one is bound to have to consider whether what the claimant did involved enough to confer originality—did it go beyond mere servile copying? Patten J held that it did. He applied this test, at para. 58:

> The question to ask in any case where the material produced is based on an existing score is whether the new work is sufficiently original in terms of the skill and labour used to produce it.

86. That seems to me to be exactly right. Of course the test involves a question of degree— mere photocopying or merely changing the key would not be enough. But a high degree of skill and labour was involved. This must be considered as a whole—it would not be right to look at each contribution and say 'that is not enough' and conclude that the same goes for the whole. The claimant started by choosing which original manuscript(s) to use (actually he used mainly two out of four, using one to correct ambiguities in the other), he checked every note and supplied 27 'corrections' (i.e. his personal evaluation as to what note Lalande really intended), supplied many suggestions for the figured bass, and put the whole into modern notation. This was not mere servile copying. It had the practical value (unchallenged) of making the work playable. He recreated Lalande's work using a considerable amount of personal judgement. His recreative work was such as to create something really new using his own original (not merely copied) work.

87. I therefore think Patten J was right and agree that this appeal should be dismissed.

[**Mance LJ** agreed with both **Mummery LJ** and **Jacob LJ**.]

Do you agree that Dr Sawkins' contribution was enough to satisfy the test as set out in *Walter v Lane*? Also, does Jacob LJ satisfactorily reconcile the tension between *Walter v Lane* and *Interlego v Tyco*? Does Jacob LJ's interpretation of *Interlego v Tyco* mean that there is now a common approach to originality for literary, musical, artistic, and dramatic works?

In looking at the UK approach to originality it is important to note the influence of EC law in relation to computer programs, photographs, and databases. With respect to these types of works, EC law stipulates that copyright will subsist where they are a result of the 'author's own intellectual creation'.[73] This formulation does not reflect the originality test from any particular Member State, however, it is probably closer to the French and German approaches of, respectively, 'imprint of the author's personality' and 'personal intellectual creation' than the UK's 'skill, judgment and labour' test.

The UK did not expressly introduce the criterion of 'author's own intellectual creation' into the CDPA for computer programs and photographs because it claimed that the UK's originality test was consistent with the EC test. However, after being criticized for this omission by the EC, the UK decided to incorporate the test into the CDPA for databases. The impact this has had on the protection of databases and compilations is discussed in Chapter 12.[74] With respect to photographs, do you think that the UK approach to originality is consistent with the test of 'author's own intellectual creation'? In order to accommodate the position of some Member States (such as Germany), Article 6 of the Term Directive allows protection for 'other photographs', i.e. those that do not meet the EC test of originality. Therefore, under EC law two types of photographs may be protected: 'original' photographs and 'other' (non-original) photographs. Can we say that UK law adequately distinguishes between original photographs and photographs which fail to meet this standard?

---

[73] See Art. 1(3) Software Directive, Art. 6 Term Directive and Art. 3 Database Directive.
[74] See p. 722.

Having considered the relevant case law, as well as EC legislation, it is worth asking whether there is a consistent approach to originality in the UK? Finally, in your view, does the requirement of originality continue to serve a useful purpose?

FURTHER READING

G. W. G. Karnell, 'European originality: A copyright chimera' in Kabel et al. (eds.), *Intellectual Property and Information Law* (The Hague: Kluwer, 1998), pp. 201–9.

2.5.3 FIXATION

Although Article 5(2) of the Berne Convention prohibits formalities, Article 2(2) states that it shall be for Union Members 'to prescribe that works in general or any specified categories of works shall not be protected unless they have been fixed in some material form'. The UK adopts a 'fixation' requirement expressly in relation to literary, dramatic, and musical works, since s. 3(2) of the CDPA stipulates that copyright will not subsist in these works 'unless and until it is recorded, in writing or otherwise'. The definition of 'writing' in s. 178 is such that this would include digital or electronic recordings. It is important to note that, according to s. 3(3) of the CDPA, someone other than the author can record the work and that it is immaterial whether the work is recorded by or with permission of the author. Where the work is recorded by someone other than the author, s. 3(3) envisages that distinct copyrights may arise—one in the content and one in the recording as such.

In relation to artistic works, there is no express requirement of fixation. However, is it possible to argue that fixation is implicit in the notion of an artistic work? In considering this question, it is worthwhile reconsidering the extracts from *Merchandising Corporation of America v Harpbond* and also *Creation Records* that were referred to above.[75]

For films, sound recordings, and typographical arrangements of published editions, fixation is inherent in their definitions. Thus, a 'film' is 'a recording on any medium from which a moving image may by any means be produced'[76] and a 'sound recording' is 'a recording of sounds, from which the sounds may be reproduced'.[77] With typographical arrangements of published editions, the notion of 'published edition' seems to assume fixation.

The only category that clearly does not have a fixation requirement is that of 'broadcast'. This is because 'broadcast' is defined as 'an electronic transmission of visual images, sounds or other information' and so by its very nature is ephemeral. However, as a matter of practice it is often the case that broadcasts, whilst they are being transmitted, are recorded.

Why is it, particularly in relation to literary, musical, and dramatic works, that UK copyright law requires fixation? What kinds of works does such a requirement exclude and is this defensible? Does it make sense to retain fixation as a requirement of protection, as opposed to, say, as an evidential requirement (which is the position in France)?

FURTHER READING

Y. Gendreau, 'The criterion of fixation in copyright law' (1994) 159 RIDA 110.

D. J. Brennan and A. F. Christie, 'Spoken words and copyright subsistence in Anglo-American law' [2000] IPQ 309.

---

[75] See p. 65–8.   [76] CDPA, s. 5B(1).   [77] Ibid., s. 5A(1)(a).

2.5.4 QUALIFICATION

Qualification is a prerequisite to copyright protection[78] and may arise via the author, the place of publication, or, in the case of a broadcast, the place from where the broadcast was made.

A work will qualify for copyright protection if, at the material time, the author was a qualifying person.[79] A qualifying person is either:

i)   a British citizen;

ii) an individual domiciled or resident in the UK or another country to which the relevant provisions of this Part extend;

iii) a body incorporated under the law of a part of the UK or of another country to which the relevant provisions of this Part extend or are applied.

The material time for literary, dramatic, musical, or artistic works is, in the case of unpublished works, when the work was made and in the case of published works, when the work was first published.[80] In the case of sound recordings, films, and broadcasts it is when the work was made. For typographical arrangements of published editions it is when the edition was first published.[81]

Literary, dramatic, musical, and artistic works; films; sound recordings; and typographical arrangements may also qualify for protection if first published in the UK or in another country to which the relevant provisions of this Part extend or are applied.

Finally, a broadcast qualifies for protection if it is made from a place in the UK or a country to which the relevant provisions of this Part extend or are applied.

Countries to which the Part extends include England, Wales, Scotland, and Northern Ireland and may include any of the Channel Islands, the Isle of Man, and any colony.[82] Countries to which the Part does not extend, but may be applied by Order in Council are Convention countries[83] and Member States of the EC.

2.5.5 PUBLIC POLICY EXCLUSION

Even if the above requirements for subsistence of copyright have been satisfied, courts retain, as part of their inherent jurisdiction, the ability to deny protection on public policy grounds. Courts may refuse to recognize the existence of copyright in a work or they may recognize copyright but deny a remedy to the owner. The public policy grounds that have warranted such intervention in the past include immorality[84] and fraudulent and deceptive works.[85] Also, in *Attorney-General v Guardian Newspapers Ltd (No 2)*[86] Lord Jauncey commented obiter that because the book *Spycatcher* was published in breach of a confidential obligation owed to the Crown, his action 'reeked of turpitude' and it was 'inconceivable

---

[78] See ibid., ss. 1(3) and 153(1). Except this does not apply to Crown or Parliamentary copyright.

[79] Ibid., s. 154.   [80] Ibid., s. 154(4).   [81] Ibid., s. 154(5).   [82] Ibid., s. 157.

[83] s. 159(4) defines 'Convention country' to mean 'a country which is a party to a Convention relating to copyright to which the United Kingdom is also a party'. This would include, for example, the Berne Convention, Rome Convention and TRIPS Agreement.

[84] *Glyn v Weston Feature Film Co* [1916] 1 Ch 261.

[85] *Slingsby v Bradford Patent Truck and Trolley Co* [1905] WN 122, [1906] WN 51.

[86] [1990] 1 AC 109. See Ch. 8, p. 388, 399.

that a United Kingdom court would afford to him or his publishers any protection in relation to any copyright which either of them may possess in the book'.[87]

FURTHER READING

A. Sims, 'The denial of copyright protection on public policy grounds' (2008) EIPR 189.

2.6 AUTHORSHIP

2.6.1 IDENTIFYING THE AUTHOR

Identifying the author of a copyright work is important for several reasons. First, as discussed in the previous section, a 'qualifying person' is linked to authorship in the case of literary, dramatic, musical, and artistic works. Secondly, for literary, dramatic, musical, and artistic works, the term of protection is calculated *post mortem auctoris*, i.e. 70 years after the death of the author. Finally, the author of the work will be its first owner according to s. 11(1) of the CDPA.

Who, then, is the author of the work? Section 9(1) of the CDPA stipulates that it is the person who *creates* the work. As such, there is a clear link between the notions of authorship and originality, a point that is aptly illustrated by *Walter v Lane*.[88] The person who contributes the relevant skill and labour will be the person who creates the work and thus its author.

In the case of sound recordings, broadcasts, typographical arrangements of published editions, and films, further guidance as to authorship is provided by s. 9(2) of the CDPA. It is the producer for sound recordings, the person making the broadcast in the case of broadcasts, the publisher in the case of typographical arrangements, and, finally, the principal director *and* producer in the case of films. 'Producer' is further defined in s. 178 of the CDPA as 'the person by whom the arrangements necessary for the making of the sound recording or film are undertaken'. For these types of works, do you think that it is possible for legal entities to be authors? What about in the case of literary, dramatic, musical, or artistic works?

For literary, dramatic, musical, or artistic works, identifying the author will involve asking who has contributed the relevant skill, judgment, and labour. But in the case of sound recordings and films, the enquiry is whether or not someone is the 'producer'. Cases, such as the one considered below, have elaborated upon who can be a 'producer'.

Bamgboye v Reed [2004] EMLR 5

The case concerned disputed ownership of copyright in the musical work and sound recording of a song called 'Bouncing Flow'. The first claimant (Mr Bamgboye) had worked as a trainee tape operator and sound engineer at a particular recording studio. The track 'Bouncing Flow' was conceived and recorded at sessions at the recording studio, during which sessions the first claimant alleged that he had contributed drum and bass-line parts and cymbal effects. After the track was recorded the first defendant (Mr Reed) used equipment at the first claimant's home to further work on and master

---

[87] *Attorney-General v Guardian Newspapers Ltd (No 2)* [1990] 1 AC 109, 294.   [88] See p. 73.

the recording. Deputy Judge Hazel Williamson QC held that Mr Bamgboye was a joint author of the musical work. However, in relation to the sound recording she found that the first defendant was the producer.

Deputy Judge Hazel Williamson QC:

47. Identifying the relevant person is said to be a matter of fact, and I have been referred helpfully to various authorities that deal with that. These show, in particular, that 'undertaking these arrangements' effectively means to be responsible for producing the sound recording in the financial sense or generally.

48. Mr Harbottle, in his closing submissions, drew my attention to certain authorities giving examples of the way in which the court had approached the question of who had undertaken the arrangements for the making of sound recordings and films, because the same principles obviously apply. He referred me to *Adventure Film Productions v Tully* [1993] EMLR 376 in which on an application for interim relief, the claimant who provided the funds for a film that was actually shot by others on its behalf, the funds coming from Channel 4, was held to be sufficiently likely to be the owner of a film copyright that a serious issue should go forward to trial. In *Mad Hat Music v Pulse 8 Records* [1993] EMLR 172, there was a claim that the second defendant owned copyright in a sound recording because, as the first claimant's manager, it had made her available for the recording sessions, although others, namely the defendants, had made other arrangements which included paying for the studio time. It was held again that this raised a serious question to be tried.

49. The case I probably found must useful was *Century Communications Ltd v Mayfair Entertainment Ltd* [1993]. This was a case in which a film had been produced by E on the Chinese mainland, but to do this it had had to bring in assistance from another company known as C, and it was held that even though C was responsible for obtaining the permissions and shooting the film, arrangements for making it had in fact been made by E, since E had initiated its making and organised the activity necessary for its making and paid for it. The particular passage that deals with this is briefly at p. 342 of the authority, where the learned judge said: 'Looking at the documents and appreciating that Era Communications could not make a film in mainland China without the help of CCP, it is plain to me that the arrangements necessary for the making of the film were undertaken by Era Communications. There never would have been a film had Era Communications not initiated its making and organised the activity necessary for its making and paid for it. To achieve that purpose they had to invoke the help of CCP and that Era Communications did. CCP made no arrangements, they simply helped Era Communications to make the film. Accordingly, I find that copyrights subsist in the film in that Era Communications was its author and, as is agreed, Era Communications is a body which qualifies for copyright protection. By documents that are not challenged, C is the present owner of the copyright and Era has distribution rights.' So the copyright in the film was given to E in that situation.

50. Finally, I should refer to the case of *Beggars Banquet Records v Carlton Television* [1993] EMLR at 349. A similar question arose as to who had undertaken the arrangements necessary for the making of a film, and it was in that case decided they do include finance, but the question arising is who, in fact, is directly responsible for the payment of the production costs rather than who is the person who might be the ultimate source of the funds. There is a passage in the judgment of Warner J which emphasises that in any case it is a question of fact who, in fact, made the arrangements.

. . .

86. The cases are often concerned with financial arrangements. No payments were involved here, so the real question, is who instigated the relevant recording and organised

the activity necessary for its making? Mr Bamgboye has agreed that he would have regarded Bouncing Flow as finished, and it was Mr Reed who decided that further editing, recording and mastering was necessary. I find that it was Mr Reed who arranged, as it were, to get Mr Bamgboye to make available the house and the equipment. If this had not happened, it could have been done elsewhere. If that had happened it would have had to have been done by payment, but nonetheless the moving force, the person who got this recording made at the end of the day, seems to me to have been Mr Reed in substance, rather than it being a joint operation by Mr Reed and Mr Bamgboye.

87. As I have said, I found the *Century Communications v Mayfair Entertainment* case helpful in this regard. Without Mr Reed there would not have been the recording because he instigated everything, and the arrangements that he got Mr Bamgboye to make were subsidiary. It is right to say that Mr Bamgboye was assisting in the recording and, indeed, possibly even contributing to parts of the recording, but I find that that was a part of the artistic, or creative element of creating a musical piece, rather than part of undertaking the necessary arrangements for the sound recording as such. In so far as Mr Bamgboye did have any input that might be described as that, it was done at Mr Reed's behest to this extent that it was even anything that he did on his own behalf, perhaps by asking his father to let them have the computer in the relevant room, it was really not significant enough, and would have effectively been done as part of having been asked by Mr Reed to get the premises, and so forth, into position to make the final recording which Mr Reed was organising.

What are the key factors for determining who is the producer of a sound recording or film? How influential is the provision of finance to this assessment?

When it comes to identifying the author of a copyright work, it is important to remember that the CDPA sets out certain presumptions.[89] Thus, in the case of literary, dramatic, musical, or artistic works, where a name purporting to be that of the author appears on copies of the work, the person named shall be presumed, until the contrary is proved, to be the author of the work.[90] The same presumption applies in the case of works of joint authorship.[91] Likewise, with respect to sound recordings, if copies of the recording as issued to the public bear a label or other mark stating that a named person is the owner of copyright in the recording, this shall be presumed to be correct until the contrary is proved.[92] In the case of films, where copies of the film as issued to the public state that a named person is the director or producer of the film this shall be presumed to be correct until the contrary is proved.[93] The provisions on presumptions in ss. 104 and 105 of the CDPA repay closer inspection. The general point to remember, however, is that these provisions create evidential presumptions that can be very valuable when it comes to litigation, a point that is highlighted by *Brighton v Jones*,[94] which is discussed below.

2.6.2 JOINT AUTHORSHIP

UK copyright law recognizes that works may be jointly authored. In s. 10(1) of the CDPA it defines 'works of joint authorship' as:

a work produced by the collaboration of two or more authors in which the contribution of each is not distinct from that of the other author or authors.

---

[89] Note that the Berne Convention, Art. 15 permits such evidential presumptions.
[90] CDPA, s. 104(2)(a).   [91] Ibid., s. 104(3).   [92] Ibid., s. 105(1)(a).
[93] Ibid., s. 105(2)(a).   [94] [2004] EMLR 26.

Notably, films are deemed to be works of joint authorship between the producer and principal director, unless these two persons are the same.[95]

2.6.2.1 Significance of joint authorship

A finding of joint authorship is significant to both duration and ownership of copyright. The term of protection, generally speaking, will be calculated according to 70 years after the death of the last remaining author.[96] Further, as a general rule, joint authorship will lead to joint ownership[97] and, as a result, this will constrain the behaviour of all co-owners in the manner described below.

Robin Ray v Classic FM [1988] FSR 622

The facts are described below at p. 102.

Lightman J, at pp. 637–8:

It is common ground that joint authors hold copyright in the subject of the joint authorship as tenants in common entitled in equal shares. The defendant contends that, if it was a joint author of the copyright in the above five documents and the catalogue, as tenant in common it was entitled to exploit the copyright in the way it has because: (1) such exploitation did no damage to the copyright; and, (2) the only right of the plaintiff as co-owner is to an account of the profits earned.

It is unnecessary to consider whether the use made of the copyright material did any damage, for it is quite clear that, even if the defendant was joint author of the five documents and the catalogue, joint ownership could not without the consent of the plaintiff justify the making of copies for the purpose of exploitation of the copyright abroad. The 1988 Act itself provides in section 16(2) that it is an infringement of copyright to do any of the restricted acts (which include making copies) without the consent of the 'copyright owner', and section 173(2) expressly provides that in case of joint owners this means the consent of all the owners. This result is in accord with the decision in *Cescinsky v George Routledge & Sons Ltd* [1916] 2 KB 325 and the view expressed by Laddie J in *Cala* (at 836). I reject the defendant's submission that the defendant as a joint owner is free to do a restricted act so long as he accounts to the plaintiff as its joint owner for a share of the profits, or that the right of the plaintiff is limited to claiming an account: the plaintiff is entitled to sue for infringement, claiming damages and an injunction.

What is the reason, do you think, for requiring all joint owners to consent to any exploitation of the work? Would it make more sense to allow each co-owner to exploit the work, but to account to each other for any profits that they make from such use?

As already mentioned, a finding of joint authorship will invariably lead to a finding of joint ownership of the copyright work. However, in *Fisher v Brooker*[98] although the claimant successfully established joint authorship of the musical work, 'A Whiter Shade of Pale', as a result of contributing the distinctive organ sections, he failed to establish joint ownership. A majority of the Court of Appeal held that the claimant's excessive delay (of 38 years) in bringing the action was unconscionable conduct that gave rise to the equitable defences

---

[95] CDPA, s. 10(1A).   [96] Ibid., s. 12(8).   [97] Ibid., s. 11(1).   [98] [2008] FSR 26.

of acquiescence and laches, which in turn allowed the court to refuse to grant a declaration of joint ownership.

2.6.2.2 Requirement of 'contribution'

Joint authorship has been raised in numerous cases. Of the requirements contained in s. 10(1) of the CDPA that of 'contribution' has received the most judicial attention. The principles for determining whether there is a relevant contribution are neatly summarized in the following case.

Brighton v Jones [2004] EMLR 26

The case involved a dispute about copyright in the play, 'Stones In His Pockets'. The defendant had written the script of the play in 1996 and had been listed as the sole author on publicity material, whilst the first claimant had directed the first production of the play. The defendant rewrote elements of the script in 1999 and exploited it in various ways, achieving major commercial success. The first claimant alleged, *inter alia*, that she was a joint author, and therefore joint owner, of the play as a result of contributions made during rehearsals of the 1996 version, including suggested changes to plot and dialogue.

Park J:

[He began by rehearsing the principles of joint authorship:]

34. ... The Act itself does not expand upon the concept of joint authorship, but there have been a number of cases which have examined it. In my opinion three propositions can be extracted from the cases which may be relevant to this case.

(i) If someone claims to be a joint author, although the contribution which he needs to have made to the creation of the work does not have to be equal in magnitude to the contribution of the other joint author or authors, it still needs to be significant. In the *Robin Ray* case...Lightman J said that he had to be someone 'who (as an author) provides a significant creative input'. In *Godfrey v Lees* [1995] EMLR 307 at 325 Blackburne J said: 'What the claimant to joint authorship of a work must establish is that he has made a significant and original contribution to the creation of the work...It is not necessary that his contribution to the work is equal in terms of either quantity, quality or originality to that of his collaborators.' In *Hadley v Kemp* [1999] EMLR 589 at 643 I noted that, where a person is a joint author, the effect was that he had an equal share in the copyright, and I added: 'It would be surprising if a slight contribution was enough to make a person a joint author and thereby make him an equal owner with another or others who had contributed far more than he had.' I should, however, add that in the recent case of *Bamgboye v Reed* [2002] EWHC 2922 (QB); [2004] EMLR 5, the claimant was held to have been a joint author by reason of his contributions, but with a one-third share, not a half share: see [77] of the judgment of Hazel Williamson QC.

(ii) The contribution which a person claiming to be a joint author makes must be a contribution towards the creation of the work. A contribution, even a significant one, of a different kind will not cause him or her to be a joint author. *Fylde Microsystems Ltd v Key Radio Systems Ltd* [1998] FSR 449 concerned the ownership of the copyright in software which, on the face of it, had been written by Fylde Microsystems (acting by its employees). Key Radio Systems argued unsuccessfully that it was a joint author because of contributions which its employees had made. They had put much skill, time and effort into testing the software and ensuring that it would achieve the performance which was intended. Laddie J accepted that their contributions were extensive and technically sophisticated, and that they had required considerable time and effort; but he held that they were not contributions to the 'authoring' of the software. The skill was like a proof reader's skill, not authorship skill. Key Radio Systems had not contributed 'the right kind of skill and labour'. *Hadley v Kemp* (*supra*) is another example of the same point, this time in the context of a pop group. One member of the group devised the songs (the musical works), and the group as a whole performed them with much skill and flair. I held that the other members of the group were not joint authors. I said (at 643): '...contributions by the plaintiffs, however significant and skilful, to the performance of the musical works are not the right kind of contributions to give them shares in the copyrights. The contributions need to be to the creation of the musical works, not to the performance or interpretation of them.' The case can interestingly be compared with *Stuart v Barrett* [1994] EMLR 449, in which the songs of another group emerged from a process of 'collective jamming', and all the members were found to be joint authors.

(iii) However, a person can become a joint author even if he has not himself put pen to paper, but someone else has done that, effectively writing what the first person had created. *Cala Homes (South) Ltd v Alfred McAlpine Homes East Ltd* [1995] FSR 818 was about the copyright in drawings for aspects of house designs. The physical drawings had been prepared by staff of a business called Crawley Hodgson. However, the Crawley Hodgson staff had been very closely instructed, verbally and sometimes by means of sketches, by the design director of Cala Homes. Laddie J held that, on the facts, Cala Homes was a joint author. In the *Robin Ray* case...Lightman J ascribed a fairly narrow ambit to this concept: 'But in my judgment what is required is something which approximates to penmanship. What is essential is a direct responsibility for what actually appears on the paper...As it appears to me the architects in that case [Cala Homes] were in large part acting as "scribes" for the director. In practice such a situation is likely to be exceptional.'

...

[**Park J** went on to apply these principles to the facts:]

55. It must be remembered that, by virtue of s. 104(2), the burden of proof rests on Miss Brighton. The person described on the script of the play as the author was Miss Jones alone. She was also billed as the sole author in publicity material and in programmes. It never occurred to Miss Brighton to say that she ought to be regarded as a joint author until she commenced this case. None of that is conclusive against her, but it does at the least raise a substantial evidential hurdle for her to overcome.

56. I agree that, on all versions of what happened in the rehearsals, changes were made to Miss Jones' original script, and that the changes resulted from the experience of the rehearsals and the discussions in the rehearsals. I agree that Miss Brighton was involved in the rehearsals throughout, and I would accept (though the point was not specifically covered) that she probably knew about all the changes before they were made and had played a part in what had led to each of them. However, there are still several reasons why, in my opinion, she was not a joint author.

(i) In terms of the dialogue of the final play, I believe that 100 per cent of the words spoken (or as near to 100 per cent as makes no difference) were actually composed by Miss Jones. Miss Brighton no doubt identified passages and places where some rewriting was desirable, but it was Miss Jones who (if she agreed that there should be some rewriting at those points) actually chose the words which the actors were to use. There is a sentence in Miss Brighton's witness statement which reads: 'In respect of each Act, I was heavily responsible for the actual form of expression of the dialogue on paper.' That appears to be saying that Miss Brighton was responsible not just for determining where some rewriting was to take place, but also for determining what the precise new words were to be. All of the other evidence is contrary to that, and I do not accept it.

(ii) The point made in (i) above concerns the actual words used, and it is not in itself decisive. Copyright can subsist in a story or a plot, so that if what happened in rehearsals was that Miss Brighton determined what the plot of the play was to be (or Miss Brighton and Miss Jones determined in collaboration what it was to be), and then Miss Jones actually wrote the words to give effect to the plot, I can see that Miss Brighton might have been a joint author. But in my opinion that was not how it was. I believe that the script which Miss Jones provided in advance of the rehearsals, plus the fairly small part which she had not written before the rehearsals began but did write before the rehearsals got round to that part, contained a complete plot for the play. It was a dramatic work, and at that stage the copyright in it was solely owned by Miss Jones. (That conclusion is not changed by the use which Miss Jones made of Miss Brighton's draft opening script, as I will explain later.) I am sure that there were some changes to the plot before the final form of the 1996 script was reached, and I accept that Miss Brighton made her own input into what those changes were; but I do not believe that the changes were nearly significant enough to mean that a different dramatic work, of which Miss Brighton and Miss Jones were joint authors, had been created.

(iii) Just focusing on the changes, Miss Brighton had played a part in what led up to them, but in my view, on the general thrust of the evidence and bearing in mind the burden of proof, she has not established that the contributions which she made were contributions to the creation of the dramatic work rather than contributions to the interpretation and theatrical presentation of the dramatic work. In the expression used in the Fylde Microsystems case (see [34(ii)] above), they were not 'the right sort of contributions'.

(iv) It cannot be said that, whenever Miss Brighton wanted a change to be made to the script, Miss Jones simply and unquestioningly made it. I accept that she expected to have suggestions for changes made to her, that she was fully prepared to consider them, that she probably expected that she would agree to many of them, and that she did agree to many of them. But it is clear from the evidence which I summarised earlier that she would not make changes to the script if she did not agree to them. The decision whether to make a change or not was hers, and that was not just a theoretical position: it was also the reality of what actually happened.

(v) It is in any case unrealistic to distinguish, so far as the present issue is concerned, between what Miss Brighton did in the rehearsals and what the two actors did. The actors do not claim to have become joint authors simply by doing well one of the things which led to them being engaged: working on the rehearsals of a newly commissioned play which had not yet been performed, and by doing so assisting in making the script better than it had been before the rehearsals. It seems to me that Miss Brighton is in essentially the same position. Miss Jones presented her with a play upon which, during the rehearsals, she was expected to exercise her director's skills, together with Mr Murphy and Mr Hill exercising their actors' skills, in order to get it ready to be performed before live audiences. The actors did not become joint authors by reason of what they did, and I do not think that Miss Brighton became a joint author by reason of what she did either.

. . .

59. For the foregoing reasons my decision on Miss Brighton's joint authorship claim is that it fails.

What are the relevant principles for assessing whether a person has made a contribution sufficient to qualify for joint authorship? Do you agree with them? Can a clear distinction be drawn between contributions to the creation of a work and contributions to its performance? Also, why is it necessary for a person to have direct responsibility for expression in order to make an appropriate contribution?

2.6.2.3 Requirement of collaboration

A work of joint authorship also requires collaboration between two or more persons. In the following case, the Court of Appeal explored whether this means an intention to be joint authors.

Beckingham v Hodgens [2003] EMLR 18

The claimant in this case was a professional fiddle player who had been hired as a session musician for the recording of the song 'Young at Heart' by the Bluebells. He claimed that he had composed the violin part that featured in the introduction to the song and recurred several times throughout the song. At first instance, the claimant was held to have contributed the violin part and, as such, was a joint author and joint owner of the musical work. On appeal, it was argued, *inter alia*, that joint authorship in s. 11(3) of the Copyright Act 1956 (which is in very similar terms to s. 10(1) of the CDPA) required an intention to create a joint work, which was absent in this case.

Jonathan Parker LJ (with whom **Laws LJ** and **Ward LJ** agreed):

49. I reject the submission that s. 11(3) requires, as one of the elements of joint authorship, the existence of a common intention as to joint authorship. I do so for essentially the reasons which the judge gave.

50. In the first place, I agree with the judge that there is nothing in the express wording of s. 11(3) which warrants the imposition of such a requirement. The only requirements for a 'work of joint authorship' expressed in s. 11(3) are that the authors should have collaborated and that their contributions should not be 'separate'.

51. As *Levy v Rutley* makes clear, these requirements will not be met unless there has been 'joint labouring in furtherance of a common design' (see ibid. p. 529, per Keating J). But the 'common design' in that context is not an intention that there should be joint authorship.

What Keating J was describing, as I read his judgment, was the process of jointly creating the work in question: as the judge in the instant case put it in para. 48 of the judgment, a 'common design to produce the work'. So much is clear, in my judgment, from the passage in Keating J's judgment which follows his reference to 'common design', where he says:

> I fail to discover any evidence that there was any co-operation of the two in the design of this piece [a play], or in its execution, or in any improvements either in the plot or the general structure... If the plaintiff and the author had agreed together to rearrange the plot, and so to produce a more attractive piece out of the original materials, possibly that might have made them joint authors of the whole. So, if two persons undertake jointly to write a play, agreeing in the general outline and design, and sharing the labour of working it out, each would be contributing to the whole production, and they might be said to be joint authors of it. But, to constitute joint authorship, there must be a common design. Nothing of the sort appears here. The plaintiff made mere additions to a complete piece, which did not in themselves amount to a dramatic piece, but were intended only to make the play more attractive to the audience.

52. As to the Canadian case of *Darryl Neudorf*, on which Mr Engelman naturally relies strongly, I agree with the judge that there is no basis in the English cases for importing the requirement of an intention as to joint authorship. In *Darryl Neudorf*, Cohen J followed the United States case of *Childress v Taylor* 945 F 2d 500. At p. 962 of the report of *Darryl Neudorf*, Cohen J said this:

> the creation of the intent to co-author requirement in *Childress v Taylor* happened despite the statutory definition of joint authorship..., not because of it. The court looked beyond the language of the section and moved on to review policy considerations in the application of the section. In particular, the court could not accept that Congress intended to extend joint authorship to, for example, editors and researchers. It was for this reason that the court created the intent to co-author requirement.

53. In my judgment, the judge in the instant case was clearly right to confine his consideration to the language of s. 11(3) and not to look beyond the section into the uncertain realms of policy. So doing, he plainly reached the correct conclusion.

54. I would accordingly refuse permission to appeal on the s. 11(3) issue, confirming my earlier refusal of permission on the papers.

Thus, we see from the above case that collaboration does not mean an intention to create a work of joint authorship, but rather acting pursuant to a 'common design'. How will that common design be shown?

2.6.2.4 Requirement of 'not distinct'

According to s. 10(1) of the CDPA contributions must be 'not distinct' from those of the other author/s. This requirement has received little attention in the case law, however, at first instance in *Beckingham v Hodgens*,[99] Deputy Judge Christopher Floyd QC commented upon the requirement of 'not separate' in the Copyright 1956 Act as follows:

> 46. Finally there is the negative requirement: non-separateness. A work will not be a work of joint authorship if the contribution of the co-authors is separate. The example often given

---

[99] [2003] ECDR 6.

> is of a literary work where separate authors contribute specific chapters, but there are other examples where the distinction made in the section may not be so easy to apply. I do not believe that a contribution to the arrangement of a song of the kind I am concerned with in this case is 'separate' in the sense in which that word is used in the section. The added part is heavily dependent on what is there already. Stripped of the voices and other instruments, the violin part would sound odd, and lose meaning. The final musical expression—what the audience will hear—is a joint one.

Does it make sense to adopt a test that asks whether or not the contribution is dependent on the other parts, in order to judge whether it is 'not distinct'? If not, what could be an alternative, workable test? What is the purpose of retaining the 'not distinct' requirement? Here, it is interesting to note that in the US a joint work requires the contribution to be 'merged into inseparable or interdependent parts of a unitary whole'.[100] Would it make sense to follow this approach instead?

FURTHER READING

J. Ginsburg, 'The concept of authorship in comparative copyright law' (2003) 52 DePaul L Rev 1063.

2.7 OWNERSHIP

The first owner of copyright in a work is its author.[101] However, in the case of literary, dramatic, musical, and artistic works and films, where the work is made by an employee in the course of his or her employment, in the absence of an agreement to the contrary, ownership will vest in the employer.[102] What is the rationale, do you think, behind such an exception to first ownership? Here, it is interesting to note the contrasting approach of civil law systems, such as France, where there is no presumed transfer of ownership of economic rights to the employer. Instead, employers have to negotiate with employees to agree a transfer of such rights.

An author must be an employee in order for s. 11(2) to apply. Section 178 of the CDPA defines this as employment under a contract of service or of apprenticeship. The indicia of a contract of service, as opposed to a contract for services, were explored in the following case.

Beloff v Pressdram [1973] FSR 33

Ms Beloff had written a memorandum, excerpts of which were used by the defendant in its 'Private Eye' publication. A key issue was whether or not Ms Beloff was an employee of *The Observer* newspaper. If so, she had created the memorandum in the course of employment and her employer owned copyright in the literary work, such that she did not have standing to bring the action against the defendant. Ungoed Thomas J held that Ms Beloff was an employee.

---

[100] US Copyright Act 1976, s. 101.   [101] CDPA, s. 11(1).   [102] Ibid., s. 11(2).

Ungoed-Thomas J, at pp. 42, 45–6:

It thus appears, and rightly in my respectful view, that, the greater the skill required for an employee's work, the less significant is control in determining whether the employee is under a contract of service. Control is just one of many factors whose influence varies according to circumstances. In such highly skilled work as that of the plaintiff it seems of no substantial significance.

...

The plaintiff writes for the Observer a weekly article headed 'Politics-Nora Beloff': it is usually on one theme. She also writes profiles, and on the major speeches of politicians, and she even writes leaders. The Editor described her as 'a very active member of the general editorial staff' and said that she shared in the editorial responsibility of the newspaper. She is a regular attendant at weekly and ad hoc editorial meetings presided over by the Editor and whose wide scope is indicated by the functions of those who attend—deputy and assistant editors, chief reporters, the Business Editor, the Leader Writer, the News Editor, and others as advisable from time to time. The plaintiff said its purpose was to plan the paper for the next issue, to look ahead and to have a general discussion and exchange ideas. She said that her article for the following issue was very often discussed. The Editor said that she tells him what she is going to write and that discussion only arises if it overlaps with something else. The Editor has certainly some strong-minded persons attending these meetings and, as might be expected from his experience and wisdom, he said that 'my government is as a rule consensual'. The plaintiff said that she was free to decline to write on a suggested topic. Of course, she could not be forced to do so, nor can I imagine Mr Astor attempting to force her. The editorial meetings are for discussion, without power of decision; that rests solely with the Editor, and not the less so, although as a rule consensually exercised by him.

I come to other recognised indications of contract of service, in addition to her substantial regular salary for her full-time job and her holidays. Apart from an electric typewriter, which the plaintiff has at home, the plaintiff does not provide any equipment of her own which she uses for her work. All the Observer's resources are available to her to carry out her job. She has an office in the Observer building, and a secretary who is provided by the Observer. She does not use her own capital for the job, nor is her remuneration affected by the financial success or otherwise of the Observer. In addition to PAYE deductions, deduction for the pension scheme to which she belongs is also made by the Observer from her salary. All these indications are in favour of her contract being a contract of service.

It is not enough that the author is an employee—he or she must also have created the work in the course of employment in order for ownership to vest in the employer. The sorts of factors relevant to determining this question are explored in the case below.

Noah v Shuba [1991] FSR 14

Dr Noah had been employed as a consultant epidemiologist at the Public Health Laboratory Service ('PHLS'). He had written 'A Guide to Hygienic Skin Piercing' at home in the evenings and weekends, but had used the PHLS library and secretarial assistance. The guide had been first published by the PHLS. The defendant had written and published an article, which reproduced substantial extracts from Dr Noah's guide. The claimant brought proceedings alleging, *inter alia*, copyright infringement under the Copyright Act 1956. The defendant argued that the owner of copyright in the guide was not Dr Noah but his employer.

Mummery J (as he then was), at pp. 25–6:

The primary submission made on behalf of Dr Noah is that the copyright in the Guide did not vest in the PHLS as his employer because he had not made it 'in the course of his employment' with PHLS. His evidence, which I accept, is that he wrote the Guide at home in the evenings and at weekends and not at the instigation of or on the direction of PHLS.

On behalf of Mr Shuba many points have been taken on the evidence as indicating that Dr Noah wrote the Guide in the course of his employment. It has been pointed out that under the terms of his conditions of service, which do not expressly deal with the matter of copyright, he was expected to report on research work by means of contributions to appropriate scientific journals and before recognised learned societies. Regulation 11 of the Staff Regulations provided that before doing so he should inform the Director of the Service and follow the normal practice of consulting colleagues who have been associated with him in collaborative investigations. It was, however, also provided in regulation 11 that the writing of scientific books or monographs, if undertaken, was 'not expected to be done in working hours'. It is also clear from regulation 3(b) and (c) that the writing of books and articles was in general to be regarded as something done 'in addition to official duties', though staff were entitled to undertake such work at the laboratory or elsewhere and to receive fees, provided that the work would not interfere with their official duties.

Mr Price, on behalf of Mr Shuba, pointed out that the PHLS functions included the provision to persons perceived as needing it information relevant to the control of infectious diseases; that the Guide fell within those functions and had been printed and published by PHLS at public expense; that Dr Noah's duties included the making of investigations and provision of information on subjects which were covered by the Guide; that the Guide had been designed to enable health authorities and other bodies to set and observe high and uniform standards in the implementation of the 1928 Act; that it could not be said that Dr Noah had undertaken the writing of the book in any private capacity and that the preparation of the Guide was part of the official duties which fell within the terms of his conditions of service. It was pointed out that the Guide could not be properly described as a 'private' venture by Dr Noah, since it was clear from the cover and the title page that it was a PHLS guide. The previous 1979 Tattooing Guide had been signed by Dr Noah in his official capacity as a consultant at the Communicable Diseases Surveillance Centre. The evidence showed that Dr Noah had used PHLS notepaper in order to send out letters to those from whom he solicited comments and views before settling on the final version of the Guide. The typescript of the Guide had been produced by his secretary at the Centre using PHLS time and equipment. In brief, it was submitted that the Guide was a PHLS venture involving the collaboration of staff at PHLS premises, including Dr Noah's colleague, Mr Peter Hoffman, who wrote one of the appendices in the Guide. Mr Price submitted that, if the court accepted Dr Noah's contention, this would result in the surprising consequence that Dr Noah, as owner of the copyright, would be in a position to invoke that copyright in order to prevent PHLS from reprinting and disseminating the Guide without his permission. This was surprising, it was argued, in view of the public functions of PHLS and the public interest in the whole question of hygiene and infectious diseases. I have not been persuaded by these points that Mr Shuba has discharged the burden of proving that Dr Noah made the Guide in the course of his employment. In my judgment, Dr Noah's position is very similar to that of the accountant in *Stevenson Jordan and Harrison Limited v McDonald and Evans* [1952] 1 TLR 101 in relation to copyright in lectures delivered by the accountant author who was employed under a contract of service. It was held that the provisions of the Copyright Act 1911 equivalent to section 4(4) did not apply. At page 111 Denning LJ pointed out that it had to be remembered that a man employed under a contract of service may sometimes perform services outside the contract. He gave the instance of a doctor on the staff of a hospital or the master on the staff of a school employed under a contract of service giving lectures or lessons orally to students. He expressed the view that if, for his own convenience, he put the lectures into writing then his written work was not done under the contract of service. It might be a useful accessory to his contracted work, but it was not part of it and the copyright vested in him and not in his employers. Morris LJ also pointed out at page 113 that, even though the employer in that case paid the expenses of the lecturer incurred in the delivery of a lecture and was prepared to type the lectures as written by any lecturer and even though it would not have been improper for that lecturer to have prepared his lecture in the company's time and used material obtained from its library, it had not been shown that the accountant could have been ordered to write or deliver the lectures or that it was part of his duty to write or deliver them. In those circumstances the lectures were not written in the course of his employment.

Assessing whether a work has been created in the course of employment is very much a question of fact, to be determined in light of the factors discussed by Mummery J. Do you think it makes sense for the overriding factor to be whether or not the employee could have been ordered to create the particular work?

It is important to remember that if there is an agreement to the contrary, ownership of copyright works created in the course of employment may remain with the employee. In *Noah v Shuba*, Mummery J commented obiter that there was an agreement to the contrary.

Mummery J (as he then was), at pp. 26–7:

Although that conclusion is sufficient to dispose of the issue on ownership of copyright, I should add that, even if I had found that the Guide had been written by Dr Noah in the course of his employment, I would have found on the evidence before me that there was an implied term of his contract of service excluding the operation of the statutory rule in section 4(4) vesting the copyright in the work so made in the employer PHLS. Evidence was given by Dr Noah and also by Dr Christine Miller, who was a consultant epidemiologist at PHLS from 1967 to 1987 and the author of numerous publications on vaccination, that it had for long been the practice at PHLS for employees there to retain the copyright in work written by them, usually in the form of articles, in the course of their employment there. If, for example, the articles were published in learned journals, it was the author of the article and not the PHLS who, at the insistence of most learned journals, assigned the copyright to the publishers of the journal in question. At no relevant time has the copyright in those articles been claimed by PHLS. It has acquiesced in a practice under which that copyright was retained and then assigned by the employee authors. The position of the PHLS in relation to this case is consistent with that practice. It has accepted that the copyright in the Guide is vested in Dr Noah. In my judgment, this longstanding practice is sufficient material from which I can and do imply that it was a term of Dr Noah's appointment as consultant that he should be entitled to retain the copyright in works written by him in the course of his employment.

Mummery J implied an agreement (or more specifically a term in his employment contract) to the contrary because of the conduct of the PHLS. For employees wishing to retain copyright in the works it would be preferable to rely on an express, rather than implied, agreement to the contrary. Yet, is it a realistic possibility that employees will be able to negotiate such an agreement? If the UK followed a civil law approach and did not presumptively transfer ownership to employers, would this lead to more employees retaining ownership of the works they create?

2.8 EXPLOITATION

2.8.1 EXPRESS ASSIGNMENTS AND LICENCES

Copyright is a property right,[103] which can be exploited in two main ways: assignment and licence. An assignment is a transfer of ownership. It may be partial, in the sense of transferring only some of the owner's exclusive rights or in transferring ownership for only a limited period, as opposed to the whole term of copyright.[104] To be effective, an assignment must be in writing signed by or on behalf of the assignor.[105] Why do you think such a requirement exists?

Unlike assignment, a licence does not involve a transfer of ownership. Rather, it is a grant of permission to carry out certain acts that fall within the exclusive rights of the owner. A variety of types of licences may be granted. An important distinction is between exclusive, sole and non-exclusive licences. An exclusive licence is one that grants to the licensee the right to carry out the right/s stipulated in the licence that would otherwise be exercisable by the copyright owner, to the exclusion of all other persons, including the person granting the licence (usually the copyright owner). By way of contrast, a sole licence differs from an exclusive licence in that the copyright owner remains free to exercise the licensed rights. Finally, a non-exclusive licence is where a licensee has the right to carry out the licensed rights, but this is not to the exclusion of third parties or the copyright owner.

Section 92 of the CDPA defines an exclusive licence as 'a licence in writing signed by or on behalf of the copyright owner'. In other words, as with assignments, exclusive licences must satisfy formal requirements. Why do you think this is the case? It is also important to note that s. 101 of the CDPA grants exclusive licensees the same rights and remedies (except as against the copyright owner) in respect of matters occurring after the grant of the licence as if the licence had been an assignment. Given the nature of an exclusive licence, why would it be preferable to obtain an assignment?

Another broad distinction that can be made in respect of licences is between contractual and gratuitous licences. The former are contractual promises to licence certain rights, while the latter are non-contractual in nature. When it comes to revocation, what do you think are the main differences between contractual and gratuitous licences?[106]

2.8.2 IMPLIED ASSIGNMENTS AND LICENCES

Where a copyright work has been commissioned, i.e. it has been created pursuant to a contract *for* services, as opposed to in the course of a contract *of* service, first ownership will vest in the author according to the general rule in s. 11(1), CDPA. Yet, the commissioning

---

103 CDPA, s. 1(1).   104 Ibid., s. 90(2).   105 Ibid., s. 90(3).
106 For the circumstances in which a gratuitous, implied licence may be revoked see *Brighton v Jones*.

party will undoubtedly want to be able to exploit or use the copyright work that it has commissioned. In this situation, what would you advise the commissioning party to do?

It sometimes happens, however, that the parties to a contract *for* services fail to mention or stipulate anything about ownership of copyright or permission to carry out certain acts in relation to the copyright work. In such situations, courts may intervene to imply terms of assignment or terms of licence in favour of the commissioning party. The principles governing the implication of such terms were set out in *Robin Ray v Classic FM*.

Robin Ray v Classic FM [1988] FSR 622

The claimant had entered into a consultancy agreement with the defendant, under which he was to provide advice on their classical musical repertoire and catalogue its recorded music library. Nothing was mentioned about intellectual property rights in any work created by the claimant when acting as a consultant for the defendant. The claimant supplied various documents and a catalogue to the defendant and these formed a crucial part of their programming database. The defendant radio station became highly successful and, as a result, proposed to grant licences to foreign radio stations to use the database. The claimant objected to this use, but the defendant nevertheless went ahead with granting these licences. The claimant then commenced proceedings for infringement of copyright in the documents and catalogue he had produced. The defendant argued, *inter alia*, that because it had commissioned the claimant to produce these works, it had been granted an implied assignment of copyright or an implied licence.

Lightman J, at pp. 640–5:

[**Lightman J** began by stating the principles governing the implication of such terms:]

The general principles governing the respective rights of the contractor and client in the copyright in a work commissioned by the client appear to me to be as follows:

(1) the contractor is entitled to retain the copyright in default of some express or implied term to the contrary effect;

(2) the contract itself may expressly provide as to who shall be entitled to the copyright in work produced pursuant to the contract. Thus under a standard form Royal Institute of British Architects ('RIBA') contract between an architect and his client, there is an express provision that the copyright shall remain vested in the architect;

(3) the mere fact that the contractor has been commissioned is insufficient to entitle the client to the copyright. Where Parliament intended the act of commissioning alone to vest copyright in the client, e.g. in case of unregistered design rights and registered designs, the legislation expressly so provides (see section 215 of the 1988 Act and section 2(1A) of the Registered Designs Act 1949 as amended by the 1988 Act). In all other cases the client has to establish the entitlement under some express or implied term of the contract;

(4) the law governing the implication of terms in a contract has been firmly established (if not earlier) by the decision of the House of Lords in *Liverpool City Council v Irwin* [1977] AC 239 ('Liverpool'). In the words of Lord Bingham MR in *Philips Electronique v British Sky Broadcasting Ltd* [1995] EMLR 472 ('Philips') at 481, the essence of much learning on implied terms is distilled in the speech of Lord Simon of Glaisdale

on behalf of the majority of the Judicial Committee of the Privy Council in *BP Refinery (Westernport) Pty Ltd v The President, Councillors and Ratepayers of the Shire of Hastings* (1978) 52 ALJR 20 at 26:

> Their Lordships do not think it necessary to review exhaustively the authorities on the implication of a term in a contract which the parties have not thought fit to express. In their view, for a term to be implied, the following conditions (which may overlap) must be satisfied: (1) it must be reasonable and equitable; (2) it must be necessary to give business efficacy to the contract, so that no term will be implied if the contract is effective without it; (3) it must be so obvious that 'it goes without saying'; (4) it must be capable of clear expression; (5) it must not contradict any express term of the contract.

Lord Bingham added an explanation and warning:

> The courts' usual role in contractual interpretation is, by resolving ambiguities or reconciling apparent inconsistencies, to attribute the true meaning to the language in which the parties themselves have expressed their contract. The implication of contract terms involves a different and altogether more ambitious undertaking: the interpolation of terms to deal with matters for which, *ex hypothesi*, the parties themselves have made no provision. It is because the implication of terms is so potentially intrusive that the law imposes strict constrains on the exercise of this extraordinary power...
>
> The question of whether a term should be implied, and if so what, almost inevitably arises after a crisis has been reached in the performance of the contract. So the court comes to the task of implication with the benefit of hindsight, and it is tempting for the court then to fashion a term which will reflect the merits of the situation as they then appear. Tempting, but wrong.

(5) where (as in the present case) it is necessary to imply the grant of some right to fill a lacuna in the contract and the question arises how this lacuna is to be filled, guidance is again to be found in Liverpool. The principle is clearly stated that in deciding which of various alternatives should constitute the contents of the term to be implied, the choice must be that which does not exceed what is necessary in the circumstances (see Lord Wilberforce at 245F–G). In short a minimalist approach is called for. An implication may only be made if this is necessary, and then only of what is necessary and no more;

(6) accordingly if it is necessary to imply some grant of rights in respect of a copyright work, and the need could be satisfied by the grant of a licence or an assignment of the copyright, the implication will be of the grant of a licence only;

(7) circumstances may exist when the necessity for an assignment of copyright may be established. As Mr Howe has submitted, these circumstances are, however, only likely to arise if the client needs in addition to the right to use the copyright works the right to exclude the contractor from using the work and the ability to enforce the copyright against third parties. Examples of when this situation may arise include: (a) where the purpose in commissioning the work is for the client to multiply and sell copies on the market for which the work was created free from the sale of copies in competition with the client by the contractor or third parties; (b) where the contractor creates a work which is derivative from a pre-existing work of the client, e.g. when a draughtsman is engaged to turn designs of an article in sketch form by the client into formal manufacturing drawings, and the draughtsman could not use the drawings himself without infringing the underlying rights of the client; (c) where the contractor is engaged as part of a team with employees of the client to produce a composite or joint work and he is unable, or cannot have been intended to be able, to exploit for his own benefit the joint work or indeed any distinct contribution of his own created in the course of his

engagement: see *Nichols Advanced Vehicle Systems Inc v Rees* [1979] RPC 127 at 139 and consider *Sofia Bogrich v Shape Machines*, unreported, November 4, 1994, Pat Ct and in particular page 15 of the transcript of the judgment of Aldous J. In each case it is necessary to consider the price paid, the impact on the contractor of assignment of copyright and whether it can sensibly have been intended that the contractor should retain any copyright as a separate item of property;

(8) if necessity requires only the grant of a licence, the ambit of the licence must be the minimum which is required to secure to the client the entitlement which the parties to contract must have intended to confer upon him. The amount of the purchase price which the client under the contract has obliged himself to pay may be relevant to the ambit of the licence. Thus in *Stovin-Bradford v Volpoint Properties Ltd* [1971] 1 Ch 1007, where the client agreed to pay only a nominal fee to his architect for the preparation of plans, he was held to have a licence to use the plans for no purpose beyond the anticipated application for planning permission. By contrast in *Blair v Osborne and Tompkins* [1971] 2 QB 78, where the client was charged the full RIBA scale fee, his licence was held to extend to using the plans for the building itself. Guidance as to the approach to be adopted is provided in a passage in the judgment of Jacobs J in *Beck v Montana Constructions Pty* [1964–5] NSWR 229 at 235 cited with approval by Widgery LJ in *Blair v Osborne and Tomkins*, supra at 87:

> it seems to me that the principle involved is this; that the engagement for reward of a person to produce material of a nature which is capable of being the subject of copyright implies a permission, or consent, or licence in the person giving the engagement to use the material in the manner and for the purpose in which and for which it was contemplated between the parties that it would be used at the time of the engagement.

(9) the licence accordingly is to be limited to what is in the joint contemplation of the parties at the date of the contract, and does not extend to enable the client to take advantage of a new unexpected profitable opportunity (consider *Meikle v Maufe* [1941] 3 All ER 144).

[**Lightman J** then applied these principles to the facts of the case:]

It is common ground that upon the true construction of the consultancy agreement some form of right in respect of the intellectual property rights in the five documents and the catalogues must have been intended in favour of the defendant, for without it the contract for the provision of his services by the plaintiff would be without purpose or value: the defendant could make no use and obtain no benefit from their product. The question raised is the content of the implication. The plaintiff says that the implication should be of a licence limited to use of the database and the making of copies for the purpose of the defendant's existing business. The defendant says that the implication should be of a grant of the copyright in the five documents and the catalogue or at least of a licence broad enough to permit the making of copies for the purposes of exploitation of the copyright abroad.

It seems quite clear to me upon the true construction of the consultancy agreement in its matrix of facts that the limits of what was contemplated at the date of the consultancy agreement were that the plaintiff's work would be used for the purpose of enabling the defendant to carry on its business as set out in recital A, namely to broadcast in the United Kingdom. The only necessary implication to give purpose and effect to the consultancy agreement is accordingly the grant of a licence to the defendant to use the copyright material for the indefinite future for this purpose and for this purpose only.

. . .

> The defendant can accordingly make copies of the database if this was reasonably required for carrying on the business of a broadcaster in the United Kingdom, but cannot do so for the purpose of exploiting the database abroad. The making of the copies in question in this case accordingly constituted an infringement of the plaintiff's copyright.

The principles governing the implication of terms of assignment or terms of licence set out in *Robin Ray* were approved and followed by the Court of Appeal in *Griggs Group Ltd v Evans & Raben Footwear*.[107] On the facts, however, the court found an implied term of assignment. In this case the claimants had commissioned an advertising agency to produce a combined logo for their 'Doc Martens' footwear. The advertising agency in turn commissioned the first defendant (a freelance artist) to produce the logo and paid him at their standard rate. Subsequently, the first defendant assigned copyright in the combined logo to the second defendant, who was an Australian footwear company. The claimants asserted that they were equitable owners of copyright in the logo and sought a declaration to that effect and an order that copyright be formally assigned to them. The claimants were successful at first instance and the defendant's appeal was dismissed. Jacob LJ (with whom Chadwick and Lloyd LJJ agreed) held at para. 19:

> If an officious bystander had asked at the time of contract whether Mr Evans was going to retain rights in the combined logo which could be used against the client by Mr Evans (or anyone to whom he sold the rights) anywhere in the world, other than in respect of point of sale material in the UK, the answer would surely have been 'of course not'. Mr Evans had no conceivable further interest in the work being created...

Do you agree with courts' implying terms of assignment or licence? If so, how can this practice be reconciled with the requirements in ss. 90(3) and 92(1) of the CDPA that assignments and exclusive licences must be in writing signed by or on behalf of the assignor/copyright owner?

2.9 DURATION

2.9.1 CALCULATION OF TERM

The rules for calculating term of protection are generally straightforward. For literary, dramatic, musical, and artistic works, copyright expires 70 years from the end of the calendar year in which the author dies.[108] In relation to sound recordings, copyright expires 50 years after the end of the calendar year in which the recording is made or, if during that period the recording is published or made available to the public by being played in public or communicated to the public, 50 years from the end of the calendar year in which first publication takes place or the work is so made available.[109] For broadcasts, copyright lasts for 50 years from the end of the calendar year when the broadcast is made[110] and for typographical arrangements, 25 years from the end of the calendar year in which the edition was first published.[111]

---

[107] [2005] FSR 31.   [108] CDPA, s. 12(2).   [109] Ibid., s. 13A(2).
[110] Ibid., s. 14.   [111] Ibid., s. 15.

Calculating the term of protection for films differs in that it does not coincide with a fixed term after the death of the author/s. Instead, s. 13B of the CDPA provides that copyright expires 70 years after the end of the calendar year in which the death of the last of the following persons to die occurs: the principal director, the author of the screenplay, the author of the dialogue, or the composer of music specially created for and used in the film. Only one of these persons—i.e. the principal director—is the author of a film. The explanation for this apparent oddity is the Term Directive,[112] which sought to harmonize the terms of protection for all copyright works.

Prior to the Term Directive, the CDPA stipulated that the author of a film was its producer and that protection would last for 50 years from the time the film was made. However, in other Member States, such as Germany, films were protected as cinematographic works and copyright expired 70 years after death of the relevant authors: these included persons who made a creative contribution to the film which was inseparably incorporated into the film work, such as the principal director, cameraman, or cutter.[113] Thus, in harmonizing the length of protection for films, the Term Directive needed to come up with a common approach to calculating term, but at the same time respect the different approaches to authorship of films. The result was partial harmonization of film authorship, whereby Article 2(1) of the Term Directive states that the principal director of a cinematographic work shall be considered as one of its authors. UK copyright law was amended accordingly. However, commentators have queried whether the UK properly implemented the provisions relating to cinematographic works, given the limited scope of protection for film works. Further, although films may now be classified as dramatic works and thus obtain a greater scope of protection,[114] it seems that Article 2(1) of the Term Directive, as implemented in s. 13B of the CDPA, does not apply to films that are protected as dramatic works.

FURTHER READING

P. Kamina, 'British film copyright and the incorrect implementation of the EC Copyright Directives' (1998) 9(3) Ent LR 109.

2.9.2 IMPACT OF TERM DIRECTIVE ON EXPIRED COPYRIGHT WORKS

When it came to harmonization of the term of protection, it was thought that upwards harmonization to 70 years *post mortem auctoris* would be least disruptive. Thus, countries like the UK, which hitherto offered 50 years *post mortem auctoris,* were required to extend the term to life of the author plus 70 years.[115] In addition, Article 10(2) of the Term Directive stated that the extended term of 70 years would apply to all works and subject matter still protected in at least one Member State. Thus, even if copyright in, say, a musical work had expired in the UK if, at the relevant time, it was still protected in Germany (which had a rule of life plus 70 years), copyright would revive in that work in *all* Member States. In other words, the Term Directive not only extended the term of protection for works in which

---

[112] The terms of protection for copyright and related rights were harmonized by Directive 93/98/EEC, which was subsequently codified by Directive 2006/116/EC of 12 Dec. 2006 on the term of protection of copyright and certain related rights ('Term Directive'), Art. 2(2).

[113] Art. 65 of German Law on Copyright and Neighbouring Rights of 9 Sept. 1965.

[114] See p. 62–4.   [115] Art. 1(1) Term Directive.

copyright still existed, it also revived copyright in works that had fallen into the public domain. To deal with the possible hardship and unfairness that third parties might suffer as a result of these rules, Article 10(3) of the Term Directive allowed Member States to 'adopt the necessary provisions to protect in particular acquired rights of third parties'.

The UK implemented the Term Directive via the Duration of Copyright and Rights in Performances Regulations 1995.[116] Of particular note are Regulations 23 and 24, which protect the interests of third parties when it comes to works in which copyright has been revived.

Regulation 23(1) states that no act done before commencement of the regulations (i.e. 1 January 1996) shall be treated as infringing revived copyright in a work. Regulation 23(2) states that it is also not infringement of revived copyright in a work to do anything 'in pursuance of arrangements made before 1 January 1995 at a time when copyright did not subsist in the work' or 'to issue to the public after commencement copies of the work made before 1st July 1995 at a time when copyright did not subsist in the work'. 'Arrangements' are defined in Regulation 23(5) to mean 'arrangements for the exploitation of the work in question'.

Regulation 24 differs insofar as it creates a form of compulsory licence. It states that in relation to works in which copyright has revived, 'any acts restricted by the copyright shall be treated as licensed by the copyright owner, subject only to the payment of such reasonable royalty or other remuneration as may be agreed or determined in default of agreement by the Copyright Tribunal'. Importantly, a person seeking to rely on this provision must give reasonable notice of his intention to the copyright owner.[117] The scope of Regulations 23 and 24 were analysed in the following case.

Sweeney v Macmillan Publishers Ltd [2002] RPC 35

James Joyce had died in 1941 and, as such, copyright in 'Ulysses' had expired in the UK as from 1 January 1992. In 1992 the second defendant (Mr Rose), a Joyce scholar, contacted the first defendant (Macmillan Publishers) with a view to him producing a Reader's Edition of 'Ulysses'. He started work on the project during 1992 and completed most of the work by the end of 1993. He entered into an agreement with the second defendant to publish the text in early 1996 and publication occurred in 1997. As a result of the Duration of Copyright and Rights in Performances Regulations 1995, SI 1995/3297, copyright in 'Ulysses' was revived, with effect from 1 January 1996, until the end of 2011. The claimants (Sweeney), who were the trustees of James Joyce's estate, commenced proceedings against the defendants alleging infringement of copyright. The defendants sought to rely on Regulations 23 and 24.

Lloyd J:

[Discussing the scope and application of Regulation 23:]

57. I do not propose to attempt a definition of 'arrangements'. I can accept Mr Burkill's proposition that they are not necessarily limited to arrangements by way of contract. Nevertheless they must be of some degree of solidity or certainty, such that it can be said that acts done later are done in pursuance of the arrangements. Regulations 23(2)(a) and (3)(b) are not so wide as to extend to anything done after commencement in consequence of anything at all

---

[116] SI 1995/3297.   [117] Regulation 24(2).

which has been done, or any steps of any kind taken, with a view to exploiting the work in question, before January 1, 1995. Apart from anything else a very wide reading of 'arrangements' would produce a very odd contrast with the fairly narrow and specific provisions of regulation 23(2)(b). That deals only with the distribution of stock in hand on July 1, 1995...

58. I accept Mr Rose's evidence that he did not start on his Reader's Edition project until after January 1, 1992. All that he did in respect of the project before January 1, 1995 was done while the 1922 edition was in the public domain. But what did that amount to? He started work on the project, and no doubt achieved a great deal of what he intended by the end of 1994. He got into discussion with Penguin, to whom he was already talking about Finnegans Wake. He told me that he was confident that Penguin would publish the Reader's Edition, but he was wrong. In 1993 he approached Macmillan, and may at that stage have showed them some sample text. They were encouraging but without any commitment. Mr Rose was again confident that they would publish the Reader's Edition, once Penguin withdrew, and this confidence was enhanced when Mr Riley moved from Penguin to Macmillan in September 1993. It does not seem to me that these limited contacts with publishers can fairly be described as amounting to 'arrangements for the exploitation of the work'. That aside, what he relies on is his having done a great deal, even the vast bulk, of the work needed to prepare his new edition. That, by itself, does not seem to me to be arrangements in pursuance of which it could be said that the eventual publication was done. If it were sufficient it is difficult to see how a distinction could be made between this case and one in which only a small amount of the work had been done before January 1, 1995, but the work was thereafter carried on, eventually brought to completion, and finally published. The publication could be said to have been done in that case too in pursuance of the work started before January 1, 1995. Such an interpretation of the regulation would, in my judgment, be far too wide, even in its own terms, and the more so with the guidance of the European Court of Justice given in the passages from *Butterfly Music* which I have quoted above. It would interfere to an excessive extent with the rights conferred by the revived copyright.

[**Lloyd J** then discussed the scope and application of Regulation 24:]

62. In order to qualify for the compulsory licence afforded by regulation 24, all that has to be done is for the person intending to avail himself of the right conferred by the regulation to give reasonable notice of his intention to the copyright owner, stating when he intends to begin to do the acts. The first question is whether Macmillan, when they told the estate, via Mr Monro, of their intention in March 1997, stated when they intended to begin the acts. The letter of 1996 does not contain that information. But it seems to me that, in the context of the exchanges that took place in March 1997, it would be wrong to regard Macmillan as not having given notice of that simply because the intended publication date of June 1997 was not stated in that letter. Normally it would be sensible for a notice which is intended to take effect under regulation 24 itself to state the intended date. But here Mr Monro already knew the intended date from the publicity which had been drawn to his attention, and this was confirmed by Mr Riley in their telephone conversation. I am not prepared to hold that no sufficient notice was given because the intended publication date was not included in the 1996 letter, as received in March 1997.

63. A puzzle about regulation 24 is the requirement for 'reasonable' notice, which must refer to the period of notice. Since the copyright owner cannot do anything to stop the intended acts once notice is given, so long as they are within the regulation, it seems to be arguable that only quite short notice needs to be given. The requirement of notice means that the acts must be open and not clandestine, and that a person who hoped to get away with publication in breach of copyright in secret cannot justify his acts retrospectively by

reference to the regulation. But on any basis notice in March for publication in June would be reasonable, and I need not say anything about what is required to make the period of notice reasonable. Mr Baldwin submitted that the notice had to include full particulars of what was to be done, including, he said, a copy of the intended publication. I cannot get that out of the text of the regulation, and it seems to me that it would not be compatible with a notice given at all well in advance, since the text may well not be finalised until near the time of publication. In my judgment Macmillan's notice was not invalid on this account.

64. The other question is whether it is open to the person seeking to take advantage of the regulation to give notice on a contingent basis, as a fall-back to, for example, an argument under regulation 23 as here…It seems to me that it would be reading a great deal too much into regulation 24(2) to say that the notice can only ever be given unequivocally, and that no such notice can be given in the alternative to an argument that it is not necessary.

….

66. Accordingly, as to whether a valid notice was given under regulation 24, I find for the defendants. If and in so far as their acts would otherwise infringe revived copyright, they would be entitled to do them but would have to pay a sum to be agreed or determined under the regulations.

Do you think Regulations 23 and 24, as interpreted in *Sweeney*, strike a fair balance between the interests of the owner of revived copyright and those of third parties? If not, what would be your suggested alternatives?

FURTHER READING

B. Lindner, 'Revival of rights v protection of acquired rights' [2000] EIPR 133.

2.9.3 FUTURE DEVELOPMENTS

A recent controversy is whether the term of protection for sound recordings and performers' rights should be increased from 50 to 95 years. This issue was examined in the context of UK law by the Gowers Review of Intellectual Property,[118] which recommended against such an increased term. In the EC context, however, the European Commission thinks otherwise and has submitted a Proposed Directive[119] that will amend the Term Directive to extend the length of protection for sound recordings and performers' rights to 95 years.

The Commission seeks to justify the increase in term on two main grounds. First, performers are generally outliving the existing 50-year period of protection for their performances and, as such, are facing an income gap at the end of their lifetimes.[120] Secondly, sound recording producers are vulnerable to revenue losses because of peer-to-peer piracy and an extra 45 years' protection will assist in maintaining a steady revenue stream necessary to invest in new talent.[121] In the extract below, the Commission explains why it favours a proposal which grants a 95-year term to performers and producers of sound recordings.

---

[118] See <http://www.hm-treasury.gov.uk/gowers_review_index.htm> at paras. 4.20–4.47.

[119] Proposal for a European Parliament and Council directive amending Directive 2006/116/EC of the European Parliament and of the Council on the term of protection of copyright and certain related rights, Brussels COM (2008) 464/3 ('Proposed Directive').

[120] Recitals 5 and 6 of Proposed Directive; pp. 2–3 of the Explanatory Memorandum to the Proposed Directive.

[121] Explanatory Memorandum, pp. 4–5.

Explanatory Memorandum to Proposal for a European Parliament and Council Directive amending Directive 2006/116/EC of the European Parliament and of the Council on the term of protection of copyright and certain related rights, Brussels COM (2008) 464/3

At pp. 8–9:

[This option] would increase the pool of A&R resources available to phonogram record producers and could thus have an additional positive impact on cultural diversity. The [Impact Assessment] also demonstrates that the benefits of a term extension are not necessarily skewed in favour of famous featured performers. While featured performers certainly earn the bulk of the copyright royalties that are negotiated with record companies, all performers, be it featured artists or session musicians, are entitled to so-called 'secondary' incomes sources, such as single equitable remuneration when the sound recording incorporating their performances is broadcast or performed in public. A term extension would ensure that these income sources do not cease during the performer's lifetime. Even incremental increases in income are used by performers to buy more time to devote to their artistic careers, and to spend less time on part time employment. Moreover, for the thousands of anonymous session musicians who were at the peak of their careers in the late fifties and sixties, 'single equitable remuneration' for the broadcasting of their recordings is often the only source of income left from their artistic career.

...

On the other hand, the impact on users would be minimal. This is true in relation to statutory remuneration claims and for the sale of CDs:

- First, the 'single equitable remuneration' due for broadcasting and performances of music in public venues would remain the same as these payments are calculated as a percentage of the broadcasters or other operators revenue (a parameter independent of how many phonograms are in or out of copyright).

- Empirical studies also show that the price of sound recordings that are out of copyright are not lower than that of sound recordings in copyright. A study by Price Waterhouse Coopers concluded that there was no systematic difference between prices of in-copyright and out-of copyright recordings. It is the most comprehensive study to date and covers 129 albums recorded between 1950 and 1958. On this basis, it finds no clear evidence that records in which the related rights have expired are systematically sold at lower prices than records which are still protected

...

Overall the extended term should have a positive impact on consumer choice and cultural diversity. In the long run, this is because a term extension will benefit cultural diversity by ensuring the availability of resources to fund and develop new talent. In the short to medium term, a term extension provides record companies with an incentive to digitize and market their back catalogue of old recordings. It is already clear that internet distribution offers unique opportunities to market an unprecedented quantity of sound recordings.

The impact on so-called public domain producers would be minimal. While those companies could [argue] that they have to wait longer to produce phonograms in which the performers and phonogram producers' rights have expired, the works performed in a phonogram would not lose protection once the term of protection for the phonogram expires. This is because the work performed on a phonogram remains protected for the life of the author (songwriter and composer) who wrote the work.

The Commission's proposal has attracted vehement and wide-ranging criticism, particularly from the academic community. One of the major criticisms is that the real problem for performers is not the length of protection, but rather their poor bargaining position such that they bargain away their rights in return for a one-off payment. Thus, scholars have argued that a means of vastly improving the position of performers would be to restrict the lawfulness of these contracts.[122] Scholars have also pointed out that the majority of performers earn an inadequate sum and a prolongation of protection will merely extend the receipt of this fairly minimal income, rather than substantially increase it.[123] Further, doubts have been expressed about whether the losses in revenue to the record industry are due to peer-to-peer piracy and indeed whether an increase from 50 to 95 years of protection will be an adequate countermeasure to alleged widespread piracy.[124] Finally, commentators are sceptical that an increase in term will not negatively impact on users, in terms of access and the price paid for recordings that would otherwise be out of copyright.[125]

The arguments on both sides of the debate repay much closer attention. However, based on what has been thus far discussed, and bearing in mind the justifications for copyright addressed in s. 3, do you support the Commission's Proposal?

FURTHER READING

S. Ricketson, 'The copyright term' (1992) 23 IIC 753.

R. Hilty et al., 'Comment by the Max-Planck Institute on the Commission's proposal for a directive to amend Directive 2006/116 concerning the term of protection for copyright and related rights' [2009] EIPR 59.

'Creativity stifled? A joint academic statement on the proposed copyright term extension for sound recordings' [2008] EIPR 341.

---

[122] R. Hilty et al., 'Comment by the Max-Planck Institute on the Commission's proposal for a directive to amend Directive 2006/116 concerning the term of protection for copyright and related rights' [2009] EIPR 59, 61.

[123] Ibid., pp. 62–3; 'Creativity stifled? A joint academic statement on the proposed copyright term extension for sound recordings' [2008] EIPR 341, 342.

[124] Hilty et al., 'Comment by the Max-Planck Institute', pp. 64–5.

[125] Ibid., p. 69; 'Creativity stifled?', pp. 343–4.

3

COPYRIGHT II:

INFRINGEMENT AND EXCEPTIONS

This chapter examines the economic rights that belong to copyright owners, along with the moral rights that authors have in their works, and the circumstances in which these rights may be infringed. It considers also some of the major exceptions that may be relied upon as a defence to a claim of copyright infringement.

3.1 ECONOMIC RIGHTS

According to s. 16 of the CDPA, the copyright owner has the exclusive right to:

- copy the work
- issue copies of the work to the public
- rent or lend the work to the public
- perform, show, or play the work in public
- communicate the work to the public
- make an adaptation of the work or do any of the above in relation to an adaptation.

These economic rights comprise the copyright owner's monopoly and allow the owner to exploit the work in a variety of ways. From the time of the Statute of Anne (1710), which prohibited only copying, it is clear that the bundle of rights granted to an owner has grown steadily. It is also interesting to note that the CDPA enumerates the exclusive rights, meaning that it specifically states the acts that belong to the copyright owner. Thus, if a new mode of exploitation arises it is a matter of seeing whether it can be encompassed within the existing rights; if not, the practice is to amend the legislation accordingly. The most recent example of this was the insertion of the right of communication to the public, particularly to include Internet transmissions.[1] This approach may be contrasted with that taken in France, where two broad rights are granted—that of reproduction and performance—and courts

---

[1] See CDPA, s. 20 and see 12.6.2.

have interpreted these rights to include new forms of exploitation as and when they have emerged, thus avoiding the need for regular legislative amendment.

The following sections discuss the scope of the exclusive rights in the CDPA in more detail.

3.1.1 REPRODUCTION

The right to copy the work is the oldest of the exclusive acts, being first recognised in the Statute of Anne 1710. Section 17 of the CDPA elaborates upon the scope of this right and emphasizes several important features. For literary, dramatic, musical, and artistic works, the right means 'reproducing the work in any material form' and this includes 'storing the work in any medium by electronic means'. As such, simply digitizing a work (for example, by scanning a document or converting an analogue musical recording to digital) will amount to a copy. In addition, for any description of work, copying includes transient or incidental copies. Thus, running a computer program or browsing an Internet webpage will involve copying since transient copies are made in the Random Access Memory (RAM) of one's computer.

In relation to artistic works, s. 17(3) of the CDPA stipulates that copying includes changes of dimension, from two-dimensional to three-dimensional form and vice versa. Thus, an owner of copyright in a drawing of, say, a cartoon character will be able to prevent an unauthorized third party from making a cuddly toy of that character. Further, an owner of copyright in sculpture will be able to prevent unauthorized photographs of it being made. The fact that copying of artistic works includes changes of dimension is particularly useful to those creating industrial or functional designs and can create a tension between copyright and designs law.[2]

An issue that has arisen is whether reproduction in a different dimension or material form is prohibited for works other than artistic works. For example, does following a set of instructions (such as a recipe or knitting pattern) and producing a resultant article according to those instructions amount to an infringement of the literary work represented by the instructions? This issue was discussed in obiter in the following case.

Autospin (Oil Seals) Ltd v Beehive Spinning [1995] RPC 683

The claimant (Autospin) had designed and developed a new type of oil seal. There were three dimensions of critical importance to manufacturing this seal and the claimant had produced charts containing instructions that allowed these dimensions to be calculated. The defendants (Beehive Spinning), who were all ex-employees of the claimant, began manufacturing oil seals, which the claimants alleged, *inter alia*, infringed copyright in the compilation of measurements in their charts. Laddie J considered whether or not a three dimensional article could reproduce a literary work, in this case the compilation.

Laddie J, at pp. 697–8, 700:

Argument in favour of a three dimensional article being a reproduction of a literary work:

The type of literary work at issue in this case is a compilation. Once again, it is not the mere form of words or notation used which justifies copyright protection for a compilation, it is the author's skill and effort expended in gathering together the information which it contains.

. . .

---

2 See 11.4.

It is well established that the copyright in a two dimensional drawing (an 'artistic work' under the relevant legislation) may be infringed by reproducing it in a three dimensional article. This was the law well before the legislation expressly provided that it was so (See *King Features Syndicate Inc v O and M Kleeman Ltd* [1941] AC 417). By parity of reasoning, since copyright in a literary work may be infringed by reproducing it in any material form, why should it not be an infringement to take a compilation of dimensions and reproduce it in the form of a three dimensional article which embodies those dimensions? After all, the alleged infringer has made use of the author's skill and effort in discovering and bringing together the relevant dimensions.

The argument can also be put another way. As I have mentioned, copyright in a drawing can be infringed by reproducing it in a three dimensional form. It is possible to define any shape in words and letters. Therefore a design in a drawing can be defined equally accurately in non-graphic notation. In fact many three dimensional articles are now designed on computers. A literary work consisting of computer code therefore represents the three dimensional article. Surely if it is an infringement of copyright in a two dimensional drawing to make a three dimensional article from it, it must follow that it should also be an infringement to produce the article from the equivalent literary work which contains the same design information and is just as much a product of the author's design skill...Against this, my attention was drawn to statements in two cases. In the Privy Council in *Interlego AG v Tyco Industries Inc* [1988] RPC 343, Lord Oliver said:

'It has always to be borne in mind that infringement of copyright by three dimensional copying is restricted to artistic copyright (section 48(1)). To produce an article by following written instructions may be a breach of confidence or an infringement of patent, but it does not infringe the author's copyright in his instructions.' [page 373]

...

The second case was *Brigid Foley Ltd v Ellott* [1982] RPC 433 in which the plaintiff was seeking to enforce the copyright in a knitting guide. Megarry V-C stated:

'I did not call upon Mr Pumphrey to argue this point, since it seems to me quite plain that there is no reproduction of the words and numerals in the knitting guides in the knitted garments produced by following the instructions. The essence, I think, of a reproduction (and I do not attempt to be exhaustive) is that the reproduction should be some copy of or representation of the original. I do not see how anyone looking at the knitted garment could then say "Well, that is a copy of, or a reproduction of, the words and numerals to be found in the knitting guide". By a process of counting up the number of stitches, and so on, in the knitted garment one might be able to work back and produce the knitting instructions; but that is a very different matter from saying that the garment is a reproduction of those instructions.' [page 434]

...In my view the court should ask the question 'is it accurate to say that the alleged infringer's article is, from a common sense point of view, a reproduction of this particular type of literary work?' In answering that question in this case, it is potentially misleading to look over one's shoulder to see what the response would have been if the compilation had been an artistic work or even a different form of literary work. Thus it may well be sensible to say that making a three dimensional article from a data file in a computer (a literary work) which precisely defines the shape of the article is to reproduce it. However, in my view, even if the plaintiff's charts in this case had included the three critical dimensions of some of the parts used for making a seal, it would not be right to say that making a seal to those dimensions is to reproduce the charts. Those dimensions say virtually nothing about the shape of the seal, they merely indicate some critical dimensions used in the manufacturing process which results in the creation of the seal.

Indeed, in my view, on the facts, this case is even weaker that that. The charts do not contain even the three critical dimensions. They contain instructions for the calculation of those dimensions...

> The charts say nothing more about how a seal is to be constructed. In my view, just as it cannot be a reproduction of literary copyright in a recipe for a cake to make a cake to the recipe, so it is not a reproduction to follow such mathematical instructions.
>
> For these reasons I hold that the claim to infringement of copyright in the charts also fails.

Do you agree with the approach taken by Laddie J? In what sorts of situations do you imagine there could be a three dimensional reproduction of a literary work?

3.1.2 ADAPTATION

It is important to note that, unlike under US copyright law, the right of adaptation in the CDPA does not amount to a right to control the creation of all adaptations or derivative works. Rather, it is restricted to certain types of works—literary, dramatic, and musical works—and is defined narrowly.[3] For example, it includes a translation of a literary or dramatic work or converting a dramatic work into non-dramatic form (and vice versa).[4] In relation to musical works, adaptation means an arrangement or transcription of the work.[5]

An adaptation of a literary, dramatic, or musical work may itself separately qualify for protection assuming the originality requirement has been satisfied. This will usually be the case and the fact that the adaptation is carried out without permission and is thus infringing will not preclude it from being protected by copyright.[6]

3.1.3 DISTRIBUTION

The right to issue copies of a work to the public was first introduced by s. 18 of the CDPA. Prior to this legislation there existed only a right to publish the work for the first time.[7] In other words, there was a shift from a right of divulgation to a right of distribution of the work. Section 18 has been amended twice, in order to implement Article 4 of the Software Directive and Article 9 of the Rental Rights Directive. These amendments have resulted in a complex provision that gives rise to several uncertainties. One of the major uncertainties, discussed in the following extract, is at what point issuing of copies to the public occurs.

J. Phillips and L. Bently, 'Copyright issues: The mysteries of section 18'
[1999] EIPR 133, 134–5

When does the Issuing Occur?

A central, and recurring, issue in the interpretative problems of section 18 is at what point in the potential chain of distribution does the issuing occur. To take a simple example, when a manufacturer (A) distributes copies to a wholesaler (B) who in turn distributes to a retailer (C), who then sells to the general public, which of these acts constitutes 'an issue to the public of copies of the work' within the meaning of section 18? The determination of this question is important, especially since those persons who deal with the copies subsequent

---

[3] CDPA, s. 21.   [4] Ibid., s. 21(3)(a).   [5] Ibid., s. 21(3)(b).

[6] See for example, *Redwood Music v Chappell* [1982] RPC 109 and *ZYX v King* [1995] FSR 566 (both involving musical arrangements).

[7] See *Infabrics Ltd v Jaytex Ltd* [1981] 1 All ER 1057, 1067.

to the first issuing to the public will not be liable for infringement as a result of the operation of section 18(3). As set out above, this specifically provides that subsequent distribution and importation of these copies will not constitute an issue to the public.

There are two possible interpretations of section 18 in this respect, which will be referred to as 'destination theory' and 'disposition theory'.

'Destination theory' draws on the idea of issuing to the 'public', which implies that the issuing occurs only when the distribution reaches its final destination, the consumer, thus suggesting that the critical act covered by the right is the act of retail sale. This meaning is supported by the fact that the phrase 'the act of putting into circulation' in section 18(2)(a) is related directly to the act of issuing copies to the public; it is expressed as being a 'reference to the issue to the public of copies of a work'. At least in the context of the subsistence of copyright, the public has generally been defined in a broad manner, rather than as a limited class. Adopting this analogy, in our example, A might not be regarded as issuing copies to the public since there is a supply only to a restricted group of wholesalers. On this view, the result is that it is the retailer C who puts the copies into circulation, generating strict liability for the retailer pursuant to section 18.

This first interpretation appears consistent with Article 9 of the Rental Rights Directive, which refers to the right as being 'to make available these objects to the public by sale or otherwise'. It is also an interpretation which would best safeguard the copyright owners' rights. Indeed, as will be seen, it will create liability for those who, prior to the enactment of the present section 18, would not have been liable for copyright infringement in English law.

Another view of the meaning of section 18, which the authors term 'disposition theory', lays emphasis on the words 'putting into circulation', which implies an act of alienation early in the chain of distribution, for example, that of a manufacturer (A) selling to a wholesaler (B), or the act of the wholesaler (B) supplying to the retailer.

Such a construction receives some support from the fact that, according to section 18(3) references to the issue to the public of copies of a work do not include 'any subsequent distribution, sale, hiring or loan of those copies previously put into circulation'. This implies that the first act is the relevant one, rather than subsequent acts. In addition, in making an exception to the rule as regards subsequent distribution when copies are introduced from outside the EEA, section 18(3)(b) seems to envisage that the very act of importation can be an act of 'issuing', suggesting that the section is targeted at acts of circulation that do not involve members of the public.

Even if section 18 is regarded as connoting the notion of supply to the public, the supply of copies by the manufacturer to the wholesaler could be regarded as an *indirect* supply of goods to the general public or, alternatively, the wholesalers could be viewed as 'the manufacturer's public' for this purpose. The latter construction derives some support from the fact that in respect of infringement by performing a work in public (s. 19) a performance given to a limited class of the public ('the owner's public') is sometimes sufficient to found liability.

This 'disposition theory' interpretation of section 18 is not without its difficulties. One result is that the right conferred by section 18 is of relatively minor significance because the 'reproduction right' conferred by section 17 operates, in most circumstances, to enable the copyright owner to control whether copies are disseminated, and, if so, when and how. But as will be seen, it is an interpretation which best serves to preserve the long-standing distinction in English law between primary and secondary infringement.

The determination of this central question of when copies of the work are first issued to the public is not an easy one. The arguments in favour of one interpretation rather than another are not compelling, yet the impact of the two possibilities may make a significant difference as regards liability in respect of the specific issues now to be considered.

Unfortunately, English courts have yet to resolve the uncertainty discussed above. They have also failed to address other difficulties identified by Phillips and Bently, including the interaction of the distribution right and the principle of exhaustion of rights.

3.1.4 PERFORMANCE IN PUBLIC

Section 19 of the CDPA grants the exclusive right to perform a literary, dramatic, or musical work in public, and the right to play or show a sound recording, film, or broadcast in public. The main difficulty with this right is identifying when the performance is *in public*. Although courts have interpreted the scope of the right on several occasions, they have not produced a consistent set of factors for determining when performances are 'in public' as opposed to private. Two cases in particular highlight the different approaches adopted by the courts.

Harms Ltd and Chappell v Martans Club Ltd [1927] 1 Ch 526

The case involved the performance of a musical work, 'That Certain Feeling' at an exclusive London club, the 'Embassy Club'. Approximately 1800 people were members of the club, but on the night in question 150 members and 50 of their guests had been present. The claimants (who were the owner and musical publisher of the work) brought an action for infringement under the Copyright Act 1911. The defendants admitted the performance but argued that it was not 'in public'. At first instance Eve J held that the claimants' right had been infringed. The defendants appealed, on the basis that he had incorrectly interpreted the words 'in public'. The appeal was dismissed.

Lord Hanworth MR, at 532–3:

In considering here whether or not there has been within s. 2, sub-s. 1, an infringement of the author's sole right, one must see whether or not, upon the facts as a whole, the true view is that there has been a representation of this composition in public. In dealing with the tests which have been applied in the cases, it appears to me that one must apply one's mind to see whether there has been any injury to the author. Did what took place interfere with his proprietary rights? As to that, profit is a very important element. Next, you must consider whether there has been admission of any portion of the public, with or without payment, and when you are considering what you mean by any portion of the public you will find in *Duck v Bates* that according to Brett MR it means the public who would go either with or without payment—the class of persons who would be likely to go to a performance if there was a performance at a public theatre for profit. Then one has also to consider whether or not the performance is a domestic one so as to exclude the notion of 'public'—domestic in the sense that it was private and domestic, a matter of family and household concern only. Then again you must consider where the performance took place, bearing in mind that the place need not be one which is kept habitually for the exhibition of dramatic entertainments. I do not say that I have catalogued all the suggestions made as tests of the facts to be considered, but it appears to me that I have tabled enough to support the conclusion that Eve J was right in his judgment.

[**Sargant** and **Lawrence LJJ** delivered concurring judgments.]

What are the factors identified by Lord Hanworth MR? Does it make sense to take all of these into account or should there be an overriding or definitive factor and, if so, which one?

Jennings v Stephens [1936] Ch 469

A play was performed without consent by a dramatic society at a meeting of the Duston Women's Institute. No guests were present at the performance, but only 62 of the 109 members of the Duston Women's Institute.

Lord Wright MR, at 479–81:

The presence or absence of visitors is thus not the decisive factor, nor does it matter whether the performance is paid or gratuitous, nor is it conclusive that admission is free or for payment, nor is the number of the audience decisive... The antithesis adopted by the cases between performances in public and performances domestic or quasi-domestic cannot be said necessarily to depend on these factors either separately or in combination. The true criterion seems to be the character of the audience. If the performance of 'The Rest Cure' in the Duston Village Institute had been before an audience of exactly the same women as constituted it in fact, drawn from the village, but they had been brought together by a general invitation or advertisement, all other conditions being the same, it cannot be doubted that it would have been a performance in public. In the actual facts, the audience was limited to members of the institute in the village, but all the adult women in the village could be members, and were invited to be members. Election if desired was, in the absence of special disability, a matter of course. If payment was to be considered, the annual 2s. subscription included such performances, and thus corresponded to a small payment for the performance. There was no other qualification for membership except residence in the village, but mere residence in the same village in different homes cannot be regarded as constituting a domestic or quasi-domestic audience. There was nothing like the fact of the hospital as the common home which gave a quasi-domestic complexion to the performance in *Duck v Bates*. Thus it would certainly be a great extension of *Duck v Bates* to apply the decision there to this case; and, as already stated, that case was, in the opinion of Brett MR a border-line and extreme case. The words of Bowen LJ quoted above with reference to a club of persons united for purposes of good fellowship seem to indicate that a dramatic performance given to its members would generally fall within the prohibition of the statute. Furthermore, the institute is a society of a quasi-public character... The Court cannot be influenced by feelings of sympathy for the Women's Institute movement, and must decide the case as if it related to an ordinary village social club open to all village women who chose to take the necessary steps to join, which gave to its members a dramatic entertainment by means of performers from outside, whether amateur or professional. Probably no one would question that the performance was in public if the audience, other circumstances being the same, had been, not sixty-two, but 600, as I suppose in one of the larger villages it might have been. If that were not a performance in public, and might be repeated indefinitely all over the country, the performing right would not be of much value. The quality of domesticity or quasi-domesticity seems to me to be absent. I think such performances are in public within the meaning of the statute. The case seems to me to be within the principle laid down in *Harms'* case rather than within the principle applied in *Duck v Bates*. With great respect to the learned judge, I have come to the conclusion that the performance in question of 'The Rest Cure' was a performance in public.

Greene LJ, at 485:

It is, I think, important, in approaching the question whether a particular performance is 'in public', to bear in mind that by s. 2, sub-s. 1, of the Copyright Act, 1911, infringement is defined by reference to the things the sole right to do which is by the Act conferred on the owner of the copyright. The owner of the copyright is by s. 1, sub-s. 2, given the sole right to perform the work in public, and any person who does this without the consent of the owner infringes his copyright. The question may therefore be usefully approached by inquiring whether or not the act complained of as an infringement would, if done by the owner of the copyright himself, have been an exercise by him of the statutory right conferred upon him. In other words, the expression 'in public' must be considered in relation to the owner of the copyright. If the audience considered in relation to the owner of the copyright may properly be described as the owner's 'public' or part of his 'public', then in performing the work before that audience he would in my opinion be exercising the statutory right conferred upon him; and any one who without his consent performed the work before that audience would be infringing his copyright.

[**Romer LJ** delivered a concurring judgment.]

Do Lord Wright MR and Greene LJ adopt the same overriding test for determining whether a performance is 'in public'? If not, how do their approaches differ and which approach is preferable? In your view, is it desirable to identify when performances are in public according to a combination of factors or a single factor?

3.1.5 COMMUNICATION TO THE PUBLIC[8]

The exclusive right to communicate a work to the public applies to all works, except for typographical arrangements of published editions.[9] A key difference between this right and that of performance *in* public is that, for the latter, the audience is in the same place at the same time (e.g. the audience at a performance of Shakespeare at the Globe Theatre); whereas, with the right of communication *to* the public, the audience may be geographically and chronologically dispersed. For example, a broadcaster may transmit the performance of the Shakespeare play to numerous people who watch it on their television in the privacy of their own home. Alternatively, the broadcaster may upload the broadcast to a website for users to watch at a time and place convenient to them.

Section 20(2) of the CDPA makes it clear that communication to the public covers both broadcasting and Internet transmissions, the latter being captured by the language of 'making available to the public of the work by electronic transmission in such a way that members of the public may access it from a place and at a time individually chosen by them'. The main uncertainty with this right is from where exactly does the communication take place? This has been resolved in the case of broadcasts, since s. 6(4) of the CDPA designates that a wireless broadcast is made from the place:

where, under the control and responsibility of the person making the broadcast, the programme-carrying signals are introduced into an uninterrupted chain of communication (including, in the case of a satellite transmission, the chain leading to the satellite and down towards earth).

---

[8] See 12.6.2.   [9] CDPA, s. 20.

However, no guidance is provided in respect of communication to the public *other* than satellite broadcasting and, in particular, in relation to making available to the public. One school of thought is to apply the 'emission theory', i.e. the applicable law in the context of the making-available right would be the law of the country from which the interactive transmission originates. This begs the question, of course, from where does the interactive transmission originate—is it the place of upload or the place where the server is located? Another school of thought is the 'communication theory', where the applicable law would be the laws of the countries where the work is accessed or accessible or the law of the country of emission (whether place of upload or place of the server) and the laws of the countries of reception. Of these two theories, which do you think is preferable for identifying where communication to the public, in respect of Internet transmissions, occurs?

FURTHER READING

T. Aplin, *Copyright Law in the Digital Society* (Oxford: Hart: 2005), pp. 131–7.

M. Makeen, *Copyright in a Global Information Society: The scope of copyright protection under international, US, UK and French law* (London: Kluwer, 2000).

3.2 INFRINGEMENT

The previous section has discussed the exclusive rights that belong to the copyright owner. This next section explores when those rights are infringed. At the outset, it is important to distinguish between primary and secondary infringement/liability. Primary infringement occurs where a person does, or authorizes another to do, without the licence of the copyright owner, one of the exclusive acts restricted by the copyright.[10] Importantly, there is no requirement of knowledge on the part of the infringer and so innocently doing one of the acts will not constitute a defence.[11] Secondary infringement, by way of contrast, occurs where a person facilitates primary infringing activities or deals in infringing copies of a work.[12] A key difference is the requirement of knowledge since a person has to know or have reason to believe that he or she was facilitating an infringement or dealing with an infringing copy of a work.

3.2.1 PRIMARY INFRINGEMENT

To establish a primary infringement it is necessary to ask whether a person has carried out one of the exclusive acts or authorized the doing of one of them. The scope of these acts has been discussed above. The main additional point to note here is that, because copyright is a territorially limited right, the infringing act must occur within the UK. However, when it comes to authorizing the doing of an exclusive act, it is possible for the act of authorization to occur outside the UK, provided the exclusive act itself occurs within the UK.[13] The next question to ask is whether or not the alleged infringing activity falls within the scope of an express or implied licence. If yes, it will not amount to an infringement and if

---

[10] Ibid., s. 16.

[11] It may, however, be relevant to an award of damages—see CDPA, s. 97(1) and Ch. 13 below.

[12] CDPA, ss. 22–6.

[13] *ABKCO Music and Records Inc v Music Collection International Ltd* [1995] RPC 657.

not, it may amount to an infringement depending on whether the remaining elements are established.

What are those remaining elements? First, there must be a causal connection or copying of the copyright work. The causal connection may be direct (e.g. copying onto one's computer a music CD) or indirect (e.g. copying drawings by copying an article that has been manufactured according to those drawings). Second, the act must be done in relation to the whole or *substantial* part of the work.

3.2.1.1 Causal connection

It is important to remember that independently creating the same or similar work will not amount to an infringement. Rather, it is essential to show that the allegedly infringing work was copied or derived from the relevant copyright work. This is described as the requirement of 'copying' or 'causal connection'.[14] Often this issue is not disputed, the defendant conceding that he/she copied from the claimant's work, but arguing that it was not a substantial part or that a relevant exception applies. But sometimes a defendant will argue that the circumstances in which they created their work had absolutely nothing to do with the claimant's copyright work, as occurred in the following case.

Designer Guild v Russell Williams [1998] FSR 803

The claimant (Designer Guild) owned copyright in a painting from which it had produced its Ixia fabric design, a design which consisted of a vertically striped pattern scattered with flowers. The claimant complained that the defendant (Russell Williams) had infringed copyright in its painting, by virtue of copying the Ixia design in its own Marguerite fabric design, i.e. this was a case of indirect copying. The defendant vigorously denied this allegation, claiming that it was not aware of the Ixia design at the time of creating its own Marguerite design. There was, however, evidence that the Ixia design had been displayed at a trade show that the defendant had attended.

Deputy Judge Lawrence Collins QC, at pp. 810–11, 813, 818, 820:

(6) There must be a causal connection between the copyright work and any infringing work; infringement may be negatived by acceptable evidence of independent design, and copying may not be an infringement if it fails to create a sufficient resemblance to amount to a reproduction: *Billhöfer Maschinenfabrik GmbH v TH Dixon & Co Ltd* [1990] FSR 105, 107, *per* Hoffmann J.

(7) There is no infringement if a person arrives by independent work at a substantially similar result to that sought to be protected; but the beginning of the necessary proof of copying normally lies in the establishment of similarity combined with proof of access to the plaintiff's productions: *LB (Plastics) Ltd v Swish Products Ltd* [1979] RPC 619, *per* Lord Wilberforce. If there is proof of access and a sufficient similarity, there will be a shift to the defendant of the evidential burden, i.e. *prima facie* evidence of copying which the party charged may refute by evidence that, notwithstanding the similarity, there was no copying but independent creation: *ibid.* at 625, *per* Lord Hailsham of St Marylebone, citing *King Features Syndicate Inc v O&M Kleeman Ltd* [1941] AC 417, 436, *per* Lord Wright.

---

14 See *Francis Day & Hunter Ltd v Bron* [1963] Ch 587.

[Applying these principles to the facts, the judge held that copying had occurred:]

The similarities are these:

1. Each fabric consists of vertical stripes, with spaces between the stripes equal to the width of the stripe, and in each fabric flowers and leaves are scattered over and between the stripes, so as to give the same general effect.

2. Each is painted in a similar neo-Impressionistic style. Each uses a brush-stroke technique, i.e. the use of one brush to create a stripe, showing the brush marks against the texture.

3. In each fabric the stripes are formed by vertical brush strokes, and have rough edges which merge into the background.

4. In each fabric the petals are formed with dryish brushstrokes and are executed in a similar way (somewhat in the form of a comma).

5. In each fabric parts of the colour of the stripes shows through some of the petals.

6. In each case the centres of the flower heads are represented by a strong blob, rather than by a realistic representation.

7. In each fabric the leaves are painted in two distinct shades of green, with similar brush strokes, and are scattered over the design.

The overall impression is very similar, but there are differences. The *Ixia* design is smaller and more delicate and the detail is different. In *Marguerite* the effect of the stripes showing through the petals is not as marked as it is in *Ixia*. The leaves in *Marguerite* are distinctly less impressionistic than those in *Ixia*. The impression of similarity is more marked on a comparison of the pink colourways.

...it is extremely improbable that the similarities between *Ixia* and *Marguerite* could be the result of coincidence. There are simply too many, and too many obvious, similarities, any one of which could of itself be coincidental, but the combination of which could not.

...In my judgment the effect of the (1) many and obvious similarities; (2) the opportunity to copy; (3) the complementary nature of the acetate and the striped artwork: and (4) the false provenance given to the acetate, is that Designers Guild has convincingly discharged the burden of proving that Russell Williams copied *Ixia*.

What of situations where a creator has been unconsciously or subconsciously influenced by the claimant's work? Will this amount to causal connection? According to *Francis Day Hunter v Bron*[15] it is possible for it to do so. The case involved alleged infringement of copyright in a musical work, 'In a Little Spanish Town', first published in 1926 and extensively exploited in the US and elsewhere since that time. The claimants alleged that the defendant's work, 'Why', published in 1959 was an infringement because it reproduced the first eight bars of the chorus of the claimants' work. The defendants denied that they had copied the claimant's work, the composer giving evidence that he had not consciously copied the claimant's song and had not heard it (accepting that if he had heard it, it must have been when he was young). The judge (Wilberforce J) found a considerable degree of similarity between the two songs, but accepted the evidence of the composer of 'Why' that there had been no conscious copying. He also found insufficient evidence to prove unconscious copying. On appeal, the Court of Appeal held that proof of similarity between the allegedly infringing work and the original, coupled with proof of access to the original, creates a prima facie case

---

[15] [1963] Ch 587.

but not an irrebuttable presumption of copying. As to the issue of subconscious or uncon-scious copying Willmer LJ stated that, 'if subconscious copying is to be found, there must be proof (or at least a strong inference) of de facto familiarity with the work alleged to be copied. In the present case, on the findings of Wilberforce J., this element is conspicuously lacking.'[16] Upjohn LJ did not stipulate the same requirement of de facto familiarity with the allegedly copied work, but stressed that strong evidence would be required in order to draw an inference of unconscious copying and that 'the possibility that the defendant had heard it, or even played it in his early youth, is quite insufficient'.[17]

3.2.1.2 Substantial part

It is prima facie infringement where a defendant, without permission of the owner, does one of the exclusive acts in relation to the whole of a copyright work. However, where the dealing is in relation to only part of the work it becomes necessary to establish that this amounts to a substantial part. What constitutes a 'substantial' part is difficult to predict and the courts have developed fairly general guidelines to assist in this assessment. Several of those guide-lines are set out in the House of Lords decision in *Designer Guild*.

Designer Guild v Russell Williams [2000] 1 WLR 2416

The facts of this case were discussed above. At first instance, the judge found that a sub-stantial part of the design had been copied; however, the Court of Appeal overturned this decision. The claimants appealed to the House of Lords.

Lord Bingham, at p. 2418:

While not accepting the judge's finding of copying, the defendant recognised the virtual impossibility of dislodging it in the Court of Appeal and did not challenge it. The defendant's challenge was accordingly directed to the judge's finding that a substantial part of the *Ixia* design had been copied. The Court of Appeal upheld this challenge. But in doing so, as it seems to me, it fell into error. First, by analysing individual features of the two designs and highlighting certain dissimilarities the court failed to give effect to the judge's conclusion, not challenged before it, that the similarities between the two designs were so marked as to war-rant a finding that the one had been copied from the other. While the finding of copying did not in theory conclude the issue of substantiality, on the facts here it was almost bound to do so. Secondly, the Court of Appeal approached the issue of substantiality more in the manner of a first instance court making original findings of fact than as an appellate court reviewing findings already made and in very important respects not challenged. It was not for the Court of Appeal to embark on the issue of substantiality afresh, unless the judge had misdirected himself, which in my opinion he had not.

There was, I conclude, no ground for interfering with the judge's conclusion.

Lord Hoffmann, at pp. 2422–3:

[**Lord Hoffmann** began by emphasizing that the question of substantiality is one of mixed law and fact and that, as such, the Court of Appeal should not have reversed the trial judge's decision unless he had made an error of principle, which he had not. He therefore allowed the appeal.]

---

[16] Ibid., p. 613.   [17] Ibid., pp. 620–1.

It is often said, as Morritt LJ said in this case, that copyright subsists not in ideas but in the form in which the ideas are expressed. The distinction between expression and ideas finds a place in the Agreement on Trade-Related Aspects of Intellectual Property Rights (TRIPS) (OJ 1994 L 336, p. 213), to which the United Kingdom is a party (see article 9.2: 'Copyright protection shall extend to expressions and not to ideas...'). Nevertheless, it needs to be handled with care. What does it mean? As Lord Hailsham of St Marylebone said in *LB (Plastics) Ltd v Swish Products Ltd* [1979] RPC 551, 629, 'it all depends on what you mean by "ideas"'.

Plainly there can be no copyright in an idea which is merely in the head, which has not been expressed in copyrightable form, as a literary, dramatic, musical or artistic work. But the distinction between ideas and expression cannot mean anything so trivial as that. On the other hand, every element in the expression of an artistic work (unless it got there by accident or compulsion) is the expression of an idea on the part of the author. It represents her choice to paint stripes rather than polka dots, flowers rather than tadpoles, use one colour and brush technique rather than another, and so on. The expression of these ideas is protected, both as a cumulative whole and also to the extent to which they form a 'substantial part' of the work. Although the term 'substantial part' might suggest a quantitative test, or at least the ability to identify some discrete part which, on quantitative or qualitative grounds, can be regarded as substantial, it is clear upon the authorities that neither is the correct test. *Ladbroke (Football) Ltd v William Hill (Football) Ltd* [1964] 1 WLR 273 establishes that substantiality depends upon quality rather than quantity (Lord Reid, at p. 276, Lord Evershed, at p. 283, Lord Hodson, at p. 288, Lord Pearce, at p. 293). And there are numerous authorities which show that the 'part' which is regarded as substantial can be a feature or combination of features of the work, abstracted from it rather than forming a discrete part. That is what the judge found to have been copied in this case. Or to take another example, the original elements in the plot of a play or novel may be a substantial part, so that copyright may be infringed by a work which does not reproduce a single sentence of the original. If one asks what is being protected in such a case, it is difficult to give any answer except that it is an idea expressed in the copyright work.

My Lords, if one examines the cases in which the distinction between ideas and the expression of ideas has been given effect, I think it will be found that they support two quite distinct propositions. The first is that a copyright work may express certain ideas which are not protected because they have no connection with the literary, dramatic, musical or artistic nature of the work. It is on this ground that, for example, a literary work which describes a system or invention does not entitle the author to claim protection for his system or invention as such. The same is true of an inventive concept expressed in an artistic work. However striking or original it may be, others are (in the absence of patent protection) free to express it in works of their own: see *Kleeneze Ltd v DRG (UK) Ltd* [1984] FSR 399. The other proposition is that certain ideas expressed by a copyright work may not be protected because, although they are ideas of a literary, dramatic or artistic nature, they are not original, or so commonplace as not to form a substantial part of the work. *Kenrick & Co v Lawrence & Co* (1890) 25 QBD 99 is a well known example. It is on this ground that the mere notion of combining stripes and flowers would not have amounted to a substantial part of the plaintiff's work. At that level of abstraction, the idea, though expressed in the design, would not have represented sufficient of the author's skill and labour as to attract copyright protection.

Generally speaking, in cases of artistic copyright, the more abstract and simple the copied idea, the less likely it is to constitute a substantial part. Originality, in the sense of the contribution of the author's skill and labour, tends to lie in the detail with which the basic idea is presented. Copyright law protects foxes better than hedgehogs. In this case, however, the elements which the judge found to have been copied went well beyond the banal and I think that the judge was amply justified in deciding that they formed a substantial part of the originality of the work.

Lord Millett, at p. 2426:

Once the judge has found that the defendant's design incorporates features taken from the copyright work, the question is whether what has been taken constitutes all or a substantial part of the copyright work. This is a matter of impression, for whether the part taken is substantial must be determined by its quality rather than its quantity. It depends upon its importance to the copyright work. It does not depend upon its importance to the defendant's work, as I have already pointed out. The pirated part is considered on its own (see *Ladbroke (Football) Ltd v William Hill (Football) Ltd* [1964] 1 WLR 273, 293, *per* Lord Pearce) and its importance to the copyright work assessed. There is no need to look at the infringing work for this purpose.

The Court of Appeal were concerned only with this second stage. They were not entitled to reverse the judge's finding that the defendant's design reproduced features of the copyright work, nor his identification of the features in question. The only issue was whether those features represented a substantial part of the copyright work. A visual comparison of the two designs was not only unnecessary but likely to mislead.

My noble and learned friend, Lord Scott of Foscote, has drawn attention to the differences between the copying of a discrete part of the copyright work and the altered copying of the whole, or the copying with or without modifications of some but not all the features of the copyright work. The distinction is not material in the present case. Whether or not it is alleged that a discrete part of the copyright work has been taken, the issues of copying and substantiality are treated as separate questions. Where, however, it is alleged that some but not all the features of the copyright work have been taken, the answer to the first question will almost inevitably answer both, for if the similarities are sufficiently numerous or extensive to justify an inference of copying they are likely to be sufficiently substantial to satisfy this requirement also.

For these reasons, as well as those given by my noble and learned friends, Lord Hoffmann and Lord Bingham of Cornhill, I would allow the appeal.

Lord Scott of Foscote, at pp. 2430–2:

Substantiality

Section 16(3) of the Act of 1988 says that copying a copyright work is a copyright infringement if the copying is of 'the work as a whole or any substantial part of it'. Section 16(3) may come into play in two quite different types of case. One type of case is, obviously, where an identifiable part of the whole, but not the whole, has been copied. For example, only a section of a picture may have been copied, or only a sentence or two, or even only a phrase, from a poem or a book, or only a bar or two of a piece of music, may have been copied: see the examples given at pp. 88–89, para. 2–102 of *Laddie, Prescott and Vitoria, The Modern Law of Copyright and Designs*, 2nd edn (1995), vol. 1 (which, for convenience, I will refer to as '*Laddie*'). In cases of that sort, the question whether the copying of the part constitutes an infringement depends on the qualitative importance of the part that has been copied, assessed in relation to the copyright work as a whole. In *Ladbroke (Football) Ltd v William Hill (Football) Ltd* [1964] 1 WLR 273 Lord Reid said, at p. 276, that: 'the question whether he has copied a substantial part depends much more on the quality than on the quantity of what he has taken'.

The present case is not a case of that type. The judge did not identify any particular part of *Ixia* and hold that that part had been copied. His finding of copying related to *Ixia* as a whole.

The other type of case in which a question of substantiality may become relevant is where the copying has not been an exact copying of the copyright work but a copying with modifications. This type of copying is referred to in *Laddie* as 'altered copying'. A paradigm of this type of case would be a translation of a literary work into some other language, or the dramatisation of a novel. The translation, or the play or film, might not have a single word in common with the original. But, assuming copyright existed in the original, the 'copy' might well, and in the case of a word-by-word translation certainly would, constitute an infringement of copyright.

The present case is an 'altered copying' case. Helen Burke put together a number of artistic ideas derived from various sources in order to produce her *Ixia* design, an original artistic design as it is accepted to be. Miss Ibbotson and Mrs Williams, as the judge found, copied the *Ixia* design in order to produce their *Marguerite* design. But they did so with modifications. The *Marguerite* design is not an exact copy of *Ixia*. Nor is any specific part of the *Marguerite* design an exact copy of any corresponding part of the *Ixia* design. It is an altered copy.

The question, then, where an altered copy has been produced, is what the test should be in order to determine whether the production constitutes a copyright infringement. If the alterations are sufficiently extensive it may be that the copying does not constitute an infringement at all. The test proposed in *Laddie*, at pp. 92–93, para. 2–108, to determine whether an altered copy constitutes an infringement is: 'Has the infringer incorporated a substantial part of the independent skill, labour etc contributed by the original author in creating the copyright work...'

My Lords, I think this is a useful test, based as it is on an underlying principle of copyright law, namely, that a copier is not at liberty to appropriate the benefit of another's skill and labour.

My noble and learned friend, Lord Millett, has made the point that once copying has been established, the question of substantiality depends on the relationship between what has been copied on the one hand and the original work on the other, similarity no longer being relevant. My Lords, I respectfully agree that that would be so in the first type of case. But in an altered copying case, particularly where the finding of copying is dependant, in the absence of direct evidence, upon the inferences to be drawn from the extent and nature of the similarities between the two works, the similarities will usually be determinative not only of the issue of copying but also of the issue of substantiality. And even where there is direct evidence of copying, as, for example, where it is admitted that the copier has produced his 'copy' with the original at his elbow, the differences between the original and the 'copy' may be so extensive as to bar a finding of infringement. It is not a breach of copyright to borrow an idea, whether of an artistic, literary or musical nature, and to translate that idea into a new work. In 'altered copying' cases, the difficulty is the drawing of the line between what is a permissible borrowing of an idea and what is an impermissible piracy of the artistic, literary or musical creation of another. In drawing this line, the extent and nature of the similarities between the altered copy and the original work must, it seems to me, play a critical and often determinative role. In particular, this must be so where there is no direct evidence of copying and the finding of copying is dependant on the inferences to be drawn from the similarities.

[**Lord Hope** agreed with **Lord Bingham**.]

According to *Designers Guild*, when will it be appropriate for an appellate court to overturn a first instance decision regarding substantiality? Where the similarities between the copyright work and allegedly infringing work are so extensive as to support a finding of copying or causal connection, to what extent will this justify a finding that a substantial part of the work has been copied? In this situation is Lord Scott of Foscote's characterization of copying as either 'discrete' or 'altered' a helpful tool? How does his approach differ from that of Lord Millett's?

Lords Hoffmann, Millett, and Scott of Foscote all held that substantiality is a qualitative assessment, a principle that was reiterated and explicated in the subsequent House of Lords decision in *Newspaper Licensing Agency v Marks & Spencer Ltd.*

Newspaper Licensing Agency v Marks & Spencer Ltd [2003] 1 AC 551

The defendant (Marks & Spencer) had obtained press cuttings from an agency licensed by the claimant (Newspaper Licensing Agency). However, it made further copies of some of the press cuttings for circulation within its organization. The claimant (who represented national and provincial newspapers) alleged infringement of copyright in the typographical arrangement of published editions of certain newspapers. At first instance, the judge held that copyright in the typographical arrangement related to both the newspaper as a whole and the individual articles. Further, that even if typographical arrangement copyright was restricted to the whole newspaper, copying individual articles amounted to a 'substantial part'. The Court of Appeal allowed the appeal, holding that typographical arrangement copyright subsisted in the newspaper as a whole and none of the individual cuttings constituted a substantial part of the newspaper from which they were derived. The claimant appealed.

Lord Hoffmann (delivering the leading speech), at pp. 559–62:

19. The House of Lords decided in *Ladbroke (Football) Ltd v William Hill (Football) Ltd* [1964] 1 WLR 273 that the question of substantiality is a matter of quality rather than quantity. The relevant passages are too well known to require citation: see Lord Reid, at p. 276, Lord Evershed, at p. 283, Lord Hodson, at p. 288 and Lord Pearce, at p. 293. But what quality is one looking for? That question, as it seems to me, must be answered by reference to the reason why the work is given copyright protection. In literary copyright, for example, copyright is conferred (irrespective of literary merit) upon an original literary work. It follows that the quality relevant for the purposes of substantiality is the literary originality of that which has been copied. In the case of an artistic work, it is the artistic originality of that which has been copied. So, in the recent case of *Designers Guild Ltd v Russell Williams (Textiles) Ltd (trading as Washington DC)* [2000] 1 WLR 2416, the House decided that although not the smallest part of a fabric design had been reproduced with anything approaching photographic fidelity, the copying of certain of the ideas expressed in that design which, in their conjoined expression, had involved original artistic skill and labour, constituted the copying of a substantial part of the artistic work.

20. In my opinion the question of substantiality in relation to typographical copyright must be decided according to the same principles. There is, however, an important difference in the definition of copying typographical arrangements which has to be taken into account. In relation to a literary, dramatic, musical or artistic work, copying means 'reproducing the work in any material form': section 17(2). In relation to the typographical arrangement of an edition, it means 'making a facsimile copy of the arrangement': section 17(5). The notion of reproduction, as demonstrated by the *Designers Guild* case, is sufficiently flexible to include the copying of ideas abstracted from a literary, dramatic, musical or artistic work, provided that their expression in the original work has involved sufficient of the relevant original skill and labour to attract copyright protection. In the case of a typographical arrangement, however, nothing less than a facsimile copy will do. It is in this context that one must ask whether there has been copying of sufficient of the relevant skill and labour to constitute a substantial part of the edition's typographical arrangement.

...

23. In the case of a modern newspaper, I think that the skill and labour devoted to typographical arrangement is principally expressed in the overall design. It is not the choice of a particular typeface, the precise number or width of the columns, the breadth of margins and the relationship of headlines and strap lines to the other text, the number of articles on a page and the distribution of photographs and advertisements but the combination of all of these into pages which give the newspaper as a whole its distinctive appearance. In some cases that appearance will depend upon the relationship between the pages; for example, having headlines rather than small advertisements on the front page. Usually, however, it will depend upon the appearance of any given page. But I find it difficult to think of the skill and labour which has gone into the typographical arrangement of a newspaper being expressed in anything less than a full page. The particular fonts, columns, margins and so forth are only, so to speak, the typographical vocabulary in which the arrangement is expressed.

25. ...The test is quantitative in the sense that, as there can be infringement only by making a facsimile copy, the question will always be whether one has made a facsimile copy of enough of the published edition to amount to a substantial part. But the question of what counts as enough seems to me to be qualitative, depending not upon the proportion which the part taken bears to the whole but on whether the copy can be said to have appropriated the presentation and layout of the edition. That is why I said earlier that I do not think it is likely to matter whether the supplements or inserts in a newspaper are separate published editions.

...

27. Your Lordships have been shown specimens of the press cuttings of which complaint has been made. I agree with the majority of the Court of Appeal that none of them sufficiently reproduces the layout of any page to amount to a substantial part of its typographical arrangement. In many cases, as I have mentioned, the changes in layout which have been made to fit the article to an A4 sheet mean that they do not even reproduce the layout of the article itself. As Mance LJ said, at p. 288c, Marks & Spencer had not 'reproduced anything that could be regarded as either resembling the newspaper concerned or having newspaper-like qualities'. For these reasons, I would dismiss the appeal. Marks & Spencer also claimed that they came within the defence of fair dealing but as your Lordships were all of opinion that there had been no infringement, no argument on the point was heard and I say nothing about it.

It is clear that substantiality is a qualitative test. But how, according to *NLA v Marks & Spencer*, is that assessment made and does it differ depending on the category of work that is allegedly infringed?

Aside from considering the originality of the part that has been copied, are there other factors relevant to determining substantiality? What is the role, for example, of the idea/expression distinction to this enquiry? In this regard, consider again Lord Hoffmann's speech in *Designers Guild*.

The idea/expression distinction and its relationship to whether the part taken is 'substantial' has been further explored by the Court of Appeal in the 'Da Vinci Code' case.

Baigent v Random House [2007] FSR 24

The case involved a dispute between two of the authors of The Holy Blood and The Holy Grail (HBHG), a work of historical conjecture, and the UK publisher of Dan Brown's Da Vinci Code (DVC), a work of fiction. The claimants alleged that a substantial part of

HBHG had been reproduced in DVC. In particular, they alleged copying of 15 elements of what was described as the 'central theme' of HBHG and very minor examples of language similarity. The defendant argued that they had copied only ideas and, as such, no infringement had occurred. At first instance, Peter Smith J dismissed the claimants' action. The claimants appealed.

Mummery LJ (Rix LJ in agreement):

153. I appreciate that the Central Theme and its elements particularised in the VSS [Voluntary Supplemental Schedule] are important to the claimants. They are by-products of their years of research, discussion and speculation. Viewed objectively, however, in the context of the necessary and sufficient conditions for infringement, they are not 'a substantial part' of HBHG. They are not substantial *in the copyright sense*, any more than a fact or theory that took a lifetime to establish, or a discovery that cost a fortune to make.

154. The position is that the individual elements of the Central Theme Points distilled from HBHG in the VSS are not of a sufficiently developed character to constitute a substantial part of HBHG. In the words of the judge they are 'too generalised' to be a substantial part of HBHG. They are an assortment of items of historical fact and information, virtual history, events, incidents, theories, arguments and propositions. They do not contain detailed similarities of language or 'architectural' similarities in the detailed treatment or development of the collection or arrangement of incidents, situations, characters and narrative, such as is normally found in cases of infringement of literary or dramatic copyright. The 11 aspects of the Central Theme in DVC are differently expressed, collected, selected, arranged and narrated.

155. Of course, it takes time, effort and skill to conduct historical research, to collect materials for a book, to decide what facts are established by the evidence and to formulate arguments, theories, hypotheses, propositions and conclusions. It does not, however, follow, as suggested in the claimants' submissions, that the use of items of information, fact and so on derived from the assembled material is, in itself, 'a substantial part' of HBHG simply because it has taken time skill and effort to carry out the necessary research.

156. The literary copyright exists in HBHG by reason of the skill and labour expended by the claimants in the original composition and production of it and the original manner or form of expression of the results of their research. Original expression includes not only the language in which the work is composed but also the original selection, arrangement and compilation of the raw research material. It does not, however, extend to clothing information, facts, ideas, theories and themes with exclusive property rights, so as to enable the claimants to monopolise historical research or knowledge and prevent the legitimate use of historical and biographical material, theories propounded, general arguments deployed, or general hypotheses suggested (whether they are sound or not) or general themes written about.

157. The reported cases in which infringement claims have succeeded in relation to historical works or semi-historical works do not assist the claimants' case. They are decisions by experienced Chancery judges at first instance correctly applying well established general principles to the particular facts of the case. For example, in *Ravenscroft v Herbert* [1980] RPC 193 Brightman J found that there was copying of a substantial part of a work of non-fiction (The Spear of Destiny) in the form of a novel. To an appreciable extent they were competing works. The defendant's novel was alleged to contain as many as 50 instances of deliberate language copying, as well as copying of the same historical characters, historical incidents and interpretation of the significance of historical events.

158. *Harman Pictures NV v Osborne* [1967] 1 WLR 723 is another well known example of a case in which the author of a historical work (The Reason Why) obtained an interlocutory

injunction in a copyright claim against the writer of a film script, which had much in common with the original copyright work in its selection of incidents and quotations supplemented by some alterations and additions attributed to other sources. Goff J found 'many similarities of detail' in John Osborne's film script (p. 735) and he was impressed by 'the marked similarity of the choice of incidents...and by the juxtaposition of ideas' for which there was a lack of explanation on the defendant's side.

159. In my judgment, the judge rightly held that the claimants have not established that a substantial part of HBHG has been copied, either as to the original composition and expression of the work or as to the particular collection, selection and arrangement of material and its treatment in HBHG.

[**Lloyd LJ** also dismissed the appeal.]

After having read and considered *Designers Guild, NLA v Marks & Spencer,* and *Baigent v Random House,* do you think originality and the idea/expression distinction are key influences on the notion of 'substantial part'?

In terms of the idea/expression distinction, is this a sufficiently precise concept to be useful to courts? How was it characterized by Lord Hoffmann in *Designer Guild* as compared with the Court of Appeal in *Baigent v Random House*? Finally, does the latter case suggest that it will be harder to establish infringement of copyright in historical works or works of non-fiction than fictional works? If so, does this seem sensible?

FURTHER READING

R. H. Jones, 'The myth of the idea/expression dichotomy in copyright law' (1990) 10 Pace LR 551.

3.2.1.3 Authorization

Where a person authorizes, without permission of the copyright owner, another to carry out one of the exclusive acts, this will amount to primary infringement. But in what circumstances will 'authorization' occur? This issue was explored at length in the following House of Lords decision.

CBS Songs v Amstrad [1988] AC 1013

The defendant (Amstrad) manufactured and sold a dual-tape cassette deck machine, which enabled high speed recording from pre-recorded cassette tapes to blank cassette tapes. The claimants (CBS Songs) sued on behalf of themselves and other owners of copyright in the music trade alleging, *inter alia*, that the defendant by making, advertising and selling its machine had authorized members of the public to infringe their copyright under the Copyright Act 1956. The defendants applied to strike out the writ and statement of claim as disclosing no cause of action. This was refused by Whitford J, but allowed by the Court of Appeal. There was an appeal to the House of Lords:

Lord Templeman (with whom the other law lords agreed), **at pp. 1052G–1055:**

Section 1(1) of the Act of 1956 confers on the copyright owners in a record the 'exclusive right...to authorise other persons' to copy the record. BPI submit that by selling a model which incorporates a double-speed twin-tape recorder Amstrad 'authorise' the purchaser of the model to copy a record in which copyright subsists and therefore Amstrad infringe the exclusive right of the copyright owner. My Lords, twin-tape recorders, fast or slow, and single-tape recorders, in addition to their recording and playing functions, are capable of copying on to blank tape, directly or indirectly, records which are broadcast, records on discs and records on tape. Blank tapes are capable of being employed for recording or copying. Copying may be lawful or unlawful. Every tape recorder confers on the operator who acquires a blank tape the facility of copying; the double-speed twin-tape recorder provides a modern and efficient facility for continuous playing and continuous recording and for copying. No manufacturer and no machine confers on the purchaser authority to copy unlawfully. The purchaser or other operator of the recorder determines whether he shall copy and what he shall copy. By selling the recorder Amstrad may facilitate copying in breach of copyright but do not authorise it.

BPI's next submission is that Amstrad by their advertisement authorise the purchaser of an Amstrad model to copy records in which copyright subsists. Amstrad's advertisement drew attention to the advantages of their models and to the fact that the recorder incorporated in the model could be employed in the copying of modern records. But the advertisement did not authorise the unlawful copying of records; on the contrary, the footnote warned that some copying required permission and made it clear that Amstrad had no authority to grant that permission. If Amstrad had considered the interests of copyright owners, Amstrad could have declined to incorporate double-tape double-speed recorders in Amstrad's models or could have advertised the illegality of home copying. If Amstrad had deprived themselves of the advantages of offering improved recording facilities, other manufacturers would have reaped the benefit. The effect of double-tape double-speed recorders on the incidence of home copying is altogether speculative. If Amstrad had advertised the illegality of home copying the effect would have been minimal. Amstrad's advertisement was deplorable because Amstrad thereby flouted the rights of copyright owners. Amstrad's advertisement was cynical because Amstrad advertised the increased efficiency of a facility capable of being employed to break the law. But the operator of an Amstrad tape recording facility, like all other operators, can alone decide whether to record or play and what material is to be recorded. The Amstrad advertisement is open to severe criticism but no purchaser of an Amstrad model could reasonably deduce from the facilities incorporated in the model or from Amstrad's advertisement that Amstrad possessed or purported to possess the authority to grant any required permission for a record to be copied.

...

In the present case, Amstrad did not sanction, approve or countenance an infringing use of their model and I respectfully agree with Atkin LJ and with Lawton LJ in the present case [1986] FSR 159, 207 that in the context of the Copyright Act 1956 an authorisation means a grant or purported grant, which may be express or implied, of the right to do the act complained of. Amstrad conferred on the purchaser the power to copy but did not grant or purport to grant the right to copy.

In *Moorhouse v University of New South Wales* [1976] RPC 151 in the High Court of Australia where the facilities of a library included a photocopying machine, Gibbs J said, at p. 159:

> a person who has under his control the means by which an infringement of copyright may be committed—such as a photocopying machine—and who makes it available to other persons, knowing, or having reason to suspect, that it is likely to be used for the purpose of committing an infringement, and omitting to take reasonable steps to limit its use to legitimate purposes, would authorise any infringement that resulted from its use.

Whatever may be said about this proposition, Amstrad have no control over the use of their models once they are sold…

In *CBS Inc v Ames Records & Tapes Ltd* [1982] Ch 91, Whitford J held that a record library which lent out records and simultaneously offered blank tapes for sale at a discount did not authorise the infringement of copyright in the records. He said, at p. 106:

> Any ordinary person would, I think, assume that an authorisation can only come from somebody having or purporting to have authority and that an act is not authorised by somebody who merely enables or possibly assists or even encourages another to do that act, but does not purport to have any authority which he can grant to justify the doing of the act.

This precisely describes Amstrad.

In *RCA Corporation v John Fairfax & Sons Ltd* [1982] RPC 91 in the High Court of Australia, Kearney J, at p. 100, approved a passage in Laddie, Prescott & Vitoria, *The Modern Law of Copyright* (1980), para. 12.9, p. 403, in these terms:

> a person may be said to authorise another to commit an infringement if the one has some form of control over the other at the time of infringement or, if he has no such control, is responsible for placing in the other's hands materials which by their nature are almost inevitably to be used for the purpose of infringement.

This proposition seems to me to be stated much too widely. As Whitford J pointed out in the *Ames* case, at p. 107:

> you can home tape from bought records, borrowed records, borrowed from friends or public libraries, from the playing of records over the radio, and indeed, at no expense, from records which can be obtained for trial periods on introductory offers from many record clubs who advertise in the papers, who are prepared to let you have up to three or four records for a limited period of trial, free of any charge whatsoever.

These borrowed records together with all recording machines and blank tapes could be said to be 'materials which by their nature are almost inevitably to be used for the purpose of an infringement'. But lenders and sellers do not authorise infringing use.

For these reasons, which are to be found also in the judgments of the Court of Appeal, at pp. 207, 210 and 217, I am satisfied that Amstrad did not authorise infringement.

CBS v Amstrad was decided at a time when the threat of music piracy came from dual-tape cassette deck machines. But today, piracy is more likely to arise from peer-to-peer file sharing activities. How would the principles stated in *CBS v Amstrad* apply to modern day piracy? Could it be argued that operators of peer-to-peer file sharing facilities authorize the infringing uploading and downloading activities of their users? This issue is explored at greater length in Chapter 12.[18]

3.2.2 SECONDARY LIABILITY

Secondary infringement occurs where, broadly speaking, a person facilitates primary infringing activities or deals in infringing copies of a work. More specifically, a person who permits a place of public entertainment to be used for an infringing performance will be liable unless there were reasonable grounds for believing that the performance would not infringe

---

[18] See 12.6.3 below.

copyright.[19] Further, a person who supplies apparatus by which an infringing public performance occurs will be liable where they knew or had reason to believe the apparatus was likely to be used to infringe copyright.[20] Importing into the UK, other than for private and domestic use, an article, which a person knows or has reason to believe is an infringing copy of a work, will amount to infringement.[21] Similarly, possessing, selling, hiring, commercially dealing with, or prejudicially distributing an article, which a person knows or has reason to believe is an infringing copy of a work, will constitute infringement. Finally, a person will be liable if they make, import, possess in the course of business, sell, or let for hire, an article specifically designed or adapted for making copies of that work, knowing or having reason to believe that it is to be used to make infringing copies.[22]

A key feature of the secondary infringement provisions is actual knowledge or having reason to believe. The requirement of 'reason to believe' was explored in the following case.

LA Gear Inc v Hi-Tec Sports Plc [1992] FSR 121

The claimant (LA Gear) sold a man's shoe (Fire shoe) and woman's shoe (Flame shoe), both of which had been manufactured in accordance with drawings made by one of its employees. The claimant became aware of a prototype shoe originating from the defendant (Hi-Tec Sports), which they alleged was an infringing copy of their drawings. The claimant's solicitors sent a letter before action in August 1989, in which they alleged copyright infringement and enclosed a drawing of the Flame shoe. In September 1989, the defendant imported 40 pairs of allegedly infringing shoes and also attended a trade show at which they advertised for sale the same shoes. The claimant's solicitors sent another letter (on 18 September 1989) and enclosed another drawing of the Flame shoe. A copy of the Fire shoe was sent on 8 October 1989 and shortly thereafter an action for infringement was commenced. The claimants then applied for summary judgment, which was granted by Morris J. The defendant appealed arguing, *inter alia*, that there was a triable issue as to secondary infringement.

Nourse LJ (with whom **Staughton LJ** and **Sir Michael Kerr** agreed), **at 138–9:**

The fourth question is whether the defendant had 'reason to believe' that its Flair shoe was an infringing copy of the Fire shoe within section 23. The defendant does not now suggest that it did not have reason to believe that the Flair shoe was an infringing copy of the Flame shoe. It now accepts that the crucial event there was its receipt of a copy of drawing 2 with the plaintiff's solicitors' letter of 29 August 1989. It is the consequential elimination of the Flame shoe from this part of the dispute which has made it unnecessary to consider section 22 of the 1988 Act. One of the plaintiff's arguments in the court below was that the defendant had reason to believe that the Flair shoe was an infringing copy of the Flame shoe at the time when the 40 pairs of the former shoe were imported into the United Kingdom.

Mr Purvis accepted that if the necessary reason to believe existed at the date of the issue of the writ, 9 October 1989, then the fourth question must be decided in favour of the plaintiff. Moreover, he accepted the judge's interpretation of the words 'reason to believe':

Nevertheless, it seems to me that 'reason to believe' must involve the concept of knowledge of facts from which a reasonable man would arrive at the relevant belief. Facts from which

---

[19] CDPA, s. 25.   [20] Ibid., s. 26.   [21] Ibid., s. 22.   [22] Ibid., s. 24.

a reasonable man might suspect the relevant conclusion cannot be enough. Moreover, as it seems to me, the phrase does connote the allowance of a period of time to enable the reasonable man to evaluate those facts so as to convert the facts into a reasonable belief.

Mr Purvis placed particular reliance on the last sentence in this passage. He emphasised that it was not until Wednesday 4 October that the defendant received a copy of drawing 1. That left insufficient time before Monday 9 October for the defendant to consider that drawing and make the necessary enquiries, for example from the employee in Korea, so as to bring it to a state of reasonable belief that its own shoe was an infringing copy of the plaintiff's.

This argument must also be rejected. Here Mr Baldwin's primary submission was that the widespread promotion of the plaintiff's shoes at fairs and exhibitions and its widespread advertising formed a sufficient basis for an inference that both the plaintiff's shoes had come fully to the defendant's attention before the end of August 1989. Alternatively, submitted Mr Baldwin, from 30 August onwards the defendant had had a copy of drawing 2 representing a shoe which was of much the same design as the Fire shoe. Moreover, in the letter of 18 September the defendant was told that the Flame shoe had been designed in conjunction with the Fire shoe and that the plaintiff's solicitors would be obtaining the early design drawings for the Fire shoe in order to show how the Flame shoe was conceived. It would in any event have been a matter of common knowledge in the trade that shoes of this kind could only be designed from drawings.

I reject Mr Baldwin's primary submission, but accept his alternative submission. I think it very clear that by 9 October at the latest the defendant had knowledge of facts from which a reasonable man would have believed that its shoe was an infringing copy of drawing 1. The key event was the defendant's receipt of the letter of 18 September. There was plenty of time between then and 9 October for the facts to be evaluated and converted into a reasonable belief. Since the test is an objective one, there is no possibility of this issue being decided in favour of the defendant at a trial. I would therefore decide the fourth question, like the first three, in favour of the plaintiff.

For these reasons, which are substantially those of Morritt J, I think that his disposal of this case was satisfactory in every respect and I would dismiss the defendant's appeal accordingly.

A crucial factor in establishing that the defendant in *LA Gear* had 'reason to believe' their shoes were infringing copies was receipt of the claimant's copyright drawings. But will it always be necessary to supply a copy of the copyright work in order to establish a 'reason to believe'? This argument was rejected by the Court of Appeal in *Pensher Security Door Co Ltd v Sunderland City Council*,[23] which held that the relevant belief may be established by the surrounding circumstances.

3.3 MORAL RIGHTS

We have examined the economic rights belonging to a copyright owner and when these may be infringed. In this section, we discuss a different set of rights—called moral rights—that inhere in authors of copyright works regardless of whether they retain ownership of the economic rights.

Moral rights were developed in the civil law countries, primarily Germany and France, during the 18th and 19th centuries. They are rights of a non-pecuniary nature and the main

---

[23] [2000] RPC 249.

ones include: the right to divulge the work, the right to be attributed as author of the work (or the right of paternity), the right of integrity in the work, and the right to withdraw the work from circulation. Article 6*bis* of the Berne Convention, however, obliges Union Members to implement only the rights of attribution and integrity. This provision was inserted into Berne at the Rome Revision Conference in 1928 and represented a compromise between civil law countries, represented by France, and common law countries of the UK and Australia. The latter countries had resisted the introduction of moral rights into the Berne Convention on the basis that it was a concept 'alien' to common law systems and that, in any event, such interests were adequately protected by the laws of contract, defamation, and passing off.

Moral rights are said to be about protecting the personality interests of the author. In the following extract, Professor Ginsburg suggests that this justification is at odds with common law systems and investigates whether or not alternative justifications may be found.

J. Ginsburg, 'Moral rights in the common law system' [1990] Ent LR 121, 122

Why Protect Moral Rights?

The denomination 'moral rights' may appear rhetorically charged. Does the 'moral' label suggest that these rights are somehow better or more sacrosanct than other rights associated with copyright? Does it cast the opponent of these rights as some kind of unethical bully? Although some moral rights advocates may subscribe to those sentiments, the derivation of the term is not so invested with 'moral' meaning. The term is a translation from the French 'droit moral', where it does not address 'morality', but rather, non-pecuniary interests. For example, the broader term 'dommage moral' denotes non-economic damages, such as psychological suffering, incurred by the victim of a tort. The justification of 'droit moral', as understood on the Continent, comes from the notion that the work incorporates the personality of the author because the authorial persona permeates and pervades the work. Therefore, when something happens to the work—such as a deformation or a mutilation—that constitutes an attack on the person or the personality of the author herself.

Such a deeply personalist justification may seem alien to copyright systems derived from the English copyright law. But that does not mean that moral rights are some kind of bizarre irruption into our intellectual property regimes. Rather, it means that an effort should be made to understand moral rights on our copyright terms. What are those terms? The 1710 English Statute of Anne enunciates a public benefit policy of copyright law. Protection is afforded because we believe it will induce authors to create works. The Statute of Anne states that its purpose is 'for the encouragement of learned men to write useful books'. Copyright creates a climate conducive to the production of works of authorship. Copyright benefits authors, and by so doing, enhances our scientific and cultural heritage.

How do moral rights fit into this socially-oriented scheme? It is often said that 'Anglo' copyright concerns only economic rights. This has generally been true, but it does not follow that our copyright laws are therefore incapable of protecting non-pecuniary personality rights. To say that a law has not yet done something does not imply that the law is inherently hostile to that goal. One strong argument for moral rights—an argument that strongly resonates with our copyright heritage—is that protection of creators' interests in attribution and integrity will improve the climate in which they create works of authorship. A writer who feels secure that she will receive name credit for her work, or an artist who can rely on the continued existence of his sculpture, may find this background knowledge more conducive to creative activity. Indeed, for some creators, the non-pecuniary rewards such as recognition and hoped-for immortality through preservation of the work, may be more important than immediate material gain. Adoption of moral rights sends a message that a society cares about creation, and about authorship. I cannot prove that the existence of moral rights would in fact make a difference to any given author, any more than I can prove that their absence forestalls creation. Nor indeed, by the same token, can I, or moral rights' detractors, prove that the existence of moral rights would in fact hurt the production of works. Adequate evidence is lacking on these issues. As a result, then, the question of moral rights should be viewed partly as a question of tone and primarily as a question of social policy.

Another argument for moral rights, which also echoes our collective copyright tradition, concerns the public benefit flowing from the enactment of moral rights. In addition to presenting the prospect of more productive creators, a moral rights regime furthers several public concerns. The right of attribution enhances the public interest because it affords, or it should afford, the fullest possible public information about who created a work, about the source of the work. The public has at least as much of an interest in knowing who the author is, as in knowing who the producer of a brand of detergent is. Moreover, the reverse side of the attribution right helps avoid public deception, as it prevents misattribution of the author's name to works the author did not create, or perhaps to works for which the author is only partially responsible, and for which she is receiving undue attribution. The integrity right promotes the public interest perhaps most strongly in the context of conservation of works of the visual arts, but it also plays an important public role to the extent that it avoids misrepresentation of deformed or altered works as those of an aggrieved artist or author.

Of course, as already indicated, these arguments do not represent the only possible vision of the relationship between moral rights and the public interest. One might contend that moral rights impede the efficient exploitation of works of authorship, and that this will discourage investment in creation. Essentially, this view articulates an investment model of copyright. In the United States we say: 'money talks'. In this 'investment' view, it also means that money writes, composes, paints and sculpts. Whatever the power of the dollar, it does not wreak these acts on its own. Indeed, the US Constitution acknowledges that the progress of learning is achieved by awarding copyright, not to publishers or investors, but to authors. But behind most works, even those in which there is third-party investment, there is a person or persons that have to do the creating. Moral rights are about society's commitment to the person. Not because she is superior, but because that commitment benefits all of us in ways not readily captured by a pure investment model of copyright.

In your view, is the personality-based justification for moral rights alien to UK copyright law? If so, do you think Professor Ginsburg's alternative justifications are a sound basis for protecting moral rights in the UK? According to her justifications, what sort of moral-rights regime would you expect to see, particularly when there is a conflict between the economic interests of the owner and the moral rights of the author?

Although Article 6*bis* of Berne was inserted in 1928, the UK did not implement this obligation until the Copyright Designs and Patents Act 1988. Prior to the adoption of the Copyright Act 1956, the Gregory Committee report took the view that the obligations in Article 6*bis* were satisfied indirectly by the common law torts of defamation and passing off, and the law of contract. However, the Whitford Committee in 1977 expressed scepticism about whether such indirect provisions in English law were adequate and recommended the express introduction of moral rights.[24] They were expressly introduced in 1988.

The moral-rights provisions are contained in ss. 77–85 and include the right to be identified as the author or director (s. 77 attribution right); the right to object to derogatory treatment of

---

[24] G. Dworkin, 'Moral rights in English law: The shape of rights to come' [1986] EIPR 329.

the work (s. 80 integrity right); the right to object to false attribution of the work (s. 84 false attribution right); and the right to privacy in certain photographs and films (s. 85 privacy right).

Although the false attribution right and privacy right are grouped under the heading 'Chapter IV Moral Rights', one needs to ask whether they are moral rights in the strict sense. This is especially so since neither right is concerned with the link between an author and his or her work, and the focus is on personal interests more generally. In the case of false attribution, it is the right to ensure that a person is not misattributed as the author of a work not created by him or her. In the case of the privacy right, it is the right to control the exploitation of photographs or films that have been commissioned for private and domestic purposes.

3.3.1 FALSE ATTRIBUTION

The false attribution right was first inserted in the Copyright Act 1956.[25] It is now contained in s. 84 of the CDPA, which states that a person has a right to object to having a literary, dramatic, musical, or artistic work or film falsely attributed to him or her. The right is only infringed, however, where there is some kind of dealing with a work or copies of the work in or on which there is a false attribution.[26] Unlike the other moral rights, which endure for as long as copyright subsists in the work, this right lasts for 20 years after a person's death.

Below we consider one of the few decisions concerning s. 84 of the CDPA.

Clark v Associated Newspapers Ltd [1998] 1 WLR 1558

The claimant (Clark) was a well-known Conservative MP, who had published diaries documenting his public and private life. The defendant (Associated Newspapers Ltd), who published the Evening Standard newspaper in London, ran a series of articles parodying the claimant's diaries. They were headed with the titles 'Alan Clark's Secret Election Diary' or 'Alan Clark's Secret Political Diaries' and were accompanied by a small masthead photograph of the claimant. Underneath the title was an introductory paragraph containing the name of the real author (Mr Peter Bradshaw) in capital letters and a statement that the author was imagining how the claimant would record the day's events. The claimant brought an action under s. 84 of the CDPA and also passing off.

Lightman J, at pp. 1564, 1568, 1571:

Legal principles

The plaintiff invokes two rights to protection from false attribution of authorship, one statutory and one common law. The plaintiff can succeed in this action if he establishes that either right has been infringed. The statutory right is that conferred by section 84(1)(a) of the Copyright, Designs and Patents Act 1988 'not to have a literary...work falsely attributed to him as author'. (Section 84 of the Act of 1988 re-enacts the provision to like effect in section 43 of the Copyright Act 1956.) An 'attribution' in relation to such a work means 'a statement (express or implied) as to who is the author', and the right is infringed 'by a person who—(a) issues to the public copies of a work of any of those descriptions in or on which there is a false attribution': see section 84(2). An example of the commission of this tort is to be found in *Moore v News of the World Ltd* [1972] 1 QB 441. The newspaper in that case

---

25 Although there was a predecessor in the Fine Arts Copyright Act 1862.
26 CDPA, s. 84(2)–(6).

published an article under the headline: 'The Girl Who Lost The Saint. When Love Turns Sour by Dorothy Squires talking to Weston Taylor.' The words attributed to the plaintiff (Dorothy Squires) were not her words: they were the words of Weston Taylor. The issue was whether the article pretended to be written by Dorothy Squires. The trial judge directed the jury to make up their minds what the impression was to the reader. The jury found that the article did pretend to be written by Dorothy Squires. The Court of Appeal approved the direction by the trial judge and affirmed the decision that the tort had been committed.

Two distinctive features of the statutory tort are: (a) that it is unnecessary that the plaintiff be a professional author and accordingly that he has any goodwill or reputation as an author to protect or which may be damaged by false attribution; and (b) consequently the tort is action-able per se without proof of damage. In short section 84 of the Act of 1988 confers a personal or civic right on everyone not to have authorship of any literary work falsely attributed to him. The plaintiff is accordingly entitled to relief under section 84 if he merely establishes the false attribution alleged.

. . .

Section 84 of the Act of 1988

The law of passing off embraces the concept that one and the same representation may mean something different to different members of the public and in order to succeed it is suf-ficient for the plaintiff to establish that one of those meanings misleads a substantial number of people. Mr Prescott has argued that the position is different under section 84 of the Act of 1988, and that upon the true construction of section 84 for the purposes of that section a representation can only have one single correct meaning and, if the tort is to be established, that meaning must be the false attribution of authorship.

Some support may be found in the direction to the jury of Cantley J approved by the Court of Appeal in *Moore v News of the World Ltd* [1972] 1 QB 441, 444d, 451g, 453. No other judi-cial or textbook guidance was cited to me.

In my judgment, Mr Prescott's submission is correct and to succeed in a claim under sec-tion 84 of the Act of 1988 a plaintiff must establish that the work in question contains what is a false attribution of authorship, and not merely what is or may be understood by some or more people to be a false attribution. The proper approach (as under the law of defamation) is to determine what is the single meaning which the literary work conveys to the notional reasonable reader: compare *Charleston v News Group Newspapers Ltd* [1995] 2 AC 65, 71. I must accordingly read the articles and decide whether they contain what would be under-stood by a reasonable reader to be a false attribution of authorship to the plaintiff.

. . .

Section 84

In my judgment (as I have already held) the headings of the articles contain a clear and unequivo-cal false statement attributing their authorship to the plaintiff, and the vice of this statement is not cured by the various counter-messages relied on by the defendant. I would be minded to accept that (as in certain cases of false trade description) the effect of such a false statement can be neutralised by an express contradiction, but (as in the case of a false trade description) it has to be as bold, precise and compelling as the false statement (consider the citation from the judgment of Lord Widgery CJ in *Norman v Bennett* [1974] 1 WLR 1229, 1232), and in this case the contradiction lacks the required prominence and is less likely to get home to the readers, as is confirmed (if confirmation is necessary) by the evidence in this case.

The plaintiff is accordingly entitled to relief in respect of the commission of the statutory tort.

The statement regarding the actual author was held to be insufficient to neutralize the false attribution of authorship to Mr Alan Clark. But if the counter-statement had been as 'bold, precise and compelling as the false statement' how effective would the parody have been? Should parodies be given greater leeway when it comes to false attribution?

3.3.2 ATTRIBUTION

We turn now to examine the first of the two proper moral rights in the CDPA. The right of attribution (also known as the paternity right) applies to authors of literary, dramatic, musical, or artistic works and directors of films and is the right to be identified as such. However, the right is only infringed where the work is dealt with in certain ways, without the proper attribution.[27]

Importantly, a precondition of establishing infringement is that the right has been asserted.[28] This can occur by including, in an instrument of assignment of copyright in the work, a statement that the author or director asserts his right of attribution in relation to that work, or by an instrument in writing signed by the author or director.[29] In the case of public exhibition of artistic works, the right may also be asserted by ensuring that the author is identified on the original or copy of the artistic work, or on a frame, mount, or other thing to which it is attached.[30] Alternatively, by including in a licence by which the making of copies of the work is authorized a statement signed by or on behalf of the person granting the licence that the author asserts his right to be identified in the event of a public exhibition of a copy of the work.[31] What is the purpose, do you think, behind an assertion requirement? Is it problematic, particularly in light of the 'no formalities' rule specified in Article 5(2) of the Berne Convention?

What if an author uses a pseudonym or indeed wishes to remain anonymous? Does this fall within the scope of his or her right of attribution? Section 77(8) makes clear that if an author or director 'specifies a pseudonym, initials or some other particular form of identification be used, that form shall be used'. For example, this means that Joanne Rowling (née Murray), who is the author of the *Harry Potter* series, can insist on being identified as 'J. K. Rowling' on her books. In the absence of a specified form of identification it is acceptable to use any reasonable form of identification. It does not appear to be the case, however, that an author can insist on anonymity. How does this aspect of the right of attribution relate to the justification/s for moral rights?

Commentators, such as Professor Ginsburg, have been critical of the UK's implementation of the attribution right. In the following extract, the main criticisms are discussed.

J. Ginsburg, 'Moral rights in the common law system' [1990] Ent LR 121, 128–9

The CDPA announces a general right of attribution benefiting authors of literary, dramatic, musical or artistic works. But the right must be 'asserted', and binds only those who receive actual or constructive notice of the assertion. This precondition derives from a peculiar, not to say perverse, reading of article 6*bis* of the Berne Convention. The Berne Convention declares that the 'author shall have the right to claim authorship of the work'. From a provision entitling authors to recognition of their status as creators, the drafters of the CDPA fashioned an *obligation* to assert authorship before the right to be recognised can take effect. Not only does

---

[27] Ibid., s. 77(2)–(7).   [28] Ibid., s. 78.   [29] Ibid., s. 78(2).   [30] Ibid., s. 78(3)(a).
[31] Ibid., s. 78(3).

the UK text torture the Berne text, but the assertion requirement may well violate the Berne Convention's rule that 'the enjoyment and exercise' of authors' rights, including moral rights, 'shall not be subject to any formality'.

Multiple exceptions qualify the attribution right, notably the exclusions of creators of computer programs and employees creating works pursuant to their employment. Similarly, unlicensed uses of the work that are non-infringing uses (for example, fair dealing for purposes of news reporting) are not subject to the attribution right. In addition, the right is subject to waiver both formal and informal. As a result, an author who fails to 'assert' the right in her contract in effect may have no attribution right, and even if she does assert the right, a court may find overall conditions pointing to a waiver of the right.

Moreover, one may inquire how the assertion requirement affects third parties. The text of the CDPA appears to leave significant gaps in coverage. The text holds two classes of persons bound by an author's assertion of attribution rights: assignees and persons 'claiming through' them, when the assignment contained an assertion; and 'anyone to whom notice is brought of an instrument in writing [containing the assertion] signed by the author or director'. The structure of the statute prompts several questions. With respect to the second class of persons, what kind of written instrument is contemplated, and how is notice brought to third parties? It appears that identification of the author on the book, on the screen credits, etc., does not satisfy the statute, because even if this form of identification gives general notice of who the author is, it is not an 'instrument in writing signed' by the author. An author might, at least in theory, execute a document proclaiming herself to be the author, but how would this document be brought to the notice of third parties? A registry of claims of authorship, like a land-title registry, might afford notice, but would clash with the Berne Convention's proscription of formalities. Presentation of the document to third parties following their failure to credit the author should oblige them in the future, but will the notice receive retroactive effect to entitle the author to damages for prior non-attribution? A contract, such as a licence agreement, would meet the signed written instrument requirement, but, again, third parties would at least initially remain unaffected.

Finally, the distinction between an assignment and other written instruments points up further anomalies. Persons 'claiming through' an assignee of copyright are bound by the assertion in the assignment, even without actual notice. (Note, however, that third-party infringers appear to escape liability for violation of attribution rights; as infringers, they certainly do not 'claim through' the assignee.) But the sub-licensee of a licensee would not be obliged to credit the author, unless the sub-licensee had known of the author's assertion of the attribution right in the original licence agreement. Thus, for example, suppose an author executes a book-publishing agreement which includes an assertion of authorship, and entitles the publisher-licensee to license film rights in the book; the publisher licenses the film rights, but the sub-licence neither mentions the original assertion, nor obligates the film production company to attribute the work to the author. It appears that the author would have no attribution right against the film company: although the film company 'claims through' the publisher, the publisher was a licensee, not an assignee. Had the publisher been an assignee, the author would have had an attribution claim against the film company. This analysis indicates that the protection of authors' moral interests could come at the expense of their economic interests: for purposes of enforcing the attribution right, authors might be better off assigning all rights under the copyright, than retaining some rights and merely granting licences.

In light of the above discussion, would it be advisable for the UK to remove the requirement of assertion? What objections do you envisage to such a reform and are these outweighed by the disadvantages of the requirement?

3.3.3 INTEGRITY

The second moral right in the CDPA, the right of integrity, has the potential to cause the greatest conflict between the interests of the author and those of the copyright owner. For example, the owner of a copyright in an artistic work (e.g. a painting) created by A may want to publish a reduced-size version of the work in a catalogue. The copyright owner is entitled to exercise the right of reproduction, but at the same time the author, A, objects that the reduction in size is a derogatory treatment of his painting because the subtleties of the brushstrokes and colours are lost. Clearly, there is a clash of interests and the question is how will these be balanced and whose interests will prevail? A closer examination of the right of integrity will indicate where the preference lies.

Section 80 of the CDPA grants authors of literary, dramatic, musical, and artistic works and directors of films the right, in certain circumstances, not to have their work subjected to derogatory treatment. Those circumstances are set out in s. 80(3)–(6) and include such things as exhibiting in public a derogatory treatment of an artistic work or commercially publishing, performing in public, or communicating to the public a derogatory treatment of a literary, dramatic, or musical work.

3.3.3.1 Treatment

Both 'treatment' and 'derogatory' are defined. 'Treatment' means 'any addition to, deletion from or alteration to or adaptation of the work' but does not include a translation of a literary or dramatic work or an arrangement or transcription of a musical work involving no more than a change of key or register.[32] Is this definition a broad one? Would it encompass uses of a work that do not change the physical structure of the work, but alter its meaning or perception, such as a portrait of the Royal Family hung amongst an exhibition of pornography or a modern piece of classical music used as part of a television advertisement selling washing powder? Arguably, the definition of 'treatment' does not embrace such instances of re-contextualization. As a result, the UK provision on 'treatment' is probably contrary to Article 6*bis*(1) of the Berne Convention, which refers to 'other derogatory action in relation to' the work.

3.3.3.2 Derogatory

Treatment of a work is 'derogatory', 'if it amounts to distortion or mutilation of the work or is otherwise prejudicial to the honour or reputation of the author or director'.[33] There are very few cases on the UK integrity right and even fewer that discuss the meaning of 'derogatory'. One of the leading cases is examined below.

Confetti Records v Warner Music UK Ltd [2003] ECDR 31

The third claimant (Mr Alcee) had composed a piece of garage music called 'Burnin', which he sold to the first claimant (Confetti Records). The defendant (Warner Music) had been in negotiations with the first claimant to use the 'Burnin' track on a compilation

---

[32] Ibid., s. 80(2).   [33] Ibid., s. 80(2)(b).

album, but these fell through late in the day, by which time the defendant had recorded and mixed their album and made a quantity of copies. The original version of 'Burnin'' comprised an insistent instrumental beat accompanied by the vocal repetition of the word 'burning'. The version produced by the defendant featured The Heartless Crewe, a garage trio of DJ Fonti and MCs Mighty Mo and Bushkin. The Heartless Crewe used the original version of 'Burnin'' as a backing track, over which they rapped lyrics. The third claimant alleged that this was a derogatory treatment of his work because the rap lyrics were suggestive of violence and drug usage.

Lewison J:

149. Mr Howe submitted that there could be no derogatory treatment unless the treatment was prejudicial to the honour or reputation of the author. Mr Shipley, on the other hand, said that treatment was derogatory if it was a distortion or mutilation of the work, even if it did not prejudice the honour or reputation of the author. Both Laddie Prescott and Vitoria on The Modern Law of Copyrights and Designs (3rd ed.) paragraph 13.18, and Copinger and Skone James on Copyright (14th ed.) paragraph 11–42, disagree with this view. So do I. Section 80 is clearly intended to give effect to Art. 6 bis of the Berne Convention. That article gives the author the right to object: 'to any distortion, mutilation or other modification of, or other derogatory action in relation to, the said work, which would be prejudicial to his honour or reputation'.

150. It is clear that in Art. 6 bis the author can only object to distortion, mutilation or modification of his work if it is prejudicial to his honour or reputation. I do not believe that the framers of the 1988 Act meant to alter the scope of the author's moral rights in this respect. Moreover, in the compressed drafting style of the United Kingdom legislature, the word 'otherwise' itself suggests that the distortion or mutilation is only actionable if it is prejudicial to the author's honour or reputation. HH Judge Overend adopted this construction in *Pasterfield v Denham* [1999] FSR 168, and in my judgment he was correct to do so. I hold that the mere fact that a work has been distorted or mutilated gives rise to no claim, unless the distortion or mutilation prejudices the author's honour or reputation.

151. The nub of the original complaint, principally advanced by Mr Pascal, is that the words of the rap (or at least that part contributed by Elephant Man) contained references to violence and drugs. This led to the faintly surreal experience of three gentlemen in horsehair wigs examining the meaning of such phrases as 'mish mish man' and 'shizzle (or sizzle) my nizzle'.

152. The 'author' in the present case is the third claimant, Mr Alcee. The assignment of his copyright to the first and/or second claimants does not affect his authorship. The first and second claimants are not entitled to complain of prejudice to their honour or reputation. Thus the evidence that I heard about the kinds of songs produced by Confetti, and in particular about the meaning of the lyrics of 'Champion Puffa', is, to my mind, irrelevant.

153. When played at normal speed the words of the rap overlying 'Burnin'' are very hard to decipher, and indeed the parties disagreed on what the words were. Even when played at half speed there were disagreements about the lyrics. The very fact that the words are hard to decipher itself militates against the conclusion that the treatment was 'derogatory' in the statutory sense.

154. Mr Pascal did not himself claim to know what street meanings were to be attributed to the disputed phrases, but said that he had been told what they were by an unnamed informant conversant with the use of drugs. Mr Howe submitted, correctly in my opinion, that the meaning of words in a foreign language could only be explained by experts. He also submitted, again correctly in my opinion, that the words of the rap, although in a form of English, were for practical purposes a foreign language. Thus he submitted that Mr Pascal's

evidence, not being the evidence of an expert, was inadmissible. I think that he is right, although the occasions on which an expert drug dealer might be called to give evidence in the Chancery Division are likely to be rare.

155. But even if I pay regard to Mr Pascal's evidence on this topic, I do not find that the meaning of the disputed words has been proved. Mr Pascal's evidence was hearsay, and the source of his information was not identified. Mr Hunter, one of the MCs with The Heartless Crew, (professionally known as MC Bushkin) had not heard of the meanings that Mr Pascal attributed to the disputed phrases. Nor had Mr Thomas. A search on the Internet discovered the Urban Dictionary which gave some definitions of 'shizzle my nizzle' (and variants) none of which referred to drugs. Some definitions carried sexual connotations. The most popular definitions were definitions of the phrase 'fo' shizzle my nizzle' and indicated that it meant 'for sure'. There were no entries for 'sizzle my nizzle' or for 'mish mish man', and Mr Hunter said that Elephant Man (the MC who uttered the disputed phrases) often made up words for their rhyming effect.

156. To be fair, Mr Shipley did not press this complaint in his closing submissions. Instead he sought to advance a new case. First he said that the treatment was derogatory because all coherence of the original work has been lost as a result of the superimposition of the rap. Secondly he said, whatever a 'mish mish man' was, the words of the rap 'string dem up one by one' was an invitation to lynching. It is by no means clear that the words on the rap are in fact 'string dem up'. Moreover, I am not at all sure that the meaning Mr Shipley attributes to the phrase 'string dem up' is the only possible meaning. A proponent of capital punishment who says that murderers should be 'strung up' would usually be taken to advocate the return of a hangman, rather than lynching.

157. However, it seems to me that the fundamental weakness in this part of the case is that I have no evidence about Mr Alcee's honour or reputation. I have no evidence of any prejudice to either of them. Mr Alcee himself made no complaint about the treatment of 'Burnin' in his witness statement. Mr Shipley invites me to infer prejudice. Where the author himself makes no complaint, I do not consider that I should infer prejudice on his behalf.

158. I do not infer any prejudice from the fact that The Heartless Crew rode the rhythm right through the track. If I am to draw any inference, the inference I would draw, having listened to the original mix of 'Burnin', is that it was designed to be the background track to a rap. Indeed the proposed mix for the single of 'Burnin' by the Ant'ill Mob (called the vocal mix) was itself a rap which rode the rhythm throughout the track.

159. There was a suggestion that Mr Alcee is the only permanent member of the Ant'ill Mob. He did not say this in his own witness statement, and Mr Pascal said in his witness statement that the Ant'ill Mob 'do not have identifiable members in the traditional sense of a group'. He also said that when they perform Confetti hire session musicians to form the group.

160. If, however, Mr Alcee is a member (or perhaps the only member) of the Ant'ill Mob, then the way in which they are presented may impinge on his own honour and reputation. It is clear to me, despite Mr Pascal's protestations to the contrary, that the Ant'ill Mob were costumed to look like 1930s gangsters. As it was put in a newspaper article in February 2002, the release of 'Burnin' was twinned 'with a video showing the Mob in true 1930s gangster style'. My own viewing of the video confirmed this impression. I do not therefore infer any prejudice from the invitation to 'string up' 'mish mish men', even if it bears the meaning that Mr Shipley attributes to it.

From reading the above extract from *Confetti Records* would you say that to establish derogatory treatment it is enough that an author objects to what has been done to his or her work? If not, what must be established and what is the relevance of both honour and reputation? Would you describe the approach for determining whether treatment is derogatory as an objective or subjective one? In France, which represents the par excellence of moral-rights protection, it is enough that the author objects to what has been done to his or her work. For example, the estate of John Huston was successful in restraining the owners of copyright in the black and white film *Ashphalt Jungle,* which he co-directed, from showing a colourized version of it in France.[34] In your view, is the French approach preferable to that adopted in the UK?

> **FURTHER READING**
>
> E. Adeney, 'The moral right of integrity: the past and future of "honour"' [2005] IPQ 111.

3.3.4 EXCEPTIONS

There are a raft of exceptions in relation to both the attribution and integrity rights, the more important of which will be mentioned here.

The rights do not apply to computer programs or any computer-generated works[35] and, in the case of the attribution right, also designs of typefaces. The rights also do not apply in relation to any work made for the purpose of reporting current events.[36] In addition, where an act would not infringe copyright because it is fair dealing for the purpose of reporting current events by means of a sound recording, film, or broadcast, the attribution right will not be infringed.[37]

The publishing industry was successful in obtaining exceptions in their favour. Thus, neither the attribution nor the integrity right applies:

> in relation to the publication in (a) a newspaper, magazine or similar periodical, or (b) an encyclopaedia, dictionary, yearbook or other collective work of reference, of a literary, dramatic, musical or artistic work made for the purposes of such publication or made available with the consent of the author for the purposes of such publication.[38]

Perhaps the most important exclusions are those relating to employee created works. The right of attribution does not apply to anything done by or with the authority of the owner of copyright in a work, where ownership originally vested in the author's/director's employer under section 11(2).[39] As such, employee authors have their right of attribution severely limited. When it comes to the right of integrity, this does not apply to anything done in relation to an employee created work unless the author or director is identified at the time of the relevant act or has previously been identified in or on published copies of the work and there is no sufficient disclaimer.[40] Given employers will usually own copyright in works created by their employees in the course of employment, does it seem fair also to deprive employees of their moral rights in relation to such works?

3.3.5 WAIVER

If an author consents to a particular act being done, it will not amount to an infringement of moral rights.[41] In addition, an author may *waive* his or her moral rights by instrument

---

[34] See *Huston v Turner Entertainment Co* [1992] ECC 334.
[35] CDPA, ss. 79(2) and 81(2).
[36] Ibid., ss. 79(5) and 81(3).
[37] Ibid., s. 79(4)(a).
[38] Ibid., ss. 79(6) and 81(4).
[39] Ibid., s. 79(3).
[40] Ibid., s. 82(1)–(2).
[41] Ibid., s. 87(1).

in writing.[42] The waiver may potentially be broad ranging, in that it can relate to works of a specified description or to works generally and to existing or future works. If it is made in favour of the owner or prospective owner of copyright in the work to which it relates, it shall be presumed to extend to his licensees and successors in title, unless a contrary intention is expressed.[43]

Does the ability to waive moral rights, particularly in the way possible under the CDPA, seriously undermine the effectiveness of those rights? If so, would it be desirable to prevent waiver or at least limit the circumstances in which it can be used?

3.3.6 ALTERNATIVE APPROACH?

As mentioned earlier, France represents the par excellence of moral-rights regimes. In the following extract, Dr Irini Stamatoudi highlights the main features of the French approach.

I. Stamatoudi, 'Moral rights of authors in England: The missing emphasis on the role of creators' [1997] IPQ 478, 498–500

The French paradigm

France was the first country in Europe to recognise the 'droit moral'. This legal concept was first formed in a piecemeal way through case law at the end of the 19th century, while in the mid-20th century moral rights were given statutory recognition. Today moral rights in France are enshrined in the 1994 CPI. There are five moral rights, namely the right of divulgation (droit de divulgation), the right of integrity (droit au respect), the right of paternity (droit de paternité), the right of revocation (droit de repentir) and the right of access to the work (droit d'accès a l'oeuvre).

The right of divulgation or publication of the work is in fact the author's right to decide whether or not to publish a work and in what form. The paternity and integrity rights have the same content as their counterparts in the Berne Convention, although the requirement in relation to the integrity right of harm to the author's honour or reputation, has been dropped. More specifically, the integrity right, apart from harm to the author's honour or reputation, also covers situations where the material integrity of a work has not been affected and no direct harm to the author's honour or reputation has ensued, but where, for example, the image of the author has suffered due to the circumstances in which the work was exhibited to the public. The right of revocation is supposed to be a corollary to the right to publication. According to this right the author of a work can withdraw it from sale because he has changed his views. That right is, of course, not unrestricted. Essentially the author has to compensate the publisher for all the expenses he has incurred in marketing the work. However, if the owner of the work at issue is affected as well, relief under the right might not be given by the court. And lastly, there is the right of access to the work. The author has the right to see his work in order to be able to make reproductions, observe details or just enjoy it. This right is to be exercised under certain rather restrictive conditions (e.g. without being a constant nuisance to the owner of the work, and with the obligation to visit the owner's residence and not expect the owner to bring the work over to him).

Contrary to common law countries, France has adopted the dualistic approach to moral rights. It distinguishes moral rights from the economic rights of authors and considers them to be separate rights. They are also said to be perpetual, imprescriptible, non-assignable and

---

[42] Ibid., s. 87(2).   [43] Ibid., s. 87(3).

discretionary. These characteristics are indicative of the degree of protection accorded to authors under French copyright law. However, these characteristics are not without restrictions. Apart from express exceptions, such as in the case of computer programs and films where certain alterations are held not to infringe the right of integrity, there are implied exceptions as well. In fact, the scope of these rights is to be interpreted purposively, which in practice includes the rights being balanced against other legal rights which other parties may hold, as well as the practical circumstances of the specific case being taken into account. First, in relation to their existence in perpetuity, one may wonder how moral rights can be exercisable when neither the author, nor members of his family are left alive. It must be mentioned here that the courts are reluctant to accept claims from people who are not family members. As Dietz points out, '[I]n spite of the recognised principle [of perpetuity] the reduced number of persons able to sue for infringement of moral rights makes the perpetuity of its protection considerably less important'.

Secondly by 'discretion' one does not mean that the author has the unrestricted right to exercise his moral rights whenever he thinks appropriate. This right is given to him, only if he exercises his moral rights in a way that is consistent with their purpose. If that is not the case the court will prevent him from exercising them abusively or to another end; for example, to get a better deal by concluding another more lucrative publishing contract after he frees himself from the one at issue.

Lastly, assertion and waiver are not provided for under French law. Moral rights constitute *ius cogens* and they cannot be contracted out of, by the parties.

Having considered the UK regime of moral rights and briefly also the French regime, would you say that the UK takes moral-rights protection seriously? What does the UK approach to moral rights tell you about its copyright system as a whole?

FURTHER READING

E. Adeney, *The Moral Rights of Authors and Performers* (Oxford: Oxford University Press, 2006).

3.4 EXCEPTIONS AND LIMITATIONS

The CDPA has a range of exceptions and limitations to copyright infringement. Exceptions are provisions that allow a person to carry out an exclusive act in relation to a copyright work, without having to remunerate the owner, whereas limitations are provisions that allow a person to do an exclusive act, in return for paying remuneration of some kind. Exceptions and limitations are important mechanisms for facilitating a balance of interests between copyright owners and users. Where to strike that balance, however, is frequently a matter of contention and is arguably influenced by the underlying rationale/s for copyright protection.

In recent times, copyright exceptions and limitations have faced several challenges. For example, developments in digital technology have led to an expansion of rights for copyright owners and this has raised concerns about the extent to which copyright exceptions and limitations should be correspondingly adapted. Following the Gowers Review of Intellectual Property in December 2006, the UK Intellectual Property Office (UK IPO) published a consultation paper entitled, 'Taking forward the Gowers Review of Intellectual Property: Proposed changes to copyright exceptions' ('Exceptions Consultation Paper').[44]

---

[44] Available at <http://www.ipo.gov.uk/c-notice-2008-exceptions.htm>.

The proposed reforms seek to provide clarity regarding the scope of certain exceptions and limitations in a digital context and also balance and flexibility in the copyright system. The relevance of some of these proposals will be discussed below, while those concerning format shifting, educational exceptions, and library privileges are considered in Chapter 12.[45]

Another challenge that has arisen is determining the impact of the Human Rights Act 1998 (HRA) on copyright exceptions, in particular, how the right to freedom of expression, contained in Article 10 of the ECHR, should be given effect in copyright law. This has been particularly relevant in the context of the public interest defence.

Finally, it is worth noting the influence of EU law, in the form of Article 5 of the Information Society Directive, which sought to harmonize copyright exceptions and limitations. Article 5(1) sets out a mandatory exception for temporary reproduction,[46] while Article 5(2) and (3) contain an optional, but exhaustive, list of exceptions and limitations. As a result of these provisions, the UK had to amend some of its exceptions and limitations. Any future reforms in this area will also be constrained by compliance with Article 5(2) and (3).

Although the CDPA features a raft of exceptions and limitations, the next section will focus on only a few of the more important ones—the fair-dealing exceptions, the incidental inclusion exception, and the defence of public interest.

3.4.1 FAIR DEALING

The CDPA contains fair-dealing exceptions in respect of certain specific uses—these are research or private study,[47] reporting current events,[48] and criticism or review.[49] It is important to remember that these specific uses or purposes are exhaustive, meaning that a defendant must bring their actions within one or more of them in order for the exception to apply. This may be contrasted with the 'fair use' exception in s. 107 of the US Copyright Act 1976, which features an illustrative open list of purposes to which the defence may apply. Given the importance in UK copyright law of fitting within the fair-dealing purposes, we turn to examine the scope of research or private study, reporting current events, and criticism or review in more detail.

3.4.1.1 Research or private study

Fair dealing for the purpose of research or private study is limited to literary, dramatic, musical, and artistic works[50] and also typographical arrangements of published editions.[51] As such, it is not applicable to films, sound recordings, or broadcasts. As part of the UK IPO's consultation on reform of copyright exceptions, there is a proposal to extend the exception to *all* types of works.[52] In your view, does this reform make sense?

What is the meaning of 'research' and 'private study'? Section 29(1) of the CDPA, as a result of implementing Article 5(2) of the Information Society Directive, stipulates that research must be for a non-commercial purpose and s. 178 states that 'private study' does not include any study which is directly or indirectly for a commercial purpose. This gives rise to some uncertainties. Is it the case that research must be wholly for a non-commercial purpose, i.e. not directly or indirectly for a commercial purpose? Also, what is meant by a 'commercial' purpose? Is it a purpose that involves direct or indirect profit-making? If so, does that mean educational purposes, such as research within universities, are excluded? Further, what is the difference between the activities of 'research' and 'private study'? The

---

[45] See 12.6.4.3–12.6.4.5.   [46] See 12.6.4.2.   [47] CDPA, s. 29.   [48] Ibid., s. 30(2).
[49] Ibid., s. 30(1).   [50] Ibid., s. 29(1) and (1C).   [51] Ibid., s. 29(2).
[52] Exceptions Consultation Paper, Recommendation 9.

latter suggests an activity carried out by individuals for their own benefit or gratification, possibly as part of pursuing a formal qualification. By way of contrast, 'research' could connote work done by an individual for the benefit of an organization or that which has some kind of public dimension, such as through being published. Even so, the distinction between the two types of activities is fairly unclear and this matters because, in the case of research for non-commercial purposes, there is a further requirement that it is accompanied by a sufficient acknowledgement unless this would be impossible for reasons of practicality.[53] Sufficient acknowledgement is defined in s. 178 as an acknowledgement identifying the work in question by its title or other description and identifying the author.

Can a person copying on behalf of researchers or students rely on this exception? According to s. 29(3) it is possible for librarians, or a person acting on behalf of a librarian, to rely on this fair-dealing exception provided they do not supply more than one copy of the same article to the same person. Further, a person cannot rely on this exception if they know or have reason to believe that copies of substantially the same material will be provided to more than one person at substantially the same time and for substantially the same purpose. Thus, this exception would not permit a lecturer to supply copies of an article that is prescribed reading to all the students in his or her class.

3.4.1.2 Reporting current events

Fair dealing for the purpose of reporting current events applies to all copyright works *except* for photographs. Why is it, do you think, that photographs have been excluded from the scope of this exception?

What exactly is meant by 'current events'? In *British Broadcasting Corporation v British Satellite Broadcasting Ltd*,[54] a case involving the scope of fair dealing with respect to broadcasters' rights, Scott J held that it is not confined to reporting of current events in general news programmes, but extends to inclusion of material in sports news programmes. The use of very short excerpts from the BBC broadcasts of 1990 World Cup football matches in the defendant's sports news programmes was held to fall within the scope of this exception.

In the following case, the Court of Appeal considered whether publication of an article can itself constitute a 'current event'.

Newspaper Licensing Agency Ltd v Marks & Spencer plc [2003] 3 WLR 1256

The facts of this case were discussed above. One of the arguments raised by the defendant was that the further copies it had made of press cuttings had been for the purpose of reporting current events to those within its organization. This argument was rejected at first instance and, on appeal, by a majority of the Court of Appeal.

Peter Gibson LJ:

40. It is common ground that in the light of the decision of this court in *Pro Sieben Media AG v Carlton UK Television Ltd* [1999] FSR 610: (1) 'for the purpose of reporting current events' in section 30(2) should be construed as a composite phrase; (2) for that phrase there could be substituted 'in the context of' or 'as part of an exercise in' [reporting current events] without

---

[53] CDPA, s. 29(1) and (1B).   [54] [1992] Ch 141.

any significant alteration of meaning, the intentions and motives of the user of another's copyright work being of little importance save for considering whether the dealing was fair; (3) the words 'reporting current events' are of wide and indefinite scope and require a liberal interpretation.

41. It is also not in dispute that the defence of fair dealing is directed, as the judge put it [1999] RPC 536, 545, to achieving a proper balance between protection of the rights of a creative author or the wider public interest, of which free speech is a very important ingredient. The judge said, at p. 546, that the publication of a report or article in the press may itself constitute a current event and a publication may constitute fair dealing for the purpose of reporting current events though it contains no analysis or comment or any matter other than use of the copyright material, but that did not mean that whatever was reported in the press was a current event. He added that the term 'current events' was narrower than the term 'news', and that reporting of current events does not extend to publishing matters of current interest, whether generally or to particular persons like M & S, but which were not current events.

42. We were shown a number of cuttings. Many were of articles in the press which referred to M & S, whether reporting a news item (e.g. the announced intention to expand the workforce) or commenting on or displaying an M & S product. Others were of articles about matters (e.g. the launch of the Euro) which could affect M & S in its business activities or about M & S's competitors. There can be no doubt but that the copying of the articles for the benefit of M & S executives was for a genuine business purpose and put before those recipients matters which they had a good commercial reason to see.

43. The fact that an article appears in the press can be said to be an event. As the cutting is copied promptly the event might be said to be current. The circulating of a copy to an M & S executive can be said to be reporting the current event of the appearance of that article. But is that what was intended by the phrase 'for the purpose of reporting current events?' I think not for two reasons. First, the language of the subsection to my mind naturally connotes the public reporting of a recent newsworthy event. It is not natural to read it as meaning that the defence applies where the dealing lies in reporting the mere fact that an article has appeared in the press, however interesting that fact may be to M & S, for example that a fashion editor of a journal has featured an M & S garment, when that event has no other significance. Although the scope of the defence has been widened in successive Acts since it first appeared in section 2(1)(i) of the Copyright Act 1911 as 'Any fair dealing with any work for the purposes of . . . newspaper summary' and willing though I am to give the phrase a liberal interpretation, I cannot see that the language, read naturally, permits a meaning as wide as Mr Silverleaf would urge on us. Second, to interpret section 30(2) as providing a defence to copyright infringement in a case like the present would seem to me to have nothing to do with the public interest and everything to do with serving the private commercial interests of M & S. I can see no public interest reason why the legislature should want to provide a defence to an infringement of copyright for the copying within a commercial organisation for commercial reasons of material subject to copyright, whereas a public interest can be discerned in the public reporting of newsworthy current events. I would therefore hold, in agreement with the judge, that if what M & S did was an infringement of copyright, it would not come within the defence of section 30(2).

[**Mance LJ** delivering a judgment in which he agreed with **Peter Gibson LJ**, while **Chadwick LJ** delivered a dissenting judgment.]

Apparent from the above extract is that 'current events' is not synonymous with 'news'. How would you describe the difference between the two concepts? Also, it seems possible for the publication of an article itself to constitute a current event, even if that was not held to be so on the facts of *NLA v Marks & Spencer*. A case in which it was successfully argued that the fact of media coverage can itself qualify as a 'current event' is *Hyde Park Residence v Yelland* [2001] Ch 143. Here, the defendants had published in *The Sun* newspaper stills from a security video, which showed Princess Diana and Dodi Al Fayed arriving and departing from a Paris villa. The claimant company, which was responsible for security at the Paris villa, brought an action alleging infringement of copyright and sought summary judgment. The defendants argued, *inter alia*, that publication of the stills was for the purpose of reporting currents events because it refuted allegations recently made by Mohammed Al Fayed that the couple had been visiting the Paris villa in order to make wedding plans. Aldous LJ (with whom Mance and Stuart-Smith LJJ agreed), accepted that use of the security video stills was for the purpose of reporting current events, in the sense that it related to the recent media coverage of Mr Al Fayed's claims about his son and Princess Diana. Although the purpose was satisfied, he went on to hold that the use was not a 'fair' dealing.

To rely on this exception, there must be sufficient acknowledgement (as discussed above). However, where the current events are reported by means of a sound recording, film, or broadcast, no acknowledgement is required where this would be impossible for reasons of practicality or otherwise.

3.4.1.3 Criticism or review

Fair dealing for the purpose of criticism or review applies to all types of works. Importantly, the criticism or review must be directed to the work that is allegedly infringed or else another work or a performance of a work—[55] it cannot be criticism or review generally. The scope of this purpose and how it is to be assessed is explained in the case below.

Pro Sieben Media AG v Carlton UK Television Ltd [1999] 1 WLR 605

Pro Sieben had broadcast a programme (the TAFF programme), which included an exclusive interview with Mandy Allwood, a woman who was pregnant with octuplets. The second defendant had produced a current affairs programme, 'The Big Story: Selling Babies', which featured a 30 second extract from the TAFF programme and this was broadcast by the first defendant. The second defendant had also copied the whole of the TAFF programme in order to select the appropriate extract to be used. The claimant alleged copyright infringement and the defendants argued that their use of the extract was fair dealing for the purpose of criticism or review, or for reporting current events. Laddie J at first instance rejected both of these defences. There was an appeal to the Court of Appeal.

Robert Walker LJ (Henry and Nourse LJJ in agreement), at 613–15:

This court has by contrast heard quite lengthy submissions as to whether the words 'for the purpose of' in section 30(1) and section 30(2) import a subjective or an objective test. The judge did not discuss this point at length, but rejected the submission made on behalf of Pro Sieben that even if the critic had the necessary purpose, the defence is not made out unless the purpose was understood by the audience.

...

---

[55] CDPA, s. 30(1).

The fact that there is no authority on the point after nearly 90 years suggests that the issue may not be of much practical importance; indeed, that it may not be a significant point of construction at all. In *Sweet v Parsley* [1970] AC 132 the House of Lords emphasised the importance of construing a composite phrase rather than a single word. It seems to me that in the composite phrases 'for the purposes of criticism or review' and 'for the purpose of reporting current events' the mental element on the part of the user is of little more importance than in such everyday composite expressions as 'for the purpose of argument' or 'for the purpose of comparison'. The words 'in the context of' or 'as part of an exercise in' could be substituted for 'for the purpose of' without any significant alteration of meaning.

That is not to say that the intentions and motives of the user of another's copyright material are not highly relevant for the purposes of the defences available under section 30(1) and section 30(2). But they are most highly relevant on the issue of fair dealing, so far as it can be treated as a discrete issue from the statutory purpose (arguably the better course is to take the first 24 words of section 30(1), and the first 16 words of section 30(2), as a single composite whole and to resist any attempt at further dissection). It is not necessary for the court to put itself in the shoes of the infringer of the copyright in order to decide whether the offending piece was published 'for the purposes of criticism or review'. This court should not in my view give any encouragement to the notion that all that is required is for the user to have the sincere belief, however misguided, that he or she is criticising a work or reporting current affairs. To do so would provide an undesirable incentive for journalists, for whom facts should be sacred, to give implausible evidence as to their intentions.

...

'Criticism or review' and 'reporting current events' are expressions of wide and indefinite scope. Any attempt to plot their precise boundaries is doomed to failure. They are expressions which should be interpreted liberally, but I derive little assistance from comparisons with other expressions such as 'current affairs' or 'news'...

Criticism of a work need not be limited to criticism of style. It may also extend to the ideas to be found in a work and its social or moral implications. So in *Time Warner Entertainments Co v Channel Four Television Corporation Plc* [1994] EMLR 1 this court, in allowing an interlocutory appeal and discharging an injunction, accepted that a television programme criticising the withdrawal of the film 'A Clockwork Orange' from distribution in the United Kingdom amounted to criticism of the film itself, since the content of the film and the decision to withdraw it were inseparable: see Henry LJ, at p. 15, and Neill LJ, at p. 13. The defendants relied on that case. Pro Sieben on the other hand pointed out that section 30(1) requires use for the purpose of criticism or review 'of that or another work' and that the judge was not persuaded that criticism of the TAFF report, as opposed to the decision to pay for an interview, was in Ms Byrne's mind when the Carlton programme was made or broadcast.

[**Robert Walker LJ** concluded that the judge had erred in principle in his approach to this defence, mainly because he had focused too much on the expressed purpose, intention, and motive of those involved in producing the programme and too little on the likely impact on the audience. He went on to consider whether the use of the clip had been for the purpose of fair dealing for criticism or review:]

The Carlton programme as a whole was, in my judgment, made for the purpose of criticism of works of chequebook journalism in general, and in particular the (then very recent) treatment by the media of the story of Ms Allwood's multiple pregnancy. Mr Clifford, the 'News of the World' and Pro Sieben were on the side of the 'haves'; other newspapers were 'have nots' and the programme vividly depicted how payments to peripheral figures (such as Ms Allwood's former husband and one of Mr Hudson's former girlfriends) could produce material for 'spoilers'. The criticism of the TAFF report was relatively mild because the

> report itself was, to use one of Ms Byrne's milder expressions, bland...Nevertheless the criticism was not, in my view, limited to what the judge called the 'throw away' comment: 'After ten days of muckraking, a sanitised version of the truth, tightly controlled by Max Clifford.' ...Mr Clifford's involvement with the TAFF report was therefore featured prominently, rather than being limited to the single 'sanitised version' remark which came at the end of the 30-second extract showing the teddy bears. The element of criticism was also strengthened by the final part of the Carlton programme, immediately after the extract, in which Mr Clifford made the very candid remarks which I have already quoted ('We lie all the time. You know, that's, that's what it's about...lying, corruption, deceit').

When it comes to assessing whether a work, or part of a work has been used for the purposes of criticism or review, the courts will adopt an objective test. When will the subjective intentions of the parties be relevant, if at all? The Court of Appeal accepted that criticism of a work includes criticism of a genre of works, in this case works of chequebook journalism. This liberal interpretation of 'criticism or review' has also been applied in *Fraser-Woodward Ltd v BBC*[56] where Mann J accepted that photographs of the Beckham family were being used for the purpose of criticism or review of works of tabloid journalism. Do you agree with such a generous approach to the scope of the purpose?

To rely on this exception, there must be sufficient acknowledgement. In *Pro Sieben* the defendants's programme included the title 'TAFF' and also the Pro Sieben logo (a stylized number seven). While it was accepted that 'TAFF' shown on the screen identified the title of the work, the question was whether or not the television transmission of the Pro Sieben logo was sufficient to identify the author of the work.

Robert Walker LJ, at 618:

Mr Silverleaf accepted that identification of an author would normally and naturally be achieved by communicating, by spoken words or writing or both, his correct name or, if the author wrote under a pseudonym, the name by which he was known as an author. But Mr Silverleaf submitted that the television transmission of a logo could also constitute identification for the purposes of section 178, especially if the logo was the means by which the author of a television programme was accustomed to identify itself, and if the use of the correct name was unlikely to have any particular significance to the bulk of the audience. In this case there was evidence, from Mr Michael von Dessauer, a vice president of Pro Sieben, that his company used the logo (of a stylised '7') as an identification. The fact that the company's correct name and postal address was used on business communications is unsurprising and does not detract from that evidence. There was also evidence that the normal audience for Pro Sieben programmes in England is, for obvious reasons, very small and not representative of the general body of Carlton viewers. I would accept Mr Silverleaf's submissions and hold that the defendants succeed in making good a defence under section 30(1).

Another prerequisite to relying on this exception is that the work has been made available to the public. This requirement was introduced in order to implement Article 5(3)(d) of the Information Society Directive. Section 30(1A) of the CDPA states that a work will have been made available to the public by a variety of means (e.g. making the work available by means of an electronic retrieval system or communicating it to the public), but importantly that act

---

[56] [2005] FSR 36.

must have been authorized. No account is to be taken of any unauthorized act of making the work available to the public. Which users of copyright do you think this requirement will affect most? Does it reflect an appropriate balance between the interests of the author/owner in divulging the work and the public interest in permitting criticism or review?

The UK does not have a separate parody exception or indeed specific principles in the case of parodies.[57] Fair dealing for the purposes of criticism or review is arguably the exception most likely to embrace acts of parody. What obstacles, however, do you think exist for a parodist to rely successfully on this exception? Are they such that in fact a separate parody exception is warranted, as was recently introduced in Australia?[58] This is an issue currently being explored by the UK IPO, which presently recommends the introduction of a separate exception for caricature, parody, or pastiche.[59] This is certainly possible within the constraints of the Information Society Directive, since Article 5(3)(k) states that exceptions or limitations may be provided for in the case of use for the purpose of caricature, parody, or pastiche. Whether it is a desirable introduction into UK copyright law is another matter.

FURTHER READING

S. McCausland, 'Protecting "a fine tradition of satire": The new fair dealing exception for parody or satire in the Australian Copyright Act' [2007] EIPR 287.

J. McCutcheon, 'The new defence of parody or satire under Australian copyright law' [2008] IPQ 163.

C. Rutz, 'Parody: A missed opportunity?' [2004] IPQ 284.

M. Spence, 'Intellectual property and the problem of parody' (1998) 114 LQR 594.

3.4.1.4 Fair-dealing factors

It is not enough that the activity satisfies the requisite purposes, the requirement of sufficient acknowledgement and, in the case of criticism or review, that the work has been made available to the public. The dealing must also be *fair*. There is no statutory guidance, however, as to what constitutes fair dealing. This may be contrasted with the approach in the US, where s. 107 of the US Copyright Act 1976 sets out factors to be included in the assessment of whether the use is a fair one. These are:

(1) the purpose and character of the use, including whether such use is of a commercial nature or is for nonprofit educational purposes;

(2) the nature of the copyrighted work;

(3) the amount and substantiality of the portion used in relation to the copyrighted work as a whole; and

(4) the effect of the use upon the potential market for or value of the copyrighted work.

The fact that a work is unpublished shall not itself bar a finding of fair use if such finding is made upon consideration of all the above factors.

---

57 See *Williamson Music Ltd v Pearson Partnership* [1987] FSR 97.

58 See Australian Copyright Amendment Act 2006, introducing separate exceptions for parody or satire in ss. 41A and 103AA of the Australian Copyright Act 1968 (Cth).

59 Exceptions Consultation Paper, Recommendation 12.

In the UK it has been left to the courts to develop guidance for determining whether or not there is fair dealing. In *Hubbard v Vosper*,[60] Lord Denning MR held that the following factors ought to be taken into account:

> It is impossible to define what is 'fair dealing'. It must be a question of degree. You must consider first the number and extent of the quotations and extracts. Are they altogether too many and too long to be fair? Then you must consider the use made of them. If they are used as a basis for comment, criticism or review, that may be fair dealing. If they are used to convey the same information as the author, for a rival purpose, that may be unfair. Next, you must consider the proportions. To take long extracts and attach short comments may be unfair. But, short extracts and long comments may be fair. Other considerations may come to mind also. But, after all is said and done, it must be a matter of impression. As with fair comment in the law of libel, so with fair dealing in the law of copyright. The tribunal of fact must decide. In the present case, there is material on which the tribunal of fact could find this to be fair dealing.[61]

How would you describe the factors discussed by Lord Denning MR?

Additional guidance on assessing fair dealing is set out in the following extract from Aldous LJ's judgment in *Hyde Park Residence v Yelland*,[62] the facts of which were discussed above.

Aldous LJ:

38. ...Thus the court must judge the fairness by the objective standard of whether a fair minded and honest person would have dealt with the copyright work, in the manner that 'The Sun' did, for the purpose of reporting the relevant current events, in this case the published untruthful statements of Mr Al Fayed.

...

40. I reject Mr Spearman's submission. I have come to the conclusion that the defence of fair dealing cannot succeed. I do not believe that a fair minded and honest person would pay for the dishonestly taken driveway stills and publish them in a newspaper knowing that they had not been published or circulated when their only relevance was the fact that the Princess and Mr Dodi Fayed only stayed the 28 minutes at the Villa Windsor—a fact that was known and did not establish that the Princess and Mr Dodi Fayed were not to be married. To describe what 'The Sun' did as fair dealing is to give honour to dishonour. Further the extent of the use was excessive. The only part of the driveway stills relevant to the alleged purpose was the information as to the timing of arrival and departure. That information could have been given in the articles by Mr Thompson stating that he had seen the photographs which proved the Princess and Mr Dodi Fayed only stayed at the Villa Windsor for 28 minutes. If he needed confirmation he could have relied upon the statement by Mr Cole. Despite that, 'The Sun' used the driveway stills so that they covered over one-third of page 4. The information as to the time of arrival and departure did not establish that Princess Diana and Mr Dodi Fayed were not going to be married or that the other statements made by Mr Al Fayed, that are said to be untrue, were false.

41. The suggestion that the use of the driveway stills was a fair dealing for the purposes of reporting the events of 30 August 1997 is, to draw upon the words of Henry LJ in *Time Warner Entertainment Co Ltd v Channel Four Television Corpn plc* [1994] EMLR 1, 14, an

---

[60] [1972] 2 QB 84. [61] Ibid., at p. 94. [62] [2001] Ch 257.

> attempt to dress up the infringement of Hyde Park's copyright in the guise of reporting an event. In my view the judge came to the wrong conclusion and the allegation of fair dealing by the defendants could not provide them a defence to the action.

How do the factors identified by Aldous LJ compare with those set out by Lord Denning MR? Which factors overlap and which are additional? In your view, should it be relevant to consider matters from the perspective of the 'fair minded and honest person' and to give weight to whether the work has been dishonestly obtained? Does this not put the media in a difficult position when it comes to bringing matters of public interest to light? Also, do you agree that the use of the driveway stills was excessive—was the alternative method of corroborating the story a realistic one?

Further guidance on the factors relevant to 'fair' dealing is to be found in the following Court of Appeal decision.

Ashdown v Telegraph Group Ltd [2002] Ch 149

This case concerned a meeting between the then Labour Prime Minister Tony Blair and the then leader of the Liberal Democrats, Mr Paddy Ashdown, five months after the Labour party came to power in 1997. The meeting was to discuss a possible coalition government between the two political parties. Mr Ashdown wrote a minute of the meeting, which he kept confidential. Two copies were made—one was kept with Mr Ashdown's diaries and the other was shown to his closest advisors and then destroyed. A couple of years later, when it was imminent that Mr Ashdown would stand down as the Liberal Democrat leader, he made it known that he was contemplating publishing his diaries. Some of his material, including the minute of the meeting, was shown confidentially to potential publishers. It transpired that a copy of the minute was leaked to the political editor of the *Sunday Telegraph* and substantial extracts from the minute were copied verbatim in several articles published in that newspaper. The claimant sued for breach of confidence and copyright infringement and brought a motion for summary judgment on the latter claim. This motion was successful at first instance before Sir Andrew Morritt V-C. The defendant newspaper appealed. The court accepted the findings of Sir Andrew Morritt V-C that the defendant's use was not for the purposes of criticism or review, because it criticized the Prime Minister's and the claimant's actions, as opposed to the minute. In terms of fair dealing for the purpose of reporting current events, it also upheld the judge's finding that this was arguable, on the basis that 'reporting current events' should be interpreted liberally and the meeting between the claimant and Prime Minister was still a matter of current interest to the public. The court then went on to consider whether the dealing was arguably a fair one.

Lord Phillips MR (delivering the judgment of the court):

70. Authority is very sparse in relation to the defence of fair dealing in the context of reporting current events: see the comment of Scott J in *British Broadcasting Corpn v British Satellite Broadcasting Ltd* [1992] Ch 141, 148. Sir Andrew Morritt V-C commented with approval, however, on the summary of the authors of *Laddie, Prescott and Vitoria, The Modern Law of Copyright and Designs*, 3rd edn (2000), para. 20.16 on the test of fair dealing in the general

context of section 30. We also have found this an accurate and helpful summary and set it out for the purpose of discussion.

> It is impossible to lay down any hard-and-fast definition of what is fair dealing, for it is a matter of fact, degree and impression. However, by far the most important factor is whether the alleged fair dealing is in fact commercially competing with the proprietor's exploitation of the copyright work, a substitute for the probable purchase of authorised copies, and the like. If it is, the fair dealing defence will almost certainly fail. If it is not and there is a moderate taking and there are no special adverse factors, the defence is likely to succeed, especially if the defendant's additional purpose is to right a wrong, to ventilate an honest grievance, to engage in political controversy, and so on. The second most important factor is whether the work has already been published or otherwise exposed to the public. If it has not, and especially if the material has been obtained by a breach of confidence or other mean or underhand dealing, the courts will be reluctant to say this is fair. However this is by no means conclusive, for sometimes it is necessary for the purposes of legitimate public controversy to make use of 'leaked' information. The third most important factor is the amount and importance of the work that has been taken. For, although it is permissible to take a substantial part of the work (if not, there could be no question of infringement in the first place), in some circumstances the taking of an excessive amount, or the taking of even a small amount if on a regular basis, would negative fair dealing.

71. These principles are based on a summary of the authorities before the Human Rights Act 1998 came into force. They are still important when balancing the public interest in freedom of expression against the interests of owners of copyright. It is, however, now essential not to apply inflexibly tests based on precedent, but to bear in mind that considerations of public interest are paramount. With that consideration in mind, we turn to consider each of the important factors identified in *Laddie, Prescott and Vitoria* in turn.

Commercial competition

72. In a passage of its defence quoted by Sir Andrew Morritt V-C [2001] Ch 685, 698, at para. 25, Telegraph Group contended that its publication 'in no or no appreciable way competed...with any publication or publications which the claimant might issue in the future'. The Vice-Chancellor rejected this assertion, and we consider that he was right to do so. There was evidence, as he pointed out, that the publication in the 'Sunday Telegraph' destroyed a part of the value of the memoirs which it had been Mr Ashdown's intention to sell, and which he did in fact sell. Equally, we are in no doubt that the extensive quotations of Mr Ashdown's own words added a flavour to the description of the events covered which made the article more attractive to read and will have been of significant commercial value in enabling the 'Sunday Telegraph' to maintain, if not to enhance, the loyalty of its readership.

Prior publication

73. In the same passage of their defence the Telegraph Group asserted that Mr Ashdown had already revealed some details of the matters covered in the articles in his radio interview about 'Resigning Issues'. Sir Andrew Morritt V-C roundly rejected this contention, at p. 699, para. 28:

> The claimant had taken great care to limit the number of people who read it and to impose on them obligations of secrecy. Moreover the 'Sunday Telegraph' knew not only that the minute had not been published, indeed Mr Murphy described it as secret, but that, as the claimant revealed on the 'Resigning Issues' interview, he was thinking of doing so in the not so distant

future. It is not the case that during the interview for 'Resigning Issues' the claimant had already disclosed the important matters covered in the articles.

74. While we endorse these conclusions, it does not seem to us that they are wholly in point. Mr Spearman, for Mr Ashdown, argued that much of the information in the minute had already been made public and that this fact made it even harder to justify the 'Sunday Telegraph' publication. We consider that there is force in this point and will return to it in due course. What is at issue in a claim for breach of copyright is publication of the form of the literary work, not the information that it contains. It is beyond any doubt that the copyright work had never been published or otherwise exposed to the public before the publication in the 'Sunday Telegraph'.

75. At the same time, the fact that the minute was undoubtedly obtained in breach of confidence is a material consideration when considering the defence of fair dealing. Sir Andrew Morritt V-C rightly attached importance to the fact that the minute was secret and had been obtained by Telegraph Group without Mr Ashdown's knowledge or approval.

The amount and importance of the work taken

76. Here again we consider that Sir Andrew Morritt V-C correctly found that this aspect of the test of fair dealing weighed against the defence of fair dealing. A substantial portion of the minute was copied and it is reasonable to conclude, for the reasons given by Sir Andrew Morritt V-C, at p. 699, para. 29, that the most important passages in the minute were selected for publication.

77. All these considerations point in one direction and satisfy us that Sir Andrew Morritt V-C was correct to conclude that if the established authorities fell to be applied without any additional regard to the effect of Article 10 there was no realistic prospect that a defence of fair dealing would be made out.

Having read the above extracts from *Hubbard v Vosper*, *Hyde Park Residence v Yelland*, and *Ashdown*, what factors would you identify as the ones that courts are most likely to take into account when assessing whether there is a 'fair' dealing? Do you think that there are additional factors that courts should consider? Jonathan Griffiths has argued that, in order to give proper effect to Article 10 of the ECHR, right to freedom of expression, courts should also weigh up the subject matter of the defendant's article and the nature of the claimant's work.

J. Griffiths, 'Copyright law after Ashdown: Time to deal fairly with the public'
[2002] IPQ 240, 257–9

Principles relating to factors not considered by the Court of Appeal in *Ashdown*

In addition, however, it is also possible to identify two further principles that could usefully be applied. These relate to significant issues that were largely overlooked by the Court of Appeal in *Ashdown*.

The subject-matter of the defendant's article

The article within which the claimant's minute was reproduced concerned matters of considerable political significance to the United Kingdom. In finding that the meeting recorded in the minute was of continuing interest at the time of the *Sunday Telegraph's* publication, the

Court of Appeal itself noted that:

> In a democratic society, information about a meeting between the Prime Minister and an opposition party leader during the then current Parliament to discuss possible close co-operation between those parties is very likely to be of legitimate and continuing public interest. It might impinge upon the way in which the public voted at the next general election.

Information about matters of public importance is strongly protected under Article 10. Indeed, the single guiding principle of the jurisprudence of the European Court of Human Rights on that Article appears to be that interference with 'public speech' requires a very high degree of justification. The Court is extremely suspicious of sanctions on publications concerning matters of legitimate public concern. This suspicion is also a feature of other areas of domestic law concerning the disclosure of information. In *Ashdown,* however, the Court of Appeal conceded only that the significance of the subject-matter of the newspaper's disclosure justified 'making limited quotation' from the minute. This grudging approach does not do justice to the crucial significance of this factor in the Strasbourg jurisprudence.

Thus, as a further principle, it can be suggested that in assessing 'fairness' under section 30, courts should apply a strong presumption in favour of a defendant where publication raises issues of legitimate public concern. Of course, the scope of 'public speech' is not clearly defined. However, guidance can be derived from case law, both domestic and at Strasbourg. The information contained in Paddy Ashdown's minute would clearly fall within any definition of such protected 'public speech'. However, disclosure should not only be favoured in high political matters, but also in other matters of legitimate public interest.

The nature of the claimant's work

The second significant aspect of the case to which the Court of Appeal failed to pay sufficient, or indeed any, attention was the nature of the claimant's work. The structure of Article 10 required the Court of Appeal to consider, first, whether the *Sunday Telegraph's* disclosure fell within the scope of Article 10(1). It was then required to decide whether it was 'necessary in a democratic society' for this right to be outweighed by the need to protect the claimant's copyright interest. In taking this decision, the Court of Appeal ought to have weighed up the relative significance of the newspaper's right to freedom of expression and of the claimant's right under copyright law. Such an exercise is, however, only possible where an appropriate value, or weight, is attributed to the copyright interest in question. Not all copyright interests have equal value. For example, entrepreneurial or related rights are not as well protected by copyright law as 'original' works. Within the category of works requiring originality, there is also an established hierarchy. Greater protection is granted to works invested with a higher degree of labour and skill and relatively simple works receive a 'thinner' form of protection. The more convincingly copyright protection can be justified in relation to a particular work, the stronger the powers granted to the copyright owner.

However, in the past, in considering the fair dealing defence, courts have been reluctant to identify different qualities of copyright protection. Copyright interests have tended to be regarded as property rights with a settled, and universally applicable value. Courts have frequently questioned the value of the *defendant's* claim, but have tended not explicitly to evaluate the significance of the competing claim of the claimant. The Court of Appeal in *Ashdown* adopted this traditional approach. Even before October 2, 2000, this omission was rather peculiar. However, under the Human Rights Act, it is quite improper. In *Ashdown* itself, it could be strongly argued that the nature of the claimant's property interest ought to have favoured a finding of 'fair dealing'. The minute did not represent the culminating expression of extensive 'labour and skill'. It was simply a factual record of a meeting attended by the claimant. Furthermore, the claimant was present at this meeting in his capacity as the leader of a national political party. He would, undoubtedly, have regarded himself as being engaged in public service at the time of the meeting. As such, his claim to be entitled to use copyright law to protect the fruits of this opportunity to secure personal financial advantage does not seem a strong one. As a further principle, then it can be suggested that, in assessing fairness under section 30, courts should pay regard to the nature of the claimant's work. The more strongly that copyright protection is justified in the case of a work, the less likely are dealings with that work to be 'fair'.

The Court of Appeal in *Ashdown* did not give effect to the right to freedom of expression in the way suggested by Jonathan Griffiths. Instead, the court used the public interest defence as the vehicle for reconciling copyright with the right to freedom of expression. This defence is considered below at 3.4.3.

3.4.2 INCIDENTAL INCLUSION

Section 31(1) of the CDPA states that the incidental inclusion of a copyright work in an artistic work, sound recording, film, or broadcast will not constitute an infringement. Further, copyright is not infringed by issuing to the public copies, or playing, showing, or communicating to the public, anything whose making was not an infringement because it was an incidental inclusion.[63]

There is little guidance regarding what is meant by 'incidental', except for s. 31(3) of the CDPA, which states that it does not encompass *deliberate* inclusion of either a musical work, words spoken or sung with music, or so much of a sound recording or broadcast as includes a musical work or such words. Further light was shed on the meaning of 'incidental' in the following decision.

Football Association Premier League Ltd v Panini UK Ltd [2004] FSR 1

The defendant (Panini) distributed for sale within the UK collectible stickers of famous football players, together with an album into which the stickers could be placed. The stickers and album in dispute was 'Panini's Football 2003 Sticker Collection'. Each sticker in the collection depicted a photographic image of a player typically in their club 'strip', but occasionally in their international 'strip', and in total 396 football players were included. On the footballer's strip the individual club badge and the Premier League emblem were depicted. The defendant's album collection was marketed as unofficial. The 'official' collection was marketed by a company, Topps Europe Ltd, which had been licensed by the first claimant (Football Association Premier League Ltd), to use and reproduce official team crests and logos in the production of stickers and albums. The first claimant, together with Topps and fourteen of the twenty clubs that are members of the Premier League, brought proceedings against Panini for infringement of copyright in the club badges and emblems (as artistic works). Panini argued that its reproduction of the claimant's copyright works in its stickers and albums was an incidental inclusion within s. 31, CDPA. This defence was rejected at first instance and also on appeal.

---

[63] CDPA, s. 31(2).

Chadwick LJ (Brooke LJ in agreement):

24. ...It is plain that the decision to leave the word 'incidental' undefined was intentional. As the minister responsible for the progress of the Bill (Lord Beaverbrook) put it (Hansard, December 8, 1987, p. 123 lhc): 'What is incidental will depend on all the circumstances of each case and it would be impossible to provide a satisfactory definition for all circumstances.' It is plain, also, that 'incidental' was not intended to mean 'unintentional'. That is clear, not only from the debate in the House of Lords but also from the explanation which was given to the House of Commons (Hansard, May 19, 1988, p. 218) in respect of the provision which has become s. 31(3) of the 1988 Act. But it is unnecessary to have resort to proceedings in Parliament in order to reach that conclusion. It is obvious, when subss. (1) and (3) of s. 31 of the Act are read together, that 'incidental', in the context of subs. (1), is not confined to unintentional, or non-deliberate, inclusion. If it were, subs. (3)—which deals with the particular case of incidental, or background, music in (say) a film or broadcast—would be unnecessary. There is, in my view, nothing else in the material which we were shown which throws light upon what Parliament meant by the word 'incidental'; and, for my part, I doubt whether there was any proper basis upon which that material could have been put before the judge. Be that as it may, we may, perhaps, take some comfort from the evident intention of the promoter of the Bill that 'What is incidental will depend on all the circumstances of each case...'; and his recognition that 'it would be impossible to provide a satisfactory definition for all circumstances'. The relevant question, as the judge pointed out, is whether, in the circumstances of this case, the inclusion on the stickers and in the album of the FAPL emblem and the individual club badges is or is not incidental.

...

26. I would accept that, in principle, there is no necessary dichotomy between 'integral' and 'incidental'. Where an artistic work in which copyright subsists appears in a photograph because it is part of the setting in which the photographer finds his subject it can properly be said to be an integral part of the photograph: if it is part of the setting in which the photographer finds his subject, it will, necessarily, appear in the photograph unless edited out. In that sense the work in relation to which copyright is said to be infringed (work 'A') is integral to the photograph (work 'B') which is said to constitute the infringement. But that does not lead to the conclusion that the inclusion of work 'A' in work 'B' is, or is not, 'incidental' for the purposes of s. 31(1) of the Act. That, as it seems to me, turns on the question: why—having regard to the circumstances in which work 'B' was created—has work 'A' been included in work 'B'? And, in addressing that question, I can see no reason why, if the circumstances so require, consideration should not be given as well to the commercial reason why work 'A' has been included in work 'B' as to any aesthetic reason. In particular, in a case (such as the present) where work 'B' is created, primarily if not exclusively, to serve a commercial purpose, it seems to me wholly artificial to test the 'incidentality' of the inclusion of work 'A' by reference (or primarily by reference) to artistic considerations—if, by that is meant aesthetic considerations. It is, I think, pertinent to keep in mind that, for the purposes of the 1988 Act, 'artistic works' are not confined to works of artistic quality—s. 4(1)(a) of the Act.

27. If, as I would hold, the relevant question, for the purposes of testing 'incidentality' in the context of s. 31(1) of the 1988 Act, is why has work 'A' been included in work 'B', the answer, in the present case, is indeed (as the judge thought) self-evident. The objective, when creating the image of the player as it appears on the sticker or in the album, was to produce something which would be attractive to a collector. That conclusion does not depend on any inquiry into the subjective intent of the individual employee who created the image—or (as I have said) of the photographer who took the photograph from which that image was derived. It depends on an objective assessment of the circumstances in which the image was created.

It is not, I think, a matter about which there can be any doubt. Nor can there be any doubt that it was of importance, in order to achieve that objective, that the player should appear in the appropriate club strip; and that the club strip be authentic. An image of a player in strip which an informed collector would recognise as not authentic would not achieve that objective. But if the strip were to be authentic it must include the club badge and (where appropriate) the FAPL emblem. That, as it seems to me, is what the judge had in mind when he described the inclusion of the badge as 'an integral part of the artistic work comprised of the photograph of the professional footballer in his present-day kit'. The authenticity of the image of the player as it appears on the sticker or in the album (work 'B') depends on the inclusion in work 'B' of the individual badge and the FAPL emblem (work 'A') in which copyright subsists. It is impossible to say that the inclusion of the individual badge and the FAPL emblem is 'incidental'. The inclusion of the individual badge and the FAPL emblem is essential to the object for which the image of the player as it appears on the sticker or in the album was created.

Is the approach to determining whether inclusion of a copyright work is 'incidental' an objective or subjective one? Is it safe to conclude that where the inclusion has a commercial purpose of some kind it can never be incidental? In what circumstances can you envisage the requirement of 'incidental' being satisfied, particularly where the inclusion is intentional or deliberate?

FURTHER READING

K. Garnett, 'Incidental inclusion under section 31' [2003] EIPR 579.

3.4.3 PUBLIC INTEREST DEFENCE

The public interest defence was originally developed in the context of the law of confidence,[64] but later appeared in copyright cases, such as *Beloff v Pressdram*[65] where Ungoed-Thomas J accepted that public interest could override copyright, although this was not the case on the facts. Earlier in this chapter, the public policy exclusion to copyright protection was briefly discussed. In reading this next section, try to identify how this exclusion differs from the public interest defence.

Section 171(3) of the CDPA arguably preserves the public interest defence since it states, 'Nothing in this Part affects any rule of law preventing or restricting the enforcement of copyright, on grounds of public interest or otherwise.' However, in *Hyde Park Residence v Yelland* the Court of Appeal held that this did not reflect a *defence* of public interest, but rather the court's inherent jurisdiction to refuse to enforce copyright in work.

Hyde Park Residence v Yelland [2001] Ch 143

The facts were discussed above at p. 150.

Aldous LJ (Stuart-Smith LJ in agreement):

Public interest

...

43. Mr Bloch's submission that no public interest defence exists starts with an analysis of the 1988 Act. As he correctly pointed out, copyright is an intellectual property right provided

---

[64] See 8.5.2.   [65] [1973] FSR 33, 57.

for by the 1988 Act. That Act contains detailed provisions in the 51 sections in Chapter III of Part I of the types of acts that are permitted to be carried out by persons without the copyright owner's consent. They range from fair dealing to use for education, by libraries and for public administration. They are, as he submitted, provisions directed towards achieving a proper balance between the protection of copyright and the wider public interest. They would therefore appear to set out in detail the extent to which the public interest overrides copyright. I agree. The 1988 Act does not give a court general power to enable an infringer to use another's property, namely his copyright in the public interest. Thus a defence of public interest outside those set out in Chapter III of Part I of the 1988 Act, if such exists, must arise by some other route.

44. The courts have an inherent jurisdiction to refuse to allow their process to be used in certain circumstances. It has long been the law that the courts will not give effect to contracts which are, for example, illegal, immoral or prejudicial to family life because they offend against the policy of the law. In my view that inherent jurisdiction can be exercised in the case of an action in which copyright is sought to be enforced, as is made clear by section 171(3) of the 1988 Act: 'Nothing in this Part affects any rule of law preventing or restricting the enforcement of copyright, on grounds of public interest or otherwise.'

...

54. There are other cases where the courts have refused to grant interlocutory injunctions to restrain a breach of confidence upon the basis of public interest. The principle is, as stated by Lord Denning MR in *Woodward v Hutchins* [1977] 1 WLR 760, 764: 'In these cases of confidential information it is a question of balancing the public interest in maintaining the confidence against the public interest in knowing the truth.'

55. That principle has particular relevance to an action for breach of confidence. Such an action is brought to enforce an obligation of confidence in respect of information of a confidential nature imparted in circumstances where the courts import an obligation of confidence: see *Coco v A N Clark (Engineers) Ltd* [1969] RPC 41. The court can therefore weigh the public interest in knowing the truth against the public interest in maintaining the confidence in the light of the facts of each case. That cannot be the test to be applied where copyright infringement has taken place for three reasons. First, copyright is a property right which is given by the 1988 Act. Chapter III of Part I of the Act provides for exceptions in the public interest. It would therefore be wrong for a court which had rejected a defence of, for example, fair dealing, because there was not a sufficient acknowledgement, to uphold a defence because publication was in the public interest. That would result in a disregard of an important requirement set out in the Act. Second, copyright is concerned with protection of the form of works in which copyright can subsist and not with protection of information. That can be illustrated with the facts of the present case. Nobody has suggested nor could it be suggested that the information recorded on the driveway stills could be the subject of copyright or that use of that information would be an infringement of the copyright which subsists in the film. It follows that the weighing operation is not apt when the information can be published even though the action for infringement of copyright succeeds. Third, the 1988 Act gives effect to the United Kingdom's obligations pursuant to the Conventions of the International Union for the Protection of Literary and Artistic Works (Berne, 9 September 1886) and the International Convention further revising the Berne Convention (Paris, 24 July 1971–31 January 1972) (Cmnd 5002) and certain EC Council Directives. Those Conventions came into being to provide for uniform and effective protection of copyright amongst the signatories. Article 10 of the Berne Convention allows quotations from copyright works provided that the quotation is compatible with fair practice. Section 30 of the 1988 Act is thought to be within the terms of that article. However there is no general power for courts of the signatories to such Conventions to refuse to enforce copyright if it is thought to be in the public

interest of that state that it should not be enforced. Thus a general defence of public interest would appear to be contrary to this country's international obligations.

...

64. I have pointed out earlier in this judgment that the basis of the defence of public interest in a breach of confidence action cannot be the same as the basis of such defence to an action for infringement of copyright. In an action for breach of confidence the foundation of the action can fall away if that is required in the public interest, but that can never happen in a copyright action. The jurisdiction to refuse to enforce copyright, which I believe has been recognised, comes from the court's inherent jurisdiction. It is limited to cases where enforcement of the copyright would offend against the policy of the law. The *Lion Laboratories* case [1985] QB 526 was such a case. Lion Laboratories sought to obtain an interlocutory injunction to restrain publication of documents which showed that they had suppressed information leading to or which might lead to the wrongful conviction of motorists. The action was based upon documents which in the circumstances reeked of turpitude. As Lord Mansfield CJ said in *Holman v Johnson* (1775) 1 Cowp 341, 343: 'No court will lend its aid to a man who founds his cause of action upon an immoral or an illegal act.'

65. To rely upon copyright to suppress documents which could exonerate motorists convicted of drink driving or which might lead to their acquittal is, in my view, to found a cause of action upon an immoral act.

66. The circumstances where it is against the policy of the law to use the court's procedure to enforce copyright are, I suspect, not capable of definition. However it must be remembered that copyright is assignable and therefore the circumstances must derive from the work in question, not ownership of the copyright. In my view a court would be entitled to refuse to enforce copyright if the work is: (i) immoral, scandalous or contrary to family life; (ii) injurious to public life, public health and safety or the administration of justice; (iii) incites or encourages others to act in a way referred to in (ii).

Mance LJ:

83. Whilst account must be taken of the different nature of the right involved in copyright, I prefer to state no more in this case than that the circumstances in which the public interest may override copyright are probably not capable of precise categorisation or definition. I would not as at present advised agree with Aldous LJ's suggestion that 'the circumstances must derive from the work in question, not ownership of the copyright'. No doubt this would normally be so. But the possibility of assignment does not appear to me to lead to a conclusion that it must always be so. Of course, if copyright has been assigned, e.g. to a purchaser having no notice of circumstances which might have affected its enforceability in the hands of the assignor, that would be a very relevant circumstance when considering whether the public interest overrode copyright. But, aside from situations of assignment, it seems to me possible to conceive of situations where a copyright document itself appeared entirely innocuous, but its publication—as a matter of fair dealing or, in circumstances outside the scope of section 30, in the public interest—was justified by its significance in the context of other facts. It might conceivably represent the relevant, though by itself apparently meaningless, piece needed to complete a whole jigsaw.

Do you find Aldous LJ's reasons for rejecting a public interest defence persuasive? Certainly, they have been heavily criticized by some commentators, such as Robert Burrell.[66] What difference, if any, is there between a defence of public interest and, as the court in *Yelland* found,

66 See R. Burrell, 'Defending the public interest' [2000] EIPR 394.

its inherent jurisdiction to refuse to enforce copyright? With respect to the circumstances in which a court can refuse to enforce copyright, do you agree with the approach of Aldous LJ or that of Mance LJ?

Subsequent to *Yelland* the Human Rights Act 1998 (UK) came into effect and the issue of how courts should give effect to Article 10 of the ECHR, the right to freedom of expression arose. At first instance in *Ashdown v Telegraph Group Ltd*[67] Sir Andrew Morritt V-C concluded:

Article 10 cannot be relied on to create defences to the alleged infringement over and above those for which the 1988 Act provides. The balance between the rights of the owner of the copyright and those of the public has been struck by the legislative organ of the democratic state itself in the legislation it has enacted. There is no room for any further defences outside the code which establishes the particular species of intellectual property in question.

The Court of Appeal took a different approach to this issue.

Ashdown v Telegraph Group Ltd [2002] Ch 149

The facts were described above at p. 155.

Lord Phillips MR (delivering the judgment of the Court):

39. We have already observed that, in most circumstances, the principle of freedom of expression will be sufficiently protected if there is a right to publish information and ideas set out in another's literary work, without copying the very words which that person has employed to convey the information or express the ideas. In such circumstances it will normally be necessary in a democratic society that the author of the work should have his property in his own creation protected. Strasbourg jurisprudence demonstrates, however, that circumstances can arise in which freedom of expression will only be fully effective if an individual is permitted to reproduce the very words spoken by another.

. . .

43. *Fressoz and Roire* was not a copyright case, but it illustrates a general principle. Freedom of expression protects the right both to publish information and to receive it. There will be occasions when it is in the public interest not merely that information should be published, but that the public should be told the very words used by a person, notwithstanding that the author enjoys copyright in them. On occasions, indeed, it is the form and not the content of a document which is of interest.

44. Where the subject matter of the information is a current event, section 30(2) of the 1988 Act may permit publication of the words used. But it is possible to conceive of information of the greatest public interest relating not to a current event, but to a document produced in the past. We are not aware of any provision of the 1988 Act which would permit publication in such circumstances, unless the mere fact of publication, and any controversy created by the disclosure, is sufficient to make them 'current events'. This will often be a 'bootstraps' argument of little merit, but on other occasions (such as disclosure by the Public Record Office under the 30-year rule) it may have a more solid basis.

45. For these reasons, we have reached the conclusion that rare circumstances can arise where the right of freedom of expression will come into conflict with the protection afforded

---

[67] [2001] Ch 658, 696.

by the 1988 Act, notwithstanding the express exceptions to be found in the Act. In these circumstances, we consider that the court is bound, in so far as it is able, to apply the Act in a manner that accommodates the right of freedom of expression. This will make it necessary for the court to look closely at the facts of individual cases (as indeed it must whenever a 'fair dealing' defence is raised). We do not foresee this leading to a flood of litigation.

46. The first way in which it may be possible to do this is by declining the discretionary relief of an injunction. Usually, so it seems to us, such a step will be likely to be sufficient. If a newspaper considers it necessary to copy the exact words created by another, we can see no reason in principle why the newspaper should not indemnify the author for any loss caused to him, or alternatively account to him for any profit made as a result of copying his work. Freedom of expression should not normally carry with it the right to make free use of another's work.

Public interest

47. In the rare case where it is in the public interest that the words in respect of which another has copyright should be published without any sanction, we have been concerned to consider why this should not be permitted under the 'public interest' exception, the possibility of which is recognised by section 171(3). Sir Andrew Morritt V-C considered that he was precluded from so holding by the decision of this court in *Hyde Park Residence Ltd v Yelland* [2001] Ch 143.

[Referring to *Yelland*:]

52. Stuart-Smith LJ agreed that the appeal should be allowed for the reasons given by Aldous LJ. It does not seem to us that those reasons depended on the precise scope of the public interest exception identified by Aldous LJ...

[Referring to *Lion Laboratories v Evans* [1985] QB 526:]

58. In the light of these judgments, we do not consider that Aldous LJ was justified in circumscribing the public interest defence to breach of copyright as tightly as he did. We prefer the conclusion of Mance LJ that the circumstances in which public interest may override copyright are not capable of precise categorisation or definition. Now that the Human Rights Act 1998 is in force, there is the clearest public interest in giving effect to the right of freedom of expression in those rare cases where this right trumps the rights conferred by the 1988 Act. In such circumstances, we consider that section 171(3) of the Act permits the defence of public interest to be raised.

59. We do not consider that this conclusion will lead to a flood of cases where freedom of expression is invoked as a defence to a claim for breach of copyright. It will be very rare for the public interest to justify the copying of the form of a work to which copyright attaches. We would add that the implications of the Human Rights Act 1998 must always be considered where the discretionary relief of an injunction is sought, and this is true in the field of copyright quite apart from the ambit of the public interest defence under section 171(3).

There are two important strands to the Court of Appeal's reasoning. The first is that rare circumstances may arise in which it is necessary to use the precise form of the copyright work, but the existing exceptions in the CDPA cannot be relied upon. In these circumstances, the court will have to apply the CDPA in a manner that accommodates the right to freedom of expression. This may occur by refusing discretionary relief (such as an injunction). Alternatively, and this constitutes the second strand of the court's reasoning, it may be appropriate to rely upon the public interest defence. Here, the court held that Aldous LJ's definition of public interest was not the *ratio decidendi* of *Yelland* and preferred to adopt the approach of Mance LJ, whereby instances of public interest are not capable of precise categorization or definition. The court also reverted to the language of public interest *defence*. It held that the defence of public interest may be invoked in those rare circumstances where the right to freedom of expression outweighs the property rights of a copyright owner.

On the facts, the Court of Appeal held that substantial parts of the minute had been reproduced 'most likely to add flavour to the article and thus to appeal to the readership of the newspaper'[68] and in furtherance of the commercial interests of the defendant. As such, the Article 10 interests of the defendant did not outweigh the copyright interests of the claimant.

Jonathan Griffiths has remarked that the Court of Appeal in *Ashdown* crafted 'an extremely elegant solution to the challenge presented by the Human Rights Act'.[69] But, as mentioned above, in his view it does not go far enough and the court, when it comes to applying the fair dealing exceptions, should take into account additional factors. Further, Robert Burrell argues that although *Ashdown* 'represents a welcome relaxation of the approach taken in *Yelland*' the judgment 'is not an unqualified boost for users' because the defence will apply only in 'rare' circumstances.[70]

> **FURTHER READING**
>
> P. Johnson, 'The public interest: Is it still a defence to copyright infringement?' (2005) Ent LR 1.

---

[68] [2002] Ch 149, para. 82.
[69] J. Griffiths, 'Copyright law after Ashdown: Time to deal fairly with the public' [2002] IPQ 240, 247.
[70] R. Burrell, 'Reining in copyright law: Is fair use the answer?' [2001] IPQ 361, 381.

PASSING OFF

4.1 INTRODUCTION

Trade marks may be either registered or unregistered. The following chapter will consider the law of registered trade marks. The subject of this chapter is the protection which the law affords to unregistered trade marks through the tort of passing off. According to Lord Oliver in the leading case on passing off, 'Jif Lemon':[1] 'The law of passing off can be summarised in one short general proposition—no man may pass off his goods as those of another.'

4.1.1 THE DEFINITION OF PASSING OFF

4.1.1.1 The classic trinity

In 'Jif Lemon', Lord Oliver then set out the three basic elements which are necessary to bring an action in passing off. These have come to be known as the classic trinity.

> **Lord Oliver, at p. 499:**
>
> First, [the claimant] must establish a goodwill or reputation attached to the goods or services which he supplies in the mind of the purchasing public by association with the identifying 'get-up' (whether it consists simply of a brand name or a trade description, or the individual features of labelling or packaging) under which his particular goods or services as offered to the public, such that the get-up is recognised by the public as distinctive specifically of the plaintiff's goods or services. Secondly, he must demonstrate a misrepresentation by the defendant to the public (whether or not intentional) leading or likely to lead the public to believe that goods or services offered by him are the goods or services of the plaintiff.
>
> ...
>
> Thirdly, he must demonstrate that he suffers or, in a *quia timet* action that he is likely to suffer, damage by reason of the erroneous belief engendered by the defendant's misrepresentation that the source of the defendant's goods or services is the same as the source of those offered by the plaintiff.

---

[1] *Reckitt & Coleman Products Ltd v Borden Inc (No 3)* [1990] 1 WLR 491, 499.

The 'classic trinity' identified in 'Jif Lemon' as necessary for a passing off action are:

1. goodwill
2. reputation
3. damage or in a *quia timet* action, the likelihood of damage.

4.1.1.2 The 'Advocaat' definition

Earlier in the 'Advocaat' case,[2] Lord Diplock had set out the general background to the tort of passing off. He also identified five elements which he held must be present in order to bring a passing off action:

> **Lord Diplock, at p. 740–2:**
>
> The action for what has become known as 'passing off' arose in the nineteenth century out of the use in connection with his own goods by one trader of the trade name or trade mark of a rival trader so as to induce in potential purchasers the belief that his goods were those of the rival trader. Although the cases up to the end of the century had been confined to the deceptive use of trade names, marks, letters or other indicia, the principle had been stated by Lord Langdale MR as early as 1842 as being: 'A man is not to sell his own goods under the pretence that they are the goods of another man'; *Perry v Truefitt*, 6 Beav 66. At the close of the century in *Reddaway v Banham* [1896] AC 199, it was said by Lord Herschell that what was protected by an action for passing off was not the proprietary right of the trader in the mark, name or get-up improperly used. Thus the door was opened to passing off actions in which the misrepresentation took some other form than the deceptive use of trade names, marks, letters or other indicia; but as none of their Lordships committed themselves to identifying the legal nature of the right that was protected by a passing off action it remained an action sui generis which lay for damage sustained or threatened in consequence of a misrepresentation of a particular kind.
>
> *Reddaway v Banham*, like all previous passing off cases, was one in which Banham had passed off his goods as those of Reddaway, and the damage resulting from the misrepresentation took the form of the diversion of potential customers from Reddaway to Banham. Although it was a landmark case in deciding that the use by a trader of a term which accurately described the composition of his own goods might nevertheless amount to the tort of passing off if that term were understood in the market in which the goods were sold to denote the goods of a rival trader, *Reddaway v Banham* did not extend the nature of the particular kind of misrepresentation which gives rise to a right of action in passing off beyond what I have called the classic form of misrepresenting one's own goods as the goods of someone else nor did it provide any rational basis for an extension.
>
> This was left to be provided by Lord Parker in *Spalding v Gamage* (1915) 32 RPC 273. In a speech which received the approval of the other members of this House, he identified the right the invasion of which is the subject of passing off actions as being the 'property in the business or goodwill likely to be injured by the misrepresentation'.
>
> . . .
>
> The goodwill of a manufacturer's business may well be injured by some-one else who sells goods which are correctly described as being made by that manufacturer but being of an inferior class or quality are misrepresented as goods of his manufacture of a superior

---

[2] *Erven Warnink BV v J Townend & Sons (Hull) Ltd* [1979] AC 731.

class or quality. This type of misrepresentation was held in *Spalding v Gamage* to be actionable and the extension to the nature of the misrepresentation which gives rise to a right of action in passing off which this involved was regarded by Lord Parker as a natural corollary of recognising that what the law protects by a passing off action is a trader's property in his business or goodwill.

The significance of this decision in the law of passing off lies in its recognition that misrepresenting one's own goods as the goods of someone else was not a separate genus of actionable wrong but a particular species of wrong included in a wider genus of which a premonitory hint had been given by Lord Herschell in *Reddaway v Banham* when, in speaking of the deceptive use of a descriptive term, he said: 'I am unable to see why a man should be allowed in this way more than any other to deceive purchasers into the belief that they are getting what they are not, and thus to filch the business of a rival.'

...

Spalding v Gamage led the way to recognition by judges of other species of the same genus, as where although the plaintiff and the defendant were not competing traders in the same line of business, a false suggestion by the defendant that their businesses were connected with one another would damage the reputation and thus the goodwill of the plaintiff's business.

...

My Lords, *Spalding v Gamage* and the later cases make it possible to identify five characteristics which must be present in order to create a valid cause of action for passing off: (1) a misrepresentation (2) made by a trader in the course of trade, (3) to prospective customers of his or ultimate consumers of goods or services supplied by him, (4) which is calculated to injure the business or goodwill of another trader (in the sense that this is a reasonably foreseeable consequence) and (5) which causes actual damage to a business or goodwill of the trader by whom the action is brought or (in a *quia timet* action) will probably do so.

Also in 'Advocaat', Lord Fraser identified five criteria which should be present for a successful passing off action. Lord Fraser's criteria are generally complementary to those of Lord Diplock, but his do emphasize the importance of goodwill subsisting in England, an issue which will be considered later in this chapter.

Lord Fraser, at p. 755:

It is essential for the plaintiff in a passing off action to show at least the following facts: (1) that his business consists of, or includes, selling in England a class of goods to which the particular trade name applies; (2) that the class of goods is clearly defined, and that in the minds of the public, or a section of the public, in England, the trade name distinguishes that class from other similar goods; (3) that because of the reputation of the goods, there is goodwill attached to the name; (4) that he, the plaintiff, as a member of the class of those who sell the goods, is the owner of goodwill in England which is of substantial value; (5) that he has suffered, or is really likely to suffer, substantial damage to his property in the goodwill by reason of the defendants selling goods which are falsely described by the trade name to which the goodwill is attached. Provided these conditions are satisfied, as they are in the present case, I consider that the plaintiff is entitled to protect himself by a passing off action.

The definitions set out by Lord Oliver in 'Jif Lemon' and Lord Diplock in 'Advocaat' are not incompatible. In many cases of passing off, the courts have preferred to adhere to Lord Oliver's 'classic trinity'. What Lord Diplock suggests in 'Advocaat' is that the types of misrepresentation which might give rise to a passing off action are constantly evolving. In some instances, the particular circumstances of a misrepresentation may make the application of Lord Diplock's five elements more appropriate. As Lord Diplock points out, the classic misrepresentation that 'A man is not to sell his own goods under the pretence that they are the goods of another man'[3] has now expanded to encompass the situation where the defendant may sell inferior goods as if they were superior[4], he may suggest a business connection with the claimant where none exists[5], and, as was the case in 'Advocaat' itself, he may claim that his goods are the goods of a limited class of traders, to which the defendant does not belong. This latter misrepresentation characterizes what has come to be known as the extended form of passing off—and it is in such cases that Lord Diplock's formulation (together with that of Lord Fraser) might be most usefully applied.[6]

4.1.2 THE RELATIONSHIP BETWEEN PASSING OFF AND UNFAIR COMPETITION

In 'Advocaat', Lord Diplock expressed his anxiety that an action for passing off might, but should not be used to, hamper legitimate competition. He took the view, for example, that it should not be available in any instance where one trader makes untrue assertions about another's goods.

> **Lord Diplock, at p. 742:**
>
> In seeking to formulate general propositions of English law, however, one must be particularly careful to beware of the logical fallacy of the undistributed middle. It does not follow that because all passing off actions can be shown to present these characteristics, all factual situations which present these characteristics give rise to a cause of action for passing off. True it is that their presence indicates what a moral code would censure as dishonest trading, based as it is upon deception of customers and consumers of a trader's wares but in an economic system which has relied on competition to keep down prices and to improve products there may be practical reasons why it should have been the policy of the common law not to run the risk of hampering competition by providing civil remedies to every one competing in the market who has suffered damage to his business or goodwill in consequence of inaccurate statements of whatever kind that may be made by rival traders about their own wares. The market in which the action for passing off originated was no place for the mealy mouthed; advertisements are not on affidavit; exaggerated claims by a trader about the quality of his wares, assertions that they are better than those of his rivals, even though he knows this to be untrue, have been permitted by the common law as venial 'puffing' which gives no cause of action to a competitor even though he can show he has suffered actual damage in his business as a result.

In fact, there are other actions which might be invoked in instances of dishonest trading. It is possible to bring actions for defamation and trade libel, both of which, unlike passing off, require that the relevant misrepresentation be deliberate or reckless, and actions under the Trade Descriptions Act 1967.

---

[3] *Perry v Truefitt* 6 Beav 66 as per Lord Langdale MR.
[4] *Spalding & Bros v AW Gamage* (1915) 84 LJ Ch 449.
[5] *Harrods Ltd v R Harrod Ltd* (1924) RPC 74.   [6] See below at 4.2.1.7.

More recently, in *Arsenal FC v Reed*,[7] Aldous LJ opined that the tort of passing off is 'perhaps best referred to as unfair competition'. It is still the case, however, despite Aldous LJ's comment, that there is no separate tort of unfair competition in the UK. Passing off does not, unlike the law in continental Europe for example, protect a trader generally against unfair conduct by a competitor. Instead, at the heart of the tort of passing off is a misrepresentation or a deception. Often, but not always, this misrepresentation or deception will be addressed to the ultimate consumer.[8] Robertson and Horton describe the relationship in the UK between passing off and unfair competition.

A. Robertson and A. Horton, 'Does the United Kingdom or the European Community need an unfair competition law' [1995] EIPR 568–9

English law does not have a tort of unfair competition. Nor has such a tort been imposed on the United Kingdom by the European Community. English law remains sceptical about the value of a law against unfair competition, despite the United Kingdom's international obligations. As Gerald Dworkin has said, the very term 'unfair competition' is paradoxical:

> law and business morality overlap and the courts must apply their own standards to determine which unethical and unfair activities constitute unlawful competition and which activities, though unethical (and in that non-legal sense unfair), must remain legally permissible. There are those who would argue that such tasks should not be undertaken lightly by the courts. English law has traditionally refused to deal in concepts such as fairness or good faith in business, leaving the market-place to determine its own morality without the force of legal sanction.

. . .

UK Law

It is accepted that there is at present no general right to restrain unfair competition. An attempt to persuade the Privy Council to develop such a concept in Pub Squash was met with judicial indifference. English law is difficult to summarise succinctly, as it depends on the interaction of a number of torts, each of which has been developed in largely piecemeal fashion. As a broad generalisation, it could be said that English law prevents unfair competition in three principal ways.

(1) *Passing off.* A may be restrained from misappropriating B's reputation in its goods by misleading B's customers, for example, by suggesting a connection or association with B's business. This is done by B bringing an action for passing off against A. The essence of this action is customer confusion. Unless B can show that its customers have been or are likely to be misled into confusing A's for B's goods or into making a false connection or association with B's business, it will not succeed.

(2) *Inducing breach of contract and unlawful interference with contractual relations.* A may be restrained from acquiring B's customers through unlawful means. This applies where A induces B's customers to break their contracts with B or otherwise unlawfully interferes with B's contractual relations.

(3) *Defamation and injurious falsehood.* A may be restrained from acquiring B's customers by telling lies to B's customers about B or B's goods. In the case of lies about B, there

---

[7] [2003] 1 All ER 137.
[8] *Hodgkinson Corby Ltd v Wards Mobility Services Ltd* [1995] FSR 169.

> is an action for defamation. In the case of lies about B's goods, there are actions for slander of goods and injurious falsehood.
>
> Seen in this way, the law emphasises the role of the customer. It is unfair competition to acquire customers by causing them to transfer their custom by (1) confusing them as to with whom they are doing business; (2) inducing them to break existing contracts with competitors, or (3) lying to them about competitors. Beyond these limits, attempts to attract customers from other competitors are considered legal.
>
> Indeed these categories may be further rationalised, and it may be seen that there are two underlying assumptions at work here. First, lying is a means of confusing customers as to reality. Hence, the essence of the law is that customers should not be confused. Secondly, the prohibition against inducing breach of contract should be seen as part of English law's regard for the 'sanctity' of contract.
>
> The focus of English law relevant to unfair competition (as distinct from contract law) is to prevent customers being confused. Provided customers have available correct information about what and with whom they are dealing, and that bargains once struck are adhered to, the law is prepared to leave the proper functioning of the market to the free play of market forces. A similar attitude is taken by US federal and state laws.
>
> In continental Europe, while civil law jurisdictions also prevent customer confusion, unfair competition law starts from the basis that its rationale is to enforce the 'honest usages' of the market-place. Beier summarises this as meaning that a trader was granted 'the right to restrain his competitors from causing him injury by unfair conduct'. Thus the focus is not just on customer confusion, but on what is fair or ethical commercial conduct. English law has eschewed this approach, and continues to focus on customer confusion...

Robertson and Horton emphasize that in the United Kingdom, the law against unfair competition has traditionally centred on the role of the consumer. But this does not necessarily mean that ultimately the law of passing off is for the benefit of the consumer. Rather, in the case of passing off, it is possible to argue that the interest protected is the trader's interest in not losing custom to a competitor as the result of customer confusion, where that confusion is brought about by that competitor's misrepresentation. Consumer interests in the UK are more directly protected by the recently implemented Unfair Commercial Practices Directive (2005/29/EC), the Trade Descriptions Act, and the Control of Misleading Advertising Regulations. On the other hand, unlike for example in France, there is no general protection against the misappropriation of one trader's goodwill by another even without customer confusion. It is perhaps worth asking why the UK has not traditionally been sympathetic to laws preventing such misappropriation, given the normative appeal of arguments against unjust enrichment. Does the answer lie in the consistent support which UK courts have given to relatively unfettered markets: support which was clearly expressed in the speech of Lord Diplock in 'Advocaat'?

FURTHER READING

H. Carty, *An Analysis of Economic Torts* (Oxford: Oxford University Press, 2001).

J. Davis, 'Unfair competition law in the United Kingdom' in R. M. Hilty and F. Henning-Bodewig (eds.), *Law Against Unfair Competition: Towards a new paradigm in Europe?* (Heidelberg: Springer, 2007), pp. 183–8.

F. Henning-Bodewig, *Unfair Competition Law: European Union and Member States* (The Hague: Kluwer Law, 2006).

4.2 THE ELEMENTS OF PASSING OFF

4.2.1 GOODWILL

4.2.1.1 The definition of goodwill

Traditionally, goodwill has been the property protected by a passing off action. For a definition of goodwill, courts commonly revert to Lord MacNaghten's famous description in *The Commissioners of Inland Revenue v Muller & Co's Margarine.*[9]

> **Lord MacNaghten:**
>
> It is the benefit and advantage of the good name, reputation and connection of a business. It is the attractive force which brings in custom...However widely extended or diffused its influence may be, goodwill is worth nothing unless it has the power of attraction sufficient to bring customers home to the source from which it emanates.

Although, in a passing off action, the misrepresentation may result from the improper use of a trader's trade name or other indicia, the claimant is generally thought to have no property in the trade name or indicia as such. This was the view taken by Millet LJ in *Harrods* in 1996.[10]

> **Millet LJ:**
>
> It is well settled that (unless registered as a trade mark) no one has a monopoly in his brand name or get-up, however familiar these may be. Passing off is a wrongful invasion of a right of property vested in the plaintiff; but the property which is protected by an action for passing off is not the plaintiff's proprietary right in the name or get-up which the defendant has misappropriated but the goodwill and reputation of his business which is likely to be harmed by the defendant's misrepresentation...

In this passage, Millet LJ appears to be using the words 'reputation' and 'goodwill' interchangeably, but the two are not the same. Passing off will protect a trader's goodwill, but it will not necessarily protect a trader's reputation. This was made clear in the *Harrods* case.

Harrods Ltd v Harrodian School Ltd [1996] RPC 697

The claimant owned the Harrods department store. The defendants ran a preparatory school under the name 'The Harrodian School'. The school was on the site of what had previously been 'The Harrodian Club', a sports club run by the claimant but which had closed in 1990. The claimant brought an action for passing off. In the course of the action, it was established that the claimant did not run a school nor did it intend to do so. Furthermore, the word 'Harrodian' had not been used for forty or fifty years in the claimant's dealings with customers, although it had been applied to the claimant's employees and some staff associations during that period. In his judgment, Millet LJ acknowledged

---

[9] [1901] AC 217, 223–4.
[10] *Harrods Ltd v Harrodian School Ltd* [1996] RPC 697, 711.

that the claimant enjoyed 'a long-established reputation and goodwill in the business of a department store, carried on under the name "Harrods"'. He also acknowledged that it offered a 'vast' range of services.

Lord Justice Millett, at p. 702:

The plaintiffs have always been very proud of the name 'Harrods'. They claim that it has come to represent an unsurpassed level of quality in the range of goods and services which they provide. But while their range is of astonishing breadth, it would be a mistake to be dazzled into thinking that the range of the plaintiffs' commercial activities is virtually unlimited, or that they have acquired a reputation for excellence in every field of activity. They are retail suppliers of goods and services of every kind; but that is all. They sell theatre tickets; they do not run a theatre: they supply medical equipment; they do not run a hospital: they act as insurance agents; they do not underwrite policies of insurance: they supply school uniforms; they do not run a school.

[The question then arose whether, given the wide reputation which resided in the name 'Harrods', any use by the defendant of the 'Harrods' name would inevitably trespass on the claimant's goodwill. **Lord Justice Millet** concluded it would not. He noted that it is goodwill, alone, that is protected by a passing off action:]

Lord Justice Millet, at p. 711:

It is this fundamental principle of the law of passing off which leads me to reject the main way in which the plaintiffs have put their case before us. 'Harrodian', they submit, is synonymous with 'Harrods'; the name 'Harrods' is universally recognised as denoting the plaintiffs' business—it has, as counsel put it (borrowing and adapting an expression used by Falconer J in *Lego System A/S v Lego M Lemelstrich Ltd* ('the *Lego* case') [1983] FSR 155 at page 187) an unlimited 'field of recognition'; the defendants were, therefore, unarguably guilty of misrepresenting their business as that of the plaintiffs; given the huge number of persons who are customers or potential customers of the plaintiffs it is a simple matter to infer that an appreciable number of them will be deceived into thinking that 'The Harrodian School' is owned by or otherwise connected in some way with Harrods; and damage may likewise easily be inferred. But in referring to the possibility of a plaintiff having only 'a limited field of recognition', Falconer J was referring to the limited field of commercial activity with which the plaintiff's reputation was associated by the public; he was not referring to the extent to which the plaintiff's reputation in that limited field was familiar to the public. The name 'Harrods' may be universally recognised, but the business with which it is associated in the minds of the public is not all embracing. To be known to everyone is not to be known for everything.

The claimant failed in its action for passing off. Harrods is obviously a widely known name. Do you think Millett LJ was correct to assume that customers or potential customers of the store would assume it was not connected with the school? Or is the name Harrods sufficiently famous that any other business trading under that name would cause customers to make such a connection with the store? This was the conclusion reached by Kerr LJ in a dissenting judgment and it raises the issue of whether goodwill can reside in the value of the name alone and not just the underlying business.[11]

[11] See below at 4.2.2.4.

4.2.1.2 The definition of a trader

In order to bring a passing off action, the claimant must be a 'trader', for it is only a trader who will have ownership of the requisite goodwill.[12] In this context, 'trader' has been given a very wide definition by the courts. Claimants in passing off actions have included a famous diarist (Alan Clark),[13] ballroom dancers,[14] and a racing car driver, Eddie Irvine, whose goodwill resided in his business of endorsing products.[15] Trade associations, such as the Society of Accountants and Auditors, have been held to have the necessary goodwill to bring a passing off action,[16] as have non-profit and charitable organizations such as the Law Society,[17] the British Legion,[18] the Association of Plastic Surgeons,[19] and the British Diabetic Associaton.[20] More recently, the Court of Appeal held that the Countryside Alliance, a non-profit political organization which had never put up a candidate for election could succeed in a passing off action against a former member of the far-right British National Party, who ran for Parliament describing himself on the ballot paper as 'Countryside Alliance'. The Countryside Alliance had significant trading activities designed to generate revenue for campaigning and lobbying. The claimants gave evidence that the reputation of the Alliance would be damaged by association with somebody with perceived racist views.[21] During the course of the action, the question arose as to whether the Alliance, being a non-commercial organization, could be said to have the requisite goodwill. According to Brooke LJ:[22]

> 61. …This line of authority shows that a claimant in a passing off action may be a charitable organisation or a professional institution which does not carry on commercial activity in the ordinary sense of the word, but which has unquestionably in the eyes of the law a valuable property in the sense of its goodwill which it is entitled to protect by bringing a passing off action if the three classic ingredients of a passing off action are present.

4.2.1.3 The location of goodwill

To bring a passing off action goodwill must be situated in the UK. It is worth remembering that having a reputation in the UK is not the same as having goodwill. This principle is clearly demonstrated by the Court of Appeal decision in the 'Budweiser' case.[23] In this case, the American brewers of Budweiser beer bought a passing off action against the defendants who supplied beer under the name 'Budweiser' in the UK. Although it was accepted that the American 'Budweiser' beer was well known in the UK, the claimant supplied its beer only to US army bases. In the

---

[12] See for example, Lord Diplock in 'Advocaat'.
[13] *Clark v Associated Newspapers Ltd* [1998] 1 WLR 1558.
[14] *Henderson v Radio Corpn Pty Ltd* [1969] RPC 218.
[15] *Irvine v Talksport Ltd* [2002] EWHC 367 (Ch).
[16] *Society of Accountants and Auditors v Goodway & London Association of Accountants Ltd* [1907] Ch 489.
[17] *Law Society of England and Wales v Society of Lawyers* [1996] RSR 739.
[18] *British Legion v British Legion Club (Street) Ltd* (1931) 48 RPC 555.
[19] *British Association of Aesthetic Plastic Surgeons v Cambright Ltd* [1987] RPC 549.
[20] *The British Diabetic Association v The Diabetic Society* [1996] FSR 1.
[21] *Burge v Haycock* [2001] EWCA Civ 900, [2002] RPC 28.
[22] Brooke LJ distinguished this case from *Kean v McGivan* [1982] FSR 119, where the claimant also ran a political party, which was held to be not sufficiently known to have the necessary goodwill.
[23] *Anheuser-Busch Inc v Budejovicky Budvar NP* [1984] FSR 413.

Court of Appeal, Oliver LJ held that the claimants did not have the goodwill necessary for a passing off action. He noted that it is not possible to assume 'the existence of the goodwill apart from the market, and that, as it seems to me, is to confuse goodwill, which cannot exist in a vacuum, with mere reputation which may, no doubt, and frequently does, exist without any supporting local business, but which does not by itself constitute a property which the law protects'.[24]

In 'Budweiser', Oliver LJ held that the claimant must have a 'market' in the UK to have the requisite goodwill. The case law is not entirely clear as to the question of what constitutes a 'market'. This lack of clarity is largely due to the decision in *Alain Bernardin et Cie v Pavilion Properties*.[25] In this case, the claimants, who carried on a restaurant business in Paris under the title 'The Crazy Horse Saloon', had for many years advertised their establishment by publicity material distributed to tourist organizations and hotels in the UK. They failed to restrain the defendants from carrying on a restaurant in London under the same name. Pennycuick J held:[26]

> That it seems to me is what one would expect: that the trader cannot acquire goodwill in this country without some sort of user in this country. His user may take many forms and in certain cases very slight activities have been held to suffice. On the other hand, I do not think that the mere sending to this country by a foreign trader of advertisements advertising his establishment abroad could fairly be treated as user in this country...He may acquire a reputation in a wide sense in the sense of returning travellers speaking highly of that establishment, but it seems to me that those matters, although they may represent reputation in some wide sense, fall far short of user in this country and are not sufficient to establish reputation in the sense material for the purpose of a passing off action.

The 'Crazy Horse' decision suggested that for goodwill to subsist, the claimant must not only have customers in the UK but also a place of business. However, the better view is almost certainly that to establish goodwill, it is sufficient for a claimant to have customers in the UK for his goods or services. This was the view taken by Browne-Wilkinson V-C in the 'Hit Factory' decision. In making his judgment in this case, the Vice-Chancellor refused to follow the reasoning in 'Crazy Horse', arguing that it neither accorded with earlier authorities nor reflected modern trading realities.

Pete Waterman v CBS United Kingdom Ltd [1993] EMLR 27

The claimants (PWL) were a successful pop record-producing organization who were known to the public as 'The Hit Factory'. The claimants did not trade under the name 'Hit Factory', but had released three compilation albums of their hits entitled 'The Hit Factory', 'The Hit Factory 2' and 'The Hit Factory 3'. The defendant was a record company which owned a recording studio in London. The defendant had entered into a joint venture agreement with the owner of a studio in New York for the refurbishment and running of the London studio. The New York studio had traded since about 1970 as 'The Hit Factory'. Under the agreement the owner of the New York studio had granted the defendant a licence to use the name 'The Hit Factory'. The defendant proposed to

---

[24] See also *The Athletes' Foot Marketing Associates Inc v Cobra Sports Ltd* [1980] RPC 343.
[25] [1967] RPC 581. [26] Ibid., p. 354; quoted by Oliver LJ in 'Budweiser'.

rename its studio in London 'The Hit Factory'. The New York studio had an international reputation and clientele, including many from the UK. Bookings had been made direct from the UK. In addition, $3.5 million of business had been done by the New York studio with US record companies relating to English artists, including bookings placed at the behest of UK companies through their US affiliates. However, all services rendered by the New York studio had been rendered in New York. The New York studio had no agent or place of business in the UK. The claimants brought an action for passing off. As part of their defence, the defendants argued that they had established their own goodwill in the UK on the basis of UK customers for their studio in New York. PWL responded that The Hit Factory, New York, had no enforceable rights in the UK since it had no place of business, nor an agent, nor did it carry on business in the UK, and all its services had been provided outside the UK. The claimants relied upon the Crazy Horse decision to argue that, as a result, The Hit Factory in New York did not have any goodwill in the UK capable of protection. One issue for the court was whether, assuming that PWL had demonstrated that the name The Hit Factory was distinctive of their goodwill, the defendant's claim to concurrent goodwill in the UK was defeated by the Crazy Horse principle. The Vice-Chancellor called that question 'the Crazy Horse issue'.

Browne-Wilkinson V-C, at p. 50:

The issue is whether the English court will protect the trade connection with the United Kingdom customers of non-UK traders. In the passage I quoted of Lord Diplock in the *General Electric* case [*GE Trade Mark* [1972] FSR 225] he demonstrated how the principle of honest concurrent use was developed in 19th century England to meet the problem where two traders using similar marks in separate areas of the United Kingdom were brought into the same market within the United Kingdom by improvements in internal communications. The changes in the second half of the 20th century are far more fundamental than those in 19th century England. They have produced worldwide marks, worldwide goodwill and brought separate markets into competition one with the other. Radio and television with their attendant advertising cross national frontiers. Electronic communication via satellite produces virtually instant communication between all markets. In terms of travel time, New York by air is as close as Aberdeen by rail. This has led to the development of the international reputation in certain names, particularly in the service fields, for example Sheraton Hotels, Budget Rent A Car.

In my view, the law will fail if it does not try to meet the challenge thrown up by trading patterns which cross national and jurisdictional boundaries due to a change in technical achievement.

The problem is particularly acute with service industries. A first division recording studio is catering to a market which treats crossing the Atlantic as an everyday incident. Similar problems arise in relation to professional and other services. For example, an internationally famous hospital in Paris or Boston, Massachusetts draws its patients from worldwide. Is it unable to protect its goodwill otherwise than in its home country?

As a matter of legal principle, I can see no reason why the courts of this country should not protect the trading relationship between a foreign trader and his United Kingdom customers by restraining anyone in this country from passing himself off as the foreign trader. The essence of a claim in passing off is that the defendant is interfering with the goodwill of the plaintiff. The essence of the goodwill is the ability to attract customers and potential customers to do business with the owner of the goodwill. Therefore any interference with the trader's customers is an interference with his goodwill. The rules under which for certain purposes a specific local situation is attributed to such goodwill appear to me to be irrelevant. Even if under such rules the situs of the goodwill is not in England, any representation made to customers in England is an interference with that goodwill wherever it may be situate. Only if English law refuses to recognise the existence of rights locally situate abroad should the English courts refuse to protect such rights. But English law in general is not so chauvinistic; it does recognise and protect rights which are locally situate abroad. The rights of a beneficiary under a New York trust in assets in England will be protected by an English court even though the situs of his right is in New York. Therefore, when a foreign trader has customers here, one would expect the English courts to protect his goodwill with those customers.

The Vice-Chancellor then rehearsed the authorities which preceded the 'Crazy Horse' decision. He concluded that in the earlier case law, 'there is no reference to the local situation of the goodwill being important. The critical questions have been (a) the use of the name in this country and (b) the presence of customers here.' He then looked at the reasoning in the 'Crazy Horse' case and went on at p. 53:

The *Crazy Horse* decision appears to establish that even if the foreign trader has customers here he cannot protect his reputation unless he has conducted some business here, even slight evidence of business activity being sufficient. If so, it is not inconsistent with The Hit Factory Inc. in this case having a protectable interest here since, in contrast to the *Crazy Horse* case, English customers of Hit Factory Inc. placed their business in this country with Hit Factory Inc. and were invoiced in this country.

In my judgment, such narrow distinctions are unsatisfactory and, with diffidence, suggest that the case was wrongly decided. Pennycuick J seems to have held... that the right to protection against passing off in this country depends upon the plaintiff having a goodwill which is locally situate here.

[The Vice Chancellor then detailed the cases which had followed the 'Crazy Horse' decision, including the 'Budweiser' case. Of the 'Budweiser' case, he noted (p. 57–8)]:

As I read the decision of the majority in the *Budweiser* case, they do treat the presence of a local goodwill as being essential to the right to protection. However, they treat the presence or absence of customers in this country as being decisive of the question whether or not the plaintiffs are carrying on a business here and therefore, it is said, having a local goodwill.

...

From this over-long review of the authorities, I reach the following conclusions:

A. As a matter of principle, the existence of a severable English goodwill attached to a place of business in this country is not the basis of a right to complain of passing off in this country. What is necessary is for the plaintiffs to show they have a trade connection here which will normally consist of customers forming part of their goodwill, wherever that goodwill is situate, which goodwill is being invaded by the acts of the defendant in this country;

B. The approach which I have set out at A above is not open to me as there is binding authority to the effect that the basis of plaintiffs' claim must be a goodwill locally situate in England; but

C. The presence of customers in this country is sufficient to constitute the carrying on of business here whether or not there is otherwise a place of business here and

> whether or not the services are provided here. Once it is found that there are customers, it is open to find that there is a business here to which the local goodwill is attached;
>
> D. To the extent that the *Crazy Horse* case is authority to the contrary, I prefer not to follow it.
>
> It follows that since at all material times The Hit Factory Inc. has had a substantial number of customers here, it would have been entitled to protect its name here against third parties and is therefore entitled to continue to use its name here concurrently with PWL even if, contrary to my view, PWL has itself acquired a goodwill in the name.

Following the decision of the Vice-Chancellor in the 'Hit Factory' case, it is submitted that the presence of customers in the UK is sufficient to constitute the carrying on of a business in the UK to which local goodwill is attached whether or not there is a place of business in the UK and whether or not the services are provided in the UK. We may take the view that in these days of global commerce, this is an eminently sensible approach to take.

4.2.1.4 Local goodwill

Within the UK, goodwill may be local rather than national. For example, in *Associated Newspapers, Daily Mail and General Trust v Express Newspapers*,[27] it was held sufficient that the publishers of the Daily Mail had goodwill in London and the south-east of England in order to stop publication of the defendant's local newspaper, the London Evening Mail. However, the local nature of the claimant's goodwill may affect the reach of any subsequent injunction circumscribing the defendant's trading activities.[28]

4.2.1.5 The timing of goodwill

Goodwill may arise before a trader has begun trading. In *My Kinda Bones v Dr Pepper*, the claimant, trading as the Chicago Rib Shack, was able to persuade the court that its business had generated sufficient goodwill for a passing off action through a pre-launch advertising campaign.[29] Goodwill may also survive the cessation of a business. In *Ad-Lib Club v Granville*,[30] the claimant ran a successful night club which had been forced to close five years previously because of complaints about noise. However, the claimant was seeking alternative premises, and succeeded in a passing off action. One question raised by such cases is what damage might be suffered by a claimant who is not actively pursuing his business. The attitude of the court has been that the value of goodwill may derive not simply from its present use, but also any advantage that it may give to a claimant's future business plans. In the recent case of *Jules Rimet v FA*, the court held that goodwill had survived over several decades.

---

[27] [2003] EWHC 1322.
[28] *Clock v Clock House Hotel* (1936) 53 RPC 269 (CA); *Associated Newspapers v Express Newspapers*.
[29] *My Kinda Bones v Dr Pepper* [1984] FSR 289.   [30] [1967] RPC 581.

Jules Rimet Cup Ltd v Football Association Ltd [2007] EWHC 2376 (Ch)

This case involved a number of intellectual property rights. The claimant, Jules Rimet Cup Ltd (JRCL), had applied to register the words 'World Cup Willie' on their own and the lion device together with the words World Cup Willie as trade marks in respect of a range of goods. The defendant, the Football Association Ltd, opposed the applications on the ground that World Cup Willie was the name of the mascot for the 1966 World Cup hosted in England by the Football Association (FA). The mascot was a cartoon-type lion dressed in a Union Flag shirt and white trousers. The FA informed at least one party that had entered into a licence agreement with JRCL that they had good grounds for opposing the trade marks and, it is alleged, threatened legal proceedings. This is alleged to have caused that party to terminate its agreement with JRCL. The FA also claimed that it owned the copyright in the original drawings of the mascot and that JRCL had infringed this copyright. Further the FA claimed that it owned the goodwill in the drawing of the 1966 mascot and in the name World Cup Willie. It argued that the trade mark applications should be refused on these grounds. Among the issues raised by the case, was whether the FA had goodwill in the name and drawing and whether that goodwill survived even though the FA had exploited neither for over forty years. FA had adduced survey evidence that the public still connected the words and mascot with the FA. This was rejected. Mr Roger Wyand QC held that the FA had both copyright and also goodwill in the marks, which had been created by the merchandising activities it had undertaken at the time of the 1966 World Cup. He then turned to the question as to whether the goodwill had survived until 2005, when this dispute began and held that it had.

Mr Roger Wyand QC:

57. In order to oppose successfully the JRCL application for registration of the two trade marks under s. 5(4)(a) of the Trade Marks Act 1994 the FA must establish that it could have prevented the use of the trade marks by JRCL at the date of the applications in 2005. That is almost 40 years since the last activities which created the goodwill. That is a long time for the goodwill to survive. It is a question of fact as to whether the goodwill has survived and, because I rejected the FA's application to be allowed to adduce evidence of a survey, there is very little evidence to assist me. This, says JRCL with some force, means that the FA must fail. The onus is on the FA to prove their case.

58. I must, however, look at all available evidence.

[**Mr Roger Wyand QC** then looked at documents originating from JRCL which among other things set out the benefits to the company of using the name and character, and another document from Granada, JRCL's licensee:]

Mr Roger Wyand QC:

65. There is another relevant document that was not produced by JRCL but by Granada, who was JRCL's licensee at the time. This is a Brand and Sports Licensing Source Book 2005 and has an entry about World Cup Willie:

World Cup Willie
We all remember 1966 as the year England won the World Cup. It was also the first time a World Cup mascot was ever used. That mascot was World Cup Willie. Now, four

decades on, he is back! On the 40th anniversary of perhaps England's greatest ever sporting achievement, World Cup Willie will once again don his boots and become the symbol of English pride. Next summer the England team heads to Germany, the nation who they beat in THAT final, to compete for football's ultimate prize, and World Cup Willie will be helping to get the nation behind our team. We are going to make World Cup Willie famous again. He is already known and loved by older generations, and now younger generations will come to know and love him too.

66. Again this was put to Mr Sutton of JRCL whose response was that he didn't agree with what the entry said but that it was Granada that was in control of that entry.

67. In addition, there are a number of references to World Cup Willie in the press from time to time and the odd approach from potential licensees seeking a licence.

68. Taking into account all of this material I think that it does establish that there was residual goodwill in the name and character World Cup Willie in 2005 and that this would have been enough for the FA to have succeeded at that time in a passing-off action. The documents show that JRCL and its licensee Granada clearly believed that there was a residual value in World Cup Willie from 1966 that would enable them to establish a very strong brand quickly. That residual value could only be a residual goodwill which belonged to the FA.

There have been a number of cases where goodwill has been held to survive over lengthy periods without use, but this is perhaps a record.[31] What distinguishes this case, it might be argued, is that JCRL's motive in adopting the word and design marks in 2005 was precisely because they still embodied valuable goodwill. On that basis, once it was held that the FA owned the goodwill in 1966, it would seem difficult to argue convincingly that the FA's goodwill had now dissipated.

> **FURTHER READING**
>
> J. Dennis, 'Passing off: Survival of goodwill—getting the benefit of the doubt' [2002] EIPR 331.
>
> R. Swindells, 'Case comment: *Jules Rimet Cup Ltd v The Football Association Ltd*' [2008] Ent LR 41.

4.2.1.6 The ownership of goodwill

Goodwill is property. As such it can be sold or assigned. It cannot, however, be separated from the business to which it attaches. This was made clear by Lord Diplock in *Star Industrial Company Limited v Yap Kwee Kor*.[32]

> **Lord Diplock, at p. 269:**
>
> Goodwill, as the subject of proprietary rights, is incapable of subsisting by itself. It has no independent existence apart from the business to which it is attached. It is local in character and divisible; if the business is carried on in several countries a separate goodwill attaches to it in each. So when the business is abandoned in one country in which it has acquired a

---

[31] *Sutherland v V2 Music Ltd* [2002] EWHC 14 (Ch).   [32] [1976] FSR 256.

> goodwill, the goodwill in that country perishes with it although the business may continue to be carried on in other countries.

There may be more than one owner of goodwill. In a partnership or a joint venture, goodwill may be shared. Alternatively, goodwill may be shared where ownership of a business has subsequently been divided, for instance between the founder's heirs (*Sir Robert McAlpine Ltd v Alfred McAlpine Plc.*[33] Alternatively, a number of traders may have goodwill in the same mark, such as the title 'mail' which is commonly attached to newspapers (*Associated Newspapers v Express Newspapers*). Goodwill may also be shared between traders in goods which have in common distinctive characteristics; goods such as champagne, advocaat, and Swiss chocolate. In these circumstances, passing off may arise when the defendant misrepresents his own goods as sharing these characteristics. Such actions have come to be known as the extended form of passing off.

4.2.1.7 Shared goodwill/the extended form of passing off

It has been argued, by at least one observer,[34] that the novelty which characterizes the extended form of passing off is that it is not concerned with an 'origin misrepresentation' but rather 'product misrepresentation'. In other words, the defendant does not misrepresent his goods as originating from a particular source, but rather he misrepresents the fact that his goods share the same characteristics as a certain category of goods. The extended form of passing off has commonly been associated with names of alcoholic drinks, since the first 'modern' case which involved the defendant selling a Spanish sparkling wine as 'Spanish champagne'.[35] Later cases involved sherry[36] and whisky.[37] In more recent times, it has, for example, expanded to include other products, such as chocolate.[38] It is 'Advocaat' which provides the authoritative definition of the extended form of passing off. In this case, Lord Diplock set out the circumstances in which a limited class of traders might share the goodwill in a particular product.

Erven Warnink BV v J Townend & Sons (Hull) Ltd [1979] AC 731

The first claimants and other Dutch traders had for many years manufactured in the Netherlands a liquor called 'advocaat,' which was exported to Britain and distributed by the second claimants. The essential ingredients were the spirit brandewijn, egg yolks, and sugar as required by statutory regulations in the Netherlands, though the British regulations were not so specific. The liquor acquired a substantial reputation in Britain as a distinct and recognizable beverage. From 1974 a drink described as 'Keeling's Old English Advocaat' composed of dried egg powder mixed with Cyprus sherry was made and marketed in England by the defendants. Though it could not be shown that it was

---

[33] [2004] EWHC 630, [2004] RPC 36.
[34] H. Carty, 'Dilution and passing off: Cause for concern' [1996] 112 (Oct.) LQR 632–66.
[35] *Bollinger v Costa Brava Wine Co Ltd* [1960] Ch 262.
[36] *Vine Products v Mackenzie* [1969] RPC 1.
[37] *John Walker & Sons Ltd v Douglas McGibbon & Co* [1975] RPC 506.
[38] *Chocosuisse Union des Fabricants Suisse de Chocolat v Cadbury Ltd* [1998] RPC 117 HC, [1999] RPC 286 (CA) ('the Swiss Chalet case').

mistaken for Dutch advocaat, it captured a substantial part of the claimants' English market. In the passing off action in the High Court, Goulding J gave judgment for the claimants. The Court of Appeal reversed his decision and the case reached the House of Lords. Having set out the facts of the case and the general background to passing off, Lord Diplock first turned to the 'Champagne' case.

Lord Diplock, at p. 743:

The Champagne case came before Danckwerts J in two stages: the first (reported at [1960] RPC 16) on a preliminary point of law, the second (reported at [1961] RPC 116) on the trial of the action. The assumptions of fact on which the legal argument at the first stage was based were stated by the judge to be:

> (1) The plaintiffs carry on business in a geographical area in France known as Champagne; (2) the plaintiffs' wine is produced in Champagne and from grapes grown in Champagne; (3) the plaintiffs' wine has been known in the trade for a long time as 'Champagne' with a high reputation; (4) members of the public or in the trade ordering or seeing wine advertised as 'Champagne' would expect to get wine produced in Champagne from grapes grown there; and (5) the defendants are producing a wine not produced in that geographical area and are selling it under the name of 'Spanish Champagne'.

These findings disclose a factual situation (assuming that damage was thereby caused to the plaintiffs' business) which contains each of the five characteristics which I have suggested must be present in order to create a valid cause of action for passing off. The features that distinguished it from all previous cases were (a) that the element in the goodwill of each of the individual plaintiffs that was represented by his ability to use without deception (in addition to his individual house mark) the word 'Champagne' to distinguish his wines from sparkling wines not made by the champenois process from grapes produced in the Champagne district of France, was not exclusive to himself but was shared with every other shipper of sparkling wine to England whose wines could satisfy the same condition and (b) that the class of traders entitled to a proprietary right in 'the attractive force that brings in custom' represented by the ability without deception to call one's wines 'Champagne' was capable of continuing expansion, since it might be joined by any future shipper of wine who was able to satisfy that condition. My Lords, in the Champagne case the class of traders between whom the goodwill attaching to the ability to use the word 'Champagne' as descriptive of their wines was shared was a large one, 150 at least and probably considerably more, whereas in the previous English cases of shared goodwill the number of traders between whom the goodwill protected by a passing off action was shared had been two . . .

. . .

[at p. 744] It seems to me, however, as it seemed to Danckwerts J, that the principle must be the same whether the class of which each member is severally entitled to the goodwill which attaches to a particular term as descriptive of his goods, is large or small. The larger it is the broader must be the range and quality of products to which the descriptive term used by the members of the class has been applied, and the more difficult it must be to show that the term has acquired a public reputation and goodwill as denoting a product endowed with recognisable qualities which distinguish it from others of inferior reputation that compete with it in the same market. The larger the class the more difficult it must also be for an individual member of it to show that the goodwill of his own business has sustained more than minimal damage as a result of deceptive use by another trader of the widely shared descriptive term. As respects subsequent additions to the class, mere entry into the market would not give any right of action for passing off; the new entrant must have himself used the descriptive term long enough on the market in connection with his own goods and have traded successfully enough to have built up a goodwill for his business.

For these reasons the familiar argument that to extend the ambit of an actionable wrong beyond that to which effect has demonstrably been given in the previous cases would open the floodgates or, more ominously, a Pandora's box of litigation leaves me unmoved when it is sought to be applied to the actionable wrong of passing off.

I would hold the Champagne case to have been rightly decided and in doing so would adopt the words of Danckwerts J where he said (at [1960] RPC 31):

> There seems to be no reason why such licence [sc. to do a deliberate act which causes damage to the property of another person] should be given to a person competing in trade, who seeks to attach to his product a name or description with which it has no natural association, so as to make use of the reputation and goodwill which has been gained by a product genuinely indicated by the name or description. In my view, it ought not to matter that the persons truly entitled to describe their goods by the name and description are a class producing goods in a certain locality, and not merely one individual. The description is part of their goodwill and a right of property. I do not believe that the law of passing off, which arose to prevent unfair trading, is so limited in scope.

> . . .

> [at p. 747] Of course it is necessary to be able to identify with reasonable precision the members of the class of traders of whose products a particular word or name has become so distinctive as to make their right to use it truthfully as descriptive of their product a valuable part of the goodwill of each of them; but it is the reputation that that type of product itself has gained in the market by reason of its recognisable and distinctive qualities that has generated the relevant goodwill. So if one can define with reasonable precision the type of product that has acquired the reputation, one can identify the members of the class entitled to share in the goodwill as being all those traders who have supplied and still supply to the English market a product which possesses those recognisable and distinctive qualities.

In 'Advocaat', Lord Diplock made it clear that the extended form of passing off is not confined to goods produced in a particular geographical area. In the more recent 'Swiss Chalet' case, the class of goods at issue was Swiss chocolate. A question raised in the High Court was whether descriptive words, such as these, could embody goodwill in the same manner as designations such as 'champagne' or 'Advocaat'. It was held that the words 'Swiss chocolate' were clearly descriptive. However, evidence from members of the public and the relevant trade sector indicated that the words indicated a smoother chocolate, of high quality and of Swiss origin. As a result, the words 'Swiss chocolate' had acquired in England a distinct reputation and manufacturers of Swiss chocolate shared the goodwill which attached to those words. In his judgment, Laddie J also observed that it is open to any trader to join the ranks of those who sell such goods, provided the term properly describes and designates his own goods (thus appearing to differ from Lord Diplock in 'Advocaat' who opined that prospective claimants would need to build up individual goodwill in relation to the products at issue). Conversely, those who already trade in these goods cannot use the term on goods which do not share their defining characteristics without misrepresentation. Or as Laddie J noted: 'it is not open to any existing user of the protected name to use it on products for which it is not an accurate description or designation. Messrs Taittinger are no more entitled to use the word Champagne on a non-alcoholic cola drink than anyone else.'[39]

---

[39] *Chocosuisse*, p. 214.

4.2.2 DISTINGUISHING CRITERIA

According to Lord Jauncey in 'Jif Lemon': 'Get-up is the badge of the plaintiff's goodwill, that which associates the goods with the plaintiff in the mind of the public.' It is a matter of fact in each case whether the mark, get-up, or trade name under which a product is sold is distinctive of the claimant's goodwill.

4.2.2.1 The definition of distinguishing criteria

Passing off protects goodwill attached to the goods or services which the claimant supplies by association with an 'identifying indicia' or get-up. A passing off action most commonly protects the claimant against deceptive use by the defendant of this identifying or distinctive indicia which attaches to the clamaint's goodwill. It is not necessary for the consumer to know the ultimate owner of the goodwill, as long as the public believes that all goods or services sold under a distinctive insignia derive from a single source which is the claimant.[40] A useful way of determining whether any particular indicia is distinctive is to ask: may only the claimant use it in relation to his goods or services without deception or misrepresentation? If that is the case, then the indicia is distinctive. It follows that when an indicia is distinctive, the claimant will have an effective monopoly on its use. As was put by Lord Jauncey in 'Jif Lemon': 'The common law will protect goodwill against misrepresentation by recognizing a monopoly in a particular get-up.' The fact that the law of passing off effectively recognizes a monopoly in the use of distinguishing insignia by the claimant has raised particular difficulties in relation to descriptive insignia and get-up which is common to the trade.

4.2.2.2 The limits to distinctiveness (1): descriptive insignia and get-up common to the trade

If any insignia, be it a word, a colour, or even a shape, is effectively descriptive of the goods or services to which it applies then it would appear to be a hard thing to prevent any other supplier from using such insignia to accurately describe his own goods and services. The same might be true of get-up which is commonly used by a number of suppliers of particular goods or services. Nonetheless, it also possible that, because of the way in which a claimant uses such insignia on the market, the insignia may come to be associated exclusively with his goods or services in the mind of the public. If it does, it will have acquired a 'secondary meaning'. In other words, it will be not just descriptive of the claimant's goods or services, but also distinctive of his goodwill. Descriptive insignia or get-up common to the trade, which has acquired a secondary meaning, will be protected against use by other traders in passing off. It is possible, therefore, once such insignia has acquired a secondary meaning that a single trader may monopolize its use. One issue which is raised by the protection such insignia is afforded under the law of passing off involves the public interest. Is competition between traders inhibited if only one trader may use a word, colour, or shape which may, *inter alia*, accurately describe the goods or services supplied by other traders or which other traders have been accustomed to use? To what extent, if at all, should descriptive insignia and get-up common to the trade be exempt from such monopolization?

The question of when such insignia may acquire a secondary meaning was central to the 'Jif Lemon' case. So too, was the issue of whether it was in the public interest to allow

---

40 *Edge (William) & Sons Ltd v William Niccolls & Sons Ltd* [1911] AC 693 HL; Lord Oliver, 'Jif Lemon'.

descriptive insignia and get-up common to the trade, which had acquired a secondary meaning, to be protected by a passing off action. In their speeches Lords Oliver and Jauncey looked at the first question. Lord Bridge considered the public-interest issue.

Reckitt & Colman Products Ltd v Borden Inc (No 3) [1990] 1 WLR 491

The claimants sold lemon juice in yellow plastic containers which were similar in size and shape to a lemon. The containers had the word 'Jif' embossed on them and also had a yellow cap and a green label. The product had been sold for over thirty years and had become known as 'Jif lemon'. In 1985, the defendants began selling lemon juice also in lemon-shaped containers with a green cap. Both the products were sold in supermarkets. The claimants began an action in passing off. They obtained an interim injunction in the High Court. The defendants' appeal was dismissed by the Court of Appeal and the defendants unsuccessfully appealed to the House of Lords.

The first issue raised in the case was whether, the claimants had proved that the get-up under which their lemon juice had been sold since 1956 had become associated in the minds of the public specifically and exclusively with the claimant's (or 'Jif') lemon juice. The defendants' first argument was that the claimants were not seeking to protect the goodwill associated with the get-up of their product, but rather the product itself. Lord Oliver addressed this issue.

Lord Oliver, at p. 503:

There is not and cannot be any proprietary right in an idea nor can a trader claim a monopoly in the manufacture or sale of a non-patented article or, in the absence of a registered design, in the configurations of shape in which an article is manufactured. What the respondents are seeking to do, it is said, is to separate the article sold from the label under which it is sold, treat the article itself as its own trade mark and, by protecting a claim to monopoly in the mark, to establishing in the manufacture and sale of the article itself a monopoly which the law does not permit.

[Second, the defendants argued that the claimants' get-up could not be protected because it was common to the trade. Thirdly, they maintained that the get-up was descriptive, albeit in shape form, of the product. **Lords Oliver** and **Jauncey** dismissed all three arguments.]

Lord Oliver, at p. 504:

It is, no doubt, true that the plastic lemon-shaped container serves, as indeed does a bottle of any design, a functional purpose in the sale of lemon juice. Apart from being a container *simpliciter*, it is a convenient size; it is capable of convenient use by squeezing; and it is so designed as conveniently to suggest the nature of its contents without the necessity for further labelling or other identification. But those purposes are capable of being and indeed are served by a variety of distinctive containers of configurations other than those of a lemon-sized lemon. Neither the appellants nor the respondents are in the business of selling plastic lemons. Both are makers and vendors of lemon juice and the only question is whether the respondents, having acquired a public reputation for Jif juice by selling it for many years in containers of a particular shape and design which, on the evidence, has become associated with their produce, can legitimately complain of the sale by the appellants of similar produce in containers of similar, though not identical, size, shape, and colouring.

So I, for my part, would reject the suggestion that the plastic lemon container is an object in itself rather than part of the get-up under which the respondents' produce is sold.

…

[at pp. 505–6] Then it is said—and again there is no disagreement as to this—that the mere fact that the produce of the appellants and that of the respondents may be confused by members of the public is not of itself sufficient. There is no 'property' in the accepted sense of the word in a get-up. Confusion resulting from the lawful right of another trader to employ as indicative of the nature of his goods terms which are common to the trade gives rise to no cause of action. The application by a trader to his goods of an accepted trade description or of ordinary English terms may give rise to confusion. It probably will do so where previously another trader was the only person in the market dealing in those goods, for a public which knows only of A will be prone to assume that any similar goods emanate from A. But there can be no cause of action in passing off simply because there will have been no misrepresentation. So the application to the defendants' goods of ordinary English terms such as 'cellular clothing' (*Cellular Clothing Co v Maxton and Murray* (1899) 16 RPC 397) or 'Office Cleaning' (*Office Cleaning Services Ltd v Westminster Window and General Cleaners Ltd* (1946) 63 RPC 39) or the use of descriptive expressions or slogans in general use such as 'Chicago pizza' (*My Kinda Town Ltd v Soll* [1983] RPC 407) cannot entitle a plaintiff to relief simply because he has used the same or similar terms as descriptive of his own goods and has been the only person previously to employ that description.

All this is accepted by the respondents. The appellants, however, starting from this undoubted base, argue that what the respondents are asking the court to protect is no more than the use by them of a descriptive term, embodied in a plastic lemon instead of expressed verbally, which is common to the trade.

…

Every case depends upon its own peculiar facts. For instance, even a purely descriptive term consisting of perfectly ordinary English words may, by a course of dealing over many years, become so associated with a particular trader that it acquires a secondary meaning such that it may properly be said to be descriptive of that trader's goods and of his goods alone, as in *Reddaway v Banham* [1896] AC 199. In the instant case, what is said is that there was nothing particularly original in marketing lemon juice in plastic containers made to resemble lemons. The respondents were not the first to think of it even though they have managed over the past 30 years to establish a virtual monopoly in the United Kingdom. It is, in fact, a selling device widely employed outside the United Kingdom. It is a natural, convenient and familiar technique—familiar at least to those acquainted with retail marketing methods in Europe and the United States. If and so far as this particular selling device has become associated in the mind of the purchasing public with the respondents' Jif lemon juice, that is simply because the respondents have been the only people in the market selling lemon juice in this particular format. Because there has been in fact a monopoly of this sale of this particular article, the public is led to make erroneous assumption that a similar article brought to the market for the first time must emanate from the same source. This has been referred to in the argument as 'the monopoly assumption'. The likelihood of confusion was admitted by the appellants themselves in the course of their evidence, but it is argued that the erroneous public belief which causes the product to be confused arises simply from the existing monopoly and not from any deception by the appellants in making use of what they claim to be a normal, ordinary and generally available selling technique.

The difficulty about this argument is that it starts by assuming the only basis upon which it can succeed, that is to say, that the selling device which the appellants wish to adopt is ordinary and generally available or, as it is expressed in some of the cases, 'common to the trade': see e.g. *Payton & Co Ltd v Snelling, Lampard & Co Ltd* (1900) 17 RPC 48. In one sense, the monopoly assumption is the basis of every passing off action. The deceit practised on the public when one trader adopts a get-up associated with another succeeds only because the latter has previously been the only trader using that particular get-up. But the so called 'monopoly assumption' demonstrates nothing in itself. As a defence to a passing off claim it can succeed only if that which is claimed by the plaintiff as distinctive of his goods and his goods alone consists of something either so ordinary or in such common use that it would be unreasonable that he should claim it as applicable solely to his goods, as for instance where it consists simply of a description of the goods sold. Here the mere fact that he has previously been the only trader dealing in goods of that type and so described may lead members of the public to believe that all such goods must emanate from him simply because they know of no other. To succeed in such a case he must demonstrate more than simply the sole use of the descriptive term. He must demonstrate that it has become so closely associated with his goods as to acquire the secondary meaning not simply of goods of that description but specifically of goods of which and he alone is the source.

...

[p. 507] In the instant case the submission that the device of selling lemon juice in a natural size lemon-shaped squeeze pack is something that is 'common to the trade' and therefore incapable of protection at the suit of a particular trader begs the essential question. If 'common to the trade' means 'in general use in the trade' then, so far as at least as the United Kingdom is concerned, the evidence at the trial clearly established that the lemon-sized squeeze pack was not in general use. If, on the other hand, it means, as the appellants submit, 'available for use by the trade' then it is so available only if it has not become so closely associated with the respondents' goods as to render its use by the appellants deceptive; and that is the very question in issue. The trial judge here has found as a fact that the natural size squeeze pack in the form of a lemon has become so associated with Jif lemon juice that the introduction of the appellants' juice in any of the proposed get-ups will be bound to result in many housewives purchasing that juice in the belief that they are obtaining Jif juice. I cannot interpret that as anything other than a finding that the plastic lemon-shaped container has acquired, as it were, a secondary significance. It indicates not merely lemon juice but specifically Jif lemon juice.

In his speech, Lord Jauncey considered the defendant's argument that the lemon shaped container was descriptive of the product.

Lord Jauncey, at p. 517:

(3) No secondary meaning.

The appellants submitted that the respondents' plastic lemon was merely the exemplification of the descriptive word 'lemon'. It was impossible to acquire a monopoly in the use of a word which accurately described the relevant goods, from which it followed that the appellants were not entitled to establish that the plastic lemon had acquired the secondary meaning of Jif lemon juice.

This submission goes too far for two reasons. In the first place there is no absolute principle of law which supports it. In *Reddaway v Banham* [1896] AC 199, relief was granted to a plaintiff who manufactured belting under the descriptive name of 'camelhair' after a jury had found that these words had acquired the secondary meaning of belting manufactured by the plaintiff. In *The Cellular Clothing Co v Maxton & Murray* [1899] AC 326, the pursuers accurately described their fabric as cellular and sought to interdict the defenders from using this description in relation to any fabric made or supplied by them. The pursuers failed in the Court of Session and in this House. Lord Shand said, at pages 340–1:

> But I confess I have always thought, and I still think, that it should be made almost impossible for anyone to obtain the exclusive right to the use of a word or term which is in ordinary use in our language and which is descriptive only—and, indeed, were it not for the decision in *Reddaway's* case [1896] AC 199, I should say this should be made altogether impossible...But where the plaintiff's proof shows that the only representation by the defendants consists in the use of a term or terms which aptly and correctly describe the goods offered for sale, as in the present case, it must be a condition of the plaintiff's success that they shall prove that these terms no longer mean what they say—or no longer mean only what they say—but have acquired the secondary and further meaning that the particular goods are goods made by the plaintiffs, and, as I have already indicated, it is in my view difficult to conceive cases in which the facts will come up to this.

Lord Shand undoubtedly considered that it was extremely unlikely that the plaintiffs would be able to adduce satisfactory evidence of descriptive words having acquired a secondary meaning but he did not go so far as to say that it was impossible in law for such an event to occur. Lord Davey said, at page 345:

> Then, that being so, what is the evidence upon which the pursuers rely for the purpose of showing that the word has acquired a secondary meaning, so that the mere simple use of the word is alone evidence of a misrepresentation by the defenders?

[p. 518] In this passage Lord Davey clearly recognised that the acquisition of a secondary meaning was possible and he implicitly recognised the important distinction between a simple representation arising from the use of descriptive words which have acquired no secondary meaning and the misrepresentation which could arise where the words have acquired such a meaning. Once again, whether such a secondary meaning has been acquired must be a question of fact.

In the second place I do not consider that it is legitimate to equiparate a plastic lemon of natural shape and size, which is unique in the market, to a word in ordinary use. Indeed I can see no reason why a trader should not obtain protection for a get-up whose shape and colour ingeniously alluded to its contents but not for a phrase containing ordinary words which described them. I agree with Slade LJ that the proper way to regard a plastic lemon is as a fanciful and attractive variant of the get-up of the ordinary plastic squeeze bottle lemon container and I can see no reason why the fact that this get-up is allusive of its contents should deprive it of protection to which it would otherwise be entitled.

Lord Jauncey then discussed two earlier cases with contrasting results: the 'Dolly Blue' case,[41] which concerned a washing blue or tint which the claimants sold in unmarked bags on a stick, but where the defendants had taken sufficient steps to distinguish their own product by placing their own name on similar get-up; and *British American Glass v Winton Products*,[42] which concerned the passing off of ornamental glass dogs. Here, the court held that the shape was distinctive of the claimant's goodwill and as a result the configuration of the article could be protected by a passing off action.

Lord Jauncey, at p. 519:

In my view these two cases are merely examples of the general principle that no man may sell his goods under the pretence that they are the goods of another. This principle applies as well to the goods themselves as to their get-up. A markets a ratchet screwdriver with a

---

[41] *Edge v Niccolls* (1911) AC 693.   [42] [1962] RPC 230.

distinctively shaped handle. The screwdriver has acquired a reputation for reliability and utility and is generally recognised by the public as being the product of A because of its handle. A would be entitled to protection against B if the latter sought to market a ratchet screwdriver with a similarly shaped handle without taking sufficient steps to see that the public were not misled into thinking that his product was that of A. It is important to remember that such protection does not confer on A a monopoly in the sale of ratchet screwdrivers not even in the sale of such screwdrivers with similarly distinctive handles if other appropriate means can be found of distinguishing the two products. Once again it will be a question of fact whether the distinguishing features are sufficient to avoid deception.

In the end of the day this is a very simple case notwithstanding the able and attractive arguments addressed to your Lordships and the plethora of authority referred to. It is not in dispute that the respondents have acquired over many years a reputation in the market for their lemon juice got up in plastic lemons. There is abundant evidence that customers would be deceived if any of the three Marks of the appellants' lemons were put on the market in their present form. No reason in law has been made out why this evidence should not have been accepted. The respondents have accordingly established the facts necessary to succeed. The decisions in the courts below and in this House do not have the effect of conferring on the respondents a monopoly right to sell lemon juice in plastic lemons. They merely decide that on the facts as found, the appellants in seeking to enter the plastic lemon market have not taken adequate steps to differentiate their get-up from that of the respondents so that consumers will not be deceived.

For the foregoing reasons and for the reasons given by my noble and learned friend, Lord Oliver of Aylmerton, I would dismiss the appeal.

In 'Jif Lemon', both Lord Oliver and Lord Jauncey raised the question of whether the claimants' victory would endow them with a monopoly of selling lemon juice in plastic lemons. They both took the view it would not. Anyone could sell their products in the same way, if they sufficiently differentiated their own product from that of the claimants. As we shall see, in the next section on misrepresentation, this is something the defendants singly failed to do. Nonetheless, both Lord Oliver and Jauncey concluded that it is in principle possible for a trader to have an effective monopoly on certain descriptive insignia or the shape of goods, in this case the shape of a plastic lemon, if it can be shown that they have acquired a secondary meaning. We may think that it would be unlikely that another trader would chose to sell his product in a lemon-shaped container given the outcome of the 'Jif Lemon' case, even if it had differentiating features. Certainly, the outcome troubled Lord Bridge who saw it as anti-competitive.

Lord Bridge, at p. 494:

When plastic containers made in the shape, colour and size of natural lemons first appeared on the market in the United Kingdom as squeeze packs containing preserved lemon juice the respondents were astute enough to realise their potential and to buy up the businesses of the two companies who first marketed preserved lemon juice in this way. They thereby acquired a de facto monopoly which, by the periodical threat or institution of passing off actions over the years, they have succeeded in preserving ever since. This is the first such action to come to trial.

The idea of selling preserved lemon juice in a plastic container designed to look as nearly as possible like the real thing is such a simple, obvious and inherently attractive way of marketing the product that it seems to me utterly repugnant to the law's philosophy with respect to commercial monopolies to permit any trader to acquire a de jure monopoly in the container as such. But, as Mr Jacob for the respondents, quite rightly pointed out, the order made by the trial judge in this case does not confer any such de jure monopoly because the injunction restrains the appellants from marketing their product 'in any container so nearly resembling the plaintiffs' Jif lemon-shaped container as to be likely to deceive *without making it clear to the ultimate purchaser that it is not of the goods of the plaintiff*' [emphasis added]. How then are the appellants, if they wish to sell their product in plastic containers of the shape, colour and size of natural lemons, to ensure that the buyer is not deceived? The answer, one would suppose, is by attaching a suitably distinctive label to the container. Yet here is the paradox: the trial judge found that a buyer reading the labels proposed to be attached to the appellants' Mark I, II or III containers would know at once that they did not contain Jif lemon juice and would not be deceived; but he also enjoined the appellants from selling their product in those containers because he found, to put it shortly, that housewives buying plastic lemons in super markets do not read the labels but assume that whatever they buy must be Jif. The result seems to be to give the respondents a de facto monopoly of the container as such which is just as effective as de jure monopoly. A trader selling plastic lemon juice would never be permitted to register a lemon as his trade mark,[43] but the respondents have achieved the result indirectly that a container designed to look like a real lemon is to be treated, per se, as distinctive of their goods.

In his speech, Lord Bridge shows his concern that the claimants were able to obtain a 'de facto' monopoly on a container (in this case a plastic lemon) through their successful passing off action. He took the view that allowing the claimants a monopoly on such an obvious and attractive way of marketing lemon juice undermined competition and, as a result, was detrimental to the public interest. Presumably, one response to such a concern would be that it is equally in the public interest that consumers should not be deceived, as would be the case were others to use the claimants' distinctive insignia. The 'Jif Lemon' case suggests that locating the public interest in passing off actions is not always straightforward.

4.2.2.3 The limits to distinctiveness (2): generic marks

A trader may introduce a new product onto the market. In doing so, the trader will give the product a name. The name chosen may be an entirely made up word. Or it might alternatively be descriptive in some way of the product. If the latter, the question arises as to whether the name will have a 'built in' secondary meaning because the trader is the only one providing the product. Or, if the name is descriptive (or indeed if it is entirely made up), will the name lose any secondary meaning it may have had and come to be seen as synonymous with the product precisely because it is the only such product on the market? Should the latter occur, then the name has become generic. A generic mark will not be protected by a passing off action. Each of these possible outcomes was rehearsed in the 'McCain Oven Chips' case.

---

[43] At the time, a shape could not be registered as a trade mark. Under the 1994 Trade Mark Act it is now possible to register shapes.

McCain International v Country Fair Foods [1981] RPC 69 CA

In 1979 the claimants introduced a new product into the UK market: chips which could be cooked in the oven. They sold the product under the name 'McCain Oven Chips'. A year later, the defendants introduced their own version of the product which they sold under the names, 'Country Fair Oven Chips' and 'Birds Eye Oven Chips'. The claimants obtained an injunction in the High Court to restrain the defendants from marketing their product under the name 'oven chips' with or without their own brand names. The defendants appealed. The defendants argued that the name 'Oven Chip' was descriptive of the product, that it had not subsequently acquired distinctiveness, and that where a descriptive name had been applied to a product by the sole supplier of that product that name could not easily acquire distinctiveness. The claimants argued that 'oven chips' was not descriptive but was a fancy name because it was an ungrammatical combination of two words which had not previously been associated together and further that by virtue of the claimants' extensive sales and advertising it had acquired a secondary meaning.

Templeman LJ, at p. 73:

The authorities, many of which, unavoidably, were not considered by the learned judge, disclose that there is a very real distinction in passing off litigation between a fancy name and a descriptive name. A fancy name which is not descriptive of a product can only indicate that the product bearing that name is, or is licensed by, or is derived from one and the same supplier. Thus in *Spalding & Bros v Gamage Ltd* (1915) 32 RPC 273, the plaintiffs described their football as 'Orb football'. Mr Harman submitted that might be a descriptive phrase, but in my judgment it was a fancy name in that nobody would have dreamed of connecting a football with an orb in normal speech, and as it was a fancy name the defendants could not use the same fancy name without thereby representing that their goods were the goods of the plaintiff. In my judgment a fancy name is an indication of a single source and that is why it is impossible, generally speaking, for a defendant to appropriate the same fancy name without committing the tort of passing off.

A descriptive name, on the other hand, does not indicate the source of the goods, but the nature of the goods. In the present case, the name 'oven chips' is a descriptive name which is not so far-fetched or fanciful as to indicate that all oven chips emanate from the same source. Indeed the plaintiffs themselves appear to have recognised that the expression 'oven chips' is not in itself a fancy name which indicates as single source or origin. That is why they have consistently referred in their literature and in their packaging to 'McCain oven chips'. In my judgment they found it necessary or prudent to do so in order to distinguish their brand of oven chips from any other brand. The expression 'oven chips' in my judgment identifies the product and the name 'McCain', identifies the manufacturer who is responsible for that particular brand of that product.

[**Templeman LJ** then distinguished the present case from *Reddaway v Banham* (1896)[44] in which it was held that the claimant's product, 'Camel-hair Belting', had acquired a secondary meaning in connection with belting, in that it did not convey to persons dealing in belting the idea that it was made of camel's hair, but rather that it was belting manufactured by the claimant. He continued at p. 73:]

[44] [1896] AC 199.

In the present case, not only is the period [of trading] only 18 months, but it seems to me that it is quite impossible for the plaintiffs to establish that a secondary meaning has been attached to anything other than that which is claimed on their own packet and what is claimed on their own packet is 'McCain oven chips'. I have no doubt that in the trade, both as regards consumers and retailers, the name 'McCain oven chips' means those oven chips made by the plaintiffs, but the words 'oven chips' *simpliciter* never have been used in isolation by the plaintiffs. There has been neither the opportunity nor the time for people to form the impression that the only makers of oven chips are and will remain McCain. It must be remembered that in the field of frozen foods the consumer is accustomed to different brands of the same or similar products and is accustomed to competing brands coming on to the market at different times.

. . .

[at p. 75] In my judgment, the distinction is between a name which is descriptive of the product and a name which is distinctive of the manufacturer. In the present case the words 'oven chips' are distinctive of the product, and the words 'McCain oven chips' refer to the brand of the product which is put on sale by the plaintiffs.

. . .

[at pp. 80–1] It does not seem to me in the light of the admitted facts and of the evidence, and in the light of the authorities to which I have referred, that the plaintiffs have established a triable issue which justifies the granting of an injunction pending trial. Shortly, the words 'oven chips' are in my judgment descriptive of the product and the defendants will not, by using those words in conjunction with their own brand name represent, and no reasonable person would infer, that the goods sold by the defendants are to have some association with the plaintiffs' goods. There is no danger of actual confusion and the plaintiffs, by their advertisements and by their evidence, have not succeeded in establishing that the words 'oven chips' mean, and must mean, potato chips supplied by the plaintiffs and nobody else.

The learned judge [in the High Court] took the view 'that the expression "Oven Chips" is not purely descriptive of the product; it is partly descriptive—"Chips"—and partly consists of a method of preparation which may be utilised by the consumer'. In my judgment the test is whether the expression 'Oven Chips' is descriptive of the product or whether it is intended to be a badge of the manufacturer. The fact that 'chips' is undoubtedly descriptive and that 'oven' is descriptive of the method of preparation does not prevent the expression being descriptive in the sense in which that term is used in passing off litigation as opposed to a fancy name.

The learned judge continued:

> It is not suggested that anyone else had used these two words in juxtaposition until the introduction of the product by the plaintiffs before which no one would have assumed you could do anything with chips in the oven except burn them.

In my judgment that is falling into the trap of saying that because the product was novel and the name was novel, therefore the plaintiffs are entitled to a monopoly in the name. As I think I have shown from the authorities, that is not the law. On the contrary if the plaintiffs introduce a novel product with novel words, but they take the risk of choosing descriptive words, then they run the risk that the defendants cannot be prevented from using those same descriptive words so long as they make it clear that their brands of the product are not the same as the brand of the plaintiffs.

The learned judge continued:

> there has been a substantial volume of sales of oven chips and I am satisfied on the evidence that 'Oven Chips' has become distinctive of the plaintiffs' product and no one else's.

> With respect it seems to me impossible to reach that conclusion when there has not been a substantial sale of oven chips, but a substantial sale of McCain oven chips and there is not, and there could not be, any evidence of what the reaction of consumers would be if what had been sold over the counter were oven chips without the name McCain.

The claimants failed in the 'McCain' case. How important to this failure is the fact that they only sold their 'oven chips' in conjunction with their brand name, 'McCain'? Do you think that the outcome would have been different if the claimants had sold their new product from its inception only under the name 'Oven Chips'?

4.2.2.4 The protection given to distinctive insignia as such

It has been noted that the property protected by an action in passing off is goodwill. There is a strong argument that more recently the courts have come to accept that a passing off action will protect not simply damage to a claimant's goodwill caused by a defendants misrepresentation, but also damage to the claimant's distinctive insignia. According to Kerr LJ in his dissenting judgment in the *Harrods* case: 'a trader's distinctive name can in some cases in itself form part of his goodwill and constitute a property interest'. From this perspective, damage can be said to occur because the defendant, by employing the claimant's insignia to misrepresent the origin or characteristics of his own goods, will 'dilute' the distinctiveness of the claimant's insignia and hence its value. For example in the 'Elderflower champagne' case, the defendant described its cheap, non-acoholic drink as 'champagne'.[45] The Court of Appeal accepted that not only would some consumers buy the defendant's product instead of champagne, but that by using the word champagne to describe its inferior product, the defendant was also 'diluting' the value of the word more generally. At the heart of this development is the question of where the damage lies. Is it damage to goodwill or damage to the insignia as such which passing off protects or both. For this reason, the issue of 'dilution' will be considered more fully in the section of this chapter which is devoted to the third element of passing off: damage.

FURTHER READING

H. Carty, 'Passing off and the concept of goodwill' [1995] JBL 139.

G. Fearon, 'The importance of goodwill' [2004] MIP 143, 24.

C. Wadlow, 'The House of Lords ruling in Jif Lemon' [1990] IPB Rev 2(2) 19.

4.2.3 MISREPRESENTATION

The second element in a passing off action is a misrepresentation. The misrepresentation must be actionable or material.

4.2.3.1 The definition

An actionable misrepresentation will be one which deceives the consumer, and as a result the claimant suffers or is likely to suffer damage. For instance, the defendant may misrepresent

---

[45] *Taittinger SA v Albev Ltd* [1993] FSR 641 (the 'Elderflower champagne' case).

to the consumer that his product originates from the claimant. As a result of that misrepresentation, the consumer may purchase the defendant's product. To be an actionable misrepresentation, a substantial number of customers must be confused. Lord Jauncey considered the nature of a misrepresentation in the 'Jif Lemon' case.

Lord Jauncey, at p. 510:

The basic underlying principle of such an action was stated in 1842 by Lord Langdale MR in *Perry v Truefitt* (1842) 6 Beav 66, 73 to be: 'A man is not to sell his own goods under the pretence that they are the goods of another man...' Accordingly, a misrepresentation achieving such a result is actionable because it constitutes an invasion of proprietary rights vested in the plaintiff. However, it is a prerequisite of any successful passing off action that the plaintiff's goods have acquired a reputation in the market and are known by some distinguishing feature. It is also a prerequisite that the misrepresentation has deceived or is likely to deceive and that the plaintiff is likely to suffer damage by such deception. Mere confusion which does not lead to a sale is not sufficient. Thus, if a customer asks for a tin of black shoe polish without specifying any brand and is offered the product of A which he mistakenly believes to be that of B, he may be confused as to what he has got but he has not been deceived into getting it. Misrepresentation has played no part in his purchase.

4.2.3.2 A misrepresentation and mere confusion

As was suggested by Lord Jauncey, there is a difference between an actionable misrepresentation in a passing off action and 'mere' confusion. The latter may affect a consumer's actions in relation to the product or service, but does not result from a deception. In *Phones 4u v Phone 4u*, Jacob LJ examined the distinction between a misrepresentation which is vital to an action for passing off and mere confusion.

Phones 4u Ltd v Phone4u.co.uk Internet Ltd [2007] RPC 5

The claimants had, since 1995, owned and operated a nationwide chain of shops under the name, 'Phones 4u', which sold mobile phones and arranged customer contracts. It also had a domain name, 'phones4u.co.uk'. In 1999, the defendant registered the domain name 'phone4u.co.uk'. It sold mobile phones from this site, although, in 2000, it offered to sell its domain name to the claimant for a considerable sum. The claimant sued for passing off. The Court of Appeal found that, by the time the defendant commenced trading, the claimant had substantial goodwill in the name 'Phones 4u'. A considerable number of people sought to contact the claimant via the defendant's website. Once on the site, the defendant offered to sell them phones, but also stated it was unconnected with the claimant's business. Among the questions for the Court of Appeal was whether the defendant's actions amounted to an actionable misrepresentation or 'mere confusion'. In his judgment, Jacob LJ examined the difference between the two.

Jacob LJ:

16. The next point of passing off law to consider is misrepresentation. Sometimes a distinction is drawn between 'mere confusion' which is not enough, and 'deception', which is. I described the difference as 'elusive' in *Reed Executive v Reed Business Information* [2004]

RPC 767 at 797. I said this, [111]:

> Once the position strays into misleading a substantial number of people (going from 'I wonder if there is a connection' to 'I assume there is a connection') there will be passing off, whether the use is as a business name or a trade mark on goods.

17. This of course is a question of degree—there will be some mere wonderers and some assumers—there will normally (see below) be passing off if there is a substantial number of the latter even if there is also a substantial number of the former.

18. The current (2005) edition of *Kerly* contains a discussion of the distinction at paragraphs 15-043–15-045. It is suggested that:

> The real distinction between mere confusion and deception lies in their causative effects. Mere confusion has no causative effect (other than to confuse lawyers and their clients) whereas, if in answer to the question: 'what moves the public to buy?', the insignia complained of is identified, then it is a case of deception.

19. Although correct as far as it goes, I do not endorse that as a complete statement of the position. Clearly if the public are induced to buy by mistaking the insignia of B for that which they know to be that of A, there is deception. But there are other cases too—for instance those in the *Buttercup* case. A more complete test would be whether what is said to be deception rather than mere confusion is really likely to be damaging to the claimant's goodwill or divert trade from him. I emphasise the word 'really'.

20. *HFC Bank v Midland Bank* [2000] FSR 176, relied upon by Miss Lane, is a case about 'mere confusion'. The claimant Bank was known, but not very well known, as HFC. It sought to restrain the Midland with its very many branches from changing its name to HSBC. That was said to be passing off. It relied upon some 1,200 instances of alleged deception. Lloyd J analysed the ten best (pp. 189–104). None really amounted to deception. And in any event, given the scale of the parties' respective operations, the totality of what was relied upon was trivial. The case was one on its facts. It decided no question of principle.

21. In this discussion of 'deception/confusion' it should be remembered that there are cases where what at first sight may look like deception and indeed will involve deception, is nonetheless justified in law. I have in mind cases of honest concurrent use and very descriptive marks. Sometimes such cases are described as 'mere confusion' but they are not really— they are cases of tolerated deception or a tolerated level of deception.

22. An example of the former is the old case of *Dent v Turpin* (1861) 2 J&H 139. Father Dent had two clock shops, one in the City, the other in the West End. He bequeathed one to each son—which resulted in two clock businesses each called Dent. Neither could stop the other; each could stop a third party (a villain rather appropriately named Turpin) from using 'Dent' for such a business. A member of the public who only knew of one of the two businesses would assume that the other was part of it—he would be deceived. Yet passing off would not lie for one son against the other because of the positive right of the other business. However it would lie against the third-party usurper.

23. An example of the latter is *Office Cleaning Services v Westminster Window and General Cleaners* (1946) 63 RPC 39. The differences between 'Office Cleaning Services Ltd' and 'Office Cleaning Association', even though the former was well-known, were held to be enough to avoid passing off. Lord Simmonds said:

> Where a trader adopts words in common use for his trade name, some risk of confusion is inevitable. But that risk must be run unless the first user is allowed unfairly to monopolise the words. The Court will accept comparatively small differences as sufficient to avert confusion. A greater degree of discrimination may fairly be expected from the public where a trade name consists wholly or in part of words descriptive of the articles to be sold or the services to be rendered (p. 43).

> In short, therefore, where the 'badge' of the plaintiff is descriptive, cases of 'mere confusion' caused by the use of a very similar description will not count. A certain amount of deception is to be tolerated for policy reasons—one calls it 'mere confusion'.

In his judgment, Jacob LJ defined the difference between an actionable confusion and confusion as: 'whether what is said to be deception rather than mere confusion is really likely to be damaging to the claimant's goodwill or divert trade from him'. In this particular case, Jacob LJ concluded that customers or potential customers of the claimant were being deceived into contacting the defendant's website and, once there, the defendant sought to take advantage of this initial deception. This was more than 'mere deception' and since the other elements of a passing off action, goodwill and damage, were also present the claimant's case was made out. An opposite conclusion was reached in the earlier case of *BP Amoco Plc v John Kelly Ltd*. In this case, the court accepted that customers might have been confused, but the confusion did not amount to an actionable misrepresentation.

BP Amoco Plc v John Kelly Ltd [2002] FSR 5

BP Amoco operated service stations in the UK under the name BP and all were decorated in a particular shade of green. According to BP Amoco, one purpose for giving the stations a uniform colour was so that approaching motorists could identify the stations even if they were too far away to be able to read the BP logo. John Kelly operated service stations in Ireland and N. Ireland, under the name 'TOP'. In 1996, it adopted green as the main colour of its service stations. BP sued for trade mark infringement (it had registered the particular colour green as a trade mark) and passing off.

Carswell CJ, at p. 48:

Deception or its likelihood lies at the heart of the tort of passing off: *Kerly's Law of Trade Marks and Trade Names* (13th ed.), para. 14-257. If consumers are not deceived by the misrepresentation, to the consequent damage of the plaintiff, the cause of action has not been established. The respondents' case, which the judge accepted, was that only 'morons in a hurry' could be deceived into thinking that they were purchasing BP petrol and not TOP when they came to the station, with its conspicuous MID and the 'top' brand name blazened all round. As Mr Golsong accepted in the course of his evidence, a customer who confused Kelly with BP at the point of buying petrol would, even if he were in a hurry, have to be fairly stupid or fairly uncaring.

   Mr Hobbs' riposte to this was to rely again on the proposition that the misrepresentation involved in the predominantly green get-up of the service stations seen from a distance was sufficient to deceive motorists into making preparations to pull off to buy petrol, and that although a normally observant person would realise by the time he actually pulled in to the station that it sold 'TOP' and not BP petrol, the damage was done when he was lured off the road. Although Mr Hobbs argued persuasively that the law should afford a remedy in such circumstances, we are not satisfied that his proposition is justified on the law as it stands. We consider that it is a necessary ingredient of the tort that the customer is deceived into making the purchase by reason of the confusion engendered by the defendant's use of a get-up similar to that of the plaintiff. As Lord Jauncey said in the Jif Lemon case at page 417, 'Mere confusion which does not lead to a sale is not sufficient.' If the customer can see sufficiently clearly when he gets close to the station that the product sold is not that of BP, he does not

> buy the petrol under the mistaken impression that he is getting BP petrol into the tank of his vehicle. In these circumstances the tort of passing off has not in our view been committed.

Because of their inability to show an actionable misrepresentation, the claimants were unable to succeed in passing off. We may wonder whether, in practice, a motorist finding himself at the petrol pump would actually leave and seek an alternative source even if he was hoping to buy BP petrol. Does this case fall on the other side of the line from the *Phones 4u* case where the defendant's actions were deemed really likely to be damaging to the claimant's goodwill or to divert trade from him?

4.2.3.3 The circumstances in which an actionable misrepresentation may arise

The question of whether or not a misrepresentation is actionable may depend upon the nature of the customers, the nature of the goods or services at issue, and the circumstances in which the misrepresentation is made or a combination of each or all of these factors.[46]

In 'Jif Lemon', Lord Oliver considered the circumstances in which customers were likely to be deceived by the sale of the defendant's product. He began by accepting that 'a careful shopper who read the labels attached respectively to the appellants and the respondents products would have no difficulty whatever in distinguishing them'.

Lord Oliver, at p. 508:

The essence of the action for passing off is a deceit practised upon the public and it can be no answer, in a case where it is demonstrable that the public has been or will be deceived, that they would not have been if they had been more careful, more literate or more perspicacious. Customers have to be taken as they are found.

[He then noted previous cases where the court had asked whether the marks at issue would deceive 'incautious' customers:]

[at p. 509] It is also the question to be asked in this case. It has, however, to be asked in every case against the background of the type of market in which the goods are sold, the manner in which they are sold, and the habits and characteristics of purchasers in that market. The law of passing off does not rest solely upon the deceit of those whom it is difficult to deceive.

In the instant case, side-by-side visual comparison does not in fact take place. Moreover the trial judge was satisfied of the fact that a substantial part of the purchasing public requires specifically Jif lemon juice, associates it with the lemon-shape, lemon-size container which is the dominant characteristic of the get-up and pays little or no attention to the label. It is no answer to say that the diversion of trade which he was satisfied would take place would be of relatively short duration, since the public would ultimately become educated to the fact that there were two brands of lemon juice marketed in such containers and would then be likely to pay more attention to the labels to be sure that they got the brand which they required. His finding was that the diversion would be likely to run into millions of units. It inevitably follows from these findings that the appellants have not in fact sufficiently and effectively distinguished their goods from those of the respondents and it is not for the respondents or for the court to suggest what more they should do, although some suggestions were made by Slade LJ in the course of his judgment in the Court of Appeal. In the light of the trial judge's

---

[46] *Cadbury-Schweppes Pty Ltd v The Pub Squash Co* [1981] 1 WLR 193.

finding, I see no escape from the proposition that the respondents were entitled to an injunction which they obtained in the form in which it was granted.

The facts of the 'Jif Lemon' case led Lord Oliver to assume that shoppers would be confused between the two products. According to Lord Oliver, it is irrelevant that the public will not be deceived if they are more careful, literate, or perspicacious. Instead, in passing off actions, customers must be taken as they are found. Generally, as it did in 'Jif Lemon', the court will assess the likelihood of the public's being deceived by reference to the type of goods or services concerned. So the public is li_ly to be more careful and less likely to be deceived when dealing with a bank[47] than when reading an evening paper on the tube during rush hour.[48] Or, indeed, when buying lemon juice in a supermarket. In *BP Amoco v John Kelly*, there was some discussion about the nature of the customers who might have been deceived by the similarity in the get-up of the parties' service stations. The defendant suggested that likely customers would not be 'morons on a hurry'[49] and therefore would not be deceived. Conversely, the claimant argued that a 'normally observant' motorist might only realize the nature of his confusion once he had pulled into the petrol station, at which point it was too late. On this point, the Court of Appeal preferred the defendant's argument.

4.2.3.4 Definition of a substantial number in passing off

In determining whether there has been an actionable misrepresentation, it is necessary to ask whether a sufficient number of customers have been misled. The general rule is that it is necessary for a *substantial* number of customers to be misled. Conversely, as Lightman J stated in the 'Alan Clark diaries' case, 'it is no defence that many people are not deceived'.[50] Indeed, it would be fair to say that the definition of 'substantial' in relation to passing off is a relative one. For example, in the 'Swiss Chalet' case, Laddie J in the High Court concluded that a 'substantial' number of potential customers need not even comprise a majority.

Chocosuisse Union des Fabricants Suisses de Chocolat v Cadbury Ltd
[1998] RPC 117

The claimants were manufacturers and retailers of chocolate made in Switzerland. The defendant manufactured its chocolate in the United Kingdom and in 1994 launched a new chocolate bar called 'Swiss Chalet'. The claimants alleged that the defendant had passed off 'Swiss Chalet' as Swiss chocolate. In the High Court, Laddie J found that there had been passing off. The defendant unsuccessfully appealed. One question that arose for the court was whether a substantial section of the public would have been confused by the defendant's misrepresentation.

Laddie J, at p. 413:

I think it is clear that for many people, including some of those for whom the words Swiss chocolate mean a product of quality from Switzerland, the prominent use of the famous Cadbury name and get-up will be enough to prevent them thinking that Swiss Chalet is a

---

47 *HFC Bank plc v HSBC Bank plc* [2000] FSR 176.
48 *Clark v Associated Newspapers Ltd* [1998] 1 WLR 1558.
49 Citing Foster J in *Morning Star v Express Newspapers* [1979] FSR 113.
50 *Clark v Associated Newspapers Ltd* at 1566.

Swiss chocolate. Furthermore there are very many for whom the origin or connections of Swiss Chalet will be irrelevant. In addition to this, I think that in some cases it is likely that the questions asked in both the plaintiffs' and defendant's surveys may have resulted in the inter- viewees entering into an area of speculation which would not normally have crossed their minds. Many people, and particularly those who are more observant, would not be confused. For them the words 'Swiss Chalet' will signify nothing but a pretty sounding name for a bar of chocolate. They will convey no other message. However I have come to the conclusion that there are some who will be struck by the largest and most prominent word on the defend- ant's packaging namely 'Swiss' and think that it is a reference to an attribute of the product itself. I think it is likely that some will think that it is an indication that the product is Swiss chocolate. Some, like Mr Crocker, may not see the reference to Cadbury. Others might not believe that all Cadbury chocolate is made in England. In fact it is not all made here. Cadbury like many other manufacturers has set up factories or formed alliances abroad. Further, for some the get-up of the packaging with its typical Swiss scene will tend to reinforce the mes- sage of the word 'Swiss'. Finally some may be left in confusion as to whether Swiss Chalet is Swiss chocolate or not.

I have found this the most difficult issue in the case. However, I have come to the con- clusion that a substantial number of members of the public who regard Swiss chocolate as the name for a group of products of repute will be confused into thinking that Swiss Chalet is a member of that group by reason of the use of the name Swiss Chalet. It is likely that the number who think that will be smaller than the number for whom there will be no confusion but, in my view, it is still likely to be a substantial number. It follows that on this issue the plaintiffs succeed.

Laddie J's conclusion that there was sufficient customer confusion for the claimants to suc- ceed in their passing off action was subsequently upheld by the Court of Appeal.

4.2.3.4 The nature of the evidence to be produced

In the 'Swiss Chalet' case, both parties initiated surveys in order to demonstrate either that customers were or were not likely to be misled. Although this is an obvious course to take for parties to a passing off action, it is by no means the norm. Such evidence is bound to be contentious and the court, as in this case, may take a view that the questions addressed to potential customers are leading ones. Furthermore, while in marginal cases evidence of confusion may help the judge to reach a conclusion,[51] the speed with which many passing off actions reach the court may make the collection of evidence impractical. Nonetheless, where passing off is alleged to have been continuing the absence of proof of confusion may be seen as telling by the court. This was the view taken by Laddie J in the case of *Arsenal v Reed*.

Arsenal Football Club plc v Reed [2001] RPC 46

Arsenal Football Club had two logos by which it was known and which were registered as trade marks: a canon device and a crest device. It had also registered the words, 'Arsenal' and the 'Gunners' as trade marks. Arsenal earned a great deal of money through mer- chandising; that is through licensing its marks for use on a variety of products. Arsenal's

[51] *Neutrogena Corpn v Golden Land* [1996] RPC 476 (CA).

products carried 'swing-tags' and other labels which indicated their origin. Arsenal also endeavoured to ensure that customers for its products knew that they were acquiring 'official' Arsenal merchandise. Mr Reed had been selling products bearing the Arsenal trade marks outside the claimant's grounds for thirty-one years. He had a large sign over his stall which carried the message that the use of the Arsenal logos on his merchandise was 'solely to adorn the product and does not imply or indicate any affiliation or relationship' with 'official' Arsenal products. Arsenal FC sued Mr Reed for both passing off and trade mark[52] infringement. In assessing the strength of the passing off claim, Laddie J turned to the lack of evidence of confusion produced by Arsenal.

Laddie J:

[at p. 24] Where the claimant brings proceedings at or before the commencement of the defendant's trade, the court must assess as best it can what is going to happen in the real world of the marketplace. That may not be easy and the court may sometimes get it wrong, but the speed with which the claimant comes to court—something which is frequently necessary to avoid substantial damage—makes this inevitable. On the other hand, where the defendant has been carrying on his trade for some time, the court can expect to be relieved of the need to speculate as to the likelihood of confusion and damage. In most cases, it will be able to see what has actually happened. If the claimant has suffered substantial damage, one can expect it to be apparent. Absence of evidence of confusion becomes more telling and more demanding of explanation by the claimant the longer, more open, and more extensive the defendant's activities are. The purchasing public may be more or less observant and less or more easily misled than might be thought when the issues are being ventilated in the rather clinical atmosphere in court.

[Here, despite the fact that the defendant had been trading in Arsenal memorabilia outside the club's stadium for many years, the claimants did not bring forward evidence of confusion. Their failure to do so was a decisive factor in the court's initial finding that there had been no passing off by the defendant. According to **Laddie J**:]

43. Since AFC has failed to prove relevant confusion, it has also failed to show that it has suffered relevant damage as a result of Mr Reed's activities. The only loss suffered is attributable to the fact that Mr Reed and AFC are in competition in the sale of memorabilia. The broad claim of passing off fails.

4.2.3.5 The common field of activity

A recurring question, which has now been definitively answered, has been whether there must be direct competition between the claimant and the defendant, in other words must they share 'a common field of activity', for a passing off action to succeed? There have been a number of authoritative decisions which have made clear that it is not necessary for there to be a common field.[53] Among the most recent was that of the Court of Appeal in *Harrods*. Millet LJ first considered the authorities.

---

52 For a discussion of the trade mark issues, see 6.2.2.1.

53 It should be noted that the need to show a common field has had greater longevity in cases involving character merchandising (see for example, *McCulloch v May* (1948) 65 RPC 58). However, in *Irvine v Talksport Ltd* [2002] FSR 60, Laddie J held that in these cases too there was no need to show a 'common field' between the parties. Both cases will be examined in Ch. 7 on character merchandising.

Millet LJ, at p. 714:

There is no requirement that the defendant should be carrying on a business which competes with that of the plaintiff or which would compete with any natural extension of the plaintiff's business. The expression 'common field of activity' was coined by Wynn-Parry J in *McCulloch v May* (1948) 65 RPC 58, when he dismissed the plaintiff's claim for want of this factor. This was contrary to numerous previous authorities (see, for example, *Eastman Photographic Materials Co Ltd v John Griffiths Cycle Corporation Ltd* (1898) 15 RPC 105 (cameras and bicycles); *Walter v Ashton* [1902] 2 Ch 282 (The Times newspaper and bicycles)) and is now discredited. In the Advocaat case Lord Diplock expressly recognised that an action for passing off would lie although 'the plaintiff and the defendant were not competing traders in the same line of business'. In the Lego case Falconer J acted on evidence that the public had been deceived into thinking that the plaintiffs, who were manufacturers of plastic toy construction kits, had diversified into the manufacture of plastic irrigation equipment for the domestic garden. What the plaintiff in an action for passing off must prove is not the existence of a common field of activity but likely confusion among the common customers of the parties.

[**Millet LJ** then went on to suggest that while a common field of activity is not necessary, it is nonetheless suggestive of passing off. He continued as follows at p. 714:]

The absence of a common field of activity, therefore, is not fatal; but it is not irrelevant either. In deciding whether there is a likelihood of confusion, it is an important and highly relevant consideration:

> whether there is any kind of association, or could be in the minds of the public any kind of association, between the field of activities of the plaintiff and the field of activities of the defendant (*Annabel's (Berkeley Square) Ltd v G Schock (trading as Annabel's Escort Agency)* [1972] RPC 838, at page 844 per Russell LJ).

In the Lego case Falconer J likewise held that the proximity of the defendant's field of activity to that of the plaintiff was a factor to be taken into account when deciding whether the defendant's conduct would cause the necessary confusion.

Where the plaintiff's business name is a household name the degree of overlap between the fields of activity of the parties' respective businesses may often be a less important consideration in assessing whether there is likely to be confusion, but in my opinion it is always a relevant factor to be taken into account.

Where there is no or only a tenuous degree of overlap between the parties' respective fields of activity the burden of proving the likelihood of confusion and resulting damage is a heavy one.

It is clear from Millett LJ's comments and also from earlier authorities, in particular the 'Lego' case, that what is needed to establish passing off is evidence of confusion and a likelihood of damage whether or not there is a common field of activity between the parties. However, both confusion (and damage) will be easier to prove if there is a common field of activity between the parties or where, as in the 'Lego' case, the claimant is a household name. Millett LJ went on in *Harrods* to assess whether, in the absence of any common field, there was a likelihood of either confusion or damage to the claimant. He concluded there was not.

Millet LJ, at p. 717:

(3) The absence of any common field of activity.

This is of particular significance in the present case. The judge correctly directed himself as to the law; he cannot be faulted in the way in which he applied it. It is not merely that the plaintiffs have never run a school and have no established reputation for doing so; or even that the nature of the parties' respective businesses are as dissimilar as can well be imagined. It is rather that the commercial reputation for excellence as a retailer which the plaintiffs enjoy would be regarded by the public as having no bearing upon their ability to run a school. Customers of the plaintiffs would be surprised to learn that Harrods had ventured into the commercial theatre; they would, I think, be incredulous if they were told that Harrods had opened a preparatory school.

The last two features must be taken together, for they reinforce each other. Nothing in the judge's decision compels the conclusion that the defendants would have been permitted to call their school 'Harrods' or 'Harrods School'; or that an enterprising trader would be permitted to set up a retail shop under the name 'The Harrodian'. The question is whether there is a real risk that members of the public will be deceived into thinking that a school called 'The Harrodian School' (not written in the distinctive Harrods' script or livery) is owned or managed by Harrods or under Harrods' supervision or control. Whether there is a real likelihood of such confusion is a question of fact. It is primarily a question of impression. The judge decided that there was not. I would have reached the same conclusion myself. More to the point, I am satisfied that the judge made no discernible error of law and that his conclusion was one to which he was entitled to come.

In *Harrods*, the Court of Appeal held that the absence of a common field between the department store and the school meant that the public would not be misled into believing that there was any connection between the parties. Nonetheless, it is also true that where there is a common field of activity between the parties, the courts will be more likely to find both an actionable misrepresentation and the likelihood of damage. To understand how, in an area of law which regulates unfair competition, there may be no direct competition between the parties, we need to examine the various types of misrepresentation which might lead to a finding of passing off.

4.2.4 TYPES OF ACTIONABLE MISREPRESENTATIONS

The very early cases of passing off generally involved a misrepresentation by the defendant that his goods were those of the claimant. Over time, the tort has expanded to encompass many other types of misrepresentation. Indeed, at its simplest, it may be argued that any misrepresentation might give rise to an action in passing off, provided that it is material and that the other constituents of the tort are also present. Below we shall look at the most common types of actionable misrepresentations. They are:

1. That the defendant's goods or services are those of the claimant or originate from him, or if they are the claimant's goods that they are, for example, of a different quality.

2. That there is a business connection between the claimant and the defendant.

3. That the defendant's goods are of the same origin or nature as the claimant's goods.

4. The defendant claims that the goods or services of the claimant are his own.

5. That there is a licensing connection between the claimant and the defendant.[54]

6. That the claimant has endorsed the defendant's goods.[55]

4.2.4.1 The defendant's goods or services are those of the claimant or are of a different quality

'Jif Lemon' is of course a classic example of a misrepresentation that the defendant's goods originated with the claimant. The early case of *Spalding v Gamage* established that a misrepresentation by the defendant as to the quality of the claimant's goods could also amount to passing off. The claimants manufactured rubber footballs which were sewn and sold as the 'Improved Sewn Orb'. The defendants obtained a stock of moulded footballs, which the claimants had manufactured and rejected, which the defendants advertised under the same name. This was held to be an actionable misrepresentation. Other cases have concerned the claimant's second-hand goods which were sold by the defendant as if they were new[56] and goods which were manufactured to the claimant's specification but sold without its authorization.[57]

4.2.4.2 There is a business connection between the claimant and the defendant

It has also been long established that passing off may occur if the defendant wrongly claims that there is a business connection between himself and the claimant. However, not all such misrepresentations will be actionable. This was made clear by Millet LJ in the *Harrods* case.

> **Millet LJ, at p. 712:**
>
> **The relevant connection**
>
> In its classic form the misrepresentation which gave rise to an action for passing off was an implied representation by the defendant that his goods were the goods of the plaintiff, but by the beginning of the present century the tort had been extended beyond this. As Lord Diplock explained in the 'Advocaat' case [1979] AC 731 at pages 741-2, it came to include the case:
>
> > where although the plaintiff and the defendant were not competing traders in the same line of business, a false suggestion by the defendant that their businesses were connected with one another would damage the reputation and thus the goodwill of the plaintiff's business.
>
> In a written summary of the plaintiffs' points in reply which was prepared by their junior counsel and presented to us at the conclusion of the argument, and to the excellence of which I would like to pay tribute, it was submitted:
>
> > In this case the belief engendered [in the minds of the public] is probably that Harrods sponsor or back the school. Obviously not every connection will found an action for passing off...but where the representation is to the effect that the plaintiff is *behind* the defendant in some way, that is a classic case.
>
> This is too widely stated. In my judgment the relevant connection must be one by which the plaintiffs would be taken by the public to have made themselves responsible for the quality

---

[54] This will be considered in Ch. 7.   [55] This will be considered in Ch. 7.

[56] *Gillette Safety Razor v Diamond Edge* (1926) 43 RPC 310.

[57] *Primark Stores Ltd v Lollypop Clothing Ltd* [2001] FSR 637; see also G. Kwan, 'Infringement of trade mark and passing off by dealing in genuine articles' [2003] EIPR 45.

of the defendant's goods or services. In *British Legion v British Legion Club (Street) Ltd* (1931) 48 RPC 555 Farwell J considered that the public would take the defendant club to be 'connected in some way' with the plaintiff. But he explained this by saying that some persons would think that it was 'either a branch of the plaintiff or a club in some way amalgamated with or under the supervision of the plaintiff *and for which the plaintiff had in some way made itself responsible*' (my emphasis).

[p. 713] This, in my opinion, is the gist of the matter.

. . .

[p. 713] It is not in my opinion sufficient to demonstrate that there must be a connection of some kind between the defendant and the plaintiff, if it is not a connection which would lead the public to suppose that the plaintiff has made himself responsible for the quality of the defendant's goods or services. A belief that the plaintiff has sponsored or given financial support to the defendant will not ordinarily give the public that impression. Many sporting and artistic events are sponsored by commercial organisations which require their name to be associated with the event, but members of the public are well aware that the sponsors have no control over and are not responsible for the organisation of the event. Local teams are often sponsored in similar fashion by local firms, but their supporters are well aware that the sponsors have no control over and are not responsible for the selection or performance of the players.

Schools and colleges are not normally sponsored or promoted in the same way, but they are often financially supported by commercial and professional organisations. Scholarships and professorial chairs are increasingly established by professional firms which stipulate that their name is publicly associated with the endowment. But it is generally recognised that those who provide financial support to such institutions do not expect to have any control over or to be held responsible for the institution or the quality of the teaching. Many ancient schools still bear the names of the guilds which founded them, not as part of their trading activities, but as charitable institutions for the benefit of children of their members. The connection is now largely if not entirely historical; but it was probably never one which was capable of adversely affecting the goodwill and business reputation of the founder.

Millet LJ believed that at the very least, the public must believe that the claimant was responsible for the quality of the defendant's goods or services. In *Harrods*, the court found there was no misrepresentation because the two businesses were too remote from each other for the public to assume that the claimant would have control of or be responsible for the quality of the defendant's goods or services. Where the claimant and the defendant are in the same line of business, such as financial services for example, the court may find there is a real risk that such a connection will be made, and as a result the claimant may lose control of its reputation.[58] Do you think that Millet LJ's approach is realistic given that today a wide variety of goods might be sold under a single 'mark' or identifying insignia? The mark, 'Virgin' springs to mind.

4.2.4.3 The defendant's goods are of the same origin or nature as the claimant's goods

This misrepresentation is characteristic of what has become known as the extended form of passing off. In the extended form, the defendant will make the misrepresentation that its goods share the same origin or nature as those of the claimant's goods, not that they originate from the claimant, as in the classic form of passing off. As we have seen, the extended

---

[58] *Dawnay Day & Co Ltd v Cantor Fitzgerald International* [2000] RPC 669 (CA).

form of passing off has commonly been associated with names of alcoholic drinks. Over the years, it has expanded to include other products, for example Swiss chocolate in the 'Swiss Chalet' case. Furthermore, although the earlier cases involved misrepresentations as to geographical origin, later cases have also encompassed misrepresentations concerning the composition of the goods as in 'Advocaat'. Indeed, it was the 'Advocaat' case which provided the authoritative definition of the extended form of passing off.

Lord Diplock, at p. 739:

the question of law for your Lordships is whether this House should give the seal of its approval to the extended concept of the cause of action for passing off that was applied in the champagne, sherry and Scotch whisky cases. This question is essentially one of legal policy.

[**Lord Diplock** then examined the facts of the case and the High Court decision that there had been passing off (in effect, by finding that the five factors were present which **Lord Diplock** identifies in this same case as necessary for a successful action in passing off). He continues at p. 739:]

True it is that it could not be shown that any purchaser of 'Keeling's Old English Advocaat' supposed or would be likely to suppose it to be goods supplied by Warnink or to be Dutch advocaat of any make. So Warnink had no cause of action for passing off in its classic form. Nevertheless, the learned judge was satisfied: (1) that the name 'advocaat' was understood by the public in England to denote a distinct and recognisable species of beverage; (2) that Warnink's product is genuinely indicated by that name and has gained reputation and goodwill under it; (3) that Keeling's product has no natural association with the word 'advocaat'; it is an egg and wine drink properly described as an 'egg flip,' whereas advocaat is an egg and spirit drink; these are different beverages and known as different to the public; (4) that members of the public believe and have been deliberately induced by Keeling to believe that in buying their 'Old English Advocaat' they are in fact buying advocaat; (5) that Keeling's deception of the public has caused and, unless prevented, will continue to cause, damage to Warnink in the trade and the goodwill of their business both directly in the loss of sale and indirectly in the debasement of the reputation attaching to the name 'advocaat' if it is permitted to be used of alcoholic egg drinks generally and not confined to those that are spirit based.

These findings, he considered, brought the case within the principle of law laid down in the champagne case by Danckwerts J and applied in the sherry and Scotch whisky cases. He granted Warnink an injunction restraining Keeling from selling or distributing under the name or description 'advocaat' any product which does not basically consist of eggs and spirit without any admixture of wine.

[The Court of Appeal, in reversing the High Court decision, had distinguished the present case from the 'Champagne' case. They had found that while champagne was a product that could only be made by a particular class of producers, advocaat was merely the description of a particular type of drink. Lord Diplock believed this was not a useful distinction.]

Lord Diplock, at p. 747:

It cannot make any difference in principle whether the recognisable and distinctive qualities by which the reputation of the type of product has been gained are the result of its having been made in, or from ingredients produced in, a particular locality or are the result of its having been made from particular ingredients regardless of their provenance; though a geographical limitation may make it easier (a) to define the type of product; (b) to establish that it has qualities which are recognisable and distinguish it from every other type of product that competes with it in the market and which have gained for it in that market a reputation and goodwill; and (c) to establish that the plaintiff's own business will suffer more than minimal damage to its goodwill by the defendant's misrepresenting his product as being of that type.

In this case, Lord Diplock took the view that although most of the 'advocaat' on the English market came from the Netherlands, this was not its distinctive feature. Rather, any drink made in conformity to the official Dutch recipe wherever it was made, had the same recognizable and distinctive features which have gained 'advocaat' recognition and goodwill on the English market. It followed that Keelings were seeking to take advantage of this goodwill by misrepresenting that their own product was of that type.

Lord Diplock, at p. 748:

My Lords, all the five characteristics that I have earlier suggested must be present to create a valid cause of action in passing off today were present in the instant case. Prima facie as the law stands today, I think the presence of those characteristics is enough, unless there is also present in the case some exceptional feature which justifies, on grounds of public policy, withholding from a person who has suffered injury in consequence of the deception practised on prospective customers or consumers of his product a remedy in law against the deceiver. On the facts found by the judge, and I stress their importance, I can find no such exceptional feature in the instant case.

I would allow this appeal and restore the injunction granted by Goulding J.

In the 'Advocaat' case, it was accepted that because members of the public believed that in buying Keeling's 'Old English Advocaat' they were in fact buying advocaat made to the Dutch recipe, this misrepresentation would cause damage to the makers of the latter both directly through loss of sales and indirectly through the 'debasement' of the reputation attaching to the name 'advocaat'. In the later 'Elderflower Champagne' case, the defendant marketed a product, 'Elderflower Champagne' in a champagne-style bottle. It was, in fact, a non-alcoholic drink which sold at £2.35 a bottle. The Court of Appeal accepted that there had been a misrepresentation that the defendant's drink was champagne or in some way associated with it. They also concluded that it was a reasonably foreseeable consequence of the misrepresentation that there would be injury to the claimant's goodwill, both in loss of sales and the debasement of champagne's reputation. However, the court went on to suggest that the misrepresentation would also dilute the exclusivity of the name 'champagne', itself. The question of whether the 'Elderflower Champagne' case and later passing off decisions have extended the tort of passing off to encompass not merely damage to goodwill but also damage to the exclusivity of the distinguishing indicia as such will be discussed at 4.2.5 below on damage. We shall also ask the question of whether this is a legitimate extension of the tort of passing off.

4.2.4.4 The defendant claims that the goods or services of the claimant are his own

Following *Bristol Conservatories Ltd v Conservatories Custom Built Ltd*,[59] it is now generally accepted that inverse or reverse passing off falls within the wider tort of passing off. A key

---

[59] [1989] RPC 455.

problem to be overcome in this situation is that characteristically the public would not be in a position to know of the claimant, and hence would not be misled into thinking there was an association between the claimant and the defendant. In *Bristol Conservatories*, the defendant's salesman showed prospective customers photographs of conservatories, as if they were samples of their own work. In fact they were photographs of the claimant's conservatories. An action for passing off failed in the High Court, because the judge held that the public would not associate the conservatory in the photographs with the claimant; that there would be no confusion; and that the claimant had no goodwill which was affected by the showing of the photographs. The decision was overturned in the Court of Appeal. Gibson LJ held that the defendants, by their misrepresentation, were seeking to induce customers to purchase their conservatories in order to get a conservatory from the commercial source which had designed and constructed the conservatories shown in the photographs. However, if a customer ordered a conservatory they would not get one from this source, but rather one made by the defendants. This was passing off. As to goodwill, by showing the photographs to prospective customers goodwill was created for the supplier (that is the claimant) and at the same time misappropriated by the defendant. In reaching his decision, Gibson LJ stated that, 'I do not intend to decide whether there is a form of the tort to be known as reverse passing-off. It is sufficient, I think, to hold that the facts alleged can properly be regarded as within the tort of passing off'.[60]

Certainly, at least one commentator has noted that, like the extended form of passing off, most commonly reverse (or inverse) passing off will be concerned with a 'quality' misrepresentation rather than a misrepresentation as to origin and argues that this has led to an expansion in the ambit of passing off.[61]

4.2.4.5 Instruments of fraud

It is possible that a defendant may make available the means of making an actionable misrepresentation to others. For example, D may register the domain name of a well-known retailer such as Marks & Spencer. While not using the domain name itself, D may offer to sell the domain name on the open market. These were the facts in the case of *BT v One in a Million Ltd*,[62] where the defendants registered a number of domain names of well-known companies including marksandspencer.co.uk. In the Court of Appeal, the defendants were found to have created an instrument of fraud.[63] In other words, unless the purchaser of the domain name was Marks & Spencer (which may well have been the defendant's hope and intention when registering the name), the use of the domain name by any other purchaser would almost certainly amount to an actionable misrepresentation in relation to Marks & Spencer's goodwill. The defendants would, therefore, have furnished the purchaser with an 'instrument of fraud'. By making an instrument of fraud available for others, the defendant was found liable in passing off. The decision in *BT v One in a Million Ltd* has been criticized as an unacceptable extension of passing off, since the questions arise where the misrepresentation lies in this situation and what would be the resulting damage? One commentator has argued that the basis of the judgment seems to be that the claimants have ownership in their names as such and are, in principle, entitled to stop any

---

[60] *Bristol Conservatories*, p. 464.

[61] H. Carty, 'Inverse passing off: A suitable addition to passing off?' [1993] 10 EIPR 370.

[62] [1999] 1 WLR 903. See further 12.7.2.2.

[63] D was also found liable for passing off, because those who checked to see who had registered the domain name, would belief that One in a Million was associated in some way with Marks & Spencer.

other party from using the same names whether or not that use might be entirely legal.[64] Do you think that this is a legitimate ground for finding passing off?[65]

FURTHER READING

J. Griffiths, 'Misattribution and misrepresentation: The claim for reverse passing off as "patenting right"' [2006] IPQ 34.

G. Kwan, 'Infringement of trade marks and passing off by dealing in genuine articles' [2003] EIPR 45.

H. Carty, 'Inverse passing off: A suitable addition to passing off?' [1993] EIPR 370.

4.2.5 DAMAGE

4.2.5.1 Introduction

Damage is the third element identified by Lord Oliver in 'Jif Lemon' as necessary to establish an action in passing off. According to Lord Oliver, at p. 499, the claimant:

> must demonstrate that he suffers or, in a *quia timet* action, that he is likely to suffer damage by reason of the erroneous belief engendered by the defendant's misrepresentation that the source of the defendant's goods or services is the same as the source of those offered by the plaintiff.

In the same case, Lord Jauncey said, at p. 510:

> It is also a prerequisite that the misrepresentation has deceived or is likely to deceive and that the plaintiff is likely to suffer damage by such deception. Mere confusion which does not lead to a sale is not sufficient.

It is, in fact, possible to state two general principles about the role of damage in a passing off action:

1. The damage must be as a consequence of the defendant's misrepresentation.

2. There is no need for actual damage, as long as the claimant can show that there is a likelihood of damage.

A third principle would seem to be implicit in these dicta—that the damage must be to the claimant's goodwill. However, a number of recent cases have suggested that passing off may also protect against loss of distinctiveness in a claimant's insignia as such. Whether this is so remains a matter of debate which is examined below. Finally, it would be fair to say that in many passing off cases, the courts will assume that there is damage, or a likelihood of damage, if the claimant is able to prove that there is goodwill and a misrepresentation.[66] The courts will be more likely to infer damage where there is a common field of activity.

---

[64] A. Sim, 'Rethinking One in a Million' (2004) 26(10) EIPR 442–6.

[65] See also the case of *L'Oreal SA v Bellure NV* [2006] EWHC 2355.

[66] C. Wadlow, *The Law of Passing Off: Unfair competition by misrepresentation* (3rd edn, London: Sweet & Maxwell, 2004), p. 244; *Stringfellow v McCain Foods (GB)* [1984] FSR 175, [1984] RPC 501; *Harrods*, as per Millet LJ, at p. 714.

In his book, *The Law of Passing Off*, Christopher Wadlow suggests that the relevant damage in passing off may be divided into two general categories: destruction and diversion. The first category, destruction, occurs when the claimant's goodwill is 'destroyed, damaged, or depreciated.' For example, where the defendant sells substandard or counterfeit goods under the claimant's insignia. Wadlow defines the second category of damage, which is more common, as occurring when 'the goodwill as such may not initially be damaged to any measurable extent, but the claimant is just as certainly deprived of its benefit: the "attractive force" which is the goodwill may draw in custom as powerfully as before, but draw it to the defendant and not to the claimant.' He notes that these two categories of damage are frequently referred to without differentiation as 'damage to goodwill'.[67] Both these categories of damage will be considered below.

In summary, it is possible to identify four key heads of damage in passing off:

1. direct loss of sales
2. loss of reputation or control over reputation
3. dilution
4. loss of a licensing opportunity.[68]

4.2.5.2 Direct loss of sales

'Jif Lemon' is an example of a situation where the claimant would have lost sales to the defendant if the latter had continued to misrepresent its goods as those of the claimant. Similar damage would have occurred in 'Advocaat'. Direct loss of sales may also occur when a defendant sells the claimant's goods but misrepresents their quality as in *Spalding v Gamage*.

4.2.5.3 Loss of reputation or control over reputation

In the leading case of *Annabel's v Schock*, the Court of Appeal held that the claimants would suffer potential loss of earnings, because of the damage to their goodwill resulting from the association which the public would make between the claimants' and the defendant's business.

Annabel's (Berkley Square) Ltd v G Schock (t/a Annabel's Escort Agency)
[1972] FSR 261

The claimants were proprietors of a well-known London club, named Annabel's. They sought an interim injunction to restrain the defendant from carrying on the business of an escort agency under the name Annabel's Escort Agency. An injunction was granted in the High Court and the defendant appealed. A key question for the Court of Appeal was what was the nature of the misrepresentation and the consequent damage.

Russell LJ, at p. 269:

Here I have no doubt at all as at present advised that there is a sufficient association between what the public would consider the field of activity in which Annabel's Club is conducted and the field of activity in which Mr Schock indulges in the course of his escort business.

---

[67] C. Wadlow, *The Law of Passing Off* p. 241.
[68] This will be discussed in relation to character merchandising in Ch. 7.

Both are concerned with what might be described as 'night life' or 'hight [sic] entertainment'. Put another way, it can be said that Annabel's Club provides facilities to men for dining and dancing with female partners—though not in the sense that they are made available on the premises, as is the case, I understand, in some or perhaps many night clubs, where they are known as 'hostesses'. Turning it round slightly, Mr Schock's business is concerned with supplying for men facilities of female partners for the purpose, among other things, of dining and dancing with them.

I should have thought there was a relevant association between the fields of activities sufficient to make it impossible to say that the general public could not be confused into thinking that Mr Schock's business under the name of 'Annabel's' was something to do with or was associated with the plaintiffs' business also under the name of 'Annabel's'.

Now it is said, as I have previously remarked, that it may be that in terms of pounds and pence between now and the trial, when the whole matter will be finally decided, it is improbable having regard to their flourishing condition, that the plaintiffs through their club will actually lose money by the activities of Mr Schock trading under the business name of 'Annabel's Escort Agency'. Indeed, I think it is fair to remark that Mr Schock said: 'It may very well be that I have had one or two members of Annabel's who have applied to me for an escort to take them there, and no doubt have taken them there.' I dare say that has swollen the takings of the plaintiffs' club, though perhaps if it had not been that escort it would have been one of Jeannie's or another girl; one does not know. This may be so; but the crucial point seems to me in this case to be this: First of all, I absolutely and entirely agree with the learned judge that on the evidence there is a probability of confusion, and that some members of the public though not all will think that there is some association between the plaintiffs' club and Annabel's Escort Agency.

Having reached that stage we are then faced with this situation which has got nothing to do with immediate possible loss of takings by Annabel's Club, or even immediate falling off in membership, both of which seem unlikely. But the fact is, as Mr Schock very properly, rightly and honestly faced and agreed with, that escort agencies have, as yet, as a general activity, to say the least but an indifferent public image. I am prepared, of course, to accept from Mr Schock that everything to do with his particular agency has always been run with the strictest regard to public and private morals, and so on. But as he says, as yet one cannot but be tarred (I am not using his words) to some extent with the brush which the general public are inclined to think is appropriate to these escort agencies, though, according to Mr Schock they are satisfying a present and increasing want, and it may be that they will come to be thought to be a good thing or a better thing than they are thought to be now.

This seems to me to be the important matter. This seems to me to entitle Annabel's Club or the proprietors to now say what in my judgment is correct at this stage, namely: 'If it is going to be thought by a sufficient number of people that we are somehow associated with the running of an escort agency, some of the tar will come off on us, and we have no tar on us at all.' This is the real ground upon which it seems to me an interlocutory injunction is justified, because it is that kind of attack, albeit unintended, on the general good will of a plaintiff that requires the protection of an interlocutory injunction, because there is never going to be any means at the end of the road to see how much harm has been done by this kind of possible reputation being acquired in the mind of the public in regard to a perfectly respectable organisation and activity such as is the plaintiffs' and as is run by the plaintiffs.

For those reasons it appears to me that the learned judge was right in coming to his conclusion that this was a case in which an interlocutory injunction should be ordered, of course with an undertaking as to damages should the matter turn out differently on the evidence given at the trial. For those reasons I would dismiss the appeal.

An interesting aspect of this judgment is that Russell LJ accepted that it might not be possible to assess the actual damage to the claimant's goodwill which might result from the defendant's misrepresentation. As a result, he held that it was appropriate to order an interim injunction. 'Anticipated' damage, through both damage to the claimant's reputation because of an association with the defendant and also through loss of control over its reputation in the future was also the issue in *McAlpine v McAlpine*.

Sir Robert McAlpine Ltd v Alfred McAlpine Plc [2004] EWHC 630

The claimant and the defendant, both construction companies, had a common source. The original company had been founded by Sir Robert McAlpine in 1869. In 1935 the business was divided along geographical lines, into two companies which until 2001 traded under the names Robert McAlpine and Alfred McAlpine respectively. Both companies were involved in construction, civil engineering and property management, although over the years the defendant began to diversify into other fields including IT. In 2001, the defendant decided to drop the word 'Alfred' from its trading and to brand itself simply as 'McAlpine'. In 2003, the claimant sued for passing off, claiming that by using the name 'McAlpine' alone, the defendant was misrepresenting, *inter alia,* that the defendant was associated with the claimant or alternatively that it was the sole owner of the goodwill in the name McAlpine. At the trial, it was agreed between the parties that they shared the goodwill in the name 'McAlpine'. The claimant suggested it might suffer damage in a number of ways: through association between the two companies; because any bad publicity which 'McAlpine' attracted might be associated with the claimant; and finally, because the defendant might be advantaged by trading on the joint goodwill of the parties. The claimant did not claim for damage for direct loss of business. Mann J held that passing off had been proved. He had the following to say in relation to the claimant's claim for damage by association and loss of control over its reputation.

Mann J:

Damage

41. This is the most difficult aspect of this case. There has been no attempt to prove that actual quantifiable damage has occurred (though there was some limited evidence that actual confusion had already occurred). That is not surprising. It is only a relatively short time since the rebranding occurred. Robert puts its case on the footing of anticipated damage. Robert seeks to establish that it is 'really likely' to suffer damage to its goodwill within the test in *Erven Warnink BV v J Townend & Sons (Hull) Ltd* [1980] RPC 31 (the Advocaat case, per Lord Fraser).

42. This case does not manifest what might be regarded as the classic passing-off damage, namely the diversion of business from one company to the other by reason of the misrepresentation that A's goods or services are B's. I have set out earlier in this judgment the nature of the business of the two groups, how they overlap and how that business is won. In the light of that evidence it is not possible to hold that there is any present likelihood of Alfred being awarded a contract in the mistaken belief that it is Robert. By the time contracts are signed, a customer (employer) is likely to be well enough informed to know that he is dealing with Alfred and not Robert, if he had ever thought otherwise. Indeed, Mr Wyand did not put his case on the footing that this was the sort of damage that his

client was likely to suffer. He said that his client was likely to suffer damage in one or more of the following ways:

(a) Robert might lose business because of an erroneous association with Alfred in the mind of a customer who has views about 'McAlpine' but at that stage is not sufficiently well informed to know that there are two and that his views in fact relate to Alfred and not Robert. Alfred might sustain some adverse publicity which is in fact attributed to 'McAlpine'. Because the name imports an association with Robert in the minds of some people, there is a risk that Robert will not get on to a tender list which it would otherwise have got on, because the people with the power of selection (who may well be non-professionals in the industry) will make a false association.

(b) Allied to this is what is said to be a general risk to its reputation and goodwill arising where Alfred does something attracting bad publicity which rubs off in a general way on Robert because of a false association between 'McAlpine' (who on this hypothesis have sustained bad publicity) and Robert. An example was given involving railway maintenance—if there were a railway accident involving McAlpine maintenance items then there might be general damage to goodwill and to the McAlpine name. Since Robert shares that name, and the attendant publicity is more likely to arise without the identifying 'Alfred', then Robert's goodwill would suffer, as (potentially) would its business.

(c) Alfred may get work it would not otherwise get (though not necessarily at Robert's expense) because of the exploitation of the joint reputation built into the name—'punching above its weight'.

43. I shall take heads (a) and (b) together. As a matter of principle they ought to amount to damage if the risk is sufficiently great. I have already set out some extracts from authority which deal with the question of damage. That authority indicates, and it indeed is accepted by Alfred, that the relevant damage, for the purposes of passing off, is not limited to loss of sales to an opponent, or cases where the defendant's goods or services are inferior to those of the claimant. As Mr Thorley put it, injurious association or dilution of exclusivity can, in an appropriate case, amount to damage....

44. I therefore have to weigh and assess the risks of damage relied on by Robert in the light of the evidence. First, there is the question of the level of risk of a tarnishing of the McAlpine name. This is impossible to quantify, but it is a possibility. With one exception, no witness suggested that Alfred enjoyed anything other than a good current reputation in terms of its work, payment record, creditworthiness, health and safety matters and all other things that would establish a good business reputation. (The one exception was Mr Kerr, who gave some evidence that Alfred had a poor payment record and a record for being confrontational in building disputes. I accept that he had that belief, but I do not think that it is shared generally in the industry, and I find that it is not a fair picture of Alfred.) There were no positive indications that its good reputation was about to change. However, that is not entirely the point. There is a risk. A number of things might plausibly happen. Alfred's business reputation in one or more of the areas might change; or its reputation might be affected by some engineering misfortune which gains some publicity. Since Alfred is involved in railway maintenance, fears were expressed by one witness that accidents in that area might affect its reputation, though it was pointed out that Alfred's railway maintenance activities related to such fixtures as embankments, and not to such things as the track and signalling, where reputations might be said to be more vulnerable. Other work was put forward as possibly causing public opprobrium, such as participating in an environmentally sensitive road building project.

45. I do not think that it can be said that any of these things are probable, but it certainly cannot be said that they are fanciful. They are a real possibility in the modern commercial world. I do not think that Warrington LJ was insisting on proof of his various items on a balance of probabilities before they could count as damage for the purposes of passing off. It seems to me to be sufficient that there is a real risk that the claimant would be affected by one or more of them, or by similar matters.

[Having pointed out that the defendant's actions risked damaging the claimant's reputation in the future, **Mann J** then looked at various ways in which the claimant might be negatively associated with the defendant. He gave an example.]

46. Mr Spencer, who heads Robert's PFI division, considered that there was a risk that members of the PFI project board, who took the ultimate decision, might be influenced by bad publicity given to Alfred (on this hypothesis known simply as 'McAlpine'),wrongly failing to distinguish between the two companies, and that as a result Robert would not get on to a bid list.

. . .

47. I bear in mind that the customers of Robert and Alfred operate in a relatively sophisticated and well-informed market. Many will be sufficiently well-informed to be able to distinguish between the two, and not to let an adverse impression attaching to one affect its judgments in relation to the other. However, I am satisfied that there is still scope for the sort of adverse effects referred to above, and that that scope presents a sufficiently high risk to the reputation of Robert as to amount to damage for the purposes of passing off. After the rebranding there is greater scope for adverse publicity and reputation to be attached to 'McAlpine' (after all, putting the name forward prominently is part of the purpose of the rebranding exercise) without a distinguishing 'Alfred', and for that to rub off on Robert because of the shared goodwill and shared name. I accept that some of the risks tend to be more speculative than others—for example, the risk of being excluded from PFI work at the pre-qualification stage—but I have to look at the matter in the round and realistically, and doing so leads me to the conclusion that the risks are real enough to amount to the sort of damage that the law of passing off is intended to prevent, as Warrington LJ stated.

In the 'McAlpine' case, Mann J concluded that the damage caused by the defendant's misrepresentation would be not only to the claimant's reputation (or goodwill) but also to value of the claimant's 'name'. Sometimes known as 'dilution', there has been considerable controversy as to what extent passing off covers this head of damage.

4.2.5.4 Damage by dilution

The case which is generally credited with recognizing damage which dilutes the value of the claimant's identifying insignia (most usually its name) rather than directly damaging its goodwill is the 'Elderflower Champagne' case.

***Taittinger v Allbev Ltd* (Discovery)** [1993] FSR 641

The claimants produced champagne and French wines. Previous actions taken by them had ensured that the name 'champagne' was used only for sparkling wine produced in the Champagne district of France. The defendants produced a cheap drink

under the name 'Elderflower Champagne'. The drink was non-alcoholic, but was car-
bonated and was sold in champagne-style bottles with labels and wired corks similar
to those used on champagne bottles. The claimants sued for passing off. They were
unsuccessful in the High Court. The court accepted that there had been a misrepresentation, but did not believe that there was a likelihood of serious damage, because
only a small number of people were likely to be confused. The claimants appealed.
In the Court of Appeal, Peter Gibson LJ in his leading judgment concluded that it
was 'at least as likely that a not insignificant number of members of the public would
think that it [the defendant's product] had some association with champagne, if it was
not actually champagne'. In addition, he held that there was ample evidence that as
a reasonably foreseeable consequence of that misrepresentation injury to the champagne houses' goodwill would result. Furthermore, even though the activities of the
defendant were on a 'small scale' leading to 'a small injury', he took the view that this
could not be ignored and that the claimants might well suffer damage through loss of
sales. He then identified an additional head of damage which might result from the
defendant's misrepresentation, but which had been rejected by Sir Mervyn Davies in
the High Court.

Peter Gibson LJ, at p. 669:

But in my judgment the real injury to the champagne houses' goodwill comes under a different head and although the judge refers to Mr Sparrow [the plaintiff's counsel] putting the
point in argument, he does not deal with it specifically or give a reason for its undoubted
rejection by him. Mr Sparrow had argued that if the defendants continued to market their
product, there would take place a blurring or erosion of the uniqueness that now attends
the word 'champagne', so that the exclusive reputation of the champagne houses would be
debased. He put this even more forcefully before us. He submitted that if the defendants
are allowed to continue to call their product Elderflower Champagne, the effect would be to
demolish the distinctiveness of the word champagne, and that would inevitably damage the
goodwill of the champagne houses.

In the Advocaat case at first instance ([1980] RPC 31 at 52) Goulding J held that one type
of damage was 'a more gradual damage to the plaintiffs' business through depreciation of the
reputation that their goods enjoy'. He continued:

Damage of [this] type can rarely be susceptible of positive proof. In my judgment, it is likely to
occur if the word 'Advocaat' is permitted to be used of alcoholic egg drinks generally or of the
defendants' product in particular.

In the House of Lords in that case Lord Diplock referred to that type of damage to goodwill as
relevant damage, which he described as caused 'indirectly in the debasement of the reputation attaching to the name "advocaat"' ([1979] AC 731 at 740).

In *Vine Products Ltd v MacKenzie & Co Ltd* [1969] RPC 1 at 23 Cross J, commenting with
approval on the decision of Danckwerts J in *Bollinger v Costa Brava Wine Co Ltd (No 2)* said:

[Danckwerts J] thought, as I read in his judgment, that if people were allowed to call sparkling
wine not produced in Champagne 'Champagne', even though preceded by an adjective denoting
the country of origin, the distinction between genuine Champagne and 'champagne type' wines
produced elsewhere would become blurred; that the word 'Champagne' would come gradually
to mean no more than 'sparkling wine'; and that the part of the plaintiffs' goodwill which consisted in the name would be diluted and gradually destroyed.

[**Peter Gibson LJ** then identified later cases in both Australia and New Zealand which had approved **Danckwert J's** approach in the 'champagne' case to the blurring of its distinctive name. He continued at p. 670:]

It seems to me inevitable that if the defendants, with their not insignificant trade as a supplier of drinks to Sainsbury and other retail outlets, are permitted to use the name Elderflower Champagne, the goodwill in the distinctive name champagne will be eroded with serious adverse consequences for the champagne houses.

In my judgment therefore the fifth characteristic identified in the Advocaat case is established. I can see no exceptional feature to this case which would justify on grounds of public policy withholding from the champagne houses the ordinary remedy of an injunction to restrain passing off. I would therefore grant an injunction to restrain the defendant from selling, offering for sale, distributing and describing, whether in advertisements or on labels or in any other way, any beverages, not being wine produced in Champagne, under or by reference to the word champagne. That injunction, I would, emphasise, does not prevent the sale of the defendants' product, provided it is not called champagne.

[Both **Mann LJ** and **Lord Bingham MR** concurred that the claimants would suffer sufficient damage, both to their goodwill and to the exclusivity of their name.]

Mann LJ, at p. 673–4:

Their case was and is, that the word 'Champagne' has an exclusiveness which is impaired if it is used in relation to a product (particularly a potable product) which is neither Champagne nor associated or connected with the businesses which produce Champagne. The impairment is a gradual debasement, dilution or erosion of what is distinctive.

. . .

The consequences of debasement, dilution or erosion are not demonstrable in figures of lost sales but that they will be incrementally damaging to goodwill is in my opinion inescapable. On this basis I would grant injunctive relief as claimed.

Bingham LJ, at p. 678:

Any product which is not Champagne but is allowed to describe itself as such must inevitably, in my view, erode the singularity and exclusiveness of the description Champagne and so cause the first plaintiffs damage of an insidious but serious kind.

As we have seen, Peter Gibson LJ had cited a number of cases, including previous drinks cases, to support his finding that damage to the exclusivity of the claimant's name fell within the parameters of a passing off action. Yet following his judgment, a number of commentators have suggested that the Court of Appeal had in fact extended the boundaries of passing off. In her commentary, 'The Elderflower Champagne Case: Is this a further expansion of the tort of passing off?',[69] Fiona Russell notes that:

this [is the] aspect of the case which is perhaps the most interesting for those studying the elasticity of the English remedy of passing off. Such damage is akin to the American concept of dilution. To date, this has not been expressly recognised by the English courts although it

[69] F. Russell, 'The Elderflower Champagne Case: Is this a further expansion of the tort of passing off?' (1993) 10 EIPR 379, pp. 380–1.

has long been thought that something similar did exist in English law. The Court of Appeal decision in the Elderflower case has in the writer's submission confirmed that such a concept is very much now part of English law.

Millet LJ in *Harrods* took the view that, following the 'Elderflower Champagne' case, the law of passing off was in danger of operating in areas which he for one found inappropriate. He expressed this view while discussing the element of damage in relation to the claimant's claim.

Millet LJ, at p. 715:

Damage

In the classic case of passing off, where the defendant represents his goods or business as the goods or business of the plaintiff, there is an obvious risk of damage to the plaintiff's business by substitution. Customers and potential customers will be lost to the plaintiff if they transfer their custom to the defendant in the belief that they are dealing with the plaintiff. But this is not the only kind of damage which may be caused to the plaintiff's goodwill by the deception of the public. Where the parties are not in competition with each other, the plaintiff's reputation and goodwill may be damaged without any corresponding gain to the defendant. In the Lego case, for example, a customer who was dissatisfied with the defendant's plastic irrigation equipment might be dissuaded from buying one of the plaintiff's plastic toy construction kits for his children if he believed that it was made by the defendant. The danger in such a case is that the plaintiff loses control over his own reputation.

In *Taittinger SA v Allbev Ltd* [1993] FSR 641 the court appears to have recognised a different head of damage. If the defendants were allowed to market their product under the name Elderflower Champagne

there would take place a blurring or erosion of the uniqueness that now attends the word 'champagne', so that the exclusive reputation of the champagne houses would be debased. (per Peter Gibson LJ at page 669)

It is self-evident that the application of the plaintiff's brand name to inferior goods is likely to injure the plaintiff's reputation and damage his goodwill if people take the inferior goods to be those of the plaintiff. That is a classic head of damage in cases of passing off. But Peter Gibson LJ may have had more in mind than this. He referred without disapproval to the submission of counsel for the plaintiffs that if the defendants were allowed to continue to call their product Elderflower Champagne 'the effect would be to demolish the distinctiveness of the word champagne, and that would inevitably damage the goodwill of the champagne houses'.

This is a reference to the debasement of the distinctiveness of the name champagne which would occur if it gradually came to be used by the public as a generic term to describe any kind of sparkling wine. Erosion of the distinctiveness of a brand name has been recognised as a form of damage to the goodwill of the business with which the name is connected in a number of cases, particularly in Australia and New Zealand; but unless care is taken this could mark an unacceptable extension to the tort of passing off. To date the law has not sought to protect the value of the brand name as such, but the value of the goodwill which it generates; and it insists on proof of confusion to justify its intervention. But the erosion of the distinctiveness of a brand name which occurs by reason of its degeneration into common use as a generic term is not necessarily dependent on confusion at all. The danger that if the defendant's product was called champagne then all sparkling wines would eventually come to be called champagne would still exist even if no one was deceived into thinking that such wine really was champagne. I have an intellectual difficulty in accepting the concept that the law insists upon the presence of both confusion and damage and yet recognises as sufficient a head of damage which does not depend on confusion. Counsel for the plaintiffs relied strongly on the possibility of damage of this nature, but it is in my opinion not necessary to consider it further in the present case. There is no danger of 'Harrods' becoming a generic term for a retail emporium in the luxury class, and if such a danger existed the use of a different name in connection with an institution of a different kind would not advance the process.

Millet LJ observed that he was uncomfortable with a head of damage in passing off which did not rely on a misrepresentation, but rather a simple association made by the public between the name of the claimant's product and that of the defendant's, which might damage the exclusivity of the former. In his dissenting judgment in the same case, Sir Michael Kerr showed no such reservations. He noted, for example, that Harman J in the High Court, appears to have given 'no or insufficient weight to the fact that a trader's distinctive name can in some cases in itself form part of his goodwill and constitute a property interest, and that this is the position here'. He then considered the issue of damage.

Sir Michael Kerr, at p. 724:

The standard remedy in passing-off actions is an injunction; an account to assess damages is rare. In the great majority of cases the relevant damage will not be measurable in pounds and pence, but consist in the probability of damage to the plaintiff's reputation and goodwill which is ultimately liable to lead indirectly to a reduction in trade. Loss of distinctiveness causes damage to a reputation for excellence, and loss of trade will ultimately follow. The authorities show two relevant propositions in this regard. First, a debasement or dilution of the plaintiff's reputation, as the result of the action of the defendant, is a relevant head of damage. Secondly, if the act which constitutes the passing-off has the effect of raising in people's minds the mistaken belief of a connection between the defendant and the plaintiff, but which is in fact non-existent, then the court will have regard to the fact that the plaintiff has, to that extent, lost control of his reputation, and that he has therefore suffered damage to his goodwill by a potentially injurious association with the defendant against which the court will protect him by injunction.

A number of passages bear out these propositions. Inevitably, the factual contexts were different, but the aspects of principle are not open to question.

[**Sir Michael Kerr** then quoted approvingly the comments of **Peter Gibson LJ**, **Bingham LJ** and **Mann LJ** in the 'Elderflower Champagne' case in which each recognized loss of distinctiveness in the name champagne as a head of damage. He continued at p. 725:]

In fairness to the defendants, it cannot of course be said in the present case that a similar consequence [to those] would necessarily follow, and indeed it is greatly to be hoped that this would not be the case. But that is not the test. The crucial point, as stated in the second of the foregoing propositions, is the plaintiff's inevitable loss of control of his reputation and the consequent risk of damage to it.

Later decisions suggest that Lord Justice Millet's suspicion of this apparent extension to passing off has not been generally shared by the judiciary. Indeed, it is submitted that it was Sir Michael Kerr's judgment which has proved to be more prescient in terms of the future direction of passing off. For example, in *Dawnay Day v Cantor Fitzgerald*,[70] which concerned the use by the defendants of the name Dawnay Day Securities where the claimant's group company was also known as Dawnay Day, Sir Richard Scott held at pp. 705–6, following 'Elderflower Champagne', that the damage suffered by the claimant was of two varieties:

> First the Dawnay Day members, collectively and individually have no control over the activities of the proprietors of Dawnay Day Securities. The Dawnay Day reputation will suffer if those activities become in any respect reprehensible. The Dawnay Day companies will be unable to prevent that happening. Secondly, the use of Dawnay Day as a trading company that is not a member of the Dawnay Day group will dilute and, potentially, may destroy the distinctiveness of the name.

The notion that passing off will protect the claimant's name against an erosion or dilution of its distinctiveness was accepted in *Irvine v Talksport* where Laddie J noted that the law 'will not allow others so to use goodwill as to reduce, blur or diminish its exclusivity'.[71] It was also accepted in *McAlpine v McAlpine*, where Mann J cited both 'Elderflower Champagne' and *Irvine* to support his conclusion that the claimants were at risk of having their name damaged by dilution.[72]

In 1996, following the *Harrods* decision, Hazel Carty argued that the extension of the tort of passing off to cover actions for dilution of a name as such was a cause for concern. She first set out to define the problem.

H. Carty, 'Dilution and passing off: Cause for concern' (1996) 112 (October) LQR 632–66

[at p. 632]

The issue

The trouble with a 'protean' tort such as passing off is that the more elastic it becomes, so the danger increases that it will lose its coherence and rationale. Over this century, the tort of passing off has developed in leaps and bounds and now, it is submitted, may be on the brink of its most radical extension yet: to give protection against 'dilution' of a trade mark. Such an extension, it will be argued, undermines the rationale of the tort, shifting the focus of the tort away from misrepresentation and customer confusion towards protection of trade values per se.

[Carty points out that the tort was developed to protect both traders and customers against the results of a misrepresentation, not to protect the 'commercial magnetism' of a trade mark as such. She continues at pp. 633–4:]

Throughout the century the tort has developed. Misrepresentations relevant to the tort have increased and this has led to an extension of the concept of 'goodwill', to include not only customer connection to a source, but customer connection to a product. However, attempts to enlarge the tort yet further continue. In particular, plaintiffs seek to expand upon the heads of damage relevant to the tort. Thus increasingly in recent years the allegation of dilution has

---

[70] *Dawnay Day & Co Ltd v Cantor Fitzgerald International* [2000] RPC 669.
[71] At p. 958.   [72] [2004] EWHC 630, para. 20.

been added to passing off claims. Perhaps the highest profile of these attempts to guard the 'exclusivity' of a name has resulted from the campaign of the champagne houses to preserve the sanctity of the name 'Champagne'. They are not satisfied simply to prevent less sophisticated purchasers buying sparkling wine wrongly labelled champagne (a standard passing off action). They want to prevent what they perceive to be the threat of erosion of the 'exclusivity' of the name champagne. Such erosion of exclusivity or distinctiveness is termed 'dilution' in American trademark law.

To an extent this campaign bore fruit in *Taittinger SA v Allbev Ltd*, where the complaint concerned the use of the word champagne in the name of a non-alcoholic beverage, 'Elderflower Champagne'. All three members of the Court of Appeal, awarding an injunction in favour of the champagne houses, used the word 'dilution' or equivalents to describe the plaintiff's potential damage. Thus Peter Gibson LJ commented on the 'blurring or erosion of the uniqueness that now attaches to the word "champagne"'. Mann LJ noted the concern that the exclusiveness of 'champagne' would be impaired, resulting in a 'gradual debasement, dilution or erosion of what is distinctive'. Sir Thomas Bingham MR accepted that the use of the word 'champagne' on a product which is not the real thing would erode the singularity of the description champagne 'and so cause the [plaintiffs]…damage of an insidious but serious kind'.

Yet to legitimise the concept of dilution without analysis and adequate definition is, with respect, dangerous. The certainties of the tort are threatened. More dangerous still is the fact that the true focal point of dilution is the protection of the uniqueness of the trade mark in itself. With a claim for dilution, the rationale of the tort of passing off and its countervailing considerations of trader protection and public interest are obscured. The real thrust of a dilution claim is to protect the name or mark as an economic asset of importance. Protecting established traders, who, given their concern to maintain an exclusive or well-known mark, are already more than successful, becomes the (dubious) rationale.

Since *Taittinger*, a differently constituted Court of Appeal in *Harrods Ltd v Harrodian School* has revealed a conflict within the court on this issue. Thus while Millett LJ cautioned against 'unacceptable extensions' of the tort, Sir Michael Kerr (in a dissenting judgment) adopted dilution terminology similar to that used in *Taittinger*. There is an urgent need for guidance from the House of Lords on this matter.

Carty goes on to argue that following the 'Elderflower Champagne' case, which recognized dilution as a head of damage, 'passing off' is in danger of being transformed into 'misappropriation' without any acknowledgement—judicial or academic—that this is so. She takes the view that confusion dilution of the sort recognized in 'Elderflower Champagne', which involves no damage to goodwill is incompatible with the public interest protected by passing off. According to the author, the relevant misrepresentation in passing off should be one that attacks the established 'customer connection', since as a result the consumer may make inefficient choices. However, if damage to goodwill is not necessary, then traders 'will be overprotected'. As a result, she goes on to say that the 'Elderflower Champagne' case introduced 'misappropriation in disguise' because it is the mark's effectiveness as an advertising tool which is being protected not its role as an indicator of origin. It is Carty's view that although a mark may have commercial value as an advertising tool, it is not necessarily in the public interest to recognize a right in it, since by protecting a mark's advertising potential, it is 'emotional' information which is being protected and not 'rational' information such as the source of origin of the goods. The advertising function of mark does not necessarily serve the consumers' interest, because consumer loyalty becomes tied to the brand not to the qualities of the goods. This is not the tradition in passing off. She then summarizes her arguments at p. 655:

Dilution: the need for caution

In light of the above discussion, it is important to summarise the problems that an acceptance of the notion of dilution into passing off actions would pose.

(1) Imprecision

As has already been noted the notion of dilution is ill-defined. It can range from an additional head of damage tagged on to no real effect in a standard passing off claim to a denial of the classic trinity in toto. Pattishall, a dilution theory supporter, called the dilution concept 'bewilderingly intangible'. Given the majority of passing off claims are interlocutory, this is all the more alarming. The need for goodwill and damage to that goodwill 'provides valuable fence posts which have hitherto marked the territory protected by passing off'.

(2) Does dilution exist and can it be proved?

How can dilution be proved? What evidence would be capable of showing that a consumer's perception of the mark has become 'blurred' by the defendant's use of the same or similar mark? Would the court not really be penalising free rider' (see below)?

Dilution theory holds that the existence of alternative uses of the mark by others will necessarily detract from the selling power of the original mark. Welkowitz contends that dilution remains undefined in American case law: where a remedy against dilution is granted, the Court assumes the presence of harm. This is also true of the leading proponents of the dilution theory. Thus Schechter in his seminal article gave an example of the progress of dilution, using the Rolls Royce mark: 'if you allow Rolls Royce restaurants and Rolls Royce cafeterias and Rolls Royce pants and Rolls Royce candy, in 10 years you will not have the Rolls Royce mark any more'. The serious flaw here, identified by Welkowitz is that 'it assumes that, at some point, there will be several Rolls Royce items of significant public consciousness. In such a circumstance, Rolls Royce candy would be sufficiently well known in comparison to Rolls Royce cars that when people hear Rolls Royce they are likely to think of a candy bar instead of a car, or luxury or other attributes symbolized by the Rolls Royce mark on cars and jet engines. No reason, however, justifies a belief in that scenario.' Why should the existence of the second mark necessarily detract from the selling power of the first mark?

(3) Dilution and misappropriation

A major concern is that the notion of dilution is simply an obscure way of claiming unfair competition or misappropriation. Welkowitz, writing on the American experience of the dilution claims (in all their diversity), believes that the courts are in fact applying a doctrine of misappropriation, but using the label of dilution. 'The best explanation for pure dilution cases appears to be that some courts view it as a way of granting protection when the evidence of confusion is weak, but the court believes the defendant's use of the mark to be unfair.' The courts' real concern is about 'free riders' attempting to harness another's success: hence they assume dilution. Misappropriation, of course, is not really a concept that is concerned about whittling away or erosion but about 'unfair' profiting. Interestingly, in *Taittinger* Sir Thomas Bingham MR commented that it would be unfair to allow others to 'cash in on the reputation that they had done nothing to establish', a dictum referred to by Sir Michael Kerr in *Harrods*, who further noted that the defendant was not entitled to 'ride on the back of' the reputation of the name Harrods.

(4) Would an acceptance of dilution as harm in the tort of passing off offer a benefit to the competitive process?

The question is whether the existing action for passing off is adequate for the perceived rationale: to promote efficient competition. The answer would appear to be in the affirmative, if tort law is not to encroach unnecessarily upon the competitive process. However, that is precisely what dilution or misappropriation does: it focuses on standards of fairness rather than the competitive order as its rationale. The rationale of Anglo-Saxon unfair competition law has always been otherwise. 'The illegality and unfairness of the individual competitor in his struggle with the other competitors is not determined by the fairness of his conduct, but by the determination as to whether or not the result of his behaviour hinders or stifles the competitive process of differentiation and imitation.'[73]

Again, it is more than debatable that well-known or successful marks need the extra help of dilution protection. Rather, they already have the advertising power and market strength to maintain their commercial success. 'If trademark owners fail to promote the mark and its products, then they run the risk that another, non-confusing use will supplant the fame of the older mark. But this is as it should be. In a competitive economy, the competitors must stay alert. A failure to advertise exemplifies a failure to compete effectively.'[74]

It is interesting to note that the 1994 Trade Marks Act (unlike its 1938 predecessor) does allow certain registered trade marks to be protected from dilution. These marks are those with a reputation, in other words, marks with exceptional advertising value and market strength.[75] Arguably, such an approach gives priority to the interest of the proprietor in protecting the investment he has made in a mark with a reputation (which is often considerable) rather than in ensuring that competition remains unhindered or even that the public is protected against confusion. Given the enormous value of certain marks and their significant role in the global economy, it is perhaps unsurprising that the tort of passing off has also evolved to give such marks additional protection. In her article, Hazel Carty would seem to suggest that as regards passing off, at least, its primary purpose should be to protect the interests of the consumer, who may be confused. However, as has been suggested at the start of this chapter, it is arguable that the primary interest protected by passing off, in the UK, is that of the trader rather than the consumer. Given this emphasis in passing off, do you think it is unrealistic to seek to prevent dilution of the distinctive insignia becoming a head of damage under the tort?

FURTHER READING

H. Carty, 'Heads of damage in passing off' [1996] EIPR 487.

A. Murray, 'A Distinct Lack of Goodwill' [1997] EIPR 345.

F. Russell, 'The Elderflower Champagne case: Is this a further expansion of the tort of passing off?' [1993] EIPR 379.

[73] P. J. Kaufmann, 'Passing off and misappropriation: An economic and legal analysis of the law of unfair competition in the United States and Continental Europe [1986] IIC Studies 15.
[74] D. Welkowitz (1994) 44 Vand LR 531, 586.   [75] See 6.1.4.

4.3 DEFENCES

The three most common defences in passing off are:

1. delay or acquiesence
2. concurrent use
3. bona fide use of the defendant's own name.

4.3.1 DELAY OR ACQUIESENCE

If a claimant delays in bringing an action for passing off, he does not forfeit his right to do so as long as the alleged passing off is continuing. However, such delay may bring other unwelcome consequences. The claimant may be unlikely to succeed in obtaining an interim injunction. Or the defendant may have built up its own goodwill in the product or services which is independent of the claimant. Thus, in *Daimler Chrysler AG v Alavi*,[76] the claimant was the owner of the Mercedes Benz motor car company. The claimant's car was often referred to by the term, 'Merc'. The defendant owned a clothes shop called 'Merc' and also sold clothes under the name 'Merc', and had been doing so since 1967. Daimler Chrysler had registered trade marks for both 'Mercedes' and 'Merc' for, *inter alia*, clothing. It sued Alavi for both passing off and trade mark infringement. The claim for passing off failed. The court held that there had been no deception by the defendant, because by 1975 the defendant had established its own goodwill trading under the name 'Merc'. In some circumstances, the court may take the claimant's delay in bringing an action as evidence of acquiesence to the defendant's conduct. According to Christopher Wadlow, 'the irreducible minimum' of the defence of acquiesence is that the defendant must have altered his position in reliance on the claimaint's action or on his failure to act, or on a representation by the claimant that 'would make it inequitable for the claimant to enforce his rights'.[77] Acquiesence was found by the Court of Appeal in *Habib Bank v Habib Bank AG Zurich*.[78] However, the court did not find acquiesence in the 'Merc' case. According to Pumfrey J at p. 850:

> It is an essential component in a defence of acquiescence that the failure of the plaintiff to act should have induced the defendant to believe that the wrong was being assented to. But in this case there was no such reliance by Mr Alavi...in any event, DaimlerChrysler (or their predecessors) were not aware of his trading activities until 1997. These facts cannot support a plea of acquiescence. But the period of trading is long. Had I found that Mr Alavi had infringed one or more of the Mercedes marks, but that there was no passing off, and that there had been no damage, perhaps the question of delay should have to be considered in the context of relief. But the question does not arise. This defence fails.

4.3.2 BONA FIDE USE OF THE DEFENDANT'S OWN NAME

Use by a defendant of his own name may provide a defence in passing off, but it is a narrow one. For example, the defence has never been held to apply to names of new companies

---

[76] [2001] RPC 42.   [77] C. Wadlow, *The Law of Passing Off*, p. 790.   [78] [1981] 1 WLR 1265.

'as otherwise a route to piracy would be obvious'.[79] The limited nature of this defence was recently confirmed by the Court of Appeal in *Reed Executive v Reed Business Information*.

Reed Executive Plc v Reed Business Information Ltd [2004] RPC 40

The claimants had operated employment agencies since 1960 and recently through a website, 'reed.co.uk'. They had a registered trade mark 'Reed' for employment agency services since 1996. The defendants published, *inter alia*, business and science journals and magazines and had used the word Reed in relation to their business since 1983. In 1999, the defendants started their own website, totaljobs.com, which, *inter alia*, advertised jobs which had traditionally been advertised in the journals. Initially, the names 'Reed Elsevier' and 'Reed Business Information' logos appeared on the website. Furthermore, the word Reed was used as a metatag for the website and as a reference word for a variety of web advertising, although none of the advertisements actually used the word Reed. In addition, the Yahoo search engine linked the search terms 'recruitment' and 'job' to the totaljobs.com website and Yahoo gave the defendants a free use of their own name. The name Reed was chosen by Yahoo rather than Reed Elsevier. There was some minor evidence of confusion, that is enquiries being made to the claimants about jobs advertised by the defendants on their website. By the date of the trial, the only use of Reed on the defendant's website was to be found in the use of the name Reed Business Information Ltd in the copyright notices on the site and the Reed Business Information logo which was on the home page when it came up on the screen. The claimants sued for both trade mark infringement and passing off. In relation to the latter, the defendants argued both that there was no actionable misrepresentation and in addition that they had a defence of bona fide use of their own name. Although the Court of Appeal found that there had been neither trade mark infringement nor passing off, Jacob LJ did go on to examine the scope of the own name defence in passing off.

Jacob LJ:

The own name defence to passing off

109. It is long and well settled that it is no defence to passing off that the defendant has or had no intention to deceive. It is also settled that there is only a very limited own name defence. It was put this way by Romer J in *Joseph Rodgers & Sons Ltd v WN Rodgers & Co* (1924) 41 RPC 277, a passage approved by the majority of the House of Lords in *Parker-Knoll Ltd v Knoll International Ltd* [1962] RPC 265:

> To the proposition of law [that no man is entitled to carry on his business in such a way as to represent that it is the business of another, or is in any way connected with the business of another], there is an exception, that a man is entitled to carry on his business in his own name so long as he does not do anything more than that to cause confusion with the business of another, and so long as he does it honestly. To the proposition of law that [no man is entitled so to describe his goods as to represent that the goods are the goods of another,] there is no exception.

110. Thus the English law of passing off abounds with cases where people have been prevented from using their own name. This particularly happens when a scion of some well-known family business has sought to cash in on his name at the expense of that business, as

---

[79] *Asprey & Garrard Ltd v WRA (Guns) Ltd and Asprey* [2002] ETMR 47 as per Peter Gibson LJ.

for instance Dunhill (*Alfred Dunhill Ltd v Sunoptic SA* [1979] FSR 337), Gucci (*Guccio Gucci SpA v Paulo Gucci* [1991] FSR 89) and Asprey (*Asprey & Garrard Ltd v WRA (Guns) Ltd* [2002] FSR 31).

111. I have already observed that the difference between mere confusion and deception is elusive. I suppose the sort of background non-damaging confusion in this case might be the sort of thing Romer J had in mind. Once the position strays into misleading a substantial number of people (going from 'I wonder if there is a connection' to 'I assume there is a connection') there will be passing off, whether the use is as a business name or a trade mark on goods.

112. The judge [in the High Court] rightly observed that the passing-off defence is narrow. Actually no case comes to mind in which it has succeeded. Because the test is honesty, I do not see how any man who is in fact causing deception and knows that to be so can possibly have a defence to passing off.

113. Thus in this case if RBI had been causing significant deception, the fact that it was using its own name would have afforded no defence to the passing-off claim, even though it had no intention to deceive. That is the admitted position as regards Version 1 [of their website]. But in relation to later versions there is at best no more than some minimal degree of confusion—significant deception is not shown and so, narrow though it is, I think RBI come within Romer J's exception.

The own-name defence in registered trade mark actions has proved more effective.[80] Do you think that the courts are interpreting this defence too narrowly? After all, the idea that there may be a defence in passing off which has never been known to succeed is an interesting one.

4.3.3 CONCURRENT USE

This defence arises when two or more traders have acquired the right to use the same name or indicia. Although such concurrent use may initially have caused confusion, it is also the case that if the trader with the earlier right does not take action, then the public may come, over time, to distinguish between them. Cases where the courts have found concurrent use, where both parties have a right to use the name, include the 'Merc' and 'Reed' cases.[81]

4.4 CONCLUSION

It was suggested at the beginning of this chapter, that the UK does not have a general law of unfair competition It is possible to generalize and say that in passing off cases, the UK courts have continued to see the social interest best served by minimal judicial intervention in the market. As a result, the tort of passing off is primarily concerned with the relationship between traders, with the interests of consumers who might be deceived of only secondary importance. Consumer protection has generally been left to other areas of the law. The recent recognition by the courts in passing off cases of misappropriation of a trader's goodwill through dilution underscores the emphasis of the law of passing off on protecting

---

[80] Jacob LJ also went on to examine the 'own name defence' in trade mark law and this will be examined in Ch. 6.

[81] See also *Habib Bank v Habib Bank AG Zurich* [1981] 2 All ER 277.

traders' interests. But it is also possible to argue that dilution protection does involve a distortion of the market, since it increases the protection given to traders whose insignia has a reputation as against other competing traders whose insignia may not. That is one key reason why a recognition of dilution within the tort of passing off has been contentious. In the following chapters on registered trade marks, we shall see that here too anti-dilution measures have raised important questions.

5

TRADE MARKS I:

JUSTIFICATIONS, REGISTRATION, AND ABSOLUTE GROUNDS FOR REFUSAL OF REGISTRATION

5.1 INTRODUCTION

For some companies, trade marks may be their most valuable commercial assets. The trade mark, 'Coca Cola' is almost universally recognizable; and in this age of global commerce, the product to which it attaches is almost universally available too. Indeed, the value of the Coca Cola brand far exceeds the worth either of the company's tangible assets or of the trade secret which is the Coca Cola recipe. An attractive trade mark may sustain the value of a medicine, even when its patent protection has expired and there are cheaper generic alternatives on the market. The difficulty of enforcing copyright in an age of digital technology and the Internet has increased the importance to rights holders of merchandising as a means of profiting from their works, whether they be movies, books, or music. Trade marks play a crucial role in merchandising, both of products and of characters.[1]

In recent years, and certainly in large measure as a consequence of the growing value of trade marks, there has been considerable legal activity concerning their protection in the European Union. The EU agreed the Trade Marks Directive in 1988.[2] In the UK, the directive was incorporated into national law with the passage of the Trade Marks Act 1994 ('TMA'). At substantially the same time, the EU introduced its Community trade mark (CTM).[3] Since the implementation of the directive across the EU and the introduction of the CTM, there has been a substantial and growing jurisprudence relating to trade marks, emanating from both domestic courts and the ECJ. Much of this jurisprudence has been concerned with establishing how the terms of the directive (and the CTM Regulation) should be interpreted and applied.

---

[1] Character merchandising is the subject of Ch. 7.
[2] First Council Directive 89/104/EEC of 21 Dec. 1988 to approximate the laws of the Member States relating to trade marks.
[3] Council Regulation (EC) 40/94 of 20 Dec. 1993 on the Community trade mark.

The Trade Mark Directive was not intended to harmonize trade mark law across the EU but rather to 'approximate' trade mark law. In fact, it has more or less had a harmonizing effect. Behind the directive was an acknowledgement that differing trade mark regimes across the EU could place barriers in the way of trade between Member States or, as it was put in the recitals to the directive:

> Whereas the trade mark laws at present applicable in the Member States contain disparities which may impede the free movement of goods and freedom to provide services and may distort competition within the common market; whereas it is therefore necessary, in view of the establishment and functioning of the internal market, to approximate the laws of Member States...

Among the key questions which have occupied the courts, and indeed legal commentators more generally in interpreting the directive, have been which signs should be registrable and what should be the scope of the legal protection afforded to them. As regards both these questions, the answers may well depend upon the role which registered trade marks are understood to play in the market. This chapter will first explore the main justifications which have been proffered for the legal protection afforded to trade marks through registration. It will then consider the substantive law relating to the subject matter of registration as well as the practicalities of the trade mark registration process. The following chapter will be concerned with the scope of the protection which is afforded by trade mark registration. It will look at the relative grounds for refusal to register a trade mark and infringement, as well as the defences to infringement and the various ways that it is possible to lose a mark. It will also examine the international protection afforded to registered trade marks.

5.2 THE JUSTIFICATIONS FOR THE PROTECTION OF REGISTERED TRADE MARKS

5.2.1 TRADE MARKS AS A BADGE OF ORIGIN

The ECJ has recognized in a number of cases that the primary function of a registered trade mark is that it acts as an indicator of origin and hence as a guarantee of quality for the consumer. This view of the origin function of registered trade marks was clearly set out by the ECJ in *Arsenal v Reed*.

Arsenal Football Club v Reed [2003] CMLR 481

> 47. Trade mark rights constitute an essential element in the system of undistorted competition which the Treaty is intended to establish and maintain. In such a system, undertakings must be able to attract and retain customers by the quality of their goods or services, which is made possible only by distinctive signs allowing them to be identified (see, inter alia, Case C-10/89 *HAG GF* [1990] ECR I-3711, paragraph 13, and Case C-517/99 *Merz & Krell* [2001] ECR I-6959, paragraph 21).
>
> 48. In that context, the essential function of a trade mark is to guarantee the identity of origin of the marked goods or services to the consumer or end user by enabling him, without any possibility of confusion, to distinguish the goods or services from others which

have another origin. For the trade mark to be able to fulfil its essential role in the system of undistorted competition which the Treaty seeks to establish and maintain, it must offer a guarantee that all the goods or services bearing it have been manufactured or supplied under the control of a single undertaking which is responsible for their quality (see, inter alia, Case 102/77 *Hoffman-La Roche* [1978] ECR 1139, paragraph 7, and Case C-299/99 *Philips* [2002] ECR I-0000, paragraph 30).

49. The Community legislature confirmed that essential function of trade marks by providing, in Article 2 of the Directive, that signs which are capable of being represented graphically may constitute a trade mark only if they are capable of distinguishing the goods or services of one undertaking from those of other undertakings (see, inter alia, *Merz & Krell*, paragraph 23).

50. For that guarantee of origin, which constitutes the essential function of a trade mark, to be ensured, the proprietor must be protected against competitors wishing to take unfair advantage of the status and reputation of the trade mark by selling products illegally bearing it (see, inter alia, *Hoffmann-La Roche*, paragraph 7, and Case C-349/95 *Loendersloot* [1997] ECR I-6227, paragraph 22).

As this extract makes clear, the ECJ sees the system of trade mark registration as designed to protect the interests of the proprietors of the marks as well as consumers. In their influential essay, written from a 'law and economics' perspective, William Landes and Richard Posner identify what they believe to be the key economic benefits offered by the legal protection of trade marks, among which the trade mark's function as an indicator of origin is, in their view, paramount.

W. Landes and R. Posner, 'Trademark law: An economic perspective' (1987) 30(2) Journal of Law and Economics 265–309, 268–70

1. Benefits of Trademarks

Suppose you like decaffeinated coffee made by General Foods. If General Food's brand has no name, then to order it in a restaurant or grocery store you would have to ask for 'the decaffeinated coffee made by General Foods'. This takes longer to say, requires you to remember more, and requires the waiter or clerk to read and remember more than if you can just ask for 'Sanka'. The problem would be even more serious if General Foods made more than one brand of decaffeinated coffee, as in fact it does. The benefit of the brand name is analogous to that of designating individuals by last as well as first names, so that instead of having to say 'the Geoffrey who teaches constitutional law at the University of Chicago Law School—not the one who teaches corporations'. You can say 'Geoffrey Stone—not Geoffrey Miller'.

To perform its economizing function a trademark or brand name (these are rough synonyms) must not be duplicated. To allow another maker of decaffeinated coffee to sell its coffee under the name 'Sanka' would destroy the benefit of the name in identifying a brand of decaffeinated coffee made by General Foods (whether there might be offsetting benefits is considered later). It would be like allowing a second rancher to graze his cattle on a pasture the optimal use of which required that only one herd be allowed to graze. The failure to enforce trademarks would impose two distinct costs—one in the market for trademarked goods and the other in the distinct (and unconventional) market in language.

a) *The Market for Trademarked Goods.* The benefit of trademarks in reducing consumer search costs requires that the producer of a trademarked good maintain a consistent quality over time and across consumers. Hence trademark protection encourages expenditures on quality. To see this, suppose a consumer has a favorable experience with brand X and wants to buy it again. Or suppose he wants to buy brand X because it has been recommended by a reliable source or because he has a favourable experience with brand Y, another brand produced by the same producer. Rather than investigating the attributes of all goods to determine which one is brand X or is equivalent to X, the consumer may find it less costly to search by identifying the relevant trademark and purchasing the corresponding brand. For this strategy to be efficient, however, not only must it be cheaper to search for the right trademark than for the desired attributes of the good, but also past experience must be a good predictor of the likely outcome of current consumption choices—that is, the brand must exhibit consistent quality. In short, a trademark conveys information that allows the consumer to say to himself, 'I need not investigate the attributes of the brand I am about to purchase because the trade mark is a shorthand way of telling me that the attributes are the same as that of the brand I enjoyed earlier.'

Less obviously, a firm's incentive to invest resources in developing and maintaining (as through advertising) a strong mark depends on its ability to maintain consistent product quality. In other words, trademarks have a self-enforcing feature. They are valuable because they denote consistent quality, and a firm has an incentive to develop a trademark only if it is able to maintain consistent quality. To see this, consider what happens when a brand's quality is inconsistent. Because consumers will learn that the trademark does not enable them to relate their past to future consumption experiences, the branded product will be like a good without a trademark. The trademark will not lower the search costs, so consumers will be unwilling to pay more for the branded than for the unbranded good. As a result, the firm will not earn a sufficient return on its trademark promotional expenditures to justify making them. A similar argument shows that a firm with a valuable trademark would be reluctant to lower the quality of its brand because it would suffer a capital loss of its investment in the trademark.

Landes and Posner argue that the legal protection of trade marks lowers consumer search costs and also affords an incentive for proprietors both to ensure that the goods which attach to their mark are of a desirable and consistent quality and to maintain that quality over time. Furthermore, without such legal protection, others might free-ride on the original trade mark and it would lose its value as an indicator of origin and a guarantee of quality for the public. Nor do Landes and Posner believe that the legal protection of trade marks has any notable costs. They continue at pp. 274–5:

We may seem to be ignoring the possibility that, by fostering product differentiation, trademarks may create deadweight costs, whether of monopoly or of (excessive) competition. We have assumed that a trademark induces its owner to invest in maintaining uniform product quality, but another interpretation is that it induces the owner to spend money on creating, through advertising and promotion, a spurious image of high quality that enables monopoly rents to be obtained by deflecting consumers from lower-price substitutes of equal or even higher quality. In the case of products that are produced according to an identical formula, such as aspirin or household liquid bleach, the ability of name-brand goods (Bayer aspirin, Clorox bleach) to command higher prices than generic (nonbranded) goods has seemed to some economists and more lawyers an example of the power of brand advertising to bamboozle the public and thereby promote monopoly. And brand advertising presupposes trademarks—they are what enable a producer readily to identify his brand to the consumer.

Besides the possibility of creating monopoly rents, trademarks may transform rents into costs, as one firm's expenditure on promoting its marks cancels out that of another firm. Although no monopoly profits are created, consumers may pay higher prices, and resources may be wasted in a sterile competition.

The short answer to these arguments is that they have gained no foothold at all in trademark law, as distinct from anti-trust law. The implicit economic model of trademarks that is used in that law is our model, in which trademarks lower search costs and foster quality control rather than create social waste and consumer deception. A longer answer, which we shall merely sketch, is that the hostile view of brand advertising has been largely and we think correctly rejected by economists. The fact that two goods have the same chemical formula does not make them of equal quality to even the most coolly rational consumer. That consumer will be interested not in the formula but in the manufactured product and may therefore be willing to pay a premium for greater assurance that the good will actually be manufactured to the specifications of the formula. Trademarks enable the consumer to economize on a real cost because he spends less time searching to get the quality he wants. If this analysis is correct, the rejection by trademark law of a monopoly theory of trademarks is actually a mark in favor of the economic rationality of that law.

The arguments made by Landes and Posner might be especially convincing if applied to fanciful trade names (such as 'Kodak' for example) because it is possible to argue that there is potentially an unlimited supply of such marks. But what of trade marks which are proper names, perhaps geographical indications or are descriptive of the goods to which they are applied? Of course the supply of such names is not unlimited. Other traders apart from the proprietor may wish to use them. We will see later in the chapter that whether and how much protection should be given to signs such as geographical indications and indeed descriptive signs is a matter of much debate.

5.2.2 THE TRADE MARK AS AN ADVERTISING TOOL

Landes and Posner also argue that there are benefits to be gained from protecting trade marks which have moved beyond their role as a badge of origin to embody other meanings. For example, they identify the added value of a trade mark which through advertising attracts consumers, even if the product to which it attaches is no different from competing products. As early as 1927, Frank I. Schechter argued in his seminal essay that the advertising functions of a mark should also be protected along with its function as a badge of origin. In his essay, Schechter equates the trade mark's role as a badge of origin to the manner in which goodwill is protected by a distinctive insignia in passing off.

F. I. Schechter, 'The rational basis for trade mark protection' (1926–7) 40 Harvard LR 813–33, 818–19

The true functions of the trademark are, then, to identify a product as satisfactory and thereby to stimulate further purchases by the consuming public. The fact that through his trademark the manufacturer or importer may 'reach over the shoulder of the retailer' and across the latter's counter straight to the consumer cannot be over-emphasized, for therein lies the key to any effective scheme of trademark protection. To describe a trademark merely as a symbol of goodwill will, without recognizing in it an agency for the actual creation and perpetuation of goodwill, ignores the most potent aspect of the nature of a trademark and that phase most in need of protection. To say that a trademark 'is merely the visible manifestation of the more important business goodwill, which is the "property" to be protected against invasion', or that 'the goodwill is the substance, the trademark merely the shadow', does not accurately state the function of a trade mark today and obscures the problem of adequate protection. The signboard of a inn in stagecoach-days, when the golden lion or the green cockatoo actually symbolized to the hungry and weary traveller a definite smiling host, a tasty meal from a particular cook, a favourite brew and a comfortable bed, was merely 'the visible manifestation' of the goodwill or probability of custom of the house; but today the trademark is not merely the symbol of goodwill but often the most effective agent for the creation of goodwill, imprinting upon the public mind an anonymous and impersonal guaranty of satisfaction, creating a desire for further satisfactions. The mark actually *sells* the goods. And, self-evidently, the more distinctive the mark, the more effective is its selling power.

Schechter then questions whether the protection afforded to trade marks, as in passing off, should apply only when the consumer may be confused as to the origin of the defendant's goods. Schechter suggests such a view is outmoded. He argues that protection should also be offered where there is likely to be no confusion as to origin, such as, for example, when a third party uses the trade mark on quite different goods from those for which it is registered. He then sets out at p. 831 what he views as the key principles relating to trade mark protection:

(I) that the value of the modern trademark lies in its selling power; (2) that this selling power depends for its psychological hold upon the public, not merely upon the merit of the goods upon which it is used, but equally upon its own uniqueness and singularity; (3) that such uniqueness or singularity is vitiated or impaired by its use upon either related or non-related goods; and (4) that the degree of protection depends in turn upon the extent to which, through the efforts or ingenuity of its owner, it is actually unique and different from other marks.

Schechter concludes that the 'preservation of the uniqueness of a trademark should constitute the only rational basis for its protection'. Or, in other words, the mark's uniqueness (or distinctiveness) should be protected from 'dilution'. In his opinion, in *Arsenal v Reed*, which as we have seen[4] concerned football merchandising, Advocate General Colomer appeared to go further and suggest that, at times, it may be the trade mark itself which the consumer seeks to own, with the underlying product simply acting as a vehicle for the mark.

Arsenal Football Club plc v Reed Case C-206/01 [2002] ECR I-10273

AG Colomer:

A46. It seems to me to be simplistic reductionism to limit the function of the trade mark to an indication of trade origin... Experience teaches that, in most cases, the user is unaware of who produces the goods he consumes. The trademark acquires a life of its own, making a statement, as I have suggested, about quality, reputation and even, in certain cases, a way of seeing life.

---

[4] See 4.2.3.4.

A47. The messages it sends out are, moreover, autonomous. A distinctive sign can indicate at the same time trade origin, the reputation of its proprietor and the quality of the goods it represents, but there is nothing to prevent the consumer, unaware of who manufactures the goods or provides the services which bear the trade mark, from acquiring them because he perceives the mark as an emblem of prestige or a guarantee of quality. When I regard the current functioning of the market and the behaviour of the average consumer, I see no reason whatever not to protect those other functions of the trade mark and to safeguard only the function of indicating the trade origin of the goods and services.

You might agree that the view of the trade mark which sees its value as greater than and not necessarily dependant upon the product to which it attaches is particularly persuasive in the context of football merchandising. It is probably true that a football fan may well purchase goods carrying his or her club's logo because they demonstrate his or her allegiance to the club, rather than because the trade mark acts as a badge of origin. However, there is a strong argument made by cultural critics and others that a great deal of modern commerce, not just that involving football merchandise, depends upon the production and consumption of attractive brands rather than of the underlying product.[5] One question that this raises for trade mark law is the extent to which legal protection should be given not just to a trade mark but to the wider brand values, or advertising qualities, which it embodies. This question is addressed by Jessica Litman. Assuming that the origin function of trade symbols is amply protected by trade mark registration, Litman raises the question of whether the 'atmospherics' (advertising functions) which are now embodied in trade symbols should also be afforded legal protection.

J. Litman, 'Breakfast with Batman: The public interest in the advertising age' (1999) 108 Yale LJ 1717, 1728–30

To say that many consumers seem to attach real value to atmospherics, however, doesn't itself demonstrate that those atmospherics should be afforded legal protection. As Ralph Brown reminded us often, the essence of any intellectual property regime is to divide the valuable stuff subject to private appropriation from the valuable stuff that, precisely because of its importance, is reserved for public use. In the law of trade symbols, for instance, it has long been the rule that functional product features may not be protected, because they have too much value, not too little. Value, without more, does not tell us whether a particular item for which protection is sought belongs in the proprietary pile or in public use.

To agree to treat a class of stuff as intellectual property, we normally require a showing that, if protection is not extended, bad things will happen that will outweigh the resulting good things. But it would be difficult to argue that the persuasive values embodied in trade symbols are likely to suffer from underprotection. Indeed, the Mattels, Disneys, and Warner Brothers of the world seem to protect their atmospherics just fine without legal assistance. Not only can their target audiences tell the difference between, say, a Barbie doll and some other thirteen-inch fashion doll, but, regardless of features, they seem well-trained in the art of insisting on the Mattel product. Nor is the phenomenon limited to the junior set. The popularity of Ralph Lauren's Polo brand shirts or Gucci handbags is an obvious example.

To the extent that consumers want to purchase the higher-priced spread, they ought to be able to be sure that they are paying the higher price for the genuine branded article. If

---

[5] This was the argument made, for example, by Naomi Klein in her best selling book, *No Logo* (London: Flamingo, 2000).

the concept of branding is itself legitimate, then we want to ensure consumers' protection against confusion or deception. Conventional trademark law does that. But, to stick with Lauren's Polo for a minute, what about consumers who want to pick up a polo shirt with some design on the chest at a good price? What if instead, they want to buy this month's issue of polo magazine (which follows the sport, not the fashion)? It seems obvious why Lauren might want to hinder the first and collect a licence fee from the second, so it would hardly be perplexing if his company threatened to sue. There seems, nonetheless, to be no good reason why we should help him.

If competition is still the American way of doing business, then before we give out exclusive control of some coin of competition, we need, or should need, a justification. Protecting consumers from deception is the justification most familiar to trademark law, but it does not support assigning broad rights to prevent competitive or diluting use when no confusion seems likely. Supplying incentives to invest in the item that's getting the protection is another classic justification for intellectual property, and it is equally unavailing here. An argument that we would have an undersupply of good commercials if advertisers were not given plenary control over the elements of their ads cannot be made with a straight face. Finally, there is the perennially popular justification of desert. Producers have invested in their trade symbols, the argument goes; they have earned them, so they're entitled to them.

But so have we. The argument that trade symbols acquire intrinsic value—apart from their usefulness in designating the source—derives from consumers' investing those symbols with value for which they are willing to pay real money. We may want our child to breakfast with Batman. It may well increase the total utils [sic] in our society if every time a guy drinks a Budweiser or smokes a Camel, he believes he's a stud. We may all be better off if, each time a woman colours her hair with a L'Oreal product, she murmurs to herself *and I'm worth it*. If that's so, however, Warner Brothers, Anheuser-Busch, R.J. Reynolds, and L'Oreal can hardly take all the credit. They built up all that mystique with their customer's money and active collaboration. If the customers want to move on, to get in bed with other products that have similar atmospherics, why shouldn't they? It's not very sporting to try to lock up the atmospherics.

Litman concludes that no useful social purpose is to be gained by protecting the advertising function of brands, even though she recognizes that a trade mark which embodies attractive 'atmospherics' can be extremely valuable. Do you agree with Litman that the public must have a role in creating the various meanings carried by a famous trade mark? And that, as a consequence, such meaning should be left in the public sphere? Or do you think that trade mark proprietors have a right to argue that since they put considerable investment into nurturing these further meanings, they should be able to protect that investment through trade mark registration? We shall see that the present law of trade marks does protect certain marks from the dilution of their distinctive character, even if there is no customer confusion. But we shall also see that the extent to which the law should go on to protect other advertising functions of trade marks remains a contentious issue.

FURTHER READING

R. S. Brown, Jr, 'Advertising and the public interest: The protection of trade symbols' (1948) 57 Yale LJ 1165, 1206.

J. Davis, 'To protect or serve? European trade mark law and the decline of the public interest' (2003) 25(4) EIPR 180–7.

A. Griffiths, 'A law-and-economics perspective on trade marks' in L. Bently, J. Davis, and J. C. Ginsburg (eds.), *Trade Marks and Brands: An interdisciplinary perspective* (Cambridge: Cambridge University Press, 2008), p. 241.

H. Rosler, 'The rationale for European trade mark protection' [2007] EIPR 100.

5.3 THE SUBJECT MATTER OF REGISTRATION

In this part of the chapter, we will look first at the practical routes to protecting a trade mark through registration. We will then turn to the substantive law of trade marks and, in particular, how the subject matter of a registered trade mark is defined in Articles 2/3 TMD.[6]

5.3.1 REGISTERING A TRADE MARK

5.3.1.1 Domestic registrations

In the UK, applications to register a trade mark are made to the Trade Mark Registry at the UK Intellectual Property Office ('UK IPO'). Applications are made to register the mark in respect of specific goods or services. There is an International Classification of Goods and Services which was drawn up under the Nice Agreement and is administered by WIPO. Applications may be made for the mark to be registered in respect of goods or services which may fall into one or a number of classes. For example, when the Jif Lemon shape was registered as a trade mark following the passage of the TMA, it was registered in respect of 'Class 29: Lemon Juice' and 'Class 32: Fruit juices and non-alcoholic fruit extracts: all being lemon flavoured'. An application is examined by the Registry to see if there are any grounds for refusing registration. Until 2008, these grounds included whether the sign to be registered conflicted with any earlier registered mark.[7] Now, the Registry will only concern itself with the question of whether the sign avoids any of the absolute grounds for refusal of registration.[8] If the Registry finds the mark acceptable it will be published in the Trade Marks Journal. This allows third parties to view the application and gives them a period of three months to oppose the registration if they believe there are grounds for doing so. For example, a third party may have an earlier identical, but unregistered mark which is protected by the law of passing off.[9] Oppositions are dealt with first by the Registrar and, if there is an appeal, by the Appointed Person. If the dispute is not settled at the Registry level, it may proceed through the courts. Trade marks are registered for ten years, but the registration may be renewed an indefinite number of times.

5.3.1.2 European and international applications

It is also possible to obtain a Community Trade Mark. This is a single mark which is valid for the entire European Community. Applications may be made through the UK IPO or directly to the CTM Office in Alicante (the OHIM). The OHIM does not examine the

---

6 TMA 1994, s. 1(1).

7 Trade Marks (Relative Grounds) Order 2007, SI 2007/1976 and the Trade Marks (Amendment) Rules 2007, SI 2007/2076.

8 See 5.3.2.   9 See 6.1.3.

mark. It will publish the mark and third parties then have three months to enter an opposition. Oppositions are dealt with firstly by the OHIM, then by the Board of Appeal. An appeal may then go to the Court of First Instance all the way to the ECJ. Infringement actions are however heard in the national courts of Member States. The CTM is valid across the EC. Therefore, if it is unregistrable because of, for example, a conflict in one Member State, then the application will fail entirely. Finally, it is possible to register an already-registered trade mark in any of the other 25 countries which are members of the Madrid Protocol, through a single application. Applications to register a UK registered trade mark in other countries which are members of the Madrid Protocol (an International Registration) are made to the UK IPO, which will forward the application to WIPO. The application will then be examined in each of the countries for which the application is made. Unlike the CTM, if the application fails in one country, it may nonetheless go on to be successfully registered in others.

5.3.1.3 Trade Marks as property

Once it is registered, a trade mark is a form of personal property (s. 22 of the TMA). Like other sorts of personal or moveable property a registered trade mark can be assigned (s. 24 of the TMA). It may also be licensed (Article 8 of the TMD; ss. 28–31 of the TMA).

FURTHER READING

L. Jaeschke, 'The quest for a superior registration system for registered trade marks in the United Kingdom and the European Union: an analysis of the current registration system in the United Kingdom, the Community Trade Mark (CTM) registration system and coming changes' [2008] EIPR 25.

E. Shah, 'The UK trademark system: New and improved?' (2008) 211 Trademark World 29.

A. Von Muhlendahl, 'Community trade mark riddles: Territoriality and unitary character' [2008] EIPR 66.

5.3.2 THE SUBJECT MATTER OF TRADE MARK REGISTRATION

This section of the chapter will look to see how the directive (and the CTM Regulation) have been interpreted by both European and domestic courts in order to delineate the universe of signs which may be the subject matter of a trade mark registration. As we shall see, a key issue for the courts has been how wide that universe of protected signs should be. On the one hand, there is a widely shared concern that allowing a broad range of signs to be registered will hamper competition by allowing a single proprietor to monopolize a sign which other traders, as well as the proprietor, may legitimately wish to use. These may include, for example, descriptive marks and colours. On the other hand, there are those who argue that offering to protect a broad category of signs will encourage traders to invest in their trade marks, maintain the quality of the products or services to which they attach, and will ensure that the public can rely on trade marks to guarantee the source and quality of their purchases. As we shall see, the ECJ has been engaged, since the implementation of the directive, in seeking to balance these two imperatives.

5.3.2.1 Registerable signs: an introduction

There are two main articles in the directive which define which signs may be registerable. Article 2 of the directive identifies the subject matter of a trade mark registration.[10]

A trade mark may consist of any sign capable of being represented graphically, particularly words, including personal names, designs, letters, numerals, the shape of goods or of their packaging, provided that such signs are capable of distinguishing the goods or services of one undertaking from those of other undertakings.

Even if a trade mark meets the criteria set out in Article 2, there may still be bars to its registration. Article 3 of the directive sets out the absolute grounds for the refusal of registration of a trade mark.[11] It states, *inter alia*, that the following signs shall not be registered or, if registered, shall be declared invalid:

(a) signs which cannot constitute a trade mark;[12]

(b) trade marks which are devoid of distinctive character;[13]

(c) trade marks which consist exclusively of signs or indications which may serve to designate the kind, quality, quantity, intended purpose, value, geographical origin, or the time of production of the goods or rendering of the service, or other characteristics of the goods or service;[14]

(d) trade marks which consist exclusively of signs or indications which have become customary in the current language or in the bona fide and established practices of the trade.[15]

There is however a proviso. According to Article 3(3) of the directive, signs which fall under categories Article 3(1)(b)–(d):

shall not be refused registration or be declared invalid . . . if, before the date of application for registration and following the use which has been made of it, it has acquired a distinctive character.[16]

There is also a further category of signs identified in Article 3 which will not be registered under any circumstances. The most important are the following:

Art. 3(1)(e) signs which consist exclusively of:
– the shape which results from the nature of the goods themselves, or
– the shape of goods which is necessary to obtain a technical result, or
– the shape which gives substantial value to the goods

Art. 3(1)(f) trade marks which are contrary to public policy or to accepted principles of morality;

Art. 3(1)(g) trade marks which are of such a nature as to deceive the public, for instance as to the nature, quality or geographical origin of the goods or service;

---

[10] TMA 1994, s. 1.   [11] Ibid., s. 3.

[12] This means signs which do not fall within the Art. 2 definition of a trade mark. The comparable section of the TMA 1994 is s. 3(1)(a).

[13] TMA 1994, s. 3(1)(b).   [14] Ibid., s. 3(1)(c).   [15] Ibid., s. 3(1)(d).   [16] Ibid., s. 3(1).

In addition, under Article 3(2)(d), a trade mark application will be rejected if it was made in bad faith.[17]

5.3.2.2 Signs which may be registered (Article 2)

Article 2 tells us what signs may be registered. They must be capable of graphic representation and they must be distinctive, that is they must be capable of acting as a badge of origin. The wording of the directive appears to leave open the possibility that any sign might be registered so long as it is distinctive and capable of graphic representation. However, the decision by the ECJ in *Dyson Ltd v Registrar of Trade Marks* shows that not all signs may constitute a trade mark.

Dyson Ltd v Registrar of Trade Marks Case C-321/03 [2007] ECR I-687

Dyson had since 1993 made and sold 'bagless' vacuum cleaners. It sought to register the following trade marks: 'a transparent bin or collection chamber forming part of the external surface of a vacuum cleaner as shown in the representation'. Illustrations of two bagless vacuum cleaners were attached to the applications. Both the Registrar and the High Court took the view that, on the face of it, the bagless illustrations were entirely descriptive of the product. The High Court went on to ask the ECJ how distinctiveness should be assessed in light of Article 3 of the TMD. But the ECJ chose to answer a different question: did the subject matter of Dyson's application meet the requirements of Article 2—i.e. was it a sign which could in principle be registered. The ECJ held that it was not.

35. In this present case it is common ground that the subject matter in the main proceedings is not a particular type of transparent collecting bin forming part of the external surface of the vacuum cleaner, but rather, in a general and abstract manner, all the conceivable shapes of such a collecting bin.

. . .

38. Given the exclusivity inherent in a trade mark right the holder of a trade mark relating to such a non-specific subject matter would obtain an unfair competitive advantage, contrary to the purpose pursued by Art. 2 of the Directive, since it would be entitled to prevent its competitors from marketing vacuum cleaners having any kind of transparent collecting bin on their external surface regardless of its shape.

39. It follows that the subject matter of the application at issue in the main proceedings is, in fact, a mere property of the product concerned and does not therefore constitute a 'sign' within the meaning of Art. 2 of the Directive.

In this case, the ECJ held that the transparent collecting bin was not a sign at all but rather a concept which other traders might wish to use. We may question whether, in this case, the ECJ's primary concern was actually with protecting competition between traders rather than limiting the universe of what constituted a sign, since the application itself did have an illustration of what was intended to be registered. Another related question that this new, open ended definition of registrable signs raises is whether marks which cannot be

---

[17] Ibid., s. 3(6). Trade marks will also not be registered if they fail the relative grounds for refusal of registration; that is they conflict with an earlier registered mark or an earlier right. These grounds are set out in Art. 4 of the TMD and are discussed in the following chapter.

perceived visually, such as sounds, smells, and tastes might be registered. Even if such intangible signs are held capable of distinguishing, their registration raises further practical difficulties of definition and of how they might be represented graphically. These questions were addressed by the ECJ in *Sieckmann v Deutsches Patent- und Markenamt*, which concerned an application to register an odour.

Sieckmann v Deutsches Patent und Markenamt Case C-273/00 [2002] ECR I-11737

The applicant sought to register a mark which it described on its application as a 'balsamically fruity odour with a slight hint of cinammon' for goods within Classes 35, 41, and 42, including advertising and business management. When making its application, apart from offering the verbal description of the smell, the applicant had also deposited with the German Patent and Trade Mark Office its chemical breakdown and the location of local laboratories where a sample of the smell could be obtained. It also submitted an odour sample in a container. The ECJ addressed itself to the question of whether an intangible sign might be registered. In making its judgment, the ECJ clearly set out why the necessity for graphic representation is so important to a system of trade mark registration, the aim of which is to enhance competition between traders.

Findings of the Court

. . .

43. The purpose of Art. 2 of the Directive is to define the types of signs of which a trade mark may consist. That provision states that a trademark may consist of 'particularly words, including personal names, designs, letters, numerals, the shape of goods or of their packaging . . .' Admittedly, it mentions only signs which are capable of being perceived visually, are two-dimensional or three-dimensional and can thus be represented by means of letters or written characters or by a picture.

44. However, as is clear from the language of both Art. 2 of the Directive and the seventh recital in the preamble thereto, which refers to a 'list [of] examples' of signs which may constitute a trade mark, that list is not exhaustive. Consequently, that provision, although it does not mention signs which are not in themselves capable of being perceived visually, such as odours, does not, however, expressly exclude them.

45. In those circumstances, Art. 2 of the Directive must be interpreted as meaning that a trade mark may consist of a sign which is not in itself capable of being perceived visually, provided that it can be represented graphically.

46. That graphic representation must enable the sign to be represented visually, particularly by means of images, lines or characters, so that it can be precisely identified.

47. Such an interpretation is required to allow for the sound operation of the trade mark registration system.

48. First, the function of the graphic representability requirement is, in particular, to define the mark itself in order to determine the precise subject of the protection afforded by the registered mark to its proprietor.

49. Next, the entry of the mark in a public register has the aim of making it accessible to the competent authorities and the public, particularly to economic operators.

50. On the one hand, the competent authorities must know with clarity and precision the nature of the signs of which a mark consists in order to be able to fulfil their obligations

in relation to the prior examination of registration applications and to the publication and main-tenance of an appropriate and precise register of trade marks.

51. On the other hand, economic operators must, with clarity and precision, be able to find out about registrations or applications for registration made by their current or potential competitors and thus to receive relevant information about the rights of third parties.

52. If the users of that register are to be able to determine the precise nature of a mark on the basis of its registration, its graphic representation in the register must be self-contained, easily accessible and intelligible.

53. Furthermore, in order to fulfil its role as a registered trade mark a sign must always be perceived unambiguously and in the same way so that the mark is guaranteed as an indication of origin. In the light of the duration of a mark's registration and the fact that, as the Directive provides, it can be renewed for varying periods, the representation must be durable.

54. Finally, the object of the representation is specifically to avoid any element of subject-ivity in the process of identifying and perceiving the sign. Consequently, the means of graphic representation must be unequivocal and objective.

55. In the light of the foregoing observations, the answer to the first question must be that Art. 2 of the Directive must be interpreted as meaning that a trade mark may consist of a sign which is not in itself capable of being perceived visually, provided that it can be represented graphically, particularly by means of images, lines or characters, and that the representation is clear, precise, self-contained, easily accessible, intelligible, durable and objective.

The ECJ then turned to the question of whether the applicant had adequately represented the odour which it wished to register. It held that neither a chemical formula nor a description of an odour is sufficiently clear and precise. In addition, neither these nor an odour sample, nor a combination of all three, is sufficiently clear and precise to constitute an adequate graphic representation. The formula devised by the ECJ in *Sieckmann* that adequate graphic representation must be 'self-contained, easily accessible, intelligible, durable and objective' has since been applied to other intangible signs and also to colours. The questions as to whether a single colour might constitute a sign and how it might be graphically represented was considered by the ECJ in a case concerning a colour.

Libertel Groep BV v Benelux-Merkenbureau Case C-104/01 [2003] ECR I-3793

Libertel was a Dutch mobile phone company. It sought to register a trade mark for the colour orange for certain telecommunications goods and services. In the space for reproducing the trade mark, the application form contained an orange rectangle and, in the space for describing the trade mark, the word 'orange' without reference to any colour code. The application was initially refused on the grounds that the proposed mark was devoid of distinctive character and would not be registered without proof that it had acquired distinctiveness through use. Libertel appealed, and the Dutch court subsequently addressed a number of questions to the ECJ concerning distinctiveness. The ECJ began by answering the question of whether a single colour could fulfil the requirements of Article 2.

27. In that regard it must be pointed out that a colour per se cannot be presumed to consti-tute a sign. Normally a colour is a simple property of things. Yet it may constitute a sign. That

depends on the context in which the colour is used. None the less, a colour per se is capable, in relation to a product or service, of constituting a sign.

[The ECJ then went on to consider whether a single colour was capable of graphic representation, in that it fulfilled the requirements set out in *Sieckmann*. It noted as follows:]

32. ...a sample of a colour may deteriorate with time. There may be certain media on which it is possible to reproduce a colour in permanent form. However with other media, including paper, the exact shade of the colour cannot be protected from the effects of the passage of time. In these cases, the filing of a sample of a colour does not possess the durability required by Art. 2 of the Directive (see Sieckmann, para. 53).

33. It follows that filing a sample of a colour does not per se constitute a graphic representation within the meaning of Art. 2 of the Directive.

34. On the other hand, a verbal description of a colour, in so far as it is composed of words which themselves are made up of letters, does constitute a graphic representation of the colour (see Sieckmann, para. 70).

35. A description in words of the colour will not necessarily satisfy the conditions set out in paras. 28 and 29 of this judgment in every instance. That is a question which must be evaluated in the light of the circumstances of each individual case.

36. A sample of a colour, combined with a description in words of that colour, may therefore constitute a graphic representation within the meaning of Art. 2 of the Directive, provided that the description is clear, precise, self-contained, easily accessible, intelligible, durable and objective.

37. For the same reasons as those set out at para. 34 of this judgment, the designation of a colour using an internationally recognised identification code may be considered to constitute a graphic representation. Such codes are deemed to be precise and stable.

38. Where a sample of a colour, together with a description in words, does not satisfy the conditions laid down in Art. 2 of the Directive in order for it to constitute a graphic representation because, *inter alia*, it lacks precision or durability, that deficiency may, depending on the facts, be remedied by adding a colour designation from an internationally recognised identification code.

[Finally, the ECJ looked at the third element for defining a trade mark as identified in Art. 2 of the TMD, and considered whether a single colour was capable of acting as a badge of origin:]

39. As to the question whether a colour per se is capable of distinguishing the goods or services of one undertaking from those of other undertakings, within the meaning of Art. 2 of the Directive, it is necessary to determine whether or not colours per se are capable of conveying specific information, in particular as to the origin of a product or service.

40. In that connection, it must be borne in mind that, whilst colours are capable of conveying certain associations of ideas, and of arousing feelings, they possess little inherent capacity for communicating specific information, especially since they are commonly and widely used, because of their appeal, in order to advertise and market goods or services, without any specific message.

41. However, that factual finding would not justify the conclusion that colours per se cannot, as a matter of principle, be considered to be capable of distinguishing the goods or services of one undertaking from those of other undertakings. The possibility that a colour per se may in some circumstances serve as a badge of origin of the goods or services of an undertaking cannot be ruled out. It must therefore be accepted that colours per se may

> be capable of distinguishing the goods or services of one undertaking from those of other undertakings, within the meaning of Art. 2 of the Directive.
>
> 42. It follows from the foregoing that, where the conditions described above apply, a colour per se is capable of constituting a trade mark within the meaning of Art. 2 of the Directive.

The decisions in *Sieckmann* and subsequent cases suggest that while intangible signs may in principle be registered, there are hurdles to be crossed in order to ensure that they are properly represented graphically. In the case of odours, tastes, and onomatopoeic sounds,[18] it may be that these hurdles are practically insurmountable. It is notable that these categories of signs are produced by nature and consequently are in limited supply. As a result, we may ask whether the ECJ has been reluctant to see them monopolized by a single trader. This would certainly appear to be the approach which the ECJ took in *Libertel* to the registration of single colours, which are also in limited supply. Turning to Article 3 and the absolute grounds for refusal of registration, we will again see that the key question for the ECJ and domestic courts has been how wide to draw the boundaries of registrable signs.

FURTHER READING

R. Burrell and M. Handler, 'Making sense of trade mark law' [2003] IPQ 388.

J. Davis, 'Between a sign and a brand: Mapping the boundaries of a registered trade mark in European Union trade mark law' in L. Bently, J. Davis, and J. C. Ginsburg (eds), *Trade Marks and Brands: An interdisciplinary critique* (Cambridge: Cambridge University Press, 2008), pp. 65–91.

J. C. Ginsburg, '"See me, feel me, touch me, hea[r] me (and maybe smell and taste me too)— I am a trademark": A US perspective', Ibid., pp. 92–105.

E. Smith, 'Dyson and the public interest: An analysis of the Dyson trade mark case' [2007] EIPR 469.

5.3.3 THE ABSOLUTE GROUNDS FOR REFUSAL OF REGISTRATION (ARTICLE 3)

Article 3(1)(a)–(d) covers signs which do not fulfil the requirements of Article 2(1) and so cannot be registered and signs which may be registered only with evidence of distinctiveness acquired through use.

5.3.3.1 Article 3(1)(a)

Article 3 begins by providing that a sign may not be registered if it fails to fulfil the requirements of Article 2. This provision seems to raise the question of whether there is a category of signs which are inherently incapable of acting as a badge of origin. It was a question put to the ECJ by the UK Court of Appeal in the *Philips* case.

---

[18] See *Shield Mark BV v Joost Kist* Case C-283/01 [2004] ECR I-14313 for onomatopoeic sounds; see *Eli Lilly's & Co's CTM Application* [2004] ETMR 4 for tastes.

Koninklijke Philips Electronics NV v Remington Consumer Products Ltd Case C-299/99 [2002] ECR I-5475.

In 1966, Philips developed a new type of three-headed rotary electric shaver. In 1985, Philips filed an application to register a trade mark consisting of a graphic representation of the shape and configuration of the head of such a shaver, comprising three circular heads with rotating blades in the shape of an equilateral triangle. In 1995, Remington, a competing company, began to manufacture and sell in the United Kingdom the DT 55, which was a shaver with three rotating heads forming an equilateral triangle, shaped similarly to that used by Philips. Philips sued Remington for infringement of its trade mark. Remington counterclaimed for revocation of the trade mark registered by Philips on the grounds, *inter alia*, that it lacked distinctiveness. In the High Court, Jacob J held that the mark was incapable of distinguishing under Article 2, in that it could only ever convey the message, 'Here is a three-headed shaver.' The Court of Appeal also took the view that the sign was incapable of distinguishing because it had no features which were of trade mark significance. Rather, the Court of Appeal held that a trade mark such as the Philips mark which consisted of the shape of the goods could only be registered if it had some addition to its shape, some capricious element, which made it capable of distinguishing. But it also decided to ask the ECJ, *inter alia*, whether there existed a category of marks which were excluded from registration under Article 3(1)(a) of the directive whether or not they had acquired distinctiveness through use and also whether there was a category of descriptive signs (in this case a shape of goods sign) which would be registered only if they incorporated a 'capricious' element. The ECJ gave the following answer:

38. ... Article 3(1)(a) of the Directive, like the rule laid down by Article 3(1)(b), (c) and (d), precludes the registration of signs or indications which do not meet one of the two conditions imposed by Article 2 of the Directive, that is to say, the condition requiring such signs to be capable of distinguishing the goods or services of one undertaking from those of other undertakings.

39. It follows that there is no class of marks having a distinctive character by their nature or by the use made of them which is not capable of distinguishing goods or services within the meaning of Article 2 of the Directive.

40. In the light of those considerations, the answer to the first question must be that there is no category of marks which is not excluded from registration by Article 3(1)(b), (c) and (d) and Article 3(3) of the Directive which is none the less excluded from registration by Article 3(1)(a) thereof on the ground that such marks are incapable of distinguishing the goods of the proprietor of the mark from those of other undertakings.

[In relation to the second question concerning the 'capricious addition' the ECJ held:]

48. ... Article 2 of the Directive makes no distinction between different categories of trade marks. The criteria for assessing the distinctive character of three-dimensional trade marks, such as that at issue in the main proceedings, are thus no different from those to be applied to other categories of trade mark.

49. In particular, the Directive in no way requires that the shape of the article in respect of which the sign is registered must include some capricious addition. Under Article 2 of the Directive, the shape in question must simply be capable of distinguishing the product of the proprietor of the trade mark from those of other undertakings and thus fulfil its essential purpose of guaranteeing the origin of the product.

50. In the light of those considerations, the answer to the second question must be that, in order to be capable of distinguishing an article for the purposes of Article 2 of the Directive,

the shape of the article in respect of which the sign is registered does not require any capricious addition, such as an embellishment which has no functional purpose.

The implication of the ECJ's judgment in *Philips* is that the directive dictates that any sign may in principle either be initially distinctive (a good example here would be an invented sign such as 'Kodak', or a sign which bears no relation to the goods and services to which it is applied, such as 'North Pole' for bananas) or else acquire distinctiveness through use (the categories of signs set out in Article 3(1)(b)–(d)). In other words, following *Philips*, there would appear to be no category of signs which by their *nature* are incapable of acting as a trade mark. It follows that when the relevant authority is judging whether a sign might be registered, it should turn first to look at whether it fails to fulfil the requirements of Article 3(1)(b)–(d) in that it has failed to acquire distinctiveness through use. If that is the case, then there is no need to measure the sign against the Article 3(1)(a) requirements. Indeed, we may ask whether the decision in *Philips* has effectively made these requirements irrelevant. Do you think that the result is an unacceptable widening of the signs which may be registered?

5.3.3.2 Signs which have acquired distinctiveness through use: an introduction

We shall now look at the second category of signs: those which may be registered only with evidence of acquired distinctiveness. As we have seen, this provision covers signs which are devoid of distinctive character, descriptive signs, and signs which are customary in the trade (including generic marks). There has been considerable case law concerned with identifying signs which fall into each of these categories (or into more than one—for example, the Philips three-headed razor mark which was held to be both descriptive and devoid of distinctive character). In the leading ECJ case of *Linde*[19] the Court noted (at para. 67) that each of these grounds for refusal listed in Article 3(1) 'is independent of the others and calls for separate examination'. In addition, the Court also noted (at para. 73) that, 'the various grounds for refusing registration set out in Article 3 of the directive must be interpreted in the light of the public interest underlying each of them'. Article 3 raises two important questions. First, what is the scope of each of the absolute grounds for refusal of registration? Second, in the case of those signs which are initially refused registration, how should acquired distinctiveness by judged? The first major case concerning both these questions is generally agreed to be *Windsurfing*, which was concerned with a descriptive sign, in this case a geographical indication. It therefore makes sense first of all to consider how the ECJ has interpreted the scope of Article 3(1) in relation to descriptive signs.

5.3.3.3 Descriptive signs

Windsurfing Chiemsee Produktions und Vertriebs GmbH v Boots und Segelzubehör Walter Huber Joined Cases C-108/97 and C-109/97 [1999] ECR I-2779

Windsurfing concerned a geographical sign, the word 'Chiemsee' which is a large Bavarian lake and tourist attraction. Windsurfing Chiemsee, based near the shores of

---

[19] *Linde AG, Winward Industries Inc, Rado Uhren AG v Deutsches Patent- und Markenamt* Joined Cases C-53/01 to C-55/01 [2003] ECR I-3161.

the Chiemsee, sold sporting goods which were manufactured elsewhere. The goods bore the designation 'Chiemsee'. Windsurfing Chiemsee had registered the word 'Chiemsee' in Germany as a picture trade mark in the form of various graphic designs, but there was no German trade mark for the word 'Chiemsee' as such because the German registration authorities had hitherto regarded the word 'Chiemsee' as an indication which might serve to designate geographical origin and which was consequently incapable of registration as a trade mark. The defendants had been selling sports clothing since 1995 in a town also near the shores of the Chiemsee. Their clothing also bore the designation 'Chiemsee', but depicted in a different graphic form from that of the trade marks which identified Windsurfing Chiemsee's products. In the main proceedings, Windsurfing Chiemsee challenged the use by the defendants of the name 'Chiemsee', claiming that, notwithstanding the differences in graphic representation of the marks on the products in question, there was a likelihood of confusion with its designation 'Chiemsee' with which, it claimed, the public was familiar and which had in any case been in use since 1990. In reply, the defendants contended that, since the word 'Chiemsee' was an indication which designated geographical origin and must consequently remain available for other traders to use, it was not capable of protection. It was this latter contention which concerned the ECJ.

Questions on Article 3(1)(c) of the Directive

19. By those questions, which may conveniently be considered together, the national court is essentially asking in what circumstances Article 3(1)(c) of the Directive precludes registration of a trade mark which consists exclusively of a geographical name. In particular, it is asking: if the application of Article 3(1)(c) depends on whether there is a real, current or serious need to leave the sign or indication free; and what connection there must be between the geographical location and the goods in respect of which registration of the geographical name for that location as a trade mark is applied for.

...

24. It should first of all be observed that Article 3(1)(c) of the Directive provides that registration is to be refused in respect of descriptive marks, that is to say marks composed exclusively of signs or indications which may serve to designate the characteristics of the categories of goods or services in respect of which registration is applied for.

25. However, Article 3(1)(c) of the Directive pursues an aim which is in the public interest, namely that descriptive signs or indications relating to the categories of goods or services in respect of which registration is applied for may be freely used by all, including as collective marks or as part of complex or graphic marks. Article 3(1)(c) therefore prevents such signs and indications from being reserved to one undertaking alone because they have been registered as trade marks.

26. As regards, more particularly, signs or indications which may serve to designate the geographical origin of the categories of goods in relation to which registration of the mark is applied for, especially geographical names, it is in the public interest that they remain available, not least because they may be an indication of the quality and other characteristics of the categories of goods concerned, and may also, in various ways, influence consumer tastes by, for instance, associating the goods with a place that may give rise to a favourable response.

...

29. Article 3(1)(c) of the Directive is not confined to prohibiting the registration of geographical names as trade marks solely where they designate specified geographical locations which are already famous, or are known for the category of goods concerned, and

which are therefore associated with those goods in the mind of the relevant class of persons, that is to say in the trade and amongst average consumers of that category of goods in the territory in respect of which registration is applied for.

30. Indeed, it is clear from the actual wording of Article 3(1)(c), which refers to '...indications which may serve...to designate...geographical origin', that geographical names which are liable to be used by undertakings must remain available to such undertakings as indications of the geographical origin of the category of goods concerned.

31. Thus, under Article 3(1)(c) of the Directive, the competent authority must assess whether a geographical name in respect of which application for registration as a trade mark is made designates a place which is currently associated in the mind of the relevant class of persons with the category of goods concerned, or whether it is reasonable to assume that such an association may be established in the future.

32. In the latter case, when assessing whether the geographical name is capable, in the mind of the relevant class of persons, of designating the origin of the category of goods in question, regard must be had more particularly to the degree of familiarity amongst such persons with that name, with the characteristics of the place designated by the name, and with the category of goods concerned.

33. In that connection, Article 3(1)(c) of the Directive does not in principle preclude the registration of geographical names which are unknown to the relevant class of persons—or at least unknown as the designation of a geographical location—or of names in respect of which, because of the type of place they designate (say, a mountain or lake), such persons are unlikely to believe that the category of goods concerned originates there.

34. However, it cannot be ruled out that the name of a lake may serve to designate geographical origin within the meaning of Article 3(1)(c), even for goods such as those in the main proceedings, provided that the name could be understood by the relevant class of persons to include the shores of the lake or the surrounding area.

35. It follows from the foregoing that the application of Article 3(1)(c) of the Directive does not depend on there being a real, current or serious need to leave a sign or indication free ('Freihaltebedürfnis') under German case law, as outlined in the third indent of paragraph 16 of this judgment.

36. Finally, it is important to note that, whilst an indication of the geographical origin of goods to which Article 3(1)(c) of the Directive applies usually indicates the place where the goods were or could be manufactured, the connection between a category of goods and a geographical location might depend on other ties, such as the fact that the goods were conceived and designed in the geographical location concerned.

37. In view of the foregoing, the answer to the questions on Article 3(1)(c) of the Directive must be that Article 3(1)(c) is to be interpreted as meaning that:

- it does not prohibit the registration of geographical names as trade marks solely where the names designate places which are, in the mind of the relevant class of persons, currently associated with the category of goods in question; it also applies to geographical names which are liable to be used in future by the undertakings concerned as an indication of the geographical origin of that category of goods;

- where there is currently no association in the mind of the relevant class of persons between the geographical name and the category of goods in question, the competent authority must assess whether it is reasonable to assume that such a name is, in the mind of the relevant class of persons, capable of designating the geographical origin of that category of goods;

- in making that assessment, particular consideration should be given to the degree of familiarity amongst the relevant class of persons with the geographical name in question,

> with the characteristics of the place designated by that name, and with the category of goods concerned; it is not necessary for the goods to be manufactured in the geographical location in order for them to be associated with it.

In *Windsurfing*, the ECJ held that the public interest behind the Article 3(1)(c) prohibition against registering geographical signs was that such signs should be kept free for others to use both now and in the future. It may seem appropriate that the leading case on descriptive signs should concern a geographical sign. While other descriptive signs may have alternative designations (for example large, big, or bumper), a geographical sign may well be a unique way of describing goods or services, which originate from a particular locale and hence there may be other traders in the area who may legitimately wish to use it. But the ECJ also held in *Windsurfing* that according to the directive (in particular, the proviso set out in Article 3(3)), any descriptive signs (including geographical signs) may be registered provided they have acquired distinctiveness through use. Of course, geographical names are not the only signs which may fall within the category of descriptive signs and it was assumed, following *Windsurfing*, that the identification of the public interest behind Article 3(1)(c) which had been made by the ECJ applied more generally to other types of descriptive signs. However, this assumption was called into question following the ECJ's judgment in 'Baby-Dry' where the ECJ appeared to contradict its stance in *Windsurfing* and to conclude that the barrier to registering descriptive trade marks without evidence of acquired distinctiveness should not, after all, be a difficult one to surmount.

Procter & Gamble v OHIM Case C-383/99 [2001] ECR I-6251

The applicants sought to register the mark, 'Baby-Dry' for nappies as a CTM. They did not present any evidence of acquired distinctiveness. The OHIM decided that the mark was descriptive of nappies and could not be registered. After a series of appeals, the issue reached the ECJ. Perhaps surprisingly, in light of the *Windsurfing* decision, the ECJ held that the mark could be registered.

> 35. Under Article 7(1) of Regulation No 40/94, trade marks are not to be registered if they are devoid of distinctive character (subparagraph (b)) or if they consist exclusively of signs or indications which may serve, in trade, to designate the kind, quality, quantity, intended purpose, value, geographical origin, time of production of the goods or of rendering of the service, or other characteristics of the goods or service (subparagraph (c)).
>
> 36. Under Article 12 of Regulation No 40/94, the rights conferred by the trade mark do not entitle the proprietor to prohibit a third party from using, in the course of trade, indications concerning the kind, quality, quantity, intended purpose, value, geographical origin, the time of production of the goods or the time of rendering the service, or other characteristics of the goods or service, provided he uses them in accordance with honest practices in industrial or commercial matters.
>
> 37. It is clear from those two provisions taken together that the purpose of the prohibition of registration of purely descriptive signs or indications as trade marks is, as both Procter & Gamble and the OHIM acknowledge, to prevent registration as trade marks of signs or indications which, because they are no different from the usual way of designating the relevant goods or services or their characteristics, could not fulfil the function of identifying the

undertaking that markets them and are thus devoid of the distinctive character needed for that function.

38. That interpretation is the only interpretation which is also compatible with Article 4 of Regulation No 40/94, which provides that a Community trade mark may consist of any signs capable of being represented graphically, particularly words, including personal names, designs, letters, numerals, the shape of goods or of their packaging, provided that such signs are capable of distinguishing the goods or services of one undertaking from those of other undertakings.

39. The signs and indications referred to in Article 7(1)(c) of Regulation No 40/94 are thus only those which may serve in normal usage from a consumer's point of view to designate, either directly or by reference to one of their essential characteristics, goods or services such as those in respect of which registration is sought. Furthermore, a mark composed of signs or indications satisfying that definition should not be refused registration unless it comprises no other signs or indications and, in addition, the purely descriptive signs or indications of which it is composed are not presented or configured in a manner that distinguishes the resultant whole from the usual way of designating the goods or services concerned or their essential characteristics.

40. As regards trade marks composed of words, such as the mark at issue here, descriptiveness must be determined not only in relation to each word taken separately but also in relation to the whole which they form. Any perceptible difference between the combination of words submitted for registration and the terms used in the common parlance of the relevant class of consumers to designate the goods or services or their essential characteristics is apt to confer distinctive character on the word combination enabling it to be registered as a trade mark.

. . .

42. In order to assess whether a word combination such as BABY-DRY is capable of distinctiveness, it is therefore necessary to put oneself in the shoes of an English-speaking consumer. From that point of view, and given that the goods concerned in this case are babies' nappies, the determination to be made depends on whether the word combination in question may be viewed as a normal way of referring to the goods or of representing their essential characteristics in common parlance.

43. As it is, that word combination, whilst it does unquestionably allude to the function which the goods are supposed to fulfil, still does not satisfy the disqualifying criteria set forth in paragraphs 39 to 42 of this judgment. Whilst each of the two words in the combination may form part of expressions used in everyday speech to designate the function of babies' nappies, their syntactically unusual juxtaposition is not a familiar expression in the English language, either for designating babies' nappies or for describing their essential characteristics.

44. Word combinations like BABY-DRY cannot therefore be regarded as exhibiting, as a whole, descriptive character; they are lexical inventions bestowing distinctive power on the mark so formed and may not be refused registration under Article 7(1)(c) of Regulation No 40/94.

In its 'Baby-Dry' judgment, the ECJ held that a sign would be distinctive if there was 'any perceptible difference' between the sign and a commonly used descriptive term. In explaining its reasoning, a factor which weighed with the Court was that under the CTM Regulation (Article 12) and the directive, it is a defence to trade mark infringement if a registered trade mark is used by a third party purely descriptively and not as a badge of origin, thus tempering the potentially strong monopoly that registration affords to the proprietors of descriptive marks. Some commentators have preferred the expansive approach to trade mark protection afforded by 'Baby-Dry' in that it allowed for a broad range of descriptive signs to be registered, with the defence of descriptive use given to competing traders. But it is also possible to argue that, as in *Windsurfing*, the courts should be slow to give such protection to words which other traders might legitimately wish to use. When a case with similar facts to the 'Baby-Dry' decision subsequently came before the ECJ, the Court took a stance much more in keeping with its earlier decision in *Windsurfing*: that case was *Wrigley*.

Office for Harmonisation in the Internal Market v Wm Wrigley Jr Company Case C-191/01 P [2003] ECR I-12447

The OHIM rejected an application from Wrigley to register as a CTM the word 'Doublemint' for various classes of goods including chewing gum, because it was held to be descriptive. The applicant appealed. The First Board of Appeal of the OHIM dismissed the appeal on the grounds that the word 'Doublemint', a combination of two English words without additional fanciful or imaginative elements, was descriptive of certain characteristics of the goods in question, namely their mint-based composition and their mint flavour. This decision was overturned by the Court of First Instance (CFI). The CFI appeared to have followed the 'Baby-Dry' decision, and held that since the term was not the ordinary English way of describing the goods (i.e. it had other meanings and was not exclusively descriptive), the mark should be registered. The ECJ however disagreed.

31. By prohibiting the registration as Community trade marks of such signs and indications, Art. 7(1)(c) of Reg. 40/94[20] pursues an aim which is in the public interest, namely that descriptive signs or indications relating to the characteristics of goods or services in respect of which registration is sought may be freely used by all. That provision accordingly prevents such signs and indications from being reserved to one undertaking alone because they have been registered as trade marks (see, inter alia, in relation to the identical provisions of Art. 3(1)(c) of First Council Directive 89/104/EEC of 21 December 1988 to approximate the laws of the Member States relating to trade marks (OJ 1989 L40, p. 1), *Windsurfing Chiemsee*, para. 25, and Joined Cases C-53/01 to C-55/01 *Linde and Others* [2003] ECR I-3161, para. 73).

32. In order for OHIM to refuse to register a trade mark under Art. 7(1)(c) of Reg. 40/94, it is not necessary that the signs and indications composing the mark that are referred to in that article actually be in use at the time of the application for registration in a way that is descriptive of goods or services such as those in relation to which the application is filed, or of characteristics of those goods or services. It is sufficient, as the wording of that provision itself indicates, that such signs and indications could be used for such purposes. A sign must therefore be refused registration under that provision if at least one of its possible meanings designates a characteristic of the goods or services concerned.

33. In the present case, the reason given by the Court of First Instance, at para. 20 of the contested judgment, for holding that the word at issue could not be refused registration under Art. 7(1)(c) was that signs or indications whose meaning goes beyond the merely descriptive are capable of being registered as Community trade marks and, at para. 31 of the contested judgment, that that term cannot be characterised as exclusively descriptive. It thus took the view that Art. 7(1)(c) of Reg. 40/94 had to be interpreted as precluding the registration of

---

[20] Equivalent to Art. 3(1)(c) of the TM Directive and s. 3(1)c) of the 1994 TMA.

trade marks which are exclusively descriptive of the goods or services in respect of which registration is sought, or of their characteristics.

34. In so doing, the Court of First Instance applied a test based on whether the mark is exclusively descriptive, which is not the test laid down by Art. 7(1)(c) of Reg. 40/94.

35. It thereby failed to ascertain whether the word at issue was capable of being used by other economic operators to designate a characteristic of their goods and services.

36. It follows that it erred as to the scope of Art. 7(1)(c) of Reg. 40/94.

It is generally accepted that the ECJ's judgment in *Wrigley* followed its earlier approach to descriptive signs set out in *Windsurfing*, rather than the more expansive approach to their registration to be found in the 'Baby-Dry' case. Later judgments concerning descriptive signs have confirmed that this is so. In *Campina Melunkunie BV v Benelux-Merkenbureau*,[21] which concerned the application 'Biomild' for a mild-flavoured yohgurt, the ECJ held that a neologism would be unregistrable if it were descriptive. In *Koninklijke KPN Nederland NV v Benelux-Merkenbureau*,[22] concerning an application to register 'Postkantoor', the Dutch word for post office, for a range of goods including stamps, paper, and advice, the ECJ held that a mark which is composed of elements, each of which is descriptive, may itself be considered descriptive unless it creates an impression far removed from its descriptive elements. The ECJ also noted that even if synonyms exist for a descriptive word, such a word might not be registered if it is the normal way of referring to the relevant goods or services. Further confirmation that the public interest grounds raised in *Windsurfing* for protecting descriptive signs from registration applies more generally, and not simply to geographical signs, is also to be found in *Linde*, which concerned not words but rather shape of goods marks.

Linde AG, Winward Industries Inc, Rado Uhren AG v Deutsches Patent und Markenamt Joined Cases C-53/01 to C-55/01 [2003] ECR I-3161

Linde applied to register a vehicle as a three-dimensional trade mark for the following goods: motorized trucks and other mobile works vehicles, particularly fork-lift trucks. Winward applied to register a torch as a three-dimensional trade mark for torches. Rado applied to register a three-dimensional trade mark consisting of the graphic representation of a wristwatch for wristwatches. All three applications were refused by the German Patent and Trade Mark Office for lack of distinctive character. Following a series of appeals, the Bundesgerichtshof asked the ECJ whether the bar on registration of descriptive marks applied to shape of goods marks. The ECJ answered in the positive.

69. In regard to Art. 3(1)(c) of the Directive in particular, there is nothing in principle to stop that provision applying to an application for a three-dimensional shape of goods trade mark. The reference to trade marks which consist exclusively of signs or indications which may serve to designate characteristics of the goods or service other than those expressly referred to in that provision is sufficiently broad to cover a wide variety of trade marks, including three-dimensional shape of goods trade marks.

The ECJ was then asked whether in interpreting Article 3(1)(c), in relation to shape of goods marks, regard should be had to the general interest of the trade in the preservation of the

---

[21] Case C-45/06 [2004] ECR I-1699.   [22] Case C-363/99 [2004] ECR I-1619.

availability of the shape of the product, so that registration was in principle excluded and as a rule only possible if such marks had satisfied Article 3(3) of the directive and had acquired distinctiveness through use. The ECJ answered in the positive. Citing *Windsurfing*, it confirmed that the public interest in leaving such signs free is that they:

> 73. ...may be freely used by all, including as collective marks or as part of complex or graphic marks. Article 3(1)(c) therefore prevents such signs and indications from being reserved to one undertaking alone because they have been registered as trade marks (see, to that effect, *Windsurfing Chiemsee*, para. 25).

The decision in *Linde* emphasizes that it is to *Windsurfing* rather than to 'Baby-Dry' that we must look to interpret the breadth of the bar to the registration of descriptive marks provided by Article 3(1)(c) of the TMD. In other words, the ECJ has taken the view that it is more important to protect the public interest in keeping descriptive signs free for others to use even though, as some believe, this may militate against market efficiency. It remains an open question, whether the ECJ has, in fact, found the correct balance between these two approaches.

5.3.3.4 Signs which are devoid of distinctive character

These signs will be registered only if there is evidence of distinctiveness acquired through use. In *Henkel KGaA v OHIM*,[23] the ECJ ruled that the particular public interest consideration underlying this absolute ground for refusal is that there is no public benefit in conferring legal protection on a trade mark which does not fulfil its essential function as a badge of origin. The criteria for deciding whether a sign is devoid of distinctive character have been examined in a number of ECJ decisions. We have already seen in *Libertel*, which concerned an application to register the colour orange, that the ECJ held that in principle single-colour marks might be registrable provided they have adequate graphic representation. Later in the *Libertel* judgment, the ECJ also addressed the question of whether and under what circumstances a colour mark may be sufficiently distinctive to satisfy Article 3(1)(b).

> 65. The perception of the relevant public is not necessarily the same in the case of a sign consisting of a colour per se as it is in the case of a word or figurative mark consisting of a sign that bears no relation to the appearance of the goods it denotes. While the public is accustomed to perceiving words or figurative marks instantly as signs identifying the commercial origin of the goods, the same is not necessarily true where the sign forms part of the look of the goods in respect of which registration of the sign is sought. Consumers are not in the habit of making assumptions about the origin of goods based on their colour or the colour of their packaging, in the absence of any graphic or word element, because as a rule a colour per se is not, in current commercial practice, used as a means of identification. A colour per se is not normally inherently capable of distinguishing the goods of a particular undertaking.
>
> 66. In the case of a colour per se, distinctiveness without any prior use is inconceivable save in exceptional circumstances, and particularly where the number of goods or services for which the mark is claimed is very restricted and the relevant market very specific.

---

[23] Case C-144/06 P [2005] ECR I-1725.

In *Libertel*, the ECJ was also asked to identify the circumstances in which it was likely such distinctiveness would be present. It noted that:

> 71. ...the reply to Question 2(b) must be that the fact that registration as a trade mark of a colour per se is sought for a large number of goods or services, or for a specific product or service or for a specific group of goods or services, is relevant, together with all the other circumstances of the particular case, to assessing both the distinctive character of the colour in respect of which registration is sought, and whether its registration would run counter to the general interest in not unduly limiting the availability of colours for the other operators who offer for sale goods or services of the same type as those in respect of which registration is sought.

In *Libertel*,[24] the ECJ makes the point that whether a mark is initially devoid of distinctive character may depend upon the nature of the goods and services to which it attaches. We might agree that the colour orange, for example, may be more readily viewed by the public as a badge of origin, if it is used in relation to telecommunications rather than, for example, foodstuffs.[25] In *Nichols Plc v Registrar of Trade Marks*, which concerned the registration of a common surname, the ECJ made a similar point. According to the Court, any name may in principle satisfy the requirements of Article 2(1)(b) and be registered. However, a common name is more likely to be viewed as a badge of origin depending upon the context in which it is used. In *Nichols*, the ECJ also parted company with the 'Baby-Dry' judgment by holding that the availability of a defence to trade mark infringement does not mean that the relevant authorities should more readily allow the registration of a sign which might otherwise lack distinctiveness. As Jacob J pointed out in his High Court judgment in *Re Nichols*, such an approach would be to the advantage of 'powerful traders' who would have the resources to 'assert their rights even in marginal cases'.[26]

A related question then arises. If there is a public interest in leaving certain signs free for others to use unless they have acquired distinctiveness, should it be more difficult for a would-be proprietor to persuade the court that such distinctiveness has indeed been achieved? In a number of cases the ECJ has made it clear that there should be no higher hurdle to proving that a mark has acquired distinctiveness through use even if it falls into one of the categories of marks which should initially be left free for others to use.[27] Thus, in *Linde*, the ECJ held:

> 46. With reference to Art. 3(1)(b) of the Directive, it must be observed that neither the scheme of the Directive nor the wording of that provision indicate that stricter criteria than those used for other categories of trade mark ought to be applied when assessing the distinctiveness of a three-dimensional shape of goods mark.
> 47. As para. 40 of this judgment makes clear, distinctive character means, for all trade marks, that the mark must be capable of identifying the product as originating from a particular undertaking, and thus distinguishing it from those of other undertakings.

Once again, the ECJ has sought to draw a balance between the need to encourage competition between traders who might legitimately wish to use the same sign and the interests of a trader whose investment in a sign has led it to acquire distinctiveness in relation to his own goods or services. Do you think the ECJ is correct to conclude that, in the latter case, the

---

[24] See also *Linde*.
[25] In fact, following the ECJ decision, Libertel succeeded with its trade mark application.
[26] *Re Nichols Plc* [2003] RPC 16, para. 14.   [27] For another example see *Windsurfing*.

public interest lies not in giving greater protection to such signs, but rather in ensuring that a distinctive sign should be registrable whatever the initial public interest in leaving it free?

5.3.3.5 Trade marks which consist exclusively of signs or indications which have become customary in the current language or in the bona fide and established practices of the trade (Article 3(1)(d))

The key case for interpreting this exclusion is the case of *Merz & Krell GmbH & Co*. In particular, in *Merz & Krell*, the ECJ discussed the difference between these signs and descriptive signs.

Merz & Krell GmbH & Co Case C-517/99 [2000] ECR I-6959

Merz & Krell sought to register the mark 'Bravo' for writing instruments at the German Patent and Trade Mark Office. Registration was refused on the basis that 'Bravo' was seen by the relevant consumers as a word of praise, and therefore devoid of distinctive character. Merz & Krell then appealed to the Bundespatentgericht. It took the view that 'Bravo' could not be registered under para. 8(2)(3) of the Markengesetz (the German trade marks act) because the word is traditionally used in advertising for a variety of goods, and therefore had become customary in the current language or in the bona fide and established practices of the trade, even if that use was for a variety of goods and not necessarily writing instruments. It went on to address the following question to the ECJ: should Article 3(1)(d) be interpreted restrictively to mean that only signs which are descriptive would be denied registration? Or alternatively, does Article 3(1)(d) also cover signs which have become customary in current language in the sector in question, for instance as a persuasive advertising tool, but which are not directly descriptive? The ECJ answered in the positive.

35. It must first of all be observed that, although there is a clear overlap between the scope of Articles 3(1)(c) and 3(1)(d) of the Directive, marks covered by Article 3(1)(d) are excluded from registration not on the basis that they are descriptive, but on the basis of current usage in trade sectors covering trade in the goods or services for which the marks are sought to be registered.

36. It follows that, in order for Article 3(1)(d) of the Directive to be effective, the scope of the provision in respect of which the Court's interpretation is sought should not be limited solely to trade marks which describe the properties or characteristics of the goods or services covered by them.

. . .

39. It also follows that, where the signs or indications concerned have become customary in the current language or in the bona fide and established practices of the trade to designate the goods or services covered by the mark, it is of little consequence that they are used as advertising slogans, indications of quality or incitements to purchase those goods or services.

40. However, registration of a trade mark which consists of signs or indications that are also used as advertising slogans, indications of quality or incitements to purchase the goods or services covered by that mark is not excluded as such by virtue of such use. It is for the national court to determine in each case whether the signs or indications have become customary in the current language or in the bona fide and established practices of the trade to designate the goods or services covered by that mark.

41. It follows that Article 3(1)(d) of the Directive must be interpreted as meaning that it subjects refusal to register a trade mark to the sole condition that the signs or indications of which the trade mark is exclusively composed have become customary in the current language or in the bona fide and established practices of the trade to designate the goods or services in respect of which registration of that mark is sought. It is immaterial, when that provision is applied, whether the signs or indications in question describe the properties or characteristics of those goods or services.

Looking back over the series of cases which have allowed the ECJ to interpret the reach of the absolute grounds for refusal of registration as it applies to descriptive, non-distinctive marks and marks that are common in the trade, it is clear that beginning with *Windsurfing*, the ECJ has generally sought to protect such marks from the monopoly afforded by registration on the basis that, in the interests of competition, they should be left available for other traders to use. But we have also seen in *Windsurfing* and successive cases, that despite these public interest considerations, the ECJ has held that there should be no higher barrier to achieving acquired distinctiveness in relation to these signs than for any other signs, including those which do not carry with them the same public interest considerations.[28] The next question to arise is how is acquired distinctiveness to be assessed.

FURTHER READING

A. Griffiths, 'Modernising trade mark law and promoting economic efficiency: An evaluation of the Baby-Dry judgment and its aftermath' (2003) 1 IPQ 1–37.

M. Handler, 'The distinctive problem of European trade mark law' [2005] EIPR 306.

D. T. Keeling, 'About Kinetic watches, easy banking and nappies that keep a baby dry: A review of recent European case law on absolute grounds for refusal to register trade marks' [2003] IPQ 131.

J. Phillips, 'Trade mark law and the need to keep free' [2005] IIC 389.

5.3.3.6 The proviso at Article 3(3): acquiring distinctive character through use

In *British Sugar*,[29] Jacob J held that mere use of a mark does not necessarily equal distinctiveness. *Windsurfing* tells us that in the case of a geographical mark which is very well known it may be that only long-standing and intensive use will endow the mark with the necessary distinctiveness to be registered. Although *Windsurfing* was specifically concerned with geographical names, in its judgment the ECJ also set out the general criteria for assessing distinctiveness under Article 3(3).

Windsurfing Chiemsee Produktions und Vertriebs GmbH v Boots und Segelzubehör Walter Huber Joined Cases C-109/97 and C-109/97 [1999] ECR I-2779

49. In determining whether a mark has acquired distinctive character following the use made of it, the competent authority must make an overall assessment of the evidence that

---

[28] The following section considers how the courts assess acquired distinctiveness.
[29] *British Sugar plc v James Robertson & Sons* [1996] RPC 281.

the mark has come to identify the product concerned as originating from a particular undertaking, and thus to distinguish that product from goods of other undertakings.

50. In that connection, regard must be had in particular to the specific nature of the geographical name in question. Indeed, where a geographical name is very well known, it can acquire distinctive character under Article 3(3) of the Directive only if there has been long-standing and intensive use of the mark by the undertaking applying for registration. *A fortiori*, where a name is already familiar as an indication of geographical origin in relation to a certain category of goods, an undertaking applying for registration of the name in respect of goods in that category must show that the use of the mark—both long-standing and intensive—is particularly well established.

51. In assessing the distinctive character of a mark in respect of which registration has been applied for, the following may also be taken into account: the market share held by the mark; how intensive, geographically widespread and long-standing use of the mark has been; the amount invested by the undertaking in promoting the mark; the proportion of the relevant class of persons who, because of the mark, identify goods as originating from a particular undertaking; and statements from chambers of commerce and industry or other trade and professional associations.

52. If, on the basis of those factors, the competent authority finds that the relevant class of persons, or at least a significant proportion thereof, identify goods as originating from a particular undertaking because of the trade mark, it must hold that the requirement for registering the mark laid down in Article 3(3) of the Directive is satisfied. However, the circumstances in which that requirement may be regarded as satisfied cannot be shown to exist solely by reference to general, abstract data such as predetermined percentages.

53. As regards the method to be used to assess the distinctive character of a mark in respect of which registration is applied for, Community law does not preclude the competent authority, where it has particular difficulty in that connection, from having recourse, under the conditions laid down by its own national law, to an opinion poll as guidance for its judgment (see, to that effect, Case C-210/96 *Gut Springenheide and Tusky* [1998] ECR I-4657, paragraph 37).

54. In the light of the foregoing, the answer to the questions on the first sentence of Article 3(3) of the Directive must be that Article 3(3) is to be interpreted as meaning that:

- a trade mark acquires distinctive character following the use which has been made of it where the mark has come to identify the product in respect of which registration is applied for as originating from a particular undertaking and thus to distinguish that product from goods of other undertakings;

- it precludes differentiation as regards distinctiveness by reference to the perceived importance of keeping the geographical name available for use by other undertakings;

- in determining whether a trade mark has acquired distinctive character following the use which has been made of it, the competent authority must make an overall assessment of the evidence that the mark has come to identify the product concerned as originating from a particular undertaking and thus to distinguish that product from goods of other undertakings;

- if the competent authority finds that a significant proportion of the relevant class of persons identify goods as originating from a particular undertaking because of the trade mark, it must hold the requirement for registering the mark to be satisfied;

- where the competent authority has particular difficulty in assessing the distinctive character of a mark in respect of which registration is applied for, Community law does not preclude it from having recourse, under the conditions laid down by its own national law, to an opinion poll as guidance for its judgment.

Crucial to the test for distinctiveness set out in *Windsurfing* is that a 'significant portion of the relevant class of persons' have come to see the mark as a badge of origin. Later cases have elaborated on the question as to how the relevant authorities might define the relevant consumer. Emerging from the case law is what has come to be known as the 'average-consumer test'.

5.3.3.7 The average-consumer test

The issue of how to judge acquired distinctiveness was a key issue in *Philips*. Specific to the case, as we have seen was that until Remington marketed their own three-headed shaver, Philips was the only company to supply such a product. The ECJ was asked 'whether, when a trader has been the only supplier of particular goods to the market, extensive use of a sign which consists of the shape of those goods is sufficient to give the sign a distinctive character for the purposes of Article 3(3) of the Directive in circumstances where, as a result of that use, a substantial proportion of the relevant class of persons associates the shape with that trader, and no other undertaking, or believes that goods of that shape come from that trader in the absence of a statement to the contrary'.

In answering this question, the ECJ first cited the *Windsurfing* test for distinctiveness, but added the following important caveat. It noted that acquired distinctiveness:

Koninklijke Philips Electronics NV v Remington Consumer Products Ltd Case C-299/99 [2002] ECR I-5475

63. ...must be assessed in the light of the presumed expectations of an average consumer of the category of goods or services in question, who is reasonably well-informed and reasonably observant and circumspect (see, to that effect, the judgment in *Gut Springenheide and Tusky*, Case C-210/96 [1998] ECR I-4657, paragraph 31).

[It then concluded:]

65. ...where a trader has been the only supplier of particular goods to the market, extensive use of a sign which consists of the shape of those goods may be sufficient to give the sign a distinctive character for the purposes of Article 3(3) of the Directive in circumstances where, as a result of that use, a substantial proportion of the relevant class of persons associates that shape with that trader and no other undertaking or believes that goods of that shape come from that trader. However, it is for the national court to verify that the circumstances in which the requirement under that provision is satisfied are shown to exist on the basis of specific and reliable data, that the presumed expectations of an average consumer of the category of goods or services in question, who is reasonably well-informed and reasonably observant and circumspect, are taken into account and that the identification, by the relevant class of persons, of the product as originating from a given undertaking is as a result of the use of the mark as a trade mark.

The ECJ first adopted the average-consumer test in trade mark law[30] in *Sabel v Puma*[31] and *Lloyd v Lkijsen*,[32] two cases which addressed the grounds for finding a 'likelihood of

---

[30] The average-consumer test originated in EU cases concerned with misleading advertising. As both *Windsurfing* and *Philips* make clear, his first appearance was in *Gut Springenheide and Tusky* Case C-210/96 [1998] ECR I-4657.

[31] *Sabel BV v Puma AG Rudolf Dassler Sport* [1998] ECR I-6191.

[32] *Lloyd Schuhfabrik Meyer & Co GmbH v Klijsen Handel BV* [1999] ECR-3819, ECJ.

confusion' between marks under Article 4(1)(b) of the Trade Marks Directive.[33] In *Philips*, as we have seen, the perceptions of the average consumer were viewed as crucial for assessing when a mark which was initially barred from registration under Article 3(1)(b)–(d) would have acquired sufficient distinctiveness through use to be registered. Of particular importance for the average-consumer test is the nature of the goods or services which attach to the mark or marks at issue. In other words, the courts will assume that the attention the average consumer will pay to the mark at issue will vary according to the nature of the goods or services: whether, for instance, they are 'everyday' goods or luxury items. This was made clear by the ECJ in the case of *Procter & Gamble v OHIM*.

Procter & Gamble v OHIM Joined Cases C-468 to C-472/01 P [2004] ECR I-5141

Procter & Gamble sought to register a CTM for various white tablets (some speckled) and some with light green layers in respect of washing machine and dishwasher cleaning products. The applications were refused by the OHIM on the grounds that the marks were devoid of distinctive character. The case was appealed to the CFI which upheld the original decision and then to the ECJ, where the appeal was refused. In its decision, the ECJ was asked a number of questions about how distinctiveness is to be judged. These included how to assess the level of attention paid by the average consumer to the particular goods at issue and whether a trade mark should be considered as a whole in assessing distinctiveness. The ECJ set out the test for distinctivenes:

> 33. That distinctive character must be assessed, first, by reference to the products or services in respect of which registration has been applied for and, second, by reference to the perception of them by the relevant public, which consists of average consumers of the products or services in question, who are reasonably well informed and reasonably observant and circumspect (see, inter alia, *Linde*, para. 41, and Case C-363/99 *Koninklijke KPN Nederland* [2004] ECR I-0000, para. 34).
>
> ...
>
> 35. The Court of First Instance, in accordance with the settled case law of the Court of Justice, assessed whether the trade marks at issue were devoid of any distinctive character by reference, first, to the products or services in respect of which their registration was sought, and, second, by reference to the perception of the relevant public, which consists, in this case, of all consumers.
>
> 36. The Court of First Instance was also correct in stating that the criteria for assessing the distinctive character of three-dimensional shape-of-products marks are no different from those applicable to other categories of trade mark. It nonetheless observed that, for the purpose of applying those criteria, the relevant public's perception is not necessarily the same in relation to a three-dimensional mark consisting of the shape and colours of the product itself as it is in relation to a word or figurative mark consisting of a sign which is independent from the appearance of the products it denotes. Average consumers are not in the habit of making assumptions about the origin of products on the basis of their shape or the shape of their packaging in the absence of any graphic or word element and it could therefore prove more difficult to establish distinctiveness in relation to such a three-dimensional mark than in relation to a word or figurative mark (see, to that effect, *Linde*, para. 48, and Case C-218/01 *Henkel* [2004] ECR I-0000, para. 52).

---

[33] See 6.1.3.3. below.

[In light of the above, the ECJ concluded that:]

37. …Only a trade mark which departs significantly from the norm or customs of the sector and thereby fulfils its essential function of indicating origin, is not devoid of any distinctive character for the purposes of that provision (see, in relation to the identical provision in Art. 3(1)(b) of First Directive 89/104, *Henkel*, para. 49).[34]

[The ECJ then addressed the question of whether in assessing distinctiveness the trade mark should be considered as a whole or whether it was correct to analyse the distinctiveness of each of its individual features. It answered:]

44. As the Court has consistently held, the average consumer normally perceives a mark as a whole and does not proceed to analyse its various details (see *SABEL*, para. 23, and *Lloyd Schuhfabrik Meyer*, para. 25). Thus, in order to assess whether or not a trade mark has any distinctive character, the overall impression given by it must be considered (see *SABEL*, para. 23, and, in relation to a word mark, *DKV v OHIM*, para. 24).

45. That does not mean, however, that the competent authority, responsible for ascertaining whether the trade mark for which registration is sought—in this instance the graphic representation of a combination of the shape of a washing machine or dishwasher tablet and the arrangement of its colours—is capable of being perceived by the public as an indication of origin, may not first examine each of the individual features of the get-up of that mark in turn. It may be useful, in the course of the competent authority's overall assessment, to examine each of the components of which the trade mark concerned is composed.

Procter & Gamble concerned an attempt to register the shape of washing-up tablets as a CTM. Since these were an everyday item, the ECJ found that the average consumer would not pay particular attention to their shape. As a result, it held that their shape would not be viewed as a badge of origin and it did not have the necessary distinctiveness to be registered. The applicants made a counter-argument which did not find favour with the ECJ, but nonetheless might persuade some readers. According to the applicants, it is precisely because the average consumer might use these items everyday that he or she might become particularly acquainted with their shape as a badge of origin. It is submitted that this opposite approach to the consumer's level of attention has much to recommend it.

5.3.3.8 Famous signs and distinctiveness

A recent question to reach the ECJ is whether if a mark is highly distinctive in one field, it may be harder to persuade the public that it is distinctive for goods and services in another, quite unrelated field. This question was examined in *Ruiz-Picasso v OHIM*.[35]

***Claude Ruiz-Picasso v Office for Harmonisation in the Internal Market (Trade Marks and Designs), DaimlerChrysler AG* Case C-361/04 P [2006] ECR I-643**

Essentially, this case concerned the proprietors of the 'Picasso' trade mark for cars who sought to prevent the registration of the mark 'Picaro' for cars on the grounds that it

---

[34] This judgment was followed in *Mag Instrument Inc v Office for Harmonisation in the Internal Market* Case C-136/02 P [2004] ECR I-9165.
[35] Case C-361/04 P [2006] ECR I-643.

was confusingly similar under Article 8(1)(b) and Article 9(1)(b) TMD. One issue which arose was whether 'Picasso' was a particularly distinctive sign. There was no argument that it was well known to the public as the name of a famous painter. However it was held by the CFI and confirmed by the ECJ that simply because 'Picasso' was well-known in one context did not mean that it possessed a highly distinctive character when applied to motor vehicles. This point was made by the AG Colomer[36] (which he combined with a heartfelt plea against the debasement of our cultural heritage). He argued:

> 69. However, it is worth making two points about the legitimate protection of names which have earned their owners prestige. In the first place, when such a name is allowed to be used in a completely different context to that in which its reputation was earned, the greater protection which must be given to marks with a highly distinctive character cannot automatically be claimed. The simple reason for this is that, in that other context, it is very doubtful whether the name gives any information about the commercial origin of the goods and services at least initially. Secondly, there is a certain general interest in protecting the names of great artists, which represent a universal cultural heritage, from insatiable commercial greed, in order to safeguard their work from trivialisation. It is sad to think the averagely informed, reasonably aware and perceptive consumer, who no longer links names such as Opel, Renault, Ford or Porsche with the outstanding engineers whose products were named after them, will, unfortunately, in the not-too-far distant future be subjected to the same process in relation to the name Picasso.

Finally, it is important to remember that the average-consumer test is a judicial test and as such does not depend on consumer surveys. Indeed, such surveys have never found much favour in UK courts unlike equivalent courts in Germany. In *Windsurfing* it was suggested that such empirical testing was by no means necessary, and perhaps only useful in particularly difficult cases. This view was endorsed in later cases such as *Lloyd* and *Philips*. It is worth asking whether the real reason that the average-consumer test has found favour not just with domestic courts but also the ECJ is that it provides a convenient measure for assessing such issues without the need to resort to costly empirical testing.

5.3.3.9 Trade mark protection and the public domain

Thus far, in discussing the TMD and its interpretation, we have suggested that a crucial concern for the ECJ has been the need to balance the public interest in offering legal protection to signs, which are acting as trade marks, against the public interest in keeping certain signs free for others to use. Before the passage of the TMA, the UK courts had taken the view that certain signs, including geographical signs, although they might be acting as a badge of origin, should never be registered because they should be free for all to use. In a famous example, *Yorkshire Copper Works Ltd v Registrar of Trade Marks*,[37] a company which manufactured most of its products in Yorkshire applied to register as a trade mark, 'Yorkshire', for copper fittings. No one else manufactured these goods in Yorkshire and the applicants produced evidence that the mark had become '100 per cent distinctive' through use. The Registrar refused registration on the grounds that certain geographical words, including this one, could never be distinctive in law of a trader's

---

36 Ibid.   37 [1954] 1 WLR 554.

goods, even though they were distinctive in fact. The House of Lords concurred that certain signs are too important to other traders for them to be reserved to a single proprietor. However, we have seen that the directive does not allow for such an approach, since following *Windsurfing*, any descriptive signs (including geographical signs) may be registered provided they have acquired distinctiveness through use. In her article, Jennifer Davis considered why, in interpreting the directive, the ECJ had not recognized a public domain or a 'trade mark commons', containing certain trade marks, which should be refused registration in the public interest.

J. Davis, 'The need to leave free for others to use and the trade mark common' in J. Phillips and I. Simon (eds.), *Trade Mark Use* (Oxford: Oxford University Press, 2005), pp. 39–45

C. The ECJ and 'Need to Keep Free': Why has the Court not Developed a Commons Theory?

3.18 The trade mark common, as demarcated by the English courts, was a protected commons. Its development had been predicated upon the assumption, made by the courts, that a number of different and competing groups had an interest in the common. It was called into existence in large measure because the English courts believed that trade mark registration endowed a monopoly which might not only be anti-competitive but might also deprive the public more generally of access to a limited supply of socially useful signs. In interpreting the Trade Marks Directive, the ECJ recognised that there are certain categories of signs which, in the public interest, should be left free for others to use both now and in the future. What it has not recognised is a core of protected signs which cannot under any circumstances be registered. The reasons why the European trade mark regime does not (indeed, cannot) encompass a protected trade mark 'common' are to be found both in the substantive law and in the social and economic principles which shaped that law and the ways in which it has been interpreted.

3.19 Most obviously, Art. 3(3) of the Directive has been interpreted in successive cases to mean that any marks identified in Arts. 3(1)(b)–(d), whatever the apparent public interest in leaving them free for other traders, may be registered if they have acquired distinctiveness through use. This interpretation of the Directive was confirmed by the ECJ in *Philips v Remington*. In *Philips*, the English courts specifically asked the ECJ whether there remained, following the implementation of the Directive, a special class of signs which even though distinctive in fact, were nonetheless incapable of distinguishing as a matter of law. The ECJ held that there was not. Since Art. 3(1)(a) was intended to exclude from registration only those signs that are not capable of distinguishing, it followed, according to the ECJ, that there is no class of marks which have distinctive character either inherently or which have acquired distinctiveness through use, but which cannot be registered. The ECJ concluded:

> Article 3(3) therefore constitutes a major exception to the rule laid down in Art. 3(1)(b), (c) and (d), whereby registration is to be refused in relation to trade marks which are devoid of any distinctive character, descriptive marks, and marks which consist exclusively of indications which have become customary in the current language or in the bona fide and established practices of the trade.

3.20 The ECJ has emphasised the public interest concerns which underlie the absolute grounds for refusal of registration set out in Art. 3(1)(b)–(d). It is, therefore, not surprising that the question has also been raised as to whether, in assessing acquired distinctiveness under Art. 3(3), account should be taken of the extent of the need to keep certain marks free for others to use. In other words, should the degree of trade acceptance (or distinctiveness) necessary to satisfy Art. 3(3) depend upon how important it is for the sign to be left free? In fact, the ECJ has affirmed in a number of cases that it is not possible to apply stricter criteria in assessing whether descriptive signs or other non-distinctive signs in limited supply have acquired sufficient distinctiveness to be registered. The Court has, however, acknowledged that as a practical matter it may be more difficult to demonstrate acquired distinctiveness in relation to such signs, since, by definition, they are unlikely to be perceived by the public, in the first instance, as a badge of origin. As we have seen, such was the ECJ's reasoning in relation to shape marks in *Linde*.

3.21 The substantive law of the Trade Marks Directive, in particular the effects of Art. 3(3) of the Directive, has not allowed the courts to recognise a core of protected signs. Furthermore, that law was adopted at a time when the idea that strong intellectual property rights enhanced rather than inhibited competition, particularly international competition, had become common currency, at least among governments in the developed world. However, it is submitted that the ECJ has not necessarily been consistent in its approach to whether trade marks should be given a wide or narrow penumbra of protection. This inconsistency is most apparent if one looks not at the application of Art. 3(3), but rather at those cases which have concerned the registrability of descriptive or non-distinctive signs without evidence of use. In BABY-DRY the ECJ seemed to accept that signs could be registered even if they had only a minimal level of distinctiveness. In this case, it allowed the registration as a Community trade mark of BABY-DRY for nappies, on the basis that Art. 7(1)(c) was designed to exclude from registration only those signs which were purely descriptive. If, on the other hand, the descriptive components of a sign were presented in such as a way that the resultant whole could be distinguished from the usual way of designating the goods at issue, as was the case with BABY-DRY, it could be registered. In retrospect, it is clear that BABY-DRY marks, at least for the present, the high water mark of the protection afforded to minimally distinctive signs. In later cases, the ECJ has sought to hold back the tide, by returning to the reasoning in *Windsurfing*, explicitly so in the case of *Wrigley*.

3.22 The question remains as to what extent the ECJ has been willing to recognise and hence to balance the different and conflicting interests which may be affected by a trade mark registration, something which we have argued was fundamental to the delineation of the English trade mark common. Clearly, the ECJ's freedom of action in this regard has been constrained by the market led approach to trade mark registration embodied in Art. 3(3) of the Directive, which determines that any sign which is acting as a trade mark, that is as a badge of origin in the market, can be registered. Furthermore, there has been some argument, put most forcefully by Advocate General Jacobs in his BABY-DRY opinion and followed by the ECJ in its ruling, that allowing proprietors to appropriate even minimally distinctive signs did not unduly impede access to the public domain, since it is a defence to trade mark infringement if a third party uses the mark descriptively. Not surprisingly it was an English judge, Jacob J, who presented what was perhaps the most cogent criticism of this view. He pointed out that such an approach inevitably favoured 'powerful traders', who will 'naturally assert their rights even in marginal cases'. Indeed, in such cases, he believed that:

> defendants, SMEs particularly, are likely to back off when they receive a letter before action. It is cheaper and more certain to do that than stand and fight, even if in principle they have a defence.

3.23 It is submitted that, since BABY-DRY, the ECJ has backed away from the robust view of registration embodied in the judgment. Without the option of creating a protected trade mark common to protect the interest of 'the public in general and weaker and less organised companies', the ECJ has instead emphasised that the relevant authorities should be more rigorous in their examination of an applicant's sign before allowing a mark to be removed from the public domain in the first place. In other words, it is the 'competent authorities' who should be the gatekeepers as to which marks are removed from the public domain, rather than trans-ferring such responsibility, *ex post facto*, to the courts. In *Libertel* the ECJ noted that:

> the large number of and detailed nature of the obstacles to registration set out in Articles 2 and 3 of the Directive, and the wide range of remedies available in the event of refusal, indicate that the exam-ination carried out at the time of the application for registration must not be a minimal one. It must be a stringent and full examination, in order to prevent trade marks from being improperly registered.

3.24 In fact, by advocating this approach, the ECJ was once again reaching a destination which had been sign-posted 90 years earlier by Lord Parker in *W & G du Gros*.[38] He stated:

> In my opinion, in order to determine whether a mark is distinctive it must be considered quite apart from the effects of registration. The question, therefore, is whether the mark itself, if used as a Trade Mark, is likely to become actually distinctive of the goods of the persons so using it. The applicant for registration in effect says, 'I intend to use this mark as a Trade Mark, i.e., for the purpose of distinguishing my goods from the goods of other persons', and the Registrar or the court has to determine, before the mark be admitted to registration, whether it is of such a kind that the applicant, quite apart from the effects of registration, is likely or unlikely to attain the object he has in view. The applicant's chance of success, in this respect, must, I think, largely depend upon whether other traders are likely, in the ordinary course of their business and with-out any improper motive, to desire to use the same mark, or some mark nearly resembling it, upon or in connection with, their own goods.

D. Conclusion: The Balance Between Leaving Marks Free for Others to Use and Recognising Distinctiveness Acquired through Use

3.25 In its White Paper preceding the implementation of the Directive, the British Government noted:

> At present it is possible for it to be established beyond doubt that a particular trade mark is distinctive in fact and yet for it to held in law to be not capable of distinguishing. Examples are geographical names and laudatory epithets. This position has been described as unattractive, but the Registry and the courts have considered themselves bound by a long history of case law, much of it dating from a period in which trading conditions were very different from today. The government intends to take the opportunity offered by a new law to clarify the position so that any trade mark which is demonstrated to be distinctive in fact will in future be regarded as distinctive in law and therefore be registrable.

3.26 As we have seen, the effect of Art. 3(3) of the Directive has been precisely to ensure that any mark which has acquired distinctiveness through use may indeed be capable of registration. As a corollary, it is also no longer possible for certain marks to be reserved for the 'English language common', so they may be left free for others to use despite acquired distinctiveness.

3.27 It can be argued that such an approach to trade mark registration has the virtue of both simplicity and consistency. In a long line of trade mark cases, many of which preceded the Directive, the ECJ has held that:

> the essential function of a trade mark is to guarantee the identity of origin of the marked goods or services to the consumer or end user by enabling him, without any possibility of confusion, to distinguish the goods or services from others which have another origin.

---

[38] *W & G Du Cros Ltd's Application* (1913) 30 RPC 661.

3.28 It follows that if a descriptive mark or a non-distinctive mark reaches the requisite level of distinctiveness through use, it will fulfil the essential function of a trade mark and should be capable of registration. Such was the simple logic followed by the ECJ in *Windsurfing* and *Philips*, for example. Indeed, it may be further argued that to allow otherwise would be precisely to allow for the possibility of such confusion. Finally, in its reference to contemporary 'trading conditions', the White Paper was surely recognising the contemporary importance of branding. It would certainly be a hard thing to deny a trader the economic rewards for the investment he has made in ensuring that his mark, which might initially have been descriptive or lacking in distinctiveness, has indeed acquired distinctiveness through use.

3.29 There is a clear public interest in allowing factually distinctive marks to be registered which goes to the heart of the justification for trade mark registration. As we have seen, in a number of decisions, the ECJ has also identified a countervailing public interest in allowing certain signs to be left free for other traders to use. It would not be surprising if, at the margins, these two public interests might appear to conflict. This essay has sought to describe the process by which the ECJ has endeavoured to balance these two areas of trade mark law. If it is no longer possible, under the Directive, to maintain a protected common of signs which other traders may wish to use; nonetheless, the ECJ has clearly recognised that it is desirable that such signs should remain available until and unless they have acquired distinctiveness through use.

FURTHER READING

M. Boote, 'What's in a name? *Claude Ruiz Picasso v OHIM*' [2006] EIPR 349.

J. Davis, 'Locating the average consumer: His judicial origins, intellectual influences and current role in European trade mark law' (2005) 2 IPQ 183–221.

A. Folliard-Monguiral, 'Distinctive character acquired through use: The law and the case law' in J. Phillips and I. Simon (eds.), *Trade Mark Use* (Oxford: Oxford University Press, 2005), pp. 49–70.

A. Niedermann, 'Surveys as evidence in proceedings before OHIM' [2006] IIC 260.

5.3.4 SIGNS WHICH MAY NEVER BE REGISTERED

5.3.4.1 Shape marks

The Trade Mark Directive allows, as we have seen, for the registration of shape marks: both fanciful shapes and also shape of goods marks which have acquired distinctiveness. However, the directive contains a prohibition against the registration of functional shapes. Article 3(1)(e) of the TMD (s. 3(2) of the TMA) prohibits registration of signs which consist exclusively of:

— the shape which results from the nature of the goods themselves
— the shape of goods which is necessary to obtain a technical result
— the shape of goods which give substantial value to the goods.

5.3.4.2 Interpreting the shapes exclusion: *Philips*

The leading case for interpreting Article 3(1)(e) is *Philips*. We have looked at the facts. Apart from arguing that the three-headed shaver lacked distinctiveness under s. 3(1)(b) and was descriptive, Remington also argued that the Philips trade mark, viewed as a three-dimensional mark, was invalidly registered because it fell within Article 3(1)(e). In the High Court,[39] Jacob J held that while the shape did not result from the nature of the goods themselves, it consisted exclusively of a shape which was necessary to obtain a technical result and which gave substantial value to the goods. It could not be registered even though it was possible to achieve the same result with other shapes. Philips appealed. The Court of Appeal[40] agreed that the shape of the razor did not result from the nature of the goods, since there was no one shape that resulted from the nature of razors. It differed from the High Court in holding that the shape did not give substantial value to the goods, since it had no eye-appeal and gave no more value to the goods than other shapes which achieved the same result. It also took a preliminary view that a shape could fall foul of Article 3(1)(e), if its shape was functional, even if there were other shapes which could obtain the same result. The Court of Appeal addressed a number of questions to the ECJ, of which the most pertinent in relation to Article 3(1)(e) was whether Article 3(1)(e) of the TMD should be interpreted to mean that a sign consisting exclusively of the shape of a product is unregistrable if it is established that the essential functional features of the shape are attributable only to the technical result. It also asked whether the ground for refusal or invalidity of the registration imposed by that provision could be overcome by establishing that there are other shapes which can obtain the same technical result.

The ECJ answered as follows:

Koninklijke Philips Electronics NV v Remington Consumer Products Ltd Case C-299/99 [2002] ECR I-5475

76. Article 3(1)(e) [thus] concerns certain signs which are not such as to constitute trade marks and is a preliminary obstacle liable to prevent a sign consisting exclusively of the shape of a product from being registrable. If any one of the criteria listed in Article 3(1)(e) is satisfied, a sign consisting exclusively of the shape of the product or of a graphic representation of that shape cannot be registered as a trade mark.

77. The various grounds for refusal of registration listed in Article 3 of the Directive must be interpreted in the light of the public interest underlying each of them (see, to that effect, *Windsurfing Chiemsee*, paragraphs 25 to 27).

78. The rationale of the grounds for refusal of registration laid down in Article 3(1)(e) of the Directive is to prevent trade mark protection from granting its proprietor a monopoly on technical solutions or functional characteristics of a product which a user is likely to seek in the products of competitors. Article 3(1)(e) is thus intended to prevent the protection conferred by the trade mark right from being extended, beyond signs which serve to distinguish a product or service from those offered by competitors, so as to form an obstacle preventing competitors from freely offering for sale products incorporating such technical solutions or functional characteristics in competition with the proprietor of the trade mark.

79. As regards, in particular, signs consisting exclusively of the shape of the product necessary to obtain a technical result, listed in Article 3(1)(e), second indent, of the Directive, that provision is intended to preclude the registration of shapes whose essential characteristics perform a technical function, with the result that the exclusivity inherent in the trade mark right would limit the possibility of competitors supplying a product incorporating such a function or at least limit their freedom of choice in regard to the technical solution they wish to adopt in order to incorporate such a function in their product.

---

[39] *Philips v Remington* [1998] RPC 283 (HC).   [40] *Philips v Remington* [1999] RPC 809 (CA).

80. As Article 3(1)(e) of the Directive pursues an aim which is in the public interest, namely that a shape whose essential characteristics perform a technical function and were chosen to fulfil that function may be freely used by all, that provision prevents such signs and indications from being reserved to one undertaking alone because they have been registered as trade marks (see, to that effect, *Windsurfing Chiemsee*, paragraph 25).

81. As to the question whether the establishment that there are other shapes which could achieve the same technical result can overcome the ground for refusal or invalidity contained in Article 3(1)(e), second indent, there is nothing in the wording of that provision to allow such a conclusion.

82. In refusing registration of such signs, Article 3(1)(e), second indent, of the Directive reflects the legitimate aim of not allowing individuals to use registration of a mark in order to acquire or perpetuate exclusive rights relating to technical solutions.

83. Where the essential functional characteristics of the shape of a product are attributable solely to the technical result, Article 3(1)(e), second indent, precludes registration of a sign consisting of that shape, even if that technical result can be achieved by other shapes.

84. In the light of those considerations...Article 3(1)(e), second indent, of the Directive must be interpreted to mean that a sign consisting exclusively of the shape of a product is unregistrable by virtue thereof if it is established that the essential functional features of that shape are attributable only to the technical result. Moreover, the ground for refusal or invalidity of registration imposed by that provision cannot be overcome by establishing that there are other shapes which allow the same technical result to be obtained.

According to the ECJ, by obtaining a monopoly on a technical design, the proprietor of such a trade mark would effectively be able to prevent other traders from offering competing products. This would undermine what we have seen to be a key aim of the directive: to promote competition. Such protection might also allow proprietors of functional shapes to find long range protection through trade mark registration, which they would not obtain through more limited patent protection. Indeed, as we have seen, Philips itself sought to register the shape of its three-headed shaver at the point at which its patent protection expired. Subsequently, the Philips' trade mark was held invalid in UK, Germany, France, and Spain. The judgment in *Philips* suggests that once again the ECJ was seeking to find the balance between protecting a public domain of useful signs and providing legal certainty for trade mark proprietors. In this case, by disallowing the registration of functional shapes even if there were other shapes that might achieve the same result, the scales would seem to have come down firmly on the side of the former interest. Following the ECJ decision in *Philips*, questions were raised whether by using the word 'exclusively' the ECJ had intended that functional shapes which were also intended to have, for example, aesthetic appeal or functional shapes which included features which were not attributable to achieving a technical result would escape the Article 3(1)(e) prohibiton. Recently, in *Koninklijke Philips v Remington*,[41] the Court of Appeal upheld the High Court decision of Rimer J who found that neither was the case, and that the ECJ had been saying that a shape could not be registered if 'every essential feature' was intended to obtain a technical result, even though parts of those features may not be so intended and even though the shape may also have aesthetic appeal. Do you agree that trade mark registration should be so limited even though it is possible to argue that some functional shapes, such as those with aesthetic appeal, might be distinctive

---

[41] *Koninklijke Philips NV v Remington Consumer Products Ltd* [2004] EWHC 2337 (HC); *Koninklijke Philips NV v Remington Consumer Products Ltd* [2006] EWCA Civ 16 (CA).

in practice and may not, in any case, be the sole means of obtaining a particular technical result?

5.3.4.3 Other grounds for the refusal of registration

Article 3 of the TMD identifies a number of further signs which will not be registered, of which the most significant are the following:

i. Article 3(1)(f) (s. 3(3)(a) of the TMA): Trademarks which are contrary to public policy or to accepted principles of morality;

ii. Article 3(1)(g) (s. 3(3)(b) of the TMA): Trademarks which are of such a nature as to deceive the public, for instance as to the nature, quality, or geographical origin of the goods or service;

iii. Article 3(2)(d) (s. 3(6) of the TMA): Trade marks for which the application is made in bad faith.

5.3.4.4 Marks contrary to public policy or morality

These may of course vary widely over time, as social mores change. The general standard against which such signs will be judged was set out by the Appointed Person on an appeal from the Trade Mark Registry against the refusal to register 'Tiny Penis' for clothing in *Ghazilian's Trade Mark Application*.[42] The Appointed Person held that mere offence to a section of the public who see the mark as distasteful is insufficient to fall foul of this provision. Rather whether a sign offends against 'accepted principles of morality' should be judged against whether a right-thinking member of the public, who may himself or herself not be outraged, would be able, objectively, to assess whether or not the mark in question is calculated to cause 'outrage' or 'censure' to others. Applying these criteria to the present case, the Appointed Person concluded that the registration should be refused under s. 3(3) (Article 3(1)(f)) for the following reason:

Ghazilian's Trade Mark Application [2002] ETMR 56

49. Mr Ghazilian has been using the word penis as part of the slang vernacular in a way in which many people would not. I must contemplate the use of the words Tiny Penis in television advertisements going out before the general public, in advertising bill boards in public places, perhaps even on the side of the well known Clapham omnibus. I do not doubt that a very large section of the public would find this distasteful but that is not enough. Would they be outraged? Would they feel that the use should properly be the subject of censure? I have found this a difficult question to answer. 20 or 30 years ago the answer would have been clear. The accepted principles of morality change with time.

50. Placing myself in the shoes of the 'right-thinking' member of the public in the way I have indicated above, I have concluded that this trade mark would cause greater offence than mere distaste to a significant section of the public. The offence resides in the fact that an accepted social and family value is likely to be significantly undermined. This value lies in

---

[42] [2002] ETMR 56.

the belief that the correct anatomical terms for parts of the genitalia should be reserved for serious use and should not be debased by use as a smutty trade mark for clothing.

51. Accordingly I have reached the conclusion that the Registrar was justified in refusing registration on the basis that registration would be contrary to an accepted principle of morality. This appeal will be dismissed. In accordance with the usual practice there will be no order as to costs of the appeal.

Although the Appointed Person took a view in this case, we might question whether in today's pluralistic society there is ever a real consensus over what constitutes offensive language. In *CDW Graphic Design's Trade Mark Application*,[43] the TMR objected to a mark on different, and possibly more solid, grounds. In this case, it refused registration to the mark 'www.standupifyouhatemanu.com' on the grounds that it was 'liable to function as a badge of antagonism' and hence to increase the incidence of football violence—although, again we might question whether the TMR was being overly cautious.

5.3.4.5 Deceptive marks

Trade marks may be found to be deceptive if they mislead the public as to the quality of the goods to which they attach. The standard necessary for deception, according to the ECJ in *Consorzio per la tutela del formaggio Gorgonzola*,[44] is that there is 'the existence of actual deceit or a sufficiently serious risk that the consumer will be deceived'. The ECJ looked at the question of deceptive marks in *Emanuel v Continental Shelf*.

Elizabeth Florence Emanuel v Continental Shelf 128 Ltd Case C-259/04 [2006] ECR I-3089

The fashion designer, Elizabeth Emanuel, who designed Princess Diana's wedding dress, registered the mark 'Elizabeth Emanuel' in 1997. She then sold her business to a third party and assigned the trade mark to them. She was also employed by them, but subsequently left. The third party then assigned the business on to Continental Shelf who sought to register a further trade mark, 'Elizabeth Emanuel'. Elizabeth Emanuel opposed the registration on the basis that it would be deceptive of the origin of the goods. Among the questions referred to the ECJ by the Appointed Person was the following: would a trade mark be refused registration because it is deceptive where the goodwill associated with that mark has been assigned together with the business making the goods to which the mark relates and that trade mark, which corresponds to the name of the designer and first manufacturer of those goods, was previously registered in a different graphic form. The ECJ found that such a registration would not be deceptive.

45. A trade mark such as 'ELIZABETH EMANUEL' may have that function of distinguishing the goods manufactured by an undertaking, particularly where that trade mark has been assigned to that undertaking and the undertaking manufactures the same type of goods as those which initially bore the trade mark in question.

46. ...in the case of a trade mark corresponding to the name of a person, the public interest ground which justifies the prohibition laid down by Art. 3(1)(g) of Directive 89/104 to register a trade mark which is liable to deceive the public, namely consumer protection,

---

[43] [2003] RPC 30.
[44] *Consorzio per la tutela del formaggio Gorgonzola v Käserei Champignon Hofmeister GmbH & Co KG* Case C-87/97 [1999] ECR I-1301.

must raise the question of the risk of confusion which such a trade mark may engender in the mind of the average consumer, especially where the person to whose name the mark corresponds originally personified the goods bearing that mark.

47. Nevertheless, the circumstances for refusing registration referred to in Art. 3(1)(g) of Directive 89/104 presuppose the existence of actual deceit or a sufficiently serious risk that the consumer will be deceived (Case C-87/97) *Consorzio per la tutela del formaggio Gorgonzola* [1999] ECR I-1301 at paragraph 41).

48. In the present case, even if the average consumer might be influenced in his act of purchasing a garment bearing the trade mark 'ELIZABETH EMANUEL' by imagining that the appellant in the main proceedings was involved in the design of that garment, the characteristics and the qualities of that garment remain guaranteed by the undertaking which owns the trade mark.

49. Consequently, the name Elizabeth Emanuel cannot be regarded in itself as being of such a nature as to deceive the public as to the nature, quality or geographical origin of the product it designates.

50. On the other hand, it would be for the national court to determine whether or not, in the presentation of the trade mark 'ELIZABETH EMANUEL' there is an intention on the part of the undertaking which lodged the application to register that mark to make the consumer believe that Ms Emanuel is still the designer of the goods bearing the mark or that she is involved in their design. In that case there would be conduct which might be held to be fraudulent but which could not be analysed as deception for the purposes of Art. 3 of Directive 89/104 and which, for that reason, would not affect the trade mark itself and, consequently, its prospects of being registered.

It is submitted that the ECJ was correct in this approach, since it would be difficult to see how a business could be assigned together with its trade mark if subsequent use of the trade mark, by the party that had acquired it, was found to be deceptive. However, others might argue that the average consumer when purchasing a gown with the label 'Elizabeth Emanuel' would assume that the gown, like Princess Diana's wedding dress, was designed by Elizabeth Emanuel herself.

5.3.4.6 Trade marks registered in bad faith

The most common circumstances in which a trade mark may be registered in bad faith are if the applicant does not intend to use the trade mark or where there are better third-party rights to the mark.[45] Where the applicant does not intend to use his mark against all the goods and services for which it is registered, the courts have not generally made a finding of bad faith.[46] In *Harrison's Trade Mark Application*[47] in the Court of Appeal, Aldous LJ defined bad faith as whether the applicant's actions fall below the standard of acceptable commercial behaviour observed by reasonable and experienced persons in the particular commercial area being examined. The bar against the registration of marks in bad faith would appear to be directed at protecting the public interest in ensuring that there is fair competition between traders. By contrast, the bar against the registration of deceptive marks is obviously relevant to a different but no less important concern, that of ensuring that the essential

---

[45] See for example, *Ferrero SpA's Trade Marks* [2004] RPC 29.
[46] *Knoll AG's Trade Mark* [2003] EWHC 899.
[47] [2005] FSR 10.

function of the mark is maintained and that it continues to act as a badge of origin for the benefit of consumers.

5.3.4.7 The absolute grounds for refusal of registration: a summary

As we have seen, some of the categories of signs identified in Article 3(1) may be registered with evidence of acquired distinctiveness. Others may not be registered under any circumstances. We have also seen in a number of cases, that the ECJ has made it clear that marks which should be left free for others to use in the first instance, should not face any greater difficulty in acquiring distinctiveness than any others. In his article, Arnaud Folliard-Monguiral considers the justification for allowing some but not all the categories of marks indentified in Article 3 to be registered upon proof of acquired distinctiveness (pp. 51–3).

A. Folliard-Monguiral, 'Distinctive character acquired through use: The law and the case law' in J. Phillips and I. Simon (eds.), *Trade Mark Use* (Oxford: Oxford University Press, 2005)

407. The underlying logic of the possibility offered by Council Directive 89/104 or Council Regulation 40/94 to 'cure' objections under certain of the absolute grounds for refusal or for invalidity is as follows: an unjustified advantage would be granted to a single trader if he were given rights over a sign which must be freely available for use by everyone due to its descriptive, generic or non-distinctive nature. It is only in the event that such a sign, because of the use to which it has been put, is actually perceived by the relevant public as an indication of trade origin of the goods or services that the economic effort made by the trade mark applicant justifies putting aside the public-interest considerations underlying Article 3(1)(b)–(d) of Council Directive 89/104 or Article 7((1)(b)–(d) of Council Regulation 40/94.

408. In contrast, by the express intention of the legislature, the signs falling within the scope of the grounds for refusal or for invalidity provided under Article 3(1)(e)-(g) of Council Directive 89/104 and Article 7(1)(e)–(k) of Council Regulation 40/94 may never acquire distinctiveness. Indeed, it is the case that these grounds for refusal or for invalidity cannot be overcome. The underlying logic for such a prohibition against acquiring distinctiveness through use differs according to the absolute ground.

409. As regards Article 3(1)(e) of Council Directive 89/104 and Article 7(1)(e) of Council Regulation 40/94, the prohibition is justified (i) by the public interest that natural, functional or ornamental shapes may be freely used by all and (ii) by the fact that trade mark protection is not meant to perpetuate a protection which could be granted for a limited period of time through a patent right, a copyright or a design right, where appropriate. The balance of interests between the public interest protected by the absolute grounds under Article 3(1)(e) and the interest of the proprietor in protecting its investment in making the mark distinctive differs from the position taken under Articles 3(1)(b)–(d). Under those Articles, the economic effort of the trademark applicant in making his mark *de facto* distinctive outweighs the interests protected by those articles. However, under Article 3(1)(e), the applicant's investment has already been potentially protected by the award of a patent, copyright or design protection: to provide trade mark protection as a result of acquired distinctiveness would involve rewarding the investment twice.

410. As regards Article 3(1)(f)–(h) of Council Directive 89/104 and Article 7(1)(f)–(k) of Council Regulation 40/94, the justification is not that the signs falling within these absolute

grounds should remain free for all, but on the contrary that the use of such signs should be prohibited to all, either without exception or to all those who are not entitled to use them.

Folliard-Monguiral suggests there is a balance to be struck between the public interest in rewarding the investment proprietors may make in nurturing the distinctiveness of their marks, which is appropriate for some categories of signs, and the public interest in leaving other marks free for others to use under all circumstances. As we have seen, the ECJ has consistently sought, in interpreting the absolute grounds for refusal of registration, to find an acceptable balance between these two interests. We have also seen that at times this balance has shifted. We might take the view that the ECJ has achieved a fair compromise between these competing claims. But we should also be aware that it is possible for that balance to shift again.

FURTHER READING

A. Firth, 'Signs, surfaces, shapes and structures: The protection of product design under trade mark law' in G. B. Dinwoodie and M. D. Janis (eds.), *Trade Mark Law and Theory: A handbook of contemporary research* (Cheltenham: Edward Elgar, 2008), pp. 498–522.

T. Hays, 'Distinguishing use versus functional use: Three dimensional marks' in J. Phillips and I. Simon (eds.), *Trade Mark Use* (Oxford: Oxford University Press, 2005), pp. 93–110.

C. Seville, 'Trade marks' [2008] ICLQ 955.

U. Suthersanen, 'The European Court of Justice in *Philips v Remington*: Trade marks and market freedom' [2003] IPQ 257.

TRADE MARKS II:

THE RELATIVE GROUNDS FOR REFUSAL OF REGISTRATION, INFRINGEMENT, DEFENCES, AND EXHAUSTION OF RIGHTS

6.1 THE RELATIVE GROUNDS FOR REFUSAL OF REGISTRATION

6.1.1 INTRODUCTION

The previous chapter was concerned with those signs which might be registered as trade marks and those signs which, in the public interest, should be left free for others to use or registered only with acquired distinctiveness. This chapter is divided into five sections, with a sixth and final section on remedies. This first section will examine the relative grounds for refusal of registration. The second section will look at the rights conferred by registration, most notably, the right to act against infringers The third section will then go on to identify the possible defences against infringement. Section four will examine the ways in which registration may be lost. Section five will look at the protection afforded to trade marks both within and outside the European Economic Area (EEA) and how trade mark rights might be exhausted. We shall see that in considering the scope of protection afforded to trade marks, the ECJ has had to consider the extent to which registration should protect not merely the trade mark's role as a badge of origin but also its wider reputation or distinctiveness. In other words, a key question for the Court has been to what extent the TMD protects against dilution.

6.1.2 ARTICLE 4

Article 4 TMD[1] identifies the circumstances in which the proprietor of a registered trade mark (or the owner of an earlier right) may prevent the registration of a later sign. Article 4 thus

---

[1] TMA 1994, s. 5.

defines the penumbra of protection which is endowed on a trade mark by registration. The grounds for finding a conflict at the time of registration are the same as the grounds for a finding of infringement. The provisions of the directive dealing with infringement will be examined below. Nonetheless, when discussing the relative grounds for refusal of registration, we shall have considerable recourse to judgments which have turned upon whether an earlier registered mark has been infringed. In the same way, we shall see later that interpretations of the infringement provisions of the directive (and the TMA) frequently derive from judgments relating to conflict at the time of registration.

6.1.3 ARTICLE 4(1): CONFUSION AS TO ORIGIN

Article 4(1)[2] reads as follows:

> a trade mark shall not be registered or, if registered, shall be liable to be declared invalid:
>
> (a) if it is identical with an earlier trade mark, and the goods or services for which the trade mark is applied for or is registered are identical with the goods or services for which the earlier trade mark is protected.
>
> (b) if because of its identity with, or similarity to the earlier trade mark and the identity or similarity of the goods or services covered by the trade marks, there exists a likelihood of confusion on the part of the public, which includes the likelihood of association with the earlier trade mark.

Article 4(2)[3] defines earlier trade marks as Community trade marks, trade marks already registered in the Member State or in a Member State via the Madrid Protocol, and well known marks as defined under the Article 6*bis* of the Paris Convention.

Article 4(4) adds other grounds for conflict, both at the registration stage and in relation to infringement which were optional for Member States to recognize. The most important are the following:

> (a) the trade mark is identical with, or similar to, an earlier national trade mark within the meaning of paragraph 2 and is to be, or has been, registered for goods or services which are not similar to those for which the earlier trade mark is registered, where the earlier trade mark has a reputation in the Member State concerned and where the use of the later trade mark without due cause would take unfair advantage of, or be detrimental to the distinctive character or the repute of the earlier trade mark
>
> (b) rights to a non-registered trade mark or to another sign used in the course of trade were acquired prior to the date of application for registration of the subsequent trade mark, or the date of the priority claimed for the application for registration of the subsequent trade mark and the non-registered trade mark or other sign confers on its proprietor the right to prohibit the use of the subsequent trade mark
>
> (c) the use of the trade mark may be prohibited by virtue of an earlier right other than the rights referred to in paragraphs 2 and 4(b) and in particular:
>
>   (i) a right to a name;
>
>   (ii) a right of personal portrayal;

---

[2] The equivalent provisions in the TMA are s. 5(1) and s. 5(2)(a)–(b).   [3] TMA, s. 6(1).

(iii) a copyright;

(iv) an industrial property right.

The UK has chosen to incorporate these provisions into the TMA 1994. Thus s. 5(4) of the TMA refuses registration to a mark whose use is liable to be prevented either by virtue of any rule of law (in particular, the law of passing off) protecting an unregistered trade mark or other sign used in the course of trade (s. 5(4)(a)) or by virtue of an earlier right (s. 5(4)(b)). The latter would include a copyright or a patent, but not a right of personality which does not exist in the UK.[4]

6.1.3.1 Article 4(1)(a):[5] identical marks on identical goods

In this case, the later sign will be refused registration, without the necessity of proving that the public would be confused if both marks are on the Register. The ECJ considered when marks should be considered identical for the purposes of conflict in the case *LTJ Diffusion v SA Sadas*.[6]

LTJ Diffusion v SA Sadas Case C-291/000 [2003] ECR I-2799

50. The criterion of identity of the sign and the trade mark must be interpreted strictly. The very definition of identity implies that the two elements compared should be the same in all respects...

51. There is therefore identity between the sign and the trade mark where the former reproduces, without any modification or addition, all the elements constituting the latter.

52. However, the perception of identity between the sign and the trade mark must be assessed globally with respect to an average consumer who is deemed to be reasonably well informed, reasonably observant and circumspect. The sign produces an overall impression on such a consumer. That consumer only rarely has the chance to make a direct comparison between signs and trade marks and must place his trust in the imperfect picture of them that he has kept in his mind. Moreover, his level of attention is likely to vary according to the category of goods or services in question (see, to that effect, Case C-342/97 *Lloyd Schuhfabrik Meyer* [1999] ECR I-3819, para. 26).

53. Since the perception of identity between the sign and the trade mark is not the result of a direct comparison of all the characteristics of the elements compared, insignificant differences between the sign and the trade mark may go unnoticed by an average consumer.

54. In those circumstances, the answer to the question referred must be that Art. 5(1)(a) of the directive must be interpreted as meaning that a sign is identical with the trade mark where it reproduces, without any modification or addition, all the elements constituting the trade mark or where, viewed as a whole, it contains differences so insignificant that they may go unnoticed by an average consumer.

A UK case which followed *LTJ Diffusion* was *Reed*. We have already looked at this case in relation to the own name defence in passing off.[7] In *Reed*, the claimants also alleged that the defendants had infringed their registered trade mark 'Reed'. In his judgment, Jacob LJ

---

[4] See Ch. 7 on Character Merchandising and Publicity Rights.   [5] TMA, s. 5(1)(a).

[6] This case arose out of an infringement action and therefore addressed the meaning of Art. 5(1)(a).

[7] See 4.3.2.

pointed out that the defendants had never used 'Reed' alone but rather in their logos and as part of the composite 'Reed Elsevier' or more frequently 'Reed Business Information'. Jacob LJ compared the word 'Reed' to the latter, and he concluded that the marks were not identical.

Reed Executive plc v Reed Business Information Ltd [2004] EWCA Civ 159, [2004] RPC 40

Jacob LJ:

38. 'Reed' is a common surname. The average consumer would recognise the additional words as serving to differentiate the defendant from Reeds in general—this one calls itself 'Reed Business Information' because it supplies information to businesses in some unspecified way or ways.

39. Putting it another way, I do not think the additional words 'Business Information' would 'go unnoticed by the average consumer'. In all uses of the phrase complained of they are as prominent as the word 'Reed'.

40. In so holding I am not saying that in some circumstances the average consumer could not assume that 'Reed Business Information' is connected with Reed Employment or an organisation called 'Reed'. But these would be cases of similarity of mark and sign, not identity.

41. It follows that in all cases complained of there is no identity of mark and sign.

There is rather less case law which relates specifically to whether the goods or services are identical for the purposes of Article 4(1)(a). Rather the question of whether goods or services are similar or identical has been addressed more frequently in cases concerned with Article 4(1)(b) of the directive, which covers, *inter alia*, similar marks on similar goods or services. It is to the interpretation of this provision that we now turn.

6.1.3.2 Article 4(1)(b):[8] identical or similar signs on identical or similar goods or services and the proviso

There are three elements which must be proved for conflict to arise under Article 4(1)(b). First, the earlier registered mark and the later sign must be identical or similar. Second the goods must be identical or similar. If both these conditions obtain, then conflict between the earlier registered mark and the sign will still only arise if, thirdly, the proviso applies and there exists a likelihood of confusion on the part of the public, which includes the likelihood of association with the earlier trade mark. In a succession of cases following the implementation of the directive, beginning with the judgment in *Sabel v Puma*,[9] the ECJ has made clear that all these conditions are interdependent. It has developed what has become known as 'the global approach' for assessing conflict under Article 4(1)(b). The global approach arose out of a debate as to what functions of a registered trade mark Article 4(1)(b) was intended to protect. The debate is looked at by Annette Wagner. Wagner points out that some Member States (such as Benelux) have interpreted the proviso to mean that in finding infringement it is sufficient that the public has associated the two marks at issue without confusion as to

---

[8] TMA, s. 5(2)(a)–(b).
[9] *Sabel BV v Puma AG and Rudolf Dassler Sport* Case C-251/95 [1998] ECR I-6191.

source. Conversely, others (such as the UK) have assumed that there must be a confusion as to source in order to find infringement. She suggests that the Benelux interpretation of the proviso derives from the view that a trade mark is not only a badge of origin but also an advertising tool, while the UK, by contrast, primarily views a trade mark as a badge of origin.

A. Wagner, 'Infringing trade marks: Function, association and confusion of signs according to the EC Trade Marks Directive' (1999) 21(3) EIPR 127–32

Implementation and interpretation of the Directive in several Member States

It is common knowledge that the Directive has been heavily influenced by Benelux trade mark law. So the infringement provisions are often referred to as a compromise between the Benelux concept and the more narrow concept of other Member States relying on the traditional importance of a 'likelihood of confusion'. However, implementations and the following interpretations of the Directive reveal considerable differences of opinions about their meaning. The Benelux countries and the United Kingdom mark the two opposite ends of the scale and will therefore serve as especially illustrative examples.

Benelux

Even after the implementation of the Directive into Benelux trade mark law, there is no mention of a 'likelihood of confusion' in Article 13A of the Uniform Benelux Law. Accordingly, the Brussels Court of Appeal in the case *Always v Regina* dismissed an argument by the defendant that in the light of the Directive a simple 'likelihood of association' as developed under Benelux case law is no longer sufficient. The wording of the Directive was used as a reason for this judgment since it included expressly the concept of likelihood of association. Furthermore, the court considered the fact that the Benelux Governments thought that the amended version of the Benelux Trade Mark Act was in compliance with the Directive.

. . .

United Kingdom

The *Wagamama* decision of the High Court, Chancery Division is a focus for the interpretation of the scope and the requirements of trade mark protection under the 1994 Trade Marks Act in Britain. Here the judge had to investigate the meaning of Article 5(1)(b) of the Directive which has the same wording as section 10(2) of the Trade Marks Act.

Laddie J found that it was necessary to restrict the provisions in the 1994 Act to classical infringement, i.e. a likelihood of confusion as to the origin of goods or services. He argued that any extension of trade mark rights above a protection of the indication of origin would be a dramatic change compared with the former situation, for which he could not see any expressed intention in the Directive nor any commercial justification. On the contrary, in his view such an interpretation would significantly restrict the freedom of traders to compete and therefore would be inconsistent with general principles of the internal market. So it was rejected.

This decision has been harshly criticised as undermining the legitimate interests of trade mark holders and frustrating the objective of the Directive to approximate the laws in the Member States. It also raised a many-voiced call for clarification.

Wagner mentions *Wagamama* as a UK case which found that there must be origin confusion for conflict to arise under Article 4(1)(b).[10] Thus, in *Wagamama*, Laddie J noted that:

Wagamama Ltd v City Centre Restaurants Plc [1996] ETMR 23, 41

The rights of the proprietor against alleged infringers may be limited to classic infringement which includes association as to origin or following the Benelux route, it could cover not only classic infringement but also non-origin association. In my view, the former construction is to be preferred.

6.1.3.3 Confusingly similar marks

In *Sabel v Puma*, it fell to the ECJ to decide whether the protection afforded to trade marks by Article 4(1)(b) was limited to their 'classic' function as indicators of origin or whether the inclusion of the term, 'including a likelihood of association' should be taken to mean that trade marks were also protected from non-origin association (or dilution).

Sabel BV v Puma AG and Rudolf Dassler Sport Case C-251/95 [1998] ECR I-6191

The applicant sought to register a mark consisting of a 'leaping cat' device together with the word 'Sabel' in Germany for a variety of goods in classes 19 and 25, including clothing and leather goods. The application was opposed by the proprietors of two German registered trade marks, each of which featured a 'leaping cat' device which was also registered for clothing and leather goods. Since the marks were clearly not identical, the application therefore fell to be decided under Article 4(1)(b). The German court asked the ECJ first whether it was sufficient for a finding of conflict that there is a likelihood of confusion between a sign composed of text and picture and a sign consisting merely of a picture, which is registered for identical and similar goods and is not especially well known to the public, where the two signs coincide as to their semantic content (in this case, a bounding feline) and second whether, in relation to this connection, does the likelihood of confusion include the likelihood that a mark may be associated with an earlier mark? The ECJ first set out the differing views of the Member States. It summarized the broad view of trade mark protection taken by the Benelux countries and then set out its own interpretation of the proviso.

18. In that connection, it is to be remembered that Article 4(1)(b) of the Directive is designed to apply only if, by reason of the identity or similarity both of the marks and of the goods or services which they designate, 'there exists a likelihood of confusion on the part of the public, which includes the likelihood of association with the earlier trade mark'. It follows from that wording that the concept of likelihood of association is not an alternative to that of likelihood of confusion, but serves to define its scope. The terms of the provision itself exclude its application where there is no likelihood of confusion on the part of the public.

...

---

[10] See judgment of Laddie J in *Wagamama*.

22. As pointed out in paragraph 18 of this judgment, Article 4(1)(b) of the Directive does not apply where there is no likelihood of confusion on the part of the public. In that respect, it is clear from the tenth recital in the preamble to the Directive that the appreciation of the likelihood of confusion 'depends on numerous elements and, in particular, on the recognition of the trade mark on the market, of the association which can be made with the used or registered sign, of the degree of similarity between the trade mark and the sign and between the goods or services identified'. The likelihood of confusion must therefore be appreciated globally, taking into account all factors relevant to the circumstances of the case.

23. That global appreciation of the visual, aural or conceptual similarity of the marks in question, must be based on the overall impression given by the marks, bearing in mind, in particular, their distinctive and dominant components. The wording of Article 4(1)(b) of the Directive—'... there exists a likelihood of confusion on the part of the public...'—shows that the perception of marks in the mind of the average consumer of the type of goods or services in question plays a decisive role in the global appreciation of the likelihood of confusion. The average consumer normally perceives a mark as a whole and does not proceed to analyse its various details.

24. In that perspective, the more distinctive the earlier mark, the greater will be the likelihood of confusion. It is therefore not impossible that the conceptual similarity resulting from the fact that two marks use images with analogous semantic content may give rise to a likelihood of confusion where the earlier mark has a particularly distinctive character, either *per se* or because of the reputation it enjoys with the public.

25. However, in circumstances such as those in point in the main proceedings, where the earlier mark is not especially well known to the public and consists of an image with little imaginative content, the mere fact that the two marks are conceptually similar is not sufficient to give rise to a likelihood of confusion.

26. The answer to the national court's question must therefore be that the criterion of 'likelihood of confusion which includes the likelihood of association with the earlier mark' contained in Article 4(1)(b) of the Directive is to be interpreted as meaning that the mere association which the public might make between two trade marks as a result of their analogous semantic content is not in itself a sufficient ground for concluding that there is a likelihood of confusion within the meaning of that provision.

The ECJ then turned its attention to the circumstances in which marks might be found to be confusingly similar and held that the marks should be viewed through the perspective of the average consumer who will take account of the overall impression created by them. In *Sabel*, the ECJ also made clear that non-origin confusion is a matter for Articles 4(3) and 5(2)[11] of the directive, which are intended to address the issue of dilution when the earlier mark has a 'reputation'. Nonetheless, in *Sabel*, the ECJ did hold that where the earlier mark is particularly distinctive or has a reputation, there will be a greater likelihood that origin confusion will arise. Such a view was confirmed in *Marca Mode CV v Adidas AG*,[12] where the ECJ stated that where it is the case that the earlier mark may be particularly distinctive, such a mark may receive broader protection under Article 4(1)(b) than a mark which is not as distinctive. However, in *Marca Mode*, the ECJ also went on to find that a likelihood of confusion cannot be assumed simply because an earlier mark has a reputation which might give rise to the possibility of it being associated with a later mark.

[11] TMA, ss. 5(3) and 10(3). See below for a discussion of the dilution provisions of the Directive.
[12] Case C-425/98 [2000] ECR I-4861.

6.1.3.4 Confusingly similar goods and services

In *Sabel*, the ECJ held that it is necessary to take a 'global approach' to finding confusion under Article 4(1)(b). In other words, whether there is confusion under this provision will depend upon the interaction between the distinctiveness of the mark and the similarity of the goods. The global approach was further elaborated by the ECJ in *Canon v MGM* in which the Court addressed the issue of when goods are confusingly similar.[13]

Canon Kabushiki Kaisha v Metro-Goldwyn-Mayer Inc Case C-39/97 [1998] ECR I-5507

MGM applied to register in Germany the mark 'Cannon' to be used, *inter alia*, on video film cassettes, production, and distribution of films. The application was opposed by Canon which had a registered trade mark 'Canon' in respect, *inter alia*, of cameras and projectors. The question before the ECJ was whether, on a proper construction of Article 4(1)(b) of the directive, the distinctive character of the earlier trade mark, and in particular its reputation, must be taken into account when determining whether the similarity between the goods or services covered by the two trade marks is sufficient to give rise to the likelihood of confusion. The ECJ first summarized the global test for conflict which had been set out in *Sabel*. It then went on to consider the issue of the similarity of goods.

> 22. It is, however, important to stress that, for the purposes of applying Article 4(1)(b), even where a mark is identical to another with a highly distinctive character, it is still necessary to adduce evidence of similarity between the goods or services covered.
>
> ...
>
> 23. In assessing the similarity of the goods or services concerned, as the French and United Kingdom Governments and the Commission have pointed out, all the relevant factors relating to those goods or services themselves should be taken into account. Those factors include, *inter alia*, their nature, their end users and their method of use and whether they are in competition with each other or are complementary.
>
> 24. In the light of the foregoing, the answer to be given to the first part of the question must be that, on a proper construction of Article 4(1)(b) of the Directive, the distinctive character of the earlier trade mark, and in particular its reputation, must be taken into account when determining whether the similarity between the goods or services covered by the two trade marks is sufficient to give rise to the likelihood of confusion.

6.1.3.5 Summarizing the global approach

In *Canon*, the ECJ had elaborated on how the global approach may be applied to assessing whether the similarity of goods will cause confusion. In the later case of *Lloyd v Klijsen*, where the goods involved were identical, the ECJ went on to apply the global approach to assessing the similarity of marks and the likelihood of confusion, including the situation where the earlier registered mark is distinctive. In doing so, the ECJ offered a summary of the global approach.

---

[13] The question of how to assess the similarity between goods had earlier been considered in the UK in *British Sugar plc v James Robertson & Sons Ltd* [1997] ETMR 118.

Lloyd Schuhfabrik Meyer & Co GmbH v Klijsen Handel BV Case C-342/97 [1999] ECR I-3819

2. ...the more similar the goods or services covered and the more distinctive the earlier mark, the greater will be the likelihood of confusion.

3. In order to determine the distinctive character of a mark and, accordingly, in assessing whether it is highly distinctive, it is necessary to make a global assessment of the greater or lesser capacity of the mark to identify the goods or services for which it has been registered as coming from a particular undertaking, and thus to distinguish those goods or services from those of other undertakings. In making that assessment, account should be taken of all relevant factors and, in particular, of the inherent characteristics of the mark, including the fact that it does or does not contain an element descriptive of the goods or services for which it has been registered. It is not possible to state in general terms, for example by referring to given percentages relating to the degree of recognition attained by the mark within the relevant section of the public, when a mark has a strong distinctive character.

Bearing in mind the cases we have looked at which discuss the global approach to a finding of infringement under Article 4(1)(b), it is possible to summarize the global approach thus:

- The three factors—similarity of marks, similarity of goods, and the application of the proviso—are interdependent.
- A greater similarity of the mark and the later sign may lead to a finding that there is a likelihood of confusion even when there is a lesser degree of similarity between the goods or services concerned.
- A greater similarity between the goods and services may lead to a finding that there is a likelihood of confusion even when there is a lesser degree of similarity between marks.
- If the earlier mark is particularly distinctive or has a reputation this may lead to a finding that there is a likelihood of confusion even when there is a lesser degree of similarity between marks or between the goods and services.

It follows that we may wonder whether in giving greater weight to a distinctive mark in assessing conflict with a later sign or mark, the ECJ has allowed in the wider Benelux approach to trade mark protection by the back door.

FURTHER READING

A. Griffiths, 'The trade mark monopoly: An analysis of the core zone of absolute protection under Article 5(1)(a)' [2007] IPQ 312.

P. L. C. Torremans, 'The likelihood of association of trade marks: An assessment in the light of the recent case law of the Court of Justice' [1998] IPQ 295.

P. Turner-Kerr 'Confusion or association under the European Trade Mark Directive' [2001] EIPR 49.

A. Wagner, 'Infringing trade marks: Function, association and confusion of signs according to the EC Trade Marks Directive' [1999] EIPR 127.

6.1.4 ARTICLE 4(4)(A): CONFLICT AND DILUTION

According to Article 4(4)(a),[14] conflict arises between a registered mark and a later sign where the mark and the sign are identical or similar and the goods are similar or dissimilar and the earlier mark has a reputation, plus the proviso applies. We have noted that it was up to Member States to decide whether they wished to adopt Article 4(4)(a) of the TMD. The UK chose to do so. While this provision originally applied only to situations in which the goods concerned were dissimilar, in *Davidoff v Gofkid*,[15] the ECJ ruled that it also applied where the goods were identical or similar. The UK amended the TMA to reflect this decision in 2004. The intent of Article 4(4)(a) is to protect trade marks with a reputation against dilution. Fundamental to anti-dilution protection is that it protects trade marks with a reputation not against confusion as to origin but rather against the damage which might result if the public 'associates' a later mark or sign with the earlier registered mark. We have seen that as early as the 1930s, Frank Schechter argued for the importance of the advertising function of trade marks and the need for the law to protect against dilution. The concept of dilution was introduced into US federal trade mark law by the 1995 Federal Trademark Dilution Act, which has now been amended by the Trademark Dilution Revision Act 2006. In 1971, the Benelux Trade Marks Act also appeared to recognize the concept of dilution. An example of a Benelux case which took this approach, before the directive, is *Claeryn*.[16] In this case, the claimant was the proprietor of a well-known trade mark, 'Claeryn', for gin. The defendant made use of the mark 'Klarein' for a toilet cleaner. The Benelux court held that the latter infringed the 'Claeryn' mark. It accepted that the value of the 'Claeryn' mark would be undermined by any negative associations which the public might make between the gin and the toilet cleaner, because of the similarity of the marks, even if the public did not assume the marks had a common origin. The result would be a lessening of the exclusivity of the 'Claeryn' mark. Following the passage of the directive, there was general agreement that Article 4(4)(a) was intended to protect trade marks with a reputation from dilution. This understanding was confirmed in a number of judgments, including *Sabel v Puma*, which made clear (at para. 20), that to find conflict under Articles 4(3) and (4)(3)(a) and 5(2) of the directive, there is no need for proof of a likelihood of confusion, even where there is no similarity between the goods in question. In *Adidas-Salomon*,[17] the ECJ elaborated further on the difference between origin confusion and association. It ruled:

> 2. The protection conferred by Art. 5(2) of Directive 89/104 is not conditional on a finding of a degree of similarity between the mark with a reputation and the sign such that there exists a likelihood of confusion between them on the part of the relevant section of the public. It is sufficient for the degree of similarity between the mark with a reputation and the sign to have the effect that the relevant section of the public establishes a link between the sign and the mark.

We shall see later in this chapter that there has been considerable controversy as to the nature of the 'link' which will give rise to conflict under Article 4(4)(a). However, the *Adidas* case is also interesting because in the course of his opinion, the Advocate General offered an excellent summary of the sorts of damage which the Article 4(4)(a) (and Article 5(2) under infringement) are intended to protect trade marks against.

---

[14] TMA 1994, s. 5(3).   [15] *Davidoff & Cie SA v Gofkid Ltd* Case C-292/00 [2003] ECR I-389
[16] *Claeryn/Klarein* NJ/1975/472 (Benelux Court of Justice, 1 Mar. 1975).
[17] *Adidas-Salomon AG and Adidas Benelux BV v Fitnessworld Trading Ltd* Case C-408/01 [2003] ECR I-12537.

Adidas-Salomon AG and Adidas Benelux BV v Fitnessworld Trading Ltd Case C-408/01 [2003] ECR I-12537

Adidas-Salomon AG had a figurative trade mark registered at the Benelux Trade Mark Office for clothing. The mark consisted of three parallel, vertical stripes, of equal width, which appeared on the side and down the whole length of the clothing. The stripes might be of different sizes and colour combinations, provided that they contrasted with the basic colour of the clothing. Adidas gave an exclusive licence for the mark to the Dutch company. Fitnessworld was a UK company which marketed clothing under the name 'Perfetto'. Some of its clothing had a motif of two parallel stripes of equal width which contrasted with the main colour and was applied to the side seams of the clothing. In proceedings before the Dutch Court, Adidas claimed that the use of the two stripes by Fitnessworld would infringe its own mark under the terms of Article 5(2) of the directive. In particular, it alleged that such marketing by Fitnessworld took advantage of the repute of the Adidas mark, such that the exclusivity of the mark would be impaired. Advocate General Jacobs looked, *inter alia*, at the scope of Article 5(2):

36. Article 5(2) protects the proprietor of a mark with a reputation against use of an identical or similar sign where use of that sign without due cause takes unfair advantage of, or is detrimental to, the distinctive character or the repute of the trade mark. There are thus in principle four types of use which may be caught: use which takes unfair advantage of the mark's distinctive character, use which takes unfair advantage of its repute, use which is detrimental to the mark's distinctive character and use which is detrimental to its repute.

37. The concept of detriment to the distinctive character of a trade mark reflects what is generally referred to as dilution. That notion was first articulated by Schechter, who advocated protection against injury to a trade mark owner going beyond the injury caused by use of an identical or similar mark in relation to identical or similar goods or services causing confusion as to origin. Schechter described the type of injury with which he was concerned as the 'gradual whittling away or dispersion of the identity and hold upon the public mind' of certain marks. The courts in the United States, where owners of certain marks have been protected against dilution for some time, have added richly to the lexicon of dilution, describing it in terms of lessening, watering down, debilitating, weakening, undermining, blurring, eroding and insidious gnawing away at a trade mark. The essence of dilution in this classic sense is that the blurring of the distinctiveness of the mark means that it is no longer capable of arousing immediate association with the goods for which it is registered and used. Thus, to quote Schechter again:

for instance, if you allow Rolls Royce restaurants and Rolls Royce cafeterias, and Rolls Royce pants, and Rolls Royce candy, in 10 years you will not have the Rolls Royce mark any more.

38. In contrast, the concept of detriment to the repute of a trade mark, often referred to as degradation or tarnishment of the mark, describes the situation where—as it was put in the well-known *Claeryn/Klarein* decision of the Benelux Court of Justice—the goods for which the infringing sign is used appeal to the public's senses in such a way that the trade mark's power of attraction is affected. That case concerned the identically pronounced marks 'Claeryn' for a Dutch gin and 'Klarein' for a liquid detergent. Since it was found that the similarity between the two marks might cause consumers to think of detergent when drinking 'Claeryn' gin, the 'Klarein' mark was held to infringe the 'Claeryn' mark.

39. The concepts of taking unfair advantage of the distinctive character or repute of the mark in contrast must be intended to encompass instances where there is clear exploitation and free-riding on the coattails of a famous mark or an attempt to trade upon its reputation. Thus by way of example Rolls Royce would be entitled to prevent a manufacturer of whisky from exploiting the reputation of the Rolls Royce mark in order to promote his brand. It is not obvious that there is any real difference between taking advantage of a mark's distinctive character and taking advantage of its repute; since however nothing turns on any such difference in the present case, I shall refer to both as free-riding.

In *Adidas*, the Advocate General identified three types of injury which may be covered by the proviso to Article 4(4)(a). These are: use which takes unfair advantage of the mark's distinctive character and use which takes unfair advantage of its repute ('free-riding'); use which is detrimental to the mark's distinctive character (blurring); and, finally, use which is detrimental to its repute (tarnishing). The concepts of blurring and tarnishing are commonly to be found in US law on dilution and are now establishing themselves firmly in EU jurisprudence.[18] It is particularly interesting to note that the Advocate General, in describing these types of injury, refers to the article written by Schechter over half a century ago, which we looked at in the previous chapter.[19] This would appear to suggest that dilution is not a new phenomenon, even if, in certain jurisdictions, the UK for example, protection against dilution is. Does it suggest, on the contrary, that what is new is a willingness by a number of European governments, including the UK, to afford broader protection to registered marks than has been true in the past?

6.1.4.1 The nature of a reputation

We have noted that anti-dilution provisions in trade mark law are intended to protect marks with a strong advertising function, or in the words of Article 4(4)(a) of the directive, marks with a 'reputation'. In *General Motors v Yplon*,[20] the ECJ was asked in essence to explain the meaning of 'reputation' for the purpose of Article 5(2) of the directive. In this case, General Motors (GMC) had registered the mark 'Chevy' in the Benelux countries, *inter alia*, for cars. Yplon had a registered the mark 'Chevy' for detergents and cleaning fluids. GMC applied for an order to prevent Yplon using the 'Chevy' mark on the basis that it would damage the value of its own. One question posed to the ECJ was how to assess whether a mark has a reputation. According to the ECJ, first, the public amongst whom the mark must have a reputation will either be the public at large or a more specialized public, depending on the type of product or service concerned. Second, there is no rule that a given percentage of the population must know of the mark. Third, the mark must be known to a significant part of the relevant public. In determining whether it is so known, the national court may take into consideration the relevant facts of the case, including the market share of the mark, and the intensity, geographical extent, and duration of its use and the size of the investment in promoting it. Finally, the ECJ held that it is not necessary for the mark to be known in the whole of the territory concerned (for example, in this case, the whole of the Benelux) as long as it is known by the public in a substantial part of that territory.

---

[18] See for example, *Premier Brands UK Ltd v Typhoon Europe Ltd* [2000] ETMR 1071.
[19] See 5.5.2.
[20] *General Motors Corporation v Yplon SA* Case C-375/97 [1999] ECR I-5421.

6.1.4.2 The meaning of the proviso

The meaning of the proviso was looked at by the Court of Appeal in two recent cases: *Intel Corporation Inc v CPM* and *L'Oreal v Bellure*.[21] The former case concerned a trade mark registration and therefore considered the proviso at Article 4(4)(a). The latter case concerned an infringement action and therefore was concerned with Article 5(2). In the course of these judgments, the Court of Appeal addressed a number of questions regarding the meaning of the proviso to the ECJ.

Intel Corp Inc v CPM United Kingdom Ltd Case C-252/07 [2008] WLR (D) 371

Intel held a number of UK and Community trade marks for the words INTEL and INTELINSIDE for, *inter alia*, computers and related products. CPM registered the mark INTELMARK for marketing and telemarketing. Intel sought a declaration of invalidity for the CPM mark. It argued that CPM's use of the INTELMARK was without due cause and would take unfair advantage of and be detrimental to the distinctive character or the repute of its own marks. The Hearing Officer rejected Intel's application for a declaration of invalidity because he was not persuaded by Intel that use by CPM of its mark on its own products would damage the distinctiveness or repute of the Intel mark. Intel appealed. Patten J dismissed the appeal. He held that in assessing whether the proviso applied it was necessary to employ a global appreciation. Thus, even if the consumer associated the two marks, it did not follow this would be detrimental to or take advantage of the Intel mark, unless it could be shown that such a 'link' would have economic consequences favourable to the CPM mark.[22] Intel appealed. In the Court of Appeal[23] Jacob LJ accepted that 'Intel' was an invented word in that it had no other meaning beyond its identification with the products of Intel Corp, that it was unique in that it had not been used by any other trader in relation to other goods or services and that it had a 'huge reputation' in the UK for computers and related products. Jacob LJ also accepted that the marks were similar and that the goods were dissimilar. Further, he assumed that the use of the INTELMARK did not suggest that there was a trade connection with Intel Corp. Jacob LJ then sought a ruling from the ECJ whether, under these circumstances, the INTELMARK should be revoked. The ECJ summarized the questions put by the Court of Appeal.

23. Accordingly, the Court of Appeal (England and Wales) (Civil Division) decided to stay the proceedings and to refer the following questions to the Court for a preliminary ruling:

(1) For the purposes of Article 4(4)(a) of the [Directive], where:

(a) the earlier mark has a huge reputation for certain specific types of goods or services,

(b) those goods or services are dissimilar or dissimilar to a substantial degree to the goods or services of the later mark,

(c) the earlier mark is unique in respect of any goods or services,

(d) the earlier mark would be brought to mind by the average consumer when he or she encounters the later mark used for the services of the later mark,

---

[21] *L'Oreal SA v Bellure NV* [2006] EWHC 2355.
[22] *Intel Corp Ltd v CPM United Kingdom Ltd* [2006] EWHC 197 (QB).
[23] *Intel Corp Ltd v CPM United Kingdom Ltd* [2007] EWCA Civ 431.

are those facts sufficient in themselves to establish (i) 'a link' within the meaning of paragraphs 29 and 30 of [*Adidas-Salomon and Adidas Benelux*], and/or (ii) unfair advantage and/or detriment within the meaning of that Article?

(2) If no, what factors is the national court to take into account in deciding whether such is sufficient? Specifically, in the global appreciation to determine whether there is a 'link', what significance is to be attached to the goods or services in the specification of the later mark?

(3) In the context of Article 4(4)(a) [of the Directive], what is required in order to satisfy the condition of detriment to distinctive character? Specifically, (i) does the earlier mark have to be unique, (ii) is a first conflicting use sufficient to establish detriment to distinctive character and (iii) does the element of detriment to distinctive character of the earlier mark require an effect on the economic behaviour of the consumer?

The ECJ then made some preliminary observations. It noted that Article 4(4)(a) provides for three types of injury to marks with a reputation, as we have seen, and held that any one of these was sufficient for the provision to apply. Such injury will occur where, because of the similarity between the marks, the public establishes a link between them. Such a link does not involve confusion—but the existence of such a link is not enough to establish that injury has occurred. The ECJ also considered the nature of the relevant public whose perceptions are relevant to assessing whether the provision applies. Not surprisingly, it concluded that this public consisted of average consumers of the goods and services in question, who are reasonably well informed, reasonably observant, and circumspect.[24] It is the perceptions of the average consumer which determines whether a mark has a reputation, whether it is distinctive and whether injury has occurred to the distinctive character and repute of the mark. Finally, the ECJ held that to obtain protection under Article 4(4)(a), the proprietor of the earlier mark must adduce proof that use of the later mark would take 'unfair advantage of, or be detrimental to, the distinctive character' of his mark. It did however accept that it might be difficult to demonstrate actual damage, and indeed that it would be wrong to expect the proprietor of the earlier mark to have to wait to bring an action until actual damage had occurred. The ECJ thus held it sufficient for the proprietor to prove 'that there was a serious risk that such an injury will occur in the future' (at para. 38). Should the proprietor of the earlier mark show actual or potential damage, then it falls to the proprietor of the later mark to establish that there was due cause for his use of the mark. The ECJ then went on to answer the questions posed by the Court of Appeal. It held first that in assessing whether there is a relevant link, it is necessary to take a global approach:

40. By point (i) of Question 1 and Question 2, the national court asks, essentially, what the relevant criteria are for the purposes of establishing whether there is a link, within the meaning of the judgment in *Adidas Salomon and Adidas Benelux* ('a link'), between the earlier mark with a reputation and the later mark in respect of which a declaration of invalidity is sought.

41. The existence of such a link must be assessed globally, taking into account all factors relevant to the circumstances of the case (see, in respect of Article 5(2) of the Directive, *Adidas-Salomon and Adidas Benelux*, paragraph 30, and *Adidas and Adidas Benelux*, paragraph 42).

42. Those factors include:

– the degree of similarity between the conflicting marks;

– the nature of the goods or services for which the conflicting marks were registered, including the degree of closeness or dissimilarity between those goods or services, and the relevant section of the public;

---

[24] For a full discussion in relation to registration and distinctiveness, see 5.3.3.6.

- the strength of the earlier mark's reputation;
- the degree of the earlier mark's distinctive character, whether inherent or acquired through use;
- the existence of the likelihood of confusion on the part of the public.

43. In that respect, the following points must be made.

44. As regards the degree of similarity between the conflicting marks, the more similar they are, the more likely it is that the later mark will bring the earlier mark with a reputation to the mind of the relevant public. That is particularly the case where those marks are identical.

45. However, the fact that the conflicting marks are identical, and even more so if they are merely similar, is not sufficient for it to be concluded that there is a link between those marks.

46. It is possible that the conflicting marks are registered for goods or services in respect of which the relevant sections of the public do not overlap.

47. The reputation of a trade mark must be assessed in relation to the relevant section of the public as regards the goods or services for which that mark was registered. That may be either the public at large or a more specialised public (see *General Motors*, paragraph 24).

48. It is therefore conceivable that the relevant section of the public as regards the goods or services for which the earlier mark was registered is completely distinct from the relevant section of the public as regards the goods or services for which the later mark was registered and that the earlier mark, although it has a reputation, is not known to the public targeted by the later mark. In such a case, the public targeted by each of the two marks may never be confronted with the other mark, so that it will not establish any link between those marks.

49. Furthermore, even if the relevant section of the public as regards the goods or services for which the conflicting marks are registered is the same or overlaps to some extent, those goods or services may be so dissimilar that the later mark is unlikely to bring the earlier mark to the mind of the relevant public.

50. Accordingly, the nature of the goods or services for which the conflicting marks are registered must be taken into consideration for the purposes of assessing whether there is a link between those marks.

51. It must also be pointed out that certain marks may have acquired such a reputation that it goes beyond the relevant public as regards the goods or services for which those marks were registered.

52. In such a case, it is possible that the relevant section of the public as regards the goods or services for which the later mark is registered will make a connection between the conflicting marks, even though that public is wholly distinct from the relevant section of the public as regards goods or services for which the earlier mark was registered.

53. For the purposes of assessing where there is a link between the conflicting marks, it may therefore be necessary to take into account the strength of the earlier mark's reputation in order to determine whether that reputation extends beyond the public targeted by that mark.

54. Likewise, the stronger the distinctive character of the earlier mark, whether inherent or acquired through the use which has been made of it, the more likely it is that, confronted with a later identical or similar mark, the relevant public will call that earlier mark to mind.

55. Accordingly, for the purposes of assessing whether there is a link between the conflicting marks, the degree of the earlier mark's distinctive character must be taken into consideration.

56. In that regard, in so far as the ability of a trade mark to identify the goods or services for which it is registered and used as coming from the proprietor of that mark and, therefore, its distinctive character are all the stronger if that mark is unique—that is to say, as regards a word mark such as INTEL, if the word of which it consists has not been used by anyone for any goods or services other than by the proprietor of the mark for the goods and services it markets—it must be ascertained whether the earlier mark is unique or essentially unique.

57. Finally, a link between the conflicting marks is necessarily established when there is a likelihood of confusion, that is to say, when the relevant public believes or might believe that the goods or services marketed under the earlier mark and those marketed under the later mark come from the same undertaking or from economically-linked undertakings (see to that effect, inter alia, Case C-342/97 *Lloyd Schuhfabrik Meyer* [1999] ECR I-3819, paragraph 17, and Case C-533/06 *O2 Holdings and O2 (UK)* [2008] ECR I-0000, paragraph 59).

58. However, as is apparent from paragraphs 27 to 31 of the judgment in *Adidas-Salomon and Adidas Benelux*, implementation of the protection introduced by Article 4(4)(a) of the Directive does not require the existence of a likelihood of confusion.

In defining the nature of the 'link' necessary for the proviso to apply, the ECJ suggested the courts take a global approach which acknowledges the importance of a mark's distinctiveness or reputation. But it also warned that the presence of a 'reputation' for certain goods, that the goods involved are dissimilar, and the earlier mark is 'unique' do not necessarily mean that there is such a 'link'. The ECJ then went on to look at the relevant criteria for assessing whether use of the later mark would be detrimental to the distinctive character of the earlier mark. It held that this also called for a global assessment based on the criteria set out in para. 42 above. It continued:

71. ...the existence of a link between the conflicting marks does not dispense the proprietor of the earlier trade mark from having to prove actual and present injury to its mark, for the purposes of Article 4(4)(a) of the Directive, or a serious likelihood that such an injury will occur in the future.

72. Lastly, as regards, more particularly, detriment to the distinctive character of the earlier mark, the answer to the second part of the third question must be that, first, it is not necessary for the earlier mark to be unique in order to establish such injury or a serious likelihood that it will occur in the future.

73. A trade mark with a reputation necessarily has distinctive character, at the very least acquired through use. Therefore, even if an earlier mark with a reputation is not unique, the use of a later identical or similar mark may be such as to weaken the distinctive character of that earlier mark.

74. However, the more 'unique' the earlier mark appears, the greater the likelihood that the use of a later identical or similar mark will be detrimental to its distinctive character.

75. Secondly, a first use of an identical or similar mark may suffice, in some circumstances, to cause actual and present detriment to the distinctive character of the earlier mark or to give rise to a serious likelihood that such detriment will occur in the future.

76. Thirdly, as was stated on paragraph 29 of this judgment, detriment to the distinctive character of the earlier mark is caused when that mark's ability to identify the goods or services for which it is registered and used as coming from the proprietor of that mark is weakened, since use of the later mark leads to dispersion of the identity and hold upon the public mind of the earlier mark.

77. It follows that proof that the use of the later mark is or would be detrimental to the distinctive character of the earlier mark requires evidence of a change in the economic behaviour of the average consumer of the goods or services for which the earlier mark was registered consequent on the use of the later mark, or a serious likelihood that such a change will occur in the future.

78. It is immaterial, however, for the purposes of assessing whether the use of the later mark is or would be detrimental to the distinctive character of the earlier mark, whether or not the proprietor of the later mark draws real commercial benefit from the distinctive character of the earlier mark.

When Jacob LJ posed the questions for the ECJ in *Intel*, he also gave his own opinion on how they should be answered. Unsurprisingly, given the general approach the UK courts have taken to circumscribing the protection afforded by trade mark registration, Jacob LJ took the view that the necessary 'link', required more than a 'tenuous association between the two marks' or 'a mere passing to mind' (at para. 29). He pointed out:

Intel Corp Ltd v CPM United Kingdom Ltd [2007] RPC 35

Jacob LJ:

29. The average consumer is a reasonably sensible individual. He is used to lots of trade marks in different fields—some of which may resemble trade marks for other fields. In this country for example, for a long time Jif lemon juice and Jif washing up liquid coexisted happily, not to mention Jiffy for padded bags and condoms. Sometimes, but perhaps not surprisingly, trade mark owners of big brands want more protection than they really need.

30. Of course where a mark is really strong and the later allegedly conflicting mark is the same, the facts may simply go beyond a mere calling to mind. They may cause the consumer to think there is a trade connection between the owner of the former mark and the user of the later mark or at least wonder whether there is such connection. Clearly the former case ought to be protected, and perhaps the latter too if the wonder is substantial as opposed to fleeting.

[In relation to assessing whether there is detriment, **Jacob LJ** suggested that among the factors which might be taken into account are:]

36. ...

(i) whether the 'pulling power' of the earlier mark for its specific goods or services is really likely to be affected by the use of the later mark for its specific goods or services;

(ii) whether the user of the later mark is likely to get a real commercial advantage from its use for its specific goods or services by reason of the repute of the earlier mark for its specific goods or services;

(iii) whether, if the earlier mark is unique, it really matters that it is used for the dissimilar goods or services of the later mark;

(iv) where the later mark is not the same as the earlier mark what difference that will make on the average consumer and in particular whether there is merely a calling to mind of the earlier mark;

(v) whether the economic behaviour of the average consumer in relation to the earlier mark when used for its goods or services is likely to be affected;

(vi) how inherently distinctive the earlier mark is; and

(vii) how strong the reputation of the earlier mark for its goods or services is.

[Jacob LJ concluded:]

37. I would not attempt to produce a comprehensive list of factors—others may occur in the overall global appreciation. In the end it must be a question of degree. I would emphasise in my answer that it is very important that the harm or prospect of harm must be real and tangible. A mere possibility or assertion of damage is just too remote and would leave trade mark owners in too monopolistic a position. Trade mark law is there to protect a proper system of competition, not to provide trade mark owners with overreaching rights which may obstruct trade.

Do you think that the ECJ heeded Jacob LJ's warning not to be too protective of trade mark proprietors who exercise considerable market power? Has it found a balance between the restrictive view of protection taken by the UK court and the interests of the proprietors of distinctive marks? It is certainly the case that the ECJ held that even if the earlier mark is unique, has a huge reputation, and the later mark calls to mind the earlier mark, this will not necessarily establish the necessary 'link'. It also agreed with Jacob LJ that for detriment there must be evidence of a change in the economic behaviour of the average consumer which has or is likely to cause injury to the earlier mark. It is not sufficient that the proprietor of the later mark gains some advantage from his use of a mark similar to the earlier mark. But, on the other hand, the ECJ also found that the use of the later mark may cause damage to the earlier mark even if it is not unique and indeed first use of the mark may be sufficient to damage the distinctive character of the earlier mark. We might also wonder quite how one is to prove that the distinctiveness of a mark has been 'injured' or indeed is likely to be so in the future. Is there an obvious economic measurement to calculate this injury? Would we need to canvass the views of the putative, average consumer?

6.1.4.3 The meaning of 'unfair advantage'

In the slightly later case, *L'Oreal v Bellure*, Jacob LJ turned his attention to the meanings of 'takes unfair advantage'.

L'Oreal SA v Bellure NV [2008] ETMR 1

The claimant manufactured expensive perfumes and cosmetics, sold under registered trade marks, including 'Tresor', 'Miracle', 'Anais Anais' and 'Noa'. These products were sold through exclusive outlets and had expensive packaging, which also had trade mark protection. The defendants manufactured and distributed perfumes under their 'Creation Lamis' range which were sold in down market outlets. These products were intended to have a 'smell-alike' relationship to the claimant's perfumes. Furthermore, the defendants' packaging was designed to call to mind the claimant's packaging. After complaints from the claimant, the defendants altered their packaging so it would be less likely to call to mind the claimant's packaging. Nonetheless, the claimant contended that the defendants had infringed its trade marks by using signs which were similar to its registered marks. The defendants also produced a product comparison list which was designed to show which of the defendants' perfumes smelt like those of the claimant and which they argued was a legitimate use of comparative advertising.[25] In the High Court, Lewison J held that two of the defendants' bottles were sufficiently similar to the claimants' marks so as to give rise to an association between them in the eyes of the relevant consumers and that, while there was no likelihood of confusion, the defendants' products took unfair advantage of the character or reputation of the claimant's registered marks. The defendants appealed arguing in particular that their use of the claimant's marks was descriptive. In the course of his decision, Jacob LJ addressed a number of questions on how the proviso to Article 5(2) should be interpreted. In particular, he examined the question of how to define 'without due cause' in relation to the proviso. He began by noting that the onus of establishing 'due cause' would lie with the defendant; something which was later confirmed by the ECJ in *Intel*. He continued:

> 83. ...As I have observed, 'without due cause' is a point of great significance in relation to the comparison list issue: realistically you cannot sell a replica fragrance—a lawful product— without such a list. But in relation to the packaging issues there is simply no necessity or cause for adopting packaging intended to 'wink at' the original. Accordingly I do not find it necessary to go further into this point here.

Jacob LJ then looked at the third element of the proviso: that the use of an identical or similar sign is detrimental to the distinctive character or the repute of the trade mark and agreed with Lewison J that there was 'no causative link between the application of the sign and the tarnishing or blurring complained of'. Finally, he turned to the definition of 'takes unfair advantage'. In particular he took the view that taking advantage need not necessarily be unfair and it was this point that he felt should be addressed by the ECJ. For his own part he took the view that 'free-riding' by a defendant was not necessarily the same as taking unfair advantage:

> 91. I am not convinced that this is necessarily correct. It amounts to saying, 'if there is an advantage, it must also be unfair'. It gives no meaning whatever to the important word 'unfair'. If it is indeed virtually meaningless, that needs to be established at ECJ level. So I would ask a question about 'unfair advantage' based on the above assumed facts. The question I would ask is:
>
> 5. Where a trader uses a sign which is similar to a registered trade mark which has a reputation, and that sign is not confusingly similar to the trade mark, in such a way that:
>
>   (a) the essential function of the registered trade mark of providing a guarantee of origin is not impaired or put at risk;
>
>   (b) there is no tarnishing or blurring of the registered trade mark or its reputation or any risk of either of these;
>
>   (c) the trade mark owner's sales are not impaired; and
>
>   (d) the trade mark owner is not deprived of any of the reward for promotion, maintenance or enhancement of his trade mark.

---

25 See 6.3.2 below for a discussion of comparative advertising.

(e) but the trader gets a commercial advantage from the use of his sign by reason of its similarity to the registered mark

does that use amount to the taking of 'an unfair advantage' of the reputation of the registered mark within the meaning of Art. 5(2) of the Trade Mark Directive?

...

93. My own view is that the answer ought to be 'no'. Clearly activities which actually harm a trade mark or its reputation ought to be caught by trade mark law. And there may be other activities which can properly be called 'unfair'. I doubt whether one can, could or should even try to spell them all out. But one can envisage some. Consider a very distinctive mark famous for a particular kind of product, perfumes say. The trade mark owner may reasonably one day contemplate a line extension—perhaps into jewellery or wines. If another used that self-same mark, or a confusingly similar one, for these different goods, then, even if no one is confused, he would foreclose the trade mark owner's future options. I do not see why that should not be regarded as 'unfair'. Similarly, if the mark is used for wholly different goods, axle grease say, in a context intended to parody, then the use may be unfair.

94. But where there is no harm, present or prospective, caused to the mark, its distinctive character or to the mark owner or his business, present or reasonably prospective, I see no reason to say that a use is 'unfair'. Again my concern is that EU trade mark law ought not to be over-protective. Freedom to compete or just to trade is an important foundation of the European Union and should only be restricted, including by trade mark law, where necessary. Trade marks need protection to play their vital part in a competitive economy, but it is very questionable whether they need more protection than for that purpose.

As we have seen, in the *Intel* judgment, the ECJ held that there must be economic harm to the earlier mark for the proviso to apply. This would seem to accord with the viewpoint taken by Jacob LJ in *L'Oreal*. In effect, might we conclude that Jacob LJ (and, by implication also the ECJ) are rejecting the idea that intellectual property rights and, more particularly, trade mark registration should protect against unjust enrichment? The *L'Oreal* and the *Intel* case raise other interesting issues. We see once again in Jacob LJ's judgment in *L'Oreal* that he believes the purpose of the Trade Mark Directive is to ensure that there is competition in the market place and this is better provided for if the protection given to registered trade marks is limited. Such competition would both reward the trader with the better product, but more importantly it would be in the interests of consumers—as it would ensure there was both a multiplicity of products on the market and that the prices of such products would not be kept artificially high. On the other hand, it has been argued equally strongly, that the 'dilution provisions' of the TMD were not intended to benefit consumers first and foremost, but rather the trade mark proprietors who have succeeded in nurturing a valuable brand. It could also be argued that in this age of brand awareness, consumers who pay a premium for branded products would feel unhappy if the brand value was not protected.

Recently, Advocate General Mengozzi has given his opinion in *L'Oreal v Bellure*.[26] In an interesting development, in defining 'unfair advantage', he has endorsed a different approach to that taken explicitly by Jacob LJ in the Court of Appeal and arguably implicitly by the ECJ in *Intel*. He has taken the view that a finding of unfair advantage need not involve any damage to the earlier registered mark with a reputation. According to Advocate General

---

[26] *L'Oreal SA, Lancome parfums et beaute & Cie SNC, Laboratoire Garnier & Cie v Bellure NV, Malaika Investments Ltd, Starion International Ltd* Case C-487/07 (ECJ 10 Feb. 2009).

Mengozzi, referring to the questions posed to the Court by Jacob LJ:

> 97. ...it cannot be ruled out on the basis of the circumstances to which the Court of Appeal refers at (a) to (d) of the question under examination—namely whether there is no effect (or likelihood of any effect) on the essential function of the mark of providing a guarantee of origin, no effect (or likelihood of any effect) on the mark's distinctive character or reputation and no impact on the sales of the products identified by the well-known mark or on the return on the investments made in connection with that mark—that the advantage which a trader gains from the use for his own products of a sign that is similar to another person's well-known mark may be classified as unfair within the meaning of Article 5(2) of Directive 89/104.

The question then arises as to when such use may be deemed unfair. According to the Advocate General, if a mark similar to the well-known mark is used with due cause, such use may or may not be unfair. But where a mark similar to the well-known mark is used without due cause, then any advantage gained by the use of the later mark will be assumed to be unfair. Thus, in the present case:

> 110. It is for the national court to verify, in particular, whether the appellant companies showed due cause for the use of the bottles and boxes similar to those of the L'Oreal trade marks and, if so, whether, taking that due cause and the relevant circumstances of the case into account, the advantage taken by those companies of the reputation of those marks is unfair.

Should the Advocate General's opinion be followed by the ECJ, it would probably be fair to say that for the first time a clear prohibition against unjust enrichment has been introduced into UK trade mark law. It will remain to be seen whether the ECJ will take such an important step.

FURTHER READING

C. Long, 'The political economy of trademark dilution' in G. B. Dinwoodie and M. D. Janis (eds.), *Trade Mark Law and Theory: A handbook of contemporary research* (Cheltenham: Edward Elgar, 2008), pp. 132–47.

M. Richardson, 'Copyright in trade marks? On understanding trade mark dilution' [2000] IPQ 66.

I. Simon, 'Dilution in the US, Europe, and beyond, Part 1: International obligations and basic definitions' (2006) 1(6) JIPLP 406–12.

I. Simon, 'Dilution in the United States and European Union (and beyond), Part 2: Testing for blurring' (2006) 1(10) JIPLP 649–59.

6.2 INFRINGEMENT

The registration of a trade mark confers upon its proprietor the right to prevent third parties from infringing his mark. The acts which constitute infringement are set out in Article 5 TMD.[27] The key provisions mirror those which give rise to conflict under Article 4

---

[27] TMA 1994, s. 10(1)–(2).

TMD. According to Article 5(1), infringement will arise when a third party uses in the course of trade:

> (a) any sign which is identical with the trade mark in relation to goods or services which are identical with those for which the trade mark is registered;
>
> (b) any sign where, because of its identity with, or similarity to, the trade mark and the identity or similarity of the goods or services covered by the trade mark and the sign, there exists a likelihood of confusion on the part of the public, which includes the likelihood of association between the sign and the trade mark.

There is also an anti-dilution provision under Article 5(2), which again is optional and which the UK incorporated into the 1994 TMA.[28] Thus, under Article 5(2):

> Any Member State may also provide that the proprietor shall be entitled to prevent all third parties not having his consent from using in the course of trade any sign which is identical with, or similar to, the trade mark in relation to goods or services which are not similar to those for which the trade mark is registered, where the latter has a reputation in the Member State and where use of that sign without due cause takes unfair advantage of, or is detrimental to, the distinctive character or the repute of the trade mark.

The global approach to finding conflict under Article 4(1)(b) is also to be applied to finding infringement under Article 5(1)(b). As a result, it follows that if the earlier registered mark has a reputation or is particularly distinctive, then the court will be more likely to find that it has been infringed by the use of the later mark. There are also a number of limitations to the rights conferred by registration, which are more commonly thought of as defences to infringement. These include use by a third party of a trade mark descriptively or to indicate the intended purpose of goods or services. These limitations will be looked at in the following section.

6.2.1 INFRINGING ACTS

The acts which constitute use of a trade mark and which may be prohibited are set out in Article 5(3) of the TMD (s. 10(4) of the TMA). They include: affixing the sign to goods or packaging; offering goods or putting them on the market or stocking them for these purposes under the sign; offering or supplying services under the sign; importing or exporting goods under the sign; and using the sign on business papers and in advertising.[29] Infringing use must also be use 'in the course of trade'. What this entailed was considered by Advocate General Colomer in his opinion in *Arsenal v Reed* Case C-206/01 [2002] ECR I-10273. He 'clarified' the concept of 'course of trade' as follows (para. 62):

> The use which the proprietor of the trade mark may prevent is not any that might constitute a material advantage for the user, or even a use which is capable of being expressed in economic

---

[28] TMA 1994, s. 10(3). Following *Davidoff v Gofkid*, infringement under Art. 5(2) also encompasses an identical or similar mark used on similar goods.

[29] For an example of what constitutes an infringing act, see *Trebor Bassett Ltd v Football Association* [1997] FSR 211.

terms, but only…use which occurs in the world of business, in trade, the subject of which is, precisely, the distribution of goods and services in the market. In short, use in trade.

[By contrast, the Advocate General identified examples of 'private use' (at para. 63) as:]

the use that someone might make of the mark BMW on a key ring, from which he gains no material advantage other than the convenience of having the keys that he habitually uses on one holder as is the use which, in the 1960s, Andy Warhol made of the Campbell brand of soup in several of his paintings, from which, obviously, he obtained an economic benefit. A radical conception of the scope of the rights of the proprietor of the trade mark could have deprived contemporary art of some eminently expressive pictures, an important manifestation of 'pop art'. Other non-trade uses, such as those for educational purposes, also fall outside the scope of the protection afforded to the proprietor.

64. Thus, the proprietor of a trade mark is not in a position to object to the use by third parties of the symbol or indication which he has made his property where it is one of the signs that cannot constitute a trade mark or, if it is a trade mark, where the use made of it by others is not intended for commercial purposes.

In *Arsenal v Reed*, the ECJ confirmed that use in the course of trade means use which 'takes place in the context of commercial activity with a view to economic advantage and not as a private matter'.[30]

6.2.2 INFRINGING USE

We have seen that trade mark registration affords the proprietor a monopoly over the use of his mark in certain circumstances. For example, it allows the trade mark proprietor to prevent third parties from using his mark in those circumstances set out in Article 5(1) and (2). There are also limitations to this monopoly. The defences to trade mark infringement circumscribe the monopoly endowed by registration. The question of how broad the monopoly afforded by registration should be is also implicit in another key question relating to a finding of infringement, which is whether a third party needs to use the registered mark as a trade mark, that is as a badge of origin, to infringe the mark.

6.2.2.1 The judgment in *Arsenal v Reed*

The ECJ examined the question of whether it is necessary for there to be trade mark use of the later sign or mark for a finding of infringement in *Arsenal v Reed*.

Arsenal Football Club plc v Reed Case C-206/01 [2002] ECR I-10273

We have already looked at the facts of the case in relation to passing off.[31] Briefly, Matthew Reed sold merchandise outside the Arsenal football ground. These goods carried a number of Arsenal's trade marks, which had been registered for the same goods. Reed had placed a notice on his stall, stating that his goods were not 'official' Arsenal merchandise. Arsenal alleged not only passing off, but also trade mark infringement by Reed. In his defence to the latter, Reed claimed, *inter alia*, that to be

---

30 *Arsenal Football Club plc v Reed* Case C-206/01 [2002] ECR I-10273.   31 See at 4.3.1.4.

infringing, his use of Arsenal's trade marks had to be trade mark use. He argued that he did not use the Arsenal marks as a badge of origin, but rather as badges of allegiance. Laddie J agreed. In his High Court judgment, he held that the Arsenal marks on Mr Reed's merchandise were viewed as badges of 'support, loyalty or affiliation' by the relevant public. However, he also noted that although in his view the directive suggested that a mark had to be used in a trade mark sense to infringe, crucially previous UK decisions, including by the Court of Appeal in *Philips*, had held the opposite. In *Philips*, for example, the Court of Appeal had held that there was nothing in ss. 9 or 10 of the TMA 1994, which required infringing use to be trade mark use. The Court of Appeal pointed out that s. 11(2) of the TMA (Article 6 of the TMD) contains a comprehensive list of the exclusions to trade mark infringement, and it took the view that any use not falling within that list would infringe, whether or not it was trade mark use. Or, to put it another way, any use which was not trade mark use would presumably fall within the list of exclusions. Laddie J therefore chose to ask the ECJ whether infringing use must be trade mark use. The ECJ held first of all that the use of the Arsenal sign was use in the course of trade and that it prima facie fell under Article 5(1)(a) of the directive, as use of an identical sign on identical goods. The ECJ then summarized Laddie J's questions in the following way:

42. To answer the High Court's questions, it must be determined whether Art. 5(1)(a) of the Directive entitles the trade mark proprietor to prohibit any use by a third party in the course of trade of a sign identical to the trade mark for goods identical to those for which the mark is registered, or whether that right of prohibition presupposes the existence of a specific interest of the proprietor as trade mark proprietor, in that use of the sign in question by a third party must affect or be liable to affect one of the functions of the mark.

[The ECJ then reiterated what it held to be the essential function of a trade mark, which is to guarantee the trade mark as an indication of origin. It went on:]

51. It follows that the exclusive right under Art. 5(1)(a) of the Directive was conferred in order to enable the trade mark proprietor to protect his specific interests as proprietor, that is, to ensure that the trade mark can fulfil its functions. The exercise of that right must therefore be reserved to cases in which a third party's use of the sign affects or is liable to affect the functions of the trade mark, in particular its essential function of guaranteeing to consumers the origin of the goods.

52. The exclusive nature of the right conferred by a registered trade mark on its proprietor under Art. 5(1)(a) of the Directive can be justified only within the limits of the application of that article.

53. It should be noted that Art. 5(5) of the Directive provides that Art. 5(1) to (4) does not affect provisions in a Member State relating to protection against the use of a sign for purposes other than that of distinguishing goods or services.

54. The proprietor may not prohibit the use of a sign identical to the trade mark for goods identical to those for which the mark is registered if that use cannot affect his own interests as proprietor of the mark, having regard to its functions. Thus certain uses for purely descriptive purposes are excluded from the scope of Art. 5(1) of the Directive because they do not affect any of the interests which that provision aims to protect, and do not therefore fall within the concept of use within the meaning of that provision (see, with respect to a use for purely descriptive purposes relating to the characteristics of the product offered, Case C-2/00 *Hölterhoff* [2002] ECR I-4187, paragraph 16).

55. In this respect, it is clear that the situation in question in the main proceedings is fundamentally different from that in *Hölterhoff*.[32] In the present case, the use of the sign takes place in the context of sales to consumers and is obviously not intended for purely descriptive purposes.

56. Having regard to the presentation of the word 'Arsenal' on the goods at issue in the main proceedings and the other secondary markings on them . . . the use of that sign is such as to create the impression that there is a material link in the course of trade between the goods concerned and the trade mark proprietor.

57. That conclusion is not affected by the presence on Mr Reed's stall of the notice stating that the goods at issue in the main proceedings are not official Arsenal FC products . . . Even on the assumption that such a notice may be relied on by a third party as a defence to an action for trade mark infringement, there is a clear possibility in the present case that some consumers, in particular if they come across the goods after they have been sold by Mr Reed and taken away from the stall where the notice appears, may interpret the sign as designating Arsenal FC as the undertaking of origin of the goods.

58. Moreover, in the present case, there is also no guarantee, as required by the Court's case law . . ., that all the goods designated by the trade mark have been manufactured or supplied under the control of a single undertaking which is responsible for their quality.

59. The goods at issue are in fact supplied outside the control of Arsenal FC as trade mark proprietor, it being common ground that they do not come from Arsenal FC or from its approved resellers.

60. In those circumstances, the use of a sign which is identical to the trade mark at issue in the main proceedings is liable to jeopardise the guarantee of origin which constitutes the essential function of the mark, as is apparent from the Court's case . . . It is consequently a use which the trade mark proprietor may prevent in accordance with Art. 5(1) of the Directive.

61. Once it has been found that, in the present case, the use of the sign in question by the third party is liable to affect the guarantee of origin of the goods and that the trade mark proprietor must be able to prevent this, it is immaterial that in the context of that use the sign is perceived as a badge of support for or loyalty or affiliation to the proprietor of the mark.

62. In the light of the foregoing, the answer to the national court's questions must be that, in a situation which is not covered by Art. 6(1) of the Directive, where a third party uses in the course of trade a sign which is identical to a validly registered trade mark on goods which are identical to those for which it is registered, the trade mark proprietor is entitled, in circumstances such as those in the present case, to rely on Art. 5(1)(a) of the Directive to prevent that use. It is immaterial that, in the context of that use, the sign is perceived as a badge of support for or loyalty or affiliation to the trade mark proprietor.

6.2.2.2 Trade mark use after *Arsenal v Reed*

The ECJ's decision in *Arsenal v Reed* aroused considerable controversy. Following the judgment, most commentators agreed that, in the words of Sunroy and Badger, 'trade mark use is not a necessary element of infringing use'.[33] Instead, the general view seemed to be, following *Arsenal*, that there was infringement with any use of the trade mark by a third party which compromised the mark's ability to function as a guarantee of origin. Others suggested if use of the later mark affected the origin function of the earlier mark, then it

---

32 *Hölterhoff* is discussed below under the exceptions to trade mark infringement.
33 R. Sunroy and C. Badger, 'Infringing "use in the course of trade": Trade mark use and the essential function of a trade mark' in J. Phillips and I. Simon (eds.), *Trade Mark Use* (Oxford: Oxford University Press, 2005), p. 180.

was by definition trade mark use. Yet others concluded that the issue was still undecided. Confusion grew when the case returned to the High Court. Laddie J took the view that the ECJ had exceeded its jurisdiction by ruling on questions of fact. These included the ECJ's conclusion that there would be confusion among those who acquired the goods after sale and who might not be aware that they were unofficial (what had become known as the 'Christmas Present Issue') and also that the use of the sign by Reed was liable to affect the origin function of the marks. Laddie J, by contrast, concluded that because the defendant's use of the mark was not intended by him nor understood by the public to be a designation of origin, there could be no infringement as such use did not prejudice the essential function of the mark. He held that Reed had not infringed the Arsenal mark. The case then proceeded to the Court of Appeal, where it is generally agreed that the court endorsed the ECJ's decision. In his judgment, Aldous LJ[34] summarized the ECJ judgment in the following terms:

> 37. It is important to note that the ECJ is not concerned with whether the use complained about is trade mark use. The consideration is whether the third party's use affects or is likely to affect the functions of the trade mark. An instance of where that will occur is given, namely where a competitor wishes to take unfair advantage of the reputation of the trade mark by selling products illegally bearing the mark. That would happen whether or not the third party's use was trade mark use or whether there was confusion.

He added that at no stage had the ECJ suggested that use of the mark which was not understood by the public as use as a badge of origin could not infringe. Instead, what was required was consideration of whether the function of the trade mark was liable to be harmed by such use, and he concluded:

> 61. Once it has been found that, in the present case, the use of the sign in question by the third party is liable to affect the guarantee of origin of the goods and that the trade mark proprietor must be able to prevent this, it is immaterial that in the context of that use the sign is perceived as a badge of support for or loyalty or affiliation to the proprietor of the mark.

Finally, Aldous LJ also held that Reed was, in any event, using the Arsenal marks in a trade mark sense, in that some of his customers would inevitably understand them as denoting the origin of the goods. Reed had infringed the Arsenal mark.

The decision of the Court of Appeal might perhaps have been expected to be the final word on the trade mark use debate, were it not for another decision on the following day by the House of Lords, in *R v Johnstone*.[35] In this case which proceeded under s. 92(1)(c) of the TMA 1994, relating to criminal sanctions for infringement, the defendant had produced bootleg CD's of performances by a number of famous performers, including Bon Jovi. The names of these artists, which were registered trade marks, were printed on the CDs. In his defence, Mr Johnstone claimed that he had used these names not as an indication of origin but to indicate who performed on the CDs. It was held by Lord Nicholls that if the mark was used exclusively as an indication of the name of the performer, that is if it was used exclusively descriptively, then there would be no infringement. According to Lord Nicholls, use of the mark as an indication of trade origin was 'an essential prerequisite to infringement'. Descriptive use was not use as an indicator of origin. Interestingly, in reaching this

---

[34] *Arsenal Football Club Plc v Reed (No 2)* [2003] RPC 39.   [35] [2004] UKHL 28.

conclusion Lord Nicholls cited in support the judgment of the ECJ in *Arsenal*. Yet, it is submitted that the ECJ *Arsenal* decision (and the following decision by the Court of Appeal) does not support this view of trade mark use and infringement.

A number of commentators have viewed the *Arsenal* decisions of the ECJ and the Court of Appeal as marking a recognition that, in contemporary commerce, trade marks may have a value beyond their role as a guarantee of origin, and that they may also be an important vehicle for the proprietor's goodwill. In their essay, Sunroy and Badger suggest that the House of Lords in *Johnstone* was 'operating on the jurisprudence of the 1938 Act' (p. 174) which needed trade mark use for infringement. Sunroy and Badger suggest that the House of Lords was reluctant to jettison the principles of the 1938 Act which, by protecting the trade mark's origin function exclusively, limited the monopoly given to a proprietor by registration. Sunroy and Badger argue that this concern is misplaced and that it is right to recognize the broader role now played by trade marks.

R. Sunroy and C. Badger, 'Infringing "use in the course of trade": Trade mark use and the essential function of a trade mark' in J. Phillips and I. Simon (eds.), *Trade Mark Use* (Oxford: Oxford University Press, 2005), pp. 179–80

(3) Anti-competitive practices

As stated, the English courts have been vocal in highlighting competition concerns in respect of the protection afforded by the registration of a trade mark. It is submitted that such fears misplace policy concerns regarding the monopolistic nature of trade marks, which are properly the terrain of competition law.

A trade mark is anti-competitive to a certain extent due to its monopolistic nature. However, the grant of that monopoly has to be earned. The proprietor is required to pay fees and go to the time and expense of prosecuting the mark. Moreover, on the basis of a protectable name, the proprietor is encouraged to invest and thereby to stimulate the market in the goods or services covered by the mark. The grant of a monopoly in a trade mark is integral to a pro-competitive economic system. However, such a grant does not release the proprietor from the body of competition law governing the exercise of that monopoly. In particular, Article 82 of the EC Treaty prohibits the abuse of a dominant position. There is little case law on this point in relation to trade marks, although it is clear that the courts will consider the competition implications of practices of proprietors in relation to their marks, such as licensing practices (including the refusal to licence).

[They conclude:]

Laddie J, in *Arsenal*, spoke of Reed's use of Arsenal's registered marks as use as a badge of 'support, loyalty or affiliation', and not therefore as being trade mark use. This phrasing is curious, since a brand manager of a non-legal persuasion might well view the phrase as describing a core goal of any brand. Investing in trade marks and building brands is about creating a relationship between consumers and the brand and encouraging consumers to support, be loyal to and feel affiliation with the values, including the lifestyle concept, that surrounds the trade mark. This applies equally to washing powder as to a football club. Football clubs are as much about profit and loss as about successes or otherwise on the pitch.

The ECJ's proposition seems clear: trade mark use is not a necessary element of infringing use. This chapter has argued that there is an apparent reluctance on the part of certain of the English judiciary to depart from the traditional, narrower view of infringing use. It is submitted that such reluctance

- is out of step with European jurisprudence, despite the requirement upon the English courts to following rulings of the ECJ as to the interpretation of the Trade Mark Directive

- introduces into English trade mark law a requirement for infringement not found in the Trade Mark Directive, thereby defeating the purpose of the Trade Mark Directive to harmonize the laws of Member States

- ignores the purpose of and value in the structure built into the Trade Mark Directive to protect unauthorized users of registered marks against their descriptive use (and other 'innocent' uses) of such signs

- misplaces policy arguments regarding the monopolistic nature of trade marks, which are properly the terrain of competition law.

It is hoped that the English courts will follow the Court of Appeal's decision in *Arsenal* and embrace the ECJ's broader view of infringing use of a registered trade mark. In the interim, trade mark owners and practitioners are left with unsettling uncertainty as to the extent of protection enjoyed in a registered mark. This is contrary to the aims of the Trade Mark Directive and serves to hamper the pro-competitive objectives of the common market. The Trade Mark Directive was implemented in December 1988 pursuant to such objectives, and it is undoubtedly time to acknowledge changes to trade mark law within the European Community that such harmonization demands.

6.2.2.3 Trade mark use: the ECJ settles the issue

In a recent case, the ECJ clarified what is meant by trade mark use in relation to infringement.

Adam Opel AG v Autec AG Case C-48/05 [2007] ECR I-1017

Adam Opel manufactures cars and has a figurative registered trade mark in Germany, *inter alia*, for cars and for toys. Autec manufactures, *inter alia*, remote-controlled scale model cars marketed under the name Catronic. This trade name is clearly indicated in their instruction literature and on the remote controller. Opel alleged trade mark infringement as one of the models was of an Opel car carrying the Opel figurative mark. Opel argued that this use of the Opel mark was infringing because it was use of an identical mark on identical goods, since it also had a registration for toys, and such use would lead the public to assume that the use of the Opel mark on the toy cars was under license from Opel. Autec countered that their use of the Opel mark was not use as a trade mark as such. They also argued that their own mark on their products made it clear to the public the cars did not originate from Opel and, furthermore, that the public is used to seeing model cars which carry a replica of a trade mark without assuming that such use is an indicator of origin. The ECJ looked back to *Arsenal v Reed* to define infringing use, that is use which affects the essential function of a mark. It went on to hold that:

1. Where a trade mark is registered both for motor vehicles—in respect of which it is well known—and for toys, the affixing by a third party, without authorisation from the trade mark

proprietor, of a sign identical to that trade mark on scale models of vehicles bearing that trade mark, in order faithfully to reproduce those vehicles, and the marketing of those scale models:

- constitute, for the purposes of Art. 5(1)(a) of First Council Directive 89/104 of 21 December 1988 to approximate the laws of the Member States relating to trade marks, a use which the proprietor of the trade mark is entitled to prevent if that use affects or is liable to affect the functions of the trade mark as a trade mark registered for toys;

- constitute, within the meaning of Art. 5(2) of that Directive, a use which the proprietor of the trade mark is entitled to prevent—where the protection defined in that provision has been introduced into national law—if, without due cause, use of that sign takes unfair advantage of, or is detrimental to, the distinctive character or the repute of the trade mark as a trade mark registered for motor vehicles.

2. Where a trade mark is registered, inter alia, in respect of motor vehicles, the affixing by a third party, without the authorisation of the proprietor of the trade mark, of a sign identical to that mark to scale models of that make of vehicle, in order faithfully to reproduce those vehicles, and the marketing of those scale models, do not constitute use of an indication concerning a characteristic of those scale models, within the meaning of Art. 6(1)(b) of Directive 89/104.

In other words, Autec's use of the Opel mark on its model cars, which faithfully reproduced the actual Opel car did not affect the origin function of the Opel marks on cars and thus was not infringing use. The ECJ's ruling that any use of a mark by a third party which affects the origin function of the earlier mark is infringing use is more expansive than, for example, the House of Lords' approach in *R v Johnstone*. Do you take the view that this gives too great a monopoly to trade mark proprietors? After all, it would stop fans buying football strip which was not (often very costly) 'official' merchandise. But such an approach does recognize that trade marks, in today's market, may have a value beyond their role as a badge of origin. It may be important for a football fan to wear 'official' merchandise as another way of showing support for his or her club.

FURTHER READING

R. Calleja, '*R v Johnstone*' (2003) 14(7) Ent LR 186–8.

P. Dyrberg and M. Skylv, 'Does trade mark infringement require that the infringing use be trade mark use and if so, what is "trade mark use"?' [2003] EIPR 229.

H. Norman, 'Time to blow the whistle on trade mark use' [2004] 1 IPQ 1–34.

A. Poulter, in 'What is "use"?: Reconciling divergent views on the nature of infringing use' (2003/4) 163 Trade Mark World 23–4.

6.3 EXCLUSIONS TO PROTECTION

Thus far, this chapter has considered the scope of trade mark protection. We will now go on to look at the limits to the protection afforded by registration. We will first consider the defences to infringement which are set out in Article 6 of the TMD/s. 11 of the TMA and then go on to consider the various ways that it is possible to lose registered trade mark protection, of which the two most important are revocation (Article 12 of the TMD/s. 46 of the TMA) and a finding of invalidity (Article 3 of the TMD/s. 47 of the TMA).

6.3.1 DEFENCES TO TRADE MARK INFRINGEMENT

There are three main defences to trade mark infringement (or as they are termed in the TMA, 'limits on the effect' of a registered trade mark). These are set out in Article 6 of the TMD.[36] They are:

1. use by a person of his own name and address (Article 6(1)(a)) (s. 11(2)(a))

2. use of indications concerning the kind, quality, quantity, intended purpose, value, geographical origin, the time of production of the goods or of rendering of services, or other characteristics of goods or services (Article 6(1)(b)) (s. 11(2)(b))

3. use of a trade mark where it is necessary to indicate the intended purpose of a product or service (in particular accessories or spare parts) (Article 6(1)(c)) (s. 11(2)(c))

4. provided the use is in accordance with honest practices in industrial or commercial matters.

6.3.1.1 The 'own name' defence (Article 6(1)(a)) (s. 11(2)(a))

In *Scandecor v Scandecor*[37], the question arose as to whether this defence covered use of both individual and company names. The House of Lords took the view that this question should be referred to the ECJ, however the case subsequently settled. In the absence of a ruling from the ECJ, the courts will apply this defence to company names. The question of when 'own name use' will fall within the proviso, was considered by the Court of Appeal in *Reed Executive v Reed Business Information*.[38] We have already considered this case in the context of the 'own name' defence in passing off.[39] As we have seen, the claimants had a registered trade mark 'Reed' for employment agency services since 1996. The defendants had published, *inter alia*, business and science journals and magazines and had used the word 'Reed' in relation to their business since 1983. In 1999, the defendants started a website on which the names 'Reed Elsevier' and 'Reed Business Information' appeared. They also used the name 'Reed' in other contexts on their website. The claimants sued for passing off and trade mark infringement. The defendants pleaded, *inter alia*, the defence of own name use in relation to both.

Reed Executive plc v Reed Business Information Ltd, Reed Elsevier (UK) Ltd, Totaljobs.com Ltd [2004] RPC 40

We have already noted that in the Court of Appeal, Jacob LJ considered the 'own name' defence in passing off and found it a very narrow one: indeed, so narrow, that it had never been known to succeed! He also considered the own name defence to trade mark infringement, as we shall see applying the ECJ decision in *Gerolsteiner Brunnen GmbH & Co v Putsch GmbH*.[40] It was accepted in *Reed* that the defendants were using 'Reed' as

---

[36] TMA, s. 11. Another defence is the use in the course of trade in a particular locality of an earlier right which applies only in that locality (s. 11(3), Art. 6(2)). This earlier sign will be protected by virtue of any rule of law (in particular the law of passing off). An example, might be a pub sign which is the subject of another's registered trade mark.

[37] [2001] 2 CMLR 30.

[38] *Reed Executive plc v Reed Business Information Ltd, Reed Elsevier (UK) Ltd, Totaljobs.com Ltd* [2004] RPC 40.

[39] See 4.3.2.   [40] Case C-100/02 [2004] ECR I-691.

their company name at all times. The question was, did their use satisfy the proviso and, in particular, would it apply if such use caused confusion?

Jacob LJ:

116. ...(ii) It would be very strange if no company could avail itself of the defence. Think, for instance, of a company formed to take over a business established under an individual's name and having his name. It would be outrageous if the defence were lost upon incorporation.

(iii) Any fear that dishonest people might form companies with misleading names so as to take advantage of the defence is easily removed by the use of the proviso—such a deliberate attempt to avail oneself of another's mark would not be an honest practice.

[**Jacob LJ** then considered the relationship between the own name defence and trade mark use:]

123. Since the oral argument before us, the ECJ has confirmed what this court held in *Premier*; that trade mark use can fall within the scope of the Art. 6.1 defence. Case C-100/02 *Gerolsteiner Brunnen GmbH & Co v Putsch GmbH* (judgment January 7, 2004) was about a conflict between the registered mark 'Gerri' (for inter alia mineral water) and an alleged infringement 'Kerry Spring' for Irish mineral water from the Kerry Spring sold by a company called Kerry Spring Water. The referring court held 'Gerri' and 'Kelly' confusingly similar (by reason of aural confusion) and that there would be infringement under Art. 5.1(b) unless there was an Art. 6.1 defence. The questions for the ECJ were:

1. Is Art. 6.1(b) also applicable if a third party uses the indications referred to therein as a trade mark?
2. If so, must that use as a trade mark be taken into account when considering, pursuant to the final clause of Art. 6.1, whether use has been in accordance with honest practices in industrial or commercial matters?

124. The Court clearly held that use as a trade mark was not 'appropriate for determining the scope of Art. 6' (para. 15). It was enough that 'Kerry' was of geographical significance to bring it within the scope of Art. 6, even though it also had some trade mark significance. Once an alleged infringement is within one of the heads of Art. 6 the only further question is whether it is 'used in accordance with honest practices etc'.

125. Quite apart from the *Premier* and Gerri/Kelly decisions, it would make no sense to exclude trade mark use from the own name defence. For when a man uses his name in connection with his goods or services he is using it as a trade mark—to tell you 'This comes from me—John Doe.' Sometimes people think that use of a name on goods or for services is not use as a trade mark. They contrast use as a trade mark with use 'just as a name'. But use of a name in connection with goods or services, even in small print, *is* trade mark use, though not of the upfront in-your-face kind the subject of vast advertising spend.

126. The Court also gave guidance on the meaning of 'honest practices etc'...It said that the 'condition of honest practices constitutes in substance the expression of a duty to act fairly in relation to legitimate interests of the trade mark owner' (para. 23). The test is for the national court to carry out an overall assessment of all the circumstances—and in particular to assess whether the defendant 'might be regarded as unfairly competing with the proprietor of the trade mark' (para. 26).

127. It is worth noting also that the Court clearly contemplated that there must be some degree of co-existence...

129. I conclude from Gerri/Kelly that a man may use his own name even if there is some actual confusion with a registered trade mark. The amount of confusion which can be tolerated is a question of degree—only if objectively what he does, in all the circumstances, amounts to unfair competition, will there also be infringement. In practice there would have to be significant actual deception—mere possibilities of confusion, especially where ameliorated by other surrounding circumstances (mere aural confusion but clearly different bottles) can be within honest practices. No doubt in some cases where a man has set out to cause confusion by using his name he will be outside the defence (*cf.* the English passing-off cases cited above)—in others he may be within it if he has taken reasonable precautions to reduce confusion. All will turn on the overall circumstances of the case.

Jacob LJ[41] concluded obiter that in this case the defendant would not have the own name defence available.

More recently in *Celine Sarl v Celine SA*,[42] the ECJ also took a look at the own name defence. Here, the claimant Celine SA marketed up-market clothing and fashion accessories. It obtained a registered trade mark in 1948. Celine Sarl began trading in 1950. The name was registered by Celine Sarl in the Commercial and Companies Register in Nancy in relation to clothing. It also used the name 'Celine' on a shop front. The question put to the ECJ by the Cour d'appel in Nancy was whether use by a third party of a registered trade mark as a company name and a shop name was use which could be stopped under Article 5(1)(a) of the TMD. This question arose because it could be argued that such use was not in relation to goods which were identical to those of the proprietor. The ECJ answered that in principle, following *Arsenal* and *Opel*, such use could be infringing if it affected the origin function of the registered mark. However, there might be an own name defence under Article 6(1)(a), as long as such use was honest. In assessing whether use is honest, first account should be taken of the extent to which the mark was understood by the relevant public, or a significant section of it, as indicating a link between the third party's goods or services and those of the trade mark proprietor and second the extent to which the third party ought to be aware of that. Another factor to take into account is whether the trade mark concerned enjoys a reputation in the Member State in which it is registered from which the third party might profit. Thus, we see in the ECJ judgment in *Celine*, that dilution is once more relevant, since it appears that if a mark has a reputation, free-riding on that reputation by a third party even while using its own name, may not be honest use.

6.3.1.2 The defence of descriptive use (Article 6(1)(b)) (s. 11(2)(b))

The availability of this defence helps to define the scope of the monopoly accorded by trade mark registration. As we have also seen, despite its decision in 'Baby-Dry', the ECJ has made clear in a number of cases, most notably *Libertel*, that the relevant authorities should not take an a posteriori view of registration. Instead, they should ensure that trade marks, whose use can be successfully challenged because for example they are descriptive, will not be registered. But there were other parallel developments which might be said to have whittled down the availability of the descriptive use defence. In *Arsenal v Reed*, the ECJ held that use which affects the origin function of a registered mark, even if it is not trade mark

[41] He considered the ECJ case, *Gerolsteiner Brunnen v Putsch* Case C-100/02 [2004] ECR I-691.
[42] Case C-17/06 [2007] ECR I-7041.

use, is infringing. On the face of it, this decision appears to envisage a situation in which descriptive use of a registered mark by a third party might be infringing if its role as a badge of origin was affected. In both the ECJ decision in *Arsenal v Reed* and the House of Lords in *Johnstone* the case of *Hölterhoff v Freiesleben* was cited as a clear example of non-infringing, descriptive use.

Michael Hölterhoff v Ulrich Freiesleben Case C-2/00 [2002] ECR I-4187

Freiesleben was the proprietor of two trade marks, 'Spirit Sun' and 'Context Cut' for precious stones of a particular cut. Hölterhoff also dealt in precious stones. He sold two garnets which were identified in a delivery note and invoice as 'rhodolites'. However, in the course of oral negotiations with the purchaser, Hölterhoff referred to the trade marks 'Spirit Sun' and 'Context Cut' and the order was for two stones in the Spirit Sun cut. Freiesleben sued for trade mark infringement. The German court held that Hölterhoff had used the names 'Sprit Sun' and 'Context Cut' purely descriptively to identify the way the stones had been cut, and not to suggest that that they had originated from him. The ECJ agreed.

16. In that regard, it is sufficient to state that, in a situation such as that described by the national court, the use of the trade mark does not infringe any of the interests which Article 5(1) is intended to protect. Those interests are not affected by a situation in which:

— the third party refers to the trade mark in the course of commercial negotiations with a potential customer, who is a professional jeweller,

— the reference is made for purely descriptive purposes, namely in order to reveal the characteristics of the product offered for sale to the potential customer, who is familiar with the characteristics of the products covered by the trade mark concerned,

— the reference to the trade mark cannot be interpreted by the potential customer as indicating the origin of the product.

In *Arsenal*, the ECJ distinguished *Hölterhoff* (where the trade marks had been used to describe a method of cutting precious stones, rather than to identify their producer) from the use of the Arsenal marks by Reed. It noted that under the directive:

54. The proprietor may not prohibit the use of a sign identical to the trade mark for goods identical to those for which the mark is registered if that use cannot affect his own interests as proprietor of the mark, having regard to its functions. Thus certain uses for purely descriptive purposes are excluded from the scope of Art. 5(1) of the Directive because they do not affect any of the interests which that provision aims to protect, and do not therefore fall within the concept of use within the meaning of that provision (see, with respect to a use for purely descriptive purposes relating to the characteristics of the product offered, Case C-2/00 *Hölterhoff* [2002] ECR I-4187, paragraph 16).

55. In this respect, it is clear that the situation in question in the main proceedings is fundamentally different from that in *Hölterhoff*. In the present case, the use of the sign takes place in the context of sales to consumers and is obviously not intended for purely descriptive purposes.

56. Having regard to the presentation of the word 'Arsenal' on the goods at issue in the main proceedings and the other secondary markings on them (see paragraph 39 above), the use of that sign is such as to create the impression that there is a material link in the course of trade between the goods concerned and the trade mark proprietor.

As we have noted, after *Arsenal* there was considerable debate over whether or not trade mark use was necessary for infringement. However, the decisions in *Arsenal* and *R v Johnstone* also demonstrate that there is a general consensus that 'purely' descriptive use will not be infringing, and that *Hölterhoff v Freiesleben* represents an apt example of such use. What the courts will not countenance is a defence where the sign is used partly in a trade mark sense and partly descriptively. This was made clear by the ECJ in *Adidas v Fitnessworld*, where it held that the public must see a mark 'purely' as an embellishment for it not to infringe the earlier mark. Given the importance of geographical names and the need to leave free, which we discussed in the previous chapter, we may not be surprised that particular concerns have been expressed when the trade mark at issue indicates the geographical origin of goods. According to the ECJ, in such cases, the registered mark may be used by a third party to indicate the origin of the goods, but not their trade origin (an example is *Gerolsteiner v Putsch*).

6.3.1.3 Use of a trade mark where it is necessary to indicate the intended purpose of a product or service (in particular accessories or spare parts) (Article 6(1)(c)) (s. 11(2)(c))

This defence allows traders to refer to a registered trade mark in order to indicate the nature of the goods or services which they offer to the public. It is frequently referred to simply as the 'spare parts defence', although its use is not limited to trade marks used by third parties in supplying spare parts. Its purpose is to ensure that competition to supply spare parts and other goods which might be identified by reference to a registered trade mark is not inhibited by the threat of an infringement action. The scope of the defence was made clear by the ECJ in *BMW v Deenik*.

Bayerische Motorenwerke AG (BMW) and BMW Nederland BV v Deenik Case
C-63/97 [1999] ECR I-905

BMW owned the trade mark 'BMW' for Benelux. It had a network of authorized dealers in the Netherlands who also repaired BMWs. They were required to meet a certain standard of competence which was set by BMW. Deenik had a business in selling and repairing BMW cars, but he was not an authorized dealer. He advertised that he sold second-hand BMWs and that he repaired them. BMW alleged that Deenik was infringing its trade mark. The case eventually reached the Hoge Raad, which asked the ECJ to define the applicability of the 'spare parts' defence under Article 6(1)(c). In particular, the ECJ was asked under what circumstances a trade mark proprietor might object to the use of its trade mark by a third party which deals with the proprietor's goods.

44. The Court is asked to rule, in particular, on the question whether the trade mark proprietor may prevent such use only where the advertiser creates the impression that his

undertaking is affiliated to the trade mark proprietor's distribution network, or whether he may also prevent such use where, because of the manner in which the trade mark is used in the advertisements, there is a good chance that the public might be given the impression that the advertiser is using the trade mark in that regard to an appreciable extent for the purpose of advertising his own business as such, by creating a specific suggestion of quality.

[The ECJ then considered the advertisements relating to repair and maintenance of BMW cars:]

59. ...Like the use of a trade mark intended to identify the vehicles which a non-original spare part will fit, the use in question is intended to identify the goods in respect of which the service is provided.

60. Furthermore, the use concerned must be held to be necessary to indicate the intended purpose of the service. It is sufficient to note, as the Advocate General did at point 54 of his Opinion, that if an independent trader carries out the maintenance and repair of BMW cars or is in fact a specialist in that field, that fact cannot in practice be communicated to his customers without using the BMW mark.

61. Lastly, the condition requiring use of the trade mark to be made in accordance with honest practices in industrial or commercial matters must be regarded as constituting in substance the expression of a duty to act fairly in relation to the legitimate interests of the trade mark owner, similar to that imposed on the reseller where he uses another's trade mark to advertise the resale of products covered by that mark.

64. In the light of the foregoing, the answer to be given [to the fourth and fifth questions] must be that Articles 5 to 7 of the directive do not entitle the proprietor of a trade mark to prohibit a third party from using the mark for the purpose of informing the public that he carries out the repair and maintenance of goods covered by that trade mark and put on the market under that mark by the proprietor or with his consent, or that he has specialised or is a specialist in the sale or the repair and maintenance of such goods, unless the mark is used in a way that may create the impression that there is a commercial connection between the other undertaking and the trade mark proprietor, and in particular that the reseller's business is affiliated to the trade mark proprietor's distribution network or that there is a special relationship between the two undertakings.

More recently, in *Gillette*, the ECJ was asked to rule, *inter alia*, upon what constitutes 'necessity' under Article 6(1)(c) and what constitutes fair use of the registered trade mark.

Gillette Co v LA-Laboratories Ltd Oy Case C-228/03 [2005] ECR I-2337

The claimants marketed razors in Finland, including replaceable blades, under the registered marks 'Gillette' and 'Sensor'. LA also manufactured razors and replaceable blades similar to the claimant's products under a different mark, 'Parason Flexor'. But LA fixed a sticker to their packaging bearing the words 'all Parason Flexor and Gillette Sensor handles are compatible with this blade'. Gillette sued for trade mark infringement. LA claimed a defence under Article 6(1)(c) of the TMD. It was Gillette's argument that the use of its mark would lead the public to assume there was a link between the two companies and that, furthermore, the defendant could state that the blade was compatible with other razors without using the Gillette mark. The questions for the ECJ, *inter alia*, were whether a trader may only refer to the third party mark if it is strictly necessary, even if such a prohibition puts the consumer at a disadvantage and, secondly, what constitutes fair use. In particular the ECJ was asked whether fair use necessarily means that the product to which the third party attaches the mark is thus presented as being of the same quality as, or having equivalent properties to, those of the proprietor's product bearing the trade mark.

39. Use of the trade mark by a third party who is not its owner is necessary in order to indicate the intended purpose of a product marketed by that third party where such use in practice constitutes the only means of providing the public with comprehensible and complete information on that intended purpose in order to preserve the undistorted system of competition in the market for that product... It is for the national court to determine whether, in the case in the main proceedings, such use is necessary, taking account of the nature of the public for which the product marketed by the third party in question is intended.

...

[The ECJ then turned its attention to the questions of what constitutes honest practices and secondly whether use of a trade mark by a third party implies its products are equivalent to those of the original proprietor:]

40. In the first part of its fourth question, the national court seeks interpretation of the requirement in Art. 6(1)(c) of Directive 89/104 that use of the trade mark by a third party within the meaning of that provision must be in accordance with honest practices in industrial or commercial matters. In the second part of that question, the national court asks whether use of the trade mark by a third party constitutes an indication that the products marketed by the latter are equivalent, both in their quality and their technical or other characteristics, to the products bearing that trade mark.

...

42. In that regard, use of the trade mark will not comply with honest practices in industrial or commercial matters where, first, it is done in such a manner that it may give the impression that there is a commercial connection between the re-seller and the trade mark proprietor (*BMW*, para. 51).

43. Nor may such use affect the value of the trade mark by taking unfair advantage of its distinctive character or repute (*BMW*, para. 52).

44. In addition, as the UK Government and the Commission have rightly pointed out in their observations, use of the trade mark will not be in accordance with Art. 6(1)(c) of Directive 89/104 if it discredits or denigrates that mark.

45. Finally, where the third party presents its product as an imitation or replica of the product bearing the trade mark of which it is not the owner, such use of that mark does not comply with honest practices within the meaning of Art. 6(1)(c).

46. It is for the national court to determine whether, in the case in the main proceedings, the use made of the trade marks owned by Gillette Company has been made in accordance with honest practices, taking account, in particular, of the conditions referred to in paras. 42 to 45 of this judgment. In that regard, account should be taken of the overall presentation of the product marketed by the third party, particularly the circumstances in which the mark of which the third party is not the owner is displayed in that presentation, the circumstances in which a distinction is made between that mark and the mark or sign of the third party, and the effort made by that third party to ensure that consumers distinguish its products from those of which it is not the trade mark owner.

47. Concerning the second part of that question, as the UK Government has rightly pointed out in its observations, the fact that a third party uses a trade mark of which it is not the owner in order to indicate the intended purpose of its product, does not necessarily mean that it is presenting that product as being of the same quality as, or having equivalent properties to, those of the product bearing the trade mark. Whether there has been such a presentation depends on the facts of the case, and it is for the referring court to determine whether it has taken place by reference to the circumstances.

48. Moreover, whether the product marketed by the third party has been represented as being of the same quality as, or having equivalent properties to, the product whose trade mark is being used, is a factor which the referring court must take into consideration when it verifies that such use is made in accordance with honest practices in industrial or commercial matters.

49. Having regard to the above considerations, the answer to the fourth question must be that the condition of 'honest use' within the meaning of Art. 6(1)(c) of Directive 89/104, constitutes in substance the expression of a duty to act fairly in relation to the legitimate interests of the trade mark owner. Use of the trade mark will not be in accordance with honest practices in industrial and commercial matters if, for example:

— it is done in such a manner as to give the impression that there is a commercial connection between the third party and the trade mark owner;

— it affects the value of the trade mark by taking unfair advantage of its distinctive character or repute;

— it entails the discrediting or denigration of that mark;

— or where the third party presents its product as an imitation or replica of the product bearing the trade mark of which it is not the owner.

In *Gillette*, the ECJ was concerned to ensure that a number of interests were acknowledged. It recognized that the trade mark proprietor should be able to protect his trade mark from any damage to its ability to act as an indicator of origin. It also sought to ensure that other enterprises should be able to compete in the market to supply spare parts and other services. Finally, it sought to protect the interest of the consumer in being able to benefit from such competition. Do you think, that through it decisions in *BMW* and *Gillette*, the ECJ has apportioned sufficient protection to all three parties? Some would say that by suggesting that the definition of necessary use was based on the public interest, the ECJ had overlooked the considerable investment that trade mark proprietors had invested in their marks as is obviously the case with well-known marks such as BMW and Gillette. We shall see that each of the three interests recognized above, that of the proprietor, his competitors, and the ultimate consumer, also come into play when we turn to the issue of comparative advertising.

FURTHER READING

J. Reed, 'Water from Kerry Spring and honest practices' [2004] EIPR 429.

T. Scourfield, 'A tale of two Celines' [2008] EIPR 71.

I. Simon, 'Nominative use and honest practices in industrial and commercial matters: A very European history' [2007] IPQ 117.

P. Yap, 'Honestly, neither Celine nor Gillette is defensible!' [2008] EIPR 286.

6.3.2 COMPARATIVE ADVERTISING

In advertising their goods and services, commercial enterprises may wish to make comparisons with the goods and services of others. As a short cut, the advertiser may choose to refer to these latter goods and services by using the registered trade mark under which they are sold. Initially, following the passage of the TMA 1994, comparative advertising was regulated under the relevant provision of the Act. More recently, the courts have held that comparative advertising is regulated by the EU Directive on Comparative Advertising (CAD).

6.3.2.1 Comparative advertising and the TMA 1994

Comparative advertising involving third-party use of a registered trade mark is explicitly allowed under s. 10(6) of the TMA 1994 which reads:

> Nothing in the preceding provisions of this section[43] shall be construed as preventing the use of a registered trade mark by any person for the purpose of identifying goods or services as those of the proprietor or a licensee.
>
> But any such use otherwise than in accordance with honest practices in industrial or commercial matters shall be treated as infringing the registered trade mark if the use without due cause takes unfair advantage of or is detrimental to, the distinctive character or repute of the trade mark mark.

Section 10(6) was not taken from the TMD or the CTM Regulation, but was a purely domestic addition to the TMA. It is possible to think of this section as an exception to infringement rather than as a defence. There have now been a number of cases which have interpreted the meaning and scope of this exception. However, recently the Court of Appeal in *O2 Holdings v Hutchinson*[44] held that the use of a registered trade mark by a third party in comparative advertising might more properly be seen as either falling within Article 6(1)(b), that is the defence of use of a trade mark descriptively, provided such use is in accordance with honest practices in industrial and commercial matters. Or, alternatively, it was suggested by the Court of Appeal, that comparative advertising is regulated by CAD. As a result, in *O2 Holdings*, Jacob LJ called for s. 10(6) of the TMA to be repealed. This has not yet happened, so it is worth briefly reviewing the key decisions by the domestic courts which interpret s. 10(6).[45] The UK court's interpretation of s. 10(6) was neatly summarized by Jacob LJ in *British Airways v Ryanair*. Among the key principles for interpreting s. 10(6) are: that the primary purpose of s. 10(6) is to permit comparative advertising; the test of honest practices is objective, i.e. would a reasonable reader of the advertisement conclude it is honest on being given the full facts; the general public is used to hyperbole in advertising; a reasonable reader would not embark on a 'minute textual examination'. It is worth noting that the proviso to s. 10(6) follows the wording of the 'dilution' provisions of the TMA, i.e. ss. 5(3) and 10(3). As a result, it has been argued that where comparative advertising might blur or tarnish the registered mark, it should not be available as a defence.

---

[43] Which, as we have seen, deals with infringement.

[44] *O2 Holdings (formerly O2 Ltd) and O2 (UK) Ltd v Hutchison 3G Ltd* [2006] EWCA Civ 1656.

[45] These are *Barclays Bank plc v RBS Advanta* [1996] RPC 307; *Vodafone v Orange* [1997] FSR 34; *Cable and Wireless v British Telecommunications* [1998] FSR 383; and *British Airways plc v Ryanair Ltd* [2001] FSR 32.

6.3.2.2 Comparative advertising and CAD

As we have noted above, since the passage of the TMA, the EU has implemented CAD.[46] The case *O2 v Hutchison 3G*, examined the relationship between the Comparative Advertising Directive and the Trade Mark Directive.

O2 Holdings Ltd v Hutchison 3G UK Ltd Case C-533/06 [2008] ECR I-4231, [2007] 2 CMLR 15

The claimant, O2, a mobile phone service provider, had various registered trade marks for bubbles used in relation to, *inter alia*, telecommunications apparatus and telecommunications services. The defendant, H3G, was also a mobile phone service provider. H3G started an advertising campaign in which it compared its services to other providers, including O2. In the case of O2, it used as a reference, bubbles which were similar but not the same as the bubbles registered by O2 as a trade mark. O2 did not contest the accuracy of the comparison, but alleged infringement of its registered trade mark, through use of a similar mark on identical goods (Article 5(1)(b)). In the High Court, Mr J Pumfrey found for the defendant, holding that the use of the bubbles fell within Article 5(1)(b); that the advertisement complied with Article 3a(1) of the Unfair Commercial Practices Directive 84/450/EEC as amended by CAD; and that such compliance provided a defence of descriptive use provided for by Article 6(1)(b) of the TMD. O2 appealed. In the Court of Appeal, Jacob LJ took the view that there were a number of issues raised by the case which should be considered by the ECJ. They were:

> 28.
> 1. Where a trader, in an advertisement for his own goods or services, uses a registered trade mark owned by a competitor for the purpose of comparing the characteristics (and in particular the price) of goods or services marketed by him with the characteristics (and in particular the price) of the goods or services marketed by the competitor under that mark in such a way that it does not cause confusion or otherwise jeopardise the essential function of the trade mark as an indication of origin, does his use fall within either (a) or (b) of Article 5[(1)] of Directive 89/104?
> 2. Where a trader uses, in a comparative advertisement, the registered trade mark of a competitor, in order to comply with Article 3a[(1)] of Directive 84/450…must that use be 'indispensable' and if so what are the criteria by which indispensability is to be judged?
> 3. In particular, if there is a requirement of indispensability, does the requirement preclude any use of a sign which is not identical to the registered trade mark but is closely similar to it?

Article 3a(1) of CAD essentially says that comparative advertising is permitted when it is not misleading; does not create confusion between the advertiser's trade mark and those of a competitor; does not take unfair advantage of the reputation of a trade mark, trade name, or other distinguishing marks; and it does not present the goods or services as imitations or replicas of goods or services bearing a protected trade mark or trade name.

---

[46] Directive 97/55/EC of 6 Oct. 1997 amending Directive 84/450/EEC concerning comparative advertising. In the UK, implementation has been achieved by the Control of Misleading Advertisements (Amendment) Regulations 2000 (SI 2000/914). Now codified as Directive 2006/114/EC of the European Parliament and of the Council of 12 Dec. 2006 concerning misleading and comparative advertising.

The ECJ began its judgment by considering the relationship between CAD and the TMD. It held that use by an advertiser of a sign identical with, or similar to, a competitor's mark constituted use within the meaning of Article 5(1) and (2) of the TMD. It would therefore be possible for an advertiser under certain circumstances to infringe the competitor's sign. On the other hand, it is an aim of the CAD to promote comparative advertising and in doing so it may allow the competitor's mark or a similar to be used in order to do so. It went on:

> 41. Under Article 2(2a) of Directive 84/450, 'comparative advertising' means any advertising which explicitly or by implication identifies a competitor or goods or services offered by a competitor.
>
> 42. According to settled case law, that is a broad definition covering all forms of comparative advertising, so that, in order for there to be comparative advertising, it is sufficient for there to be a statement referring even by implication to a competitor or to the goods or services which he offers (see *Toshiba Europe*, paragraphs 30 and 31; Case C-44/01 *Pippig Augenoptik* [2003] ECR I-3095, paragraph 35; and Case C-381/05 *De Landtsheer Emmanuel* [2007] ECR I-3115, paragraph 16).
>
> 43. The test for determining whether an advertisement is comparative in nature is thus whether it identifies, explicitly or by implication, a competitor of the advertiser or goods or services which the competitor offers (*Toshiba Europe*, paragraph 29, and *De Landtsheer Emmanuel*, paragraph 17).
>
> 44. Therefore, when the use, in an advertisement, of a sign similar to the mark of a competitor of the advertiser is perceived by the average consumer as a reference to that competitor or to the goods and services which he offers—as in the case in the main proceedings—there is comparative advertising within the meaning of Article 2(2a) of Directive 84/450.
>
> 45. Consequently, in order to reconcile the protection of registered marks and the use of comparative advertising, Article 5(1) and (2) of Directive 89/104 and Article 3a(1) of Directive 84/450 must be interpreted to the effect that the proprietor of a registered trade mark is not entitled to prevent the use, by a third party, of a sign identical with, or similar to, his mark, in a comparative advertisement which satisfies all the conditions, laid down in Article 3a(1) of Directive 84/450, under which comparative advertising is permitted.

In effect, a comparative advertisement will not satisfy Article 3a(1) of CAD if such use presents a risk of origin confusion because of the way the comparative advertiser deploys the competitor's mark. Rather such use will fall within Article 5(1)(b) of the TMD. It will be infringing use. The ECJ then turned to the first question asked by the Court of Appeal which is whether the proprietor of a registered trade mark is entitled to prevent the use by a third party in comparative advertising of a sign similar to his own for identical or similar goods where there is no likelihood of confusion. It answered:

> 57. As is apparent from the Court's case law (*Arsenal Football Club*; C-245/02 *Anheuser-Busch* [2004] ECR I-10989; *Medion*; *Adam Opel*; and *Céline*), the proprietor of a registered mark may prevent the use of a sign by a third party which is identical with, or similar to, his mark under Article 5(1)(b) of Directive 89/104 only if the following four conditions are satisfied:
>
> – that use must be in the course of trade;
>
> – it must be without the consent of the proprietor of the mark;

- it must be in respect of goods or services which are identical with, or similar to, those for which the mark is registered, and

- it must affect or be liable to affect the essential function of the trade mark, which is to guarantee to consumers the origin of the goods or services, by reason of a likelihood of confusion on the part of the public.

...

60. It is clear that, in the case in the main proceedings, H3G used the sign similar to the bubbles trade marks in the course of a commercial activity with a view to gain and not as a private matter. The mark was therefore being used in the course of trade (see, by analogy, *Céline*, paragraph 17).

61. It is also clear that H3G used that sign without the consent of O2 and O2 (UK), the proprietors of the bubbles trade marks.

62. Furthermore, that sign was used for services identical with those for which those marks are registered.

63. By contrast, in accordance with the referring court's own findings, the use by H3G, in the advertisement in question, of bubble images similar to the bubbles trade marks did not give rise to a likelihood of confusion on the part of consumers. The advertisement, as a whole, was not misleading and, in particular, did not suggest that there was any form of commercial link between O2 and O2 (UK) on the one hand, and H3G, on the other.

64. In that regard, contrary to the submission of O2 and O2 (UK), the referring court was right to limit its analysis to the context in which the sign similar to the bubbles trade marks was used by H3G, for the purpose of assessing the existence of a likelihood of confusion.

...

66. Article 4(1)(b) of Directive 89/104, however, concerns the application for registration of a mark. Once a mark has been registered its proprietor has the right to use it as he sees fit so that, for the purposes of assessing whether the application for registration falls within the ground for refusal laid down in that provision, it is necessary to ascertain whether there is a likelihood of confusion with the opponent's earlier mark in all the circumstances in which the mark applied for might be used if it were to be registered.

67. By contrast, in the case provided for in Article 5(1)(b) of Directive 89/104, the third-party user of a sign identical with, or similar to, a registered mark does not assert any trade mark rights over that sign but is using it on an ad hoc basis. In those circumstances, in order to assess whether the proprietor of the registered mark is entitled to oppose that specific use, the assessment must be limited to the circumstances characterising that use, without there being any need to investigate whether another use of the same sign in different circumstances would also be likely to give rise to a likelihood of confusion.

68. Thus, the fourth condition required before the proprietor of a registered mark is authorised to prevent the use of a sign similar to his trade mark for goods and services identical with, or similar to, those for which that mark is registered is not satisfied in the case in the main proceedings.

69. Consequently, the answer to the first question must be that Article 5(1)(b) of Directive 89/104 is to be interpreted as meaning that the proprietor of a registered trade mark is not entitled to prevent the use, by a third party, in a comparative advertisement, of a sign similar to that mark in relation to goods or services identical with, or similar to, those for which that mark is registered where such use does not give rise to a likelihood of confusion on the part of the public, and that is so irrespective of whether or not the comparative advertisement satisfies all the conditions laid down in Article 3a of Directive 84/450 under which comparative advertising is permitted.

Since the ECJ answered the first question put to them in the affirmative, it held that there was no need to address the other two. *L'Oreal v Bellure* was also a case of comparative advertising (see the facts at p. 288 above).[47] In this case, Jacob LJ addressed the same questions to the ECJ which he had raised in the *O2* case. He also sought from the ECJ a definition of what constituted 'honest practices'. Despite the fact that the ECJ has now elucidated the correct approach to comparative advertising, a key question remains: is it more important for competitors to have the opportunity to give consumers relevant information about two competing products than it is to protect the 'reputation' of the trade mark with which comparisons are to be made? Clearly, like the UK courts, the ECJ holds that comparative advertising is beneficial as it enhances competition. The only caveat is that it will not be allowed if it causes origin confusion. Brand holders may well disagree, holding that use of their marks in comparative advertising is in effect taking advantage of their attractiveness. Do you think that the ECJ's approach to comparative advertising is compatible with its approach to dilution? This was precisely the issue considered by Clair Howell in her comment on the *O2* case.

C. Howell, '*O2 v Hutchison 3G* comparative advertising: European trade mark law beyond compare?' [2008] Comms Law 155–8

Long, long ago a trade mark allowed a craftsman to be identified and held accountable for shoddy goods. Today in the era of the 'Lovemark,' due to extensive advertising hopes and aspirations a lifestyle can be purchased with a brand. For many products a trademark is no longer merely a badge of origin but has a commercial value of its own. Through advertising an emotional attachment is created in the heart of the consumer for particular brands. Brand owners are determined that the value of this attachment be preserved and protected against any encroachment into the aura that has been painstakingly created. Comparative advertising, the allusive use of a mark, is seen by the owners of such emotive brands as likely to jeopardise the character of the brand that they have so carefully nurtured. As they have invested so heavily in creating their concept these owners want to control its use by others. There is an issue however as to how far this control ought to extend when the image is used in the marketing of a rival's goods or services.

On June 12 the European Court of Justice (ECJ) gave its judgment on a reference for a preliminary ruling regarding comparative advertising in relation to *O2 Holdings v Hutchison 3G* (the 'Bubbles' case). The Court of Appeal had asked for clarification on three questions on the interpretation of the Trade Mark Directive 89/104 and the Directive on Misleading and Comparative Advertising 84/450. The ECJ ruled that Comparative Advertising under Article 5(1)(b) Trade Mark Directive (similar marks and identical or similar goods/services, identical marks and similar goods or services) is lawful where there is no confusion as to the origin of the goods created in the mind of the public. The ruling does not relate however to Article 5(1)(a) or 5(2) (identical marks and identical goods or marks with a reputation).

The Trade Mark Directive gives the proprietor of a registered trademark the right to prevent other traders using in the course of trade a mark which is the same or confusingly similar to

---

[47] In his recent opinion, Advocate General Mengozzi has suggested that use of an identical sign on identical goods is permissible in comparative advertising if such use does not affect the origin function of the registered mark; that it is not necessarily an unfair advantage for a third party to use a well-known mark in a comparison with his own product; an advertisement is not prohibited only on the grounds that it states that the advertiser's product has an essential characteristic that is identical with that of a product bearing a protected trade mark, including a well-known mark. *L'Oreal SA v Bellure NV* Case C-487/07 (ECJ, 10 Feb. 2009).

their mark on the same or similar goods. As Advocate General Sharpston describes the right in her opinion on the *Intel* case:

> around each trade mark there is an 'exclusion zone' which other marks may not enter. The extent of the zone will vary according to circumstances. An identical or extremely similar mark must be kept at a greater distance in terms of the goods or services covered. Conversely, a mark used for identical or extremely similar products must be kept at a greater distance in terms of similarity with the protected mark.

Traditionally the essential function of a trade mark is as a badge of origin. The mark indicates trade source between the goods or services and the proprietor of the mark. Other functions of a trade mark have been recognised as highly important in promoting and marketing a brand, for example the portrayal of luxury as in the Tiffany or Rolls Royce brands, or the cheeky independence embedded in the image of the Mini car. This decision of the ECJ does not however expand the protection of such other functions. It instead emphasises that the essential function of a trademark is not to facilitate the creation of a 'Lovemark' but is as an indicator of origin as stated in the *Arsenal* case.

If a rival uses a competitor's trade mark in a comparative advertisement for identical or similar products without the consent of the proprietor, such use would prima facie infringe the rights of the proprietor of the mark. Such advertising was not permitted under the 1938 Trade Mark Act, but by 1989 it had come to be recognised that advertising was a very important means of creating genuine outlets for goods and services. The laws of Member States in this respect differed widely but as advertising is cross border the basic provisions governing comparative advertising needed to be uniform throughout the community. The objective of both the Trade Mark Directive and the Comparative Advertising Directive was to enable harmonisation and ensure equal treatment of competitors throughout the community. Although there were some, especially the Benelux countries and Germany, who did not welcome comparative advertising and who were in opposition to the new Directive which allowed it, such advertising was regarded as necessary. By objectively demonstrating the merits of competing products, comparative advertising can be used to stimulate competition between suppliers of goods and services and this should be to the consumer's advantage thus making the best possible use of the internal market.

In 1994 following the Trade Mark Directive, section 10(6), which allowed comparative advertising, was incorporated into the Trade Mark Act 1994. Comparative advertising is defined in the Comparative Advertising Directive (CAD) as 'any advertising, which explicitly or by implication, identifies a competitor or goods or services offered by a competitor'. The main objective of such advertising is to differentiate the advertiser's product from those of its target competitor and then to demonstrate that in some respect the advertiser's product is better, cheaper, easier to use or in some way superior to the rival product.

Comparative advertising is not intended to cause confusion between the competing goods. If confusion does occur the medium has failed to produce the desired result, namely affecting the consumers' buying decision and causing them to purchase the goods of the advertiser B rather than the goods of the target rival A. Such failure has in the past led to a successful action in passing off as can be seen in the case of *Macdonalds Hamburgers Ltd v Burger King*.[48] By saying 'this is not just a Big Mac' Burger King attempted but failed to differentiate the competing products. The failure resulted in a finding that a misrepresentation had been made as consumers would think that the two burger products were related rather than competing. Despite some difficulties, comparative advertising is a widely used method

---

48 [1987] FSR 112.

of advertising and common in industries where there is a lack of true differentiation between products, such as the telecommunications sector.

[Howell then goes on to look at the judgments of successive courts, including the ECJ and concludes:]

We are left with the conclusion that for Article 5(1)(b) if there is no confusion on the part of the public the conditions laid down in the Comparative Advertising Directive are irrelevant. It would seem that a comparative advertisement can be misleading, can discredit or denigrate the trade marks of the target, or even take unfair advantage of the reputation of their brand as long as there is no confusion as to origin. However, if there is an identical sign used even if the advertisement is successful and does truly differentiate the products there is a presumption of confusion. It would seem to follow that the requirements of Article 3 of the Comparative Advertising Directive relating to objective treatment and honest practice etc. would then come into effect. A bizarre result! In addition, if a similar mark is used and confusion exists the trade mark owner can bring an infringement case against the advertiser but if an identical mark is used and confusion results he can merely hope that the Advertising Standards Authority steps in. It would seem therefore that any comparative advertiser in the future would be wise to make sure that the mark he uses in his advertisement is merely similar rather than identical to the mark of his target. Apparently as long as his comparative advertisement does what it is supposed to do and differentiates the competing products, the advertiser is free to be as nasty as he likes about his target's goods and as destructive of the carefully nurtured image or 'Lovemark' of his rival as his marketing team can manage to be.

FURTHER READING

H. Carty, 'Registered trade marks and permissible comparative advertising' [2002] EIPR 294.

P. Reeskamp, 'Is comparative advertising a trade mark issue?' [2008] EIPR 130.

P. Yap, 'Essential function of a trade mark: From BMW to O2' [2009] EIPR 81.

6.4 THE LOSS OF A REGISTERED TRADE MARK

The two key routes to losing a trade mark registration are either through revocation or a finding of invalidity. According to the TMA, any person may seek a declaration of invalidity (s. 47(3)) or make an application for revocation (s. 46(4)).[49] In practice, a declaration of invalidity is most likely to be sought and an application for revocation made by a defendant in infringement proceedings.

6.4.1 INVALIDITY

For the most part the grounds for a finding of invalidity are the same as the absolute and relative grounds for refusal of registration. They are set out in Articles 3 and 4 of the TMD (s. 47 of the TMA). A trade mark may be declared invalid because it is in breach of the absolute

---

[49] Trade marks may also be voluntarily surrendered in respect to some or all of the goods and services for which it is registered (s. 45).

grounds for registration, for example that it is not sufficiently distinctive; that there is an earlier registered mark; or that it was registered in bad faith. In relation to lack of distinctiveness, a trade mark which is found not to have had the requisite distinctiveness when it was registered, may not be found to be invalid if subsequent to registration it has acquired distinctiveness through use. According to Jacob J in *British Sugar v James Robertson*, the onus is on the proprietor of the mark to prove that it has done so.[50] If a mark is found to be invalidly registered the effect is as if the mark had never been registered. As a result, infringement proceedings may cover the period during which it was on the Register. However, any past or closed proceedings relating to the expunged trade mark are not reopened.

6.4.2 REVOCATION

Article 12 of the TMD sets out the grounds for revocation. If a trade mark is revoked, the mark ceases to have protection from that date or earlier if the Registrar believes that the conditions for revocation were present at an earlier date. There are three main reasons for revocation. A trade mark may be revoked for non-use (Article 12(1)),[51] or it may be revoked because, as a consequence of the way it has been used, it has become either generic or misleading (Article 12(2)(a)–(b)).[52] We have considered misleading marks and generic marks above. We will now turn to the third circumstance which may give rise to revocation: that is non-use of the registered mark (Articles 10 and 12 of the TMD). Article 10 states:

> 1. If, within a period of five years following the date of the completion of the registration procedure, the proprietor has not put the trade mark to genuine use in the Member State in connection with the goods or services in respect of which it is registered, or if such use has been suspended during an uninterrupted period of five years, the trade mark shall be subject to the sanctions provided for in this Directive unless there are proper reasons for non-use.

Article 12(1) states that if the above conditions apply, the registered trade mark shall be liable to revocation.

In her essay, Belinda Isaac sets out the justification for this provision.

B. Isaac, 'Use for the purpose of resisting an application for revocation for non-use' in J. Phillips and I. Simon (eds.), *Trade Mark Use* (Oxford: Oxford University Press, 2005), pp. 223

> It is a fundamental principle of trade mark law, and indeed it is expressly stated in European law, that registered trade marks must actually be used if the proprietor is to continue to benefit from the exclusive rights granted by virtue of registration. In Europe, if a registered trade mark is not used, it will become liable to revocation unless legitimate reasons for non-use exist.

---

50 See 5.3.3.6; *British Sugar plc v James Robertson & Sons Ltd* [1997] ETMR 118.

51 TMA, s. 46(1). The wording of the directive and s. 46(1) in relation to revocation for non-use differ slightly. It was held by the Court of Appeal that the relevant provisions should be given the same meaning (*Laboratoires Goemar SA v La Mer Technology Inc* [2005] EWCA Civ 978).

52 TMA, s. 46(1)(c)–(d).

...

One of the reasons for the necessity to use a registered trade mark given by the Directive is:

to reduce the total number of trade marks registered and protected in the Community and, consequently, the number of conflicts which arise between them...

A consequence of the sheer number of trade marks being registered within the Community and the number of conflicts (oppositions) encountered is that there is a strong public interest in the removal from the register of marks that are not being used. Indeed, some would argue that there are only a finite number of useful or valuable marks and that revocation therefore helps to ensure that unused marks are recycled. If such unused marks were not removed the register would become clogged and the number of conflicts would soon make the system unworkable. Revocation therefore restricts the protection conferred by registration to the proprietor's legitimate and actual trade requirements, avoiding the inconvenience, cost and interference with trade that would result from allowing trade marks to be registered by traders who have no intention of using them, but only wish to prevent other traders from using them.

The key questions posed by Article 10 are first what constitutes genuine use and second what are to be considered proper reasons for non-use.[53] The first question was addressed in the ECJ decision *Ansul v Ajax*.[54] It was also considered by the UK Court of Appeal in *Laboratoires Goemar v La Mer Technology*.[55] When the *Goemar* case, which concerned the revocation of trade mark for non-use, had been heard by the High Court, Jacob J referred a number of questions to the ECJ regarding the definition of genuine use. These were answered by the ECJ in a Reasoned Order, in which it stated generally that the definition of what constituted genuine use had been given in the *Ansul* case. *Goemar* then returned to the High Court and subsequently it reached the Court Appeal. In the Court of Appeal, Mummery LJ set out the proper understanding of what constitutes 'genuine use' of a trade mark following *Ansul* and the ECJ's order on *Goemar*.

Laboratoires Goemar SA v La Mer Technology Inc [2005] EWCA Civ 978, [2006] FSR 5

Goemar was a French company which made seaweed-based products. Goemar's goods were sold under the registered mark, 'Laboratoire de la Mer'. The mark had been registered in 1989. La Mer Technology (a US company) sought to have the mark revoked for non-use. Initially, the Registrar refused to revoke the mark. But in the High Court, Blackburne J revoked the mark for non-use as of 1998. Goemar appealed to the Court of Appeal. The use relied upon by Goemar was described by Mummery LJ in the Court of Appeal judgment.

Mummery LJ:

9. It [Goemar] appointed a small enterprise with which it had no connection, Health Scope Direct Ltd (formerly Meadow Breeze Ltd) of the Old Brewery, Banff on the Moray Firth in Scotland as its agent in the United Kingdom. The agent traded as 'Health Scope

---

[53] It is possible to avoid revocation for non-use of a mark if the proprietor uses a mark which incorporates the distinctive features of the registered mark (Art. 10(2) TMD; s. 46(2), TMA). See *Elle Trade Marks, Re* [1997] FSR 529 and below, *Cabañas Habana (Device) Trade Mark, Re* [2000] RPC 26.

[54] *Ansul BV v Ajax Brandbeveiliging BV* Case C-40/01 [2003] ECR I-2439.

[55] *Laboratoires Goemar SA v La Mer Technology Inc* [2005] EWCA Civ 978.

Direct' until it ceased business and was struck off the register of companies on 21 October 1997.

10. Limited sales of the relevant products bearing the mark were made by Goemar pursuant to five separate repeat orders placed by Health Scope Direct. The orders amounted to £8,000 in all. The sales took place over the six-month period between 14 November 1996 and 16 May 1997. There were five deliveries of goods. The products imported were within the Class 3 registration...

11. There was no evidence of any sales of the goods to members of the public or consumers and end-users. The agent has been making preparations to sell the products by appointing members of the public as sub-agencies via private parties, based on the 'Tupperware' model, but there was no evidence that this method of sale to the public ever got off the ground.

[In his judgment, **Mummery LJ** considered the ECJ authority on genuine use. He noted, in particular, the issues concerning what criteria or factors should be taken into account in deciding whether a mark has been put to genuine use, what types of use can be considered and specifically whether importation by a single importer could count as genuine use.]

Ansul

18. Let us begin with *Ansul*, to which the Court of Justice looked in answering the questions posed in the *La Mer* reference. The Court of Justice said (para. 35 of *Ansul*) that 'Genuine use means actual use of the mark.' This is not altogether surprising, as trade marks are made for and matter in markets, in which goods and services are bought and sold and in which their different origins need to be identified and distinguished.

19. The Court of Justice expounded the concept of genuine use:

36. 'Genuine use' must therefore be understood to denote use that is not merely token, serving solely to preserve the rights conferred by the mark. Such use must be consistent with the essential function of a trade mark, which is to guarantee the identity of the origin of the goods or services to the consumer or end-user by enabling him, without any possibility of confusion, to distinguish the product or service from others which have another origin.

37. It follows that 'genuine use' of the mark entails use of the mark on the market for the goods or services protected by the mark and not just internal use by the undertaking concerned. The protection the mark confers and the consequences of registering in terms of enforceability *vis-a-vis* third parties cannot continue to operate if the mark loses its commercial *raison d'etre*, which is to create and preserve an outlet for the goods or services that bear the sign of which it is composed, as distinct from the goods or services of other undertakings. Use of the mark must therefore relate to goods or services already marketed or about to be marketed and for which preparations by the undertaking to secure customers are under way, particularly in the form of advertising campaigns. Such use may be either by the trade mark proprietor or, as envisaged in Article 10(3) of the Directive, by a third party with authority to use the mark.

38. Finally when assessing whether there has been genuine use of the trade mark, regard must be had to all the facts and circumstances relevant to establishing whether the commercial exploitation of the mark is real, in particular whether such use is viewed as warranted in the economic sector concerned to maintain or create a share in the market for the goods or services protected by the mark.

39. Assessing the circumstances of the case may thus include giving consideration, *inter alia*, to the nature of the goods or service at issue, the characteristics of the market concerned and the scale and frequency of use of the mark. Use of the mark need not therefore always be quantitatively significant for it to be deemed genuine, as that depends on the characteristics of the goods or service concerned on the corresponding market.

Reasoned order in *La Mer*

20. The questions in *La Mer*, which were, of course, framed without the benefit of the subsequent judgment in *Ansul*, sought rulings about the extent of use, the amount of use and types of use that can be considered when deciding whether a mark has been put to genuine use in a Member State. The Court of Justice considered the questions together on the basis of paras. 35 to 39 of *Ansul* (see paras. 18 and 19 of *La Mer*) and continued:

20. It follows from those considerations that the preservation by a trade mark proprietor of his rights is predicated on the mark being put to genuine use in the course of trade, on the market for the goods or services for which it was registered in the Member State concerned.

21. Moreover, it is clear from para. [39] of Ansul that use of the mark may in some cases be sufficient to establish genuine use within the meaning of the Directive even if that use is not quantitatively significant. Even minimal use can therefore be sufficient to qualify as genuine, on condition that it is deemed to be justified, in the economic sector concerned, for the purpose of preserving or creating market share for the goods or services protected by the mark.

22. The question whether use is sufficient to preserve or create market share for those products or services depends on several factors and on a case by case assessment which is for the national court to carry out. The characteristics of those products or services, the frequency or regularity of the use of the mark, whether the mark is used for the purpose of marketing all the identical products or services of the proprietor or merely some of them, or evidence which the proprietor is able to provide, are among the factors which may be taken into account.

23. Similarly, as emerges from paras. [35]–[39] of *Ansul* set out above, the characteristics of the market concerned, which directly affect the marketing strategy of the proprietor of the mark, may also be taken into account in assessing genuine use of the mark.

24. In addition, use of the mark by a single client which imports the products for which the mark is registered can be sufficient to demonstrate that such use is genuine, if it appears that the import operation has a genuine commercial justification for the proprietor of the mark.

Mummery LJ then summarized the judgment of Blackburne J in the High Court. Blackburne J had found that the use of the mark in the five years preceding the application did not constitute genuine use. He held that the lack of advertising, the limited number of sales, and the fact that none of these had been to the public did not constitute genuine use. Instead, it should be seen as 'internal use' (i.e. the goods were paid for by an importer and not exposed for sale) and so did not begin to establish a market share for the goods. Mummery LJ then went on to consider Blackburne J's reasoning. In relation to the idea of 'token use', he found that it was wrong to assume that any 'non-token use was therefore genuine use'. Thus internal use of the trade mark might be non-token but would still not qualify as genuine use for the purposes of maintaining a registration. Mummary LJ held that the sales and importation of the claimant's products into the UK was not internal use as argued by the defendant. He then went on to look at the issue of market use by the claimant in light of the *Ansul* decision, which held that use must be 'sufficient to preserve or create a market share' for a product. Having considered the arguments of both the claimant and the defendant as to what constituted genuine use, Mummery LJ, unlike Blackburne J, came down on the side of the claimant. He took the view that Blackurne J had wrongly interpreted the *Ansul* decision, in that he had applied a qualitative and quantitative test based on the number of end-users of the product, for assessing whether there had been sufficient market use to comprise genuine use.

Mummery LJ:

33. Trade marks are not only used on the market in which goods bearing the mark are sold to consumers and end-users. A market exists in which goods bearing the mark are sold by foreign manufacturers to importers in the United Kingdom. The goods bearing the LA MER mark were sold by Goemar and bought by Health Scope Direct on that market in arm's length transactions. The modest amount of the quantities involved and the more restricted nature of the import market did not prevent the use of the mark on the goods from being genuine use on the market. The Court of Justice made it clear that, provided the use was neither token nor internal, imports by a single importer could suffice for determining whether there was genuine use of the mark on the market.

34. There was some discussion at the hearing about the extent to which Goemar was entitled to rely on its intention, purpose or motivation in the sales of the goods bearing the mark to Health Scope Direct. I do not find such factors of much assistance in deciding whether there has been genuine use. I do not understand the Court of Justice to hold that subjective factors of that kind are relevant to genuine use. What matters are the objective circumstances in which the goods bearing the mark came to be in the United Kingdom. The presence of the goods was explained, as Dr Trott found, by the UK importer buying and the French manufacturer selling quantities of the goods bearing the mark. The buying and selling of goods involving a foreign manufacturer and a UK importer is evidence of the existence of an economic market of some description for the goods delivered to the importer. The mark registered for the goods was used on that market. That was sufficient use for it to be genuine use on the market and in that market the mark was being used in accordance with its essential function. The use was real, though modest, and did not cease to be real and genuine because the extinction of the importer as the single customer in the United Kingdom prevented the onward sale of the goods into, and the use of the mark further down, the supply chain in the retail market, in which the mark would come to the attention of consumers and end-users.

...

Result

37. I would allow the appeal, set aside the order for the revocation of the registration of the mark and restore the order of the Registrar.

According to Lord Justice Mummery in *Goemar*, the decision as to whether use of a mark has been genuine should be based on objective factors, most notably whether the goods bearing the mark have been placed on the market, even if there have been no final consumers for the goods. Furthermore, use of the mark can be modest. Other circumstances which might give rise to non-use and hence to the revocation of the registered mark are: that the mark as it is used does not incorporate the distinctive features of the registered mark, as was argued in *Bud and Budweiser Budbrau Trade Marks*,[56] or that the mark is not used on the goods for which it is registered. Recently, in *Silberquelle GmbH v Maselli-Strickmode GmbH*,[57] the ECJ held that it was not genuine use of a mark where it was used on promotional items which were handed out free as a reward for the purchase of other goods or to encourage the sale of the latter.

There are also defences to an application for revocation for non-use. It is possible to argue that the proprietor has used a mark which incorporates the distinctive elements of the

[56] [2002] RPC 747.   [57] Case C-495/07 (ECJ, 15 Jan. 2009).

registered mark (s. 46(2)), or that there are 'proper reasons' for non-use. An interesting case which considered both these defences was *Cabañas Habana (Device) Trade Mark*, which concerned an application for revocation for non-use. In his decision, the Registrar set out the principles for a finding that there are proper reasons for non-use.

Cabañas Habana (Device) Trade Mark [2000] RPC 26, 31–4

The Consolidated Cigar Corporation had a trade mark 'Cabañas Habana' registered in respect of cigars. In 1996, the applicants, Corporation Habanos SA, sought to have it revoked, under s. 46(1)(a) of the TMA, because of non-use for the previous five years and three months. The respondents claimed that they had used a mark which incorporated the distinctive elements of the registered mark (Article 10(2) of the TMD) (s. 46(2) of the TMA), an argument that was rejected by the Registrar. In the alternative, they argued that there were proper reasons for non-use. Thus, the respondents argued that because of the expropriation of land and factories by the Cuban government and the US trade embargo which followed, the company had been unable to sell Cuban cigars and were unwilling to use the mark on cigars manufactured elsewhere, because to do so would be misleading since the mark incorporated the word Habana, the capital city of Cuba. They had, however, used a mark which incorporated the word Cabañas. The Registrar first considered the s. 46(2) defence.

The Registrar

I have said earlier that section 100 of the Act places the onus for proving use on the pro-prietor. Having conceded that they have not used the trade mark but that there are proper reasons for non-use, the onus in my view stays with the proprietor to establish this.

The reasons for non-use are that the United States' trade embargo with Cuba 'precludes the corporation from manufacturing cigars bearing the mark in Cuba, or dealing with any Cuban entity for the manufacture'. The cause of the non-use of the trade mark is not so much the embargo restrictions, but the fact that the mark contains the name 'Havana', a location with a strong reputation for cigars. They say that the embargo regulations prevent them from using the mark on goods of Cuban origin, and they cannot use the mark on goods of non-Cuban origin as this would be deceptive. I have some sympathy with their position in relation to the use of the mark on goods not of Cuban origin as to do so would potentially leave them open to attack under section 46(1)(d) as being '...liable to mislead the public, particularly as to the nature, quality or geographical origin of these goods...'.

...

In question, therefore, is whether the trade embargo constitutes proper reasons for non-use. In *Invermont Trade Mark* [1997] RPC 125 at 130, the Registrar's hearing officer considered the meaning of the words 'proper reasons for non-use', and drawing a distinction between the wording of section 26(3) of the Trade Marks Act 1938 and the provisions of section 46(1)(a) of the 1994 Trade Marks Act said:

Moreover, the word 'proper' appears, rather than the slightly more restrictive word 'special'. The reasons do not have to be special, it seems merely 'proper'. As can be seen in any English dictionary, 'proper' is a word with many meanings. But bearing in mind the need to judge these things in a business sense, and also bearing in mind the emphasis which is, and has always been placed on the requirements to use a trade mark or lose it, I think the word proper in the context of section 46 means: 'apt, acceptable, reasonable, justifiable in all the circumstances...

He describes difficulties which by his own admission are normal in the industry concerned and in the relevant market place. I do not think that the term 'proper' was intended to cover normal situations or routine difficulties. I think it much more likely that it is intended to cover abnormal situations in the industry or market, or even in perhaps some temporary but serious disruption affecting the registered proprietor's business. Normal delays occasioned by some unavoidable regulatory requirement, such as the approval of a medicine might be acceptable but not, I think, the normal delays found in the marketing function. These are matters within the businessman's own control and I think he should plan accordingly . . .

. . .

The language used above [in *Invermont*] seems to suggest that factors beyond the immediate cause should be taken into account, and if as it stated, it is necessary to judge matters in a business sense, it is in my view wholly appropriate to take into account reasonable alternatives that may have enabled the mark to be used, if those alternatives are commercially viable or established practice in trade. It is not uncommon for some regulatory requirement to have to be met before goods can be used, imported or exported, and it would be nonsensical to accept as proper reasons for non-use, a claim to having been prevented from using the mark where the reason exists because the proprietor did not bother to obtain the necessary authorisation.

[The Registar noted that the embargo came into force in 1962, some 26 years after the registration of the mark.]

If the proprietors have been precluded from using the mark from the date of the embargo, by the relevant date the mark cannot have been used for approximately 33 years. Such a period of time stretches the boundaries of what might be considered a temporary disruption to the extent that the embargo restrictions could now be considered to be the normal conditions in the trade. With the trade mark having been absent from the market for such a period there is unlikely to be any residual goodwill from any use which may have taken place prior to the embargo. Certainly there was no material before me to suggest that might be the case.

I have no evidence to show that there is any immediate prospect of the embargo being lifted and normal trade relations with Cuba being re-established, and as matters stand, there does not seem to be much likelihood of the mark being used by the proprietor in the foreseeable future. While it may well be that the situation is out of the proprietors control (although this has not been established), trade marks on the register are intended to be used, not sit there unused as an impediment to others. As the hearing officer in *Invermont* said, '. . . the emphasis which is, and has always been placed on the requirements to use a trade mark or lose it.'

For the reasons set out above I find that the registered proprietors have not discharged the onus placed upon them in establishing that there are proper reasons for non-use of the trade mark, and consequently, that the application for revocation under section 46(1) succeeds.

We may think it harsh that the respondent was unable to save its mark, despite the fact that the effects of the embargo were clearly beyond its control. Furthermore, it is also the case that while being under a trade embargo might be 'normal' for Cuba, it is scarcely a 'normal' condition for international trade overall. In response, you might think that the alternative imperative, as suggested by the Registrar, that a trade mark should only be accorded the advantage of registration if it is to be used, also has its merits. Registration accords the proprietor a monopoly over the use of the mark in the course of trade and hence prevents its use by competitors in the market. In answer to this latter point, it was of course open to the respondent to say, as it did, that even were it to lose the mark still no other trader would be able to use it for cigars which did not emanate from Cuba without deceiving consumers. In other words, it was not actually available for other traders to use.

FURTHER READING

C. Howell, 'Trade marks: What constitutes "genuine use"? *Laboratoires Goemar SA v La Mer Technology*' [2006] EIPR 118.

B. Isaacs, 'Use of the purpose of resisting an application for revocation for non-use' in J. Phillips and I. Simon (eds.), *Trade Mark Use* (Oxford: Oxford University Press, 2005), 223–38.

6.5 TRADE MARKS AND THE EXHAUSTION OF RIGHTS

Article 7 of the TMD (s. 12 of the TMA) deals with the exhaustion of those rights which are endowed on a trade mark by registration. It reads:

> Art. 7(1) The trade mark shall not entitle the proprietor to prohibit its use in relation to goods which have been put on the market in the Community under that trade mark by the proprietor or with his consent.
> Art. 7(2) Paragraph 1 shall not apply where there exist legitimate reasons for the proprietor to oppose further commercialisation of the goods, especially where the condition of the goods is changed or impaired after they have been put on the market.

This provision, like the defences to trade mark infringement and the grounds for invalidity and revocation, is concerned with setting the limits to the monopoly afforded by registration. Article 7 primarily deals with the parallel importation of goods from one Member State to another by a party other than the trade mark proprietor. It has been suggested that Article 7 exhaustion marks a recognition that, under conditions of resale, the trade mark will continue to play its role as an indication of origin and quality. Its use will not deceive the public and might well serve the public interest by encouraging competition and hence lower prices. On the other hand, if the mark is used by the third party in such a way that its value is diminished, Article 7(2) affords the proprietor the power to prevent such an outcome.

6.5.1 INTERPRETING ARTICLE 7

The interpretation of both parts of Article 7 has caused considerable controversy. In interpreting Article 7(1), the key issue has been whether a trade mark proprietor is entitled to prohibit use of his mark in relation to goods which were put on the market *outside* the EEA (European Economic Area) with his consent but are then imported into the EEA by a third party. In relation to Article 7(2), the debate has focused on what constitutes legitimate reasons for a proprietor to oppose the resale of his goods which have been put on the market with his consent within the EEA. Before turning to these two questions, it is worth considering more closely the practical reasons for applying the principle of exhaustion to parallel imports of trade marked goods. In his book on parallel imports, Thomas Hays sets out the arguments for and against the exhaustion of rights in relation to parallel trade both at the national and international level.

T. Hays, *Parallel Importation Under European Union Law* (London: Sweet & Maxwell, 2004), p. 7

The Legal Nature of Parallel Importation

Intellectual property owners sue parallel importers or those merchants supplied by parallel importers for infringement in the market where the importers and merchants sell protected goods without permission even though the goods are genuine and not counterfeit. Intellectual property owners argue that although they or their licensees may have sold the goods in a foreign market they did not give permission for parallel importers to sell the particular goods at issue in the market of importation. Parallel importers argue that any rights the owners had to control the further commercialisation of the goods based on intellectual property ended when they sold the goods, that where the intellectual property rights have ended there can be no infringement, and that intellectual property owners are improperly trying to extend their control over formerly protected goods to protect their own higher prices.

As a legal problem, parallel importation points the way to another greater question, that of the exhaustion of rights: what effect, if any, does a particular sale of protected goods have upon an intellectual property owner's ability to control those goods? Depending upon the circumstances, some or all of an intellectual property owner's rights may be exhausted by the first sale. Other rights may survive the sale to allow the intellectual property owner to exercise full control over who may resell the goods and where they may resell them. This continued, post-sale control may not be readily apparent to subsequent purchasers of the goods, who presume that they have taken the goods free of any restrictions of resale and are surprised when the intellectual property owner's control resurfaces, perhaps as the basis for accusing the reseller of infringement and to deny him the right to dispose of his purchases as he would have wished. To a degree resellers are supported by general national property rules, particularly under the common law, favouring the free alienability of property. Where these rules are expressed in general bodies of commercial law, like that on contract, parallel importation continues to generate legal conflicts, even after the core issues concerning parallel importation have been litigated.

Intellectual property owners argue that a volitional sale in a particular jurisdiction will exhaust their intellectual property rights in that jurisdiction only; that the exhaustion of rights is confined to the jurisdiction where a sale takes place. Parallel importers and consumer advocates argue that a first sale of the goods anywhere in the world should be effective in exhausting an intellectual property owner's control. Both arguments have points to recommend them.

National Exhaustion of Rights

Jurisdictionally specific exhaustion, the intellectual property owner's position, has the advantage of compartmentalisation. Intellectual property rights are created under the laws of individual countries or groups of countries in the case of the EC Treaty. One nation's intellectual property laws are legally distinct from any other nation. Therefore, it is logical that actions taken in one country should have an automatic legal effect only under that nation's laws. Any intellectual property rights that might arise under the laws of other nations would be unaffected. Thus, if protected goods moved across jurisdictional borders after a sale, intellectual property based on control in the second jurisdiction, unaffected by that sale, would apply to the goods. This argument has the disadvantage of disrupting international trade. It calls into question the alienability of all branded goods on world markets and gives brand owners the ability to partition and isolate markets on the basis of intellectual property rights.

Multinational Exhaustion of Rights

Under a regime of global first sale exhaustion, the parallel importer's position, a subsequent purchaser of goods would be justified in presuming that any intellectual property rights in those goods were exhausted when the goods are encountered in free circulation. Global exhaustion has the advantage of commercial definiteness. A volitional sale of the underlying goods by an intellectual property owner or his licensee would be sufficient to exhaust intellectual property based control in those goods, regardless of the location of that sale. This position has the disadvantage that it is not able to take account of differences in intellectual property regimes, nor of the policy decisions that favour isolated markets.

Community Exhaustion

At the practical level, those who favour limited, Community-wide exhaustion argue that it provides intellectual property owners with higher economic rewards for their investment in research, marketing and distribution, making possible investment in the maintenance or improvement of the quality of existing products and services and the development of new products and brands. It aids the entry of foreign products and lesser-known brands into the overall Community market, an undertaking that might otherwise be seen as too expensive or risky. Also, it allows Community based firms to sell intellectual property protected goods at lower prices abroad, providing goods too external consumers, increased production with the associated employment within the internal market, and giving consumers within the market some benefits in the form of lower intra-market prices resulting from a larger volume of overall sales.

Furthermore, those who favour a more restrictive exhaustion regime argue that apart from designating the origin of products, trade marks function to guarantee the quality of branded products to protect consumers from disappointing purchases of inferior goods. They argue that the guarantor of quality function of marks is best served when distribution systems are strengthened by the ability to oppose goods of lesser or diminished quality that are being sold by parallel importers, or where otherwise identical branded goods are being sold outside of authorised channels with the benefit of after-sales services. Furthermore, they argue that the composition, quality, and style of branded goods should be allowed to vary between markets, with the same mark representing different product characteristics to different groups of consumers, depending on the consumers' expectations as derived from their experiences with a local variety of a product and the representation of the brand owner about the product through advertising. They argue that the consumer protection function of marks, if such a function exists, is best served where brand owners, their licensees, or their distribution systems can be responsible through a retention of brand based control for complying with any applicable technical or safety standards.

6.5.2.1 International exhaustion of rights

The TMD has introduced regional exhaustion, applying the principle to trade both within Member States and between them. However, given the global nature of trade (and more particularly of branding), it is not surprising that shortly after the directive was incorporated into the national law of Member States, the issue of international exhaustion (i.e. in relation to goods placed on the market outside the EEA) was raised. The general approach to this question, which remains authoritative today, was set out by the ECJ in *Silhouette*.

Silhouette International Schmied GmbH & Co KG v Hartlauer Handelsgesellschaft mbH Case C-355/96 [1998] ECR I-4799

Silhouette is an Austrian company producing expensive spectacle frames which it sells worldwide under the name 'Silhouette', a registered trade mark in Austria and many other countries. In Austria, Silhouette supplies its frames directly to opticians. Elsewhere, it distributes them through subsidiary companies or distributors. Hartlauer sells spectacles among other cut-priced goods through its Austrian subsidiaries. As noted by the ECJ, Hartlauer 'is not supplied by Silhouette because that company considers that distribution of its products by Hartlauer would be harmful to its image as a manufacturer of top-quality fashion spectacles'. In 1995, Hartlauer purchased 21,000 Silhouette spectacle frames. These spectacles had originally been supplied by Silhouette to a Bulgarian company which had been instructed only to sell the frames in Bulgaria or the former USSR. It is not clear from whom Hartlauer had purchased the frames. In Austria, Silhouette sought an injunction to prevent Hartlauer from selling the frames under its trade mark as they had not been put on the market in the EEA by Silhouette or with its consent. In other words, it argued that it had not exhausted its trade mark rights in the EEA. In the course of the proceedings, the Austrian courts referred to the ECJ the question of whether Article 7(1) should be understood to mean that the trade mark entitles a proprietor to prohibit a third party from using the mark for goods which have been put on the market in a state which is not part of the EEA.

18. Like the rules laid down in Article 6 of the Directive, which set certain limits to the effects of a trade mark, Article 7 states that, in the circumstances which it specifies, the exclusive rights conferred by the trade mark are exhausted, with the result that the proprietor is no longer entitled to prohibit use of the mark. Exhaustion is subject first of all to the condition that the goods have been put on the market by the proprietor or with his consent. According to the text of the Directive itself, exhaustion occurs only where the products have been put on the market in the Community (in the EEA since the EEA Agreement entered into force).

19. No argument has been presented to the Court that the Directive could be interpreted as providing for the exhaustion of the rights conferred by a trade mark in respect of goods put on the market by the proprietor or with his consent irrespective of where they were put on the market.

...

23. In that respect, although the third recital in the preamble to the Directive states that 'it does not appear to be necessary at present to undertake full-scale approximation of the trade mark laws of the Member States', the Directive nonetheless provides for harmonisation in relation to substantive rules of central importance in this sphere, that is to say according to that same recital, the rules concerning those provisions of national law which most

directly affect the functioning of the internal market, and that that recital does not preclude the harmonisation relating to those rules from being complete.

24. The first recital in the preamble to the Directive notes that the trade mark laws applicable in the Member States contain disparities which may impede the free movement of goods and freedom to provide services and may distort competition within the common market, so that it is necessary, in view of the establishment and functioning of the internal market, to approximate the laws of Member States. The ninth recital emphasises that it is fundamental, in order to facilitate the free movement of goods and services, to ensure that registered trade marks enjoy the same protection under the legal systems of all the Member States, but that this should not prevent Member States from granting at their option more extensive protection to those trade marks which have a reputation.

25. In the light of those recitals, Articles 5 to 7 of the Directive must be construed as embodying a complete harmonisation of the rules relating to the rights conferred by a trade mark. That interpretation, it may be added, is borne out by the fact that Article 5 expressly leaves it open to the Member States to maintain or introduce certain rules specifically defined by the Community legislature. Thus, in accordance with Article 5(2), to which the ninth recital refers, the Member States have the option to grant more extensive protection to trade marks with a reputation.

26. Accordingly, the Directive cannot be interpreted as leaving it open to the Member States to provide in their domestic law for exhaustion of the rights conferred by a trade mark in respect of products put on the market in non-member countries.

27. This, moreover, is the only interpretation which is fully capable of ensuring that the purpose of the Directive is achieved, namely to safeguard the functioning of the internal market. A situation in which some Member States could provide for international exhaustion while others provided for Community exhaustion only would inevitably give rise to barriers to the free movement of goods and the freedom to provide services.

30. Finally, the Community authorities could always extend the exhaustion provided for by Article 7 to products put on the market in non-member countries by entering into international agreements in that sphere, as was done in the context of the EEA Agreement.

31. In the light of the foregoing, the answer to be given to the first question must be that national rules providing for exhaustion of trade mark rights in respect of products put on the market outside the EEA under that mark by the proprietor or with his consent are contrary to Article 7(1) of the Directive, as amended by the EEA Agreement.

The decision in *Silhouette* that the directive neither allowed for international exhaustion nor enabled states within the EEA to adopt their own approach was criticized by a number of commentators. It was suggested that by not endorsing international exhaustion, the ECJ was allowing trade mark rights to be used as a barrier to international trade, with the result that prices of goods put on the market in the EEA might be kept artificially high if they were protected from competition from goods with the same trade mark but put on the market at a lower price outside the EEA. It was also suggested by some commentators that difficulties would arise around the question of when a trade mark owner will be deemed to have consented to the distribution of his goods in the EEA and when he will be deemed to have withheld consent. And it is this problem which preoccupied the case law dealing with parallel imports after the decision in *Silhouette*. Following *Silhouette*, the question of consent was examined in *Sebago*.[58] In this case, the ECJ held that for there to be consent, such

58 *Sebago Inc and Ancienne Maison Dubois et Fils SA v GB-Unic SA* Case C-173/98 [1999] ECR I-4103.

consent must relate to each individual item of the product imported and sold in the EEA by the parallel importer. However, perhaps the key case dealing with consent is *Zino Davidoff v A & G Imports*.

Zino Davidoff SA v A & G Imports Ltd; Levi Strauss & Co Ltd v Tesco Stores Ltd, Tesco Plc and Costco Wholesale UK Ltd Joined Cases C-414/99 to C-416/99 [2001] ECR I-8691

Zino Davidoff was the proprietor of two trade marks, 'Cool Water' and 'Davidoff Cool Water' registered in the UK for toiletries and other cosmetic products. Davidoff sold its products in the EEA and outside. In 1996, it contracted with a trader in Singapore to sell its products to distributors in a defined territory outside the EEA and to impose on these distributors a contractual term not to resell outside the defined territory. A & G acquired these products (identified by batch code numbers placed on them by Davidoff) and then imported and sold them in the UK. Davidoff alleged that its trade mark had been infringed by this importation and sale. A & G argued that given the circumstances in which the goods had been placed on the market in Singapore, Davidoff should be deemed to have given consent to the importation and sale of the goods in the UK. Davidoff denied it had given consent. Levi Strauss sold jeans under the marks 'Levis' and '501'. It distributed its goods in the UK through a selective distribution system, which did not include the defendants. Tesco and Costco obtained Levi jeans which had been manufactured and sold outside the EEA. The contracts by which they had acquired the jeans did not contain any terms which would prevent their sale in the UK. Indeed, the jeans had originally been sold to authorized dealers outside the UK and acquired by a third party. Levis alleged trade mark infringement. Among the questions addressed to the ECJ by the High Court was whether and in what circumstances it was possible to imply consent by a trade mark proprietor for the importation and sale of his goods in the EEA. In its judgment, the ECJ first looked at whether consent could be implied, noting that, different Member States had differing definitions of consent.

43. It therefore falls to the Court to supply a uniform interpretation of the concept of 'consent' to the placing of goods on the market within the EEA as referred to in Article 7(1) of the Directive.

...

45. In view of its serious effect in extinguishing the exclusive rights of the proprietors of the trade marks in issue in the main proceedings (rights which enable them to control the initial marketing in the EEA), consent must be so expressed that an intention to renounce those rights is unequivocally demonstrated.

46. Such intention will normally be gathered from an express statement of consent. Nevertheless, it is conceivable that consent may, in some cases, be inferred from facts and circumstances prior to, simultaneous with or subsequent to the placing of the goods on the market outside the EEA which, in the view of the national court, unequivocally demonstrate that the proprietor has renounced his rights.

47. The answer to the first question referred in each of Cases C414/99 to C-416/99 must therefore be that, on a proper construction of Article 7(1) of the Directive, the consent of a trade mark proprietor to the marketing within the EEA of products bearing that mark which have previously been placed on the market outside the EEA by that proprietor or with his

consent may be implied, where it is to be inferred from facts and circumstances prior to, simultaneous with or subsequent to the placing of the goods on the market outside the EEA which, in the view of the national court, unequivocally demonstrate that the proprietor has renounced his right to oppose placing of the goods on the market within the EEA.

[Having concluded that consent could be implied, the ECJ then went on to consider whether consent may be inferred from the mere silence of a trade mark proprietor:]

53. It follows from the answer to the first question referred in the three cases C-414/99 to C-416/99 that consent must be expressed positively and that the factors taken into consideration in finding implied consent must unequivocally demonstrate that the trade mark proprietor has renounced any intention to enforce his exclusive rights.

54. It follows that it is for the trader alleging consent to prove it and not for the trade mark proprietor to demonstrate its absence.

55. Consequently, implied consent to the marketing within the EEA of goods put on the market outside that area cannot be inferred from the mere silence of the trade mark proprietor.

56. Likewise, implied consent cannot be inferred from the fact that a trade mark proprietor has not communicated his opposition to marketing within the EEA or from the fact that the goods do not carry any warning that it is prohibited to place them on the market within the EEA.

57. Finally, such consent cannot be inferred from the fact that the trade mark proprietor transferred ownership of the goods bearing the mark without imposing contractual reservations or from the fact that, according to the law governing the contract, the property right transferred includes, in the absence of such reservations, an unlimited right of resale or, at the very least, a right to market the goods subsequently within the EEA.

58. A rule of national law which proceeded upon the mere silence of the trade mark proprietor would not recognise implied consent but rather deemed consent. This would not meet the need for consent positively expressed required by Community law.

59. In so far as it falls to the Community legislature to determine the rights of a trade mark proprietor within the Member States of the Community it would be unacceptable on the basis of the law governing the contract for marketing outside the EEA to apply rules of law that have the effect of limiting the protection afforded to the proprietor of a trade mark by Articles 5(1) and 7(1) of the Directive.

60. The answer to be given to the second question and to Question 3(a)(i), (vi) and (vii) in Cases C-415/99 and C-416/99, and to the second question in Case C-414/99, must therefore be that implied consent cannot be inferred:

— from the fact that the proprietor of the trade mark has not communicated to all subsequent purchasers of the goods placed on the market outside the EEA his opposition to marketing within the EEA;

— from the fact that the goods carry no warning of a prohibition of their being placed on the market within the EEA;

— from the fact that the trade mark proprietor has transferred the ownership of the products bearing the trade mark without imposing any contractual reservations and that, according to the law governing the contract, the property right transferred includes, in the absence of such reservations, an unlimited right of resale or, at the very least, a right to market the goods subsequently within the EEA.

[The ECJ then turned to the final question which was what were the consequences of ignorance on the part of the importing trader. It held:]

— that the importer of goods bearing the trade mark is not aware that the proprietor objects to their being placed on the market in the EEA or sold there by traders other than authorised retailers, or

— that the authorised retailers and wholesalers have not imposed on their own purchasers contractual reservations setting out such opposition, even though they have been informed of it by the trade mark proprietor.

It is submitted that the judgment in *Zino Davidoff* came down firmly on the side of the trade mark proprietor on the question of consent. Although consent might be implied, according to the ECJ, strict conditions need to be met in order to infer implied consent. Do you think that the ECJ was correct to favour the proprietor in this regard, or does this approach give too much power to proprietors to control the cost of their products, which may be sold more cheaply abroad at the expense of the consumer? Two later ECJ cases concerning parallel imports also looked at the issue of consent. In the first, *Van Doren + Q GmbH v Lifestyle Sports + Sportswear*,[59] the ECJ appeared to shift the balance somewhat towards that of the importer by holding that where a third party succeeds in establishing that there is a real risk of partitioning of national markets if he himself bears that burden of proof, particularly where the trade mark proprietor markets his products in the EEA using an exclusive distribution system, it is for the proprietor of the trade mark to establish that the products were initially placed on the market outside the EEA by him or with his consent. If such evidence is adduced, it is for the third party to prove the consent of the trade mark proprietor to subsequent marketing of the products in the EEA. In *Peak Holding AB v Axolin-Elinor AB*,[60] the emphasis shifted to defining the meaning of 'put on the market' as a factor in finding that exhaustion had occurred. In this case Peak Holding had imported their own goods, carrying their trade mark, into the EEA where they had been offered for sale to the public but had remained unsold. This was held by the ECJ not to constitute putting the goods on the market for the purpose of exhaustion. According to the ECJ (para. 43): importing the goods or offering them for sale in the EEA cannot be equated to putting them on the market there.

6.5.2.2 Free movement of trade marked goods within the EU

Article 30 (previously Article 36) of the Treaty of Rome protects the specific subject matter of industrial property rights. In the case of trade marks, the ECJ has identified this to be the guarantee to the proprietor of a trade mark that he has the exclusive right to use the trade mark for the purpose of putting the product into circulation for the first time, and therefore to protect him against competitors wishing to take advantage of the status and the reputation of the mark by selling products illegally bearing the mark.[61] But Article 30 also states that 'prohibitions or restrictions on imports between Member States which are justified on grounds of protection of industrial and commercial property are permissible, provided they do not constitute a means of arbitrary discrimination or a disguised restriction on trade between Member States'.[62] Typically, early cases which dealt with the parallel importation of trade marked goods within the EU concerned the situation where a proprietor may have

---

[59] *Van Doren + Q GmbH v Lifestyle Sports + Sportswear Handelsgesellschaft GmbH* Case C-244/00 [2003] ECR I-3051.

[60] Case C-16/03 [2005] ECR I-11313.

[61] *Centrafarm BV and Adriaan De Peijper v Sterling Drug Inc* Case 15/74 [1974] ECR 1147.

[62] *Bristol-Myers Squibb v Paranova A/S* (Case C-427/93) [1996] ECR I-3457, para. 3.

marketed the same goods under different registered marks in different Member States. In *Centrafarm BV v American Home Products*,[63] the ECJ held that a proprietor could not rely on its trade mark registrations to prevent parallel import of goods from one Member State to another if its intention was to artificially partition the market. In *Bristol-Myers Squibb v Paranova*, the ECJ held that Article 7 should be understood in light of Article 36.

6.5.2.3 Reasons to oppose further dealings 1: changing the physical condition of the goods

The specific question raised by Article 7 is under what circumstances a proprietor may object to the further marketing of his goods because of the way they are being marketed by the parallel importer. This was the issue raised in *Bristol-Myers Squibb v Paranova*, which concerned changes to the physical condition of the goods.

Bristol-Myers Squibb v Paranova A/S Case C-427/93 [1996] ECR I-3457

Paranova sold pharmaceuticals in Denmark which Bristol-Myers Squibb (BMS) had first placed on the market in other EU states. Paranova repackaged the drugs in a design which was distinctive of its own goods but also retained the design of the original packaging. Paranova left the original trade mark on the packaging, but stated that the goods had been 'imported and repackaged by Paranova'. In some cases, Paranova also changed the size of the packaging. In others it relabelled the drugs, so that they carried both the BMS marks and its own trade mark. BMS brought an action in the Danish courts claiming that Paranova had infringed its trade marks. The Danish court asked the ECJ a number of questions. The first was whether Article 7(1) precludes a proprietor from objecting to goods put on the market and with his consent where the importer has repackaged the product and reaffixed the trade mark without the proprietor's consent.

34. The Court's case law on Article 36 of the Treaty shows that the owner's exclusive right to affix a trade mark to a product must in certain circumstances be regarded as exhausted in order to allow an importer to market under that trade mark products which were put on the market in another Member State by the owner or with his consent (see Case 102/77 *Hoffmann-la Roche v Centrafarm* [1978] ECR 1139; Case 3/78 *Centrafarm v American Home Products Corporation* [1978] ECR 1823; and the judgment given today in *Eurim-Pharm Arzeneimittel GmbH v Beiersdorf AG* (Joined Cases C-71-73/94) [1996] ECR I-3603 and *MPA Pharma GmbH v Rhone-Poulenc Pharma GmbH* (Case C-232/94) [1996] ECR I-3671).

35. To accept the argument that the principle of exhaustion under Article 7(1) cannot apply if the importer has repackaged the product and reaffixed the trade mark would therefore imply a major alteration to the principles flowing from Articles 30 and 36 of the Treaty.

36. There is nothing to suggest that Article 7 of the Directive is intended to restrict the scope of that case law. Nor would such an effect be permissible, since a Directive cannot justify obstacles to inter-Community trade save within the bounds set by the Treaty rules. The Court's case law shows that the prohibition on quantitative restrictions and measures having equivalent effect applies not only to national measures but also to those emanating from Community institutions (see, most recently, Case C-51/93 *Meyhui v Schott Zwiesel Glaswerke* [1994] ECR I-3879, paragraph 11).

---

[63] *Centrafarm BV v American Home Products Corpn* Case 3/78 [1978] ECR 1823.

37. The answer to the first question in Cases C-427/93 and C-429/93 must therefore be that, save in the circumstances defined in Article 7(2), Article 7(1) of the Directive precludes the owner of a trade mark from relying on his rights as owner to prevent an importer from marketing a product which was put on the market in another Member State by the owner or with his consent, even if that importer repackaged the product and reaffixed the trade mark to it without the owner's authorisation.

[The second question addressed to the ECJ was when might a proprietor fall back on Art. 7(2) to prevent the re-marketing of its goods? The ECJ first pointed out that earlier cases had found that a trade mark owner could not rely upon its trade mark rights to artificially partition the market. The ECJ went on to identify those situations when artificial partitioning might occur:]

Artificial partitioning of the markets between Member States

52. Reliance on trade mark rights by their owner in order to oppose marketing under that trade mark of products repackaged by a third party would contribute to the partitioning of markets between Member States in particular where the owner has placed an identical pharmaceutical product on the market in several Member States in various forms of packaging, and the product may not, in the condition in which it has been marketed by the trade mark owner in one Member State, be imported and put on the market in another Member State by a parallel importer.

53. The trade mark owner cannot therefore oppose the repackaging of the product in new external packaging when the size of packet used by the owner in the Member State where the importer purchased the product cannot be marketed in the Member State of importation by reason, in particular, of a rule authorising packaging only of a certain size or a national practice to the same effect, sickness insurance rules making the reimbursement of medical expenses depend on the size of the packaging, or well-established medical prescription practices based, inter alia, on standard sizes recommended by professional groups and sickness insurance institutions.

54. Where, in accordance with the rules and practices in force in the Member State of importation, the trade mark owner uses many different sizes of packaging in that State, the finding that one of those sizes is also marketed in the Member State of exportation is not enough to justify the conclusion that repackaging is unnecessary. Partitioning of the markets would exist if the importer were able to sell the product in only part of his market.

55. The owner may, on the other hand, oppose the repackaging of the product in new external packaging where the importer is able to achieve packaging which may be marketed in the Member State of importation by, for example, affixing to the original external or inner packaging new labels in the language of the Member State of importation, or by adding new user instructions or information in the language of the Member State of importation, or by replacing an additional article not capable of gaining approval in the Member State of importation with a similar article that has obtained such approval.

56. The power of the owner of trade mark rights protected in a Member State to oppose the marketing of repackaged products under the trade mark should be limited only in so far as the repackaging undertaken by the importer is necessary in order to market the product in the Member State of importation.

57. Finally, contrary to the argument of the plaintiffs in the main actions, the Court's use of the words 'artificial partitioning of the markets' does not imply that the importer must demonstrate that, by putting an identical product on the market in varying forms of packaging in different Member States, the trade mark owner deliberately sought to partition the markets

between Member States. By stating that the partitioning in question must be artificial, the Court's intention was to stress that the owner of a trade mark may always rely on his rights as owner to oppose the marketing of repackaged products when such action is justified by the need to safeguard the essential function of the trade mark, in which case the resultant partitioning could not be regarded as artificial.

[Key to the ECJ judgment is that repackaging undertaken by a parallel importer must be 'necessary' in order for the latter to enter the market. In the judgment, the ECJ also set out the conditions which must be met by a parallel importer so as not to fall foul of Art. 7(2). They include, *inter alia*, that:]

79. ...

(c) the new packaging clearly states who repackaged the product and the name of the manufacturer in print such that a person with normal eyesight, exercising a normal degree of attentiveness, would be in a position to understand; similarly, the origin of an extra article from a source other than the trade mark owner must be indicated in such a way as to dispel any impression that the trade mark owner is responsible for it; however, it is not necessary to indicate that the repackaging was carried out without the authorisation of the trade mark owner;

(d) the presentation of the repackaged product is not such as to be liable to damage the reputation of the trade mark and of its owner; thus, the packaging must not be defective, of poor quality, or untidy; and

(e) the importer gives notice to the trade mark owner before the repackaged product is put on sale, and, on demand, supplies him with a specimen of the repackaged product.

We should not be surprised that following the *Bristol-Myers Squibb v Paranova* decision, the question was raised of when repackaging or relabelling was 'necessary' and therefore acceptable under Article 7. The leading case on the scope of necessity is *Boehringer Ingelheim KG v Swingward Ltd*.

Boehringer Ingelheim KG and Boehringer Ingelheim Pharma KG v Swingward Ltd
Case C-143/00 [2002] ECR I-3759

The pharmaceutical products involved in this action had been marketed by the claimants in the EU, and the defendants had imported them into the UK. The defendants had altered the packaging of the products in various ways. For example, they attached labels to the original packets which identified themselves and the licence number of the product but left the original trade mark visible. Alternatively, the defendant had repackaged the products but reproduced the original trade mark. Finally, in other cases, the product had been repackaged without the original trade mark visible on the outside, although the original trade mark was visible inside the box but 'over stickered' with a label giving the product's generic name and identifying the manufacturer and the parallel importer. All the packages also included an information leaflet bearing the claimants' trade marks but translated into English. The claimants argued that such changes were not 'necessary' to market the products in the UK. A key question addressed to the ECJ was whether repackaging is by definition detrimental to the specific subject matter of a trade mark even if it does not affect the essential function of the mark. The ECJ answered by reference to its finding in *Bristol-Myers Squibb v Paranova*.

34. Thus it is clear from settled case law that the change brought about by any repackaging of a trade marked pharmaceutical product—creating by its very nature the risk of interference with the original condition of the product—may be prohibited by the trade mark proprietor unless the repackaging is necessary in order to enable the marketing of the products imported in parallel and the legitimate interests of the proprietor are also safeguarded (see, to that effect, *Bristol-Myers Squibb and Others*, para. 57).

35. The answer to the first, second, fourth and eighth questions must therefore be that Article 7(2) of the Directive must be interpreted as meaning that a trade mark proprietor may rely on its trade mark rights in order to prevent a parallel importer from repackaging pharmaceutical products unless the exercise of those rights contributes to artificial partitioning of the markets between Member States.

[The UK court also asked the ECJ in *Boehringer* about the scope of the necessity test.]

The need for repackaging

36. By its third question, the national court asks the Court in what circumstances repackaging by a parallel importer in order to market pharmaceutical products in the importing State may be considered to be necessary for the purposes of the Court's case law. It seeks more specifically to ascertain whether repackaging may be considered necessary on the sole ground that, without it, the commercial success of the product would be adversely affected on the market of the importing State because a significant proportion of the consumers in that State mistrust pharmaceutical products which are manifestly intended for the market of another State.

37. The national court considers that repackaging should be regarded as necessary where it enables a real or potential impediment to the marketing of the products to be overcome. That issue is important since the claimants contend that repackaging by parallel importers, which consists in replacing the packaging of the products, is not necessary because marketing would still be possible simply by relabelling the products. According to the national court, there is real market resistance to relabelling and replacement of packaging is necessary to overcome that resistance.

[In answer to that question, the ECJ held the following:]

Findings of the Court

45. According to the Court's case law, where a trade mark proprietor relies on its trade mark rights to prevent a parallel importer from repackaging where that is necessary for the pharmaceutical products concerned to be marketed in the importing State, that contributes to artificial partitioning of the markets between Member States, contrary to Community law.

46. The Court has found in that respect that it is necessary to take account of the circumstances prevailing at the time of marketing in the importing Member State which make repackaging objectively necessary in order that the pharmaceutical product can be placed on the market in that State by the parallel importer. The trade mark proprietor's opposition to the repackaging is not justified if it hinders effective access of the imported product to the market of that State (see, to that effect, *Upjohn*, para. 43).

47. Such an impediment exists, for example, where pharmaceutical products purchased by the parallel importer cannot be placed on the market in the Member State of importation in their original packaging by reason of national rules or practices relating to packaging, or where sickness insurance rules make reimbursement of medical expenses depend on a certain

packaging or where well-established medical prescription practices are based, inter alia, on standard sizes recommended by professional groups and sickness insurance institutions. In that regard, it is sufficient for there to be an impediment in respect of one type of packaging used by the trade mark proprietor in the Member State of importation (see *Bristol-Myers Squibb and Others*, paras. 53 and54).

48. In contrast, the trade mark proprietor may oppose the repackaging if it is based solely on the parallel importer's attempt to secure a commercial advantage (see, to that effect, *Upjohn*, para. 44).

49. In that context, it has also been held that the trade mark proprietor may oppose replacement packaging where the parallel importer is able to reuse the original packaging for the purpose of marketing in the Member State of importation by affixing labels to that packaging (see *Bristol-Myers Squibb and Others*, para. 55).

50. Thus, while the trade mark proprietor may oppose the parallel importer's use of replacement packaging, that is conditional on the relabelled pharmaceutical product being able to have effective access to the market concerned.

51. Resistance to relabelled pharmaceutical products does not always constitute an impediment to effective market access such as to make replacement packaging necessary, within the meaning of the Court's case law.

52. However, there may exist on a market, or on a substantial part of it, such strong resistance from a significant proportion of consumers to relabelled pharmaceutical products that there must be held to be a hindrance to effective market access. In those circumstances, repackaging of the pharmaceutical products would not be explicable solely by the attempt to secure a commercial advantage. The purpose would be to achieve effective market access.

53. It is for the national court to determine whether that is the case.

54. The answer to the third question must therefore be that replacement packaging of pharmaceutical products is objectively necessary within the meaning of the Court's case law if, without such repackaging, effective access to the market concerned, or to a substantial part of that market, must be considered to be hindered as the result of strong resistance from a significant proportion of consumers to relabelled pharmaceutical products.

In *Boehringer*, the ECJ found that a trade mark proprietor could rely on its trade mark rights to prevent repackaging unless to do so would artificially partition the market. However, repackaging is necessary if simply relabelling goods would lead consumers to resist their purchase. Do you think the ECJ was correct to assume, in making this judgment, that consumers might be wary of purchasing goods (especially, pharmaceuticals) which may appear to have been interefered with? Or is the average consumer generally aware that pharmaceuticals may well be imported from abroad without any risk to their quality? When *Boehringer* returned to the Court of Appeal,[64] Jacob LJ interpreted the ECJ decision to mean that repackaging or rebranding is not necessary if it affects the condition of the goods or if it damages the reputation of the mark. However, because the Court of Appeal felt the situation was still unclear despite the earlier findings of the ECJ, it addressed a further question to the ECJ. It asked whether the test of necessity was relevant only to repackaging or whether it extended to the way the repackaged product was presented. It is submitted that in its judgment,[65] which was relevant solely to pharmaceutical products, the ECJ took a stance favourable to the trade mark proprietors. It held, *inter alia*, that a trade mark owner may legitimately oppose the re-marketing of its product where an external label has been applied unless to do so would contribute to the

---

[64] *Boehringer Ingelheim KG, Ingelheim Pharma GmbH & Co KG v Swingward Ltd* [2004] ETMR 65 (CA).
[65] *Boehringer Ingelheim KG v Swingward Ltd* Case C-348/04) [2007] ECR I-3391.

artificial partitioning of the market or unless the new label does not affect the original condition of the product or damage the reputation of the original trade mark, and notice is given. However, the right of a proprietor to oppose the re-marketing of a product, which has been repackaged or relabelled, because it damages the reputation of the mark is not confined to instances where the repackaging is of poor quality, defective, or untidy. It might arise when, for example, the parallel importer prints its own mark in capital letters or fails to affix the original trade mark to the new exterior packaging ('de-branding'). It is up to the national courts to decide in light of the particular circumstances whether the mark's reputation has been damaged. And, it is for the parallel importer to prove not only the existence of the conditions which made such repackaging necessary but also that the repackaging will not affect the original condition of the product or the reputation of the mark.

6.5.2.4 Reasons to oppose further dealings 2: changing the 'mental' condition of the goods

The *Boehringer* case raised the issue of when the parallel imports could be resisted by a trade mark proprietor if the way they were re-marketed damaged the reputation of the mark. In *Bristol-Myers Squibb v Paranova*, the ECJ suggested that an Article 7(2) objection might be raised where the poor presentation of the goods after repackaging damaged the mark's reputation. This was the specific issue in the *Dior* case, where the ECJ was asked whether legitimate reasons for opposing further dealing in parallel imports extended to use of the trade mark which would impair or change the 'mental' condition of the goods rather than their physical condition.

Parfums Christian Dior SA v Evora BV Case C-337/95 [1997] ECR I-6013

Dior France, which sold a number of high-profile perfumes, sought to protect the high prices paid for its goods and their luxurious image by distributing them only through exclusive outlets. Evora operated a chain of chemist shops in the Netherlands. It sold Dior perfumes which it had obtained through parallel imports. It advertised the perfumes in leaflets which reproduced Dior's marks and which also advertised other perfumes which were not of a similar quality. The ECJ was asked whether a reseller may use the marks attached to the goods for advertising purposes.

34. On the one hand, Article 5 of the Directive, which determines the rights conferred by a trade mark, provides, in paragraph (1), that the proprietor is to be entitled to prevent all third parties from using his trade mark in the course of trade and, in paragraph (3)(d), that he may prohibit all third parties from using the trade mark in advertising.

35. On the other hand, Article 7(1) of the Directive, which concerns the exhaustion of the rights conferred by a trade mark, provides that a trade mark is not to entitle its proprietor to prohibit its use in relation to goods which have been put on the market in the Community under that trade mark by its proprietor or with his consent.

36. If the right to prohibit the use of his trade mark in relation to goods, conferred on the proprietor of a trade mark under Article 5 of the Directive, is exhausted once the goods have been put on the market by himself or with his consent, the same applies as regards the right to use the trade mark for the purpose of bringing to the public's attention the further commercialisation of those goods.

[The ECJ ruled that:]

...on a proper interpretation of Articles 5 and 7 of the Directive, when trade-marked goods have been put on the Community market by the proprietor of the trade mark or with his consent, a reseller, besides being free to resell those goods, is also free to make use of the trade mark in order to bring to the public's attention the further commercialisation of those goods.

[Having held that a parallel importer can make use of the original trade mark to market the goods, the ECJ then considered the question of whether the proprietor could object to the way the mark was used by the reseller because it might endanger the advertising function or reputation of the mark. It held the following:]

42. According to the case law of the Court, Article 7 of the Directive comprehensively regulates the question of the exhaustion of trade mark rights in relation to goods put on the market in the Community and the use of the word 'especially' in paragraph (2) indicates that alteration or impairment of the condition of trade-marked goods is given only as an example of what may constitute legitimate reasons (see *Bristol-Myers Squibb*, cited above, paragraphs 26 and 39). Moreover, that provision is intended to reconcile the fundamental interest in the protection of trade mark rights with the fundamental interest in the free movement of goods within the common market (*Bristol-Myers Squibb*, cited above, paragraph 40).

43. The damage done to the reputation of a trade mark may, in principle, be a legitimate reason, within the meaning of Article 7(2) of the Directive, allowing the proprietor to oppose further commercialisation of goods which have been put on the market in the Community by him or with his consent. According to the case law of the Court concerning the repackaging of trade-marked goods, the owner of a trade mark has a legitimate interest, related to the specific subject-matter of the trade mark right, in being able to oppose the commercialisation of those goods if the presentation of the repackaged goods is liable to damage the reputation of the trade mark (*Bristol-Myers Squibb*, cited above, paragraph 75).

44. It follows that, where a reseller makes use of a trade mark in order to bring the public's attention to further commercialisation of trade-marked goods, a balance must be struck between the legitimate interest of the trade mark owner in being protected against resellers using his trade mark for advertising in a manner which could damage the reputation of the trade mark and the reseller's legitimate interest in being able to resell the goods in question by using advertising methods which are customary in his sector of trade.

45. As regards the instant case, which concerns prestigious, luxury goods, the reseller must not act unfairly in relation to the legitimate interests of the trade mark owner. He must therefore endeavour to prevent his advertising from affecting the value of the trade mark by detracting from the allure and prestigious image of the goods in question and from their aura of luxury.

46. However, the fact that a reseller, who habitually markets articles of the same kind but not necessarily of the same quality, uses for trade-marked goods the modes of advertising which are customary in his trade sector, even if they are not the same as those used by the trade mark owner himself or by his approved retailers, does not constitute a legitimate reason, within the meaning of Article 7(2) of the Directive, allowing the owner to oppose that advertising, unless it is established that, given the specific circumstances of the case, the use of the trade mark in the reseller's advertising seriously damages the reputation of the trade mark.

47. For example, such damage could occur if, in an advertising leaflet distributed by him, the reseller did not take care to avoid putting the trade mark in a context which might seriously detract from the image which the trade mark owner has succeeded in creating around his trade mark.

48. In view of the foregoing, the answer to be given to the third, fourth and fifth questions must be that the proprietor of a trade mark may not rely on Article 7(2) of the Directive to oppose the use of the trade mark, by a reseller who habitually markets articles of the same kind, but not necessarily of the same quality, as the trade-marked goods, in ways customary in the reseller's sector of trade, for the purpose of bringing to the public's attention the further commercialisation of those goods, unless it is established that, given the specific circumstances of the case, the use of the trade mark for this purpose seriously damages the reputation of the trade mark.

[Finally, the ECJ was asked whether such damage to the reputation of the mark constitutes a legitimate reason which would allow the proprietor to oppose a mark's use for further commercialization. According to the ECJ:]

59. The answer to be given to the sixth question must therefore be that, on a proper interpretation of Articles 30 and 36 of the Treaty, the proprietor of a trade mark or holder of copyright may not oppose their use by a reseller who habitually markets articles of the same kind, but not necessarily of the same quality, as the protected goods, in ways customary in the reseller's sector of trade, for the purpose of bringing to the public's attention the further commercialisation of those goods, unless it is established that, having regard to the specific circumstances of the case, the use of those goods for that purpose seriously damages their reputation.

Following *Dior*, in two cases, *Zino Davidoff v A & G Imports*[66] and *Glaxo Group Ltd v Dowelhurst Ltd*,[67] the High Court took a broad view as to what constituted unacceptable commercialization by a parallel importer. In the former case it was held that damage to the registered trade mark must be 'substantial'. In the latter it was held that damage must be to the specific subject matter of the trade mark (i.e. to its ability to act as a badge of origin).

6.5.2.5 Conclusion

Like many of the key issues raised by the TMD, the interpretation of Article 7 concerns the scope of the monopoly which should be afforded through trade mark registration. In the case of parallel imports, the courts have again been bound to weigh the interests of the proprietor against those of his competitors and consumers at large. It can be argued that where changing the physical condition of the goods is an issue, the ECJ, and indeed the domestic courts, have sought to circumscribe the ability of the proprietor to use his registration to interfere with parallel importation. In relation to re-marketing which affects the mental condition of the goods, the ECJ has been more willing to protect the proprietor's interest. This approach would seem to accord with the more general view taken by commentators that while the origin function of a mark is essentially for the benefit of consumers, the dilution provisions of the directive are primarily concerned with protecting the proprietor's investment in nurturing the advertising functions of his mark. Perhaps the most interesting question to emerge from the ECJ's judgments on exhaustion of rights and particularly its interpretation of Article 7(2), is why it was ready in 1997 in the *Dior* case to recognize the need for very broad protection for marks against dilution in relation to re-marketing, but waited another decade before defining the scope of dilution more generally, and in a far more limited way. Could it be because, in relation to parallel imports, such goods can always be re-marketed in such a

---

[66] *Zino Davidoff SA v A & G Imports Ltd* [2000] Ch 127.   [67] [2004] ETMR 39.

way that does not dilute the trade mark's reputation and hence the interest of the consumer in having access to cheaper goods need not inevitably be disturbed?

FURTHER READING

W. R. Cornish, 'Trade marks: Portcullis for the EEA?' [1998] EIPR 172.

P. Dyrberg, 'For EEA exhaustion to apply, who has to prove the marketing of the trade marked goods in the EEA: The trade mark owner or the defendant' (2004) 26(2) EIPR 81–4.

L. Harrold, 'National courts will have final word on pharmaceutical repackaged parallel imports' [2007] EIPR 395.

T. Hays, 'The free movement (or not) of trademark protected goods in Europe' in G. B. Dinwoodie and M. D. Janis (eds.), *Trademark Law and Theory: A handbook of contemporary research* (Cheltenham: Edward Elgar, 2008), pp. 204–28.

6.6 REMEDIES

The general remedies for trade mark infringement and the prohibition against groundless threats are considered later in this volume.[68] It is, however, worth noting that infringement proceedings in trade mark cases cannot begin until the date upon which the trade mark is first registered, although damages for infringement will be recoverable from the mark's priority date. In all legal proceedings relating to a registered trade mark, the registration of a person as proprietor of a trade mark shall be prima facie evidence of the validity of the original registration (s. 72 of the TMA). Specific remedies for trade mark infringement include an order for the erasure of an infringing sign (s. 15) or for the delivery up of goods, materials or articles which bear it (s. 16). There are also criminal sanctions for trade mark infringement. The prerequisite to finding an offence has been committed is that the defendant must have acted with a view to gain to himself or another or with intent to cause loss to another and without the consent of another (s. 92 of the TMA). This is an offence of strict liability, in that there is no need to show that at the time the defendant knew that there was a registered trade mark (*Torbay Council v Satnam Singh*[69]). It is a defence for the accused to show that he believed or that he had reasonable grounds to believe that the use of the sign in the manner in which it was used or was to be used was not an infringement of the registered trade mark (s. 92(5)). On the other hand, it is not a defence to an action that the quality of the infringing goods was so poor that the public would not be confused into believing they were legitimate merchandise.[70]

---

[68] In Ch. 13.   [69] [2000] FSR 158.   [70] *R v Boulter (Gary)* [2008] EWCA Crim 2375.

7

CHARACTER MERCHANDISING
AND PUBLICITY RIGHTS

7.1 INTRODUCTION

Character merchandising is not a new phenomenon, but for some time now it has been very big business indeed. The evidence is all around us. There has been the ubiquity of footballer David Beckham on advertising hoardings over the past decade. It has been estimated that Beckham has earned up to $30 million a year in product endorsement. There is also the strategy of 'product placement' in some of our most popular movies. The last two James Bond movies, 'Casino Royale' and 'Quantum of Solace' saw product placements for, among other things, Omega watches, Heineken beer, Sony Ericsson mobile phones and most notably Smirnoff vodka for the spy's signature martinis (think 'shaken not stirred'). One observer has dubbed this latter phenomenon, 'James Bond: Licensed to Sell'[1] and another has questioned whether we are dealing with 'James Bond or James Brand'?[2] The examples of Beckham and Bond highlight one important aspect of character merchandising: that it includes the marketing both of actual personalities as well as fictional characters. This chapter is concerned with how the law will protect the interests of both real celebrities and those who seek to exploit the fame of fictional ones. We will begin by seeking to define character merchandising. We will then turn to consider how UK law has developed to protect character merchandising, whether it is of sporting heroes such as David Beckham or literary heroes like James Bond. Finally, we will ask whether there should be stronger legal protection offered to character merchandising in the UK including, as some have argued, the introduction of a right of publicity.

7.1.1 DEFINING CHARACTER MERCHANDISING

7.1.1.1 The WIPO definition

In 1994, the World Intellectual Property Organization (WIPO) commissioned a study of character merchandising. The distinctions which it identifies between merchandising

---

[1] L. Rose, 'James Bond: Licensed to Sell', Forbes, 16 Nov. 2006, available at <http://www.forbes.com/2006/11/16/bond-movie-advertising-tech-media-cx_lr_1116bond.html>.

[2] R. Frankel, 'James Bond or James Brand', 17 Nov. 2006, available at <http://robfrankel.blogspot.com/2006/11/james-bond-or-james-brand.html>.

relating to fictional characters and merchandising involving real people, which is often described as personality merchandising, remain relevant today.

'Character Merchandising' Report Prepared by the International Bureau of the World Intellectual Property Organization (WIPO) WO/INF/108, 1994

(c) Types of Character Merchandising [p. 8]

From a commercial or marketing point of view, character merchandising can probably be dealt with in a single category. However, from the legal point of view it is important to differentiate between the various subjects of merchandising since the scope and duration of legal protection may vary according to the subject involved.

Two main categories exist depending on whether the merchandising involves the use of fictional characters or of real personalities (generally referred to as 'personality merchandising'). Between these two categories, a third hybrid category exists which is generally referred to as 'image merchandising'.

(i) *Merchandising of fictional characters*

This is the older and best-known form of merchandising. It involves the use of the essential personality features (name, image, etc.) of fictional characters in the marketing and/or advertising of goods or services.

Originally, the practice of character merchandising, as an organised system of promotion, developed as a means of exploiting the popularity of cartoon characters, drawings of attractive figures and the like.

The report then goes on to give examples of such fictional characters. These include literary works adapted as cartoons for films or comic strips such as Pinocchio; original cartoon characters from films and comics, such as Mickey Mouse and Batman respectively; cartoon characters created as a marketing tool, for example, in advertisements, 'the jolly green giant'; and puppets or doll characters created for film or TV, such as the Muppets. It adds 'that character merchandising with cartoon characters involves mainly the use of the name, image and appearance of the character'.

The WIPO Report continues by looking at the marketing of real individuals:

(ii) *Personality Merchandising* [p. 9]

This more recent form of merchandising involves the use of the essential attributes (name, image, voice and other personality features) of real persons (in other words, the true identity of an individual) in the marketing and/or advertising of goods and services. In general, the real person whose attributes are 'commercialised' is well known to the public at large; this is the reason why this form of merchandising has sometimes been referred to as 'reputation merchandising'. In fact, from a commercial point of view, merchandisers believe that the main reason for a person to buy low-priced mass produced goods (mugs, scarves, badges, T-shirts, etc.) is not because of the product itself but because the name or image of a celebrity appealing to that person is reproduced on the product.

This category can be subdivided into two forms. The first form consists in the use of the name, image (in two or three dimensions) or symbol of a real person. This form relates mainly to famous persons in the film or music industries. However, persons connected with other fields of activity may be concerned (for example, members of a royal family). As indicated above, it is not so much the product which is of principal importance to the consumer, but rather that the name or image that it bears is the marketing and advertising vehicle. The second form occurs where specialists in certain fields, such as famous sports or music personalities, appear in advertising campaigns in relation to the goods or services. The appeal for the potential consumer is that the personality represented endorses the product or service concerned and is regarded as an expert. Of course, the more the product or service advertised is linked with the activity of the personality, the more the potential consumer will consider that the said product or service is endorsed and approved by that personality (advertising for tennis shoes or rackets by a tennis champion, advertising for an energy drink by a cross-country runner or advertising for high-fidelity equipment or musical instruments by a pop star).

(iii) *Image Merchandising* [pp. 9–10]

This is the most recent form of merchandising. It involves the use of fictional film or television characters played by real actors, in the marketing and advertising of goods or services. In those cases, the public sometimes finds it difficult to differentiate the actor (real person) from the role he plays (character portrayed). Sometimes, however, there is complete association and the real person is referred to and known by the name of the character. The following examples can be given to illustrate this notion:

[The Report's authors then give examples from the film and television industries, including unsurprisingly, James Bond, as well as Crocodile Dundee, Tarzan, Colombo, J.R. in 'Dallas', and McGyver.]

In the case of image merchandising, goods or services will be marketed with the merchandising of distinctive elements of a film or series (appearance and dress of the actor when playing the character coupled with memorable aspects of a scene (for example, introductory scenes of the James Bond films, the appearance and weapons of Rambo or the 'knife scene' in Crocodile Dundee).

The authors of the WIPO report make the point that character merchandising as it is exploited commercially may be taken as a single category, whether or not it involves real or fictional characters. It then goes on to assert that from a legal perspective it is important to differentiate the two, since the protection given to them may vary according to the relevant law. Interestingly, in the UK, the term 'character merchandising' has, with some few exceptions, most prominently in relation to product endorsement, been understood by the courts and many legal commentators as encompassing both merchandising involving fictional characters and also personality merchandising.

7.1.1.2 The protection of personality: commercial and dignitary rights

It may seem surprising that the UK courts make so little distinction between personality and character merchandising. After all, is it not easy to identify interests which real personalities might have in exploiting their images, which will not be shared by fictional characters? To take just one example, real personalities, such as Beckham, might feel the need to separate their public images from their private lives: James Bond will not. In the following extract, Huw Beverley-Smith addresses the elision, in the English courts, of the distinction between character merchandising and the commercial exploitation of personality, arguing that the two should not be confused.

H. Beverley-Smith, *The Commercial Appropriation of Personality* (Cambridge: Cambridge University Press, 2002), pp. 5–6

The problem of appropriation of personality is commonly discussed as an aspect of 'character merchandising', with a distinction usually being drawn between real persons and fictitious characters, although the problem is also commonly referred to as 'personality merchandising', or endorsement. Without dwelling too long on the semantics, it should be noted that each of these phrases is somewhat misleading.

First, a human being is not a 'character', other than in a colloquial sense. Second, the underlying basis for legal liability is substantially different in each case. Character merchandising is a compendious term covering a variety of activities and underlying rights such as copyright, trade marks and business goodwill. In most systems, protection for a fictitious character can often be secured through copyright law which is based on some degree of original creative effort or investment on the part of the creator, or through unfair competition law in its various forms. A 'real' person's image does not usually result from such original or physical effort, and the basis of, and justification for, legal protection are not the same. A third, and related point is that while the unauthorised exploitation of fictitious characters usually results in damage to the creator's purely economic interests, appropriation of personality can affect non-pecuniary or dignitary interests, in addition to any injury to economic interests... Use of the terms 'character merchandising' or 'personality merchandising' reinforces the perception that a person's image is purely an asset, when, in truth, there is a complex interaction between economic and dignitary interests. The fourth point relates to the use of the term 'endorsement'. As will become apparent, the legal notion of an endorsement is rather nebulous and uncertain. Moreover, many unauthorised uses of a person's name or image are made in circumstances, which do not imply that the plaintiff has endorsed products. Consequently, reliance on the term 'endorsement' is unhelpful and liable to be misleading. Finally, it is rare to describe a legal wrong in terms of a particular commercial practice. It is more common to describe a wrong by reference to the interest protected or the nature of a particular kind of conduct such as trespass, negligence, deceit or appropriation of personality. One does not, generally, speak of an infringement of a person's right to merchandise his character.

Since appropriation of personality is better viewed as an autonomous problem and cause of action, it is important to draw a clear distinction between appropriation of personality and the business of character merchandising.

In this extract, Beverley-Smith refers to the contrast between economic interests and dignitary interests. Broadly, economic interests that attach to personalities would cover the right of an individual to exploit his personality, for instance in advertising or product endorsement. By contrast, Beverley-Smith identifies dignitary interests as the interest an individual may have in his reputation, personal privacy, and freedom from mental distress.[3] Interestingly, in other jurisdictions, individuals have rights, which cover both economic and dignitary interests in various combinations.

7.1.1.3 The protection of personality: Germany and the United States

German law has recognized rights to one's own name and image since the early twentieth century. In 1954, the German Federal Supreme court (BGH) also recognized a general

---

[3] H. Beverley-Smith, *The Commercial Appropriation of Personality* (Cambridge: Cambridge University Press, 2002), p. 8.

personality right. It has been suggested that these rights were initially intended to be dignitary rights, that is, designed primarily to protect privacy and to prevent the unwanted or unauthorized use of a person's name or image. However, over the years the German courts have also been increasingly willing to stretch these rights to protect the economic value of those same images. Indeed, in the *Marlene Dietrich* case, in 1999, which concerned unauthorized merchandising of the late actress's name and image, the German courts determined that the economic interests of personality rights might survive after the death of the personality.[4] Nonetheless, it is also generally agreed that the German personality right falls short of offering a general publicity right, a property right in the economic value of one's image such as is available in the United States. In that jurisdiction, there is both a right to privacy and a right to publicity, the latter having been recognized by the Supreme Court in 1977 in the case of *Zacchini v Scripps-Howard Broadcasting Co.*[5] In the United States, the publicity right is seen as primarily concerned with preventing the commercial appropriation of a person's name or image in a way which would cause damage to that image and it is treated as a fully assignable property right. The right to publicity has been given a statutory basis in a number of states including New York and California. Recently, the ECtHR in the case of *Reklos and Davourlis v Greece*[6] recognized that individuals have a right to control their images by virtue of Article 8 of the ECHR, that is the right to respect for private and family life.

7.1.1.4 The protection of personality: the UK

It is generally accepted[7] that in the UK there is no recognition of a right to privacy: although the courts are moving towards the definition of a tort of invasion of privacy. Nor, in the UK, is there a personality right, although, again, some have suggested that the House of Lords decision in *Douglas v Hello!*[8] was tantamount to establishing an 'image right' in the UK since it appeared to allow celebrities and others to licence their images to third parties for their exclusive use.[9] Furthermore, despite the widespread practice of celebrity endorsement and licensing, the domestic courts have been cautious about widening the legal avenues through which an individual might protect the economic worth of his or her image. In particular, as is the case with a right to privacy, the courts have been reluctant to introduce a right of publicity through case law, when the legislature has declined to do so itself. The fact that the Whitford Committee in 1977 considered, but did not regard as feasible, the introduction of a new 'character right' which would fill a perceived gap between the law of copyright and that of passing off, has been cited by the courts, for example by Walker LJ in the *Elvis Presley Trade Marks* case,[10] as support for this cautious approach. Later in this chapter we will consider whether the UK should introduce a publicity or personality right. But it is worth asking ourselves as we go on to look at the law as it applies to character merchandising whether the courts are right to suggest that such a development should be left to legislators. As we have seen, the German courts were willing to take the initiative themselves. Some would argue that by refusing to take similar action, the domestic courts have left real personalities seriously under protected. We should bear this in mind as we go on to look at the relevant law.

---

[4] *Marlene Dietrich* (BGH, 1 Dec. 1999).
[5] *Zacchini v Scripps-Howard Broadcasting Co* 433 US 562 (1977).
[6] App No 1234/05, (ECtHR, 15 Jan. 2009).   [7] See 8.3.4.1.
[8] [2007] UKHL 21.   [9] This is discussed at 8.3.4.1.
[10] [1999] RPC 567 (CA), 581.

FURTHER READING

H. Beverley-Smith, *The Commercial Appropriation of Personality* (Cambridge: Cambridge University Press, 2002), Chapters 2–5, 7.

H. Beverley-Smith, A. Ohly, and A. Lucas-Schloetter, *Privacy, Property and Personality: Civil law perspectives on commercial appropriation* (Cambridge: Cambridge University Press, 2005).

S. Lettmaier, 'Conceptual approaches to protecting the publicity value of athletes in Germany and the United States' (2007) 1(2) International Sports Law Journal (ISLJ) 114–18.

A. McGee and G. Scanlan, 'Phantom intellectual property rights' (2000) 3 IPQ 264.

7.2 THE LEGAL GROUNDS FOR PROTECTING CHARACTER MERCHANDISING

There is the potential for character merchandising to be protected by different intellectual property rights whether the character is real or imagined. Under UK law, an action for passing off and trade mark registration are the most common routes to protecting character merchandising (including personality merchandising). In this section, we will look at both. But first it is necessary to make a brief comment about copyright and character merchandising.

7.2.1 CHARACTER MERCHANDISING AND COPYRIGHT

The limited potential for copyright to protect character merchandising was underlined very early on in *Du Boulay v Du Boulay*,[11] which held that there is no copyright in a name. Subsequent case law in the UK has made it clear that this is the case whether it is the name of a real person or a made-up name of a fictional character.[12] Furthermore, as was pointed out by Laddie J, in the *Elvis Presley Trade Marks* case,[13] no one owns his own likeness, apart from any copyright, which might subsist in a particular reproduction. Perhaps the only circumstance in which copyright may protect character merchandising is if the defendant reproduces the image of a fictional character without permission from the copyright holder (an issue which we will consider later in this chapter).[14]

7.2.2 PASSING OFF AND CHARACTER MERCHANDISING

7.2.2.1 The relationship between passing off and trade mark protection

Until the passage of the 1994 Trade Marks Act, character merchandising, involving both real and fictional characters, was primarily protected against unfair competition by the law of passing off. The previous trade mark regime had offered little in the way of protection for character merchandising primarily because, under the 1938 TMA, it was forbidden

---

[11] (1867–69) LR 2 PC 430; see also *Burberrys v J C Cording & Co Ltd* (1909) 26 RPC 693.
[12] *Elvis Presley Trade Marks*, CA; see also *Mirage Studios v Counter-Feat Clothing* [1991] FSR 145.
[13] *Elvis Presley Trade Marks* [1997] RPC 543 HC.   [14] See below at 7.2.2.5.

for trade mark proprietors to 'traffic' in their marks. The relevance of this prohibition to character merchandising was made clear by the House of Lords decision in the 'Holly Hobbie' case.

American Greetings Corp's Application [1984] 1 WLR 189

The claimant, American Greetings Corporation (AGC), was appealing against a decision by the Trade Mark Registry not to register the mark, 'Holly Hobbie', for a range of products including toiletries and toys. Holly Hobbie was designed by the claimant, which produced greetings cards. She was a child dressed in a pinafore and bonnet and the image had considerable popularity both in the US and the UK. Although Lord Brightman in his decision noted that 'Holly Hobbie' might be registrable for greetings cards and related goods, he believed that to allow the trade mark to be registered for a wider range of goods would constitute trafficking and would therefore not be possible under the 1938 TMA.

> **Lord Brightman, p. 203:**
>
> ...the notion of dealing in a trade mark primarily as a commodity in its own right and not primarily for the purpose of identifying or promoting merchandise in which the proprietor of the mark is interested. If there is no real trade connection between the proprietor of the mark and the licensee or his goods, there is room for the conclusion that the grant of the licence is trafficking in the mark.

One of the more interesting aspects of the 'Holly Hobbie' decision is to be found in the judgment of Lord Bridge. Although he 'reluctantly' agreed with Lord Brightman's decision on trafficking, he also noted that the trafficking provisions of the 1938 TMA were 'apt descriptions of the commercial activity now widely known as "character merchandising"'. He saw as the genesis of the anti-trafficking provisions a concern that were such marks to be registered, the public might be 'hoodwinked' into thinking that the reputation attaching to the registered mark might not be upheld, 'by a mere purchaser of the right to use the mark'. However, his own view was that there was no such danger.

> **Lord Bridge, p. 202:**
>
> Character merchandising deceives nobody. Fictional characters capture the imagination, particularly of children, and can be very successfully exploited in the marketing of a wide range of goods. No one who buys a Mickey Mouse shirt supposes that the quality of the shirt owes anything to Walt Disney Productions.
>
> ...
>
> It is bad enough, in my view, that the whole field of character merchandising will now be wide open to piracy. The protection, if any, of the original inventor of the character will lie in the uncertain remedy of a passing off action. This situation seems likely to generate a mass of difficult and expensive litigation, which cannot be in the public interest. In short, though I can find no escape from section 28(6) of the Act of 1938 [the trafficking provision], I do not hesitate to express my opinion that it has become a complete anachronism and that the sooner it is repealed the better.

It may now seem remarkable that as recently as 1984, the majority of the House of Lords doubted the commercial importance of character merchandising through the mechanism of trade mark licensing. However, it is also worth recognizing that Lord Brightman, in his judgment, was seeking to protect what he considered to be a key function of a trade mark: that is, to guarantee the quality of the goods to which it attaches. In his view, this guarantee would be lost if a trade mark proprietor simply licensed his mark for others to place on merchandise, over which the proprietor had no quality control. In retrospect, it is of course also easy to see that Lord Bridge was being remarkably prescient. But was he being realistic or unduly pessimistic when he concluded that passing off was no barrier against piracy? We will seek to answer this question in the next section of this chapter. Later on, we will go on to consider the extent to which the 1994 TMA has broadened the protection offered to character merchandising.

7.2.2.2 Goodwill and a misrepresentation: 'Uncle Mac', 'Kojak', 'Abba', and the 'Wombles'

One reason for Lord Bridge's pessimism may have been that in 1984, indeed until relatively recently, it was necessary for there to be a common field of activity between the claimant and the defendant for a successful passing off action in relation to character merchandising. This was made clear in the 'Uncle Mac' case decided in 1947. It is also interesting to note, when considering 'Uncle Mac', that although the WIPO report stated that personality marketing came later to the field than the marketing of fictional characters, this has certainly not been the experience in the UK.

McCulloch v Lewis A May (Produce Distributors) Ltd [1947] 2 All ER 845 ('Uncle Mac')

The claimant was a well-known radio personality, who presented the programme, Children's Hour, and was known to his listeners as 'Uncle Mac'. He sued the defendant for passing off when it began marketing a breakfast cereal, aimed at children, under the name 'Uncle Mac'. His claim failed.

Wynn-Parry J, at p. 851:

On the postulate that the plaintiff is not engaged in any degree in producing or marketing puffed wheat, how can the defendant, in using the fancy name used by the plaintiff, be said to be passing off the goods or the business of the plaintiff? I am utterly unable to see any element of passing off in this case. If it were anything, it were libel, as to which I say nothing. Passing off, in my judgment, it certainly is not. If I were to accede to the plaintiff's claim I should, as I see it, not merely be extending quite unjustifiably the scope of the action of passing off, but I should be establishing an entirely new remedy, and that I am quite unprepared to do.

In this case, the court could see no common field between Uncle Mac's activities as a radio presenter and the defendants' trade as manufacturers of cereals. As a result, Uncle Mac lacked the requisite goodwill to bring an action in passing off. Uncle Mac, although a nickname, nonetheless involved the commercial exploitation of a real person. In two later cases,

Tavener Rutledge v Trexapalm[15] and *Wombles v Wombles Skips*,[16] the courts made clear that the need to show a common field of activity was also relevant to fictional characters with made-up names. In addition, the case of *Lyngstad v Anabas*[17] provided a further example of the limits of passing off for the protection of the merchandising of real people. We shall go on to examine each of these cases. As we shall see, the same concerns which led the courts to seek a common field of activity in cases concerning character merchandising have also made it difficult for claimants to prove the presence of a misrepresentation and hence have continued to limit the tort's role in protecting character merchandising.

Tavener Rutledge Ltd v Trexapalm Ltd [1975] FSR 479 ('Kojak')

The case arose out of the well-known (at the time) television show, Kojak, which featured the eponymous New York detective, who had a liking for lollipops. The claimants had been selling 'Kojakpops' for over a year and had considerable goodwill in the products. The defendants had been granted an exclusive licence by Universal Studios, which produced the series, to manufacture and sell confectionary under the name 'Kojak' in the UK. In particular, the defendants sold lollies under the name 'Kojak Lollies', but unlike the claimants had not yet made substantial sales in the UK. The claimants sought an injunction to prevent the defendants from passing off their lollies as those of the claimant. The defendants claimed that their licence was a defence to accusations of passing off. They also argued that since the licence contained provisions for quality control, there was a common field of activity between themselves, the claimant, and Universal Studios, so that, in effect, the claimants would be trading on the studios' goodwill. Walton J noted first that there is no copyright in a word or a name. He went on to say that for the defendants to succeed they had to show that there was a common field of activity between Universal Studios and the claimant.

Walton J, at pp. 483–4:

The relevant activity of the licensor, Universal City Studios, is the production of television serials, doubtless, and one would imagine similar things, films, photographs, possibly cassettes and things of that nature, whereas the relevant field of activity of the plaintiffs in the present action is the production of lollipops. Do those two fields of activity intersect in any such way as would enable the Universal City Studios to claim that, by putting out their lollipops as 'Kojakpops', the plaintiffs were infringing any right of Universal City Studios? In my judgment, the answer to that is in the negative, because there is no relevant field of activity either actual or existing in the mind of the public, which is common to both of them.

[**Walton J** was not persuaded by the defendant's argument that the 'business of what he calls character merchandising has become very well known in our present times and everybody who has a character, whether real or fictional, to exploit, does so by the grant of licences to people who wish to use the name of the real or fictional character'. He commented, at p. 485:]

...there may come a time when the system of character merchandising will have become so well known to the man in the street that immediately he sees 'Kojakpops' he will say to

---

[15] *Tavener Rutledge Ltd v Trexapalm Ltd* [1975] FSR 479.
[16] *Wombles Ltd v Wombles Skips Ltd* [1975] RPC 99.
[17] *Lyngstad v Anabas Products* [1977] FSR 62.

himself: 'They must have a licence from the person who owns the rights in the television series'; but that, by itself, so far as I can see would not be of any assistance to Mr Morcom at all, because that does not carry him home at all. What he would have to go on to show is that it had also become so well known that people in the situation of licensors of these names exercised quality control over any product bearing their name, so that as soon as anybody in the street came to the conclusion that a product was licensed by the owners of some series, such as the 'Kojak' series, he would say to himself not only, 'This must have been licensed by them,' but also, 'and that is a guarantee of its quality.' That point we are miles away from reaching and there is not really a shred of evidence in front of me to that effect.

It followed from this that the claimants succeeded in obtaining an injunction. Two years later, in the 'Abba' case, the court showed a similar unwillingness to accept that there was a wide recognition amongst the public of merchandising activity by famous personalities. In this case, the court's caution in this regard undermined the ability of the claimants to argue that there had been an actionable misrepresentation.

Lyngstad v Anabas Products [1977] FSR 62 ('Abba')

The action was brought by the well-known pop group Abba. Their action for passing off was in respect of the defendants' use of their name and image on a variety of articles: T-shirts, badges, key rings, and so on. Although Oliver J in this case cited the 'Kojak' decision, his approach differed from Walton J in that he focused less on a common field of activity and more on whether there was an actionable misrepresentation. In his judgment, Oliver J noted that the images shown were not those for which the group had a copyright, and therefore the law of copyright did not assist their case. The group was also unsuccessful in its claim in passing off.

Oliver J, at p. 65:

There is no question that the plaintiffs themselves or indeed I think any company connected with them, have at any time marketed in this country any of the articles to which the notice of motion refers...It cannot be claimed on the evidence that what the defendants are doing is causing goods of their manufacture to be confused with goods of the plaintiffs' manufacture, and that indeed is not claimed. What is said here is that the plaintiffs, as entertainers, have built up a reputation which is associated in the public mind with the name and image of the plaintiffs, and that the defendants are exploiting that reputation for their own commercial purposes. This, it is said, is properly the subject matter of an action for passing off.

[In effect, **Oliver J** is suggesting that what the group was complaining of was not passing off but pure unfair competition or misappropriation in the sense that the defendant was reaping what it had not sown. In **Oliver J's** view this was different from a claim in passing off, where claimants are obliged to show goodwill, misrepresentation and damage—he continued at p. 66:]

Essentially what the plaintiffs complain of here is not that there is a possibility of confusion between the defendants' business activities and their activities as singers, but that their activities as singers have generated a public interest which has enabled the defendants to exploit for their own purposes the use of the plaintiffs' photographs and names, and they say that the effect of the defendants doing that is to give to the public the impression that the goods which are being disseminated are in some way associated with, to use a broad term, the plaintiffs, in the sense that the plaintiffs have either licensed them or in some way endorsed them as being proper goods for distribution. It is said that this is something the defendants ought not to do because it may prejudice the plaintiffs' opportunities of doing the same thing themselves, although they have not yet done it or attempted to do it except in the three respects which have been mentioned, that is to say, the distribution of posters, the fan club (if that has anything to do with the plaintiffs, as to which there is no real evidence) and the jigsaw puzzle, which was in any event the subject of a licence negotiated after, I think, the commencement of the conduct complained of in this action.

While citing the 'Kojak' case, as we have seen, Oliver J suggested that the key reason for his decision was that there is no actionable misrepresentation by the defendants, rather than that a common field of activity was absent. In other words, on the facts, the claimants were unable to persuade the court that the public would be confused into thinking that the goods they purchased with the 'Abba' name or image were the result of a licensing arrangement with the claimants. The third case we shall examine, the 'Wombles' case, highlights the difficulty a claimant will have in a character-merchandising case of showing both that it has the requisite goodwill and can prove that there has been an actionable misrepresentation.

Wombles Ltd v Wombles Skips Ltd [1975] RPC 99 (the 'Wombles')

The 'Wombles' are mythical creatures who live on Wimbledon common and help to keep it clean. The Wombles were the subject of a popular book and television series. The author of the original book had assigned her copyright to the claimants, who in turn had licensed a number of firms to produce goods carrying the name and/or image of the Wombles. The defendant provided skips for rubbish and debris under the name 'Wombles'. It had deliberately chosen 'Wombles' as a name because of its connection with 'cleaning up'. The claimant's passing off action failed because of the absence of a common field of activity.

Walton J, at pp. 101–2:

It seems to me that where what is alleged is that one person is passing off his goods or business—and here it would be the business—as the business of somebody else, there must be a common field of activity. It seems to me that that common field of activity may be one which is actual, in which case there is no room for any possibility or argument at all, or it may be one—and this is very frequently the case—which is not actual, but which is reasonably assumed by the reasonable man from the use of the same or a similar name...

In the current case is there a common field of activity in the sense in which I have above-defined it between the plaintiff Wombles Limited and the defendant Wombles Skips Limited? I regret to say that in my opinion there is no such common field of activity. What the plaintiff is doing is to license people use of some of the copyright material comprised in and surrounding the Wombles. That in most cases, if indeed not in all of them, involves the use of a picture of one of the Wombles, whether it be a picture of Great Uncle Bulgaria, Tobermory, or any of the other well-known Wombles. But there is no such similar picture on any of the skips...

It seems to me that the only conceivable ground for suggesting any business connection between the plaintiff and the defendant is that the characters, albeit mythical, are characters who clean up premises, but I do not think that anybody seeing a 'Womble' skip, albeit in the

> road, albeit on one of the defendant's lorries, would think that there really was any connection between that and any business carried on by the plaintiff. The plaintiff's business is simply to licence copyright reproductions. It may be a defect in the law that, having invented the characters known as the 'Wombles', the authoress has not a complete monopoly of the use of that invented word, which she could then assign to the plaintiffs, but such is the law and that being so its seems to me I must in fact dismiss this motion.

Although his decision was grounded firmly on the fact that there was no common field of activity between the parties, Walton J also noted that as a result there was no actionable misrepresentation. It is certainly true that Walton J appears to have retreated from his view, set out in the 'Kojak' case, that any widespread public understanding of character merchandising, especially of fictional characters, was 'a long way off'. Yet, he still felt unable to fashion a judgment which would enable the claimant to prevent the misappropriation of the 'Wombles' name by the defendant. Does this seem a fair result for the claimant? Certainly, to Walton J, the result implied that there might be a 'defect' in the law. We now turn to the question of whether and to what extent this 'defect' has been remedied by subsequent judgments.

7.2.2.3 The need for a misrepresentation and damage: *Stringfellow*

We have seen in the chapter on passing off,[18] that by the time of the decisions in the 'Abba' and 'Wombles' cases, the courts were beginning to focus on finding an actionable misrepresentation rather than searching for a common field of activity in order to prove passing off. Indeed, shortly after these decisions, Lord Diplock in the 'Advocaat' case[19] confirmed that there could be passing off even though 'the plaintiff and the defendant were not competing traders in the same line of business'. The *Stringfellow* case in 1984 was perhaps the first case concerning character merchandising which explicitly made the break from seeking a common field and instead held that an actionable misrepresentation and damage or the likelihood of damage were key to a successful action in passing off.

Stringfellow v McCain Foods (GB) Ltd [1984] RPC 501

Peter Springfellow (S) had for several years run nightclubs. In 1980, he opened a London nightclub and restaurant called 'Stringfellows' using a distinctive butterfly logo accompanied by the name 'Stringfellows' in signature form. 'Disco dancing' took place on a floor of black glass accompanied by flashing lights. Stringfellows attracted wide publicity from the outset. As a result, by 1983, the club was widely known amongst a large cross-section of the population as a nightclub and restaurant with a high-class reputation. The defendants made and sold frozen foods and were pioneers in the field of oven ready chips. They developed a long, thin oven-ready chip called 'Stringfellows' which they claimed was a cross between the names 'Shoestring' and 'Longfellows'. The defendants advertised their product on television against a background of music and disco dancing taking place in a 'suburban' kitchen. The claimant sued for passing off. There was some evidence that people thought S had lent his name to the chips for money.

---

18 At 4.2.3.5.
19 *Erven Warnink BV v J Townend & Sons (Hull) Ltd* [1979] AC 731, 742.

In the High Court, Whitford J found that there was passing off because the club had a reputation, a significant number of the public might be confused, and, because as it was a high-class club, its reputation would be damaged if it was associated with oven-ready chips. The defendants appealed. Slade LJ agreed that the club had a wide reputation. He also accepted the choice of name by the defendants was honest. According to Slade LJ, the crucial questions were: (1) whether McCain could be said to have been guilty of any misrepresentation and (2) if so, whether it was a reasonably foreseeable consequence of such misrepresentation that it would cause actual damage to the claimant's business or goodwill (p. 535). Slade LJ applied Lord Diplock's five-part definition of passing off in 'Advocaat'. In relation to McCain's use of the word 'Stringfellows', he held there was no passing off because by itself such use was unlikely to lead to a reasonable belief amongst the public that S and his club were associated with chips in any way. Slade LJ accepted that the television advert did give rise to some confusion because of the night-club setting.

Slade LJ, at p. 538:

Accordingly, albeit with some misgivings, I would accept that, on the evidence, this form of advertisement did, unwittingly, involve a degree of misrepresentation alleged in the statement of claim, in that its form would lead a number of persons who knew the name of the Club—though I cannot think a large number—into the mistaken belief that the chips were connected in the course of trade with the plaintiffs or that the plaintiffs were collaborating with McCain in marketing them.

S had succeeded in persuading the court that of the three conditions needed for passing off—goodwill, a misrepresentation, and damage—the first two had been proved. But a crucial question remained: had S persuaded the court that as a result of the misrepresentation there was actual damage or the likelihood of damage? It was noted by Slade LJ (at p. 541) that no evidence of actual damage, such as a fall in numbers visiting the club, had been adduced by the claimant. So the question revolved on whether there was a likelihood of damage.

Evidence of three 'experts' in merchandising suggested that with regard 'to modern practices' including franchising, merchandising, sponsorship, and endorsement, the association of the club with a 'hard baked' oven chip, would damage its potential to profit from such activities. Slade LJ noted that there were two questions to address. First, would the claimant now be able to merchandise the mark if there had been no television commercial? Secondly, did the television advertisement prejudice the claimant's ability to profit from such advertising in the future? Slade LJ gave the following answers (pp. 544–6):

As to (i), presumably in view of their fears of tarnishing their image, the plaintiffs would only wish to grant licences (if at all) in connection with goods of a luxury or 'up-market' variety, such as clothes or jewelry. But how many, if any, persons marketing goods of this nature would expect to derive any potential benefit from the use of the name of a nightclub, albeit a celebrated nightclub? The name 'Stringfellows' is not a fancy name. It is a surname which, at least in some parts of the country, is not an uncommon one. Nor is it a name connected with a person, such as a sportsman who has a particular expertise and for the purpose of his job requires particular equipment, the quality of which he can endorse by lending his name. So far as the evidence shows, the plaintiffs possess no relevant copyright (save perhaps their logo) in connection with which they can grant licences. In all the circumstances I do not think it surprising that Mr Stringfellow, for all his business acumen, had never contemplated the exploitation of the name in this manner until the present dispute arose... In my opinion, the evidence as a whole gives no solid basis for inferring that, but for the television advertisement, the plaintiffs would have been in a position profitably to exploit merchandising rights in the name 'Stringfellows'.

However, even if that conclusion were unjustified, I would still take the view that there is not sufficient evidence that the mere showing of the television advertisement has prejudiced, or is really likely to prejudice, such chances of profitable exploitation of merchandising rights as the plaintiffs may possess. It seems to me that, in regard to this head of alleged potential damage, one is in the field of pure speculation and that this is not enough to ground an action for passing off, particularly against an innocent defendant...

If, however, one has regard to the broader aspects of this claim, there is another side of the coin. The plaintiffs, as a matter of law, can claim no monopoly in the use of the surname Stringfellow, or indeed in the use of the unregistered word 'Stringfellows'. The law does not encourage any such monopoly. McCain or any other persons (albeit with full knowledge of the plaintiffs' prior use) are perfectly free to use that same word in marketing or advertising their goods, provided only that they are not thereby in breach of contract or guilty of passing off, within the principles laid down by the Advocaat case, or of some other tort. Any such use may well lead some uninformed, perhaps unreflective, members of the public to the mistaken belief that there is some connection between the goods in question and the Club, however far apart from that of a high-class nightclub the nature of the goods may be. Experience in the present case has shown that much. Nevertheless, even if it considers that there is a limited risk of confusion of this nature, the court should not, in my opinion, readily infer the likelihood of resulting damage to the plaintiffs, as against an innocent defendant in a completely different line of business. In such a case the onus falling on plaintiffs to show that damage to their business reputation is in truth likely to ensue and to cause them more than a minimal loss is in my opinion a heavy one. I have said nothing about the position which might have arisen in this case if there had been any reason to question the reputability of McCain or of their new product, since these have never been in doubt. As things are, the onus has not in my opinion been discharged.

On these grounds he rejected the claimants' appeal. Once again, we see the UK courts, as in so many other areas of intellectual property law, loathe to grant a monopoly where one has not hitherto existed. In this case, Slade LJ seemed to be suggesting that by accepting there had been passing off, the court would effectively be granting the claimant a monopoly in the use of his name 'Stringfellow' for marketing goods and services other than those provided by his nightclub. To justify his finding that there had been no passing off, Slade LJ doubted that the claimant had been able to show an actionable misrepresentation and was clear that there was no evidence of or likelihood of damage. Does this seem a reasonable judgment today, when we are inured to the idea that individuals who find fame in one area of commercial endeavor are often quick to exploit it in others? Furthermore, as was pointed out by Carty,[20] were Slade LJ to have found otherwise and allowed Stringfellow to protect the reputation in his name *tout court*, would this have been tantamount to recognizing dilution as a head of damage in passing off: an outcome which as we have seen continues to be controversial?[21]

[20] H. Carty, 'Dilution and passing off: Cause for concern' [1996] LQR 632.
[21] See 4.2.5.4.

7.2.2.4 Character merchandising in Australia: a different approach to passing off

The outcome of the *Stringfellow* case seemed to confirm Lord Bridge's comment in 'Holly Hobbie', decided that same year, that without a remedy in trade mark infringement, character merchandisers were left with 'the uncertain remedy of a passing off action'. A number of key judgments by the Australian courts, concerning both real personalities and fictional characters, demonstrated that passing off might be sufficiently flexible to protect character merchandising. Starting with a case concerning real personalities, *Henderson v Radio Corp*,[22] the Australian court rejected the need to show a common field of activity and in *Pacific Dunlop v Hogan*[23] (which was a hybrid case of character and personality merchandising), it jettisoned the need to show an actionable misrepresentation.

Henderson v Radio Corporation Pty Ltd [1969] RPC 218

The claimants were well known professional ballroom dancers. They sued for passing off when the defendant without their authorization reproduced their image on the cover of a gramophone record entitled, 'Strictly for Dancing'. The case reached the Appellate Jurisdiction of the High Court of NSW. In its judgment, the Court (at p. 234) criticized the proposition in *McCulloch v May*, that to succeed in passing off it was necessary to show a common field of activity.

> The present case provides an illustration of the unjust consequences of such a principle. For the purposes of this part of the argument, the appellant concedes that it is falsely representing that the respondents recommend, favour or support its dance music record, but it claims that because the respondents are not engaged or likely to be engaged in making or selling gramophone records, it is entitled to appropriate their names and reputations for its own commercial advantage and that the court has no power to prevent it doing so. It would be a grave defect in the law if that were so.
>
> In our view, once it is proved that A. is falsely representing his goods as the goods of B., or his business to be the same as or connected with the business of B, the wrong of passing off has been established and B. is entitled to relief.

Having rejected the need for a common field of activity,[24] the Australian courts in the later case, *Pacific Dunlop v Hogan*, went on to consider the nature of the misrepresentation necessary in cases of character merchandising.

Pacific Dunlop v Hogan (1989) 87 ALR 14

Hogan had starred in the popular film 'Crocodile Dundee'. His role in the film was an extension of his own personality, which was widely known, not least through his appearances in television commercials. The defendants had produced a television

---

[22] *Henderson v Radio Corporation Pty Ltd* [1969] RPC 218.
[23] (1989) 87 ALR 14.
[24] This principle was extended to fictional characters in *Hogan v Koala Dundee Pty Ltd* (1988) 83 ALR 187.

advertisement for a make of shoes which 'parodied' a scene from the film, known as the 'knife scene'. Hogan claimed for passing off. The Federal Court of Australia found for Hogan, even though the character in the advert and the scene itself, although evocative of the film, were obviously not the real thing and were being used by the defendant to 'grab peoples attention' rather than to suggest that Hogan was advertising their shoes (at p. 32). As held by Beaumont J, it was not fatal to the case that Hogan had been unable to show any causal connection between the misrepresentation by the defendant and damage to his own reputation. Rather, according to Burchett J, the cause of action for passing off is complete as soon as the relevant misrepresentation is made, even though no actual deception and damage to the claimant can be shown.

> ### Burchett J, at p. 47:
>
> In my opinion, the vagueness of the suggestion conveyed in this case is not sufficient to save it. The vagueness is not incompatible with great effectiveness. It would be unfortunate if the law merely prevented a trader using the primitive club of misrepresentation, while leaving him free to employ the more sophisticated rapier of suggestion, which may deceive more completely. In my opinion, the deployment in circumstances of the present kind of techniques of persuasion, designed to influence prospective customers in favour of the trader or his products upon the basis of some underlying assumption that is false, may be held to be misleading or deceptive or likely to mislead or deceive... may [also] be held to be passing off.

There may be an argument that the 'Hogan' decision, by rejecting the necessity of showing that the defendant's misrepresentation would lead consumers to believe that there is in fact a connection between its goods and the claimant, goes some way to transforming the law of passing off into a new tort of unfair competition based on the principle of unjust enrichment. But does the case actually go any further than later decisions by the English courts, for instance as in the 'Elderflower Champagne' case?[25] After all, in this case it was held that passing off might occur even if the damage is caused merely by the association of the claimant's mark with the defendant's mark. In other words, does the 'Hogan' decision embrace the idea of dilution, which was rejected by the judge in *Stringfellow*? If so, it is an interesting question as to why the English courts thus far have not applied the judgment in 'Elderflower Champagne' and its apparent recognition of dilution as a head of damage to cases involving character merchandising.

Another Australian case relevant to the marketing of fictional characters was *Children's Television Workshop Inc v Woolworths (New South Wales) Limited*.[26] Here the courts were willing to accept that the unauthorized use by the defendants of the 'Muppets' amounted to passing off because there would be public awareness that the goods would have been created and licensed by someone who had a business interest in putting them on the market. In this case, licensing would extend both to the copyright in the characters image as well as to the use of the characters' names. This decision differed as we know from that in the 'Kojak' case, where the court doubted that the public's awareness of the use of licensing in character merchandising was sufficient to lead to an actionable misrepresentation. It also differed from the 'Wombles' case in which it was held that there would be no passing off if only a name is taken. As we shall now see, the limited approach taken by the English courts apparently changed with the decision in *Mirage Studios v Counter-Feat Clothing*, which cited with approval the Australian decisions.

---

[25] *Taittinger SA v Albev Ltd* (Discovery) [1992] FSR 647.   [26] [1981] RPC 187.

7.2.2.5 The UK courts recognize character merchandising: the case of the 'Ninja Turtles'

Mirage Studios v Counter-Feat Clothing Company Limited [1991] FSR 145 (the 'Ninja Turtles' case)

An interim injunction was sought by the claimants to restrain the use of four cartoon characters on the grounds that their reproduction constituted either a breach of copyright or passing off. The characters, the Teenage Mutant Ninja Turtles, were at the time 'a marketing phenomenon' (at p. 147), earning hundreds and millions of dollars in the US. They achieved similar success in the UK. The creators of the cartoon had formed a company, Mirage Studios, to exploit the marketing potential of the turtles. The defendants, the Counter-Feat Clothing Company Limited (CCL) licensed characters from the owners of copyrights and appointed 'manufacturing agents'. They asked for a licence to merchandise the Ninja Turtles when the phenomenon began, but the licence had already been awarded elsewhere. CCL then sought to merchandise turtles without infringing the rights of the claimants, by commissioning an artist to design humanoid turtles which were not identical to the claimant's own. The claimant produced evidence that there had been confusion with the defendants' T-shirts, which the public believed had been licensed. The judgment of Sir Nicolas Browne-Wilkinson V-C addressed the action both in relation to copyright and passing off.

> **Sir Nicolas Browne-Wilkinson V-C, at p. 148:**
>
> Character merchandising is an industry which has grown in sophistication over the comparatively recent past. The owners of the copyright in such cartoon characters as the Mutant Turtles licence their use and the use of the name of these fictitious characters and the reproduction of them on merchandise and goods. The return to the owner of the copyright, the creator of the character, is normally in the form of royalty payments. Those rights are extremely valuable in a case where the success of the underlying cartoon, video and television is as great as it has been in the present case; the royalties run into hundreds of millions of dollars.

The V-C then described how the creators of the Ninja Turtles, 'following a well-known path', had appointed 'worldwide' agents to licence the exploitation of the Turtles. At the time of the action, 150 licenses had been granted in the UK for the use of the Turtles' name and image. The V-C then employed the principles of *American Cyanamid*[27] to decide whether or not a pre-trial injunction should be granted. He believed that the claimants did have an arguable case in both copyright and passing off. He then considered whether in the absence of a pre-trial injunction, damages would be an adequate remedy if the claimants were to succeed at trial, continuing at p. 152:

> The loss likely to be suffered by the plaintiffs is of two kinds... First, they will lose royalties in the sense that goods which would be or might be manufactured under licence from them will go elsewhere and also the amount of royalties that they can seek to get from those who do take licenses from them is likely to be reduced since the market will not be an exclusive one.

---

[27] *American Cyanamid Co v Ethicon* [1974] FSR 312 (see 13.5.1).

The second type of damage they will suffer will, it is said, be loss of control over the quality of the garments on which reproductions of the Ninja Turtles and related pictures are used. The evidence is (and I think this is uncontroversial) that the value of a name or characters such as these is linked to maintaining the quality of the goods to which it is attached. If the goods go down-market or are poorly made, that rubs off on the value of the copyright in the character and thereby reduces its value. The loss of royalties head of damage, though possibly difficult to quantify, is certainly capable of quantification. The loss of reputation through bad quality products is more difficult. Certainly, I have been shown products which do not indicate that the Turtle characters licensed by the defendants are always being applied to very high-class products. It is difficult to know how one would set about at the trial quantifying that.

[The V-C then continued, at p. 154:]

The defence put forward, if I may say so with great skill by Miss Vitoria on behalf of the defendant, is primarily a legal one. She says that the plaintiffs have not shown even an arguable case, either in copyright or in passing off. In the event, I do not mean to say much about the claim based on copyright. The difficulties surrounding any claim by the plaintiff based in copyright are primarily two. First, there is the rule in copyright that you can have no copyright in a name, and on that basis it is said that Teenage Mutant Ninja Turtles, or Ninja Turtles, are names and not subject to any copyright. The point seems to me not altogether easy to say whether a descriptive invented name is to be categorised as a name or as a description. The second and more fundamental difficulty in copyright is the saying that 'there is no copyright in ideas'. For myself, I find it difficult to determine what that phrase means in the present context. As I have said, although there are similarities in the graphic reproduction of the defendants' product to those in the plaintiffs' product, they are mainly reproductions of a concept, of the humanoid turtle of an aggressive nature. But whether that permits a claim in copyright or not seems to me to be a very open question; there is certainly an arguable case in copyright. I would not like to say what the final outcome of any case based in copyright would be.

[The V-C concluded that the claimants' case was stronger in relation to passing off. He then applied (at p. 155), **Lord Diplock's** five elements of passing off as set out in the 'Advocaat' case.]

Applying those requirements to the present case, first, has there been a misrepresentation? The critical evidence in this case is that a substantial number of the buying public now expect and know that where a famous cartoon or television character is reproduced on goods, that reproduction is the result of a licence granted by the owner of the copyright or owner of other rights in that character. Mr Smith, the defendant, accepted that evidence subject to this: he said that was only true where the reproduced matter was an exact reproduction of the character in the cartoon or television show, whereas in his case the defendants' turtles were different. I cannot accept that. If, as the evidence here shows, the public mistake the defendants' turtles for those which might be called genuine plaintiffs' Turtles, once they have made that mistake they will assume that the product in question has been licensed to use the Turtles on it. That is to say, they will connect what they mistakenly think to be the plaintiffs' Turtles with the plaintiffs. To put on the market goods, which the public mistake for the genuine article, necessarily involves a misrepresentation to the public that they are genuine. On the evidence in this case, the belief that the goods are genuine involves a further misrepresentation, namely that they are licensed.

[The V-C then asked (at p. 155) whether it was reasonably foreseeable that the defendant's actions would cause injury to the claimants' goodwill.]

In my judgment, that is the critical question in the present case. What is the plaintiffs' business or goodwill? Mirage Studios are plainly in business as the creators and marketers of cartoons, videos and films of their characters, the Ninja Turtles. But the evidence is quite clear that that is only part of their business: their business also includes the turning to profit of those characters by licensing the reproduction of them on goods sold by other people. A major part of their business income arises from royalties to be received from such licensing enterprise. In relation to the drawings of Ninja Turtles as they appear in cartoons, *etc.*, there is a copyright which can be infringed. If one wishes to take advantage of the Ninja character it is necessary to reproduce the Ninja Turtle and thereby the concept, bizarre and unusual as it is, of the Teenage Mutant Turtle becomes a marketable commodity. It is in that business that the plaintiffs are engaged.

That dual nature of the plaintiffs' business (namely both the creation and exploitation of the cartoons and films themselves and the licensing of the right to use those creations) is in my judgment important. As I have said, if others are able to reproduce or apparently reproduce the Turtles without paying licence royalties to the plaintiffs, they will lose the royalties. Since the public associates the goods with the creator of the characters, the depreciation of the image by fixing the Turtle picture to inferior goods and inferior materials may seriously reduce the value of the licensing right. This damage to an important part of the plaintiffs' business is therefore plainly foreseeable.

The fifth of Lord Diplock's requirements is that foreseen damage actually occurs, or will probably do so. Again, in my judgment that is manifestly clear in the present case.

[The V-C then looked at the relevant case law. He approved the approach taken to character merchandising in Australia in *Children's Television Workshop v Woolworths*, at p. 157:]

In my judgment, the law as developed in Australia is sound. There is no reason why a remedy in passing off should be limited to those who market or sell the goods themselves. If the public is misled in a relevant way as to a feature or quality of the goods as sold, that is sufficient to found a cause of action in passing off brought by those people with whom the public associate that feature or that quality which has been misrepresented.

The V-C then turned to the relevant UK decisions in relation to character merchandising. He noted that the 'Wombles' case differed from the present case, because in the former only the name, which had no copyright protection, had been appropriated by the defendants. By contrast, here, the claimants were licensing copyright works. He then differentiated the present case from the 'Kojak' decision both because the latter had turned on the fact that there was no common field of activity and also because Walton J did not accept that the public was sufficiently aware of the licensing business. Finally, the V-C considered the decision in 'Abba'. Once again he held that there were crucial differences with the present action because, in the 'Abba' case it was simply the use of the name which had been relied on by the claimant.

Sir Nicolas Browne-Wilkinson V-C, at p. 159:

In my judgment the three English cases do not touch on a case such as the present where the plaintiff clearly has copyright in the drawings and is in business on a large scale in this country in licensing the use of the copyright in those drawings. The defendant is misrepresenting to the public that his drawings are the drawings of the plaintiffs or are licensed by the plaintiffs. I can see no reason why, in those circumstances, the defendants should be allowed to misrepresent his goods in that way. I therefore consider that if the case went to trial, the plaintiffs' case in passing off would succeed.

Following the decision in the 'Ninja Turtles' case, there was a widespread belief amongst those involved with character merchandising that the courts had finally recognized its value and were affording it commensurate legal protection. However, there were two assumptions underlying the judgment which suggested this was not necessarily the case. First, what differentiated this action from earlier cases was that it involved the licensing of a specific intellectual property right: copyright. The V-C made it clear that if the case had involved only a name, then the principles in the 'Kojak', 'Abba', and 'Wombles' cases would have been applied. The second assumption made by the V-C was that the public was sufficiently aware of character merchandising so that there would be an actionable (and damaging) misrepresentation following the defendant's sale of the T-shirts. The Court of Appeal addressed the 'Ninja Turtles' decision in the *Elvis Presley Trade Marks* case.[28] It made clear that the V-C's judgment stood on the particular facts: first that the claimants were licensing a copyright work rather than simply a name and second that a claim that the public was aware of the practice of licensing, while perhaps true in this case, could not simply be assumed in all situations.

The limits of the 'Ninja Turtles' decision were amply illustrated by the 'Spice Girls' case.[29] This case mirrored the facts of the 'Abba' case, in that the Spice Girls, a pop group, were unsuccessful in preventing the defendant from publishing an 'unofficial' sticker collection which carried the name and photographs of the group. The court did not believe that the public would assume that the pop group had authorized the merchandising of the stickers. Is it surprising that despite the extraordinary growth in the value of character merchandising, which has certainly been acknowledged by the courts in successive judgments, traders may still appropriate others' fame for their own profit without cost? Once we are aware of the limits of the 'Ninja Turtles' decision for character merchandising, we may also understand why this is possible, but we may not approve.[30] Certainly, it seems possible to maintain that, even following 'Ninja Turtles' the UK courts have scarcely travelled as far as those in Australia in adapting passing off to the needs of character merchandising.

7.2.2.6 Passing off and false endorsement

We pointed earlier to the fact that the English courts generally elide the distinction between fictional and real personalities when deciding cases involving character merchandising. Exceptionally, Laddie J's decision in *Irvine v Talksport* drew a clear distinction between the two. In the same decision, Laddie J markedly increased the protection which passing off would afford in cases of false endorsement.

Irvine v Talksport Ltd [2002] EWHC 367 (Ch)

Eddie Irvine, the claimant, was a well-known and successful Formula 1 (F1) racing car driver, whose most successful year was 1999. The defendant, Talksport, ran an eponymous radio station in the UK. In the past it had been known as 'Talk Radio' but in 1999 it decided to concentrate on sport and hence its change of name. In that same year it obtained the rights to live broadcast coverage of the F1 Grand Prix World

---

[28] *Elvis Presley Trade Marks* [1999] RPC 567 (CA).
[29] *Halliwell v Panini SpA*, an unreported case mentioned at (1997) 8(5) Ent LR E94–5.
[30] See for example, J. Davis, 'The king is dead: Long live the king' [2000] CLJ 33.

Championship. It also embarked on a promotional campaign. Part of this campaign involved the production of a number of boxed packs which were sent to 1,000 individuals who were likely advertisers on the station. One of these boxed packs concentrated on F1 racing. It contained, *inter alia*, a brochure. On the front of the brochure Eddie Irvine was shown holding a radio carrying the words, 'Talk Radio'. In fact, in the original photograph he had been holding a mobile phone, but the photograph had been manipulated by the advertising agency retained by Talksport. Irvine alleged that the distribution of the photograph was an actionable passing off (he did not have any rights in the photograph) and sued for damages, since the defendant had already undertaken not to distribute the photograph further. At the start of his judgment, Laddie J drew a distinction between endorsement, which was the concern of the current action, and other kinds of merchandising.

Laddie J:

9. When someone endorses a product or service he tells the relevant public that he approves of the product or service or is happy to be associated with it. In effect he adds his name as an encouragement to members of the relevant public to buy or use the service or product. Merchandising is rather different. It involves exploiting images, themes or articles which have become famous. To take a topical example, when the recent film, *Star Wars Episode 1* was about to be exhibited, a large number of toys, posters, garments and the like were put on sale, each of which bore an image of or reproduced a character or object in the film. The purpose of this was to make available a large number of products which could be bought by members of the public who found the film enjoyable and wanted a reminder of it. The manufacture and distribution of this type of spin-off product is referred to as merchandising. It is not a necessary feature of merchandising that members of the public will think the products are in any sense endorsed by the film makers or actors in the film. Merchandised products will include some where there is a perception of endorsement and some where there may not be, but in all cases the products are tied into and are a reminder of the film itself. An example of merchandising is the sale of memorabilia relating to the late Diana, Princess of Wales. A porcelain plate bearing her image could hardly be thought of as being endorsed by her, but the enhanced sales which may be achieved by virtue of the presence of the image is a form of merchandising.

In this case, counsel for Mr Irvine argued that as a 'false endorsement case', it fell 'squarely within the modern application of the law of passing off'. Conversely, counsel for the defence relied on the Court of Appeal decision in *Elvis Presley*, to the effect that the claimant was attempting to argue that he had an independent 'character right' that should be protected. This was something which Simon Brown LJ had rejected as a cause of action in the 'Elvis' case.[31]

Laddie J then went on to ask whether the claimant did have a case in passing off stemming from the false endorsement. He began by suggesting that over the years, the law of passing off had responded to changes in the nature of trade. Remarkably, given its advanced age, it was agreed by Laddie J and counsel for the claimant, that the most recent case of false endorsement in England was the 'Uncle Mac' case which, as we have seen, foundered on lack of a common field of activity between the claimant and the defendant. Laddie J also noted

---

[31] See below at 7.2.3.3.

that this finding had been considered but had not been followed in *Henderson v Radio Corp*, where, as we have also seen, the court had held that there was no need for a common field of activity. The Australian case, according to Laddie J, illustrated the growing importance of passing off when applied to character merchandising.

Laddie J:

38. ...the law of passing off now is of greater width than as applied by Wynne-Parry J in *McCulloch v May* that if someone acquires a valuable reputation or goodwill, the law of passing off will protect it from unlicensed use by other parties. Such use will frequently be damaging in the direct sense that it will involve selling inferior goods or services under the guise that they are from the claimant. But the action is not restricted to protecting against that sort of damage. The law will vindicate the claimant's exclusive right to the reputation or goodwill. It will not allow others to so use goodwill as to reduce, blur or diminish its exclusivity. It follows that it is not necessary to show that the claimant and the defendant share a common field of activity or that sales of products or services will be diminished either substantially or directly, at least in the short term. Of course there is still a need to demonstrate a misrepresentation because it is that misrepresentation which enables the defendant to make use or take advantage of the claimant's reputation.

39. Not only has the law of passing off expanded over the years, but the commercial environment in which it operates is in a constant state of flux. Even without the evidence given at the trial in this action, the court can take judicial notice of the fact that it is common for famous people to exploit their names and images by way of endorsement. They do it not only in their own field of expertise but, depending on the extent of their fame or notoriety, wider afield also. It is common knowledge that for many sportsmen, for example, income received from endorsing a variety of products and services represent a very substantial part of their total income. The reason large sums are paid for endorsement is because, no matter how irrational it may seem to a lawyer, those in business have reason to believe that the lustre of a famous personality, if attached to their goods or services, will enhance the attractiveness of those goods or services to their target market. In this respect, the endorsee is taking the benefit of the attractive force which is the reputation or goodwill of the famous person.

Laddie J believed that manufacturers and retailers recognized the realities of the marketplace when they paid for well-known personalities to endorse their goods, and in his view the law of passing off should do likewise. He then went on to assert that the three elements needed to support an action in passing off were entirely compatible with a case of false endorsement. Irvine could be said to have a substantial reputation or goodwill because of the popularity of F1 motor racing, the amount of publicity which surrounded it and following from that, the considerable extent to which drivers were paid to endorse products. In particular, 1999 had been a highly successful year for Mr Irvine whose professional and personal life had attracted an immense amount of press coverage, thus enabling him to earn considerable sums from endorsing products. Laddie J concluded on the first point:

57. ...that the only reasonable inference is that those who designed this promotion knew of Mr Irvine's fame and wanted it to be attached to the launch of the new sports-related programme.

Moving on to the misrepresentation, Laddie J held that the actions of the defendant created a false message which would be understood by a not insignificant section of its market to mean that its radio programme or station had been endorsed, recommended, or approved of by Mr Irvine, and in particular would 'convey the message to the audience that Talk Radio was so good that it was endorsed and listened to by Mr Irvine'. As for damage, although the defendants argued that the brochure had only gone to 1,000 recipients, the damage to Mr Irvine's reputation might be 'negligible in direct money terms but the potential for long term damage' was considerable. Passing off against the defendant was proved.

7.2.2.7 False endorsement and damages

Following the judgment in *Irvine v Talksport*, Laddie J held a further hearing to assess the amount of damages owed by the defendant.[32] Mr Irvine told the court that he had entered into four endorsement agreements in 1999, including one with Tommy Hilfiger. That agreement alone had netted him £75,000. According to Mr Irvine:[33]

> ...although I am relatively keen to endorse products, there is and was in 1999 a price below which I would not consider endorsing the product. This is because I would not want it to be known that my endorsement fee was a low figure. Word would soon get around and it could devalue my image and market rate.

Mr Irvine then calculated the cost of an actual endorsement by him for Talksport which took into account both the false endorsement as well as 'the non-fashionable image of Talk Radio' and produced evidence to support his claim. He argued that a 'reasonable company' in the defendant's position would have been prepared to spend by agreement £50.00 per brochure. Laddie J rejected this line of argument. Instead, he held that the correct approach to finding a reasonable royalty or licence fee would be to treat the parties as if they were negotiating at arms length and to try to find an amount that would have served both their legitimate interests. Even though he accepted that Eddie Irvine 'would not get out of bed' to make such an endorsement, he went on to conclude that 'erring, as it appears to me on the generous side, I would have thought a reasonable figure is £2,000 and I will so order'.[34]

Following the judge's findings, the defendant appealed regarding the finding of liability and the claimant cross appealed on the issue of damages. The Court of Appeal upheld Laddie J's judgment on passing off, but allowed the claimant's cross appeal on damages. It agreed that the approach to be followed in assessing damages was to arrive at a reasonable fee for Irvine's endorsement of the defendant's radio station. Furthermore, Laddie J was correct to set the level of damages at what the defendant's would have to pay 'to do lawfully what was done unlawfully'. However, as the Court of Appeal noted, Laddie J had declined to accept the claimant's evidence as to what that fee should be. Accepting that evidence, the Court of Appeal found that Eddie Irvine would have expected at least £25,000 to endorse a product in 1999 and this should be the level of damages paid by the defendant.

There are at least two interesting issues that arise from the *Irvine* decision. The first concerns who might take exception to a false endorsement. In his judgment Laddie J differentiated cases of false endorsement from the facts in *Elvis Presley*. In relation to the singer, he

---

[32] *Irvine v Talksport Ltd* (Damages) [2002] EWHC 539 (Ch), [2003] EMLR 6.
[33] Quoted in *Irvine v Talksport Ltd* [2003] FSR 35 (CA), 60.
[34] *Irvine v Talksport* (Damages), 557.

noted (at para. 46) that: 'There could be no question of the performer endorsing anything since he had been dead for many years.' He went on to make a similar point about the marketing of fictional characters, suggesting that they too would not be understood by the public to be endorsing products. Do you agree? You may remember that the WIPO report defined 'image marketing' as concerned with linking well-known fictional characters to merchandise. Taking the case of James Bond, but there are many others, we may well assert that although he is a fictional character he does indeed endorse products. Would brand owners pay so handsomely to have their products associated with the fictional spy if they did not believe his qualities would enhance the reputation of their products? We might argue that this investment deserves to be protected. The second point derives from first. If we accept that fictional characters can endorse products, should not the Court of Appeal's method of assessing damages in *Irvine* apply to character merchandising more generally and not simply to cases of false endorsement brought by real personalities.

FURTHER READING

C. Barton, 'Celebrity image rights: An international comparison' (2003) 5(8) WLLR 22–4.

H. Carty, 'Character merchandising and the limits of passing off' (1993) 13(3) Legal Studies 289.

F. Robinson, 'How image conscious is English law?' [2004] Ent LR 151.

G. Scanlan, 'Personality, endorsement and everything: The modern law of passing off and the myth of the personality right' [2003] EIPR 563.

7.2.3 TRADE MARKS AND CHARACTER MERCHANDISING

7.2.3.1 Introduction

You may recall that when discussing the 'Holly Hobbie' case, we quoted Lord Bridge as saying that because of the trafficking provisions in the 1938 TMA, the 'whole field of character merchandising will now be wide open to piracy' or 'left to the uncertain remedy of a passing off action'.[35] It is not surprising that many of those involved in character merchandising looked forward to a definite change of direction following the passage of the TMA, which allowed relatively unconditional licensing of trade marks. Certainly, the new Act eased the position for those marketing fictional characters. Thus, 'Teenage Mutant Ninja Turtles' is now a registered trade mark for a range of goods, including computer games and clothing. But would the protection of personality merchandising also become more certain?

7.2.3.2 *Elvis Presley Trade Marks*: the High Court

The first test of the impact of the TMA on personality merchandising was the *Elvis Presley Trade Marks* case.

Elvis Presley Trade Marks [1997] RPC 543 (HC), [1999] RPC 567 (CA)

Elvis Presley Enterprises Inc. ('Enterprises') applied to register three trade marks under the 1938 Trade Marks Act for toiletries including perfume and anti-perspirants.

---

[35] 'Holly Hobbie', 202.

One was a manuscript version of the name 'Elvis A. Presley', which in the proceedings was referred to as the 'signature mark'. One was for the word 'Elvis' and the third for the words 'Elvis Presley'. The application was opposed by Mr Sid Shaw who, for many years, had traded in Elvis memorabilia and who had the registered trade mark 'Elvisly Yours' for a wide range of goods including toiletries. Mr Shaw based his opposition on the assertion that the names 'Elvis' and 'Elvis Presley' lacked the distinctiveness needed for registration. He failed on this argument in the Trade Mark Registry, which held that the three marks were sufficiently distinctive to act as a badge of origin, and he appealed. Although the case was brought under the 1938 Act, any judgment would be relevant to the interpretation of the TMA, since it would be under the terms of the latter act that, for example, any infringement action would be decided. In the High Court, Laddie J identified the two questions raised by the appeal.

Laddie J, at p. 546:

...(a) can anyone claim the exclusive right under the 1938 Act to the names Elvis and Elvis Presley or the signature as a trade mark for a range of common retail products and, if so, (b) who?

[**Laddie J** then pointed out that it was not possible for Enterprises to 'own' the names Elvis and Elvis Presley as there is no copyright in a name. He went on, at p. 547:]

Even if Elvis Presley was still alive, he would not be entitled to stop a fan from naming his son, his dog or goldfish, his car or his house 'Elvis' or 'Elvis Presley' simply by reason of the fact that it was a name given to him at birth by his parents. To stop the use of the whole or part of his name by another he would need to show that as a result of such use, the other person is invading some legally recognised right. This is also reflected in many cases in the law of passing off.

Laddie J then made a similar point about Elvis' likeness, noting that, even during his lifetime, Elvis did not own his appearance. It was open to anyone to make a likeness of Elvis Presley, say as a tattoo or a painting, unless by doing so he or she invaded a legally recognized right, such as copyright. Turning, then, to the two questions posed, Laddie J looked first at the application for the name 'Elvis'. Under the 1938 Act, the mark, to be distinctive and therefore registrable, had to act as a badge of origin either by 'nature' or 'nurture'. He pointed out (at p. 549) that:

The more a proposed mark alludes to the character, quality or non-origin attributes of the goods on which it is used or proposed to be used, the lower its inherent distinctiveness.

In this case, counsel for Mr Shaw, Mr Meade, argued that the fact that Elvis had a high level of fame, would not make the mark more distinctive, but less so. For his part, counsel for Enterprises argued that Elvis would certainly have been able to register his name either before he became famous or during his lifetime and the position should be no different just because the singer had died. Laddie J rejected this latter argument. He cited the case, *Tarzan Trade Mark*[36] where the author of the Tarzan stories failed in his attempt to register the mark 'Tarzan' for films and other merchandise because by the time of the application 'the

---

[36] *Tarzan Trade Mark* [1970] FSR 245.

word "Tarzan" had passed into the language and had become a household word' and indeed a descriptive word. It followed from the 'Tarzan' decision that the registrability of a mark must be addressed at the time of the application for registration. Instead Laddie J agreed with counsel for Mr Shaw that the word 'Elvis' had very low inherent distinctiveness. Not only was it a well-known given name, it would also be taken by many members of the public to refer back to Elvis Presley. He went on (at p. 552):

> ...the more a mark has come to describe the goods to which [it] is...to be applied or to indicate some quality of those goods, the less it is inherently adapted to carry out the trade mark function of distinguishing the trade origin of the proprietor's goods from the origin of similar goods from other sources. This is consistent with Mr Meade's argument that the more famous Elvis Presley, the less inherently distinctive are the words 'Elvis' and 'Presley'. They are peculiarly suitable for use on the wide range of products sold as Elvis Presley memorabilia. He therefore does not contest but adopts Enterprises' assertion that 'Elvis is about as famous a name as could be, made famous by the efforts of Elvis Presley...Why else do members of the public wish to [purchase] Elvis merchandise?' Just as members of the public will go to see a Tarzan film because it is about Tarzan, so they will purchase Elvis merchandise because it carries the name or likeness of Elvis and not because it comes from a particular source...there is no reason why Mr Shaw or anyone else for that matter should not sell memorabilia and mementoes of Elvis Presley, including products embellished with pictures of him, and such traders are likely, in the ordinary course of their business and without any improper motive, to desire the name Elvis or Elvis Presley upon or in connection with their own such goods.

Laddie J also rejected the argument of the applicant's counsel, Mr Prescott that as the public became more aware of character merchandising they would expect to acquire a 'genuine' article (i.e. one that resulted from a licence given by the rights-holder in the character to the manufacturer) when they purchased memorabilia. Laddie J noted (at p. 554):

> That type of inference appears to have been drawn by the Vice-Chancellor in the *Mirage* case. But, as I have already said, there is no reason to assume that it would be drawn in all cases for all products. In particular there is nothing here which indicates that any significant section of the public seeing any of Enterprises' products would associate them with Enterprises by reason of the use of the words 'Elvis' or 'Elvis Presley'. On the contrary, everything is consistent with the words being used and recognised as what the relevant public want not because of any source they may indicate but because they are a reminder of the famous musician. That does not indicate distinctiveness of trade origin...As Mr Prescott put it during his submissions, the motivation for buying Elvis Presley aftershave must have something to do with Elvis Presley. That does not indicate distinctiveness of trade origin...I note in passing, that although Mr Shaw has sold millions of pounds worth of memorabilia bearing the name Elvis or Elvis Presley over the last 18 or so years, it has not been suggested that anyone has ever thought they emanated from Enterprises.
>
> It follows that I have come to the conclusion that there is very little inherent distinctiveness in the mark 'Elvis'.

Laddie J then looked to see whether the names 'Elvis' and 'Elvis Presley' had acquired distinctiveness through use, and concluded that they had not, at least in relation to the goods cited in the application. Perhaps most importantly, he noted that there was not a single instance to show that the public took the names 'Elvis' and 'Elvis Presley' marked on the goods sold by the applicants as indications of trade origin. He concluded that the applications to register both 'Elvis and 'Elvis Presley' should be rejected. Finally, turning to the signature mark, Laddie J concluded that that too was not registerable because the manner in which it was written was not sufficiently distinctive and, furthermore, if registered, it would conflict with Shaw's registered trade mark, which like the signature was written in cursive script. The applicant appealed.

7.2.3.3 *Elvis Presley Trade Marks*: the Court of Appeal[37]

The Court of Appeal found for the respondent, Mr Shaw, on much the same grounds as Laddie J in the High Court, save on the issue of the signature. The majority of the Court of Appeal accepted that the signature was genuine, but that it should not be registered because this would cause confusion with the 'Elvisly Yours' mark. Walker LJ gave the leading judgment. He began by confirming that all the products involved in this action were being marketed primarily on the strength of their bearing the name or image of Elvis Presley. He also cited *Tarzan* to the effect that words which once have been distinctive can in time become descriptive. Walker LJ then went on to survey the case law relating to character merchandising both in passing off and registered trade marks, up to and including 'Uncle Mac', 'Kojak', 'Abba', 'Holly Hobbie', and the 'Ninja Turtles'. He suggested that what differentiated the 'Ninja Turtles' case was that the claimant was in the business of not only licensing a name, but also a copyright work (that is the drawings of the turtles).

Walker LJ then looked at the arguments of the respective counsel. For Enterprises, Mr Prescott argued: (i) that the 'Tarzan' decision should be restricted to its special facts, i.e. a fictitious character whose name had once been an invented word and was no longer of wide significance; (ii) other traders could not legitimately wish to use the names 'Elvis' and 'Elvis Presley'; (iii) the law had now evolved to a point where there is a general rule that a trader may not make unauthorized use of the name of a celebrity in order to sell his own goods (he asserted that this principle applied to 'Elvis' who although deceased was of enduring fame); (iv) there may be some instances where it would be 'fair dealing' to allow use by others of these marks, such as in biographical material, but 'in those instances—the "product" is really text or information about the celebrity', unlike in this case where the concern is with 'consumable commercial items like soap, toothpaste and perfume'; (v) that it was a matter of 'everyday experience, that reputable traders do not use the name of a living person in connection with their merchandise' without authorization; and finally (vi) that the use by others of these marks would not cause confusion with Mr Shaw's mark, because the rights clearly belonged to Enterprises.

The arguments on behalf of Mr Shaw presented by his counsel Mr Meade, were that: (i) it was a 'bold contention' that, in any instance of the use of a well-known name, either living or dead, fictional or real, the public would assume that the name had been 'franchised'; (ii) such an assumption must be proved by real evidence pertaining to that name; (iii) Laddie J was right to conclude that the 'Elvis' and 'Elvis Presley' marks had little inherent distinctiveness, especially when applied to memorabilia or as decoration; (iv) the singer had become an important part of popular culture whose name and image other traders might legitimately wish to use; (v) that the more famous a 'man becomes, the harder it will be to register his name' if that name is used on memorabilia of Elvis Presley, as the average consumer will be buying

---

[37] *Elvis Presley Trade Marks* [1999] RPC 567 (CA).

such goods because they carry a likeness of the singer rather than as a product from a particular source; (vi) that Enterprises could not rely on the fact that it had specific intellectual property rights that they owned which were being infringed (such as copyright); and finally, (vii) Enterprises had failed to educate the public that the names 'Elvis' and 'Elvis Presley' were being used by them as a badge of origin.

Walker LJ then canvassed the judgment of Laddie J. He endorsed Laddie J's conclusions.

Walker LJ, at p. 585:

...the public purchase Elvis Presley merchandise not because it comes from a particular source, but because it carries the name or image of Elvis Presley. Indeed the judge came close to finding (although he did not in terms find) that for goods of the sort advertised by Elvisly Yours (or by Enterprises in the United States) the commemoration of the late Elvis Presley is the product, and the article on which his name or image appears (whether a poster, a pennant, a mug or a piece of soap) is little more than a vehicle. I consider that the judge was right to treat all these goods as memorabilia or mementoes, and not to treat some as being in a different class of consumable commercial goods.

As a result, Laddie J had been right to conclude that the marks had 'very low inherent distinctiveness'.

Morrit LJ also supported the findings by Laddie J in respect of the 'Elvis' and 'Elvis Presley' marks. As to the 'Elvis' mark, he suggested that the 'Tarzan' decision should be followed in this case.

Morrit LJ, at p. 593–4:

I agree with counsel for Mr Shaw that the ['Tarzan'] case is indistinguishable from this. It is true that the goods of which registration is sought, for instance soap, are consumer items. To market those goods under the mark Elvis would obviously seek to turn to account the name and memory of Elvis Presley; but it would seek to do so as descriptive of a popular hero not as distinctive of the connection between the soap and EPEI [Enterprises] as the proprietor of the mark. The soap would be sold as Elvis soap. The character of the soap would be Elvis soap.

As a result, the mark would not act as a badge of origin but rather would be 'a direct reference to the character of the soap'.

With respect to the 'Elvis Presley' mark, Morrit LJ also concluded that it lacked inherent or factual capability to act as a badge of origin. In particular, he noted that 'the fame of Elvis Presley was as a singer. He was not a producer of soap. There is no reason why he or any organization of his should be concerned with toiletries so as to give rise to some perceived connection between his name and the product.'

Morritt LJ, at p. 594:

Counsel for EPEI forcefully contended that such a conclusion would leave the door wide open to unscrupulous traders seeking to cash in on the reputations of others. This is true if, but only if, the mark has become so much a part of the language as to be descriptive of the goods rather than distinctive of their source. But in that event I can see no objection to any trader being entitled to use the description. In the field of memorabilia, which I consider includes consumer items bearing the name or likeness of a famous figure, it must be for that person to ensure by whatever means may be open to him or her that the public associate his or her name with the source of the goods. In the absence of evidence of such association in my view the court should be very slow to infer it.

Like Walker LJ and Morritt LJ, Simon Brown LJ took the view that one could not just assume that the public would be aware of character merchandising, as had been argued by the applicant. According to Simon Brown LJ whether this was true in each case must turn on its facts. He noted that here there was no connection between toiletries and those attributes for which Elvis Presley was and remained famous; that Elvis memorabilia in the UK had not been primarily marketed by Enterprises; and that, in any event, the public who consumed such items would not assume that the use of the names had been officially licensed.

Simon Brown LJ, at pp. 597–8:

On analysis, as it seems to me, all the English cases upon which Enterprises seeks to rely (Mirage Studios not least) can be seen to have turned essentially upon the need to protect copyright or to prevent passing off (or libel). None creates the broad right for which in effect Mr Prescott contends here, a free standing general right to character exploitation enjoyable exclusively by the celebrity. As Robert Walker LJ has explained, just such a right, a new 'character right' to fill a perceived gap between the law of copyright (there being no copyright in a name) and the law of passing off was considered and rejected by the Whitford Committee in 1977. Thirty years earlier, indeed, when it was contended for as a corollary to passing off law, it had been rejected in *McCulloch v Lewis A. May* [1947] 2 AER 845. I would assume to reject it. In addressing the critical issue of distinctiveness there should be no a priori assumption that only a celebrity or his successors may ever market (or licence the marketing) of his own character. Monopolies should not be so readily created.

In the *Elvis* case, the Court of Appeal had to weigh two persuasive but quite incompatible arguments. The one put by counsel for Mr Shaw was that since the public had contributed to the fame of Elvis Presley (and hence the value inherent in his name) it would be wrong for it to be monopolized by a single undertaking. Or as Jeremy Phillips has written, 'since it is the public who make people celebrities during their lifetimes, it is the public who should be able to enjoy in common the greatest freedom to cherish those celebrities after death'.[38] The other argument, put by counsel for Enterprises, was that since Elvis Presley had accrued such a high degree of fame through his own efforts (and hence the value inherent in his name) it would be wrong if his estate could not profit from it. Which do you think is the more persuasive? We might also ask whether Simon Brown LJ was correct in his assumption that the public that bought Elvis Presley merchandise would not think it had been licensed. Indeed, was the Court of Appeal perhaps underestimating the extent to which the public may seek to buy 'official', rather than often cheaper 'unofficial', merchandise as a way of demonstrating their loyalty to the personality involved?

7.2.3.4 Trade marks and the registration of famous names following Elvis

Taken at face value, the *Elvis* decision suggests that the more famous a personality, the less likely he will be able to obtain trade mark protection for his name. Indeed, this point

---

[38] J. Phillips, 'Life after death' [1998] EIPR 201.

of view has been buttressed by the ECJ's more recent decision in the *Picasso* trade mark case.[39] As we have seen, such an outcome is particularly problematic for those involved in character merchandising because the law of passing off will not protect a name as such, except in cases of false endorsement. The decision in the 'Princess Diana' trade mark application appears to confirm that this is a correct understanding of the *Elvis* decision.[40]

Diana, Princess of Wales Trade Mark [2001] ETMR 25

The Trustees of the late Princess Diana's estate applied to register 'Diana, Princess of Wales' as a trade mark to cover a wide range of goods and services. The Registrar refused registration on the grounds that the mark did not fulfil the conditions of s. 3 of the TMA in that it lacked distinctive character and had not acquired distinctiveness through use.

The Registrar began by clearing up some 'red herrings': 'The first is that whilst she was alive Diana, Princess of Wales owned her name and therefore had an exclusive and unqualified right to the use of it for commercial purposes. No such "personality right" exists under UK law.' The second red herring, according to the Registrar, citing the Court of Appeal in *Elvis Presley*, 'is that a name which is unique to a particular person must by definition have distinctive character as a trade mark. This is not necessarily so.' He then went on to conclude: 'Accordingly, the use of a famous name for product endorsement purposes is not trade mark use unless the proprietor of the "mark" takes responsibility for the quality of the goods/services to which it is applied.'[41]

Turning to the particular facts of this case, the Registrar noted that the evidence for the Estate showed it had licensed the use of Diana's signature on a wide range of products, largely relating to cards and prints, but also on other less obvious products such as margarine. The Estate also produced survey evidence which supported the view that when the public saw the name and signature of Diana on goods they would assume it was related to the Diana Memorial Fund and that the proceeds were meant for charity. The Registrar then turned to the applicable law. In particular, he asked whether the average consumer would see the 'message' sent by these marks as a badge of origin. In other words, were these words acting as a trade mark?

The Registrar

40. There cannot be any doubt that the late Diana, Princess of Wales was one of the most famous people in the world. I believe that I am entitled to take notice of this and that the name and face of Diana, Princess of Wales has, since her marriage to Prince Charles in 1981, continuously featured on the covers of countless magazines, books and in TV programmes. She was probably one of the most photographed people in the world. None of this use indicated any trade connection between the source of these goods/services and the Princess. The average consumer would be aware of this and that there has long been a trade in this

---

[39] *Ruiz-Picasso v OHIM (Trade Marks and Designs)* Case C-361/04 P) [2006] ECR I-643; see 5.3.3.8.
[40] See also, *Jane Austen Trade Mark* [2000] RPC 879.
[41] *Diana, Princess of Wales Trade Mark* [2001] ETMR 25, para. 14.

country in souvenirs and mementoes featuring members of the Royal Family without any significance as to the trade source of the goods.

[Noting that her name and signature had not been used as a trade mark before her death, the Registrar concluded:]

55. In the light of the use made of the Princess' name whilst she was alive—which could not have been further from a trade mark for products—I do not believe that, at the date of application, the average consumer who was reasonably well informed and circumspect, would have expected all commemorative articles bearing the Princess' name to be commercialised under the control of a single undertaking. The applicants' evidence confirms what one would in any event have suspected, that the average consumer would like some or all of the proceeds of the sale of products bearing the Princess' name to go to charity. It does not establish that the mere appearance of the Princess' name is sufficient to guarantee to the average consumer that all such commemorative products are commercialised under the control of a single undertaking which is responsible for their quality. The fact that the Estate has, in practice, seen it necessary to use other signs (i.e. the official logo and hallmark) to signify 'official' authorisation rather suggest that the applicants themselves were not confident that the Princess' name *per se* was capable of guaranteeing their connection in trade with the goods. I conclude that, at the relevant date, the name lacked the necessary trade mark character for the goods listed in the application.

[The Registrar then turned to the question of whether the name and signature had acquired distinctiveness through use (s. 3(1)(b) of the TMA):]

61. I believe that the answer to this question is straightforward. There is no evidence of any use of the name DIANA, PRINCESS OF WALES as a trade mark. Much of the use shown in the evidence falls under the heading of 'authorised' use in respect of goods such as calendars, cards, books, reproduction prints, a lily and fund raising events over which the applicants appear to have no relevant control, or is merely descriptive use (such as the Tribute CD). In the case of the commemorative stamps produced by the Royal Mail, the Princess' name is not actually used at all, and the images of her which are used clearly did not perform a trade mark function. The same can be said of the commemorative postmarks which did bear her name.

62. There is some evidence of trade mark use in respect of commemorative enamel boxes, a memorial tartan and possibly a 'Beanie Baby' product, but in each case it is noticeable that it is the official Diana 'signature' logo (with the words 'Princess of Wales Memorial Fund') and the hallmark of the Estate which are used to identify a trade connection with the Estate have been accepted for registration by the Registrar for a wide range of goods on the basis that these signs are capable of distinguishing 'official' commemorative products from others. This is not evidence that the words DIANA, PRINCESS OF WALES *per se* have come to perform this function.

7.3.3.5 Famous names and Registry practice: a cause for optimism

Celebrities and their legal representatives might have been forgiven for believing that the law relating to the registrations of famous names had not moved on in the way they had expected following the implementation of the TMA. However, if we look at the practice of the Trade Mark Registry, we may conclude that their gloom is to some extent misplaced. The Manual of Trade Marks Practice suggests that it will mainly be the representatives of 'deceased celebrities', such as Princess Diana, and 'defunct groups' rather than living celebrities who will have cause for concern.

'Manual of Trade Marks Practice' UK IPO (www.ipo.gov.uk/pro-types/pro-tm/t-law/t-manual.htm)

Chapter 3

21. Famous Names

Where a famous name is concerned (and where the reputation does not stem from a trade in the goods/services applied for) it is possible that, when used in relation to certain goods/services, the name may appear to the average consumer as an indication that the goods/services are *about* the person whose name it is rather than as an indication that the goods/services are supplied by, or under the control of, one undertaking.

The Court of Appeal decided that 'Elvis Presley' was not registrable under the 1938 Act for memorabilia products in Class 3: see [1997] RPC 543.

In the case of *Arsenal v Reed* [2002] EWHC 2695 (Ch), Laddie J held that the trade mark 'Arsenal' was validly registered under the 1994 Act, even though it could and had been used by others in a non-trade mark sense. He concluded that this did not automatically make the trade mark ARSENAL non-distinctive for scarves etc.

Although Arsenal is the name of a famous football club rather than the name of an individual or group, a similar point arises; namely, whether the name of a person or organisation which others wish to use in order to demonstrate their support/allegiance should be registrable as a trade mark for relevant goods. The decision in the *Arsenal* case indicates that such protection should not be automatically refused or invalidated in these circumstances.

Accordingly, the correct approach appears to be to consider whether the famous name put forward for registration is so descriptive in relation to the goods/services for which registration is sought that it could not be perceived by consumers as anything more than a description of the subject matter of the goods/services. The following paragraphs are directed at the main areas of uncertainty.

21.1 Media

The names of famous persons or groups may serve as trade marks for printed publications, recorded sounds, films, videos, TV programmes, musical or live performances etc as use of the mark on such goods or services would be likely to imply some form of control of, or guarantee from, the holder. Consequently, there will not usually be an objection to the registration of a famous name for these goods.

21.2 Mere Image Carriers

The name of a famous person or group is likely to be perceived as merely descriptive of the subject matter of posters, photographs, transfers and figurines. Names of famous persons or groups are therefore unlikely to be accepted by consumers as trade marks for these goods because they will usually be seen as mere descriptions of the subject matter of the product. Objections will arise under Section 3(1)(b) & (c) of the Act.

21.3 Badges of Allegiance

The name of a famous person or group may serve to identify the trade source of badges of allegiance (including T-shirts, mugs, scarves etc) even if the possibility of other traders producing unofficial merchandise cannot be ruled out. Consequently, such marks will normally be accepted for such goods unless there is a particular reason to believe that the mark in question cannot fulfil the function of a trade mark, for example, the names of some members of the Royal Family may be incapable of performing a trade mark function for such goods because of the widespread historical trade in Royal souvenirs.

21.4 Names of Deceased Famous Individuals or Defunct Groups

In these circumstances the name is more likely to be seen by consumers as merely an historical reference to the subject matter of the goods or services, rather than to the trade source of the goods. However, each such case must be judged on its own facts taking account of the length of time that has passed since the person concerned died, or the group became defunct, and the relationship (if any) between the goods/services in the application and those associated with the dead person or defunct group. A Team Leader will be involved in each case.

21.5 Pictures of Famous Persons (living and deceased) and Groups

Pictures of famous persons/groups present similar issues to famous names. However, depending upon the goods, they may be more likely (compared to a name) to be taken as mere decoration and therefore to lack a trade mark character. Each case will be judged on its own merits and a Hearing Officer will be involved in each case.

21.6 Section 3(6)—Bad Faith

Where third parties apply to register the name of a famous individual or a recently deceased famous individual an objection under Section 3(6) of the Act may be appropriate. However, this will depend upon whether the application covers goods and/or services with which the famous individual is associated. For example, an application to register the name of a famous fashion model for 'clothing' or 'cosmetics' would be liable to an objection because it is an obvious attempt to take unfair advantage of the person's reputation. Conversely, an application to register a name [which corresponded to that] of a famous fashion model for 'agricultural machinery' would not, *prima facie,* be liable to a bad faith objection. However, the application may still be successfully opposed, under Section 5(4)(a) of the Act, if it can be proven that use of the mark could be restrained under the law of passing off.

   Care should however be taken where the reputation of a famous individual is not commercial. For example Tony Blair, whose fame stems from politics, should not be accepted for any goods/services without his consent.

   Applications to register the names of famous musical groups will not normally at the examination stage face an objection. This is because to firmly establish who are the rightful owners of the names of musical groups often requires evidence and is therefore best left to be determined in opposition proceedings.

   Bad faith objections can be overcome if permission to the registration of the mark is obtained from the individual or his/her legal representative.

There are a number of points of interest in the above excerpt. We shall isolate just two. The first is the importance of the *Arsenal v Reed*[42] decision to character merchandising. The Manual makes clear that a famous name (or in this case the name of a famous football club) on merchandise may be viewed as a badge of origin and be protected by trade mark registration rather than simply viewed as a badge of allegiance. Second, the Registry may take a different approach to registering celebrity names depending upon the type of goods specified

---

[42] *Arsenal Football Club plc v Reed (No 2)* [2003] EWCA Civ 696; see 6.2.2.1.

in the application. The Registry will almost certainly accept applications for celebrity names for goods which the public would buy as 'official merchandise', and which may be a very wide-ranging category. But the Registry will reject applications for those same names on goods, such as posters, where they would not be understood as acting as a badge of origin. In other words, as the Manual puts it, such goods would be seen as 'mere image carriers' and the celebrity name as descriptive. A recent example of this approach is to be found in Linkin Park's trade mark application.[43]

Linkin Park LLC's Application O/035/05 [2006] ETMR (74) 1017

Linkin Park LLC, the corporate vehicle of the American rock group called Linkin Park, applied to register the trade mark 'Linkin Park' for a wide range of goods and services. The application was successful except for the goods: 'printed matter, posters and poster books'. The Registrar maintained that a registration for these goods would be contrary to s. 3(1)(b) of the TMA as placed on these goods the name 'Linkin Park' would be devoid of distinctive character and descriptive. He described the goods as 'mere image carriers' to differentiate such goods and others for which the applicant had obtained registration. The applicants appealed. The Appointed Person set out the basis for the applicant's appeal. Thus the applicants maintained that:

> 22. The hearing officer erred in principle on four main grounds. First, that the hearing officer wrongly failed to take into account the fact that the Mark was coined by the Group and was therefore an invented word. Secondly, that the Mark was not descriptive because subject matter was not a 'characteristic' of the Goods within the meaning of s. 3(1)(c). Thirdly and most fundamentally, that the hearing officer was wrong, and the Registrar's practice is wrong, to differentiate between goods such as posters and other goods. In particular, the applicant contends that the Mark is no more descriptive for posters and the like than it is for the goods in relation to which the application had been accepted; but on the contrary is just as distinctive for posters and the like as it is for the other goods. Fourthly, that the hearing officer's decision was inconsistent with certain other registrations.
>
> [Looking at the applicants' first ground for appeal, that the mark consisted of invented and therefore meaningless words, the Appointed Person made the following findings:]
>
> 42. What matters, [however], is its meaning at the application date. By the application date, the Mark was no longer meaningless, but on the contrary had acquired a well-established meaning of denoting the Group. This was particularly so in the perception of the relevant average consumer.
>
> 43. The applicant's attorney argued that this led to a paradox, which was that the applicant was worse off than if it had sought to register the Mark when the Group was unknown. He said that it ought to have a stronger case for registration once the Group was well known. In my judgment there is no such paradox, for two reasons. First, there is no evidence that the Group is (or was at the application date) well known as a trade source of posters and the like. If there was, it could gain registration on that basis. Secondly, as the Registrar's representative observed, a mark may by becoming distinctive for one class of goods or services (here

---

[43] See also *Sir Alexander Chapman Ferguson's Application* No. 2323092B [2005] Trade Mark Decisions available at: <http://www.ipo.gov.uk/o09406.pdf>.

musical performances) become descriptive for another class of goods or services (here the Goods).

[The Appointed Person then turned to the second contention which was that the mark did not denote a characteristic of the goods, because the subject matter was not characteristic of them.]

47. First, if one imagines a consumer who wants a poster depicting LINKIN PARK asking a shop assistant whether that shop stocks such things, he would be very likely to say 'Do you have any LINKIN PARK posters?' I accept that he might use the alternative formulation, but in my judgment this is less likely. In the question 'Do you have any LINKIN PARK posters?' the Mark is clearly being used to describe a characteristic of the Goods being sought, namely their subject matter.

The applicants' third argument was that the hearing officer wrongly distinguished between the goods at issue here, posters etc. which the trade mark registrar termed 'mere image carriers' and the goods (e.g. clothes) for which the mark has been accepted. In particular, the applicants argued that the group should be able to stop any use of its name without its consent in relation to all goods and services. Here the Appointed Person noted that to obtain such protection there would need to be a recognized personality right in the UK, which there was not. The Appointed Person then cited the Court of Appeal decision in *R v Johnstone*[44] which held that the use of trade marks such a 'Bon Jovi' and the 'Rolling Stones' on compact discs was descriptive use.

60. Considered as a matter of principle, the position in this type of case is as follows. If the name of the artist or group affixed to the compact disc and displayed on the packaging is *exclusively* an indication of the name of the performer whose performance is recorded on the compact disc, and if this use of the name of the performer is not likely to be understood as indicating any other connection between the performer and the compact discs, then such use would be descriptive only.

. . .

66. The applicant's attorney argued that the relevant consumers in the present case, being mainly fans of the Group, would be knowledgeable about intellectual property rights and would expect merchandise relating to the Group, including posters, to be licensed by the Group or its vehicle the applicant. I am not satisfied that this is correct. As the hearing officer held and the Registrar's representative submitted, consideration of the copyright position suggests the opposite. The first owner of copyright in a photograph of the Group will be the photographer or the photographer's employer. Accordingly, exploitation of photographs of the Group will not necessarily require the Group's licence. Accordingly, even if performers' or authors' names may be registered in respect of compact discs and books on the basis that members of the public would expect such items to be authorised by the performer or author (contrary to what is suggested above), that would not mean that such marks were registrable for posters.

He concluded that the decision by the Registrar, that the posters were 'mere image carriers' and therefore that the use of mark 'Linkin Park' on these goods was descriptive, was correct.

Is the Registry right to view a celebrity name used on posters and other printed matter as descriptive rather than a badge of origin? When seeking to buy official merchandise,

[44] [2003] 1 WLR 1736; see 6.2.2.2.

will fans really differentiate between, for example, T-shirts, and posters? What we can say is that such an approach is compatible with the decision in the earlier 'Spice Girls' case. But this would suggest that in some areas of character merchandising at least, in particular that concerned with real personalities, trade mark law still offers the same 'uncertain protection' that Lord Bridge believed was available through the law of passing off.

FURTHER READING

S. Bains, 'Personality rights: Should the UK grant celebrities a proprietary right in their personality? Part 1' (2007) 18(5) Ent LR 165–9; 'Part 2' (2007) 18(6) Ent LR 205–11; 'Part 3' (2007) 18(7) Ent LR 237–40.

P. Jaffey, 'Merchandising and the law of trade marks' [1998] IPQ 240.

C. Macleod and A. Wood, 'The Picasso case, famous names and branding celebrity' [2006] Ent LR 44.

I. Simon, 'CDs, celebrities and merchandise: The Trade Mark Registry's hybrid theory' [2005] EIPR 265.

7.3 THE FUTURE OF CHARACTER MERCHANDISING

7.3.1 INTRODUCTION

This last section of the chapter will look at how commentators view the present state of the law protecting character merchandising in the UK. In fact, the changes wrought by the 1994 Act in relation to the marketing of fictional characters have received relatively little comment. A consensus seems to have emerged that the increased ability to protect such characters now that the trafficking provisions of the 1938 TMA no longer apply is a fair reflection of the substantial economic value of character merchandising. On the other hand, there has been a great deal of academic debate regarding the extent to which the law should be fashioned to protect both the ability of real persons (or their estates) to exploit their fame and also to prevent others from doing so without their permission.

7.3.2 SHOULD THE UK HAVE A PUBLICITY OR PERSONALITY RIGHT?

In *The Commercial Appropriation of Personality*, Huw Beverley-Smith, considers how a tort of appropriation of personality, which would protect both the dignitary rights of the famous as well as their commercial interest in exploiting their fame, might be justified.

H. Beverley-Smith, *The Commercial Appropriation of Personality* (Cambridge: Cambridge University Press, 2002), pp. 314–5

By its very nature, a hybrid cause of action such as a *sui generis* tort of appropriation of personality invites a number of different possible justifications. The first option noted above, a personal tort remedy based on infringement of privacy, may be justified on the broad basis that it provides protection for personal privacy and dignity against unauthorized commercial exploitation. Few people wish to be treated as commodities, and many would resent being involuntarily enlisted to help further the commercial interests of advertisers and merchandisers. The privacy perspective, viewing appropriation of personality as a dignitary wrong, focuses on the loss of privacy, indignation and distress that may result from such conduct. As such, damages would tend to be modest, intended to soothe injured feelings, rather than compensate for any specific pecuniary loss, apart from exceptional cases where the defendant's conduct might require an award of punitive damages.

When the focus shifts towards the invasion of essentially proprietary interests, a corresponding shift in underlying justification seems to be required. This certainly seems to be true for the American experience, where the development of an essentially dignitary interest in privacy into an essentially economic interest in publicity has resulted in the invocation of different and more sophisticated justifications. If a person is to enjoy an extensive property right in his personality or image which allows him to prevent unauthorized commercial exploitation by others, and secure substantial profits for himself, then standard arguments justifying property rights should apply. However, as noted above, the standard arguments (to the extent that they can be regarded as paradigm examples), primarily the utilitarian and natural rights of labour arguments, apply rather uneasily in the case of property rights in personality. The degree of labour and the level of incentive required to develop commercially valuable attributes in personality are generally much less than in the case of more orthodox intangibles such as patentable inventions and artistic and literary works. Attempts to draw analogies between economic interests in personality and the interests protected under the core areas of intellectual property law such as copyright and trade marks somehow seem strained.

At the broadest level, claims for property rights in personality are but one manifestation of the proprietarian creed, which some see as increasingly pervasive in intellectual property law, whereby property rights have a moral priority over other rights and interests, and activities that first give rise to economic value also necessarily create property rights. Property rights trump the wider community interests and everything is capable of private ownership. On the other hand, and equally broadly, the dignitary aspects of appropriation of personality reflect the increased value that modern societies place on personal privacy, sensibilities and autonomy. Ultimately, we are left with a new remedy that is rather difficult to justify on orthodox grounds. Of course, arguments of the kind outlined above rarely play any significant part in the decisions made by courts as to whether to allow claims for the protection of new interests, and such decisions are made without any consideration of extra-legal philosophical, economic or moral argument. It remains to be seen whether the formal legal authorities provide support for such a tort.

Beverley-Smith concludes that a tort of the appropriation of personality might be difficult to justify. However, he suggests that judges may well reach something similar by an accretion of case law and, indeed, without giving any thought as to how such a development might be justified. In this final extract, Hazel Carty argues that the judgments in *Irvine*, both in the High Court and the Court of Appeal, have indeed set the law on course to recognize a right of publicity, although this would be an unjustifiable extension of the tort of passing off.

H. Carty, 'Advertising, publicity rights and English law' [2004] IPQ 209, 210

The celebrity industry argues that the magnetism of the celebrity persona is a valuable intangible that 'belongs' to the celebrity or those commercial partners who have 'bought into' that celebrity, through contract so that only they may profit by the use of their celebrity persona in advertising or promotion generally. However, those who deny this argue that celebrity magnetism is public property (and part of popular culture) rather than a private right. In other words, that exploitation is fine, provided no specific harm is inflicted. The celebrity image—which may also involve lookalikes or soundalikes of the celebrity—may be used to convey endorsement or for eye-catching effect, including parodic use of the celebrity image. It may also be used for allegiance appeal, where rather than advertising another product the celebrity is the product itself (as is the case in souvenir or memorabilia merchandising).

Those who support a publicity right argue that the celebrity or those who are commercially linked to that celebrity should have legal control over all the above uses of the celebrity link. Their argument is that the magnetism of the celebrity persona is a valuable intangible that 'belongs' to the celebrity or those commercial partners who have 'bought into' that celebrity, through contract. It is claimed that these parties should have the protection of the law over unauthorised use of the celebrity magnet so that only they may profit by the use of their celebrity persona in advertising or promotion generally...

...

[at p. 211] The industry would obviously prefer a general protection against unauthorised use of the celebrity image, based on an allegation of misappropriation...

But what of those who seek to exploit celebrity magnetism without authorisation (and, therefore, without payment)? They would argue that, in the absence of specific wrongs such as trade mark infringement or defamation, the use of the celebrity magnet is open to all. That, in effect, celebrity magnetism is public property (and part of popular culture) rather than a private right. Rather than view fame as bestowing a new form of intellectual property right, those outside the celebrity industry could argue that the price of fame is public interest and commercial free-riding. In other words, that exploitation is fine, provided no specific harm is inflicted. And to raise the banner of 'misappropriation' is to seek the moral high ground where none in fact exists.

...

[at p. 253]

False endorsement as passing off

The celebrity industry can scent blood: *Irvine v Talksport* signals a marked advance in their quest for image rights...An action for misappropriation appears to be on the horizon.

If, as this article suggests, English law is in danger of moving towards a publicity right, the need for clarity and the need to avoid the wrong turnings of other jurisdictions is stark. Misappropriation, personality rights and economic incentives are all discredited rationales for a free-standing publicity right.

Carty then goes on to suggest that a review of the possible justifications for a publicity or image right leads to the conclusion that 'legal control should only arise where there is an unauthorized use of a celebrity image which involves a misrepresentation affecting consumer choice', in particular through false endorsement. She argues that passing off provides both a legitimate and an adequate remedy for such unauthorized use. However, she believes that the judgments in the *Irvine* case go well beyond the need for a claimant to prove goodwill, a misrepresentation, and damage or the likelihood of damage. She continues at 254–5:

Goodwill involves trading activity—where trading in an image is concerned the celebrity is asserting goodwill in his endorsement potential. That potential can be harmed by injurious association and by lost licensing opportunities. However, the goodwill at the heart of a false endorsement claim is not the standard 'customer connection' goodwill found in the tort. The established forms of goodwill—source goodwill and product goodwill—do not encapsulate what a celebrity like Irvine is concerned about. Source goodwill protects against a misleading connection between the claimant's and defendant's products; product goodwill protects against misleading claims concerning the inherent characteristics of the defendant's product (it is genuine Advocaat or Parma Ham, etc.). But celebrity 'goodwill' is a different animal: it is promotional goodwill in a wide sense. Murumba calls this 'radiant' business reputation rather than the traditional linear business reputation.

Promotional goodwill—and the type of harm that goes with it—involves an extension of the tort. And indeed Laddie J in *Irvine* appeared to acknowledge this. However it would appear that such an extension would still fall within the rationale of the tort. By protecting promotional goodwill, harmed by the defendant's false indication of celebrity endorsement, the tort (as it always does) protects 'deserving claimants' by protecting against consumer misinformation. So it would still be protecting traders where it is clearly in the public interest so to do.

However this viable extension of the tort rests on the presence of an endorsement that turns out to be false. To prevent this extension from masking a reworking of the tort at the expense of the public interest element, there must be an endorsement in a real sense. Without a real message of endorsement there will be no material reliance and no harm to promotional goodwill. If this central requirement is applied in a vague way to mean a false implication that there is 'some association' or financial link between the celebrity and the advertised product or service or indeed if the requirement for a misrepresentation is dropped in favour of protecting against unpaid use of the celebrity for attention-grabbing then true passing off is not involved. In all these cases the use of the celebrity image, rather than telling the public anything about the product or service involved, simply involves the defendant cashing in on the feel-good factor or magnetism of the celebrity. Rather than misconveying product information, the defendant is merely placing the celebrity image with the product, without paying. In such circumstances we are closer to what Laddie J termed 'merchandising rights' ('exploiting images') rather than endorsement. And it should be remembered that Laddie J rejected liability in passing off for mere merchandising.

. . .

So the need to find apparent endorsement must be strictly applied. What then should be necessary, for liability to apply, in line with the tradition of the tort of passing off? To endorse is defined as 'to declare one's approval'. It requires that something is being said about the nature or quality of the product/service with which the celebrity is being associated. That, in other words, the product is being endorsed, rather than simply the celebrity is being 'used'.

[While **Carty** believes that the decision in *Irvine* was justified on the facts, she points out that **Laddie J** defined 'endorsement' in an open ended way which went beyond protecting the public from a misrepresentation caused by a false endorsement. She identifies (at p. 256) a number of ways **Laddie J** characterized 'endorsement' in *Irvine*, including:]

. . . 'happy to be associated'; 'he adds his name as an encouragement to members of the relevant public to buy or use the service or product'; the advertisement was designed 'with the intention of grabbing the attention of the audience'.

[**Carty** goes on to argue that in discussing the harm in *Irvine*, **Laddie J** recognized that damage might be caused by 'dilution'; which results from the misappropriation of the fame of

> the claimant by the defendant and not from any harm which the misrepresentation of false
> endorsement might cause to the public. She continues, at p. 256:]
>
> To sum up: there is a need to apply the 'endorsement' requirement strictly. The tort should
> only protect the celebrity where the unauthorised use of his image conveys a false message
> about the product to consumers. Otherwise the other extensions to the tort—to encom-
> pass promotional goodwill and lost licensing opportunities—become unacceptably wide.

In this extract, Carty argues that in passing off cases involving the famous, 'dilution' of the attractiveness of the claimant's name or image is not an appropriate head of damage. Is it possible to answer that Carty is swimming against the current in making this argument? We have seen that, since the 'Elderflower Champagne' case was decided, judges have increasingly begun to accept that a misrepresentation which 'dilutes' the value of the claimant's name or image rather than directly misleads the public, constitutes an actionable misrepresentation.[45] So why should this approach not also apply to celebrity names? On the other hand, is it possible to distinguish passing off involving a famous person from passing off as it relates to goods and services?

7.3.3 CONCLUSION

It has been widely argued, not least by Carty in the above extract and by Sid Shaw's counsel in the *Elvis* case, that fame should be seen as a product of popular culture or the result of an interaction between the public and the famous, and as such it should not be wholly 'owned' by the person who becomes famous. As Michael Madow has put it: 'The question "Who owns Madonna?" is not just a question about who gets to capture the immense economic values that attach to her persona. The question is also, even chiefly, about who gets to decide what "Madonna" will mean in our culture: what meaning(s) her image will be used to generate and circulate, and what meaning(s) she will have for us.'[46] One danger in giving both celebrities and fictional characters intellectual property protection may be that their meanings become fixed and popular culture is impoverished as a result. In contemporary society, perhaps the most prominent example of the interaction between fame and popular culture is to be found on the Internet site, YouTube. Individuals who are not known to the public might find immediate fame or notoriety through an appearance on YouTube. Sometimes, as is the case with the popular singer Lily Allen, individuals will use YouTube to acquire fame. At other times, fame will be thrust upon them. A recent example of the latter process was an interview with a contestant in a beauty pageant which millions of people watched on YouTube. In this case, the fame earned by the contestant derived not from her beauty but instead from a hilariously inept answer which she gave to one of the judge's questions. Should the fame earned by the contestant on YouTube 'belong' to her or to the public who enjoyed her performance? Would your answer be different if, like Lily Allen, the individual set out to acquire such fame or conversely if, like Miss Teenage South Carolina, she became famous for reasons she had not intended?

---

[45] See 4.2.5.4.

[46] M. Madow, 'Private ownership of public image: Popular culture and publicity rights' (1993) 81(125) Cal LR 134.

FURTHER READING

R. J. Coombe, 'Authorizing the celebrity: Publicity rights, postmodern politics, and unauthorized genders' (1991–2) 10 Cardozo Arts & Ent LJ 365.

J. Klink, '50 years of publicity rights in the United States and the never ending hassle with intellectual property and personality rights in Europe' [2003] IPQ 363–87.

8

BREACH OF CONFIDENCE

8.1 INTRODUCTION

The action for breach of confidence emerged fairly recently, in the mid-19th century.[1] Since that time, the action has evolved to protect a variety of confidential information, whether it is personal, commercial, artistic, or governmental in nature. The action is thus a flexible one that embraces diverse interests. Most recently, and under the impetus of the Human Rights Act 1998 (UK), courts have reshaped the action for breach of confidence to explicitly, and more effectively, protect privacy. This has created uncertainty about how other types of confidential information and interests, particularly commercial in nature, will be regulated and has also raised the question of whether a separate tort of privacy should be recognized. The law of confidence is thus at an important juncture in its development. This chapter will discuss the key features of the law of confidence, those areas in which it has been significantly reshaped and also the areas of uncertainty.

8.2 CONTRACTUAL AND EQUITABLE ACTIONS

There has been significant scholarly debate about the jurisdictional basis of the action for breach of confidence. More specifically, whether it is grounded in contract, property, or equity or is sui generis in nature. It is submitted, however, that English courts have tended to characterize the action as either contractual or equitable.

Parties may enter into express *contractual* duties of confidence. Courts have also been willing to imply obligations of confidence into contracts, particularly in the employment field. There are two main advantages to relying upon express contractual duties of confidence as opposed to the equitable action for breach of confidence. First, it allows parties to agree on the scope of the obligation and also the information to be protected. Secondly, the protected subject matter may be defined more broadly than is possible under the equitable doctrine of confidence. In particular, information that is *not* confidential can be the subject

---

[1] The beginnings of the law of confidence are frequently traced back to the case of *Prince Albert v Strange* (1849) 1 MacN & G 25, 41 ER 1171.

of protection. This is illustrated by *Attorney General v Blake*[2] where the defendant, who had published an autobiography in which he recounted his activities as a British secret service officer, was held in breach of his promise not to disclose official government information, even though the information was no longer secret.

Aside from contractual obligations, there is also the possibility of establishing *equitable* duties of confidence. This was recognized by the Court of Appeal in *Saltman Engineering v Campbell Engineering*[3] and reiterated by Megarry J in the following seminal case.

Coco v AN Clark (Engineers) Ltd [1969] FSR 415

The claimant had designed a new 'Coco' moped, which featured special engine parts and had entered into negotiations with the defendants with a view to them ultimately manufacturing it. He showed the defendants a prototype and also supplied them with information, drawings, and other aids towards the production of the moped. After several months of discussions, the defendants broke off negotiations and subsequently began manufacturing and selling their own 'Scamp' moped, which was highly successful. The defendants admitted that the piston and carburettor were of the same types as the 'Coco' moped. The claimant then sought an injunction against the manufacture and sale of any machines in which the defendants had made use, directly or indirectly, of any confidential information which was the property of the claimant. This was refused by Megarry J.

Megarry J, at p. 419:

The equitable jurisdiction in cases of breach of confidence is ancient; confidence is the cousin of trust. The Statute of Uses, 1535, is framed in terms of 'use, confidence or trust'; and a couplet, attributed to Sir Thomas More, Lord Chancellor avers that;

> Three things are to be helpt in Conscience; Fraud, Accident and things of Confidence.

(See 1 Rolle's Abridgement 374). In the middle of the last century, the great case of *Prince Albert v Strange* (1849) 1 MacN & G 25 reasserted the doctrine. In the case before me, it is common ground that there is no question of any breach of contract, for no contract ever came into existence. Accordingly, what I have to consider is the pure equitable doctrine of confidence, unaffected by contract. Furthermore, I am here in the realms of commerce, and there is no question of any marital relationship such as arose in *Duchess of Argyll v Duke of Argyll* [1967] Ch 302. Thus limited, what are the essentials of the doctrine?

Of the various authorities cited to me, I have found *Saltman Engineering Co Ltd v Campbell Engineering Co Ltd* (1948) 65 RPC 203; *Terrapin Ltd v Builders' Supply Co (Hayes) Ltd* [1960] RPC 128 and *Seager v Copydex Ltd* [1967] 1 WLR 923; [1967] RPC 349; of the most assistance. All are decisions of the Court of Appeal. I think it is quite plain from the *Saltman* case that the obligation of confidence may exist where, as in this case, there is no contractual relationship between the parties. In cases of contract, the primary question is no doubt that of construing the contract and any terms implied in it. Where there is no contract, however, the question must be one of what it is that suffices to bring the obligation into being; and there is the further question of what amounts to a breach of that obligation.

In my judgment, three elements are normally required if, apart from contract, a case of breach of confidence is to succeed. First, the information itself, in the words of Lord Greene MR in the *Saltman* case on page 215, must 'have the necessary quality of confidence about

---

[2] [2001] 1 AC 268.   [3] (1948) 65 RPC 203.

it'. Secondly, that information must have been imparted in circumstances importing an obligation of confidence. Thirdly, there must be an unauthorised use of that information to the detriment of the party communicating it.

Megarry J outlines a three-limb test—known as the *Coco v Clark* test—for establishing an equitable breach of confidence. However, Megarry J refused to grant the injunction since he was not satisfied that the claimant had made out the first and third limbs.

The House of Lords has approved the *Coco v Clark* test in subsequent cases.[4] The remainder of this chapter examines the elements for establishing an equitable breach of confidence in more detail. As we shall see, in the field of personal or private information, the *Coco v Clark* test has been significantly altered.

FURTHER READING

R. G. Hammond, 'The origins of the equitable duty of confidence' (1979) 8 Anglo-American LR 71.

S. Ricketson, 'Confidential information: A new proprietary interest? Part I' (1977) 11 Melbourne University LR 223.

8.3 CONFIDENTIAL INFORMATION

8.3.1 TYPE OF INFORMATION THAT IS PROTECTABLE

The flexibility of the action for breach of confidence is demonstrated by the width of the information that it encompasses. This includes literary and artistic material, such as ideas for a television series,[5] photographic images of articles assembled for the purpose of a record album cover,[6] and the costumes and design of a film set.[7] It also embraces government information, such as Cabinet discussions and advice,[8] and details of the security services.[9] Confidential commercial information, including trade secrets, may be protected, such as the design of a carpet grip,[10] the design of prefabricated portable buildings,[11] and a moulding system for decorative gas fires.[12] Finally, personal information may qualify as confidential, including marital secrets,[13] private telephone conversations,[14] details of a homosexual affair,[15] photographic images of a wedding reception,[16] details of narcotics addiction therapy,[17] and details of a sadomasochistic sex party.[18]

---

[4] e.g. *Attorney-General v Observer Ltd* [1990] 1 AC 109, 268, per Lord Griffiths and *Douglas v Hello! Ltd* [2008] 1 AC 1, paras. 111–15, per Lord Hoffmann.
[5] *Fraser v Thames TV* [1984] 1 QB 44.
[6] *Creation Records Ltd v News Group Newspapers Ltd* [1997] EMLR 444.
[7] *Shelley Films v Rex* [1994] EMLR 134.   [8] *Attorney-General v Cape* [1976] QB 752.
[9] *Attorney-General v Observer Ltd* [1990] 1 AC 109.
[10] *Seager v Copydex (No 1)* [1967] 2 All ER 415.
[11] *Terrapin Ltd v Builders' Supply Company (Hayes) Ltd* [1967] RPC 375.
[12] *Lancashire Fires v SA Lyons* [1966] FSR 629.
[13] *Argyll (Duchess) v Argyll (Duke)* [1967] 1 Ch 302.
[14] *Francome v Mirror Group Newspapers Ltd* [1984] 2 All ER 408.
[15] *Barrymore v News Group Newspapers Ltd* [1997] FSR 600.
[16] *Douglas v Hello! (No 3)* [2006] QB 125.
[17] *Campbell v Mirror Group Newspapers Ltd* [2004] 2 AC 457.
[18] *Mosley v News Group Newspapers Ltd* [2008] EMLR 20.

8.3.2 INFORMATION MUST BE IDENTIFIABLE, ORIGINAL, NOT TRIVIAL NOR IMMORAL

Although a wide range of information may be capable of protection, important threshold requirements, as outlined in the following case, must be satisfied.

Fraser v Thames TV [1984] 1 QB 44

The claimants had developed a well-formed idea for a television series concerning the formation of a female rock group and their subsequent experiences and adventures. It was to be partly fictional and partly based upon the experiences of the second claimants, who had formed a group, called 'Rock Bottom' in 1973. The idea for the series was orally communicated in confidence by one of the claimants to the second defendant (the scriptwriter), who in turn communicated the idea to the third defendant (the producer). The first defendant television company were also made aware of the idea for the series and decided to make the series, *Rock Follies* except using different actresses. The claimants claimed, *inter alia*, damages for breach of confidence. The defendants argued that while confidence can, in principle, protect a literary or dramatic idea, it can only do so when it is fully developed in the form of a synopsis or embodied in a material form.

Hirst J, at pp. 65–6:

In my judgment there is no reason in principle why an oral idea should not qualify for protection under the law of confidence, provided it meets the other criteria I discuss below. Neither the originality nor the quality of an idea is in any way affected by the form in which it is expressed. No doubt both the communication and the content of an oral idea may be more difficult to prove than in the case of a written idea, but difficulties of proof should not affect the principle any more than in any other branches of the law where similar problems arise (e.g. contract and defamation).

...

I accept that to be capable of protection the idea must be sufficiently developed, so that it would be seen to be a concept which has at least some attractiveness for a television programme and which is capable of being realised as an actuality: see *per* Harris J in *Talbot v General Television Corporation Pty Ltd* [1981] RPC 1, 9, lines 20–22. But I do not think this requirement necessitates in every case a full synopsis. In some cases the nature of the idea may require extensive development of this kind in order to meet the criteria. But in others the criteria may be met by a short unelaborated statement of an idea. In *Talbot's* case itself I do not think the detailed submission, quoted at p. 5, added very much of substance to the idea which is set out in one sentence starting at line 10 on p. 5.

Unquestionably, of course, the idea must have some significant element of originality not already in the realm of public knowledge. The originality may consist in a significant twist or slant to a well known concept (*Talbot's* case). This is, I think, by analogy, consistent with the statements in *Saltman Engineering Co Ltd v Campbell Engineering Co Ltd* 65 RPC 203 and *Coco v AN Clark (Engineers) Ltd* [1969] RPC 41, that novelty in the industrial field can be derived from the application of human ingenuity to well known concepts.

...

This of course does not mean that every stray mention of an idea by one person to another is protected. To succeed in his claim the plaintiff must establish not only that the occasion of communication was confidential, but also that the content of the idea was clearly identifiable, original, of potential commercial attractiveness and capable of being realised in actuality.

[**Hirst J** accepted that these requirements were satisfied on the facts and that the scriptwriter, producer, and Thames were fixed with an obligation of confidence.]

How does the type of information that can be protected by confidence differ from the subject matter that can be protected by copyright? Further, what are the requirements for protection set out in *Fraser*? An example of where these requirements were not satisfied is *De Maudsley v Palumbo*.[19] In this case, the claimant had revealed to the defendant, during a dinner party at the defendant's flat, his idea for a new nightclub. Subsequently, a nightclub—the Ministry of Sound—was opened by the defendants, in which the claimant had no involvement. The claimant argued, *inter alia*, breach of confidence. Knox J held that the information disclosed by the claimant was not capable of protection. The information included the idea that the club would legally operate all night long; that top disc jockeys from the UK and worldwide would appear at the club; that there would be separate areas for dancing, resting, and socializing; and that the club would be big, decorated in a 'high-tech industrial' warehouse style. Knox J described the information as either too general or vague, or lacking in originality, to constitute confidential information.

Information of a grossly immoral nature will not be the subject of a confidential obligation.[20] It seems, however, that what can be regarded as grossly immoral is judged according to a fairly high standard and courts are unlikely to characterize sexual activities as such because '[t]here is no common view that sexual conduct of any kind between consenting adults is grossly immoral'.[21]

8.3.3 INFORMATION MUST BE SECRET

A crucial threshold requirement for protection is that the information is secret or confidential, i.e. not in the public domain. This general principle was set out by Lord Greene MR in *Saltman Engineering v Campbell Engineering*:[22]

The information, to be confidential, must, I apprehend, apart from contract, have the necessary quality of confidence about it, namely, it must not be something which is public property and public knowledge. On the other hand, it is perfectly possible to have a confidential document, be it a formula, a plan, a sketch, or something of that kind, which is the result of work done by the maker on materials which may be available for use of anybody; but what makes it confidential is the fact that the maker of the document has used his brain and this produced a result which can only be produced by somebody who goes through the same process.

As Lord Greene MR emphasizes, information must not be in the public domain, but confidentiality can arise where materials in the public domain are developed or processed as a result of human skill or creativity.[23] An example of where information was held to have entered the public domain is *Mustad & Son v Dosen*.

---

[19] [1996] FSR 447.   [20] *Stephens v Avery* [1988] Ch 449.
[21] Ibid., 449, 453.   [22] (1948) 65 RPC 203, 215.
[23] See also *Coco v Clark* [1969] FSR 415, 420, per Megarry J.

O Mustad & Son v Dosen and Allcock [1963] 3 All ER 416

The appellants, Mustad, had purchased a company called Thoring and Co and with it the benefit of Thoring's trade secrets, which included confidential information relating to a machine for the manufacture of fish hooks. The first respondent, Dosen, had originally been employed by Thoring and had come under an express contractual obligation of confidence. The appellants commenced proceedings and sought an injunction against Dosen from communicating confidential information relating to the machine to Dosen's new employer, the second respondents, Allcock & Co Ltd.

The appellant had filed a patent application in respect of the information alleged to be confidential in Germany in 1925 and the patent specification was published in 1926. The respondents contended that, as such, the information was no longer secret. The appellant argued that Dosen possessed more information than appeared in the patent specification. A final injunction was granted by Rowlatt J, which was set aside by the Court of Appeal. The appeal to the House of Lords was dismissed.

Lord Buckmaster (the other law lords in agreement), **at p. 418:**

Of course, the important point about the patent is not whether it was valid or invalid, but what it was that it disclosed, because after the disclosure had been made by the appellants to the world, it was impossible for them to get an injunction restraining the respondents from disclosing what was common knowledge. The secret, as a secret, had ceased to exist. But the appellants say—and I think say with considerable force—that it might well have been that in the course of the experience which Dosen had gained in their service he had obtained knowledge of ancillary secrets connected with the patented invention which were not in fact included in the invention but which would be of very great service to any person who proceeded to make the machine to which the invention related.

[The onus of showing this knowledge ancillary to the patent specification lay with the appellants, who failed to adduce this evidence.]

Cases show that the secrecy requirement, unlike in patent law, is not an absolute one. Thus, in *Prince Albert v Strange*,[24] an injunction was granted even though the confidential information, in the form of etchings of Queen Victoria and Prince Albert, had been circulated amongst friends of the claimant. Further, in *Exchange Telegraph Co Ltd v Central News Ltd*[25] Stirling J rejected the argument that race information was no longer protected because it had become public to those present at the racecourse. As he explained: 'the information was not made known to the whole world; it was no doubt known to a large number of persons, but a great many more were ignorant of it'.[26] In the following case, an obligation of confidence was maintained even though the allegedly confidential information could have been obtained from public sources.

Schering Chemicals Ltd v Falkman Ltd [1982] QB 1

The claimant made and marketed a drug, Primodos, as a pregnancy test. Subsequently, it was suspected that the drug was responsible for causing abnormalities in unborn

---

[24] (1849) 1 MacN & G 25, 41 ER 1171. [25] [1897] 2 Ch 48.
[26] *Exchange Telegraph Co Ltd v Central News Ltd* [1897] 2 Ch 48, 53.

children and, unsurprisingly, this attracted large media coverage. The claimant engaged the services of the first defendant to provide training sessions for their executives to assist them in handling the adverse publicity. For the purpose of training the claimant's executives, a great deal of information was disclosed to the first defendant, which they agreed to keep confidential. The instructors also accepted that the information was confidential. One of the instructors, the second defendant, came up with the idea of making a documentary on Primodos, which the claimant rejected. Nevertheless, the second defendant went ahead with making the documentary. The claimant issued proceedings against the defendants and obtained an interim injunction to prevent the broadcasting of the film. A majority of the Court of Appeal dismissed the appeal against the award of an injunction, rejecting the argument that the information was not confidential because it could be derived from public domain sources.

Shaw LJ, at pp. 27–8:

The second proposition put forward on behalf of Mr Elstein and Thames was to this effect. When Mr Elstein undertook as an associate of Falkman to participate in the course for Schering, he had no intimate knowledge of the controversy and contentions which surrounded Primodos. By that time there had been numerous articles in scientific papers and journals and the first Sunday Times article had given publicity to the matter in the popular press. Mr Elstein's mind had, however, not been prompted to look in that direction. What he learned at the course came new to him. It is now said that all the information upon which the programme of the projected documentary is based could have been derived from sources available to the public before the Schering course with Executive Television Training. It is asserted also that Mr Elstein, with the assistance of a colleague at Thames, has assiduously explored and collated all those sources. The relevant facts and opinions are all to be found in what has been described as 'the public domain' or 'the public sector'. No principle of confidentiality can apply, so it is contended, to matters which have become notorious. Whatever may have been the fiduciary duty on the part of Mr Elstein not to disclose anything of a confidential nature that he had learned on the course it had been entirely dissipated when the Primodos affair emerged into public view. What obligation of reticence can apply to what has long been an open secret? So the argument ran.

It is an argument which at best is cynical; some might regard it as specious. Even in the commercial field, ethics and good faith are not to be regarded as merely opportunist or expedient. In any case, though facts may be widely known, they are not ever-present in the minds of the public. To extend the knowledge or to revive the recollection of matters which may be detrimental or prejudicial to the interests of some person or organisation is not to be condoned because the facts are already known to some and linger in the memories of others.

Templeman LJ, at pp. 37–8:

In my judgment, when Mr Elstein agreed for reward to take part in the training course and received and absorbed information from Schering, he became under a duty not to use that information and impliedly promised Schering that he would not use that information for the very purpose which Schering sought to avoid, namely, bad publicity in the future, including publicity which Schering reasonably regarded as bad publicity. Schering reasonably regard the film 'The Primodos Affair' as bad publicity based on information which they supplied to Mr Elstein to enable him to advise Schering. Mr Elstein could have made a film based on Primodos if he had not taken part in the training programme, but 'The Primodos Affair' film only came into existence because Mr Elstein received from Schering information for one purpose and used that information for another purpose, for his own gain and to the detriment, as they reasonably believe, of Schering.

The information supplied by Schering to Mr Elstein had already been published, but it included information which was damaging to Schering when it was first published and which could not be republished without the risk of causing further damage to Schering. Any republication and recycling by Mr Elstein of any of the information supplied to him by Schering could be unwelcome to Schering, could be inimical to the best interests of Schering and could reasonably be regarded by Schering as further bad publicity. Mr Elstein must have realised that if he revived and recycled and republished information which he received from Schering, that action on his part was liable to be damaging. Mr Elstein must have realised that Schering would not supply Mr Elstein with any information at all if they thought for one moment that there was any possibility that he might make use of that information for his own purposes and in a manner which Schering might find unwelcome or harmful. That Mr Elstein realised and accepted this is shown by his letter dated July 4, 1979. As between Schering and Mr Elstein, if Mr Elstein had obtained information from sources other than Schering, then it would of course not have been confidential in his hands but, by agreeing to advise Schering and by accepting information from them to enable him to advise Schering, Mr Elstein placed himself under a duty, in my judgment, not to make use of that information without the consent of Schering in a manner which Schering reasonably considered to be harmful to their cause. As between Schering and Mr Elstein, the information which Mr Elstein received from Schering was confidential and cannot be published by Mr Elstein in the film 'The Primodos Affair'. Thames made the film 'The Primodos Affair' with full knowledge of all the circumstances and with knowledge of the claim by Schering that the film would constitute a breach of confidentiality and could not be broadcast without the prior consent of Schering.

[**Lord Denning MR** delivered a dissenting judgment, holding that an injunction should be refused because the information was not confidential and it was in the public interest to disclose the information.]

The majority in *Schering* found that even though the information previously had been the subject of extensive media coverage this did not preclude the information from being confidential and subject to an obligation of confidence. Does this mean that information will fall into the public domain only when it is generally accessible on a large scale? Or is the test of confidentiality tied to whether or not further prejudice or harm can be suffered by further circulation? Are either of these approaches a desirable way to determine confidentiality? Another view of the case is that, even though much of the information was already in the public domain, the defendants had contractually promised not to disclose the information and this had been defined in the agreement as 'information, some of which is public and some of which is private'. It could be argued that, even though much of the information used by the defendants *was* in the public domain, they had been privy to some information that was still secret and, as such, were in breach of their obligation. Alternatively, it could be argued that the defendants' obligation was not dependent on the information being secret and was simply a promise not to use the information that had been disclosed to them. Such an approach, however, would mean that contractual obligations of confidence could be created in respect of information that was not confidential. Is this acceptable?

It appears that there is no 'bright line' test for determining when information enters the public domain. Nevertheless, courts have sought to provide guidance on this issue, as illustrated by the House of Lords decision in *Attorney-General v Observer Ltd*.

Attorney-General v Observer Ltd [1990] 1 AC 109

The case concerned the publication of the memoirs of former senior MI5 agent, Peter Wright. The book, entitled *Spycatcher*, was published in Australia, the United States, Canada, the Republic of Ireland, and elsewhere. Although the book had not been published in the UK, it could be readily imported into the country. Litigation in England was commenced in relation to the activities of certain newspapers. *The Guardian* and *Observer* newspapers had published articles about the litigation in Australia to restrain the publication of the work and the *Sunday Times* had published the first extract of an intended serialization of *Spycatcher*. At first instance and in the Court of Appeal, it was held that the Attorney-General was not entitled to an injunction against the newspapers. A majority of the House of Lords dismissed the appeal.

Lord Keith, at pp. 259–60:

In relation to Mr Wright, there can be no doubt whatever that had he sought to bring about the first publication of his book in this country, the Crown would have been entitled to an injunction restraining him. The work of a member of MI5 and the information which he acquires in the course of that work must necessarily be secret and confidential and be kept secret and confidential by him. There is no room for discrimination between secrets of greater or lesser importance, nor any room for close examination of the precise manner in which revelation of any particular matter may prejudice the national interest. Any attempt to do so would lead to further damage. All this has been accepted from beginning to end by each of the judges in this country who has had occasion to consider the case and also by counsel for the respondents…The question whether Mr Wright or those acting for him would be at liberty to publish *Spycatcher* in England under existing circumstances does not arise for immediate consideration. These circumstances include the world-wide dissemination of the contents of the book which has been brought about by Mr Wright's wrongdoing. In my opinion general publication in this country would not bring about any significant damage to the public interest beyond what has already been done. All such secrets as the book may contain have been revealed to any intelligence services whose interests are opposed to those of the United Kingdom. Any damage to the confidence reposed in the British Security and Intelligence Services by those of friendly countries brought about by Mr Wright's actions would not be materially increased by publication here…I have not been persuaded that the effect of publication in England would be to bring about greater damage in the respects founded upon than has already been caused by the widespread publication elsewhere in the world. In the result, the case for an injunction now against publication by or on behalf of Mr Wright would in my opinion rest upon the principle that he should not be permitted to take advantage of his own wrongdoing.

…For the reasons which I have indicated in dealing with the position of Mr Wright, I am of the opinion that the reports and comments proposed by *The Guardian* and the *Observer* would not be harmful to the public interest, nor would the continued serialisation by *The Sunday Times*. I would therefore refuse an injunction against any of the newspapers. I would stress that I do not base this upon any balancing of public interest nor upon any considerations of freedom of the press, nor upon any possible defences of prior publication or just cause or excuse, but simply upon the view that all possible damage to the interest of the Crown has already been done by the publication of *Spycatcher* abroad and the ready availability of copies in this country.

It is possible, I think, to envisage cases where, even in the light of widespread publication abroad of certain information, a person whom that information concerned might be entitled to restrain publication by a third party in this country. For example, if in the *Argyll* case the Duke had secured the revelation of the marital secrets in an American newspaper, the Duchess could reasonably claim that publication of the same material in England would bring it to the attention of people who would otherwise be unlikely to learn of it and who were more closely interested in her activities than American readers. The publication in England would be more harmful to her than publication in America. Similar considerations would apply to, say, a publication in America by the medical adviser to an English pop group about diseases for which he had treated them. But it cannot reasonably be held in the present case that publication in England now of the contents of *Spycatcher* would do any more harm to the public interest than has already been done.

Lord Brightman, at p. 265:

A member of the Security Service is under a lifelong duty of confidence towards the Crown. The purpose of that duty is to preserve intact the secrets of the service which it would be against the public interest to disclose. If the member departs abroad and publishes his memoirs there, he breaches his lifelong duty of confidence. Thereafter such duty is incapable of existing *quoad* the matter disclosed. The reason why the duty of confidence is extinguished is that the matter is no longer secret and there is therefore no secrecy in relation to such matter remaining to be preserved by the duty of confidence. It is meaningless to talk of a continuing duty of confidence in relation to matter disclosed world-wide. It is meaningful only to discuss the remedies available to deprive the delinquent confidant or his successors in title of benefits flowing from the breach, or in an appropriate case to compensate the confider.

Lord Goff, at p. 281:

I start with the broad general principle (which I do not intend in any way to be definitive) that a duty of confidence arises when confidential information comes to the knowledge of a person (the confidant) in circumstances where he has notice, or is held to have agreed, that the information is confidential, with the effect that it would be just in all the circumstances that he should be precluded from disclosing the information to others.

. . .

To this broad general principle, there are three limiting principles to which I wish to refer. The first limiting principle (which is rather an expression of the scope of the duty) is highly relevant to this appeal. It is that the principle of confidentiality only applies to information to the extent that it is confidential. In particular, once it has entered what is usually called the public domain (which means no more than that the information in question is so generally accessible that, in all the circumstances, it cannot be regarded as confidential) then, as a general rule, the principle of confidentiality can have no application to it. I shall revert to this limiting principle at a later stage.

The second limiting principle is that the duty of confidence applies neither to useless information, nor to trivia. There is no need for me to develop this point.

Attorney-General v Observer Ltd illustrates that confidentiality will be destroyed by information entering the public domain. But in what circumstances, broadly speaking, will this be the case? Will the assessment differ depending on the type of information involved, i.e. whether it is personal or not and, if so, should this matter?

8.3.4 THE IMPACT OF THE HUMAN RIGHTS ACT 1998

8.3.4.1 Protection of private information

Cases subsequent to the Human Rights Act 1998 ('HRA') have further relaxed the requirement of confidentiality when it comes to personal information. The HRA makes it unlawful for a public authority (which includes a court) to act in a way that is incompatible with a Convention right. The Convention rights include Articles 8 and 10 of the European Convention on Human Rights ('ECHR'). The former establishes the right to respect for private and family life, while the latter sets out the right to freedom of expression. The House of Lords first considered the impact of Articles 8 and 10 on the law of confidence in *Campbell v Mirror Group Newspapers Ltd*.

Campbell v Mirror Group Newspapers Ltd [2004] 2 AC 457

The case concerned a series of articles published by *The Mirror* newspaper in February 2001. The articles disclosed that the claimant, Naomi Campbell, had a drug addiction (which she had previously denied) and was receiving therapy with Narcotics Anonymous ('NA') and gave details of the meeting she was attending. Two of the articles were accompanied by photographs of Ms Campbell, dressed casually, leaving a NA meeting in Chelsea, London. The first of the articles was sympathetic to Ms Campbell, but the later articles were not, in light of the fact that she had commenced proceedings against *The Mirror*. At first instance Morland J held that Ms Campbell had established entitlement to damages for breach of confidence and breach of duty under the Data Protection Act 1998 and awarded her £2,500 in compensatory damages and £1,000 in aggravated damages, for the racist and hurtful remarks contained in the later articles. This was overturned by the Court of Appeal, but upheld by the House of Lords.

Lord Nicholls:

Breach of confidence: misuse of private information

17. The time has come to recognise that the values enshrined in articles 8 and 10 are now part of the cause of action for breach of confidence. As Lord Woolf CJ has said, the courts have been able to achieve this result by absorbing the rights protected by articles 8 and 10 into this cause of action: *A v B plc* [2003] QB 195, 202, para. 4. Further, it should now be recognised that for this purpose these values are of general application. The values embodied in articles 8 and 10 are as much applicable in disputes between individuals or between an individual and a non-governmental body such as a newspaper as they are in disputes between individuals and a public authority.

18. In reaching this conclusion it is not necessary to pursue the controversial question whether the European Convention itself has this wider effect. Nor is it necessary to decide whether the duty imposed on courts by section 6 of the Human Rights Act 1998 extends to questions of substantive law as distinct from questions of practice and procedure. It is sufficient to recognise that the values underlying articles 8 and 10 are not confined to disputes between individuals and public authorities.

. . .

20. I should take this a little further on one point. Article 8(1) recognises the need to respect private and family life. Article 8(2) recognises there are occasions when intrusion into

private and family life may be justified. One of these is where the intrusion is necessary for the protection of the rights and freedoms of others. Article 10(1) recognises the importance of freedom of expression. But article 10(2), like article 8(2), recognises there are occasions when protection of the rights of others may make it necessary for freedom of expression to give way. When both these articles are engaged a difficult question of proportionality may arise. This question is distinct from the initial question of whether the published information engaged article 8 at all by being within the sphere of the complainant's private or family life.

21. Accordingly, in deciding what was the ambit of an individual's 'private life' in particular circumstances courts need to be on guard against using as a touchstone a test which brings into account considerations which should more properly be considered at the later stage of proportionality. Essentially the touchstone of private life is whether in respect of the disclosed facts the person in question had a reasonable expectation of privacy.

22. Different forms of words, usually to much the same effect, have been suggested from time to time. The American Law Institute, Restatement of the Law, Torts, 2d (1977), section 652D, uses the formulation of disclosure of matter which 'would be highly offensive to a reasonable person'. In *Australian Broadcasting Corpn v Lenah Game Meats Pty Ltd* (2001) 208 CLR 199, 226, para. 42, Gleeson CJ used words, widely quoted, having a similar meaning. This particular formulation should be used with care, for two reasons. First, the 'highly offensive' phrase is suggestive of a stricter test of private information than a reasonable expectation of privacy. Second, the 'highly offensive' formulation can all too easily bring into account, when deciding whether the disclosed information was private, considerations which go more properly to issues of proportionality; for instance, the degree of intrusion into private life, and the extent to which publication was a matter of proper public concern. This could be a recipe for confusion.

Lord Hope:

86. The language has changed following the coming into operation of the Human Rights Act 1998 and the incorporation into domestic law of article 8 and article 10 of the Convention. We now talk about the right to respect for private life and the countervailing right to freedom of expression. The jurisprudence of the European Court offers important guidance as to how these competing rights ought to be approached and analysed. I doubt whether the result is that the centre of gravity, as my noble and learned friend, Lord Hoffmann, says, has shifted. It seems to me that the balancing exercise to which that guidance is directed is essentially the same exercise, although it is plainly now more carefully focussed and more penetrating. As Lord Woolf CJ said in *A v B plc* [2003] QB 195, 202, para. 4, new breadth and strength is given to the action for breach of confidence by these articles.

...

92. The underlying question in all cases where it is alleged that there has been a breach of the duty of confidence is whether the information that was disclosed was private and not public. There must be some interest of a private nature that the claimant wishes to protect: *A v B plc* [2003] QB 195, 206, para. 11(vii). In some cases, as the Court of Appeal said in that case, the answer to the question whether the information is public or private will be obvious. Where it is not, the broad test is whether disclosure of the information about the individual ('A') would give substantial offence to A, assuming that A was placed in similar circumstances and was a person of ordinary sensibilities.

93. The trial judge applied the test which was suggested by Gleeson CJ in Australian *Broadcasting Corpn v Lenah Game Meats Pty Ltd* (2001) 208 CLR 199. In that case the respondent sought an interlocutory injunction against the broadcasting of a film about its operations at a bush tail possum processing facility. It showed the stunning and killing of

possums. Gleeson CJ said, at p. 204, paras. 34–5, that information about the respondent's slaughtering methods was not confidential in its nature and that, while the activities filmed were carried out on private property, they were not shown, or alleged, to be private in any other sense. He observed, at p. 226, para. 42, that there was a large area in between what was necessarily public and what was necessarily private:

> An activity is not private simply because it is not done in public. It does not suffice to make an act private that, because it occurs on private property, it has such measure of protection from the public gaze as the characteristics of the property, the nature of the activity, the locality, and the disposition of the property owner combine to afford. Certain kinds of information about a person, such as information relating to health, personal relationships, or finances, may be easy to identify as private; as may certain kinds of activity, which a reasonable person, applying contemporary standards of morals and behaviour, would understand to be meant to be unobserved. The requirement that disclosure or observation of information or conduct would be highly offensive to a reasonable person of ordinary sensibilities is in many circumstances a useful practical test of what is private.

Applying to the facts of the case the test which he had described in the last sentence of this paragraph, he said in para. 43 that the problem for the respondent was that the activities secretly observed and filmed were not relevantly private.

94. The test which Gleeson CJ has identified is useful in cases where there is room for doubt, especially where the information relates to an activity or course of conduct such as the slaughtering methods that were in issue in that case. But it is important not to lose sight of the remarks which preceded it. The test is not needed where the information can easily be identified as private...

95. I think that the judge was right to regard the details of Miss Campbell's attendance at Narcotics Anonymous as private information which imported a duty of confidence. He said that information relating to Miss Campbell's therapy for drug addiction giving details that it was by regular attendance at Narcotics Anonymous meetings was easily identifiable as private. With reference to the guidance that the Court of Appeal gave in *A v B plc* [2003] QB 195, 206, para. 11(vii), he said that it was obvious that there existed a private interest in this fact that was worthy of protection. The Court of Appeal, on the other hand, seem to have regarded the receipt of therapy from Narcotics Anonymous as less worthy of protection in comparison with treatment for the condition administered by medical practitioners. I would not make that distinction. Views may differ as to what is the best treatment for an addiction. But it is well known that persons who are addicted to the taking of illegal drugs or to alcohol can benefit from meetings at which they discuss and face up to their addiction. The private nature of these meetings encourages addicts to attend them in the belief that they can do so anonymously. The assurance of privacy is an essential part of the exercise. The therapy is at risk of being damaged if the duty of confidence which the participants owe to each other is breached by making details of the therapy, such as where, when and how often it is being undertaken, public. I would hold that these details are obviously private.

96. If the information is obviously private, the situation will be one where the person to whom it relates can reasonably expect his privacy to be respected. So there is normally no need to go on and ask whether it would be highly offensive for it to be published.

Baronness Hale:

[Referring to the test as stated by **Gleeson CJ** in *Lenah*.]

136. It is apparent, therefore, that Gleeson CJ did not intend those last words to be the only test, particularly in respect of information which is obviously private, including information

about health, personal relationships or finance. It is also apparent that he was referring to the sensibilities of a reasonable person placed in the situation of the subject of the disclosure rather than to its recipient.

137. It should be emphasised that the 'reasonable expectation of privacy' is a threshold test which brings the balancing exercise into play. It is not the end of the story. Once the information is identified as 'private' in this way, the court must balance the claimant's interest in keeping the information private against the countervailing interest of the recipient in publishing it. Very often, it can be expected that the countervailing rights of the recipient will prevail.

...

154. ...We have not so far held that the mere fact of covert photography is sufficient to make the information contained in the photograph confidential. The activity photographed must be private. If this had been, and had been presented as, a picture of Naomi Campbell going about her business in a public street, there could have been no complaint. She makes a substantial part of her living out of being photographed looking stunning in designer clothing. Readers will obviously be interested to see how she looks if and when she pops out to the shops for a bottle of milk. There is nothing essentially private about that information nor can it be expected to damage her private life. It may not be a high order of freedom of speech but there is nothing to justify interfering with it. (This was the view of Randerson J in *Hosking v Runting* [2003] 3 NZLR 385, which concerned a similarly innocuous outing; see now the decision of the Court of Appeal [2004] NZCA 34.)

[**Lord Carswell** agreed that the information was private for the reasons given by **Lord Hope** and **Baroness Hale**. Although **Lord Nicholls** was in the minority, his statements of principle were consistent with the majority. Where he differed was in the application of those principles to the facts of the case.]

In *Campbell* did the House of Lords ask whether the information was confidential in nature or did they simply ask whether it was private and thus engaged Article 8 of the ECHR? Does it therefore seem that, in so far as personal information is concerned, the enquiry is directed at the private nature of the information, i.e. whether there is a 'reasonable expectation of privacy'?

Several, subsequent Court of Appeal decisions have adopted the test of 'reasonable expectation of privacy'.[27] Determining whether a person has a reasonable expectation of privacy will entail a detailed examination of all the circumstances of the case.[28] The relevant factors include:

...the attributes of the claimant, the nature of the activity in which the claimant was engaged, the place at which it was happening, the nature and purpose of the intrusion, the absence of consent and whether it was known or could be inferred, the effect on the claimant and the circumstances in which and the purpose for which the information came into the hands of the publisher.[29]

---

[27] *Douglas v Hello! (No 3)* [2006] QB 125, 161 per Lord Phillips MR (delivering the judgment of the court); *McKennitt v Ash* [2007] 3 WLR 194, 123 per Buxton LJ (with whom Latham LJ and Longmore LJ agreed); *Associated Newspapers v HRH Prince of Wales* [2007] 3 WLR 222, 276–7 per Lord Phillips MR (delivering the judgment of the court); *Lord Browne of Madingley v Associated Newspapers Ltd* [2007] 3 WLR 289, 298, per Sir Anthony Clarke MR (delivering the judgment of the court); and *Murray v Express Newspapers Plc* [2008] ECDR 12, para. 35, per Sir Anthony Clarke MR (delivering the judgment of the court).
[28] *Lord Browne of Madingley v Associated Newspapers Ltd* [2007] 3 WLR 289, 301; *Murray v Express Newspapers Plc* [2008] ECDR 12, para. 36.
[29] *Murray v Express Newspapers Plc* [2008] ECDR 12, para. 36 per Sir Anthony Clarke MR (delivering the judgment of the court).

What do you envisage are the main consequences of asking whether information is private, as opposed to asking whether the information is secret or confidential? In particular, will it matter to the former enquiry that information has been published or the activities concerned have occurred in a public location?

Jurisprudence from the European Court of Human Rights (ECtHR) will be highly relevant to determining whether information is private and thus engages Article 8 of the ECHR. An important, and controversial, case on the scope of Article 8 is *Von Hannover v Germany*.[30] The case was the culmination of a ten year campaign by Princess Caroline against various German magazine publishers to restrain them from publishing photographs of her going about her daily business (many of which were innocuous). The German courts held that as a 'figure of contemporary society' the applicant had to tolerate photographs of herself in a public place, even where she was not engaged in public duties. The exception to this was if she was in a 'secluded place' out of the public eye. However, the notion of 'secluded place' did not extend to activities such as her leaving her home, going shopping, engaging in sporting activities, or being on holiday. The applicant complained to the ECtHR that the lack of adequate state protection of her private life was an infringement of Article 8. The Court accepted that Article 8 conferred both negative and positive obligations on states and that the claimant's right had been infringed. It pointed out that, although the claimant was a public figure, she did not exercise any public or official functions and her private activities were not relevant to any political or public debate. The publication of the photographs did not have the purpose of contributing to any debate of general interest to society, but were solely to satisfy the curiosity of readers. Further it held that the public 'does not have a legitimate interest in knowing where the applicant is and how she behaves generally in her private life even if she appears in places that cannot always be described as secluded and despite the fact that she is well known to the public'.[31] The Court also referred to the fact that the photographs were often taken 'in a climate of continual harassment that induces in the persons concerned a very strong sense of intrusion into their private life.'[32]

Does *Von Hannover* suggest an extremely broad scope for Article 8? If so, can this be reconciled with the English courts' test of 'reasonable expectation of privacy' and the comments obiter of Lady Hale in *Campbell* at para. 154, extracted above? The potential tension between *Von Hannover* and the English authorities was explored in the context of deciding whether a child of a public figure, who was being pushed in a pram along a public street, had a reasonable expectation of privacy.

Murray v Express Newspapers Plc [2008] ECDR 12

The case involved innocuous photographs taken on a public street of a child of famous author J K Rowling (whose real name is Joanne Murray). The colour photograph, which was taken covertly by a photographer, showed the claimant's face in profile, his clothes, size, hair style and colour, and skin colour. The photograph appeared in the *Sunday Express* magazine (published by the first defendant), alongside an article that included quotations from the claimant's mother on her approach to parenting and family life. The claimant issued proceedings against the defendants (the first defendant was a photographic agency which licensed out the use of photographs) for breach of confidence,

---

[30] (2005) 40 EHRR 1.   [31] *Von Hannover v Germany* (2005) 40 EHRR 1, 28.
[32] Ibid., 25.

infringement of his right to privacy and misuse of private information. At first instance, Patten J struck out the claim based on breach of confidence or invasion of privacy for two reasons. The first was that according to the law (including *Von Hannover*) there remains an area of innocuous conduct in a public place which does not raise a reasonable expectation of privacy. The second reason was that, even if *Von Hannover* conflicted with *Campbell*, he was bound to follow *Campbell* and the New Zealand decision of *Hosking v Runting*,[33] which was cited with approval in *Campbell* and was on all fours with the facts of the case at hand, denied a privacy claim. An appeal to the Court of Appeal was allowed. In the course of its decision, the Court explored the relationship between *Von Hannover* and *Campbell*.

Sir Anthony Clarke (delivering the judgment of the Court):

47. Neither *Campbell* nor *Von Hannover* is a case about a child. There is no authoritative case in England of a child being targeted as David was here.

...

55. We recognise that there may well be circumstances in which there will be no reasonable expectation of privacy, even after *Von Hannover*. However, as we see it, all will (as ever) depend upon the facts of the particular case. The judge suggests that a distinction can be drawn between a child (or an adult) engaged in family and sporting activities and something as simple as a walk down a street or a visit to the grocers to buy the milk. This is on the basis that the first type of activity is clearly part of a person's private recreation time intended to be enjoyed in the company of family and friends and that, on the test deployed in *Von Hannover*, publicity of such activities is intrusive and can adversely affect the exercise of such social activities. We agree with the judge that that is indeed the basis of the ECtHR's approach but we do not agree that it is possible to draw a clear distinction in principle between the two kinds of activity. Thus, an expedition to a café of the kind which occurred here seems to us to be at least arguably part of each member of the family's recreation time intended to be enjoyed by them and such that publicity of it is intrusive and such as adversely to affect such activities in the future.

56. We do not share the predisposition identified by the judge in [66] that routine acts such as a visit to a shop or a ride on a bus should not attract any reasonable expectation of privacy. All depends upon the circumstances. The position of an adult may be very different from that of a child. In this appeal we are concerned only with the question whether David, as a small child, had a reasonable expectation of privacy, not with the question whether his parents would have had such an expectation. Moreover, we are concerned with the context of this case, which was not for example a single photograph taken of David which was for some reason subsequently published.

57. It seems to us that, subject to the facts of the particular case, the law should indeed protect children from intrusive media attention, at any rate to the extent of holding that a child has a reasonable expectation that he or she will not be targeted in order to obtain photographs in a public place for publication which the person who took or procured the taking of the photographs knew would be objected to on behalf of the child. That is the context in which the photographs of David were taken.

58. It is important to note that so to hold does not mean that the child will have, as the judge puts it in [66], a guarantee of privacy. To hold that the child has a reasonable expectation of privacy is only the first step. Then comes the balance which must be struck between the child's rights to respect for his or her private life under Art. 8 and the publisher's rights to freedom of expression under Art. 10. This approach does not seem to us to be inconsistent with that in *Campbell*, which was not considering the case of a child.

---

[33] [2004] NZCA 34.

59. In these circumstances we do not think that it is necessary for us to analyse the decision in *Von Hannover* in any detail, especially since this is not an appeal brought after the trial of the action but an appeal against an order striking the action out. Suffice it to say that, in our opinion, the view we have expressed is consistent with that in *Von Hannover*, to which, as *McKennitt v Ash* makes clear, it is permissible to have regard . . .

60. The context of *Von Hannover* was therefore different from this but we have little doubt that, if the assumed facts of this case were to be considered by the ECtHR, the Court would hold that David had a reasonable expectation of privacy and it seems to us to be more likely than not that, on the assumed facts, it would hold that the Art. 8/10 balance would come down in favour of David. We would add that there is nothing in the Strasbourg cases since *Von Hannover* which in our opinion leads to any other conclusion: see, e.g. *Reklos v Greece* (petition no. 1234/05), September 6, 2007.

61. In these circumstances, the judge was in our judgment wrong to strike out David's claim on the ground that he had no arguable case that he had a reasonable expectation of privacy. Understandably, the judge did not consider whether, if Art. 8 was engaged, David had an arguable case that the balance should be struck in his favour. In our opinion David has an arguable case on both points and his parents should be permitted to take his claim to trial on his behalf.

Does *Murray* satisfactorily reconcile *Von Hannover* and *Campbell* or does it side-step the issue? What view would an English court take, do you think, of a situation where an adult public figure is surreptitiously photographed whilst going about their ordinary business in a public location?

8.3.4.2 Classifying information as private and commercial

An interesting question is whether information can be classified as *both* private and commercial and thus be subjected to the two different tests—'reasonable expectation of privacy' and 'confidentiality'? The *Douglas v Hello!* litigation undoubtedly supports the dual characterization of information. The litigation was prompted by *Hello!* magazine's threatened publication of surreptitiously taken photographs of the high-profile celebrity wedding between Michael Douglas and Catherine Zeta-Jones, in advance of *OK!* magazine's exclusive coverage of the event. The claimants were unsuccessful in obtaining an interim injunction to prevent the threatened publication,[34] but at trial Lindsay J found in favour of the claimants on the basis of an actionable breach of confidence[35] and awarded the first and second claimants (the Douglases) £3,750 each in respect of the distress caused by publication of the unauthorized photographs and £7,000 combined for wasted costs incurred by their having to bring forward preparation, approval, and provision of the authorized photographs to the third claimant, *OK!* magazine. A sum of £1,033,156 was awarded to *OK!* magazine in respect of lost profits and wasted costs.[36] The Court of Appeal dismissed *Hello!* magazine's appeal against the first and second claimants but allowed their appeal against *OK!* magazine.[37] In the House of Lords, *OK!* magazine's appeal was upheld and the order of Lindsay J restored.[38]

The Court of Appeal held that photographs of the Douglases at their wedding plainly portrayed aspects of their private life, which was not affected by the fact that they had contracted

---

[34] *Douglas v Hello! Ltd (No 1)* [2001] QB 967. [35] *Douglas v Hello! Ltd* [2003] EMLR 31 (Ch).
[36] *Douglas v Hello!* [2004] EMLR 2 (Ch). [37] *Douglas v Hello! (No 3)* [2006] QB 125.
[38] *Douglas v Hello! Ltd* [2008] 1 AC 1.

with *OK!* to give it the exclusive right to publish photographs of the event. However, the Court of Appeal accepted that, 'To the extent that an individual authorizes photographs taken on a private occasion to be made public, the potential for distress at the publication of other, unauthorized, photographs, taken on the same occasion, will be reduced.'[39]

However, the Douglases were also treated as having a *commercial* interest in the photographic images of their wedding. The Court of Appeal recognized that the award of damages for the labour and expense of editing the photographs that were to be provided to *OK!* was a head of damage that related to the Douglases commercial exploitation of their wedding and had nothing to do with their private life.[40] The Court saw: 'Recognition of the right of a celebrity to make money out of publicizing private information about himself, including his photographs on a private occasion [as breaking] new ground.'[41] But it could see 'no reason in principle why equity should not protect the opportunity to profit from confidential information about oneself in the same circumstances that it protects the opportunity to profit from confidential information in the nature of a trade secret'.[42]

The appeal to the House of Lords concerned only the claim of *OK!* magazine and whether or not an obligation of confidence was owed by the defendants towards them. This aspect of the decision is considered below at 8.4. For the present purposes, it is important to note that a majority of the lords rejected the argument that publication of the approved photographs in *OK!* magazine meant that the information was now in the public domain.

Douglas v Hello! Ltd [2008] 1 AC 1

Lord Hoffmann (delivering the leading speech of the majority):

[117] The point of which one should never lose sight is that *OK!* had paid 1 million for the benefit of the obligation of confidence imposed upon all those present at the wedding in respect of *any* photographs of the wedding. That was quite clear. Unless there is some conceptual or policy reason why they should not have the benefit of that obligation, I cannot see why they were not entitled to enforce it. And in my opinion there are no such reasons. Provided that one keeps one's eye firmly on the money and why it was paid, the case is, as Lindsay J held, quite straightforward.

...

[120] My noble and learned friends, Lord Nicholls of Birkenhead and Lord Walker of Gestingthorpe, are troubled by the fact that the information in the photographic images was not intended to be kept secret but to be published to the world by *OK!* and was so published at much the same time as the unauthorized photographs in *Hello!* But I see no reason why there should not be an obligation of confidence for the purpose of enabling someone to be the only source of publication if that is something worth paying for.

...

[122] Whether there is still a point in enforcing the obligation of confidence depends on the facts. If the purpose of publishing the pictures was simply to convey the information that the Douglases had married, the bride wore a wedding dress and so forth, then the publication of any photographs would have put that information in the public domain. So would a description of the event. In this case, however, the point of the transaction was that each picture would be treated as a separate piece of information which *OK!* would have the exclusive right to publish. The pictures published by *OK!* were put into the public domain and it would have

---

[39] *Douglas v Hello! (No 3)* [2006] QB 125, para. 107.   [40] Ibid., para. 111.
[41] Ibid., para. 113.   [42] Ibid., para. 113.

had to rely on the law of copyright, not the law of confidence, to prevent their reproduction. But no other pictures were in the public domain and they did not enter the public domain merely because they resembled other pictures which had.

Can we say that Lord Hoffmann properly applied the accepted tests for determining whether information is to be protected as confidential? Should the fact that *OK!* was prepared to pay large sums of money to acquire photographic images of the Douglases wedding have been enough to establish confidentiality? Finally, should the confidential information have been defined to include each and every visual image of the wedding? Does this risk protecting an event as a whole and, as such, begin to resemble a right of publicity?

8.4 OBLIGATION OF CONFIDENCE

8.4.1 TRADITIONAL PRINCIPLES

The second element required to establish an equitable breach of confidence is that the information is imparted in circumstances importing an obligation of confidence. How to establish this second limb is explained in *Coco v Clark*.

Coco v AN Clark (Engineers) Ltd [1969] FSR 415

The facts were described above at p. 381.

Megarry J, at pp. 420–1:

The second requirement is that the information must have been communicated in circumstances importing an obligation of confidence. However secret and confidential the information, there can be no binding obligation of confidence if that information is blurted out in public or is communicated in other circumstances which negative any duty of holding it confidential. From the authorities cited to me, I have not been able to derive any very precise idea of what test is to be applied in determining whether the circumstances import an obligation of confidence. In the *Argyll* case at page 330, Ungoed-Thomas, J concluded his discussion of the circumstances in which the publication of marital communications should be restrained as being confidential by saying 'If this was a well-developed jurisdiction doubtless there would be guides and tests to aid in exercising it.' In the absence of such guides or tests he then in effect concluded that part of the communications there in question would on any reasonable test emerge as confidential. It may be that that hard-worked creature, the reasonable man, may be pressed into service once more; for I do not see why he should not labour in equity as well as at law. It seems to me that if the circumstances are such that any reasonable man standing in the shoes of the recipient of the information would have realised that upon reasonable grounds the information was being given to him in confidence, then this should suffice to impose upon him the equitable obligation of confidence. In particular, where information of commercial or industrial value is given on a business-like basis and with some avowed common object in mind, such as a joint venture or the manufacture of articles by one party for the other, I would regard the recipient as carrying a heavy burden if he seeks to repel a contention that he was bound by an obligation of confidence: see the

Saltman case at page 216. On that footing, for reasons that will appear, I do not think I need explore this head further. I merely add that I doubt whether equity would intervene unless the circumstances are of sufficient gravity; equity ought not to be invoked merely to protect trivial tittle-tattle, however confidential.

Does the above passage establish an objective or subjective test for determining whether information has been communicated in circumstances importing an obligation of confidence? To what extent can the subjective views of the parties involved be taken into account? Later cases support the view that courts should consider whether the parties regarded themselves as being under an obligation to preserve confidence.[43]

On whom will the equitable obligation of confidence be imposed? More specifically, what if A communicates confidential information to B, who in turn and without authorization communicates it to C? The position of third-party recipients of confidential information was discussed in obiter dicta in *Attorney-General v Observer Ltd*.

Attorney-General v Observer Ltd [1990] 1 AC 109

The facts were discussed above at p. 388.

Lord Keith, at p. 260:

The newspapers which are the respondents in this appeal were not responsible for the world-wide dissemination of the contents of *Spycatcher* which has taken place. It is a general rule of law that a third party who comes into possession of confidential information which he knows to be such, may come under a duty not to pass it on to anyone else. Thus in *Duchess of Argyll v Duke of Argyll* [1967] Ch 302 the newspaper to which the Duke had communicated the information about the Duchess was restrained by injunction from publishing it.

Lord Griffiths, at p. 268:

The duty of confidence is, as a general rule, also imposed on a third party who is in possession of information which he knows is subject to an obligation of confidence: see *Prince Albert v Strange* (1849) 1 Mac & G 25 and *Duchess of Argyll v Duke of Argyll* [1967] Ch 302. If this was not the law the right would be of little practical value: there would be no point in imposing a duty of confidence in respect of the secrets of the marital bed if newspapers were free to publish those secrets when betrayed to them by the unfaithful partner in the marriage. When trade secrets are betrayed by a confidant to a third party it is usually the third party who is to exploit the information and it is the activity of the third party that must be stopped in order to protect the owner of the trade secret.

Lord Goff, at p. 281:

I start with the broad general principle (which I do not intend in any way to be definitive) that a duty of confidence arises when confidential information comes to the knowledge of a person (the confidant) in circumstances where he has notice, or is held to have agreed, that the

---

[43] *De Maudsley v Palumbo* [1996] FSR 447, 457 and *Carflow Products UK Ltd v Linwood Securities* [1996] FSR 424, 428.

information is confidential, with the effect that it would be just in all the circumstances that he should be precluded from disclosing the information to others. I have used the word 'notice' advisedly, in order to avoid the (here unnecessary) question of the extent to which actual knowledge is necessary; though I of course understand knowledge to include circumstances where the confidant has deliberately closed his eyes to the obvious. The existence of this broad general principle reflects the fact that there is such a public interest in the maintenance of confidences, that the law will provide remedies for their protection.

I realise that, in the vast majority of cases, in particular those concerned with trade secrets, the duty of confidence will arise from a transaction or relationship between the parties—often a contract, in which event the duty may arise by reason of either an express or an implied term of that contract. It is in such cases as these that the expressions 'confider' and 'confidant' are perhaps most aptly employed. But it is well settled that a duty of confidence may arise in equity independently of such cases; and I have expressed the circumstances in which the duty arises in broad terms, not merely to embrace those cases where a third party receives information from a person who is under a duty of confidence in respect of it, knowing that it has been disclosed by that person to him in breach of his duty of confidence, but also to include certain situations, beloved of law teachers—where an obviously confidential document is wafted by an electric fan out of a window into a crowded street, or where an obviously confidential document, such as a private diary, is dropped in a public place, and is then picked up by a passer-by. I also have in mind the situations where secrets of importance to national security come into the possession of members of the public—a point to which I shall refer in a moment.

In what circumstances will third parties be bound by an obligation of confidence? In what circumstances will persons who are strangers to a confidential relationship or communication and who accidentally or unintentionally encounter confidential information come under a duty of confidence?

Cases subsequent to *Attorney-General v Observer Ltd* have also envisaged that an equitable obligation of confidence might arise in the absence of a confidential relationship or communication. Thus, in *Hellewell v Chief Constable of Derbyshire*[44] Laws J commented obiter:[45]

If someone with a telephoto lens were to take from a distance and with no authority a picture of another engaged in some private act, his subsequent disclosure of the photograph would, in my judgment, as surely amount to a breach of confidence as if he had found or stolen a letter or diary in which the act was recounted and proceeded to publish it. In such a case, the law would protect what might reasonably be called a right of privacy, although the name accorded to the cause of action would be breach of confidence. It is, of course, elementary that, in all such cases, a defence based on the public interest would be available.

In *Shelley Films v Rex Features Ltd*[46] Deputy Judge Martin Mann QC held, in an application for an interlocutory injunction, that it was seriously arguable that the defendant's knowledge of the circumstances in which the photograph was taken was sufficient to place it under an obligation of confidence. In this case, a photograph from a scene of the (then forthcoming) film *Mary Shelley's Frankenstein* was credited to the defendant and published

---

[44] [1995] 1 WLR 804.   [45] Ibid., 807.   [46] [1994] EMLR 134.

in the *The People* newspaper. In granting the injunction the judge referred to the obiter dicta of Lord Goff and took into account the following circumstances: the film studio was fenced, with security guards at the main gate; there were signs clearly stating that the property was private and entry was by permission only; there were notices that photography within the studios was permitted and the set itself was patrolled by security guards and featured signs at the entrance prohibiting entrance to other than authorized persons.

A similar conclusion to that in *Shelley Films* was reached in *Creation Records*.

Creation Records Ltd v News Group Newspapers Ltd [1997] EMLR 444

The case concerned a photographic shoot for the cover of a forthcoming record album. The shoot was directed at a scene outside a country hotel. A freelance photographer took photographs of the same scene and these were published in *The Sun* newspaper. In considering whether to grant an interim injunction, Lloyd J accepted that while the freelance photographer was permitted to view the scene, he was not authorised to photograph it.

Lloyd J, at p. 455:

Here, while admittedly Mr Seeburg was lawfully at the hotel and with others was able to gain access to the restricted area and his presence there was tolerated and even the taking of photographs was tolerated before the shoot as such began, the plaintiff's evidence, if accepted, shows that thereafter a tighter regime of security was imposed as regards preventing photography, the tight ring of security men and minders of which the *Sun's* first article spoke. It would of course have been clearer if each of the strangers to the shoot who were allowed to stay in the restricted area had been told that they may not take photographs thereafter. But what the plaintiff's witnesses depose to amounts to much the same as that, although in a more general and less explicit form. I accept also that they were of course allowed to observe the scene and could therefore have gone away and told the world the ingredients of the picture, or even made a sketch of it from memory. But being lawfully there does not mean that they were free to take photographs and its seems to me that to be able to record it as a photographic image is different in kind, not merely in degree, from being able to relate it verbally or even by way of a sketch. That is above all because it was in photographic form that it was intended to be preserved for the group. It is the photographic record of the scene, the result of the shoot in fact, that was to be confidential.

I accept it as well arguable that the nature of the operation together with the imposition of security measures as described by the plaintiffs' witnesses made it an occasion of confidentiality at any rate as regards photography. In that context I also accept it as sufficiently arguable that in order to get his picture Mr Seeburg must have conducted himself a good deal less openly than he suggests and indeed surreptitiously, as the plaintiffs suggest. If so, it is an easy inference that he did so because he knew that photography was not permitted and that he was being allowed to remain in the restricted area only on the basis that photographs would not be taken of the actual shoot.

On that footing it seems to me that the plaintiffs do have a sufficiently arguable case for saying that the taking of the photograph and its publication is in breach of confidence and that future publication can be restrained by injunction at any rate until the image is fully released into the public domain, presumably on publication of the album, if it does come out with this cover.

In summary, the second limb of *Coco v Clark* requires that information be communicated in circumstances importing an obligation of confidence. There have, however, been inroads into this principle when it comes to third party recipients of confidential information or where persons are strangers to a confidential relationship or have not had the information communicated to them. These inroads, represented by dicta in *Attorney-General v Observer Ltd*, and *Hellewell* and the decisions in *Shelley Films* and *Creation Records*, have been relied upon in cases following the Human Rights Act 1998 to justify imposing obligations of confidence in respect of personal or private information in a wider variety of situations. As such, this has created greater scope for the protection of privacy than was previously the case, which we turn now to consider.

FURTHER READING

G. Phillipson and H. Fenwick, 'Breach of confidence as a privacy remedy in the Human Rights Act era' (2000) 63 Modern Law Review 660.

M. Richardson, 'Breach of confidence, surreptitiously or accidentally obtained information and privacy: Theory versus law' (1994) 19 Melbourne University LR 673.

8.4.2 THE IMPACT OF THE HUMAN RIGHTS ACT

That the second limb of *Coco v Clark* is no longer relevant or necessary, at least in relation to personal or private information, is starkly illustrated by the House of Lords decision in *Campbell*.

Campbell v Mirror Group Newspapers Ltd [2004] 2 AC 457

The facts were described above at p. 390.

Lord Nicholls:

13. The common law or, more precisely, courts of equity have long afforded protection to the wrongful use of private information by means of the cause of action which became known as breach of confidence. A breach of confidence was restrained as a form of unconscionable conduct, akin to a breach of trust. Today this nomenclature is misleading. The breach of confidence label harks back to the time when the cause of action was based on improper use of information disclosed by one person to another in confidence. To attract protection the information had to be of a confidential nature. But the gist of the cause of action was that information of this character had been disclosed by one person to another in circumstances 'importing an obligation of confidence' even though no contract of non-disclosure existed: see the classic exposition by Megarry J in *Coco v A N Clark (Engineers) Ltd* [1969] RPC 41, 47–48. The confidence referred to in the phrase 'breach of confidence' was the confidence arising out of a confidential relationship.

14. This cause of action has now firmly shaken off the limiting constraint of the need for an initial confidential relationship. In doing so it has changed its nature. In this country this development was recognised clearly in the judgment of Lord Goff of Chieveley in *Attorney-General v Guardian Newspapers Ltd (No 2)* [1990] 1 AC 109, 281. Now the law imposes a 'duty of confidence' whenever a person receives information he knows or ought to know is

fairly and reasonably to be regarded as confidential. Even this formulation is awkward. The continuing use of the phrase 'duty of confidence' and the description of the information as 'confidential' is not altogether comfortable. Information about an individual's private life would not, in ordinary usage, be called 'confidential'. The more natural description today is that such information is private. The essence of the tort is better encapsulated now as misuse of private information.

Lord Hoffmann:

46. In recent years, however, there have been two developments of the law of confidence, typical of the capacity of the common law to adapt itself to the needs of contemporary life. One has been an acknowledgement of the artificiality of distinguishing between confidential information obtained through the violation of a confidential relationship and similar information obtained in some other way. The second has been the acceptance, under the influence of human rights instruments such as article 8 of the European Convention, of the privacy of personal information as something worthy of protection in its own right.

47. The first development is generally associated with the speech of Lord Goff of Chieveley in *Attorney-General v Guardian Newspapers Ltd (No 2)* [1990] 1 AC 109, 281, where he gave, as illustrations of cases in which it would be illogical to insist upon violation of a confidential relationship, the 'obviously confidential document... wafted by an electric fan out of a window into a crowded street' and the 'private diary... dropped in a public place'. He therefore formulated the principle as being that:

> a duty of confidence arises when confidential information comes to the knowledge of a person... in circumstances where he has notice, or is held to have agreed, that the information is confidential, with the effect that it would be just in all the circumstances that he should be precluded from disclosing the information to others.

48. This statement of principle, which omits the requirement of a prior confidential relationship, was accepted as representing current English law by the European Court of Human Rights in *Earl Spencer v United Kingdom* (1998) 25 EHRR CD 105 and was applied by the Court of Appeal in *A v B plc* [2003] QB 195, 207. It is now firmly established.

49. The second development has been rather more subtle. Until the Human Rights Act 1998 came into force, there was no equivalent in English domestic law of article 8 of the European Convention or the equivalent articles in other international human rights instruments which guarantee rights of privacy. So the courts of the United Kingdom did not have to decide what such guarantees meant. Even now that the equivalent of article 8 has been enacted as part of English law, it is not directly concerned with the protection of privacy against private persons or corporations. It is, by virtue of section 6 of the 1998 Act, a guarantee of privacy only against public authorities. Although the Convention, as an international instrument, may impose upon the United Kingdom an obligation to take some steps (whether by statute or otherwise) to protect rights of privacy against invasion by private individuals, it does not follow that such an obligation would have any counterpart in domestic law.

50. What human rights law has done is to identify private information as something worth protecting as an aspect of human autonomy and dignity. And this recognition has raised inescapably the question of why it should be worth protecting against the state but not against a private person. There may of course be justifications for the publication of private information by private persons which would not be available to the state—I have particularly in mind the position of the media, to which I shall return in a moment—but I can see no logical ground for saying that a person should have less protection against a private individual

than he would have against the state for the publication of personal information for which there is no justification. Nor, it appears, have any of the other judges who have considered the matter.

51. The result of these developments has been a shift in the centre of gravity of the action for breach of confidence when it is used as a remedy for the unjustified publication of personal information. It recognises that the incremental changes to which I have referred do not merely extend the duties arising traditionally from a relationship of trust and confidence to a wider range of people. As Sedley LJ observed in a perceptive passage in his judgment in *Douglas v Hello! Ltd* [2001] QB 967, 1001, the new approach takes a different view of the underlying value which the law protects. Instead of the cause of action being based upon the duty of good faith applicable to confidential personal information and trade secrets alike, it focuses upon the protection of human autonomy and dignity—the right to control the dissemination of information about one's private life and the right to the esteem and respect of other people.

52. These changes have implications for the future development of the law. They must influence the approach of the courts to the kind of information which is regarded as entitled to protection, the extent and form of publication which attracts a remedy and the circumstances in which publication can be justified.

Although Lord Nicholls and Lord Hoffmann were in the minority, the House was unanimous on important points of principle reflected in the above extracts. Thus, Lord Hope held that a confidential relationship is not required but that a duty will arise where a person knows or ought to know that there is a reasonable expectation of privacy.[47] Baroness Hale cited with approval comments in *Hosking v Runting*[48] that English courts have 'recognised that no pre-existing relationship is required in order to establish a cause of action'.[49] Her ladyship then engaged in a balancing exercise between Articles 8 and 10 of the ECHR, rather than applying the three-limb test of *Coco v Clark*. According to Baroness Hale, the basis upon which the confidential obligation is imposed is that 'the person publishing the information knows or ought to know that there is a reasonable expectation that the information in question will be kept confidential'.[50] Lord Carswell was in agreement.

Campbell emphasizes that, when it comes to protection of personal information or privacy, the 'traditional' action for breach of confidence (as represented by *Coco v Clark*) has been supplanted by an 'extended' action. Courts will enquire whether the information is private and, where a person knows or ought to know the information is private, impose an obligation of confidence. A claimant's Article 8 rights will then be balanced against the Article 10 rights of the defendant.[51]

The jettisoning of the *Coco v Clark* test raises the question of whether a separate tort of privacy should be introduced? Here it is interesting to note that the New Zealand Court of Appeal in *Hosking v Runting* chose to recognize a limited tort of privacy, relating to wrongful publicity

---

[47] *Campbell v Mirror Group Newspapers Ltd* [2004] 2 AC 457, 480.   [48] [2003] 3 NZLR 385.
[49] *Campbell v Mirror Group Newspapers Ltd* [2004] 2 AC 457, 495.   [50] Ibid.
[51] This shift in approach is also highlighted by obiter dicta in the House of Lords decision in *Douglas v Hello! Ltd* [2008] 1 AC 1. Lord Hoffmann, at para. 118, commented: 'English law has adapted the action for breach of confidence to provide a remedy for unauthorized disclosure of personal information.' Similarly, Lord Nicholls stated at para. 255: 'As the law has developed breach of confidence, or misuse of confidential information, now covers two distinct causes of action, protecting two different interests: privacy, and secret ("confidential") information.' Although Lord Nicholls dissented on the issue of whether *OK!* could recover damages for breach of commercial confidentiality, his statement of general principle is consistent with the comments of Lord Hoffmann (who delivered the leading majority speech).

of private facts.[52] Gault and Blanchard JJ stated that the same result could have been achieved by developing the action for breach of confidence along similar lines to English courts; however, a separate tort was favoured because it would be 'conducive of clearer analysis'.[53] Australian courts have also been invited to recognize a tort of privacy; however, they have thus far refused to do so, preferring to protect privacy interests through the law of confidence.[54]

The main arguments in favour of recognizing a tort of privacy is that this would avoid distorting the principles of breach of confidence, recognize what the courts are already doing, and provide certainty and more effective protection. The key objections to a separate tort are its uncertain limits and that this would be inappropriate judicial law-making.[55] In your view, which is the preferable way for English courts to proceed—recognizing a separate, albeit limited, tort of privacy or continuing to develop the action for breach of confidence?

FURTHER READING

T. Aplin, 'The future of breach of confidence and the protection of privacy' (2007) 7 OUCLJ 137.

R. Mulheron, 'A potential framework for privacy? A reply to *Hello!*' (2006) 69(5) MLR 679.

J. Morgan, '*Hello!* again: Privacy and breach of confidence' [2005] CLJ 549.

G. Phillipson, 'The "right" of privacy in England and Strasbourg' in A. Kenyon and M. Richardson (eds.), *New Dimensions in Privacy Law* (Cambridge: Cambridge University Press, 2006), pp. 184–228.

P. Stanley, *The Law of Confidentiality: A restatement* (Oxford: Hart, 2008), Appendix C: Confidence and Privacy

---

8.4.3 STANDING TO SUE

It is well established that it is only the person to whom the duty of confidence is owed who is able to sue for breach of confidence.[56] Standing to sue was particularly crucial in *Douglas v Hello!* where *OK!* magazine had, by virtue of contract, acquired exclusive rights to the coverage of the Douglases' wedding. At first instance Lindsay J found that *Hello!* Magazine owed an obligation of confidence to the Douglases *and also* to *OK!*.[57] He explained:

> They knew that *OK!* had an exclusive contract; as persons long engaged in the relevant trade, they knew what sort of provisions any such contract would include and that it would include provisions intended to preclude intrusion and unauthorized photography. Particularly would that be so where, as they knew, a very considerable sum would have had to have been paid for the exclusive rights which had been obtained. As to their knowledge of steps taken to protect the secrecy of the event, their own written text in their Issue 639 spoke of 'elaborate security procedures'. The surrounding facts were such that a duty of confidence should be inferred from them... The unauthorized pictures themselves plainly indicated they were

---

[52] See *Hosking v Runting* [2005] 1 NZLR 1, 32, per Gault and Blanchard JJ.

[53] *Hosking v Runting* [2005] 1 NZLR 1, 15, per Gault and Blanchard JJ. See also Tipping J, at p. 59.

[54] See for example *Giller v Procopets* [2008] VSCA 236, especially paras. 167–8, per Ashley JA and paras. 447–52, per Neave JA.

[55] T. Aplin, 'The future of breach of confidence and the protection of privacy' (2007) 7 OUCLJ 137.

[56] *Fraser v Evans* [1969] 1 QB 349.   [57] *Douglas v Hello! Ltd* [2003] EMLR 31, para. 198.

> taken surreptitiously. Yet these defendants firmly kept their eyes shut lest they might see what they undeniably knew would have become apparent to them. Breach of confidence apart, had the *Hello!* defendants opened their eyes they would have seen that the taking of the photographs which they bought had involved at least a trespass.

According to Lindsay J the benefit of the obligation of confidence could be shared between the claimants and, in support of this view, he cited *Gilbert v The Star Newspaper Co Ltd*[58] and *Mustad v Dosen*.[59]

It was on this point that the Court of Appeal overturned Lindsay J. The court held that Lindsay J had incorrectly 'treated the information about the wedding as if it were property when he referred to its benefit being 'shared between and...enforceable by co-owners or by a successor in title'.[60] Further *Gilbert* and *Mustad v Dosen* were said to be distinguishable because the *OK!* contract only purported to transfer or share with *OK!* the right to use *approved* photographs and not *any* photographs of the wedding and any rights not expressly granted to *OK!* were retained by the Douglases.[61] The Court of Appeal explained:

> The grant to *OK!* of the right to use the approved photographs was no more than a licence, albeit an exclusive licence, to exploit commercially those photographs for a nine-month period. This licence did not carry with it any right to claim, through assignment or otherwise, the benefit of any other confidential information vested in the Douglases.[62]

On appeal to the House of Lords, Lord Hoffmann (who delivered the leading speech of the majority) held that Lindsay J had been correct in holding that the obligation of confidence was also owed to *OK!* Magazine on the basis that 'everyone knew that the obligation of confidence was imposed for the benefit of *OK!* as well as the Douglases'.[63] Further, the obligation was owed in respect of *any* photographs and not just the authorized photographs:

> The point of which one should never lose sight is that *OK!* had paid £1 million for the benefit of the obligation of confidence imposed upon all those present at the wedding in respect of *any* photographs of the wedding. That was quite clear. Unless there is some conceptual or policy reason why they should not have the benefit of that obligation, I cannot see why they were not entitled to enforce it. And in my opinion there are no such reasons. Provided that one keeps one's eye firmly on the money and why it was paid, the case is, as Lindsay held, quite straightforward.[64]

Lord Brown also shared Lord Hoffmann's view that the obligation of confidence owed to *OK!* included all photographs and not just the approved photographs.[65]

This aspect of the House of Lords decision is perplexing for several reasons. First, it did not address the reasoning of the Court of Appeal. Second, the basis for the duty being owed to *OK!* is unclear. It appears that it is simply that *Hello!* had knowledge that the wedding was being kept secret for the benefit of *OK!*. If so, this approach is a considerable extension of Lord Goff's dicta in *Attorney-General v Observer Ltd* and opens up a broad spectrum of situations in which persons for whose benefit confidentiality is sought will be owed an

---

[58] (1894) 11 TLR 3.   [59] [1963] 3 All ER 416.
[60] *Douglas v Hello! (No 3)* [2006] QB 125, para. 128.   [61] Ibid., para. 132.
[62] Ibid., para. 134.   [63] *Douglas v Hello! Ltd* [2008] 1 AC 1, para. 114.   [64] Ibid., para. 117.
[65] Ibid., para. 327.

obligation of confidence. As Richard Arnold QC comments: 'the effect of it will be to give many exclusive, and indeed non-exclusive, licensees of confidential information a right of action. Whether this is a good thing or not remains to be seen'.[66] Finally, the majority decision completely sidesteps the issue of whether and in what circumstances obligations of confidence can be assigned.[67]

8.4.4 DURATION OF THE OBLIGATION: SPRINGBOARD DOCTRINE

The 'springboard' doctrine deals with situations where a person uses confidential information to get an illegitimate head start, yet the information has subsequently become public. The doctrine was first articulated in the case below.

Terrapin Ltd v Builders' Supply Co (Hayes) Ltd [1967] RPC 375

The defendant made prefabricated portable buildings to the claimant's design as part of a joint venture. For this purpose, the claimant communicated information concerning manufacturing details, technical information, and know-how to the defendant. After the joint venture came to an end, the defendant offered prefabricated buildings incorporating many of the features of the claimant's design for sale. The defendant argued that sale of the claimant's buildings, together with publication of brochures, had disclosed all the relevant design features to the public and, since the information was no longer secret, their obligation of confidence had been discharged.

Roxburgh J at p. 391:

[Referring to **Lord Greene MR's** judgment in *Saltman Engineering*.]

As I understand it, the essence of this branch of the law, whatever the origin of it may be, is that a person who has obtained information in confidence is not allowed to use it as a spring-board for activities detrimental to the person who made the confidential communication, and spring-board it remains even when all the features have been published or can be ascertained by actual inspection by any member of the public. The brochures are certainly not equivalent to the publication of the plans, specifications, other technical information and know-how. The dismantling of a unit might enable a person to proceed without plans or specifications, or other technical information, but not, I think, without some of the know-how, and certainly not without taking the trouble to dismantle. I think it is broadly true to say that a member of the public to whom the confidential information had not been imparted would still have to prepare plans and specifications. He would probably have to construct a prototype, and he would certainly have to conduct tests. Therefore, the possessor of the confidential information still has a long start over any member of the public. The design may be as important as the features. It is, in my view, inherent in the principle upon which the *Saltman* case rests that the possessor of such information must be placed under a special disability in the field of competition in order to ensure that he does not get an unfair start; or, in other words, to

---

[66] R. Arnold, 'Confidence in exclusives: *Douglas v Hello!* in the House of Lords' [2007] 29 EIPR 339, 343.
[67] This issue has been extensively analysed in the New South Wales Supreme Court decision, *Mid-City Skin Cancer & Laser Centre v Zahedi-Anarak* [2006] NSWSC 844.

> preclude the tactics which the first defendants and the third defendants and the managing director of both of those companies employed in this case.

The above passage from *Terrapin* has been the subject of considerable debate and discussion. In particular, subsequent cases have struggled to reconcile the statement by Roxburgh J that 'spring-board it remains even when all the features have been published' with the House of Lords decision in *Mustad v Dosen*. Refer back to the discussion of *Mustad v Dosen* at 8.3.3 above—what is the apparent conflict between this decision and *Terrapin*?

Courts have sought to resolve the tension between *Terrapin* and *Mustad v Dosen* in various ways. One such example is illustrated by *Cranleigh Precision Engineering Ltd v Bryant*.

Cranleigh Precision Engineering Ltd v Bryant [1965] 1 WLR 1293

The claimant company manufactured above-ground swimming pools to a design invented by the defendant, Bryant, its managing director. Bryant learned from the company's patent agent of a British patent owned by a third party which covered features of the Cranleigh design. Instead of informing the claimant, Bryant took steps to set up a rival business and he purchased the patent for this purpose. The claimant sued, *inter alia*, for an injunction against the defendant making use of confidential information obtained while a managing director of Cranleigh. To this, Bryant pleaded that the relevant information, the existence of the patent, was in the public domain and that, in accordance with *Mustad v Dosen*, it could not be protected as confidential.

Roskill J, at pp. 1318–19:

[Referring to *Terrapin*.]

The judgment of Roxburgh J was strongly criticised by counsel for the defendants in the Court of Appeal. Although Sellers LJ dissented from the majority judgments of Lord Evershed MR and of Romer LJ dismissing the appeal, the ground of dissent was not that the judge had misstated the law. Whilst it is true that nowhere in the judgments of the Court of Appeal is there any approval of the passage which Mr Sieghart criticised, there is equally no indication of disapproval. It is difficult to believe that had anyone thought that the judge's statement of the law was wrong in principle, some criticism would not have been advanced since it would have afforded an easy way of securing the reversal of the judge's order. Furthermore, the language of the judge appears to me to echo certain language used earlier by Luxmoore J in *Reid & Sigrist v Moss & Mechanism Ltd* a case to which I have already referred.

The question whether this passage in the judgment of Roxburgh J was correct also arose in a very recent case before Pennycuick J, *Peter Pan Manufacturing Corporation v Corsets Silhouette Ltd*, but that judge found it unnecessary to determine the point. The passage was also cited by Havers J in *Ackroyds (London) Ltd v Islington Plastics Ltd* a case to which I have already referred—not only without disapproval but as stating the law which he proceeded to apply. It may be that, strictly speaking, Mr Sieghart is right in saying that in those circumstances it would be open to me to hold that the passage in Roxburgh J's judgment misstated the law. I apprehend that it would be my duty to so do if I were convinced that it conflicted with the decision in the *Mustad* case, but in my judgment there is no such conflict because the two matters are separate and distinct. I would respectfully borrow and adopt the passage as correctly stating the law which I have to apply, and I respectfully agree with the judge in stating that the principle, as he stated it, is a logical consequence of the decision of the Court of Appeal in *Saltman's* case. *Mustad* was, as I have said, a case where the employer made the publication in question. In the present case, Bryant, as possessor of what I have held to be the plaintiffs' confidential information, is seeking to free himself from his obligations of confidence, not because of what the plaintiffs have published, for they have published nothing, but because of what Bischoff published—a publication of which Bryant only became aware because of his contractual and confidential relationship with the plaintiffs.

I have dealt with this question at length for the matter was argued at length before me. Applying the law as I conceive it to be, I have no doubt that Bryant acted in grave dereliction of his duty to the plaintiffs in concealing from the plaintiffs' board the information which he received from the plaintiffs' patent agents, and in taking no steps whatsoever to protect the plaintiffs against the possible consequences of the existence and publication of the Bischoff patent. I also have no doubt that Bryant acted in breach of confidence in making use, as he did as soon as he left the plaintiffs, of the information regarding the Bischoff patent which he had acquired in confidence and about its various effects on the plaintiffs' position, for his own advantage and for that of the defendant company. Any other conclusion would involve putting a premium on dishonesty by managing directors.

Is the type of distinction drawn by Roskill J a defensible one? If information has entered the public domain, should whether an obligation of confidence arises depend upon *who* disclosed the information to the public? The Court of Appeal in *Speed Seal Products Ltd v Paddington*[68] found this type of approach acceptable, however, Lord Goff in *Attorney-General v Observer Ltd* was much more sceptical. Lord Goff's dicta shed helpful light on the 'springboard' doctrine and its relationship to information entering the public domain.

Attorney-General v Observer Ltd [1990] 1 AC 109

The facts were described above at p. 388.

Lord Goff, at pp. 285-287:

As I have already indicated, it is well established that a duty of confidence can only apply in respect of information which is confidential: see *Saltman Engineering Co Ltd. v Campbell Engineering Co Ltd* 65 RPC 203, 215, *per* Lord Greene MR. From this it should logically follow that, if confidential information which is the subject of a duty of confidence ceases to be confidential, then the duty of confidence should cease to bind the confidant. This was held to be so in *O Mustad & Son v Dosen* (Note) [1964] 1 WLR 109. That was however a case in which the confidential information was disclosed by the confider himself; and stress was placed on this point in a later case where the disclosure was not by the confider but by a third party and in which *O Mustad & Son v Dosen* was distinguished: see *Cranleigh Precision Engineering Ltd v Bryant* [1965] 1 WLR 1293. It was later held, on the basis of the *Cranleigh Precision Engineering* case, that, if the confidant is not released when the publication is by a third party, then he cannot be released when it is he himself who has published the information: see *Speed Seal Products Ltd v Paddington* [1985] 1 WLR 1327. I have to say however that, having studied the judgment of Roskill J in the *Cranleigh Precision Engineering* case

---

[68] [1986] FSR 309, 313, per Fox LJ.

[1965] 1 WLR 1293, it seems to me that the true basis of the decision was that, in reliance on the well known judgment of Roxburgh J in the 'springboard' case, *Terrapin Ltd v Builders' Supply Co (Hayes) Ltd* [1967] RPC 375, the defendant was in breach of confidence in taking advantage of his own confidential relationship with the plaintiff company to discover what a third party had published and in making use, as soon as he left the employment of the plaintiff company, of information regarding the third party's patent which he had acquired in confidence: see [1965] 1 WLR 1293, 1319. The reasoning of Roskill J in this case has itself been the subject of criticism (see e.g. Gurry, *Breach of Confidence*, at pp. 246–7); but in any event it should be regarded as no more than an extension of the springboard doctrine, and I do not consider that it can support any general principle that, if it is a third party who puts the confidential information into the public domain, as opposed to the confider, the confidant will not be released from his duty of confidence. It follows that, so far as concerns publication by the confidant himself, the reasoning in the *Speed Seal* case [1985] 1 WLR 1327 (founded as it is upon the *Cranleigh Precision Engineering* case [1965] 1 WLR 1293) cannot, to my mind, be supported. I recognise that a case where the confider himself publishes the information might be distinguished from other cases on the basis that the confider, by publishing the information, may have implicitly released the confidant from his obligation. But that was not how it was put in *O Mustad & Son v Dosen* (Note) [1964] 1 WLR 109, 111, in which Lord Buckmaster stated that, once the disclosure had been made by the confider to the world, 'The secret, as a secret, had ceased to exist.' For my part, I cannot see how the secret can continue to exist when the publication has been made not by the confider but by a third party.

...On this approach, it is difficult to see how a confidant who publishes the relevant confidential information to the whole world can be under any further obligation not to disclose the information, simply because it was he who wrongfully destroyed its confidentiality. The information has, after all, already been so fully disclosed that it is in the public domain: how, therefore, can he thereafter be sensibly restrained from disclosing it? Is he not even to be permitted to mention in public what is now common knowledge? For his wrongful act, he may be held liable in damages, or may be required to make restitution; but, to adapt the words of Lord Buckmaster, the confidential information, as confidential information, has ceased to exist, and with it should go, as a matter of principle, the obligation of confidence.

From the above passage it is apparent that Lord Goff found the reasoning in *Speed Seal Products* unpersuasive and that *Cranleigh Precision Engineering v Bryant* does not support a continuing duty of confidence even where the information has been made public, whether by a third party or the defendant. Rather, Lord Goff characterized *Cranleigh* as an application of the *Terrapin* 'springboard' doctrine. Do you agree with his view of *Cranleigh*?

Another view of the *Terrapin* decision is that it was not in fact a 'springboard' case because the information had not entered the public domain. Although *some* of the confidential information had become public, there was a considerable amount of other information—in the form of technical specifications and know-how—that was not apparent from either sales of the buildings or publication of the brochures. In other words, there was still confidential information that could be the subject of protection. *Cranleigh Precision v Bryant* can also be viewed in the same way, namely, that because of Bryant's position as managing director of the claimant company and his intimate knowledge of the claimant's business, he knew the relevance and impact of the patent specification on the claimant's business. If these two cases are viewed in this way, the 'springboard' is the fact that use of the confidential information *enabled* much faster or more effective use of information that was already in the public domain.

Where a defendant has obtained an unfair advantage according to the springboard doctrine what is the appropriate remedy? Courts have frequently favoured an injunction. This in turn raises, however, the question of how long the injunction should last. In *Roger Bullivant v Ellis*[69] the Court of Appeal indicated that the injunction should not 'normally extend beyond the period for which the unfair advantage may reasonably be expected to continue'.[70]

8.4.5 EMPLOYEE OBLIGATIONS

Employees are frequently entrusted with, or are privy to, the secrets of their employer's business. Thus, an important topic is the extent to which obligations of confidence may be applicable to employees, both during and after employment. Confidential obligations may be imposed via the express terms of the employment contract, but in the absence of such express terms, courts may imply various duties. These will be invariably more stringent in relation to employees than ex-employees and for very good reason, namely, the need for ex-employees to be able to work freely and use the skills they have acquired.

8.4.5.1 Obligations during employment

Courts will readily imply a duty of fidelity on employees, the scope of which will depend on the facts of the case. An early case in which the duty of fidelity was held to cover action by employees to build up a rival business is *Hivac Ltd v Park Royal*.

Hivac Ltd v Park Royal Scientific Instruments Ltd [1946] 1 Ch 169

The claimant company was the sole manufacturer of small thermionic valves for use in hearing aids. Five of its skilled manual employees worked on Sundays for the defendant company, which had been established to make hearing aids with valves that competed with the claimant's. The claimant could not dismiss the five employees without following a complex statutory procedure, thus, it instead sought interlocutory relief enjoining the defendant from procuring breach by the workers of their employment contracts.

Lord Greene MR (Bucknill LJ in agreement**), at 174–5:**

It has been said on many occasions that an employee owes a duty of fidelity to his employer. As a general proposition that is indisputable. The practical difficulty in any given case is to find exactly how far that rather vague duty of fidelity extends. Prima facie it seems to me on considering the authorities and the arguments that it must be a question on the facts of each particular case. I can very well understand that the obligation of fidelity, which is an implied term of the contract, may extend very much further in the case of one class of employee than it does in others. For instance, when you are dealing, as we are dealing here, with mere manual workers whose job is to work five and a half days for their employer at a specific type of work and stop their work when the hour strikes, the obligation of fidelity may be one the operation of which will have a comparatively limited scope.

---

[69] [1987] FSR 172.   [70] Ibid., 183, per Nourse LJ (May LJ in agreement).

The law would, I think, be jealous of attempting to impose on a manual worker restrictions, the real effect of which would be to prevent him utilising his spare time. He is paid for five and a half days in the week. The rest of the week is his own, and to impose upon a man, in relation to the rest of the week, some kind of obligation which really would unreasonably tie his hands and prevent him adding to his weekly money during that time would, I think, be very undesirable. On the other hand, if one has employees of a different character, one may very well find that the obligation is of a different nature. A manual worker might say: 'You pay me for five and a half days work. I do five and a half days work for you. What greater obligation have I taken upon myself? If you want in some way to limit my activities during the other day and a half of the week, you must pay me for it.' In many cases that may be a very good answer. In other cases it may not be a good answer because the very nature of the work may be such as to make it quite clear that the duties of the employee to his employer cannot properly be performed if in his spare time the employee engages in certain classes of activity. One example was discussed in argument, that of a solicitor's clerk who on Sundays it was assumed went and worked for another firm in the same town. He might find himself embarrassed because the very client for whom he had done work while working for the other firm on the Sunday might be a client against whom clients of his main employer were conducting litigation, or something of that kind. Obviously in a case of that kind, by working for another firm he is in effect, or may be, disabling himself from performing his duties to his real employer and placing himself in an embarrassing position. I can well understand it being said: 'That is a breach of the duty of fidelity to your employer because as a result of what you have done you have disabled yourself from giving to your employer that undivided attention to his business which it is your duty to give.' I merely put that forward, not for the purpose of laying down the law or expressing any concluded opinion, but merely as illustrating the danger of laying down any general proposition and the necessity of considering each case on its facts.

[**Morton LJ** delivered a short concurring judgment.]

Lord Greene MR went on to conclude that the deliberate and secret action by the employees was a prima facie breach of their duty of fidelity.

The relationship of an implied contractual duty of fidelity to an express contractual duty of confidence was explored in the following case.

Thomas Marshall (Exporters) Ltd v Guinle [1979] Ch 227

The defendant was managing director of the claimant company. His appointment was for ten years and his service agreement provided that during his employment he was not to engage in other business without the company's consent; that during and after his employment he was not 'to disclose' confidential information relating to the company; and that after ceasing to be managing director he was neither 'to use or disclose' confidential information about the suppliers and customers of the group nor, for a period of five years, employ any person who had worked for the company during the last two years of his appointment.

Unbeknown to the claimant, the defendant began to trade on his own account and on behalf of his two companies in competition with the claimant. He bought from the claimant's suppliers and sold to the claimant's customers. He also employed several former employees of the claimant. He purported to resign part way through his contract. The claimant brought proceedings against the defendant and his companies and sought interim injunctions against them.

Megarry V-C, at 244–6:

[**Sir Robert Megarry V-C** considered, *inter alia*, whether there was a breach of the defendant's implied duty of fidelity and also his contractual duty not to disclose confidential information relating to the company.]

First, then, there is the servant's implied duty of fidelity and good faith. For this, Mr Morritt cited two decisions of the Court of Appeal, *Wessex Dairies Ltd v Smith* [1935] 2 KB 80 and *Hivac Ltd v Park Royal Scientific Instruments Ltd* [1946] Ch 169. In the Wessex case, a milk roundsman employed by a company solicited the company's customers to transfer their custom to him when he ceased to be employed by the company. The Court of Appeal held that, apart from any express term of his employment, to do this was a breach of the servant's implied obligation to serve his master with good faith and fidelity, and to look after his master's interests and not his own, and he was held liable in damages. I need not set out the rather more complex facts of the *Hivac* case, which related to skilled workers secretly working in their spare time for a trade rival of their employers. I need only say that in it the Court of Appeal reaffirmed the servant's implied duty of fidelity, and applied it to acts done by the servant outside his hours of work for his employer, in addition to acts done within those hours. An interlocutory injunction was granted to restrain the rival firm from employing the workers in question.

...It is impossible to deny that the defendant has been guilty of gross and repeated breaches of his implied obligation to be faithful to the company. While still in office as managing director of the company he travelled abroad, ostensibly on the company's business, and without the company's knowledge placed orders for the benefit of himself and his companies with the company's suppliers. He also, while still managing director and without the company's knowledge, sold goods for the benefit of himself and his companies to customers of the company. In the *Boston* case, 39 Ch D 339, the receipt by the managing director of what may have been a single secret commission was said in the Court of Appeal to be dishonest and a fraud. I can apply no milder description to the defendant's prolonged duplicity. His contention is that he is entitled to go on doing this, and that the company is not entitled to any injunction restraining him from doing it. The injunctions claimed do not seek to restrain him from carrying on a similar business: all that is claimed is that he should not solicit orders from the company's customers or suppliers, or otherwise deal with them, and that he should not disclose or use any confidential information or trade secrets of the company. Subject to what I shall say later, particularly about confidential information, I think it clear that injunctions to this effect ought to be granted.

...

Third, there is clause F.7 of the service agreement. The obligation of the defendant not to 'disclose any confidential information relating to the affairs customers or trade secrets of the group' of which he became possessed while in the company's service is clear enough; and it plainly continues after the service agreement terminates. However, Mr Hutchison contended, as I have mentioned, that this provision did not justify the injunctions claimed. He contended that the only obligation was against disclosure.

...

I return, then, to Mr Hutchison's distinction between 'disclose' and 'use or disclose'. Mr Morritt contended that the obligation in clause F.7 not to 'disclose' any confidential information should be read as including an obligation not to use that information: the words 'or use' ought, he said, to be implied into it. I can see no basis upon which such an implication could be made, especially in view of the contrast with the 'use or disclose' of the first proviso to clause J.2. I think 'disclose' means what it says, and does not extend to 'use'. Of course, I can conceive of methods of use which would amount to making a disclosure. If an employee were to use his secret knowledge in such a way as to make it plain to others what the secret process or information was, that might well amount to a disclosure. The mode and circumstances of use may be so ostentatious that they plainly constitute a disclosure. But apart from such cases, I do not think that a prohibition on disclosure prevents use. It therefore seems to me that clause F.7 provides no basis for granting an injunction to restrain the defendant from using confidential information or trade secrets, as distinct from disclosing them.

...

With that, I turn to the injunctions sought by the company. First, there is the soliciting order, to restrain the defendant from soliciting orders from, or otherwise dealing with, any of the company's customers for goods of the nature of those sold by the company, and from soliciting orders for the supply of such goods from, or otherwise dealing with, any of the company's suppliers. From what I have said it can be seen that in my judgment the implied duty of fidelity and good faith plainly warrants the grant of an injunction in such terms.

...

Second, there is the breach of confidence order. This, in its wide form, restraining the disclosure or use of confidential information or trade secrets, seems to me to be fully supported by the implied duty of fidelity and good faith... [Also] clause F.7 fully supports the breach of confidence order so far as disclosing is concerned, but not as to using.

As the above case highlights, express contractual duties of confidence must be interpreted according to their terms. However, this does not inhibit courts from implying duties of fidelity that extend wider than those contractual terms. Do you think it is appropriate for courts to place more onerous obligations on employees than those that were explicitly agreed in the employment contract?

8.4.5.2 Obligations post-employment

In determining the scope of any implied duty of good faith for ex-employees an important policy consideration is ensuring that they can use and put at the disposal of their new employers all of their acquired skill, knowledge, and experience. As is apparent from the case below, this had led to a narrower duty of good faith—one that is restricted to 'trade secrets' rather than confidential information.

Faccenda Chicken Ltd v Fowler [1987] Ch 117

The claimant company (Faccenda) carried on the business of rearing, slaughtering, and selling fresh chickens in Northampton. The first defendant (Fowler) was engaged as a sales manager and had instituted a 'van sales operation', namely, selling fresh chickens from itinerant refrigerated vans. The first defendant resigned from the claimant and proceeded to set up his own business of selling fresh chickens from refrigerated vans in the same area. Several employees of the claimant left to join the first defendant's new business. The claimant brought a claim against the first defendant and former employees claiming, *inter alia*, an injunction and damages for breach of confidence. None of the employees' contracts of employment contained express terms dealing with unauthorized use of confidential information gained during their employment. The allegedly confidential information was 'sales information', which comprised the contact details of customers, the most convenient routes to reach them, the usual orders of customers, the usual delivery days and times, and the prices customers were charged. Goulding J dismissed the claimant's claim and an appeal to the Court of Appeal was dismissed.

Neill LJ (delivering the judgment of the Court), at 135–9:

Having considered the cases to which we were referred, we would venture to state these principles:

(1) Where the parties are, or have been, linked by a contract of employment, the obligations of the employee are to be determined by the contract between him and his employer: cf. *Vokes Ltd v Heather* (1945) 62 RPC 135, 141.

(2) In the absence of any express term, the obligations of the employee in respect of the use and disclosure of information are the subject of implied terms.

(3) While the employee remains in the employment of the employer the obligations are included in the implied term which imposes a duty of good faith or fidelity on the employee. For the purposes of the present appeal it is not necessary to consider the precise limits of this implied term, but it may be noted: (a) that the extent of the duty of good faith will vary according to the nature of the contract (see *Vokes Ltd v Heather* 62 RPC 135); (b) that the duty of good faith will be broken if an employee makes or copies a list of the customers of the employer for use after his employment ends or deliberately memorises such a list, even though, except in special circumstances, there is no general restriction on an ex-employee canvassing or doing business with customers of his former employer: see *Robb v Green* [1895] 2 QB 315 and *Wessex Dairies Ltd v Smith* [1935] 2 KB 80.

(4) The implied term which imposes an obligation on the employee as to his conduct after the determination of the employment is more restricted in its scope than that which imposes a general duty of good faith. It is clear that the obligation not to use or disclose information may cover secret processes of manufacture such as chemical formulae (*Amber Size and Chemical Co Ltd v Menzel* [1913] 2 Ch 239), or designs or special methods of construction (*Reid & Sigrist Ltd v Moss and Mechanism Ltd* (1932) 49 RPC 461), and other information which is of a sufficiently high degree of confidentiality as to amount to a trade secret. The obligation does not extend, however, to cover all information which is given to or acquired by the employee while in his employment, and in particular may not cover information which is only 'confidential' in the sense that an unauthorised disclosure of such information to a third party while the employment subsisted would be a clear breach of the duty of good faith. This distinction is clearly set out in the judgment of Cross J in *Printers & Finishers Ltd v Holloway* [1965] 1 WLR 1; [1965] RPC 239 where he had to consider whether an ex-employee should be restrained by injunction from making use of his recollection of the contents of certain written printing instructions which had been made available to him when he was working in his former employers' flock printing factory. In his judgment, delivered on 29 April 1964 (not reported on this point in [1965] 1 WLR 1), he said [1965] RPC 239, 253:

> In this connection one must bear in mind that not all information which is given to a servant in confidence and which it would be a breach of his duty for him to disclose to another person during his employment is a trade secret which he can be prevented from using for his own advantage after the employment is over, even though he has entered into no express covenant with regard to the matter in hand. For example, the printing instructions were handed

to Holloway to be used by him during his employment exclusively for the plaintiffs' benefit. It would have been a breach of duty on his part to divulge any of the contents to a stranger while he was employed, but many of these instructions are not really 'trade secrets' at all. Holloway was not, indeed, entitled to take a copy of the instructions away with him; but in so far as the instructions cannot be called 'trade secrets' and he carried them in his head, he is entitled to use them for his own benefit or the benefit of any future employer.

The same distinction is to be found in *E Worsley & Co Ltd v Cooper* [1939] 1 All ER 290 where it was held that the defendant was entitled, after he had ceased to be employed, to make use of his knowledge of the source of the paper supplied to his previous employer. In our view it is quite plain that this knowledge was nevertheless 'confidential' in the sense that it would have been a breach of the duty of good faith for the employee, while the employment subsisted, to have used it for his own purposes or to have disclosed it to a competitor of his employer.

(5) In order to determine whether any particular item of information falls within the implied term so as to prevent its use or disclosure by an employee after his employment has ceased, it is necessary to consider all the circumstances of the case. We are satisfied that the following matters are among those to which attention must be paid:

(a) The nature of the employment. Thus employment in a capacity where 'confidential' material is habitually handled may impose a high obligation of confidentiality because the employee can be expected to realise its sensitive nature to a greater extent than if he were employed in a capacity where such material reaches him only occasionally or incidentally.

(b) The nature of the information itself. In our judgment the information will only be protected if it can properly be classed as a trade secret or as material which, while not properly to be described as a trade secret, is in all the circumstances of such a highly confidential nature as to require the same protection as a trade secret *eo nomine*. The restrictive covenant cases demonstrate that a covenant will not be upheld on the basis of the status of the information which might be disclosed by the former employee if he is not restrained, unless it can be regarded as a trade secret or the equivalent of a trade secret: see, for example, *Herbert Morris Ltd v Saxelby* [1916] 1 AC 688, 710 *per* Lord Parker of Waddington and *Littlewoods Organisation Ltd v Harris* [1977] 1 WLR 1472, 1484 *per* Megaw LJ.

We must therefore express our respectful disagreement with the passage in Goulding J's judgment at [1984] ICR 589, 599E, where he suggested that an employer can protect the use of information in his second category, even though it does not include either a trade secret or its equivalent, by means of a restrictive covenant. As Lord Parker of Waddington made clear in *Herbert Morris Ltd v Saxelby* [1916] 1 AC 688, 709, in a passage to which Mr Dehn drew our attention, a restrictive covenant will not be enforced unless the protection sought is reasonably necessary to protect a trade secret or to prevent some personal influence over customers being abused in order to entice them away.

In our view the circumstances in which a restrictive covenant would be appropriate and could be successfully invoked emerge very clearly from the words used by Cross J in *Printers & Finishers Ltd v Holloway* [1965] 1 WLR 1, 6 (in a passage quoted later in his judgment by Goulding J [1984] ICR 589, 601):

If the managing director is right in thinking that there are features in the plaintiffs' process which can fairly be regarded as trade secrets and which their employees will inevitably carry away with them in their heads, then the proper way for the plaintiffs to protect themselves would be by exacting covenants from their employees restricting their field of activity after they have left their employment, not by asking the court to extend the general equitable doctrine to prevent breaking confidence beyond all reasonable bounds.

It is clearly impossible to provide a list of matters which will qualify as trade secrets or their equivalent. Secret processes of manufacture provide obvious examples, but innumerable other pieces of information are *capable* of being trade secrets, though the secrecy of some information may be only short-lived. In addition, the fact that the circulation of certain information is restricted to a limited number of individuals may throw light on the status of the information and its degree of confidentiality.

(c) Whether the employer impressed on the employee the confidentiality of the information. Thus, though an employer cannot prevent the use or disclosure *merely* by telling the employee that certain information is confidential, the attitude of the employer towards the information provides evidence which may assist in determining whether or not the information can properly be regarded as a trade secret. It is to be observed that in *E Worsley & Co Ltd v Cooper* [1939] 1 All ER 290, 307D, Morton J attached significance to the fact that no warning had been given to the defendant that 'the source from which the paper came was to be treated as confidential'.

(d) Whether the relevant information can be easily isolated from other information which the employee is free to use or disclose. In *Printers & Finishers Ltd v Holloway* [1965] RPC 239, Cross J considered the protection which might be afforded to information which had been memorised by an ex-employee. He put on one side the memorising of a formula or a list of customers or what had been said (obviously in confidence) at a particular meeting, and continued, at p. 256:

> The employee might well not realise that the feature or expedient in question was in fact peculiar to his late employer's process and factory; but even if he did, such knowledge is not readily separable from his general knowledge of the flock printing process and his acquired skill in manipulating a flock printing plant, and I do not think that any man of average intelligence and honesty would think that there was anything improper in his putting his memory of particular features of his late employer's plant at the disposal of his new employer.

> For our part we would not regard the separability of the information in question as being conclusive, but the fact that the alleged 'confidential' information is part of a package and that the remainder of the package is not confidential is likely to throw light on whether the information in question is really a trade secret.

These then are the principles of law which we consider to be applicable to a case such as the present one. We would wish to leave open, however, for further examination on some other occasion the question whether additional protection should be afforded to an employer where the former employee is not seeking to earn his living by making use of the body of skill, knowledge and experience which he has acquired in the course of his career, but is merely selling to a third party information which he acquired in confidence in the course of his former employment.

...

But in the present case the following factors appear to us to lead to the clear conclusion that neither the information about prices nor the sales information as a whole had the degree of confidentiality necessary to support the plaintiffs' case. We would list these factors as follows. (1) The sales information contained some material which the plaintiffs conceded was not confidential if looked at in isolation. (2) The information about the prices was not clearly severable from the rest of the sales information. (3) Neither the sales information in general, nor the information about the prices in particular, though of some value to a competitor, could reasonably be regarded as plainly secret or sensitive. (4) The sales information, including the information about prices, was necessarily acquired by the defendants in order that they could do their work. Moreover, as the judge observed in the course of his judgment, each salesman could quickly commit the whole of the sales information relating to his own area to memory. (5) The sales information was generally known among the van drivers who were employees, as were the secretaries, at quite a junior level. This was not a case where the relevant information was restricted to senior management or to confidential staff. (6) There was no evidence that the plaintiffs had ever given any express instructions that the sales information or the information about prices was to be treated as confidential. We are satisfied that, in the light of all the matters set out by the judge in his judgment, neither the sales information as a whole nor the information about prices looked at by itself fell within the class of confidential information which an employee is bound by an implied term of his contract of employment or otherwise not to use or disclose after his employment has come to an end.

Faccenda Chicken attempts to reconcile the interests of employers in preserving their confidential information with the interests of former employees in being able to work freely and utilize their accumulated experience and knowledge. Do you think the principles articulated by the Court of Appeal achieve an appropriate balance and in a way that has sufficient clarity to be useful?

FURTHER READING

FSS Travel and Leisure Systems Ltd v Johnson [1999] FSR 505.

Helmet Integrated Systems Ltd v Tunnard [2007] FSR 16.

P. Goulding (ed.), *Employee Competition: Covenants, confidentiality and garden leave* (Oxford: Oxford University Press, 2007).

8.5 UNAUTHORIZED USE

8.5.1 REQUIREMENT OF DETRIMENT

The third element of *Coco v Clark* requires an unauthorized use of the information to the detriment of the person communicating it. However, Megarry J in *Coco v Clark* expressed doubt about whether detriment is in fact necessary:

Thirdly, there must be an unauthorised use of the information to the detriment of the person communicating it. Some of the statements of principle in the cases omit any mention of detriment; others include it. At first sight, it seems that detriment ought to be present if equity is to be induced to intervene; but I can conceive of cases where a plaintiff might have substantial motives for seeking the aid of equity and yet suffer nothing which could fairly be called detriment to him, as when the confidential information shows him in a favourable light but gravely injures some relation or friend of his whom he wishes to protect. The point does not arise for decision in this case, for detriment to the plaintiff plainly exists. I need therefore say no more than that although for the purposes of this case I have stated the proposition in the stricter form, I wish to keep open the possibility of the true proposition being that in the wider form.[71]

Determining whether the information has been used in an unauthorized manner will depend on the purpose for which it has been confided or communicated—in other words, the scope of the obligation.

8.5.2 PUBLIC INTEREST DEFENCE

It is a well-recognized principle that unauthorized use or disclosure of confidential information may be excused on the grounds of public interest. But what constitutes 'public interest'? Is it where information will be of interest to the public or must the information relate to an act or issue of a sufficiently serious nature?

Lion Laboratories v Evans [1985] QB 526

The claimant was a company which manufactured and sold the Lion Intoximeter 3000, an instrument for measuring blood-alcohol levels. The device was one of two devices approved by the Home Office for police use in carrying out breathalyzer tests in drivers of motor vehicles. The first and second defendants, who were former employees of the claimant, leaked confidential documents to a journalist at the *Daily Express* (the fourth defendant), in breach of the duty of confidence owed to their former employer. An ex parte injunction was granted against the *Daily Express* and its editor (the third defendant) restraining them from publishing the contents of the confidential documents. Nevertheless, the *Daily Express* published an article, in which it alleged that the Intoximeter was liable to serious error and could lead to wrongful conviction. The interim injunction was confirmed at an inter partes hearing. The defendants appealed. There was no dispute that the documents were confidential and that publication of the documents would be in breach of confidence. However, the defendants contended that publication was justified on the grounds of public interest. The Court of Appeal discharged the injunction.

Stephenson LJ (O'Connor LJ in agreement), at 536–7:

...The problem before the judge and before this court is how best to resolve, before trial, a conflict of two competing public interests. The first public interest is the preservation of the right of organisations, as of individuals, to keep secret confidential information. The courts will restrain breaches of confidence, and breaches of copyright, unless there is just cause or excuse for breaking confidence or infringing copyright. The just cause or excuse with which this case is concerned is the public interest in admittedly confidential information. There is confidential information which the public may have a right to receive and others, in particular the press, now extended to the media, may have a right and even a duty to publish, even if the information has been unlawfully obtained in flagrant breach of confidence and irrespective of the motive of the informer. The duty of confidence, the public interest in maintaining it, is a restriction on the freedom of the press which is recognised by our law, as well as by article 10(2) of the Convention for the Protection of Human Rights and Fundamental Freedoms

---

71 *Coco v Clark*, 421.

(1953) (Cmd 8969); the duty to publish, the countervailing interest of the public in being kept informed of matters which are of real public concern, is an inroad on the privacy of confidential matters. So much is settled by decisions of this court, and in particular by the illuminating judgments of Lord Denning MR in *Initial Services Ltd v Putterill* [1968] 1 QB 396; *Fraser v Evans* [1969] 1 QB 349; *Hubbard v Vosper* [1972] 2 QB 84; *Woodward v Hutchins* [1977] 1 WLR 760; and *per* Lord Denning MR (dissenting) in *Schering Chemicals Ltd v Falkman Ltd* [1982] QB 1. I add to those the speeches of Lord Wilberforce, Lord Salmon and Lord Fraser of Tullybelton in *British Steel Corporation v Granada Television Ltd* [1981] AC 1096.

There are four further considerations. First, 'there is a wide difference between what is interesting to the public and what it is in the public interest to make known' said Lord Wilberforce in *British Steel Corporation v Granada Television Ltd*, at p. 1168. The public are interested in many private matters which are no real concern of theirs and which the public have no pressing need to know. Secondly, the media have a private interest of their own in publishing what appeals to the public and may increase their circulation or the numbers of their viewers or listeners; and I quote from Sir John Donaldson MR in *Francome v Mirror Group Newspapers Ltd* [1984] 1 WLR 892, 898B, 'they are peculiarly vulnerable to the error of confusing the public interest with their own interest'. Thirdly, there are cases in which the public interest is best served by an informer giving the confidential information, not to the press but to the police or some other responsible body, as was suggested by Lord Denning MR in *Initial Services Ltd v Putterill* [1968] 1 QB 396, 405–6 and by Sir John Donaldson MR in *Francome v Mirror Group Newspapers Ltd* [1984] 1 WLR 892, 898. Fourthly, it was said by Wood V-C in 1856, in *Gartside v Outram* (1856) 26 LJ Ch 113, 114, 'there is no confidence as to the disclosure of iniquity'; and though Mr Hoolahan concedes on the plaintiffs' behalf that, as Salmon LJ said in *Initial Services Ltd v Putterill* [1968] 1 QB 396, 410, 'what was iniquity in 1856 may be too narrow or…too wide for 1967', and in 1984 extends to serious misdeeds or grave misconduct, he submits that misconduct of that kind is necessary to destroy the duty of confidence or excuse the breach of it, and nothing of that sort is alleged against the plaintiffs in the evidence now before the court.

Mr Alexander, on behalf of the third and fourth defendants, and Mr Bloch on behalf of the first and second defendants, have not been able to find any case where a defendant has been able to rely on public interest in defence of a claim for breach of confidence and the plaintiff has not also been guilty of such misconduct, and there are passages in the speeches of Lord Wilberforce and Lord Fraser of Tullybelton in *British Steel Corporation v Granada Television Ltd* [1981] AC 1096, 1165, 1195 in which they appear to be satisfied with describing the 'public interest rule' as the 'iniquity rule'. But I nowhere find any authority for the proposition, except perhaps in the judgment of Ungoed-Thomas J in *Beloff v Pressdram Ltd* [1973] 1 All ER 241, 260, that some modern form of iniquity on the part of the plaintiffs is the only thing which can be disclosed in the public interest; and I agree with the judge in rejecting the 'no iniquity, no public interest' rule; and in respectfully adopting what Lord Denning MR said in *Fraser v Evans* [1969] 1 QB 349, 362, that some things are required to be disclosed in the public interest, in which case no confidence can be prayed in aid to keep them secret, and '[iniquity] is merely an instance of just cause or excuse for breaking confidence'.

Griffiths LJ put this case in argument. Suppose the plaintiffs had informed the police that their Intoximeter was not working accurately nor safe to use, and the police had replied that they were nevertheless going to continue using it as breath test evidence. Could there then be no defence of public interest if the defendants sought to publish that confidential information, simply because the plaintiffs themselves had done nothing wrong but the police had? There would be the same public interest in publication, whichever was guilty of misconduct; and I cannot think the right to break confidence would be lost, though the public interest remained the same. Bearing this last consideration in mind, in my opinion we cannot say that the defendants must be restrained because what they want to publish does not show misconduct by the plaintiffs.

...

The issue raised by the defendants is a serious question concerning a matter which affects the life, and even the liberty, of an unascertainable number of Her Majesty's subjects, and though there is no proof that any of them has been wrongly convicted on the evidence of the plaintiffs' Intoximeter, and we certainly cannot decide that any has, we must not restrain the defendants from putting before the public this further information as to how the Lion Intoximeter 3000 has worked, and how the plaintiffs regard and discharge their responsibility for it, although the information is confidential and was unlawfully taken in breach of confidence.

[**Griffiths LJ** delivered a concurring judgment.]

As the Court of Appeal emphasized, the public interest defence does not equate to that which is of interest to the public. Neither does it have to relate necessarily to wrongful or iniquitous conduct on the part of the claimant. But the matter or issue that is sought to justify the unauthorized disclosure must be of sufficient importance or gravity. Thus, we see that the public interest defence has succeeded where publication concerned disclosure of criminal or other unlawful activities[72] or protected the public from medically dangerous practices[73] or from a potentially dangerous mental patient likely to be discharged into the community.[74] However, the defence has, on occasion, succeeded in relation to matters of lesser importance, such as where the disclosure sought to correct a misleading public image that famous pop stars were wholesome.[75]

8.5.3 THE IMPACT OF THE HUMAN RIGHTS ACT 1998

In *Lion Laboratories* Stephenson LJ noted that upholding a duty of confidence is a restriction on the freedom of the press, as recognized by Article 10(2) of the ECHR. Since the enactment of the HRA the role of Article 10 has come into sharper focus. This is because s. 6 of the HRA makes it unlawful for a public authority (including a court) to act in a manner incompatible with a Convention right and this includes Article 10 of the ECHR, which sets out a right to freedom of expression. A significant amount of recent case law has been concerned with weighing a claimant's Article 8 right to privacy against a defendant's Article 10 right to freedom of expression. The House of Lords decision in *Campbell* aptly illustrates this balancing exercise.

Campbell v Mirror Group Newspapers Ltd [2004] 2 AC 457

The facts were described above at p. 390.

Lord Hope:

[His Lordship stated that the Court of Appeal wrongly held that details of Ms Campbell's therapy was not confidential and thus had failed to carry out the required balancing exercise between Arts. 8 and 10.]

---

[72] *Malone v Metropolitan Police Commissioner* [1979] Ch 344; *Initial Services v Putterill* [1968] 1 QB 396.
[73] *Hubbard v Vosper* [1972] 2 QB 84.   [74] *W v Edgell* [1990] 1 Ch 359.
[75] *Woodward v Hutchins* [1977] 1 WLR 760.

105. The context for this exercise is provided by articles 8 and 10 of the Convention. The rights guaranteed by these articles are qualified rights. Article 8(1) protects the right to respect for private life, but recognition is given in article 8(2) to the protection of the rights and freedoms of others. Article 10(1) protects the right to freedom of expression, but article 10(2) recognises the need to protect the rights and freedoms of others. The effect of these provisions is that the right to privacy which lies at the heart of an action for breach of confidence has to be balanced against the right of the media to impart information to the public. And the right of the media to impart information to the public has to be balanced in its turn against the respect that must be given to private life.

...

Striking the balance

112. There is no doubt that the presentation of the material that it was legitimate to convey to the public in this case without breaching the duty of confidence was a matter for the journalists. The choice of language used to convey information and ideas, and decisions as to whether or not to accompany the printed word by the use of photographs, are pre-eminently editorial matters with which the court will not interfere. The respondents are also entitled to claim that they should be accorded a reasonable margin of appreciation in taking decisions as to what details needed to be included in the article to give it credibility. This is an essential part of the journalistic exercise.

113. But decisions about the publication of material that is private to the individual raise issues that are not simply about presentation and editing. Any interference with the public interest in disclosure has to be balanced against the interference with the right of the individual to respect for their private life. The decisions that are then taken are open to review by the court. The tests which the court must apply are the familiar ones. They are whether publication of the material pursues a legitimate aim and whether the benefits that will be achieved by its publication are proportionate to the harm that may be done by the interference with the right to privacy. The jurisprudence of the European Court of Human Rights explains how these principles are to be understood and applied in the context of the facts of each case. Any restriction of the right to freedom of expression must be subjected to very close scrutiny. But so too must any restriction of the right to respect for private life. Neither article 8 nor article 10 has any pre-eminence over the other in the conduct of this exercise. As Resolution 1165 of the Parliamentary Assembly of the Council of Europe (1998), para. 11, pointed out, they are neither absolute nor in any hierarchical order, since they are of equal value in a democratic society.

The article 10 right

...

115. The first question is whether the objective of the restriction on the article 10 right—the protection of Miss Campbell's right under article 8 to respect for her private life—is sufficiently important to justify limiting the fundamental right to freedom of expression which the press assert on behalf of the public. It follows from my conclusion that the details of Miss Campbell's treatment were private that I would answer this question in the affirmative. The second question is whether the means chosen to limit the article 10 right are rational, fair and not arbitrary and impair the right as minimally as is reasonably possible. It is not enough to assert that it would be reasonable to exclude these details from the article. A close examination of the factual justification for the restriction on the freedom of expression is needed if the fundamental right enshrined in article 10 is to remain practical and effective.

The restrictions which the court imposes on the article 10 right must be rational, fair and not arbitrary, and they must impair the right no more than is necessary.

116. In my opinion the factors that need to be weighed are, on the one hand, the duty that was recognised in *Jersild v Denmark* (1994) 19 EHRR 1, para. 31 to impart information and ideas of public interest which the public has a right to receive, and the need that was recognised in *Fressoz and Roire v France* (1999) 31 EHRR 28, para. 54 for the court to leave it to journalists to decide what material needs to be reproduced to ensure credibility; and, on the other hand, the degree of privacy to which Miss Campbell was entitled under the law of confidence as to the details of her therapy. Account should therefore be taken of the respondents' wish to put forward a story that was credible and to present Miss Campbell in a way that commended her for her efforts to overcome her addiction.

117. But it should also be recognised that the right of the public to receive information about the details of her treatment was of a much lower order than the undoubted right to know that she was misleading the public when she said that she did not take drugs. In *Dudgeon v United Kingdom* (1981) 4 EHRR 149, para. 52 the European court said that the more intimate the aspects of private life which are being interfered with, the more serious must be the reasons for doing so before the interference can be legitimate. *Clayton & Tomlinson, The Law of Human Rights* (2000), para. 15.162, point out that the court has distinguished three kinds of expression: political expression, artistic expression and commercial expression, and that it consistently attaches great importance to political expression and applies rather less rigorous principles to expression which is artistic and commercial. According to the court's well-established case law, freedom of expression constitutes one of the essential foundations of a democratic society and one of the basic conditions for its progress and the self-fulfilment of each individual: *Tammer v Estonia* (2001) 37 EHRR 857, para. 59. But there were no political or democratic values at stake here, nor has any pressing social need been identified: contrast *Goodwin v United Kingdom* (1996) 22 EHRR 123, para. 40.

118. As for the other side of the balance, Keene LJ said in *Douglas v Hello! Ltd* [2001] QB 967, 1012, para. 168, that any consideration of article 8 rights must reflect the fact that there are different degrees of privacy. In the present context the potential for disclosure of the information to cause harm is an important factor to be taken into account in the assessment of the extent of the restriction that was needed to protect Miss Campbell's right to privacy.

The article 8 right

119. Looking at the matter from Miss Campbell's point of view and the protection of her article 8 Convention right, publication of details of the treatment which she was undertaking to cure her addiction—that she was attending Narcotics Anonymous, for how long, how frequently and at what times of day she had been attending this therapy, the nature of it and extent of her commitment to the process and the publication of the covertly taken photographs (the third, fourth and fifth of the five elements contained in the article)—had the potential to cause harm to her, for the reasons which I have already given. So I would attach a good deal of weight to this factor.

120. As for the other side of the balance, a person's right to privacy may be limited by the public's interest in knowing about certain traits of her personality and certain aspects of her private life, as L'Heureux-Dubé and Bastarache JJ in the Supreme Court of Canada recognised in *Aubry v Éditions Vice-Versa Inc* [1998] 1 SCR 591, paras. 57–58. But it is not enough to deprive Miss Campbell of her right to privacy that she is a celebrity and that her private life is newsworthy. A margin of appreciation must, of course, be given to the journalist. Weight must be given to this. But to treat these details merely as background was to undervalue the importance that was to be attached to the need, if Miss Campbell was to be protected, to

keep these details private. And it is hard to see that there was any compelling need for the public to know the name of the organisation that she was attending for the therapy, or for the other details of it to be set out. The presentation of the article indicates that this was not fully appreciated when the decision was taken to publish these details. The decision to publish the photographs suggests that greater weight was being given to the wish to publish a story that would attract interest rather than to the wish to maintain its credibility.

121. Had it not been for the publication of the photographs, and looking to the text only, I would have been inclined to regard the balance between these rights as about even. Such is the effect of the margin of appreciation that must, in a doubtful case, be given to the journalist. In that situation the proper conclusion to draw would have been that it had not been shown that the restriction on the article 10 right for which Miss Campbell argues was justified on grounds of proportionality. But the text cannot be separated from the photographs. The words 'Therapy: Naomi outside meeting' underneath the photograph on the front page and the words 'Hugs: Naomi, dressed in jeans and baseball hat, arrives for a lunchtime group meeting this week' underneath the photograph on p. 13 were designed to link what might otherwise have been anonymous and uninformative pictures with the main text. The reader would undoubtedly make that link, and so too would the reasonable person of ordinary sensibilities. The reasonable person of ordinary sensibilities would also regard publication of the covertly taken photographs, and the fact that they were linked with the text in this way, as adding greatly overall to the intrusion which the article as a whole made into her private life.

[**Baroness Hale** delivered a concurring speech; **Lord Carswell** was in agreement. **Lord Nicholls** and **Lord Hoffmann** delivered dissenting opinions.]

The House of Lords were divided on the issue of where the balance lay between Ms Campbell's rights under Article 8 and the rights of *The Mirror* under Article 10. A majority of their lordships concluded that, while the defendant was justified in disclosing the fact of the claimant's addiction, it was not particularly compelling for the public to receive details of her therapy and such disclosure would cause significant harm to the claimant. Whereas the minority took the view that, given it was acceptable to disclose the claimant's drug addiction, publication of the details of her therapy represented a fairly minor intrusion into her private life and was part of the journalistic latitude in reporting the fact of her addiction.[76] Do you agree with the view of the majority or the minority of their lordships?

When it comes to balancing Articles 8 and 10 of the ECHR neither of these rights have presumptive priority over the other—why is this? How did Lord Hope in *Campbell* structure the approach to balancing the competing rights and to what extent is the weight of the Articles 8 and 10 interest relevant to the assessment? How does this approach differ, if at all, from the public interest defence?

An important issue that arises is the relationship between the public interest defence and Article 10—are they synonymous concepts or interrelated ones? Courts have been frustratingly opaque on this issue. Another significant issue is the extent to which the fact a person is a public figure or in the public eye affects the balancing exercise. The initial trend post-HRA, as represented by *A v B plc*,[77] was to interpret 'public interest' very broadly, such that public figures had to expect and accept close media scrutiny, even in relation to trivial facts. In *A v B plc*, the claimant, simply by virtue of being a professional footballer, was held to be a role

---

[76] *Campbell v Mirror Group Newspapers Ltd* [2004] 2 AC 457, 468, per Lord Nicholls, 476–7, per Lord Hoffmann.

[77] [2003] QB 195.

model whose off-field behaviour was deemed to be of 'public interest'. However, in recent cases (including *Campbell*) courts have retreated from this broad approach. Also, while they have not clarified the exact relationship between Article 10 and the defence of public interest, it appears that 'public interest' is being subsumed within Article 10 considerations. Both of these points are illustrated by the Court of Appeal decision in *McKennitt v Ash*.

McKennitt v Ash [2007] 3 WLR 194

In this case, the first defendant (Ash), who had been a close friend and associate of the claimant (McKennitt), a famous folk musician, published a book in which various personal revelations relating to the claimant were disclosed. The claimant brought proceedings based upon breaches of privacy and/or obligations of confidence, seeking a declaration, injunction, and damages. At first instance, Eady J held that the claimant had a reasonable expectation of privacy, such as to engage Article 8 of the ECHR, and this was not outweighed by the Article 10 rights of the first defendant. He granted a declaration and an injunction to restrict further publication of the infringing passages of the book, along with £5,000 damages for hurt feelings and distress. On appeal, Eady J's decision was upheld.

Buxton LJ (with whom **Lathan LJ** and **Longmore LJ** agreed):

The public interest: and the first claimant as a public figure

56. One might instinctively think that there was little legitimate public interest in the matters addressed by the book, and certainly no public interest sufficient to outweigh the first claimant's article 8 right to private life. That is what the judge thought and, as already pointed out, in the absence of error of principle his view will prevail. That conclusion was contested under this head in two respects, which it is necessary to keep separate. First, there was a legitimate public interest in the affairs of the first claimant because she was a public figure, *and for that reason alone*. Second, if a public figure had misbehaved, the allegation in the present case being of hypocrisy, the public had a right to have the record put straight. The parallel for that argument was the case of Ms Campbell, who could not retain privacy for the fact that she was a drug addict because she had lied publicly about her condition.

57. The first of these arguments involves consideration of two recent authorities, already introduced, *Von Hannover v Germany* (2005) 40 EHRR 1 and *A v B plc* [2003] QB 195, to which I must now return.

Von Hannover v Germany

58. There is no doubt that the European Court of Human Rights has restated what were previously thought to be the rights and expectations of public figures with regard to their private lives. The court recognised the important role of the press in dealing with matters of public interest, and the latitude in terms of mode of expression there provided: 40 EHRR 1, para. 58. But a distinction was then drawn between a watchdog role in the democratic process and the reporting of private information about people who, although of interest to the public, were not public figures. The European Court of Human Rights said, at paras. 63–64:

63. The court considers that a fundamental distinction needs to be made between reporting facts—even controversial ones—capable of contributing to a debate in a democratic society relating

to politicians in the exercise of their functions, for example, and reporting details of the private life of an individual who, moreover, as in this case, does not exercise official functions. While in the former case the press exercises its vital role of 'watchdog' in a democracy by contributing to 'impart[ing] information and ideas on matters of public interest' it does not do so in the latter case.

64. Similarly, although the public has a right to be informed, which is an essential right in a democratic society that, in certain special circumstances, can even extend to aspects of the private life of public figures, particularly where politicians are concerned, this is not the case here. The situation here does not come within the sphere of any political or public debate because the published photos and accompanying commentaries relate exclusively to details of the applicant's private life.

59. There is more in the same sense. If we follow in this case the guidance given by the English courts, that the content of the law of confidence is now to be found in articles 8 and 10 (see para. 10 above), then it seems inevitable that the first defendant's case must fail. Even assuming that the first claimant is a public figure in the relevant sense (which proposition I suspect the European Court of Human Rights would find surprising), there are no 'special circumstances' apart from the allegation of hypocrisy dealt with in the next section to justify or require the exposure of her private life. But the first defendant argued that English courts could not follow or apply *Von Hannover's* case to the facts of the present case because we were bound by the contrary English authority of *A v B plc* [2003] QB 195. That effectively required the first claimant's private affairs to be exposed to the world, hypocrite or not.

A v B plc

60. The facts have already been set out. The judgment of this court is notable for the detailed guidance that it contains as to how a court should address complaints about invasion of privacy by public or allegedly public figures. The first defendant placed particular reliance on the court's para. 11(xii):

Where an individual is a public figure he is entitled to have his privacy respected in the appropriate circumstances. A public figure is entitled to a private life. The individual, however, should recognise that because of his public position he must expect and accept that his actions will be more closely scrutinised by the media. Even trivial facts relating to a public figure can be of great interest to readers and other observers of the media. Conduct which in the case of a private individual would not be the appropriate subject of comment can be the proper subject of comment in the case of a public figure. The public figure may hold a position where higher standards of conduct can be rightly expected by the public. The public figure may be a role model whose conduct could well be emulated by others. He may set the fashion. The higher the profile of the individual concerned the more likely that this will be the position. Whether you have courted publicity or not you may be a legitimate subject of public attention. If you have courted public attention then you have less ground to object to the intrusion which follows. In many of these situations it would be overstating the position to say that there is a public interest in the information being published. It would be more accurate to say that the public have an understandable and so a legitimate interest in being told the information. If this is the situation then it can be appropriately taken into account by a court when deciding on which side of the line a case falls. The courts must not ignore the fact that if newspapers do not publish information which the public are interested in, there will be fewer newspapers published, which will not be in the public interest. The same is true in relation to other parts of the media.

61. The first defendant relied on two parts of this account. First, that 'role models', voluntary or not, have less expectation of privacy. That was reinforced by a later passage in

the judgment, at para. 43(vi): 'Footballers are role models for young people and undesirable behaviour on their part can set an unfortunate example. While [the trial judge] was right to say on the evidence which was before him that A had not courted publicity, the fact is that someone holding his position was inevitably a figure in whom a section of the public and the media would be interested.' The first claimant, it was said, was inevitably a figure in whom a section of the public would be, and was, interested. Second, the general interest in supporting the 'media' in the publication of the sort of material that sells newspapers should extend to biographies and literary works generally, such as the book was claimed to be.

62. The width of the rights given to the media by *A v B plc* cannot be reconciled with *Von Hannover's* case. Mr Price said that whether that was right or wrong, we had to apply *A v B plc*, in the light of the rule of precedent laid down by the House of Lords in *Kay v Lambeth London Borough Council* [2006] 2 AC 465, in particular by Lord Bingham of Cornhill, at paras. 43–45. Put shortly, the precedential rules of English domestic law apply to interpretations of Convention jurisprudence. Where, for instance, the Court of Appeal has ruled on the meaning or reach of a particular article of the Convention, a later division of the Court of Appeal cannot depart from that ruling simply on the basis that it is inconsistent with a later, or for that matter an earlier, decision of the European Court of Human Rights.

63. I would respectfully and fully agree with the importance of that rule. The alternative, as an earlier constitution of this court said, is chaos. But I do not think that the rule inhibits us in this case from applying *Von Hannover's* case. If the court in *A v B plc* had indeed ruled definitively on the content and application of article 10 then the position would be different; but that is what the court did not do. Having made the important observation that the content of the domestic law was now to be found in the balance between articles 8 and 10, the court then addressed the balancing exercise effectively in the former English domestic terms of breach of confidence. No Convention authority of any sort was even mentioned. It may well be that aspect of the case that caused a later division of this court to comment, per Lord Phillips of Worth Matravers MR in *Campbell v MGN Ltd* [2003] QB 633, paras. 40–41:

> 40. ...When Lord Woolf CJ spoke of the public having 'an understandable and so a legitimate interest in being told' information, even including trivial facts, about a public figure, he was not speaking of private facts which a fair-minded person would consider it offensive to disclose. That is clear from his subsequent commendation of the guidance on striking a balance between article 8 and article 10 rights provided by the Council of Europe Resolution 1165 of 1998.
>
> 41. For our part we would observe that the fact that an individual has achieved prominence on the public stage does not mean that his private life can be laid bare by the media. We do not see why it should necessarily be in the public interest that an individual who has been adopted as a role model, without seeking this distinction, should be demonstrated to have feet of clay.

64. However that may be, and wherever that leaves courts that would have to apply the guidance given in *A v B plc*, it seems clear that *A v B plc* cannot be read as any sort of binding authority on the content of articles 8 and 10. To find that content, therefore, we do have to look to *Von Hannover's* case. The terms of that judgment are very far away from the automatic limits placed on the privacy rights of public figures by *A v B plc*.

65. But, in any event, even if we were to follow *A v B plc*, the guidance that that case gives does not produce the outcome in our case that is sought by the first defendant. First, as to the position of the first claimant, she clearly does not fall within the first category mentioned by Lord Woolf CJ, and 'hold a position where higher standards of conduct can be rightly expected by the public': that is no doubt the preserve of headmasters and clergymen, who according to taste may be joined by politicians, senior civil servants, surgeons and journalists. Second, although on one view the first claimant comes within Lord Woolf CJ's second

class, of involuntary role models, I respectfully share the doubts of Lord Phillips MR, set out in para. 63 above, as to the validity of that concept; and it would in any event seem difficult to include in the class a person such as the first claimant, who has made such efforts not to hold herself out as someone whose life is an open book. Third, it is clear that Lord Woolf CJ thought that role models were at risk, or most at risk, of having to put up with the reporting of *disreputable* conduct: such as was the conduct of the claimant before him. The first claimant does not fall into that category; but to make that good I need to go on to the second part of this argument, that exposure is legitimate to demonstrate improper conduct or dishonesty.

66. In so doing I have not overlooked Lord Woolf CJ's second general point, that weight must be given to the commercial interest of newspapers in reporting matter that interests the public. That view has also received criticism, and it seems clear that this court in *Campbell's* case, in the passage cited above, was not entirely happy with it. It is difficult to reconcile with the long-standing view that what interests the public is not necessarily in the public interest, a view most recently expressed by Baroness Hale in *Jameel (Mohammed) v Wall Street Journal Europe Sprl* [2007] 1 AC 359, para. 147:

> The public only have a right to be told if two conditions are fulfilled. First, there must be a real public interest in communicating and receiving the information. This is, as we all know, very different from saying that it is information which interests the public—the most vapid tittle-tattle about the activities of footballers' wives and girlfriends interests large sections of the public but no one could claim any real public interest in our being told all about it.

It is fortunately not necessary to pursue that issue further, because it is merely a general factor that cannot be said to have any significant impact on the present case.

Hypocrisy

67. This is the charge brought against the first claimant, which is said to justify telling the world about her private behaviour and attitudes. Much of the book (for instance the matters about health or bereavement) does not fall into this category in any event. The complaint is that the first claimant treated the first defendant, and others, badly in two main respects, in the Irish cottage and in connection with the property dispute, and that that was inconsistent with her public position about proper behaviour and respect for others.

68. Once again, this argument simply fails on the facts. The judge made findings, at paras. 98–100, about the material on which the first claimant's alleged announcement of her principles was based, the 'compass points'. He found them, as I do, a fragile basis for any public interest defence; and indeed said, at para. 100, that they were 'simply being used as an excuse by Ms Ash to enable her to escape her obligations of confidence and, in her own phrase, 'unqualified loyalty'. And the judge concluded that in any event the first claimant had not behaved disreputably or insincerely in any way.

69. Some criticism is made of the judge having said, at para. 97, that 'a very high degree of misbehaviour must be demonstrated' to trigger a public interest defence. As an entirely general statement, divorced from its context, that may well go too far. But the judge was speaking of the particular situation argued before him, where not the conduct in itself, but the fact that it had previously been lied about or treated with hypocrisy, was said to be the basis for disclosure. In *Campbell v MGN Ltd* [2004] 2 AC 457 it was the fact that Ms Campbell had not merely said that she did not take drugs but had gone out of her way to emphasise that she was in that respect unlike other fashion models that deprived otherwise private material of protection: see per Lord Nicholls, at para. 24. By contrast, as the judge clearly thought, at para. 97, the conduct complained of in the case of the first claimant fell well below the level that would justify complaint on the ground of hypocrisy.

The Court of Appeal considered at length both *Von Hannover* and *A v B plc*. In what ways do these decisions differ when it comes to assessing the legitimate scrutiny of public figures and how did the court in *McKennitt v Ash* reconcile the tension between them?

According to both *Campbell* and *McKennitt v Ash* the balancing exercise will be between Articles 8 and 10, rather than the public interest in maintaining confidentiality versus the public interest in disclosure. It therefore seems that Article 10 replaces the public interest defence, at least insofar as personal information is concerned. Can we say that although the terminology is different the outcome is unlikely to be so? Here it is important to note that in both *Campbell* and *McKennitt v Ash* the House of Lords and Court of Appeal, respectively, saw it as extremely important to interpret the scope of Article 10 in the light of ECtHR jurisprudence. Whether or not English courts will find earlier case law on the public interest defence helpful in interpreting Article 10 remains to be seen, although it is likely that it will become increasingly irrelevant.

In relation to commercial confidences, courts are unlikely to carry out a balancing exercise between Articles 8 and 10 of the ECHR because Article 8 is unlikely to be engaged. As the successful claims of Mr Douglas and Ms Catherine Zeta-Jones in *Douglas v Hello!* illustrate, private information that has been commercialized can engage Article 8. However, this does not mean that Article 8 is triggered where purely commercial information is concerned. Further, it is doubtful, at least at this stage, that a corporation could establish that it has Article 8 rights.[78] Where a confider is seeking to restrain a confidant from using or disclosing (confidential) commercial information, the confidant may argue that this infringes his or her right to freedom of expression. If Article 10 is the only Convention right to be engaged it is arguable that a confidant's right to freedom of expression will take precedence and courts will have to assess whether upholding a duty of confidence is a justified interference with a confidant's Article 10 rights. Because the structure of the enquiry is different, arguably it no longer makes sense to think of the 'public interest' defence in relation to commercial confidences as well. As such, while previous case law on the 'public interest' defence may be useful in judging the importance of the disclosure, it will not be determinative since ECtHR jurisprudence will have an important role to play in considering the weight of Article 10.

FURTHER READING

T. Aplin, 'A right of privacy for corporations?' in P. Torremans (ed.), *IP & Human Rights* (The Hague: Kluwer, 2008) pp. 475–505.

T. Aplin, 'Commercial confidences after the Human Rights Act' (2007) 10 EIPR 411.

G. Phillipson, 'Judicial reasoning in breach of confidence cases under the Human Rights Act: Not taking privacy seriously' (2003) EHRLR 53.

8.6 REMEDIES

Remedies are examined in detail in Chapter 13. Nevertheless, they are also considered here, specifically in relation to breach of confidence, because of the nuances and special issues that arise in this particular context.

---

[78] T. Aplin, 'A right of privacy for corporations?' in P. Torremans (ed.), *IP & Human Rights* (The Hague: Kluwer, 2008), pp. 475–505.

8.6.1 DAMAGES

8.6.1.1 Compensatory damages

Where there is a breach of a *contractual* obligation of confidence, the normal contractual principles of recovery apply. Where, however, an *equitable* duty of confidence has been breached, one basis for awarding monetary compensation is s. 2 of the Chancery Amendment Act 1858 (Lord Cairns's Act), which was subsequently re-enacted as s. 50 of the Supreme Court Act 1981. Section 2 of Lord Cairns's Act stated:

> In all cases in which the Court of Chancery has *jurisdiction to entertain an application for an injunction against* a breach of any covenant, contract, or agreement, or against the commission or continuance of *any wrongful act*, or for the specific performance of any covenant, contract, or agreement, it shall be lawful for the *same court, if it shall think fit, to award damages to the party injured, either in addition to or in substitution for such injunction* or specific performance, and such damages may be assessed in such manner as the Court shall direct.[79]

The objective of this provision appears to have been to permit the Court of Chancery to award damages at common law where a litigant sought equitable relief as well as damages. However, the provision was subsequently interpreted as creating a jurisdiction to award damages for purely equitable rights ('equitable damages'). More specifically, 'wrongful act' was interpreted as including wrongful acts at law as well as in equity.[80]

Another basis for awarding monetary compensation is equity's inherent jurisdiction, which permits the award of monetary restitution for breach of purely equitable duties ('equitable compensation').[81]

English courts have tended not to explore the legal basis for awarding equitable damages or equitable compensation for breach of confidence.[82] Rather, they have concentrated on issues to do with assessing quantum, as illustrated by the following case.

Seager v Copydex Ltd (No 2) [1969] 1 WLR 809

The claimant invented and patented a carpet grip, called the 'Klent', and had negotiated with the defendants with a view to their marketing the Klent grip. In the course of negotiations, the claimant disclosed to the defendants his idea for another type of carpet grip, whose spikes were V shaped prongs, which the defendants realized had been disclosed to them in confidence. After a year, the negotiations amounted to nothing. Subsequently, the defendants developed their own carpet grip that embodied the very idea of the claimant's alternative grip. The Court of Appeal held that the defendants had unconsciously made use of the confidential information disclosed to them by the claimant and that they were infringing a duty of confidence (see *Seager v Copydex (No 1)*

---

[79] Emphasis supplied.

[80] See *Saltman Engineering v Campbell Engineering* (1948) 65 RPC 203, 219, per Lord Greene MR; *Attorney-General v Observer Ltd* [1990] 1 AC 109, 286 per Lord Goff; *Giller v Procopets* [2008] VSCA 236, paras. 397–403, 406–7, per Neave JA.

[81] See D. Capper, 'Damages for breach of the equitable duty of confidence' (1994) 14 Legal Studies 313 and also *Giller v Procopets* [2008] VSCA 236.

[82] Contrast the judgment of Neave JA in the recent decision of the Supreme Court of Victoria in *Giller v Procopets* [2008] VSCA 236.

[1967] 1 WLR 923.) In relation to the award of damages for this breach, Lord Denning MR (with whom Salmon and Winn LJJ agreed) set out the relevant principles.

Lord Denning MR, at p. 813:

Now a question has arisen as to the principles on which the damages are to be assessed. They are to be, assessed, as we said, at the value of the information which the defendants took. If I may use an analogy, it is like damages for conversion. Damages for conversion are the value of the goods. Once the damages are paid, the goods become the property of the defendant. A satisfied judgment in trover transfers the property in the goods. So here, once the damages are assessed and paid, the confidential information belongs to the defendants.

The difficulty is to assess the value of the information taken by the defendants. We have had a most helpful discussion about it. The value of the confidential information depends on the nature of it. If there was nothing very special about it, that is, if it involved no particular inventive step, but was the sort of information which could be obtained by employing any competent consultant, then the value of it was the fee which a consultant would charge for it: because in that case the defendants, by taking the information, would only have saved themselves the time and trouble of employing a consultant. But, on the other hand, if the information was something special, as, for instance, if it involved an inventive step or something so unusual that it could not be obtained by just going to a consultant, then the value of it is much higher. It is not merely a consultant's fee, but the price which a willing buyer—desirous of obtaining it—would pay for it. It is the value as between a willing seller and a willing buyer. In this case Mr Seager says the information was very special. People had been trying for years to get a carpet grip and then he hit upon this idea of a dome-shaped prong. It was, he said, an inventive step. And he is supported in this issue by the fact that the defendants themselves have applied for a patent for it. Furthermore, if he is to be regarded as a seller, it must be remembered that he had a patent for another carpet grip called Klent: and, if he was selling the confidential information (which I will call the Invisigrip information), then the sales of Klent might be adversely affected. The sales of the Klent would be reduced owing to the competition of the Invisigrip. So he would ask for a higher price for the confidential information in order to compensate him for the reduction in the Klent.

In these circumstances, if Mr Seager is right in saying that the confidential information was very special indeed, then it may well be right for the value to be assessed on the footing that in the usual way it would be remunerated by a royalty. The court, of course, cannot give a royalty by way of damages. But it could give an equivalent by a calculation based on a capitalisation of a royalty. Thus it could arrive at a lump sum. Once a lump sum is assessed and paid, then the confidential information would belong to the defendants in the same way as if they had bought and paid for it by an agreement of sale. The property, so far as there is property in it, would vest in them. They would have the right to use that confidential information for the manufacture of carpet grips and selling of them. If it is patentable, they would be entitled to the benefit of the patent as if they had bought it. In other words, it would be regarded as a real outright purchase of the confidential information. The value should, therefore, be assessed on that basis: and damages awarded accordingly.

In these circumstances, I do not think we should make any such declaration as Copydex Ltd ask. It is sufficient for us to say that, on a satisfied judgment for damages, the confidential information belongs to the defendants.

What are the different methods of assessing damages for breach of confidence? Do you agree with the Court of Appeal's finding that, upon payment of damages, the confidential information should belong to the defendant?

Seager v Copydex (No 2) was concerned with unauthorized use of confidential *commercial* information. Where personal or private information is involved a claimant undoubtedly will desire an injunction to restrain publication or further publication of the information. This is discussed below at 8.6.3. However, the claimant may also wish to recover damages for mental distress or injured feelings. Prior to the HRA, the only authority supporting such an award was *Cornelius v De Taranto*.

Cornelius v De Taranto [2001] EMLR 12

The defendant had been instructed by the claimant to prepare a confidential medico-legal report concerning the claimant. Without permission, the defendant sent the report to the claimant's GP and a consultant psychiatrist and, as a result, it became permanently part of the NHS records. The claimant brought proceedings against the defendant for, *inter alia*, breach of an implied contractual duty of confidence. Morland J held that a breach had occurred and that damages for injury to feelings was recoverable.

Morland J:

Damages for Breach of Confidence (including damages for injury to feelings)

65. Under Article 8 of the European Convention for the Protection of Human Rights everyone has the right to respect for his private and family life and there shall be no interference by a public authority with the exercise of this right except such as is in accordance with the law and is necessary in a democratic society for the protection of health.

66. In my judgment it would be a hollow protection of that right if in a particular case in breach of confidence without consent details of the confider's private and family life were disclosed by the confidant to others and the only remedy that the law of England allowed was nominal damages. In this case an injunction or order for delivery up of all copies of the medico-legal report against the defendant will be of little use to the claimant. The damage has been done. The details of the claimant's private and family life are within the archives of the National Health Service and she has been unable to retrieve them.

67. In cases of commercial or business breach of confidence the powers of the court are not barren. Such remedies as injunction, delivery-up, account of profits and damages may be available (see chapter X of *Toulson on Confidentiality*, 1996); similarly in the case of personal confidences exploited for profit or peddled to the media (see chapter VI of Toulson, page 72).

...

69. In the present case in my judgment recovery of damages for mental distress caused by breach of confidence, when no other substantial remedy is available, would not be inimical to considerations of policy but indeed to refuse such recovery would illustrate that something was wrong with the law. Although the object of the contract was the provision of a medico-legal report, that object could not be achieved without the defendant's examination and assessment of confidential material relating to the claimant's private and family life. The duty of confidence was an essential indeed fundamental ingredient of the contractual relationship between the claimant and the defendant which she breached.

Morland J went on to acknowledge that his conclusion was at odds with the view expressed by Scott J in *W v Egdell*.[83] Scott J cited the House of Lords decision in *Addis v Gramaphone*

---

[83] [1990] 1 Ch 359, 398A–G.

Co Ltd,[84] where it was held impermissible to award general damages for frustration, mental distress, injured feelings, or annoyance occasioned by a breach of contract. Scott J also commented that the exception to this general rule—i.e. where the contract itself is to provide peace of mind or freedom from distress—did not apply to the facts of the case. Morland J then cited the views of Professor Cornish.

> 73. Toulson at page 126 says:
>
> Professor Cornish has commented: 'There remains the question as yet unexplored in the case-law, whether damages for injury to feelings are available for breach of confidence as they are for defamation and copyright infringement. All that can usefully be said is this. Breach of confidence is slowly becoming one of the ways in which the law accords protection to privacy and those aspects of personal reputation that are associated with it. Infringement of copyright and defamation fulfil the same function in ways that are differently limited. But since both allow damages for injured feelings, it would seem quixotic to bar this form of monetary compensation from the third field, for the sake of yet another historical point. It may be argued that, in a case where a duty of confidentiality exists to protect personal privacy, its object is to protect the feelings of the confider, and therefore it would be in accordance with principle to allow damages for injury to feelings caused by breach of that duty. But whether the courts will adopt that approach remains to be seen.
>
> . . .
>
> 77. My conclusion is that I am entitled to award damages for injury to feelings caused by breach of confidence. Although it is a novel instance of such a remedy, it is in accord with the movement of current legal thinking. My decision is incremental rather than revolutionary.
> 78. In my assessment of damages I must be careful to ensure that the claimant is only compensated for the injury to her feelings caused by the defendant's unauthorised disclosure of the medico-legal report.

Morland J recognized the possible jurisdictional difficulties in awarding damages for mental distress caused by breach of contractual or equitable duties of confidence, but held that these were outweighed by the need to give proper protection to a person's Article 8 rights.

Since the HRA courts have been willing to grant damages for mental distress or injury to feelings where there is a breach of confidence (whether contractual or equitable) relating to personal information or a misuse of private information. This has occurred with scant attention to, or discussion of, jurisdictional difficulties. For example, in *Campbell v MGN* Morland J awarded £2,500 compensatory damages for the claimant's distress and injury to feelings caused by the unjustified revelation of the details of her therapy and a further £1,000 in aggravated damages for increased distress and injury to feelings caused by the publication of a follow-up article in which the claimant was disparaged in harsh and racist terms. In the House of Lords, Morland J's order was restored, but none of their lordships discussed the basis for awarding damages for mental distress. In *Archer v Williams*[85] the defendant was in breach of express and implied contractual duties of confidence. Jackson J, citing *Cornelius* and also *Campbell* held that:

> where a breach of confidence causes injury to feelings this court has power to award general damages. General damages for injury to feelings should be kept to a modest level and should

[84] [1909] AC 488.   [85] [2003] EMLR 38.

> be proportionate to the injury suffered. Such awards should be well below the level of general damages for serious physical or psychiatric injury.[86]

With this in mind, Jackson J awarded the claimant £2,500 damages. In *Douglas v Hello!* Lindsay J cited *Cornelius, Campbell,* and *Archer v Williams* and awarded £3,750 pounds to each of the Douglases in respect of the distress caused by publication of the unauthorized photographs of their wedding (a finding which was not challenged on appeal).[87] In *McKennitt v Ash,* Eady J declared (without giving reasons or citing authority) that the claimant was entitled, in addition to the grant of an injunction, to damages for hurt feelings and distress in the sum of £5,000.[88] Most recently, in *Giller v Procopets*[89] the Supreme Court of Victoria followed *Cornelius, Douglas v Hello!,* and *Campbell* in the context of an action for breach of confidence based on unauthorized disclosure of video tapes of the claimant and defendant having sex.[90] The court awarded compensatory damages of 40,000 AUS dollars.

Guidance on how damages for misuse of private information should be calculated was laid down in a recent decision, *Mosley v News Group Newspapers Ltd.*[91] In this case, the *News of the World* had published, in its newspaper and via its website, graphic and extensive details about a sado-masochistic sex party at which the claimant, the president of the Formula 1 governing body, was present. The defendant had alleged (incorrectly as the judge found) that the sex party had a Nazi theme. Eady J held that where infringement of privacy is concerned, the law is 'concerned to protect such matters as personal dignity, autonomy and integrity'.[92] He further commented that, unlike defamation actions, in which 'reputation can be vindicated by an award of damages, in the sense that the claimant can be restored to the esteem in which he was previously held, that is not possible where embarrassing personal information has been released for general publication'.[93] As such, Eady J considered the only realistic course was to 'select a figure which marks the fact that an unlawful intrusion has taken place while affording some degree of *solatium* to the injured party'.[94] With regards to the facts of the case, the judge found that the appropriate award of damages, taking into account the severe embarrassment and distress caused and in order to acknowledge the infringement, was £60,000.

FURTHER READING

D. Capper, 'Damages for breach of the equitable duty of confidence' (1994) 14 Legal Studies 313.

I. E. Davidson, 'The equitable remedy of compensation' (1982) 13 Melbourne University LR 349.

L. Clarke, 'Remedial responses to breach of confidence: The question of damages' [2005] 24 CJQ 316.

N. Witzleb, 'Monetary remedies for breach of confidence in privacy cases' (2007) 27(3) Legal Studies 430.

---

[86] *Archer v Williams* [2003] EMLR 38, para. 76.   [87] *Douglas v Hello!* [2004] EMLR 2 (Ch).
[88] *McKennitt v Ash* [2006] EMLR 10.   [89] [2008] VSCA 236.
[90] See especially the judgment of Neave JA in *Giller v Procopets* [2008] VSCA 236.
[91] [2008] EMLR 20.   [92] *Mosley v News Groups Newspapers Ltd* [2008] EMLR 20, para. 214.
[93] Ibid., para. 230.   [94] Ibid., para. 231.

8.6.1.2 Aggravated and exemplary damages

Aggravated damages are compensatory, rather than punitive, in nature and seek to compensate a claimant where the harm caused by a wrongful act is aggravated by the manner in which the act was done. *Campbell* supports the ability of courts to award aggravated damages where there has been misuse of private information, as does the Australian decision of *Giller v Procopets*.[95]

By way of contrast, exemplary damages are punitive in nature and, as such, anomalous in the context of civil litigation. Recently, Mr Justice Eady ruled in *Mosley* that exemplary damages were not available in a claim for infringement of privacy/breach of confidence.[96] This was because there was no authority to support such an award. Further, it would act as an unjustified restriction on the right to freedom of expression, as contained in Article 10 of the ECHR.

8.6.2 ACCOUNT OF PROFITS[97]

An alternative financial remedy to damages is an account of profits. This focuses on the gain made by the defendant as a result of the infringing behaviour, as compared with damages which focuses on the loss or harm suffered by the claimant. An order for an account of profits is an equitable remedy and thus is clearly available for breach of an equitable obligation of confidence.[98] When it comes to contractual duties of confidence, however, such an award will be available only in exceptional circumstances, where the normal remedies of damages, specific performance, and injunction are inadequate and the justice of the case demands it.[99]

According to Lord Keith and Lord Brightman in *Attorney-General v Observer Ltd*[100] the rationale for this type of remedy is that no one should be able to profit from their wrongdoing or be unjustly enriched.[101] The main difficulty with an order for an account of profits is calculating the profits attributable to the wrongful act. Where the profits are made as a result of illegitimate and legitimate behaviour, courts will do their best to apportion profits attributable to the wrongful act. No apportionment will occur, however, where the profits are entirely attributable to the breach of confidence.[102]

8.6.3 INTERIM INJUNCTIONS

Prior to the HRA, the House of Lords decision in *American Cyanamid v Ethicon*[103] set out the rules governing the grant of interim injunctions. However, s. 12(3) of the HRA provides that interim relief is not to be granted, 'unless the court is satisfied that the applicant is likely to establish that publication should not be allowed'. The meaning of 'likely to establish' and whether the approach in *American Cyanamid v Ethicon* was consistent

---

[95] [2008] VSCA 236.   [96] *Mosley v News Group Newspapers Ltd* [2008] EMLR 20.

[97] For further discussion of this remedy, refer to 13.6.4.

[98] *Peter Pan Manufacturing v Corsets Silhouette* [1963] 3 All ER 402.

[99] See *Attorney-General v Blake* [2001] 1 AC 268.   [100] [1990] 1 AC 109.

[101] *Attorney-General v Observer Ltd* [1990] 1 AC 109, 262, per Lord Keith, and p. 266, per Lord Brightman.

[102] As in *Peter Pan Manufacturing v Corsets Silhouette* [1963] 3 All ER 402.

[103] [1975] AC 396. This is further discussed at 13.5.1.

with this language were issues that were settled by the House of Lords in *Cream Holdings Ltd v Banerjee.*

Cream Holdings Ltd v Banerjee [2005] 1 AC 253

The claimants were Liverpool-based companies, whose business included running nightclubs, organizing dance festivals, and franchising and merchandising their brand name and logo. The first defendant, a chartered accountant, following her dismissal took with her copies of documents, which she claimed showed illegal and improper activity by the Cream group. She passed these to the second defendant, who published articles about alleged corruption within the Cream group. The claimants then sought injunctive relief to restrain further publication of any confidential information disclosed by the first defendant. At first instance, Lloyd J granted the injunction and the appeal was dismissed by a majority of the Court of Appeal. The House of Lords allowed the defendants' appeal.

Lord Nicholls (delivering the leading speech with which the other law lords agreed):

Section 12(3) and 'likely'

13. The legal background against which this statutory provision has to be interpreted is familiar. In the 1960s the approach adopted by the courts to the grant of interlocutory injunctions was that the applicant had to establish a prima facie case. He had to establish this before questions of the so-called 'balance of convenience' fell to be considered. A prima facie case was understood, at least in the Chancery Division, as meaning the applicant must establish that as the evidence currently stood on the balance of probability he would succeed at the trial.

14. The courts were freed from this fetter by the decision of your Lordships' House in *American Cyanamid Co v Ethicon Ltd* [1975] AC 396. Lord Diplock said, at pp. 407–408, that the court must be satisfied the claim 'is not frivolous or vexatious; in other words, that there is a serious question to be tried'. But it is no part of the court's function at this stage of litigation to try to resolve conflicts of evidence on affidavit nor to decide difficult questions of law calling for detailed argument and mature consideration. Unless the applicant fails to show he has 'any real prospect of succeeding in his claim for a permanent injunction at the trial', the court should proceed to consider where the balance of convenience lies. As to that, where other factors appear to be evenly balanced, 'it is a counsel of prudence' for the court to take 'such measures as are calculated to preserve the status quo'.

15. When the Human Rights Bill was under consideration by Parliament concern was expressed at the adverse impact the Bill might have on the freedom of the press. Article 8 of the European Convention, guaranteeing the right to respect for private life, was among the Convention rights to which the legislation would give effect. The concern was that, applying the conventional *American Cyanamid* approach, orders imposing prior restraint on newspapers might readily be granted by the courts to preserve the status quo until trial whenever applicants claimed that a threatened publication would infringe their rights under article 8. Section 12(3) was enacted to allay these fears. Its principal purpose was to buttress the protection afforded to freedom of speech at the interlocutory stage. It sought to do so by setting a higher threshold for the grant of interlocutory injunctions against the media than

the *American Cyanamid* guideline of a 'serious question to be tried' or a 'real prospect' of success at the trial.

16. Against this background I turn to consider whether, as the 'Echo' submits, 'likely' in section 12(3) bears the meaning of 'more likely than not' or 'probably'. This would be a higher threshold than that prescribed by the *American Cyanamid* case. That would be consistent with the underlying parliamentary intention of emphasising the importance of freedom of expression. But in common with the views expressed in the Court of Appeal in the present case, I do not think 'likely' can bear this meaning in section 12(3). Section 12(3) applies the 'likely' criterion to all cases of interim prior restraint. It is of general application. So Parliament was painting with a broad brush and setting a general standard. A threshold of 'more likely than not' in every case would not be workable in practice. It would not be workable in practice because in certain common form situations it would produce results Parliament cannot have intended. It would preclude the court from granting an interim injunction in some circumstances where it is plain injunctive relief should be granted as a temporary measure.

17. Take a case such as the present: an application is made to the court for an interlocutory injunction to restrain publication of allegedly confidential or private information until trial. The judge needs an opportunity to read and consider the evidence and submissions of both parties. Until then the judge will often not be in a position to decide whether on balance of probability the applicant will succeed in obtaining a permanent injunction at the trial. In the nature of things this will take time, however speedily the proceedings are arranged and conducted. The courts are remarkably adept at hearing urgent applications very speedily, but inevitably there will often be a lapse of some time in resolving such an application, whether measured in hours or longer in a complex case.

18. What is to happen meanwhile? Confidentiality, once breached, is lost for ever. Parliament cannot have intended that, whatever the circumstances, section 12(3) would preclude a judge from making a restraining order for the period needed for him to form a view on whether on balance of probability the claim would succeed at trial. That would be absurd. In the present case the 'Echo' agreed not to publish any further article pending the hearing of Cream's application for interim relief. But it would be absurd if, had the 'Echo' not done so, the court would have been powerless to preserve the confidentiality of the information until Cream's application had been heard. Similarly, if a judge refuses to grant an interlocutory injunction preserving confidentiality until trial the court ought not to be powerless to grant interim relief pending the hearing of an interlocutory appeal against the judge's order.

19. The matter goes further than these procedural difficulties. Cases may arise where the adverse consequences of disclosure of information would be extremely serious, such as a grave risk of personal injury to a particular person. Threats may have been made against a person accused or convicted of a crime or a person who gave evidence at a trial. Disclosure of his current whereabouts might have extremely serious consequences. Despite the potential seriousness of the adverse consequences of disclosure, the applicant's claim to confidentiality may be weak. The applicant's case may depend, for instance, on a disputed question of fact on which the applicant has an arguable but distinctly poor case. It would be extraordinary if in such a case the court were compelled to apply a 'probability of success' test and therefore, regardless of the seriousness of the possible adverse consequences, refuse to restrain publication until the disputed issue of fact can be resolved at the trial.

20. These considerations indicate that 'likely' in section 12(3) cannot have been intended to mean 'more likely than not' in all situations. That, as a test of universal application, would set the degree of likelihood too high. In some cases application of that test would achieve the antithesis of a fair trial. Some flexibility is essential. The intention of Parliament must be taken to be that 'likely' should have an extended meaning which sets as a normal prerequisite to the

grant of an injunction before trial a likelihood of success at the trial higher than the common-place *American Cyanamid* standard of 'real prospect' but permits the court to dispense with this higher standard where particular circumstances make this necessary.

After *Banerjee,* is the test of 'serious question to be tried', as set out in *American Cyanamid,* still applicable? If not, what test will an applicant for an interim injunction have to satisfy? Is this a rigid test or may courts apply it flexibly in certain circumstances?

8.6.4 CONSTRUCTIVE TRUSTS

Whether proprietary remedies, in the form of a remedial constructive trust, can be awarded for breach of confidence is a difficult issue that has been touched upon by English courts in only a few cases. The most detailed consideration of this issue thus far was in *Ocular Sciences v AVCL.*

Ocular Sciences v AVCL [1997] RPC 289

In this case, the claimants were seeking, *inter alia*, a declaration that the defendant held such part of its business and assets as were derived from or acquired by reason of its breach of confidence on trust for them.

Laddie J, at pp. 414–16:

[As there was little English case law on this issue, **Laddie J** referred to the Supreme Court of Canada decision in *Lac Minerals Ltd v International Corona Resources Services Ltd*,[104] where the Court imposed a constructive trust over land which the defendant had bought because he had been told in confidence that it might be gold bearing.]

As Goff & Jones says, and Mr Males accepted, in determining whether to grant a proprietary remedy, the court should consider whether it is the appropriate remedy in the circumstances of the case. In considering this, the court must bear in mind the possible effects of imposing a constructive trust. Not only will the plaintiff obtain priority over general creditors, he may recover profits made by the defendant, limitation periods may be different and the plaintiff may be able to obtain compound interest. It seems to me that in the *Lac Minerals* case there were special and very good reasons why the imposition of a constructive trust was appropriate. La Forest J said that in breach of confidence cases there is considerable flexibility in remedy. He explained the imposition of a constructive trust in that case as follows:

The appropriate remedy in this case can not be divorced from the findings of fact made by the courts below. As I indicated earlier, there is no doubt in my mind that but for the actions of Lac in misusing confidential information and thereby acquiring the Williams property, that property would have been acquired by Corona. That finding is fundamental to the determination of the appropriate remedy...The issue then is this. If it is established that one party, (here Lac), has been enriched by the acquisition of an asset, the Williams property, that would have, but for the actions of that party been acquired by the plaintiff, (here Corona), and if the acquisition of that asset amounts to a breach of duty to the plaintiff, here either a breach of fiduciary obligation or a breach of a duty

---

[104] (1989) 61 DLR (4th) 14, 16 IPR 27.

of confidence, what remedy is available to the party deprived of the benefit? In my view the constructive trust is one available remedy, and in this case it is the only appropriate remedy.

...Much of the difficulty [in deciding whether the imposition of a constructive trust is appropriate] disappears if it is recognised that in this context the issue of the appropriate remedy only arises once a valid restitutionary claim has been made out. The constructive trust awards a right in property, but that right can only arise once a right to relief has been established. In the vast majority of cases a constructive trust will not be the appropriate remedy. Thus in *Hunter* [an unreported Canadian case], had the restitutionary claim been made out, there would have been no reason to award a constructive trust, as the plaintiff's claim could have been satisfied simply by a personal monetary award; a constructive trust should only be awarded if there is reason to grant to the plaintiff the additional rights that flow from recognition of a right of property. Among the most important of these will be that it is appropriate that the plaintiff receive the priority accorded to the holder of the right of property in a bankruptcy. More important in this case is the right of the property holder to have changes in value accrue to his account rather than the account of the wrongdoer. Here as well it is justified to grant a right of property since the concurrent findings below are that the defendant intercepted the plaintiff and thereby frustrated its efforts to obtain a specific and unique property that the courts below held would otherwise have been acquired. The recognition of a constructive trust simply redirects the title of the Williams property to its original course. The moral quality of the defendants' act may also be another consideration in determining whether a proprietary remedy is appropriate. Allowing the defendant to retain a specific asset when it was obtained through conscious wrongdoing may so offend a court that it would deny to the defendant the right to retain the property. This situation will be more rare, since the focus of the inquiry should be upon the reasons for recognising the right of property in the plaintiff, not on the reason for denying it to the defendant.

Lac Minerals does not purport to set out all the factors which should be taken into account in deciding whether or not to impose a constructive trust as a form of relief. But it does indicate some which are of significance. Although not binding, it makes eminent sense. None of the parties suggested to me that it was wrong.

What the plaintiffs are asking for is the imposition of a constructive trust over a part of the defendants' business and assets. Unlike *Lac Minerals*, there is no question here of the defendants having diverted their business or assets, or any part of them, from the plaintiffs. Furthermore even if it is said that part of the defendants' business and assets have been contaminated by breaches of confidence, that contamination is small and technically inconsequential. In my view it would be quite wrong to impose a constructive trust over such a minor fraction. It was not clear to me how a constructive trust imposed on such a fraction would work. Who would decide what repairs or modifications should be carried out to equipment, who should pay for them, who should decide what to do with obsolete equipment and if AVCL was to be floated on the stock exchange, who would decide at what price and on what terms? I can see attractions in a suitable case of imposing a constructive trust over a complete discrete item of property but imposing such a trust over a part only raises additional problems. On the above grounds alone I would come to the conclusion that this is not a proper case for the imposition of a constructive trust.

However, since the imposition of a constructive trust is part of the equitable armoury of the court, the considerations which may affect the court's willingness to grant an injunction also have a part to play. Mr Males suggested that if the court was unwilling to grant an injunction against use of confidential information, the imposition of a constructive trust becomes all the more necessary. I do not agree. Most of the reasons which have led me to refuse that type of injunctive relief, have made me come to the conclusion that this is not a case where it would be right for the court to exercise its discretion in the plaintiffs' favour by imposing a trust.

Laddie J indicated that a breach of confidence, independent of a breach of fiduciary duty, *could* give rise to a constructive trust over the property acquired as a result of the breach. The sorts of factors relevant to making such a declaration included those identified in *Lac Minerals*. However, consideration of these factors did not lead him to declare a constructive trust on the facts of the case. Particularly important was the fact that the defendants' breach of confidence did not result in them acquiring particular property or assets, which the claimants would otherwise have acquired.

The Court of Appeal in *United Pan-Europe v Deutsche Bank*,[105] relying on *Lac Minerals*, also supported the availability of a constructive trust in respect of breach of confidence. Despite this (rather limited) authority, it seems that it will be only in extremely rare cases that an English court will impose a constructive trust where there has been a breach of confidence.

FURTHER READING

M. Conaglen, 'Thinking about proprietary remedies for breach of confidence' [2008] IPQ 82.

P. Stanley, *The Law of Confidentiality: A restatement* (Oxford: Hart, 2008), Appendix B: Information & Property.

T. H. Wu, 'Confidence and the constructive trust' (2003) 23 Legal Studies 135.

8.7 FUTURE ISSUES

Undoubtedly, significant changes have occurred to the equitable action for breach of confidence insofar as it relates to personal or private information. While the way in which the law of confidence protects privacy has become much clearer, there is still considerable uncertainty about the impact of these privacy developments on the law of confidence generally. There is also the lingering question of whether it would be preferable for courts to recognize a separate tort of misuse of private information, rather than continuing to rely upon breach of confidence. The interrelationship between 'traditional' breach of confidence and the 'new' or 'extended' action is another issue that has yet to be explored in any depth. The current indication from the Court of Appeal is that, even where a confidential obligation in respect of personal information exists, a court should approach liability for unauthorized use or disclosure of such information according to a balancing exercise between Articles 8 and 10 of the ECHR.[106] Finally, in light of the House of Lords decision in *Douglas v Hello!*, there are concerns about the possibility of protecting publicity interests in addition to privacy.

The above are crucial issues, from both doctrinal and policy perspectives, with which scholars and judges are only beginning to grapple. We can only hope that the next few years will bring much needed clarification and resolution.

FURTHER READING

T. Aplin, 'Commercial confidences after the Human Rights Act' (2007) 10 EIPR 411.

T. Aplin, 'The future of breach of confidence and the protection of privacy' (2007) 7 OUCLJ 137.

---

[105] [2000] 1 BCLC 461.
[106] See *McKennitt v Ash* [2007] 3 WLR 194 and *Associated Newspapers v HRH Prince of Wales* [2007] 3 WLR 222.

T. Aplin, 'The relationship between breach of confidence and the "tort of misuse of private information"' (2007) 18(2) King's Law Journal 329.

R. Bagshaw, 'Obstacles on the path to privacy torts' in Birks (ed.), *Privacy and Loyalty* (Oxford: Clarendon, 1997), pp. 1–28.

P. Jaffey, 'Privacy, confidentiality, and property' in P. Torremans (ed.), *Copyright and Human Rights* (The Hague: Kluwer Law International, 2004), pp. 447–73.

9

PATENTS I:

JUSTIFICATIONS, REGISTRATION, AND VALIDITY

9.1 INTRODUCTION

A patent may be understood as a monopoly right over the commercial exploitation of an invention, granted for a limited time (usually 20 years). Patents may relate to all manner of inventions, including those in the chemical, mechanical engineering, pharmaceutical, biotechnology, and information technology fields. Thus, the medicines we take, the cars we drive, the bicycles we ride, the portable electronic devices or telephones we use, even the food that we consume, is likely to involve a patented product or process somewhere along the line. For some businesses, the difference between owning patents or not can mean the difference between millions, even billions, of pounds. But that is not to say that patent law is entirely the province of big business. It can, and does, have a relevance also to small and medium enterprises. However, one of the struggles for patent law is creating a system that is equally accessible and valuable to all participants.

Patent law grants a territorial right, yet the global significance of patents is without doubt. This has led to international and regional agreements that ensure basic consistencies in the substantive and, to a lesser extent, procedural law relating to patents. The focus of the next two chapters will be on elucidating UK patent law principles. However, it should be remembered that, like so much of intellectual property law today, patent law sits firmly within an international context.

9.2 HISTORY

The following section will provide an overview of the history of UK patent law. This is important, not only because it contextualizes the existing law, but also because it highlights that some of the present-day controversies in patent law are not in fact new.

The UK patent system can be traced back to at least the 14th century, when the Crown granted royal privileges to foreign craftsmen (mainly weavers, salt-makers, and glass-makers) with a view to encouraging them to live in England and practice their trade, thereby transferring skills to the local population. These privileges were granted by a document known as a 'letters patent'[1] and, initially, did not confer any exclusive rights. Further, 'letters patent' were not confined to granting privileges for inventions, but were also used by the Crown to grant land, honours, liberties, and franchises.[2]

In the middle of the 16th century the practice of granting letters patent to attract superior Continental technology was revived on a larger scale, with a key difference being that this time the privileges did confer exclusivity, an idea which seems to have been borrowed from the Venetians.[3] Although the transfer of manufacturing knowledge and skills was the predominant motive for the issue of patents under Elizabeth I, this royal practice was also used to assist in paying off political debts and in raising revenue. These monopolies became the source of discontent because they artificially raised prices, gave patent holders wide powers of enforcement of their rights, and were granted for questionable material. The popular outcry reached such a pitch that in 1601 Elizabeth I agreed to revoke many of the worst patents, by issuing the Proclamation Concerning Monopolies of 1601. This revoked the majority of monopoly grants and, more importantly, allowed matters concerned with such grants to be contested in the common law courts. The next year, Edward Darcy, who had been granted letters patent in the importation, making, and selling of playing cards, attempted to enforce his right against an infringer named Allen. The court held that the monopoly was illegal and the patent was declared invalid.[4]

Elizabeth I's successor, James I, continued to use the patent system in an arbitrary and abusive manner and, as a result, Parliament introduced in 1624 the Statute of Monopolies. This legislation imposed a general prohibition on the grant of patents by the Crown. However, an exception was created by s. 6, which stated:

> Provided . . . that any declaration before mentioned shall not extend to any letters patent and grants of privilege for the term of fourteen years or under . . . of the sole working or making of any manner of new manufactures within this Realme, to the true and first inventor and inventors of such manufactures which others at the time of making such letters patent and grants shall not use, so as also they be not contrary to the law, or mischevious to the State, by raising prices of commodities at home, or hurt of trade, or generally inconvenient . . .

Section 6 of the 1624 Statute of Monopolies was declaratory of the previous practice and common law.[5] Yet, it is often regarded as laying the foundations of patent law. The tendency to trace patent law back to the 1624 Statute of Monopolies is something that Sherman and Bently warn against, mainly because it encourages us to gloss over the history of the patent

---

[1] Since the Patents Act 1977 ('PA 77'), letters patent are no longer used to grant patents for inventions in the UK. Rather, the Comptroller-General of Patents, Designs and Trade Marks (i.e. UK Intellectual Property Office) sends the proprietor a certificate in the prescribed form stating that the patent has been granted to him: see s. 24(2), PA 1977; Patents Rules, SI 2007/3291, r. 34.

[2] C. Macleod, *Inventing the Industrial Revolution: The English patent system 1660–1800* (Cambridge: Cambridge University Press, 1988), p. 10.

[3] The Venetian law of 1474 provided for 10-year exclusive privileges to be granted to inventors of new arts and machines.

[4] *Darcy v Allen* (1602) 77 ER 1260.

[5] C. Macleod, *Inventing the Industrial Revolution*, pp. 17–19 and J. Pila, 'The common law invention in its original form' (2001) IPQ 209.

system between 1624 to the present day and to treat patent law as predestined and timeless, as opposed to open and historically contingent.[6]

The 17th century 'provided no more than a germ of a functioning patent system'.[7] However, it is interesting to note that in the 17th century, the essential consideration for the grant of the patent was not the filing of a patent specification which sufficiently disclosed the knowledge of the invention, but rather the introduction of the new industry or trade, in other words the putting into practice of the invention.[8]

The requirement that a patent owner provide a written description of the invention did not emerge until the 18th century and was one that grew out of common practice. In the latter half of the 18th century, it effectively became a requirement as courts insisted upon a written description of the invention as 'consideration' for the monopoly granted.[9] An example of such judicial insistence is *Liardet v Johnson*.[10] In this case Liardet brought an action for infringement against Johnson in relation to a patent for a newly invented stucco, or composition, to imitate stone for covering the outside of buildings. Lord Mansfield, in instructing the jury at the end of the trial, emphasized that the specification had to instruct others in how to make the invention. The shifting of the 'consideration' of the patent grant from practising the invention to disclosure of the invention led to a corresponding change in the conception of novelty. In assessing novelty, it was now pertinent also to ask if the trade already knew of the invention through publication?[11]

At the beginning of the 19th century there was deep dissatisfaction with the patent system. Three main complaints emerged:[12] first, that the administrative machinery for securing a patent was excessively unwieldy; second, that the cost of obtaining patents was too high, particularly since separate patents had to be registered for England, Scotland, and Ireland; third, the grounds on which a patent could be declared invalid were too harsh—judges would set aside patents as invalid because of minor errors in the patent specification and yet inventors were not entitled to correct such errors once the specification had been enrolled. In 1829, Thomas Lennard called on Parliament to establish a Select Committee to inquire into the state of patent law. The grievances mentioned above, along with others, were aired before the Select Committee. The main proposal to emerge was the establishment of a scientific commission to examine inventions. It was thought that such an examination process would reduce the number of faulty specifications and the risk of them being set aside by the courts. Unfortunately, the Select Committee's findings were inconclusive and little by way of concrete reform was achieved. Sherman and Bently argue that the Select Committee nonetheless, 'still played an important role in bringing about the emergence of modern patent law: it both operated to expose the confused and uncertain nature of the law and drew together many of the divergent criticisms that existed at the time.'[13]

---

[6] B. Sherman and L. Bently, *The Making of Modern Intellectual Property Law* (Cambridge: Cambridge University Press, 1999), pp. 208–9.

[7] W. R. Cornish and D. Llewelyn, *Intellectual Property: Patents, copyright, trade marks and allied rights* (6th edn., London: Sweet & Maxwell, 2007) 3–06.

[8] See D. Seaborne Davies, 'The early history of the patent specification' (1934) LQR 86, 97, 99–100; and E. Wyndham Hulme, 'On the consideration of the patent grant, past and present' (1897) LQR 313, 313–14.

[9] See E. Wyndham Hulme, 'On the history of patent law in the seventeenth and eighteenth centuries' (1902) 18 LQR 280.

[10] (1778) 62 Eng Rep 1000.   [11] According to Hulme, 'On the history of patent law' (1902), p. 287.

[12] See H. I. Dutton, *The Patent System and Inventive Activity during the Industrial Revolution, 1750–1852* (Manchester: Manchester University Press, 1984), pp. 34–6.

[13] Sherman and Bently, *The Making of Modern Intellectual Property Law*, p. 103.

After the Select Committee, enthusiasm for reform continued. A bill in 1833 was brought before Parliament by Godson,[14] but failed. This highlighted that although reformers were keen to improve the position of inventors, there was much disagreement about the best way to achieve this.[15] A bill was introduced in 1835, this time by Lord Brougham. While the 1835 bill was successful, it brought about modest changes. It was now possible for patentees to amend their specifications to correct minor errors and for patentees to obtain a further seven years protection upon petitioning the Judicial Committee of the Privy Council.[16] Other minor amendments were achieved by legislation in 1839 and 1844.

Due to other, more pressing domestic concerns, calls for patent law reform declined during the 1840s. However, interest in patent reform was revived in the late 1840s/early 1850s and culminated in the Patent Law Amendment Act 1852. This Act brought about substantial reform of the patent system. The administration of the system was simplified; an index of patents that could be consulted by the public was introduced; a single patent for the UK replaced the separate patents for England, Scotland, and Ireland; and, perhaps most importantly, the cost of patenting was reduced.[17]

Whereas the first half of the 19th century saw repeated calls and attempts to reform the patent system, the latter half saw calls for its abolition with the controversy reaching its peak between 1850 and 1875.[18] Political economists were key opponents of the patent system and linked the ills of tariff protectionism in trade with those of patent protectionism and the patent monopoly.[19] In order to distance the issue of patent protection from monopoly and free trade issues, the pro-patent lobby sought to justify patents according to natural law and utilitarian rationales. These rationales, which are discussed in the next section on justifications, have a continuing relevance. In the end, the anti-patent movement waned and the pro-patent lobby prevailed. Even so, the attempts to abolish the patent system were critical to a transformation in the legal image of the invention, providing the foundations of modern patent law.[20]

In 1883, the Patents, Designs and Trade Marks Act was passed and gave effect to the Paris Convention for the Protection of Industrial Property 1883 (discussed below). There were several important consequences of this Act. First, patent actions were now tried by a single judge. Second, patentees were obliged to include in their specifications at least one claim delineating the scope of their monopoly and judges came to insist that claims mark out the full range of protection for patentees. Finally, the Patent Office began to examine applications, albeit mainly for formal defects and sufficiency of description.

In the 20th century, various patent statutes were passed. However, the most important of these were the Patents Act 1902, the Patents Act 1949, and the Patents Act 1977. The Patents Act 1902 saw a change in the examination process. A Select Committee in 1901 (the Fry Committee) had shown that 40 per cent of patents granted were for inventions already described in earlier British patent specifications. Thus, the 1902 Act introduced into the examination process a novelty search, but not a test of obviousness (although, this was a ground on which a patent might be revoked). The Patents Act 1949 represented a codification of incremental changes that had occurred via the common law. It also introduced obviousness as a ground of pre-grant opposition and removed the restrictions on patentability of chemical substances that had been introduced in 1919. The Patents Act 1977 ('PA 77') was introduced to implement the European Patent Convention 1973 ('EPC') and as such

---

14 For a discussion see Dutton, *The Patent System and Inventive Activity*, pp. 46–8.

15 See ibid., p. 48.   16 For a discussion see ibid., pp. 48–51.   17 Ibid., p. 63.

18 See F. Machlup and E. Penrose, 'The patent controversy in the nineteenth century' (1950) 10 Journal of Economic History 1, 1–10.

19 Ibid., p. 9.   20 Sherman and Bently, *The Making of Modern Intellectual Property Law*, pp. 152–7.

represented a landmark change for UK patent law. The PA 77 (as amended) is the law which today regulates patents in the UK.

From the above historical account, it is interesting to note the sorts of concerns that arose during the development of the patent system. These include the detrimental effects of granting a monopoly right, the need for an accessible and efficient patent system, and avoiding the grant of patents for unmeritorious inventions. In reading this and the next chapter consider the extent to which these are also problematic for modern patent law.

FURTHER READING

H. I. Dutton, *The Patent System and Inventive Activity during the Industrial Revolution, 1750–1852* (Manchester: Manchester University Press, 1984).

P. W. Grubb, *Patents for Chemicals, Pharmaceuticals and Biotechnology* (4th edn., Oxford: Oxford University Press, 2004), pp. 8–14.

F. Machlup and E. Penrose, 'The patent controversy in the nineteenth century' (1950) 10 Journal of Economic History 1.

C. Macleod, *Inventing the Industrial Revolution: The English patent system 1660–1800* (Cambridge: Cambridge University Press, 1988).

J. Pila, 'The common law invention in its original form' (2001) IPQ 209.

D. Seaborne Davies, 'The early history of the patent specification' (1934) LQR 86.

B. Sherman and L. Bently, *The Making of Modern Intellectual Property Law* (Cambridge: Cambridge University Press, 1999).

E. Wyndham Hulme, 'The history of the patent system under the prerogative and at common law' (1896) 12 LQR 141.

E. Wyndham Hulme, 'On the consideration of the patent grant, past and present' (1897) LQR 313.

E. Wyndham Hulme 'The history of the patent system under the prerogative at common law: A sequel' (1900) 16 LQR 44.

E. Wyndham Hulme, 'On the history of patent law in the seventeenth and eighteenth centuries' (1902) 18 LQR 280.

9.3 JUSTIFICATIONS

Of all the intellectual property rights, a patent grants a true monopoly, insofar as it gives the owner (i.e. a patentee or patent proprietor) an exclusive right to make and sell the invention, even where a third party may have independently developed the same innovation. This will enable the patentee to charge a monopoly price in respect of his or her invention, and is the reason why owning a patent is so valuable. What justifications exist for bestowing this type of privilege on those who invent? As we have seen, in the late 19th century there were fierce opponents of the patent system. To counter this opposition, pro-patent advocates developed four main arguments in support of retaining patent rights, justifications that are often invoked today. The following extract from Machlup and Penrose explores these arguments in detail.

F. Machlup and E. Penrose, 'The patent controversy in the nineteenth century'
(1950) 10 Journal of Economic History 1, 9–26

The arguments for patents, formulated in these terms and opposed and defended during the controversy of the nineteenth century, are still used today whenever the patent system is debated. Indeed, little, if anything, has been said for or against the patent system in the twentieth century that was not said equally well in the nineteenth.

The Four Main Arguments

It is possible to distinguish four fundamentally different lines of argument to justify the creation of patent rights...

Argument Type One: A man has a natural property right in his own ideas. Their appropriation by others must be condemned as stealing. Society is morally obligated to recognize and protect this property right. Property is in essence exclusive. Hence enforcement of exclusivity in the use of a patented invention is the only appropriate way for society to recognize this right.

Argument Type Two: Justice requires that a man receive, and therefore that society secure to him, reward for his services in proportion as these services are useful to society. Inventors render useful services. The most appropriate way to secure to inventors rewards commensurate with their services is by means of exclusive patent rights in their inventions.

Argument Type Three: Industrial progress is desirable to society. Inventions and their exploitation are necessary to secure industrial progress. Neither invention nor exploitation of invention will be obtained to any adequate extent unless inventors and capitalists have hopes that successful ventures will yield profits which make it worth their while to make their efforts and risk their money. The simplest, cheapest, and most effective way for society to hold out these incentives is to grant exclusive patent rights in inventions.

Argument Type Four: Industrial progress is desirable to society. To secure it at a sustained rate it is necessary that new inventions become generally known as part of the technology of society. In the absence of protection against immediate imitation of novel technological ideas, an inventor will keep his invention secret. The secret will die with him, and society will thereby lose the new art. Hence it is in the interest of society to induce the inventor to disclose his secret for the use of future generations. This can best be done by granting exclusive patent rights to the inventor in return for public disclosure of his invention.

The four types of argument are independent of one another. Any one of them may be upheld if the other three should be rejected. The first two are based on ethical norms, the last two on political expediency. The first is anchored in concepts of natural law, giving the inventor a natural right to protection; the second calls for protection in the name of fairness to secure the inventor his just reward. The third, resting on the assumption that not enough inventions would be made and utilized without adequate inducements, recommends patent protection as the best inducement. The fourth, fearing the loss of inventions through secrecy, recommends patent protection as a means of inducing disclosure and publicity.

The Natural Property Right in Ideas

...

One of the favourite formulations of the property argument by the patent advocates was in terms of man's natural right to the fruits of his labor. The product of one's labor must be recognized as one's property. This form of the argument was challenged by Rodriguez, a Spanish economist, as follows:

> Labor, in fact, is not the *title* to it [the invention], but only the rational *method* of acquiring it....Labor results in property when it results in an *exclusive appropriation*; when the product can only belong to him who has done the work; when it would be necessary to take the article or utility created away from its possessor before it can be used by another person.

But, as Chevalier emphasized, 'an idea can belong to an unlimited number of persons; it is indeed the essence of an idea that, once published, it belongs to all the world...'

...

Wirth's position—accepting the theory of property rights in ideas but denying its applicability to technological inventions—was also Chevalier's, who said:

> Literary and artistic works have a perfectly decided character of individuality, and on this account they constitute a distinct property, which the law can recognize. In contrast to this, the character of individuality is wanting in real or supposed inventions, which are the object of patents, since what one man made today, another—a hundred others—may make tomorrow.

R. A. Macfie, the most vocal patent abolitionist in England and a severe critic of the theory of natural property rights in inventions, declared that if there were any 'natural rights' in connection with inventions it would be the inventor's 'right to use his own invention'. But just this right, he argued, was frequently denied under the patent system: all too often an inventor would find himself barred from using his own idea because somebody else had obtained a patent on it; this might happen even if his idea were better than the patented one but was considered a version of it.

...

The whole notion of natural rights of property in ideas in general, and in invention in particular, makes sense only to those who recognize 'natural law' and accept private property as part of it. To others, private property in anything is merely an institution given the sanction of positive law for a social purpose; hence it should be confined to areas where the purpose is good.

...During the third quarter of the nineteenth century, chiefly in Germany, the patent opposition was able to weaken the cause of patent protection partly by demolishing its shaky construction as a natural property right. German patent advocates found it expedient to abandon this position and retreat to stronger ones.

The Just Reward for the Inventor

A safer and sounder defense of the claims of inventors was founded on their moral rights to receive reward for services rendered. Many of those who rejected the notion of private property in ideas saw justice in securing a reward to the inventor for his labor and accepted the institution of the patent as the best method of doing it.

...

Other participants in the patent controversy did not deny the inventor's moral right to be rewarded for his work but held that such reward would come without intervention. If an inventor was really ahead of others, the time interval between his use of the invention and its imitation by his competitors would secure him temporary profits or rents sufficient to reward him for his contribution.

...One might recognize that pecuniary rewards for the inventors' efforts were required as a matter of justice...yet one might still reject patent privileges and support a system of cash prizes or bonuses paid to meritorious inventors. This was the conclusion many economists had reached. They were in favour of rewards for inventors but opposed to the patent system.

...

The alternatives most frequently recommended in lieu of patents were bonuses granted to inventors (a) by the government, (b) by professional associations financed through voluntary contributions by private industries, (c) by an intergovernmental agency, or (d) by an international association maintained through contributions from industries of all countries. Proposals along these lines were discussed in the professional journals and conferences almost everywhere.

The proposals for bonus systems of rewarding inventors did not receive great support. The chief objection was that their administration would give rise to partiality, arbitrariness, or even corruption—the dangers of all institutions giving discretionary power to administrators. Bentham had written, many years earlier: 'An exclusive privilege is of all rewards the best proportioned, the most natural, and the least burthesome.' John Stuart Mill clung to this view. He was still convinced that

> an exclusive privilege, of temporary duration is preferable; because it leaves nothing to anyone's discretion; because the reward conferred by it depends upon the invention's being found useful, and the greater the usefulness, the greater the reward; and because it is paid by the very persons to whom the service is rendered, the consumers of the commodity.

This became the standard argument in the defense of the patent system as the most adequate method of securing just rewards to inventors.

...

The Best Incentive to Invent

...

To say that patents are effective incentives to inventive activity is one thing; it is another to contend that they are necessary for inducing an adequate amount of such activity.

...

Even if the need for a special incentive through 'legislative interference' is accepted, the question whether patents are the best or cheapest means to that end arises just as it arose in connection with the method of doing justice to the inventor. There was the same argument, some claiming that money grants were cheaper and more effective incentives than patents.

The counterclaim that patents were the cheapest means of providing effective incentives turned attention to the comparison between the social benefits and social costs of the patent system.

...

To the extent that the stimulus of the patent system is effective, in the sense of causing people to do what they would not do otherwise, its effectiveness may consist chiefly in diverting existing activity into different, perhaps less productive, channels. This is one of the main contentions of the economists opposing the patent system. The diversion may be from ordinary productive pursuits into 'inventing', or from innovation or research activities in one field to the same kind of activities in another field in which the results enjoy patent protection.

The sacrifice of the production that would otherwise have occurred through the alternative uses of the productive resources steered into different channels by the patent incentive must of course be considered a social cost of the patent system. But three other factors were counted among the cost: First, the cost of the bureaucracy administering the patent system: the court personnel, lawyers, agents, and others engaged in prosecuting patent applications and litigations. Second, the economic disadvantages connected with the extension of the monopoly power of certain firms, an extension that often goes far beyond the scope of an individual patent grant. And, third, the social loss involved in the temporary prevention of the use of the most efficient processes by most, if not all, other producers.

It was this social loss that some writers felt was the worst effect of the patent system, and they emphasized the obstacles that the system put in the way of improvement by others of patented inventions...

...

Very often the advocates as well as the opponents of patents discussed the economic effects of the system on the assumption that the inventor was also the owner of the firm using the patent. It was not overlooked, however, that most inventors are either 'employed by a manufacturer or capitalist' or must sell their patents to them for a 'pittance'. This separation and possible conflict of interests between the inventor and exploiter not merely added to the arguments against the 'just-reward' theory but weighed heavily also against the theory that inventive activity requires a special incentive. If the inventors could not hope to reap the fruits of their work, the patent system could hardly be the incentive to their activity that it was represented to be. But another theory could be substituted for the weakened theory of the patent as an incentive to invent: a theory of the patent as an incentive to venture capital for the financing of the development and pioneer exploitation of inventions...

The Best Incentive to Disclose Secrets

...A supplementary or substitute argument in support of patents for inventions was advanced proposing that patents were necessary as incentives to induce inventors to disclose their new inventions instead of keeping them secret. Perhaps there would be enough inventive activity without patents, but could one count on disclosure of inventions so that they would become part of society's general fund of technological knowledge?

The 'incentive-to-disclose' theory of patent protection was often formulated as a social-contract theory...The patent was represented not as a privilege granted by society but as the result of a bargain between society and inventor, a contract in which the inventor agreed to disclose his secret and the state agreed, in exchange, to protect the inventor for a number of years against imitation of his idea. Why should anybody object to such a fair bargain with such a reasonable *quid pro quo*?

But there were objections and rather serious ones. They were based on the following lines of reasoning: (1) If inventors should prefer to keep their ideas secret and if they should succeed in doing so, society would not lose much, if anything, because usually the same or similar ideas are developed simultaneously and independently in several quarters. (2) It is practically impossible to keep inventions secret for any length of time; new products, new tools, and new processes are soon found out by eager competitors. (3) Where an inventor thinks he can succeed in guarding his secret, he will not take out a patent; hence, patent protection does not cause disclosure of concealable inventions but serves only to restrict the use of inventions that could not have been kept secret anyway. (4) Since patents are granted only on inventions developed to a stage at which they can be reduced to practical use, the patent system encourages secrecy in the developmental stage of inventions; without patents, inventors would hurry the publication of their ideas at earlier stages in order to secure recognition and fame, and this would hasten technological progress on all fronts.

The arguments discussed in the above extract from Machlup and Penrose arose in the context of a 19th-century controversy about whether to retain the patent system. For many developed countries, the debate is no longer about the existence of a patent system, but its scope and whether the rationales identified above justify certain features of patent law. For some developing countries, however, the question remains whether patent systems should be introduced at all. This has been particularly controversial in the light of the Agreement on Trade Related Aspects of Intellectual Property Rights 1994 (TRIPS Agreement), which is discussed below.[21] Commentators have questioned whether the incentive-based arguments used to justify a patent system are indeed applicable to developing countries. The following extract from a *Report of the Commission on Intellectual Property Rights* illustrates this concern:

Report of the Commission on Intellectual Property Rights, *Integrating Intellectual Property Rights and Developmental Policy* (London, Sept 2002), pp. 14–15

Patents are one way of addressing…market failure. By conferring temporary market exclusivities, patents allow producers to recoup the costs of investment in R&D and reap a profit, in return for making publicly available the knowledge on which the invention is based. However, someone else can only put that knowledge to potential commercial use with the authorisation of the patentee. The costs of investment in R&D and the return on that investment are met by charging the consumer a price based on the ability to exclude competition.

Protection is therefore a bargain struck by society on the premise that, in its absence, there would be insufficient invention and innovation. The assumption is that in the longer run, consumers will be better off, in spite of the higher costs conferred by monopoly pricing, because the short term losses to consumers are more than offset by the value to them of the new inventions created through additional R&D. Economists take the view that the patent system improves dynamic efficiency (by stimulating technical progress) at the cost of static efficiency (arising from the costs associated with monopoly).

This rationale for patent protection is relatively straightforward, but it is dependent on a number of simplifying assumptions that may not be borne out in practice. For instance, the optimal degree of patent protection cannot be accurately defined. If protection is too weak, then the development of technology may be inhibited through insufficient incentives for R&D. If too much protection is conferred, consumers may not benefit, even in the long run, and patentees may generate profits far in excess of the overall costs of R&D. Moreover, further innovation based on the protected technology may be stifled because, for instance, the length of the patent term is too long or the scope of the protection granted is too broad.

The length of the monopoly granted is one determinant of the strength of patent protection. Another is the scope of the patent…Broad patents can tend to discourage subsequent innovation by other researchers in the general area of the patent.

…

The optimal degree of protection (where the social benefits are judged to exceed the social costs) will also vary widely by product and sector and will be linked to variations in demand, market structures, R&D costs and the nature of the innovative process. In practice IPR regimes cannot be tailored so precisely and therefore the level of protection afforded in practice is necessarily a compromise. Striking the wrong compromise—whether too much or too little—may be costly to society, especially in the longer term.

One underlying assumption is that there is a latent supply of innovative capacity in the private sector waiting to be unleashed by the grant of the protection that the IP system provides. That may be so in countries where there is substantial research capacity. But in most

---

[21] At 9.4.1.4.

developing countries local innovation systems (at least of the kind established in developed countries) are weak. Even where such systems are stronger, there is often more capacity in the public than the private sectors. Thus, in such contexts, the dynamic benefit from IP protection is uncertain. The patent system may provide an incentive but there may be limited local capacity to make use of it. Even when technologies are developed, firms in developing countries can seldom bear the costs of acquisition and maintenance of rights and, above all, of litigation if disputes arise.

Economists are also now very aware of what they call *transaction costs.* Establishing the infrastructure of an IPR regime, and mechanisms for the enforcement of IP rights, is costly both to governments, and private stakeholders. In developing countries, where human and financial resources are scarce, and legal systems not well developed, the opportunity costs of operating the system effectively are high. Those costs include the costs of scrutinising the validity of claims to patent rights (both at the application stage and in the courts) and adjudicating upon actions for infringement. Considerable costs are generated by the inherent uncertainties of litigation. These costs too need to be weighed against the benefits arising from the IP system.

Thus the value of the patent system needs to be assessed in a balanced way, acknowledging that it has both costs and benefits, and that the balance of costs and benefits is likely to differ markedly in diverse circumstances.

Do you agree with the view expressed in the Report that some of the assumptions underlying the 'incentive' rationale for patent protection are not entirely applicable to developing countries? A more sceptical and strident position is taken by commentators, such as Vandana Shiva, who argue that developing countries are being forced to introduce patent systems at the behest of developed countries (via international agreements, such as the TRIPS Agreement) and that the justifications put forward for doing so are untenable.

V. Shiva, *Protect or Plunder?: Understanding intellectual property rights* (London, Zed books, 2001) pp. 21–3, 26

The Myth of Stimulating Creativity

The myth that patents contribute to the stimulation of creativity and inventiveness and their absence to lack of creativity and ingenuity is based on an artificial construction of knowledge and innovation—that of knowledge being isolated in time and space, without being connected to the social fabric and contributions from the past. Based on this construct, knowledge is thus seen as capital, a commodity and as a means for exclusive market control.

. . .

Knowledge, however, by its very nature is a collective, cumulative enterprise. It is based on exchange within a community. It is an expression of human creativity; both individual and collective. Since creativity has diverse expressions, science is a pluralistic enterprise which refers to different 'ways of knowing'. The term 'science' cannot be used to refer only to modern western science. It should include the knowledge systems of diverse cultures in different periods of history. But patents are granted for private intellectual property, built on the fiction of totally individualistic scientific innovation. There is then an intrinsic conflict built into the granting of patents as private rights for individual innovation and creativity and the view of knowledge as a collective endeavour.

. . .

This interpretation of creativity, as unleashed only when formal regimes of IPR protection are in place, is a total negation of creativity in nature and creativity generated by non-profit motives in both industrial and non-industrial societies. It is a denial of the role of innovation in traditional cultures, as well as in the public domain.

...

Central to the ideology of IPRs is this fallacy... that people are creative only if they can make profits and such profits are guaranteed through IPR protection. This negates the scientific creativity of those not spurred by the search for profits, i.e. the majority of scientists in universities and public research systems. It negates the creativity of traditional societies and the modern scientific community in which the free exchange of ideas is the very condition for creativity, not its anti-thesis.

...

The Myth of Technology Transfer, Innovation and R&D

The argument frequently promoted for a uniform worldwide IPR system is that such a system will promote investment, research and technology transfer in developing countries. The 'disclosure' clauses in patent laws which are related to medieval incentives for 'revealing the mysteries of the art' are now conveniently projected as necessary for the transferring of knowledge to society. However, the opposite is true. When companies can import products under import monopolies granted by patents, they have no incentive to set up domestic manufacture, or set up local R&D, or transfer technology to local production.

To what extent do you sympathize with the views expressed by Vandana Shiva? Does patent law invoke artificial notions of the way innovation occurs? And is there little likelihood that the introduction of patent systems in developing countries will encourage local investment in research and development?

Aside from whether traditional justifications for patent protection are universal and thus appropriate to developing countries, there is also the issue of whether patents have deleterious effects on indigenous communities. The argument is that a patent system encourages and legitimizes the unauthorized appropriation and commercial exploitation of traditional knowledge, sometimes referred to as 'bio-piracy'. Further, that indigenous communities are not in a position to pursue the benefits that a patent system may offer. These issues were alluded to in Chapter 1, in an extract from Daniel Gervais.[22] In the following extract, Graham Dutfield explores the inter-relationship between patents and traditional knowledge in greater detail.

G. Dutfield, 'Indigenous peoples, bioprospecting and the TRIPs agreement: Threats and opportunities' in P. Drahos and M. Blakeney (eds.), *IP in Biodiversity and Agriculture: Regulating the biosphere* (London: Sweet & Maxwell, 2001), pp. 135–49, at pp. 140–5

Are IPRs inimical to indigenous and local people's rights?

Defenders of strong patent systems are likely to argue that companies holding patents derived from knowledge acquired from local communities cannot prevent members of these communities from continuing to use their knowledge, and moreover such companies have

[22] See at 1.4.2.

never attempted to do so. For example, just because a United States company holds a patent for, say, a stable storage form of neem pesticide, this does not prevent Indian farmers from continuing to use neem as a pesticide as they have done for generations. Defenders may also assert that as long as the patent requirements of usefulness, novelty and inventive step are strictly upheld by patent offices there is no reason for local communities to feel exploited since if their knowledge were simply copied there would be no invention to patent. Both of these arguments are essentially correct, although the turmeric patent case referred to below shows how the theory and practice of patenting may sometimes differ.

A recent study by two political philosophers, Anthony Stenson and Tim Gray, took the controversial position that moral entitlement theories do not justify indigenous peoples' IPRs over their knowledge. The problem with their analysis is that they based it on a simplistic conception of traditional knowledge, assuming that it is *by definition* collectively held and generated *and* part of the public domain. This makes their argument appear more plausible than it should. To argue that *traditional* knowledge when defined this way should enjoy a privileged legal status *vis-á-vis* other public domain knowledge originating from *non-traditional* sources such as public or private sector research programmes does indeed prima facie seem problematic from a moral entitlement-based perspective.

However, what should not be overlooked is the question of *how* traditional knowledge usually falls into the public domain. Indigenous peoples have for centuries endured abuses of their basic human rights, and they still tend to be politically, economically and socially marginalised. It would therefore be naïve to suppose that it has ever been normal practice for their knowledge to be placed in the public domain and disseminated, with their prior informed consent *and* with respect for their customary laws and regulations concerning access, use and distribution of knowledge. It can plausibly be argued, then, that unconsented placement of knowledge into the public domain does not in itself extinguish the legitimate entitlements of the holders and may in fact violate them.

Secondly, while Stenson and Gray's argument is relevant to cases of widely-distributed and long-documented traditional knowledge such as that which is related to neem, a great deal of knowledge is more localised in its distribution and may be held only by small numbers of people or even an individual (see below).

Thirdly, it is unreasonable to suggest that indigenous peoples have no reason to complain as long as their knowledge is not directly copied in a patented invention. The outrage felt by many indigenous peoples in South America about the US plant patent on a sacred plant, aya-huasca, is legitimate, and makes clear that resorting to the arguments of Western thinkers who justify IPRs, like Hegel and Locke, is not always fruitful or even relevant.

Nevertheless, Stenson and Gray usefully demonstrate that advocates of indigenous peoples and local communities' rights need to be consistent in their argumentation. For example, let us assume that the traditional knowledge about neem had been forgotten by most Indians so that only a few farmers still held the knowledge. Would the use of their knowledge by a company as a lead for a patented invention make these people victims of intellectual piracy? If the farmers were identifiable one could possibly build a strong case that the company's act was economically exploitative by using some of the arguments provided earlier. But—unlike the turmeric case—it is more difficult to argue that it is intellectual piracy. This is because to be consistent one would also have to argue that a temporary monopoly right to an incremental improvement (which is what a patent essentially is) is inherently exploitative of *all* people past and present that had contributed to the state of the art (or more accurately all the states of the arts) relevant to the patent. Such a position is difficult to sustain and is highly inappropriate in this case. The state of the art includes not only the knowledge that neem seed extracts are an effective pesticide, but also the industrial techniques that can be applied to produce neem derivatives that are in one way or another more useful than the natural product.

Following a more critical perspective, it is tempting to draw an analogy between the taking of indigenous peoples' knowledge without permission and patenting inventions based upon this knowledge, and seizing their territories and displacing them from their homelands. In each case, it seems that territories, ecosystems, plant varieties (whether domesticated or not) and traditional knowledge, are treated as if they are *res nullius* (the property of nobody) before their 'discovery' by explorers, scientists, governments, corporations, and conservation organisations. During the Colonial period, sparsely populated 'wildernesses' were regarded as being to all legal intents and purposes vacant prior to colonisation. Settler societies, such as in Australia, built up legal systems based upon the *terra nullius* (the land of nobody) doctrine. According to such a view, open access is the rule for land, traditional knowledge and resources, whereas enclosure is the rule as soon as these are proved to have economic value.

The analogy is powerful and persuasive even if it is conceded that whereas lands and territories are finite, new knowledge is constantly being generated and is, at least in theory, inexhaustible. Nevertheless, the analogy does seem to reflect indigenous peoples' views— based as they are upon bitter historical experience—more accurately than the rights for holders of useful knowledge. Also, it accurately reflects the sentiments of indigenous peoples who see Western law as an imposition which seems to cancel out their own custom based regulations. After all, if indigenous peoples in WTO members states are required to accept the existence of patents that they are economically prevented from availing themselves of, why shouldn't their own knowledge-related regimes be respected by others? *It is perhaps this point, that one type of IPR system is being universalised and prioritised to the exclusion of all others, that causes the most legitimate disquiet among those peoples and communities that are least able to benefit from what to them is an imposed system.*

Comparing so-called 'biopiracy' cases such as the recently-revoked turmeric patent (US Patent No. 5,401,504: 'Use of Turmeric in Wound Healing'), the neem patents (of which over 150 exist in the world) and the (lapsed) quinoa patent exemplify some of the various ways that inventions may be derived from traditional knowledge and how the just entitlements of traditional knowledge holders may vary as a result. In the turmeric case, the 'invention' *was* the traditional use of the plant, and it is because this traditional use had been documented that the invention was ultimately deemed to lack novelty. At least some (and possibly most) of the neem-related inventions embody uses identical to those of Indian farmers but the products and/or methods of extraction are different. In such cases it can safely be assumed that the existence of relevant traditional knowledge was *a* (but not *the*) *sine qua non* for the inventions. In the case of the quinoa patent (US Patent No. 5304718: 'Cytoplasmic Male Sterile Quinoa'), traditional knowledge was not a *sine qua non* for the invention except in the sense that the development and continued existence of quinoa varieties can be attributed to the efforts of past and present Andean peoples. The main problem with this patent is that it seems to appropriate part of the public domain by dint of the excessive breadth of what it claims rather than that it 'pirates' traditional knowledge. Even so, it is understandable that local communities should object when patent claims include names of their own folk varieties (as did the quinoa patent) especially when these communities depend on exporting these varieties to countries where such a patent is held. A strong case can still be made for compensating the Andean farmers when their knowledge and resources are used in such patent applications, but patent law is unlikely to be the best possible mechanism for benefit sharing given that most patented inventions are not commercially viable while many natural products may not even be IPR-protected.

Even if it is still debatable whether strong patent systems modelled on those of Europe or the United States are *inherently* harmful to the indigenous peoples and local communities, arguments that such systems *reinforce* existing injustices are convincing. The question to be asked, then, is whether perverse characteristics of the system are integral to IPRs or whether they could be mitigated by rigorous patent examinations or by careful drafting or interpretation of IPR laws.

...

Can IPRs protect traditional biodiversity-related knowledge?

IPR law does not enable all creative or inventive expressions to be protected by IPRs. With respect to patents, only inventions that can be dated and attributed to an individual or small group of people can be protected. In traditional societies, the sources of traditional knowledge may be attributable to individuals, kinship or gender-based groups, or to single communities. In theory such knowledge may be patentable. However, a great deal of traditional knowledge is not traceable to a specific community or geographical area and is ineligible for patent protection. Whether widely known or not, once traditional knowledge is recorded and publicly disseminated, it use and application is beyond the control of the original knowledge providers. As we saw earlier, if a researcher investigates a piece of published traditional knowledge and then improves upon it in a practical way, the result may well become a patentable 'invention' that this researcher can own.

Patents are essentially blunt instruments that cannot be expected to accommodate the subtleties and complexities of many non-western proprietary systems. These systems are sometimes assumed to be collective or communally-based, but in fact any assumption that there exists a generic form of non-western, traditional collective intellectual rights ignores the intricacies and sheer diversity of indigenous and traditional proprietary systems. Implicit in some criticisms of patents is an assumption that collective and individual *ownership* and *property rights*, including intellectual property rights, are necessarily alien concepts in all traditional societies which are characterised by a strong sharing ethos. In fact, reviews of anthropological literature reveal that such concepts (or at least close equivalents to them) are quite common. Any laws that aim to protect property rights, including IPRs, should not therefore be dismissed out of hand. Even so, the strong tendency among many traditional communities is to exchange seeds freely rather than to treat them as commodities to be bought and sold.

At the practical level, critics of patents are certainly correct in asserting that the lack of economic self-sufficiency of many traditional communities, the unequal power relations between them and the corporate world, and the high cost of litigation, would make it very difficult for them to protect their IPRs through the patent system. In the United States, for example, it costs about $20,000 to prepare a patent application. This is clearly beyond the financial means of local communities (as well as many independent inventors and small companies) in most parts of the world, especially when we take into account the fact that most patents do not result in the development of a profitable product anyway. How could this situation be justified? First, one could argue that the high expenses of acquiring and enforcing patents do not make the system inherently unfair just because patent examinations and legal challenges are unavoidably expensive. Secondly, it might be asserted that the patent system cannot be blamed because many potential users either lack sufficient financial resources or are unwilling to take the risks of applying for patents in exchange for future gains that may never materialise. Besides, many countries have low-cost petty patent systems that are more accessible to less wealthy rights claimants, and TRIPS does not prohibit these systems. For these reasons, a case could be made for arguing that it is not the fault of the patent system *per se* that the main beneficiaries from the trade in products derived from genetic resources appear to be corporations located mainly in the technologically advanced countries. In the absence of a patent system, corporations would most probably still dominate this trade.

When considering later the rules relating to patentable subject matter, novelty, inventive step, and ownership, bear in mind the points canvassed by Dutfield and ask to what extent are these rules predicated on particular conceptions of invention and progress? Further, should patent law accommodate different understandings of invention and progress and is it possible for it to do so? If not, do we need to question the TRIPS approach of making minimum standards of patent protection universal? Finally, to what extent should the patent system be affordable and accessible to all and how can this be achieved?

FURTHER READING

W. M. Landes and R. A. Posner, 'The economics of patent law' in *The Economic Structure of Intellectual Property Law* (Cambridge, MA: Harvard, 2003), pp. 294–333.

E. Kitch, 'The nature and function of the patent system' (1977) 20 Journal of Law and Economics 265.

Sir Arnold Plant, 'The economic theory concerning patents for inventions' in *Selected Economic Essays and Addresses* (London: Routledge, 1974), pp. 35–56.

9.4 SOURCES OF LAW

9.4.1 INTERNATIONAL

A collection of international conventions and treaties exists to regulate patent law and thus it is important to understand the extent of the obligations imposed by these instruments. The main conventions are considered below.

9.4.1.1 Paris Convention for the Protection of Industrial Property 1883 ('Paris Convention')

The Paris Convention, signed in 1883 and revised on several occasions,[23] was the first international convention covering industrial property, i.e. patents, utility models, industrial designs, trademarks, service marks, trade names, indications of source or appellations of origin, and unfair competition.[24] The Convention is administered by the World Intellectual Property Organization ('WIPO') and, as at 26 January 2009, 173 countries were party to it.[25] The UK has been a party since 7 July 1884.

A fundamental principle of the Paris Convention is that of national treatment.[26] This means that a Paris Union country cannot discriminate between its nationals and the nationals of other Paris Union countries when it comes to protection of industrial property. In other words, Paris Union countries are obliged to grant nationals of other Paris Union countries the same protection, in respect of industrial property, as they grant to their own nationals. Paris Union countries can, however, subject nationals of other Union countries to the same conditions and formalities that they impose on their own nationals, except for requirements as to domicile or establishment in the country in which protection is claimed.

---

[23] In 1900 (Brussels); 1911 (Washington); 1925 (The Hague); 1934 (London); 1958 (Lisbon); and 1967 (Stockholm) and amended in 1979 (Paris Union).

[24] Paris Convention, Art. 1(2).   [25] See <http://www.wipo.int/> for details.

[26] Paris Convention, Art. 2.

An important related principle is that of independence of patents. This means that patents applied for in various Paris Union countries by nationals of the Union countries shall be independent of patents obtained for the same invention in other countries, whether members of the Union or not.[27]

Another key principle in the Paris Convention is that of priority, which is relevant to the patent application process. Where a person has duly filed an application for a patent in one of the countries of the Union, that person, or his successor in title, shall enjoy, for the purpose of filing in the other Union countries, a 12-month period of priority, calculated from the date of filing of the first application.[28] The benefit of claiming priority is that the substantive requirements of patentability, such as novelty and inventive step, will be measured against the prior art as it stood at the date of the earlier application. To claim priority based on a previous filing, a person must make a declaration indicating the date of such filing and the country in which it was made and these particulars must be mentioned in the patent specification.[29] Where priority is claimed under the Paris Convention, the duration of the patent obtained will be the same as if that patent had been applied for or granted without the benefit of priority.[30]

The Paris Convention contains very few obligations concerning the substantive law of patents. The major one is that relating to compulsory licences. Article 5A(2) states that each Union country shall have the right to provide for the grant of compulsory licences in their legislation, where this is to prevent abuses which might result from exercise of the exclusive rights conferred by the patent, such as failure to work. Article 5A(4) stipulates that an application for a compulsory licence on the basis of failure to work or insufficient working may not be made until the end of four years from the date of filing of the patent application or three years from the date of the grant of the patent, whichever is later. The compulsory licence shall be refused if the patentee justifies his inaction by legitimate reasons and the form of the compulsory licence must be non-exclusive and non-transferable. Forfeiture of the patent shall only be provided for where the grant of a compulsory licence would not have been sufficient to prevent the said abuses. Proceedings for the forfeiture or revocation of a patent may not occur until expiration of two years from the grant of the first compulsory licence.[31]

There are two other obligations worthy of note: first, the right of the inventor to be mentioned in the patent;[32] second, that a patent shall not be refused or invalidated on the basis that the sale of the patented product or of a product obtained by means of a patented process is subject to restrictions or limitations resulting from the domestic law.[33]

9.4.1.2 Patent Cooperation Treaty ('PCT')

The PCT, signed at Washington on 19 June 1970 and amended on subsequent occasions,[34] creates a mechanism for making an international patent application. Importantly, it does not establish an international patent, but rather allows for the filing of an international patent application, which in turn enables protection for an invention to be simultaneously sought in any of the Contracting States to the PCT. Under the PCT, an applicant can make an international application and obtain an international search and an international preliminary examination (the international phase), before the patent is forwarded to the patent offices of

[27] Ibid., Art. 4*bis*(1).   [28] Ibid., Arts. 4A(1) and 4C(1)–(2).   [29] Ibid., Art. 4D(2).
[30] Ibid., Art. 4*bis*(5).   [31] Ibid., Art. 5A(3).   [32] Ibid., Art. 4*ter.*
[33] Ibid., Art. 4*quater.*   [34] Amended on 28 Sept. 1979, and modified on 3 Feb. 1984 and 3 Oct. 2001.

the designated Contracting States (the national phase). Like the Paris Convention, the PCT is administered by WIPO and as at 26 January 2009 there were 139 Contracting States to the PCT.[35] The UK has been bound by the PCT since 24 January 1978.

Any person who is a resident or national of a Contracting State may file an international application,[36] which must contain the following: a request; a description; one or more claims; one or more drawings (where required); and an abstract.[37] The request must designate the Contracting State or States in which protection for the invention is desired on the basis of the international application. Where the applicant is claiming priority under the Paris Convention, the international application must contain a declaration to this effect.[38] The application is filed at the prescribed Receiving Office,[39] which is either a national Office of one of the Contracting States or the International Bureau of WIPO.[40] Provided the prescribed formal requirements have been satisfied, the Receiving Office designates the date of receipt of the international application as the international filing date.[41] The international application shall then have the effect of a regular national application in each designated state as of the international filing date and the international filing date will be considered to be the actual filing date in each designated state.[42] The international application will also be equivalent to a regular national filing within the meaning of the Paris Convention.[43] Thus, it will be possible to claim Paris Convention priority on the basis of a PCT international application.

The next step is the international search conducted by the International Searching Authority,[44] which may be either a national Office or an intergovernmental organization.[45] Presently, there are twelve International Searching Authorities: the Patent Offices of the European Patent Organization, USA, Japan, Sweden, Republic of Korea, Australia, China, Canada, Austria, Spain, Russian Federation, and Finland. The purpose of the International Search is to discover relevant prior art.[46] Once the international search report is produced it must be transmitted to the applicant and the International Bureau of WIPO.[47] It must also, along with the international application, be communicated to each designated Office.[48] After 18 months from the priority date of the international application, the International Bureau of WIPO shall publish the application and the international search report.[49]

Unless the applicant requests an International preliminary examination (which is not obligatory), the international application moves to its national phase. This must occur not later than 30 months from the priority date and occurs by the applicant furnishing a copy of the international application and a translation thereof and paying the national fee (if any) to each designated Office.[50] If the applicant fails to do this, then the effect of the international application shall cease in the designated state with the same consequences as the withdrawal of any national application in that state.[51] The designated Office shall not process or examine the international application prior to the expiration of 30 months from the priority date. However, any designated Office may, on the express request of the applicant, process or examine the international application at any time.[52]

For applicants from countries which have adopted Chapter II of the PCT, it is possible to demand an international preliminary examination. By this demand, which is made separately from the international application, the applicant elects the Contracting State or

35 See <http://www.wipo.int/> for details.　　36 PCT, Art. 9(1).　　37 Ibid., Art. 3(2).
38 Ibid., Art. 8(1).　　39 Ibid., Art. 10.　　40 Ibid., Art. 2.　　41 Ibid., Art. 11(1).
42 Ibid., Art. 11(3).　　43 Ibid., Art. 11(4).　　44 Ibid., Art. 15.　　45 Ibid., Art. 16(1).
46 Ibid., Art. 15(2).　　47 Ibid., Art. 18(2).　　48 Ibid., Art. 20(1)(a).
49 Ibid., Art. 21(1)–(2)(a).　　50 Ibid., Art. 22.
51 Ibid., Art. 24(1)(iii).　　52 Ibid., Art. 23.

States for which the results of the examination will be used.[53] International preliminary examination is carried out by an International Preliminary Examining Authority[54] and, at present, there are 12 such authorities (the same Patent Offices listed above that are also International Searching Authorities). The purpose of the international preliminary examination is to 'formulate a preliminary and non-binding opinion on the questions whether the claimed invention appears to be novel, to involve an inventive step (to be non-obvious), and to be industrially applicable'.[55] An international preliminary examination report is produced and transmitted to the applicant and the International Bureau of WIPO.[56] The International Bureau in turn communicates the report to each elected Office. Provided the election of any Contracting State has been effected within 19 months after the priority date, the national Office of that state shall not proceed to the examination and other processing of the international application prior to the expiration of 30 months from the priority date.[57] In other words, for an applicant to take advantage of both the 30-month time delay before the application enters its national phase and the facility for international preliminary examination, the latter must be instigated within 19 months of the priority date.

There are three main advantages to filing an international application according to the PCT. First, applications in numerous countries may be initiated by a single mechanism. Second, the applicant has 30 months from the priority date in which to decide whether to move to the national phase. This extra time is useful in deciding whether it is worthwhile to obtain a patent in that country and also in delaying the costs associated with pursuing a national patent application (e.g. official fees and translation costs). Third, the international preliminary examination may provide a useful resource for countries that lack an examination system.

According to WIPO the PCT has been a great success. The number of international applications that are filed annually has grown significantly—from 19,809 in 1990 to 158,400 in 2007. The largest number of PCT applications in 2007 came from the USA, followed by Japan, Germany, France, and the UK.[58]

9.4.1.3 Patent Law Treaty ('PLT')

The PLT was adopted at Geneva on 1 June 2000 and came into force on 28 April 2005. It currently has 14 contracting parties, including the UK. The UK ratified the PLT on 22 December 2005 and it entered into force on 22 March 2006. The PLT is administered by WIPO and aims to harmonize and streamline formal procedures in respect of national and regional patent applications and patents. It does not seek to regulate substantive patent law.[59] For the most part, the PLT stipulates maximum requirements, which means that a Contracting State may provide more favourable requirements for applicants and owners. These requirements concern, *inter alia*, the use of PCT Request Forms and establishment of Model Forms; exceptions from mandatory representation before the relevant patent office; relief in respect of procedural time limits and restrictions on revocation or invalidation of a patent for formal defects; and the implementation of electronic filing. An important minimum requirement relates to the filing date. Article 5 stipulates that a Contracting State shall accord a filing date on receipt of three key elements: an indication that the elements received by the

---

[53] Ibid., Art. 31(3)–(4)(a).   [54] Ibid., Art. 32.   [55] Ibid., Art. 33(1).
[56] Ibid., Art. 36(1).   [57] Ibid., Art. 40.
[58] See WIPO, *World Patent Report: A statistical review 2008*, available from <http://www.wipo.int/>.
[59] Art. 2(2) PLT.

Office are intended to be an application; indications that would allow the Office to identify or contact the applicant; and a part which appears to be a description of the invention.

9.4.1.4 Substantive Patent Law Treaty ('SPLT')

In November 2000, the WIPO Standing Committee on the Law of Patents initiated discussions on the harmonization of the substantive law of patents. At the fifth session of the Standing Committee, in May 2001, a first draft of the SPLT was considered. Revised drafts have been discussed at subsequent sessions of the WIPO Standing Committee on the Law of Patents, most recently at the 12th Session in June 2008. Agreement in principle has been reached on several issues, including the scope of the SPLT (e.g. it does not deal with infringement); and the requirements of novelty, inventive step, industrial applicability/utility, and of sufficient disclosure of the invention. However, discussions remain live on matters such as patentable subject matter, exceptions to patentability, the first-to-file versus first-to-invent rule, the exact scope of the prior art, and the introduction of a grace period.[60] Responsibility for progressing matters on the issue of sufficiency of disclosure and a Contracting State's freedom to take action in relation to protecting genetic resources has shifted to the Intergovernmental Committee on Intellectual Property and Genetic Resources. The issues of prior art, grace period, novelty, and inventive step will continue to be pursued by the Standing Committee on the Law of Patents.[61]

9.4.1.5 Agreement on Trade Related Aspects of Intellectual Property Rights 1994 ('TRIPS')

The TRIPS Agreement forms part of the Agreement establishing the World Trade Organization (WTO) and thus binds all WTO members, including the UK and EC who have been WTO members since 1 January 1995.

TRIPS incorporates, *inter alia*, the key provisions of the Paris Convention,[62] but also goes much further in laying down minimum standards with respect to substantive patent law.[63] Article 27(1) stipulates that patents shall be available for inventions, whether products or processes, in all fields of technology, which are new, involve an inventive step, and are capable of industrial application; further, that 'patents shall be available and patent rights enjoyable without discrimination as to the place of invention, the field of technology and whether products are imported or locally produced'. However, TRIPS members may exclude three types of inventions from patentability: first, inventions whose commercial exploitation would be contrary to *ordre public* or morality;[64] second, diagnostic, therapeutic, and surgical methods for the treatment of humans or animals;[65] finally, plants and animals other than micro-organisms, and essentially biological processes for the production of plants or animals other than non-biological and microbiological processes.[66] Article 27(3)(b) stipulates that this last exclusion be reviewed four years after the date of entry into force of the WTO Agreement. The Ministerial Declaration of the Fourth Ministerial Conference, held at Doha on 9–14 November 2001, instructed the TRIPS Council to consider, whilst reviewing

---

[60] See the documents relating to the Standing Committee at: <http://www.wipo.int/meetings/en/topic.jsp?group_id=61>.

[61] Which met again for its 13th session on 23–7 Mar. 2009.

[62] Art. 2(1) TRIPS.

[63] These minimum standards are set out in s. 5, Art. 27–34 TRIPS.

[64] TRIPS, Art. 27(2).

[65] Ibid., Art. 27(3)(a).

[66] Ibid., Art. 27(3))(b).

Article 27(3)(b), the relationship between the TRIPS Agreement and the Convention on Biological Diversity. This work is ongoing.[67]

Article 29(1) provides that members shall require a patent application to disclose the invention in a manner sufficiently clear and complete for it to be carried out by a person skilled in the art. The exclusive rights conferred by a patent are set out in Article 28. For patented products, this is the right to prevent a person making, using, offering for sale, selling, or importing the product without the owner's consent. For patented processes, this is the right to prevent a person using the process and from using, offering for sale, selling, or importing the product directly obtained by that process. The minimum duration of protection is 20 years from the filing date.[68]

Member states may provide for exceptions, however, these must be limited, and not unreasonably conflict with a normal exploitation of the patent and must not unreasonably prejudice the legitimate interests of third parties.[69] Article 31 permits TRIPS members to provide for compulsory licences. Such use may only be permitted where the proposed user has 'made efforts to obtain authorisation from the right holder on reasonable commercial terms and conditions and that such have not been successful within a reasonable period of time'. This requirement may be waived in situations of national emergency, extreme urgency, or in cases of public non-commercial use. The grant of a compulsory licence is subject to several other conditions, including that the use shall be non-exclusive and non-assignable and predominantly for the supply of the domestic market of the member authorizing such use and that the right holder is paid adequate remuneration.

The scope of Article 31, and whether it may be invoked to avoid public health crises, such as the HIV/AIDS virus, has been the focus of controversy in recent years. In particular, for WTO members with limited or no capacity to manufacture pharmaceuticals, difficulties may arise in seeking to rely on the compulsory licence provision in Article 31. A WTO member who is not able to produce a pharmaceutical will seek to import it from a foreign manufacturer according to the compulsory licence. However, the foreign manufacturer may fall foul of its domestic patent law if a patent for that pharmaceutical is also owned there. This means that a WTO member with insufficient manufacturing ability would be forced to licence foreign manufacturers in countries where patent protection is unavailable and these may be very few indeed.[70]

At the Fourth Ministerial Conference held at Doha on 9–14 November 2001, a Declaration on the TRIPS Agreement and Public Health was adopted (the 'Doha Declaration').[71] This dealt, *inter alia*, with the right to grant compulsory licences pursuant to Article 31. The Doha Declaration, para. 6, instructed the TRIPS Council to find an expeditious solution to the above problem by the end of 2002. A solution was not found, however, until 30 August 2003 when the TRIPS General Council finally issued a decision.[72] The decision created a 'waiver', which facilitates WTO members, in reliance on a compulsory licence, exporting pharmaceutical products to other members with no manufacturing capacity in the pharmaceutical sector.[73] A subsequent decision of 6 December 2005 agreed to amend the TRIPS Agreement

[67] See <http://www.wto.org/english/tratop_e/trips_e/art27_3b_e.htm> for details.

[68] TRIPS, Art. 33.   [69] Ibid., Art. 30.

[70] P. Rott, 'The Doha Declaration: Good news for public health' [2003] IPQ 284, 293.

[71] This may be found at: <http://www.wto.org/english/thewto_e/minist_e/min01_e/mindecl_trips_e.htm>.

[72] For the decision see <http://www.wto.org/english/tratop_e/trips_e/implem_para6_e.htm>.

[73] C. Tuosto, 'The TRIPs Council decision of August 30, 2003 on the import of pharmaceuticals under compulsory licences' [2004] EIPR 542.

along the lines of the 2003 'waiver'. This will become a permanent amendment to the TRIPS Agreement once two-thirds of the WTO's members have ratified the change. They have until 31 December 2009 to do so.[74]

FURTHER READING

M. Blakeney, *Trade Related Aspects of Intellectual Property Rights: A concise guide to the TRIPs Agreement* (London: Sweet & Maxwell, 1996).

D. Gervais, *TRIPS Agreement* (3rd edn., London: Sweet & Maxwell, 2008).

P. Rott, 'The Doha Declaration: Good news for public health' [2003] IPQ 284.

C. Tuosto, 'The TRIPs Council decision of August 30, 2003 on the import of pharmaceuticals under compulsory licences' [2004] EIPR 542.

9.4.1.6 Convention on Biological Diversity ('CBD')

The CBD was signed at Rio de Janeiro on 5 June 1992. According to Article 1, its aims are 'the conservation of biological diversity, the sustainable use of its components and the fair and equitable sharing of the benefits arising out of the utilisation of genetic resources, including by access to genetic resources and by appropriate transfer of relevant technologies ... and by appropriate funding.'

Article 15 of the CBD affirms that states have sovereign rights over their natural resources and the authority to determine access to genetic resources. Nonetheless, each Contracting State 'shall endeavour to create conditions to facilitate access to genetic resources for environmentally sound uses by other Contracting Parties'.[75] Access shall be on mutually agreed terms and subject to the prior informed consent of the Contracting State providing such resources.[76] Further, 'each Contracting State shall take legislative, administrative or policy measures, as appropriate ... with the aim of sharing in a fair and equitable way the results of research and development and the benefits arising from the commercial and other utilisation of genetic resources with the Contracting State providing such resources.'[77]

Contracting Parties undertake to provide and/or facilitate access for and transfer to other Contracting Parties of technologies, including biotechnology, that are relevant to the conservation and sustainable use of biological diversity.[78] Access and transfer of technology shall be provided and/or facilitated under fair and most favourable terms. Where the technology is protected by patents or another intellectual property right, 'such access and transfer shall be provided on terms which recognise and are consistent with the adequate and effective protection of intellectual property rights.'[79] Article 19(2) stipulates that Contracting parties, 'shall take all practicable measures to promote and advance priority access on a fair and equitable basis by Contracting Parties, especially developing counties, to the results and benefits arising from biotechnologies based upon genetic resources provided by those Contracting Parties. Such access shall be on mutually agreed terms.'

The role of traditional knowledge in conservation of biological diversity is also covered by the CBD. The preamble recognizes the 'close and traditional dependence of

---

[74] Amendment of the TRIPS Agreement—Extension of the Period for the Acceptance by Members of the Protocol Amending the TRIPS Agreement, Decision of 18 Dec. 2007 WT/L/711—see <http://www.wto.org/english/tratop_e/trips_e/pharmpatent_e.htm>.

[75] CBD, Art. 15(2).   [76] Ibid., Art. 15(4)–(5).   [77] Ibid., Art. 15(7).

[78] Ibid., Art. 16(1).   [79] Ibid., Art. 16(2).

many indigenous and local communities embodying traditional lifestyles on biological resources, and the desirability of sharing equitably benefits arising from the use of traditional knowledge, innovations and practices relevant to the conservation of biological diversity and the sustainable use of its components.' Further, Article 8(j) states that Contracting Parties shall, as far as possible and as appropriate respect, preserve, and maintain traditional knowledge.

Professor Michael Blakeney has commented that, 'Reflecting the uncomfortable political deal which was struck in bringing the CBD to conclusion, the language of the Convention is unfortunately vague.'[80] Meanwhile, Peter Drahos has characterized the relationship between the CBD and TRIPS as an opposition of principles, namely, the principle of sustainable development and the principle of economic growth. The TRIPS Agreement does not mention conservation of biodiversity, while the CBD obliges members to ensure that intellectual property rights do not undermine the objectives of the Convention.[81] The relationship between the CBD and TRIPS is a continuing source of tension and thus has been placed on the TRIPS review agenda, in the context of reviewing Article 27(3)(b), which deals with patentability of plant and animal inventions and plant varieties.[82]

FURTHER READING

M. Blakeney, 'Intellectual property aspects of traditional agricultural knowledge' in P. Drahos and M. Blakeney (eds.), *IP in Biodiversity and Agriculture: Regulating the biosphere* (London: Sweet & Maxwell, 2001), pp. 31–52.

P. Drahos, 'The TRIPS Reviews and the CBD' in P. Drahos and M. Blakeney (eds.), *IP in Biodiversity and Agriculture: Regulating the biosphere* (London: Sweet & Maxwell, 2001), pp. 57–67.

N. S. Gopalakrishnan, 'TRIPS and protection of traditional knowledge of genetic resources: New challenges to the patents system' [2005] EIPR 11.

9.4.2 REGIONAL

A collection of conventions and EC instruments exists to regulate patent law at the European level and thus it is important to understand the extent of the obligations imposed by them. The main instruments are considered below.

9.4.2.1 European Patent Convention ('EPC')

The European Patent Convention (EPC) was signed in Munich in 1973 and came into operation on 1 June 1978. It is an intergovernmental treaty and *not* an instrument of the European Community. The aim of the EPC was to establish a centralized system of obtaining patents in Contracting States. There are at present 35 Contracting States (of which the UK is one).[83]

---

[80] M. Blakeney, 'Intellectual property aspects of traditional agricultural knowledge' in P. Drahos and M. Blakeney (eds.), *IP in Biodiversity and Agriculture: Regulating the biosphere* (London: Sweet & Maxwell, 2001), pp. 31–52, at p. 40.

[81] P. Drahos, 'The TRIPS Reviews and the CBD' in P. Drahos and M. Blakeney (eds.), *IP in Biodiversity and Agriculture*, 57–67, at pp. 59–60.

[82] See <http://www.wto.org/english/tratop_e/trips_e/art27_3b_e.htm>.

[83] For details see <http://www.epo.org/about-us/epo/member-states.html#contracting>.

The EPC does not provide for the granting of a single pan-European patent but rather offers a mechanism for obtaining a bundle of national patents. The EPC established the European Patent Office (EPO), which is the executive arm of the European Patent Organization, which is an intergovernmental body set up under the EPC and whose members are the EPC Contracting States. Applications for a European patent are made to the Examining Division of the EPO in Munich and must designate the Contracting States in which protection is sought. EPC applications must be in one of three official languages (English, German, or French) and the text of the patent must be in that language. If the application is successful, there is a grant of a European patent for each of the designated Contracting States, which take effect as national patents. It is possible, however, centrally to challenge the grant of a European patent by instigating opposition proceedings in the Opposition Division nine months after grant. The Technical Boards of Appeal hear appeals from the decisions of, *inter alia*, the examining and opposition divisions of the EPO. Important questions of law may be referred to the Enlarged Board of Appeal either by a Board of Appeal or by the President of the EPO.

9.4.2.2 Revised European Patent Convention ('EPC 2000')

A Diplomatic Conference held in Munich in November 2000 produced the Act Revising the Convention on the Grant of European Patents ('EPC 2000'). This was signed at Munich on 29 November 2000 and extensively amends the EPC. The EPC 2000 entered into force on 13 December 2007 (i.e. two years after the 15th Contracting State—which was Greece—deposited its instrument of ratification). Accompanying it are new implementing regulations, which were adopted by the Administrative Council on 7 December 2006.[84]

The underlying aim of the EPC 2000 was to modernize the European patent system, in the light of the various political, legal, and technical changes that have occurred since the signing of the EPC in 1973. Thus, the EPC 2000 aims to make the EPO procedures more effective and efficient and to bring the EPC into line with international developments such as TRIPS and the PLT. The following is a summary of the major changes that have come into effect as a result of the EPC 2000:

1. A Conference of Ministers will be held at least every five years, in order for Contracting States to exercise greater political responsibility over the European Patent Organization.

2. The Administrative Council is now competent to amend the EPC in order to bring it into line with international patent treaties or EC legislation relating to patents.

3. Several amendments aim to simplify and streamline the patent grant procedure before the EPO. For example, it is possible to file patent applications in any language and a translation into one of the official languages of the EPO is not required until a later date. Further, search and examination occur in the same location, whereas previously search and examination were spread over a number of different locations.

4. A central procedure before the EPO for amendment of the patent is available, so that proprietors do not have to go through the national patent offices.

5. The Protocol on the Interpretation of Article 69 of the EPC has been amended to include the doctrine of 'equivalents'.

---

[84] See <http://www.epo.org/patents/law/legal-texts/epc2000/regulations.html>.

6. The content of European applications as filed now form part of the prior art for all EPC Contracting States.

7. There is the legal basis for special agreements between Contracting States to introduce a central court system for the enforcement of European patents.

At the Diplomatic Conference it was resolved that the exclusion from patentability of computer programs per se should remain, but that this exclusion, along with the patentability of biotechnological inventions, should be revisited at future Diplomatic Conferences.

9.4.2.3 Community Patent Convention ('CPC')

The CPC is an intergovernmental treaty that was signed in Luxembourg in 1975 and which aimed to establish a single Community patent obtainable via one central procedure and binding in all Contracting States. It also sought to rationalize patent administration and thus reduce the costs of patenting. Unlike the EPC, the CPC has never come into force since not all signatories have ratified it. Interest in the CPC is unlikely to be renewed, particularly in the light of attempts by the European Community to establish a single Community-wide patent.

9.4.2.4 Supplementary Protection Certification Regulation ('SPC Regulation')

The European Community's intervention in the field of patent law has been fairly limited, especially when compared with its activity in the fields of copyright and trade marks. One such intervention is Council Regulation (EEC) 1768/92 of 18 June 1992, which created the Supplementary Protection Certificate ('SPC') for the benefit of medicinal products for which regulatory approval has been obtained. The purpose behind the SPC is to provide adequate protection to patented medicinal products, whose marketing has been delayed by the need to obtain regulatory approval, in order to encourage pharmaceutical research.[85] This is achieved by granting an SPC, for a maximum duration of five years, at the expiry of the 20-year patent term. The protection granted is strictly confined to the medicinal product for which regulatory approval was obtained.

9.4.2.5 Directive on the legal protection of biotechnological inventions ('Biotechnology Directive')

A second, and rather controversial, intervention by the European Community is reflected in the Biotechnology Directive, which sought to harmonize the patent law protection of biotechnological inventions 'in order to maintain and encourage investment in the field of biotechnology'.[86] The path to adoption of the Biotechnology Directive was beset with difficulties. It was first proposed by the European Commission in 1988, but was vetoed by the European Parliament in 1995, due to the intense opposition from the Green Party, animal welfare activists, and environmentalists. The central objection to the proposed directive was that it failed adequately to address the ethical concerns of patenting biotechnological inventions.[87] The European Commission introduced a revised version of the Biotechnology

---

[85] Recital 3, SPC Regulation.   [86] Recital 3, Biotechnology Directive.
[87] See D. Curley and A. Sharples, 'Patenting biotechnology in Europe: The ethical debate moves on' [2002] 24 EIPR 565.

Directive in 1995. After further debate and numerous amendments, the European Council of Ministers eventually adopted the directive in June 1998 and its deadline for implementation was 30 July 2000. The controversy, however, did not end there. Shortly after the adoption of the Biotechnology Directive, the Netherlands government brought an action for annulment of the directive before the European Court of Justice. The grounds of the challenge were varied, but mainly procedural in nature.[88] The Opinion of Advocate General Jacobs rejected the arguments for annulment and in October 2001, the ECJ affirmed the Advocate General's Opinion.[89] As at June 2005, the Biotechnology Directive had been implemented in 21 Member States.

The directive is divided into four chapters. Chapter I harmonizes the rules relating to patentability of biotechnological inventions. For example, Article 3 iterates that inventions concerning biological material are patentable if they are new, involve an inventive step, and are capable of industrial application. However, plant and animal varieties, and essentially biological processes for the production of plants or animals are not patentable.[90] Simple discoveries of the elements of the human body, including the sequence or partial sequence of a gene cannot constitute a patentable invention.[91] However, Article 5(2) stipulates that 'an element isolated from the human body or otherwise produced by means of a technical process, including the sequence or partial sequence of a gene, may constitute a patentable invention, even if the structure of that element is identical to that of a natural element'. Where the commercial exploitation of an invention would be contrary to *ordre public* or morality, such inventions shall be considered unpatentable.[92] These rules will be discussed in more detail later in this chapter.

Chapter II of the Biotechnology Directive deals with the scope of protection conferred by patents on certain biotechnological inventions. For example, Article 8 states that 'a patent on a biological material possessing specific characteristics as a result of the invention shall extend to any biological material derived from that biological material through propagation or multiplication in an identical or divergent form and possessing those same characteristics'. However, this protection is exhausted where the biological material is placed on the market in the territory of a Member State by the holder of the patent or with his consent.[93] Further, Article 11 contains derogations from the protection set out in Article 8 and 9.

Chapter III provides for compulsory cross-licensing in respect of patents and plant-variety rights. In circumstances where a breeder cannot acquire or exploit a plant-variety right without infringing a prior patent, he may apply for a compulsory licence for non-exclusive use of the invention protected by a patent. This is subject to payment of an appropriate royalty. Similarly, where the holder of a patent concerning a biotechnological invention cannot exploit it without infringing a prior plant variety right, he may apply for a compulsory licence for non-exclusive use of the plant variety protected by that right, subject to payment of an appropriate royalty. Applicants must show that they have applied unsuccessfully to the holder of the patent or plant-variety right to obtain a contractual licence and, further, that the plant variety or invention constitutes significant technical progress of considerable economic interest compared with the invention claimed in the patent or the protected plant variety.

---

[88] For a discussion of these grounds see A. Scott, 'The Dutch challenge to the bio-patenting directive' [1999] EIPR 212.

[89] See *Netherlands v European Parliament and Council of the European Union* Case C-377/98 [2001] ECR I-7079.

[90] Biotechnology Directive, Art. 4(1). [91] Ibid., Art. 5(1).

[92] Ibid., Art. 6. [93] Ibid., Art. 10.

Chapter IV allows the sufficiency requirement under patent law to be satisfied by the deposit of biological material at a recognized depositary institution. This is applicable where an invention involves the use of or concerns biological material which is not available to the public and which cannot be described in a patent application such that a person skilled in the art can work the invention.[94] Article 13 also stipulates that access to the deposited biological material shall be provided through the supply of a sample.

The Biotechnology Directive also includes obligations on the Commission to report to the European Parliament and Council on various matters, including on the development and implications of patent law in the field of biotechnology and genetic engineering.[95] The first such report was issued in 2002 and the latest in 2005.[96]

FURTHER READING

D. Curley and A. Sharples, 'Patenting biotechnology in Europe: The ethical debate moves on' [2002] 24 EIPR 565.

D. Wood, 'European patents for biotechnological inventions: Past, present and future' (2001) 23 World Patent Information 339P.

In recent years, the European Community has sought to extend its harmonization efforts in the patent-law area to include harmonization of the substantive law of patents generally and also specifically in the field of computer-related inventions. The attempt to harmonize the patentability of computer-related inventions failed after a protracted and controversial legislative process. A proposal for a Community patent was introduced by the European Commission in 2000,[97] but has thus far made little headway.

9.4.3 NATIONAL

9.4.3.1 Patents Act 1977 ('PA 77')

The PA 77 established the UK Patent Office, now known as the UK Intellectual Property Office (UK IPO), its procedure, and the substantive law of patents in the UK. The Patents Rules 2007, SI 2007/3291 are the main piece of secondary legislation made under the PA 77 and they regulate the business and procedure of the UK IPO.

The PA 77 saw the UK's entry into the EPC. As such, it brought about numerous substantive and procedural changes to UK patent law. Section 130(7) of PA 77 states that certain provisions of the Act 'are so framed as to have, as nearly as practicable, the same effects in the United Kingdom as the corresponding provisions of the European Patent Convention'. UK courts must therefore have regard to this legislative intention when interpreting these provisions. The importance of avoiding divergent interpretations between the EPO and UK,

---

94 Ibid., Art. 13(1).   95 Ibid., Art. 16(c).

96 See Report from the Commission to the European Parliament and the Council: Development and implications of patent law in the field of biotechnology and genetic engineering, Brussels 14 July 2005, COM (2005) 312 final, OJ C211 of 30 Aug. 2005.

97 Proposal for a Council Regulation on a Community Patent COM ʼ(2000) 412 final OJ C337E of 28 Nov. 2000.

together with the considerable persuasive authority of decisions of the Boards of Appeal and Enlarged Board of Appeal of the EPO, has been stressed on a number of occasions.[98]

9.4.3.2 Patents Act 2004 ('PA 2004')

The PA 2004 was enacted primarily with a view to implementing the EPC 2000, but also with the aim of generally modernizing the PA 77. The PA 2004 has now come into force[99] and, consequently, the PA 77 has been amended in a variety of ways. Broadly speaking, the changes that it brought about can be divided into four areas: (i) changes necessary to give effect to the EPC 2000; (ii) changes related to or consequential upon EPC 2000 revisions but not required for its implementation; (iii) changes related to enforcement and post-grant issues; and (iv) general modernization of the PA 77. Where relevant, the changes brought about by the PA 2000 will be discussed later in the chapter in relation to specific topics.

9.5 OBTAINING A PATENT

9.5.1 PRELIMINARY QUESTIONS

In deciding whether to apply for a patent, a company or individual will take into account various considerations. These include the relative advantages and disadvantages of patent protection as compared with other forms of protection, such as the law of confidence or contract law, and the strategic or commercial value of owning a patent.

Briefly, there are two key advantages to relying on patent law, as opposed to the law of confidence or contract law, to protect one's invention. First, patent law confers a property right, i.e. a right enforceable *in rem* rather than *in personam*. Thus, a patent owner can exercise her exclusive monopoly right against third parties and is not restricted to enforcing her right against the party/parties to the contract or to the person who is under an obligation to keep the commercial information secret. The second advantage of relying on patent law is that it protects those inventions that do not lend themselves to secrecy. The law of confidence (which relies upon the invention not being in the public domain) is not useful when an invention can be easily discovered from studying a product incorporating the invention that has been released onto the market.

There are, however, certain disadvantages associated with patenting an invention, as opposed to relying on contract or confidentiality. First, there is the bureaucratic process of registering a patent, which is both time consuming and costly. Second, the *quid pro quo* for obtaining a patent is disclosing the invention to the rest of the world. If a person wishes to keep their invention entirely secret from their competitors this disclosure will be

---

[98] See *Gale's Application* [1991] RPC 305, 322–23 per Nicholls LJ, cited with approval in *Re Fujitsu Limited's Application* [1997] RPC 608, 611, per Aldous LJ; *Merrell Dow v Norton* [1996] RPC 76, 82, per Lord Hoffmann; *Biogen v Medeva* [1997] RPC 1, 34, per Lord Hoffmann; *Generics (UK) Ltd v H Lundbeck A/S* [2009] UKHL 12, para. 35, per Lord Walker, para. 46, per Lord Mance, and para. 86, per Lord Neuberger.

[99] The Patents Act 2004 (Commencement No. 1 and Consequential and Transitional Provisions) Order 2004, SI 2004/2177 came into force on 22 Sept. 2004; The Patents Act 2004 (Commencement No. 2 and Consequential, etc. and Transitional Provisions) Order 2004, SI 2004/3205 came into force on 1 Jan. 2005; the Patents Act 2004 (Commencement No. 3 and Transitional Provisions) Order 2005, SI 2005/2471 came into force on 1 Oct. 2005; The Patents Act 2004 (Commencement No. 4 and Transitional Provisions) Order 2007, SI 2007/3396 came into force 13 Dec. 2007.

counter-productive, and it may be preferable to rely on the law of confidence. Finally, patent protection lasts for 20 years whereas protection may be longer under contract (depending on the terms of the contract) or the law of confidence (depending on whether the information is still secret).

The strategic or commercial value of owning a patent will also be a relevant consideration. Aside from the obvious value in having an exclusive monopoly right to make or use the invention, there are other, consequential benefits. For example, obtaining a patent will allow the owner to value that asset more easily from an accounting point of view. Further, a patent operates as a visible public identification of one's intellectual property rights and this may serve as a disincentive to others to produce competing products for fear of possible infringement. Finally, owning a patent may be strategically valuable when it comes to negotiating with other patent owners in the same field to obtain licences to use their patented technology.

Having decided to apply for a patent, rather than rely on contract law or the law of confidence, the applicant will need to ask further questions, such as: in which countries do I want a patent and how much am I prepared to spend on patent protection? The latter question is tied to the first since the more countries in which patent protection is sought, the higher will be the costs of obtaining and maintaining protection. As we will see from the discussion below, there are three possible routes to obtaining patent protection. The first is to apply for a national patent, e.g. apply to the UK IPO for a UK patent or to the US Patent Office for a US Patent. The second is to apply to the EPO for a European Patent, designating the Contracting States in which protection is sought (e.g. UK and Germany). The third is to make a PCT application designating the Contracting States in which protection is sought (e.g. UK, Germany, and the US). As was stressed above at 9.4.1.2, this does not lead to an international or global patent. Rather, it allows for an international patent application, which enables protection for an invention to be simultaneously sought in any of the PCT Contracting States.

9.5.2 REGISTRATION PROCESS

This section will provide a general overview of the registration process and its function. We begin with a brief discussion of the value of a registration system before turning to describe the application process.

What is the value of having a registration system for patents? Several benefits may be pointed out. First, operating a central register allows competitors and other third parties to search for patents that might impact upon their commercial decisions and activities, thus minimizing the risk of inadvertent infringement. Second, it assists third parties in ascertaining the ambit of the patented invention, which in turn may help them to invent around the patent. Finally, the successful applicant can feel reasonably secure of the validity of the patent granted to them, because their application has gone through an examination process. This last point, however, depends on the rigour or quality of the examination process. Further, it is still possible for third parties to challenge the validity of the granted patent, right up until its expiry.

As mentioned above, there are three possible application routes: national, via the EPO, and via the PCT. The following is an overview of the application process via the national and EPO routes. The PCT application process is not discussed here since it was already dealt with above at 9.4.1.2.

9.5.2.1 Filing an application

Any person may make an application;[100] however, the person entitled to the grant of a patent is generally speaking the inventor.[101] An application for a UK patent should be made to the UK IPO and, for a European Patent, to the EPO designating the particular Contracting States in which patent protection is sought.[102] For a European patent application, the application may proceed in any of the official languages, i.e. English, French, or German.[103]

Filing an application is important because it establishes the 'priority date' of the application, i.e. the date at which the validity requirements (of novelty, inventive step, etc.) for a patent will be assessed. The general rule is that the filing date is the priority date *unless* an applicant is claiming 'Convention priority'. Convention priority refers to where the applicant has filed, within the previous 12 months, an earlier application in a Paris Convention country. The result is that the priority date is treated as the date of filing of the earlier application. To claim Convention priority, the applicant must file a declaration of priority at the time of filing the application.[104]

To make a full application, the following elements must be included: a request for the grant of a patent; a specification containing a description of the invention, a claim or claims, and any drawing referred to in the description or any claim; and an abstract.[105]

It is possible, prior to making a full application, to file an early 'informal' application. This occurs where a person files documents indicating that a patent is sought, information identifying the applicant and a description of the invention.[106] The applicant then has 12 months in which to file the remaining documents—i.e. the abstract and claims. The advantage of early filing is that it establishes a priority date and also gives the applicant 12 months in which to decide whether to pursue a patent. Importantly, however, the later documentation must be 'supported' by the earlier application.

9.5.2.2 Preliminary examination and search

The next step is that the applicant should request, within 12 months of the date of filing, a preliminary examination and search.[107] The preliminary examination involves the examiner or, for the EPO, the Receiving Section, determining whether the application has complied with certain formal requirements. These are that: (i) the application contains the relevant documents; (ii) the fees have been paid; (iii) the inventors have been identified; and (iv) for the EPO, the application designates the Contracting States in which patents are sought. The applicant receives a preliminary examination report, which will list any problems and allow an applicant to respond to them.

A limited search is then conducted by the examiner or, at the EPO, the Search Division.[108] The search will identify relevant prior art (i.e. documents published before the priority date that contain similar inventions to the one applied for), which will be used at the substantive examination stage. The applicant receives an Examiner's Report or, from the EPO, a European Search Report.

Finally, at this stage, the application will be examined to ensure that it relates to one invention or to a group of inventions so linked as to form a single inventive concept.[109]

---

[100] PA 77, s. 7(1); Art. 58 EPC.   [101] PA 77, s. 7(2)(a); Art. 60 EPC.
[102] EPC, Art. 79.   [103] Ibid., Art. 14(1).
[104] PA 77, s. 5(2); r. 6(1), Patents Rules; Art. 88(1) EPC.   [105] PA 77, s. 14(2); Art. 78 EPC.
[106] PA 77, s. 15; Art. 80 EPC.   [107] PA 77, s. 17; Art. 90 EPC.
[108] PA 77, s. 17(1)–(2); Art. 92 EPC.   [109] PA 77, s. 14(5)(d) and (6); PA 77, s. 17(6); Art. 82 EPC.

This requirement is important because two patents should not be obtained for the cost of one and also it simplifies the classification and search of patent specifications.[110] Where the application relates to more than one invention, the applicant can divide it into multiple new applications, but still rely on the priority date of the original application.

9.5.2.3 Publication of patent application

The patent application, including any amended claims, is published 18 months from the date of filing or, in the case of the EPO and where Convention priority has been claimed, from the priority date.[111] The examiner's report or European search report is also published, as an annex to the application.

Publication has three significant consequences. First, it prevents the applicant from relying on the law of confidentiality to protect their invention. Second, if the patent is granted, the date of publication is the date from which the patentee is able to claim for damages for any infringement of the patent.[112] For a European patent application, an applicant will need to translate the claims into the languages of the designated Contracting States if they want to obtain protection from the publication date to the date of grant.[113] Finally, following publication of an application it is possible for third parties to submit observations as to whether the invention is patentable.[114] The observations must be filed in writing and include appropriate reasons. The comptroller of the UK IPO must consider the observations whereas the EPO need only communicate those observations to the applicant, who may comment on them. The person submitting observations does not become a party to proceedings.

9.5.2.4 Substantive examination

Within six months from the date of publication of the application, or at the EPO the publication of the Search Report, the applicant must request a substantive examination.[115] The purpose of the substantive examination is for the examiner to consider whether the requirements of the PA 77 or EPC have been satisfied,[116] and in particular, to assess whether the invention does not consist of subject matter excluded from patentability, and is novel, inventive, and capable of industrial application. The examiner also considers whether the claims are clear and concise and supported by the description, and whether the specification discloses the invention in a manner which is clear and complete enough for the invention to be performed by a person skilled in the art.

The examiner issues a report in which any objections are raised. It is then up to the applicant to persuade the examiner that the objections are unfounded or to amend the application so as to comply with the requirements.[117]

If the examiner is satisfied with the application, the patent will be granted.[118] If the objections raised by the examiner have not been resolved, the applicant may have a hearing before the Senior Examiner in the UK or the full Examining Division of the EPO. From there it is possible to appeal to the UK Patents Court or the Technical Board of Appeal of the EPO.[119]

---

[110] Cornish and Llewelyn, *Intellectual Property*, para. 4–15.
[111] PA 77, s. 16; Art. 93 EPC.   [112] PA 77, s. 69; Art. 67 EPC.
[113] Art. 67(3) EPC.   [114] PA 77, s. 21; Art. 115 EPC.   [115] PA 77, s. 18(1); Art. 94 EPC.
[116] PA 77, s. 18(2); Art. 94(1) EPC.   [117] PA 77, s. 18(3); Art. 96 EPC.
[118] PA 77, s. 18(4); Art. 97(2) EPC.   [119] PA 77, s. 97(1); Arts. 106 and 110 EPC.

9.5.2.5 Grant of the patent

The patent will be granted where the UK IPO or EPO is satisfied that all the necessary requirements have been satisfied. If they are not, the application will be refused. A notice that the patent has been granted must be published in the UK IPO Official Journal or the European Patent Bulletin.[120] It is from this date that the patent takes effect and protection lasts for up to 20 years from the date of filing, provided the requisite renewal fees are paid.[121]

Once a European patent is granted and takes effect, it transforms into a bundle of national patents corresponding to the designated Contracting States. For example, a European patent designating the UK, as from the publication of its grant in the European Patent Bulletin, will be treated as a patent under the PA 77, as if it had been granted by the UK IPO.[122] Upon grant, the patent claims must be translated into the other official languages of the EPC.[123] In addition, Contracting States may require the whole specification to be translated into the language of that Contracting State within three months of grant.[124] However, Contracting States that have ratified or acceded to the London Agreement (the UK being one)[125] may waive entirely or partially the requirement for translations of European patents.[126]

9.5.2.6 Revocation

Although the UK IPO and EPO operate a reasonably stringent examination process, it is not comprehensive and therefore cannot be treated as conclusive. Thus, it is possible for the validity of a patent to be challenged following its grant upon the following grounds:[127]

(i)   The invention is not a patentable invention.

(ii) The patent was granted to the wrong person, i.e. the person who was not entitled to the patent.

(iii) The patent specification does not disclose the invention clearly and completely enough for it to be performed by a person skilled in the art.

(iv) The matter disclosed in the specification extends beyond that disclosed in the patent application as filed.

(v)   The protection conferred by the patent has been extended by an amendment which should not have been allowed.

---

[120] PA 77, s. 24(1); Art. 97(4) EPC.   [121] PA 77, s. 25; Art. 63(1) EPC.
[122] PA 77, s. 77(1).   [123] EPC, r. 71(3) and (7).   [124] Art. 65 EPC.
[125] Agreement on the application of Art. 65 of the Convention on the Grant of European Patents, 17 Oct. 2000 (OJ EPO 2001, 549). The UK ratified the London Agreement on 15 Aug. 2005 and it entered into force on 1 May 2008.
[126] A state which has an official language in common with one of the official languages of the EPO shall dispense entirely with the translation requirements, whereas a state which does not have an official language in common with one of the official languages of the EPO shall dispense with the translation requirements if the European patent has been granted in the official language of the EPO prescribed by that State, or translated into that language and supplied under the conditions provided for in Art. 65(1) EPC. These States may, however, require a translation for the claims into one of their official languages.
[127] PA 77, s. 72; Art. 138 EPC.

In the UK, the court or comptroller may revoke a patent on any of the above grounds, on the application of any person.[128] In addition, the comptroller may on his own initiative revoke the patent.[129]

In the EPO, once a European patent is granted it transforms into a bundle of national patents. Thus, it can be revoked according to the provisions set out in the relevant national law. However, it is possible centrally to challenge the validity of a European patent through a process called 'opposition'. Any person, within nine months of the grant of the patent, may give notice to the EPO of opposition to the European patent granted.[130] The grounds of opposition are:

(i) The invention is not a patentable invention.

(ii) The patent specification does not disclose the invention clearly and completely enough for it to be performed by a person skilled in the art.

(iii) The matter disclosed in the specification extends beyond that disclosed in the patent application as filed.[131]

The Opposition Division examines the grounds of opposition and the patent proprietor is given the opportunity to contest the opposition, make observations, and/or make amendments. The Opposition Division will decide whether or not the European patent should be revoked, maintained, or maintained in an amended form.[132]

Opposition proceedings arguably provide a cheaper and more convenient way of initiating a single attack, as compared with instigating revocation proceedings in each of the Contracting States where the patent was granted. However, experience has shown that opposition proceedings can often take many years. The availability of opposition proceedings in the EPO, along with revocation proceedings in a Contracting State, gives rise to the possibility that parallel proceedings may occur. In such circumstances, the national court may stay revocation proceedings until the outcome of the opposition proceedings is determined. The UK Court of Appeal in *Glaxo Group Ltd v Genentech Inc*[133] held that the Patents Court has a wide discretion whether to stay proceedings, having regard to the balance of justice between the parties. Further, it held that no presumption exists that the duplication of proceedings in it and the EPO is, by itself, a ground for stay of proceedings in the Patents Court. Considerations that affect the balance of justice include the additional costs in the duplication of proceedings and the order in which the proceedings were commenced. However, the factor that usually will carry most weight is if commercial certainty will be achieved at a considerably earlier date in one forum rather than the other.[134] As the Court of Appeal explained:[135]

> The length of the stay of proceedings, if granted, is, in general, the most significant factor in the discretion. Both the parties' legitimate interests and the public interest are in dispelling the uncertainty surrounding the validity of the monopoly rights conferred by the grant of a patent and the existence or non-existence of the exclusive proprietary rights on a public register... If the likelihood is that proceedings in the Patents Court would achieve this resolution significantly sooner than the proceedings in the EPO, it would normally be a proper exercise of discretion to decline to stay the Patents Court proceedings.

---

[128] PA 77, s. 72. [129] Ibid., s. 73.
[130] Art. 99 EPC. [131] Art. 100 EPC. [132] Arts. 101–2 EPC.
[133] [2008] FSR 18. [134] Ibid., paras. 79–88.
[135] Ibid., para. 84.

Aside from the possibility of parallel opposition and revocation proceedings, another potential conflict may arise where a person initiates opposition proceedings in the EPO, but before these have been concluded the patent proprietor successfully sues for patent infringement in the UK Patents Court. This is indeed what occurred in *Unilin Beheer BV v Berry Floor*[136] where the patent had been declared valid and infringed by the defendants. The defendants sought a stay of proceedings for an account of profits, on the basis that their opposition proceedings in the EPO were still pending and might eventually succeed. The Court of Appeal held that the defendants were estopped from challenging the claimant's entitlement to an account of profits, whatever the ultimate result in the EPO. This outcome was an inevitable consequence of the EPC permitting opposition nine months after the date of grant of the patent, along with proceedings in the national courts. As Jacob LJ stated: 'No one pretends that the compromise is satisfactory—it was a fudge at the time and remains so. Unless and until sensible judicial arrangements are put in place, the litigation of European patents in various national courts and the EPO will remain a messy, expensive and prolix business.'[137]

9.5.2.7 Amendment

During the application process, it is possible for an applicant to amend their application in order to address objections that have been raised during the preliminary and substantive examination stages.[138] There is also a general power to amend the patent application at any time before a patent is granted.[139]

Once a UK patent is granted, it is possible for the owner to amend the patent, although this is at the discretion of the comptroller or court (whichever is applicable).[140] Under the EPC, amendment of a patent can only occur in opposition proceedings, otherwise it is a matter for national law.[141]

9.5.2.8 Correction of errors

Errors of translation or transcription or clerical mistakes in a patent specification may be corrected, upon request to the comptroller or the EPO.[142] The correction must be obvious in the sense that it is immediately evident that nothing else would have been intended other than what is suggested as the correction.[143]

9.5.3 PATENT SPECIFICATION

A crucial document in the application process, and indeed also in relying upon a granted patent, is the patent specification. In the UK and EPO systems the specification comprises two main parts: the *description* (which may be accompanied by diagrams) and the *claims*. Pages from a sample patent specification are extracted below, in order to give a better sense of this document.

---

[136] [2007] FSR 25.
[137] Ibid., para. 17. Arden LJ and Mummery LJ were in agreement.
[138] PA 77, ss. 15A(6) and 18(3); Art. 123(1) EPC, r. 86.
[139] PA 77, s. 19(1); Art. 123(1) EPC, r. 86.   [140] PA 77, ss. 27(1) and 75.
[141] Arts. 102(3) and 123 EPC, r. 57a.   [142] PA 77, s. 117(1); EPC, r. 88.
[143] Patents Rules, SI 2007/3291, r. 50; EPC, r. 88.

(12) **UK Patent Application** (19) **GB** (11) **2 266 045** (13) **A**

(43) Date of A publication **20.10.1993**

(21) Application No 9207766.8

(22) Date of filing 07.04.1992

(71) Applicant
Mandy Nicola Haberman
Dove Cottage, 44 Watford Road, Radlett,
Hertfordshire, WD7 8LR, United Kingdom

(72) Inventor
Mandy Nicola Haberman

(74) Agent and/or Address for Service
Lloyd Wise, Tregear & Co
Norman House, 105-109 Strand, London, WC2R 0AE,
United Kingdom

(51) INT CL⁵
A47G 19/22

(52) UK CL (Edition L)
A4A ALN
A5X X5E
U1S S1787 S2409

(56) Documents cited
GB 2169210 A   US 5050758 A   US 4946062 A
US 4782975 A   US 4441624 A   US 4245752 A
US 4190174 A   US 4184604 A

(58) Field of search
UK CL (Edition K) **A4A ALC ALN ALQ ALX AN ASA**
ASB ASX, A5X X5E X5X
INT CL⁵ **A47G, A61J**
Online database: **WPI**

(54) **Drinking vessel suitable for use as a trainer cup**

(57) A drinking vessel suitable for use as a trainer cup or cup for the elderly comprises an open-mouthed generally cup-shaped container (2) and a lid (5) for covering the open mouth of the container (2). The lid (5) has an associated mouthpiece (6). Valve means (10) are provided to prevent flow of liquid from the interior of the container (2) through the mouthpiece (6) unless a predetermined level of lip pressure and suction is applied to the mouthpiece (6). Other embodiments of the valve mechanism are described (see Figures 4, 10, 13 and 15).

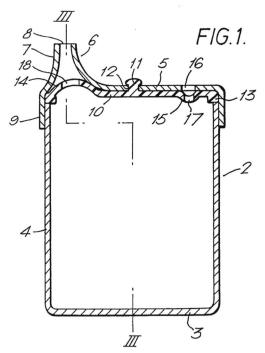

FIG.1.

At least one drawing originally filed was informal and the print reproduced here is taken from a later filed formal copy.

GB 2 266 045 A

1/6

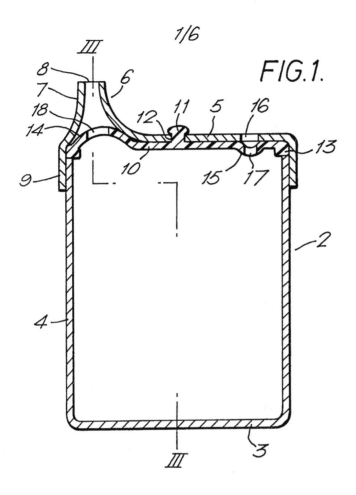

FIG.1.

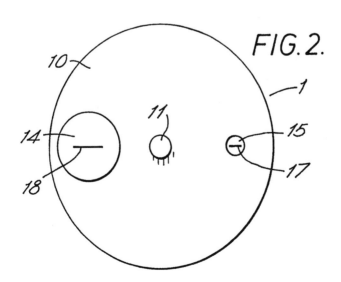

FIG.2.

1

DRINKING VESSEL SUITABLE FOR USE
AS A TRAINER CUP OR THE LIKE

This invention relates to drinking vessels and more particularly to drinking vessels suitable for use as a trainer cup or the like.

Trainer cups (that is a cup or mug provided with a lid having a mouthpiece - usually a spout - associated therewith) are well known and have been designed to bridge the gap between use of a baby's feeding bottle and use of a normal cup or glass by a young child. Such a trainer cup will often be a child's first step in learning to feed itself. As this period in a child's development will usually coincide with the cutting of its first teeth, quite apart from the child's inherent difficulty in handling what is new to it which may lead to the cup inadvertently being knocked over, the irritability characteristic of teething allied with the natural exuberance of young children tends to exacerbate what is frequently a noisy and messy experience.

The existence of the lid may reduce or at least delay the effect of knocking the cup over, but will not deter a child from shaking the cup violently up and down. Neither will the lid delay spillage for very long if the cup is knocked over. Notwithstanding that trainer cups of this kind have been known for a very lengthy period of time, I am unaware of any practical arrangement for overcoming these self-evident problems.

In the somewhat different field of babies feeding bottles, I have myself designed arrangements in which a valve interrupts the flow of fluid from the interior of the bottle through a teat or other mouthpiece (see for example my Patent Specifications Nos: 2 131 301 and

2

2 169 210). Bottles to my design have achieved some
commercial success particularly in the rather specialised
field of feeding of babies with_sucking problems. Other
arrangements proposing valved feeding bottles such as US
Patents 4 135 513, 3 704 803 and 4 339 046 and UK Patents
460 274 and 1 253 398 have been proposed in the patent
literature but I am not aware that any of these proposals
have proved of practical utility. I am not aware of any of
them having been marketed. Nevertheless, it is clear that
there have been a series of proposals by different workers
for the valving of babies feeding bottles. Notwithstanding
this, I am not aware of any previous proposal for valving
training cups or the like. As will become clear from the
detailed description hereinbelow of a presently preferred
embodiment of training cup or the like constructed in
accordance with my present invention, the present invention
enables the production of practical embodiments of trainer
cups which neatly and effectively overcome the problems of
accidental spillage or of child-generated deliberate
attempts at spilling the contents of the trainer cup.
Moreover, my practical embodiment achieves this desirable
end, never previously achieved, so far as I am aware, in a
simple, neat construction which is cheap and simple to
manufacture and facilitates easy cleaning. It has no
moving parts.

In broad terms, my invention in its broadest context
provides a drinking vessel suitable for use as a trainer
cup or the like, comprising: an open-mouthed generally cup-
shaped container; and a lid for the open mouth of said
container, the lid having a mouthpiece associated
therewith; the vessel being provided with valve means
adapted to prevent flow of liquid from the interior of the
container through the mouthpiece unless a predetermined
level of lip pressure and suction is applied to the mouthpiece.

3

The valve may be a separate valve member located in use between the container and the lid. Alternatively the valve may be integrally formed with the lid.

Suitably the lid is apertured to allow for the ingress of air to make up for the liquid sucked via the valve through the mouthpiece. To prevent the possibility of liquid issuing through this aperture, that is also suitably provided with a valve, preferably a non-return valve allowing flow of air from the exterior into the container but preventing flow of liquid from the interior of the container outwardly through the aperture.

Conveniently the two valves are provided by a single valve member which may be attached to the lid. The valve member may comprise a single piece of latex, silicone rubber, plastics or other suitable flexible material integrally moulded with two valves, one adapted to underlie the lid in the region of the mouthpiece and the other underlying the aperture. The two valves may comprise dome-shaped regions, the larger underlying the lid in the region of the mouthpiece and being concave towards the interior of the container, and the smaller underlying the aperture and being convex towards the interior. These dome-shaped regions are provided with a simple slit or cross-cut which in effect is self-closing, in each case the slit or cross-cut allowing flow from the concave to the convex side but not in the reverse direction. Other valve formations (e.g., a so-called "duck-bill" or a flap valve) are feasible. The valve member may be held in place between the lid and a valve member support plate.

In an alternative arrangement in which the valve is integrally formed with the lid, the lid itself may be made of a material listed above as a candidate for the separate valve member. The exit valve may comprise several dome-

12

CLAIMS

1. A drinking vessel suitable for use as a trainer cup or the like, comprising: an open-mouthed generally cup-shaped container; and a lid for the open mouth of said container, the lid having a mouthpiece associated therewith; the vessel being provided with valve means adapted to prevent flow of liquid from the interior of the container through the mouthpiece unless a predetermined level of lip pressure and suction is applied to the mouthpiece.

2. A drinking vessel according to Claim 1, wherein said valve means is a separate valve member located in use between the container and the lid.

3. A drinking vessel according to Claim 1, wherein said valve means is integral with the lid.

4. A drinking vessel according to Claims 1 or 3, wherein the valve means is at the extreme end of the mouthpiece.

5. A drinking vessel according to any preceding claim, wherein the lid is provided with an aperture to allow for the ingress of air.

6. A drinking vessel according to Claim 5, wherein said vessel is provided with additional valve means to prevent flow of liquid from the interior of the container through said aperture.

7. A drinking vessel according to both Claim 2 and Claim 6, wherein both said valve means are provided on the same said valve member located in use between the lid and the container.

The front page or title page is the least important part of the specification. Nevertheless, it contains some significant information. The first is the date of filing (in this example 7 April 1992) which will serve as the priority date, unless the applicant is claiming Convention priority. However, it seems that the applicant is not claiming priority from an earlier application since, if she had been, this would have been listed on the title page as 'priority data'. The names of the applicant and inventor are also listed on the title page. In this example, Mandy Nicola Haberman is both the applicant and the inventor and, as such, will be entitled to grant of the patent if the application is successful. The date of publication of the application is listed as 20 October 1993. As was mentioned above, the significance of publication is that, once the patent is granted, the patentee will be able to sue for any infringing acts that occur after this date. Finally, the title page contains the *abstract* listed under 'Drinking vessel suitable for use as a trainer cup'. The abstract is one of the documents required in order to make a full application. It is a brief summary of the important technical features of the invention and is a crucial element in facilitating searches of the patent register and alerting third parties to the existence of the application. Importantly, the abstract is only a source of technical information and does not form part of the state of the art.[144]

The subsequent pages contain *drawings* of the invention; these must be included in making an application where they are referred to in either the claims or the description. Along with the description, the drawings may be used to interpret the claims.

Next there is the *description* of the invention, which is also a necessary part of filing an application. The purpose of the description is to teach the notional skilled person in the relevant technological field (i.e. the person skilled in the art) about the invention. The specification must disclose the invention in a manner which is clear and complete enough for the person skilled in the art to perform the invention,[145] and the description is a key means of making such disclosure. The description will usually set out the background to the invention, summarizing any relevant prior art, and set out the technical problem which the invention seeks to solve. For example, in the patent application extracted above the background is that drinking cups for toddlers, known as trainer cups, are crucial in the developmental stage of children learning to drink from normal cups. However, the description tells us that existing trainer cups are prone to spillage when shaken or knocked over. In the field of baby feeding bottles, it is said that the use of certain 'valve means' has been helpful in interrupting the flow of liquid, but that such 'valve means' have not yet been used in relation to trainer cups. The invention, as described, is a trainer cup which uses 'valve means adapted to prevent flow of liquid from the interior of the container through the mouthpiece unless a predetermined level of lip pressure and suction is applied to the mouthpiece.' The valve means is then described in more detail with reference to the drawings.

Another important aspect of the application is the *claims*. Whereas the purpose of the description is to teach the reader about the invention and ensure that it is of some practical use, the purpose of the claims is to define the scope of the patent owner's monopoly. As such, the claims have a key role in determining whether or not a patent is infringed and difficult questions of interpretation of the language of the claims may arise. Usually, the claims are arranged hierarchically, with the broadest or principal claim listed first and the narrower or subsidiary claims listed subsequently. The advantage of doing this is that, if the principal claim is rejected or declared invalid, the patentee can still rely on the narrower claims. The types of the claims that may be encountered are various, but it is important to appreciate two key types of claims—product claims and process claims. Product claims are to inventions

---

[144] PA 77, s. 14(7); Art. 85 EPC.   [145] PA 77, s. 14(3); EPC.

concerning products, articles, machines, compounds, or substances. Process claims are to inventions relating to processes, methods, or uses.

As should be apparent from the excerpted patent application and discussion above, the patent specification is a highly technical document which requires specialist knowledge and expert drafting skills. For this reason, they are often drafted with the assistance of experts, called patent agents (in the UK) or European patent agents (for the EPC). These persons normally have knowledge of the patent administration process, patent law, and a particular branch of science.

9.6 PATENTABLE SUBJECT MATTER

9.6.1 INTRODUCTION

Section 1(1) of the PA 77 states that a patent may be granted for an *invention* which is new, involves an inventive step, and is capable of industrial application.[146] Each of these requirements will be examined in detail in later sections.[147] Section 1(1)(d) of the PA 77 also requires that the grant of a patent is not excluded by sub-ss. (2) and (3) or s. 4A. Section 1(3) excludes inventions which are contrary to public policy or morality, while s. 4A excludes methods of medical and veterinary treatment. Both of these exclusions are discussed later in this chapter.[148]

Notably, s. 1(2) of the PA 77 declares that certain things are *not inventions*, including:

(a) a discovery, scientific theory, or mathematical method;

(b) a literary, dramatic, musical, or artistic work or any other aesthetic creation whatsoever;

(c) a scheme, rule, or method for performing a mental act, playing a game, or doing business, or a program for a computer;

(d) the presentation of information

but only to the extent that a patent or patent application relates to that thing *as such*.[149]

Prior to the PA 77, inventions were defined positively as a 'manner of new manufacture'—a test which had its origins in s. 6 of the Statute of Monopolies 1624.[150] However, ss. 1(1)(d) and 1(2) of the PA 77 reflect a new approach to defining inventions, which accords with Article 52(2)–(3) of the EPC, namely to define them in a negative sense. The issue of whether there is a residual positive requirement of invention has been left open.[151]

FURTHER READING

J. Pila, 'Article 52(2) of the Convention on the Grant of European Patents: What did the framers intend? A study of the *travaux preparatoires*' (2005) 36 IIC 755.

---

[146] For European patents see Art. 51(1) EPC.

[147] See at 9.8 for industrial application, 9.10 for novelty, and 9.11 for inventive step.

[148] At 9.9 for methods of medical and veterinary treatment and 9.7.6 for the public order and morality exclusion.

[149] The EPC equivalent is to be found in Art. 52(2)–(3).   [150] Discussed above at 9.2.

[151] See comments obiter of Lord Hoffmann in *Biogen Inc v Medeva Plc* [1997] RPC 1, 41–2, and those of Lord Mustill, at pp. 31–2.

9.6.2 APPLYING SECTION 1(2) PA 77/ ARTICLE 52(2)–(3) EPC

As mentioned above, previously UK patent law defined 'invention' positively as a 'manner of new manufacture'. Under the PA 77 and EPC, however, the approach is to define 'invention' negatively, stipulating certain categories of subject matter that are *not* inventions. Is there an explanation for why these particular categories are excluded? Do they share a common objection or can the exclusion of each category be justified for different reasons? In *Aerotel*, the Court of Appeal explored these questions.

Aerotel Ltd v Telco Holdings Ltd [2007] RPC 7

The facts are discussed below at p. 501.

Jacob LJ (giving the judgment of the court):

8. The provisions about what are not to be 'regarded as inventions' are not easy. Over the years there has been and continues to be much debate about them and about decisions on them given by national courts and the Boards of Appeal of the EPO. They form the basis of a distinct industry of conferences and are the foundation of a plethora of academic theses and publications. There has also been much political debate too: some urging removal or reduction of the categories, others their retention or enlargement. With the political debate we have no concern—it is our job to interpret them as they stand.

9. As the decisions show this is not an easy task. There are several reasons for this:

i) In the first place there is no evident underlying purpose lying behind the provisions as a group—a purpose to guide the construction. The categories are there, but there is nothing to tell you one way or the other whether they should be read widely or narrowly.

ii) One cannot form an overall approach to the categories. They form a disparate group—no common, overarching concept, for example, links rules for playing games with computer programs or either of these with methods for doing business or aesthetic creations.

iii) Some categories are given protection by other intellectual property laws. Most importantly, of course, aesthetic creations and computer programs have protection under the law of copyright. So the legislator may well have formed the view that additional protection by way of patentability was unnecessary or less appropriate.

iv) Further, some categories are so abstract that they are unnecessary or meaningless. For instance a scientific theory as such is excluded. But how could a scientific theory ever be the subject of a patent claim in the first place? Einstein's special theory of relativity was new and non-obvious but it was inherently incapable of being patented. A patent after all is to a legal monopoly over some commercial activity carried out by human beings such as making or dealing in goods or carrying out a process. A scientific theory is not activity at all. It simply is not the sort of thing which could be made the subject of a legal monopoly.

Nor can the presence of the exclusion be explained on the narrower basis that it was intended to exclude woolly and general claims such as 'Any application of $E = mc^2$'. For such a claim would be bad for the more conventional reason that it does not disclose the invention 'in a manner sufficiently clear and complete for it to be carried out by a person skilled in the art' (Arts 83 and 100(b)).

v) There is or may be overlap between some of the exclusions themselves and between them [and] the overall requirement that an invention be 'susceptible of industrial application'. The overall requirement is, perhaps surprisingly, hardly ever mentioned in the debate about the categories of 'non-invention' (no-one relied upon it before us) but it is clearly a factor lying behind some of the debate.

...

11. So, one asks, what help can be had from the *travaux préparatoires* to the EPC? The answer is not a lot. The debates amongst the framers of the Convention which lead to the excluded categories were the subject of two fascinating and valuable articles in 2005 by Dr Justine Pila of the Oxford University Intellectual Property Research Centre ('Dispute over the meaning of "invention" in Art. 52(2) EPC—The patentability of computer-implemented inventions in Europe' 36 IIC 173; 'Art. 52(2) of the Convention on the Grant of European Patents: What did the framers intend?' 36 IIC 755). She shows that the *travaux* provide no direct assistance to any of the categories we have to consider. 'Only a bull's-eye counts' (per Lord Steyn in *Effort Shipping Co Ltd v Linden Management SA* [1988] AC 605 at 625) and there are no bull's-eyes in the *travaux* for present purposes. What does emerge is that the various categories are the result of various compromises and distinct discussions about each of them. So one can at least find confirmation that no overarching principle was intended. What was done was to formulate the language of each of the categories independently of one another, add the 'as such' rider to all of them and leave it to the EPO and European patent judges to work out the detail.

12. Perhaps one other thing emerges—by its absence. There is no indication of any intention as to how the categories should be construed—either restrictively or widely. In EU law exceptions to a general principle are generally interpreted restrictively, see, e.g. per La Pergola A-G at [8] in Case C-12/98 *Amengual Far v Amengual Far* [2002] STC 382 (a VAT case): 'This criterion has been consistently followed in the case law of this court.' The EPO Boards of Appeal have applied that principle to the interpretation of Art. 53. See, e.g. *HARVARD/Onco-mouse* (1990) T 0019/90 [1990] OJ EPO 376, T 356/93 *Plant Genetic Systems/Glutamine Synthetase Inhibitors* (1995) [1995] OJ EPO 545; [1995] EPOR 357. But Art. 53 is not the same as Art. 52(2). It is expressly entitled 'Exceptions to patentability'. The exceptions are clearly specified as such and the exception principle of construction can and does apply to them. But Art. 52(2), by contrast, is not expressed as an exception to patentability—it sets out positive categories of things which are not to be regarded as inventions.

What are the difficulties, according to *Aerotel*, of interpreting s. 1(2) of the PA 77? Further, is the correct approach for courts to interpret each category of excluded subject matter according to its particular underlying purpose and legislative background?

In assessing whether an invention falls foul of s. 1(2) PA 77, courts will look at the invention as a *whole*, even where it is a mix of patentable and non-patentable elements. However, this can create difficulties around establishing whether the invention as claimed falls within the excluded categories of subject matter. To assist in determining whether the invention falls within the exclusions, courts have developed the test of 'technical effect', 'technical contribution', or 'technical character'. If the invention has a technical effect, or makes a technical contribution or features a technical character, the logic is that it must fall outside s. 1(2) of the PA 77 or Article 52(2)–(3) of the EPC because these provisions are concerned with categories of subject matter that are non-technical in nature. Brad Sherman describes the advantage of this test:

> One of the main advantages of this way of approaching Article 52(2) is that by shifting atten-
> tion towards the idea of 'technical character', the Board of Appeal is able to avoid having to
> formulate a workable definition of 'computer program', a task which is not only technically
> problematic but also one that changes in technology are likely to render obsolete. Indeed one
> of the major problems with specific formulations such as Article 52(2) is that because they
> are drafted in the light of contemporary technology they are prone to obsolescence or, at
> least, convoluted interpretations. Whatever advantages this approach to Article 52 may have,
> it still leaves the Board of Appeal with two further questions: first, the need to characterise
> the invention; second, the task of having to formulate and understand what is meant by the
> term 'technical'...[152]

Examining the invention as a whole and asking whether it produces a 'technical effect' or
'technical contribution' was first introduced by the Technical Board of Appeal in *Vicom/
Computer-related invention* T208/84.[153] This case involved a European patent application
for a method of digitally processing images using a device called an operator matrix, which
aimed at producing enhanced images. The Examining Division rejected the application on
the ground that it was for a mathematical method and/or a computer program as such. The
applicants appealed to the Technical Board of Appeal, arguing that the invention conferred
a technical benefit, in the form of a substantial increase in processing speed compared with
the prior art and, further, that digital image processing was not an abstract process, 'but the
physical manipulation of electrical signals representing the picture in accordance with the
procedures defined in the claims'. As such, the invention reflected a new and valuable contribution which was not excluded by Article 52(2)–(3) of the EPC.

The Technical Board of Appeal set aside the decision of the Examining Division, stating
that:

> Generally speaking, an invention which would be patentable in accordance with conven-
> tional patentability criteria should not be excluded from protection by the mere fact that for
> its implementation modern technical means in the form of a computer program are used.
> Decisive is what technical contribution the invention as defined in the claim when considered
> as a whole makes to the known art.[154]

The Board also commented that where the method is 'carried out on a physical entity
(which may be a material object but equally an image stored as an electric signal) by some
technical means implementing the method and provides as its result a certain change in
that entity'[155] this could amount to a technical result. In your view, is this guidance from the
Board as to what constitutes a 'technical result' or 'technical contribution' helpful?

In a subsequent case the approach in *Vicom* was challenged. However, as we shall see,
the Technical Board of Appeal reiterated the 'technical effect' test for determining whether
the invention as a whole falls foul of the excluded subject matter in Article 52(2)–(3) of
the EPC.

---

152 B. Sherman, 'The patentability of computer-related inventions in the United Kingdom and the
European Patent Office' [1991] 13 EIPR 85, 87–8.
153 [1987] EPOR 74.   154 Ibid., para. 16.   155 Ibid., para. 5.

Koch & Sterzel/X-Ray Apparatus T26/86 [1988] EPOR 72

Claim 1 of the patent in suit was directed to X-ray apparatus for radiological imaging. The apparatus had a data processing unit which stored the X-ray tube rating curves for different exposure parameters and used these to set the tube voltage values for the exposure parameters selected, characterized in that the data-processing unit determined by a specified method the tube voltage and exposure parameters which ensured optimum exposure with sufficient protection against overloading of the X-ray tube.

The opponents argued that the subject matter of the patent was not patentable, being covered by Article 52(2) of the EPC. The opponents submitted that the approach in *Vicom* should not be followed, but rather the approach of the German Federal Supreme Court, which involved applying Article 52(2) of the EPC whenever the essence of the subject matter was not of a technical character, such as when the essence of the teaching was a computer program. The oppositions were rejected. The Technical Board of Appeal dismissed the appeal and refused to refer proceedings to the Enlarged Board.

Technical Board of Appeal, at pp. 74–6:

3.1 To decide whether the subject-matter of Claim 1 is or is not an invention within the meaning of Article 52(1) EPC, it is necessary to determine whether or not it is a computer program as such and hence falls under Article 52(2)(c) and (3) EPC. Claim 1 relates neither to a computer program on its own and divorced from any technical application, nor a computer program in the form of a recording on a data carrier, nor a known, general-purpose computer in combination with a computer program. It is in fact an X-ray apparatus incorporating a data processing unit operating in accordance with a routine which produces a technical effect in the X-ray apparatus.

This emerges clearly from the characteristics (a), (b) and (c) of Claim 1, which states that the X-ray tubes are controlled by the routine so that by establishing a certain parameter priority, optimum exposure is combined with adequate protection against overloading of the X-ray tubes.

The subject-matter of Claim 1 is therefore an invention within the meaning of Article 52(1) EPC and patentable irrespective of whether or not the X-ray apparatus without this computer program forms part of the state of the art.

. . .

3.3 Appellant 0II objects that the position taken in the Guidelines (CIV, 2.2) and in Decision T208/84 delivered by Board 3.5.1 (OJ 1/1987, p. 14, VICOM) would render Article 52(2)(c) EPC totally ineffectual because even an ordinary computer program used in a general-purpose computer could then be regarded as an invention under Article 52(1) EPC since each computing operation is carried out with the aid of natural, that is, electromagnetic, forces. The Board takes the view that, while an ordinary computer program used in a general-purpose computer certainly transforms mathematical values into electric signals with the aid of natural forces, the electric signals concerned amount to no more than a reproduction of information and cannot in themselves be regarded as a technical effect. The computer program used in a general-purpose computer is thus considered to be a program as such and hence excluded from patentability by Article 52(2)(c) EPC. But if the program controls the operation of a conventional general-purpose computer so as technically to alter its functioning, the unit consisting of program and computer combined may be a patentable invention.

[Rejecting the approach of the German Federal Court of Justice:]

3.4 ... The Board is unable to share this view because it makes the field in which an invention essentially lies crucial to the issue of whether that invention is or is not technical in nature. The Board holds that an invention must be assessed as a whole. If it makes use of both technical and non-technical means, the use of non-technical means does not detract from the technical character of the overall teaching. The European Patent Convention does not ask that a patentable invention be exclusively or largely of a technical nature; in other words, it does not prohibit the patenting of inventions consisting of a mix of technical and non-technical elements.

Apart from the fact that the Board fails to find any legal basis in the European Patent Convention for the theory of the Federal Court of Justice concerning the essence of inventions, it also sees practical objections to a need to give a weighting to technical and non-technical aspects because according to the Federal Court of Justice the criterion to be applied is which aspect makes the essential contribution to the invention's success. Not only is such a decision fraught with difficulties in practice; it also has the effect of making the teaching unpatentable in its entirety if the greater part is non-technical and even though the technical aspect which is found to be subordinate is in fact judged to be novel and to involve inventive step.

On what basis did the Board decide that the invention in *Koch & Sterzel* had a technical effect or contribution? Further, why is it that use of an ordinary computer program or computer will not produce the requisite technical effect? Finally, are the Board's reasons for rejecting the approach of the German Federal Supreme Court, by asking whether the essence of the invention had technical character, convincing?

Shortly after *Vicom* and *Koch & Sterzel*, the UK Court of Appeal had an opportunity to consider how to approach s. 1(2) of the PA 77.

Merrill Lynch Inc's Application [1989] RPC 561

The invention related to an improved data processing system for implementing an automated trading market for securities. The principal examiner held that the invention was unpatentable pursuant to s. 1(2) of the PA 77. The applicants appealed and the appeal was dismissed by Falconer J in the Patents Court. Falconer J held that the principal examiner had correctly construed the qualification in s. 1(2). On appeal to the Court of Appeal, the appeal was dismissed. The approach of Falconer J was not followed, but rather the approach in *Vicom*.

Fox LJ (with whom Stocker and Taylor LJJ agreed), at p. 569:

The position seems to me to be this. *Genentech* decides that the reasoning of Falconer J is wrong. On the other hand, it seems to me to be clear, for the reasons indicated by Dillon LJ, that it cannot be permissible to patent an item excluded by section 1(2) under the guise of an article which contains that item—that is to say, in the case of a computer program, the patenting of a conventional computer containing that program. Something further is necessary. The nature of that addition is, I think, to be found in the *Vicom* case where it is stated: 'Decisive is what technical contribution the invention makes to the known art.' There must, I think, be some technical advance on the prior art in the form of a new result (e.g., a substantial increase in processing speed as in *Vicom*).

Now let it be supposed that claim 1 can be regarded as producing a new result in the form of a technical contribution to the prior art. That result, whatever the technical advance may be, is simply the production of a trading system. It is a data-processing system for doing a specific business, that is to say, making a trading market in securities. The end result, there-fore, is simply 'a method of doing business', and is excluded by section 1(2)(c). The fact that the method of doing business may be an improvement on previous methods of doing busi-ness does not seem to me to be material. The prohibition in section 1(2)(c) is generic; quali-tative considerations do not enter into the matter. The section draws no distinction between the method by which the mode of doing business is achieved. If what is produced in the end is itself an item excluded from patentability by section 1(2), the matter can go no further. Claim 1, after all, is directed to 'a data processing system for making a trading market'. That is simply a method of doing business. A data processing system operating to produce a novel technical result would normally be patentable. But it cannot, it seems to me, be patentable if the result itself is a prohibited item under section 1(2). In the present case it is such a pro-hibited item.

The *Vicom* approach was followed in *Merrill Lynch*, however, the Court of Appeal added the 'rider' that where the technical contribution relates to excluded subject matter (e.g. is a method of doing business) it will still be excluded. In other words, the technical contribu-tion must not reside in the excluded subject matter. Although the applicability of the 'rider' to the 'technical effect' approach was subsequently questioned,[156] it has since been reiterated in *Aerotel*.

Implicit in the 'technical effect' or 'technical contribution' approach is that the court looks to what is *new* and/or *inventive* about the invention (i.e. the contribution) to judge whether it is technical in nature. In *PBS Partnership/Pension Benefit Systems* T931/95,[157] the Technical Board of Appeal rejected this approach because, *inter alia*, it confused the requirements of 'invention', 'novelty', and 'inventive step'. Instead, the Board held that:

a computer system suitably programmed for use in a particular field, even if that is the field of business and economy, has the character of a concrete apparatus in the sense of a phys-ical entity, man-made for a utilitarian purpose and is thus an invention within the meaning of Article 52(1) EPC.[158]

Thus, the invention was held *not* to be excluded subject matter because it had a technical character by virtue of being embodied in physical apparatus, i.e. computer hardware. The approach in *Pension Benefit Systems* has thus been referred to as the 'any hardware' approach.[159] Later decisions of the Technical Board of Appeal (in *Hitachi/Auction Method* T258/03[160] and *Microsoft/Clipboard Formats I* T424/03[161]) have also rejected the 'technical effect' approach to Article 52(2)–(3) of the EPC in favour of the 'any hardware' approach. These decisions, along with *Pension Benefit Systems*, are discussed in more detail below at 9.6.3.2.

The divergence of approaches in the jurisprudence of the Technical Boards of Appeal has put the UK in an awkward position when it comes to pursuing uniformity with the EPO. In *Aerotel* the Court of Appeal declined to follow the EPO approach to Article 52(2)–(3) of the EPC, as reflected in *Pension Benefit Systems* T0931/95, *Hitachi* T258/04, and *Microsoft/*

---

[156] As a result of a comment by Aldous LJ in *Fujitsu* [1997] RPC 608, 614.
[157] [2002] OJ EPO 441. Discussed further at 9.6.3.2.   [158] Ibid., p. 530.
[159] *Aerotel*, para. 26: 'ask whether the claim involves the use of or is to a piece of physical hardware, how-ever mundane'.
[160] [2004] EPOR 55.   [161] [2006] EPOR 39.

Clipboard Formats I T424/03. The court stated:[162]

> We are conscious of the need to place great weight on the decisions of the Boards of Appeal, but, given the present state of conflict between the old (*Vicom* etc) and the new (*Hitachi* etc) approaches, quite apart from the fact that there are three distinct new approaches each to some extent in conflict with the other two, it would be premature to do so. If and when an Enlarged Board rules on the question, this Court may have to re-consider its approach…All we decide now is that we do not follow any of the trio. The fact that the BGH has already declined to follow *Pension Benefits* reinforces this view—doing so will not lead to European consistency.

In its subsequent decision in *Symbian Ltd*[163] the Court of Appeal reiterated this position. Thus, until the Enlarged Board of Appeal rules on this issue,[164] UK courts will continue to adopt a 'technical effect' approach to s. 1(2) of the PA 77, in contrast to the 'any hardware' approach of the EPO.

To what extent do these approaches differ and will this have an impact in practice? Deputy Judge Peter Prescott QC in *CFPH LLC's Application*[165] explored this very question and made the following observations:

> 44. Let me first outline the practice of the UK Patent Office. They look at the applicant's claim, and ask themselves: what is his 'technical contribution'? If there is none—as in my tax-planning example—they reject the application. They hold that is not an 'invention'. If there is some 'technical contribution', they still have to decide whether to reject it for being old, or obvious. It is an 'invention', but it may be an old invention, or an obvious one.
>
> 45. Now let me outline the practice of the European Patent Office. They look at the applicant's claim, and ask themselves: does it have any 'technical features'? If there are no 'technical features' at all they reject the application, for not being an 'invention'. But they consider it is an invention if there is any 'technical feature' at all. They take it very far. Even paper, or ink, can count as a technical feature. I suppose a detective story, written on paper with ink, would pass that part of their test. What they then go on to do is to ask themselves, 'Yes, but is it old, or obvious?' And in deciding if it is old or obvious, they *ignore* anything that is not a 'technical feature'.
>
> 46. In short, the difference between the two approaches is that the EPO filters out excluded subject-matter at the stage of considering obviousness—at the last stage—while the UK Patent Office does so at the first stage (when considering excluded subject-matter). Or to put it a little more precisely, what the UK Patent Office does is to consider the exclusion under the description 'novelty', but the EPO does so under the description 'inventive step'.

Does It Matter?

> 47. Do both approaches lead to the same end-result in practice? I asked counsel if they could come up with a clear concrete example, real or imaginary, where it made all the difference, but they were not able to think of one. Not a convincing one, anyway.
>
> 48. So why is it that the difference may matter all the same? It is because, as Renan and Lord Hoffmann said in other contexts, *la verité est dans une nuance*. Even if the two approaches are the same functionally they may, conceivably, produce different results when

---

[162] [2007] RPC 7, at para. 29.   [163] [2008] EWCA Civ 1066. For a further discussion see at 12.3.2.1.

[164] Which looks likely given the recent reference by the President of the EPO dated 22 Oct. 2008—see <http://www.epo.org/index.html> for details.

[165] [2006] RPC 5.

it comes to matters of evaluation. That is because cases have to be decided by human beings; but the human mind is affected by the context in which a question is posed. And technological invention cannot reliably be divorced from business context.

Would it be fair to say that the UK takes the 'invention' requirement more seriously than the EPO? On the other hand, if the EPO considers only *technical* contributions when assessing inventive step, is it not the case that inventions simply get refused at a later stage of the examination process? Even so, do you agree with Deputy Judge Prescott QC that it remains possible for different outcomes to occur? It is important to bear these questions in mind in the discussion that ensues about particular categories of excluded subject matter. We turn now to examine the exclusions for methods for performing mental acts and methods of doing business. The exclusion relating to computer programs as such is considered in a subsequent chapter.[166]

9.6.3 METHOD FOR PERFORMING A MENTAL ACT

The reason for incorporating this exclusion into Article 52(2)–(3) is not apparent from the *travaux preparatoires* of the EPC. This may explain why both narrow and broad interpretations of this exclusion have emerged in EPO and UK jurisprudence. It is also worth noting that the exclusion for a method for performing a mental act is closely related to the exclusion concerning computer programs.[167] This is because computer-related inventions may represent an automated, and therefore more efficient way, of carrying out a mental process. An example of computer software being used in this manner is the following case.

IBM/Text Clarity Processing T38/86 [1990] EPOR 606

The European patent application concerned a method for automatically detecting and replacing linguistic expressions which exceeded a predetermined understandability level in a list of linguistic expressions in a text-processing system. The text-processing system comprised a dictionary section storing linguistic expressions each with an appended grade-level code and a synonym section storing a list of synonymic expressions for said dictionary section each with an appended grade-level code, a keyboard, and a display. The method comprised the steps of: (1) inputting into the system a code reflecting a predetermined understandability level; (2) comparing the linguistic expressions to the dictionary section and highlighting on the display those linguistic expressions that exceeded the stored understandibility level code; (3) retrieving in said synonym section the linguistic expressions which are synonyms for the highlighted expressions and match the stored understandability code; and (4) displaying those synonyms, whereby the operator is enabled to replace the highlighted linguistic expression with the synonym.

The application was refused by the Examining Division on the basis that the subject matter of the claims was excluded from patentability by Article 52(2)–(3) of the EPC and for lack of inventive step. On appeal the appellants argued, *inter alia*, that the subject matter did not relate to a method for performing a mental act since the mental acts were not performed by a human being but were performed automatically by the system and produced technical effects, such as the automatic provision and display of synonyms.

---

[166] See 12.3.   [167] Discussed ibid.

Technical Board of Appeal (dismissing the appeal), **at pp. 611–12:**

12. The Board recognises that the use of technical means for carrying out a method, partly or entirely without human intervention, which method if performed by a human being, would require him to perform mental acts, may, having regard to Article 52(3) EPC, render such a method a technical process or method and therefore an invention within the meaning of Article 52(1) EPC, that is, one which is not excluded from patentability under Article 52(2)(c) EPC. This is because paragraph 3 of Article 52 EPC makes it clear that patentability is excluded only to the extent to which the patent application relates to excluded subject-matter or activities as such. In the opinion of the Board, while it follows that the EPC does not prohibit the patenting of inventions consisting of a mix of excluded and non-excluded features (in conformity with T26/86 OJ EPO 1988, 19), it does not necessarily follow that all such mixes are patentable. Since patentability is excluded only to the extent to which the patent application relates to excluded subject-matter or activities as such, it appears to be the intention of the EPC to permit patenting only in those cases in which the invention involves a contribution to the art in a field not excluded from patentability.

13. However, this seems not to be the case here. Once the steps of the method for performing the mental acts in question (enumerated under the foregoing item 11) have been defined, the implementation of the technical means to be used in those steps, at least at the level of generality specified in Claim 1, involves no more than the straightforward application of conventional techniques and must therefore be considered to be obvious to a person skilled in the (technical) art, so that the method according to Claim 1 of the present application does not contribute to the art anything involving an inventive step within the meaning of Article 56 EPC in a field not excluded from patentability by Article 52(2)(c) EPC.

14. Although a computer program is not expressly recited in Claim 1, it is clear to a reader skilled in the art that the claim covers the case in which a computer program is used and, indeed, in the only embodiment disclosed in the application the text processing system is controlled by a set of programs and data stored in the memory.

15. It can be seen from the analysis in paragraphs 4 to 10 above that the operations performed in the method claimed in Claim 1 of the present application do not go beyond the processing of data relating to a list of linguistic expressions and codes representing their understandability level. The overall effect of the method is that signals representing one linguistic expression in the list are replaced with signals representing another linguistic expression. These signals are not different from a technical point of view. They differ only in that they represent different linguistic expressions, which are purely abstract expressions without any technical significance. The overall effect of the method is thus not technical.

16. The fact that the claimed method involves a new method of operating, as pointed out by the appellant, cannot by itself confer patentability on the method, since the specified hardware is conventional, the data processed has no technical significance and the processing of this data involves only conventional techniques of entering, storing, retrieving, comparing, displaying, highlighting and selecting from a menu. The Board cannot find anything in the claimed method, considered as a whole, or in any of its details, which could involve an inventive step in a field which is not excluded from patentability by Article 52(2) EPC.

In *IBM* T38/86 the Technical Board of Appeal followed the 'technical effect' or 'technical contribution' approach. It considered that the new and inventive part of this claim (i.e. the 'contribution') related to excluded subject matter (a mental act) and was not of a technical nature. Using technical means to implement the method (i.e. a computer program running on conventional hardware) did not supply the requisite technical contribution because these technical means were obvious to a person skilled in the art (and therefore were not a 'contribution'). A similar approach and conclusion was reached in *IBM/Text Processing* T65/86,[168] where the European patent application concerned a method of automatically detecting and correcting contextual homophone errors.

In the UK, the *Fujitsu* decision highlights the close relationship between the exclusions relating to a computer program and a method for performing a mental act.

Fujitsu Ltd's Application [1996] RPC 511

The UK patent application related to a method and apparatus for modelling a synthetic crystal structure for designing inorganic materials. It involved a computer programmed so that an operator could select an atom, a lattice vector, and a crystal face in each of two crystal structures displayed on the computer. The computer then converted data representing the physical layouts of the two crystal structures into data representing the crystal structure that would have been obtained by combining the original two structures in that way. The resulting data was then displayed to give an image of the resulting combined structure. Conventionally, the modelling of such structures occurred by assembling plastic models.

The examiner objected that the application was a method for performing a mental act or a program for a computer as such. The Hearing Officer rejected the application on the same basis. On appeal to the Patents Court, Laddie J held that, in form at least, the claims were not programs as such, but that they did relate to a method for performing a mental act.

Laddie J, at pp. 532–3:

In this case, Fujitsu's application leaves it to the operator to select what data to work on, how to work on it, how to assess the results and which, if any, results to use. The process is abstract and the result of use of it is undefined. What is produced is not an inevitable result of taking a number of defined steps but is determined by the personal skill and assessment of the operator. As such it consists in substance of a scheme or method for performing a mental act and is unpatentable.

...

I should mention that both before me and before Mr Haselden, particular emphasis was placed on the fact that the steps to be carried out with the assistance of the programmed computer matched steps which, prior to Fujitsu's development, were done manually by workers in this field. For example physical models of crystals were built and manipulated to help visualise new hybrid structures. However the fact that a new process is the electronic equivalent of what has been done manually before goes primarily to the issue of novelty (a matter not before me) not the question of whether the application falls within section 1(2). I would have come to the same conclusion that this invention was not patentable even if all the steps set out in the claims had been novel.

In the Court of Appeal, the basis for rejecting the application was that it was a computer program as such.[169] On the issue of whether the claim was a method of performing a mental act as such, the appellant argued that the words in s. 1(2)(c) of the PA 77 should be

---

[168] [1990] EPOR 181.   [169] See 12.3.2.

construed as covering methods which the human mind *actually* carries out and not the sort of acts which a human mind could carry out. Aldous LJ concluded that there was no need to decide this issue. Nevertheless, he commented obiter that this 'narrow construction' of the exclusion should be rejected:

> There are good reasons to reject the narrow construction. First, a decision as to whether an invention is patentable as consisting of a method of performing a mental act as such should be capable of determination without recourse to evidence as to how the human mind actually works. If it were to the contrary, the section would pose an extremely difficult problem. Second, the narrow interpretation appears to introduce a consideration of novelty which is covered in section 1(1)(a). Third, the words used as 'a mental act' suggest any mental act whether done before or not.[170]

Do you agree with the view expressed by Aldous LJ and his reasons for reaching it? Interestingly, in *Aerotel*, the Court of Appeal commented obiter that 'we are by no means convinced that Aldous LJ's provisional view is correct. There is no particular reason to suppose that "mental act" was intended to exclude things wider than, for instance, methods of doing mental arithmetic...or remembering things.'[171]

9.6.4 METHOD FOR DOING BUSINESS

9.6.4.1 Rationale

It was uncontroversial that methods for doing business would form part of the excluded subject matter when it came to drafting Article 52(2)–(3) of the EPC.[172] This is because historically business schemes had been unpatentable in the UK and other Contracting States to the EPC. The reason for this could have been that methods for doing business were considered inherently unsuitable to patents. Alternatively, it could have been because patents were thought unnecessary in this field, given that commercial innovation had flourished in the absence of patents.[173]

It is fair to say, however, that nowadays there is significant pressure for the EPO and the UK (along with other jurisdictions) to allow patents for methods of doing business. This pressure has arisen for at least two reasons. First, the development of information technologies, including software and the Internet, has facilitated new types of innovation to occur in the way that business is conducted. Second, since the US Court of Appeals for the Federal Circuit decision in *State Street Bank & Trust Co v Signature Financial Group, Inc*,[174] the US has recognized the patentability of business methods—although, it is important to note that the recent decision of the US Court of Appeals for the Federal Circuit in *Re Bilski*[175] signals a shift in approach. A majority of the court eschewed the test of 'useful, concrete and tangible result' adopted in *State Street Bank* in favour of the 'machine-or-transformation' test. This test requires that a process must be tied to a 'particular machine' or else involve the transformation of an article from one thing or state to another thing or state. On the facts, the patent application in *Re Bilski*, which was for a method of hedging risk in the field

---

[170] *Fujitsu Ltd's Application* [1997] RPC 608, 620.   [171] *Aerotel*, para. 97.
[172] See J. Pila, 'Article 52(2) of the Convention on the Grant of European Patents: What did the framers intend? A study of the *travaux preparatoires*' (2005) 36 IIC 755.
[173] See *CFPH LLC's Application* [2006] RPC 5, para. 41.   [174] 149 F 3d 1368 (Fed Cir, 1993).
[175] 545 F 3d 943 (CA Fed, 2008).

of commodities trading, did not satisfy this test. Thus, while the US Court of Appeals did not reject business methods as being unpatentable, the 'machine-or-transformation' test is apparently stricter than the *State Street Bank* test of 'useful, concrete and tangible result'. Whether this, more cautious, approach to business method patents in the United States impacts upon other jurisdictions is yet to be seen.

In this area we must ask whether the patenting of business methods can be justified? Is it the case that an incentive, in the form of patent protection, is needed to encourage business innovation? Would the grant of patents for business methods (particularly ones of dubious merit) unduly restrict the activities of competitors and stifle further innovation? On the other hand, if patents are viewed as a means of rewarding innovation, should a business innovation be excluded if it satisfies the requirements of novelty and inventive step? In this respect it is important to note that TRIPS Article 27 provides that patents should be available in all fields of technology. In the extract below, the authors explore the key arguments in favour of, and against, business method patents.

J. McNamara and L. Cradduck, 'Can we protect how we do what we do? A consideration of business methods patents in Australia and Europe' (2008) IJL & IT 96, 113–16

4.1.1 Philosophical Objections

Business method patents are claimed to be a 'soft' area of intellectual property where the usefulness of patents as a tool is questioned. It is argued that patents over *business methods* are not justified on an economic basis because the implementation of *business methods* merely involves market risk as opposed to technological risk as all enterprises implementing a new product take market risk. The developer of any new product faces the risk that the product will not achieve market acceptance and developers of *business methods* should not receive any special shelter from this risk.

Other commentators expressed concern that by enabling the registration of *business method patents* the way has been '...*paved*...*for patenting developments in the liberal arts, social sciences, the law, and other indeterminate areas of human activity*'.

An argument that patents generally do not encourage innovation, but are merely wealth creation or protection devices (not necessarily to the benefit of the true inventors) also has been raised. Detailed consideration of this argument is beyond the scope of this paper, however, it is noted that it may be particularly apposite for *business method patents* because monopolies in *business methods* may lead to far greater stifling of competition than in other more technical fields.

As some commentators have suggested, the underlying questions to be asked in respect of *business method patents* are—'*Do these methods serve the purpose of patent law? Do they promote innovation?*' Without international harmonisation however it is submitted that internationally these questions are difficult to answer as the underlying premise of patent law varies from jurisdiction to jurisdiction.

4.1.2 Lack of rigour in granting business method patents

The lack of a prior art database and the inexperience of patent examiners in business fields means that it can be difficult for patent examiners to assess whether the alleged innovation is actually new. As a result it is argued that many *business method patents* have been granted that, if tested in the courts, would be found to be invalid. If too many *business method patents* are ultimately found to be invalid, the integrity of the patent system will be undermined. In addition, businesses may be uncertain as to whether they are infringing patent rights because *business methods* are difficult to define in patent claims.

4.1.3 Effects on Competition

During the ACIP Review, the Australian Consumers' Association raised concerns with the compliance costs that *business method patents* impose on small to medium enterprises ('SMEs'). They identified that firstly, the payment of royalty fees is an added expense to be passed on to the consumers; and secondly, that protection of intellectual property diverts SMEs from their core activity, resulting in a less efficient industry.

Expensive and protracted patent disputes may be a significant threat to the development of e-commerce. While *business method patents* may be challenged on the grounds of lack of novelty or obviousness, the cost of such a challenge may be prohibitive for SMEs. Patents therefore may be used as a tool to stifle legitimate competition. Worse still '...*knowledge that was...freely exchanged between researchers will...be tied...posing a big danger to innovation*'.

It is possible that patents may be used by SMEs to protect their own business assets, which is to their advantage. Overall however, as patents are traditionally used by big business to stifle competition, it is argued that small businesses cannot afford to obtain and maintain a sufficient number of patents to obtain bargaining leverage.

4.2 In Defence of Business Method Patents

Submissions to the ACIP Review suggested various ways of ensuring that *business methods* are not patentable, including by imposing a requirement that a patentable advance must be technology rather than merely use technology. Such a requirement is not justifiable and would discriminate against innovations in the business as opposed to scientific fields. In any event, many scientific patents simply use technology rather than advance it. Also, it is suggested that discrimination between scientific methods and *business methods* would cause confusion in patent law.

Other submissions were concerned not to deny the patentability of *business methods* but rather to ensure that *business method patents* that are granted are properly examined to ensure that they are novel and involve an inventive step. The majority of submissions to the ACIP Review supported the patentability of *business method patents*. Other commentators support *business method patents* on the grounds that they '...*in fact encourage innovation...and therefore serve consumer interest by enhancing choice...*'

To exclude *business methods* from patentability would be in breach of Australia's obligations under TRIPS which requires *business methods* to be patentable. The field of technology requirement in Article 27(1) of TRIPS is meant to be expansive, i.e. it indicates that patents are to be granted in all fields of technology (unless the specific exclusions in Art 27(2) and (3) apply), rather than limiting. It is submitted that as the European exception predates TRIPS, it is not justified and cannot be sustained. Further, even if a *business method* exception is allowable under TRIPS, *business methods* are patentable in the US and, except in narrow circumstances, in the EU. Accordingly, Australia should not implement an exception in relation to *business methods* that would be contrary to its TRIPS obligations.

Intellectual property protection is crucial to the growth of Australia's information and communications technology sector. Without patent protection, there would be little incentive for businesses to continue to develop their business ideas, as those ideas could simply be exploited by others with whom the developer must share their idea in order to develop their business. Barriers to entry for Internet based businesses are relatively few and lack of patent protection for new business innovations would be an unfair advantage to the imitator over the innovator. However, if Australia did implement an exception that was out of step with our ICT trading partners it would be damaging to our ICT industry.

Supporters of *business method patents* argue that problems that have arisen with some *business method patents* are because the patents granted were not novel or inventive. A particular problem arises where known business ideas are applied in a new medium such as the Internet. Accordingly, most of the recommendations made for change by those who support *business method patents* in principle relate to closer examination of patents by IP Australia. It is clear however that business believes that to ignore *business methods* would be to be '… *left behind*'.[176]

Having considered the arguments raised in the above extract, do you consider there to be sound, principled objections to allowing patents for methods of doing business or is the problem essentially how to effectively examine business method patents so that unmeritorious ones do not make it onto the register? If the latter, is this a problem that can be adequately addressed?

We turn now to consider the different ways in which the EPO and the UK approach the 'method for doing business *as such*' exclusion. In reading the following material, it is worth keeping in mind two questions: (1) do the divergent approaches lead to a different result; and (2) to what extent is the approach adopted by the US Court of Appeals in *Re Bilski* similar to that taken in the EPO or UK?

FURTHER READING

V. M. Janich, 'Sui generis rights for business methods' (2004) IIC 376.

A. Kalpakidou, 'Business method patents: Should they survive in Europe?' (2005) IJL & IT 243.

R. Stern, 'Being within the useful arts as a further constitutional requirement for US patent-eligibility' [2009] EIPR 6.

X. Yu and Y. Zhang, 'The patent protection for business method inventions in China' [2008] EIPR 412.

9.6.4.2 EPO approach

In this field the EPO first adopted the 'technical effect' approach that it had enunciated in *Vicom* and subsequent cases.[177] However, in *Pension Benefit System*, the Technical Board of Appeal applied the 'any hardware' approach, at least in relation to apparatus claims.

PBS Partnership/Pension Benefit System T931/95 [2002] OJEPO 441, [2002] EPOR 522

Claim 1 of the European patent application related to a method of controlling a pension-benefits program, comprising the successive steps of providing employee personal and employment information to data-processing means; determining the average age of all

---

[176] Original references and footnotes omitted.
[177] *Petterson/Queuing System* T1002/92 [1996] EPOR 1.

enrolled employees by average-age computing means; determining the periodic cost of life insurance for all enrolled employees by life-insurance cost computing means; and estimating all administrative, legal, trustee, and government premium yearly expenses for said subscriber employer by administrative-cost computing means, the method producing for the employer information as to his relevant financial liability. Claim 5 was to an apparatus for controlling a pension benefits system comprising a data-processing means and a processor which includes average-age computing means; life insurance-cost computing means; and administrative-cost computing means.

The application was rejected as being non-patentable under Article 52(2)–(3) of the EPC since the subject matter, considered as a whole, related to a method for doing business and lacked any technical character or contribution. The applicant appealed to the Technical Board of Appeal.

Technical Board of Appeal, at pp. 528, 530:

[The Board began by reiterating that 'technical character' is an implicit requirement of patentability under Art. 52 of the EPC. It turned first to consider the method claim:]

Claim 1 of the main request is, apart from various computing means mentioned in that claim, directed to a 'method for controlling a pension benefits program by administering at least one subscriber employer account'. All the features of this claim are steps of processing and producing information having purely administrative, actuarial and/or financial character. Processing and producing such information are typical steps of business and economic methods.

Thus the invention as claimed does not go beyond a method of doing business as such and, therefore, is excluded from patentability under Article 52(2)(c) in combination with Article 52(3) EPC; the claim does not define an invention within the meaning of Article 52(1) EPC.

The appellant referred to the data processing and computing means defined in the method claim, arguing that the use of such means conferred technical character to the method claimed. However, the individual steps defining the claimed method amount to no more than the general teaching to use data processing means for processing or providing information of purely administrative, actuarial and/or financial character, the purpose of each single step and of the method as a whole being a purely economic one.

The feature of using technical means for a purely non-technical purpose and/or for processing purely non-technical information does not necessarily confer technical character to any such individual steps of use or to the method as a whole: in fact, any activity in the non-technical branches of human culture involves physical entities and uses, to a greater or lesser extent, technical means.

Arguments or facts which indicate that the individual steps of the method or the method itself solve any particular technical problem or achieve any technical effect, are not derivable from the patent application and have not been submitted to the board.

The board notes that the mere occurrence of technical features in a claim does thus not turn the subject-matter of the claim into an invention within the meaning of Article 52(1). Such an approach would be too formalistic and would not take due account of the term 'invention'.

[The Technical Board then went on to consider the apparatus claim:]

In the board's view a computer system suitably programmed for use in a particular field, even if that is the field of business and economy, has the character of a concrete apparatus in the sense of a physical entity, man-made for a utilitarian purpose and is thus an invention within the meaning of Article 52(1) EPC.

This distinction with regard to patentability between a method for doing business and an apparatus suited to perform such a method is justified in the light of the wording of Article 52(2)(c) EPC, according to which 'schemes, rules and methods' are non-patentable categories in the field of economy and business, but the category of 'apparatus' in the sense of 'physical entity' or 'product' is not mentioned in Article 52(2) EPC.

This means that, if a claim is directed to such an entity, the formal category of such a claim does in fact imply physical features of the claimed subject-matter which may qualify as technical features of the invention concerned and thus be relevant for its patentability.

Did the Technical Board of Appeal approach the method claim differently to the apparatus claim? If so, how? As mentioned previously, the 'technical contribution' test was jettisoned when the Board considered the apparatus claim because it considered that this confused the requirement of 'invention' with the requirements of novelty and inventive step. But why then did the Board apply this test to the method claim?

Although the apparatus claim in *Pension Benefit System* was not excluded under Article 52(2)–(3) EPC, the Technical Board of Appeal found that it lacked an inventive step. This is because inventive step had to involve technical subject matter and here the improvement on the prior art was non-technical in nature: 'the improvement envisaged by the invention according to the application is an essentially economic one, i.e. lies in the field of economy, which, therefore, cannot contribute to inventive step'.[178] Any technical contribution lay in the programming of a computer system for carrying out the invention; however, that programming and information processing would have been well known and therefore obvious, according to a person skilled in the art (software developer or application programmer).

A later decision of the Technical Board of Appeal entirely rejected the 'technical effect' or 'technical contribution' approach to Article 52(2)–(3) of the EPC, in favour of the 'any hardware' approach. In *Hitachi/Auction Method* T258/03[179] the European patent application claimed an automatic auction method executed in a server computer. It comprised the following series of steps: information about a product to be auctioned is transmitted to bidders; bidders then enter a desired price and a maximum price; the auction price is started high and then lowered until it corresponds with a bid (i.e. desired price); and if it corresponds with more than one bid then the auction price proceeds upwards until there is a singe highest bidder (taken from the maximum price). The application also claimed a 'computerised auction apparatus for performing an automatic auction via a network'.

The Examining Division refused the application on the grounds, *inter alia*, that the method and corresponding apparatus claim fell foul of Article 52(2)–(3) of the EPC for being a method of doing business. On appeal, the Technical Board of Appeal held that Article 52(2)–(3) of the EPC did not exclude the apparatus claim since it comprised technical features such as a 'server computer', 'client computers', and a 'network'. This conclusion was said to be in conformity with *Pension Benefit System* T931/95.

On the question of the method claim, however, the Board departed from its earlier decision in *Pension Benefit System*, finding that the justification for rejecting the 'technical effect'

---

[178] *Pension Benefit System*, p. 532.   [179] [2004] EPOR 55.

approach for apparatus claims was equally applicable to method claims:

> in order to be consistent with the finding that the so-called 'contribution approach', which involves assessing different patentability requirements such as novelty or inventive step, is inappropriate for judging whether claimed subject-matter is an invention within the meaning of Art. 51(2) EPC, there should be no need to further qualify the relevance of technical aspects of a method claim in order to determine the technical character of the method.[180]
>
> [The Board added that it was:]
>
> …not convinced that the wording of Art. 52(2)(c) EPC, according to which 'schemes, rules and methods for performing mental acts, playing games or doing business' shall not be regarded as inventions within the meaning of Art. 52(1) EPC, imposes a different treatment of claims directed to activities and claims directed to entities for carrying out these activities. What matters having regard to the concept of 'invention' within the meaning of Art. 52(1) EPC is the presence of technical character which may be implied by the physical features of an entity or the nature of an activity, or may be conferred to a non-technical activity by the use of technical means. In particular, the Board holds that the latter cannot be considered to be a non-invention 'as such' within the meaning of Arts. 52(2) and (3) EPC. Hence, in the Board's view, activities falling within the notion of non-invention 'as such' would typically represent purely abstract concepts devoid of any technical implications.
>
> The Board is aware that its comparatively broad interpretation of the term 'invention' in Art. 52(1) EPC will include activities which are so familiar that their technical character tends to be overlooked, such as the act of writing using pen and paper. Needless to say, however, this does not imply that all methods involving the use of technical means are patentable. They still have to be new, represent a non-obvious technical solution to a technical problem, and be susceptible of industrial application.[181]

Thus, in *Hitachi* the Technical Board of Appeal adopted the 'any hardware' approach for *both* apparatus and method claims and recognized that a broad interpretation should be given to 'invention'.[182] Do you agree with the Board's view that the same approach must be applied regardless of whether apparatus or method claims are involved? Further, did the Board adopt too generous a view of what can confer 'technical character', i.e. any hardware? Does a generous interpretation matter given that an invention must still satisfy the other validity requirements?

In *Microsoft/Clipboard Formats I* T424/03[183] the approach in *Hitachi* was taken even further in that a computer program stored on a carrier (e.g. a disk) was held to feature technical character. In other words, the technical character was provided by the mere fact that the claim related to a computer-readable medium.

9.6.4.3 UK Approach

The UK courts have thus far refused to follow *Pension Benefit System*, *Hitachi*, or *Microsoft* as the Court of Appeal decision in *Aerotel* illustrates.

---

[180] Ibid., para. 4.3.   [181] Ibid., paras. 4.5 and 4.6.

[182] The divergence in approach to method claims in *Pension Benefit System* and *Hitachi* has yet to be reconciled by the EPO, since the EPO Guidelines still reflect the *Pension Benefit System* approach (see Ch. IV, Part C, para. 2.3.6).

[183] [2006] EPOR 39.

Aerotel Ltd v Telco Holdings Ltd [2007] RPC 7

The case concerned two appeals—the 'Aerotel' appeal and the 'Macrossan' appeal. In the first appeal, Aerotel were appealing the decision of Lewison J to grant summary judgment for revocation of their patent. The invention related to a new method of making telephone calls and a new apparatus for making such calls. The essence of the invention was the use of an extra piece of equipment, called a 'special exchange'. The caller would have an account with the owner of that special exchange and deposit credit with him. The caller also had a code and, to make a call, the caller would dial the number of the special exchange, input the code, and then the caller's number. If the code was verified and there was enough credit the call was connected.

In the second appeal, an application for a UK patent had been made in relation to an automated method of acquiring the documents necessary to incorporate a company. It involved the user sitting at a computer and communicating with a remote server, answering questions. By posing questions, enough information was gleaned from the user's answers to produce the required documents. This application had been rejected by the Patent Office on the ground that the subject matter was unpatentable. The objection was upheld and an appeal to Mann J dismissed.

Jacob LJ (delivering the judgment of the court):

38. The fact is that this court is bound by its own precedent: that decided in *Merill Lynch*, *Gale* and *Fujitsu*—the technical effect approach with the rider. We think we must apply it as we understand it, namely as set out above. That we will proceed to do.

39. However before doing so we must consider the approach which the Comptroller, through Mr Birss, urges upon us. We must in particular consider whether it is consistent with that which has already been decided.

40. The approach is in 4 steps:

(1) properly construe the claim;

(2) identify the actual contribution;

(3) ask whether it falls solely within the excluded subject matter;

(4) check whether the actual or alleged contribution is actually technical in nature.

41. The Comptroller submits that this approach is structured and thus helpful to the public and examiner alike and is consistent with the principles enunciated in *Merrill Lynch*. He further submits:

A structured approach needs to be workable across the whole field of Section 1(2). This is important because although the policy behind different exclusions is not uniform, the structure of the legislation requires that they ought to work the same way. A structured approach will also allow the examiners and hearing officers applying this area of law to follow a consistent scheme and will allow the public to see how a decision has been arrived at. A problem the Comptroller is often confronted with is reliance by applicants on broad observations from earlier decisions which work well in the particular circumstances in which they were made but break down when applied elsewhere. (Mr Birss' skeleton argument).

We think this structured approach is indeed consistent with what has been decided by this court. It is a re-formulation in a different order of the *Merill Lynch* test.

42. No-one could quarrel with the first step—construction. You first have to decide what the monopoly is before going on the question of whether it is excluded. Any test must involve this first step.

43. The second step—identify the contribution—is said to be more problematical. How do you assess the contribution? Mr Birss submits the test is workable—it is an exercise in judgment probably involving the problem said to be solved, how the invention works, what its advantages are. What has the inventor really added to human knowledge perhaps best sums up the exercise. The formulation involves looking at substance not form—which is surely what the legislator intended.

44. Mr Birss added the words 'or alleged contribution' in his formulation of the second step. That will do at the application stage—where the Office must generally perforce accept what the inventor says is his contribution. It cannot actually be conclusive, however. If an inventor claims a computer when programmed with his new program, it will not assist him if he alleges wrongly that he has invented the computer itself, even if he specifies all the detailed elements of a computer in his claim. In the end the test must be what contribution has actually been made, not what the inventor says he has made.

45. The third step—is the contribution solely of excluded matter?—is merely an expression of the 'as such' qualification of Art. 52(3). During the course of argument Mr Birss accepted a re-formulation of the third step: Ask whether the contribution thus identified consists of excluded subject matter as such? We think either formulation will do—they mean the same thing.

46. The fourth step—check whether the contribution is 'technical'—may not be necessary because the third step should have covered that. It is a necessary check however if one is to follow *Merrill Lynch* as we must.

Applying the 'technical effect' structured approach to the Aerotel invention the court held that the contribution was a new system. Although it used conventional computers, the key to it was a new physical combination of hardware and, as such, there was more than just a method of doing business as such. Finally, the system was clearly technical in nature.[184]

In relation to the Macrossan application, the court dismissed the appeal on the basis that this was a method of doing business, or a computer program, as such. The contribution was an interactive system which would do the job otherwise done by a solicitor or company formation agent. This method was for the very business of advising upon and creating appropriate company formation documents. Further, there was nothing technical about the contribution beyond the mere fact of the running of a computer program.[185]

9.6.5 CONCLUSION

Most recently, the Court of Appeal in *Symbian Ltd*[186] followed the *Aerotel* approach to s. 1(2) of the PA 77. Thus, the divergence between the UK and EPO in this area is likely to continue for the foreseeable future, unless a ruling from the Enlarged Board of Appeal clarifies matters in a manner that UK courts see fit to follow.

Between the UK 'technical effect' and the EPO 'any hardware' approaches which in your view is preferable? Or are both undesirable? Is a viable alternative simply to delete the exclusions contained in s. 1(2) of the PA 77 and Article 52(2)–(3) of the EPC and allow courts flexibly to interpret 'invention' to cover new forms of technology?

---

[184] Aerotel, paras. 51–4.   [185] Ibid., paras. 63–72.   [186] [2008] EWCA Civ 1066.

FURTHER READING

J. Pila, 'Dispute over the meaning of "invention" in Article 52(2) EPC: The patentability of computer-implemented inventions in Europe' (2005) 36 IIC 173.

9.7 BIOTECHNOLOGICAL INVENTIONS

9.7.1 INTRODUCTION

In the next section we consider exclusions from patentability that are particularly relevant to biotechnological inventions. These are discoveries as such; plant and animal varieties and non-microbiological processes for their production; and inventions which are contrary to ordre public or morality. It should be stressed that these exclusions are not confined to biotechnological inventions. Nevertheless, it is fair to say that they have assumed increased significance in the light of modern biotechnological research. Indeed, the Biotechnology Directive sought to harmonize the approach to these exclusions.[187]

Before turning to examine the exclusions in detail, it is worth pausing to consider how classical biotechnology differs from modern biotechnology, since it is the latter that has caused most problems for patent law in recent years. Phillip Grubb explains the difference thus:[188]

Classical biotechnology may be defined loosely as the production of useful products by living micro-organisms, and as such it has been with us for a long time. The production of ethanol from yeast cells is as old as history, and over 50 years ago the production of various industrial chemicals such as acetic acid and acetone by fermentation processes was well known.

. . .

What may be described as modern biotechnology, as distinct from the classical fermentation technology, began in the 1970s with the two basic techniques of recombinant DNA technology and hybridoma technology. In the first of these, also referred to as gene splicing or genetic engineering, genetic material from an external source is inserted into a cell in such a way that it causes the production of a desired protein by the cell; in the second, different types of immune cell are fused together to form a hybrid cell line producing monoclonal antibodies. More recently, the techniques of genetic engineering have been applied to higher organisms to produce transgenic animals and plants, and even to humans (gene therapy) for example to replace missing or defective genes coding for a protein required by the body, or to introduce genes into cancer cells which will render them easier to kill.

9.7.2 DISCOVERIES

According to s. 1(2) of the PA 77 and also Article 52(2)–(3) of the EPC, a discovery as such is not an invention. In the context of biotechnological research it has been argued that identification of a gene[189] is simply a discovery because the gene already exists in nature. By way

---

[187] Discussed above at 9.4.2.5.
[188] P. Grubb, *Patents for Chemicals, Pharmaceuticals and Biotechnology* (4th edn., Oxford: Oxford University Press, 2004), p. 246.
[189] A gene is a discrete segment of DNA molecules that contain the information necessary for producing specific proteins.

of response, it has been argued that the invention is not the naturally occurring gene but rather an isolated form of that gene and thus it has technical character. The following decision of the Technical Board of Appeal illustrates the approach the EPO has taken to these arguments.

Howard Florey/Relaxin [1995] EPOR 541

The patent granted related to a process for obtaining H2-relaxin and the complementary DNA sequence coding for H2-relaxin. H2-relaxin is a naturally occurring hormone in the human ovaries that relaxes the uterus during childbirth. The complementary DNA sequence coding for this hormone had been isolated from ovarian tissue removed in the treatment of an ectopic pregnancy. The Green Party opposed the grant of the patent on several grounds, including that it was a discovery and thus not patentable under Article 52(2)(a) EPC. The Opposition Division of the EPO rejected this argument.

> 5.1 …This argument ignores the long-standing practice of the European Patent Office concerning the patentability of natural substances. As explained in the Guidelines, C-IV, 2.3, to find a substance freely occurring in nature is mere discovery and therefore unpatentable. However, if a substance found in nature has first to be isolated from its surroundings and a process for obtaining it is developed, that process is patentable. Moreover, if this substance can be properly characterised by its structure and it is new in the absolute sense of having no previously recognised existence, then the substance *per se* may be patentable.
>
> 5.2 The above guideline is highly appropriate in the present case. Human H2-relaxin had no previously recognised existence. The proprietor has developed a process for obtaining H2-relaxin and the DNA encoding it, has characterised these products by their chemical structure and has found a use for the protein. The products are therefore patentable under Article 52(2) EPC.

The logic reflected in the above passage—that isolating a substance found in nature gives it sufficient technical character to avoid being a mere discovery—was adopted in the Biotechnology Directive, Articles 3 and 5.[190] Thus, Article 3(2) provides:

> (2) Biological material which is isolated from its natural environment or produced by means of a technical process may be the subject of an invention even if it previously occurred in nature.

Similarly, in the context of the human body, Article 5 of the Biotechnology Directive provides:

> (1) The human body, at the various stages of its formation and development, and the simple discovery of one its elements, including the sequence or partial sequence of a gene cannot constitute patentable inventions.
>
> (2) An element isolated from the human body or otherwise produced by means of a technical process, including the sequence or partial sequence of a gene, may constitute a patentable invention, even if that element is identical to that of a natural element.

---

[190] Which have been implemented in the PA 77, Sch. A2.

Do you find convincing the view that technical character is conferred either via the process of isolating a gene sequence or because an artificial molecule of that gene sequence has been created? Does such a view give proper weight to the exclusion of discoveries *as such*?

FURTHER READING

Nuffield Council, *Discussion Paper on The Ethics of Patenting DNA* (July 2002), pp. 27–8.

9.7.3 PLANT VARIETIES

Article 53(b) of the EPC provides that a European patent shall not be granted in respect of plant varieties or essentially biological processes for the production of plants.[191] The origin of this exclusion may be explained in the light of sui generis plant breeder's protection that had been established in accordance with the International Convention for the Protection of New Varieties of Plants 1961 ('UPOV Convention'). It was desired that plant breeders be prevented from obtaining dual protection under both plant breeder's legislation and patent law. To that end, a prohibition on double protection was included in Article 2(1) of the UPOV Convention (although subsequently deleted when the Convention was revised in 1991). Article 53(b) of the EPC was included to give effect to this aim.[192]

The concept of 'plant variety' is not defined in the EPC and there is no generally recognized taxonomic definition of 'variety' as there is for 'species' and 'genus'. The concept of 'plant variety' was considered by the Boards of Appeal of the EPO on a few occasions[193] and subsequently harmonized by the Biotechnology Directive. Article 2(3) of the Biotechnology Directive defines 'plant variety' according to Article 5 of Regulation (EC) 2100/94 on Community plant variety rights, which states that 'plant variety':

> shall be taken to mean a plant grouping within a single botanical taxon of the lowest known rank, which grouping...can be:
>
> - defined by the expression of the characteristics that results from a given genotype or combination of genotypes,
> - distinguished from any other plant grouping by the expression of at least one of the said characteristics, and
> - considered as a unit with regard to its suitability for being propagated unchanged.

This definition has been implemented into UK law as para. 11 of Sch. A2 of the PA 77.

The first case involving a genetically engineered plant to come before the Technical Board of Appeal was *Plant Genetic Systems/Glutamine synthetase inhibitors* T356/93.[194]

---

[191] Prior to the implementation of the Biotechnology Directive, this exclusion was contained in s. 1(3)(b), PA 77. It is now contained in para. 3(f) of Sch. A2, PA 77.

[192] For a more detailed discussion of the historical background to Art. 53(b) see the decision of the Enlarged Board of Appeal in *Novartis/Transgenic plant* [2000] EPOR 303, 315–18.

[193] Including *Ciba Geigy/Propagating material* T49/83 [1979–85] EPOR C758; *Lubrizol/Hybrid plants* T320/87 [1990] EPOR 173; *Plant Genetic Systems/Glutamine synthetase inhibitors* T356/93 [1995] EPOR 357.

[194] [1995] EPOR 357.

It concerned a European patent relating to plants and plant cells that possessed a foreign gene which made them resistant to a type of herbicide. This allowed farmers to spray their crops with the herbicide safe in the knowledge that it would only affect the unmodified weeds. The claims related to processes for producing the modified plants and plant cells and also to the modified plants and plant cells themselves. In opposition proceedings it was contended, *inter alia*, that the claims were not patentable according to Article 53(b) of the EPC. The Technical Board of Appeal held that the claim relating to modified plant cells was not excluded as a 'plant variety'. However, the claim relating to modified plants *was* held to fall within the 'plant variety' exclusion. This was so, even though the claim was not drafted in terms of a variety description (because there was no reference to a single botanical taxon of the lowest-known rank). Rather, the claim was in general directed to a plant which possessed, integrated in its genome in a stable manner, a heterologous DNA containing a foreign nucelotide sequence encoding a protein having a non-variety specific enzymatic activity capable of neutralizing or inactivating a glutamine synthetase inhibitor. The working examples of the patent, however, showed that the practical forms of realization of the invention according to this claim were genetically transformed plant varieties. Thus, since the claim *encompassed* plant varieties (even though it was not drafted in terms of a variety description), it was held to fall within the plant variety exclusion in Article 53(b). The Technical Board of Appeal reasoned that this had to be the case otherwise the Article 53(b) exclusion could be evaded too easily.

This aspect of the *Plant Genetic Systems* decision was particularly controversial because it meant that, in most cases, plants produced as a result of genetic engineering would be unpatentable. A referral of the case to the Enlarged Board by Appeal by the President of the EPO was rejected and it was not until the *Novartis* decision (considered below) that the Enlarged Board of Appeal overruled the approach taken in *Plant Genetic Systems*. Prior to *Novartis*, however, the Biotechnology Directive had been adopted and addressed this particular issue in Article 4. Specifically, Article 4 states:

1. The following shall not be patentable:
   (a) plant and animal varieties;
   (b) ...
2. Inventions which concern plants or animals shall be patentable if the technical feasibility of the invention is not confined to a particular plant or animal variety.

Article 4(1) of the Biotechnology Directive corresponds to Article 53(b) of the EPC. However, Article 4(2) allows claims to plants which embrace more than one variety. This is made clear from recital 31, which states:

Whereas a plant grouping which is characterised by a particular gene (and not its whole genome) is not covered by the protection of new varieties and is therefore not excluded from patentability even if it comprises new varieties of plants.

As a result of Article 4(2) of the Biotechnology Directive, a discrepancy existed between the approach taken in the directive and that taken in *Plant Genetic Systems*. This discrepancy was, however, resolved by the Enlarged Board of Appeal in *Novartis*.

Novartis/Transgenic plant G01/98 [2000] EPOR 303

The European Patent application in suit contained claims to genetically modified plants, and methods for producing such plants, comprising in their genomes specific recombinant DNA sequences, the expression of which resulted in the plants becoming pathogen-resistant (i.e. resistant to fungi). The Examining Division refused the application on the basis that several of the claims did not satisfy Article 53(b) of the EPC. It followed *Plant Genetic Systems* on the issue of whether a claim to genetically engineered plants and seeds generally, but which encompassed plant varieties, was not allowable under Article 53(b). On appeal, the Technical Board of Appeal decided to refer questions to the Enlarged Board of Appeal.[195] The Enlarged Board emphasized that the claimed invention neither expressly nor implicitly encompassed a plant variety and went on to consider whether a claim that encompassed a plant variety, but was not to a plant variety per se, was caught by Article 53(b) of the EPC.

Enlarged Board of Appeal:

3.3.1 . . . whereas the exclusion for processes is related to the production of plants, the exclusion for products is related to plant varieties. The use of the more specific term 'variety' within the same half-sentence of the provision relating to products is supposed to have some meaning. If it was the intention to exclude plants as a group embracing in general varieties as products, the provision would use the more general term plants as used for the processes.

The Enlarged Board then examined in detail the history of Article 53(b) of the EPC and its origins in Article 2(b) of the Strasbourg Patent Convention, which in turn sought to implement the ban on dual protection in the UPOV Convention. Thus, the intention was that the exclusion in the EPC should correspond to the availability of protection in the UPOV Convention. It continued:

3.8 . . . Whereas in the case of a plant variety, the breeder has to develop a plant grouping fulfilling in particular the requirements of homogeneity and stability, this is not the case with a typical genetic engineering invention in a claim such as that referred to in question 2. The inventor in the latter case aims at providing tools whereby a desired property can be bestowed on plants by inserting a gene into the genome of those plants. Providing these tools is a step which precedes the further step of introducing the gene into a specific plant. Nevertheless, it is the contribution of the inventor in the genetic field which makes it possible to take the second step and insert the gene into the genome of any appropriate plant or plant variety. Choosing a suitable plant for this purpose and arriving at a specific, marketable product, which will mostly be a plant variety, is a matter of routine breeding steps which may be rewarded by a plant breeders' right. The inventor in the genetic engineering field would not obtain appropriate protection if he were restricted to specific varieties for two reasons: first, the development of specific varieties will often not be in his field of activity and, secondly he would always be limited to a few varieties even though he had provided the means for inserting the gene into all appropriate plants.

3.10 In summary, according to Article 53(b) EPC, a patent is 'in respect of plant varieties' and shall not be granted if the claimed subject-matter is directed to plant varieties. In the

---

[195] See *Novartis/Transgenic plant* T1054/96 [1999] EPOR 123 for the referring decision of the TBA.

absence of the identification of a specific plant variety in a product claim, the subject-matter of the claimed invention is not directed to a plant variety or varieties within the meaning of Article 53(b) EPC. This is why it is, contrary to the conclusions of the referring Board, in agreement with the rules of logic that a patent shall not be granted for a single plant variety but can be granted if varieties may fall within the scope of its claims. The conclusion of the referring Board is based on the premise that a claim is necessarily 'in respect of' a certain subject if it may comprise this subject. For Article 53(b) EPC, this interpretation is, as set out above, at odds with the purpose of the provision. It disregards the fact that Article 53(b) EPC defines the borderline between patent protection and plant variety protection. The extent of the exclusion for patents is the obverse of the availability of plant variety rights. The latter are only granted to specific plant varieties and not for technical teachings which can be implemented in an indefinite number of plant varieties…It is not sufficient for the exclusion of Article 53(b) EPC to apply that one or more plant varieties are embraced or may be embraced by the claims.

Was the Enlarged Board's narrow construction of Article 53(b) of the EPC heavily influenced by the purpose of that provision to prohibit dual protection under plant variety rights and patent law? If so, why is it that an invention relating to a genetically engineered plant, but not specifically claiming a plant variety, would not be adequately protected by plant variety rights?

Should the decision of the Enlarged Board of Appeal in *Novartis* be welcomed on the grounds that it engenders consistency between Article 53(b) of the EPC and the Biotechnology Directive? If so, do any residual difficulties remain, such as attempts by patent applicants to avoid the Article 53(b) exclusion by the way in which they draft their claims? Finally, as has been suggested by Margaret Llewelyn, would it make sense to delete the exclusion altogether? Or, alternatively, to extend the exclusion to cover all plant material, thus leaving plant variety rights, and not patent law, to govern this type of subject matter?[196]

FURTHER READING

M. Llewelyn, 'The patentability of biological material: Continuing contradiction and confusion' [2000] EIPR 191.

S. Bostyn, 'The patentability of genetic information carriers' [1999] IPQ 1.

9.7.4 ANIMAL VARIETIES

Article 53(b) of the EPC provides that a European patent shall not be granted in respect of animal varieties or any essentially biological processes for the production of animals.[197] The scope of this exclusion has been considered on several occasions by the EPO in relation to the *Harvard/Onco-Mouse* patent.

A European patent application was filed on 24 June 1985 by the President and Fellows of Harvard College in respect of the (now infamous) onco-mouse. The patent application

---

[196] M. Llewelyn, 'The patentability of biological material: Continuing contradiction and confusion' [2000] *EIPR* 191.

[197] Prior to the implementation of the Biotechnology Directive, this exclusion was contained in s. 1(3)(b), PA 77. It is now contained in para. 3(f), Sch. A2, PA 77.

claimed a method for producing a transgenic[198] non-human mammalian animal having an increased likelihood of developing cancer, which would prove useful in cancer research. The method involved introducing an activated oncogene into a non-human mammalian animal. The application also claimed the transgenic non-human mammalian animals produced by this method, in particular transgenic rodents. The Examining Division of the EPO refused the application on the basis that the claims fell foul of Article 53(b).[199] The Examining Division took the view that Article 53(b), as it relates to animal varieties, should not be interpreted restrictively as had been done for plant varieties. This was because the plant-variety exclusion existed to avoid double protection (of patents and plant varieties) and a similar situation did not exist in relation to animal varieties. The Examining Division therefore interpreted Article 53(b) 'to refer not only to these cases where a specifically designated variety is claimed but also to cases where varieties are covered by a claim'.[200] Since the claims covered an animal variety they were excluded by Article 53(b) of the EPC.

On appeal, the Technical Board of Appeal set aside the decision and remitted the case back to the Examining Division for the reasons expressed below.

Harvard/Onco-mouse T19/90 [1990] OJ EPO 476, [1990] EPOR 501

Technical Board of Appeal:

4.2 As pointed out by the Examining Division, the three texts of Article 53(b) EPC differ in terminology as to the non-patentable area. In particular, the German term 'Tierarten' is broader than the English 'animal varieties' and the French 'races animales'.

4.3 Article 177(1) EPC lays down that the English, French and German texts of the EPC are all equally authentic. In the present case, there is obviously a need to establish their common meaning through interpretation of the Convention in order to determine to what extent animals are excluded form patentability under Article 53(b), first half-sentence, EPC.

4.4 In the Decision under appeal the Examining Division interpreted Article 53(b) EPC as excluding not only certain groups of animals from patentability but, in fact, animals as such. The Board is unable to accept this interpretation.

4.5 Firstly, the Examining Division did not take duly into account that Article 53(b) EPC is an exception, for certain kinds of inventions, to the general rule under Article 52(1) EPC that European patents 'shall be' granted for all inventions which are susceptible of industrial application, which are new and which involve an inventive step. Any such exception must, as repeatedly pointed out by the Boards of Appeal, be narrowly construed (cf. in particular T320/87, point 6, OJ EPO 1990, 76). The Examining Division has given no convincing reasons for deviating in this particular case from this principle of interpretation, nor are any such reasons apparent to the Board.

4.6 The possibility that the reference to certain categories of animals rather than to animals as such was simply a mistake by the legislators can be ruled out. Nothing in the legislative history of either the EPC or the Strasbourg Convention of 27 November 1963 on the Unification of Certain Points of Substantive Law on Patents for Invention, whose Article 2(b) was taken over and incorporated into Article 53(b) EPC, supports such an assumption. On the contrary, a clear indication that the terms 'animal varieties', 'races animales' and 'Tierarten' were not intended to cover animals as such is the wording of Article 53(b) EPC itself. The very same

---

[198] i.e. genetically modified.
[199] *Harvard/Onco-Mouse Application* No. 85 304 490.7 [1990] EPOR 4.   [200] Ibid., para. 7.1.2.

provision also contains, as appears from paragraph 4.1 above, a reference to 'animals' (in general). In using the different terms 'animal varieties' ('races animales', 'Tierarten') and 'animals' ('animaux', 'Tiere') in this way, the legislators cannot have meant 'animals' in both cases.

4.7 In contrast to the exclusion of 'plant varieties' from patentability under Article 53(b) EPC (cf. T320/87—see above), the preparatory documents to this provision are completely silent as to the purpose of excluding 'animal varieties' from patentability. However, the purpose of a law (*ratio legis*) is not merely a matter of the actual intention of the legislators at the time when the law was adopted, but also of their presumed intention in the light of changes in circumstances which have taken place since then. It is now the task of the European Patent Office to find a solution to the problem of the interpretation of Article 53(b) EPC with regard to the concept of 'animal varieties', providing a proper balance between the interest of inventors in this field in obtaining reasonable protection for their efforts and society's interest in excluding certain categories of animals from patent protection. In this context it should, *inter alia*, be borne in mind that for animals—unlike plant varieties—no other industrial property right is available for the time being.

4.8 To sum up, the Board concludes that the Examining Division was wrong in refusing the present application on the ground that Article 53(b) EPC excludes the patenting of animals as such. The proper issue to be considered is, therefore, whether or not the subject-matter of the application is an 'animal variety' ('race animale', 'Tierart') within the meaning of Article 53(b) EPC. On this point the contested decision is for obvious reasons entirely silent. In view of the importance of this matter and the desirability of having it considered by at least two instances, the Board will exercise its powers under Article 111(1) EPC to remit the case to the department of first instance for further prosecution. It should also be noted that a number of questions outlined below and not yet dealt with by the Examining Division now need to be considered.

In its resumed examination with regard to Article 53(b) EPC, the Examining Division must, as indicated above, first consider whether the subject-matter of the present application constitutes an 'animal variety', 'race animale' or 'Tierart' within the meaning of that provision. If it comes to the conclusion that the subject-matter is not covered by any of these three terms, then Article 53(b) EPC constitutes no bar to patentability. If, however, it considers that any of these terms applies, then refusal of the application would only be justified if that specific term represents the proper interpretation of Article 53(b) (see point 4.3 above). This would also presuppose that Article 53(b) EPC can be applied at all in respect of animals which are genetically manipulated, given that neither the drafters of the Strasbourg Convention nor those of the EPC could envisage this possibility.

What were the main reasons given by the Technical Board of Appeal for rejecting the argument that Article 53(b) of the EPC excludes the patenting of animals as such?

The case was remitted back to the Examining Division, which considered whether the application constituted an 'animal variety', '*race animale*' or '*Tierart*' within the meaning of Article 53(b) of the EPC. The Examining Division[201] held that the exact scope of 'animal variety' was not clear given the differing wording in the three official languages of the EPC. Nevertheless, it concluded that rodents constituted a taxonomic classification unit much higher than species and thus it was unnecessary to determine whether Article 53(b) of the EPC referred to species or sub-unit of a species. The patent was granted in favour of the applicants on 15 May 1992.

---

[201] *Harvard/Onco-mouse Application* No. 85 304 490.7 [1991] EPOR 525.

After grant, 17 oppositions were filed against the patent on a variety of grounds, including that the patent was contrary to Article 53(b) of the EPC. In the meantime, the Biotechnology Directive had been adopted. Between the time when the oppositions were filed and the opposition proceedings were decided, the Administrative Council of the European Patent Organization had implemented the relevant provisions of the Biotechnology Directive by adding r. 23b–e of the EPC to Part II of the Implementing Regulations.[202] Relevantly, Article 4(1)(a) of the Biotechnology Directive states that animal varieties shall not be patentable. However, Article 4(2) provides that 'Inventions which concern…animals shall be patentable if the technical feasibility of the invention is not confined to a particular…animal variety.'

The Opposition Division considered whether new r. 23b–e of the EPC, implementing the Biotechnology Directive, was applicable to the opposition proceedings in hand.[203] It held that '[a]s a general rule, in the absence of transitional provisions, administrative and judicial bodies have to apply the law as it stands at the date when a decision is taken' and that this applied to pending patent cases, whether in examination or in opposition. Only in exceptional circumstances would this not be the case.[204] Given that the new r. 23b–e of the EPC did not constitute a major departure from the previous law, but merely interpreted relevant provisions of the EPC, there was no need to restrict the applicability of the new rules.

The Opposition Division went on to consider patentability of animals under Article 53(b) of the EPC as it relates to animal varieties. It followed the earlier Technical Board of Appeal decision in *Onco-mouse*. It also referred to the decision of the Enlarged Board in *Novartis* and stated that the holding could be transferred to the interpretation of the exclusion of animal varieties. More specifically, it held that claims to animals that encompassed an animal variety or varieties would not be caught by the exclusion, but only claims directed to an animal variety or varieties per se. On the facts, the Opposition Division held that the invention as claimed was applicable to more than just varieties of mice and thus Article 53(b) of the EPC was not a bar to patentability.

9.7.5 ESSENTIALLY BIOLOGICAL PROCESSES FOR THE PRODUCTION OF PLANTS AND ANIMALS

Article 53(b) of the EPC, in addition to excluding animal and plant varieties from patentability, also excludes essentially biological processes for the production of plants or animals. This exclusion was reiterated in the Biotechnology Directive, Article 4(1)(b). The exclusion is limited to *processes* where those processes are *essentially* biological. This, of course, begs the question: when is a process *essentially* biological in nature? The Technical Board of Appeal considered this issue in *Novartis* and identified three possible approaches to determining when a process is essentially biological.

Novartis/Transgenic plant T1054/96 [1999] EPOR 123

Technical Board of Appeal:

26. One approach is analogous to that used under Article 52(4) EPC relating to methods of treatment by surgery and therapy. As stated for example in Decision T820/92 (OJ EPO

---

[202] These Rules entered into force on 1 Sept. 1999.   [203] In its Decision [2003] 10 OJ EPO 473.
[204] Ibid., para. 9.7.2.

1995, 113) 'in the case of a method involving administration of two or more substances, the question for the purposes of Article 52(4) EPC is not whether the main or even the only reason for carrying out the whole of the claimed method is non-therapeutic. Rather, a method claim falls under the prohibition of Article 52(4) EPC if the administration of one of the substances is a treatment by therapy, and the administration of this substance is a feature of the claim.'

27. The consequences of such an approach would be that to be considered as 'non essentially biological', the claimed process for producing plants should only comprise clearly identified non-biological process steps and no 'essentially biological' steps (whatever uncertainties may be attached to the term). A process involving the crossing of two existing plants such as in Claim 24 would not be allowable. This approach would have the advantage that it would be clear to applicants what steps to mention in a claim.

28. A second approach would be that adopted in Decision T320/87 (OJ EPO 1990, 71) where it was held that whether or not a process is to be considered as 'essentially biological' has to be judged on the basis of the essence of the invention, taking into account the totality of human intervention and its impact on the result achieved (see point 6 of the Reasons). The consequences of such an approach, as discussed in T356/93 (see above, point 28 of the Reasons), would be that 'a process for the production of plants comprising at least one essential technical step, which cannot be carried out without human intervention and which has a decisive impact on the final result does not fall under the exceptions to patentability under Article 53(b) EPC first half sentence'. Following such an approach leaves it to the instances of the EPO to assess whether a claim as a whole is directed to an 'essentially biological process for the production of plants'. Its outcome could be relatively uncertain.

29. Yet another approach would require, for a process for the production of plants to escape the prohibition of Article 53(b) EPC with regard to essentially biological processes, at least one clearly identified 'non-biological' process step but allow any number of additional 'essentially biological steps' which would be carried into allowability by the 'non-biological' process step. The definition given in the proposed EU Directive, Art. 2(2) adopts this approach. The definition is 'A process for the production of plants or animals is essentially biological if it consists entirely of natural phenomena such as crossing or selection'. This approach would be that most favourable to applicants. It is not the approach so far adopted by the Boards of Appeal.

Article 2(2) of the Biotechnology Directive, as adopted, states that, 'a process for the production of plants or animals is essentially biological if it consists entirely of nature phenomena such as crossing or selection'.[205] This interpretation reflects the third approach identified by the Technical Board of Appeal in *Novartis*. Thus, following the Biotechnology Directive, it seems that if a process of production of plants or animals includes a technical intervention it will no longer consist *entirely* of natural phenomena and thus will not be classed as essentially biological.

9.7.6 MICROBIOLOGICAL PROCESSES FOR THE PRODUCTION OF PLANTS AND ANIMALS

Notably, Article 53(b) of the EPC contains a qualification to the exclusion for plant or animal varieties or essentially biological processes for the production of plants or animals. This is where the process is a microbiological process or the product thereof.

---

[205] This has been implemented in para. 11 of Sch. A2 of PA 77.

Prior to the Biotechnology Directive, the issue arose whether technical processes *including* a microbiological step could be equated with microbiological processes. In *Plant Genetic Systems* the Technical Board of Appeal opined that the process had to be judged as a whole and that, where it was really a technical process that included a microbiological step, it would not constitute a microbiological process.

Subsequently, the Biotechnology Directive was adopted. Article 4(3) of the Biotechnology Directive states that the exclusion in Article 4(1) (for plant or animal varieties and essentially biological processes), 'shall be without prejudice to the patentability of inventions which concern a microbiological or other technical process or a product obtained by means of such a process.' Article 2 of the Biotechnology Directive defines 'microbiological process' as 'any process involving or performed upon or resulting in microbiological material.' Given that Article 4(3) refers to microbiological *or other technical processes* it seems that technical processes which include a microbiological step (e.g. manipulation of micro-organisms by genetic engineering or fusion techniques) will be covered by the qualification and thus held not to fall foul of the exclusion set out in Article 4(1). However, it is worth remembering that product claims for plant or animal varieties cannot be allowed, even if the variety is produced by means of a microbiological process. This is because the exception to patentability in Article 53(b) relating to plant or animal varieties applies *irrespective* of the way in which they are produced.

9.7.7 *ORDRE PUBLIC* AND MORALITY

9.7.7.1 Pre Biotechnology Directive

Since the Statute of Monopolies 1624, it has been a principle of UK patent law that inventions which are contrary to law or morality are excluded from protection. Prior to UK implementation of the Biotechnology Directive, the *ordre public* and morality exclusion was contained in s. 1(3)(a) of the PA 77. This section provided that a patent 'shall not be granted...for an invention the publication or exploitation of which would be generally expected to encourage offensive, immoral or anti-social behaviour'. Section 1(4) of the PA 77 then went on to qualify that behaviour would not be offensive, immoral, or anti-social simply because it was illegal in the UK. These provisions were intended to give effect to the comparable exemption in the EPC, Article 53(a) which states that European patents shall not be granted in respect of:

> inventions the publication or exploitation of which would be contrary to 'ordre public' or morality, provided that the exploitation shall not be deemed to be so merely because it is prohibited by law or regulation in some or all of the Contracting States.[206]

With the advent of biotechnological research and subsequent attempts to patent genetically engineered inventions, this exclusion has been invoked with reasonable frequency and its scope interpreted on a number of occasions.

The first such occasion was in the *Onco-mouse* decision. As already discussed above, the application claimed a non-human mammal (such as a mouse), into which an oncogene had been inserted which would make it susceptible to cancer. The Examining Division

---

206 Note that the wording of Art. 53(a) has changed as a result of the EPC 2000. It now refers to 'inventions the commercial exploitation of which would be contrary to "ordre public" or morality'.

considered that patent law was an inappropriate legislative tool for assessing the ethical and environmental considerations associated with the patenting of genetically modified animals and thus did not refuse the application on the basis of Article 53(a) of the EPC.[207] On appeal, the Technical Board of Appeal directed the Examining Division to apply this exclusion for the reasons expressed in the following passage:[208]

> The Board considers, however, that precisely in a case of this kind there are compelling reasons to consider the implications of Article 53(a) EPC in relation to the question of patentability. The genetic manipulation of mammalian animals is undeniably problematical in various respects, particularly where activated oncogenes are inserted to make an animal abnormally sensitive to carcinogenic substances and stimuli and consequently prone to develop tumours, which necessarily cause suffering. There is also a danger that genetically manipulated animals, if released into the environment, might entail unforeseeable and irreversible adverse effects. Misgivings and fears of this kind have been expressed by a number of persons who have filed observations with the Board under Article 115 EPC. Considerations of precisely this kind have also led a number of Contracting States to impose legislative control on genetic engineering. The decision as to whether or not Article 53(a) EPC is a bar to patenting the present invention would seem to depend mainly on a careful weighing up of the suffering of animals and possible risks to the environment on the one hand, and the invention's usefulness to mankind on the other. It is the task of the department of first instance to consider these matters in the context of its resumed examination of the case.

Do you agree with the view of the Technical Board of Appeal that Article 53(a) of the EPC should be considered in relation to inventions involving genetically modified animals or with the view of the Examining Division that the EPO is an inappropriate forum in which to assess such ethical issues? Further, would you describe the Technical Board's approach to Article 53(a) as utilitarian? If so, is this an appropriate ethical framework by which to determine whether certain kinds of invention should be patentable?

The case was later remitted back to the Examining Division, which sought to weigh up the risks and benefits to mankind of the onco-mouse.[209] The Examining Division found that the invention's usefulness to mankind could not be doubted, given that cancer is a frequent cause of death and suffering in many countries. Further, the use of genetically engineered rodents in cancer research was likely to involve fewer animals than was the case with conventional research and thus contribute 'to a reduction of the overall extent of animal suffering'. There was also evidence to suggest that animal testing was indispensable to cancer research. The Examining Division did not consider that the invention would pose risks to the environment, given that it would be used in controlled laboratory conditions by qualified staff. Further, it commented that exclusion from patentability could not be justified 'merely because a technology is dangerous' and that the regulation of dangerous activity was the task of specialist government authorities and not that of the EPO. Thus, the Examining Division concluded that the invention could not be considered as contrary to public order or morality.

Did the Examining Division's assessment of whether the invention fell foul of Article 53(a) of the EPC take into account general objections in principle to the patenting of transgenic

---

[207] *Harvard/Onco-mouse* [1990] EPOR 4, para. 10.3.
[208] *Harvard/Onco-mouse* T19/90 [1990] EPOR 501, 513.
[209] *Harvard/Onco-mouse* [1991] EPOR 525, 527–8.

animals or were the moral considerations limited to the special circumstances of the case? If the latter, does this reflect a failure to engage in a comprehensive moral assessment?[210]

Transgenic plants have also been subjected to scrutiny according to Article 53(a) of the EPC, as illustrated by *Plant Genetic Systems*.[211] In this case, which involved transgenic plants and plant cells resistant to herbicide, the Technical Board of Appeal did not adopt a balancing exercise of advantages and disadvantages of the invention. This was because no sufficient evidence of actual disadvantages had been adduced and the 'balancing' approach was seen as just one possible way of assessing patentability according to Article 53(a).[212] The Board began by articulating the scope of the concepts of *ordre public* and morality under Article 53(a) of the EPC:

> It is generally accepted that the concept of 'ordre public' covers the protection of public security and the physical integrity of individuals as part of society. This concept encompasses also the protection of the environment. Accordingly, under Article 53(a) EPC, inventions the exploitation of which is likely to breach public peace or social order (for example, through acts of terrorism) or seriously to prejudice the environment are to be excluded from patentability as being contrary to 'ordre public'.
>
> The concept of morality is related to the belief that some behaviour is right and acceptable whereas other behaviour is wrong, this belief being founded on the totality of the accepted norms which are deeply rooted in a particular culture. For the purposes of the EPC, the culture in question is the culture inherent in European society and civilisation. Accordingly, under Article 53(a) EPC, inventions the exploitation of which is *not* in conformity with the conventionally-accepted standards of conduct pertaining to this culture are to be excluded from patentability as being contrary to morality.
>
> The second half-sentence of Article 53(a) EPC contains the qualification 'that the exploitation shall not be deemed to be so contrary merely because it is prohibited by law or regulation in some or all of the Contracting States'. This qualification makes clear that the assessment of whether or not a particular subject-matter is to be considered contrary to either 'ordre public' or morality is not dependent on any national laws or regulations. Conversely and by the same token, the Board is of the opinion that a particular subject-matter shall not automatically be regarded as complying with the requirements of Article 53(a) EPC merely because its exploitation is permitted in some or all of the Contracting States. Thus, approval or disapproval of the exploitation by national law(s) or regulation(s) does not constitute per se a sufficient criterion for the purposes of examination under Article 53(a) EPC.[213]

How useful is the above guidance of the Technical Board? Importantly, what sort of evidence will go to establish whether an invention is contrary to *ordre public* or morality?

To support their objections under Article 53(a) of the EPC, the opponents in *Plant Genetic Systems* sought to rely on survey and opinion poll evidence as probative of public opinion. For example, they submitted a survey conducted among Swedish farmers, according to which a large majority were opposed to genetic engineering; and an opinion poll carried out in Switzerland, according to which the majority of those surveyed were opposed

[210] A. Warren, 'A mouse in sheep's clothing: The challenge to the patent morality criterion posed by "Dolly"' (1998) 20 EIPR 445, 447–8 suggests that it does.

[211] *Plant Genetic Systems/Glutamine synthetase inhibitors (Opposition by Greenpeace)* T356/93 [1995] EPOR 357.

[212] Ibid., at p. 373.   [213] Ibid., at pp. 366–7.

to patenting animals and plants. The Technical Board of Appeal rejected this evidence for the following reasons:[214]

The results of surveys or opinion polls can scarcely be considered decisive per se when assessing patentability of a given subject-matter with regard to the requirements of Article 53(a) EPC, for the following reasons:

— Surveys and opinion polls do not necessarily reflect 'ordre public' concerns or moral norms that are deeply rooted in European culture.

— The results of surveys and opinion polls can fluctuate in an unforeseeable manner within short time periods and can be very easily influenced and controlled, depending on a number of factors, including the type of questions posed, the choice and the size of the representative sample, and so on.

— Surveys of particular groups of people (for example, farmers) tend to reflect their specific interests and/or their biased beliefs.

— As stated above, the question whether Article 53(a) EPC constitutes a bar to patentability is to be considered in each particular case on its merits. Consequently, if surveys and opinion polls were to be relied on, they would have to be made ad hoc on the basis of specific questions in relation to the particular subject-matter claimed. For obvious reasons, such a procedure is scarcely feasible.

— Like national law(s) and regulation(s) approving or disapproving the exploitation of an invention (see point 7 above), a survey or an opinion poll showing that a particular group of people or the majority of the population of some or all of the Contracting States opposes the granting of a patent for a specified subject-matter, cannot serve as a sufficient criterion for establishing that the said subject-matter is contrary to 'ordre public' or morality.

Was the Technical Board ruling out completely the use of surveys or opinion polls? If so, what sort of evidence can be relied upon when it comes to mounting a challenge on the grounds that an invention is contrary to *ordre public* or morality?

In *Plant Genetic Systems* the Technical Board of Appeal concluded that the invention was neither contrary to morality or *ordre public*. On the morality point, the Board held that the claimed subject matter did not relate to a misuse or destructive use of plant biotechnology because it concerned activities or products which could not be considered wrong in the light of conventionally accepted standards of conduct of European culture.[215] A factor which seemed to influence the Board's decision was that plant biotechnology was similar in its goals to traditional selective breeding.[216] With regards to *ordre public*, the Board held that there must be evidence sufficiently substantiating that the patent would seriously prejudice the environment and that no such conclusive evidence had been presented. Evidence of possible, but not yet conclusively documented hazards was insufficient.[217]

Again, the question must be asked, what type of evidence *will* be accepted in order conclusively to show serious prejudice to the environment or that an invention offends the norms of European culture? In *Howard Florey/Relaxin*[218] the opponents requested that the EPO carry out a referendum, in order to determine whether the process for obtaining the hormone H2-relaxin and the complementary DNA sequence coding for H2-relaxin,

---

[214] Ibid., at pp. 368–9.   [215] Ibid., p. 370.
[216] Ibid., pp. 369–370.   [217] Ibid., p. 372.
[218] [1995] EPOR 541.

was contrary to morality. The Opposition Division refused this request on the basis that the opponent had the burden of proof and it was thus their responsibility to adduce such evidence. Further, the Opposition Division doubted the weight of such evidence, commenting that it would be 'only in those very limited cases in which there appears to be an overwhelming consensus that the exploitation or publication of an invention would be immoral may an invention be excluded from patentability under Article 53(a).'[219] In your view, is it fair to place such a heavy, and apparently vague, evidential burden on opponents of granted patents?

FURTHER READING

M. Llewelyn, 'Article 53 Revisited' [1995] 17 *EIPR* 506.

P. Drahos, 'Biotechnology Patents, Markets and Morality' [1999] *EIPR* 441.

L. Bently and B. Sherman, 'The Question of Patenting Life' in Bently & Maniatis (eds.), *Intellectual Property and Ethics* (London: Sweet & Maxwell, 1998), pp. 111–25.

Nuffield Council on Bioethics, *Report on Human Tissue: Ethical and Legal Issues* (April 1995), pp. 97–8.

9.7.7.2 Post Biotechnology Directive

Article 6 of the Biotechnology Directive sought to clarify the application of the *ordre public* and morality exclusion to biotechnological inventions. Article 6(1) provides:

> Inventions shall be considered unpatentable where their commercial exploitation would be contrary to ordre public or morality; however, exploitation shall not be deemed to be so contrary merely because it is prohibited by law or regulation.

Section 1 of the PA 77 was amended to be consistent with Article 6 of the Biotechnology Directive. Thus, s. 1(3), PA 77 now provides:

> A patent shall not be granted for an invention the commercial exploitation of which would be contrary to public policy or morality.[220]

Article 6(2) of the Biotechnology Directive sets out an illustrative list of inventions which are deemed unpatentable under Article 6(1):

> (a) processes for cloning human beings;
>
> (b) processes for modifying the germ line genetic identity of human beings;
>
> (c) uses of human embryos for industrial or commercial purposes;
>
> (d) processes for modifying the genetic identity of animals which are likely to cause them suffering without any substantial medical benefit to man or animal, and also animals resulting from such processes.

---

[219] *Howard Florey/Relaxin* [1995] EPOR 541, para. 6.5.

[220] As a result of EPC 2000, Art. 53(a) EPC was also amended to be consistent with Art. 6(1) Biotechnology Directive.

Article 6(2) of the Biotechnology Directive has been incorporated into the PA 77 as para. 3(f) of Sch. A2 and into the EPC as part of its implementing regulations. Previously it was r. 23(d) of the Implementing Regulations, but is now r. 28 of the Implementing Regulations to the EPC 2000.

In the action for annulment of the Biotechnology Directive[221] the applicant pleaded that the directive exacerbated the legal ambiguities identified in the recitals, and thus was in breach of the principle of legal certainty. In particular, the applicant argued that Article 6 gave national authorities too much discretion in applying concepts expressed in general and ambiguous terms. The ECJ rejected this argument. It held that while Article 6 gave national authorities a wide scope for manoeuvre in applying the exclusion, this was necessary in order to take into account the particular difficulties that may arise from a patent in the social and cultural context of each Member State. Further, the type of provision reflected in Article 6 was well known in patent law. Finally, the provision was not discretionary because it was limited by well-known concepts of *ordre public* and morality and because it gave four examples of processes or uses which are not patentable. 'Thus, the Community legislature gives guidelines for applying the concepts at issue which do not otherwise exist in the general law on patents.'[222]

Do you agree that Article 6(2) of the Biotechnology Directive provides clear and useful guidance on the scope of the *ordre public* and morality exclusion? What ambiguities and controversies could arise in relation to the illustrative list contained in Article 6(2)?

FURTHER READING

S. Bostyn 'The patentability of genetic information carriers' [1999] IPQ 1.

Two aspects of Article 6(2) of the Biotechnology Directive that have caused particular difficulties of interpretation are sub-paras. (c) (uses of human embryos for industrial or commercial purposes) and (d) (processes for modifying the genetic identity of animals etc).

Article 6(2)(c) of the Biotechnology Directive, which prohibits as contrary to *ordre public* or morality uses of human embryos for industrial or commercial purposes has recently been the subject of interpretation by the Enlarged Board of Appeal in *WARF/Thomson stem cell application* G2/06.[223]

WARF/Thomson stem cell application G2/06

Wisconsin Alumni Research Foundation (WARF) filed a European patent application for an invention by James Thomson which claimed the cultures of human embryonic stem cells. The application was refused by the Examining Division as contrary to r. 28(c) of the EPC (formerly r. 23(d)(c)) because, in order to generate the human embryonic stem-cell cultures, human embryos were used as starting material. The Technical Board of Appeal decided to refer questions to the Enlarged Board. Question 1 asked whether r. 28(c) of the EPC (formerly r. 23(d)(c)) applied to an application filed before the entry into force of the rule? If yes, question 2 asked whether the rule forbade claims directed

---

[221] *Netherlands v European Parliament and Council of the European Union* Case C-377/98 [2001] ECR I-7079.

[222] Ibid., para. 39.

[223] Decision of the Enlarged Board of Appeal of 25 Nov. 2008.

to products (here human embryonic stem cells) which at the date of filing could only be prepared by a method that necessarily involved the destruction of human embryos? Question 3 asked whether Article 53(a) of the EPC in any event forbade the patenting of such claims. Question 4 asked whether it was relevant to r. 23d(c) or Article 53(a) of the EPC that, after the filing date, the same products could be obtained without having to use a method that necessarily involved the destruction of human embryos?

Enlarged Board of Appeal:

[On question 1, the Board indicated that the EPC provisions implementing the Biotechnology Directive had been introduced without any transitional provisions.]

13. ...[this] can only be taken as meaning that this detailed guidance on what was patentable and unpatentable was to be applied as a whole to all then pending applications.

14. In view of the above, the answer to referred Question 1 must be that Rule 28(c) (formerly 23d(c)) EPC applies to all pending applications, even those filed before the entry into force of the rule. As the Appellant itself agrees with this answer, as does the President of the EPO and the vast majority of the *amicus curiae* briefs, nothing more need be said.

[On question 2, the appellant contended that embryos referred to embryos 14 days or older, which were not involved in the method that produced the human embryonic stem cells.]

20. Neither the EU legislator nor the EPC legislator have chosen to define the term 'embryo', as used in the Directive or now in Rule 28 (formerly 23d) EPC. This contrasts with the German law...where embryo is defined as including a fertilized egg, or the UK law...where embryo includes the two cell zygote and an egg in the process of fertilisation. The EU and the EPC legislators must presumably have been aware of the definitions used in national laws on regulating embryos, and yet chose to leave the term undefined. Given the purpose to protect human dignity and prevent the commercialization of embryos, the Enlarged Board can only presume that 'embryo' was not to be given any restrictive meaning in Rule 28 (formerly 23d) EPC, as to do so would undermine the intention of the legislator, and that what is an embryo is a question of fact in the context of any particular patent application.

[The appellant also contended that use of human embryos must be claimed.]

21. However, this Rule (as well as the corresponding provision of the Directive) does not mention claims, but refers to 'invention' in the context of its exploitation. What needs to be looked at is not just the explicit wording of the claims but the technical teaching of the application as a whole as to how the invention is to be performed. Before human embryonic stem cell cultures can be used they have to be made. Since in the case referred to the Enlarged Board the only teaching of how to perform the invention to make human embryonic stem cell cultures is the use (involving their destruction) of human embryos, this invention falls under the prohibition of Rule 28(c) (formerly 23d(c)) EPC...To restrict the application of Rule 28(c) (formerly 23d(c)) EPC to what an applicant chooses explicitly to put in his claim would have the undesirable consequence of making avoidance of the patenting prohibition merely a matter of clever and skilful drafting of such claim.

[The appellant also argued that the use of human embryos to make the stem cell cultures was not for industrial or commercial purposes.]

25. A claimed new and inventive product must first be made before it can be used. Such making is the ordinary way commercially to exploit the claimed invention and falls within the monopoly granted, as someone having a patent application with a claim directed to this product has on the grant of the patent the right to exclude others from making or using such product. Making the claimed product remains commercial or industrial exploitation of

the invention even where there is an intention to use that product for further research. On the facts which this Board must assume in answering the referred Question 2, making the claimed product involves the destruction of human embryos. This use involving destruction is thus an integral and essential part of the industrial and commercial exploitation of the claimed invention, and thus violates the prohibition of Rule 28(c) (formerly 23d(c)) EPC.

Question 3 did not need answering in light of the answer to Question 2. In relation to question 4, the Enlarged Board concluded that technical developments which became available after the filing date could not be taken into consideration.

Do you agree with the Enlarged Board's interpretation of r. 28(c) of the EPC?

FURTHER READING

S. Sterckx, 'The European Patent Convention and the (non) patentability of human embryonic stem cells: The WARF case' (2008) IPQ 478.

The scope of Article 6(2)(d) of the Biotechnology Directive reared its head in the *Onco-mouse* proceedings. Earlier it was discussed how the Examining Division did not deny granting a patent in *Onco-mouse* on the basis of Article 53(a) of the EPC. This was because the benefits to mankind outweighed any risks. However, after the patent was granted seventeen parties filed opposition proceedings on various grounds, including that the patent was contrary to Article 53(a) of the EPC. By the time of the decision of the Opposition Division, Article 6(2)(d) of the Biotechnology Directive had been implemented as r. 23(d)(d) of the Implementing Regulations to the EPC. At this point, you should refer back to this provision to see how it differs, if at all, from the utilitarian approach adopted by the Examining Division in *Onco-mouse*.

The Opposition Division in *Onco-mouse* considered both Article 53(a) of the EPC and r. 23(d)(d). In terms of its approach to Article 53(a) of the EPC it followed the Technical Board of Appeal's decision in *Plant Genetic Systems*.

For the purposes of Article 53(a) EPC, 'ordre public' and morality have to be assessed primarily by looking at laws or regulations which are common to most of the European countries because these laws and regulations are the best indicator about what is considered right or wrong in European society. In so far as such laws or regulations concerning the relevant issue exist, it appears neither necessary nor appropriate to rely on other possible means of assessment such as public opinion polls which were relied upon or requested by several Opponents.

In applying the above principles to the assessment of 'ordre public' and morality under Article 53(a) EPC for an invention which is concerned with test animals in medicinal research, statutory law regulating the use of such animals for testing is highly indicative because it shows whether the exploitation of the invention is de facto prohibited or not. The use of animals for experimental or other scientific purposes is allowed under certain conditions in most if not all of the states being party to the EPC...It is therefore concluded that patenting of those animals of the present invention being useful as test animals in the sense of this Directive complies with the principle requirement of morality because the exploitation of the invention is explicitly allowed.[224]

---

224 *Onco-mouse* [2003] OJ EPO 473, 502–3.

Insofar as the Opposition Division rejected the use of public opinion polls, is this in line with *Plant Genetic Systems*? To the extent that the Opposition Division also relied upon compliance with European laws and regulations to indicate that the invention was not excluded by Article 53(a) of the EPC is this also consistent with *Plant Genetic Systems*?

The Opposition Division then considered the relevance of r. 23(d)(d). It held that it superseded the balancing approach in the first *Onco-mouse* decision. Further, that it should be applied as a second round in the assessment of patentability. The Opposition Division also dealt with when the questions of 'suffering' and 'substantial medical benefit to man or animal' would have to be assessed. The assessment of suffering would occur *after* the filing date, whereas substantial medical benefit would be assessed *at* the filing date, without taking into account later evidence as to actual outcome of the exploitation. Further, the question would be whether at the filing date the inventor had a bona fide reason to believe that his invention would have a substantial medical benefit. The Opposition Division concluded:

> In the present case, it cannot be denied that the animals of the invention were made for a good cause, namely, progress in cancer research. In view of the new approach the inventor took vis-à-vis the problem of medical cancer testing at the time, there were bona fide reasons at the effective date to expect a substantial medical benefit. Rule 23(d)(d) EPC is therefore no bar to patentability of those animals covered by the patent which were found to be allowable under Article 53(a) EPC above.[225]

The approach of the Opposition Division of applying r. 23(d)(d) as a second round in the assessment of patentability is curious since it is meant to reflect instances of when Article 53(a) of the EPC is contravened. Arguably, the better approach is to begin by applying the illustrative list in Article 6(2) of the Biotechnology Directive/r. 23(d) EPC, and then to consider Article 53(a) of the EPC.

FURTHER READING

D. Thomas and G. A. Richards, 'The importance of the morality exception under the European Patent Convention: The *Onco-mouse* case continues' [2004] 26 EIPR 97.

9.7.7.3 Conclusion

Having considered the scope of Article 53(a) of the EPC and the guidance sought to be provided by Article 6(2) Biotechnology Directive, as implemented in r. 28 EPC, do you consider that it is appropriate for patent law to exclude inventions the commercial exploitation of which are contrary to *ordre public* or morality? If so, is the EPO approach to this assessment satisfactory? If not, what alternatives could be pursued?

9.8 INDUSTRIAL APPLICATION

For an invention to be patentable it must be capable of industrial application[226] and an invention shall be capable or susceptible of industrial application 'if it can be made or used in any kind of industry, including agriculture'.[227] This requirement ensures that patents are

---

225 *Onco-mouse* [2003] OJ EPO 473, 504.   226 PA 77, s. 1(1)(c); Art. 52(1) EPC.
227 PA 77, s. 4(1); Art. 57 EPC.

not granted for abstract creations and emphasizes that inventions should have a practical or concrete application.[228]

Generally speaking, most inventions will be capable of industrial application. However, in the case of biotechnological inventions this requirement may prove difficult to satisfy where the function of substances (such as a protein or DNA sequence) that have been identified and isolated is unknown. For example, in *Chiron Corporation v Murex Diagnostics Ltd*,[229] the patent in suit claimed an almost infinite number of polypeptides[230] of the Hepatitis C Virus, which were useless for any known purpose. The proprietor of the patent sued the defendants, who manufactured and sold kits to test for the Hepatitis C Virus, for infringement and the defendants alleged that the patent was invalid on the grounds, *inter alia*, that the invention was not capable of industrial application. This argument was rejected at first instance, but accepted on appeal. Morritt LJ explained:

> We accept that the polypeptides claimed in the second part of claim 11 can be made, for as will become apparent from the section of our judgment dealing with insufficiency, it is a routine task to see whether one polynucleotide will hybridise with another. But the sections require that the invention can be made or used 'in any kind of industry' so as to be 'capable' or 'susceptible of industrial application'. The connotation is that of trade or manufacture in its widest sense and whether or not for profit. But industry does not exist in that sense to make or use that which is useless for any known purpose.[231]

The EPO has adopted a similar approach to the industrial application requirement for biotechnological inventions, as the following case illustrates.

Max-Planck/BDP1 Phosphatase T870/04 [2006] EPOR 14

The application in suit disclosed the means and method of making Brain Derived Phosphatase 1 (BDP-1) polypeptide, which was one of a class of enzymes called protein tyrosine phosphatases (PTPases), and suggested that BDP-1 polypeptides were possible anti-cancer proteins.

Legal Board of Appeal:

> 19. The case law indicates that the notion of 'industry' has to be interpreted broadly to include all manufacturing, extracting and processing activities of enterprises that are carried out continuously, independently and for financial (commercial) gains (*cf.* e.g. T144/83 [1986] OJ EPO 301, see point 5 of the reasons).
>
> 20. The requirement of Art. 57 EPC that the invention 'can be made or used' in at least one field of industrial activity emphasises that a 'practical' application of the invention has to be disclosed. Merely because a substance (here: a polypeptide) could be produced in some ways does not necessarily mean that this requirement is fulfilled, unless there is also some profitable use for which the substance can be employed.
>
> . . .

---

228 *Max-Planck/BDP1 Phosphatase* T870/04 [2006] EPOR 14, para. 20.   229 [1996] RPC 535.
230 Polypeptides are amino acids joined together by peptide bonds, and amino acids are constituent units of proteins.
231 *Chiron Corporation v Murex Diagnostics Ltd* [1996] RPC 535, 607.

22. In cases where a substance, naturally occurring in the human body, is identified, and possibly also structurally characterised and made available through some method, but either its function is not known or it is complex and incompletely understood, and no disease or condition has yet been identified as being attributable to an excess or deficiency of the substance, and no other practical use is suggested for the substance, then industrial applicability cannot be acknowledged. While the jurisprudence has tended to be generous to applicants, there must be a borderline between what can be accepted, and what can only be categorised as an interesting research result which per se does not yet allow a practical industrial application to be identified. Even though research results may be a scientific achievement of considerable merit, they are not necessarily an invention which can be applied industrially.

The Legal Board of Appeal held that although there were suggestions that BDP1 polypeptide might be used to target cancer these were rather speculative and would require further research. As such, the invention lacked industrial application. Do you agree with the view expressed by the Board of Appeal that patents should not be granted simply for meritorious research results that point in the direction of further research, as opposed to those which can be usefully applied in some kind of industry?

FURTHER READING

N.-L. Wee Loon, 'Patenting of genes: A closer look at the concepts of utility and industrial applicability' (2002) IIC 393.

9.9 METHODS OF MEDICAL AND VETERINARY TREATMENT

Until recently, methods of medical and veterinary treatment were regarded as unpatentable on the ground that they were not associated with trade or manufacture and thus were not capable of industrial application.[232] Subsequently, however, this was thought to be a legal fiction which masked the real policy and public-health considerations underpinning the exclusion.[233] Thus, the EPC 2000 retained the exclusion for methods of medical and veterinary treatment, but as a stand-alone provision in Article 53 EPC (deleting Article 52(4)). Section 4(2) of the Patents Act 1977 was deleted and replaced by s. 4A, which provides:

(1) A patent shall not be granted for the invention of—

    a. A method of treatment of the human or animal body by surgery or therapy, or

    b. A method of diagnosis practised on the human or animal body.

(2) Subsection (1) above does not apply to an invention consisting of a substance or composition for use in any such method.

The public-policy justification for this exclusion has been described by the Enlarged Board of Appeal as allowing freedom to medical and veterinary practitioners to 'take the actions they consider suited to diagnose illnesses by means of investigative methods' without being

---

[232] See previous s. 4(2), PA 77 and Art. 52(4) EPC (now repealed).
[233] *Diagnostic Methods* G1/04 [2006] EPOR 15, para. 7.

inhibited by patents or the fear of infringing them.[234] Not everyone, however, agrees with this rationale, as the following extract indicates.

S. Bostyn, 'No cure without pay? Referral to the Enlarged Board of Appeal concerning the patentability of diagnostic methods' [2005] 28 EIPR 412, 415

The rationale of Art. 52(4) EPC, as it has been expressed by the Technical Boards of Appeal, and also in national case law, has been that medical personnel should not be hindered in performing their medical (health care) activities. It can be doubted whether this rationale is still of value today. All features of medicine are patentable, except for medical treatment and diagnostic methods. It is difficult to understand why a method of diagnosis on the human body should be excluded from patentability, while the products used therein, and the products used for the treatment are perfectly patentable. It cannot be readily seen why, from an ethical point of view, there would be more reasons to deny patent protection for medical treatment methods than there would be for patenting medical products and medicaments. The latter categories are not contested, however. It seems that relics from the past, from times when the judiciary and the legislator had difficulties in dealing with these types of problems, have succeeded in surviving the stone-ages of patent law. Maybe it is time to lay this ill-conceived exclusion to rest. The consequences of this exclusion on doubtful grounds are to be felt in all fields of medical technology, including treatment and diagnosis. The consequences are probably more severe for medical treatment methods than they are for diagnostic methods.

Other commentators, however, fiercely defend the method of medical and veterinary treatment exclusion. For example, Alexandra Sims[235] argues that patents for methods of treatment of this kind are unnecessary because, unlike pharmaceuticals, they do not involve the same vast expenditure to develop. Further, she doubts whether patenting such methods would lead to disclosure of important technical knowledge because there is no requirement in patent law to disclose the best method for performing the invention and medical practitioners already operate within a culture of sharing. Sims is also sceptical that patents would encourage more innovation with respect to methods of medical treatment since there are other types of incentives within the medical community, such as recognition, promotion, prizes, and publication in prestigious journals. In fact, she suggests that patents might stifle innovation in this field, rather than promote it, as well as increase the cost to society of providing medical care and, thus, in turn reduce patient access to such care.

Of the two positions described above which would you favour? In considering this issue, it is worth noting that newly discovered pharmaceutical substances are patentable and, as we shall see at 9.10.6 below, known pharmaceutical substances that are used for different therapeutic purposes along with known substances that feature a novel dosage regime. Given the scope of protection that is available to pharmaceuticals, one might query whether it is justified to exclude methods of medical and veterinary treatment. One might also ask whether, in light of the narrow construction of this exclusion and the generous approach to novelty for pharmaceutical substances, this exclusion still serves a useful purpose. We turn now to consider the ways in which the exclusions for methods of medical and veterinary treatment have been interpreted.

---

[234] *Diagnostic Methods* G1/04 [2006] EPOR 15, para. 7.
[235] A. Sims, 'The case against patenting methods of medical treatment' [2007] 29 EIPR 43.

9.9.1 TREATMENT BY SURGERY

'Treatment…by surgery' does not include methods that ultimately lead to the death of the living beings under treatment. For example, in *Shell/Blood Flow* T182/90,[236] the application related to a method for measuring blood-flow to a specific tissue in an animal; however, it ultimately led to the animal being killed. On this basis, the Technical Board of Appeal set aside the Examining Division's decision that this was excluded as a method of surgical treatment. It commented that 'methods consciously ending in the laboratory animal's death…are not in their nature methods of surgical treatment, even if some of the steps they involve may have a surgical character'.[237]

It is also the case that where a method of treatment includes at least one surgical step, this will be caught by the exclusion.

Georgetown University/Pericardial access T35/99 [2001] EPOR 21

The patent application claimed a method for transvenously accessing the pericardial space between a heart and its pericardium in preparation for a medical procedure, using a catheter device. The application had been refused on the basis that it was a method of treatment by surgery. The applicant appealed, arguing that the presence of a surgical step within a method did not constitute a method of treatment by surgery. The Technical Board of Appeal dismissed the appeal.

Technical Board of Appeal, at pp. 174–5:

[It reiterated the policy reasons behind the conclusion and then concluded as follows:]

In the light of this clear and deliberate choice on the part of the legislator, the terms 'treatment' and 'surgery' in Article 52(4) EPC cannot be considered as constituting two distinct requirements for the exclusion. For a given patient, the optimal or only available treatment could not be administered if even a single part or step thereof—and most treatments comprise several steps—were covered by patent protection. In the extreme, the physician would have to deny life-saving assistance in order not to infringe a patent. Indeed, as a matter of principle the patent protection for a method as defined by the features of a claim includes its use (or 'carrying out') without having regard to the intentions of the user. Moreover, it would be quite difficult if not impossible to define clearly whether a surgical method is a complete or a non-insignificant treatment per se, or as carried out in an individual case. Therefore such criteria would run counter to clarity and legal certainty.

…Consequently…a claim is not allowable…if it includes at least one feature defining a physical activity or action (e.g. a method step) which constitutes a 'method for treatment of the human body by surgery or therapy'; and it is irrelevant whether the method in question is susceptible of being carried out in isolation or only in combination with other methods which together achieve the intended medical effect.

9.9.2 TREATMENT BY THERAPY

The scope of 'treatment…by therapy' has been interpreted in the following Board of Appeal decision.

---

[236] [1994] EPOR 320. [237] Ibid., at p. 324.

Salminen/Pigs III T58/87 [1989] EPOR 125

The case involved a patent for a method for preventing piglets from suffocating under the dam (i.e. mother) in a brooding pen. Newborn piglets have a tendency to creep under the dam whilst standing up, in order to feed, and they risk being suffocated when the dam lies down. The method thus involved using a sensor to detect when the dam was standing and lying down and, when the dam was standing up, triggering unpleasant conditions for the piglets by blowing hot air under the dam. The appellant opposed the grant of the patent on the basis, *inter alia*, that it was not capable of industrial application pursuant to Article 52(4) of the EPC. The TBA dismissed the appeal, indicating the scope of 'therapy' in Article 52(4), and finding that the method did not constitute a therapeutic method.

Technical Board of Appeal, at pp. 127–8:

2.1 The Board agrees in that the word 'therapy'

— covers any non-surgical treatment which is designed to cure, alleviate, remove or lessen the symptom of, or prevent or reduce the possibility of contracting any malfunction of the animal body (cf. *Patent Law of Europe and the United Kingdom* by A. M. Walton, H. I. L. Laddie, J. P. Baldwin and D. J. T. Kitchin, 1983, page II [684]), and also

— relates to the treatment of a disease in general or to a curative treatment in the narrow sense as well as the alleviation of the symptoms of pain and suffering (cf. *Chambers Twentieth Century Dictionary*, 1399, 'Therapy'; The Oxford English Dictionary, Vol. XI, 280, 'Therapy'; and, for example, T144/83 (Point 3); OJ, EPO 1986, 301).

2.3 The behaviour of newborn piglets to creep under the dam standing up to eat and drink either during or after farrowing cannot be fairly regarded as a malfunction of piglets whose instinct is not adequately developed. Furthermore, as far as the language of Claim 1 is concerned, it clearly covers a method for protection of piglets from the disadvantageous consequences of this behaviour, such as suffocating under the dam, by blowing air under the standing dam thus creating unpleasant conditions for the piglets. This cannot reasonably be called a treatment by therapy, which is practised on the bodies of piglets, within the meaning of Article 52(4) EPC. As the Opposition Division rightly considered, the invention is concerned with preventing accidents, analogous to a method of preventing a worker from trapping his hand in machinery.

2.4 Consequently, the Claims 1 and 2 comply with the requirements of Article 57 EPC.

On what basis did the Technical Board of Appeal find that the invention was *not* a method of treatment by therapy? Therapeutic treatment will often be linked to that which is targeting disease. Here it is interesting to note that pregnancy is not regarded as a disease and therefore inventions for methods of treatment that prevent pregnancy are not caught by the exclusion.[238]

Where a method of treatment is claimed that provides both therapeutic and cosmetic benefits this will still be caught by the exclusion. For example, in *ICI/Cleaning Plaque (Opposition by Blendax)* T290/86[239] the patent in question was a method of using water-soluble

---

[238] *British Technology Group/Contraceptive Method* T74/93 [1995] EPOR 279.
[239] [1991] EPOR 157.

lanthanum salts as an agent for cleaning plaque and/or stains from human teeth. The Technical Board of Appeal held that this was directed both to therapeutic benefits (i.e. reducing plaque) and cosmetic benefits (the teeth looking cleaner). This was distinguished from *Du Pont/Appetite Suppressant* T144/83,[240] where the claim was clearly directed to a method of treatment of the human body for cosmetic purposes only (i.e. weight loss).

9.9.3 DIAGNOSTIC METHODS

The Enlarged Board of Appeal has ruled upon the scope of the exclusion for methods of diagnosis practised on the human or animal body.

Diagnostic Methods G1/04 [2006] EPOR 15

The reference to the Enlarged Board on the scope of the exclusion for 'diagnosis practised on the human or animal body' arose out of two conflicting decisions in the area. In one decision, *Bruker/Non-invasive Measurement* T385/86,[241] the Technical Board of Appeal held that the exclusion applied only to those diagnostic methods whose results immediately made it possible to decide on a particular course of medical treatment. However, in *Cygnus/Diagnostic Method* T964/99,[242] the Technical Board of Appeal held that the exclusion applied to all methods practised on the human or animal body which relate to diagnosis or which are of value for the purposes of diagnosis.

Enlarged Board of Appeal:

6.1 As a starting point, Article 52(4) EPC mentions 'diagnostic methods practised on the human or animal body'. The provision does not make reference to particular steps pertaining to such methods, nor does it contain a wording such as 'relating to diagnosis' or 'of value for diagnostic purposes'. Thus, the text of the provision itself already gives an indication towards a narrow interpretation in the sense that, in order to be excluded from patentability, the method is to include all steps relating to it. Furthermore, if the aim of the exclusion of such methods is to prevent medical or veterinary practitioners being inhibited by patents from taking the actions they consider appropriate to diagnose illnesses (*cf.* point 4 above), it will indeed be necessary to define the persons that are considered to be such practitioners. However, it is difficult, if not altogether impossible, to give such a definition on a European level within the framework of the EPC. From this it follows that, for reasons of legal certainty, which is of paramount importance, the European patent grant procedure may not be rendered dependent on the involvement of such practitioners. Since a comprehensive protection of medical and veterinary practitioners may be achieved by other means if deemed necessary, in particular by enacting legal provisions on the national level of the Contracting States of the EPC, introducing a right to use the methods in question, a narrow interpretation of the scope of the exclusion from patentability referred to above is therefore equitable. On the national level, it will also be more appropriate to define what a medical or veterinary practitioner is. Moreover, such a narrow interpretation is also justified by the fact that recent developments in the field of diagnostics for curative purposes render these methods more and more complex and technically sophisticated so that it is becoming increasingly difficult for medical or

---

240 [1987] EPOR 6.   241 [1988] EPOR 357.   242 [2002] EPOR 26.

veterinary practitioners to have the means to carry them out. In this respect, they will hardly be hampered in their work by the existence of patents related to such methods. It is therefore difficult to see why applicants and inventors in the field of diagnostics should be deprived of a comprehensive patent protection.

. . .

6.2.2 The method steps to be carried out prior to making a diagnosis as an intellectual exercise (*cf.* point 5.2 above) are related to examination, data gathering and comparison (*cf.* point 5 above). If only one of the preceding steps which are constitutive for making such a diagnosis is lacking, there is no diagnostic method, but at best a method of data acquisition or data processing that can be used in a diagnostic method (*cf.* T385/86, point 3.3 of the Reasons). It follows that, whilst the surgical or therapeutic nature of a method claim can be achieved by a single method step (*cf.* point 6.2.1 above), several method steps are required to define a diagnostic method within the meaning of Article 52(4) EPC due to the inherent and inescapable multi-step nature of such a method (*cf.* point 5 above). Consequently, the restrictive interpretation of the patent exemption for diagnostic methods adopted by decision T385/86 does not amount to setting a different standard for diagnostic methods than that established for methods of surgery or therapy, as has been asserted in decision T964/99, point 3.6 of the Reasons.

The Enlarged Board of Appeal preferred the narrower interpretation of the exclusion, as reflected in *Bruker*. As such, diagnostic methods practised on the animal or human body are only excluded 'if all of the preceding steps which are constitutive for making a diagnosis as an intellectual exercise…are performed on a living human or animal body'.[243] Those steps are: '(i) the examination phase involving the collection of data (ii) the comparison of these data with standard values; (iii) the finding of any significant deviation, i.e. a symptom, during the comparison; and (iv) the attribution of the deviation to a particular clinical picture, i.e. the deductive medical or veterinary decision phase'.[244]

Do you agree with the reasons expressed by the Enlarged Board as to why the exclusion relating to diagnostic methods had to be construed more narrowly than that relating to methods of surgical or therapeutic treatment?

9.10 NOVELTY

9.10.1 INTRODUCTION

A crucial requirement for patentability is that the invention is *new*[245] or, in other words, is not anticipated. An invention is new if it does not already form part of the state of the art and the 'state of the art' is defined broadly to include all matter that is available to the public before the priority date of the invention.[246]

The rationale behind the novelty requirement is twofold: first, to ensure that patents are not used to prevent people doing what they did before the patent was granted (the 'right to work' rationale); second, to make certain that a patent is being given in relation to technical information that is not otherwise accessible to the public (the 'information disclosure' rationale).

[243] *Diagnostic Methods*, para. 6, p. 172.
[244] Ibid., para. 5, pp. 171–2.
[245] PA 77, s. 1(1) Art. 52(1) EPC.
[246] PA 77, s. 2 Art. 54 EPC.

9.10.2 THE STATE OF THE ART

9.10.2.1 General rule

Given that an invention will not be new if it forms part of the state of the art (also known as the prior art), it is important to ascertain what comprises this body of knowledge. According to s. 2(2) of the PA 77:

> The state of the art in the case of an invention shall be taken to comprise all matter (whether a product, process, information about either, or anything else) which has at any time before the priority date of that invention been made available to the public (whether in the United Kingdom or elsewhere) by written or oral description, by use or in any other way.[247]

As is apparent from this definition, the *priority date* is essential to establishing the prior art. The priority date is usually the date on which the application was filed; however, it may be an earlier date where the applicant is claiming Convention priority.[248]

The state of the art comprises all matter made available to the public before the priority date *whether in the UK or elsewhere*. In other words, the prior art is not territorially restricted and can comprise material that is available anywhere in the world (referred to as 'absolute' novelty). Thus, a document published in the United States or Brazil, or a prior use in India, for example, could anticipate the invention. This is in contrast to the position under earlier UK patent law where the prior publication or use had to occur *within* the UK (referred to as 'local' novelty). It is also stricter than a 'relative' novelty approach according to which acts of prior use are limited to those occurring within a particular territory, but prior documentary disclosures are territorially unrestricted.[249] What is the purpose, do you think, of adopting an absolute, as opposed to local or relative approach to novelty and is it preferable?

It is not required that the material has been disseminated at large in order for it to form part of the state of the art. For example, it suffices that a document is placed in a library or other place in the UK for consultation as of right by any person (with or without paying a fee).[250] Further, giving away or selling a single item will be sufficient for it to form part of the prior art,[251] as will limited use in a remote area.[252]

The form of disclosure to the public is unrestricted since s. 2(2) of the PA 77 refers to matter made available to the public 'by written or oral description, by use or in any other way'. Thus, the prior art may include material such as patent applications or specifications, journal articles, photographs, conference presentations, conversations, product samples, or sales.

It is worth noting that s. 2(2) does not distinguish between whether the matter has been made available to the public by the inventor or by a third party. Thus, it is possible for the inventor to anticipate his or her own invention by disclosing it before he or she applies for a patent. It is therefore unwise for an inventor to discuss his or her invention, or to show it to anyone, unless done under strict conditions of confidentiality. Even so, there is the risk that the person to whom the inventor has confided may breach that obligation of confidence. If that happens, as we shall see below, such disclosures may be excluded from the prior art if they occur six months prior to the filing date. In several jurisdictions,

---

[247] For the EPC equivalent see Art. 54(2).   [248] See above at 9.4.1.1.
[249] As is the case in the US and Australia, for example.   [250] PA 77, s. 130(1).
[251] *Fomento v Mentmore* [1956] RPC 87.
[252] See *Windsurfing International Inc v Tabur Marine (Great Britain) Ltd* [1985] RPC 59.

including Australia, Japan, and Canada, 'grace periods' are used to mitigate the harshness of a bright line novelty rule. A grace period refers to where publications by the inventor occurring during a limited time before the date of filing are excluded from the state of the art. In your view, should inventors in the UK and under the EPC be able to rely on a grace period? In this respect, it is worth considering the types of inventors that a grace period is likely to favour and the inevitable complication that will arise when it comes to the novelty assessment.

9.10.2.2 Material deemed excluded from the state of the art

According to s. 2(4) of the PA 77 certain disclosures shall be disregarded in determining novelty, i.e. they will be excluded from the prior art where they occur during the six months prior to the date of filing of the patent application. It is important to note that the six months is judged *not* from the priority date but from the *date of filing*.[253] This may be significant where, due to Convention priority, the date of filing and the priority date differ.

The disclosures that will be disregarded relate to two situations. The first is where the information was obtained unlawfully or in breach of confidence either from the inventor or from any third party who had obtained it in confidence from the inventor.[254] The second situation is where the disclosure was due to, or made in consequence of the inventor displaying the invention at an 'international exhibition', as prescribed by the Convention on International Exhibitions 1928.[255] The applicant must, on filing the application, state that the invention has been so displayed.[256] According to the Convention an 'international exhibition' is one that is non-commercial, with a duration of more than three weeks, and which is officially organized by a nation and to which other nations are invited.[257] The frequency and quality of international exhibitions so defined is regulated by the Bureau International des Expositions.[258]

9.10.2.3 Material deemed included in the state of the art

Importantly, certain matter is deemed to form part of the state of the art *even though it is published after the priority date.* Section 2(3) of the PA 77 provides that the state of the art includes matter contained in other patent applications where that other application is published on or after the priority date of the invention. This is provided the priority date of the other application pre-dates that of the invention and that the matter was contained in the other application, both as filed and as published.[259]

The reason for this provision, and its scope, was considered in *Woolard's Application.*[260] In this case the applicant had filed an application on 1 December 1995. He decided to withdraw this application and his patent agents wrote to the Patent Office abandoning the 1995 application. This letter was received by the Patent Office on 12 May 1995 and became

---

[253] *University Patents/Herpes Simplex Virus* [2001] EPOR 33.

[254] PA 77, s. 2(4)(a)–(b) Art. 55(1)(a) EPC.   [255] PA 77, s. 130 Art. 55(1)(b) EPC.

[256] PA 77, s. 2(4)(c) Art. 55(1)(b) EPC.

[257] See Arts. 1–2 of the Convention on International Exhibitions 1928.

[258] See <http://www.bie-paris.org/>.

[259] For the equivalent EPC provision see Art. 54(3). Note that prior to the EPC 2000, later published European patent applications having earlier priority or filing dates were only considered part of the state of the art to the extent that the same Contracting States were designated in the earlier and later applications. This restriction has been dropped as a consequence of the EPC 2000 coming into effect.

[260] [2002] RPC 39.

effective on that date; however, the application was nevertheless published on 4 June 1997. The applicant later filed a fresh application on 3 June 1997 but this was refused on the ground of lack of novelty due to the earlier application that he had filed and which formed part of the state of the art by virtue of s. 2(3) of the PA 77. The applicant's appeal was allowed. Laddie J held that the purpose of s. 2(3) was to 'avoid the potential co-existence of two patents for the same subject matter'[261] and, as such, the two applications need to be made in the same country. Further, he held that if the earlier application is withdrawn before it is published it should not be treated as prior art for any purpose.[262]

9.10.3 INTERPRETING THE PRIOR ART

The prior art is interpreted according to the perspective of a notional person, known as the person skilled in the art. For more details of the characteristics of this person see the discussion under inventive step at 9.11 below.

9.10.3.1 Documents

A person skilled in the art will interpret a document forming part of the prior art 'as at the date of its publication, having regard to the relevant surrounding circumstances which then existed, and without regard to subsequent events'.[263] This may be contrasted with other forms of prior art, which will be interpreted as at the date of priority. This special rule for documentary disclosure thus seems somewhat out of place and the justifications for it are not entirely clear.

Importantly, it is not possible for documents to be combined or read together, i.e. to 'mosaic' documents, except in limited circumstances. Thus, in *ICI/Latex Composition* T77/87,[264] the Technical Board of Appeal held that the abstract of a document, which conveyed conflicting data to that contained in the original document, had to be interpreted by reference to the original document, so that the data stipulated in the original document prevailed. Similarly, in *Scanditronix/Radiation Beam Collimation* T56/87[265] the Technical Board of Appeal emphasized that:

> the technical disclosure in a prior art document should be considered in its entirety, as it would be done by a person skilled in the art. It is not justified arbitrarily to isolate parts of such document from their context in order to derive therefrom a technical information, which would be distinct from or even in contradiction with the integral teaching of the document.[266]

9.10.3.2 Products and prior use

Determining what information a product, substance, or prior use contributes to the prior art depends on what information a person skilled in the art can derive from that product or prior use. This includes information that can be ascertained from analysing the substance

---

[261] [2002] RPC 39, para. 17, p. 772.   [262] Ibid.

[263] *General Tire & Rubber v Firestone Tyre & Rubber* [1971] FSR 417, 443.

[264] [1989] EPOR 246.   [265] [1990] EPOR 352.   [266] Ibid., at p. 358.

or product, even if there is no motivation for doing so. This is highlighted by the following extract from the Enlarged Board of Appeal decision in *Availability to the Public*.[267]

> 1.4 An essential purpose of any technical teaching is to enable the person skilled in the art to manufacture or use a given product by applying such teaching. Where such teaching results from a product put on the market, the person skilled in the art will have to rely on his general technical knowledge to gather all information enabling him to prepare the said product. Where it is possible for the skilled person to discover the composition or the internal structure of the product *and to reproduce it without undue burden*, then both the product and its composition or internal structure become state of the art.
>
> ...
>
> 2. There is no support in the EPC for the additional requirement referred to by Board 3.3.3 in Case T93/89 (cf. point II above) that the public should have particular reasons for analysing a product put on the market, in order to identify its composition or internal structure. According to Article 54(2) EPC the state of the art shall be held to comprise everything made available to the public. It is the fact that direct and unambiguous access to some particular information is possible, which makes the latter available, whether or not there is any reason for looking for it.

9.10.4 DETERMINING WHETHER THE INVENTION IS NEW

Under the old law (Patents Act 1949), the courts placed particular emphasis on the 'right to work' rationale of novelty. They did this by using what was known as a 'reverse infringement' test for novelty. More specifically, if a prior use would have constituted an infringement if it had occurred *after* the priority date, then it was treated as an anticipation of the invention if it occurred *before* the priority date. As such, prior use of an invention, whether it was secret, inherent, or unknown at the time, would anticipate. The new law, as reflected in the Patents Act 1977, takes a different approach to novelty, which is aptly illustrated by the House of Lords decision in *Merrell Dow Pharmaceuticals Inc v Norton*.

Merrell Dow Pharmaceuticals Inc v Norton [1996] RPC 76

Merrell Dow (MD) obtained a patent in the UK in 1972 for an antihistamine drug called terfenadine. MD later conducted research into the way in which the drug actually worked. They discovered that the drug passed through the stomach to be absorbed in the small intestine and was then 99.5 per cent metabolized in the liver, which explained why the drug did not produce any side effects such as drowsiness. In 1980, MD obtained a second patent, this time in respect of the acid metabolite which was formed in the liver. After the first patent expired, pharmaceutical companies began manufacturing and selling terfenadine. MD brought an action for infringement of the second patent against the defendant. It claimed that the defendant was a contributory infringer under s. 60(2) of the PA 77 by virtue of knowingly supplying consumers with the means for putting the invention in the second patent (i.e. the acid metabolite) into effect.

---

[267] [1993] OJ EPO 277.

The defendant applied to strike out the infringement action as disclosing no cause of action. Aldous J dismissed the action on the basis of lack of novelty and the Court of Appeal affirmed his decision on this ground. On appeal to the House of Lords, the appeal was dismissed.

Lord Hoffmann (delivering the leading speech), **at pp. 85–91:**

8. Anticipation by Use

...

It is important to notice that anticipation by use relies solely upon the fact that the volunteers in the clinical trials took terfenadine and therefore made the acid metabolite. There is no suggestion in the Agreed Statement of Facts and Issues that the volunteers were also at liberty to analyse the terfenadine to discover its composition. If it was open to them to have done so, they would have been in the same position as if they had read the terfenadine specification and the arguments for anticipation by use would have been the same as for anticipation by disclosure.

...

(a) The Old Law

I think that there can be no doubt that under the Patents Act 1949, uninformative use of the kind I have described would have invalidated the patent. One of the grounds for revocation in section 32(1) was (e): 'the invention...is not new having regard to what was *known or used*, before the priority date of the claim, in the United Kingdom'. (Emphasis added) Ground 32(1)(i) was that before the priority date the invention was 'secretly used' in the United Kingdom. In *Bristol-Myers Co (Johnson's) Application* [1975] RPC 127 this House decided that use included secret or otherwise uninformative use. (I distinguish between secret and uninformative use because the House decided by a majority that 'secret' meant that information about the invention had been deliberately concealed. It did not include a case in which the manufacturer was also unaware of the relevant facts.) Bristol-Myers had applied for a patent with a product claim for an ampicillin compound which was found to be more stable than alternative forms. Beechams were able to show, from samples providentially retained, that before the priority date they had made some quantities of that particular compound, although at the time they did not know or care which ampicillin compound it was and were unaware of the advantages discovered by Bristol-Myers. Furthermore, they had marketed the ampicillin in a form which made it impossible to discover what the original compound had been. Thus the anticipation upon which Beechams relied conveyed no relevant information about the product to the general public. The compound in the hands of the reasonably skilled member of the public told him nothing about its distinctive chemical form or how he could make it or what the advantages of that form would be. Nevertheless, the compound was anticipated by use.

The reasoning of the House was founded upon two principles of the old United Kingdom patent law. The first, to which I have already referred, was that the Crown could not grant a patent which would enable the patentee to stop another trader from doing what he had done before. It did not matter that he had been doing it secretly or otherwise uninformatively. The second was that the test for anticipation before the priority date was in this respect co-extensive with the test for infringement afterwards. If the use would have been an infringement afterwards, it must have been an anticipation before. For the purpose of infringement, it was not necessary that the defendant should have realised that he was doing an infringing act. Such knowledge was therefore equally unnecessary for anticipation.

(b) The New Law

...This provision [Art. 54 EPC] makes it clear that to be part of the state of the art, *the invention* must have been made available to the public. An invention is a piece of information. Making matter available to the public within the meaning of section 2(2) therefore requires the communication of information. The use of a product makes the invention part of the state of the art only so far as that use makes available the necessary information.

The 1977 Act therefore introduced a substantial qualification into the old principle that a patent cannot be used to stop someone doing what he has done before. If the previous use was secret or uninformative, then subject to section 64, it can. Likewise, a gap has opened between the tests for infringement and anticipation. Acts done secretly or without knowledge of the relevant facts, which would amount to infringements after the grant of the patent, will not count as anticipations before.

This construction of section 2(2) is supported by a number of authorities both in the courts of this country and the EPO. I shall refer to only two. In *PLG Research Ltd. v. Ardon International Ltd* [1993] FSR 197, 225, Aldous J. said:

> Mr Thorley submitted that if a product had been made available to the public, it was not possible thereafter to patent the product whether claimed as a product claim or a product-by-process claim. That submission is too broad. Under the 1977 Act, patents may be granted for an invention covering a product that has been put on the market provided the product does not provide an enabling disclosure of the invention claimed. In most cases, prior sale of the product will make available information as to its contents and its method of manufacture, but it is possible to imagine circumstances where that will not happen. In such cases a subsequent patent may be obtained and the only safeguard given to the public is section 64 of the Act.

And in *MOBIL/Friction reducing additive Decision* G02/88 [1990] EPOR 73 the Enlarged Board of Appeal of the EPO said (at page 88):

> [T]he Enlarged Board would emphasise that under Article 54(2) EPC the question to be decided is what has been 'made available' to the public: the question is not what may have been 'inherent' in what was made available (by a prior written description, or in what has previously been used (prior use), for example). Under the EPC, a hidden or secret use, because it has not been made available to the public, is not a ground of objection to [the] validity of a European patent. In this respect, the provisions of the EPC may differ from the previous national laws of some Contracting States, and even from the current national laws of some non-Contracting States. Thus, the question of 'inherency' does not arise as such under Article 54. Any vested right derived from prior use of an invention is a matter for national law...

Mr Thorley is therefore right in saying that his claim cannot be dismissed simply on the ground that making the acid metabolite is something which has been done before. To that extent, the intuitive response is wrong.

9. Anticipation by disclosure

I turn therefore to the ground upon which the respondents succeeded before Aldous J and the Court of Appeal, namely that the disclosure in the terfenadine specification had made the invention part of the state of the art. This is different from the argument on anticipation by use because it relies not upon the mere use of the product by members of the public but upon the communication of information. The question is whether the specification conveyed sufficient information to enable the skilled reader to work the invention.

Mr Thorley says that no one can know about something which he does not know exists. It follows that if he does not know that the product exists, he cannot know how to work an invention for making that product in any form. The prior art contained in the terfenadine specification gave no indication that it would have the effect of creating the acid metabolite in the human body. Therefore it did not contain sufficient information to enable the skilled reader to make the substance in that or any other form. It did not make the acid metabolite available to the public.

What does Mr Thorley mean when he says that no one knew that the acid metabolite existed? What Merrell Dow's research revealed was that something was created in the liver which could be given a chemical description. But the same thing may be known under one description and not known under another.

...

My Lords, I think that on this point the Patents Act 1977 is perfectly clear. Section 2(2) does not purport to confine the state of the art about products to knowledge of their chemical composition. It is the *invention* which must be new and which must therefore not be part of the state of the art. It is therefore part of the state of the art if the information which has been disclosed enables the public to know the product under a description sufficient to work the invention.

For most of the purposes of a product claim, knowledge of its chemical composition will be necessary to enable the public to work the invention. It is something they will need to know in order to be able to make it. So in *Availability to the Public Decision* G01/92 [1993] EPOR 241 the President of the EPO referred to the Enlarged Board of Appeal the question of the circumstances in which making a product available to the public would count as making available its chemical composition. The Board answered that the composition or internal structure of a product becomes part of the state of the art if it is possible for a skilled person to discover it and reproduce it without undue burden. Mr Thorley took this case to mean that in no context can a product be part of the state of the art unless its chemical composition is readily discoverable. But that is not what the case says. The Board was asked about the circumstances in which the chemical composition of a product becomes part of the state of the art. It was not asked about the circumstances in which knowing its chemical composition was necessary for the purpose of treating the product as part of the state of the art.

Other decisions of the EPO seem to me to make it clear that, at least for some purposes, products need not be known under their chemical description in order to be part of the state of the art. In *BAYER/Diastereomers Decision* T12/81 [1979–85] EPOR Vol. B. 308, 312, the Technical Board of Appeal said:

> [T]he concept of novelty must not be given such a narrow interpretation that only what has already been described in the same terms is prejudicial to it. The purpose of Art. 54(1) EPC is to prevent the state of the art being patented again. Art. 54(2) EPC defines the state of the art as comprising everything made available to the public before the date of filing in any way, including by written description. There are many ways of describing a substance in chemistry and this is usually done by giving its precise scientific designation. But the latter is not always available on the date of filing... [It] is the practice of a number of patent offices to accept the process parameter, in the form of a product-by-process claim, for closer characterisation of inventions relating to chemical substances. To the Board's knowledge this is also the practice at the European Patent Office. If inventions relating to chemical substances defined by claims of this kind are patented, it necessarily follows that the resulting patent documents, once they enter the state of the art, will be prejudicial to the novelty of applications claiming the same substance although in a different and perhaps more closely defined form.

In other words, if the recipe which inevitably produces the substance is part of the state of the art, so is the substance as made by that recipe. *CPC/Flavour Concentrates Decision* T303/86 [1989] 2 EPOR 95 was a case about actual recipes for cooking. The application was to patent a process for making flavour concentrates from vegetable or animal substances by extraction with fat solvents under pressure in the presence of water. The claim specified certain parameters for the ratio between the vapour pressure of the water in the meat or vegetables and the vapour pressure of the free water. Opposition was based upon two cook-book recipes for pressure-frying chickens and making stews which in non-technical terms disclosed processes having the same effect. The Technical Board of Appeal said (at page 98):

> It is sufficient to destroy the novelty of the claimed process that this process and the known process are identical with respect to starting material and reaction conditions since processes identical in these features must inevitably yield identical products.

Furthermore, it did not matter that the cook did not realise that he was not only frying a chicken, but also making a 'flavour concentrate' in the surplus oil. It was enough, as the Board said, that 'some flavour of the fried chicken is extracted into the oil during the frying process even if this is not the desired result of that process'.

Mr Thorley said that *CPC/Flavour Concentrates* can be explained on the ground that the flavour concentrates as made according to the cooking recipes could have been analysed and chemically identified. Perhaps they could. But this was not the ground for the Board's decision. It proceeded on the basis that for the purpose of being part of the state of the art, a process for making flavour concentrates was sufficiently described by a recipe for cooking food which did not expressly refer to the flavour concentrates but would inevitably have the effect of making them.

In this case, knowledge of the acid metabolite was in my view made available to the public by the terfenadine specification under the description 'a part of the chemical reaction in the human body produced by the ingestion of terfenadine and having an anti-histamine effect'. Was this description sufficient to make the product part of the state of the art? For many purposes, obviously not. It would not enable anyone to work the invention in the form of isolating or synthesising the acid metabolite. But for the purpose of working the invention by making the acid metabolite in the body by ingesting terfenadine, I think it plainly was. It enabled the public to work the invention by making the acid metabolite in their livers. The fact that they would not have been able to describe the chemical reaction in these terms does mean that they were not working the invention. Whether or not a person is working a product invention is an objective fact independent of what he knows or thinks about what he is doing...

It may be helpful at this point to highlight the similarities and the distinctions between the case for anticipation by use, which I have rejected, and the case for anticipation by disclosure, which I have accepted. In both cases no one was aware that the acid metabolite was being made. In the case of anticipation by use, however, the acts relied upon conveyed no information which would have enabled anyone to work the invention, i.e. to make the acid metabolite. The anticipation in this form relies solely upon the fact that the acid metabolite was made, as the anticipation in *Bristol-Myers Co (Johnson's) Application* relied solely upon the fact that ampicillin trihydrate had been made and sold to the public. It disavows any reliance upon extraneous information, such as the formula for making terfenadine and the instructions to take it for its anti-histamine effect. Anticipation by disclosure, on the other hand, relies upon the communication to the public of information which enables it to do an act having the inevitable consequence of making the acid metabolite. The terfenadine specification teaches that the ingestion of terfenadine will produce a chemical reaction in the body and for the purposes of working the invention in this form, this is a sufficient description of the making of the acid metabolite. Under the description the acid metabolite was part of the state of the art.

What is the shift in approach to novelty that has occurred under the new law? Would you say that there is now more emphasis placed on the 'information disclosure' rationale than the 'right to work' rationale? Why is it that the patent for the acid metabolite was anticipated by the patent specification for terfenadine but *not* by the prior use of the antihistamine ingested by clinical volunteers? Is the distinction made between the two types of prior art convincing? In this respect, it is important to note the limited basis upon which anticipation by use in *Merrell Dow* was alleged, namely, the ingestion of a substance which did not actually contain the acid metabolite, but which produced it in the body, and the fact that the clinical volunteers were not at liberty to analyse the terfenadine pills. This may be contrasted with the case of *Evans Medical Ltd's Patent*[268] where the patent in suit was for a particular protein, pertactin, which helped immunize against the whooping cough. Laddie J held that the patent was invalid for lack of novelty because, before the priority date, a whooping cough vaccine had been used in Japan which, unknown to the person skilled in the art, contained the protein pertactin. Laddie J distinguished *Merrell Dow* on the ground that, unlike the terfenadine pills ingested by the clinical volunteers, the vaccine was open to anyone to analyse it and thus the information within it (i.e. the protein) formed part of the prior art.

In *Merrell Dow* Lord Hoffmann refers to an invention lacking novelty where there exists information available to the public that would enable the working of the invention. Another way of describing this requirement is as 'enabling disclosure'. However, as we shall see from the decision below, the House of Lords has insisted that 'enabling disclosure' in fact reflects two distinct, but related, requirements of 'disclosure' and 'enablement'.

Synthon BV v SmithKline Beecham Plc (No 2) [2006] RPC 10

Paroxetine is a chemical compound that has been successfully marketed in the form of its hydrochloride hemihydrate salt as a treatment for depression. The patent in suit in an application for revocation related to a different paroxetine salt, i.e. paroxetine methanesulfonate (PMS) in a particular crystalline form, which had properties making it more suitable for pharmaceutical use. The applicant for revocation, Synthon, had filed an application for a patent which claimed a broad class of sulfonic acid salts including PMS. The specification identified PMS as a compound which had good stability and high solubility and described how to make PMS in crystalline form. SmithKline Beecham, before the Synthon application was published, filed a patent application which claimed PMS in a particular crystalline form. Both patents were granted. However, Synthon subsequently sought to revoke the SmithKline patent, on the ground that the crystalline form of PMS described in the claims was not new. Synthon argued that its application formed part of the state of the art, pursuant to s. 2(3) of the PA 77 and thus anticipated the SmithKline patent. The first instance judge, Jacob J, held that the SmithKline patent lacked novelty but the Court of Appeal upheld the validity of the patent. On appeal, the House of Lords allowed the appeal, restoring the order of the judge.

Lord Hoffmann (delivering the leading speech), at paras, 19–33:

The law

19. Before I discuss what the Court of Appeal made of these findings, I must say something about the law. I have said that there are two requirements for anticipation: prior disclosure and enablement.

---

[268] [1998] RPC 517.

(a) Disclosure

20. The concept of what I have called disclosure has been explained in two judgments of unquestionable authority. The first is Lord Westbury LC in *Hill v Evans* (1862) 31 LJ Ch (NS) 457, 463:

> I apprehend the principle is correctly thus expressed: the antecedent statement must be such that a person of ordinary knowledge of the subject would at once perceive, understand and be able practically to apply the discovery without the necessity of making further experiments and gaining further information before the invention can be made useful. If something remains to be ascertained which is necessary for the useful application of the discovery, that affords sufficient room for another valid patent.

21. The second authoritative passage is in the judgment of the Court of Appeal (Sachs, Buckley and Orr LJJ) in *General Tire and Rubber Co v Firestone Tyre and Rubber Co Ltd* [1972] RPC 457, 485–6:

> To determine whether a patentee's claim has been anticipated by an earlier publication it is necessary to compare the earlier publication with the patentee's claim . . . If the earlier publication . . . discloses the same device as the device which the patentee by his claim . . . asserts that he has invented, the patentee's claim has been anticipated, but not otherwise . . .
>
> When the prior inventor's publication and the patentee's claim have respectively been construed by the court in the light of all properly admissible evidence as to technical matters, the meaning of words and expressions used in the art and so forth, the question whether the patentee's claim is new . . . falls to be decided as a question of fact. If the prior inventor's publication contains a clear description of, or clear instructions to do or make, something that would infringe the patentee's claim if carried out after the grant of the patentee's patent, the patentee's claim will have been shown to lack the necessary novelty . . . The prior inventor, however, and the patentee may have approached the same device from different starting points and may for this reason, or it may be for other reasons, have so described their devices that it cannot be immediately discerned from a reading of the language which they have respectively used that they have discovered in truth the same device; but if carrying out the directions contained in the prior inventor's publication will inevitably result in something being made or done which, if the patentee's claim were valid, would constitute an infringement of the patentee's claim, this circumstance demonstrates that the patentee's claim has in fact been anticipated.
>
> If, on the other hand, the prior publication contains a direction which is capable of being carried out in a manner which would infringe the patentee's claim, but would be at least as likely to be carried out in a way which would not do so, the patentee's claim will not have been anticipated, although it may fail on the ground of obviousness. To anticipate the patentee's claim the prior publication must contain clear and unmistakeable directions to do what the patentee claims to have invented . . . A signpost, however clear, upon the road to the patentee's invention will not suffice. The prior inventor must be clearly shown to have planted his flag at the precise destination before the patentee.

22. If I may summarise the effect of these two well-known statements, the matter relied upon as prior art must disclose subject-matter which, if performed, would necessarily result in an infringement of the patent. That may be because the prior art discloses the same invention. In that case there will be no question that performance of the earlier invention would infringe and usually it will be apparent to someone who is aware of both the prior art and the patent that it will do so. But patent infringement does not require that one should be aware that one is infringing: 'whether or not a person is working [an] . . . invention is an objective fact independent of what he knows or thinks about what he is doing': *Merrell Dow*

Pharmaceuticals Inc v H N Norton & Co Ltd [1996] RPC 76, 90. It follows that, whether or not it would be apparent to anyone at the time, whenever subject-matter described in the prior disclosure is capable of being performed and is such that, if performed, it must result in the patent being infringed, the disclosure condition is satisfied. The flag has been planted, even though the author or maker of the prior art was not aware that he was doing so.

23. Thus, in *Merrell Dow*, the ingestion of terfenadine by hay-fever sufferers, which was the subject of prior disclosure, necessarily entailed the making of the patented acid metab-olite in their livers. It was therefore an anticipation of the acid metabolite, even though no one was aware that it was being made or even that it existed. But the infringement must be not merely a possible or even likely consequence of performing the invention disclosed by the prior disclosure. It must be necessarily entailed. If there is more than one possible consequence, one cannot say that performing the disclosed invention will infringe. The flag has not been planted on the patented invention, although a person performing the invention disclosed by the prior art may carry it there by accident or (if he is aware of the patented invention) by design. Indeed, it may be obvious to do so. But the prior disclosure must be construed as it would have been understood by the skilled person at the date of the disclos-ure and not in the light of the subsequent patent. As the Technical Board of Appeal said in T-396/89 *UNION CARBIDE/high tear strength polymers* [1992] EPOR 312 at [4.4]:

> It may be easy, given a knowledge of a later invention, to select from the general teachings of a prior art document certain conditions, and apply them to an example in that document, so as to produce an end result having all the features of the later claim. However, success in so doing does not prove that the result was inevitable. All that it demonstrates is that, given knowledge of the later invention, the earlier teaching is capable of being adapted to give the same result. Such an adaptation cannot be used to attack the novelty of a later patent.

24. Although it is sometimes said that there are two forms of anticipatory disclosure: a disclosure of the patented invention itself and a disclosure of an invention which, if per-formed, would necessarily infringe the patented invention (see, for example, Laddie J in *Inhale Therapeutic Systems Inc v Quadrant Healthcare Plc* [2002] RPC 21 at [43]) they are both aspects of a single principle, namely that anticipation requires prior disclosure of subject-matter which, when performed, must necessarily infringe the patented invention.

25. As I have indicated by reference to the quotation from *UNION CARBIDE*, it is this requirement that performance of an invention disclosed in the prior art must necessarily infringe the patent which distinguishes novelty from obviousness. If performance of an invention disclosed by the prior art would not infringe the patent but the prior art would make it obvious to a skilled person how he might make adaptations which resulted in an infrin-ging invention, then the patent may be invalid for lack of an inventive step but not for lack of novelty. In the present case, the Synthon application is deemed to form part of the state of the art for the purposes of novelty (s. 2(3)) but not for the purpose of obviousness (s. 3). As Synthon rely solely upon s. 2(3) matter as prior art, they do not rely and cannot succeed on obviousness.

(b) Enablement

26. Enablement means that the ordinary skilled person would have been able to per-form the invention which satisfies the requirement of disclosure. This requirement applies whether the disclosure is in matter which forms part of the state of the art by virtue of s. 2(2) or, as in this case, s. 2(3). The latter point was settled by the decision of this House in *Asahi Kasei Kogyo KK's Application* [1991] RPC 485.

27. *Asahi's* case was decided on the assumed facts that there had been a prior disclosure of the same invention (a particular polypeptide) but that neither the disclosed information

nor common general knowledge would have enabled the skilled man to make it. The House therefore did not have to consider the test for deciding what degree of knowledge, skill and perseverance the skilled man was assumed to have. But the concept of enablement is used in other contexts in the law of patents (see *Biogen Inc v Medeva Plc* [1997] RPC 1, 47) and in particular as a ground for the revocation of a patent under s. 72(1)(c): 'the specification of the patent does not disclose the invention clearly enough and completely enough for it to be performed by a person skilled in the art'. The question of what will satisfy this test has been discussed in a number of cases. For example, in *Valensi v British Radio Corp* [1973] RPC 337, 377 Buckley LJ said:

> the hypothetical addressee is not a person of exceptional skill and knowledge, that he is not to be expected to exercise any invention nor any prolonged research, inquiry or experiment. He must, however, be prepared to display a reasonable degree of skill and common knowledge of the art in making trials and to correct obvious errors in the specification if a means of correcting them can readily be found.

There is also a valuable and more extended discussion in the judgment of Lloyd LJ in *Mentor Corp v Hollister Incorporated* [1993] RPC 7. In the present case the Court of Appeal was reluctant to say that the test of enablement of a prior disclosure for the purpose of anticipation was the same as the test of enablement of the patent itself for the purpose of sufficiency. But I can think of no reason why there should be any difference and the Technical Board of Appeal has more than once held that the tests are the same: see T-206/83 *ICI/Pyridine Herbicides* [1986] 5 EPOR 232, [2]; *COLLABORATIVE/Preprorennin* [1990] EPOR 361, [15]. In my opinion, therefore, the authorities on s. 72(1)(c) are equally applicable to enablement for the purposes of ss. 2(2) and (3). There may however be differences in the application of this test to the facts; for example, because in the case of sufficiency the skilled person is attempting to perform a claimed invention and has that goal in mind, whereas in the case of prior art the subject-matter may have disclosed the invention but not identified it as such. But no such question arises in this case, in which the application plainly identified crystalline PMS as an embodiment of the invention.

(c) Keeping the concepts distinct

28. It is very important to keep in mind that disclosure and enablement are distinct concepts, each of which has to be satisfied and each of which has its own rules. As Laddie J said in relation to sufficiency in *University of Southampton's Applications* [2005] RPC 11, [46]:

> In my view, devising an invention and providing enabling disclosure are two quite different things. Although both may be necessary to secure valid protection, as section 14 of the Act shows, they relate to different aspects of the law of patents. It is very possible to make a good invention but to lose one's patent for failure to make an enabling disclosure. The requirement to include an enabling disclosure is concerned with teaching the public how the invention works, not with devising the invention in the first place.

29. For a similar point, see Jacob J in *Beloit Technologies Inc v Valmet Paper Machinery Inc* [1995] RPC 705, 739. Of course the same disclosure may satisfy both requirements. The prior art description may be sufficient in itself to enable the ordinary skilled man, armed with common general knowledge of the art, to perform the subject-matter of the invention. Indeed, when the prior art is a product, the product itself, though dumb, may be enabling if it is 'available to the public' and a person skilled in the art can discover its composition or internal structure and reproduce it without undue burden: see the decision

of the Enlarged Board of Appeal in GO1/92 *Availability to the Public* [1993] EPOR 241, GO1/92 [1.4].

30. Nevertheless, in deciding whether there has been anticipation, there is a serious risk of confusion if the two requirements are not kept distinct. For example, I have explained that for the purpose of disclosure, the prior art must disclose an invention which, if performed, would necessarily infringe the patent. It is not enough to say that, given the prior art, the person skilled in the art would, without undue burden, be able to come up with an invention which infringed the patent. But once the very subject-matter of the invention has been disclosed by the prior art and the question is whether it was enabled, the person skilled in the art is assumed to be willing to make trial and error experiments to get it to work. If, therefore, one asks whether some degree of experimentation is to be assumed, it is very important to know whether one is talking about disclosure or about enablement.

31. An example of laying oneself open to misunderstanding in this way is the famous statement by Lord Westbury LC in *Hill v Evans* (1862) 31 LJ Ch (NS) 457, 463, which I have quoted above. Lord Westbury said that the person skilled in the art must be able practically to apply the discovery 'without the necessity of making further experiments and gaining further information before the invention can be made useful'. Was he referring to disclosure or enablement? I rather think he meant disclosure and was saying the same as the Court of Appeal did later in *General Tire* when it said that the prior disclosure must have planted the flag on the invention. On the other hand, by speaking of the man skilled in the art being 'able practically to apply the discovery' he certainly gave the impression that he was talking about enablement, and was so understood by Lord Reid in *C Van der Lely NV v Bamfords Ltd* [1963] RPC 61, 71, when he said, correctly in relation to enablement:

> Lord Westbury must have meant experiments with a view to discovering something not disclosed. He cannot have meant to refer to the ordinary methods of trial and error which involve no inventive step and are generally necessary in applying any discovery to produce a practical result.

32. Likewise, the role of the person skilled in the art is different in relation to disclosure and enablement. In the case of disclosure, when the matter relied upon as prior art consists (as in this case) of a written description, the skilled person is taken to be trying to understand what the author of the description meant. His common general knowledge forms the background to an exercise in construction of the kind recently discussed by this House in *Kirin-Amgen Inc v Hoechst Marion Roussel Ltd* [2005] RPC 9. And of course the patent itself must be construed on similar principles. But once the meanings of the prior disclosure and the patent have been determined, the disclosure is either of an invention which, if performed, would infringe the patent, or it is not. The person skilled in the art has no further part to play. For the purpose of enablement, however, the question is no longer what the skilled person would think the disclosure meant but whether he would be able to work the invention which the court has held it to disclose.

33. There is also a danger of confusion in a case like *Merrell Dow Pharmaceuticals Inc v H N Norton & Co Ltd* [1996] RPC 76, in which the subject-matter disclosed in the prior art is not the same as the claimed invention but will, if performed, necessarily infringe. To satisfy the requirement of disclosure, it must be shown that there will necessarily be infringement of the patented invention. But the invention which must be enabled is the one disclosed by the prior art. It makes no sense to inquire as to whether the prior disclosure enables the skilled person to perform the patented invention, since ex hypothesi in such a case the skilled person will not even realise that he is doing so. Thus in *Merrell Dow* the question of enablement turned on whether the disclosure enabled the skilled man to make terfenadine and feed it to hay-fever sufferers, not on whether it enabled him to make the acid metabolite.

In what ways do the 'disclosure' and 'enablement' requirements differ and why is it important to treat them as distinct? Here, it is worth noting Lord Walker's comments (in a concurring speech) that the practical importance of keeping the inquiries distinct may depend on whether low-tech or high-tech inventions are involved. For low-tech inventions 'the simple disclosure of the invention will probably be enough to enable the skilled person to perform it', but this is unlikely to be the case for high-tech inventions.[269]

How did the requirements of 'disclosure' and 'enablement' apply to the facts of *Synthon*? To establish disclosure, Synthon relied on the fact that their patent application had disclosed PMS in crystalline form. The problem was that the crystalline form disclosed in their application was different to the crystalline form disclosed in SmithKline's application. To address this problem Synthon established at trial that the crystalline form of PMS was in fact monomorphic, rather than polymorphic. In other words, that PMS had only one crystalline form, rather than several crystalline forms, so that performance of their invention would inevitably have infringed the SmithKline patent. In seeking to establish enablement, the difficulty for Synthon was that the method described in their application, when performed, did not produce seeding crystals. However, they argued that a person skilled in the art would engage in reasonable trial and error and subsequently be able to crystallize the PMS. Jacob J (as he then was) accepted these arguments at first instance. They were also accepted by the House of Lords, which held that the Court of Appeal had fallen into error by confusing the requirements of disclosure and enablement.

In stating in *Synthon* that 'the matter relied upon as prior art must disclose subject matter which, if performed, would necessarily result in an infringement of the patent', was Lord Hoffmann retreating from the approach taken in *Merrell Dow* where the reverse-infringement test was rejected for the purpose of assessing whether secret or uninformative use anticipated the invention? Further, in *Merrell Dow* Lord Hoffmann held, in relation to anticipation by prior use, that 'the acts relied upon conveyed no information which would have enabled anyone to work the invention, i.e. to make the acid metabolite'.[270] In the light of *Synthon* can this objection be characterized as one of lack of disclosure or lack of enablement? Here it is interesting to note that Lord Hoffmann in *Synthon* commented that the disclosure requirement in *Merrell Dow* had been satisfied because the patent specification for terfenadine disclosed the ingestion of the antihistamine and this 'necessarily entailed the making of the patented acid metabolite in their livers'. There was also enablement because the specification enabled the skilled person to make terfenadine and feed it to hay-fever sufferers. Given this was Lord Hoffmann's view of anticipation via the patent specification, do you think prior use in *Merrell Dow* failed for lack of disclosure or lack of enablement?

FURTHER READING

C. Floyd, 'Novelty under the Patents Act 1977: The state of the art after *Merrell Dow*' [1996] 9 EIPR 480.

9.10.5 NOVELTY IN RELATION TO PHARMACEUTICALS

Although new pharmaceutical substances or drugs may be patentable, the pharmaceutical industry has directed much of its research not towards the creation of new substances or

---

[269] *Synthon*, para. 64, pp. 343–4.   [270] *Merrell Dow*, at p. 91.

drugs but to discovering new uses or new benefits of known ones. It seems there are two main explanations for this trend. First, the difficulty of coming up with truly new substances and, secondly, the ability to satisfy regulatory approval more easily if there is new use of an already existing substance, for which approval has already been obtained. The difficulty, however, with patenting a new use of a known substance is that it risks being caught by the method of medical treatment exclusion that was discussed above at 9.9. As the Enlarged Board of Appeal in *Eisai/Second Medical Indication* G05/83[271] explained, this is because:

> a claim directed to the 'use of a substance or composition for the treatment of human or animal body by therapy' was in no way different in essential content from a claim directed to 'a method of treatment of the human or animal body by therapy with the substance or composition'. The difference between the two claims is one of form only and the second form of claim is plainly in conflict with Article 52(4) EPC [now Art. 53(c) EPC].

The solution to the difficulty was to include Article 54(5) EPC, which provided:

> The provisions of paragraphs 1 to 4 shall not exclude the patentability of any substance or composition, comprised in the state of the art, for use in a method referred to in Article 52, paragraph 4, provided that its use for any method referred to in that paragraph is not comprised in the state of the art.

Following the coming into force of the EPC 2000, however, the relevant provisions of Article 54 EPC now read:

> (4) Paragraphs 2 and 3 shall not exclude the patentability of any substance or composition, comprised in the state of the art, for use in a method referred to in Article 53(c), provided that its use for any such method is not comprised in the state of the art.
> (5) Paragraphs 2 and 3 shall also not exclude the patentability of any substance or composition referred to in paragraph 4 for any specific use in a method referred to in Article 53(c), provided that such use is not comprised in the state of the art.

In the Patents Act 1977 the equivalent provision to the previous Article 54(5) of the EPC was s. 2(6). Now the corresponding provisions to the new Article 54(4)–(5) of the EPC are reflected in s. 4A(3)–(4) of the PA 77. The effect of the old Article 54(5) of the EPC was considered at length by the Enlarged Board of Appeal in *Eisai*.

Eisai/Second Medical Indication G05/83 [1979–1985] EPOR B241

In the course of examining seven separate appeals against refusals of European patent applications, the Technical Board of Appeal referred to the Enlarged Board of Appeal a question of law regarding medical use claims. It is worth noting that the Enlarged Board of Appeal refers in its decision to the old provision excluding methods of medical treatment (Article 52(4) of the EPC), which was expressed in terms of lack of industrial application.

---

[271] [1979–1985] EPOR B241, para. 13.

Enlarged Board of Appeal:

15. Furthermore, Article 54(5) EPC provides that the general rules of law relating to novelty (Article 54(1) to (4) EPC) shall not exclude the patentability of any substance or compositions, comprised in the state of the art, for use in a method referred to in Article 52(4) EPC, provided that its use for any such method is not comprised in the state of the art. Thus the inventor of a 'first medical indication' can obtain purpose-limited product protection for a known substance or composition, without having to restrict himself to the substance or composition when in a form technically adapted to a specified therapeutic purpose. The appropriate protection for him is, therefore, in its broadest form, a purpose-limited product claim. No problem arises over its susceptibility of industrial application, within the meaning of Article 57 EPC.

16. Claims directed to the use of a substance or composition for the preparation of a pharmaceutical product are equally clearly directed to inventions which are susceptible of industrial application, within the meaning of Article 57 EPC.

In the above extract, the Enlarged Board of Appeal referred to the exception to novelty for pharmaceutical substances created by Article 54(5) of the EPC, namely, that use of an existing substance in a method of medical treatment satisfies the novelty requirement. However, this is provided that use of the substance for any such method is not already known and also that the invention is claimed as a purpose-limited product. This latter requirement is necessary to avoid the prohibition on patenting of methods of medical treatment.

The Enlarged Board of Appeal also had to consider the situation where subsequent or second medical uses are discovered for known substances. This type of invention had been claimed in the Swiss Intellectual Property Office as follows: the 'use of a substance or composition for the manufacture of a medicament for a specified (new) therapeutic application'. The Enlarged Board of Appeal then considered the patentability of these 'Swiss-type' claims:

19. As indicated in the Enlarged Board of Appeal's communication dated 31 July 1984, having regard to the statement of practice of the Swiss Federal Intellectual Property Office, the Enlarged Board has also given careful consideration to the possibility of protecting second (and subsequent) medical indications by means of a claim directed to the use of a substance or composition for the manufacture of a medicament for a specified (new) therapeutic application. Such claims do not conflict with Article 52(4) EPC or Article 57 EPC but there may be a problem concerning the novelty of the invention.

20. Where the medicament itself is novel in the sense of having novel technical features, for example, a new formulation, dosage or synergistic combination, the ordinary requirements of Article 54(1) to (4) EPC will be met and there will in principle be no difficulty over the question of novelty, whether the claim be directed to the medicament *per se* or to the use of the active ingredient to prepare the medicament. The critical case is, however, that in which the medicament resulting from the claimed use is not in any way different from a known medicament.

21. As is rightly recognised by the Federal Court of Justice, Article 52(1) EPC expresses a general principle of patentability for inventions which are industrially applicable, new and inventive and it is clear that in all fields of industrial activity other than those of making products for use in surgery, therapy and diagnostic methods, a new use for a known product can be fully protected as such by claims directed to that use.

> This is in fact the appropriate form of protection in such cases as the new and non-obvious use of the known product constitutes the invention and it is the clear intention of the European Patent Convention that a patent be granted for the invention to which a European patent application relates (cf. Articles 52(1), 69, 84 and Rule 29 EPC read together). Article 54(5) EPC provides an exception to this general rule, however, so far as the first use of medicaments is concerned, in respect of which the normal type of use claim is prohibited by Article 52(4) EPC. In effect, in this case the required novelty for the medicament which forms the subject-matter of the claim is derived from the new pharmaceutical use.
>
> It seems justifiable by analogy to derive the novelty for ·the process which forms the subject-matter of the type of use claim now being considered from the new therapeutic use of the medicament and this irrespective of the fact whether any pharmaceutical use of the medicament was already known or not. It is to be clearly understood that the application of this special approach to the derivation of novelty can only be applied to claims to the use of substances or compositions intended for use in a method referred to in Article 52(4) EPC.
>
> 22. The intention of Article 52(4) EPC, again as recognised by the Federal Court of Justice, is only to free from restraint non-commercial and non-industrial medical and veterinary activities. To prevent the exclusion from going beyond its proper limits, it seems appropriate to take a special view of the concept of the 'state of the art' defined in Article 54(2) EPC. Article 54(5) EPC alone provides only a partial compensation for the restriction of patent rights in the industrial and commercial field resulting from Article 52(4) EPC, first sentence. It should be added that the Enlarged Board does not deduce from the special provision of Article 54(5) EPC that there was any intention to exclude second (and further) medical indications from patent protection other than by a purpose-limited product claim. The rule of interpretation that if one thing is expressed the alternative is excluded (*expressio unius (est) exclusio alterius*), is a rule to be applied with very great caution as it can lead to injustice. No intention to exclude second (and further) medical indications generally from patent protection can be deduced from the terms of the European Patent Convention; nor can it be deduced from the legislative history of the articles in question. On this last point, after conducting its own independent studies of the preparatory documents, the Enlarged Board finds itself also in accord with the conclusion of the Federal Court of Justice.
>
> 23. For these reasons, the Enlarged Board considers that it is legitimate in principle to allow claims directed to the use of a substance or composition for the manufacture of a medicament for a specified new and inventive therapeutic application, even in a case in which the process of manufacture as such does not differ from known processes using the same active ingredient.

As is apparent from the above extract, the Enlarged Board of Appeal considered that with Swiss-form claims novelty arose by virtue of the new therapeutic or pharmaceutical use and this was the case even if other therapeutic uses had already been discovered. The justification for this special approach to novelty was the terms of Article 54(5) of the EPC and the fact that it ensured that the exclusion in Article 52(4) of the EPC did not go beyond its proper limits.

The *Eisai* approach to novelty of Swiss-type claims to second medical uses of known substances was followed by the English courts in *John Wyeth's Application; Schering AG's Application*,[272] largely because of the desirability of achieving conformity with the EPO. The correctness of *Eisai* and *John Wyeth's Application*, along with when a second

---

[272] [1985] RPC 545.

medical use of a known substance may be regarded as novel, was considered by the Court of Appeal in the following two cases.

Bristol Meyers Squibb Co v Baker Norton Pharmaceuticals [2001] RPC 1

The patent in dispute was for a particular regime covering the dosage and infusion duration of the known anti-cancer drug taxol. One inevitable side effect of the use of taxol is that it leads to a fall in the patient's white blood cell count (which is known as 'neutropenia'). Claim 1 of Bristol-Meyer's patent, which was in Swiss form, sought protection for:

> Use of taxol and sufficient medications to prevent severe anaphylactic reactions, for manufacturing a medicamentation for simultaneous, separate, or sequential application for the administration of from 135mg/m2 up to 175mg/m2 taxol over a period of about 3 hours or less as a means for treating cancer and simultaneously reducing neutropenia.

Bristol-Myers claimed that the novelty of their invention lay in the discovery of a regime of dosage/infusion of taxol that reduced the side effect of neutropenia, without losing any of the benefits of the taxol. In addition, a shorter dosage time meant that the supply of taxol could be extended and it would minimize patient discomfort and expense. In an action for infringement with a counterclaim for revocation of the patent, the defendants alleged, *inter alia*, that the claim was merely to a method of medical treatment and thus unpatentable under Article 52(4) of the EPC and that the patent lacked novelty. In support of the latter claim, the defendants relied upon a public lecture (the Winograd lecture) given before the priority date, in which the initial stages of a clinical study comparing 24-hour continuous infusion with short, three-hour continuous infusion with different dosages were revealed. The lecture indicated that three-hour infusion was as feasible and safe as 24-hour infusion, but did not indicate that neutropenia was less. At first instance, Jacob J (as he then was) found that the claim was not to a method of medical treatment, but that it lacked novelty. There was an appeal to the Court of Appeal.

Aldous LJ:

34. The appellants accept that taxol had by the priority date been made available to the public as an effective treatment for cancer when administered over a period of 24 hours. Their case for novelty depended upon the last part of claim 1, namely that the medicament was for administration at the claimed dosage over about three hours as a means for treating cancer and simultaneously reducing neutropenia. Thus the claim in broad terms was for the use of two known products to produce a medicament with the novelty relied on being provided by the alleged new application. The appellants submitted that such a claim was novel according to the principles laid down by the Enlarged Board in the *Eisai* case which concluded in paragraph 23 of their reasons:

> the Enlarged Board considers that it is legitimate in principle to allow claims directed to the use of a substance or composition for the manufacture of a medicament for a specified new and inventive therapeutic application, even in a case in which the process of manufacture as such does not differ from the known processes using the same active ingredient.

35. A claim of the type considered to be legitimate by the Enlarged Board has become known as a 'Swiss-type' claim.

36. The conclusion reached in *Eisai* was at the time and has since been the subject of considerable discussion amongst patent lawyers. Its importance was recognised by Whitford J and Falconer J who sat en banc to decide whether it should be followed in this country. They held in *John Wyeth and Brothers Ltd's Application* and *Schering AG's Application* [1985] RPC 545 that it should...Having referred in detail to the reasoning of the Enlarged Board in *Eisai*, they held at page 567:

> That approach to the novelty of the Swiss type of use claim directed to a second, or subsequent, therapeutic use is equally possible under the corresponding provisions of the 1977 Act and, not withstanding the opinion expressed earlier as to the better view of the patentability of such a Swiss type claim under the material provisions of the Act considered without regard to the position, as it has developed under the corresponding provisions of the EPC, having regard to the desirability of achieving conformity, the same approach should be adopted to the novelty of Swiss-type of claim now under consideration under the material provisions of the Act.

37. The patent judges in the *John Wyeth* case correctly summarised the approach of the Enlarged Board and I believe that they came to the right conclusion in the cases before them.

...

44. Mr Waugh submitted that claim 1 contained two novel features over the Winograd lecture. First, there was no disclosure that taxol was suitable for treating cancer when infused in the claimed amount over a period of three hours. Secondly, that there was no disclosure of reduction of neutropenia.

45. In my view the judge was right to reject the first submission. The claim requires the medicament to be suitable for treating cancer. Anybody listening to the lecture would have realised that the three-hour arm of the trial had not shown adverse hypersensitivity and was safe and that a response had been shown which Dr Winograd categorised as in the ballpark of what had been published up to now. No doubt it would have been sensible to await the conclusion of the trials, but the lecture disclosed that taxol was suitable for trying to treat cancer using a three-hour treatment.

46. The second submission depends upon the discovery that less neutropenia occurred during the three-hour infusion than during a 24-hour infusion. That was not mentioned in the lecture, but it was, as I have already pointed out, a discovery not a second therapeutic use as considered in *Eisai*. Further it is an inevitable consequence of the three-hour, 135mg/m2 infusion, described in the lecture and as such cannot impart novelty to the claim. As the judge held, the public could, using the information in the lecture, carry out the disclosed and claimed three-hour infusion with premedication without the need of any information from the patent. Such a person would inevitably monitor the patient's blood and would inevitably find the extent of neutropenia that occurred. The lecture contained clear and unmistakable directions to carry out such a three-hour infusion and the result would inevitably be that which was claimed. The information given in the lecture enabled the public to carry out an act which would have the inevitable consequence of less neutropenia. That conclusion is consistent with the attitude expressed by the Technical Boards in *Dow Chemical Company* T.90/0958 and *American Cyanamid* T.93/0279. In my view the judge came to the right conclusion. Claim 1 lacks novelty.

...

48. It is not necessary to come to any concluded view as to whether Mr Thorley's submissions as to the correctness of *Eisai* were right and I decline to do so. However, it is relevant to point out that *Eisai* has been applied by the EPO since at least 1985 and was accepted as

correctly stating the law in 1985 by the Patents Court in the *John Wyeth* case. It has also, I believe, been applied by the members of the EPC, except perhaps France. There are therefore strong reasons for maintaining the view expressed by the patent judges in the *John Wyeth* case.

...

63. In my view the form of claim 1 does not disguise its effect. The invention was the discovery that by changing the treatment from a 24-hour infusion to three hours a similar effect was obtained with less neutropenia. That was a discovery that a change in the method of treatment provided the result. The claim is an unsuccessful attempt to monopolise the new method of treatment by drafting it along the lines of the Swiss-type claim. When analysed it is directed step-by-step to the treatment. The premedication is chosen by the doctor, and administered prior to the taxol according to the directions of the doctor. The amount of taxol is selected by the doctor as is the time of administration. The actual medicament that is said to be suitable for treatment is produced in the patient under supervision of the medical team. It is not part of a manufacture. In my view Mr Thorley is correct. The invention made and claimed was a method of treatment precluded from patentability by section 4(2) (Article 52(4)). That is emphasised by the way the allegations of infringement were pleaded.

Buxton LJ:

82. The conclusion that we ought to adopt the approach of the Board in *Eisai* requires us to look closely at what *Eisai* in fact decided; and in particular at what was meant by in *Eisai* by new 'pharmaceutical' use; new 'therapeutic' use; and new 'therapeutic application': all of these expressions appearing to carry the same meaning.

83. It is important in this enquiry to remember the emphasis placed by the Board on justification by analogy from cases of first medical use. Recognition of first medical use as a subject of patentability necessarily entails the use of the substance for new and completely different purposes from that in relation to which it is already known. If the Board's analogy is to hold, therefore, the relationship between the first and the second medical use must be of the same nature: the second medical use must be for an end-purpose distinctively different from the first, albeit also medical, purpose for which the substance was used. That not only follows from the structure of the Board's argument, but also from the need to respect the exclusion of methods for treatment from patentability. If the novelty can lie in the nature of use, rather than in the end-result at which that use aims, then it is indeed the method of treatment on which patentability rests.

...

88. Judged by the test just set out, I cannot agree that the patent in suit claims an invention that is new in the terms of Article 54 of the EPC as it was understood in *Eisai*. The inventive step is to find that in the use of taxol for the treatment of cancer three-hour infusion, when compared with longer infusion, achieves antineoplastic effect with reduced myelosuppression. That is an improvement in the method of administering an existing treatment; it is not a new therapeutic purpose. The judge was right to hold, at paragraph 66, that

> This is not a case of a second or other medical use. It is a case of mere discovery about an old use.

The invention is therefore not patentable.

...

93. ...As my Lord has described, the mixing is of amounts and types of premedication, and of amounts of taxol, all determined by the doctor in relation to the specific patient. It is in reality not a self-standing operation, but subordinate and incidental to the doctor's treatment

of the patient. True it is that, in treating the patient, the doctor will, or at least may, administer the drugs according to the guidance contained in the patent. But that merely underlines that what the patent teaches is not how to manufacture a drug for use in the treatment of the patient, which would be in form at least a Swiss-type claim, but how to treat the patient: which is the teaching that the Swiss-type claim is designed to avoid.

94. The invention in the patent in suit is, therefore, of a method of medical treatment, which is not patentable.

[**Holman J** agreed with both **Aldous LJ** and **Buxton LJ** and added:]

107. I respectfully disagree with the view of the judge that this patent was not a claim to a method of treatment of the human body by therapy. In my view it clearly was . . . It is clear that the clinician must make a decision as to, and prescribe, the actual quantities of premedication to be given to, and taxol to be infused into the particular patient and as to the period of infusion . . .

. . .

111. In the present case, however, the drug, taxol, is exactly the same; the method of administration, by injection and infusion, is exactly the same; and the therapeutic application or purpose, namely the attempt to treat cancer, is exactly the same. The only difference is the discovery that if the drug is infused over a shorter period an undesirable side-effect, neutropenia, is less than it otherwise would be, while the therapeutic effect remains. No 'previously unrecognised advantageous properties in [the] chemical compound' have been discovered. All that has been discovered (important though that discovery is) is that if the compound is administered over a shorter period, one of its disadvantageous side-effects will be less than it otherwise would be.

How would you describe the ratio of *Bristol Meyers v Norton*? Is it that the claim was in effect a method of medical treatment, given the interventions and steps that would have to be taken by medical staff to implement the invention? Or is it that the Swiss-form claim lacked novelty because it did not disclose a new and distinct therapeutic purpose but simply disclosed that an old use would reduce the side effects associated with taxol? Alternatively, is the ratio that the invention lacked novelty because the Winograd lecture contained clear and unmistakeable directions to carry out the new infusion regime and an inevitable consequence of doing so would have been to reduce neutropenia? The exact ratio of *Bristol Meyers v Norton* was crucial to a later decision of the Court of Appeal, in which it considered the novelty of a new dosage regime.

Actavis UK Ltd v Merck & Co Inc [2008] EWCA Civ 444

Merck had obtained a patent in respect of the following:

The use of [finasteride] for the preparation of a medicament for oral administration useful for the treatment of androgenic alopecia in a person and wherein the dosage amount is about 0.05 to 1.0mg. (Claim 1)

The substance finasteride was known and as at the priority date it was also known that it could be used to treat androgenic alopecia (i.e. male pattern baldness). Nevertheless, Merck claimed that the particular dosage regime was new. Warren J rejected this argument at first instance, holding that claim 1 was invalid for lack of novelty. On appeal, the Court of Appeal considered whether a new dosage regime could be novel according to *Eisai* and subsequent Board of Appeal authority and whether *Bristol Meyers v Norton* precluded a finding of novelty.

Jacob LJ (delivering the judgment of the court):

22. Next the Board [in *Eisai*] puts on one side cases where it sees no novelty objection:

[20] Where the medicament itself is novel in the sense of having novel technical features—e.g. a new formulation, dosage or synergistic combination—the ordinary requirements of Article 54(1) to (4) EPC will be met and there will in principle be no difficulty over the question of novelty, whether the claim be directed to the medicament *per se* or to the use of the active ingredient to prepare the medicament.

23. In the course of argument Rimer LJ noted that the Board considered that a new *dosage* form would be enough to confer novelty. Mr Prescott seized upon that, submitting that the Board clearly contemplated that a new dosage — even for treating a disease previously treated with the same substance in a different dosage was regarded as novel. We agree. A claim to a pill containing a 1mg dose of finasteride would be a claim to a new thing. No-one had made or proposed such a thing, so why should it not be novel? Whether it would be obvious is a quite different matter. Since the patent in fact has no claim to a pill with a 1 mg dose is not necessary to pursue this further, though in view of our conclusion on obviousness it may be that such a claim would have stood as valid on its own.

[Referring to Swiss-form claims:]

28. Does this mean only treatment of a different disease ('second medical indication' in a narrow sense), or does it also extend to a different method of using a compound for treatment of a particular disease when it was already known for use in treating that disease but by a different method?

29. We think that the latter should be the answer is fairly clear from policy. The Enlarged Board clearly had policy in mind for it went on to say:

[22] The intention of Article 52(4) EPC…is only to free from restraint non-commercial and non-industrial medical and veterinary activities.

So the method of treatment exception to patentability should be construed restrictively. When Mr Thorley was asked what policy reason there should be for on the one hand allowing Swiss form second medical treatment claims for different diseases but not allowing them for the same disease, the only answer he could devise was that the treatment might cost more. Why, he said, should you have to pay more for a 1mg pill than for an out of patent 5mg pill? The reason is obvious—the 1mg pill has only come about because of expensive unpredictable research. Patented things often cost more. And the reason is because the monopoly has been given as result of the research which led to it. Research into new and better dosage regimes is clearly desirable—and there is simply no policy reason why, if a novel non-obvious regime is invented, there should not be an appropriate patent reward. Such a reward cannot extend to covering the actual treatment but a Swiss form claim which specifies the new, inventive, regime is entirely in accordance with policy.

…

31. Accordingly on the basis of *Eisai* alone we would hold that Swiss form claims are allowable where the novelty is conferred by a new dosage regime or other form of administration of a substance.

32. So holding is far from saying that in general just specifying a new dosage regime in a Swiss form claim can give rise to a valid patent. On the contrary nearly always such dosage

regimes will be obvious—it is standard practice to investigate appropriate dosage regimes. Only in an unusual case such as the present (where, see below, treatment for the condition with the substance had ceased to be worth investigating with any dosage regime) could specifying a dosage regime as part of the therapeutic use confer validity on an otherwise invalid claim.

33. The EPO takes the same view about the effect of *Eisai* as us. For there is now clear Board of Appeal authority holding, as we do, that it follows from *Eisai* that a novel dosage regime can confer novelty to a Swiss form claim. In *Genentech/method of administration* of IFG-I, T1020/03 [2006] EPOR 9 a Legal Board of Appeal specifically so held in an unusually detailed and carefully crafted reasoned opinion. It said:

[72] ...the Board interprets decision G 5/83 [*Eisai*] allowing Swiss form claims directed to the use of a composition for manufacture of a medicament for a specified new and inventive thera-peutic application, where the novelty of the application might lie only in the dose to be used or the manner of application. This Board allowed such a claim, where only the manner of applica-tion was new, already eleven years ago in T 0051/93 of 8 June 1994. The discussion in decision G 0005/83 concerning further medical indications did indeed refer to use for treating a new ill-ness. But the Board regards this significant only of the fact that most further medical use claims will refer to a new illness, as in that case novelty and inventive step are more likely to exist than in the case of a minor modification of the treatment known for an existing illness. The logic of deci-sion G 0005/83 allowing claims to further medical uses of known compositions, seems equally applicable to any use of such known composition for a new and inventive treatment which can-not be claimed as such because of Article 54(4) EPC first sentence.

34. *Genentech* was hardly a new departure in some respects, even though it disapproved certain earlier decisions. The quoted passage refers to T0051/93, an important case not cited in *BMS*. It was about a claim to 'use of X for the manufacture of a medicament for use in the treatment by subcutaneous administration of [an identified disorder]'. The prior art disclosed the use of X *for the same disorder* but by intramuscular administration. The difference in the method of treatment was enough to confer novelty because the purpose of manufacture was different. There cannot be any sensible difference between different dosage regimes and different methods of administration: either they confer novelty or they do not. The EPO has decided both do.

The court referred also to the fact that Germany and New Zealand permitted Swiss-form claims whose novelty depends on a new treatment by a different dosage regime or method of administration. The court went on to conclude that, subject to the binding effect, if any, of *Bristol Meyers v Norton*, it would follow the EPO and hold that a new dosage regime is enough to confer novelty on a Swiss-form claim.

The court then turned to analyse the Court of Appeal decision in *Bristol Meyers v Norton* and concluded that the ratio was that the claim was essentially to a method of medical treat-ment and *not* that a Swiss-form claim lacks novelty if the only difference between it and the prior art is a new dosage regime for a known medical condition. The court went on to con-sider the conclusions of Warren J at first instance:

74. The Judge held the claim lacked novelty and was for a method of treatment. In both cases he considered that *BMS* required him so to do. As to novelty for the reasons we have given we think he was wrong because there is no clear *ratio* of *BMS* on the point.

75. As to the method of treatment point, the Judge dealt with it briefly. He accepted Mr Thorley's submission that the dosing regime was a matter of choice for the doctor and

that as far as the prior art was concerned it would make no difference whether the patient was given five 1 mg tablets a day or one 5mg tablets per day. But that is not enough in our view to mean that the claim is in substance to a method of treatment. There is nowhere near the degree of involvement of medical personnel which turned the case in *BMS*. In its essence the claim here is to the use of finasteride for the preparation of a medicament of the specified dosages. It is not aimed at and does not touch the doctor—it is directed at the manufacturer. Putting it another way, even if *BMS* is right on this point, it cannot be extended to cover every case where novelty depends on a specified dosage regime. After all every prescription medicine must be prescribed—that does not mean they are all for methods of treatment.

76. Accordingly we think the Judge was wrong on both aspects. We should record in fairness that he did not have the benefit of the sustained argument we have had before us on these points.

...

84. Since we are satisfied that there is no clear *ratio* of *BMS* governing this case, we are free therefore to hold, and do hold, that we should follow *Genentech* and, subject to the cross-appeal on obviousness, allow the appeal.

The court then considered what the position would be if it were wrong and *Bristol Meyers v Norton* did in fact contain a clear ratio precluding the novelty of new dosage regimes. Rather remarkably, it created a further exception to the rule in *Young v Bristol Aeroplane Company*[273] that the Court of Appeal is bound to follow previous decisions of its own.

107. So we hold that there ought to be, and is, a specialist and very limited exception to the rule in *Young v The Bristol Aeroplane Company*. Spelling it out it is that this court is free but not bound to depart from the *ratio decidendi* of its own earlier decision if it is satisfied that the EPO Boards of Appeal have formed a settled view of European Patent law which is inconsistent with that earlier decision. Generally this court will follow such a settled view.

The decision of the Enlarged Board of Appeal in *Eisai* and the Legal Board of Appeal in *Genentech* supports a Swiss-form claim having novelty where it contains a new dosage regime. But do you agree with the Court of Appeal that this approach makes sense from a policy perspective? Does it effectively render impotent the exclusion for methods of medical treatment?[274] Further, do you agree with the court's interpretation of the ratio of *Bristol Meyers v Norton*? Finally, is it desirable for the UK Court of Appeal to be able to depart from its own precedent in circumstances where the Boards of Appeal of the EPO have expressed a settled view that is inconsistent with that previously taken by the court?

The dispute in *Actavis v Merck* concerned the law in force before the EPC 2000 came into effect.[275] In an intriguing twist to the story, the Technical Board of Appeal in *Kos Life Sciences* T1319/04[276] has referred the following questions to the Enlarged Board of Appeal relating to the amendments brought about by the EPC 2000.

---

[273] [1944] KB 718.

[274] Cornish and Llewelyn, *Intellectual Property*, para. 5–70 suggest not, given that 'the employment of known medical equipment for new treatments' still remain unpatentable.

[275] Following the EPC 2000 the semantic difficulties associated with the Swiss-form claim may be avoided by formulating claims as 'compound X for use in treating disease Y'. See new Art. 54(5) EPC, and Grubb, *Patents for Chemicals, Pharmaceuticals and Biotechnology*, p. 243.

[276] [2008] EPOR 27.

1. Where it is already known to use a particular medicament to treat a particular illness, can this known medicament be patented under the provisions of Articles 53(c) and 54(5) EPC 2000 for use in a different, new and inventive treatment by therapy of the same illness?

2. If the answer to question 1 is yes, is such patenting also possible where the only novel feature of the treatment is a new and inventive dosage regime?

3. Are any special considerations applicable when interpreting and applying Articles 53(c) and 54(5) EPC 2000?

Before the formal handing down of the judgment in *Actavis v Merck* the Court of Appeal became aware of the referral in *Kos Life Sciences* and heard submissions on whether the court should give a preliminary judgment and stay all further proceedings pending the decision of the Enlarged Board of Appeal. The court decided that final judgment in *Actavis v Merck* should be delivered, but that, to allow for the remote possibility that *Kos Life Sciences* might affect the case at hand, it extended leave to appeal to the House of Lords to 28 days after the Enlarged Board delivers its decision. The outcome of *Kos Life Sciences* is eagerly awaited and will no doubt have a major bearing on the shape of UK patent law in this particular area.

9.10.6 NOVELTY OF PURPOSE

It has long been the case that new things, as well as new uses of an old thing, are patentable. But is a claim to an old substance used in an old way but for a new purpose patentable? This might seem very plausible in the light of what has been discussed in the previous section. However, this question is different insofar as it deals with novelty of purpose generally, as opposed to on the restricted basis of use of an existing pharmaceutical substance for a new therapeutic purpose, which is justified by specific statutory provisions. Whether novelty of purpose is permissible beyond the pharmaceutical sphere was considered by the Enlarged Board of Appeal in the following case.

Mobil/Friction Reducing Additive G2/88 [1990] EPOR 73

The patent application related to a compound for use as an additive for lubricating oils. The purpose of the additive was to reduce friction between sliding surfaces in an engine. However, a prior US patent disclosed the same compound as an additive for motor oils, except with the purpose of reducing rust formation. Mobil amended their patent to claim the use of the compound as a 'friction-reducing additive'. Several questions of law were referred to the Enlarged Board of Appeal, including whether novelty can exist where there is a known use of a known compound but for a new purpose.

Enlarged Board of Appeal

6.1 ...The question of law which was referred to the Enlarged Board in G05/83 [*Eisai*] arose essentially because of the particular exclusion from patentability in relation to 'methods of treatment of the human or animal body' set out in the first sentence of Article 54(5) EPC, and the exception to that exclusion set out in Article 54(5) EPC. The reasoning in G05/83 is therefore primarily directed to answering a question of law concerning the allowability of claims whose subject-matter is a particular kind of medical or veterinary invention. The *ratio decidendi* of that decision is essentially confined to the proper interpretation of Articles 52(4) and 54(5) EPC in their context.

...

In contrast, the question of law which has been referred to the Enlarged Board in the present case is not related to medical inventions but is of a general nature, being primarily concerned with the question of interpretation of Article 54(1) and (2) EPC.

6.2 Question (iii) assumes that the only novel feature in the claim under consideration is the purpose for which the compound is to be used. However, in so far as the question of interpretation of Article 54(1) and (2) EPC and the question of the allowable scope of protection (if any) of inventions concerning a further non-medical use are matters of general importance, it will be appropriate for this Board to consider the question raised more generally, and in particular to consider other possible constructions for such use claims.

[We can see that the Enlarged Board of Appeal refused to draw analogies with *Eisai* on the basis that this decision was concerned with a specific question of law, namely, the proper interpretation of Article 54(5) EPC, whereas the question of law in the present case was of a general nature. The Board went on to consider this question:]

7.1 ...In relation to a claim to a use of a known entity for a new purpose, the initial question is again: what are the technical features of the claimed invention? If the new purpose is achieved by a 'means of realisation' which is already within the state of the art in association with the known entity, and if the only technical features in the claim are the (known) entity in association with the (old) means of realisation, then the claim includes no novel technical feature. In such a case, the only 'novelty' in the claimed invention lies in the mind of the person carrying out the claimed invention, and is therefore subjective rather than objective, and not relevant to the considerations that are required when determining novelty under Article 54(1) and (2) EPC.

7.2 It follows that in the Enlarged Board's judgment, in relation to a claim to a new use of a known compound (the new purpose of such use being the only potentially novel feature), if on its proper construction the claim contains no technical feature which reflects such new use, and the wording of the claim which refers to such new use is merely mental in nature and does not define a technical feature, then the claim contains no novel technical feature and is invalid under Article 54(1) and (2) EPC (because the only technical features in the claim are known).

[At this point, one might be forgiven for thinking that the Enlarged Board was about to conclude that the patent in question lacked novelty. However, the Board went on to hold that the *fact* that the substance achieved the new purpose would result in an objective technical feature of the invention, not residing in the mind of the user.]

10.3 The answer to question (iii) may therefore be summarised as follows: with respect to a claim to a new use of a known compound, such new use may reflect a newly discovered technical effect described in the patent. The attaining of such a technical effect should then be considered as a functional technical feature of the claim (for example, the achievement in a particular context of that technical effect). If that technical feature has not been previously made available to the public by any of the means as set out in Article 54(2) EPC, then the claimed invention is novel, even though such technical effect may have inherently taken place in the course of carrying out what has previously been made available to the public.

The same conclusion was reached by the Enlarged Board of Appeal in *Bayer/Plant Growth Regulating Agent* G06/88.[277] Here the patent application was directed to the use of a compound as a fungicide, whereas the prior art described the use of the same compound as an agent for influencing plant growth. The claim in question was held to include a functional technical feature, namely, 'that the named compounds, when used in accordance with the described means of realisation, in fact achieve the effect (that is, perform the function) of controlling fungus'.[278]

In the UK concerns have been expressed about the approach in *Mobil Oil* and *Bayer*. For example, Lord Hoffmann in *Merrell Dow v Norton*[279] commented obiter:

> I think it is fair to say that, in the United Kingdom at least, this aspect of the Enlarged Board's decision has been criticised on the ground that a patent for an old product used in an old way for a new purpose makes it difficult to apply the traditional United Kingdom doctrine of infringement. Liability for infringement is, as I have said, absolute. It depends upon whether the act in question falls within the claims and pays no attention to the alleged infringer's state of mind. But this doctrine may be difficult to apply to a patent for the use of a known substance in a known way for a new purpose. How does one tell whether the person putting the additive into his engine is legitimately using it to inhibit rust or infringing by using it to reduce friction? In this appeal, however, we are not concerned with this aspect of the case.

The difficulties which novelty of purpose claims pose for determining infringement were most likely not in the forefront of the minds of the members of the Enlarged Board of Appeal because the EPO is concerned only with issues of validity.[280] The difficulty identified by Lord Hoffmann is particularly real for English courts, however, because they deal with *both* validity and infringement. One might ask why the Swiss-form claims discussed in the previous section have not given rise to similar difficulties with regards to infringement? In *Actavis v Merck* the Court of Appeal suggested that this had not caused problems, 'because manufacturers, particularly those for prescription medicine and probably many others, have to provide detailed instructions and information about the use(s) and dosage(s) of their products. So in practice you can tell whether someone has used X for the manufacture of a medicament for the treatment of Y.'[281]

9.10.7 SELECTION PATENTS

We have seen that, in relation to pharmaceutical substances, there is a statutory exception for novelty that has been broadly interpreted by UK courts and also the Enlarged Board of Appeal. The area of selection patents has traditionally been considered as another (albeit judge made) exception to the novelty requirement, although recent jurisprudence suggests otherwise.[282]

The concept of selection patents was developed in response to the problem caused by patenting compounds. More specifically, an earlier disclosure might have referred to an

---

[277] [1990] EPOR 257.   [278] *Bayer/Plant Growth Regulating Agent* G06/88 [1990] EPOR 257, para. 7.
[279] [1996] RPC 76, 92.
[280] In *Bristol Meyers Squibb Co v Baker Norton Pharmaceuticals Inc* [1999] RPC 253, 272, Jacob J (as he then was) commented at first instance that it is not helpful for the EPO 'to take a view on validity (particularly novelty) which simply leaves intractable problems for an infringement court'.
[281] *Actavis UK Ltd v Merck & Co Inc* [2008] EWCA Civ 444, para. 10.
[282] *Dr Reddy's Laboratories (UK) Ltd v Eli Lilly and Co Ltd* [2008] EWHC 2345.

extremely broad class of compounds (i.e. a generic disclosure), yet later it may have been discovered that an individual compound within that class had a particular quality or advantage that was not previously known. Did the earlier generic disclosure (which would have included that individual compound) anticipate the individual compound? In *IG Farbenindustrie's Patent*,[283] Maugham J held that where the individual compounds had not been previously made, the patent might be valid if the following three requirements were satisfied:

> First, a selection patent to be valid must be based on some substantial advantage to be secured by the use of the selected members (the phrase will be understood to include the case of a substantial disadvantage to be thereby avoided). Secondly, the whole of the selected members must possess the advantage in question. Thirdly, the selection must be in respect of a quality of a special character which can fairly be said to be peculiar to the selected group.[284]

This decision was followed and the notion of selection patents further explored by the House of Lords in *EI Du Pont de Nemours & Co's (Witsiepe's) Application*.

EI Du Pont de Nemours & Co's (Witsiepe's) Application [1982] FSR 303

Du Pont sought a patent for co-polyesters made of three ingredients: (1) terephthalic acid, (2) polyalkylene oxide, and (3) 1, 4 butanediol. These co-polyesters were described as especially effective in injection moulding because of their improved hardening rates. Du Pont's application was opposed on the basis, *inter alia*, of anticipation by an earlier patent specification published in 1952. The published specification claimed a class of co-polyesters that had an enhanced absorptive capacity for water, thus enabling them to be more readily dyed in the form of fibres for textiles. The specification mentioned the first two ingredients of the applicant's invention, together with a series of nine glycols defined by a general formula, of which 1, 4 butanediol was named as one. However, the working examples described the use only of the first member of the series, namely, ethylene glycol. It was argued that the earlier patent specification gave sufficient directions to enable a chemist to make any of the indicated nine co-polyesters and that each and all of these was therefore available to the public and anticipated Du Pont's invention. The hearing officer accepted this objection, but was reversed by Whitford J in the Patents Court. The Court of Appeal upheld Whitford J's judgment and an appeal to the House of Lords was dismissed.

Lord Wilberforce (delivering the leading speech), at pp. 309–12:

In order to consider whether [the opponent's] argument is correct, or whether it is too simplistic, it is necessary to look more closely at the process by which an invention is disclosed in a document, and the nature of the identification required. There are several principles here involved. First, it may be true to say as a general rule that where an invention for a substance is specifically disclosed, with a claim for particular advantages, or where a substance is already known, a discovery that the disclosed or known substance has some advantage or useful quality not previously recognised does not give a right to a patent. The difficulty

---

[283] (1930) 47 RPC 289.   [284] Ibid., pp. 322–3.

arises when disclosure is made of a group or class of substances for which some advantage is claimed, and later it is found that one or more of this group or class possesses special advantages not belonging to the rest of the group or class, and not previously identified. This situation arises particularly in relation to inventions in the chemical field, particularly where molecular combinations are involved. In many fields, of which those concerned with poly-meric chains are a good example, the number of combinations of chains, sub-chains, rings, individual molecules, may be very large. When a researcher is able to discover that a particu-lar combination produces advantageous results he will most probably be able to assert, and will assert in the specification of his invention, that the same qualities will be produced by a number of variants or homologues described by a formula, or formulae. Moreover, having described how to produce the particular combination, he may well be able to assert, with truth, that productions of any of the combinations can be made by any skilled chemist, follow-ing the indications he has given. Is, then, the mere fact that he has disclosed or published in general terms the possibility of these combinations, in such a way that they can be made, a disclosure or publication of unrecognised advantages which may be found to be possessed by one or some of them?

The law regarding selection patents has been developed to deal with this problem. It has done so in the direction of recognising two objectives, first to protect the original inventor, as regards the invention which he has made, but secondly, to encourage other researchers in the field to use their inventive powers so as to discover fresh advantages and to treat the dis-covery of such advantages as inherent in selected members of the group or class as a patent-able invention. The modern statement of this part of the law as regards chemical patents is the judgment of Maugham J in *I G Farbenindustrie A.G.'s Patents* (1930) 47 RPC 289, a case concerned with chemical combinations for the production of dyes.

...

In the first place, in order to leave open a field for selection by a subsequent inventor, it does not matter whether the original field is described by formula or by enumeration. A skilled chemist could, in most cases, quite easily transform the one into the other and the rights of the subsequent inventor cannot depend upon the notation used. In the present case, the I.C.I. specification uses both a formula, and, to some extent, an enumeration: it does not matter to which one directs attention.

Secondly, the size of the initial group or class is not in itself decisive as to a question of prior publication of an invention related to a selected member or members. A selection patent might be claimed for one or several out of a class of 10 million (*cf. I G Farbenindustrie A.G.'s Patents* v.s. p. 321) or for one out of two (*cf.* the selection of one of two epimers of a synthetic penicillin combination). The size of the class may be relevant to a question of obviousness, and that question in turn may depend, in part, upon whether the later invention relates to the same field as that occupied by the prior invention, or to a different field. If an ordinary unin-ventive man would not be likely to look for the advantages he desires to produce in the area occupied by the prior invention, a decision to do so may well amount to the beginning of an inventive step. Here, to look for a product possessing special thermoplastic and elastomeric qualities in a 20-year old patent concerned with producing dyable fibres involves, *prima facie*, an inventive approach.

Thirdly, disclosing a prior invention does not amount to prior publication of a later invention if the former merely points the way which might lead to the latter...

It is the absence of the discovery of the special advantages, as well as the fact of non-making, that makes it possible for such persons to make an invention related to a member of the class.

Applying the law as I have endeavoured to state it, I have no doubt that the invention made by Du Pont was not disclosed or published by I.C.I. The latter merely indicated that

> the use, with other ingredients, of one preferred glycol would produce a compound with particular qualities, suggesting at the same time that use of any one of the other eight glycols would produce the same result. There was no statement that any of these others had in fact been used or that the product resulting therefrom had been found to have any particular advantages. That left it open to Du Pont to select one of them, to exercise upon it inventive research, and to discover that the product so made had valuable properties in a different field. I do not therefore understand how it can be claimed that this product, with its advantages, had been anticipated by I.C.I.

Is it justified or, indeed, desirable to create special rules, such as those stated in *IG Farbenindustrie* and *Du Pont* when it comes to assessing the novelty of chemical compounds? Could the existing general rules of novelty be applied in such a way to deal with the problem highlighted by 'selection patents'? Recently, Floyd J in *Dr Reddy's Laboratories (UK) Ltd v Eli Lilly and Co Ltd*,[285] has suggested that Maugham J in *IG Farbenindustrie* was in fact dealing with the issue of inventive step, and not that of novelty and, further, that *Du Pont* can be read in way that is consistent with the application of general novelty principles, as opposed to carving out special rules for selection patents. More specifically, Floyd J pointed to the EPO practice of not denying the novelty of a claim to a specific compound unless the compound is disclosed in 'individualized form'. He favoured this principle for the following reasons:

> 92. Firstly, a general formula is an extremely powerful way of covering a large number of chemical compounds: hence their frequent use in patent disclosure. It is, of course possible that someone could write down in succession all the compounds covered by all possible permutations of the variable substituents of the formula: but it is wholly artificial to suppose that anyone would. Attention would focus on compounds actually described, the remainder of the class being no more than a theoretical penumbra around those compounds.
>
> 93. Secondly, in those circumstances, I do not think it can be said that the prior document 'contains a clear description of, or clear instructions to do or make, something which would infringe the patentee's claim'. The description is not clear because of the need to make a combination of substituents before the compound could be regarded as 'unalterably established'.

Floyd J stated that *Du Pont* could be seen as consistent with the EPO approach: that is, the earlier patent specification did not contain a sufficiently individualized disclosure of the co-polyester containing 1, 4 butanediol. Floyd J also took the view that *Du Pont* did not require Maugham J's criteria in *IG Farbenindustrie* to be satisfied in order to be new. Rather, these criteria were treated as relevant to the issue of obviousness. It remains to be seen whether *Dr Reddy's Laboratories* will be followed by subsequent and higher courts in the UK. In your view, what are the advantages of adopting Floyd J's view in this area?

9.11 INVENTIVE STEP

9.11.1 INTRODUCTION

To be patentable, an invention must feature an inventive step. According to s. 3 of the PA 77 an invention will involve an inventive step 'if it is not obvious to a person skilled

---

[285] [2008] EWHC 2345.

in the art, having regard to any matter which forms part of the state of the art'. Failure to satisfy this requirement is variously described as 'lack of inventive step', 'lack of inventiveness', or 'obviousness'. An invention that surmounts this hurdle is described as 'inventive' or 'non-obvious'.

The requirement of inventive step in the UK emerged from case law at the end of the 19th century. It was put on a statutory footing (as a ground for revocation of a patent) in 1932 and as a ground for opposing the award of a patent in 1949. The requirement of inventive step was included in the Patents Act 1977 in terms similar to the equivalent provision in the EPC (Article 56).[286]

Whereas novelty is a quantitative requirement, inventive step is qualitative in nature.[287] More specifically, it ensures that patents are granted for meritorious inventions, as opposed to obvious extensions and modifications of the prior art.[288] Inventive step is a question of fact and, as such, precedents have limited value in relation to this inquiry (aside from setting out the relevant principles of law) and it will be difficult to predict the outcome of a challenge based on obviousness.[289] Further, appeal courts will be reluctant to overturn decisions of lower courts on this issue.[290]

9.11.2 STATE OF THE ART

The inventive step inquiry asks whether the invention is obvious to a person skilled in the art, having regard to what forms part of the state of the art. What comprises the prior art is essentially the same as for novelty, but with two key differences. First, matters specified in s. 2(3) of the PA 77, i.e. earlier unpublished patent applications, are excluded from the prior art for the purpose of obviousness. Presumably this is because the aim of s. 2(3) is to avoid double patenting and, as this function is carried out at the novelty stage, it is unnecessary to apply this principle at the stage of inventive step. Second, it is possible to combine together different pieces of prior art, i.e. to 'mosaic' prior art, where it is natural and logical or obvious to do so (e.g. where there are cross references).

The person skilled in the art is expected only to have scrutinized the information available in their own or closely related fields.[291] We turn now to consider the characteristics of this hypothetical person.

9.11.3 PERSON SKILLED IN THE ART

Central to the inventive step inquiry is the person skilled in the art, variously referred to as the hypothetical skilled addressee or notional skilled addressee. The attributes of this hypothetical person have been expounded in numerous cases and are helpfully summarized below by Laddie J.

---

[286] For further details of the history of this requirement see: Beier, 'The inventive step in its historical development' (1986) 17 IIC 301; S. Gratwick, 'Having regard to what was known and used' (1972) 88 LQR 341; J. Bochnovic, *The Inventive Step: Its evolution in Canada, the United Kingdom and the United States* (Munich: Max Planck, 1982).

[287] *Molnlycke AB v Proctor & Gamble Ltd* [1994] RPC 49, 112.

[288] A. Griffiths, 'Windsurfing and the inventive step' [1999] IPQ 160, 163–4.

[289] *Molnlycke AB v Proctor & Gamble Ltd* [1994] RPC 49, 114.

[290] *Biogen v Medeva* [1997] RPC 1, 45.   [291] See *John Manville Corporation's Patent* [1967] RPC 327.

Pfizer Ltd's Patent [2001] FSR [16] 201

Laddie J, at pp. 226–227:

62. …The question of obviousness has to be assessed through the eyes of the skilled but non-inventive man in the art. This is not a real person. He is a legal creation. He is supposed to offer an objective test of whether a particular development can be protected by a patent. He is deemed to have looked at and read publicly available documents and to know of public uses in the prior art. He understands all languages and dialects. He never misses the obvious nor stumbles on the inventive. He has no private idiosyncratic preferences or dislikes. He never thinks laterally. He differs from all real people in one or more of these characteristics. A real worker in the field may never look at a piece of prior art—for example he may never look at the contents of a particular public library—or he may be put off because it is in a language he does not know. But the notional addressee is taken to have done so. This is a reflection of part of the policy underlying the law of obviousness. Anything which is obvious over what is available to the public cannot subsequently be the subject of valid patent protection even if, in practice, few would have bothered looking through the prior art or would have found the particular items relied on. Patents are not granted for the discovery and wider dissemination of public material and what is obvious over it, but only for making new inventions. A worker who finds, is given or stumbles upon any piece of public prior art must realise that that art and anything obvious over it cannot be monopolised by him and he is reassured that it cannot be monopolised by anyone else.

63. Of particular importance in this case, in view of the way that the issue has been developed by the parties, is the difference between the plodding unerring perceptiveness of all things obvious to the notional skilled man and the personal characteristics of real workers in the field. As noted above, the notional skilled man never misses the obvious nor sees the inventive. In this respect he is quite unlike most real people. The difference has a direct impact on the assessment of the evidence put before the court. If a genius in a field misses a particular development over a piece of prior art, it could be because he missed the obvious, as clever people sometimes do, or because it was inventive. Similarly credible evidence from him that he saw or would have seen the development may be attributable to the fact that it is obvious or that it was inventive and he is clever enough to have seen it. So evidence from him does not *prove* that the development is obvious or not. It may be valuable in that it will help the court to understand the technology and how it could or might lead to the development. Similarly evidence from an uninspiring worker in the field that he did think of a particular development does not prove obviousness either. He may just have had a rare moment of perceptiveness. This difference between the legal creation and the real worker in the field is particularly marked where there is more than one route to a desired goal. The hypothetical worker will see them all. A particular real individual at the time might not. Furthermore, a real worker in the field might, as a result of personal training, experience or taste, favour one route more than another. Furthermore, evidence from people in the art as to what they would or would not have done or thought if a particular piece of prior art had, contrary to the fact, been drawn to their attention at the priority date is, necessarily, more suspect. Caution must also be exercised where the evidence is being given by a worker who was not in the relevant field at the priority date but has tried to imagine what his reaction would have been had he been so.

64. This does not mean that evidence from those in the art at the relevant time is irrelevant. It is not. As I have said, it may help the court to assess the possible lines of analysis and deductions that the notional addressee might follow. Furthermore, sometimes it may be very persuasive. If it can be shown that a number of ordinary workers in the relevant field

at the relevant time who were looking for the same goal and had the same prior art, missed what has been patented then that may be telling evidence of non-obviousness.

Why is it that obviousness is evaluated according to a hypothetical person, as opposed to an expert in the particular field of the invention, and what does this indicate about the level of inventiveness required by patent law? Given that much of the evidence relating to inventive step comes from witnesses who are leading experts in their field, how predictable will this assessment be?

The person skilled in the art is also imputed with the *common general knowledge* of the particular art or technical field in question. The common general knowledge is an important source of information in its own right and also forms the basis from which the hypothetical addressee will consider the prior art. It must be stressed that common general knowledge does not equate to the prior art or what is public knowledge. Rather, 'it is part of the mental equipment necessary for competency in that art or science concerned'.[292] What may comprise this body of knowledge was helpfully summarized by the Court of Appeal in the case below.

Beloit Technologies Inc v Valmet Paper Machinery Inc [1997] RPC 489

Aldous LJ (with whom Schiemann and Hirst LJJ agreed), at pp. 494–5:

It has never been easy to differentiate between common general knowledge and that which is known by some. It has become particularly difficult with the modern ability to circulate and retrieve information. Employees of some companies, with the use of libraries and patent departments, will become aware of information soon after it is published in a whole variety of documents; whereas others, without such advantages, may never do so until that information is accepted generally and put into practice. The notional skilled addressee is the ordinary man who may not have the advantages that some employees of large companies may have. The information in a patent specification is addressed to such a man and must contain sufficient details for him to understand and apply the invention. It will only lack an inventive step if it is obvious to such a man.

It follows that evidence that a fact is known or even well-known to a witness does not establish that that fact forms part of the common general knowledge. Neither does it follow that it will form part of the common general knowledge if it is recorded in a document. As stated by the Court of Appeal in *General Tire & Rubber Co v Firestone Tyre & Rubber Co Ltd* [1972] RPC 457, at page 482, line 33:

> The two classes of documents which call for consideration in relation to *common general* knowledge in the instant case were individual patent specifications and 'widely read publications'.
>
> As to the former, it is clear that individual patent specifications and their contents do not normally form part of the relevant *common general* knowledge, though there may be specifications which are so well known amongst those versed in the art that upon evidence of that state of affairs they form part of such knowledge, and also there may occasionally be particular industries (such as that of colour photography) in which the evidence may show that all specifications form part of the relevant knowledge.

---

[292] *Terrell*, at p. 125.

As regards scientific papers generally, it was said by Luxmoore, J in *British Acoustic Films* (53 RPC 221 at 250):

'In my judgment it is not sufficient to prove common general knowledge that a particular disclosure is made in an article, or series of articles, in a scientific journal, no matter how wide the circulation of that journal may be, in the absence of any evidence that the disclosure is accepted generally by those who are engaged in the art to which the disclosure relates. A piece of particular knowledge as disclosed in a scientific paper does not become common general knowledge merely because it is widely read, and still less because it is widely circulated. Such a piece of knowledge only becomes general knowledge when it is generally known and accepted without question by the bulk of those who are engaged in the particular art; in other words, when it becomes part of their common stock of knowledge relating to the art.'

And a little later, distinguishing between what has been written and what has been used, he said:

'It is certainly difficult to appreciate how the use of something which has in fact never been used in a particular art can ever be held to be common general knowledge in the art.'

Those passages have often been quoted, and there has not been cited to us any case in which they have been criticised. We accept them as correctly stating in general the law on this point, though reserving for further consideration whether the words 'accepted without question' may not be putting the position rather high: for the purposes of this case we are disposed, without wishing to put forward any full definition, to substitute the words 'generally regarded as a good basis for further action'.

How does the common general knowledge of a person skilled in the art differ from the state of the art? What sorts of things might you expect to see included in the latter that would not be included in the former?

The person skilled in the art asks whether the invention is technically or practically obvious, as opposed to whether it is commercially worthwhile or obvious to pursue.[293] As we shall see, this means that evidence of the commercial success of an invention is not essential to proving its inventiveness and, indeed, is very cautiously approached when it comes to this inquiry. Even so, courts have taken commercial considerations into account when determining the mindset of a person skilled in the art. For example, in *Dyson Appliances Ltd v Hoover Ltd*[294] the Court of Appeal held that the trial judge had been correct to take into account, as part of the mindset of the person skilled in the art, commercial considerations that made it extremely unlikely that a particular line of inquiry would be pursued. More specifically, the invention related to a vacuum cleaner which operated by virtue of cylindrical and conical cyclone units, such that the dirt could be emptied directly from the units and filter bags were not required. The trial judge had imputed to the notional addressee an aversion to cyclone units and an addiction to the use of filter bags, on the basis that the vacuum cleaner industry was steeped in usage of the latter. The fact that this prejudice was commercially influenced did not matter. As Sedley LJ commented:[295]

it remains the case that the perceived limits of technical practicability are a matter of mindset, and that mindset is characteristically affected by awareness of need, of which commercial potential is both a function and an index.

. . .

---

[293] *Hallen Co v Brabantia (UK) Ltd* [1991] RPC 195, 213, per Slade LJ.   [294] [2002] RPC 22.
[295] Ibid., at paras. 87–8. See also Aldous LJ, at paras. 56–7 and Arden LJ, at para. 95.

> If then the intellectual horizon of practical research and innovation is in part set by the economic milieu, commercial realities cannot necessarily be divorced from the kinds of practical outcome which might occur to the law's skilled addressee as potentially worthwhile.

How does taking commercial realities into account as part of the mindset of the person skilled in the art differ from asking whether an invention is commercially worthwhile or obvious?

9.11.4 UK APPROACH

The way in which UK courts have approached the obviousness inquiry was established by the Court of Appeal in *Windsurfing v Tabur*, and later restated by the Court of Appeal in *Pozzoli*.

9.11.4.1 *Windsurfing v Tabur*

Windsurfing International v Tabur Marine [1985] RPC 59

The patent in suit related to the basic equipment employed in windsurfing. It comprised a surfboard with a spar attached. The spar was connected to the surfboard by a joint having three axes of rotation. A triangular sail was attached to the spar by a pair of arcuate (i.e. wishbone) booms, which were also used as a handle to steer and manipulate the sail. The inventive concept was the 'free sail concept', i.e. the unstayed spar which was free to move in any direction under the direct control of the user.

The claimants commenced infringement proceedings under the Patents Act 1949 against the defendants, who in turn counterclaimed contesting the validity of the patent on the grounds of, *inter alia*, novelty and obviousness. The claim of obviousness was based primarily on prior publication of an article written for an American periodical, which was reproduced in the UK in October 1966 in a publication produced by the Amateur Yacht Research Society (the Darby article). The article described essentially the same basic concept as the claimant's invention, namely, the use of an unstayed sail, which is used to steer the vehicle and which can be jettisoned in case of trouble. However, the sailboard described in the article used a square sail, and the unstayed spar was attached by a socket from which it could be removed, not by a movable joint. The article described how to build the sail and board, with diagrammatical illustrations. The defendants also relied on the prior use of a 12-year-old child (Chilvers), who had made a sailboard similar to the patent in suit, except that it employed straight booms, rather than arcuate booms. The prior use had occurred at an inlet at Hayling Island on summer weekends during 1958.

Oliver LJ (delivering the judgment of the court), **at pp. 73–4:**

There are, we think, four steps which require to be taken in answering the jury question. The first is to identify the inventive concept embodied in the patent in suit. Thereafter, the court has to assume the mantle of the normally skilled but unimaginative addressee in the art at the priority date and to impute to him what was, at that date, common general knowledge in the art in question. The third step is to identify what, if any, differences exist between the matter cited as being 'known or used' and the alleged invention. Finally, the court has to ask itself whether, viewed without any knowledge of the alleged invention, those differences constitute steps which would have been obvious to the skilled man or whether they require any degree of invention. As regards the first step, we respectfully agree with the learned judge that the inventive concept of the patent is the free-sail concept. It is that which constitutes the essential difference between the patent in suit and other conventional vehicles propelled by sail. Going back, then, to the priority date, anyone familiar with sailing and sailing craft would then have known, as part of his general knowledge, the difference between square sail and Bermuda rigs and the disadvantages as regards manoeuvrability presented by the former. He would also have been familiar with twin booms arcuate in shape known as 'wishbone' booms which, though not in wide use in the 1960s, were well known to anyone interested in constructing light craft. Darby's article was addressed initially to the knowledgeable handyman for whom the American journal *Popular Science Monthly* (in which it first appeared) was designed and, so far as the publication in this country was concerned, was directed to members of a society dedicated to amateur research into yachts. It in fact disclosed, and disclosed to persons knowledgeable in the art, the self-same inventive step claimed by the patent in suit, the only difference of any substance being the use of the kite rig held by the crossed spar and boom instead of a Bermuda rig with a wishbone boom. We agree, of course, that one must not assume that the skilled man, casting his experienced eye over Darby, would at once be fired with the knowledge that here was something which had a great commercial future which he must bend every effort to develop and improve, but he must at least be assumed to appreciate and understand the free-sail concept taught by Darby and to consider, in the light of his knowledge and experience, whether it will work and how it will work. In the light of the evidence, it seems to us inescapable that anyone skilled in the art and contemplating Darby's article in 1966 would immediately recognise, as the witnesses did, that the kite rig suggested for this very simple and elementary device would suffer from the disadvantages that it would perform poorly upwind and would require to be manipulated from the lee side of the sail. It does not, in our judgment, require the attribution to the skilled addressee of any inventive faculty to say that, if he applied his mind to it at all, it would be immediately obvious to him that these disadvantages would disappear if the rig were changed to Bermuda, a change which, as would also be obvious to him, required the sail to be stretched by means of a wishbone boom. It may well be that nobody in the United Kingdom at that time would have considered that there was a commercial future in this interesting beach novelty, but that is not as we conceive the question which has to be answered. One has, in our judgment, to postulate a person who comes to Darby knowing of the advantages of a Bermuda rig over a square rig and who is at least sufficiently interested to read the article and consider how the vehicle described would work on the water. All the evidence suggests that such a person would immediately see, by application of his own general knowledge, the adoption of a Bermuda rig as an obvious way of improving the performance of the Darby vehicle.

Obviousness based on prior publication—i.e. the Darby article—was enough to dispose of the appeal. However, the court went on to consider the obviousness challenge based on prior use of the Chilvers sailboard. It held that, although the use was of a short duration and had only a limited audience, it nonetheless formed part of the prior art and, further, that a person skilled in the art, on seeing the Chilvers sailboard, would have at once considered it obvious to replace the unconventional straight boom with an arcuate boom.

Although *Windsurfing v Tabur* was decided in relation to the Patents Act 1949, the structured approach to obviousness that it sets out has been followed in subsequent Court of Appeal decisions concerning the Patents Act 1977.[296] While the House of Lords has not expressly followed *Windsurfing v Tabur*, neither has it disapproved of the approach taken in that case.[297]

Most recently, the Court of Appeal in *Pozzoli SPA v BDMO SA*[298] has restated the four-step *Windsurfing* approach as follows:

1. (a) Identify the notional 'person skilled in the art';

   (b) Identify the relevant common general knowledge of that person;

2. Identify the inventive concept of the claim in question or if that cannot readily be done, construe it;

3. Identify what, if any, differences exist between the matter cited as forming part of the 'state of the art' and the inventive concept of the claim or the claim as construed;

4. Viewed without any knowledge of the alleged invention as claimed, do those differences constitute steps which would have been obvious to the person skilled in the art or do they require any degree of invention?

The difference between the *Windsurfing* four-step approach and the restatement in *Pozzoli* is marginal. Basically, the order of the first two questions in *Windsurfing* have been switched, so that the first step involves identifying the person skilled in the art and imputing to him the common general knowledge in the field, rather than identifying the inventive concept. Jacob LJ explained that the reason for the switch was that the inventive concept could only be understood through the eyes of the skilled addressee.[299] In the second step Jacob LJ has also sought to emphasize that the inventive concept is not some generalized concept to be derived from the patent specification as a whole, but that which is reflected in the patent claim/s. Finally, the third step refers to the 'state of the art' rather than what was 'known or used' in order to make it consistent with the EPC and PA 77.

In your view, is the approach set out in *Windsurfing* and restated in *Pozzoli* helpful in determining obviousness? Does it make the outcome of this inquiry more predictable?

FURTHER READING

G. Grant and D. Dibbins, '"Inventive concept": Is it a good idea' [2005] EIPR 170.

S. Gratwick, 'Having regard to what was known and used: Revisited' [1986] LQR 403.

A. Griffiths, 'Windsurfing and the inventive step' [1999] IPQ 160.

9.11.4.2 The importance of identifying the inventive concept: the approach to collocation

What is the situation where the alleged inventiveness comes from combining known features? Previously, courts have applied the so-called 'law of collocation' as set out by Lord

---

[296] See for example, Court of Appeal decisions in *Molnlycke AB v Proctor & Gamble Ltd* [1994] RPC 49; *Wheatley (Davina) v Drillsafe Ltd* [2001] RPC 133; and *Dyson Appliances Ltd v Hoover Ltd* [2002] RPC 22.

[297] See *Biogen v Medeva* [1997] RPC 1 and *Sabaf SpA v MFI Furniture Centres Ltd* [2005] RPC 10.

[298] [2007] FSR 37, 23, per Jacob LJ (Keene and Mummery LJJ in agreement).   [299] Ibid., para. 15.

Tomlin in *British Celanese Ltd v Courtaulds Ltd*:[300]

> a mere placing side by side of old integers so that each performs its own proper function independently of any of the others is not a patentable combination, but that where the old integers when placed together have some working inter-relation producing a new or improved result then there is patentable subject-matter in the idea of a working interrelation brought about by the collocation of the integers.

Guidance on this issue is also to be found in the EPO Guidelines for Substantive Examination (December 2003 edition) in Ch IV:

> 9.5 Combination vs. juxtaposition or aggregation. The invention claimed must normally be considered as a whole. When a claim consists of a 'combination of features', it is not correct to argue that the separate features of the combination taken by themselves are known or obvious and that 'therefore' the whole subject-matter claimed is obvious. However, where the claim is merely an 'aggregation or juxtaposition of features' and not a true combination, it is enough to show that the individual features are obvious to prove that the aggregation of features does not involve an inventive step. A set of technical features is regarded as a combination of features if the functional interaction between the features achieves a combined technical effect which is different from, e.g. greater than, the sum of the technical effects of the individual features. In other words, the interactions of the individual features must produce a synergistic effect. If no such synergistic effect exists, there is no more than a mere aggregation of features.

The House of Lords in *Sabaf SpA v MFI Furniture Centres Ltd*[301] clarified that there is no law of collocation in the sense of some kind of qualification to the test of inventive step stated in the PA 77. In other words, where the invention involves a combination of elements the proper test to apply is that contained in s. 3. However, Lord Hoffmann (who delivered the leading speech) noted that in determining the invention, the court must decide whether it is dealing with a single inventive concept or a collocation of separate inventions. He added:

> If the two integers interact upon each other, if there is synergy between them, they constitute a single invention having a combined effect and one applies s. 3 to the idea of combining them. If each integer 'performs its own proper function independently of any of the others', then each is for the purposes of s. 3 a separate invention and it has to be applied to each one separately. That, in my opinion, is what Laddie J meant by the law of collocation.

Thus, where several known integers are combined, the court must determine whether this reflects a single invention or separate inventions and apply the test of inventive step accordingly. In other words, properly identifying the inventive concept is crucial. Lord Hoffmann held that Laddie J had adopted this approach and, having determined that two separate inventions were involved, had found that there were pieces of prior art that rendered each of the inventions obvious.[302]

The approach to inventiveness of a collocation of elements in *Sabaf* makes sense, although it is puzzling why a claim would in fact feature two or more separate inventions given the procedural requirement in s. 14(5)(d) of the PA 77 that a claim shall 'relate to

---

[300] (1935) 52 RPC 171, 193.   [301] [2005] RPC 10.   [302] Ibid., para. 27.

one invention or to a group of inventions which are so linked as to form a single inventive concept'. Could it be that examiners sometimes fall into error in this respect or that the courts subsequently take a different view to that adopted by the examiner?

FURTHER READING

M. Wilkinson, 'Patents: Inventive step—collocation, validity and infringement' [2005] 27 EIPR N47–50.

9.11.4.3 The importance of identifying the inventive concept and its relationship to sufficiency

In a recent decision, the House of Lords emphasized that inventive step and sufficiency (discussed below at 9.12) are separate enquiries that should not be conflated. In *Conor Medsystems Incorporated v Angiotech Pharmaceuticals Inc*[303] Angiotech and the University of British Columbia had obtained a European patent (UK) for a stent coated with taxol for treating restenosis. Stents are tubular metal scaffolds inserted into an artery to keep it open. When stents are inserted there is often injury to the inner layer of the artery, which in turn produces an exaggerated healing response that tends to constrict the artery (known as restenosis). The patentees discovered that a known cancer treating drug, taxol, had properties which could be used to inhibit or prevent tissue growth in restenosis and thus claimed taxol-coated stents. At trial, counsel for Conor Medsystems argued that the inventive step was not the taxol coated stent but rather the *idea* of trying to treat or prevent restenosis by coating a stent with taxol. As such, the invention was obvious because it was known that taxol was worth a try. Further, it was unnecessary to show that it was obvious actually to use a taxol-coated stent to treat restenosis because the patent did not teach that it would work.

Lord Hoffmann, delivering the leading speech in the House of Lords, regarded Conor's argument 'as an illegitimate amalgam of the requirements of inventiveness (Article 56 of the EPC) and either sufficiency (Article 83) or support (Article 84) or both'[304] and that 'the invention is the product specified in the claim' as opposed to 'some vague paraphrase based upon the extent of his disclosure in the description'.[305] His lordship held that if the patent specification had not taught that a taxol-coated stent would treat or prevent restenosis, the patent would have been insufficient.[306] But once 'a specification passes the threshold test of disclosing enough to make the invention plausible' there was no reason to apply a different test of obviousness. Thus, the question was whether it was obvious that a taxol-coated stent would treat restenosis as opposed to whether it was obvious that taxol (among many other products) might have this effect.[307]

FURTHER READING

A. Carter, '*Conor Medsystems Inc v Angiotech Pharmaceuticals Inc*: House of Lords judgment clarifying the assessment of "inventive step"' [2008] EIPR 429.

---

[303] [2008] UKHL 49. [304] Ibid., para. 17. [305] Ibid., para. 18.
[306] Ibid., paras. 27, 37. [307] Ibid., para. 28.

9.11.4.4 'Obvious-to-try': *Conor v Angiotech*

Although the UK approach to obviousness is that set out in *Windsurfing v Tabur* as restated in *Pozzoli*, UK courts have nevertheless developed certain 'sub-tests' that may be applicable in appropriate circumstances. One such 'sub-test' is the 'obvious-to-try' test. This 'sub-test' may be particularly applicable where at the priority date the inventor had several technical options that could have been pursued in order to arrive at his invention. In *Conor v Angiotech* the House of Lords held that the refusal of the Court of Appeal to apply the 'obvious-to-try' sub-test to the patent in suit was erroneous.

Conor Medsystems Incorporated v Angiotech Pharmaceuticals Inc
[2008] UKHL 49

The facts were discussed at 9.11.4.3 above.

Lord Hoffmann (delivering the leading speech):

42. In the Court of Appeal, Jacob LJ dealt comprehensively with the question of when an invention could be considered obvious on the ground that it was obvious to try. He correctly summarised the authorities, starting with the judgment of Diplock LJ in *Johns-Manville Corporation's Patent* [1967] RPC 479, by saying that the notion of something being obvious to try was useful only in a case in which there was a fair expectation of success. How much of an expectation would be needed depended upon the particular facts of the case. As Kitchin J said in *Generics (UK) Ltd v H Lundbeck A/S* [2007] RPC 32, para 72:

> The question of obviousness must be considered on the facts of each case. The court must consider the weight to be attached to any particular factor in the light of all the relevant circumstances. These may include such matters as the motive to find a solution to the problem the patent addresses, the number and extent of the possible avenues of research, the effort involved in pursuing them and the expectation of success.

43. But Jacob LJ rejected this approach (at paragraph 48) on the grounds that 'this is not an "obvious to try" case of the Johns-Manville type' because 'the patent has not in any way demonstrated that taxol actually works to prevent restenosis'. I agree with the Dutch court that patent law does not require such a demonstration. It was not a sufficient reason for not applying the ordinary principles of obviousness to the claimed invention. I would therefore allow the appeal.

Apparent from the above extract is the point referred to in the previous section, namely, that the issues of obviousness and sufficiency should be treated separately. Further, when it came to obviousness it was appropriate to ask whether a person skilled in the art would have a fair expectation of success sufficient to induce him to incorporate taxol in a drug-eluting stent? Lord Hoffmann concluded that if Pumfrey J had applied this test at first instance the patent would have been found to be inventive.[308]

FURTHER READING
P. England, 'Obvious to try, one year on' (2009) 4 JIPLP 114.

---

[308] *Conor v Angiotech*, at paras 40–1.

9.11.5 THE EPO APPROACH

9.11.5.1 'Problem & solution' analysis

The EPO has adopted a different approach to assessing 'inventive step' than the UK courts. This 'problem and solution' approach was first espoused in the *Bayer/Carbonless Copying Paper.*[309]

The case involved a chemical invention, namely, microcapsules for carbonless copying paper which contained something called dyestuff-intermediate. The Examining Division refused the European Patent application for lack of inventive step. This was because a German unexamined application disclosed the manufacture of carbonless copying papers containing the micro-encapsulated dyestuff solution. However this paper was not impermeable to water, which meant that the paper had problems with storage stability, which in turn affected its duplicating capacity. In their appeal to the Technical Board, the applicant narrowed its claims to refer to the use of a more precise chemical element (which was water-repelling) to create special walls on the microcapsule containing the dyestuff-intermediate.

The Technical Board of Appeal allowed the appeal. It found that the applicant had defined the problem, vis-á-vis the nearest prior art as not just preparing other copying papers but improved copying papers. In order to solve the problem of storage stability the applicant proposed to encapsulate the dyestuff-intermediate as solution within capsule walls made up of the more precisely described chemical element. It was known from the German application that in principle a range of chemical elements could be used for the capsule walls. But, from the point of view of the problem of preparing copying paper that had improved storage stability, it did not indicate the more precisely prescribed chemical element. Thus, a person skilled in the art who had tried to improve copying papers would not, on the basis of the prior art cited, have arrived at the solution claimed in the application.

9.11.5.2 Criticisms

The problem-and-solution approach to inventive step has been widely accepted by the EPO. Even so, it was criticized by the Technical Board of Appeal in *Alcan/Aluminium Alloys Case* T465/92[310] for several reasons. First, the approach is inherently based on hindsight because it relies on the results of a search made with actual knowledge of the invention. Second, it is difficult to apply the approach to fields where new ground is broken, and thus no close prior art exists from which to formulate the problem. Third, it can lead to formulations of unrealistic and artificial technical problems, especially where there is no close prior art (or no problem in mind). Fourth, the benefit of the approach is said to be its 'objective-ness'. However, the problem-and-solution analysis does not remove the element of judgment inherent in the assessment of inventiveness, but rather displaces it from the task set by the EPC to another task, which is inessential to Article 56 of the EPC.

Despite *Alcan,* the EPO and Technical Board of Appeal have continued to use the problem-and-solution approach, which involves asking whether the solution to a problem that an invention provides would have been obvious.

---

[309] [1981] OJ EPO 206.   [310] [1995] EPOR 501.

9.11.5.3 Following the EPO?

The problem-and-solution approach has found limited support in the UK. In *Biogen v Medeva*[311] the House of Lords seemingly expressed support for it. Lord Hoffmann, delivering the leading speech in *Biogen,* commented obiter on the issue of inventive step. He took the view that the first-instance judge had, following the *Windsurfing* approach, formulated the inventive concept too broadly as 'the idea or decision to express a polypeptide displaying HBV antigen specificity in a suitable host'.[312] Formulated in this way, the inventive concept was the idea of making hepatitis B virus antigens by recombinant DNA technology, yet this was obvious because several people shared this idea at the relevant time. Lord Hoffmann commented that, 'A proper statement of the inventive concept needs to include some express or implied reference to the problem which it required the invention to overcome.'[313] His lordship went on to re-characterize the inventive concept with more particularity as, 'the idea of trying to express unsequenced eukaryotic DNA in a prokaryotic host'.[314] Reformulated in this way, the argument for the existence of an inventive step was stronger. Although the Court of Appeal had differed from the first-instance judge on obviousness, his lordship did not believe that it was necessary to pursue this issue since he was content to assume that what the inventor did was not obvious. Moreover, the key issue in the case was whether or not the disclosure in the priority document supported the claims of the patent.[315]

Lord Hoffmann's comment about inventive concept has been described as the 'nearest he came to criticism of the *Windsurfing* test'.[316] It is a far cry, however, from an eschewal of *Windsurfing* and may, in fact, only indicate that a problem-and-solution analysis is helpful to identifying the inventive concept.[317]

In your view, how important is it that the UK and EPO adopt a uniform approach to the question of inventive step? Which, out of the two approaches, do you consider preferable?

FURTHER READING

P. G. Cole, 'Inventive step: Meaning of the EPO problem and solution approach, and implications for the United Kingdom: Part 1' [1998] EIPR 214.

P. G. Cole, 'Inventive sep: Meaning of the EPO problem and solution approach, and implications for the United Kingdom: Part 2' [1998] EIPR 267.

9.11.6 EVIDENCE OF INVENTIVE STEP

9.11.6.1 Primary evidence

Parties will call evidence from experts in the particular field about whether or not an invention was obvious. This is primary evidence and all other evidence is secondary in nature.[318] As mentioned above, the views of experts cannot be equated to those of the person skilled

---

[311] [1997] RPC 1. [312] Ibid., at p. 43. [313] Ibid., at p. 45.
[314] Ibid., at p. 45. [315] Discussed below, at 9.12.3.
[316] G. Grant and D. Dibbins, ' "Inventive concept": Is it a good idea' [2005] EIPR 170, 172.
[317] P. G. Cole, 'Inventive step: Meaning of the EPO problem and solution approach, and implications for the United Kingdom: Part 2' [1998] EIPR 267, 271.
[318] *Hoechst Celanese Corporation v BP Chemicals Ltd* [1997] FSR 547, 563; *Molnlycke AB v Proctor & Gamble Ltd* [1994] RPC 49, 113.

in the art. Nonetheless, courts will find expert evidence helpful in assessing the possible lines of analysis and research avenues a notional addressee might follow.

9.11.6.2 Secondary evidence

Secondary evidence is an aid to assessing primary evidence. It includes evidence concerning the commercial success of the invention, the failure of others to find a solution to the problem which the invention solves, and whether there has been a long felt want for that particular invention. UK courts have been sensitive to the pitfalls of relying on secondary evidence and thus cautious about when it is relied upon.[319] What do you consider the pitfalls of secondary evidence to be?

In the following case, Laddie J explored the way in which courts should approach secondary evidence, particularly that relating to commercial success.

Haberman v Jackel International Ltd [1999] FSR 683

The case involved a UK patent for a trainer cup, the specification for which was discussed above at 9.5.3. A trainer cup is a feeding device for use by toddlers to help wean them off the mother's nipple or a feeding bottle, and to transfer to using a normal cup. A key difference between trainer cups and feeding bottles is that a feeding bottle uses a synthetic nipple-like teat, whereas a training cup uses a spout made out of soft or flexible material. The inventor of the patent in suit, Mrs Haberman, had observed that children were prone to knocking over their trainer cups, or shaking them violently, and that the contents of the cup would leak out as a result. She subsequently developed a trainer cup involving a conventional design, except for the use of a slit valve in the spout, which ensured that there was no leakage of fluid between sips. After obtaining a patent, Mrs Haberman granted an exclusive licence for the UK to V&A Marketing Ltd. The trainer cup, marketed as the Anywayup Cup, was immensely successful. Sales commenced in March 1996 and by the end of the year 20,000 cups were being sold per month. After 12 months of the launch, the cups were selling at 685,000 per annum and in the first nine months of 1998 sales had reached nearly 2 million cups. Both parties sued the defendant for infringement of the patent and the defendant counterclaimed for revocation of the patent on the ground, *inter alia*, of obviousness.

Laddie J, at pp. 699–701:

In most cases this type of evidence is of little or no value because it does no more than show that a particular item or process which employs the patented development has sold well. The mere existence of large sales says nothing about what problems were being tackled by those in the art nor, without more, does it demonstrate that success in the market place has anything to do with the patented development nor whether it was or was not the obvious thing to do. After all, it is sometimes possible to make large profits by selling an obvious product well. But in some circumstances commercial success can throw light on the approach and thought processes which pervade the industry as a whole. The plaintiffs rely on commercial

---

[319] e.g. see *Hoechst Celanese Corporation v BP Chemicals Ltd* [1997] FSR 547, 563; *Molnlycke AB v Proctor & Gamble Ltd* [1994] RPC 49, 113.

success here. To be of value in helping to determine whether a development is obvious or not it seems to me that the following matters are relevant:

(a) What was the problem which the patented development addressed?...

(b) How long had that problem existed?

(c) How significant was the problem seen to be? A problem which was viewed in the trade as trivial might not have generated much in the way of efforts to find a solution. So an extended period during which no solution was proposed (or proposed as a commercial proposition) would throw little light on whether, technically, it was obvious... On the other hand evidence which suggests that those in the art were aware of the problem and had been trying to find a solution will assist the patentee.

(d) How widely known was the problem and how many were likely to be seeking a solution? Where the problem was widely known to many in the relevant art, the greater the prospect of it being solved quickly.

(e) What prior art would have been likely to be known to all or most of those who would have been expected to be involved in finding a solution? A development may be obvious over a piece of esoteric prior art of which most in the trade would have been ignorant. If that is so, commercial success over other, less relevant, prior art will have much reduced significance.

(f) What other solutions were put forward in the period leading up to the publication of the patentee's development? This overlaps with other factors. For example, it illustrates that others in the art were aware of the problem and were seeking a solution. But it is also of relevance in that it may indicate that the patentee's development was not what would have occurred to the relevant workers. This factor must be treated with care. As has been said on more than one occasion, there may be more than one obvious route round a technical problem. The existence of alternatives does not prevent each or [sic] them from being obvious. On the other hand where the patentee's development would have been expected to be at the forefront of solutions to be found yet it was not and other, more expensive or complex or less satisfactory, solutions were employed instead, then this may suggest that the *ex post facto* assessment that the solution was at the forefront of possibilities is wrong.

(g) To what extent were there factors which would have held back the exploitation of the solution even if it was technically obvious? For example, it may be that the materials or equipment necessary to exploit the solution were only available belatedly or their cost was so high as to act as a commercial deterrent. On the other hand if the necessary materials and apparatus were readily available at reasonable cost, a lengthy period during which the solution was not proposed is a factor which is consistent with lack of obviousness.

(h) How well has the patentee's development been received? Once the product or process was put into commercial operation, to what extent was it a commercial success. In looking at this, it is legitimate to have regard not only to the success indicated by exploitation by the patentee and his licensees but also the commercial success achieved by infringers. Furthermore, the number of infringers may reflect on some of the other factors set out above. For example, if there are a large number of infringers it may be some indication of the number of members of the trade who were likely to be looking for alternative or improved products...

(i) To what extent can it be shown that the whole or much of the commercial success is due to the technical merits of the development, i.e. because it solves the problem?

Success which is largely attributable to other factors, such as the commercial power of the patentee or his license, extensive advertising focusing on features which have nothing to do with the development, branding or other technical features of the product or process, says nothing about the value of the intention.

I do not suggest that this list is exhaustive. But it does represent factors which taken together may point towards or away from inventiveness. Most of them have been addressed in this case.

[**Laddie J**, at pp. 701–2, went on to consider these factors in relation to the evidence and concluded that the patent disclosed an inventive step.]

There is no dispute that the problem which Mrs Haberman's patent seeks to solve, namely the leakage of fluids from feeding containers, has existed for a very long time. Nor is there any doubt that it was seen to be significant...The industry as a whole appears to have wanted to produce spill-proof trainer cups.

. . .

The variety of solutions put forward to meet the leakage problem is impressive not only in number but because they all appear to suffer from significant disadvantages when compared with Mrs Haberman's design...if one looks at what was on the market before April 1992 the multitude of difficult and partially ineffective designs is apparent. Although the objective of making a leak-proof cup was known, by and large it had not been achieved. There were numerous designs of products which could be rendered leak proof by parental intervention. But in all these cases the parent turned the cup on or off.

. . .

These efforts should be set against the simplicity of what Mrs Haberman suggested. All the raw materials were readily available. The simplest of valves, used frequently in the same trade, could be used to make a product which had all the virtues which anyone designing a product would want to achieve. The advantages of the use of such a design would have been immediately apparent, once it was thought of. There was nothing which was holding anyone back.

It is against this background that the claim to commercial success has to be gauged...Mrs Haberman's product was cheap, simple, effective and a remarkable commercial success.

. . .

The point to be made about this evidence is that the only selling feature relied upon was that the product was leak resistant. I have already noted that its appearance was dull and unexceptional. In other words it was only the effect of Mrs Haberman's design which was used to promote the Anywayup cup and it was only that which achieved the sales.

To what extent was Laddie J in *Haberman v Jackel* sensitive to the fact that commercial success may be attributable to factors other than the technical merits of the invention? Further, how does evidence of the failure of others and long felt want interact with evidence of commercial success? Is it fair to say the latter type of evidence is only meaningful where in fact there has been a long felt want and others, working from the same or similar prior art, have failed? Finally, do you agree with the conclusion reached by Laddie J about the inventiveness of the Anywayup trainer cup?

FURTHER READING

R. P. Merges, 'Commercial success and patent standards: Economic perspectives on innovation' (1988) 76 Cal LR 803.

9.12 SUFFICIENCY AND SUPPORT

9.12.1 INTRODUCTION

In addition to showing that an invention is patentable subject matter, new, inventive, and capable of industrial application, an applicant must satisfy certain disclosure requirements. Section 14(3) of the PA 77 provides that the *specification* of an application must disclose the invention in a manner that is clear and complete enough for it to be performed by the person skilled in the art.[320] This requirement is known as *sufficiency* of disclosure. Whereas s. 14(5)(c) of the PA 77 provides that the *claims* must be clear and concise and supported by the description.[321] This requirement is known as the claims being *supported* by the description.

Each of these requirements is distinct, but interrelated. They are distinct insofar as they have differing purposes. Sufficiency of disclosure is aimed at ensuring that the consideration for granting the patent is extracted, i.e. ensuring that practical information about working the invention is disclosed to the public. Whereas the requirement of the description supporting the claims is seeking to ensure that the patentee is not claiming a monopoly that is wider than the invention they have disclosed. The requirements are interrelated insofar as lack of sufficiency is explicitly a basis upon which a patent may be revoked;[322] however, lack of support is not. Even so, it has been held that failure to comply with the requirement of claims being supported by the description *is* a ground on which a patent can be revoked. In *Biogen v Medeva*[323] Lord Hoffmann, who delivered the leading speech of the House of Lords, held that the substantive effect of s. 14(5)(c) of the PA 77 (i.e. sufficiency of disclosure) is that the description should constitute an 'enabling disclosure' and given that s. 72(1)(c) of the PA 77 gives effect to this requirement, it must also include lack of support as a ground for revocation. The logic is that a description would not support claims for the purpose of s. 14(5)(c) unless the specification contained sufficient material to constitute an enabling disclosure under s. 14(3).

The interrelationship between s. 14(3) and s. 14(5)(a) was explored again by the House of Lords in *Generics (UK) Ltd v H Lundbeck A/S*.[324] The House confirmed the view taken in *Biogen v Medeva*, namely, that the requirements are closely connected, albeit that 'section 14(3) relates to the specification as a whole, whereas section 14(5)(c) relates to the claims which define the monopoly sought by the inventor' and the provisions 'operate together...to spell out the need for an "enabling disclosure"'.[325]

9.12.2 SUFFICIENCY

9.12.2.1 General principles

What amounts to sufficiency of disclosure was elucidated by the Court of Appeal in *Mentor v Hollister*.[326]

---

[320] See also Art. 83 EPC.   [321] See also Art. 84 EPC.   [322] See PA 77, s. 72(1).
[323] *Biogen Inc v Medeva Plc* [1997] RPC 1.   [324] [2009] UKHL 12.
[325] Lord Walker at paras. 19–20.   [326] [1993] RPC 7.

Mentor v Hollister [1993] RPC 7

Mentor had patented a new type of male incontinence device, which they marketed as the Freedom Catheter. The invention incorporated a layer of adhesive in a rolled-up sheath of latex rubber, such that when the sheath was unrolled the adhesive would be released onto the inside of the sheath and come into contact with the skin. This in turn created a leak-proof seal. At the other end of the sheath there was a tube leading to a bag for the collection of urine. The claimant's device achieved substantial commercial success in the UK and elsewhere. Hollister copied the device and, when sued for infringement, counterclaimed that the patent was invalid on the ground that it lacked sufficiency. More specifically, Hollister argued that the specification did not disclose the invention clearly and completely enough for it to be performed by a person skilled in the art because it failed to disclose which adhesive would be suitable for making the device, nor how to select a latex rubber to release the adhesive as the sheath was unrolled. The first-instance judge found that the patent was valid. The defendants appeal was dismissed.

Lloyd LJ (with whom **Stuart-Smith** and **Scott LJJ** agreed), at pp. **10–13:**

...Disclosure of an invention does not have to be complete in every detail, so that anyone, whether skilled or not, can perform it. Since the specification is addressed to the skilled man, it is sufficient if the addressee can understand the invention as described, and can then perform it. In performing the invention the skilled man does not have to be told what is self-evident, or what is part of common general knowledge, that is to say, what is known to persons versed in the art. But then comes the difficulty. How much else may the skilled man be expected to do for himself? Is he to be able to produce what Mr Thorley called a workable prototype of the invention at his first attempt? Or may he be required to carry out further research or at least make some further enquiries before achieving success? And how does one draw the line between production of the so-called workable prototype and the subsequent development or 'optimisation' of the commercial product?

. . .

The parameters within which the skilled man is entitled to look for instruction were authoritatively stated by Cotton LJ in *Edison & Swan v Holland*, supra at page 277, and have often been repeated and paraphrased. On the one hand the addressee must be able to perform the invention without any further inventive step on his part. On the other hand it is not required that he should be able to perform the invention without any trial or experiment at all, in particular where the subject matter is new or especially delicate. Lindley LJ, at page 282, put the matter with somewhat different emphasis. He acknowledged that practice might be necessary, but added that he felt great difficulty in defining the amount of practice which might be required without affecting the validity of the patent. Nevertheless he was clear that practice was one thing; experiment and trial was another.

. . .

But if a working definition is required then one cannot do better than that proposed by Buckley LJ in giving the judgment of the Court of Appeal in *Valensi v British Radio Corporation* [1973] RPC 377. After referring to a number of earlier authorities, including *Edison & Swan v Holland*, he said:

We think that the effect of these cases as a whole is to show that the hypothetical addressee is not a person of exceptional skill and knowledge, that he is not to be expected to exercise any

> invention nor any prolonged research, inquiry or experiment. He must, however, be prepared to display a reasonable degree of skill and common knowledge of the art in making trials and to correct *obvious* errors in the specification if a means of correcting them can readily be found.

Then a little later:

> Further, we are of the opinion that it is not only inventive steps that cannot be required of the addressee. While the addressee must be taken as a person with a will to make the instructions work, he is not to be called upon to make a prolonged study of matters which present some initial difficulty: and, in particular, if there are actual errors in the specification—if the apparatus really will not work without departing from what is described—then, unless both the existence of the error and the way to correct it can quickly be discovered by an addressee of the degree of skill and knowledge which we envisage, the description is insufficient.

> In that case there was a mistake in the specification. But Buckley LJ's language is equally apt to cover an omission. Aldous J held that the *Valensi* test is as apposite under the 1977 Act as it was under the 1949 Act. I agree.

The court found that the judge had not erred in principle and that, on the facts, there was no lack of sufficiency. Although several tests had been performed in order to produce a workable prototype of the invention, this was routine trial and error and did not involve prolonged experimentation.

Do you agree that sufficiency of disclosure should mean that a person skilled in the art is neither required to exercise inventiveness or to carry out prolonged research or experimentation, even if that research is straightforward (i.e. non-inventive) in nature? Should there be an additional aspect to the sufficiency requirement, namely that the specification discloses the *best* mode of performing the invention? This used to be the case under the Patents Act 1949,[327] but is no longer so under the PA 77.

9.12.2.2 *Biogen* insufficiency

In the field of biotechnology lack of sufficiency has arisen as a particular concern. This is apparent from the House of Lords decision in *Biogen v Medeva*.[328] The principal claim of the patent in suit was for an artificially constructed molecule of DNA carrying a genetic code which, when introduced into a suitable host cell, would cause that cell to make antigens of the virus hepatitis B (HBV). At the application date, the inventiveness of this invention lay in the fact that it permitted an artificially constructed molecule of DNA to be constructed *prior* to when the sequencing of DNA was known. The invention involved taking fragments of DNA (cut with the use of restriction enzymes) and using standard plasmids to create a recombinant molecule inserted into a host bacterium that would produce HBV antigens.

The patent in suit generalized this invention in two ways: in terms of the result achieved and the method that had been used. It claimed *any* recombinant DNA molecule which expressed the genes of any HBV antigen in any host cell, and *any* method of manufacture that would achieve the necessary expression. Lord Hoffmann commented obiter that the reasoning that led to lack of support (discussed below) also led to lack of sufficiency.[329] Thus, the disclosure in the specification (which was of *one* particular method of creating a particular recombinant DNA molecule) was not clear and complete enough to

---

[327] See PA 1949, s. 32(1)(h).   [328] [1997] RPC 1.   [329] Ibid., at p. 53.

enable a person skilled in the art to work the broad monopoly that was claimed (i.e. *any* recombinant DNA molecule which expressed the genes of any HBV antigen in any host cell or *any* method of creating such a molecule). To amount to sufficient disclosure, the specification would have had to disclose a general principle for the making of recombinant DNA capable of producing HBV antigens.

In a subsequent decision, *American Home Products Corporation v Novartis Pharmaceuticals UK Ltd*,[330] the Court of Appeal had occasion to consider sufficiency in relation to a biotechnological invention and sought to apply the *Biogen* principles. The claimants in the case held a second medical-use patent for a product called rapamycin, which was useful in suppressing transplant rejection (and which had previously been used for its antifungal and anti-tumour properties). Novartis also produced an immunosuppressant, referred to as SDZ RAD, which is a derivative of rapamycin. They were sued for infringement by the claimants who argued that the patent claim covered both rapamycin *and* its derivatives. The defendants counterclaimed, alleging that, if the patent claim was construed in that way, the patent was invalid for insufficiency. This was because the specification disclosed only the beneficial property of rapamycin and not a beneficial property of a *class* of products (i.e. rapamcyin and its derivatives). Laddie J at first instance held that the patent was valid and infringed.

On appeal, Aldous LJ (with whom Sedley and Simon Brown LJJ agreed) held that the principles relating to sufficiency had been settled by *Biogen v Medeva*. Applying those principles, he concluded that a person skilled in the art, looking at the patent specification, would not have been able to predict *which* rapamycin derivatives would have beneficial immunosuppressant qualities. Instead, it would require the person skilled in the art to engage in prolonged tests in order to ascertain if the derivative did have the appropriate qualities. Thus, the patent specification did not provide an enabling disclosure across the breadth of the claim, but only a starting point for further research.[331]

In your view, does *American Home Products* illustrate a lack of sufficiency according to *Biogen* principles or can the lack of sufficiency be explained according to the general principles stated in *Mentor v Hollister*?

Most recently, the House of Lords has clarified the nature and scope of *Biogen* insufficiency.

Generics (UK) Ltd v H Lundbeck A/S [2009] UKHL 12

Lundbeck had previously held a patent for an organic compound, citalopram, which operates as an anti-depressant. After the patent expired its competitors began marketing citalopram. Citalopram is a racemate, meaning that it is a combination of two types of molecules, called enantiomers, each being a mirror image of each other. It was not known which of the (+) and (–) enantiomers of citalopram was responsible for its anti-depressant quality. Lundbeck devised a novel and inventive means of separating the (+) and (–) enantiomers and discovered that it was the (+) enantiomer that had the desired effect. They then applied for and obtained a European patent (UK) for the (+) enantiomer, known as escitalopram.

The generic pharmaceutical companies, Generics (UK) Ltd, Arrow Generics Ltd, Teva UK Ltd, and Teva Pharmaceutical Industries Ltd, brought an action for

---

[330] [2001] RPC 8.   [331] Ibid., paras. 40–4.

revocation of the Lundbeck patent, claiming that it lacked novelty, inventive step, and sufficiency. The attacks based on lack of novelty and obviousness failed at first instance. However, Kitchin J held that claims 1 and 3 were invalid for insufficiency. Claim 1 was to the (+) enantiomer itself and claim 3 was to a pharmaceutical composition comprising as an active ingredient the (+) enantiomer. Kitchin J based his conclusion on insufficiency on the House of Lords decision in *Biogen*.

On the issue of insufficiency, the Court of Appeal took a different view. It concluded that the claim was to a patented product, the enantiomer of the anti-depressant drug citalopram, and not to a class of products, as was in *Biogen*. As such, there was sufficiency of disclosure given that the patent specification disclosed at least one way of making the enantiomer. Jacob LJ noted that product claims provide extensive protection in at least two ways.[332] The first is that product claims are infringed whenever the product is made even if it is made by a method which is inventive and quite different from the patentee's route. Second, a product claim will provide a monopoly to the patentee over all uses of the product, even those which he has not discovered. Nevertheless, the court concluded that this was the nature of product claims and Parliament had seen fit to allow them.[333]

Generics (UK) Ltd et al. appealed to the House of Lords, but the appeal was dismissed.

Lord Neuberger (with whom **Lord Phillips** and **Lord Scott** agreed; **Lord Walker** and **Lord Mance** delivered concurring opinions):

74. Of course, sections 1 and 14 are concerned with the grant of patents, whereas it is section 72 (reflecting art 100 of the EPC) which is concerned with the revocation of patents, and which is therefore the section directly in point on this appeal. Section 72(1) provides that a patent can 'only' be revoked on certain specified grounds. These grounds include '(a) the invention is not a patentable invention', and '(c) the specification...does not disclose the invention clearly enough and completely enough for it to be performed by a person skilled in the art'. Section 72(1)(a) reflects section 1(1) though it may also go further. Section 72(1)(c) appears only to reflect section 14(3), but, as explained by Lord Hoffmann in *Biogen* [1997] RPC 1, 47, it also extends to what is covered by section 14(5)(c).

The reasoning of the courts below

75. In a sense, it was at this point that the reasoning of the Court of Appeal in this case ended. At [2008] RPC 19, para 36, Lord Hoffmann said that '[w]hen a product claim satisfies the requirements of section 1 of the 1977 Act, the technical contribution to the art is the *product* and not the process by which it was made, even if that process was the only inventive step'. Accordingly, as sections 1 and 14 appeared to be satisfied by the patent, he concluded that the claim to escitalopram was valid.

76. To the same effect, Jacob LJ said at [2008] RPC 19, para 52, that, as at June 1988, the pure (+)-enantiomer, as a product, was 'novel and non-obvious', and if 'one asks the straightforward question "Does the patent enable the skilled man to make it?" the answer is an equally straightforward "Yes". So, in the language of art 83, the patent "discloses the invention in a manner sufficiently clear and complete for it to be carried out."'

---

[332] *H Lundbeck A/S v Generics (UK) Ltd* [2008] RPC 437, Jacob LJ, at paras. 54–5.
[333] Ibid., Lord Hoffmann, at para. 46, and Jacob LJ, at para. 57.

77. The different view formed by Kitchin J was not based on any disagreement with this approach as far as it goes, but on reasoning which is helpfully summarised in his judgment at [2007] RPC 32, paras 264 and 265. He described the obtaining of the purified enantiomers as 'an obviously desirable goal', and said that, accordingly, the 'inventive step' was 'not deciding to separate the enantiomers . . . but finding a way it could be done'. He went on to say that the technical contribution made by the Patent was not to find a new product, but to find a way of making a product, namely a single enantiomer of citalopram, through the medium of isolating the diol intermediate.

78. Accordingly, the Judge concluded that, as the specification disclosed that the respondent had found only one way to make the (+)-enantiomer, it would be a monopoly disproportionate to the technical contribution if the Patent effectively covered all ways of making the enantiomer, which would be the effect of the product claim. The principle he relied on was succinctly encapsulated in a short sentence virtually at the end of his judgment, namely 'The first person to find a way of achieving an obviously desirable goal is not permitted to monopolise every other way of doing so.'

79. The sole authority upon which Kitchin J relied in support of this analysis was the speech of Lord Hoffmann in *Biogen* [1997] RPC 1. I propose first to consider whether his conclusion is justified on the basis of any principle or authority other than what was said in this House in *Biogen* [1997] RPC 1, and then to address the reasoning in *Biogen* [1997] RPC 1.

The insufficiency argument apart from *Biogen* [1997] RPC 1

80. The starting point must, of course, be the 1977 Act and the EPC. I have already identified and discussed the centrally relevant provisions of the 1977 Act, namely section 72(1)(a) and (c), which reflect art 100 of the EPC and refer back to sections 1(1), 14(3), and 14(5), which in turn reflect arts. 52, 83, and 84 of the EPC. It is hard to discern any statutory provision (or, by the same token, any provision in the EPC) to support the proposition that, once it has been established that a product claimed in a patent is novel and non-obvious, and the specification sufficiently explains to the person skilled in the art how to make it, the claim can nonetheless be rejected because there may be other ways of making the product which owe nothing to the teaching of the patent.

81. Mr Simon Thorley QC, for the appellants, relied on section 14(5)(c): he said that where, as in this case, a product was a known *desideratum*, the first person to make it could rely on his way of making it as 'support' for a claim for that process, but not for a claim for the product, as the single process did not support a claim for the product. I think that that argument ascribes an effect to section 14(5)(c) which it does not have. In *Asahi Kasei Kogyo KK's Application* [1991] RPC 485, 536, Lord Oliver of Aylmerton explained that 'a description would not "support" the claims for the purpose of subsection (5)(c) unless it contained sufficient material to enable the specification to constitute the enabling disclosure which subsection (3) required' (to quote Lord Hoffmann's summary in *Biogen* [1997] RPC 1, 47). That brings one straight back to section 14(3), and, as already mentioned, the specification of the Patent clearly sets out the diol method of manufacturing escitalopram, and therefore it plainly satisfies section 14(3).

84. Subject, at any rate, to *Biogen* [1997] RPC 1 (and some cases purportedly following it), your Lordships have not been referred to any decided case in this jurisdiction which calls into question the approach of Lord Hoffmann and Jacob LJ in this case, as summarised in paras 74 and 75 above.

. . .

86. While, as my noble and learned friend Lord Mance says, no real help in this case can be obtained from judicial decisions in countries which are not signatories to the EPC,

quite different considerations apply to decisions of the Board. Your Lordships' House has frequently emphasised that the principles of patent law adopted by courts in this jurisdiction should, if at all possible, be the same as those adopted by the Board—see for instance *Merell Dow Pharmaceuticals Inc v H N Norton & Co Ltd* [1996] RPC 76, 82, *Kirin-Amgen Inc v Hoechst Marion Roussel Ltd* [2004] UKHL 46, [2005] RPC 9, para 101, and *Conor Medsystems Inc v Angiotech Pharmaceuticals Inc* [2008] UKHL 49, [2008] 4 All ER 621, para 3.

87. In that connection, the approach of the Board has been consistently along the same lines as that of the Court of Appeal in this case. Thus, in T595/90 *Grain-orientated silicon sheet/Kawasaki* [1994] OJEPO 695, 703, the Board said:

> [A] product which can be envisaged as such with all characteristics determining its identity together with its properties in use, i.e. an otherwise obvious entity, may become nevertheless non-obvious and claimable as such if there is no known way or applicable (analogy) method in the art to make it and the claimed methods for its preparation are therefore the first to achieve this in an inventive manner.

(See also the decisions cited by Lord Hoffmann at [2008] RPC 19, paras 38 and 39.)

88. Indeed, specifically in relation to the type of question arising in this case, the Board has held on more than one occasion that the fact that 'the two enantiomers . . . actually exist unseparated in the racemate . . . [and generally] can also be separated . . .' are 'considerations [which] are immaterial to the question of novelty . . . and will be more usefully applied to the examination as to inventive step' (quoted from T0296/87, *Hoechst*, 30 August 1988, para 6.5, and see also, for example, T1046/97, *Enantiomer/Zeneca*, 2 December 1999, para 2.1.1.4). That would suggest that Kitchin J's conclusion on novelty was correct and that he rightly addressed the issue of obviousness, but that, having decided those issues in favour of the respondent, he should have upheld the claim to escitalopram.

89. It is true that in none of these decisions of the Board was any consideration given to whether the product claim failed on the ground of insufficiency for the reason given by Kitchin J in this case at [2007] RPC 32, paras 264 to 265. However, the argument based on obviousness considered by the Board is very similar to the insufficiency reason given by Kitchin J. It also seems to me that, in the light of the expertise and experience of the members of the Board, and the number of decisions where the insufficiency reason could have been raised, it is fanciful to suggest that, if the reason had been arguable, it would not have been raised before or by the Board by now. As mentioned below, much of the reasoning in *Biogen* [1997] RPC 1 was based on decisions of the Board, and members of the Board appear to be well aware of their previous decisions, and, at least in general, anxious to have a consistent approach. Further, the decision in *Biogen* [1997] RPC 1 was well known in the world of patents, and it did not cause the Board to change its view on the issue of product claims, as is demonstrated by the reasoning in *Enantiomer/Zeneca* in relation to enantiomers, and, more generally, in T1195/00 *Alcan International Ltd*, 24 May 2004.

90. In the light of this discussion, it appears clear to me that, unless precluded by the reasoning in *Biogen* [1997] RPC 1, on which Kitchin J primarily relied in his decision and on which Mr Thorley primarily relies in his argument, the product claim in the present case is valid. I appreciate that this means that, by finding one method of making a product, a person can obtain a monopoly for that product. However, that applies to any product claim. Further, where (as here) the product is a known *desideratum*, it can be said (as Lord Walker pointed out) that the invention is all the more creditable, as it is likely that there has been more competition than where the product has not been thought of. The role of fortuity in patent law cannot be doubted: it is inevitable, as in almost any area of life. Luck as well as skill often determines, for instance, who is first to file, whether a better product or process is soon discovered, or whether an invention turns out to be valuable. Further, while the law must be principled, it must also be clear and consistent.

The insufficiency argument based on *Biogen* [1997] RPC 1

91. As I have mentioned, the principal plank in the appellants' argument is the opinion of Lord Hoffmann in *Biogen* [1997] RPC 1, no doubt for the reasons just discussed. Mr Thorley was able to point to a number of observations in that opinion which, at least if read on their own, might at first sight be said to support his contention that, given that the (+)-enantiomer was known to be a desirable goal, the only technical contribution of the Patent was the diol method of making the enantiomer, and accordingly it is that process, and not the enantiomer, which should have been claimed.

92. Of the seven passages in the speech of Lord Hoffmann Mr Thorley particularly relied on, I shall limit myself to three, although the observations which follow apply equally to the other passages. At [1997] RPC 1, 48, Lord Hoffmann said that 'if the claims include a number of discrete methods or products, the patentee must enable the invention to be performed in respect of each of them'. But in this case the claim is to a single product, and it is clear that the product is enabled by the disclosure in the Patent.

93. At [1997] RPC 1, 50, there is this: '[The issue] is not whether the claimed invention could deliver the goods, but whether the claims cover other ways in which they might be delivered: ways which owe nothing to the teaching of the patent or any principle which it disclosed'. This is perhaps the most important of the three passages for present purposes. The vital point is that Lord Hoffmann was not dealing with a simple product claim, as is involved in this Patent. As he explained at [1997] RPC 1, 40, the claim in that case was 'to a product, a molecule identified partly by the way in which it has been made . . . and partly by what it does'. In that case, the patentee could claim neither the product (a DNA fragment of the so-called Dane particle), as it had already been made (see per Aldous J at first instance at [1995] RPC 25, 57), nor the process (recombinant DNA technology enabling expression in a cell), as it had already been invented (see at [1995] RPC 25, 58 and 65). Nor could he identify the product in any other way, as it had not been mapped or sequenced (see e.g. at [1995] RPC 25, 65).

94. Accordingly, the invention claimed in *Biogen* [1997] RPC 1 was, as it were, the notion of subjecting the product (the unsequenced DNA fragment from the Dane particle) to the process (recombinant DNA technology) in order for it to be expressed to produce HBV antigens. It was therefore at least as much as a process claim as a product claim. In those circumstances, one can well see why the claim was held to be insufficient. The patent disclosed one way in which the DNA fragments could produce HBV antigens, but the claim 'cover[ed] other ways in which they might be delivered, ways which owed nothing to the teaching of the patent or any principle which it disclosed'—[1997] RPC 1, 50. Accordingly, the claim was very different from a simple product claim as in the present case. This analysis of the facts in *Biogen* [1997] RPC 1 also explains why Lord Hoffmann said at pp. 51–52 that 'the excessive breadth' of the patent in that case was due 'to the fact that the same results could be produced by different means' from that disclosed by the patent.

95. Finally, at [1997] RPC 1, 54, Lord Hoffmann emphasised that 'the extent of the monopoly claimed [should not] exceed . . . the technical contribution to the art made by the invention as described in the specification'. As already explained, in the context of a simple product claim such as the present (especially where the claim is to a single chemical product), the technical contribution is (at least in the absence of special factors) the product itself. As I have suggested, the technical contribution can often be equated with non-obvious novelty—what is new to the art and not obvious is really another way of identifying the technical contribution.

96. The notion that Lord Hoffmann was not seeking to depart from the established approach of the Board is supported by the weight he placed on the reasoning in its decisions, especially *Genentech/Polypeptide expression* [1989] OJEPO 275 and T409/91 EXXON/Fuel

Oils to which I have referred—see at [1997] RPC 1, 48–53. The fact that he took a different view from the Board on the patent in suit does not detract from this point: he was considering an argument which had not been raised in the opposition proceedings—see section 12 of his judgment at [1997] RPC 1, 52–53. Indeed, at the end of that section Lord Hoffmann was at pains to point out that there was no 'divergence between the jurisprudence of this court and that of the EPO'.

97. It is perhaps worth referring to one passage in the Board's decision in T409/91 *EXXON/ Fuel Oils*, which was relied on by Mr Thorley, and was quoted in *Biogen* [1997] RPC 1, 49. The quotation, taken from para 3.3 of the decision, concludes with the statement that there is a 'general legal principle that the extent of the patent monopoly, as defined by the claims, should correspond to the *technical contribution* to the art in order for it to be supported, or justified'. However, the passage continues:

> This means that the definitions in the claims should essentially correspond to the scope of the invention as disclosed in the description. In other words...the claims should not extend to subject-matter which, after reading the description, would still not be at the disposal of the person skilled in the art.

98. Thus, it is clear that, in that paragraph the Board was discussing insufficiency and support in the normal sense, and there is nothing to suggest that, in the case of a product claim, once it is decided that the product is novel, the technical contribution may not be the product itself, if it is a known *desideratum*.

99. In my opinion, therefore, in agreement with the Court of Appeal, the opinion of Lord Hoffmann in *Biogen* [1997] RPC 1, though a *tour de force* as Lord Walker says, is of no assistance to the appellants in this case. It applied in the light of the very unusual nature of the claim in that case. Far from being a straightforward product claim (as in this case) or even a product-by-process claim (as discussed in *Kirin-Amgen* [2005] RPC 9, paras 86–91 and 101), the claim was to a product identified in part by how it was made and in part by what it did— almost a process-by-product-by-process claim.

In the above extract, Lord Neuberger emphasizes the importance of UK courts' taking an approach consistent with the EPO. How significant were the EPO Board of Appeal decisions to Lord Neuberger's reasoning in the case?

With regard to the scope of *Biogen* insufficiency what was the main point of distinction made between *Biogen* and the Lundbeck patent? Is it now fair to say that *Biogen* insufficiency will apply only where there are unusual claims and not in the case of simple product claims?

At first instance, Kitchin J's concern was that Lundbeck had acquired a patent for a product (as opposed to merely a process for obtaining escitalopram) and that this would give it the exclusive right to, *inter alia*, make the product and to prevent others from doing so, even if they made escitalopram by a different method to the one developed by Lundbeck. The Court of Appeal and House of Lords took the view that this was simply a consequence of having product claims. Does this seem like a fair outcome? Should Parliament provide for a different scope of protection for patented products depending on the type of technical contribution that has been made?

FURTHER READING

A. Batteson and I. Karet, *'Lundbeck v Generics*: "Biogen insufficiency" explained' [2009] EIPR 51.

9.12.3 SUPPORT

The leading case on when claims will be supported by the description is *Biogen v Medeva*.

Biogen v Medeva [1997] RPC 1

The facts were described above at 9.12.2.2. The issue of lack of support arose because Biogen were claiming an earlier priority date, by virtue of an earlier application.[334] As such, they needed to show that the patent claim was supported by matter disclosed in the earlier application. The earlier priority date was crucial because otherwise their invention would have lacked inventive step.

Lord Hoffmann (delivering the leading speech), **at pp. 51–2:**

As I have said, I accept the judge's findings that the method was shown to be capable of making both antigens and I am willing to accept that it would work in any otherwise suitable host cell. Does this contribution justify a claim to a monopoly of *any* recombinant method of making the antigens? In my view it does not. The claimed invention is too broad. Its excessive breadth is due, not to the inability of the teaching to produce all the promised results, but to the fact that the same results could be produced by different means. Professor Murray had won a brilliant Napoleonic victory in cutting through the uncertainties which existed in his day to achieve the desired result. But his success did not in my view establish any new principle which his successors had to follow if they were to achieve the same results. The inventive step, as I have said, was the idea of trying to express unsequenced eukaryotic DNA in a pro-karyotic host. Biogen 1 discloses that the way to do it is to choose the restriction enzymes likely to cleave the Dane particle DNA into the largest fragments. This, if anything, was the original element in what Professor Murray did. But once the DNA had been sequenced, no one would choose restriction enzymes on this basis. They would choose those which digested the sites closest to the relevant gene or the part of the gene which expressed an antigenic fragment of the polypeptide. The metaphor used by one of the witnesses was that before the genome had been sequenced everyone was working in the dark. Professor Murray invented a way of working with the genome in the dark. But he did not switch on the light and once the light was on his method was no longer needed. Nor, once they could use vectors for mammalian cells, would they be concerned with the same problem of introns which had so exercised those skilled in the art in 1978. Of course there might be other problems, but Biogen 1 did not teach how to solve them. The respondents Medeva, who use restriction enzymes based on knowledge of the HBV genome and mammalian host cells, owe nothing to Professor Murray's invention.

It is said that what Professor Murray showed by his invention was that it could be done. HBV antigens could be produced by expressing Dane particle DNA in a host cell. Those who followed, even by different routes, could have greater confidence by reason of his success. I do not think that this is enough to justify a monopoly of the whole field. I suppose it could be said that Samuel Morse had shown that electric telegraphy could be done. The Wright Brothers showed that heavier-than-air flight was possible, but that did not entitle them to a monopoly of heavier-than-air flying machines. It is inevitable in a young science, like electricity in the early nineteenth century or flying at the turn of the last century or recombinant

---

[334] See PA 77, s. 5(2)(a).

DNA technology in the 1970s, that dramatically new things will be done for the first time. The technical contribution made in such cases deserves to be recognised. But care is needed not to stifle further research and healthy competition by allowing the first person who has found a way of achieving an obviously desirable goal to monopolise every other way of doing so. (See Merges and Nelson, 'On the complex economics of patent scope' (1990) 90 Columbia LR 839.)

I would therefore hold that Biogen 1 did not support the invention as claimed in the European Patent and that it is therefore not entitled to the priority date of Biogen 1. As it is conceded that the invention was obvious when the patent application was filed, it is invalid.

[His lordship also gave two examples of where the description would not support the claims:]

The patent may claim results which it does not enable, such as making a wide class of products when it enables only one of those products and discloses no principle which would enable others to be made. Or it may claim every way of achieving a result when it enables only one way and it is possible to envisage other ways of achieving that result which make no use of the invention.

As *Biogen* demonstrates, this type of lack of support may arise particularly in situations where new areas of technology are emerging and the patent obtained is one of the first in the field. Do you think that it is important, as Lord Hoffmann said, to ensure that further research and healthy competition are not stifled? Or does this approach to the requirement of support act as a disincentive for those to engage in ground-breaking areas of research?

Where there is a lack of support of the type indicated in *Biogen* will the specification invariably lack sufficiency? If so, does *Biogen* risk conflating the requirements of support and sufficiency or does it merely highlight how closely connected are the requirements?

FURTHER READING

M. Spence, 'Patents and biotechnology' (1997) LQR 368.

PATENTS II:

INFRINGEMENT AND ENTITLEMENT

10.1 INFRINGEMENT

10.1.1 INTRODUCTION

Broadly speaking, assessing whether or not a patent has been infringed involves a three-stage inquiry. First, the patent claims must be construed to see whether the defendant's activities fall within the scope of the monopoly. Second, it is necessary to identify the infringing acts which the defendant is alleged to have carried out. Third, the applicability of exceptions to infringement must be considered. Each of these topics will be discussed in turn.

Before we do so, however, it is worth noting a practical consequence of commencing an action for infringement. Not only is litigation an expensive process, but perhaps more importantly, it also makes one's patent vulnerable to an invalidity challenge. This is because a defendant will usually counterclaim, arguing that even if they have infringed the patent it is in fact invalid. Moreover, in contesting the validity of the patent, particularly on the grounds of novelty or sufficiency, the defendant will force the patent proprietor to put forward an interpretation of the scope of the claims that is not overreaching for the purposes of infringement. This is because UK courts adopt a consistent interpretation of the claims for both validity and infringement purposes and if a proprietor advances too wide a construction of the claims this will increase the risk of his patent being anticipated by the prior art or lacking sufficiency.[1]

10.1.2 CONSTRUCTION OF THE CLAIMS

The claims are a crucial feature of the patent specification for the reasons expressed in the following extract.

---

[1] See the discussion of the 'Rapamycin' case at 9.12.2.2 to illustrate this point.

D. Chisum, 'Common law and civil law approaches to Patent claim interpretation' in Vaver and Bently (eds.), *Intellectual Property in the New Millennium* (Cambridge: CUP, 2004), at p. 97

Whether patent law ought to require a written claim to an invention is debatable, but the requirement is conventionally accepted as sound. Under the conventional view, the claiming requirement serves two purposes. First, the claim defines the invention for purposes of determining patentability, during both examination by a patent office and judicial assessment. Second, the claim provides notice to the public, usually, a business entity seeking to avoid a patent, of what the patent covers. The notice supposedly provided by a written claim enables the entity not only to determine whether to engage in potentially infringing conduct but also how to develop alternative technology ('design around').

But words are only words, and a claiming requirement can fully serve its intended purposes only if there is reasonably predictable certainty as to how the words of a claim will be interpreted by critical decision-makers. Thus arises a central problem for every patent system that requires a verbal definition of a protected invention: how to achieve consistency in the interpretation of the claims in patents.

Thus, claims are important because they help define the invention and because they provide notice to the public of the scope of the monopoly that the patentee has been granted. This dual role of claims developed relatively recently, from the early 20th century onwards,[2] and makes it imperative that they can be interpreted with reasonable certainty. Traditionally, however, the UK and Germany have adopted divergent approaches to the interpretation of claims, which posed difficulties when it came to drafting the EPC, as the following extract from Chisum explains.[3]

The framers of European patent law harmonization were faced with a specific national conflict (or at least the perception of a conflict) on judicial patent claim interpretation: Germany versus the United Kingdom. The former has a civil law tradition; the latter a common law tradition. Resolution of the conflict was essential: the two countries had the largest volume of litigation over patent infringement in Europe. On the one hand, German courts were deemed to view the language of a patent claim as a guide to determining what the patented invention is—only a guide, the invention and whether it has been misappropriated by an accused infringer being determined by a plenary consideration of the patent's disclosure and the relationship between the invention and the prior art. On the other hand, United Kingdom courts were deemed to view patent claim language as the exclusive and restricting definition of the invention. For example, if a patent claim required that a component be 'vertical', the German courts would assess the reason for the 'vertical' limitation—did the nature of the invention as an advance over the prior art require strict verticality or merely substantial verticality that would perform the function of the invention?—and deem the patent to cover any structure or method that appropriated the invention. This approach, in theory, assured a fair scope of protection for patent owners: allowing a slight variation from the literal requirement of 'vertical' might authorize appropriation of the invention's essence. The United Kingdom courts would define 'vertical' and deem the patent to cover only structures or methods that met the definition. This approach, in theory, assured certainty and predictability of the scope of patent protection.

Professor William Cornish, in his characteristic lucid manner, described the conflict as between 'fence post' claiming and 'sign post' claiming.

---

[2] D. J. Brennan, 'The evolution of English patent claims as property definers' [2005] IPQ 361.
[3] At p. 98.

The UK 'literal' or 'fence post' approach to interpretation of claims was driven by the desire for certainty[4] and meant that even if some of the integers of the claim were omitted or replaced by mechanical equivalents infringement would not occur. That said, the courts later developed the doctrine of 'pith and marrow' to deal with situations where there were simply colourable or immaterial variations of the claimed invention.[5] Where that occurred, a person could still infringe if he had taken the substance or 'pith and marrow' of the invention.

The approach taken in the EPC was to set out the main norm for determination of the patent's scope in Article 69, which provides:

> The extent of the protection conferred by a European patent or a European patent application shall be determined by the terms of the claims. Nevertheless, the description and drawings shall be used to interpret the claims.

A Protocol to Article 69 of the EPC was also inserted and was intended to be a compromise between the UK and German traditions of interpretation to claims.[6] The Protocol to Article 69 provides:

> Article 69 should *not be interpreted* in the sense that the extent of the protection conferred by a European patent is to be understood as that defined *by the strict, literal meaning* of the wording used in the claims, the description and the drawings being employed only for the purpose of resolving an ambiguity found in the claims. *Neither* should it be *interpreted* in the sense that the *claims serve only as a guideline* and that the actual protection conferred may extend to what, from a consideration of the description and drawings by a person skilled in the art, the patentee has contemplated. On the contrary, it is to be *interpreted* as defining a position *between these extremes* which combines a *fair protection* for the patentee with a *reasonable degree of certainty* for third parties. [emphasis supplied]

Both Article 69 and the Protocol were given effect in UK law via s. 125 of the PA 77. Following the EPC 2000, the Protocol to Article 69 was amended to include the above provision as Article 1 and to introduce a new provision, Article 2, dealing with equivalents. Article 2 of the Protocol states:

> For the purpose of determining the extent of protection conferred by a European patent, due account shall be taken of any element which is equivalent to an element specified in the claims.

The impact of Article 2 of the Protocol will be discussed later at 10.1.2.3.

10.1.2.1 *Catnic*

As has been mentioned, the Protocol to Article 69 sought to move UK courts away from a 'literal' or 'fence post' approach to construction of the patent claims. In fact, however, this shift had already begun to occur, as shown by the landmark House of Lords decision in *Catnic*.

---

[4] *Electrical and Musical Industries Ltd v Lissen Ltd* (1939) 56 RPC 23 at 39 per Lord Russell.
[5] *Marconi v British Radio Telegraph and Telephone Company Ltd* (1911) 28 RPC 181, 217; *Van der Lely v Bamfords* [1963] RPC 61.
[6] For a brief discussion of the history of the Protocol see *Kirin Amgen Inc v Hoechst Marion* [2005] RPC 9.

Catnic v Hill and Smith [1982] RPC 183

The claimant's invention was a steel lintel for use in spanning the spaces above window and door openings. Part of the reason for the claimant's success was that previous, solid, much heavier lintels had been used (i.e. timber and heavy gauge metal girders). With the claimant's invention the necessary strength and rigidity was obtained, but with lightness, economy of material and ease of handling. The invention had a vertical back plate and an angled front plate. Specifically, the claims referred to 'a second rigid support member extending vertically from or near the rear edge of the first horizontal plate or part'. The defendants produced a lintel that had a back plate that was inclined to a slight angle of six degrees from the vertical. This was done to avoid infringement of the claimant's patent and in response to customer feedback. The claimant sued for infringement under the Patents Act 1949. At first instance, Whitford J held that although the defendant's lintel did not 'extend vertically' and thus was not a literal (or textual) infringement of the claims, the defendants had taken all the essential features of a number of the claims and thus the defendants' lintels constituted an infringement. On appeal, the Court of Appeal held that there had been no literal infringement of the claims; further the court held that it was an essential feature of the claims that the rear support member should 'extend vertically', and accordingly there could be no infringement of the 'pith and marrow' of the invention. The claimant appealed to the House of Lords.

Lord Diplock (with whom the other Law Lords agreed), **at pp. 242–3:**

My Lords, in their closely reasoned written cases in this House and in the oral argument, both parties to this appeal have tended to treat 'textual infringement' and infringement of the 'pith and marrow' of an invention as if they were separate causes of action, the existence of the former to be determined as a matter of construction only and of the latter upon some broader principle of colourable evasion. There is, in my view, no such dichotomy; there is but a single cause of action and to treat it otherwise, particularly in cases like that which is the subject of the instant appeal, is liable to lead to confusion.

The expression 'no textual infringement' has been borrowed from the speeches in this House in the hay-rake case, *Van der Lely v Bamfords*, where it was used by several of their Lordships as a convenient way of saying that the word 'hindmost' as descriptive of rake wheels to be dismounted could not as a matter of linguistics mean 'foremost': but this did not exhaust the question of construction of the specification that was determinative of whether there had been an infringement of the claim or not. It left open the question whether the patentee had made his reference to the 'hindmost' (rather than any other wheels) as those to be dismounted, an essential feature of the monopoly that he claimed. It was on this question that there was a division of opinion in this House and in the Court of Appeal in the hay-rake case.

My Lords, a patent specification is a unilateral statement by the patentee, in words of his own choosing, addressed to those likely to have a practical interest in the subject matter of his invention (i.e. 'skilled in the art'), by which he informs them what he claims to be the essential features of the new product or process for which the letters patent grant him a monopoly. It is those novel features only that he claims to be essential that constitute the so-called 'pith and marrow' of the claim. A patent specification should be given a purposive construction rather than a purely literal one derived from applying to it the kind of meticulous verbal analysis in which lawyers are too often tempted by their training to indulge. The question in each case is: whether persons with practical knowledge and experience of the kind of work in which the invention was intended to be used, would understand that strict compliance with a particular descriptive word or phrase appearing in a claim was intended by the patentee to be an essential requirement of the invention so that *any* variant would fall outside the monopoly claimed, even though it could have no material effect upon the way the invention worked.

The question, of course, does not arise where the variant would in fact have a material effect upon the way the invention worked. Nor does it arise unless at the date of publication of the specification it would be obvious to the informed reader that this was so. Where it is not obvious, in the light of then-existing knowledge, the reader is entitled to assume that the patentee thought at the time of the specification that he had good reason for limiting his monopoly so strictly and had intended to do so, even though subsequent work by him or others in the field of the invention might show the limitation to have been unnecessary. It is to be answered in the negative only when it would be apparent to any reader skilled in the art that a particular descriptive word or phrase used in a claim cannot have been intended by a patentee, who was also skilled in the art, to exclude minor variants which, to the knowledge of both him and the readers to whom the patent was addressed, could have no material effect upon the way in which the invention worked.

...

...Put in a nutshell the question to be answered is: Would the specification make it obvious to a builder familiar with ordinary building operations that the description of a lintel in the form of a weight-bearing box girder of which the back plate was referred to as 'extending vertically' from one of the two horizontal plates to join the other, could *not* have been intended to exclude lintels in which the back plate although not positioned at precisely 90 degrees to both horizontal plates was close enough to 90 degrees to make no material difference to the way the lintel worked when used in building operations? No plausible reason has been advanced why any rational patentee should want to place so narrow a limitation on his invention. On the contrary, to do so would render his monopoly for practical purposes worthless, since any imitator could avoid it and take all the benefit of the invention by the simple expedient of positioning the back plate a degree or two from the exact vertical.

It may be that when used by a geometer addressing himself to fellow geometers, such expressions descriptive of relative position as 'horizontal', 'parallel', 'vertical' and 'vertically' are to be understood as words of precision only; but when used in a description of a manufactured product intended to perform the practical function of a weight-bearing box girder in supporting courses of brickwork over window and door spaces in buildings, it seems to me that the expression 'extending vertically' as descriptive of the position of what in use will be the upright member of a trapezoid-shaped box girder, is perfectly capable of meaning positioned near enough to the exact geometrical vertical to enable it in actual use to perform satisfactorily all the functions that it could perform if it were precisely vertical; and having regard to those considerations to which I have just referred that is the sense in which in my opinion 'extending vertically' would be understood by a builder familiar with ordinary building operation. Or, putting the same thing in another way, it would be obvious to him that the patentee did not intend to make exact verticality in the positioning of the back plate an essential feature of the invention claimed.

My Lords, if one analyses line by line the ways in which the various expressions are used in the specification, one can find pointers either way as to whether in particular lines various adjectives and adverbs descriptive of relative position are used as words of precision or not. Some of these are discussed in the judgments of the majority of the Court of Appeal who found the pointers in favour of precision stronger than those to the contrary, of which one example is the description of the two 'horizontal' plates as being only '*substantially* parallel'. For my part I find the result of such analysis inconclusive and of little weight as compared with the broad considerations to which I have referred and which are a consequence of giving as I think one should, a purposive construction to the specification.

It follows that I have reached the same conclusion as the trial judge and Sir David Cairns, although not by the route of drawing a distinction between 'textual infringement' and infringement of the 'pith and marrow' of the invention. Accordingly I would allow the appeal.

Did Lord Diplock in *Catnic* reject the previous tests of 'literal construction' and 'pith and marrow', in favour of a purposive construction of the claims? What does purposive construction entail and do you agree that this approach is preferable?

10.1.2.2 *Improver*

As *Catnic* was a decision under the Patents Act 1949, the issue subsequently arose whether purposive construction was consistent with the Protocol to Article 69 of the EPC. This issue was considered in *Improver*.

Improver Corporation v Remington Consumer Products Limited [1990] FSR 181

The claimants European Patent (UK) was for an electrical device for plucking hairs from the body. Its principal element consisted of a helical spring bent to the form of an arc which was rotated at a high speed. Because of the arcuate form, on the convex side the spring would open out, while on the concave side it would close together. Hairs would accordingly be captured and then plucked with the rotation of the spring. The result was less painful than waxing and more long-lasting than shaving. The claimants' device, the 'Epilady', was a great commercial success. The defendants' device was designed as a less painful alternative to 'Epilady'. In place of a helical spring it had a tube of synthetic rubber, partly cut through by slits. When rotated, hair was drawn into the slits and then plucked, as the slits squeezed together. It was marketed as 'Smooth and Silky' with additional tubes for replacement after some seven hours use. The claimants sued for infringement of their patent.

Hoffmann J (as he then was), at pp. 188–90:

[**Hoffmann J** began by setting out the general principles of construction with reference to *Catnic*:]

The proper approach to the interpretation of patents registered under the Patents Act 1949 was explained by Lord Diplock in *Catnic Components Ltd v Hill & Smith Ltd* [1982] RPC 183, 242. The language should be given a 'purposive' and not necessarily a literal construction. If the issue was whether a feature embodied in an alleged infringement which fell outside the primary, literal or a contextual meaning of a descriptive word or phrase in the claim ('a variant') was nevertheless within its language as properly interpreted, the court should ask itself the following three questions:

(1) Does the variant have a material effect upon the way the invention works? If yes, the variant is outside the claim. If no—

(2) Would this (i.e. that the variant had no material effect) have been obvious at the date of publication of the patent to a reader skilled in the art. If no, the variant is outside the claim. If yes—

(3) Would the reader skilled in the art nevertheless have understood from the language of the claim that the patentee intended that strict compliance with the primary meaning was an essential requirement of the invention. If yes, the variant is outside the claim.

On the other hand, a negative answer to the last question would lead to the conclusion that the patentee was intending the word or phrase to have not a literal but a figurative meaning (the figure being a form of synecdoche or metonymy) denoting a class of things which included the variant and the literal meaning, the latter being perhaps the most perfect, best-known or striking example of the class.

Thus in *Catnic* itself the claim of a patent for a lintel of box construction required that the upper plate be supported upon the lower plate by two rigid supports, one in the front and the other 'extending vertically' from the one plate to the other at the rear. The defendant's lintel had a rear support which was inclined 6° or 8° from the vertical. The House of Lords decided that this variation had no material effect upon the load-bearing capacity of the lintel or the way it worked and that this would have been obvious to the skilled builder at the date of publication of the patent. It also decided that the skilled reader would not have understood from the language of the claim that the patentee was insisting upon precisely 90° as an essential requirement of his invention. The conclusion was that 'extending vertically' meant 'extending with the range of angles which give substantially the maximum load-bearing capacity and of which 90° is the perfect example'.

In the end, therefore, the question is always whether the alleged infringement is covered by the language of the claim. This, I think, is what Lord Diplock meant in *Catnic* when he said that there was no dichotomy between 'textual infringement' and infringement of the 'pith and marrow' of the patent and why I respectfully think that Fox LJ put the question with great precision in *Anchor Building Products Ltd v Redland Roof Tiles Ltd* (CA), unreported, 23 November 1988, transcript at p. 18. when he said the question was whether the absence of a feature mentioned in the claim was 'an immaterial variant which a person skilled in the trade would have regarded as being *within the ambit of the language*' (My emphasis). It is worth noticing that Lord Diplock's first two questions, although they cannot sensibly be answered without reference to the patent, do not primarily involve questions of construction: whether the variant would make a material difference to the way the invention worked and whether this would have been obvious to the skilled reader are questions of fact. The answers are used to provide the factual background against which the specification must be construed. It is the third question which raises the question of construction and Lord Diplock's formulation makes it clear that on this question the answers to the first two questions are not conclusive. Even a purposive construction of the language of the patent may lead to the conclusion that although the variant made no material difference and this would have been obvious at the time, the patentee for some reason was confining his claim to the primary meaning and excluding the variant. If this were not the case, there would be no point in asking the third question at all.

[**Hoffmann J** observed that, even though *Catnic* was a decision according to the Patents Act 1949, subsequent courts had regarded Lord Diplock's speech as indicating the same approach to construction as that laid down in the Protocol. Thus, he regarded *Catnic* as binding authority and went on to apply the *Catnic* test, as reformulated into three questions, at pp. 192–7:]

(1) Does the variant have a material effect on the way the invention works?

The answer to this question depends upon the level of generality at which one describes the way the invention works.

...

...It seems to me that the right approach is to describe the working of the invention at the level of generality with which it is described in the claim of the patent. As I have said, Dr Laming agreed that there was no difference between the descriptions in Mr Gross's patent and the patent in suit of the way the inventions worked. The differences lay entirely in the descriptions of the hardware. In my judgment, at the appropriate level of description, the rubber rod works in the same way as the helical spring and the differences I have mentioned, so far as they exist, are not material.

(2) Would it have been obvious to a man skilled in the art that the variant would work in the same way?

...

In my view the question supposes that the skilled man is told of both the invention and the variant and asked whether the variant would obviously work in the same way.

...

Dr Laming and Dr Sharp, the eminent engineer called as an expert by the plaintiff, agreed that it would have been obvious to the skilled man that the attributes which enabled the helical spring to function in the way described in the specification were that it was capable of rotating, capable of transmitting torque along its length to resist the forces involved in plucking hairs, *bendy* (to form an arc) and *slitty* (to entrap hairs by the opening and closing effect of rotation). They also agreed that it would have been obvious that any rod which had these qualities in sufficient degree and did not have other defects such as overheating or falling to bits would in principle work in the same way and that the rubber rod plainly belonged to that class. On this evidence the second question must in my judgment be answered yes. I express no view on whether the rubber rod was also an inventive step.

...

(3) Would the skilled reader nevertheless have understood that the patentee intended to confine his claim to the primary meaning of a helical spring?

This brings one to the question of construction. Since the question is what the skilled reader would have understood, I set out the views of the rival experts.

...

In my judgment the difference between the experts depends upon how one construes the equivalents clause. The first part of the clause merely says that the description should not be used to restrict the meaning of the language used in the claims. That is not the question here. What matters is the final words: *'and all variations which come within the meaning and range of equivalency of the claims are therefore intended to be embraced therein'*. If this means: 'whatever contrary impression the skilled man may be given by the language of the claims read in the context of the rest of the description, all references in the claims to hardware are deemed to include any other hardware which would in any circumstances function in the same way' then I think Dr Sharpe must be right. In my judgment, however, the clause does not have so wide an effect. The words I have quoted say that the variation must still come within the *meaning* of the claims and the reference to 'range of equivalency' means in my judgment no more than 'don't forget that the claims must be interpreted in accordance with *Catnic* and the Protocol'.

Thus interpreted, I do not think that 'helical spring' can reasonably be given a wide generic construction and I accept Dr Laming's reasons for thinking that a skilled man would not understand it in this sense. This is not a case like *Catnic* in which the angle of the support member can be regarded as an approximation to the vertical. The rubber rod is not an approximation to a helical spring. It is a different thing which can in limited circumstances work in the same way. Nor can the spring be regarded as an 'inessential' or the change from metal spring to rubber rod as a minor variant. In *Catnic* Lord Diplock asked rhetorically whether there was any reason why the patentee should wish to restrict his invention to a support angled at precisely 90°, thereby making avoidance easy. In this case I think that a similar question would receive a ready answer. It would be obvious that the rubber had problems of hysteresis which might be very difficult to overcome. The plaintiff's inventors had done no work on rubber rods. Certainly the rubber rod cannot be used in the loop configuration which is the plaintiff's preferred embodiment. On the other hand, drafting the claim in wide generic terms to cover alternatives like the rubber rod might be unacceptable to the patent office. I do not think that the hypothetical skilled man is also assumed to be skilled in patent law and he would in my judgment be entitled to think that patentee had good reasons for limiting himself, as he obviously appeared to have done, to a helical coil. To derive a different meaning solely from the equivalents clause would in my view be denying third parties that reasonable degree of certainty to which they are entitled under the Protocol.

Hoffmann J reformulated the *Catnic* test into three questions, known as the *Improver* questions. These were subsequently renamed the Protocol questions on the basis that they were consistent with the Protocol to Article 69 of the EPC.[7] In your view, do the *Improver* questions accurately reflect Lord Diplock's speech in *Catnic*?

The patent in *Improver* contained an equivalents clause. How did Hoffmann J treat this clause in the context of construing the claims? Here it is worth noting that Lord Hoffmann (as he then became) returned to this issue in *Kirin-Amgen*, discussed below.

Finally, the European patent in *Improver* was litigated in several European states where, in Germany at least, the infringement proceedings met with success. This fact was drawn to the attention of Hoffmann J, who took the view that his colleagues in Germany were adopting an interpretation 'closer to treating the language of the claims as a "guideline" than the median course required by the Protocol'.[8] Given the different outcomes in the *Improver* litigation in different Contracting States, does this suggest that the Protocol is not enough to unify the distinct and long-standing traditions to infringement reflected in the UK and Germany?[9]

10.1.2.3 *Kirin-Amgen*

Subsequent decisions of the Court of Appeal affirmed that the *Catnic* test and the *Improver* questions (later known as the Protocol questions) were consistent with the Protocol to Article 69 of the EPC.[10] However, it was not until *Kirin Amgen Inc v Hoechst Marion* that the House of Lords had an opportunity to consider this issue.

---

[7] See *Wheatly v Drillsafe* [2001] RPC 133, 142, per Aldous LJ.   [8] *Improver*, p. 198.

[9] See further B. Sherman, 'Patent claim interpretation: The impact of the protocol on interpretation' (1991) 54 Modern Law Review 499.

[10] See for example, *Kastner v Rizla* [1995] RPC 585; *Union Carbide Corp v BP Chemicals Ltd* [1999] RPC 409; *Wheatly v Drillsafe* [2001] RPC 133.

Kirin Amgen Inc v Hoechst Marion [2005] RPC 9

Kirin-Amgen ('Amgen') sued Transkaryotic Therapies Inc ('TKT') for infringement of its European patent (UK) relating to the production of erythropoietin ('EPO') by recombinant DNA technology. EPO is a hormone made in the kidney which stimulates the production of red blood cells by the bone marrow. Amgen's method of making EPO artificially for use as a drug was a significant advance in the treatment of anaemia, particularly when associated with kidney failure. Amgen's method involved an exogenous DNA sequence coding for EPO which had been introduced into a host cell. TKT had also developed a method for making EPO, however, it used a different process, called 'gene activation'. This involved an endogenous DNA sequence coding for EPO naturally present in a human cell, into which an exogenous upstream control sequence had been inserted, thereby 'activating' the production of DNA. On the issue of infringement, the key question was construction of the claims. Would a person skilled in the art understand 'host cell' to mean a cell which is host to the DNA sequence which coded for EPO? Or would a person skilled in the art understand 'host cell' to include a cell in which the DNA sequence coding for EPO is endogenous, provided the cell is host to some exogenous DNA? At first instance, Neuberger J held, *inter alia*, that claim 19 was invalid for insufficiency and that claim 26 was valid and infringed. However, the Court of Appeal found both claims to be valid, but that TKT had not infringed. Both sides appealed.

Lord Hoffmann (delivering the leading speech):

[**Lord Hoffmann** took the opportunity to review the history and background of Art. 69 of the EPC and the Protocol, before moving on to consider whether *Catnic* was consistent with the Protocol.]

Is *Catnic* consistent with the Protocol?

47. The Protocol, as I have said, is a Protocol for the construction of art. 69 and does not expressly lay down any principle for the construction of claims. It does say what principle should not be followed, namely the old English literalism, but otherwise it says only that one should not go outside the claims. It does however say that the object is to combine a fair protection for the patentee with a reasonable degree of certainty for third parties. How is this to be achieved? The claims must be construed in a way which attempts, so far as is possible in an imperfect world, not to disappoint the reasonable expectations of either side. What principle of interpretation would give fair protection to the patentee? Surely, a principle which would give him the full extent of the monopoly which the person skilled in the art would think he was intending to claim. And what principle would provide a reasonable degree of protection for third parties? Surely again, a principle which would not give the patentee more than the full extent of the monopoly which the person skilled in the art would think that he was intending to claim. Indeed, any other principle would also be unfair to the patentee, because it would unreasonably expose the patent to claims of invalidity on grounds of anticipation or insufficiency.

48. The *Catnic* principle of construction is, therefore, in my opinion, precisely in accordance with the Protocol. It is intended to give the patentee the full extent, but not more than the full extent, of the monopoly which a reasonable person skilled in the art, reading the claims in context, would think he was intending to claim.

Can we say with certainty that the purposive construction approach in *Catnic* is consistent with the Protocol to Article 69? What about the Protocol questions?

Lord Hoffmann also considered the role of 'equivalents' under the EPC and PA 77. He began by explaining the doctrine of equivalents and that it does not form part of the EPC.

The doctrine of equivalents

36. At the time when the rules about natural and ordinary meanings were more or less rigidly applied, the United Kingdom and American courts showed understandable anxiety about applying a construction which allowed someone to avoid infringement by making an 'immaterial variation' in the invention as described in the claims. In England, this led to the development of a doctrine of infringement by use of the 'pith and marrow' of the invention (a phrase invented by Lord Cairns in *Clark v Adie* (1877) 2 App Cas 315, 320) as opposed to a 'textual infringement'. The pith and marrow doctrine was always a bit vague ('necessary to prevent sharp practice' said Lord Reid in *C Van Der Lely NV v Bamfords Ltd* [1963] RPC 61, 77) and it was unclear whether the courts regarded it as a principle of construction or an extension of protection outside the claims.

37. In the United States, where a similar principle is called the 'doctrine of equivalents', it is frankly acknowledged that it allows the patentee to extend his monopoly beyond the claims. In the leading case of *Graver Tank & Manufacturing Co Inc v Linde Air Products Co* 339 US 605, 607 (1950), Jackson J said that the American courts had recognised:

> that to permit imitation of a patented invention which does not copy every literal detail would be to convert the protection of the patent grant into a hollow and useless thing. Such a limitation would leave room for—indeed encourage—the unscrupulous copyist to make unimportant and insubstantial changes and substitutions in the patent which, though adding nothing, would be enough to take the copied matter outside the claim, and hence outside the reach of law.

...

41. There is often discussion about whether we have a European doctrine of equivalents and, if not, whether we should. It seems to me that both the doctrine of equivalents in the United States and the pith and marrow doctrine in the United Kingdom were born of despair. The courts felt unable to escape from interpretations which 'unsparing logic' appeared to require and which prevented them from according the patentee the full extent of the monopoly which the person skilled in the art would reasonably have thought he was claiming. The background was the tendency to literalism which then characterised the approach of the courts to the interpretation of documents generally and the fact that patents are likely to attract the skills of lawyers seeking to exploit literalism to find loopholes in the monopoly they create. (Similar skills are devoted to revenue statutes.)

42. If literalism stands in the way of construing patent claims so as to give fair protection to the patentee, there are two things that you can do. One is to adhere to literalism in construing the claims and evolve a doctrine which supplements the claims by extending protection to equivalents. That is what the Americans have done. The other is to abandon literalism. That is what the House of Lords did in the *Catnic* case, where Lord Diplock said (at [1982] RPC 183, 242):

> Both parties to this appeal have tended to treat 'textual infringement' and infringement of the 'pith and marrow' of an invention as if they were separate causes of action, the existence of the former to be determined as a matter of construction only and of the latter upon some broader principle of colourable evasion. There is, in my view, no such dichotomy; there is but a single cause of action and to treat it otherwise . . . is liable to lead to confusion.

43. The solution, said Lord Diplock, was to adopt a principle of construction which actually gave effect to what the person skilled in the art would have understood the patentee to be claiming.

44. Since the *Catnic* case we have art. 69 which, as it seems to me, firmly shuts the door on any doctrine which extends protection outside the claims. I cannot say that I am sorry because the *Festo* litigation suggests, with all respect to the courts of the United States, that American patent litigants pay dearly for results which are no more just or predictable than could be achieved by simply reading the claims.

[**Lord Hoffmann** goes on to explain that while there is no doctrine of equivalents in the EPC, equivalence *is* a relevant factor in the construction of claims and to discuss how the Protocol questions operate as guidelines for applying the principle of purposive construction to equivalents.]

Equivalents as a guide to construction

49. Although art. 69 prevents equivalence from extending protection outside the claims, there is no reason why it cannot be an important part of the background of facts known to the skilled man which would affect what he understood the claims to mean. That is no more than common sense. It is also expressly provided by the new art. 2 added to the Protocol by the Munich Act revising the EPC, dated November 29, 2000 (but which has not yet come into force):

For the purpose of determining the extent of protection conferred by a European patent, due account shall be taken of any element which is equivalent to an element specified in the claims.

50. In the *Catnic* case [1982] RPC 183, 243 Lord Diplock offered some observations on the relevance of equivalence to the question of construction:

The question in each case is: whether persons with practical knowledge and experience of the kind of work in which the invention was intended to be used, would understand that strict compliance with a particular descriptive word or phrase appearing in a claim was intended by the patentee to be an essential requirement of the invention so that any variant would fall outside the monopoly claimed, even though it could have no material effect upon the way the invention worked.

The question, of course, does not arise where the variant would in fact have a material effect upon the way the invention worked. Nor does it arise unless at the date of publication of the specification it would be obvious to the informed reader that this was so. Where it is not obvious, in the light of then-existing knowledge, the reader is entitled to assume that the patentee thought at the time of the specification that he had good reason for limiting his monopoly so strictly and had intended to do so, even though subsequent work by him or others in the field of the invention might show the limitation to have been unnecessary. It is to be answered in the negative only when it would be apparent to any reader skilled in the art that a particular descriptive word or phrase used in a claim cannot have been intended by a patentee, who was also skilled in the art, to exclude minor variants which, to the knowledge of both him and the readers to whom the patent was addressed, could have no material effect upon the way in which the invention worked.

51. In *Improver Corp v Remington Products Ltd* [1990] FSR 181, 189, I tried to summarise this guidance:

If the issue was whether a feature embodied in an alleged infringement which fell outside the primary, literal or a contextual meaning of a descriptive word or phrase in the claim ('a variant') was nevertheless within its language as properly interpreted, the court should ask itself the following three questions:

(1) Does the variant have a material effect upon the way the invention works? If yes, the variant is outside the claim. If no?

(2) Would this (ie that the variant had no material effect) have been obvious at the date of publication of the patent to a reader skilled in the art? If no, the variant is outside the claim. If yes?

(3) Would the reader skilled in the art nevertheless have understood from the language of the claim that the patentee intended that strict compliance with the primary meaning was an essential requirement of the invention? If yes, the variant is outside the claim.

On the other hand, a negative answer to the last question would lead to the conclusion that the patentee was intending the word or phrase to have not a literal but a figurative meaning (the figure being a form of synecdoche or metonymy) denoting a class of things which include the variant and the literal meaning, the latter being perhaps the most perfect, best-known or striking example of the class.

52. These questions, which the Court of Appeal in *Wheatley v Drillsafe Ltd* [2001] RPC 133, 142 dubbed 'the Protocol questions' have been used by English courts for the past 15 years as a framework for deciding whether equivalents fall within the scope of the claims. On the whole, the judges appear to have been comfortable with the results, although some of the cases have exposed the limitations of the method. When speaking of the '*Catnic* principle' it is important to distinguish between, on the one hand, the principle of purposive construction which I have said gives effect to the requirements of the Protocol, and on the other hand, the guidelines for applying that principle to equivalents, which are encapsulated in the Protocol questions. The former is the bedrock of patent construction, universally applicable. The latter are only guidelines, more useful in some cases than in others.

Having read the above passages from Lord Hoffmann's speech, how would you describe the difference between the *Catnic* principle of purposive construction and the Protocol questions?

The key issue of construction in *Kirin Amgen* was whether a person skilled in the art would understand 'host cell' to mean a cell which is host to the DNA sequence which coded for EPO or whether it included an EPO sequence endogenous to the cell, provided the cell hosted some exogenous DNA. Lord Hoffmann held that, in light of the evidence of expert witnesses and the language of the specification, Neuberger J at first instance had construed the claims correctly to mean the former.[11] However, his lordship held that the first-instance judge had erred in classifying his construction as 'literal' and then moving on to apply the Protocol questions.

The judge's application of the Protocol questions

63. …The judge's construction could not possibly be described as acontextual. It was entirely dependent on context and reflected the evidence of how the claim would have been understood by men skilled in the art.

…

66. …the present case illustrates the difficulty of applying the Protocol questions when no such question arises. No one suggests that 'an exogenous DNA sequence coding for EPO' can have some looser meaning which includes 'an endogenous DNA sequence coding

---

[11] *Kirin-Amgen*, paras. 54–8.

for EPO'. The question is rather whether the person skilled in the art would understand the invention as operating at a level of generality which makes it irrelevant whether the DNA which codes for EPO is exogenous or not. That is a difficult question to put through the mangle of the Protocol questions because the answer depends entirely upon what you think the invention is. Once you have decided that question, the Protocol questions answer themselves.

. . .

69. . . . The determination of the extent of protection conferred by a European patent is an examination in which there is only one compulsory question, namely that set by art. 69 and its Protocol: what would a person skilled in the art have understood the patentee to have used the language of the claim to mean? Everything else, including the Protocol questions, is only guidance to a judge trying to answer that question. But there is no point in going through the motions of answering the Protocol questions when you cannot sensibly do so until you have construed the claim. In such a case—and the present is in my opinion such a case—they simply provide a formal justification for a conclusion which has already been reached on other grounds.

70. I agree with the Court of Appeal that the invention should normally be taken as having been claimed at the same level of generality as that at which it is defined in the claims. It would be unusual for the person skilled in the art to understand a specification to be claiming an invention at a higher level of generality than that chosen by the patentee. That means that once the judge had construed the claims as he did, he had answered the question of infringement. It could only cause confusion to try to answer the Protocol questions as well.

71. No doubt there will be patent lawyers who are dismayed at the notion that the Protocol questions do not provide an answer in every case. They may feel cast adrift on a sea of interpretative uncertainty. But that is the fate of all who have to understand what people mean by using language. The Protocol questions are useful in many cases, but they are not a substitute for trying to understand what the person skilled in the art would have understood the patentee to mean by the language of the claims.

Why was the trial judge's reliance on the Protocol questions held to be erroneous? Given that the Protocol questions will always be secondary to the *Catnic* principle of purposive construction, when does it make sense to utilize them? Here it is interesting to note that post-*Kirin-Amgen* courts have been unwilling to apply the Protocol questions. Instead, they have either applied the general principles set out in *Kirin-Amgen*[12] or relied upon a 'practical working guide' based on the decision, as laid down by Jacob LJ in *Mayne Pharma v Pharmacia Italia*.[13]

One of the more controversial aspects of *Kirin-Amgen* was Lord Hoffmann's approach to equivalents, particularly in light of the new Article 2 of the Protocol and the fact that in other Contracting States, notably Germany, a doctrine of equivalence (although not in the US sense) is recognized. Some commentators have argued that, in practice, there are no substantial differences between the UK approach to claim construction and the German determination of the scope of protection. But the fact that equivalence in the UK merely forms 'an important part of the background of facts known to the skilled man which would affect what he understood the claims to mean' is said to mask important aspects of equivalence that need to be addressed and discussed at a pan-European level.[14] Others

---

[12] *Merz Pharma GmbH v Allergan Inc* [2006] EWHC 2686.   [13] [2005] EWCA Civ 137, para. 5.
[14] N. Hölder, 'Exogenous equals endogenous? Claim construction after the *Amgen* decision' (2006) 37 IIC 662, 669.

have argued that Lord Hoffmann painted an unfair picture of the doctrine of equivalence, which (incorrectly) assumes that protection for equivalents automatically means that the scope of the claims is unbounded.[15]

FURTHER READING

C. Von Drathen, 'Patent scope in English and German law under the European Patent Convention 1973 and 2000' (2008) IIC 384.

N. Hölder, 'Exogenous equals endogenous? Claim construction after the *Amgen* decision' (2006) 37 IIC 662.

M. Fisher, *Fundamentals of Patent law: Interpretation and scope of protection* (Oxford: Hart, 2007), Chs. 1, 9, and 10.

H. Laddie, 'Kirin Amgen—the end of equivalence in England?' (2009) IIC 3.

B. Sherman, 'Patent claim interpretation: The impact of the protocol on interpretation' (1991) 54 Modern Law Review 499.

10.1.2.4 Relevance of prosecution history to construction

Can the documents, in particular the correspondence between patent applicants and the examiner, which are generated during the examination process be used by courts as an aid to construction of the patent as granted? In the UK, the answer is generally no,[16] although there have been exceptional cases where this has happened. For example, in *Furr v Truline (Building Products) Ltd*[17] the judge relied upon documents evidencing the prosecution history. However, these were submitted by the patentee to support a narrow construction of the patent claim and thus could be seen as an admission against interest.[18] Another example is *Rohm & Haas v Collag Ltd*[19] where the Court of Appeal accepted that a letter between the patentee and the EPO 'could be of assistance in resolving some puzzling features of the specification'.[20]

The resistance of the UK courts to admitting evidence relating to the prosecution history may be contrasted with the approach taken in the US, where courts regularly consider such evidence, alongside the language of the claim and the specification. The reasons for doing so are explored below.

N. Fox, 'Divided by a common language: A comparison of patent claim interpretation in the English and American courts' [2004] 26 EIPR 528, 531

In the United States, although comments in the prosecution file will not be taken to override the content of the claims or the description, the prosecution file is considered to be 'intrinsic'

---

[15] M. Fisher, *Fundamentals of Patent law: Interpretation and scope of protection* (Oxford: Hart, 2007), pp. 363, 373.

[16] See *Bristol-Meyers Squibb Co v Baker Norton Pharmaceuticals Inc* [1999] RPC 253, 274–5; *Taylor v Ishida (Europe) Ltd* [2001] EWCA Civ 1092.

[17] [1985] FSR 553.

[18] N. Fox, 'Divided by a common language: A comparison of patent claim interpretation in the English and American courts' [2004] 26 EIPR 528, 532.

[19] [2002] FSR 28.   [20] Ibid., pp. 457–8.

evidence and is favoured over 'extrinsic' evidence. It is easy to understand why prosecution history should be given this favoured status as it is the prosecution history that enables the court to interpret a claim in a manner matching the construction which caused a claim to be granted. This should ensure that any patent will be valid over the prior art considered by the USPTO during prosecution and hence will complement the liberal interpretation which is most likely to maintain an inventor's rights.

Additionally, the content of 'intrinsic' evidence is ultimately under the control of the patentee. It is the patentee who drafts the specification and formulates the wording of the claims. It is also the patentee who is responsible for making claim amendments and for presenting arguments to persuade the USPTO to allow a patent to be granted. If during the course of patent prosecution a patentee wishes to argue in favour of broader protection, that option is open to him. In contrast, if a patentee argues that certain wording should be narrowly construed, reference to the prosecution file will ensure that the same wording is consistently construed when the scope of a patent is considered in the context of a potential infringement. Since all these matters are under the control of the patentee, statements and amendments made during a prosecution can reasonably be taken to reflect the patentee's view as to the extent of the patentee's invention.

It is principally these arguments in favour of consistency and fairness that justify the status of prosecution history in US claim interpretation. The wording of the claims and specification as granted reflect the scope of monopoly that the USPTO considered acceptable. The prosecution file is then a record of both the reasons why the granted claims were considered acceptable and a history of rejected wording which was not considered acceptable. Admitting the prosecution history as evidence therefore achieves the dual aims of trying to maintain an inventor's rights while limiting those rights to the true extent of a claimed invention.

Are the reasons for considering prosecution history when it comes to interpreting the patent claims in the US equally as applicable in the UK? What would be the obstacles or disadvantages to UK courts taking this approach? Jacob J (as he then was) discussed some of these in obiter in *Bristol-Meyers Squibb Co v Baker Norton Pharmaceuticals Inc*.

Bristol-Meyers Squibb Co v Baker Norton Pharmaceuticals Inc [1999] RPC 253

See above at p. 546 for the facts.

Jacob J, at pp. 274–5:

Now there are several points to be made about a claim construction argument based on the prosecution history. First, whether that history can, and if so how, be used as an aid to construction would not be governed by national rules of construction. Claim construction is no longer a matter for national law but is governed by Article 69 and the Protocol. Thus, by way of example, specific English law notions of estoppel, cannot, as such, be used to construe the claim. Preventing him from asserting such a wide construction may be different— a specific English law defence. Second, there is an obvious important practical difference between merely referring to the specification as originally filed as an aid to construction and referring to detailed matter (e.g. contentions in correspondence or evidence) as contained in the EPO file. The specification as filed is a published document (the 'A' specification) and is referred to in the specification as granted. The intermediate processing correspondence with the examiner is different in volume and character, not least because it is not normally translated. Thirdly, there is another obvious difference between using the prosecution his-tory to *widen* the claim and using that history to *narrow* it. It would be unfair on the public if material they would not normally look at could serve as a basis for supporting a wide con-struction of the claim. But there is not the same sort of unfairness if a patentee having con-tended for a narrow construction of his claim during prosecution is held to that construction later (cf. *Furr v Truline (Building Products) Ltd* [1985] FSR 553, an English case). Fourthly there is a difference between merely resolving a puzzle in the specification (though not the claim) by reference to the specification as filed and using the specification as filed as an aid to con-struction of the claim itself...All these are matters to be considered, perhaps by the Enlarged Board of Appeal or, if current proposals were to proceed, by a European Patent Court.

Having considered the comments of Jacob J in *Bristol-Meyers*, do you regard the UK position on prosecution history as justifiable? Would allowing reference to prosecution history create the potential for unfairness as well as risk increasing the costs of litigation?

10.1.3 INFRINGING ACTS

Once the claims have been properly construed and it is established that a person is doing something which falls within their scope, the next issue to consider is whether one of the exclusive acts has been carried out. The exclusive acts are stipulated in s. 60 of the PA 77 and divide into acts of direct infringement and those of contributory (or indirect) infringe-ment. The key difference between the two types is that knowledge is an essential element of contributory infringement. The following sections will examine the scope of acts amount-ing to direct infringement; contributory infringement will be considered in a later section.

10.1.3.1 Introduction

To directly infringe a patent, a person must carry out one of the prescribed exclusive acts *in the United Kingdom* in relation to the invention *without the consent* of the proprietor of the patent.[21] In other words, acts of infringement are territorially limited and if the proprietor has granted a licence to carry out the particular exclusive acts liability will not ensue.

For product inventions, the exclusive acts are to make, dispose of, offer to dispose of, use, or import the product or keep it whether for disposal or otherwise.[22] For process inventions, the exclusive acts are to dispose of, offer to dispose of, use, or import any product *obtained directly* by means of that process or keep any such product whether for disposal or other-wise.[23] In addition, where the invention is a process, it is an infringement for a person to use the process or offer it for use in the UK when he knows, or it is obvious to a reasonable per-son in the circumstances, that its use there without the consent of the proprietor would be an infringement of the patent.[24] This is the only act of direct infringement that involves an element of knowledge. The following sections will discuss the scope of these exclusive acts.

10.1.3.2 Right to make the patented product

The most fundamental exclusive act for product inventions is making the patented prod-uct. The main issue that has arisen is whether repairing a patented product amounts to

---

[21] PA 77, s. 60(1).   [22] Ibid., s. 60(1)(a).   [23] Ibid., s. 60(1)(c).   [24] Ibid., s. 60(1)(b).

making it. The following House of Lords decision has provided helpful clarification on this issue.

United Wire Ltd v Screen Repair Services [2001] RPC 24

The case involved an action for infringement of two UK patents. The inventions related to improvements to sifting screens used to recycle drilling fluid in the offshore drilling industry. When drilling fluid is pumped down the shaft and brought back to the surface, it contains quantities of foreign solids which must be filtered out. The fluid is filtered by being passed through mesh screens vibrating at high speed in a vibrating sifting machine. The claimant's patented inventions were 'screens' and consisted of a frame to which meshes were bonded or adhesively secured at the edge so as to be different tensions. The meshes of the screens had a relatively short life, but the frames to which they were bonded often remained serviceable. The claimant enjoyed a captive and profitable aftermarket in selling replacement screens. The defendants sought to break into this market by selling reconditioned screens made from the claimant's own frames. The defendant would acquire the frames from the claimant's customers, strip them down to the bare metal, recoat them with adhesive polyethylene, and attach the two layers of mesh (coarse and fine) with differential tensions. The screens were then on-sold to the customers, who received a credit for supplying the frames.

The defendants argued, *inter alia*, that the repaired screens did not infringe because they 'repaired' a screen, rather than 'made' it within the meaning of s. 60(1)(a) of the PA 77. This succeeded at first instance, but the Court of Appeal allowed an appeal on this issue. The Court of Appeal held that the trial judge had erred in focussing on whether or not the actions were in fact repair: the issue was whether the acts amounted to a manufacture of the product, taking into the account the nature of the repair claimed. The defendants appealed, but this was dismissed by the House of Lords.

Lord Hoffmann (with whom the other law lords agreed):

65. The defendants say that although the product which they sell is a screen in accordance with the invention, they do not infringe because they do no more than repair screens which have been marketed with the consent of the plaintiffs. The grounds upon which this is said not to constitute an infringement is put in various ways. First, it is said that, in marketing the screens, the plaintiffs impliedly licence anyone who acquires a screen to prolong its life by repair. Secondly, it is said that the marketing of the screens constitutes an exhaustion of any rights which a repair might infringe. Thirdly, it is said that a person who repairs a screen does not 'make' that screen within the meaning of the definition of an infringement in section 60(1)(a) of the Patents Act 1977.

...

68. My Lords, the point is a very short one and in my opinion the Court of Appeal was right. The concept of an implied licence to do various acts in relation to a patented product is well established in the authorities. Its proper function is to explain why, notwithstanding the apparent breadth of the patentee's rights, a person who has acquired the product with the consent of the patentee may use or dispose of it in any way he pleases. The traditional Royal Command in the grant of a patent forebade others not only to 'make' but also to 'use, exercise or vend' the invention. Similarly, s. 60(1)(a) provides that a person infringes a patent for a product not only if he 'makes' it but also if, without the consent of the proprietor, he 'disposes

of, offers to dispose of, uses or imports the product or keeps it whether for disposal or otherwise'. Put shortly, the problem is to explain why, for example, a patentee cannot complain when someone to whom he had sold the patented product then, without any further consent, uses it or disposes of it to someone else. The answer given by Lord Hatherley LC in the leading case of *Betts v Willmott* (1871) LR 6 Ch App 239, 245 (which concerned the resale of a patented product) was that he did so by virtue of an implied licence:

I apprehend that, inasmuch as [the patentee] has the right of vending the goods in France or Belgium or England, or in any other quarter of the globe, he transfers with the goods necessarily the licence to use them wherever the purchaser pleases. When a man has purchased an article he expects to have the control of it, and there must be some clear and explicit agreement to the contrary to justify the vendor in saying that he has not given the purchaser his licence to sell the article, or to use it wherever he pleases as against himself.

69. An alternative explanation, adopted in European patent systems, is that of exhaustion of rights. The patentee's rights in respect of the product are exhausted by the first sale: see *Merck & Co Inc v Primecrown Ltd* [1997] 1 CMLR 83 at page 119. The difference in the two theories is that an implied licence may be excluded by express contrary agreement or made subject to conditions while the exhaustion doctrine leaves no patent rights to be enforced.

70. Where however it is alleged that the defendant has infringed by *making* the patented product, the concepts of an implied licence or exhaustion of rights can have no part to play. The sale of a patented article cannot confer an implied licence to make another or exhaust the right of the patentee to prevent others from being made. A repair of the patented product is by definition an act which does not amount to making it: as Lord Halsbury LC said of the old law in *Sirdar Rubber Co Ltd v Wallington, Weston & Co* (1907) 24 RPC 539 at page 543:

you may prolong the life of a licensed article but you must not make a new one under the cover of repair.

71. Repair is one of the concepts (like modifying or adapting) which shares a boundary with 'making' but does not trespass upon its territory. I therefore agree with the Court of Appeal that in an action for infringement by making, the notion of an implied licence to repair is superfluous and possibly even confusing. It distracts attention from the question raised by section 60(1)(a), which is whether the defendant has made the patented product. As a matter of ordinary language, the notions of making and repair may well overlap. But for the purposes of the statute, they are mutually exclusive. The owner's right to repair is not an independent right conferred upon him by licence, express or implied. It is a residual right, forming part of the right to do whatever does not amount to making the product.

. . .

73. …in this case the Court of Appeal was in my opinion entitled to substitute its own evaluation because I think, with great respect to the judge, that he did not correctly identify the patented product. He said that the frame was an important part of the assembly and that the defendants had prolonged 'the screen's useful life'. It is quite true that the defendants prolonged the useful life of the *frame*. It would otherwise presumably have been scrapped. But the *screen* was the combination of frame and meshes pre-tensioned by attachment with adhesive according to the invention. That product ceased to exist when the meshes were removed and the frame stripped down to the bare metal. What remained at that stage was merely an important component, a skeleton or chassis, from which a new screen could be made.

According to *United Wire,* is there ever any point in asking whether a product has been repaired as opposed to made? Also, what is the relationship between the right to make a patented product and the concepts of implied licence and exhaustion of rights?[25] To which acts would an implied licence or the doctrine of exhaustion of rights apply?

10.1.3.3 Right to dispose of or offer to dispose of the product

The right to dispose of the product includes the right to sell (or vend) the product. As such, an offer to dispose of a product includes an offer of sale. Importantly, the sale or offer of sale must occur within the UK. *Kalman v PCL Packaging*[26] illustrates these points. In this case the second defendant was a corporation operating in the USA, with no place of business in the UK and no regular trading activities outside the USA. The second defendant had sold and delivered to the first defendant two allegedly infringing articles within the USA. Falconer J held that the second defendant had not disposed of the products within the UK, given that the allegedly infringing articles had been sold in the USA. Neither had it offered to dispose of an infringing product, since this would have required an offer *made in the UK* to dispose of filters *within* the UK. Whilst the second defendant had arguably made an offer in the UK, it was not an offer to dispose of the filters within the UK.

10.1.3.4 Right to keep the product whether for disposal or otherwise

In relation to the PA 77, it was unclear whether passively storing a patented product, or the product directly obtained from a patented process, would constitute keeping the product for disposal or otherwise. Oliver J considered this issue in *SKF v Harbottle*.[27] In this case, British Airways were in the process of transporting, at the request of the first defendant, an antihistamine drug called cimetidine from Italy to Nigeria. The quantity of drugs had not been cleared through customs and was stored at their bonded warehouse. The claimants, who held a UK patent covering the drug cimetidine, brought an infringement action against the importer of the drug, Harbottle. British Airways was joined as a co-defendant and was thereby restrained from disposing of the drug. The claimants claimed that British Airways had infringed their right to keep the product.

Oliver J declined to arrive at a definitive meaning of 'keep'. However, he held that the act of passively storing a patented drug in a warehouse in London could *not* be construed as 'keeping of a product' within the meaning of s. 60(1) of the PA 77. In coming to this conclusion he was strongly influenced by the lack of positive language to effect such a significant change. Prior to PA 77, a carrier or warehouseman who did no more than innocently carry or store infringing goods for a consignor/consignee was not liable as an infringer. Oliver J reasoned:

> But if it had been the intention of Parliament to bring within the category of infringers a new and extensive class of persons who by the very nature of their trade or calling would be unlikely to have any knowledge, either actual or potential, of any patent protection affecting the goods which were only transitorily in their control, one would have expected so revolutionary a change in the common law to be effected by a pronouncement of a less Delphic nature.[28]

In addition, Oliver J was strongly influenced by the 'very much more limited' terms employed in Article 29(a) of the Community Patent Convention, which refers to 'stocking'

---

[25] For a discussion see 1.3.2.1.   [26] [1982] FSR 406.
[27] [1980] RPC 363.   [28] Ibid., p. 371.

of the patented product. The intention of the framers of the PA 77 was to give effect to the provisions of the Community Patent Convention.[29] Thus, 'keep' implied 'keeping in stock' rather than acting as a custodian.[30] Subsequently, the Court of Appeal followed this interpretation in *McDonald v Graham*.[31]

10.1.3.5 Right to import the product

According to the House of Lords decision in *Sabaf SpA v MFI Furniture Centres Ltd*[32] where goods have been sold outside the UK, arranging transport of the goods from outside the UK to the UK does not constitute importation.

10.1.3.6 Direct infringement of a patented process

Section 60(1)(c) of the PA 77 stipulates that a person will infringe a *process* patent if they dispose of, offer to dispose of, use, or import any product *obtained directly* by means of that process or keep any such product whether for disposal or otherwise. The stipulation that the product must be obtained *directly* from the patented process is a way of ensuring that the scope of the monopoly is kept within justifiable limits. If it did not exist, the provision might cover those products which were only tangentially or partly derivative from the patented process.

The Court of Appeal in *Pioneer Electronics Capital Inc v Warner Music*[33] shed light on when a product will be obtained directly from a process. The case concerned a European patent, which designated the UK, involving processes used in the manufacture of optical discs, otherwise known as compact disks (CDs). The defendants applied to strike out the writs and statements of claim. This application succeeded before Aldous J (as he then was), who held that the products complained of could not be said to have been obtained directly by means of the patented processes. The claimants appealed. Nourse LJ (with whom Leggatt and Schiemann LJJ agreed) turned to German authorities in particular to interpret s. 60(1)(c) of the PA 77. This was because there were no relevant UK authorities and s. 130(7) of the PA 77 requires that s. 60(1)(c) be interpreted in conformity with the corresponding provisions of the EPC and CPC. From German jurisprudence Nourse LJ extracted the principle:[34]

> that the product obtained directly by means of a patented process is the product with which the process ends; it does not cease to be the product so obtained if it is subjected to further processing which does not cause it to lose its identity, there being no such loss where it retains its essential characteristics.

Nourse LJ was of the view that authorities from other European countries did not differ from the German approach and that the 'loss of identity test' could be taken to reflect the test adopted by European law. The question of whether a product had retained its essential characteristics such that it had not lost its identity and could be said to be directly obtained from the patented process was a question of fact and degree. On the facts of this case, however, it was clear that the product had not retained its identity.

---

[29] See PA 77, s. 130 (7).   [30] *SKF v Harbottle* [1980] RPC 363, 373.
[31] [1994] RPC 407, 431, per Ralph Gibson LJ.   [32] [2005] RPC 10, para. 40, per Lord Hoffmann.
[33] [1997] RPC 757.   [34] Ibid., p. 771.

Do you agree that a test of 'loss of identity' is an appropriate way in which to measure whether a product has been obtained directly from a patented process?

10.1.3.7 Indirect or contributory infringement

Section 60(2) of the PA 77 creates a form of indirect or contributory infringement. This subsection provides:

> Subject to the following provisions of this section, a person (other than the proprietor of the patent) also infringes a patent for an invention if, while the patent is in force and without the consent of the proprietor, he supplies or offers to supply in the United Kingdom a person other than a licensee or other person entitled to work the invention with any of the means, relating to an essential element of the invention, for putting the invention into effect when he knows, or it is obvious to a reasonable person in the circumstances, that those means are suitable for putting, and are intended to put, the invention into effect in the United Kingdom.

Thus, to establish indirect infringement, one must show that:

1. without the consent of the proprietor of the patent, a person supplies or offers to supply means relating to an *essential element* of the invention; and

2. there must be *actual or constructive knowledge* on the part of the supplier, both that the means are 'suitable' for and are 'intended' to be used in putting the invention into effect.

Importantly, the territorial limitation applies both to where the supply or offer to supply is made *and* also to where the invention is put into effect. In other words, if a person were to supply an essential element of a patented invention in the UK, but the invention was put into effect outside the UK (say, in Italy), this provision would not be infringed.

What is an essential element of the invention will depend on how the claims are construed. Further, whether there is actual or constructive knowledge will depend on the facts of the case. However, it is important to note that according to s. 60(3) of the PA 77, supply or offer of a *staple commercial product* will not constitute an indirect infringement under s. 60(2), unless the supply or offer is made for the purpose of inducing a direct infringement under s. 60(1).

10.2 EXCEPTIONS TO INFRINGEMENT

There are a limited number of exceptions to patent infringement. The following section will focus on three key exceptions within the PA 77: acts done for experimental purposes ('experimental use'); acts done for private and non-commercial purposes ('private use'); and the right to continue use begun before the priority date ('prior use').

10.2.1 EXPERIMENTAL USE

We have seen that one of the justifications for the patent system is that it encourages disclosure of inventions[35] and this, in turn, benefits society because others can learn from

---

[35] See 9.3.

and build upon existing innovations. We have also seen that the requirements of novelty and sufficiency emphasize the disclosure rationale of patent law. However, if patent proprietors have the exclusive right to make a patented product or products directly resulting from a patented process does this mean that third parties will have to wait until the 20-year grant expires before they can utilize the knowledge disclosed in the specification? To the extent that their activities fall within the scope of the claims, this will constitute infringement. But should a person be liable where they are conducting research or experiments in order to understand how the invention works or to develop ways of improving it or to acquire knowledge that will be beneficial to other technological areas? Professor Cornish has succinctly noted the tension that arises:

> If they may engage in such experiments as they please, the initial incentive of the patent may to a degree be diminished. But if they may not, the original patentee may control the further progress of a particular technology for the duration of his exclusive right.[36]

Section 60(5)(b) of the PA 77 seeks to balance the competing interests of the patentee and third parties by exempting from infringement acts done for experimental purposes relating to the subject matter of the invention. The origin of this exception is Article 27(b) of the CPC.[37] Although it was intended to exclude only academic or non-commercial research from infringement, the terms of Article 27(b) of the CPC did not make this distinction.[38] As we shall see, the courts have interpreted the exception generously, in a manner that does not restrict it to purely non-commercial or academic research.

Monsanto Co v Stauffer Chemical Co [1985] RPC 515

The claimants were proprietors of a patent relating to herbicides for agricultural use and marketed a herbicide under the trademark 'Roundup'. The defendants devised their own herbicide which performed substantially the same function as the claimants' herbicide, which they marketed under the trademark 'Touchdown'. The claimants brought an action for infringement against the defendants and obtained interlocutory relief restraining the defendants from further using or selling their allegedly infringing product. The defendants applied to modify the injunction to permit them to undertake certain experimental uses. Falconer J dismissed the application and the defendants appealed.

Dillon LJ (with whom **Watkins LJ** and **Sir Denys Buckley** agreed), at pp. 537–9:

Section 60 was, as section 130(7) shows, enacted to bring UK patent law into line with the corresponding provisions of the Community Patent Convention and I have no reason to suppose that the signatories of that Convention were concerning themselves with the minutiae of earlier UK patent law. Beyond that, however, the word 'experiment' is an ordinary word in the English language and has never been a term of art in UK patent law.

---

[36] W. R. Cornish, 'Experimental use of patented inventions in the EC states' (1998) 29 IIC 735, 735.
[37] See PA 77, s. 130(7).
[38] Cornish, 'Experimental use of patented inventions in the EC states', p. 736.

Mr Gratwick further submits that the words 'for experimental purposes' are limited to experiments in the privacy of a laboratory or glasshouse. I cannot, however, see why that should be so. What may legitimately be the subject of experiment may perhaps depend upon the nature of the product but, with herbicides or compositions to stimulate plant growth, it must surely be a legitimate area for experiment to see if results obtained in the laboratory or glasshouse can also be achieved in natural conditions in the open air where the product will have to be used.

Mr Gratwick urges that the words in section 60(5)(b) 'relating to the subject-matter of the invention' ought to be narrowly construed so as to exclude experiments directed to the commercial exploitation of the invention. For my part, however, I find it difficult to draw any such hard and fast line. The distinction between the wording of sub-head (a) and the wording of sub-head (b) in section 60(5) indicates that experimental purposes in sub-head (b) may yet have a commercial end in view, as do all the activities of companies such as the parties to this dispute. I would regard the sort of experimental activity which was considered by the Supreme Court of Canada in *Micro-Chemicals Ltd v Smith Kline and French Inter-American Ltd* (1971) 25 DLR 79 at the top of page 89, viz. a limited experiment to establish whether the experimenter could manufacture a quality product commercially in accordance with the specification of a patent, as being covered by the words 'for experimental purposes relating to the subject-matter of the invention'.

The defendants' farm in Essex is described in the evidence as a research farm, and that makes sense in the context of all that is disclosed on the evidence about the defendants' activities. Accordingly, I would modify the injunction by providing that it shall not extend to acts done for experimental purposes relating to the subject-matter of the invention in laboratories or glasshouses in the United Kingdom or on the defendants' farm in Essex.

The second category of field trials for which the defendants seek a relaxation covers trials to be carried out by the second defendant's personnel on land rented by the second defendant on other farms. What the defendants want to do, by arrangement with farmers in different parts of the country, is to use TOUCHDOWN on different crops, and at different stages of the year, and at different concentrations, on small areas, of perhaps a couple of acres each, on some 20 or 25 farms in different parts of the country and to tabulate the results. They submit with obvious force that, if it is necessary to experiment to see if what is successful in the laboratory or glasshouse works successfully out of doors, it is necessary that the experiments should be carried out in different soil conditions and in different climatic conditions. What works in California will not necessarily work in England and what works on their farm in Essex may not necessarily work in Wales or Cumbria.

The real problem here, however, is whether, in the light of all they have already done which culminated in the commercial launch of TOUCHDOWN in August 1983, what they want to do now by these field trials can fairly be classified as experimental, or is in truth merely a matter of amassing statistics to further the commercial exploitation, after 22 October 1987, of a product whose qualities they already know. It is therefore necessary to look at some of the evidence.

[After reviewing the evidence, **Dillon LJ** concluded:]

Trials carried out in order to discover something unknown or to test a hypothesis or even in order to find out whether something which is known to work in specific conditions, e.g. of soil or weather, will work in different conditions can fairly, in my judgment, be regarded as experiments. But trials carried out in order to demonstrate to a third party that a product works or, in order to amass information to satisfy a third party, whether a customer or a body such as the PSPS or ACAS, that the product works as its maker claims are not, in my judgment, to be regarded as acts done 'for experimental purposes'. The purposes for which tests or trials are carried out may in some cases be mixed and may in some cases be difficult to discern; indeed, in the present case, if fuller evidence is given at the trial, a different result may then be reached. On the affidavit evidence before this court, it is not clear to me what the defendants are still wanting to find out about TOUCHDOWN. On that, evidence, if I ask, in relation to the defendant's proposed field trials of category (2) to be carried out by the second defendant's personnel on land rented on other farms, the broad question whether those trials would be carried out, or done, for experimental purposes, my answer is that they would not; they would be carried out in order to obtain the approval of the PSPS and ACAS.

I therefore agree with Falconer J that the injunction should not be modified to permit the defendants to carry out field trials of category (2).

By the same reasoning, the injunction should not be modified to permit the defendants to carry out field trials of category (3), trials to be carried out on their own lands, albeit for the defendants, by ACAS, the Forestry Commission, certain Water Authorities and others.

It is worth noting that courts in other European states, notably Germany and the Netherlands, have adopted a similar approach to that taken by the Court of Appeal in *Monsanto*.[39] Do you agree that it makes sense to permit experiments where there is a commercial end in view? Or should the exception be confined to activities that are strictly noncommercial? Why is it, do you think, that trials carried out to amass information in order to obtain regulatory approval do not fall within the scope of the exception?

As well as establishing an experimental purpose, a defendant must show that the purpose relates to the *subject matter of the invention*. The meaning of this requirement was explored in the following case.

SKF v Evans [1989] FSR 513

The claimants, Smith Kline & French, were proprietors of three patents relating to the drug, cimetidine. The patents were described as the generic patent, the master patent, and the polymorph patent. SK&F applied to the patent comptroller to amend the polymorph patent. The defendant, Evans, opposed this application to amend and, to support their case, carried out an experiment which SK&F alleged infringed all three patents. SK&F applied for summary judgment against Evans and Evans sought to strike out the action. Evans did not dispute that they had used over 30 kg of cimetidine and had proceeded to make it into tablets and that they had done an act falling within s. 60(1)(a) of the PA 77. However, they argued, *inter alia*, that their acts were exempted as experimental use.

Aldous J:

Section 60(5)(b) not only requires the act to be done for experimental purposes, but also that the purposes relate to the subject matter of the invention. The invention referred to appears to me to be an invention of the patent in respect of which infringement is alleged. In the present case there are three patents, and SK&F contend that even if the acts were done for experimental purposes, they did not relate to the subject matter of the generic or master

---

[39] See Cornish, 'Experimental use of patented inventions in the EC states'.

610 | INTELLECTUAL PROPERTY LAW: TEXT, CASES, AND MATERIALS

patents. They only related to the subject matter of the polymorph patent. This requires a determination of the meaning of the words 'purposes relating to the subject matter of the invention'.

First it should be noted that the words 'the invention' are used, and not 'an invention'. Secondly, section 130(7) states that section 60 of the Patents Act 1977 was framed as to have as nearly as practical the same effect in the United Kingdom as the corresponding provisions of *inter alia* the Community Patent Convention has in other Convention countries. Articles 29 and 31 of the CPC suggest that the subject-matter of an invention is to be found in the claims of the patent. Thus I believe that if an act is to fall within subsection (5)(b) it must be done for purposes relating to the subject-matter of the invention found in the claims of the patent alleged to be infringed.

So far so good, but the real difficulty arises as to what nexus is required by the words 'relating to'. Can it be an indirect relationship, or must it be a direct relationship? The difficulty is best illustrated by an example which was canvassed before me in argument. Supposing a company seeking to investigate a chemical patent either for the purposes of challenging its validity or for the purposes of improving upon the invention of that patent, carries out the process of the patent using a reagent which is made and marketed by a third party who has patented that reagent. In such circumstances can the experimenter, relying on sub-section (5)(b), manufacture the reagent without the consent of the patentee of the reagent patent, thereby depriving him of the sale. In my view he cannot. I believe that in the circumstances outlined the experimental purposes relate to the chemical patent and not to the reagent patent. A contrary conclusion would, in practice, deprive the words 'relating to the subject-matter of the invention' of any meaning as subsection (5)(b) would apply in all cases where experiments were carried out which involve the use of an invention. Such an act would be protected as it would inevitably involve and therefore relate to the subject-matter of the invention.

Further, the words I have quoted suggest that some acts done for experimental purposes do not have the required relationship. It therefore seems to me that the relationship must be a real and direct one. I am therefore of the view that section 60(5)(b) covers acts done for experimental purposes including experiments with a commercial end in view, but the purposes must relate to the claimed subject-matter of the patent in suit in the sense of having a real and direct connection with that subject-matter.

It is clear that Evans carried out their experiment for the purposes of the amendment proceedings. In so doing they carried out an example of the master patent with a view of challenging the polymorph patent. They do not contend that the experiment was carried out to invalidate the generic patent, but say that all three patents relate to the same subject matter and therefore subsection (5)(b) applies. However, this disregards the fact that each of the patents relates to a separate invention. Thus upon my view of the correct construction of subsection (5)(b), I believe that this subsection does not provide a defence to infringement of at least the generic patent. However I believe that the relationship between the experiment and the master patent is sufficiently direct as to be covered by the subsection.

Why it is important that the experimental purpose relates to the subject matter of the invention in the claims of the patent allegedly infringed, and that the relationship is a real and direct one?

Finally, it should be noted that the experimental use exception does not apply to acts of indirect infringement.[40] Commentators have queried 'why there should be such a limitation on supplying for the purpose of permitting others to perform excepted

[40] See PA 77, s. 60(6).

experiments'.[41] However, Professor Cornish has argued that this has not arisen as a problem in the cases because the defendant who procures the experiment is usually liable directly and not indirectly and is thus able to rely on the exception.[42]

FURTHER READING

F. Bor, 'Exemptions to patent infringement applied to biotechnology research tools' [2006] EIPR 5.

W. R. Cornish, 'Experimental use of patented inventions in the EC states' (1998) 29 IIC 735.

T. Cook, 'Responding to concerns about the scope of the defence from patent infringement for acts done for experimental purposes relating to the subject matter of the invention' (2006) IPQ 193.

R. Eisenberg, 'Patents and the progress of science: Exclusive rights and experimental use' (1989) 56 U Chicago LR 1017.

10.2.2 PRIVATE USE

Acts which are done privately, and for purposes that are not commercial, are exempt from infringement pursuant to s. 60(5)(a) of the PA 77. The scope of this exception was first considered in *SKF v Evans*.

SKF v Evans [1989] FSR 513

For the facts see above at p. 609. SKF alleged that Evans had infringed all three of their patents and applied for summary judgment. Evans sought to rely on the defence for private and non-commercial use.

Aldous J, at pp. 517–18:

The first matter that needs to be established is that the act is done privately. As this subsection goes on to exclude acts done for commercial purposes the word 'privately' includes commercial and non-commercial situations. This word is not, in my view, synonymous with 'secret' or 'confidential' and would include acts which were secret or confidential or were not. This word appears to me to be used as the opposite of 'publicly' and to be used in the sense of denoting that the act was done for the person's own use. This construction of the word 'privately' is consistent with the rest of the subsection which provides that even if the acts are done privately in the sense of for the person's own use, there will be infringement if the acts are done for commercial purposes.

As I have said, the subsection excludes acts which, even if done privately, are done for purposes which are not commercial. The court is therefore required to consider the purpose of the alleged infringing act and then decide whether that purpose was commercial or not. The word 'commercial' does not need explanation and clearly includes any commercial purpose. The more difficult question is whether acts done primarily for purposes which are not commercial, but do have a commercial benefit, are infringing acts. For instance, in the present

---

41 Cornish, 'Experimental use of patented inventions in the EC states', p. 751.　　42 Ibid., pp. 751–2.

case Evans contend that the only purpose of their experiment was private, but accept that in carrying out those experiments they may have acquired information which would be of commercial use to them. I believe that in such circumstances the court is required to consider what the purposes of the acts were. It is a subjective test and if, on the evidence, the court should find that there was a dual purpose, then in those circumstances there would be infringement. If, however, all the purposes were not commercial, the fact that knowledge gained could and might be of commercial benefit would not preclude the act from falling within section 60(5)(a) and therefore be an act which was not an infringement.

In the present case it is accepted that the experiment carried out by Evans was done privately. The dispute turns on whether it was done for purposes which were commercial. Evans says that the only purpose of the experiment was to produce evidence for the amendment proceedings but, as I have said, accept that in carrying out the experiment it can be assumed that they acquired information which would be useful in commercial production.

If they are right on the facts, then I believe that the acts alleged fall within section 60(5)(a). Experiments done for legal proceedings in the High Court or in the Patent Office are not, in my view, done for a commercial purpose. However, SK&F say that from the nature of the experiment it is clear that Evans had a dual purpose, namely to provide evidence for the amendment proceedings and to obtain commercial experience. If they are right as a matter of fact then it seems to me that section 60(5)(a) does not apply.

Under Order 14 summary judgment should only be given if the plaintiff can prove his claim clearly and the defendant is unable to set up a *bona fide* defence. Leave to defend must be given unless it is clear that there is no real substantial question to be tried. In the present case I consider that there is a substantial issue to be tried, namely whether the alleged infringing acts were done for the sole purpose of the amendment proceedings, or whether there was a dual purpose, one of which was a commercial purpose.

Does it make sense that 'private' use is the opposite of 'public', but yet this does not necessarily mean 'secret' or 'confidential'? If the use has both commercial and non-commercial purposes will it still come within the exception? Finally, is the distinction between a commercial purpose and a purpose which is non-commercial but which may have a commercial benefit an easy one to draw?

10.2.3 PRIOR USE

According to *Merrell Dow v Norton*, secret, inherent, or uninformative use before the priority date does not amount to anticipation since the invention must have been 'made available to the public'.[43] As a result of this shift in approach to novelty, third parties may infringe a patent if they continue to carry out such activities. In recognition of the 'right to work' principle, namely, that it would be unfair if patents were used to prevent persons from carrying out activities that they were doing before the priority date, s. 64 of the PA 77 gives prior users a personal defence. Section 64(1) provides:

Where a patent is granted for an invention, a person who in the United Kingdom before the priority date of the invention—

(a) does in good faith an act which would constitute an infringement of the patent if it were in force, or

---

[43] See 9.10.4.

(b) makes in good faith effective and serious preparations to do such an act,

has the right to continue to do the act or, as the case may be, to do the act, notwithstanding the grant of the patent; but this right does not extend to granting a licence to another person to do the act.

In the following case, Jacob J (as he then was) commented obiter on the scope of the prior use defence.

Lubrizol Corporation v Esso Petroleum Co Ltd [1997] RPC 195

The patent in suit was granted under the PA 1949 and related to lubricant oil containing a particular additive produced by reacting an amine or other active compound with a defined succinic acylating agent. In an action for infringement, the defendants challenged the validity of the patent on grounds of ambiguity and lack of novelty. They also sought to rely on s. 64 of the PA 77 in relation to acts of infringement occurring after 1977. Jacob J found the patent bad for ambiguity and lack of novelty under the PA 1949. In obiter, he commented on the scope of s. 64 of the PA 77 and found that it did not apply to the defendants.

Jacob J, at pp. 215–16:

In earlier proceedings in the present case, *Lubrizol Corp v Esso Petroleum Co Ltd (No 1)* [1992] RPC 281 at page 285, Laddie J disagreed with this, also *obiter*

> I think it is only right to say that I have some doubts, with great respect to Aldous J, as to whether *Helitune* is correct. The act which the alleged infringer is entitled to continue to conduct by virtue of section 64(2) is the act which he was committing before the priority date. It is that specific act of commerce which he is entitled to continue. I have difficulty in accepting that by, for example, manufacturing product A before the priority date, he was thereby given a right to manufacture any product after the priority date. In my view, section 64 is intended to safeguard the existing commercial activity of a person in the United Kingdom which is overtaken by the subsequent grant of a patent. It is not meant to be a charter allowing him to expand into other products and other processes.

I agree with Laddie J for all the reasons he gave in his decision, and because I do not think the actual language of section 64 is appropriate were Aldous J correct. It is 'the doing of that act' which is protected, not 'any act which would otherwise be an infringement'.

However there was a slight gloss. I think Laddie J's reference to 'existing commercial activity'—the protected 'act' of the section—means an activity which is substantially the same as the prior act or act for which substantial and effective preparations were made. In deciding whether the activity is substantially the same all the circumstances must be considered. Both technical and commercial matters must be taken into account. That is important in a case such as the present where there are inherent minor variations in starting materials or the like. If the protected act has to be *exactly* the same (whatever that may mean) as the prior act then the protection given by the section would be illusory. The section is intended to give a practical protection to enable a man to continue doing what in substance he was doing before. In so holding I reject Mr Young's suggestion that the nature of the protected act depends in some way on the claims of the patent specification. I cannot see

how that can be: an act is protected or not depending on what it was, not on the somewhat
adventitious manner in which the patentee may have chosen to cast his monopoly.

Jacob J concluded that the defence did not apply since preliminary planning did not constitute 'effective and serious preparations' to do an act.

Based on the terms of s. 64 of the PA 77 and *Lubrizol* the following should be noted about
the prior-use exception:

1. It only applies where the prior acts were committed in the UK and the acts were carried out in good faith.

2. The defendant must have done acts or made 'serious and effective preparations'
   before the priority date of the patent to do an act which would be infringing if it was
   carried out after the grant of the patent.

3. The defence allows a prior user to do an act which is the *same* or *substantially* the
   same as the prior act or act for which substantial and effective preparations were made.
   Substantial and effective preparations to do an act do not include acts of preliminary
   planning.

4. The continued use must be by the same person. However, where the act or preparations were done in the course of business, the prior user has the right to authorize the
   doing of the act by their partners for the time of the business: s. 64(2) of the PA 77. The
   defence does not extend to granting a licence to another to do the act.

Does the prior use defence give sufficient weight to the 'right to work' rationale that was pre-
viously protected by allowing secret or uninformative prior use to anticipate an invention?
Further, does the defence provide any protection against those inventions, such as in *Mobil
Oil*, where novelty is established by a new purpose?

10.3 ENTITLEMENT

10.3.1 INTRODUCTION

Although any person may apply for a patent,[44] only certain persons are entitled to the
grant of a patent. These are: (1) the inventor or joint inventors;[45] (2) the employer of the
inventor when the invention is made in the course of employment; or (3) a person who by
virtue of any foreign law, treaty, or international convention is entitled to the grant.[46] In
addition, a patent may be granted to any successor in title of any of these persons.[47] The
person entitled to the grant of a patent will be the first owner, i.e. proprietor, of the patent.
The proprietor may then assign, licence, or mortgage the patent[48] and is able to sue for
infringement.[49]

Where there are joint proprietors, each has an equal, undivided share in the patent
(unless otherwise agreed) and a co-proprietor may carry out any of the exclusive acts for
his own benefit *without* the consent of the other co-proprietor/s and without having to

---

[44] PA 77, s. 7(1)(a).   [45] Ibid., s. 7(2)(a).   [46] Ibid., s. 7(2)(b).   [47] Ibid.
[48] Ibid., s. 30. Note that according to s. 30(6), PA 77 assignments and mortgages must be in writing
signed by or on behalf of the assignor or mortgagor.
[49] Ibid., s. 61. Note that exclusive licensees are also entitled to sue for infringement: ibid., s. 30(7).

compensate them.[50] However, consent must be obtained from the other co-proprietor/s in order to assign the patent, mortgage a share in the patent, or to grant a licence.[51] Where a deadlock between co-proprietors arises, the comptroller has jurisdiction to grant or to order a co-proprietor to grant a licence to third parties.[52]

10.3.2 DETERMINING ENTITLEMENT

It is possible to have the question of entitlement determined *before* or *after* the grant of a patent for an invention. Section 8(1)(a) of the PA 77 provides that at any time *before* a patent has been granted (whether or not an application has been made for it):

> (a) any person may refer to the comptroller the question whether he is entitled to be granted a patent for the invention (either alone or with any other person) or has or would have any right in or under any patent so granted or any application for such a patent; or
>
> (b) any of two or more co-proprietors of an application for a patent for that invention may so refer the question whether any right in or under the application should be transferred or granted to any other person;
>
> and the comptroller shall determine the question and may make such order as he thinks fit to give effect to the determination.

After a patent has been granted, s. 37(1) of the PA 77 states that any person having or claiming a proprietary interest in or under the patent may refer to the comptroller the question:

> (a) who is or are the true proprietor or proprietors of the patent;
>
> (b) whether the patent should have been granted to the person or persons to whom it was granted; or
>
> (c) whether any right in or under the patent should be transferred or granted to any other person or persons;
>
> and the comptroller shall determine the question and make such order as he thinks fit to give effect to the determination.

Importantly, the reference must be made before the end of two years after the date of grant of the patent.[53] Where the reference initially claims joint entitlement, but then is amended to claim sole entitlement, this does not constitute a new reference and, provided the initial reference was made within the limitation period, the fact that the amendment occurred after the limitation period will not bar the claim.[54]

---

[50] Ibid., s. 36(1)–(2).

[51] Ibid., s. 36(3). In support of such rules for joint proprietors see R. P. Merges and L. A. Locke, 'Co-ownership of patents: A comparative and economic view' (1990) 72 J Pat & Trademark Off Soc 586, 592–6.

[52] *Hughes v Paxman* [2007] RPC 2. This discretion must be exercised rationally, fairly, and proportionately and must have regard to all the circumstances of the case.

[53] PA 77, s. 37(5).

[54] *Rhone-Poulenc Rorer International Holdings Inc v Yeda Research and Development Co Ltd* [2007] UKHL 43.

10.3.3 DETERMINING THE INVENTOR

It is important to determine the inventor or joint inventors since they are the persons who are generally entitled to the grant of a patent. Further, the inventor or joint inventors must be identified in any published application for a patent or in any patent granted for an invention, unless they have waived their right to be so mentioned.[55]

The courts have developed a basic, two-step approach to identifying the inventor/s. First, it is necessary to identify the inventive concept and then, secondly, to determine who was responsible for the inventive concept.[56]

In terms of the first step, identifying the inventive concept, courts have considered how this should be approached when there is a patent *application*, as opposed to a granted patent. More specifically, courts have considered whether the patentability of the invention should be taken into account. It seems that, in general, the patentability or validity of the invention should be ignored.[57] However, the Court of Appeal in *Markem Corporation v Zipher Ltd*[58] held that:

> [i]f the patent or part of it is clearly and unarguably invalid, then we see no reason why as a matter of convenience, the Comptroller should not take it into account in exercising his wide discretion. The sooner an obviously invalid monopoly is removed, the better from the public point of view. But we emphasise that the attack on validity should be clear and unarguable.[59]

In identifying the inventive concept, the Court of Appeal in *Markem v Zipher* emphasized that in determining entitlement (in this case under s. 8 of the PA 77) the court is not restricted to the claims. This is because s. 8 applies to situations where there may not even be a patent application and because patent applications are not required to have claims. Jacob LJ held that:

> s. 8 is referring essentially to information in the specification rather than the form of the claims...s. 8 calls for identification of information and the rights in it. Who contributed what and what rights if any they had in it lies in the heart of the inquiry, not what monopolies were actually claimed....What one is normally looking for is 'the heart' of the invention.[60]

In relation to the second step, determining who is responsible for, or who devised, the inventive concept, the PA 77 provides little guidance. Section 7(3) of the PA 77 defines 'inventor' in relation to an invention to mean the 'actual deviser of the invention' and 'joint inventor' is to be construed accordingly.

---

[55] See PA 77, ss. 13(1) and 24(3).

[56] See *Henry Bros v Ministry of Defence* [1999] RPC 442, 448 (Robert Walker LJ); *Collag Corp v Merck & Co Inc* [2003] FSR 16, 291 (Pumfrey J); *Minnesota Mining and Manufacturing Co's International Patent Application* [2003] RPC 28, 555–6 (Mr Peter Hayward); *University of Southampton's Applications* [2006] RPC 21, 575, per Jacob LJ (with whom Wilson and Ward LJJ agreed); *Rhone-Poulenc Rorer International Holdings Inc v Yeda Research and Development Co Ltd* [2007] UKHL 43, para. 20, per Lord Hoffmann.

[57] *Minnesota Mining and Manufacturing Co's International Patent Application* [2003] RPC 28, paras. 32 and 44 (Mr Peter Hayward).

[58] [2005] RPC 31.

[59] Ibid., at p. 796, para. 88, per Jacob LJ (Mummery and Kennedy LJJ in agreement).

[60] At p. 798, paras. 101, 102. This approach was followed in *University of Southampton's Applications* [2006] RPC 21, 575, per Jacob LJ (Wilson and Ward LJJ in agreement).

In the following case, one of the issues was whether there was a sole inventor or joint inventors.

Staeng Ltd's Patent [1996] RPC 183

A Mr Neely applied to the Comptroller to be named as the sole inventor and proprietor of UK and European patents which had been granted in favour of Staeng and which named one of their employees, a Mr Robertson, as inventor. The invention in question concerned securing electric-cable sheathing to the body portion of a 'connector backshell adaptor'. Mr Neely worked for Hellermann, whose business was primarily aimed at the provision of cable markers and heat-shrink products for use in the cable industry. Staeng's business was designing and developing cable harnesses and backshell adaptors. The two companies worked in close collaboration in the development of connector kits and the invention had arisen from this collaboration.

Dr P. Ferdinando (Superintending Examiner), at pp. 188–90:

As part of the usual collaboration between the two companies Mr Robertson visited Mr Neely at Hellermann's Plymouth premises in May 1987, as was apparently his common practice. At some point in the discussion Mr Robertson showed Mr Neely a backshell adaptor which Staeng had been developing.

...

Mr Robertson asked Mr Neely if he could think of an alternative way of holding the cable screen to the adaptor without the use of specialised machinery. The question was apparently posed very casually. As Mr Robertson put it, it was along the lines of 'wouldn't it be nice if there was a better way...' or 'is there a better way...' or 'there must be a better way...' of securing the braid to the adaptor.

Both men agree that Mr Neely suggested the use of a constant tension spring, as he had seen one only a short time earlier being used to attach an earth strap for a power cable to the cable armour. He went to the office of a Mr Isaac, who was investigating the use of springs in this context, and obtained a few sample springs to try in place on top of the braid over the groove in the body of the adaptor which Mr Robertson had produced. They appeared to work well, Mr Neely being especially surprised that the spring was not dislodged when the cable braid was tugged. Both Mr Robertson and Mr Neely together then tested the electrical resistance between the braid and adaptor of the assembly and found it to be more than satisfactory.

...

Section 7 of the Patents Act 1977 defines the inventor as 'the actual deviser of the invention', and states that 'joint inventor shall be construed accordingly'. The evidence leaves me in no doubt that, as is now conceded on behalf of Staeng, Mr Neely contributed to the invention the idea of using a spring coiled around the body of the adaptor over the sheathing to secure the latter to the former, and that to this extent at least, as accepted by Mr Wilson, I find that he was the actual deviser, and as such the inventor, or [sic] the invention the subject matter of both GB049 and EP266.

Mr Neely's claim, however, goes further than this, since he claims to have been the *sole* inventor, and seeks to *replace* Mr Robertson in this respect.

...

...the onus lies with Mr Neely to establish his claim to sole inventorship.

> I conclude on this limited basis that Mr Neely has failed to establish that Mr Robertson has no right to continue to be named as an inventor. It seems clear on the evidence that Mr Neely did not come up with the idea of using a spring unprompted, and, indeed, that he is unlikely to have done so had Mr Robertson not spoken to him about the problem in the first place. Mr Neely himself has said on several occasions that he was not skilled in the art of backshell adaptor construction. His background experience was in the field of cable markers and heatshrink products. Mr Robertson alerted Mr Neely to the notion that the method of attaching cable braids to backshell adaptors which Staeng had been using until then might in some way be improved. Mr Robertson posed the question, and Mr Neely came up with a suggested solution. Tests on that solution surpassed their expectations. In these circumstances, and especially in view of the onus upon Mr Neely to persuade me to alter Mr Roberston's present status as inventor, I find that Mr Neely and Mr Robertson jointly invented the invention which is the subject of GB049 and EP266.

Do you agree that Mr Robertson was partly responsible for the inventive concept, such as to make him a joint inventor? Relevant here is s. 43(3) of the PA 77 which states that, 'references to the making of an invention by an employee...do not include references to his merely contributing advice or other assistance in the making of an invention by another employee'. Could the question posed by Mr Robertson about whether there was an improved way of securing cable braids to backshell adaptors be characterized as little more than advice? Or was Mr Robertson's contribution that he identified a problem to be solved? But can this be inventive if all he did was articulate a known problem that was regularly encountered in the field?[61]

The *Staeng* decision highlights that the burden of proof lies on the person claiming joint or sole inventorship. This has been emphasized by the House of Lords in *Rhone-Poulenc Rorer International Holdings Inc v Yeda Research and Development Co Ltd*[62] where Lord Hoffmann stated:

> The effect of section 7(4) is that a person who seeks to be added as a joint inventor bears the burden of proving that he contributed to the inventive concept underlying the claimed invention and a person who seeks to be substituted as sole inventor bears the additional burden of proving that the inventor named in the patent did not contribute to the inventive concept.[63]

The following case is an example of where this burden of proof was discharged and sole inventorship established on the basis of suggesting an idea.

University of Southampton's Applications [2006] RPC 21

The University of Southampton (along with the second and third respondents) filed a patent application for a method for controlling pests by trapping or killing them by exposing the pest to a composition consisting of magnetic particles. The second respondent, Professor Howse, had been contacted by Mr Metcalfe of IDA (the appellants) who had read about another of Professor Howse's inventions for pest control which involved the use of electrostatic talcum powder. Mr Metcalfe suggested to Professor Howse

---

[61] See P. Chandler, 'Employees' inventions: Inventorship and ownership' [1997] EIPR 262, 262–3.
[62] [2007] UKHL 43.   [63] Ibid., para. 21.

the idea of using magnetic powders instead, their advantages over electrostatic powder being that they would not lose their stickiness over time. Professor Howse pursued Mr Metcalfe's suggestion and through routine trial and experimentation learned that magnetic particles worked successfully. IDA brought a reference under s. 8 of the PA 77 and the hearing officer found that it were entitled to ownership of the patent. On appeal, Laddie J in the Patents Court held that IDA and the University of Southampton were jointly entitled. IDA then appealed to the Court of Appeal.

Jacob LJ (with whom Wilson and Ward LJJ agreed):

[Jacob LJ began by stating the general principles in this area:]

23. In *Henry Brothers (Magherafelt) Ltd v Ministry of Defence and Northern Ireland Office* [1997] RPC 693 at 706 I said:

One must seek to identify who in substance made the combination. Who was responsible for the inventive concept, namely the combination?

24. The Court of Appeal in [1999] RPC 442 agreed with this approach, although on the facts did not accept there was a combination. See *per* Robert Walker LJ at 449. Moreover, in *Markem* it was held that:

S.8 is referring essentially to information in the specification rather than the form of the claims…s.8 calls for identification of information and the rights in it. Who contributed what and what rights, if any, lies in the heart of the inquiry, not what monopolies were actually claimed, [101].

25. Later we said:

What one is normally looking for is 'the heart' of the invention. There may be more than one 'heart' but each claim is not to be considered as a separate 'heart' on its own, [102].

[Jacob LJ then went on to consider the application of these principles to the facts:]

31. The parallel with Claim 1 of Professor Howse's 1994 patent is exact. In 1994 the exposure was 'to particles carrying an electrostatic charge'; in the patent in suit the exposure is 'to a composition comprising particles containing or consisting of at least one magnetic material'. In short: magnetic particles for electrostatic particles. To my mind, that is the sole key to the information in the patent in suit. That key was provided solely by Mr Metcalfe. Putting it another way, insofar as there is anything inventive in the patent, it was provided only by him.

32. It is true that he did not know whether his idea would work and it is true that he had not realised that if it did work it would be by adhesion to the legs of the insects, or that because of that insects could be made to pick up insecticide (what Laddie J called the 'sticky poison concept'). Neither of these matters prevents Mr Metcalfe from being the sole devisor of the invention. For neither of these matters involve the contribution of anything inventive to his idea. So far as finding out whether or not his idea worked that was a matter of simple and routine experimentation—mere verification.

33. So far as the sticky poison concept is concerned that would follow by adding that which any ordinary skilled worker in the field of insect killing would have known. All that Professor Howse added to Mr Metcalfe's idea is the common general knowledge of those in the art. There was nothing inventive about it and I do not see how Professor Howse could fairly be described as an inventor. The 'heart' was Mr Metcalfe's idea and his alone.

…

> 38. Next, it should be noted that this is a case where what was needed to get a patent was only disclosure of an idea. Disclosure of a means of enablement was not necessary: given the idea, the skilled man could readily practice the invention, as the graduate students did...
>
> 39. In the context of entitlement to a patent a mere, *non-enabling* idea, is probably not enough to give the patent for it to solely the devisor. Those who contribute enough information by way of *necessary* enablement to make the idea patentable would count as 'actual devisors', having turned what was 'airy-fairy' into that which is practical (see the discussion about the co-inventors in *Markem* at [36]–[37]). On the other hand those who contribute no more than essentially unnecessary detail cannot on any view count as 'actual devisors' as Laddie J rightly said: see his [45].

What was the inventive concept in *University of Southampton's Applications* and why did it not include the sticky poison concept? Further, why did disclosure of an idea amount to an inventive contribution in this case? Will disclosure of an idea usually be enough to make a person an inventor or joint inventor?

The House of Lords in *Rhone-Poulenc Rorer International Holdings Inc v Yeda Research and Development Co Ltd*[64] held that the key question under s. 7(2)(a) of the PA 77 is always who is the inventor or joint inventors and there is no additional requirement that a person must show that a proprietor is not entitled to a patent because he or she obtained it as a result of breach of confidence.[65] Thus, if person A discloses in confidence an invention to person B and person B then makes an unauthorized use of that information and patents the invention, all that person A has to establish is that he was in fact the inventor. It is not necessary for person A also to show that person B was granted the patent as a result of a breach of confidence. What about the situation where person A discloses information to person B that is *not* an invention, but which enables person B to come up with an invention? In this situation, Lord Walker in *Yeda Research* suggested in obiter that this may give person A the right to claim an injunction or damages, or an account of profits, but not to claim entitlement to the invention.[66]

10.3.4 EMPLOYEE INVENTORS

Article 60 EPC provides that the right to a European patent shall belong to the inventor or his successor in title. However, the EPC does *not* regulate the position of employee inventors. Instead, this is governed by the law of the Contracting State in which the employee is mainly employed or, if that cannot be determined, the law of the state in which the employer has his place of business to which the employee is attached. To ensure that the EPO does not have to investigate entitlement, Article 60(3) of the EPC provides that the applicant shall be deemed to be entitled to exercise the right to the European patent.

The Proposed Community Patent Regulation[67] adopts the same approach to employee inventors.[68] Thus, ownership of employee inventions, along with compensation of

---

[64] [2007] UKHL 43.

[65] Ibid., per Lord Hoffmann (delivering the leading speech) at paras. 18–24 and per Lord Walker, at para. 62.

[66] Ibid., per Lord Walker, at para. 62.

[67] Proposal for a Council Regulation on a Community Patent COM (2000) 412 final OJ C337E of 28 Nov. 2000.

[68] See Art. 4(2) of the Proposal.

employee inventors, would fall within the jurisdiction of national courts rather than the proposed Community Intellectual Property Court.[69]

In the UK, the position of employee inventors is governed by ss. 39–43 of the PA 77. Previously, this area was developed and regulated by the common law.[70] Although guidance may be obtained from pre-77 cases, the PA 77 has superseded the previous common law and it is the language of the relevant statutory provisions that must be interpreted and applied.[71]

According to s. 39 of the PA 77 an invention made by an employee mainly employed in the UK shall belong to his employer in two situations. The first is where the invention is made *in the course of normal duties* or *specifically assigned duties* and an invention might *reasonably be expected to result* from the carrying out of his duties.[72] The second situation is where the invention is made in the *course of the employee's duties* and, because of the nature of his duties and associated responsibilities, the *employee has a special obligation* to further the interests of his employer's undertaking.[73] Otherwise, an invention made by an employee will belong to the employee.[74] Importantly, s. 42 of the PA 77 makes unenforceable any term in a contract between employee and employer or an employee and a third party (at the request of the employer) which diminishes the employee's rights in inventions made by him. Thus, it would not be possible to include a term in a contract of employment legally requiring the employee to assign to the employer all inventions which he may make, since the only inventions which belong to an employer are those set out in s. 39.

Where an employer owns an employee invention pursuant to s. 39 of the PA 77 there is no question of the employee retaining beneficial ownership as against the employer. As held by Pumfrey J in *French v Mason*:[75]

> Where the section speaks of the invention being 'taken to belong to his employer for the purposes of this Act and for all other purposes' it is in my view plainly talking about ownership in a sense which is not technical, and which does not distinguish between legal and equitable ownership. It is talking of the ownership which permits the owner to deal with the patent and to work under it.

We turn to consider the first limb of s. 39.

10.3.4.1 In the course of normal duties or specifically assigned duties: s. 39(1)(a)

Harris' Patent [1985] RPC 19

The patent in suit concerned a slide valve for controlling the flow of material, in particular powdery and erosive material such as coal dust, through a duct into which the

---

[69] See Opinion of the Economic and Social Committee on the 'Proposal for a Council Regulation on the Community Patent' [2001] OJ C155/80, 29 May 2001, at para. 6.2.7.2.

[70] As reflected in cases such as *Worthington Pumping Engine Company v Moore* (1903) 20 RPC 41; *Patchett v Stirling Engineering Co Ltd* (1955) 72 RPC 50; *British Syphon Co Ltd v Homewood* (1956) RPC 225; and *Electrolux Ltd v Hudson* [1977] FSR 312.

[71] *Harris' Patent* [1985] RPC 19, 28 (Falconer J); *Liffe v Pinkava* [2007] RPC 30, para. 57, per Morritt V-C, and para. 92, per Jacob LJ.

[72] PA 77, s. 39(1)(a).   [73] Ibid., s. 39(1)(b).   [74] Ibid., s. 39(2).   [75] [1999] FSR 597, 604.

valve plate is slid to stop the flow and from which it is withdrawn to permit the flow. The invention was thought to be an improvement on known slide valves—i.e. 'Wey' valves (so-called after the inventor Joseph Wey)—in that it reduced problems of jamming of the valve plate and erosion of seals.

Reiss Engineering sold Wey valves and provided an after-sales service. Harris was employed as a manager of the Wey valve department and made the invention whilst he was working for them (after he received notice of his redundancy but prior to his departure) and filed a patent application. Reiss Engineering sought an order under s. 8 of the PA 77 that the patent application should proceed in their name; however, as the patent had been granted, the matter came to be decided pursuant to s. 37 of the PA 77. This was an appeal from the decision of the superintending examiner, who found that Harris was the inventor and proprietor of the patent.

Falconer J, at p. 29, 31–2:

As to the second requirement in the paragraph, that is to say, whether the circumstances were such that an invention might reasonably be expected to result from his carrying out those duties, Miss Vitoria submitted that the circumstances referred to in paragraph (a) must be the circumstances in which the invention was made; and it seems to me that submission must be right. Mr Pumfrey, in the course of his argument, pointed out that the wording of the paragraph was 'an invention might reasonably be expected to result' and not 'the invention might' and so on. But plainly, the wording 'an invention' cannot mean any invention whatsoever; it is governed by the qualification that it has to be an invention that 'might reasonably be expected to result from the carrying out of his duties' by the employee. That wording applies equally to the second alternative in paragraph (a), that of 'specifically assigned' duties falling outside the employee's normal duties; and, therefore, in my judgment the wording 'an invention might reasonably be expected to result from the carrying out of his duties' must be referring to an invention which achieves, or contributes to achieving, whatever was the aim or object to which the employee's efforts in carrying out his duties were directed, in the case of alternative (i) of paragraph (a) his normal duties being performed at the time; in the case of alternative (ii) of paragraph (a) the specifically assigned duties, that is to say, such an invention as that made, though not necessarily the precise invention actually made and in question.

Thus, it seems the court must ask whether an invention *of the type that was made* would have been expected to result from the carrying out of the employee's normal duties or specifically assigned duties.

Falconer J went on to consider the business of Reiss Engineering in order to ascertain Mr Harris's normal duties at the material time.

Reiss Engineering did not themselves manufacture valves until after Mr Harris left their employ. It is also to be noted that Reiss Engineering sold only valves made by Sistag or to Sistag drawings. Reiss Engineering had no research laboratory or primary design office and only one of its two draughtsmen was employed in their valve division ... In promoting the sale of their valves, Reiss Engineering, of course, advised customers and made recommendations as to the type of valve to use and as to what body material and seal material would be supplied for the customer's particular application. They were concerned to see satisfactory installation of any valve they sold and provided after-sale service. But during the period when Mr Harris was employed by them Reiss Engineering never themselves designed a valve or an improvement or a modification to a valve… It is quite clear from the evidence that, when a problem developed with a valve they had sold to a customer, the practice was that Reiss Engineering would investigate and report on the problem to Sistag, but it was for Sistag to deal with any such problem and find a solution.

…

…There is, it seems to me, great force in Miss Vitoria's submission that, as Reiss Engineering never took it upon themselves to solve design problems in the valves but restricted their role in regard to such problems to reporting any such problem to Sistag for Sistag to consider and solve, it cannot have been part of Mr Harris's normal duties to provide solutions to problems relating to the design of the valves; there was no reason why they should, and no evidence that they did, impose on Mr Harris, their employee, as part of his normal duties, an obligation they never assumed themselves. His duty in regard to any such problems was to report them for transmission to Sistag for Sistag's consideration and solution.

Falconer J concluded that the invention was not made in the course of Mr Harris's normal duties, nor were the circumstances such that such an invention might reasonably be expected to have resulted from carrying out his normal duties.

In *Harris* no contract of employment had been put before the superintending examiner. As such, Harris's duties were determined by looking at the nature of the various tasks that he undertook whilst employed by Reiss Engineering. But what is the position where a written contract of employment exists? Will this be determinative of what constitutes an employee's normal duties? This issue was considered in *Greater Glasgow Health Board's Application*.[76] In this case, Dr Montgomery was the sole inventor of an optical spacing device for use with an indirect ophthalmoscope, which allowed for more effective measuring of the retina to be carried out. At the time of making the invention, Dr Montgomery was employed by the Greater Glasgow Health Board (GGHB) as a registrar in the Department of Ophthalmology. GGHB filed a PCT application in respect of the invention and a reference under s. 12 of the PA 77 was made. The superintending examiner found that the invention in the application in suit was made in the course of Dr Montgomery's normal duties in circumstances such that an invention might reasonably have been expected to result from the carrying out of those duties. As such, it was owned by GGHB pursuant to s. 39(1)(a) of the PA 77. An appeal from the examiner's decision was allowed by Laddie J. In assessing the 'normal duties' of Dr Montgomery, Laddie J thought it instructive to look not only at the contract of employment, which indicated that the doctor had clinical responsibilities, teaching duties, and an expectation to avail himself of the research facilities, but also to look at the *duties actually carried out by the employee*. In looking at what Dr Montgomery actually did, Laddie J found that research and invention were not in fact part of his normal duties. Rather, he was mainly involved in clinical treatment, with some involvement in teaching.[77]

The Court of Appeal in *Liffe v Pinkava*[78] has reiterated that the court must look at what the employee actually does, as well as his or her contract of employment. As such, it is possible for the normal duties of an employee to exceed those stipulated in the employment contract, as was the case in *Liffe v Pinkava*.

We turn now to consider the second limb of s. 39 of the PA 77.

[76] [1996] RPC 207.   [77] Ibid., pp. 221–3.
[78] [2007] RPC 30, para. 58, per Morritt V-C, with whom Longmore and Jacob LJJ agreed.

10.3.4.2 In the course of duties where the employee has a special obligation: s. 39(1)(b)

Where the employee's status within the employer's business creates a special obligation to further the interests of the employer, the invention will be owned by the employer. Section 39(1)(b) has only been considered in *Harris's Patent* and also, in obiter, in *Staeng's Patent*. In *Harris* the employee was held not to owe his employer a special obligation, whereas an opposite conclusion was reached in *Staeng's Patent*. The reasons for these differing conclusions are dealt with in the following extract.

Staeng Ltd's Patent [1996] RPC 183

For the facts see above at p. 617.

> **Dr P Ferdinando, at pp. 200–3:**
>
> Although my findings under section 39(1)(a) make it strictly unnecessary for met [sic] to decide whether Mr Neely's employers are also entitled to the invention by virtue of section 39(1)(b), much time was occupied at the hearing on the issue of the seniority of Mr Neely's status within Hellermann, with a view, as I understood it, to persuading me that he either did or did not have the special obligation to further the interests of his employers' undertaking required under section 39(1)(b). I will therefore address this question.
>
> Following *Harris*, I note that there are two conditions to be fulfilled under section 39(1)(b). The first is that the invention was made in the course of the duties of the employee. Since I have already found that the invention in suit met the narrower condition of section 39(1)(a) of having been made as part of Mr Neely's *normal* duties, it follows that it also meets the broader first condition of 39(1)(b).
>
> The second condition is that, at the time of making the invention, because of the nature of his duties and the special responsibilities arising from their nature, the employee had a special obligation to further the interests of the employers' undertaking.
>
> In *Harris* it was held that the extent of an employee's obligation to further the interest of his employer's undertaking was dependent on his status and the duties and responsibilities associated with that status. In *Harris'* case he only had to sell Wey valves and ensure after-sales service; his powers as a manager did not extend to hiring or firing staff or agreeing holiday dates and he did not attend board meetings even when his own department was under discussion. His status was not such that his obligations would take him within the confines of section 39(1)(b).
>
> ...Mr Neely was employed under contract directly by the holding company, rather than by Hellermann, and such contracts were reserved for senior executives. Mr Neely's was a 'Category V(1)' contract, which again was reserved for Directors and other senior executives within the various divisions of Bowthorpe...There were then five senior executives, including Mr Neely as Business Development Manager...Mr Neely was to receive a bonus of 1% of the subsidiary company or division's annual trading profit above a certain level. This was presumably in addition to the basic salary, set at £22,000 per annum when Mr Neely took up employment.
>
> ...
>
> I am satisfied that, within the framework of Hellermann at the time of Mr Neely's employment there, he enjoyed a position of high status and responsibility. His involvement in the profit bonus scheme and his direct employment by the parent company identified him

specifically as a senior executive, and he was plainly perceived as such by his colleagues...In particular it is clear that he operated at a significantly more senior level than did Harris within his employer company. Harris' duties were confined solely to sales. He was described as a 'trouble-shooter' to deal with problems that customers experienced with their installations, not by solving their problems directly but by passing them on to another company for solution. He thus had no opportunity for developing his employer's product, whereas Mr Neely was charged with the need to identify new products; his job title—Product Development Manager—encapsulated that intention. Moreover, Mr Neely was given the highly responsible task of streamlining and restructuring the Hellermann product range, and had sufficient authority to achieve a major reform in this respect within a short time of joining the company. Harris did not attend board meetings, whereas Mr Neely was involved in the sort of meetings and engaged in the sort of discussion that were also the province of directors. Although there were constraints on Mr Neely's ability to hire and fire and to spend, his powers clearly exceeded those of Harris in this respect.

...

In all these circumstances it is clear to me, therefore, that the invention was made by Mr Neely under the second condition set out in the section 39(1)(b), namely in which the nature of his duties and the particular responsibilities arising from them were such that he had a special obligation to further the interests of his employer's undertaking.

I therefore find that, under both sections 39(1)(a) and (b) as between Mr Neely and his employers, the invention in suit must be taken to belong to his employers for all purposes.

Which factors contributed to Mr Neely owing a special obligation to his employer and how did his situation differ from the employee in *Harris*?

10.3.5 COMPENSATION FOR EMPLOYEE INVENTIONS

10.3.5.1 UK approach

Section 40 of the PA 77 introduced a statutory right of compensation to employee inventors in two instances. The first instance is set out in s. 40(1) of the PA 77. This section provides that compensation is payable where the patent is owned by the employer[79] and it can be shown that 'having regard among other things to the size and nature of the employer's undertaking, the invention or the patent for it (or the combination of both) is of outstanding benefit to the employer and by reason of those facts it is just that the employee should be awarded compensation to be paid by the employer'.[80] It should be noted that the language of this section was recently amended[81] and previously referred only to the *patent* being of outstanding benefit to the employer.

The second instance is set out in s. 40(2) of the PA 77 and applies where the employee invention has been assigned or exclusively licensed to the employer and it can be shown that the benefit received by the employee from the assignment or exclusive licence was inadequate in relation to the benefit derived by the employer from the patent and by reason of those facts it is just that the employee should be awarded compensation to be paid by the employer.[82]

---

79 By virtue of PA 77, s. 39.
81 As a result of s. 10 of Patents Act 2004.

80 Ibid., s. 40(1).
82 PA 77, s. 40(2).

The amount of compensation in both instances is to be determined in accordance with s. 41 of the PA 77. The award is meant to secure for the employee a fair share of the benefit which the employer has derived, or may reasonably be expected to derive from: the invention in question; the patent for the invention; the assignment or grant of the property or any right in the invention or the property in, or any right in or under, an application for the patent to a person connected with the employer.

Where the invention has always belonged to the employer (pursuant to s. 39), the following matters shall be taken into account in determining the award of compensation: the nature of the employee's duties, his remuneration, and other advantages he derives or has derived from his employment (e.g. ex gratia payments); the effort and skill which the employee has applied to making the invention; the effort and skill which any other person has contributed to making the invention jointly with the employee; and the contribution made by the employer to the making, developing, and working of the invention.[83] Where the invention originally belonged to the employee, the following matters shall be taken into account: any licence conditions in respect of the invention or the patent for it; the extent to which the invention was made jointly by the employee with another person; and the contribution made by the employer to the making, developing, and working of the invention.[84] Any order of payment may be for a lump sum or for periodical payment or both.[85] Where any order for compensation is refused, this does not preclude a later application being made.[86]

Thus far, the only applications for statutory compensation have related to the first instance (i.e. s. 40(1) of the PA 77).[87] One of the early authoritative decisions on s. 41(1) is *Memco-Med Ltd's Patent*.

Memco-Med Ltd's Patent [1992] RPC 403

Mr Trett was a former employee of Memco-Med. Whilst in their employment he invented a new model (the 'R' model) of detector unit for use in lifts. The 'R' model of detector would sense if a person was near the lift doors and prevent the doors from closing on people. Memco-Med had a long-standing business relationship with the Otis Elevator Company and had been supplying detectors to them for a considerable time. Sales from 1982 to 1989 of the 'R' model of detector to Otis totalled just over £4 million out of a total sales of £11.5 million. Mr Trett brought an application for compensation under s. 40(1) of the PA 77. The superintending examiner refused the application and there was an appeal to the Patents Court.

Aldous J (as he then was), at pp. 412–13:

Section 40 draws a distinction between the patent and the invention; thus the task of the court is to ascertain whether the patent, not the invention, is of outstanding benefit to the employer, that benefit being a benefit in money or money's worth.

The benefit from the patent may be readily recognisable where the patent is licensed and royalties are paid. However, the task of the court will be more difficult in cases where

---

[83] See ibid., s. 41(4).   [84] Ibid., s. 41(5).   [85] Ibid., s. 41(6).   [86] Ibid., s. 41(7).

[87] See *GEC Avionics Ltd's Patent* [1992] RPC 107 (Superintending examiner Mr Vivian); *British Steel Plc's Patent* [1992] RPC 117 (Superintending Examiner Dr Ferdinando); and *Memco-Med Ltd's Patent* [1992] RPC 403 (Aldous J, Patents Court).

> an employer exploits the patent by manufacturing articles in accordance with the invention of the patent. In such cases, the court will need to differentiate between the benefit from using the inventive advance and that from the patent. It is also possible to imagine a case where the patent is not licensed and the invention is never put into practice, but the patent is of great benefit to the patentee to prevent activities which would compete with those carried on by the patentee.

Aldous J emphasizes that the benefit must be derived by virtue of having a patent and not from the inventive advance and that this may be a difficult distinction to make. However, this distinction has been removed by the amendments to s. 40(1) of the PA 77, which now provides that the benefit may derive from the *invention* or the *patent* or *both*.

Aldous J went on to consider the meaning of 'outstanding' benefit. In doing so, he referred to *GEC Avionics Ltd's Patent*[88] in which the superintending examiner held that 'outstanding' connoted 'something out of the ordinary and not such as one would normally expect to arise from the results of the duties that the employee is paid for'.[89] He referred also to the decision in *British Steel Plc's Patent*[90] in which the superintending examiner held that 'outstanding' implies a superlative and considered that the test must be correspondingly stiff. After having considered these decisions Aldous J concluded:

> I do not disagree with the approaches of those superintending examiners. The word 'outstanding' denotes something special and requires the benefit to be more than substantial or good. I believe that it is unwise to try to redefine the word 'out-standing'. Courts will recognise an outstanding benefit when it occurs.
>
> The section requires the court to assess whether the benefit is outstanding, having regard among other things to the size and nature of the employer's undertaking. Thus the court must look at the employer's undertaking, which may be the whole or a division of the employer's business, and ascertain the benefit to the employer taking into account the size and nature of that business and all the surrounding circumstances.

Aldous J then considered who bears the onus of proof in establishing a claim under s. 40 of the PA 77. In *GEC Avionics Ltd's Patent*[91] the superintending examiner held that where the patentee does not license his product or is not paid compensation but is a manufacturer who negotiates contracts for his products which are protected by patent, the initial evidential burden of showing that no benefit is derived from the patent rests with the patentee. Aldous J, however, at p. 415 rejected this approach:

> I cannot agree with that approach. The onus of proof lies upon the person seeking to invoke the provisions of section 40, namely the employee. Thereafter the onus may shift to the employer, but this will depend upon the evidence before the court and will not depend upon any inference of law or presumption. Each case must be decided upon its own facts using the normal standard of proof in civil proceedings, namely the balance of probabilities.
>
> [Finally, **Aldous J** at p. 417 considered whether an outstanding benefit had been conferred on Memco-Med by virtue of the patent over the 'R' model detector:]
>
> The fact that a company only sells a patented product to one customer and therefore its existence depends on sales of that product does not mean that the patent is of any benefit.

---

[88] [1992] RPC 107.   [89] Ibid., p. 115.   [90] [1992] RPC 117, 122.   [91] [1992] RPC 107.

I suspect that there are companies which depend for their existence upon sales of one product which is not covered by a patent. If so the sales are of vital importance and of great benefit, but they could not be attributable to a non-existing patent. The fact that the sales of the 'R' model were vital is a relevant consideration to decide whether the patent is of outstanding benefit but cannot be determinative. The existence of those sales is consistent with the case of Memco-Med, namely that all the sales were to Otis, that the sales resulted from the price and quality of the product and the good relationship Memco-Med had with Otis, and that the patent played no part in obtaining sales, let alone the profit from those sales.

The superintending examiner first considered whether the benefit to Memco-Med was outstanding on the assumption that the benefit was derived from that patent. He concluded that there were strong pointers to the conclusion that the benefits were not outstanding. Upon the evidence, including the evidence I admitted *de bene esse*, sales of detectors substantially increased when the 'R' model was introduced, but that does not mean the monetary benefit was outstanding. The development to produce the 'R' model was funded by Memco-Med, encouraged by Otis, and therefore it is not surprising that Otis would give increased orders for the new model. No doubt sales of about £4m, between 1982 and 1989, were good but the evidence does not establish that the profit, being the monetary benefit was also good. Discovery would have thrown light on this, but Mr Trett must have had a general idea of the position up to August 1983 and did not give any relevant evidence on this matter. In any case, the important matter to decide is whether the benefit, if any, was obtained from the patent and, if so, was it outstanding.

The superintending examiner decided that Memco-Med had not derived an outstanding benefit from the patent. I agree with his conclusion and reasoning. I have found it helpful when considering the evidence filed by the parties to look for indications as to whether Memco-Med would have sold any fewer detectors if the patent had not been granted. Although Mr Trett did suggest in his reply evidence that the patent had some effect upon other manufacturers and himself, I did not find that evidence convincing. The evidence does not establish that the patent has been of substantial benefit to Memco-Med, let alone of outstanding benefit.

The appeal was dismissed.

The application in *Memco-Med* was unsuccessful, as were the earlier applications in *GEC Avionics* and *British Steel*. It therefore appeared that the right to statutory compensation under UK patent law was more theoretical than real, leading one commentator to describe the provisions on compensation as 'a dead letter'.[92] However, significant awards of employee compensation were recently made in *Kelly and Chiu v GE Healthcare Ltd*, to which we now turn.

Kelly and Chiu v GE Healthcare Ltd [2009] EWHC 181 (Pat)

Dr Kelly and Dr Chiu had been employed as research scientists at Amersham International Plc, which company was taken over by GE Healthcare Ltd. They were co-inventors of a radioactive imaging agent, which was the subject of two European (UK) patents. The patented agent was marketed under the trade mark 'Myoview'. Myoview was a tremendous success, with sales to 2007 exceeding £1.3 billion sterling,

---

[92] P. Grubb, *Patents for Chemicals, Pharmaceuticals and Biotechnology* (4th edn., Oxford: Oxford University Press, 2004), p. 393.

and accounted for a large proportion of Amersham's profits. The claimants brought an action under s. 40 of the Patents Act 1977 seeking an award of compensation. The law applicable was that prior to the amendment resulting from s. 10 of the Patents Act 2004. Thus, the outstanding benefit had to be shown to result from the patent.

Floyd J:

[**Floyd J** began by considering the existing case law on s. 40, including *Memco-Med Ltd's Patent*, and the terms of s. 41. He summarized the law as follows:]

60. Drawing this material together:

i) Section 40 is available to an inventor in the sense of the 'actual deviser' of the invention, but not to those who merely contribute to the invention without being joint inventors;

ii) Section 40 is available to an employee who makes an invention (which is subsequently patented by the employer) in the ordinary course of his employment or in the course of duties specifically assigned to him;

iii) Under the section prior to its amendment, it is the patent (as opposed to the invention) which must be of outstanding benefit to the employer, having regard to the size and nature of the employer's undertaking;

iv) 'Outstanding' means 'something special' or 'out of the ordinary' and more than 'substantial', 'significant' or 'good'. The benefit must be something more than one would normally expect to arise from the duties for which the employee is paid;

v) On the other hand it is not necessary to show that the benefit from the patent could not have been exceeded;

vi) Section 40 is not concerned with whether the invention is outstanding, although the nature of the employee's contribution may fall to be considered at the section 41 stage, if it is reached;

vii) It will normally be useful to consider what would have been the position of the company if a patent had not been granted, and compare this with the company's position with the benefit of the patent;

viii) The patent must have been a cause of the benefit, although it does not have to be the only cause. The existence of multiple causes for a benefit does not exclude the benefit from consideration, although the benefit may have to be apportioned to isolate the benefit derived from the patent;

ix) 'Patent' in section 40 does not include regulatory data exclusivity. Thus the scenario without patent protection is one where RDE nevertheless exists;

x) It must be 'just' to make an award: the consideration of what is just is not limited to the facts set out in section 40;

xi) It is not a requirement of obtaining compensation that the employee can prove a loss (for example by reference to inadequate remuneration for his employment) or by the expenditure of effort and skill beyond the call of duty. These are nevertheless factors to take into account under section 41;

xii) The valuation of any benefit is to be performed *ex-post* and in the light of all the available evidence as to benefit derived from the patent: not '*ex-ante*';

xiii) Where the employee shows that the invention has been of outstanding benefit, the amount of compensation is to be determined in the light of all the available evidence in accordance with section 41 so as to secure a just and fair reward to the employee, neither limiting him to compensation for loss or damage, nor placing him in as strong a position as an external patentee or licensor.

[**Floyd J** went on to consider whether the patents were of outstanding benefit to Amersham:]

148. I have come to the conclusion that the patents were of outstanding benefit to Amersham having regard to all the circumstances, including the size and nature of its undertaking. The benefits went far beyond anything which one could normally expect to arise from the sort of work the employees were doing.

149. The first and most obvious contribution the patents have made to Amersham is in protecting the business against generic competition and reduced profits after the expiry of RDE. The expiry of the patents in about 2008 and the advent of generic competition was one of the major issues facing the company from 2000 onwards. If the patents had not existed in 2000, and Amersham had been facing the expiry of RDE in 2002, this would not simply have been a major issue, it would have been a crisis for Amersham.

150. The benefit of patent protection is not limited to profits from sales. As I have held, the fact that Amersham had a patented blockbuster radiopharmaceutical has been a major factor in achieving the corporate deals. In this way the patents have helped transform Amersham. Considering the totality of the evidence I had no difficulty in recognising that the patents were of outstanding benefit to Amersham.

Floyd J then concluded that it was just to make an award of compensation in favour of the employees. The defendant argued that it was invidious to single out individual inventors for an award where there had been a truly corporate research effort and much work by others in order to develop Myoview. In response to this argument Floyd J stated that it was inherent in ss. 40–1 that employees who have contributed to the invention and its development but who are not joint inventors will not receive an award. Further, Floyd J held that it was immaterial that Dr Kelly and Dr Chiu had waited until the end of 2003 to make a claim because the statute permits the employee to wait until the patent expires before raising any claim.[93]

Having found an outstanding benefit resulting from the patent and that it was just to award compensation to the claimants, Floyd J then considered the value of the benefit of the patents to Amersham. He found as follows:

168. Nevertheless I have held that generic competition would have caused price cutting after the expiry of RDE. A significant part of Amersham's US sales would have been protected to some extent from generic competition, but other parts of their market would not. In my judgment the evidence justifies the conclusion that, at a minimum, generic competition would have caused the price of Myoview to drop by 10% (at least but probably a lot more) on about half of its sales.

. . .

170. Taking a round figure of £1 billion, a price cut of only 10% on only half of Myoview's sales over that period would have reduced Amersham's revenues by £50 million. I consider that I have been very conservative in arriving at these figures. I think that prices would have fallen by much more than this over the course of the post RDE period.

. . .

---

[93] More specifically, r. 91, Patents Rules 2007, SI 2007/3291 stipulates that an employee can make a claim for compensation anytime after the date of grant of the patent and before 1 year after the patent expires.

172. I think I am justified in taking a figure of £50 million pounds as the absolute rock bottom figure for the benefit from the patents.

[**Floyd J** then examined the factors under s 41 relevant to determining the amount of compensation:]

188. In the present case I think the following are important factors favouring the employee:

i) the overall costs of R&D in the present case are extremely small in relation to the profits generated: some £2.4 million as reported in the Queen's Award document;

ii) neither Dr Kelly nor Dr Chiu were carrying out routine operations: their jobs involved significant thought and creativity.

189. On the other hand the following factors help the employer:

i) Dr Chiu's and Dr Kelly's work was to a significant degree dependent on the opportunity provided by the employer to make inventions;

ii) the downstream work was well executed, and involved the solution of some problems: Dr Kelly's contribution to this was limited;

iii) the development of the market in the United States was also a major factor of assistance in working the invention;

iv) overall it was the employer who accepted the risk for the project.

Amersham contended that the factors pointed to a nominal award or, alternatively, a bonus by reference to the employee's annual remuneration as at 1989, the year after the patents were granted. Scaled for inflation this would have resulted in a payment of about £100,000 for Dr Kelly and £60,000 for Dr Chiu. The claimants argued that a fair share of the benefit was to be determined by external licensing arrangements in the field, which pointed to 6 per cent of turnover. There was evidence before the judge of a consultancy agreement, whereby the consultant would receive royalties of 0.25–1 per cent for technology involving a 'minimal degree of innovation' and 1–3 per cent for technology involving a 'significant degree of innovation'. There was also evidence that the rate paid by universities to academic inventors was 33 per cent. After considering this evidence Floyd J concluded:

202. I think, aside from the facts of this case, from the materials I have reviewed, the employee's share of the value of a patent might in principle lie somewhere in the broad range from nil to as much as 33% or beyond. In the present case I think the employee's share lies towards the bottom of the scale, having regard to the factors which I have considered at length above. I have taken a very conservative figure for the valuation of the benefit. Taking the same approach to the share of the benefit, I consider that 3% of the value of the benefit represents a just and fair award to the employee claimants.

203. As between the two inventor claimants, I think Dr Kelly should receive more than Dr Chiu. Dr Kelly should receive 2% and Dr Chiu 1% of the £50 million figure I have taken as the value of the patents. Thus Dr Kelly receives £1 million and Dr Chiu £500,000.

204. These combined figures represent about 0.1% of turnover. I am confident that none of the comparators show this figure to be unreasonable. Whilst it is far from perfect, the closest comparable is the Goldman licence. The lowest figure in the Goldman licence was 0.25% of turnover. Standing back, and looking at these sums in the light of all the evidence I have heard, I consider them to be just and fair. It represents about three days' of the profits from Myoview at current rates.

205. Whilst I have had in mind the fact that the context of the award is employment, I have not thought it right to limit the award by reference to one year's salary. The benefit to Amersham has extended well beyond a single year.

206. Although the Act contemplates that the employee can make more than one application, I was invited to make a once and for all award, which is what I have done.

As mentioned above, *Kelly and Chiu v GE Healthcare Ltd* was a decision concerning s. 40 of the Patents Act 1977 before it was amended by the Patents Act 2004 to include reference to the outstanding benefit arising from the invention, and not just the patent. Do you think that if the new s. 40 applied, the claimants would have had an easier task of establishing an outstanding benefit?

Floyd J concluded that a fair share of the benefit of the patent received by Amersham was 3 per cent, to be shared between Dr Kelly and Dr Chiu. In your view, was this about the right figure?

Following the decision in *Kelly and Chiu v GE Healthcare Ltd* can we say that the provisions on employee compensation are no longer a 'dead letter'? Or were the facts of this case so unusual that it is difficult to envisage many other instances where statutory compensation will be awarded to employee inventors?

FURTHER READING

Y. Lee and M. Langley, 'Employees' inventions: Statutory compensation schemes in Japan and the UK' [2005] EIPR 250.

10.3.5.2 Alternative approaches

The limited success of the statutory compensation scheme in the UK begs the question whether it should be retained in its current form or at all. In addressing this question, it is useful to consider how other jurisdictions approach the issue of employee inventions.

The Japanese Patent Law distinguishes between 'service' and 'free inventions'. 'Service' inventions are those which fall within the scope of the employer's business and were made as a result of efforts which were part of the present or past duties of the employee and were performed on behalf of the employer. 'Free' inventions are those inventions which do not fall within the scope of the employer's business or are not made as a result of the employee's present or past duties. Ownership of both types of invention vests in the employee inventor. The major difference is that 'service inventions' are pre-assignable through contract, whereas 'free inventions' are not capable of pre-assignment. Where an employee has pre-assigned to his employer the rights to his service invention, s. 35(3) of the Japanese Patent Law provides that an employee should receive 'reasonable remuneration'. Such remuneration is calculated by reference to the profits made by an employer from an invention less the extent of the contribution made by the employer towards the invention.

Companies, however, developed the practice of stipulating, within contracts of employment or company regulations, the amount payable to employees as 'reasonable remuneration'. These awards were rarely challenged before the courts until the decision in *Olympus Corporation v Shumpei Tanaka*[94] opened the way for doing so. In *Olympus*, the

---

[94] (JYU) 1256 (Jap Sup Ct, 22 Apr. 2003).

Supreme Court of Japan ruled that employees can challenge the remuneration paid or payable under a company's internal policy. Thereafter followed a series of claims in which former employees successfully challenged the remuneration received from their former employers and the court ordered substantially increased sums of money to be paid to these employees.[95] Companies argued that unpredictable and exorbitant court awards of remuneration would undermine confidence in ongoing investment in R&D and reduce the international competitiveness of Japanese industry.[96] In response, legislation was passed in 2004, which took effect on 1 April 2005. The 2004 amendment aims to recognize and uphold the contractual provisions, or internal policies, of employers for payment of remuneration to employees as binding and not unreasonable under certain circumstances. These circumstances are where consultation between employers and employees has taken place in order to set standards for determining the remuneration; where these standards have been disclosed to the employees; and where the opinions of employees on the calculation of the amount of the remuneration have been taken into account.

Employee inventions in Germany are regulated by the Employees' Invention Law 1957 ('1957 Law'). The 1957 Law distinguishes between 'service inventions' and 'free inventions'. 'Service inventions' are inventions which originate in the course of the employee's duties, or which are essentially based upon the experience or activities of the company. All other inventions are 'free inventions'. The basic rule is that inventions made by employees belong to them, and it is only by special action that the invention can become the property of the employer. In the case of service inventions, an employee has a duty to immediately and completely notify any such invention made by it to the employer in writing. In the case of free inventions, the employee has to inform the employer in such a manner which allows the employer to decide whether the respective invention is a free or service invention. In each case, the employer has a two-month term in which to object to the notification or information as being incomplete. In the case of a free invention, the employer has a three-month period in which to object to the characterization of the invention as 'free'. Where the employer does not object, the employer can make no further claim to the invention and the employee is entitled to deal with it in any manner he/she wishes. In the case of a service invention, the employer has four months in which to declare either an unrestricted claim or a limited claim or to lay no claim to the invention. An unrestricted claim will result in ownership of the invention being automatically transferred to the employer and the employee has no further interest in the invention, except a claim to reasonable remuneration. However, an employer has a duty immediately to file a patent application in Germany (or an EPC application designating Germany or a PCT application designating Germany). A limited claim has the effect that ownership of the invention remains with the employee, but the employer will be entitled to a non-exclusive licence to use the invention on payment of an adequate royalty to the employee. The advantage of a limited claim to an employer is that it does not incur any costs associated with patent protection. If the employer fails to make a claim or decides not to make a claim to the invention within the four-month period, then the invention becomes free and the employee can deal with the invention in any manner he wishes.[97]

According to Article 9 of the 1957 Law an employee is entitled to reasonable remuneration where an employer has claimed the invention unrestrictedly. Pursuant to Article 11 of the 1957 Law, Guidelines for calculating remuneration ('Guidelines') have been laid

[95] For further details see Y. Lee and M. Langley, 'Employees' inventions: Statutory compensation schemes in Japan and the UK' [2005] EIPR 250.

[96] Ibid., p. 251.

[97] See Grubb, *Patents for Chemicals, Pharmaceuticals and Biotechnology*, pp. 390–1.

down by the Ministry of Labour. These Guidelines establish three methods of calculating remuneration. There is the 'licence analogy' method which is the royalty which the employer would have had to pay a third party for an exclusive licence, based on the net sales made by the employer. This is the most commonly used method of calculation. Second, there is the method of granting employees a certain percentage of the internal cost savings which the employer achieves by using the invention. This method is useful, say, where the invention relates to a process improvement which reduces costs. Third, there is a free estimation of the value of the invention, in which the inventor has the right to participate. This method is useful where the patent is not actually worked, but is used 'defensively', such as for cross-licensing purposes. Disputes regarding the amount of remuneration can be brought before the Board of Arbitration at the Germany Patent and Trademark Office (GPTO) in Munich or Berlin and also before the German courts.[98] According to the GPTO approximately 90,000 employees' inventions are made in Germany and only about 200–300 cases per year are brought before the Arbitration Board and less than 20 cases before the German Courts.[99]

The Guidelines on remuneration are fairly complex and for this reason have been criticized. Consequently, the German government has been considering a substantial review of the 1957 Law which would, *inter alia*, simplify the remuneration system. Fixed amounts would be paid on a staggered basis. On notification of the invention a basic remuneration of €800 would be paid. When the employer first uses the invention, a further remuneration of €2,000 would be paid. A further payment to the employee inventor would be made if the invention proves to be a huge commercial success. This would entail the payment of further fixed lump-sum payments once certain turnover thresholds had been met. These proposed amendments have been dropped from the current legislative agenda, in the light of the failed negotiations between the government, trade unions, and employer organizations. However, such proposed changes may reappear on the legislative agenda in the future.

In contrast to the United Kingdom, Japan, and Germany, the US has no statutory compensation scheme for employees' inventions (except in relation to federal government employees). Various attempts to introduce pro-inventor compensation schemes, including one along German lines, have failed.[100] In the US, ownership of employee inventions is typically regulated by contract, i.e. employers will routinely require their employees to pre-assign title to future inventions.[101] In the absence of a contractual arrangement, there are default common-law rules about ownership of inventions. Where an employee has been 'hired to invent' (i.e. an R&D employee), the employer owns the inventive output. Where there is a non R&D employee who creates an invention related to her duties or using employer resources, entitlement is split. The employee owns the patent, but the company has a limited, non-transferable

---

[98] See further Grubb, *Patents for Chemicals, Pharmaceuticals and Biotechnology*, pp. 394–5 and H. Goddar, 'Current status of employees' invention law in Germany', delivered at 13th Annual Intellectual Property Conference at Fordham University School of Law, New York, 31 Mar.–1 Apr. 2005 (a copy on file with the author).

[99] See Goddar, 'Current status of employees' invention law in Germany'.

[100] See W. P. Hovell, 'Patent ownership: An employer's rights to his employee's invention' (1983) 58 Notre Dame LR 863, 883–7.

[101] For criticism of pre-invention assignment agreements see: A. Bartow, 'Inventors of the world unite! A call for collective action by employee-inventors' (1997) 37 Santa Clara LR 673.

licence (referred to as a 'shop right'). Where an employee creates an invention unrelated to their duties or without employer resources, the employee will own it outright.[102]

Rather than a statutory compensation scheme, the US relies on the private sector utilizing internal reward schemes for their employees. These include promotion, spot bonuses for significant inventions, output-based bonus schemes, and more elaborate rewards systems based on an administrative assessment of various factors such as invention value and individual employee contribution.[103] Merges argues that a complex system of compensation, such as that in Germany, is 'deeply flawed and that internal reward schemes are preferable:

> Compensation plans administered by firms no doubt encounter similar problems, but the decisionmakers under intra-firm reward plans, unlike government bureaucrats, are intimately familiar with the industry, the technology, the firm, and perhaps even the individual inventors. This knowledge, together with the freedom from a cumbersome administrative structure, permits each firm to experiment and adapt its reward plan to produce the optimal incentives. Employees benefit more from this diversity of reward schemes than they would benefit from a 'one size fits all' solution, as found in Germany.[104]

In conclusion, we have seen different ways in which to regulate employee inventions. At one end of the scale is the US approach which is to leave matters to contract and, in the absence of contract, create default rules in favour of employer ownership, *without* any right to remuneration for the employee. At the other end of the scale is the German approach in which ownership of service and free inventions rests with the employee, but which can be automatically transferred to employers in respect of service inventions where the employer gives notice. However, there is an obligation on the employer to patent the invention and to pay reasonable remuneration to the employee. In the middle are the Japan and UK approaches. In Japan, employee service inventions are owned by the employer, subject to the employee receiving reasonable remuneration. What constitutes reasonable remuneration can be pre-agreed between employer and employee. In the UK, employee inventions are owned by the employer in two instances and it is possible for employees to claim remuneration where the inventions are owned by the employer or where the employee has granted the employer an assignment or exclusive licence. Either the patent or the invention (or both) has to have been of outstanding benefit to the employer or the benefit received by the employee from the contract of assignment or licence is inadequate in relation to the benefit derived by the employer from the patent.

Broadly speaking, each of the jurisdictions considered above accepts the importance of employer ownership of certain types of inventions created by employees. However, the jurisdictions differ as to whether compensation should be paid to employees and the system for awarding such compensation. Out of the various approaches that have been described, which do you consider the most desirable?

---

[102] See R. P. Merges, 'The law and economics of employee inventions' (1999) 13 Harvard Journal of Law & Technology 1, 6–9; and for a more detailed discussion see Hovell, 'Patent ownership': An employer's rights to his employee's invention.

[103] For a discussion see Merges, 'The law and economics of employee inventions', pp. 38–42.

[104] Ibid., p. 45.

FURTHER READING

P. Grubb, *Patents for Chemicals, Pharmaceuticals and Biotechnology* (4th edn., Oxford: Oxford University Press, 2004), Ch. 21.

W. P. Hovell, 'Patent ownership: An employer's rights to his employee's invention' (1983) 58 Notre Dame LR 863.

Y. Lee and M. Langley, 'Employees' inventions: Statutory compensation schemes in Japan and the UK' [2005] EIPR 250.

R. P. Merges, 'The law and economics of employee inventions' (1999) 13 Harvard Journal of Law & Technology 1.

C. G. Stallberg, 'The legal status of academic employees' inventions in Britain and Germany and its consequences for R&D agreements' (2007) IPQ 489.

INDUSTRIAL DESIGN

11.1 INTRODUCTION

Industrial designs may seem like the poor relations of other intellectual property. For the most part, they lack the glamour of a good brand, the creative genius of a best selling novel, and the outstanding inventiveness of many patents. Nonetheless, it is important not to underestimate the value of industrial designs. Some, like the design of the Apple iPod, might achieve iconic status. Others, such as the design of spare parts for motor vehicles may have considerable economic value. Perhaps the latter fact explains why the protection for industrial designs after an early life as being purely local in character has recently been given a makeover by the European Union. It is also noteworthy that for the most part, purely functional industrial designs are afforded much less protection than other sorts of intellectual property. This is not because functional industrial designs are deemed to have any lesser worth. Indeed, quite the reverse. The short term of protection accorded to functional designs stems from a recognition that a monopoly of such designs, for example of motor vehicle spare parts, would run counter to achieving market efficiency through genuine competition between suppliers.

11.1.1 DESIGN PROTECTION IN THE UK AND THE EU

Until the implementation of the Community Design Directive[1] and the Community Design Regulation,[2] there were two ways in which an industrial design, depending upon its character, might be protected against copying in the UK. These were as a registered design (RD) or by unregistered design right (UDR). The UDR had been introduced by the Copyright, Designs and Patents Act 1988 ('CDPA') which removed copyright protection from almost all industrial designs.[3] The registered design regime was regulated by the Registered Designs Act 1949. Historically, registered designs offered protection for industrial designs which had 'eye appeal'. By contrast the UDR offered protection for functional

---

[1] Design Directive 98/71/EC of the European Parliament and of the Council of 13 Oct. 1998 on the legal protection of designs.

[2] Council Regulation (EC) 6/2002 of 12 Dec. 2001 on Community designs.

[3] See 11.4 below.

designs which did not. As we shall see, such a clear distinction has been eroded by the implementation of the Design Directive and Regulation.

The Design Directive was intended to approximate national laws relating to the registration of industrial designs as a means of facilitating trade between Member States. However, four years later the Community agreed that the mere approximation of design law in Member States had failed to open up the market as had been hoped. The subsequent Design Regulation, which created a Community registered design (RCD) and a Community unregistered design (CUDR), were the result. The purpose in creating these new rights is identified in the recital to the regulation.

Recitals

(3) The substantial differences between Member States' design laws prevent and distort Community-wide competition. In comparison with domestic trade in, and competition between products incorporating a design, trade and competition within the Community are prevented and distorted by the large number of applications, offices, procedures, laws, nationally circumscribed exclusive rights and the combined administrative expense with correspondingly high cost and fees for the applicant. Directive 98/71/EC of the European Parliament and of the Council of 13 October 1998 on the legal protection of designs [the Design Directive] contributes to remedying this situation.

(4) The effect of design protection being limited to the territory of the individual Member States whether or not their law are approximated, leads to a possible division of the internal market with respect to products incorporating a design which is the subject of national rights held by different individuals, and hence constitutes an obstacle to the free movement of goods.

(5) This calls for the creation of a Community design which is directly applicable in each Member State, because only in this way will it be possible to obtain, through one application made to the Office for the Harmonisation of the Internal Market (Trade Marks and Designs) in accordance with a single procedure under one law, one design right for one area encompassing all Member States.

(6) Since the objectives of the proposed action, namely the protection of one design right for one area encompassing all the Member States, cannot be sufficiently achieved by the Member States by reason of the scale and the effects of the creation of a Community design authority and can therefore be better achieved at Community level, the Community may adopt measures, in accordance with the principle of subsidiarity as set out in Article 5 of the Treaty. In accordance with the principle of proportionality, as set out in that Article, this Regulation does not go beyond what is necessary in order to achieve these objectives.

As we see from the recital to the regulation, the introduction of an RCD and a CUDR was intended to simplify the protection for industrial designs in the EC, something which the Design Directive had singly failed to do. However, it is certainly questionable whether the implementation of the regulation has had a simplifying effect in the protection of industrial designs in the UK. In fact, there are now five ways in which an industrial design might be protected in the UK—as opposed to the pre-regulation era when there were only three. They are:

- as a Community registered design (RCD)
- as a UK registered design (RD)
- as a Community unregistered design (CUDR)
- as a UK unregistered design (UDR)
- by copyright.

11.1.2 THE HISTORY OF INDUSTRIAL DESIGN

The muddled and overlapping protection which in the UK is afforded to industrial designs results in large measure from the piecemeal way in which industrial design protection evolved over the last century. During the 19th and early 20th century, the push to protect industrial designs came from the textile industry. The Copyright Act 1911, which was the first to define infringement in its recognizable present form, excluded from copyright protection designs which were reproduced or intended to be reproduced in more than 50 single articles or were to be applied, for example, to carpets and textiles. Instead, the latter were protected by registration under the Patents and Designs Act 1907. This Act evolved into the Registered Designs Act 1949, which has now been amended to accord with the EU Design Directive and Regulation. Until the implementation of the Design Directive, only designs with 'eye appeal' could be registered.

The problem however remained as to how designs which did not have eye appeal would be protected. This problem was not solved by the Copyright Act 1956 which in effect granted copyright protection to designs which did not have eye appeal, but not to designs which did and so could be registered.[4] The result was that industrial designs that lacked eye-appeal received the full term of copyright protection, while the maximum term of protection for registered designs was 25 years. The Design Copyright Act 1968 addressed part of this problem by allowing copyright protection for artistic works which were registerable designs, but only for 15 years. However, the more entrenched problem of what many saw as the over-protection of industrial designs lacking eye-appeal remained. This issue was finally addressed by the creation of the unregistered design right in the CDPA. The CDPA also restricted the extent to which industrial designs would be protected by copyright.

11.1.3 INDUSTRIAL DESIGNS AND THE MARKET FOR SPARE PARTS

The motive behind granting legal protection to industrial designs in the 19th and early 20th century was to protect the flourishing UK textile industry. The industrial design regime introduced by the CDPA 1988 had another agenda fit for an age when free markets were worshipped. It was designed in large measure to open up the UK market to makers of automobile spare parts. As things stood, automobile makers had a virtual monopoly in the provision of spare parts for their cars, because of the lengthy copyright protection afforded to the original designs. The issue was addressed by the House of Lords in *British Leyland v Armstrong Patents Co Ltd*.

British Leyland Motor Corpn Ltd v Armstrong Patents Co Ltd [1986] AC 577

The claimant manufactured cars and the defendant manufactured spare parts for the claimant's cars. The House of Lords found that the defendant had infringed copyright in the claimant's design documents. However, it went on to hold that the benefits of having a competitive market in the provision of spare parts overrode the claimant's right to copyright protection. Looking at the competing interests between automobile makers and the ultimate consumers of the spare parts, Lord Bridge held that 'there is no halfway-house solution' as to which interest should prevail.

---

[4] *Dorling v Honnor Marine* [1965] Ch 1.

640 | INTELLECTUAL PROPERTY LAW: TEXT, CASES, AND MATERIALS

Lord Bridge, at p. 626:

Either the court must allow the enforcement of the copyright claim to maintain a monopoly in the supply of spare parts for the copyright owner and his licensees, regardless of any adverse effect of the monopoly on car owners; or the right of car owners to a free market in spare parts necessary for economical repair should prevail and the court should accordingly decline to enforce copyright claims as against the manufacturer of spare parts intended exclusively, as are Armstrong's exhaust systems, to be available as replacement parts for cars in need of repair. As I have already indicated, the first alternative would be unacceptable at one end of the spectrum of possible consequences. But, apart from this, it seems to me that there are sound reasons in principle why the second alternative should be preferred. By selling cars fitted with exhausts based on their copyright drawings BL have already enjoyed the primary benefit which their copyright protects. By selling those same cars BL have also created a large community of car owners who, quite independently of any contractual rights derived from BL, enjoy the inherent right as owners to repair their cars by replacing the exhaust whenever necessary in the most economical way possible. To allow BL to enforce their copyright to maintain a monopoly for themselves and their licensees in the supply and replacement of exhausts is, to a greater or lesser extent, to detract from the owner's rights and, at least potentially, the value of their cars. There is an inconsistency between marketing cars and thereby creating whatever rights attach to their ownership on the one hand and acting to restrain the free exercise of those rights on the other. The law does not countenance such inconsistencies. It may be a novel application of the principle to preclude a plaintiff from enforcing a statutory right to which he is *prima facie* entitled. But, as my noble and learned friend Lord Templeman demonstrates, the application of the principle to the relationship between the mass car manufacturer and those who at any time acquire cars of his manufacture is no more than an extension to a non-contractual relationship of the considerations which underlie the classical doctrine of the law that a grantor may not derogate from his grant.

In effect, the House of Lords decided to introduce a new economic policy, the freeing up of the market for spare parts, in the face of the government's failure to act. Two years later the UDR was introduced, arguably making the decision in *British Leyland* redundant. Indeed, 11 years later, the Privy Council decided, in *Canon Kabushiki Kaisha v Green Cartridge*, not to follow the House of Lords' judgment in *British Leyland*.

Canon Kabushiki Kaisha v Green Cartridge Co (Hong Kong) Ltd [1997] AC 728

This was a Privy Council decision. Like *British Leyland*, the *Canon* case concerned the conflicting interests of the manufacturer of, in this case, printers and photocopiers and a defendant who manufactured ink cartridges for the same equipment. It was noted by the court that the claimant, Canon, earned a significant profit from its monopoly of supplying replacement cartridges for its equipment.

Lord Hoffmann, at p. 732:

The issue in this appeal is the scope of the spare parts exception recognised by the House of Lords in *British Leyland Motor Corporation Ltd v Armstrong Patents Co Ltd* [1986] AC 577. In particular, the question is whether that doctrine entitles the defendant to infringe the plaintiff's copyright in drawings of parts of the cartridges used with its photocopiers and laser printers.

[**Lord Hoffmann** then went on to characterize, at p. 736, **Lord Bridge's** judgment in *British Leyland*, as 'unorthodox':]

This reasoning involves a somewhat unorthodox extension of what would normally be understood by the inherent right to repair one's motor car. Of course one has a right to repair one's car, as one has the right to cultivate one's garden and indulge in all kinds of harmless activities. But such a right is not usually treated as entitling one to invade the property rights of others; for example, by taking a neighbour's dahlias on the ground that this is the most economical way of going about it. It is hard to see why the appropriation of intellectual property rights should be any different...

It is hard to escape the conclusion that although Lord Bridge felt driven to accept that Parliament had created intellectual property rights which covered the manufacture of three-dimensional parts by reverse engineering, he felt free to remedy what he saw as a legislative error by treating such rights as an inferior species of property which could be subordinated to the right to repair one's motor car. Such prepotency over statute has not yet been accorded in this country even to human rights such as free speech.

[**Lord Hoffmann** was similarly dismissive of **Lord Templeman's** view in *British Leyland* that 'a grantor may not derogate from his grant'. And he was unhappy that in *British Leyland*, the House of Lords had trespassed outside its legal domain to make public policy. He continued at pp. 737–8:]

Their Lordships think the *British Leyland* spare parts exception cannot be regarded as truly founded upon any principle of the law of contract or property. It is instead an expression of what the House perceived as overriding public policy, namely the need to prevent a manufacturer from using copyright (as opposed to patents or design right) in order to control the aftermarket in spare parts. This appears clearly from the emphasis on the need for an 'unrestricted market' as opposed to the right of the manufacturer to 'use his copyright in such a way as to maintain a monopoly in the supply of spare parts' (Lord Bridge at page 625) and the danger of the car owner who 'sells his soul to the company store' being enmeshed in the 'tentacles of copyright' (Lord Templeman at pages 628–629).

It is of course a strong thing (not to say constitutionally questionable) for a judicially-declared head of public policy to be treated as overriding or qualifying an express statutory right. Their Lordships therefore think that the prospect of any extension of the *British Leyland* exception should be treated with some caution. The question of whether it is contrary to the public interest for a manufacturer to be able to exercise monopoly control over his aftermarket cannot usually be answered without some inquiry into the relevant market. For example, if customers are in a position to reckon the lifetime cost of one product (including purchases such as cartridges which will have to be made in the aftermarket) as against the lifetime cost of a competing product, then control of the aftermarket will not be anti-competitive. A manufacturer who charges too much for his cartridges will sell less of his machines. The figures which their Lordships have already quoted for expenditure on the machine itself and on cartridges make it likely that purchasers with any degree of sophistication will be comparing machines on a lifetime cost basis.

Furthermore, the ability to control the aftermarket and price the machines on the assumption that the purchasers will buy one's cartridges may actually enhance competition and provide greater choice to consumers, because it will enable manufacturers to compete not only on quality and price but also on the way they divide the cost of their products between

> the initial outlay and the aftermarket. For example, as Rogers J [the trial judge] pointed out, expenditure in the aftermarket may be treated by the tax authorities as revenue costs and more fully deductible than the capital cost of the machine. Thus a manufacturer who prices the machines lower and the cartridges higher may secure a competitive advantage as against a rival who charges the same lifetime cost in different proportions.

Lord Hoffmann went on to differentiate between the supply of spare parts for automobiles where the need for repair would be irregular and unpredictable, and the supply of replacement cartridges where the need to have a regular supply would have been foreseen by the consumer at the time of purchase. It followed that the regular need to purchase ink cartridges could not really be described as a 'repair'. Indeed, differences in the costs of ink cartridges for different machines meant, in effect, that the consumer would bear this in mind when purchasing a printer or copier, ensuring that the supply of ink cartridges took place in a competitive market. Lord Hoffmann suggested the same competitive market would not automatically arise in relation to automobile spare parts and was willing to accept that the decision in *British Leyland* could be justified on its facts. In fact, by the time the Privy Counsel undermined the decision in *British Leyland*, the transformation in the protection of industrial designs under the CDPA had arguably already made the decision in *British Leyland* otiose.

11.1.4 CONCLUSION

This chapter will examine the law relating to industrial designs following the introduction of the UDR and later the new Community industrial designs regime ushered in by the EU Design Directive and Regulation. It is therefore informative to hear what one informed observer, T. A. Blanco White, made of the proposed changes to the protection of industrial designs on the eve of the introduction of the UDR by the CDPA (which Blanco White refers to as the Copyright Bill).

T. A. Blanco White, 'Intellectual property: A future for British concepts' (1988) EIPR 229, 232–3

Industrial Designs

Forty years ago the UK had a system of registered designs little altered since it was reorganised in 1907. It was a sort of compromise between a copyright system and something analogous to what the UK had for patents: the idea being to provide protection for the artistic aspects of industrial design. It had been decided early in the century that usable articles were not necessarily excluded from design registration, but by and large the system was directed at what the current UK Copyright Bill calls surface decoration. Even in those industries that did regard themselves as artistic, design registrations had little commercial importance.

When in 1949 patent law was tidied up, there was a new Registered Designs Act too, tending towards a patent-type rather than a copyright system.[5] This was probably not intentional, rather designs were not considered important enough for anyone to bother about it; nor did

---

[5] According to the Registered Designs Act 1949 a registered design might be infringed without proving that it had been copied.

things work out that way. Whatever the Act said, the really important question in an action on a registered design still was, whether there had been copying or not. So there remained after 1949 what was essentially a copyright system, but with the inconveniences of the need for registration and the remaining uncertainties over the extent to which the system extended beyond unnecessary decoration. In those industries that depend on novelty of design this state of affairs was widely reckoned unsatisfactory.

...

The next stage is the UK Copyright Bill, excluding from the protection of the copyright system proper the shaping and configuration of an article, but creating a new unregistered design right, in parallel with the registered design system, to cover shape and configuration. (The term 'configuration' is taken from the Registered Designs Act and its predecessor, but even after 80 years there is little authority as to just what it covers, and a good deal may turn on how the courts understand it.) The new design right is to be wider than registration can give, to the extent that it covers purely functional designs (except, perhaps, those of spare parts); but surface decoration is excluded, being left to registration on the one hand and copyright on the other. This then leaves the UK with three overlapping systems to protect industrial design; copyright covering ornamentation and two-dimensional patterning; the new design right covering shape and configuration but not ornamentation; and the registration system, with minor changes, covering everything but the purely functional. They all have different periods of protection, varying from the life-plus-50-years of the copyright system, through 25 years for registered designs, to 10 years, only 5 of them undisturbed for the new design right.

The question of spare parts has, of course, some history behind it. It would not have been surprising, as things stand, if it had been decided to remove all protection from spare parts, other than patent protection. In fact, it seems that the intention of the Bill was to allow spare parts the limited period of protection of the design right system; yet its language seems designed to exclude them—and if the new Act does not do that, the Courts will, judging by the recent *Lego* case.[6] Furthermore, there have been mutterings from the European Commission on the point: it takes the view that monopolies in spare parts are inherently anti-competitive.

Looking to the future, two points stand out: that this is far too complicated, and that it is anti-European. A unique national system allowing a monopoly in certain goods necessarily tends to hamper trade between that nation and the others. Foreign manufacturers will find that goods in general circulation outside this country cannot be marketed there, while manufacturers in the country, with a protected market for particular products, will tend to be less competitive elsewhere. The author's feeling is that in the not too distant future the people in Brussels are going to demand a uniform European system of protection for industrial designs of one sort or another, and that the UK tripartite system will by then have been found so clumsy that it will not be defended very vigorously. How long this will take the author will not guess; the process could start quite quickly, following the European Commission's deliberations over monopolies in spare parts.

Nor is it easy to say what such a European design law would look like. There is always the tension between the desire to free competition and the desire to reward innovation, and between those concerned to avoid the problems of registration and those insistent that monopolies should be matters of public record. The author would guess at a registration system, with a firm requirement of originality. And he would expect something more like a 'utility model' system than the UK registration system, which with its emphasis on decorative features has never been satisfactory.

---

6 *Interlego AG v Tyco Industries Inc* [1988] RPC 343 (PC).

It was the view of T. A. Blanco White that the introduction of the new UDR would complicate the legal protection of industrial designs in the UK still further and would exacerbate the tensions within the EU between Member States with disparate industrial design regimes. The reader must judge from the remainder of this chapter the extent to which Blanco White's pessimism was justified.

FURTHER READING

J. Rawkins, 'British Leyland spare part defence: *Canon Kabushiki Kaisha v Green Cartridge Company (Hong Kong) Ltd* [1998] EIPR 674.

Russell-Clarke & Howe on Industrial Designs (7th edn., London: Sweet & Maxwell, 2005).

11.2 REGISTERED DESIGNS

11.2.1 OBTAINING REGISTRATION

The Registered Design regime in the UK is now regulated by the Registered Designs Act (RDA) 1949, as amended by CDPA, the Registered Design Regulations 2001, SI 2001/3949 and the Registered Design Regulations 2003, SI 2003/550. As a result, the law applying to RCDs and RDs is the same. The regulation of registered designs thus mirrors that of registered trade marks. In both cases the EU has created a Community right, and the law which applies to these rights also applies to the UK registered design and registered trade mark respectively.

Applications for an RCD are made to the Office for Harmonization of the Internal Market (OHIM) in Alicante, which also deals with the Community trade mark. The process of registration calls for the applicant to indicate the products into which 'the design is intended to be incorporated'. The applicant may also choose to indicate the class of goods for which the design will be used, by reference to the Locarno Agreement.[7]

It is also possible to register a design in the UK by application to the UK IPO. Both UK registered designs and RCDs will be protected for five years in the first instance and may be renewed thereafter for a total of 25 years. As with patents, the RCD and the RD endow an absolute monopoly. It is not necessary for a registered design to be copied for it to be infringed. Both at the OHIM and the UK IPO, design registration follows the same procedures as for trade mark registration. There will be no substantive examination of the design by the registering authority either for novelty or individual character.[8] There will however be an examination of the design to see if it falls within the exclusions to registration, for instance if it is functional or offends against public morality.

While the OHIM is concerned with the process of registering an RCD, domestic courts, designated as Community Design Courts, deal with issues of infringement and counterclaims of invalidity. As regards domestic registered designs, these are governed by the same legal conditions as the RCD. Thus, UK examiners and judges will look to the examiners, the First Board of Appeal in Alicante, and on to the Court of First Instance up to the ECJ to see how to interpret the Community Design Directive and Regulation as they apply to both RCDs and UK RDs.

---

[7] The Locarno Agreement Establishing an International Classification for Industrial Designs, 1968.
[8] For trade marks, see 5.3.1.

11.2.2 THE DEFINITION OF A REGISTRABLE DESIGN

Because the Design Regulation has been in force for a relatively brief period of time, there are relatively few cases either at the domestic or Community level which have sought to interpret it. Hence, this chapter will look first at the Design Regulation, itself, before going on to consider the relevant case law.

11.2.2.1 A registrable design

We have noted that until the implementation of the Design Directive and Regulation only industrial designs with eye-appeal could be registered. This requirement was understood to mean that the appearance of the registered design was a material factor in attracting consumers. In particular, the article's appeal was seen to reside in its shape, pattern, or ornamentation.[9] Under the new European law, an RD no longer needs to have eye appeal. Instead, a 'design' is defined, more broadly, as:

> the appearance of the whole of the product resulting from the features of, in particular, the lines, contours, colours, shapes, texture of the product or its ornamentation.[10]

It is possible to argue that the requirement that a registered design have eye-appeal justified the longer protection it was given in contrast to an unregistered design which did not. The fact that the new law does not make eye-appeal a necessary prerequisite for registration represents for some a worrying extension of design protection. The regulation then goes on to define a product as:

> any industrial or handicraft item other than computer programs; and in particular includes packaging, get-up, graphic symbols, typographic type faces and parts intended to be assembled into a complex product.[11]

Here too we might detect an increased measure of protection offered to designs. Under the new law, a registerable design does not have to be applied to a product by an industrial process. In addition, it is no longer necessary, as before, to register the design in respect of a specific article or group of articles. This change opens the way, some have argued, to registering the 'get up' of a branded product to protect it, for example, from supermarket 'lookalikes'. A complex product is defined in Article 3(c) of the CDR as 'being composed of multiple components which can be replaced permitting disassembly and re-assembly of the product' and by s. 1(3) of the RDA 1949 as amended as 'composed of at least two replaceable parts permitting disassembly and reassembly of the product'. This definition will, according to the UK IPO, stretch the protection offered by the registration of a design to products which are 'costly, long lasting and complex': an automobile but not a teapot.

The definition of a registrable design is then set out:

> A design shall be protected by a right in a registered design to the extent that the design is new and has individual character.[12]

---

[9] *Interlego AG v Tyco Industries Inc* [1988] AC 217.
[10] Art. 3(a) Community Design Regulation (CDR) (s. 1(2), RDA 1949).
[11] Art. 3(b) CDR (s. 1(3), RDA 1949).
[12] Art. 4(1) CDR (s. 1B(1), RDA 1949).

According to the CDR a design will be considered novel:[13]

> if no identical design has been made available to the public before the relevant date.

By contrast, according to the RDA as amended, a design will be considered new:

> if no identical design or no design whose features differ only in immaterial details has been made available to the public before the relevant date.[14]

The design must also have individual character.[15] The regulation defines individual character, as whether:

> the overall impression it produces on the informed user differs from the overall impression produced on such a user by any design which has been made available to the public before the relevant date.

The relevant date will most commonly be the date on which the application for the registration of the design was made or is treated as having been made. An exception would be if a design has been substantially modified since an application was first made. In judging the extent to which a design has individual character:

> The degree of freedom of the author in creating the design shall be taken into consideration. Designs shall be deemed to be identical if their features differ only in immaterial details.[16]

Although only novel designs are registrable, it is important to be aware that a design will retain its novelty if disclosure of the design occurred during a 12-month period preceding the date of filing or, if a priority date is claimed, the date of priority.[17] This gives the originator of the design a crucial period in which to decide whether there is sufficient economic justification for registering his design. Such a justification may be absent, for instance, if the design is for a fashion fabric which may only bring economic rewards over a short period. Furthermore, such ephemeral designs might find sufficient protection as a Community unregistered design right.

11.2.2.2 Exceptions to registration

There are also exceptions to the protection of registered designs set out in the regulation. The most important of these, which also apply to the Community unregistered designs, are:

> 1. A Community design shall not subsist in features of the appearance of a product which are solely dictated by the product's technical function[18]
>
> [and]

---

[13] Art. 5(1) CDR. The relevance of immaterial details is at Art. 5(2) CDR.   [14] RDA, s. 1B(2).
[15] Art. 6(1) CDR (s. 1B(2), RDA 1949).
[16] Art. 6(2) CDR (s. 1B(3), RDA 1949).   [17] Art. 7(2)(b), CDR.
[18] Art. 8(1) CDR (s. 1C(1), RDA 1949).

> 2. A right in a registered design shall not subsist in features of the appearance of a product which must necessarily be reproduced in their exact form and dimensions so as to permit the product in which the design is incorporated or to which it is applied to be mechanically connected to, or placed in, around or against, another product so that either product may perform its function.[19]

Otherwise known as the 'must fit' exception, this second exception does not prevent a right in a registered design subsisting in a design serving the purpose of allowing a multiple assembly or connection of mutually interchangeable products within a modular system.

Finally, the regulation defines infringement, by identifying the rights which a registration endows on its proprietor. Most notably, it is:[20]

> the exclusive right to use it [the RD] and to prevent any third party not having his consent from using it.[21]

According to s. 7A of the RDA 1949, a registered design would therefore be infringed by a person who, without the consent of the registered proprietor, does anything which by virtue of Article 12 (s. 7 of the RDA 1949) is the exclusive right of the registered proprietor.[22] Other rights given to the proprietor include: the making, offering, putting on the market, importing, exporting, or using a product in which the design is incorporated or to which it is applied; or stocking such a product for those purposes. There are however defences to an allegation of infringement of a registered design. These are set out at Article 20 (s. 7A(2) of the RDA 1949), of which the most notable are that a registered design is not infringed if it is used privately for non-commercial or for experimental purposes. In addition, the right to protect a registered design is exhausted once a product embodying that design has been put on the market in the EEA by the proprietor or with his consent.[23]

11.2.3 REGISTERED DESIGNS: THE CASE LAW

11.2.3.1 The 'informed user', different overall impression and individual character

There have been no authoritative judgments dealing with the exceptions to infringement of an RD.[24] In the two cases which have reached the Court of Appeal, the court has looked at the issue of whether or not an RCD (and therefore a UK RD) should be revoked for lack of novelty.[25] The Court of Appeal has also sought to interpret some of the key concepts in the law relating to RCDs (and UK RDs). Thus in *Procter & Gamble v Reckitt Benckiser*[26] the court considered the definitions of 'the informed user', 'different overall impression', and 'individual character'.

---

[19] Art. 8(2) CDR (s. 1C(2), RDA 1949).

[20] Art. 19 CDR (s. 7A, RDA 1949).

[21] Art. 19(1) CDR (s. 7A(1), RDA 1949).   [22] There is no equivalent article in the CDR.

[23] Art. 21 CDR (s. 7A(2), RDA 1949).

[24] The issue was raised by the defendants in the High Court case of *Rolawn Ltd v Turfmech Machinery Ltd* [2008] ECDR 13 but not pursued.

[25] See 11.2.3.4 below.

[26] *Woodhouse UK Plc v Architectural Lighting Systems* [2006] ECDR 1 was an earlier High Court decision involving a UK registered design which had centred on questions of ownership.

Procter & Gamble Co v Reckitt Benckiser (UK) Ltd [2008] ECDR 3

This was an appeal by Procter & Gamble ('P&G') from a judgment of Lewison J in 2007.[27] P&G had an RCD which was intended to apply to 'sprayers'. P&G had used the design in a number of countries for an air freshener product called 'Febreze'. The claimants alleged that a Reckitt spray canister for their 'Air Wick' room air conditioner infringed their RCD. In return, the defendants claimed that P&G's design had been invalidly registered. In the High Court Lewison J held that P&G's design was validly registered and was infringed by the defendants' design. The defendants appealed. Jacob LJ agreed with the High Court that the design was validly registered and so concentrated on the infringement claim. In his judgment, Jacob LJ began by noting that P&G had won an award for their design in their three-dimensional embodiment and, citing the first instance judge, he described the award winning design.

Jacob LJ:

7. ... 'Febreze Air Effects is packaged in a uniquely shaped aerosol can that breaks category norms, stands out on the shelf, is easy to use and delivers a superb scent experience for consumers. Febreze redefines the difference a great product and a unique package can make in a customized container and actuator.'

On the other hand, the allegedly infringing design, unlike the Febreze container (which had a slightly tapered top to the can which blended with the top), had a top which fitted onto a standard cylindrical canister.

We have already noted that design registration gives the proprietor the exclusive right to use the design and any design which does not produce on the informed user a different overall impression. In judging whether a defendant's design was infringing, Jacob LJ considered how the 'informed user' would judge the two designs. But first, he needed to identify the 'informed user' and define what was meant by a 'different overall impression'. And, since both these terms are also relevant to judging whether a design has individual character, Jacob LJ's judgment in *P&G* covers both the registration and infringement of an RD. We shall see that Jacob LJ held that the definition of the informed user was the same for both registration and infringement. However, for policy reasons, he suggested this was not true of the 'different overall impression'.

Jacob LJ:

16. The [Design] Regulation does not tell us much about the notional 'informed user'. He/she is clearly not quite the same sort of person as the 'person skilled in the art' of patent law. The equivalent to that person in the field of design would be some sort of average *designer*, not a *user*. Recital 14 [of the regulation] assists a bit. It says:

14. The assessment as to whether a design has individual character should be based on whether the overall impression produced on an informed user viewing the design clearly differs from that produced on him by the existing design corpus, taking into consideration the nature of the product to which the design is applied or in which it is incorporated, and in particular the industrial sector to which it belongs and the degree of freedom of the designer in developing the design.

---

[27] *Procter & Gamble Co v Reckitt Benckiser (UK) Ltd* [2008] FSR 8.

17. The recital is actually framed around the requirement for registrability—whether the design has 'individual character'—rather than the test for infringement. Curiously the reference to the 'existing design corpus, taking into consideration the nature of the product to which the design is applied' is not expressly carried over into the text of any of the actual Articles of the Regulation. But self-evidently it is relevant to their interpretation. What it tells us is that for the purposes of registrability the notional informed user is to be taken as aware of other similar designs which form part of the 'design corpus'. Further, the 'overall impression' to the 'informed user' is also a key ingredient of the infringement test. So for that test too the notional informed user must be taken to be aware of the 'existing design corpus'.

[**Jacob LJ** then went on to assess what was meant in the recital to the regulation by the phrase 'different overall impression':]

18. ...Only if the 'overall impression' 'clearly differs' from that of the 'existing design corpus' will the design have an 'individual character'. Plainly that is relevant for registrability, even if Art. 6(1) does not expressly use 'clearly differs'. Does the phrase also apply to the infringement test? Does an accused design escape infringement only if its overall impression 'clearly differs' from the registered design? All Art. 10(1) says is 'different overall impression'. Does that really mean 'clearly different'—the word 'clearly' requiring much blue water between the accused and registered design for non-infringement?

19. The judge [Lewison J] thought it did...But I do not. Different policies are involved. It is one thing to restrict the grant of a monopoly right to designs which are shown 'clearly' to differ from the existing design corpus. That makes sense—you need clear blue water between the registered design and the 'prior art', otherwise there is a real risk that design monopolies will or may interfere with routine, ordinary, minor, everyday design modifications—what patent lawyers call 'mere workshop modifications'. But no such policy applies to the scope of protection. It is sufficient to avoid infringement if the accused product is of a design which produces a 'different overall impression'. There is no policy requirement that the difference be 'clear'. If a design differs, that is enough—an informed user can discriminate.

...

21. I move on to mention another point. The right conferred applies to any sort of product even though the registration contains an indication of the type of article for which it is intended, see Art. 36(2). Where the alleged infringement is a quite different sort of product from that indicated as being the intended type, there may be problems about identifying the attributes of the informed user—is he a user of the kind of article such as the alleged infringement or a user of the kind of intended article? Or both? But none of that applies here.

22. Here the 'design corpus' of which the informed user is taken [to] be aware are other sprayers generally known—not just sprayers for air fresheners or even those of the kind purchased by ordinary consumers. There was no dispute about this.

23. The 'informed user' test makes sense: a user who has experience of other similar articles will be reasonably discriminatory—able to appreciate enough detail to decide whether a design creates an overall impression which has individual character and whether an alleged infringement produces a different overall impression.

Jacob LJ thus concluded that the test for registration of a RCD (and therefore a UK RD) should be more discriminating in terms of the overall impression made on the informed user than the test for infringement, because registration endows a monopoly which is only warranted for a design which is some distance removed from other designs in the same field. He believed that the same was not true for infringement. By contrast, Article 10(2), which states that the scope of protection for a RCD depends upon the degree of freedom the designer has in developing the design, and is, according to Jacob LJ, 'a narrowing provision. Smaller differences will be enough to create a different overall impression where freedom of design is limited.'[28] Returning to the informed user, Jacob LJ adopted the definition given by the Austrian court in a 2006 case[29] which concerned the same parties:

26. 'The 'informed user' will, in the view of the Appeals Court, have more extensive knowledge than an 'average consumer in possession of average information, awareness and understanding'…in particular he will be open to design issues and will be fairly familiar with them.

It is important to note that the 'informed user' identified here is not the same as the 'average consumer' in trade mark law. The difference arises in large measure from the fact that an RCD (and a UK RD) does not get the same protection as a registered trade mark, since the latter is to protect against customer confusion, while the point of the former is, according to Jacob LJ:

27. ….to protect that design *as a design*. So what matters is the overall impression created by it: will the user buy it, consider it or appreciate it *for its individual design*? That involves the user looking at the article, not half-remembering it. The motivation is different from purchasing or otherwise relying on a trade mark as a guarantee of origin.

28. So the informed user is alert to design issues and is better informed than the average consumer in trade mark law. Things which may infringe a registered trade mark may not infringe a corresponding registered design. I cannot think of any instance where the reverse might be so.

[**Jacob LJ** then moved on to consider the 'different overall impression' test:]

34. This test is inherently rather imprecise: an article may reasonably seem to one man to create 'a different overall impression' and yet to another not to do so. It is always so with the scope of rights in a visual work. You need to cover not only exact imitations, but also things which come 'too close'. Whatever words you choose, you are bound to leave a considerable margin for the judgment of the tribunal.

Jacob LJ found that the test of 'substantiality' in copyright law 'leaves just the same sort of margin as the 'overall impression' test. However, he added: 'Whether it is the same test or not I leave for others to consider.' He nonetheless went on to make a number of general observations about both the 'informed user' and the 'different overall impression' in relation to infringement of an RCD. Among them were the following:

35. …

(ii) The notional informed user is 'fairly familiar' with design issues, as discussed above.

---

[28] For a number of OHIM decisions on this point see: *Eredu v Arrmet* (OHIM ref: ICD000000024; 27 Apr. 2004 concerning a bar stool); *Sunstar Suisse SA v Dentaid SL* (OHIM ref: ICD000000420; 20 Jun. 2005, concerning an interdental brush); *Built NV Inc v I-Feng Kao* (OHIM ref: ICD 0000002103; 3 May 2006, a bottle carrier); *Honda Motor Co Ltd v Kwang Yang Motor Co Ltd* (OHIM ref: ICD 000001006; 30 Aug. 2006, concerning an internal combustion engine, intended principally for lawnmowers).

[29] *Bulling/Langöhrig/Hellwig, Gemeinschaftsgeschmackmuster [Community designs], Rz 56.*

(iii) Next is not a proposition of law but a statement about the way people (and thus the notional informed user) perceive things. It is simply that if a new design is markedly different from anything that has gone before, it is likely to have a greater overall visual impact than if it is 'surrounded by kindred prior art'. (HH Judge Fysh's pithy phrase in *Woodhouse* at [58]).[30] It follows that the 'overall impression' created by such a design will be more significant and the room for differences which do not create a substantially different overall impression is greater. So protection for a striking novel product will be correspondingly greater than for a product which is incrementally different from the prior art, though different enough to have its own individual character and thus be validly registered.

(iv) On the other hand it does not follow, in a case of markedly new design (or indeed any design) that it is sufficient to ask, 'is the alleged infringement closer to the registered design or to the prior art', if the former infringement, if the latter not. The tests remains, 'is the overall impression different?'

(v) It is legitimate to compare the registered design and the alleged infringement with a reasonable degree of care. The court must 'don the spectacles of the informed user' to adapt the hackneyed but convenient metaphor of patent law. The possibility of imperfect recollection has a limited part to play in this exercise.

(vi) The court must identify the 'overall impression' of the registered design with care. True it is that it is difficult to put into language, and it is helpful to use pictures as part of the identification, but the exercise must be done.

(vii) In this exercise the level of generality to which the court must descend is important. Here, for instance, it would be too general to say that the overall impression of the registered design is 'a canister fitted with a trigger spray device on the top'. The appropriate level of generality is that which would be taken by the notional informed user.

(viii) The court should then do the same exercise for the alleged infringement.

(ix) Finally the court should ask whether the overall impression of each is different. This is almost the equivalent to asking whether they are the *same*—the difference is nuanced, probably, involving a question of onus and no more.

11.2.3.2 *Procter & Gamble v Reckitt*: the judgment

In turning to the particular facts in this case, the defendants argued that Lewison J had been 'wrong in principle', for not directly comparing the 'different overall impression' that was created when looking at the claimants' and the defendants' products. Had he done so, claimed the defence, he would have found that the products created a different overall impression. In fact, Lewison J had found that: 'Overall, the shape of the [claimant's] design had a smooth and dynamic feel, flowing lines, and an elegant sense of movement.' By contrast, the defendants' design was described by its own expert as 'a common canister with a plastic cap stuck on top'; and was 'not in the same league as regards quality'. Given these findings, the defence argued that 'surely' the two designs created a different overall impression. This claim was underlined by the fact that the judge had compared various general aspects of the two designs which were not necessarily the most original aspects of

---

[30] *Woodhouse UK Plc v Architectural Lighting Systems* [2006] ECDR 1.

the claimants' design, enabling him to hold that the designs differed only in 'insignificant detail', and so to conclude that the defendants' design was infringing. For their part, the claimants argued, *inter alia*, both that the policy behind the regulation as set out in recital 7 was to encourage the development of innovative products and designs and that the Febreze design was particularly innovative and unlike any earlier designs. This suggested that there was considerable design freedom in the field. The claimants also submitted that, assuming there should be a broad scope of protection, infringement should arise when a design gives a 'slightly cheaper, or slightly coarser impression' than the registered design, as had been found by Lewison J. Jacob LJ disagreed and indentified six areas where the judge had 'erred', which included the following:

> 59....
>
> (iii) in failing, at the point where he was considering infringement, to state what the overall impression of the alleged infringement was;
>
> (iv) in applying by implication a requirement that the accused product should give the informed user a *clearly* different impression;
>
> (v) in applying a 'stick in the mind' test rather than 'what would impress now' test; and
>
> (vi) in approaching the 'dominant features' of the design at too general a level, a level such as not to convey in words the overall impression which would be given to an informed observer.

Perhaps one of the most interesting aspects of the case is that the defence argued and Jacob LJ accepted that a 'poor quality imitation' would escape infringement. Indeed, Jacob LJ considered that such an outcome was within the spirit of the regulation:

> 60. We are here considering monopolies in designs, not trade marks. A 'poor quality' imitation if it does not convey the same impression as the 'original' will fail on its own design merits, or rather the lack of them. If it conveys the 'same impression' then it can hardly be a 'poor quality imitation' and will succeed for the same reason as the 'original'...
>
> [He concluded:]
>
> 61. ...I think the impression which would be given to the informed user by the Air Wick product is different from that of the registered design...
>
> 62. The similarities between the products are at too general a level for one fairly to say that they would produce on the informed user the same overall impression. On the contrary, that user would get a different overall impression.
>
> 63. Accordingly I would allow the appeal on infringement, but dismiss the appeal on validity.

It is submitted that the idea that a poor quality design will be unlikely to infringe a registered design is an interesting one. As we have seen, with trade marks it is possible for there to be infringement of a distinctive mark if an association with a later mark tarnishes its reputation.[31] In this case, the court appears to be arguing the opposite: that the more the later design is of poor quality, the more likely it is to be found non-infringing. Surely, such a result would appear to run counter to the idea that the Design Regulation was intended to

---

[31] See 6.2 and 6.3.

nurture high-class and original industrial designs? On the other hand, Jacob LJ seems to be following trade mark law by suggesting that it should be harder to register a design than to find it has been infringed once it is registered. Clearly he is seeking to limit the monopoly offered by registration of a design. Given that the overall impression is measured against not the average consumer as in trade mark law, but rather a design specialist, is it necessary for him to be so cautious?

11.2.3.3 The relevant evidence

In the *P&G* case Jacob LJ also identified the crucial evidence to consider in registered design cases.

Jacob LJ:

3. …

    1. the registered design;

    2. the accused object; and

    3. the prior art.

And the most important thing about each of these is what they look like. Of course parties and judges have to try to put into words why they say a design has 'individual character' or what the 'overall impression produced on an informed user' is. But 'it takes longer to say than to see' as I observed in *Philips Electronics NV v Remington Consumer Products Ltd (No 1) [1998] RPC 283* at 318. And words themselves are often insufficiently precise on their own.

    4. It follows that a place for evidence is very limited indeed. By and large it should be possible to decide a registered design case in a few hours. The evidence of the designer, e.g. as to whether he/she was trying to make, or thought he/she had made, a breakthrough, is irrelevant. The evidence of experts, particularly about consumer products, is unlikely to be of much assistance: anyone can point out similarities and differences, though an educated eye can sometimes help a bit. Sometimes there may be a piece of technical evidence which is relevant—e.g. that design freedom is limited by certain constraints. But even so, that is usually more or less self-evident and certainly unlikely to be controversial to the point of a need for cross-examination, still less substantial cross-examination.

We might think that this is a surprising observation. It is now taken as axiomatic that a judge can play the role of the 'average consumer' in trade mark cases.[32] But it is less clear that a judge can adopt the mantle of the 'informed user' in industrial design cases, which is what Jacob LJ appears to be suggesting.

11.2.3.4 Prior art in design registration

In his judgment in *P&G v Reckitt*, Jacob LJ considered the contrast between the protection given to registered trade marks and to registered designs respectively. In *Green Lane Products v PMS*, which also reached the Court of Appeal, Jacob LJ compared the meaning of prior art for patent and registered design protection. In *Green Lane Products*, the court was specifically asked how the Design Regulation views 'prior art' and, in particular, when, under the terms of the regulation, a design would have been made available to the public and

---

[32] See 5.3.3.7.

hence lack the novelty and individual character which is required both for registration and infringement. The particular article of the regulation for which the parties in the case sought elucidation was Article 7 and the phrase, 'the circles specialised in the sector concerned'. Article 7 reads:

> For the purpose of applying Articles 5 [on novelty) and 6 [on individual character], a design shall be deemed to have been made available to the public if it has been published following registration or otherwise, or exhibited, used in trade or otherwise disclosed... except where these events could not reasonably have become known in the normal course of business to the circles specialised in the sector concerned, operating within the Community.

Green Lane also arose as an appeal from a judgment given by Lewison J in the High Court.[33]

Green Lane Products v PMS International Group, PMS International Far East Limited, Poundland Limited [2008] FSR 28

Green Lane made and sold spiky plastic balls to be used in tumble driers under the trade mark 'Dryerballs'. In 2004, Green Lane had registered the design of the Dryerballs as a CDR. The application date was 24 August 2004. The purpose of the balls was to soften the fabrics and to separate the laundry in the drier. Some of the balls were pink with rounded nodes. Others were green with square nodes. PMS also marketed spiky plastic balls, although these were intended as massage balls not laundry balls. The balls were made in China and had been extensively marketed in the EU since 2002. In 2006, PMS sold its massage balls for other pruposes, including as a laundry ball but also as a hand exerciser and a dog trainer. Green Lane alleged that PMS would infringe its CRD unless they sold their product only as massage balls. In return, PMS alleged that Green Lane's CRD was invalid because of the prior sale of their massage balls. The claimant replied that (a) that such prior art is irrelevant as a matter of law and (b) even if it is relevant, their CRDs are nonetheless valid. In beginning his judgment, Jacob LJ set out the arguments of the parties as to how Article 7 should be construed.

Jacob LJ:

6. Green Lane says that the extent of its rights under its CRDs are defined by Art. 10—*any* article, whatever its intended purpose, will infringe unless it does not produce on the informed user a different overall impression. The only reason why continued sales by PMS of balls for massage purposes do not infringe is that such sales are protected by Art. 22.[34] Even then such sales are protected only to the extent provided by that Article.

7. PMS says the design registrations are not 'new' within the meaning of Art. 5 or do not have 'individual character' within the meaning of Art. 6. They say this is so because of their own prior sales in the EU of what, for all practical purposes is the very design complained of. In short they say the design is old.

---

[33] *Green Lane Products v PMS International Group, PMS International Far East Limited, Poundland Limited* [2008] FSR 1.

[34] Art. 22 raises a defence of prior use if use of a design had been undertaken by a third party in good faith before the application for a registered design is filed.

8. Now absent Art. 7 one would say that PMS are right: that a design cannot be 'new' or have 'individual character' if it is the same or practically the same as an article previously used in trade. But, say Green Lane, a design may be new or have individual character even if it is fact old: Art. 7 says that a prior design is not taken to be made available to the public, even if it in reality was, where 'these events [i.e. prior use in trade] could not reasonably have become known in the normal course of business to the circles specialised in the sector concerned, operating in the Community'.

9. And, says Green Lane, the 'sector concerned' means the sector for which the design was registered, not the sector of the alleged prior art.

As identified by Jacob LJ, the exact question being asked by the parties was whether when judging the novelty of a registered design, one looks only at the class of goods for which it is registered, as argued by Green Lane. Or, alternatively, one looks at the class of goods of the allegedly infringing party. Or, indeed, does one, as in patent law, look at all 'prior' art. According to Lewison J, in his judgment, the sector concerned under Article 7 is the sector which consists of or includes the sector of the alleged prior art. The circles specialized in the sector consist of those individuals who trade in the products in the relevant sector, including those who, *inter alia*, design, make, and market such products in the EC. Jacob LJ upheld the ruling of Lewison J as 'clearly right'. He pointed to the fact that such a ruling is supported by the language of the regulation, its recitals, and the *travaux préparatoires*. He also compared the language of the regulation with the relevant patent law regarding prior art and concluded that the meaning of the prior art is the same for both patents and registered designs—albeit in the case of RCDs, the relevant prior art is confined to the EU.

Jacob LJ:

19. Turning now to the requirements for protection, the basic rule, is that a design must be 'new' and have 'individual character' (Art. 4.1). Art. 5 elaborates on what is meant by 'new' and Art. 6 on what is meant by 'individual character'. In both cases the test involves consideration of an earlier design, that is a design which 'has been made available to the public'.

20. This is a clear incorporation of a key concept and well-known language of patent law defining the prior art which may be used to attack validity of a patent. An invention is 'new' if it is not part of the 'state of the art'. The 'state of the art shall be held to comprise everything made available to the public by means of a written or oral description, by use, or in any other way before [the relevant date]' (see Art. 54 of the European Patent Convention). I shall use the expression conventionally used for this test: 'absolute novelty'.

...

23. This clear rule, which so far as I am aware, is virtually standard for patent systems throughout the world, not only for identifying prior art available to attack novelty but also that for basing an obviousness attack...

24. Both sides accept that 'made available to the public' in the conventional patent law sense is also the basic rule for identifying prior art which may be considered for the purpose of attacking the validity of designs...

...

27. It is particularly important to realise that the scope of protection covers any use of the design for an article, whatever its intended purpose. The scope provision, unlike for instance the previous law of the UK (s. 7 of the Registered Designs Act 1949) does not limit infringement to 'articles for which the design is registered' or anything like that. So if you register a

> design for a car you can stop use of the design for a brooch or a cake or a toy, or if you register a textile design you can stop its use on wallpaper, a shirt or a plate.

Jacob LJ then considered the *travaux préparatoires* in relation to Article 7 which he found as supporting the view that prior art in relation to designs mirrored the meaning of prior art in patent law—save that in the case of RCDs, the prior art was confined to the Community. He took the view that there would be 'absurd' consequences for the law relating to the RCD if the Green Lane contention was correct, and the relevant prior art was to be found only in the type of products on which the RCD was to be used. To illustrate these 'absurd' consequences, Jacob LJ reproduced some possible scenarios which in the first instance had been described by Lewison J. The following is a fair example:

Jacob LJ:

75. There are a number of potential consequences of Green Lane's interpretation which suggest that it is wrong. First, consider the form of the application. Suppose a designer produces a design of a product which can be used for a multitude of purposes or products, each of which is in a different product class. Call the classes A, B, C and D; and assume that circles specialised in one class do not know about designs in the other classes. The design is both old and well-known in circles specialising in class D. If Dr Lawrence [for Green Lane] is right, then the registration will be invalid if the applicant for registration specifies all four classes (or class D alone); but it will be valid if he only specifies class A. Yet once registered, the registration gives him a monopoly extending across all four classes. So the canny applicant will specify the products to which the design is intended to be applied in the narrowest possible way, so as to avoid exposing his design to prior art, confident in the expectation that once the design has been registered he will obtain the wide protection given to him by the registration.

...

77. These examples are realistic. Mr Vaughan [for Green Lane] did not really contend otherwise. And he could not find any fault with them. His answer was to suggest that the alternative construction also produced absurd results. First it would involve difficult questions of searching and second that the right holder might find his registration lost by reason of prior art which he could not reasonably learn about because the validity of a design could be challenged on the basis of any prior art in any field unless it was obscure in its own field.

78. I do not accept either point as absurd. As to the practicalities of searching, it has always been the case that design searches are not easy—most prior designs are not registered and so not readily searchable as, for instance, patent literature is. Yet the system has worked well for a long time with absolute novelty in many countries, for instance under the prior UK system.

79. But of even more fundamental significance is this: the right gives a monopoly over any kind of goods according to the design. It makes complete sense that the prior art available for attacking novelty should also extend to all kinds of goods, subject only to the limited exception of prior art obscure even in the sector from which it comes.

In this instance, in interpreting the scope of protection afforded to RDs, the UK courts have sought to limit the monopoly afforded by registration. It is possible to sympathize with Green Lane's argument that it will be extremely difficult for an applicant to ensure that there is no prior art when seeking to register a design, if that prior art might arise in any sector of goods. But is it not a stronger argument that to limit prior art to the sector concerned would allow for design registrations in one sector which could then be used to stifle designs in other sectors? Certainly, in this case, the courts found such an outcome not only logically 'absurd' but also offering too great a penumbra of protection to registered designs.

11.2.3.5 Registered design right and the defence of innocent infringement

J Choo (Jersey) Ltd v Towerstone Ltd[35] is an interesting RCD case which applies the principles of interpretation of the Design Regulation arising from the judgments in *Procter & Gamble* and *Green Lane*. In this case, the claimant had an RCD for its handbag, 'Ramona', which it sold from its Oxford Street store and which it was agreed was the 'it' bag of the moment. The defendants also sold bags. J. Choo's claim that the defendants' bags infringed its RCD was upheld, despite the fact that they were of poorer quality. However, the defendants argued that they were 'innocent infringers', having acquired their bags from third parties, not being aware that the bags were infringing. On this point, the court found that although when the Design Regulation had been introduced, the UK law on registered designs had allowed for a defence of innocent infringement for UK RDs, this was not the case either for RCDs or CUDRs. The defence failed.

> **FURTHER READING**
>
> A. Carboni, 'Design validity and infringement: Feel the difference' [2008] EIPR 111–17.
>
> J. J. Izquierdo Peris, 'OHIM practice in the field of invalidity of registered Community designs' (2008) 30(2) EIPR 56–65.
>
> K. Starks and H. Padley, 'Registered design: Modernisation of a system' [2007] Ent LR N8.

11.3 UNREGISTERED DESIGN RIGHT

11.3.1 THE COMMUNITY UNREGISTERED DESIGN RIGHT (CUDR)

The Design Regulation as well as introducing a Community registered design also introduced a Community unregistered design right (CUDR). For the most part the regulation treats both the RCD and the CUDR in essentially the same manner. Thus, the meaning of a 'design', 'product', and 'complex product' are the same for both Community designs. So too are the requirements for protection: most notably, the need for novelty (Article 5) and individual character (Article 6). Similarly, the rights endowed on proprietors are the same for both Community designs, so that the scope of protection extends to any design that does not produce on the informed user a different overall impression (Article 10(1)). And, in assessing whether this is so, the designer's degree of freedom will be taken into account (Article 10(2)). As a result, it is likely that the Court of Appeal decisions in *Procter & Gamble* and *Green Lane*, which defined the various terms used in the Design Regulation, for example, the informed user in relation to RCDs should apply equally to CUDRs. Furthermore, the limitations on the rights conferred by an RCD, most notably that there will be no protection for designs

---

[35] *J Choo (Jersey) Ltd v Towerstone Ltd* [2008] FSR 19.

dictated by their technical functions or their need to fit with a product which allows the product to function, also applies to both Community designs (Article 8). There are however two key differences between the RCD and the CUDR. The first is that a CUDR will only be infringed if infringement results from direct or indirect copying (as is the case in copyright law). Secondly, a CUDR is only protected for three years from the date on which the design was first made available (or disclosed) to the public within the Community (Article 11). In his article, 'The unregistered community design', Victor Saez identifies the circumstances in which the Community unregistered design may be of use.

V. Saez, 'The unregistered community design'
[2002] EIPR 585–9, 585

Why an Unregistered Design?

The introduction of a short-term protection system which dispenses with red tape is one of the foundations of this novel form of design protection. In order properly to understand the role played by the unregistered design within the Community system under the Regulation, however, it is necessary to bear in mind that the intention is not to create an alternative system parallel to that of the registered design. Instead, the goal is a system of subsidiary protection which helps to overcome the inevitable shortcomings of the Community regis-tered design.

The main reasons for including this form of protection in the Regulation on Community designs may be summarised as follows:

— Providing industry with prompt design protection, permitting it to market test the prod-ucts into which the design is incorporated immediately and at no extra cost, while still maintaining the option of more lasting, comprehensive protection by registration. Protection as an unregistered Community design thus complements the 12-month period of grace provided by the Regulation.

— Providing protection for designs which are not intended to remain on the market for very long and for which registration was never contemplated.

At this stage it is not possible to assess in economic terms the real impact that the unregis-tered design right may have. On the one hand, by the very nature of this right it is not possible to say how many designs will make use of the protection it provides. On the other, this right will provide protection for many designs for which registration has been ruled out from the outset and which, for this reason are not currently protected by any design right.

Saez is of course right to suggest that it will be difficult to measure the value of a CUDR, since by its very nature it subsists in qualifying designs automatically and will only come into play if a proprietor believes his unregistered design has been infringed. It is certainly possible that the existence of the CUDR may act as a deterrent against copying. But it also has to be recognized that such a right might have a chilling effect on the emergence of new designs. However, once again, this effect would be difficult to substantiate.

11.3.2 THE UK UNREGISTERED DESIGN RIGHT (UDR)

Unlike the situation with registered designs, where UK law has been amended to reflect the Community Design Directive and Regulation, the same is not true for the unregistered design right (UDR) in the UK. The UDR was introduced by the CDPA and the courts look to domestic rather than Community legislation when interpreting the relevant law. Nonetheless, the UK UDR does share a number of features with the Community UDR. These include the fact that for both the UK UDR and the Community UDR, protection arises automatically without the need for registration. Also, a UDR does not confer a 'monopoly right'. Rather, as with copyright, a UDR—like the Community UDR—will be infringed only by copying. There are also major differences between a Community UDR and a UK UDR. Unlike a Community UDR which is protected for three years, protection for a UK UDR will run for 15 years from when it was first recorded or, if the design is marketed within the first five years, ten years from when it was first made available for sale (s. 216 of the CDPA). Secondly, and this is perhaps the key difference between the UK UDR and the Community UDR, the former has a 'must match' exclusion from protection, while the latter does not. As we shall see, the inclusion of a must match exception for the UK UDR is explained by the impetus which gave rise to the creation of the right in the first place—which was a need to rationalize the relationship between copyright protection and protection for functional designs.[36]

11.3.2.1 The statutory definitions

Section 213 of the CDPA[37] defines a UDR:

> Design right is a property right which subsists in accordance with this Part in an original design [s. 213(1)]
>
> [and]
>
> In this Part 'design' means the design of any aspect of the shape or configuration (whether internal or external) of the whole or part of an article [s. 213(2)].

There are also exceptions to protection which are identified in s. 213(3). Thus:

> Design Right does not subsist in—
>
> (a) a method or principle of construction,
>
> (b) features of shape or configuration of an article which—
>
>   (i) enable the article to be connected to, or placed in, around or against, another article so that either article may perform its function, or
>
>   (ii) are dependant upon the appearance of another article of which the article is intended by the designer to form an integral part, or
>
> (c) surface decoration.

Originality is defined in s. 213(4):

> A design is not 'original' for the purposes of this Part if it is commonplace in the design field in question at the time of its creation.

---

[36] This is discussed at 11.4.1 below.   [37] At Part III.

11.3.2.2 Unregistered design right: authorship, ownership, and duration

The designer is the person who creates the design (s. 214 (1) of the CDPA). In a similar approach to copyright, a UDR will not subsist unless or until the design has been recorded in a design document, or an article has been made to that design (s. 213(6)). A design document can range from a drawing to data stored in a computer. The designer need not be the same person who records the design.[38]

The designer is the first owner of a UDR. However, if the design was produced in the course of employment or for commission, ownership will reside with the employer or the commissioner (s. 215)). Furthermore the design must be a 'qualifying' design. Whether or not it is qualifying will depend upon a number of factors including the nationality or residence of the designer.[39] A UDR lasts for a total of 15 years from when it is first recorded; or for ten years from when it was made available for sale, if it was marketed within the first five years (s. 216). During the final five years of the ten-year period of protection (in other words from the date of first marketing) licences of right may be granted through an application to the UK IPO (s. 237).

11.3.2.3 The relationship between the 'design' and the 'article'

According to its definition, a design may include the shape or configuration of individual parts of an article or of the whole of the article. The relationship between a design and an article is explained by *Russell-Clarke & Howe on Industrial Designs*—an explanation which was quoted with approval by Jacob LJ in *Fulton v Totes Isotoner*[40]:

> unlike a registered design, which protects the design applied to a whole article, unregistered design right subsists in the shape or configuration of part of an article, or indeed in 'any aspect' of the shape or configuration of the whole or part of the article. Thus, a single article (or a design document recording the design of an article) will normally embody not a single design right, but a large bundle of different design rights subsisting in the whole and every part and every aspect of the shape and configuration of the article, provided that the part or aspect concerned is original and is not otherwise excluded from enjoying design right by one of the exceptions considered in the following paragraphs. This concept of a bundle of design rights becomes significant when the question of infringement is considered, because, except in the case of slavish copying of the whole article, the design right proprietor will seek to match a design right which he can contend subsists in a part or aspect of the design of his article with the features of the alleged infringing article which he contends have been copied.

Or as was put by Laddie J in *Ocular Sciences Ltd v Aspect Vision Care Ltd*:[41]

> If the right is said to reside in the design of a teapot, this can mean that it resides in the design of the whole pot, or in a part such as the spout, the handle or the lid, or, indeed, part of the lid.

---

[38] For a computer-generated design, the designer is the individual who makes the arrangements necessary for the creation of the design (s. 214(2)).

[39] CDPA, ss. 217–20.   [40] *Fulton Co Ltd v Totes Isotoner (UK) Ltd* [2004] RPC 16, at para. 20.

[41] *Ocular Sciences Ltd v Aspect Vision Care Ltd (No 2)* [1997] RPC 289. See also Jacob LJ in *Dyson Ltd v Qualtex (UK) Ltd* [2006] RPC 31.

The idea that a single article might embody a number of UDRs was criticized by counsel in *Fulton v Totes* in that, until a defendant receives a letter before action, it is not possible for him to know in which parts of an article a UDR is said to subsist.

Fulton Co Ltd v Totes Isotoner (UK) Ltd [2004] RPC 16

Fulton designed and manufactured umbrellas and cases. Fulton alleged that the defendant had infringed its UDR (and its RDs) which resided in its cases for folding umbrellas, described as types A to E. The claimants also argued that UDRs subsisted in both the entire design of these cases and also in aspects of their design, most notably a 'cuff', which had a 'cut out' design and was integral to all the umbrella cases. In the High Court, the RDs of types A and B (that is the designs of the entire cases) were held by Laddie J to be valid and infringed. The High Court also held that while the UDRs of types C to E of the cases had not been infringed by the defendant's case designs as a whole, the UDR of the 'cut out' design in cases A to E was infringed. The defendant appealed on the basis that it was incorrect to hold that there was a separate UDR in the cut out design. They argued that in designing the cases, the claimant had never envisaged the cut out actually constituted a separate design. And, indeed, they argued that the 'cut out' design was a 'chimera' not least because it was not clear that it had an identifiable designer. Certainly, in an earlier case, *Farmers Build v Carier Bulk Materials Handling*, the Court of Appeal had held that, to be protected, an unregistered design must have originated from an author in that it was his original creation.[42] Jacob LJ did not find merit in this argument.

Jacob LJ:

34. Fifthly, there is Mr Thorley's argument based upon qualification for design right. Who, he asked forensically, is the creator of the design chimera? And is he 'a qualifying individual' within the meaning of s. 217? I think this all misses the point. Indeed I think the whole notion of a 'design chimera' is somewhat misleading. The Act is not concerned with any chimera. It is merely telling you that 'design' covers not just any aspect of the design of the whole article but also any aspect of the design of part of it. There is no chimera. The designer of the whole thing necessarily also designs all its parts. For the same reason I do not fully go along with Laddie J's suggestion that what the proprietor can do is to 'trim his design right claim'. It is not really a question of 'trimming'—it is just identifying the part of his overall design which he claims has been taken exactly or substantially. And although Laddie J was right in saying that the defendant will not know in what the *alleged* (my emphasis) monopoly resides until the letter before action or the claim form, that does not mean the defendant does not know where he stands before then. The man who copies a part of an article, exactly or substantially, will know what he has taken. It is true that it will be for the designer to formulate his claim properly in any proceedings, but the subsistence of his rights does not depend on how he frames his claim.

Recently, in *Dyson v Qualtex*,[43] the Court of Appeal revisited the question of how to obviate the disadvantage to an alleged infringer who will not know where in an article the claimant's UDRs might subsist until accused of infringing them.

---

[42] *Farmers Build v Carier Bulk Materials Handling Ltd* [1999] RPC 461.
[43] *Dyson Ltd v Qualtex (UK) Ltd* [2006] RPC 31.

Jacob LJ:

122. First it will be important that the claimant should identify with precision each and every 'design' he relies upon. Just claiming design rights in parts, for instance, will not do— each aspect said to constitute a 'design' should be spelt out. This will focus minds from the outset. Well-advised claimants will confine themselves to their best case 'designs'. In principle the defendant should then plead to each, raising challenges to originality or alleging commonplace and saying, if it is so contended, that one of the exclusions of must-match or must-fit apply. There may be cases where, either by agreement at that early stage, or by application to court pre-defence, the issues can be limited to sample issues even at that stage.

123. In those cases where there is no earlier identification of such issues, there should be a case management conference at which such issues are identified. They should be such that they will in principle determine the whole case. Such an approach will obviate the evidence covering unnecessary detail, and very likely much else. It will considerably shorten the trial…

124. Following identification of the sample issues the parties should produce a sort of Scott schedule, identifying each design relied upon, and each of the defences raised to that design. In that way it should be possible for all to keep the case within proportionate bounds.

We may see a parallel here with the issue of prior art in relation to registered designs. You may recall that in *Green Lane v PMS*, the defendant argued that it was difficult to gauge whether a design was infringing if what constituted the relevant prior art was broadly defined.[44] You may also recall that Jacob LJ took a typically robust approach to the issue. In *Fulton*, the defendant raised a similar concern, although in this case it was the difficulty of identifying the allegedly infringing UDR, especially if the design might be the whole or only a part of an object. Once again, Jacob LJ gave the argument short shrift. Nor, it may be suggested, does the subsequent judgment in *Dyson* give a defendant a great deal of comfort. The judgment does not address the issue of how to identify an unregistered design at the time of copying, even though the claimant will need to be precise in identifying his design once he believes it to have been infringed.

11.3.2.4 Unregistered design right and originality

A UDR will not subsist unless the design is original. A design is not original if it is 'commonplace in the design field in question at the time of its creation' (s. 213(4) of the CDPA). *C & H Engineering v Klucznik & Sons*[45] was an early case to consider the meaning of 'original'. In this case, which involved the design of a 'pig fender', Aldous J defined originality at p. 421:

The word 'original' in section 213(1) is not defined, but I believe that it should be given the same meaning as the word 'original' in section 1(1)(a) of the Act,[46] namely not copied but the independent work of the designer. It should be contrasted with novelty which is the requirement for registration of a registered design: see section 265(4) of the Act.

---

[44] See 11.2.3.4 above.   [45] *C & H Engineering v F Klucznik & Sons Ltd* [1992] FSR 421.
[46] The CDPA.

Section 213(4) says that the design is not original if it is commonplace in the design field in question. The word 'commonplace' is not defined, but this subsection appears to introduce a consideration akin to novelty. For the design to be original it must be the work of the creator and that work must result in a design which is not commonplace in the relevant field. The designer is the creator and no design right will subsist until the design has been recorded in a document or in an article. Thus the creator is not necessarily the person who records the design but usually will be.

11.3.2.5 The definition of commonplace

The questions of what is meant by 'original' and 'commonplace' and how these concepts are related were looked at again but this time by the Court of Appeal in *Farmers Build v Carier Bulk Materials Handling*.

Farmers Build Ltd v Carier Bulk Materials Handling Ltd [2000] ECDR 42

The claimants owned the IP rights in a slurry separator, a machine which separates manure into solid and liquid parts for use as a fertilizer. The machine, the 'Target' had been designed in 1991 by the defendants, for the claimants. The Target's design was an improvement on the designs of two previous separators. In 1992, the defendants began manufacturing and marketing their own separator, the 'Rotoscreen'. The Rotoscreen was different to the Target in appearance, but the two separators were almost identical inside. The claimants sued the defendants for infringement of their UDRs which they claimed subsisted in various component parts of the Target individually and in combination and in the overall design of the machine. The defendants replied that the design of the Target was not original and, indeed, was commonplace in the design field in question at the time of its creation. In the High Court, the judge held, *inter alia*, that design right subsisted in the Target as a whole and in a number of its component parts and that these had been infringed. The defendants appealed. Among their counter-arguments was the claim that a hopper (a chamber within the slurry) had long existed as a part of agricultural machinery in general and that its design variants were limited. The defendants also maintained that the Target as a whole was commonplace, since its improved performance was simply due to the combining of parts of the two earlier machines. In reply the claimants maintained that the design of the Target was original, being significantly better than the earlier machines. They also argued that an original machine could be made out of 'trite' ingredients and, in any event, the relevant field for judging originality was not that of agricultural instruments generally but rather the infinitely more restricted field of slurry separators. In his judgment, Mummery LJ considered the meaning of the terms 'original', 'novel', and 'commonplace' (s. 213(4) of the CDPA). According to Mummery LJ, it was significant that the UDR had been created to replace copyright protection for functional designs.

Mummery LJ, at 64–6:

The overall purpose of the provision was not to impose a requirement of novelty in order to secure the limited protection enjoyed by unregistered designs, but to guard against situations in which even short term protection for functional designs would create practical difficulties.

Substantial similarity of design might well give rise to a suspicion and an allegation of copying in cases where substantial similarity was often not the result of copying but an inevitable consequence of the functional nature of the design. All that is meant by 'original designs' in the context of section 213 is (a) that the design for which protection is claimed must have been originated by the designer in the sense that it is not simply a copy by him of a previous design made by someone else (like a photocopy) and (b) that where it has not been slavishly copied from another design, it must in some respects be different from other designs, so that it can be fairly and reasonably described as not commonplace. The context is important. Design right, like copyright, is informally acquired and affords weaker protection, as only copying is actionable. Copying may be inferred from proof of access to the protected work, coupled with substantial similarity. This may lead to unfounded infringement claims in the case of functional works, which are usually bound to be substantially similar to one another. On the other hand, a registered design, like a patent, is a stronger right, is harder to obtain, but it is vulnerable to challenge on the ground that it is lacking in novelty and it would not be novel if it was well known and used by others. To introduce a requirement of novelty into unregistered designs would effectively remove from the limited new right a large measure of the protection that the right must have been intended to confer on designers to protect their work from plagiarism. It cannot have been the purpose of section 213(4) to take away by one provision all the protection given by another.

Commonplace—conclusion

In the light of the language, context and purpose of section 213(4), what is the proper approach of the court faced with the issue that the design of an article is not original because it is alleged to be 'commonplace'?

(1) It should compare the design of the article in which design right is claimed with the design of other articles in the same field, including the alleged infringing article, as at the time of its creation.

(2) The court must be satisfied that the design for which protection is claimed has not simply been copied (e.g. like a photocopy) from the design of an earlier article. It must not forget that, in the field of designs of functional articles, one design may be very similar to, or even identical with, another design and yet not be a copy: it may be an original and independent shape and configuration coincidentally the same or similar. If, however, the court is satisfied that it has been slavishly copied from an earlier design, it is not an 'original' design in the 'copyright sense' and the 'commonplace' issue does not arise.

(3) If the court is satisfied that the design has not been copied from an earlier design, then it is 'original' in the 'copyright sense'. The court then has to decide whether it is 'commonplace'. For that purpose it is necessary to ascertain how similar that design is to the design of similar articles in the same field of design made by persons other than the parties or persons unconnected with the parties.

(4) This comparative exercise must be conducted objectively and in the light of the evidence, including evidence from experts in the relevant field pointing out the similarities and the differences, and explaining the significance of them. In the end, however, it is for the court and not for the witnesses, expert or otherwise, to decide whether the design is commonplace. That judgment must be one of fact and degree according to the evidence in each particular case. No amount of guidance given in this or in any other judgment can provide the court with the answer to the particular case. The closer the similarity of the various designs to each other, the more likely it is that the designs are commonplace, especially if there is no causal link, such as copying, which accounts

for the resemblance of the compared designs. If a number of designers working independently of one another in the same field produce very similar designs by coincidence the most likely explanation of the similarities is that there is only one way of designing that article. In those circumstances the design in question can fairly and reasonably be described as 'commonplace'. It would be a good reason for withholding the exclusive right to prevent the copying in the case of a design that, whether it has been copied or not, it is bound to be substantially similar to other designs in the same field.

(5) If, however, there are aspects of the plaintiff's design of the article which are not to be found in any other design in the field in question, and those aspects are found in the defendant's design, the court would be entitled to conclude that the design in question was not 'commonplace' and that there was good reason for treating it as protected from misappropriation during the limited period laid down in the 1988 Act. That would be so, even though the design in question would not begin to satisfy any requirement of novelty in the registered designs legislation.

[**Mummery LJ** then went on to apply these concepts to the facts of the case. At p. 70, he rejected the contention of the defendant that:]

there was no design right in the whole of the TARGET machine. It is true that design right may not exist in the whole of the TARGET machine in the sense of the shape or configuration of *each and every part* of the whole machine. For example, in these proceedings Farmers Build have only claimed design right in parts and in combinations of parts which make up a small part of the entire machine. But that does not prevent there being a design right in the overall shape and configuration of the combination of parts which make up the whole. A whole assembly of parts, even if all the individual parts are commonplace, is not itself commonplace if the result is to produce a slurry separator of an overall design different from the overall design of other slurry separators. The position is that there were detailed design changes in a number of the parts. The combination of those parts, even with other parts in which Farmers Build do not claim any design right, produced a whole which could properly be regarded as an original design of an article which was not commonplace.

Clearly Mummery LJ took the view that functional designs should have less protection than both copyright works and registered designs which at that time had to have eye-appeal. In this view, the danger was that too-strong protection for functional designs might inflate their value, especially if the designs were for spare parts, for example for cars. If the UDRs were 'overprotected', there was a danger that the original manufacturers could command monopoly rents on the supply of spare parts. Nonetheless, it still seems fair to ask whether, in terms of their relative social value, it is obvious that a UDR should have less protection than a registered design.

Another issue also arises in relation to originality and commonplace. What if a design is unique to a particular product, but the product itself becomes widely known and used? It is clear that such a result would not render the design commonplace. As was put by Jacob LJ in *Dyson v Qualtex*:

108. …There can be no question of a very good design which becomes very well known losing design right by reason of becoming well known. *Ex hypothesi* at the time of its creation such a design would not be commonplace on any view. What happens thereafter could not affect the subsistence of the right. What would be 'lost' would be a protection by way of any further design right in an aspect of a variant of the original design which was only different from the original in a commonplace manner.

In an earlier case, *Lambretta Clothing v Teddy Smith*,[47] Jacob LJ made the same point about the design of the iPod. Surely he is right to hold that really attractive, and therefore popular, designs should not suffer for their popularity by being deemed commonplace?

11.3.2.6 The definition of the 'design field in question'

In *Farmers Build*, Mummery LJ agreed with counsel for the claimant that:

> the relevant design field in question was that of slurry separators and that evidence relating to agricultural machinery generally or engineering fields other than slurry separators was irrelevant to the question of what was commonplace within the meaning of section 213(4).

Farmers Build thus gave a relatively narrow interpretation of the 'design field in question' when compared to the broader interpretation of the related concept of prior art in the law of both patents and registered designs.[48] The definition of the 'design field in question' was further elaborated in the case of *Scholes Windows v Magnet*. In this case, the Court of Appeal endorsed a more generous definition of the 'design field in question' but still one that falls short of the definition of prior art for design registration.

Scholes Windows Ltd v Magnet [2002] FSR 10

The claimants manufactured UPVC casement windows in which they argued design right subsisted. The designs were adapted from earlier Victorian window designs, in particular by including a 'horn' in their designs, and the windows were sold under the name 'Nostalgia'. The defendants manufactured windows which embodied these same features. At first instance, the judge agreed that the claimant's design was original (in the sense of not copied) but it was commonplace in the design field in question if that was understood to include all windows, whether plastic or wooden, and also to include surviving Victorian windows. The claimants appealed on the basis that the judge had defined the design field in question too broadly and should have confined it to casement windows including UPVC casement windows. In particular, the claimants challenged the inclusion of Victorian windows, which were of course a century old, arguing that only designs 'in use' should be included and not 'historical' designs. In his judgment Mummery LJ approved Underhill J's definition of the design field in question.

Mummery LJ:

The design field point

31. The expression 'design field in question' is not legally defined in the 1988 Act. It must accordingly be understood in its ordinary and natural meaning, bearing in mind that the purpose of the provision in subsection (4) is to withhold legal protection from commonplace designs. The expression is obviously intended to set sensible limits to the inquiry whether a design is 'commonplace'. The making of comparisons with other designs is the essence

---

[47] *Lambretta Clothing Co Ltd v Teddy Smith (UK) Ltd* [2005] RPC 6.
[48] See 11.2.3.4 above.

of that inquiry. The outer bounds of the limits on comparisons with pre-existing designs are matters of fact and degree to be assessed by the tribunal of fact in taking account of all the relevant circumstances of the particular case.

32. Magnet contended that the design field in question is window design simpliciter, regardless of the materials used or the nature and purpose of the design. The initial position of Scholes at the trial was that the design field in question was PVC window design and that the designer is presented with different design problems according to the materials used— wood, steel, aluminium or PVC. By the close of the trial, however, it was the judge's understanding that it had been conceded that the design field extended to mock sash windows in any material, including timber as well as PVC.

33. The deputy judge accordingly posed the relevant question as follows:

was the design of the Nostalgia horn commonplace in the field of window design in July 1994?

34. He held that it was. His conclusion was based on a comparison with the design of window horns in the built environment, using as comparators horns on sash windows made of wood.

35. It was submitted on behalf of Scholes that this approach involved a misdirection or an error of principle. It ignored the fact that there are two primary considerations in ascertaining what is meant by the term 'the design field in question'. They are: (i) the nature and purpose of the article; and (ii) the material structure of the article.

. . .

37. In my judgment, there was no misdirection or error of principle in the approach of the deputy judge to the 'design field in question'. It is necessary to examine the submissions of Scholes by reference to the statutory language and by relating it to a correct appreciation of the concept of a design. The definition of 'design' in subsection (2) covers any aspect of the shape or configuration of the whole or part of an article. The definition of design does not incorporate, either expressly or by implication, the nature or purpose of the article itself or the material structure of the article.

38. The submissions advanced on behalf of Scholes confuse the design of the aspect of the shape or configuration of the window horn with (a) the nature of the particular article to which the design is applied and (b) the idea of using horns as a decorative feature on top opening windows with frames made of U-PVC. The property right is in the design of any aspect of the shape or configuration of the horn. It is not a right in the article itself. It is not a right in the idea of a particular construction, use or application of the article itself. Thus the fact that part of the article is made out of U-PVC does not make that material a part of the design of an aspect of the shape or configuration of the Nostalgia horn. The fact that the purpose of the article is to decorate a mock sash casement window, rather than the genuine article, does not make that a design of an aspect of the shape or configuration of the Nostalgia horn. As those matters are not part of the design they are irrelevant to the delineation of the 'design field in question'.

[**Mummery LJ** also approved **Underhill J's** approach of including 'historical designs' in the design field in question.]

The time of creation point

44. In my judgment, there is no misdirection or error of principle in the approach of the deputy judge to 'old' designs of horns. The statutory question does not depend on when other designs in the design field with which comparison is to be made were first produced or on when they were in use or whether they have fallen into disuse and become 'historical

designs'. The relevant question is 'Is the design in which the right is claimed commonplace?' That question is to be determined by having regard to the 'design field in question at the time of creation'. There is nothing in these provisions which expressly or impliedly excludes from consideration existing designs, which were first produced at an earlier time than the design in suit, if they can be fairly and reasonably regarded as included in the design field in question at the time of the creation of the design in suit. The fact that they could still be seen by designers and interested members of the public as a feature of windows on many houses in July 1994 is a relevant factor in deciding whether or not they were in the design field at the date of creation and were commonplace within the meaning of subsection.

By suggesting that there is no time limit for designs to be included in the design field in question, Mummery LJ could be said to be approaching the patent/registered design definition of prior art. It is possible to question whether such a definition is too broad. UDRs are given only short-lived protection. It may be no bad thing that such protection should be available to those who imaginatively adopt 'historical designs'. After all, UDRs only protect against direct copying. In other words, if a third party were inspired to adopt the same design from the same historical source this would not be infringing—he could do so with impunity.

11.3.3 EXCLUSIONS TO UNREGISTERED DESIGN RIGHT PROTECTION

There are four exclusions to UDR protection set out in s. 213(3) of the CDPA. Design right does not subsist in:

1. a method or principle of construction (s. 213(3)(a))
2. the 'must fit' exclusion (s. 213(3)(b)(i))
3. the 'must match' exclusion (s. 213(3)(b)(ii))
4. surface decoration (s. 213(3)(c)).

11.3.3.1 Exception 1: a method or principle of construction

This exclusion was considered by the Court of Appeal in *Landor & Hawa v Azure Designs Ltd*.[49]

Landor & Hawa International Ltd v Azure Designs Ltd [2007] FSR 9

The dispute was over the design of a type of suitcase which expanded if one panel was unzipped. Suitcases embodying this design, known as the 'Expander', had been sold by the claimants since 2002. The claimants discovered that the defendants were marketing a suitcase made in China which they argued infringed their UK UDR and their Community UDR in the Expander design. The High Court found for the claimant and the defendants appealed arguing, *inter alia*, that the Expander design constituted a

---

[49] Other earlier cases which considered this exception are *Fulton v Grant Barnett & Co Ltd* [2001] RPC 257 and *Baby Dan AS v Brevi Srl* [1999] FSR 377.

method or principle of construction. In his judgment, Neuberger LJ (as he then was) considered this argument both as a matter of principle and fact.

Neuberger LJ:

9. This contention has given rise to two main arguments, one of principle and one essentially of fact. The argument of principle concerns the meaning and effect of s. 213(3)(a) of CDPA 1998 ('s. 213(3)(a)'). The judge held that the provision should be relatively narrowly construed, and that it did not apply merely because a design serves a functional purpose: it would not apply unless it can be shown that that purpose cannot be achieved by any other means. Although this formulation was challenged by Azure at least in its initial skeleton argument, it was not by any means the main focus of the well-sustained submissions of Mr Alastair Wilson QC (who appears with Mr Michael Edenborough) on behalf of Azure.

10. In my opinion, the judge's interpretation of s. 213(3)(a) is correct. First, the section does not, as a matter of ordinary language, preclude a design [from] being protected merely because it has a functional purpose. The language is perhaps a little opaque, but the words 'method or principle' are important, and serve, in my view, to emphasise that mere functionality is quite insufficient to exclude a design from protection. Tempting though it may be to seek to redefine or expand on those words, I think it would normally be unhelpful in practice, and arguably wrong in principle, to do so, save to explain in a particular case why they do or do not apply.

11. Secondly, as Mr Daniel Alexander QC, who appears with Mr David Wilkinson for Landor, says, it would be wrong in principle to conclude that a design is incapable of protection merely because it serves a functional purpose. There is no simply no justification in policy or principle for such a conclusion. It would mean that a design which had only aesthetic features would be favoured over one with both aesthetic and functional features, a curious consequence of legislation one of whose main functions is to reward imagination and inventiveness.

12. As Park J rightly observed in *A Fulton Co Ltd v Grant Barnett & Co Ltd* [2001] RPC 16 at [70]:

> The fact that a special method or principle of construction may have to be used in order to create an article with a particular shape or configuration does not mean that there is no design right in the shape or configuration. The law of design right will not prevent competitors using that method or principle of construction to create competing designs...as long as the competing designs do not have the same shape or configuration as the design right owner's design has.

13. Thirdly, the textbooks support this approach to interpretation. The judge quoted a passage from *Russell-Clarke on Copyright in Industrial Designs* (7th edn), at para. 3–80, which analyses the effect of s. 213(3)(a) in these terms:

> A method or principle of construction is a process or operation by which a shape is produced, as opposed to the shape itself. To say that a shape is to be denied registration because it amounts to a method or principle of construction is meaningless. The real meaning is this: that no design shall be construed so widely as to give to its proprietor a monopoly in a method or principle of construction. What he gets is a monopoly for one particular individual and specific appearance. If it is possible to get several different appearances, which all embody the general features which he claims, then those features are too general and amount to a method or principle of construction. In other words, any conception which is so general as to allow several different specific appearances as being made within it, it is too broad and will be invalid.

14. The judge agreed with that analysis, and so do I. It is a view which is supported by the editors of *Copinger and Skone-James on The Law of Copyright* (15th edn). At para. 13–55, they state that the purpose of the section is 'to ensure that designers cannot create an

effective monopoly over articles made in a particular way'. Jacob J appears to have taken the same view in paras. 14 and 15 in *Isaac Oren v Red Box Toy Factory Ltd* [1999] FSR 785. Having decided that 'it is possible to make a device visually very different from Mr Oren's designs but which works the same way', he went on to hold that '[i]t follows that there is no principle monopolised here—only a visual embodiment of a device constructed in accordance with a principle'.

Essentially, as held by Neuberger LJ, a design would only fall within this exception if it constituted the *only* way of achieving a particular function. Applying this approach to the facts in *Landor & Hawa v Azure*, Neuberger LJ held that, since it was possible to achieve the same design advantage with designs which were different from the Expander design, the claimants did indeed have a valid UDR in the Expander design. The attention of the court then turned to the issue of whether the claimant had a valid Community UDR in the Expander design, albeit one that had expired. Interestingly, both parties had sought to argue that the ECJ's interpretation of Article 3(1)(e)(ii) of the Trade Mark Directive, which excludes the registration for functional designs as trade marks,[50] was a model for interpreting Article 8(1) of the Design Regulation.

Neuberger LJ:

35. In my judgment, the judge was right to hold that decisions on the Trademark Directive cannot be safely relied on in a case involving the Designs Directive. Article 3.1(e)(ii) of the Trademark Directive refers to 'signs that consist exclusively of . . . the shape of goods which is necessary to obtain a technical result'. It will be seen at once that the wording is not by any means identical to that of art. 8.1.

36. Indeed, as pointed out by the judge, the opinion of Advocate General Colomer in the *Phillips* case (reported at [2001] RPC 38)[51] contains in [34], an instructive comparison between the two provisions: 'The wording used in the Designs Directive for expressing that ground for refusal does not entirely coincide with that used in the Trade Marks Directive. That discrepancy is not capricious. Whereas the former refuses to recognise external features "which are solely dictated by its technical function", the latter excludes from its protection "signs which consist exclusively of the shape of goods which is necessary to obtain a technical result". In other words, the level of "functionality" must be greater in order to be able to assess the ground for refusal in the context of designs; the feature concerned must not only be necessary but essential in order to achieve a particular technical result: form follows function. This means that a functional design may, none the less, be eligible for protection if it can be shown that the same technical function could be achieved by another different form.'

37. Nothing in the reasoning of the ECJ in its subsequent decision, which agreed with the ultimate conclusions reached by the Advocate-General, in that case calls into question those observations. Further, as Mr Alexander says, there are real differences between the nature and purpose of trademark protection and design right. Trademarks are badges of origin, and the purpose of (and therefore the regime for) protecting the owner is different from the purpose for protecting designs, which have nothing to do with demonstrating origin.

Neuberger LJ concluded that the High Court was correct in finding that the Expander design was neither at such a level of generality nor was it the only design which would

---

[50] For functional designs and trade marks, see 5.3.4.1.
[51] *Koninklijke Philips Electronics NV v Remington Consumer Products Ltd* [2001] RPC 38.

achieve the same technical result. As a result, it was a valid UDR. The judgment in *Landor & Hawa v Azure* once again underlines the fact that a UK UDR and a CUDR, unlike a patent, are not intended to be monopoly rights. It is also interesting to compare the protection afforded to the functional aspects of UK UDRs and CUDRs and to a registered trade mark. As we have seen, a trade mark will not be registered if it achieves a technical result, even if the same technical result may be achieved by other means.[52] In *Landor & Hawa v Azure*, the Court of Appeal took the reverse position, finding that a UDR will be valid as long as there are other designs which would achieve the same technical result. One reason for this divergence is almost certainly that a trade mark may be renewed indefinitely, whereas protection for UDRs lasts only a relatively short period of time. There is therefore a danger, which was pointed out by the High Court in *Philips v Remington*,[53] that trade mark registration might allow indefinite protection for a functional design once its protection as a UDR has lapsed. This result would certainly appear to contradict the spirit of the UDR, whose short period of protection is generally understood to be a reflection of the fact that it will protect functional designs. But are the UK courts correct to think that the public interest is best served by ensuring that such designs are relatively quickly made available for other traders to use? Or might one take the opposing view that it is precisely because these designs are functional that they have value?

11.3.3.2 The 'must fit' exclusion

The 'must fit' and 'must match' exclusions have been described as the 'interface' exclusions. The 'must fit' exclusion is defined in s. 213(3)(b) of the CDPA as excluding from design right protection:

> features of shape or configuration in an article which enable the article to be connected to, or placed in, around or against, another article so that either article may perform its function.

Again like the 'must match' exclusion, this exclusion was directly aimed at undermining the monopolies which some manufacturers, such as automobile makers, were able to establish in the field of spare parts. While in the 1980s the prevailing mood was to free up the market for spare parts as much as possible, the recent decision by the Court of Appeal in *Dyson v Qualtex* suggests that this aim will not be pursued at all costs.

Dyson Ltd v Qualtex (UK) Ltd [2006] RPC 31

The claimant, Dyson, manufactured vacuum cleaners. The defendant manufactured spare parts (or 'pattern parts' as they are known), including for the Dyson vacuum cleaner. Dyson claimed that the defendant's spare parts copied parts of the vacuum cleaner which were protected by UDRs. Among the arguments raised by the defendant was that these parts were covered by both the 'must fit' and 'must match' exclusions, and further that the designs not covered by this exception were commonplace. The claimant succeeded in the High Court and as we shall see also in the Court of Appeal. In the High Court, the claimant alleged that 14 of its UDRs had been infringed. In the Court of Appeal, the number of UDRs at issue had been reduced to six, and the Court focused on

---

[52] *Koninklijke Philips Electronics NV v Remington Consumer Products* [2003] RPC 2.
[53] *Philips Electronics v Remington Consumer Products* [1998] RPC 283.

particular features of the UDRs which both parties claimed illustrated its arguments. In considering *Dyson v Qualtex* we will focus, in the first instance, on the Court of Appeal's finding with regards to the 'must fit' exception. The arguments relating to the 'must match' exclusion will be considered below. But first it is useful to look at the general points made by Jacob LJ at the start of this judgment. Jacob LJ began by summarizing the conflicting concerns of the claimant and the defendant.

Jacob LJ:

2. The original designers and manufacturers of consumer items, (often known as original equipment manufacturers ('OEMs'), not surprisingly sometimes desire to control the trade in spare parts for their machines. The independent manufacturers or dealers generally wish to imitate the original manufacturer's part as closely as they can—they will sell better than a part which works as well but looks different. The reasons why they will sell better are complicated. One factor though is self-evident: a consumer is likely to have more confidence in a part which looks exactly the same as the broken one. One can readily imagine the consumer going into a shop with his broken part and saying 'can I have another of these?' If the part looks different there will be sales resistance.

[**Jacob LJ** then went on to look at the history of the UDR, primarily to ascertain whether the UDR was intended clearly to protect either the interests of the OEMs or the contrasting interests of the makers of pattern parts, as the claimant and defendant claimed respectively. He concluded that it was difficult to approach the 'must fit' exception with, as he put it, 'a clear purpose in mind', and noted:]

14. …neither the language used nor the context of the legislation give any clear idea what was intended. Time and time again one struggles but fails to ascertain a precise meaning, a meaning which men of business can reasonably use to guide their conduct. The amount of textbook writing and conjecture as to the meaning is a testament to its obscurity. We just have to do the best we can, trying to arrive at 'an interpretation which the reasonable reader would give to the statute read against its background' per Lord Hoffmann in *R (Wilkinson) v IRC* [2005] UKHL 30; [2006] 1 All ER 529 at [18]. The absence of any clear policy, as to where the line of compromise was intended to run, means that brightline rules cannot be deduced.

It is certainly interesting that Jacob LJ asserts that the interpretation of the law relating to the UDR and its exceptions should be left to the 'reasonable reader'. It is submitted that this fails to take account of the fact that a 'reasonable reader' in an age which lauded free markets might have a different view of the UDR, than when, for the sake of argument, such a clear ideological conviction no longer obtains. In other words, we might question whether what seems 'reasonable' in one context will continue to appear reasonable once that context changes. Nonetheless, having made these general points, Jacob LJ turned to considering the breadth of what he dubbed the 'so called must fit' exception.

Jacob LJ:

27. I say this sub-section is 'so-called' because that is the term by which it is known. Mr Arnold[54] rightly said that its language did not actually say 'must-fit' (just as the next sub-section, so-called 'must-match' does not actually say that). I agree that one must go by the actual language and not by the epithet or even the notion behind the epithet…

---

54 Counsel for the defendant.

[**Jacob LJ** also reproduced with approval the interpretation of the 'must fit' exception given by **Mann J** in the High Court.]

28. In his general consideration of the law, the judge used the decisions of Laddie J in *Ultraframe UK Ltd v Fielding* [2003] RPC 23 at [73] and *Ocular Sciences Ltd v Aspect Vision Care Ltd* [1997] RPC 289 at p. 424 to extract three propositions [34]:

(i) It does not matter if there are two ways of achieving the necessary fit or connection between the subject article (the first one referred to in the sub-section) and the article to which it fits or with which it interfaces. If the design chosen by the design right owner is a way of achieving that fit or interface, then it does not attract design right no matter how many alternative ways of achieving the same 'fit' might be available.

(ii) For the purposes of the sub-section, the article with which the subject article is interfacing can be part of the human body. This might have had relevance in the present case because some of the parts (triggers and a catch) are designed to interface with the human finger or thumb. However, Mr Arnold disclaimed reliance on this—he did not rely on the finger or thumb as a must fit item in the context of any article in the present case.

(iii) The sub-section operates to exclude design right even if the relevant part of the design performs some function other than the function described in the sub-section—for example, it is decorative, or has an additional function not falling within the provision. This additional function does not exclude the operation of the provision.

Counsel for the defendant posed a number of questions to the court. The first was whether the 'must fit' exception excludes parts that do not touch each other. It was argued that because the High Court had excluded parts that do not touch from the 'must fit' exception, Mann J had been wrong in law. Indeed, the defence then gave concrete examples of aspects of the design of the cleaner which, while not touching, would be crucial to the overall functioning of other parts of the machine. Jacob LJ approved the approach taken in the High Court:

38. Any working part must of course be so located so as not to interfere with the working of other parts—that does mean that any spacing between parts is a feature which enables function.

Secondly, the defendants argued that Mann J had been wrong to construe the 'must fit' exception as not being satisfied by a feature which merely makes an article function more effectively. Once again the defence gave examples taken from the vacuum cleaner design which it argued should have been included in the 'must fit' exceptions. In this case, it identified the 'bleed holes' in the upper knob of the cleaner whose function was to prevent excessive vacuum if the whole end of the tube was blocked. Mann J had held these were not aspects of the design which 'must fit' since they were safety features not features which had to be touching other aspects of the design (in this case the handle) to function. However, the defence went on to ague that the bleed holes did function to enable the handle to function better as they enabled the handle to be placed against another article (e.g. a stair carpet) in order to vacuum effectively. On this point, Jacob LJ agreed with defence:

43. I think Mr Arnold is right here. The judge focussed on the effect on a third object (the motor) but overlooked the function of the wand handle itself. I think the bleed holes fall within the exception: they enable the handle to be placed against a flat surface so as to perform its function as a vacuum cleaner handle.

Thirdly, the defence alleged that the exclusion should apply even where the articles are designed sequentially, for example, in this case, to allow the vacuum cleaner to function. The defence gave the illustration of the curve of a handle which formed a 'wall' underneath to 'fit' the release catch. The claimant argued that in order to function the handle did not need to be curved. Jacob LJ accepted this contention which meant that the handle 'wall' design did not fall with the UDR exclusions:

> 45. I do not think that it is necessarily relevant whether the underlying wall had to be that shape. The fact is that it is that shape. However, I think that there is a different reason why the catch is must fit and the handle is not. Looking at the matter realistically I think that while it can be said that the catch is the shape it is to enable the catch to perform its function, I do not think that the evidence allows me to say that the *handle* is the way it is to enable the catch to perform its function. Accordingly this aspect of the handle is not must fit. The design history of the parts showed that the handle was designed first and the catch was designed later. The handle had its first expression in a design drawing in February 1992 and the catch found its first expression in a drawing in April 1992. While those are formal drawings which do not necessary reflect the precise form of the order of designs, in my view they are likely to do so, thus making the catch must fit but this part of the body of the handle not must fit.

Finally, the defence argued that Mann J had failed to 'adopt a practical approach to the "must fit" exclusion'. In other words, it was wrong that the UDR would be understood to cover even 'minor matters' of design such as those adopted by the defendant. Jacob LJ disagreed:

> 48. The trouble with that is that is not what the section says. On the contrary it has gone out of its way to create UDR in any aspect of any part of an article. That is indeed an odd way of going about things but it is what it says. There is no limitation to aspects which have no practical significance. As I have said, the lower limit is where one cannot really say there is an 'aspect' at all.

In *Dyson v Qualtex*, the Court of Appeal looked at a number of issues raised by the 'must fit' exception. On the whole, it sided with the OEMs rather than the spare-parts manufacturers. There is certainly no doubt that by recognizing unregistered design right protection in minor matters of design or parts which are needed for the machine to function but are not touching, the Court of Appeal has made it more difficult for makers of pattern parts to avoid treading on the UDRs of the OEMs. Interestingly, this is not the result we might have expected were we to think back to the original impetus for introducing the UDR: that was to free up the market in spare parts. We shall see, moreover, as we now come to look at the 'must match' exception, that the Court of Appeal is set upon giving OEMs a generous settlement in that area too.

11.3.3.3 The 'must match' exception

Along with the 'must fit' exception, the 'must match' exception is known as an 'interface exception'. The 'must match' exception speaks directly to the concerns which led to the creation of a UDR—that is, the perceived need to free up the competition between OEMs and the suppliers of pattern parts—for the ultimate benefit of the consumer. As we have seen, the 'must match' exception is not a part of the Community UDR nor do all other EU countries recognize this exception.

The 'must match' exception is set out at s. 213(3)(b)(ii). It states that design right does not subsist in features of the shape or configuration of an article:

> which are dependent upon the appearance of another article of which the article is intended by the design to form an integral part.

An obvious example of a design which would fall under this exclusion would be a replacement of a body panel for a car. What would not be covered would be wing mirrors whose designs can be changed without compromising the integrity of the car's design over all.[55] In the case of *Ultraframe UK Ltd v Clayton (No 2)*,[56] which concerned components for a conservatory roof, it was held by Laddie J, in the High Court, that the fact that certain features of the components helped to achieve a 'consistent theme' for the conservatory as a whole, did not mean that they 'were dependent upon the appearance of another article'. Indeed the fact that the components had 'little visual impact' meant that they were less likely to be dependent upon similar features on other articles. The 'must match' exception was considered in some detail by the Court of Appeal in *Dyson v Qualtex*. In his judgment, Jacob LJ endorsed the approach taken by Mann J in the High Court in interpreting the 'must match' exception, quoting Mann J's judgment extensively. Thus, as Mann J put it:

> 53. 'Accordingly, when considering "must match", I shall apply section 213(3)(b)(ii) by considering whether there is dependency of the kind, or to the extent, which would make the overall article in question (article 2) radically different in appearance if article 1 were not the shape it is. That is not to substitute, or superimpose, a test different from that appearing in the statute. It is to explain how the statute works. This sort of consideration is inevitably one of fact and degree, and of impression. It will doubtless be less than straightforward to apply in relation to various parts or aspects, but that is the nature of the beast. The saleability of the item can be used as a sort of guide to assessment or a cross-check in any particular case.'
>
> **[Jacob LJ** continued:]
>
> 54. Mr Arnold [for the defendants] attacked the 'radically different in appearance' test. His principal submission was that any feature of the whole article which was externally visible was 'dependent' on the appearance of the whole article. The concept of 'dependency' is concerned with the relationship between the appearance of the part and the appearance of the whole. He pointed to the fact that a Dyson machine was 'a design icon'—the integrity of the design of the whole article, depended on the external shape of each article forming part of that integral design. His submission went so far (as it had to in respect of at least some features) as to cover aspects of parts which, viewed from the point of view of the machine as a whole, were minor (such as the outward portions of the lower hose cuff). The submission also extended to accessories.

Like Jacob LJ held in relation to the 'must fit' exception, Mann J held that the interpretation of the 'must match' exception was not notably aided by a consideration of the legislative context in which it was framed. Nor were there any binding authorities. He suggested that the only case which offered some assistance was *Ford Motor Co Ltd's Design Application*, which concerned an attempt to register design parts for motor vehicles. From that case came the approach that 'one must ask whether there is a feature of shape of the part which is dependent on the appearance of the whole machine'. He went on to approve the argument

---

[55] See *Ford Motor Co. Ltd's Design Application* [1993] RPC 399.   [56] [2003] RPC 23.

put forward by counsel for the claimant as being largely consistent with the approach taken in *Ford Motor Co.* Essentially this was a 'radically different in appearance' test. Under this test, if substitutions could be made without radically affecting the appearance or identity of the vehicle then the design would fall outside the exclusion. According to Mann J this was 'another way of looking at dependency. If there is, as a practical matter, design freedom for the part, then there is no dependency.' He continued:

> 64. I accept this latter proposition. One has to approach the provision bearing in mind that Parliament did not intend to exclude all spare parts, or even all externally visible portions of spare parts, yet such was the substance of Mr Arnold's submission. 'Dependency' must be viewed practically. In some cases the answer is obvious—the paradigm example being body parts of cars. In others it may be necessary to examine the position more carefully. But unless the spare parts dealer can show that as a practical matter there is a real need to copy a feature of shape or configuration because of some design consideration of the whole article, he is not within the exclusion. It is not enough to assert that the public 'prefers' an exact copy for it will always do so for the reason I gave in [2] above. The more there is design freedom the less is there room for the exclusion. In the end it is a question of degree—the sort of thing where a judge is called upon to make a value judgment. Unless wrong in principle, his evaluation will not be interfered with on appeal.

For example, Mann J considered and rejected the defence argument that changing the design of the handle would undercut the design of the whole, in much the same way as if a car door panel did not match the car design as a whole. According to Mann J:

> 67. To my mind and eye the must-match provision does not apply to this part. Changing one or more or all of the design features of this handle would not necessarily make the whole machine (including the handle) look "radically different" within the guidance that appears from the cases. I do not think that this part is like the door panels in *Ford*. It is of course true that one *could* make the handle so different that the overall appearance of the machine would be radically different, but that is not necessarily the case ... So far as one can make a cross-check by inquiring what sort of a market there is or would be for a non-replica handle, while it is true that there was no evidence of any such market, there is no evidence that there would not be one. In the absence of solid and reasoned evidence (which in the circumstances would have had to have been opinion evidence) I do not think it is possible to say that no-one would buy a non-replica handle, and I would be a little sceptical of assertions to that effect. It is conceivable they might, if there were a price differential which made it worthwhile. As I have said, I do not think the handle is like a car body part. Cars have a certain public display element to them. They are seen in public, and customer choice is likely to be affected, at least in part, by the design and the customer's willingness to be associated with the design by driving in it or having it parked in his driveway. The same cannot be said of vacuum cleaners. A Dyson vacuum cleaner may well be purchased at least in part because of its design, but I would require some evidence were it to be said that the design preference of the customer for this piece of household utilitarianism would lead the customer to require it to keep its looks after a repair in the same way as a car is required to keep its looks. This is, I accept, somewhat speculative in the absence of solid evidence, but it is plausible and I certainly cannot find that that is wrong and Qualtex has not discharged its burden of showing it is right.

As was noted above, Jacob LJ, in his judgment, approved the 'radically different' test set out by Mann J. He also accepted the claimant's contention that if there were design freedom for the part, it was not dependent on the overall appearance of the product and therefore it fell outside the exclusion. When Jacob LJ applied this interpretation of the exclusion to the facts of this case, notably the handle, he once again endorsed Mann J's finding. Like Mann J, Jacob LJ asked:

> 68. …how much does the design of the wand handle really matter to the overall design? Would it matter, for instance, if there were a ribless handle? The more I looked the less I thought it mattered. From the point of view of a consumer, I doubt, as did the judge, whether he/she would care whether his/her Dyson cleaner, if repaired with a ribless wand handle, looked a bit different from as new. There was no evidence of any such concern by a consumer. Such inference as one could get from the sales of the DC02 wand handles suggest otherwise (see above). This is just the sort of area where the judge has made a value judgment, here as to dependency, upon which a court of appeal should not interfere unless there is an error of principle.

Jacob LJ noted, 'That is really all that need be said as regards the "must match" exclusion.' Nor did he find any of the defendant's other examples of designs which fell within the exclusion convincing. In sum, he approved the High Court's decision that none of the pattern spares produced by the defendant were covered by the 'must match' exclusion. As we noted earlier in the *Dyson v Qualtex* decision, the Court of Appeal here threw its weight behind the OEMs to a greater extent than might have been envisaged when the UDR was first introduced. Perhaps it is simply reflecting common sense. We might ourselves ask the question as to whether a consumer, who is willing to pay a premium price for a Dyson vacuum cleaner in part because of its novel and attractive appearance, will really be content with a spare part that alters the overall appearance of the machine, even in minor aspects?

11.3.3.4 The surface decoration exclusion (s. 213(3)(c))

Design right will not subsist in surface decoration. Before the Design Directive, it was this exclusion which set unregistered design right apart from a registered design. Now there is no longer such a clear division. As we have seen, with the implementation of the Design Directive, it is no longer necessary for a design to possess eye-appeal to be registered. This exclusion was considered in two recent Court of Appeal decisions, *Lambretta v Teddy Smith* and *Dyson v Qualtex*.

Lambretta Clothing Co Ltd v Teddy Smith (UK) Ltd [2005] RPC 6

The claimant designed and produced fashion clothes. In particular, it produced a track-top in a striking range of colours. The top itself was of a standard design. The design had been recorded in two documents which included, *inter alia*, instructions as to the colours to be used and also the fabric. It was successfully marketed in 2002. That same year, the defendants, Teddy Smith and Next plc, marketed track tops in a similar fabric and colour combinations. The claimant alleged that the defendants' tops infringed its design right and also its copyright in the design documents. The defendants argued, relying on s. 51 of the CDPA,[57] that the design documentation did not record an artistic work, and therefore it was not an infringement of copyright to copy the design of the tops. The High Court found that no design right subsisted in the tops, as the originality of the design lay in its surface decoration or colourways.[58] The claimant appealed arguing, *inter alia*, that the colourways were not surface decoration because they were dyed through the garment. The Court of Appeal, Mance LJ dissenting, approved the approach taken by the High Court.

Jacob LJ:

30. …It is true that the parts of the garment are dyed right through, but any realistic and practical construction of the words 'surface decoration' must cover both the case where a surface is covered with a thin layer and where the decoration, like that in Brighton rock, runs throughout the article. To hold otherwise would mean that whether or not UDR could subsist in two different articles, having exactly the same outward appearance, depended on how deep the colours went. Parliament cannot have intended anything so capricious.

31. I should also deal with an incidental argument arising from the exclusion of surface decoration. It is suggested that 'shape or configuration' would otherwise include surface decoration—that the exclusion is a pointer to the width of those words without it. It is not an argument which could really help Lambretta—for it necessarily concedes that the colourways are surface decoration. But in any event I do not think it right. Surface decoration can be more than essentially flat—you can decorate a thing with three dimensional decoration—for instance the 'cock beading' considered by Jonathan Parker J in *Mark Wilkinson Furniture Ltd v Woodcraft Designs (Radcliffe) Ltd* [1998] F.S.R. 63. The point of the exclusion is obviously to avoid problems of this sort—three-dimensional embellishments of an article are intended to be excluded. They may have an independent artistic copyright—that depends on the rules for artistic copyright and s. 51.

32. Accordingly I think the judge was right to conclude that UDR cannot subsist in the design of the Lambretta top.

The Court of Appeal also considered the surface decoration exclusion in *Dyson v Qualtex*. In the High Court, the judge had found that the pattern parts produced by the defendant did not fall within the surface decoration exclusion. On appeal, the defence argued that Mann J had wrongly construed surface decoration as limited to decorating a surface that was already there. Instead the defence argued that, 'the exclusion necessarily encompassed, indeed only encompassed, three-dimensional surface decoration'. The defence also argued that a UDR 'is only created in an aspect of the shape or configuration of the whole or part of an article. So it only subsists in 3D shapes. So the exclusion must be dealing with 3D shapes only.' Jacob LJ did not accept this argument for two reasons:

74. First, you can have 2D features of shape or configuration, e.g. one produced by cutting one out from a piece of paper. Secondly, exclusion (a) (to a method or principle of construction) is an exclusion which is probably not necessary—a method or principle of construction can hardly be a mere feature of shape or configuration. Mr Arnold's implied premise that the exclusion does not extend beyond the definition of the right is false—an exclusion can go further than is necessary and clearly does so in the case of (a).

---

[57] See 11.4 below.
[58] *Lambretta Clothing Co Ltd v Teddy Smith (UK) Ltd* [2003] RPC 41.

> 75. Next it seems clear that the exclusion will cover what are essentially 2D designs on a 3D article. A willow-pattern plate, or a painted vase, have what can fairly be described as 2D decoration on a 3D article—and the painting is merely 'surface' even though it has a 3D nature. And you can also clearly have a surface decoration of just a flat part of a 3D article.

Applying these principles, Jacob LJ held that Mann J had not limited surface decoration to a surface which was already there (in other words, 2D decoration) as the defence claimed. Instead, he found on the facts that Mann J was correct to conclude that the ribbing above the handle of the vacuum cleaner would not be viewed by a consumer as surface decoration and thus it fell outside the exclusion. Jacob LJ also considered a further question raised by the defence as to whether the exception would apply if the surface features had a function. He held that surface features which had a significant function and were not merely surface decoration would not fall within the exclusion.[59]

11.3.3.5 The balance between OEMs and pattern parts manufacturers revisited

As we have seen, in *Dyson v Qualtex*, Jacob LJ found that the context in which the UDR was created by Parliament did not give an obvious guide to how the law relating to exclusions from protection should be interpreted. Instead, he left it up to the 'reasonable man' to interpret the issue of how broadly the boundaries to UDR protection should be drawn. We have submitted that because the relative importance one gives to a free market in pattern parts will be ideologically determined, it is not a suitable question to address to the reasonable man. In their article, Smith and Burke argue that in *Dyson v Qualtex*, Jacob LJ came down heavily on the side of original equipment manufacturers ('OEMs').

J. Smith and K. Burke, 'Design rights: Original manufacturers maintain control of unregistered design rights' (2006) 28(6) EIPR N110–11

The overall lesson here is that the exceptions to UDR created by the Act do not give a carte blanche for pattern spares. Those who wish to make spares during the period of design right must design their own spares and cannot just copy every detail of the OEM's part.

The decision is to be welcomed by designers as it brings much needed clarification to the thorny issue of whether spare parts, in particular, replica or so-called 'pattern parts' (replicas) should be afforded UDR protection in the United Kingdom.

Jacob LJ delivered the leading judgment, narrowly construing the statutory exceptions to UDR infringement (as set out in s. 213 of the Copyright, Designs and Patents Act 1988 'CDPA'), finding that Qualtex was not entitled to rely on them.

[**Burke** and **Smith** welcome the fact that **Jacob LJ** was broadly supportive of the OEM's rather than the spare-part manufacturers. They conclude, at N111:]

Comment: The main message to take from *Dyson v Qualtex* is that UDR cannot be ignored. 'Pattern part' spare parts manufacturers must design their own spares and cannot simply copy the OEMs' parts. The statutory exceptions to UDR will be construed narrowly and so

---

[59] For a High Court case which considered this issue, see *Hi Tech Autoparts Ltd v Towergate Two Ltd (No 2)* [2002] FSR 16.

third-party manufacturers must be extremely careful, as in the words of Jacob LJ:

> To be on the safe side they will have to make them different as far as is possible—for trying to navigate by the chart provided by this crude statute is a risky business.

Should the balance of interest in interpreting the UDR exclusions fall on the side of the OEMs? After all, it might be argued that, since the UDR was introduced, the design of even functional articles has become much more visually sophisticated. As a result, it might be difficult for spare-part manufacturers to offer competition to OEMs if they cannot market spare parts which fit visually with the original articles.

11.3.3.6 Primary infringement (s. 226)

The owner of a UDR has the exclusive right to reproduce the design for commercial purposes (s. 226(1)). The design owner also has the right to reproduce the design by making articles to that design exactly or substantially to the design (s. 226(2)). Design right is infringed by a person who without the licence of the owner does or authorizes another to do anything which is the exclusive right of the owner. Infringement may consist of direct or indirect copying. The issue of what constitutes infringing use was considered by the High Court in *C & H Engineering v Klucznik* which, as we have seen, involved the design of a pig fender.

C & H Engineering v Klucznik & Sons Ltd [1992] FSR 421

The claimants manufactured agricultural equipment including 'lamb creep fenders' and pig fenders. A pig fender is a pen outside a pigpen low enough for a sow, but not her piglets, to step over. The claimant sued the defendants for infringing the design of its fenders and the defendants counter-sued, alleging that the claimant had infringed their design in a novel pig fender which, based on suggestions from a customer, had a bar along the top in order to prevent the sow from injuring her teats when she stepped over the fender. The claimant subsequently supplied pig fenders to the same customer, although their design had tubes around the top edge of the fender and was designed to be stackable. A key question for Aldous J to determine was what constitutes an infringing design in the field of UDRs, and in particular whether it was the same test as applied to copyright infringement. He held that it was not.

Aldous J, at p. 428:

Section 226 appears to require the owner of a design right to establish that copying has taken place before infringement can be proved; that is similar to copyright. However the test of infringement is different. Under section 16 copyright will be infringed if the work, or a substantial part of the work, is copied. Under section 226 there will only be infringement if the design is copied so as to produce articles exactly or substantially to the design. Thus the test for infringement requires the alleged infringing article or articles be compared with the document or article embodying the design. Thereafter the court must decide whether copying took place and, if so, whether the alleged infringing article is made exactly to the design or substantially to that design. Whether or not the alleged infringing article is made substantially to the plaintiff's design must be an objective test to be decided through the eyes of the person to whom the design is directed. Pig fenders are purchased by pig farmers and I have no doubt that they purchase them taking into account price and design. In the present case, the plaintiff's alleged infringing pig fenders do not have exactly the same design as shown in the defendant's design document. Thus it is necessary to compare the plaintiff's pig fenders with the defendant's design drawing and, looking at the differences and similarities through the eyes of a person such as a pig farmer, decide whether the design of the plaintiff's pig fender is substantially the same as the design shown in the drawing.

[On the facts, **Aldous J** held that the claimant's pig fender did not infringe the design document for the defendant's pig fender. He continued at pp. 428–9:]

By 1990 pig fenders were commonplace and had been made in metal and wood. In essence Mr Butler wanted a commonplace pig fender with a metal roll bar on the top. He had seen fenders with a wooden roll bar. He gave Mr Jackson the basic measurements needed and the only part of the pig fender shown in the drawing which was not commonplace was the 2 inch tube on the top. Thus the design is the incorporation of the 2 inch pipe into a commonplace pig fender.

. . .

I have no doubt that the idea of having a tube as the roll bar came from the defendant's pig fender and therefore copying did take place. However, the plaintiff's pig fenders are not made exactly to the defendant's design, and I do not believe that they are made substantially to that design. Metal pig fenders must have an overall similarity due to the function they have to perform, but a person interested in their design would appreciate that the plaintiff's pig fender was of a different design to that of the defendant, although they have in common a tube as the roll bar. In that respect the two designs are substantially the same, but taken as a whole the two designs are not substantially the same. An interested man would be struck by the design features which enable the plaintiff's pig fender to be stacked. Those features not only attract the eye, but would also be seen by an interested person as being functionally significant. They contrast with the overall design features of the defendant's pig fender. The interested man looking at the plaintiff's and the defendant's pig fenders would consider the two designs to be different, but with a similar design feature—namely, the bar around the top. Therefore the defendant's claim for infringement of a design right fails.

The approach to judging infringement taken by Aldous J in *C & H Engineering* was approved by the Court of Appeal in *L Woolley Jewellers Ltd v A & A Jewellery Ltd*.[60]

In *C & H Engineering*, Aldous J defined the test for infringement as whether the allegedly infringing design had been copied from the earlier UDR and if so whether it was 'not substantially different'. On this basis the claimant's design was not infringing. Interestingly, the case was decided relatively soon after the introduction of the UDR. The approach to UDR infringement taken by Aldous J ensures that it will be more difficult to infringe a UDR than to infringe a copyright work, where the test is whether a substantial part has been taken. If, as we suggested earlier, the introduction of the UDR had been designed to free up the market for spare parts and functional designs generally, this outcome is not surprising. On the other hand, given the relatively favourable treatment which has been given to OEMs in more recent cases involving UDRs, it is worth speculating whether, if the question of what constitutes infringement were to be decided today, would the outcome be quite so sympathetic to the copier of the earlier design?

---

[60] [2003] FSR 15.

11.3.3.7 Secondary infringement (ss. 227–8)

Design right is infringed by a person who, without the licence of the design right owner, imports or has in his possession for commercial purposes or sells an article which he knows or has reason to believe is infringing.

11.3.3.8 Remedies (ss. 277–82)

Like copyright infringement, it is possible to obtain additional damages if an infringement is particularly flagrant. Otherwise the usual remedies are available including damages or an account of profits, delivery up, or destruction of the articles.[61] However, it is worth noting that where a defendant at the time of infringement did not know and had no reason to believe that the design right subsisted in the design to which the action relates, the claimant will not be entitled to damages, although the other remedies identified here will be available. Surely it is correct that innocent infringers should be excluded from having to pay damages given that, as has been noted, it is often difficult to indentify a UDR until it become the subject of a court action?

FURTHER READING

I. Connor, 'The design trigger: Case comment on *Procter & Gamble v Reckitt Benckiser*' (2007) 29(7) EIPR 293–7.

A. Gerdau de Borja, 'Exceptions to design rights: The potential impact of Article 26(2) TRIPS' [2008] EIPR 500.

P. Groves, 'Design protection for spare parts' (2005) 26(12) Bus LR 291–3.

R. Plaistowe and M. Heritage, 'Europe versus the world: Does unregistered Community design right only protect designs first made available in Europe?' (2007) 29(5) EIPR 187–90.

G. Scanlan and S. Gale, 'Industrial design and the Design Directive: Continuing and future problems in design rights?' [2005] JBL 91.

D. Wilkinson, 'Case closed: Functional designs protected by design right' [2007] EIPR 118.

11.4 THE RELATIONSHIP BETWEEN COPYRIGHT AND INDUSTRIAL DESIGNS

The changes in industrial design protection ushered in by the CDPA did not entirely result in the uncoupling of copyright protection from the protection given to industrial designs. According to s. 51(1) of the CDPA, it is not an infringement of any copyright in a design document or a model recording or embodying a design for anything other than an artistic work or a typeface to make an article to that design or to copy an article made to that design. In addition, s. 52(1)–(2) holds that if an artistic work is exploited by the copyright owner by making and marketing it on an industrial scale (the Act defines this as making 50

---

[61] See Ch. 13.

or more articles to that design), copyright protection would be reduced to 25 years after it is first marketed. As a result, while full copyright protection would continue to be given to the artistic work which embodied this design (for example, a painting or a statue) it would not be an infringement to copy the industrial articles embodying that design once the 25-year period had expired.

11.4.1 INDUSTRIAL DESIGNS AND COPYRIGHT: SECTION 51 OF THE CDPA

In brief, this section ensures that while the copying of a design document will continue to be a straightforward infringement of copyright, it will not infringe copyright to make an article to the design recorded in the document or to copy an article made to that design. For the purposes of s. 51, 'design' means any aspect of shape or configuration other than surface decoration. However, the making of an object to a design recorded in a design document or the copying of an object embodying that design may well be an infringement of any UDR embodied in the finished articles. Two cases which looked at s. 51 were *BBC Worldwide v Pally Screen Printing*[62] and *Mackie Designs Inc v Behringer.*[63] *BBC Worldwide*, concerned a company which was making tee shirts carrying unauthorized images of the 'Teletubbies', well-known television characters. The company was sued by the BBC for copyright infringement. The High Court held that there was an arguable defence under s. 51 because the images were indirect copies of articles which had been made to original three-dimensional designs, which were not themselves works of artistic craftsmanship. *Mackie Designs* concerned circuit diagrams which the claimant alleged had been copied. It was held by Pumfrey J in the High Court that these diagrams were design documents within the meaning of s. 51(3) and therefore their copying did not constitute copyright infringement. Instead, they fell to be protected as UDRs.

More recently, the Court of Appeal considered the relationship between s. 51 and design right protection in *Lambretta v Teddy Smith*. We have rehearsed the facts of the case when looking at the exceptions to UDR protection, more specifically surface decoration. It is worth noting however that the claimant did not argue that the overall design of its track-top was new. Rather, the claimant argued that the design's originality lay in its colourways which had been recorded in design documents. The claimant alleged that the defendants had not only infringed its UDRs (and as we have seen failed in this claim) but also that the defendants had infringed its artistic copyright in the design documents. The defendants argued, *inter alia*, that s. 51 of the CDPA provided a defence against copyright infringement. In the High Court, Etherton J held that Teddy Smith but not Next had copied the claimant's tracktops, but that design right could not subsist in the design and in any event s. 51 offered a defence to infringement. The claimant appealed arguing, *inter alia*, that Etherton J had wrongly applied s. 51. Jacob LJ held, in a majority judgment, that he had not:

Jacob LJ:

34. Section 51 does not apply if the design document is itself for an artistic work. So if it is for, say a sculpture, the defence does not apply. And in relation to certain kinds of artistic works, Parliament has decided that even if s. 51 does not apply, the term of protection

[62] *BBC Worldwide Ltd v Pally Screen Printing Ltd* [1998] FSR 665.
[63] *Mackie Designs Inc v Behringer Specialised Studio Equipment (UK) Ltd* [2000] ECDR 445.

(normally 70 years from year of author's death) is reduced if there is industrial production of the work. The details of this are to be found in s. 52 and the statutory instrument made thereunder. The provision broadly carries on the regime formerly existing under s. 10 of the Copyright Act 1956 but only for those artistic works for which s. 51 does not provide a total defence. For present purposes the significance is the period of protection. Even for artistic works identified in the statutory instrument which are reproduced industrially the period is much greater than that for UDR—25 years from first marketing in the case of works within s. 52. For other artistic works the period is 70 years from the year of death of the author.

35. Mr Wyand [for the claimant] submits that if Lambretta do not have UDR, then they must have rights in artistic copyright—that Parliament cannot have intended to leave a 'hole' between UDR and ordinary copyright rights. He relies on what was said by Jonathan Parker J in *Mark Wilkinson*:

> s. 51 of the 1988 Act removes copyright protection from designs which are protected by design right. The twin concepts of copyright and design right are thus rendered mutually exclusive.

36. He suggests that Jonathan Parker J was thereby saying you get UDR or ordinary copyright—there are no gaps. Now it is generally the case that that is so—but I do not think Jonathan Parker J was intending to say that it was always and necessarily so. Whether or not there is a 'gap' or 'hole' on the facts of a particular case must in the end depend solely upon the language used to create the rights concerned.

[According to **Jacob LJ**, to accept the contention that there could never be a 'gap' between copyright protection and protection as a UDR would be to accept the principle that anything worth copying was worth protecting, an axiom he said which 'goes too far' and, in any event, is not unequivocally supported by the case law. He continued:]

38. Accordingly I approach the question of whether s. 51 provides a defence with no pre-conceived bias one way or the other and without regard to the fact that I have concluded that there is no UDR in the colourways as such. All depends on the meaning of s. 51 in context. And as the judge rightly observed s. 51 is obviously not simply saying 'anything protected by UDR is not protected by artistic copyright', as it has the other way round in s. 236.

39. Now, apart from the colourways, there is no doubt that Mr Harmer's drawing is a 'design document'. Does the fact that 'surface decoration' is excluded from the definition of 'design' for the purpose of s. 51 make any difference? I think not. For these colourways are not just colours in the abstract: they are colours applied to shapes. Neither physically nor conceptually can they exist apart from the shapes of the parts of the article. It is not as though this surface decoration could subsist on other substrates in the same way as, for instance, a picture or logo could. If artistic copyright were to be enforced here, it would be enforced in respect of Mr Harmer's whole design drawing. But that is not allowed by s. 51. I think the judge put it elegantly when he said ([74]):

> Such an approach...would appear to give rise...to an impossible task. It would require the Court to consider the existence and infringement of copyright in respect of the juxtaposition of colourways divorced from the shape or configuration of the article in question, even though the shape and configuration of Lambretta's garment provide the borders of the colourways and the means by which the colourways are juxtaposed.

40. Accordingly I think Etherton J was right to hold that s. 51 barred the claim here. I am reinforced in this view by the bizarre oddity that would otherwise arise—that Lambretta would have a much longer period of protection (25 years from first marketing) than if they have a proper UDR, for instance by actually designing a new garment rather than just (for I here ignore the stripes and logos) colouring an old one.

Flashing Badge Co Ltd. v Groves also looked at the meaning of s. 51.

Flashing Badge Co Ltd v Groves [2007] FSR 36

The applicant applied for summary judgement alleging copyright infringement by the defendant of its designs for a number of badges and of the backing cards which gave instructions as to how safely to attach the 'flashing badges', which carried messages such as 'happy birthday', to garments. The defendant had offered for sale copies of these badges. There was no dispute among the parties that the designs for these badges were artistic works in which copyright subsisted. However, the defendants argued that s. 51 of the CDPA offered them a defence. The claimants disputed this argument by claiming that what was at issue here was not the design of the articles themselves (the copying of which the claimant conceded would fall within the s. 51 defence), but rather of the artistic work which was applied to the surface of the badges. In its turn, the defendant argued that the drawings embodying the decoration of the badges also ensured that the decoration was shaped to fit the badges and hence was a design document for the badge itself and so fell within the meaning of s. 51. Rimer J preferred the claimant's argument. He followed the judgment in *Lambretta v Teddy Smith*.

Rimer J:

22. In my judgment the facts of the present case fall squarely on that side of the line on which are to be found Jacob LJ's 'picture or logo'. It is true that the design of the shape of the badge follows the outline of the design for the artistic work on the face of each badge. But the latter design is in the nature of a graphic design which is in no sense something which (unlike the *Lambretta* colourways) can only exist as part of the shape of the badge. It is a design which can be applied to any other substrate and which, if so applied, would enjoy copyright protection for the infringement of which s. 51 would afford no defence.

23. I hold, therefore, that s. 51 affords the defendant no defence to this claim.

Finally, ss. 51–2 were recently considered in *Lucasfilm Ltd v Ainsworth*.[64] In this case, the director of the Star Wars movies alleged, *inter alia*, copyright infringement in the helmets and armour worn by the Imperial storm troopers in the Star Wars films. Ainsworth had played a part in their design and manufacture and was now offering replicas for sale to the public. The High Court held that the helmets and the armour were neither sculptures nor works of artistic craftsmanship. It followed that the original drawings on which they were based were not artistic works but design documents. As a result, Ainsworth had a defence under s. 51. Furthermore, because of the time that had elapsed since the original design was made, there was also a defence available under s. 52. The judgment in *Lambretta v Teddy Smith* and, indeed, in *Lucasfilm* suggest that ss. 51–2 do provide a substantial defence to copyright infringement in the field of industrial designs. As a result, it is possible to maintain that the provisions relating to industrial designs in the CDPA, most notably ss. 51–2 have gone some way to addressing the anomaly which saw functional designs 'over protected' under previous copyright regimes. Given that it was for this very reason that the

---

[64] [2008] ECDR 17.

UDR was created, we might wonder why it took roughly 20 years for the courts to confirm that this was indeed the case.

11.5 CONCLUSION

In the present decade, a number of significant cases have reached the Court of Appeal which have raised questions concerning the interpretation of the legal rules protecting industrial designs. Within the Court of Appeal, Jacob LJ has given many of these judgments. So it is interesting to return to 1987 and to the eve of the introduction of the modern legal regime relating to industrial designs, to see how Sir Robin Jacob then a QC saw the law developing.

R. Jacob, 'Reform of the UK copyright law: Do the necessary' [1987] EIPR 123

My father tells of a fellow officer at the War Office. He had three trays marked 'in', 'out' and 'too difficult'. Such a technique is less than ideal. But it helped win the war. And it embodies a valuable pragmatic rule: don't let the complicated jobs hold up the easy jobs which need to be done now.

[**Sir Robin** was expressing his concern that the government of the day might not introduce what became the 1988 Copyright Act. In particular, he saw a pressing need to eliminate the 'over representation' of functional designs.]

Fifty Years for Functional Designs

Trying to explain to foreigners or businessmen fortunate enough not to have met UK industrial design law before that you get 15 years' protection for designs which have eye appeal but 50 years' plus life of author for non-eye-appeal designs is difficult. They do not at first believe that such a daft law can exist. The result of the rule (now firmly established, and equally firmly criticised, in *Leyland*) is very serious. No-one in the UK can safely copy any purely functional article made in this century! Moreover 'copying' includes cases of substantial reproduction, particularly cases where the copy contains improvements made by the defendant. So again business simply goes abroad. Only recently I was selecting which drawings from the 1930s a plaintiff should sue on. The defendant will be less than prudent if he defends, although the design is pre-war.

The solution is again simple. Amend the appalling section 10 of the Copyright Act so that it is a defence to any action for infringement of copyright that three-dimensional articles substantially of the design (whether registrable or not) complained of were first marketed more than 15 years ago. I say 'substantially' so as to prevent fresh claims based on slighly modified drawings of essentially the same design. This amendment must be retrospective or it will take another 50 years or more before it has any useful effect!

Now it is true that the argument rages as to whether there should be an unregistered design right lasting 10 years. But whichever way the argument is resolved, the existence of the argument does not justify the retention for a moment of the present period of protection for functional articles. As it stands the law is a serious hindrance to manufacture and trade.

Both of my suggested amendments could be incorporated in a short and uncontroversial Act. Why not get on with it?

It is interesting to note, that at the time Sir Robin wrote this article, he was more concerned with the obstacles that spare parts manufacturers faced in plying their trade than with protecting the interests of the original manufacturers. Would it be fair to say that, since 1988, Sir Robin has taken a different, and some would say, more balanced view of the differing interests of the original manufacturers and the spare part producers? And how might we explain this change of view? One possible explanation is that aesthetic considerations have become more important to even functional designs. Another might be that, with globalization, the economic context in which the law operates has changed, with the markets now dominated by large, multinational manufacturers.

FURTHER READING

E. Derclaye, 'Flashing Badge Co Ltd v Groves: A step forward in the clarification of the copyright/design interface' [2008] EIPR 251.

G. Dworkin and R. Taylor, 'By accident or design? The meaning of "design" under section 51 Copyright, Designs and Patents Act 1988' [1990] EIPR 33.

G. Scanlan, 'The future of design right: Putting s. 51 Copyright Designs & Patents Act 1988 in its place' [2005] Stat LR 146.

INTELLECTUAL PROPERTY AND INFORMATION TECHNOLOGIES

12.1 INTRODUCTION

The constant development of new technologies frequently creates challenges for intellectual property law. Broadly speaking, three main issues tend to arise. The first is whether or not the new technology gives rise to subject matter that is protected by existing law (e.g. can computer software be copyrighted or patented?). Secondly, there is the question of whether exploitation of intellectual creations using a new technology gives rise to an infringing activity (e.g. peer-to-peer file-sharing of music or the use of domain names that include a trade mark). Finally, there is the problem of enforcing intellectual property rights where technology enables infringements to occur more easily, in multiple jurisdictions and with reduced risk of detection (e.g. the Internet, which has posed many difficulties when it comes to copyright enforcement).

In addressing these issues intellectual property lawyers and scholars seek to apply existing laws and debate the need for reforms. This, in turn, raises questions of what is the purpose of intellectual property rights, their appropriate scope, and how best to preserve their value. In other words, the process of adapting to new technologies creates a valuable opportunity for reflection about the role of intellectual property law in society.

This chapter considers a range of information technologies—in particular software, databases, computer video games, peer-to-peer file-sharing, and the Internet—and examines the ways in which they have been accommodated by intellectual property law.

12.2 COMPUTER PROGRAMS AND COPYRIGHT PROTECTION

12.2.1 INTRODUCTION

Computer programs (or computer software) are crucial to many activities that we carry out during our daily lives, whether that is operating a computer, listening to an MP3 player, travelling to work, or accessing the Internet. Computer programs are also a staple component of most businesses. The first stored program computers were developed in the 1950s; however, these were machines that filled entire rooms and computer programs were individualized to the particular hardware. It was not until the 1970s and 1980s that the phenomenon of computer programs emerged in full force, largely due to the advent of personal computers. How this technology was to be regulated by intellectual property law, if at all, was a matter of considerable debate. As we shall see below, software producers initially turned to copyright law for protection, but in recent times, patent law has become increasingly important.

To understand the challenges of protecting computer programs by copyright requires at least a rudimentary understanding of the technology. Computer programs may be thought of as instructions for a computer, which bring about a certain result. They are frequently written in source code, i.e. a programming language that bears resemblance to natural language and is human-readable. The source code is then converted into object code or machine code, via a compiler. Object or machine codes tend not to be human-readable, but are the instructions, in binary form, that are executed by the computer. Importantly, computer programs can achieve the same or similar functions or results without having the same or similar source code. Thus, it is readily conceivable that two programs with similar functions and appearances will feature very different underlying source code.

12.2.2 HISTORY

Although the World Intellectual Property Organization in 1977 initially proposed sui generis protection for computer programs, there was considerable pressure at the national level to rely upon copyright law to protect this new type of subject matter. Software manufacturers were keen to obtain quick and effective protection, and copyright law represented an established and 'ready-made' solution, for which the benefit of national treatment and minimum rights under the Berne Convention could be claimed.

Even so, it was controversial whether computer programs could be classed as 'literary works' within Article 2(1) of the Berne Convention. Those against the inclusion of computer programs argued that while source code was superficially analogous to literary works, machine code was not, and the final addressee of the instructions was a computer (which then carried out a function) and not an individual. Further, they argued that computer programs lacked the intellectual creativity (i.e. originality) required for 'literary and artistic works' and the length of protection (50 years *post mortem auctoris*) was excessive for works with such a short life cycle. The counter-arguments to these objections were as follows. First, computer programs were writings and should be protected provided they were intellectual creations. Second, there was sufficient room for creativity in making computer programs. Further, the fact that programs were stored in object code should not preclude their protection since other literary and artistic works could be stored in computer systems as machine-readable code. Finally, while the duration of protection was arguably too long, this could be said for other types of subject matter protected as 'literary and artistic works'.[1]

While debates occurred about whether the Berne Convention extended to computer programs, national laws began to accept copyright law as an appropriate means of protection. Thus, the US amended its Copyright Act 1976 in 1980 (via the Computer Software Copyright Act 1980) to protect computer programs and France, Germany, and the UK

---

[1] M. Ficsor, *The Law of Copyright and the Internet: The 1996 WIPO Treaties, their interpretation and implementation* (Oxford: Oxford University Press, 2002), pp. 472–3.

followed suit in relation to their respective laws in 1985. Gradually, the concerns about copyright protection of computer programs disappeared and the WIPO Copyright Treaty 1996, Article 4 clarified that computer programs are protected as literary works within the meaning of Article 2 of the Berne Convention. The TRIPS Agreement 1996, Article 10(1) is to the same effect. Thus, it is now well accepted at an international level that software is protected by copyright.

12.2.3 EUROPEAN COMMUNITY

The area of computer programs was the first to be harmonized by EC law, in the form of the Software Directive.[2] As the recitals indicate, there was a concern that the considerable investment made in developing software could be 'copied at a fraction of the cost needed to develop them independently',[3] and the sentiment that computer programs were increasingly fundamental to the Community's industrial development.[4] Further, it was envisaged that the differences in legal protection of computer programs in Member States would be detrimental to the smooth functioning of the internal market.[5]

The Software Directive harmonized copyright law protection of computer programs in a range of areas—the subject matter of protection, the originality requirement, authorship and ownership, the exclusive rights available, along with the relevant exceptions, and copy-protection devices. We will look at these areas in turn and, where relevant, the UK implementation via the Copyright (Computer Programs) Regulations 1992.[6]

12.2.3.1 Subject matter

Article 1(1) of the Software Directive makes clear that Member States must protect computer programs as literary works within the meaning of the Berne Convention and the term 'computer program' shall include preparatory design material. As stated in recital 7, this means 'preparatory design work leading to the development of a computer program provided that the nature of the preparatory work is such that a computer program can result from it at the later stage'. Article 1(2) states that protection extends 'to the expression in any form of a computer program', but not to the ideas and principles underlying any element of a computer program. Aside from stipulating that a computer program includes preparatory design material, there was no attempt to provide a harmonized exhaustive definition of what constitutes a computer program.

According to a Report from the European Commission,[7] it seems that all Member States have implemented the requirement that 'computer programs' be protected as literary works. The vast majority of Member States have also included preparatory design materials as a 'computer program'. However, this is not the case in the UK where s. 3(1) of the CDPA treats preparatory design materials as a sub-category of literary work but not as a computer program. The European Commission took the view, however, that this did not make the UK

---

[2] Directive 91/250/EEC on the legal protection of computer programs (OJ L122 17 May 1991) ('Software Directive').
[3] Ibid., recital 2.   [4] Ibid., recital 3.   [5] Ibid., recitals 4 and 5.   [6] SI 1992/3233.
[7] Report from the Commission to the Council, the European Parliament and the Economic and Social Committee on the implementation and effects of Directive 91/250/EEC on the legal protection of computer programs, Brussels 10 Apr. 2000, COM (2000) 199 final ('Report').

non-compliant with the Software Directive.[8] Even so, oddities could arise when it comes to applying the exceptions that are specific to computer programs since these refer only to computer programs and not preparatory design materials.

In the UK, the scope of what constitutes a 'computer program' was partially clarified by the following case.

Navitaire v Easyjet Airline Co [2006] RPC 3

The case concerned software for an airline booking system that was 'ticketless' and used primarily by low-cost airlines. The claimant's software was called OpenRes, while the software used by the first defendant was called eRes and had been produced for them by the second defendant. It was not disputed that the defendants had not had access to the source code of OpenRes and that there was no similarity between the source codes of the two programs. However, the claimant alleged that the user interfaces of both programs were virtually indistinguishable. In particular, the claimant alleged that there had been detailed copying of many of the individual commands and complex commands used in the OpenRes system, copying of the screen displays, and also the overall look and feel of the software. The following extract deals with what Pumfrey J held in respect of the claim that each of the individual commands and complex commands in OpenRes were copyright works in their own right and that the collection of commands was protectable as a compilation.

Pumfrey J:

79. In my judgment, it is not possible to suggest that a copyright subsists in the individual command names as literary works. They do not have the necessary qualities of a literary work. The *Exxon* case wisely skirts the problem of providing a test for a literary work. There was no definition of literary work in the 1956 Act (s. 48 merely stated that it included any written table or complation) and the definition in the 1988 Act is new. When one considers the modern definition (anything written spoken or sung which is not a dramatic or musical work—[75] above) it becomes essential to eschew any attempt at further definition. A single command name, or the word Exxon, is certainly written, and is plainly neither a musical nor a dramatic work. So why is it not a literary work? Laddie, Prescott & Vitoria, *The Modern Law of Copyright and Designs* (3rd edn) (hereinafter 'The Modern Law') suggests that *Exxon* decides that the word is not a work, but warn that it is the composite phrase 'original literary work' which is what matters. There is obviously no bright line test. To attempt definitions ad hoc (such as, does it convey information or emotion?) is ultimately unhelpful. With great respect, this is particularly the case with old *dicta* from a different world, such as that of Davey LJ in *Hollinrake v Truswell* (1894) 3 Ch D 420, albeit that it was relied on by Stephenson LJ in the *Exxon* case:

Now, a literary work is intended to afford either information and instruction, or pleasure, in the form of literary enjoyment. The sleeve chart before us gives no information or instruction. It does not add to the stock of human knowledge or give, and is not designed to give, any instruction by way of description or otherwise; and it certainly is not calculated to afford literary enjoyment or pleasure.

---

[8] Report, p. 9.

80. In the 1988 Act, the phrase 'literary work' embraces tables or compilations, computer programs, preparatory design material for computer programs and databases. To concentrate on the word 'literary' may mislead, but it must not be ignored. In the end, the question is merely whether a written artefact is to be accorded the status of a copyright work having regard to the kind of skill and labour expended, the nature of copyright protection and its underlying policy. It is not sufficient to say that the purpose of the act is to protect original skill and labour: there was plenty of that in *Exxon*. Nor is it of much weight that other forms of protection may be available. I think however, that it is clear that single words in isolation are not to be considered as literary works. The individual command words and letters do not qualify.

81. The second possible class arises from concentrating on the 'complex' commands alone. These are the commands that have a syntax, or, put another way, have one or more arguments that must be expressed in a particular way . . . To describe a command as complex is just to describe its syntax, not its implementation nor its effects. It is possible to divide the commands up in this way. In such a classification, a command with two variants would be a complex command.

. . .

83. In my judgment, the 'command word + syntax' approach to the complex commands in this case is not a valid one. I do not consider that the individual complex commands are distinct copyright works at all. The corresponding work cannot be identified. As pleaded, they are said to be literary works: that is, they must be written—see s. 3(1). This aspect of the case turns, it seems to me, on whether and to what extent they have been recorded. They are recorded, in so far as they can be said to be recorded, in the manner I have described in [36] and [37]. In other words, the source code records them in the sense that it is possible to analyse the code to ascertain that a machine operating according to that code will 'recognise' the command A13JUNLTNAMS . . . as requiring the display of available seats on June 13 between Luton and Amsterdam. But this 'syntax' is recorded without being stated. The reason it is recorded rather than stated is that the reader, in effect, has to turn him or herself into a machine in order to work out what the machine will recognise when operating according to this program.

84. This is a feature of all computer programs in what are often called procedural languages, which are the kind of languages with which this case is primarily concerned. It cannot be too strongly emphasised that a computer program controls a machine, and the result of that control may not appear from the program at all. Accordingly this part of the claim falls at the first hurdle.

85. However, I am acutely conscious that this may not be a satisfactory answer to the problem. It depends too much upon the way in which OpenRes was written.

. . .

87. I think the problem should be approached in the following way. To define a series of commands and their syntax to be recognised by the computer is to define a computer language. It is exactly the same as defining a language such as BASIC or a simple language to control a calculator program. A program consists of a statement or series of statements in that 'language'. Thus, to take the availability command as an example, one would say that the language includes an availability statement that starts with the letter 'A' and one of the permissible forms of which is A[date][City-Pair]. (An example of a statement that will be parsed as an allowable statement to control the computer in accordance with this language is A13JUNLTNAMS). Recitals 13, 15 and 14 of the Software Directive are as follows:

[13] Whereas, for the avoidance of doubt, it has to be made clear that only the expression of a computer program is protected and that ideas and principles which underlie any element of a program, including those which underlie its interfaces, are not protected by copyright under this Directive.

[14] Whereas, in accordance with this principle of copyright, to the extent that logic, algo-rithms and programming languages comprise ideas and principles those ideas and principles are not protected under this Directive.

[15] Whereas, in accordance with the legislation and jurisprudence of the Member States and the international copyright conventions, the expression of those ideas and principles is to be protected by copyright.

88. The Software Directive is a harmonising measure. I must construe any implement-ing provision in accordance with it: if the implementing provision means what it should, the Directive alone need be consulted: if it departs from the Directive, then the latter has been incorrectly transposed into UK law. The recitals quoted are said by Laddie, Prescott & Vitoria, *Modern Law of Copyright and Designs*, (3rd edn), para. 34.19 to make it clear that 'computer languages are not included in the protection afforded to computer programs'. With this con-clusion I agree, although the point cannot be said to be entirely clear and will require to be referred to the Court of Justice. In my view, the principle extends to ad hoc languages of the kind with which I am here concerned, that is, a defined user command interface. It does not matter how the 'language' of the interface is defined. It may be defined formally or it may be defined only by the code that recognises it. Either way, copyright does not subsist in it. This is of course not to suggest that the expression of a program in a particular language is not entitled to copyright. Quite the reverse. What this recital, and the associated dispositive provision of Art. 1(2), appear to be intended to do, is to keep the language free for use, but not the ideas expressed in it:

(2): Protection in accordance with this Directive shall apply to the expression in any form of a com-puter program. Ideas and principles which underlie any element of a computer program, includ-ing those which underlie its interfaces, are not protected by copyright under this Directive.

89. There is here more than an echo of a conceptual distinction between idea and expres-sion, but it is unprofitable to pursue this approach in the light of the express reference to computer languages and interfaces in the recital and to the interfaces in Art. 1(2).

The compilation of commands

. . .

92. In my view, the answer to the compilation point is the same as that as I have given in respect of the individual commands. They are a computer language, not a program, and they should not be entitled to copyright.

On what basis did Pumfrey J hold that the individual commands were not literary works? Does his reasoning make sense, or would it be preferable to utilize a test, such as that stated in *Hollinrake v Truswell*? Pumfrey J classified the complex commands and the compilation of these commands as a computer language. Why are computer languages excluded from copyright protection and does this seem sensible?

The European Commission continues to disfavour inserting a definition of 'computer program' into the Software Directive. In your view, is this something that ought to be pursued?

12.2.3.2 Originality

Article 1(3) of the Software Directive stipulates that '[a] computer program shall be pro-tected if it is original in the sense that it is the author's own intellectual creation'. This was the first time the originality threshold was harmonized and it was thought necessary because of the differences between the UK, France, and Germany. The UK used its traditional, 'labour, skill, and judgment' test, while France applied 'imprint of the author's personality'. Germany applied the strictest standard, as evidenced in *Inkasso-Program*,[9] where the German Federal Supreme Court applied a test of 'significant level of creativity' that required comparison with what could have been achieved by the average programmer.

The requirement of 'author's own intellectual creation' was not expressly incorporated into six Member States' laws (the UK being one) on the basis that it was an implied condition of their laws. The European Commission, however, took issue with the UK because of its lower standard of originality and because the standard subsequently was incorporated for databases in the CDPA. In Germany, Article 69(a) was introduced into the German Copyright Law 1965 in order to implement the originality criterion and reject the 'level of creativity' approach previously taken.

12.2.3.3 Authorship and ownership

In terms of authorship, Article 2(1) of the Software Directive recognizes that a natural person or persons may be the author or co-authors of a computer program. It also states that the author of a computer program shall be 'where the legislation of the Member State permits, the legal person designed as the rightsholder by that legislation'.

For Member States, such as France, that recognize collective works, 'the person considered by the legislation of the Member State to have created the work shall be deemed to be its author'.[10] For example, in France, a collective work is defined in Article L113–2 of the French Intellectual Property Code 1992 as:

> a work created at the initiative of a natural or legal person who edits it, publishes it, and discloses it under his direction and name and in which the personal contributions of the various authors who participated in its production are merged in the overall work for which they were conceived, without it being possible to attribute to each author a separate right in the work as created.

Does this mean that a legal person can be an author under French law? Article L113–1 of the French Intellectual Property Code 1992 suggests so because it provides that authorship shall belong to the person/s under whose name the work has been disclosed and it is conceivable that a legal person can disclose a collective work. On the other hand, such an interpretation is at odds with the natural rights basis of French authors' rights law, which protects 'works of the mind'. In addition, Article L113–5 states that 'a collective work shall be the property, unless proved otherwise, of the natural or legal person under whose name it has been disclosed' and the authors' rights shall vest in this person. This suggests that under French authors' rights law it is only ownership of the work that is held by a legal person and not authorship. As such, it seems strange that Article 2(1) of the Software Directive would permit Member States to designate legal persons as authors, as opposed to rightsholders.

In the UK, authorship of computer programs was considered in *Fylde Microsystems Ltd v Key Radio Systems Ltd*.[11] In this case, the claimant's business was the development and manufacture of telecommunications equipment and related computer software. The defendant's business involved the importation and manufacture of mobile and portable

---

[9] (1986) 17 IIC 681.   [10] Software Directive, Art. 2(1).   [11] [1998] FSR 449.

radios. The claimants and defendants had cooperated in the design of software to be used in a new generation of radios to be sold by the defendant. In an action for infringement of copyright in the software, the defendant argued, *inter alia*, that the software was a work of joint authorship and thus jointly owned by them. It was not disputed that the claimant had written the relevant software. However, the defendant argued that it had made significant contributions to the development of the software. These contributions included testing the software and reporting faults, making suggestions as to what was causing some of the faults, error fixing, providing technical information about the hardware into which the software would be fitted, setting the specification for what the software was supposed to achieve, and setting the parameters and timings within the software. Laddie J held that the defendant's contributions were 'extensive and technically sophisticated' and 'took a lot of time and were very valuable', but they were not contributions to the *writing* of the computer program.[12] As such, the defendant could not be classed as a joint author of the computer program.

When it comes to computer programs created by employees, Article 2(3) states that where this occurs 'in the execution of his duties or following the instructions given by his employer' it is the employer who will have the exclusive economic rights. This default rule may, however, be altered by contract. The UK did not have to do anything to implement this provision, given its approach to employee created works in s. 11(2) of the CDPA (discussed at 2.7). However, in France and Germany, where ownership rests with authors even where they are employees, changes to the respective legislation were necessary. Thus, Article L113–9 of the French Intellectual Property Code 1992 provides that:

> Unless otherwise provided by statutory provision or stipulation, the economic rights in the software and its documentation created by one or more employees in the execution of their duties or following the instructions given by their employer shall be the property of the employer and he exclusively shall be entitled to exercise them.

Likewise, Article 69b of German Copyright Law 1965 implements Article 2(3) of the directive.

12.2.3.4 Exclusive rights

According to Article 4 of the Software Directive rightsholders of copyright in computer programs are given the exclusive right to do the following acts:

a. the permanent or temporary reproduction of a computer program by any means and in any form, in part or in whole

b. the translation, adaptation, arrangement, and any other alteration of a computer program

c. any form of distribution to the public, including the rental, of the original computer program or copies thereof.

The reproduction right is extremely broad and covers the situation where a program is loaded into the RAM of a computer in order to operate. This interpretation is clearly catered for by the UK notion of 'reproduction', defined in s. 17(6) of the CDPA to include 'the making of copies which are transient'. Thus, running a computer program will involve its reproduction.

---

[12] *Fylde Microsystems Ltd v Key Radio Systems Ltd* [1998] FSR 449, 459–60.

The adaptation right is implemented in s. 21(ab) of the CPDA, which states that 'adaptation' in relation to a computer program means 'an arrangement or altered version of the program or a translation of it'. According to s. 21(4) of the CDPA, a 'translation' of the program includes where a version of the program in one language or code is converted into another language or code.

The distribution right for computer programs also includes rental. According to recital 16 of the Software Directive, rental does not include public lending and refers to 'making available for use, for a limited period of time and for profit-making purposes' a computer program or copy thereof. This is implemented in s. 18A of the CDPA. Importantly, the distribution right is subject to the exhaustion principle. Thus, where a rightsholder sells a copy of a program (or consents to such as sale) in the Community, this will exhaust the distribution right within the Community of that copy. This does not apply, however, to the rental right.

What about where software is transmitted or distributed over the Internet? Does this fall within the rightsholder's exclusive rights? The European Commission has expressed the view that a generous interpretation on the distribution right would include such activities. However, the right of communication to the public in Article 3 of the Information Society Directive (discussed below) certainly covers this activity and it is arguable that it is applicable to computer programs.

12.2.3.5 Exceptions

When it comes to exceptions, the Software Directive draws a distinction between reverse engineering that involves studying the operation of a computer program and reverse engineering that involves decompilation. Article 5(3) deals with the former situation whereas Article 6 deals with the latter.

Studying a computer program involves running it and this in turn involves reproduction of the program in the RAM of the computer. As such, unless the person running a computer program (or copy thereof) has the copyright owner's permission to do so, this temporary reproduction will constitute a prima facie infringement of copyright. It may also amount to an infringing adaptation (because the source code will be converted to object code in order to operate). Yet, the purpose in running the computer program is simply to observe what it does and how it functions, in other words to understand the ideas and principles underlying the program, and it is clear from Article 1(2) that such matter is not protected by copyright. Thus, an exception was crafted to deal with the apparent conflict between a prima facie infringement (through copying) and the need to ensure underlying ideas and principles are not protected. Article 5(3) was the solution. This provision states:

> The person having a right to use a copy of a computer program shall be entitled, without the authorisation of the rightholder, to observe, study or test the functioning of the program in order to determine the ideas and principles which underlie any element of the program if he does so while performing any of the acts of loading, displaying, running, transmitting or storing the program which he is entitled to do.

Only the person having a 'right to use a copy of a computer program' can rely on this exception. There has been uncertainty about what this phrase means, given that Article 5(1) refers to a 'lawful acquirer' and Article 5(2) refers to 'a person having a right to use the computer program'. However, it is now understood that all three expressions mean the same concept of 'lawful user': that is, a person who *lawfully* acquires the program (for example, via purchase, gift, public lending, or rental contracts).[13] Thus, where an illicit or pirated copy of the program is used the exception cannot be relied upon.

Article 9(1) of the Software Directive emphasizes that any contractual provision contrary to Article 5(3) will be null and void. Thus, it seems that the owner of copyright in the program cannot override the user's right to reverse engineer. However, the terms of Article 5(3), which state that reverse engineering has to occur 'while performing any of the acts of loading, displaying, running or transmitting or storing the program *which he is entitled to do*' (emphasis supplied), read in combination with recital 19, which provides that the acts of reverse engineering 'do not infringe copyright in the program', suggest that the copyright owner could license the use of the program in such a way that restricted the user's ability to carry out acts of reverse engineering.

The UK did not insert an express provision into the CDPA corresponding to Article 5(3) of the Software Directive and was criticized by the Commission for failing to do so. As a result of the Copyright and Related Rights Regulations 2003,[14] however, a new s. 50BA was inserted into the CDPA, which provision mirrors Article 5(3) and Article 9(1).

Decompilation allows a software engineer or programmer to access the original source code, or a version as near as possible to the source code, so that he can appreciate the ideas and principles underlying a computer program, how the program functions and its interfaces. This may allow a competitor to imitate the program, design a competing program that improves upon the existing program, or create a program or hardware device that complements the program. However, decompilation necessarily involves either a reproduction or adaptation of the underlying source code (or code written in another higher level language) and, in the absence of an applicable exception or express licence, will constitute an infringement of copyright.

Article 6(1) creates a fairly detailed and complex exception for decompilation. It provides that a rightsholder's permission is not required for reproduction or translation of a computer program where these acts are '*indispensable* to obtain the information necessary to achieve the *interoperability* of an *independently created computer program* with other programs'.[15] Indispensability means, for example, that the information needed to achieve interoperability cannot already be obtained by reverse engineering in reliance on Article 5(3). The purpose of decompilation must be to achieve interoperability and it is clear that the independently created program may be one that competes with the program that is decompiled.

Certain circumstances have to exist before a person can rely on Article 6 of the Software Directive. First, pursuant to Article 6(1)(a), the person performing the acts of reproduction or translation must be the licensee, or another person having a right to use a copy of a program, or a person authorized by the licensee or a person having a right to use the program. Second, Article 6(1)(b) requires that the information necessary to achieve interoperability has not previously been readily available to the persons just mentioned. It is unclear, however, what will constitute 'readily available'. Finally, Article 6(1)(c) states that the acts of reproduction and translation must be 'confined to the parts of the original program which are necessary to achieve interoperability'. The difficulty with this requirement is that it is not always possible to ascertain at the beginning of the decompilation process which parts of the work are essential to achieving interoperability.

---

[13] T. Aplin, *Copyright Law in the Digital Society: The challenges of multimedia* (Oxford: Hart, 2005), p. 164.
[14] SI 2003/2498.   [15] Emphasis supplied.

Once information necessary to achieve interoperability has been obtained, Article 6(2) imposes further obligations on what may be done with this information. First, the information obtained cannot be used for purposes other than to achieve interoperability of the independently created computer program. Second, the information cannot be passed on to others, except for the purposes of interoperability. Finally, the information cannot be used to create a substantially similar computer program, 'or for any other act which infringes copyright'.

Article 9(1) of the Software Directive makes clear that any contractual provision contrary to Article 6 will be null and void. Even so, it seems that Article 9(1) does not prohibit Article 6 from being overridden by other forms of legal protection, such as the law of confidence.

Article 6 is implemented in the UK via s. 50B of the CDPA. This provision departs from the language of Article 6 in two respects. First, 'decompiling' is not described as 'reproduction of the code and translation, of its form' but rather in terms of converting a copy of a computer program expressed in a low level language into a version in a higher level language; or, incidentally while doing so, copying the program. Arguably the UK language has a more restricted meaning. Second, s. 50B refrains from using the term 'interoperability' and instead refers to obtaining the information necessary *to create an independent program* which can be operated with the program decompiled or another program. It seems, therefore, that under the UK provision a person will not be able to decompile another program in order to obtain information that could lead to the interoperability of a program that already exists.

Aside from the complexity of the decompilation exception, another criticism is that it does not permit the reproduction of data tables that do not form part of the computer program, but which are frequently necessary to achieve interoperability. This may be contrasted with the position under Australian law, where a person is able to reproduce data tables in order to achieve interoperable software. This is because, for the purposes of decompilation, the Australian Copyright Act 1968 defines 'computer program' to include any literary work that is incorporated or associated with a computer program and essential to the effective operation of a function of that program.

Article 5(2) of the Software Directive creates an exception for back-up copies. This was implemented in the UK by s. 50A(1) of the CDPA. Section 50A(1) creates an exception for a lawful user of a copy of a computer program, 'to make any back up copy of it which it is necessary for him to have for the purposes of his lawful use'. The right to make a back-up copy cannot be excluded by contract.[16] However, what amounts to a 'back-up copy' is not defined in the Software Directive or CDPA, but seems to include a copy made by a user as a reserve in case of loss or damage to the original. While it may be desirable to make a back-up copy, it is questionable whether it is generally necessary to do so. The requirement of 'necessity' probably limits the lawful user to making only one back-up copy.

Article 5(1) of the Software Directive provides that a lawful acquirer of a computer program may carry out the acts of reproduction, translation, adaptation, and any other alteration of a computer program, 'where they are necessary for use of the computer program by the lawful acquirer in accordance with its intended purpose, including for error correction'. Unlike the other exceptions, Article 5(1) states that the exception applies in the absence of specific contractual provisions, thus it appears permissible to override via contract. This provision is implemented in the UK in s. 50C of the CDPA.

---

[16] ss. 50A(3) and 296A, CDPA.

12.2.3.6 Technical protection measures

Software producers frequently use technical 'locks' or devices to stop unintended copying of their programs. However, this protection will be of limited use if there is no sanction against those who circumvent such devices. Article 7(1)(c) of the Software Directive thus provides for sanctions, insofar as it obliges Member States to provide remedies against a person committing:

> any act of putting into circulation, or the possession for commercial purposes of, any means the sole intended purpose of which is to facilitate the unauthorised removal or circumvention of any technical device which may have been applied to protect a computer program.

This provision does not prohibit circumvention per se, but rather commercially dealing in circumvention means.

The UK implemented the above provision in s. 296 of the CPDA. The section was amended, however, in 2003 and the revised version is much broader than the original and more in keeping with Article 7(1)(c).

The new s. 296 applies where a technical device has been applied to a computer program and 'technical device' means any device intended to prevent or restrict acts that are restricted by copyright and not authorized by the owner. A person will infringe the provision if they make for sale or hire, import, distribute, sell or let for hire, offer for sale or hire, advertise for sale or hire, or possess for commercial purposes *any means the sole intended purpose* of which is to facilitate the unauthorized removal or circumvention of the technical device; or publish information intended to enable or assist persons to remove or circumvent the technical device. The person must, however, know or have reason to believe that the means or information will be used to make infringing copies.

This provision is broader than the old s. 296 in that it covers technical devices that would prevent *any act* that would infringe copyright and not just devices intended to prevent or restrict copying of the work. In addition, previously only the person issuing copies of the work to the public in an electronic, copy-protected form could sue for infringement of s. 296. By contrast, revised s. 296(2) gives standing to sue to three types of persons:

1. the person issuing to the public copies of or communicating to the public the computer program to which the technical device has been applied

2. the copyright owner or exclusive licensee of the computer program

3. the owner or exclusive licensee of any intellectual property right in the technical device applied to the computer program.

Whether the means has the *sole intended purpose* of facilitating the unauthorized removal or circumvention of the technical device was considered in the case below.

Kabushiki Kaisha Sony Computer Entertainment Inc v Ball [2004] ECDR 33

The case concerned Sony Playstation 2 consoles and Sony games, which are embedded with special codes that are read by the console. The defendants were involved in the design, manufacture, and sale of an electronic chip called Messiah 2. This chip could be fitted into a Playstation 2 console, enabling the authorization process to be bypassed. Using this chip, legitimate Sony games designed for different world regions, along with unauthorized copies of Sony games, could be played on the Playstation 2 console. In an action for infringement of s. 296, the first defendant argued that it was not the sole intended purpose of the Messiah 2 chip to facilitate unauthorized removal or circumvention of the technical device. This was because the chip was designed to enable any necessary back-up copies of the original game to be played, or to enable playing UK (PAL) games on non-European (non PAL) Playstation 2 consoles imported into the UK.

Laddie J:

30. Mr Mellor says that Mr Ball does not begin to raise an arguable defence under this provision. One of the advantages of CDs and DVDs is that they are robust and cannot be wiped clean. There is no necessity, as required by s. 50A, to make back ups. Mr Ball has not pleaded anything which could justify him saying that it is necessary. Furthermore here it is quite clear that no such necessity could arise. Sony says that it makes replacement CDs or DVDs available to users in the unlikely event that theirs are damaged or destroyed. Since there is no necessity to make a back up, there is no justification for having one. Playing such a disc is unauthorised and the resultant creation of transitory copies of the program (or other data) in RAM is unauthorised. The copy protection system implemented by Sony is designed to prevent this type of activity. Even assuming that the Messiah2 chip was designed, in part at least, to facilitate the use of 'back up' copies of Sony games, there is no authorisation from Sony for such use (or indeed the making of such copies in the first place). It follows that this purpose of the chip amounts to an unauthorised circumvention of the Sony copy-protection system and falls within the section.

31. The other point raised by Mr Kime is as follows. Each of the PS2 games intended for the United Kingdom market has marked on it the words 'for home use only'. This is said to give the user a licence to use in the countries in which they were issued, i.e. in the United Kingdom. It follows that it is permissible to run games purchased in the United Kingdom on PS2 consoles imported from a non-PAL country. Such use must be treated as authorised by Sony. The Messiah2 chip, so it is argued, is designed to allow owners of non-PAL consoles to operate under this licence. Even if one accepts that this is one of the purposes for which the Messiah2 chip was designed and marketed—and I will not venture an opinion as to the likelihood of the court doing so—in my view this argument is hopeless. The label on each PAL PS2 game not only says that it is for home use only but also includes the following words:

> This software is only compatible with the PlayStation®2 computer entertainment system displaying the PAL logo.

32. In other words the purchaser of the PAL game is told in clear language that it is not designed to be played on a non-PAL machine. There is no support for the suggestion of licence or authorisation. Once again the copy protection system adopted by Sony is designed to prevent just such use of a non-PAL game on a PAL console. In this respect as well the Messiah2 chip is designed to facilitate unauthorised removal or circumvention of the copy protection system. None of this provides a defence to Mr Ball.

33. In summary, Sony's copy protection system is designed to prevent all uses of copied PS2 game CDs and DVDs on PS2 consoles and all uses of non-PAL games on PAL consoles (and vice versa), The Messiah2 chips' sole purpose is to circumvent this. Such circumvention is not authorised expressly or impliedly by Sony, nor is it suggested that Sony must be deemed to have authorised it.

As we shall see in the discussion below at 12.6.5, Article 6(1)–(2) of the Information Society Directive[17] obliges Member States to prohibit circumvention of technological protection measures applied to any copyright work (other than a computer program) *and* commercially dealing in circumvention devices. This protection is wider than that available under Article 7(1)(c) of the Software Directive. Does it make sense to have differing levels of protection for circumvention of technical devices, depending on the copyright works to which they are attached?

12.2.4 INFRINGEMENT

Although the Software Directive achieved considerable harmonization of copyright law protection of computer programs, difficult issues remain. In particular, where the functionality and visual appearance manifested by a computer program is copied (i.e. the non-literal features), but not the underlying source or object code (i.e. the literal elements), the line between infringement and non-infringement is not always obvious.

The issue of when copying of the non-literal elements of a computer program will amount to infringement was explored in the early cases of *John Richardson Computers Ltd v Flanders*[18] and *IBCOS Computers Ltd v Barclays Mercantile Highland Finance Ltd.*[19] In *Flanders*, Ferris J adopted the US 'abstraction-filtration-comparison' test in order to determine whether non-literal similarities amounted to copying a substantial part of a computer program. The 'abstraction-filtration-comparison' test was adopted by the US Court of Appeals for the Second Circuit in *Computer Associates International Inc v Altai Inc.*[20] It requires that first the non-literal elements of a program, at varying degrees of abstraction, are ascertained. The next step is to filter out those elements that are not protected by copyright, such as unprotectable ideas, features that are dictated by considerations of efficiency or by external factors, or which are taken from the public domain. After this process, the court should be left with a core of protectable expression which can be compared with the defendant's program. Although Ferris J was in favour of the *Altai* test, he admitted that it was difficult to apply to the facts of the case before him.[21]

In the later case of *IBCOS* Jacob J (as he then was) expressed his agreement with Ferris J in *Flanders* that consideration of copyright in computer programs extends beyond the literal text of the code to encompass non-literal features. However, he disagreed that the *Altai* test should be invoked to determine whether there has been copying of a substantial part. Rather, he suggested the question of substantial part 'is a question of degree where a good guide is the notion of over-borrowing of skill, labour and judgment which went into the copyright work'.[22]

The most recent consideration of when non-literal copying of a computer program will infringe is *Navitaire v Easyjet*. Here the claimant argued that, even though the defendants had not copied the source code of their computer program, they had copied its 'look and feel'. In other words, they alleged non-literal (or non-textual) copying of the computer program.

---

[17] Directive 2001/29/EC on the harmonization of certain aspects of copyright and related rights in the information society, OJ L167 22 June 2001, 10–19.
[18] [1993] FSR 497.   [19] [1994] FSR 265.   [20] 23 USPQ 2d 1241 (1992).
[21] *Flanders*, p. 527.   [22] *IBCOS*, p. 302.

Navitaire v Easyjet Airline Co [2006] RPC 3

For the facts, see p. 691 above.

Pumfrey J:

The OpenRes System: 'Business Logic' and Non-Textual Copying in eRes

107. As I have indicated above, the case advanced by Navitaire is based on the fact that the functions of OpenRes and eRes are identical to the user so far as the aspects of the system of interest to easyJet are concerned. The case had its origin in the suggestion that what was called the 'business logic' of OpenRes had been appropriated.

. . .

109. As will appear from what I have said, I agree that the commands were really quite a limited feature. The question is whether the 'something else that has been copied' over and above the limited features of commands and screens is something Navitaire may protect from being copied. It seems to me that the following list sets out the matters copied over and above the comparatively limited aspects of the user interface:

i) The relationship between the commands and the screens. No doubt this is obvious, but it is worth pointing out that the screens and commands do not exist in a vacuum. They are connected by invisible chains, and I do not think that in this context they should be considered separately.

ii) The ability to carry out the operations of reservation, check-in, irregular operations and so on, with much the same commands and screens with a successful result.

iii) Making the same data about all transactions as OpenRes provides available, and in substantially the same form.

iv) At easyJet, at least, accordingly providing a 'drop-in' replacement for OpenRes.

. . .

113. There is no doubt that easyJet and BulletProof had no access to the source code of OpenRes, and it is not in dispute that in languages used, actual code and architecture (subject to the claim in respect of the database) the systems are quite different. There is no suggestion that the eRes code represents a translation or adaptation of the OpenRes code. The term 'non-textual copying' might be replaced by the more accurate 'copying without access to the thing copied, directly or indirectly'.

. . .

118. The problem, therefore, if one is to arrive at a finding of infringement is to settle on a level of abstraction that describes something that is not merely inherent in the nature of the business function to be performed by the software, is taken by the defendants, represents the skill and labour of the designers and programmers but goes wider than the details of the command set and the screen displays, acknowledged by Dr Hunt to be a limited feature. Since copyright in computer programs is a literary copyright, the natural approach for Navitaire is to base its contentions on the analogy between the function of a computer program and the plot of a literary work.

. . .

122. . . . Two other cases are particularly relied on by Mr Carr. The first is *John Richardson Computers Ltd v Flanders* [1993] FSR 497 (Ferris J). This is a difficult case to summarise, but for present purposes I need only refer to a few salient facts. Mr Flanders, the defendant, had written the program the copyright in which was asserted against his new program. It was

accepted that he did not have access to a copy of his earlier work when he wrote the later; and the judge rejected any contention of deliberate copying. He said this [at p. 548]:

> In short, I do not accept the evidence I have discussed under heads (i) and (ii) in this section of my judgment as establishing deliberate copying of the [earlier] program by Mr Flanders. But the fact remains that he had, as I have said, an intimate knowledge of the [earlier] program at all levels of abstraction (to use the term employed in *Nichols v Universal Pictures Corp* (1930) 45 F (2d) 119 and other United States authorities that I have mentioned) and *it is possible that he has, unconsciously or unintentionally or in some other way which he did not consider to be objectionable, made use of that* knowledge in a way that amounts to copying in the context of breach of copyright. It is that possibility that I must evaluate in appraising the particular similarities that I have identified. (my emphasis)

123. Seventeen similarities were relied on. Nearly all of them were rejected, but the ones which survived included the 'line editor'. Ferris J dealt with this feature in the following way at [p. 553]:

> I find it impossible not to conclude that the line editor in the [later] program has substantially been copied from the line editor in the [earlier] program. If all that had been copied was the concept of a line editor that would not have mattered for present purposes, being a mere adoption of an idea. But similarities such as the obscuration of the text which is to be amended, the message 'Insert to edit' in one case and 'Copy to edit' in the other and, above all, the idiosyncratic restoration of text which is merely deleted and not replaced demonstrate that there has been copying of expression as well as idea.

124. The reference to 'copying of expression as well as idea' is a clear echo of the United States authorities discussed at length by Ferris J elsewhere in his judgment whose employment for this purpose was criticised by Jacob J in the *Ibcos* case, itself relied on by Mr Carr. But it is quite correct, as he submits, that it is possible to read the foregoing passage as stating that the concept of 'expression' as distinct from 'idea' extended to the manner in which the programmed machine worked, in detail. If this was what Ferris J was saying, then I would respectfully suggest that it is based upon a misapprehension as to the meaning of 'expression' in this context. But I do not need to go into this in detail, because I would with respect accept what is said by Jacob J in *Ibcos* [at p. 291]:

> The true position is that where an 'idea' is sufficiently general, then even if an original work embodies it, the mere taking of that idea will not infringe. But if the 'idea' is detailed, then there may be infringement. It is a question of degree. The same applies whether the work is functional or not, and whether visual or literary. In the latter field the taking of a plot (i.e. the 'idea') of a novel or play can certainly infringe—if that plot is a substantial part of the copyright work. As Judge Learned Hand said (speaking of the distinction between 'idea' and 'expression'): Nobody has ever been able to fix that boundary and nobody ever can.

125. This does not answer the question with which I am confronted, which is peculiar, I believe, to computer programs. The reason it is a new problem is that two completely different computer programs can produce an identical result: not a result identical at some level of abstraction but identical at any level of abstraction. This is so even if the author of one has no access at all to the other but only to its results. The analogy with a plot is for this reason a poor one. It is a poor one for other reasons as well. To say these programs possess a plot is precisely like saying that the book of instructions for a booking clerk acting manually has a plot: but a book of instructions has no theme, no events, and does not have a narrative flow. Nor does a computer program, particularly one whose behaviour depends upon the history of its inputs in any given transaction. It does not have a plot, merely a series of pre-defined operations intended to achieve the desired result in response to the requests of the customer.

...

128. I think that the answer to the problem is to be gathered from the passage in Lord Hoffmann's speech immediately following that quoted above ([119]) from the *Designers' Guild* case:

> My Lords, if one examines the cases in which the distinction between ideas and the expression of ideas has been given effect, I think it will be found that they support two quite distinct propositions. The first is that a copyright work may express certain ideas which are not protected because they have no connection with the literary, dramatic, musical or artistic nature of the work. It is on this ground that, for example, a literary work which describes a system or invention does not entitle the author to claim protection for his system or invention as such. The same is true of an inventive concept expressed in an artistic work. However striking or original it may be, others are (in the absence of patent protection) free to express it in works of their own: see *Kleeneze Ltd v DRG (UK) Ltd* [1984] FSR 399. The other proposition is that certain ideas expressed by a copyright work may not be protected because, although they are ideas of a literary, dramatic or artistic nature, they are not original, or so commonplace as not to form a substantial part of the work. *Kenrick & Co v Lawrence & Co* (1890) 25 QBD 99 is a well known example. It is on this ground that the mere notion of combining stripes and flowers would not have amounted to a substantial part of the plaintiff's work. At that level of abstraction, the idea, though expressed in the design, would not have represented sufficient of the author's skill and labour as to attract copyright protection.
>
> Generally speaking, in cases of artistic copyright, the more abstract and simple the copied idea, the less likely it is to constitute a substantial part. Originality, in the sense of the contribution of the author's skill and labour, tends to lie in the detail with which the basic idea is presented. Copyright law protects foxes better than hedgehogs. In this case, however, the elements which the judge found to have been copied went well beyond the banal and I think that the judge was amply justified in deciding that they formed a substantial part of the originality of the work.

129. The questions in the present case are both a lack of substantiality and the nature of the skill and labour to be protected. Navitaire's computer program invites input in a manner excluded from copyright protection, outputs its results in a form excluded from copyright protection and creates a record of a reservation in the name of a particular passenger on a particular flight. What is left when the interface aspects of the case are disregarded is the business function of carrying out the transaction and creating the record, because none of the code was read or copied by the defendants. It is right that those responsible for devising OpenRes envisaged this as the end result for their program: but that is not relevant skill and labour. In my judgment, this claim for non-textual copying should fail.

130. I do not come to this conclusion with any regret. If it is the policy of the Software Directive to exclude both computer languages and the underlying ideas of the interfaces from protection, then it should not be possible to circumvent these exclusions by seeking to identify some overall function or functions that it is the sole purpose of the interface to invoke and relying on those instead. As a matter of policy also, it seems to me that to permit the 'business logic' of a program to attract protection through the literary copyright afforded to the program itself is an unjustifiable extension of copyright protection into a field where I am far from satisfied that it is appropriate.

When it comes to determining whether there has been non-literal copying of a computer program would you agree with Pumfrey J that drawing an analogy with the plot of a novel or play is unhelpful? Is it more useful to focus, as Pumfrey J did, on whether relevant skill and labour has been copied by the defendant? Finally, as a matter of policy, is it sensible to reject protection for the 'business logic' of a program?

Clearly, a large part of the value of a computer program is what it *does* and yet it seems that under copyright law, unless the underlying program code is copied, this can only be protected in a limited fashion. Some commentators argue that this shows the inherent unsuitability of copyright law for this type of creation and the desirability of a sui generis right for computer programs. Would you agree?

In a bid to better protect the behaviour of a computer program, software producers have sought to rely on patent law, in addition to copyright. We turn now to examine this form of protection.

FURTHER READING

A. Christie, 'Designing appropriate protection for computer programs' [1994] 11 EIPR 486.

J. Ginsburg, 'Four reasons and a paradox: The manifest superiority of copyright over *sui generis* protection of computer software' (1994) 94 Columbia LR 2559.

J. H. Reichman, 'Legal hybrids between the patent and copyright paradigms' (1994) 94 Columbia LR 2432.

P. Samuelson et al, 'A manifesto concerning the legal protection of computer programs' (1994) 94 Columbia LR 2308.

12.3 COMPUTER PROGRAMS AND PATENT PROTECTION

12.3.1 INTRODUCTION

Patent law, on the face of it, has very little to offer when it comes to protection of computer programs. This is because Article 52(2)–(3) of the European Patent Convention ('EPC') and s. 1(2) of the UK Patents Act 1977 exclude 'computer programs as such' from being inventions. The policy reasons for this prohibition are neatly summarized in the following extract.

CFPH LLC's Application [2006] RPC 5

Deputy Judge Peter Prescott QC:

35. ...The reason why computer programs, as such, are not allowed to be patented is quite different. Although it is hotly disputed now by some special interest groups, the truth is, or ought to be, well known. It is because at the time the EPC was under consideration it was felt in the computer industry that such patents were not really needed, were too cumbersome (it was felt that searching the prior art would be a big problem), and would do more harm than good. I shall not go into details here but it is worth noting that the software industry in America developed at an astonishing pace when no patent protection was available. Copyright law protects computer programs against copying. A patent on a computer program would stop others from using it even though there had been no copying at all. So there would have to be infringement searches. Furthermore you cannot have a sensible patent system unless there exists a proper body of prior art that can be searched. Not only are most computer programs supplied in binary form—unintelligible to humans—but most of the time it is

actually illegal to convert them into human-readable form. A patent system where it is illegal to search most of the prior art is something of an absurdity.

12.3.2 UK APPROACH

Importantly, it is computer programs *as such* that are excluded from patentability. Thus, even though an invention may include a computer program, if it does not claim a computer program *as such* it will be patentable. As we shall see from the following case, UK courts have determined this issue by using the test of 'technical effect' or 'technical contribution'.

Fujitsu Limited's Application [1997] RPC 608

The application related to a method and apparatus for modelling a synthetic crystal structure for designing inorganic materials. It involved a computer programmed so that an operator could select an atom, a lattice vector, and a crystal face in each of two crystal structures displayed on the computer. The computer then converted data representing the physical layouts of the two crystal structures into data representing the crystal structure that would have been obtained by combining the original two structures in that way. The resulting data was then displayed to give an image of the resulting combined structure. Conventionally, the modelling of such structures occurred by assembling plastic models.

The examiner objected that the application was a method for performing a mental act or a program for a computer as such. The Hearing Officer rejected the application on the same basis. On appeal to the Patents Court, Laddie J held that, in form at least, the claims were not to programs as such, but that they did relate to a method for performing a mental act as such. In the Court of Appeal, the appeal was dismissed.

Aldous LJ (with whom Roch and Leggatt LJJ agreed), at pp. 614–19:

The law

Section 1(2)(c) of the Act has been considered by this court in *Merrill Lynch's Application* [1989] RPC 561 and in *Gale's Application*. In both those cases the court drew attention to the proviso to section 1(2) which states that the 'things', referred to in the subsection, should only be excluded 'to the extent that a patent or an application for a patent relates to that thing as such'.

In *Merrill Lynch* the applicants submitted that the question for the court was to decide whether the subject matter of the claim was a computer program. If it was, it was not patentable. If it was not, then the invention was not excluded from patentability by section 1(2). Thus it was said that a piece of machinery (a computer) which follows the instructions of a computer program was patentable, although the program itself would be excluded from patentability by the section. That was rejected by the Court of Appeal. Fox LJ said at page 569:

It seems to me to be clear, . . . that it cannot be permissible to patent an item excluded by section 1(2) under the guise of an article which contains that item—that is to say, in the case of a computer program, the patenting of a conventional computer containing that program. Something further is necessary. The nature of that addition is, I think, to be found in the *Vicom* case where it is stated: 'Decisive is what technical contribution the invention makes to the known art.' There must, I think, be some technical advance on the prior art in the form of a new result (eg. a substantial increase in processing speed as in *Vicom*).

By that statement Fox LJ was making it clear that it was not sufficient to look at the words of the claimed monopoly. The decision as to what was patentable depended upon substance not form. He also went on to point out the importance of considering whether the invention made a technical contribution, despite the fact that neither the statute nor Article 52 of the Convention lays down that the matter, which would result in the invention not relating to the thing as such, must provide a technical contribution. It would therefore seem that as a matter of words, if for instance the patent was not confined to a computer program, then it could not be excluded under subsection (2), as to an extent the patent would not relate to the computer program as such. However it is and always has been a principle of patent law that mere discoveries or ideas are not patentable, but those discoveries and ideas which have a technical aspect or make a technical contribution are. Thus the concept that what is needed to make an excluded thing patentable is a technical contribution is not surprising. That was the basis for the decision of the Board in *Vicom*. It has been accepted by this court and by the EPO and has been applied since 1987. It is a concept at the heart of patent law.

...

The reasoning in Vicom as to what was the technical contribution is not easy to ascertain. However, I do not read the decision as concluding that all claims to processing real images are patentable and I can see no reason why, if they are, the same reasoning should not apply to all useful images. As I read the decision, the Board saw a technical contribution, namely the generation of the enhanced picture. As the Principal Examiner pointed out:

the numbers which are mathematically processed in *Vicom* do not merely determine the intellectual content of the images which are displayed, but are also the technical means which cause the display to operate to a technical level. Thus in *Vicom* manipulating numbers in the manner described affects the technical quality of the image. So in *Vicom*, the invention concerned the technical representation, or technical control of what is displayed and not the information content of what is displayed.

In my view *Vicom* does not support the submission that claims to processing of real images are allowable. The technical contribution was not the fact that an image was being produced. It was the way the enhanced image was produced.

In *Gale* this court had to consider a patent application for a ROM programmed to carry out a method of calculating a square root of a number. Nicholls LJ who gave the leading judgment described the working of a computer and said:

In principle, the instructions in a computer program do no more than prescribe a particular manner of operation for which it was constructed. Thus writing a fresh set of instructions for use in a computer in particular circumstances or for particular purposes cannot in itself be regarded as inventive.

He went on to point out that, to be used in a computer, a series of instructions had to be recorded in some physical form perhaps on a disc in a ROM. He said that if the instructions *qua* instructions were not patentable, they were not patentable merely because they were recorded on or in a known piece of apparatus. The disc on ROM was 'merely the vehicle used for carrying' the instruction.

the physical differences are not material for patent purposes, because they constitute no more than the use of a compact disc for its intended purpose. Likewise with a disc or ROM which records or reproduces a new set of instructions, if those instructions are recorded on a conventional disc, or are stored in a ROM using conventional methods. To decide otherwise would be to exalt form over substance.

He went on to conclude that the application before him did not contain a technical contribution and therefore was a computer program which was excluded from patentability.

I, like Nicholls LJ, have difficulty in identifying clearly the boundary line between what is and what is not a technical contribution. In *Vicom* it seems that the Board concluded that the enhancement of the images produced amounted to a technical contribution. No such contribution existed in *Gale's Application* which related to a ROM programmed to enable a computer to carry out a mathematical calculation or in *Merrill Lynch* which had claims to a data processing system for making a trading market in securities. Each case has to be decided upon its own facts.

...

There is only one invention. The fact that it is claimed as a method, a way of manufacture or an apparatus having appropriate features is irrelevant. Further there is no dispute as to what the invention is. In summary it uses a computer program so that an operator can select an atom, a lattice vector and a crystal face in each of two crystal structures displayed. The computer, upon instruction and using the program, then converts data representing the physical layouts of the two crystal structures into data representing the physical layout of the structure that is obtained by combining the original two structures in such a way that the selected atoms, the selected lattice vectors and the selected faces are superposed. The resulting data are then displayed to give a picture of the resulting combined structure. Clearly the whole operation revolves around the computer program and the question for decision is whether there is a technical contribution so that it cannot be said that the invention consists of a computer program as such.

...

I believe that the application is for a computer program as such. I agree in general with the reasons of the Principal Examiner which I have quoted. In *Vicom* the technical contribution was provided by the generation of the enhanced display. In the present case the combined structure is the result of the directions given by the operator and use of the program. The computer is conventional as is the display unit. The two displays of crystal structures are produced by the operator. The operator then provides the appropriate way of superposition and the program does the rest. The resulting display is the combined structure shown pictorially in a form that would in the past have been produced as a model. The only advance is the computer program which enables the combined structure to be portrayed quicker.

I conclude that the application does not relate to a patentable invention as it is excluded by section 1(2)(c) as being a program for a computer as such.

Although Aldous LJ followed the approach set out in *Vicom/Computer Related Invention* T208/84[23] and *Merrill Lynch's Application*[24] (discussed at length at 9.6.2), he commented on the difficulty of identifying a 'technical contribution'. He distinguished *Vicom* on its facts, stating that the technical contribution in that case was the generation of an enhanced display, whereas, in *Fujitsu*, the only real contribution was the computer program (enabling images to be displayed faster) and this was excluded subject matter. The Court of Appeal in *Symbian Ltd v Comptroller of Patents*[25] has commented 'while the test applied by the court in *Fujitsu* was ostensibly consistent with that in *Vicom* and *Gale*, the outcome is a little hard to reconcile with the view taken in those two cases to the question of what constitutes a

---

[23] [1987] OJ EPO 14.   [24] [1989] RPC 561.   [25] [2008] EWCA Civ 1066.

"technical" contribution'.[26] Would you agree? If so, does that mean the decision in *Fujitsu* was incorrect? The Court of Appeal in *Symbian* suggests not, on the basis of the alternative ground that the alleged invention was a 'method for performing a mental act'.

12.3.2.1 Divergence with EPO

As was discussed at 9.6.2, the current EPO approach to determining whether there is a patentable invention differs from that adopted in the UK. Although both the UK Intellectual Property Office ('UK IPO') and EPO take the approach that if subject matter exhibits a technical contribution or effect then it is not a computer program *as such*, they differ as to what constitutes a *technical* contribution or effect. The EPO, following the Board of Appeal decisions in *Pension Benefit System Partnership* T931/95,[27] *Hitachi/Auction Method* T258/03,[28] and *Microsoft/Clipboard formats I* T424/03,[29] does not treat subject matter as excluded where it has technical features and these are interpreted very broadly to include hardware of most kinds (e.g. storing a computer program on a carrier or a computer). In other words, the EPO takes a formalistic approach to Article 52(2)–(3) and leaves it to the inventive step stage to filter out excluded subject matter. Whereas, in the UK, the approach in *Vicom*, *Merrill Lynch*, and *Fujitsu* is followed and the question is whether there is a technical contribution. If no technical contribution exists, then the subject matter is not an invention and the enquiry goes no further (into novelty or inventive step).

The divergence between the EPO and UK approaches is clearly undesirable. However, the UK Court of Appeal has stated in *Aerotel Ltd v Telco Holdings Ltd*[30] that it will not reconsider its approach until the Enlarged Board of Appeal rules on the question. This view was recently reiterated in *Symbian Ltd v Comptroller of Patents*,[31] where the Court of Appeal held that it would not adopt the EPO approach. This was for several reasons: (i) there was no decision of the Enlarged Board on this issue; (ii) the decisions of the Boards of Appeal are not consistent; (iii) the approach of the EPO may lead to the computer exclusion losing its meaning; (iv) other jurisdictions, notably Germany, have expressed concerns about the EPO approach to the computer programs 'as such' exclusion; and (v) if the Court of Appeal 'is seen to depart too readily from its previous, carefully considered, approach, it would risk throwing the law into disarray'.[32] The Court of Appeal, however, reiterated the 'strong desirability of the approaches and principles in the two offices marching together as far as possible' and that this meant the 'need for a two-way dialogue between national tribunals and the EPO, coupled with a degree of mutual compromise'.[33] The likelihood of the Enlarged Board of Appeal ruling on the patentability of computer programs, and thus hopefully clarifying the inconsistent decisions of the Boards of Appeal, has been given a boost by the recent reference from the President of the EPO.[34] If a ruling ensues then we may see the UK Court of Appeal revisiting its approach to the computer programs 'as such' exclusion.

12.3.2.2 Convergence with the EPO

It is important to note that there is a strand of consistency between the UK and the EPO on one particular aspect of patentability of computer programs, i.e. claims to computer programs on suitable storage media (or 'program on carrier' claims). The UK Patent Office

---

[26] Ibid., para. 42.   [27] [2002] EPOR 52.   [28] [2004] EPOR 55.   [29] [2006] EPOR 39.
[30] [2007] RPC 7.   [31] [2008] EWCA Civ 1066.   [32] Ibid., para. 46.
[33] Ibid., para. 61.   [34] <http://www.epo.org/topics/news/2008/20081024.html>.

(as it then was) had previously rejected this form of claim, but later changed its practice—given certain decisions of the EPO Boards of Appeal, the persuasive value of this jurisprudence, and the desirability of maintaining consistency.[35] However, after the Court of Appeal decision in *Aerotel* the UK IPO (as it is now known) reverted to its original practice of disallowing 'program on carrier' claims. This change in practice was challenged in the following case.

Astron Clinica Ltd v Comptroller General of Patents, Designs and Trade Marks
[2008] EWHC 85 (Pat), [2008] RPC 14

This was an appeal from the decision of the Hearing Officer, Mr Peter Marchant, that in respect of various patent applications (from five different applicants) the claims to computer programs on suitable storage media were not allowable. In each of the applications (except for that of Cyan Technology), there were independent apparatus and method claims, which the patent examiner found acceptable. The applications also included claims to computer programs on storage media that referred back to the earlier claims, i.e. 'a storage medium storing computer implementable instructions to cause a programmable computer to become configured as an information processing apparatus [in accordance with earlier claims]' and 'a storage medium storing computer implementable instructions for causing a programmable computer to perform a method [in accordance with earlier claims]'. In the case of Cyan Technology, the claims were self-contained and did not refer back to earlier independent apparatus or method claims, but nevertheless were of equivalent scope to the 'computer program on storage medium' claims in the other applications and could be considered alongside them.

The issue before Kitchin J was whether claims to computer programs on suitable storage media were prohibited by s. 1(2) of the PA 77/Article 52(2)–(3) of the EPC, for being 'computer programs as such'.

Kitchin J:

47. In considering this question I believe the following points are material. First, the point did not arise in *Aerotel Ltd v Telco Holdings Ltd; In re Macrossan's Application* [2007] Bus LR 634. The Court of Appeal allowed the *Aerotel* appeal because the contribution of the invention was a new combination of apparatus for making telephone calls. The *Macrossan* appeal was a little more complicated. It concerned an automated method for acquiring the documents necessary to incorporate a company. The application had been rejected as being a method of performing a mental act and a computer program as such, but not as a method of doing business. The Court of Appeal did not address the first finding, upheld the second and reversed the third. It considered the contribution of Mr Macrossan's method was for the business of advising upon and creating company formation documents and there was nothing technical about it. Similarly the program provided no more than an interactive website and so was also excluded as a computer program as such. In both appeals the contribution fell wholly within the exclusions. The court was not required to consider what claims were permissible in the case of a computer related invention which made a contribution extending beyond excluded subject matter.

48. Second, I do not detect anything in the reasoning of the Court of Appeal which suggests that all computer programs are necessarily excluded. I have identified the key aspects

---

[35] See UK Patent Office Practice Notice of 19 Apr. 1999 reported in [1999] RPC 563.

of the decision which relate to computer related inventions and they undoubtedly criticise the reasoning of the EPO Board of Appeal in each of the 'trio' of cases. But the criticism is directed at the 'any hardware will do' approach and the return to form over substance with the drawing of a distinction between a program as a set of instructions and a program on a carrier. I do not understand the court to have doubted the earlier decisions of the board in *IBM/ Computer programs* [2000] EPOR 219 and *IBM/Computer programs II* [1999] RPC 861.

49. Third, I believe that in any particular case the application of the new approach should produce the same result as did the old. Indeed the Court of Appeal considered it was doing no more than applying a reordering of the *Merrill Lynch* test and that it was bound by the *Merrill Lynch* [1989] RPC 561, *Gale* [1991] RPC 305 and *Fujitsu* [1997] RPC 608 cases. Thus, in the case of a computer related invention which produces a substantive technical contribution, the application of step (ii) will identify that contribution and the application of step (iii) will lead to the answer that it does not fall wholly within excluded matter. Any computer related invention which passes step (iii) but does not involve a substantive technical contribution will fail step (iv). The answer to these questions will be the same irrespective of whether the invention is claimed in the form of a programmed computer, a method involving the use of that programmed computer or the program itself. The *Aerotel case* [2007] Bus LR 634 requires the analysis to be carried out as a matter of substance not form, just as did the *Genentech* [1989] RPC 147, *Merrill Lynch* [1989] RPC 561, *Gale* [1991] RPC 305 and *Fujitsu* [1997] RPC 608 cases. True it is that the first step requires the scope of the monopoly to be determined and, in the case of a program, that will necessarily be limited. However the contribution of that monopoly must still be assessed by reference to the process it will cause a computer to perform.

50. Fourth, and as I have recognised earlier in this judgment, it is highly undesirable that provisions of the Convention are construed differently in the EPO from the way they are construed in the national courts of a contracting state. Moreover, decisions of the Board of Appeal are of great persuasive authority. In the light of the *Aerotel* case [2007] Bus LR 634 it is not open to this court to follow the decisions in the 'trio'. However the new approach can be interpreted to produce a result consistent with that obtained by applying the reasoning of the Boards of Appeal in *IBM/Computer programs* [2000] EPOR 219 and *IBM/Computer programs II* [1999] RPC 861—decisions which, I would add, are still followed in the EPO as shown, for example, by the decision of the Board of Appeal in *Tao Group Ltd* (Decision T 121/06) (unreported) 25 January 2007. Significantly, much the same approach has been adopted in Germany following the decision of the Bundesgerichtshof—the German Federal Supreme Court—in *Suche fehlerhafter Zeichenketten* (Case No XZB 16/00) [2002] IIC 753.

51. In all these circumstances I have reached the conclusion that claims to computer programs are not necessarily excluded by article 52. In a case where claims to a method performed by running a suitably programmed computer or to a computer programmed to carry out the method are allowable, then, in principle, a claim to the program itself should also be allowable. I say 'in principle' because the claim must be drawn to reflect the features of the invention which would ensure the patentability of the method which the program is intended to carry out when it is run.

It is important to understand why the applicants in the case included 'computer program on storage medium claims'. The reason is that they exploited their inventions by selling them as computer programs stored on disks and other media and also by Internet download. As such, there were practical and commercial benefits to including 'computer program on storage medium' claims since otherwise the applicants would have been confined to protecting their inventions by the contributory infringement provisions of s. 60(2) of Patents

Act 1977. This provision requires that the alleged infringer must supply or offer to supply in the UK any of the means relating to an essential element of the invention for putting the invention into effect in the UK. In other words, it has the disadvantage that the substantive infringement is territorially limited to the UK, and this provides no protection against persons producing and selling programs in the UK for use abroad. There is another disadvantage (not raised before the Hearing Officer), namely, the requirement of actual or constructive knowledge.

The UK IPO issued a new Practice Note on 7 February 2008 implementing the *Astron Clinica* decision. However, it is questionable whether it will engender greater consistency between the EPO and UK IPO.[36] This is because the 'any hardware' approach, particularly as reflected in *Microsoft/Data Transfer*, has the potential to render redundant the *IBM* decisions. If the technical effect can arise simply by virtue of the program being stored on a carrier then it is unlikely such claims will fail because they lack the potential to produce a technical effect. That said, the Guidelines for Examination in the EPO, Part C, Chapter IV, para. 2.3.6 still refer to *IBM* T1173/97; however, confusingly, they also refer to *Hitachi*.

12.3.3 REFORM

The 'computer programs as such' exclusion has been the focus of reform efforts. At the Diplomatic Conference to revise the EPC, held in Munich in November 2000, it was proposed to delete this exclusion from Article 52(2)(c). The reason was that the exception had become de facto obsolete, given Board of Appeal decisions holding that computer programs that produced a technical effect were patentable subject matter. However, delegates to the Diplomatic Conference voted against the proposal and the exclusion remains.

Subsequently, the debate about how best to regulate inventions involving computer programs shifted to the European Commission and Parliament. The European Commission, believing that the legal situation concerning patenting of computer-related inventions was ambiguous and uncertain, and that the approaches of Member States were divergent, presented a Proposed Directive on the patentability of computer-implemented inventions in February 2002.[37] The Proposed Directive sought to harmonize the rules relating to patentability of computer-implemented inventions. A key feature was retaining the requirement of 'technical contribution' and ensuring that it was included in the patent legislation of Member States in relation to computer-implemented inventions.

Although the proposed reforms were fairly minimal, largely seeking to codify the EPO practice at the time, the Proposed Directive proved controversial and ran into difficulties during its legislative passage. On 24 September 2003, the European Parliament voted for preliminary approval to an amended version of the Proposed Directive. On 7 March 2005, the Council, by a qualified majority, adopted a common position. However, the European Parliament rejected the Common Position on 7 July 2005, thus bringing the legislative procedure to an end. As such, the patentability of computer-related inventions remains governed by the national law of Member States and the EPC.

It is clear that computer programs are patentable subject matter, provided a relevant technical effect or contribution can be shown. But the likelihood of establishing that technical effect will differ depending on whether one is applying via the EPO or the UK IPO.

---

[36] See T. Aplin, 'Patenting of computer programs: A glimmer of convergence' (2008) 9 EIPR 379–82.

[37] COM (2002) 92 final (20 Feb. 2002).

Of course, even if the invention is characterized as protectable subject matter, the hurdles of novelty and inventive step must still be surmounted and this may be difficult given the incremental developments that tend to occur in the information technology field. Certainly, we need to ask whether it makes sense to retain the 'computer programs as such' exclusion. If so, which approach is preferable—that of the EPO or the UK IPO, or should we adopt an entirely different approach? Further, how important is it that the same approach be used in all Member States and should this be achieved through harmonization?

FURTHER READING

R. M. Ballardini, 'Software patents in Europe: The technical requirement dilemma' (2008) 3 JIPLP 563.

D. Booton and P. Mole, 'The action freezes? The Draft Directive on the patentability of computer implemented inventions' [2002] IPQ 289.

J. Pila, 'Dispute over the meaning of "invention" in Article 52(2) EPC: The patentability of computer-implemented inventions in Europe' (2005) 36 IIC 173.

P. Leith, *Software and Patents in Europe* (Cambridge: Cambridge University Press, 2007).

12.4 COMPUTER VIDEO GAMES

12.4.1 INTRODUCTION

Computer video games first emerged as commercial products in the early 1970s.[38] Since then the video-game industry has grown phenomenally and is hugely lucrative. For example, it is estimated that 267.8 million video games were sold in 2007, amounting to 9.5 billion US dollars in revenue.[39] In simple terms a video game involves interaction with a user interface to generate visual data on a display device. Video games may be played on a variety of platforms, including personal computers, consoles, arcade machines, hand-held devices, and mobile phones. Producers of computer video games are concerned about piracy and the losses that it causes (estimated to be 3 billion US dollars in 2007).[40] We turn to consider the way in which copyright law has protected this type of intangible creation in the UK.

12.4.2 COPYRIGHT PROTECTION OF THE UNDERLYING PROGRAM

Given that a computer program underlies any video game it makes sense that copyright law has been heavily relied upon to protect this type of creation. Thus, as early as 1982 Goulding J in *Sega Enterprises Ltd v Richards*[41] granted interlocutory relief in respect of the video game, 'Frogger', which he characterized as a computer program and held was protected as a literary work under the Copyright Act 1956 (UK).

---

[38] e.g. 'Computer Space' and Atari's 'Pong'.

[39] According to the Entertainment Software Association: <http://www.theesa.com/facts/salesandgenre. asp>.

[40] See Entertainment Software Association: <http://www.theesa.com/policy/antipiracy_faq.asp>.

[41] [1983] FSR 73.

Computer video game producers continue to rely on protection of the underlying computer program as a literary work. However, as the case extracted below demonstrates, there are limits to this kind of protection.

Nova Productions Ltd v Mazooma Games Ltd [2007] RPC 25

The claimant produced a computer video game (in particular an arcade game) called 'Pocket Money', which was based on pool. The defendants' games, 'Jackpot Pool' and 'Trick Shot', allegedly infringed copyright in the claimant's game as, *inter alia*, a literary work. At first instance, Kitchin J found that the defendants had not had access to the source code of 'Pocket Money'. Further, that the games were visually very different, although certain similarities existed, namely, the presence of a power meter, a visual indication of the direction of the shot, the fact that the cue rotated around the cue ball via a rotary controller, the fact that the pool table was shown in plain view, and the values associated with particular pockets. Kitchin J held that copyright in the computer program was not infringed because ideas, rather than expression, had been copied. On appeal, the Court of Appeal upheld Kitchin J's decision.

Jacob LJ (with whom Lloyd LJ and Sir Andrew Morritt agreed):

Mere idea, not expression

31. Mr Howe had to face the formidable objection created by Art. 1.2 of the Directive and recitals 13 and 15. To my mind these provisions are abundantly clear. The well-known dichotomy between an idea and its individual expression is intended to apply and does to copyright in computer software...

32. Mr Howe suggested that the dichotomy was intended to apply only to ideas which underlie an element of a program—what he called a 'building block'. He cited (as did the judge) what Lord Hoffmann said about the dichotomy outside the context of computer programs in *Designers Guild*:

...

34. Mr Howe then submitted that the 'idea' of the cue pulsing with the power-meter could not be discounted within Lord Hoffmann's first category because here we are concerned with copyright in a computer program. You cannot say the 'idea' has no connection with the nature of the work. Nor did it fall within the second category because it was not held 'commonplace', merely 'obvious'. He sought to bolster the argument by reference to the *travaux préparatoires* to the Directive. At the very least, he submitted, the position was unclear and that we should refer some questions to the European Court of Justice pursuant to Art. 234 of the Treaty.

35. I reject all of that. First I think the fact that we are considering a computer program copyright does not in any way preclude a mere 'idea' as to what the program should do from being excluded as having nothing to do with the nature of the work. The nature of the work is a computer program having all the necessary coding to function. The general idea is only faintly related to that—no different from the relationship of the general idea of a plastic letterbox draught excluder to the artistic works consisting of the drawings for a particular excluder in the *Kleeneze* case. Indeed I have to say that, as Mr Howe waxed lyrical about the combination of features in the animation, he sounded more like counsel in a patent case than one in a copyright case. Not all of the skill which goes into a copyright work is protected—the obvious example being the skill involved in creating an invention which is then described in a literary

work. An idea consisting of a combination of ideas is still just an idea. That is as true for ideas in a computer program as for any other copyright work.

36. Nor am I impressed by Mr Howe's attempt to limit the dichotomy to 'building blocks'. He sought to do this by reference to recital 14 which refers to 'logic, algorithms and programming languages' as comprising 'ideas and principles'. I see no reason to suppose that recital 13 is thereby limited. Recital 14 is clearly drawn on the basis that the basic position of recital 13—no protection for ideas and principles—applies also to those specified matters.

. . .

44. Accordingly I think the appeal on literary copyright fails on the simple ground that what was found to have inspired some aspects of the defendants' game is just too general to amount to a substantial part of the claimants' game. The judge's evaluation, far from being wrong in principle, was right when he said:

> They are ideas which have little to do with the skill and effort expended by the programmer and do not constitute the form of expression of the literary works relied upon.

45. I also think the appeal fails on the more specific basis (also accepted by the judge) of the principles applied by Pumfrey J in *Navitaire Inc v easyJet Airline Co* [2004] EWHC 1725 (Ch); [2006] RPC 3.

[**Jacob LJ** then quoted extensively from *Navitaire* and went on to deal with Counsel for the claimant's disagreement with the case.]

. . .

49. He further developed the argument basing himself on recital 7 of the Directive. This says:

> 'computer program'…also includes preparatory design work leading to the development of a computer program provided that the nature of the preparatory work is such that a computer program can result from it at a later stage.

He asked us to suppose a case where there are two clear stages in the making of a program— a first stage where the designer sets out all the things he wants the program to be able do and a second stage (which may be by a different person) where the actual program code is written. Mr Howe contended that the first stage was intended to be protected as such, even if it consisted only of ideas as to what the program should do. Going back to the analogy, the 'preparatory work' for the program is like the skill of devising the recipe and the actual program writing like the reduction of the recipe to written form. The difference, he submitted, is that for computer programs, unlike the recipe, the preparatory work is to be protected.

50. I reject the argument. The reason is simple. The Directive does not say that mere ideas by way of preparatory design work are to be protected. As I have said it makes it clear that for computer programs as a whole (which includes their preparatory design work) ideas are not to be protected. What is protected by way of preparatory design work is that work as a literary work—the expression of the design which are to go into the ultimate program, not the ideas themselves.

51. So for example, if Mr Jones had actually written a description of the pulsing, rotating cue, and synchronised power meter his description would (if not too trivial at least) be protected as a literary work. People could not copy that. But they could use the same idea. Similarly and more generally, a written work consisting of a specification of the functions of an intended computer program will attract protection as a literary work. But the functions themselves do not. Of course to someone familiar with the prior English law it is self-evident that copyright could subsist in such a description. The fact that a work can get copyright even if mundane, is old and familiar to an English lawyer. But the Directive needed to say that

protection as a literary work should be provided for preparatory design work because not all Member States under their existing laws necessarily provided that. That is the whole point of the Directive—and the clear reason for it is recited in Art. 1.

52. So I think Mr Howe's attack on *Navitaire* fails. The reasoning in *Navitaire* provides a second reason for dismissing this appeal. Pumfrey J was quite right to say that merely making a program which will emulate another but which in no way involves copying the program code or any of the program's graphics is legitimate.

...

54. I would only add this. Both sides submitted that this case had significance for the computer games (and computer program writing) industry. Mr Howe submitted that if the decision below is upheld there is no effective protection for games against copying of the game where a party copies the rules of a game but not its graphics. Mr Carr submitted that that not all things are covered by copyright, that most if not every work is, to some extent, influenced or derived from other works. So it is very important that copyright is not allowed to intervene to stifle the creation of works that are actually very different, as the individual games are here.

55. I agree with Mr Carr. If protection for such general ideas as are relied on here were conferred by the law, copyright would become an instrument of oppression rather than the incentive for creation which it is intended to be. Protection would have moved to cover works merely inspired by others, to ideas themselves.

Nova Productions reiterates that the idea/expression principle applies to computer programs protected as literary works and emphasizes that the behaviour or appearance generated by a program falls within the realm of 'idea'. As such, it will not be possible to prevent a competitor from producing a visually similar game, with similar game play in reliance on copyright in the underlying computer program. Are there alternative means of protecting these creative aspects of computer video games? This is explored in the next section.

12.4.3 COPYRIGHT PROTECTION OF THE VISUAL APPEARANCE

In order to protect the visual appearance of a video game, it may be possible to rely on different categories of works, such as artistic, dramatic, and film works. The ability of relying on the artistic work category was also explored in *Nova Productions*.

Nova Productions Ltd v Mazooma Games Ltd [2007] RPC 25

For the facts, see p. 714 above.

Jacob LJ (with whom Lloyd LJ and Sir Andrew Morritt agreed):

12. First then, what is the artistic work? It was common ground that the individual frames stored in the memory of a computer were 'graphic works' with the meaning of the Act (judgment [100]–[104]). But the actual appearance of individual frames between Pocket Money and the alleged infringements are very different (see Judgment Annex). Regarded just as

pictures—as 'graphic works' in the words of the Act—they are obviously very different. Save for the fact that they are of a pool table with pocket, balls and a cue, nothing of the defendants' screens as single frames can be said to be a substantial reproduction of a corresponding screen in Pocket Money. Both before the judge and us Mr Howe accepted that 'each of the defendants had done their own drawings of cues and billiard balls' and did not contend for infringement at the level of individual screen graphics.

13. Mr Howe invited us to find that there was in effect a further kind of artistic work, something beyond individual freeze-frame graphics. This was said to be because there is a series of graphics which show the 'in-time' movement of cue and meter. So, it was said, that what the defendants had done was to:

create a dynamic 're-posing' of the Claimant's version—one in which the detail of the subjects had changed, but an essential artistic element of the original was carried through to the Defendants.

This was said to involve extra skill and labour beyond just that involved in creating the individual frames.

14. The judge was prepared to accept:

that 'in time' movement of the cue and meter must be considered as being reflected in a series of still shots and like must be compared with like,

but nonetheless held there was no infringement.

15. Mr Carr, by a respondents' notice, challenged that assumption. He submitted that a series of still images, whether created by drawing for a cartoon film or by a computer, was not in itself anything more than a series of frames, each of which would have its own copyright and no more. No 'extra' copyright work or protection is created by having a series. Putting it another way, a series of stills is just that.

16. I think that must be right. 'Graphic work' is defined as including all the types of thing specified in s. 4(2) which all have this in common, namely that they are static, non-moving. A series of drawings is a series of graphic works, not a single graphic work in itself. No-one would say that the copyright in a single drawing of Felix the Cat is infringed by a drawing of Donald Duck. A series of cartoon frames showing Felix running over a cliff edge into space, looking down and only then falling would not be infringed by a similar set of frames depicting Donald doing the same thing. That is in effect what is alleged here.

17. This reasoning is supported by the fact that Parliament has specifically created copyright in moving images by way of copyright in films. If Mr Howe were right, the series of still images which provides the illusion of movement would itself create a further kind of copyright work protecting moving images. It is unlikely that Parliament intended this.

18. So I think the case on artistic works falls at the first hurdle, given the concession that there is no frame-for-frame reproduction.

As mentioned in passing in the above extract, it is possible for a series of screen displays or frames to be protected as a film. However, as seen in *Norowzian v Arks Ltd (No 1)* [1998] FSR 394, protection as a film work extends only to *literal* copying. Thus, where a competitor produces a similar-looking game, as opposed to making unauthorized or pirated copies of the copyright owner's video game, this type of protection will be of no assistance. Protection as a dramatic work, however, would extend to non-literal copying, as was established in *Norowzian v Arks (No 2)*. Whether a series of screen displays can be protected as a dramatic work was considered at first instance in *Nova Productions*.

Nova Productions Ltd v Mazooma Games Ltd [2006] RPC 14

For the facts, see p. 714 above.

Kitchin J:

116. I have reached the conclusion that it is quite impossible to say that the Pocket Money game is in any sense a dramatic work for all the following reasons. First, it will be apparent from the nature of the game that I have described earlier in this judgment that it is not a work of action which is intended to be or is capable of being performed before an audience. On the contrary, it is a game. Although the game has a set of rules, the particular sequence of images displayed on the screen will depend in very large part on the manner in which it is played. That sequence of images will not be the same from one game to another, even if the game is played by the same individual. There is simply no sufficient unity within the game for it to be capable of performance.

117. Secondly, Nova relies in support of its claim for copyright infringement on various particulars of similarity. I deal with these in detail later in this judgment. However, it will be apparent from those particulars that Nova has sought to identify a number of distinctive features in the Pocket Money game which, it contends, have been reproduced in the defendants' games. In my judgment these features can no more be described as features of a dramatic work than could the features that Mr Green sought to rely upon in his case against the Broadcasting Corporation of New Zealand. They are not capable of performance. They are simply aspects of the Pocket Money game. Nor do they have the certainty needed in order to avoid injustice to third parties. As I will explain later in this judgment, they are drawn at a very high level of generality.

118. Thirdly, I understand it was contended that the dramatic work is recorded in the original development notes produced by Mr Jones and in the program code. As far as the development notes are concerned, I have accepted that these are a literary work. Accordingly, they cannot be a dramatic work. Further, they contain a whole series of different ideas, only some of which found their way into the finished game. They do not constitute a single work which is capable of being performed before an audience.

119. Fourthly, so far as the code is concerned, Nova sought to contend that the literary copyright subsists in the source code and the dramatic work is recorded in the object code. Nevertheless Nova has not explained how the dramatic work upon which it relies is recorded in the code. It has given no evidence about the code and indeed the source code was not provided to the defendants until shortly before the trial. As I explain below in considering the issue of infringement of the code as a literary work, it seems to me inevitable that the code contains not a record of any dramatic work but rather a set of instructions which dictates the way in which the game may be played and what will appear on the screen in response to the various inputs made by the person playing the game.

Given the views of Kitchin J in the above extract do you think it will be possible ever to protect the visual appearance of a video game as a dramatic work? In particular, consider the situation where the visual features that a claimant is seeking to protect are more specific than that in *Nova Productions*. Or does the very fact that a video game is interactive, thus giving rise to different moving images on each playing, mean that it will always lack sufficient unity to be capable of performance? Finally, is Kitchin J saying that the underlying program code can never record or fix a dramatic work? If so, how else could a dramatic work (reflected in the moving images on screen) be recorded?

In conclusion, copyright law appears to offer limited protection to video game manufacturers in the sense that it will not prevent competitors from producing and selling similar types of computer video games. However, copyright law may be used against those who make unauthorized or pirated copies. This type of protection is bolstered by the ability to apply technical protection measures to copies of computer video games and the provisions prohibiting circumvention or commercially dealing in circumvention devices. For a discussion on the unlawfulness of circumvention see 12.2.3.6 above and 12.6.5 below. We may therefore ask whether the protection of computer video games under copyright law is sufficient and, if not, can this be remedied?

FURTHER READING

S. G. McKnight, 'Substantial similarity between video games: An old copyright problem in a new medium' (1983) 36 Vand LR 1277.

T. M. S. Hemnes, 'The adaptation of copyright law to video games' (1982–83) 131 U Pa LR 171.

12.5 DATABASES

12.5.1 INTRODUCTION

Copyright law has long protected compilations or collections of information. In the UK, for example, trade directories,[42] indexes of information,[43] betting coupons,[44] and football fixture lists,[45] have qualified for protection as literary works. In determining whether compilations are 'original' literary works, English courts have taken a generous approach and there have been cases where compilations featuring marginal skill or judgment in their selection or arrangement of materials, but which have involved considerable labour or expense, have been protected.[46] Further, courts have been prepared to consider the skill and effort applied in collecting, gathering, or calculating data for a compilation, as opposed to that expended in its selection or arrangement.[47] Finally, the scope of protection given to compilations has been extensive, in that copying information, as opposed to its selection or arrangement, has been treated as infringing.[48]

Catalogues, directories, and other sorts of compilations have also been protected in other jurisdictions, such as the US, France, and Germany. In the US, compilations resulting from the 'sweat of the brow' (i.e. labour) were eligible for copyright protection until the landmark decision of the US Supreme Court in *Feist Publications Inc v Rural Telephone Service Co.*[49] In this case, the Supreme Court unequivocally repudiated the 'sweat of the brow' test of originality and replaced it with a test of 'independent creation' plus 'minimal level of creativity'. The court emphasized that the 'requisite level of creativity is extremely

---

[42] *Morris v Ashbee* (1868–69) LR 7 Eq 34; *Kelly v Morris* (1865–66) LR 1 Eq 697.

[43] *Blacklock v Pearson* [1915] 2 Ch 376.

[44] *Ladbroke (Football) Ltd v William Hill (Football) Ltd* [1964] 1 WLR 273.

[45] *Football League v Littlewoods* [1959] Ch 637.   [46] Ibid.

[47] *Ladbroke (Football) Ltd v William Hill (Football) Ltd* [1964] 1 WLR 273.

[48] e.g. see *Waterlow Directories Ltd v Reed Information Services Ltd* [1992] FSR 409; *Waterlow Publishers Ltd v Rose* [1995] FSR 207; and *Elanco Products Ltd v Mandops Ltd* [1979] FSR 409.

[49] (1991) 499 US 340.

low; even a slight amount will suffice'.[50] However, on the facts, the 'white pages' telephone directory in issue did not evidence the requisite creativity because it was comprehensive (therefore no selection was involved) and the arrangement was entirely typical of that genre of work (i.e. alphabetical).

France adopts an originality test of 'author's imprint of their personality', while in Germany the test is whether the work is a 'personal intellectual creation'. In both jurisdictions, courts are reasonably generous in their application of these tests to tables and compilations. However, they are less willing than English courts to protect very mundane compilations. Thus, in Germany, telephone directories were held not to satisfy the test of 'personal intellectual creation'[51] and, in France, a table of wine information (listing wines by region, year, and quality) was held not to reflect the author's 'imprint of personality'.[52]

12.5.2 INTERNATIONAL PROTECTION OF DATABASES

The development of software led to a transformation in compilations. In particular, collections of information were no longer limited to physical formats, but could be stored in electronic or digital form. As a result, it became possible to store larger quantities of data and to search and retrieve information in a variety of ways. These electronic collections, known popularly as 'databases', took considerable investment to develop, yet because of their format were vulnerable to piracy. Database producers, therefore, were keen to protect their works and sought to rely on copyright law to do so. However, it was unclear whether there was an international obligation to protect databases as copyright works. This is because Article 2(5) of the Berne Convention stipulates:

> Collections of literary or artistic works such as encyclopaedias and anthologies which, by reason of the selection and arrangement of their contents, constitute intellectual creations shall be protected as such, without prejudice to the copyright in each of the works forming part of such collections.

The problem with databases falling within this provision is that they do not necessarily include collections of 'literary and artistic' *works*, but are frequently collections of *information*. This problem, however, was solved by the TRIPS Agreement, Article 10(2), which states:

> Compilations of data or other material, whether in machine readable or other form, which by reason of the selection or arrangement of their contents constitute intellectual creations shall be protected as such. Such protection, which shall not extend to the data or material itself, shall be without prejudice to any copyright subsisting in the data or material itself.

Article 5 of the WIPO Copyright Treaty 1996 is in virtually identical terms and the Agreed Statement confirms that this provision is consistent with Article 2 of the Berne Convention. Thus, it is now clear that an international obligation exists to protect databases by copyright where the selection or arrangement of their contents constitutes an intellectual creation. However, a key feature of databases is their comprehensive nature, and as such it may be difficult to show that the 'selection and arrangement' of their contents is an intellectual

---

[50] Ibid., p. 345.

[51] *Unauthorised Reproduction of Telephone Directories on CD-Rom* [2002] ECDR 3.

[52] *Compagnie des Courtiers Jures Piqueurs de Vins de Paris v Société DDB Needham* [2000] ECC 128.

creation. There is also the problem that different approaches to originality are adopted in various jurisdictions.

12.5.3 EU DATABASE DIRECTIVE

In the early 1990s the European Commission became extremely keen to nurture and protect the European database industry. However, it saw the differences between Member States when it came to the protection of databases, as well as the lack of appropriate protection, as obstacles to achieving this goal. The result was a directive harmonizing the legal protection of databases[53] ('Database Directive'), which was adopted on 11 March 1996. The directive adopted a twofold approach to protecting databases: first, it sought to harmonize copyright protection and secondly, it introduced a new, sui generis right.

12.5.3.1 Copyright protection

According to recitals 2 to 4 of the Database Directive the variances in copyright protection of databases in Member States was believed negatively to impact on the functioning of the internal market and prevent the free movement of goods. Thus, harmonization of copyright protection occurred in most areas, including the definition of subject matter, originality, authorship, exclusive rights, and exceptions. Notably absent, however, were provisions harmonizing copyright ownership of databases created by employees and also moral rights. This next section will briefly examine the degree of copyright harmonization and the extent to which the UK successfully implemented its obligations.

Turning first to the definition of subject matter, Article 1(2) of the Database Directive states that a 'database' is:

> a collection of independent works, data or other materials arranged in a systematic or methodical way and individually accessible by electronic or other means.

The definition allows for a wide range of materials to comprise a database. This view is confirmed by recital 17 of the Database Directive, which states that databases include 'literary, artistic, musical or other collections of works or collections of other material such as texts, sounds, images, numbers, facts, and data'. However, it seems that a database does not extend to collections of tangible objects, such as a group of artworks in a gallery. This is because the purpose of the directive was to protect databases as informational works.[54]

The collection must comprise independent works, data, or other materials, but what is meant by independent? Some guidance is provided by recital 17, which states that a 'recording or an audiovisual, cinematographic, literary or musical work as such does not fall within the scope of this Directive'. Further, the ECJ has indicated that 'independent' materials refers to those materials 'which are separable from one another without their informative, literary, artistic, musical or other value being affected'.[55] Works, data, or other material will be arranged in a systematic or methodical way where they are presented in an

---

[53] Directive 96/9/EC of the European Parliament and of the Council of 11 Mar. 1996 on the legal protection of databases.

[54] See recital 9 and also E. Derclaye, 'What is a database? A critical analysis of the definition of a database in the European Database Directive and suggestions for an international definition' (2002) 5 Journal of World Intellectual Property 281, 998–1003.

[55] *Fixtures Marketing Ltd v Organismos prognostikon agonon podosfairou AE (OPAP)* Case C-444/02 [2004] ECR I-10549, para. 29.

organized manner as opposed to being physically stored as such.[56] This includes presentation in an alphabetical, chronological, or subject order. Also, it is clear from the words 'individually accessible by electronic or other means' that both electronic and non-electronic (or hard copy) databases are included. As for the requirement that materials are 'individually accessible' this is best understood as where the collection of materials is searchable and the materials can be perceived distinctly.[57]

Importantly, Article 1(3) of the Database Directive provides that protection shall not apply to 'computer programs used in the making or operation of databases accessible by electronic means'. It thus appears that computer programs cannot be protected as databases. This assumes that it is a straightforward matter to distinguish databases from computer programs. However, this may be questioned, not least because there is no accepted definition of 'computer program' at an EC level, as was explained at 12.2.3.1 above. The difficulty of separating out the database elements from the underlying computer program is further complicated by recital 20, which states that protection 'may also apply to the material necessary for the operation or consultation of certain databases such as thesaurus and indexation systems'. In the case of electronic databases, the underlying computer program will be responsible for such systems. Does this mean that computer programs are protected to the extent that they operate as a database?

The UK implemented verbatim Article 1(2) in s. 3A of the CDPA, but in s. 3(1) 'databases' are characterized as 'literary works'. This classification of 'databases' as literary works suggests that in the UK a narrower range of works may comprise a 'database'. However, the better view is that the amendments implementing the Database Directive should be construed as far as possible to comply with that directive, so that the broad definition of 'database' contained in s. 3A be given its full effect. Article 1(3) was not explicitly incorporated into the CDPA; however, it seems that computer programs will not amount to a 'database' because s. 3(1) of the CDPA draws a clear distinction between computer programs and databases and the legislation should be construed in conformity with the Database Directive.

At 12.5.1 above, we saw that a different originality test is used in the UK, as compared with France and Germany. As such, the Database Directive sought to harmonize the test of originality for databases and did so by including Article 3, which states 'databases, which by reason of the selection or arrangement of their contents, constitute the author's own intellectual creation shall be protected as such by copyright'. This was implemented in s. 3A(2) of the CDPA and represents the first time the originality test has been explicated in UK legislation. According to s. 3(1)(a) of the CDPA, tables or compilations *other than a database* appear to remain subject to the traditional originality test of 'labour, skill, and judgment'. A question that arises is whether this test differs from that of 'author's own intellectual creation' applicable to databases and, if so, to what extent? One view is that 'author's own intellectual creation' reflects the civil law standards of originality in France and Germany. Alternatively, it has been suggested that the standard is synonymous with the 'minimal level of creativity' test in the US *Feist* decision. Whichever view is taken, it seems that extremely mundane works, which reflect little skill or judgment in their selection or arrangement, will not be protected as 'databases' under UK copyright law. Could it be that they are alternatively protected as compilations? The answer seems to be no since s. 3 of the CDPA distinguishes between 'databases' and 'tables or compilations other than databases'. In other words, if a collection satisfies the definition of 'database' in s. 3A, it will be classified as such and, as a result, will not be capable of qualifying as a table or compilation. Given the breadth of the

---

[56] See recital 21.   [57] Aplin, *Copyright Law in the Digital Society*, p. 51.

definition of 'database' it seems fair to say that few collections will fall outside it. Thus, there will be a minimal number of works that are tables or compilations and subject to the traditional originality test.

When it comes to authorship of a copyright database, Article 4 of the Database Directive states that this will be the natural person or persons who created the work. However, where the legislation of a Member State allows for a legal person to be the rightsholder, that legal person may be an author. Again, it may be queried whether such a provision was necessary given that the Member States to which it seems directed (such as France) arguably do not permit legal persons to be authors, as opposed to rightsholders. In contrast to the Software Directive, there is no provision in the Database Directive governing ownership of copyright in databases created by employees. Rather, this is left to the discretion of Member States and nothing prevents a Member State from providing that the employer shall be entitled to exercise all economic rights in the database created by an employee in the execution of his duties for the employer, unless otherwise provided by contract.[58]

According to Article 5 of the Database Directive, the author of a database protected by copyright shall have the exclusive right to carry out or authorize:

(a) temporary or permanent reproduction by any means and in any form, in whole or in part;

(b) translation, adaptation, arrangement and any other alteration;

(c) any form of distribution to the public of the database of copies thereof...;

(d) any communication, display or performance to the public;

(e) any reproduction, distribution, communication, display or performance to the public of the results of the acts referred to in (b).

It was unnecessary to amend the UK law in order to provide the protection stipulated in Article 5 since these exclusive acts were already contained in s. 16 of the CDPA. However, the Database Directive significantly narrowed the scope of protection for databases in the UK, insofar as infringement can no longer occur simply by copying the information within a database. Instead, the whole or a substantial part of the *selection* or *arrangement* of the contents must be copied. This may be illustrated by a simple example. Company A publishes a directory of practising barristers and solicitors in England and Wales. The directory contains 10,000 names and is arranged geographically by city, then according to area of expertise and then alphabetically by name. Assume that the directory satisfies the originality requirement of 'author's own intellectual creation' because skill and judgment has been used in classifying the practitioners according to their area of expertise. Company B then publishes a competing directory, in which it copies the names of 5,000 lawyers listed in Company A's directory, but arranges the information solely in alphabetical order. Under the previous UK law, there was authority that suggested this would amount to an infringement. However, post implementation of the Database Directive it appears that Company B would not infringe since they have not copied the arrangement of contents in Company A's directory.[59] Nor have they copied a substantial part of Company

[58] Database Directive, recital 29.

[59] See recital 38 of the Database Directive: 'Whereas the increasing use of digital recording technology exposes the database maker to the risk that the contents of his database may be copied and rearranged electronically, without his authorization, to produce a database of identical content which, however, does not infringe any copyright in the arrangement of his database.'

A's selection of data since this selection is not an intellectual creation, but merely the result of being comprehensive.

When it comes to exceptions to copyright infringement, Article 6 contains one mandatory and four optional exceptions. The mandatory exception is contained in Article 6(1) and states that the performance by a lawful user of any of the exclusive acts 'which is necessary for the purpose of access to the contents of the databases and normal use of the contents by the lawful user' shall not require authorization. Any contractual provision that seeks to override this exception will be null and void according to Article 15 of the Database Directive. Importantly, the exception applies only to the *lawful user* of a database, the meaning of which is not entirely certain. However, it has been argued that the preferable interpretation of 'lawful user' is that it refers to any person who lawfully acquires the database (for example, via sale, gift, public lending, and rental contracts).[60] Article 6(1) has been implemented in the CDPA as s. 50D. This provision is similar in terms to Article 6(1), except that instead of referring to 'lawful user' it refers to 'a person who has a right to use the database or any part of the database (whether under a licence to do any of the acts restricted by the copyright in the database or otherwise)'. This wording is possibly inconsistent with the concept of 'lawful user' in the Database Directive insofar as it may include persons who rely upon an implied licence.

Member States, according to Article 6(2), may also provide for exceptions in the following cases:

a. in the case of reproduction for private purposes of a non-electronic database;

b. where there is use for the sole purpose of illustration for teaching or scientific research, as long as the source is indicated and to the extent justified by the non-commercial purpose to be achieved;

c. where there is use for the purposes of public security or for the purposes of an administrative or judicial proceeding;

d. where other exceptions to copyright which are traditionally authorised under national law are involved, without prejudice to points (a), (b) and (c).

The scope of the above exceptions is discussed in the following extract.

T. Aplin, *Copyright Law in the Digital Society: The Challenges of Multimedia*
(Oxford: Hart, 2005), pp. 179–80

The first optional exception is limited, in that it exempts only the act of reproduction carried out in relation to non-electronic databases. It reflects a private use type exception for hardcopy databases. This exception was not implemented into the CDPA probably because a private use exception does not exist in UK copyright law, as compared with certain civil law Member States.

The scope of the second optional exception is difficult to ascertain. It is unclear, for example, what will amount to '*illustration* for teaching or scientific research'. Does 'illustration' confine the use to providing examples of what is being taught or researched? If so, this would not allow a teacher or researcher to use the database simply in preparing their teaching or as an

---

[60] Aplin, *Copyright Law in the Digital Society*, p. 177.

aid to their research. Further, does 'illustration for teaching' mean that use for the purpose of learning, in other words, private study, is excluded? Finally, illustration for teaching or scientific research must be the sole purpose and must not exceed the non-commercial purpose. Thus, it appears that the use must be non-commercial, which may be a difficult requirement to satisfy in the light of realities of education and research institutions. This exception was not specifically implemented in UK law. However, the exception of fair dealing for the purpose of (non-commercial) research and private study, along with the exceptions relating to copying by educational establishments in sections 32–36 of the CDPA will embrace the sorts of activities contemplated by Article 6(2)(b) of the Database Directive.

The third optional exception, namely, Article 6(2)(c) concerning the purposes of public security and administrative and judicial proceedings, would appear to be catered for by sections 45–50 of the CDPA. These provisions create exceptions relating to public administration.

The fourth optional exception, namely, exceptions to copyright traditionally authorised under national law, was the subject of consideration in *Mars v Teknowledge* (discussed above in relation to computer programs). In *Mars*, Jacob J considered that such exceptions had to be adopted by Member States and did not encompass judge-made exceptions, such as the common law 'right to repair' or 'spare parts' exception that originated in *British Leyland v Armstrong,* and was subsequently narrowed by the Privy Council in *Canon Kabushiki Kaisha v Green Cartridge.* In relation to Article 6(2)(d) of the Database Directive, Jacob J commented—

> that provision is an option for Member States to adopt by way of limitation of database rights. It can hardly be for the judges of a particular Member State of their own to act as though they are exercising the option on behalf of that State. If Parliament had wanted to adopt an option in relation to the use of database rights for updating equipment, that is a matter for it, not the judges. I cannot regard section 173(2) [sic] as adopting such an option. Moreover it is far from certainly the case that the use of copyright in databases (which, before the Directive, were generally protected in the UK as literary works in the form of compilations) was 'traditionally authorised' in this country.

Jacob J's comments about Article 6(2)(d), strictly speaking, are obiter dicta since the case concerned the applicability of the 'spare parts' defence to the *database right* and Article 6(2)(d) relates only to copyright databases.

Would you agree with the comments made in the above extract about the scope of exceptions in Article 6(2)(a)–(b) of the Database Directive? If so, how would you seek to broaden the scope of these exceptions?

12.5.3.2 Sui generis protection

The Database Directive introduced a new sui generis right for databases, also referred to as the 'database right'. This was implemented in the UK via the Copyright and Rights in Databases Regulations 1997.[61] As the recitals to the directive indicate,[62] databases were seen as vital components of an information market within the Community, but as vulnerable to piracy. Protection additional to that offered by copyright was thought necessary in order to prevent the unauthorized extraction and reuse of database contents and hence to safeguard the considerable investment required to produce databases. It was seen as particu-

---

[61] SI 1997/3032.   [62] See especially, recitals 6–12, 38–40.

larly important to encourage this type of investment because of the 'very great imbalance in the level of investment in the database sector both as between the Member States and between the Community and the world's largest database-producing third countries'.[63] A sui generis right was adopted as the form of protection, rather than unfair competition law, because of the difficulties of harmonizing the law of unfair competition (not least because some countries, such as the UK and Ireland, do not have this type of protection). Thus, it is now the case that a database may be protected both by copyright *and* the sui generis right and this protection is irrespective of the eligibility of individual contents for protection by copyright or related rights.[64] Copyright protects the selection or arrangement of the contents in a database, while the sui generis right protects the contents of the database as a whole.

The definition of 'database' is the same for the sui generis right as it is for copyright.[65] As such, the scope of that definition and its difficulties, discussed in the previous section (12.5.3.1), also apply here.

Chapter III of the Database Directive sets out the sui generis right. According to Article 7(1) the maker of a database only acquires the right where there has been 'qualitatively and/or quantitatively a substantial investment in either the obtaining, verification or presentation of the contents'. Where that threshold is met, the database maker will have the right to prevent extraction and/or reutilization of the whole or a substantial part of the database contents.

The exact nature of the threshold requirement of substantial investment etc. has been the source of uncertainty and so it was that several references on the same issue were made to the ECJ.[66] For our purposes, it suffices to focus on the reference from the Court of Appeal of England and Wales, which is dealt with below.

British Horseracing Board Ltd v William Hill Organization Ltd Case C-203/02 [2004] ECR I-10415

The British Horseracing Board ('BHB') is the governing authority for the British racing industry, formed in 1993. Its functions include compiling data related to horseracing, establishing the dates and programme contents for race fixtures, and creating the fixture list for each year's racing. William Hill is one of the leading providers of off-course betting services in the UK and elsewhere and mainly provides fixed-odds bets on sporting and other events from its licensed betting offices. It also provides online betting services.

Racing information in the BHB database was distributed in two main ways. First, via a company called Racing Pages Ltd, which operated a declarations feed. The declarations feed contained a list of races, declared runners and jockeys, distance and name of races, race times, and number of runners in each race together with other information and this data was forwarded to subscribers usually the day before the race. The second form of distribution was via Satellite Information Services, one of Racing Pages' subscribers, who supplied this data to its own subscribers in the form of a raw-data feed.

---

[63] Recital 11.   [64] Database Directive Art. 7(4).   [65] Ibid., Art. 1(2).
[66] *Fixtures Marketing Ltd v Svenska Spel AB* Case C-338/02 [2004] ECR I-10497; *Fixtures Marketing Ltd v Organismos prognostikon agnon podosfairou AE (OPAP)* Case C-444/02 [2004] ECR I-10549; *Fixtures Marketing Ltd v Oy Veikkaus Ab* Case C-46/02 [2004] ECR I-10365; *British Horseracing Board Ltd v William Hill Organization Ltd* Case C-203/02 [2004] ECR I-10415.

William Hill subscribed to both the declarations feed and the raw-data feed, for the purpose of its betting operations from its licensed betting offices.

The dispute arose from William Hill's use of data from the raw-data feed in relation to its online betting services. BHB claimed that William Hill's activities amounted to unauthorized extraction or reutilization of a substantial part of the contents of its database, contrary to Article 7(1), or else repeated and systematic extraction or reutilization of insubstantial parts of the contents contrary to Article 7(5). BHB succeeded in the High Court before Laddie J.[67] The Court of Appeal referred a series of questions to the ECJ for interpretation.[68]

> 28. By its second and third questions the referring court seeks clarification of the concept of investment in the obtaining and verification of the contents of a database within the meaning of Art. 7(1) of the directive.
>
> 29. Article 7(1) of the directive reserves the protection of the *sui generis* right to databases which meet a specific criterion, namely to those which show that there has been qualitatively and/or quantitatively a substantial investment in the obtaining, verification or presentation of their contents.
>
> 30. Under the 9th, 10th and 12th recitals of the preamble to the directive, its purpose, as William Hill points out, is to promote and protect investment in data 'storage' and 'processing' systems which contribute to the development of an information market against a background of exponential growth in the amount of information generated and processed annually in all sectors of activity. It follows that the expression 'investment in... the obtaining, verification or presentation of the contents' of a database must be understood, generally, to refer to investment in the creation of that database as such.
>
> 31. Against that background, the expression 'investment in... the obtaining... of the contents' of a database must, as William Hill and the Belgian, German and Portuguese Governments point out, be understood to refer to the resources used to seek out existing independent materials and collect them in the database, and not to the resources used for the creation as such of independent materials. The purpose of the protection by the *sui generis* right provided for by the directive is to promote the establishment of storage and processing systems for existing information and not the creation of materials capable of being collected subsequently in a database.
>
> 32. That interpretation is backed up by the 39th recital of the preamble to the directive, according to which the aim of the *sui generis* right is to safeguard the results of the financial and professional investment made in 'obtaining and collection of the contents' of a database. As the Advocate General notes in points AG41 to AG46 of her Opinion, despite slight variations in wording, all the language versions of the 39th recital support an interpretation which excludes the creation of the materials contained in a database from the definition of obtaining.
>
> 33. The 19th recital of the preamble to the directive, according to which the compilation of several recordings of musical performances on a CD does not represent a substantial enough investment to be eligible under the *sui generis* right, provides an additional argument in support of that interpretation. Indeed, it appears from that recital that the resources used for the creation as such of works or materials included in the database, in this case on a CD, cannot be deemed equivalent to investment in the obtaining of the contents of that database and cannot, therefore, be taken into account in assessing whether the investment in the creation of the database was substantial.

---

[67] *British Horseracing Board Ltd v William Hill Organization Ltd* [2001] CMLR 12.
[68] *British Horseracing Board Ltd v William Hill Organization Ltd* [2002] ECDR 4.

34. The expression 'investment in…the…verification…of the contents' of a database must be understood to refer to the resources used, with a view to ensuring the reliability of the information contained in that database, to monitor the accuracy of the materials collected when the database was created and during its operation. The resources used for verification during the stage of creation of data or other materials which are subsequently collected in a database, on the other hand, are resources used in creating a database and cannot therefore be taken into account in order to assess whether there was substantial investment in the terms of Art. 7(1) of the directive.

35. In that light, the fact that the creation of a database is linked to the exercise of a principal activity in which the person creating the database is also the creator of the materials contained in the database does not, as such, preclude that person from claiming the protection of the *sui generis* right, provided that he establishes that the obtaining of those materials, their verification or their presentation, in the sense described in [31] to [34] of this judgment, required substantial investment in quantitative or qualitative terms, which was independent of the resources used to create those materials.

36. Thus, although the search for data and the verification of their accuracy at the time a database is created do not require the maker of that database to use particular resources because the data are those he created and are available to him, the fact remains that the collection of those data, their systematic or methodical arrangement in the database, the organisation of their individual accessibility and the verification of their accuracy throughout the operation of the database may require substantial investment in quantitative and/or qualitative terms within the meaning of Art. 7(1) of the directive.

37. In the case in the main proceedings, the referring court seeks to know whether the investments described in [14] of this judgment can be considered to amount to investment in obtaining the contents of the BHB database. The plaintiffs in the main proceedings stress, in that connection, the substantial nature of the above investment.

38. However, investment in the selection, for the purpose of organising horse racing, of the horses admitted to run in the race concerned relates to the creation of the data which make up the lists for those races which appear in the BHB database. It does not constitute investment in obtaining the contents of the database. It cannot, therefore, be taken into account in assessing whether the investment in the creation of the database was substantial.

39. Admittedly, the process of entering a horse on a list for a race requires a number of prior checks as to the identity of the person making the entry, the characteristics of the horse and the classification of the horse, its owner and the jockey.

40. However, such prior checks are made at the stage of creating the list for the race in question. They thus constitute investment in the creation of data and not in the verification of the contents of the database.

41. It follows that the resources used to draw up a list of horses in a race and to carry out checks in that connection do not represent investment in the obtaining and verification of the contents of the database in which that list appears.

Do you agree with the distinction made by the ECJ between investment in creating data (which is irrelevant) and investment in obtaining or verifying existing data (which is relevant)? Will this be a straightforward distinction to apply in practice?

Importantly, the ECJ decision in *British Horseracing* held that the only test for determining whether the sui generis right subsists is that contained in the directive. As such the spin-off doctrine that had emerged in certain Member States case law (particularly the Netherlands) was rejected. According to the spin-off doctrine, a database that is a consequence or spin-off of commercial activity not aimed at producing a database cannot be considered to have met the standard of 'substantial investment'. This is because the 'investment' must be a conscious act directed towards a particular end, namely, the creation of a database. The ECJ rejected the spin-off doctrine, for the reasons expressed in para. 35 of the above extract. In short, the spin-off doctrine focuses on who has invested in the *creation* of the materials in the database, however, this is not relevant investment according to the ECJ.

In terms of investment in the presentation of contents, this issue was not addressed in *British Horseracing*, but it was dealt with in the other three references to the ECJ. The ECJ held in *Fixtures Marketing v Svenska, Fixtures Marketing v OPAP*, and *Fixtures Marketing v Veikkaus*, that investment in presentation of the database contents refers to 'the resources used for the purpose of giving the database its function of processing information, that is to say those used for the systematic or methodical arrangement of the materials contained in that database and the organization of their individual accessibility'.[69] The Court held that in relation to the database in issue, i.e. football fixtures, there was no relevant investment because the presentation of the list was too closely linked to the creation of the data.[70]

An issue that none of the ECJ rulings addressed is, what constitutes *substantial* investment? The Advocate General in her Opinion in *Fixtures Marketing v Svenska* took the view that substantial investment should be construed in relative terms 'first in relation to costs and their redemption and secondly in relation to the scale, nature and contents of the database and the sector to which it belongs'.[71] However, the Advocate General went on to explain that 'the criterion "substantial" cannot be construed only in relative terms. The directive requires an absolute lower threshold for investments worthy of protection as a sort of *de minimis* rule. That is implied by the 19th recital, according to which the investment must be "substantial enough".'[72] Further, that this threshold should be set at a low level, consistent with the purpose of the directive to create incentives for investment in databases. In its ruling in *Svenska*, the ECJ observed that 'the quantitative assessment refers to quantifiable resources and the qualitative assessment to efforts which cannot be quantified, such as intellectual effort and energy, according to the 7th, 39th and 40th recitals'.[73] Unfortunately, however, the Court did not express any views on whether substantial investment is to be measured in absolute or relative terms or whether the threshold of investment is low or high. In your view, what would be the preferable approach bearing in mind the objectives of the directive?

When it comes to ownership of the sui generis right this lies with the maker of a database who, according to recital 41 of the Database Directive, is 'the person who takes the initiative and the risk of investing'. The directive is silent on the position of employees, however, reg. 14(2) of the UK Database Regulations provides that the employer shall be regarded as the maker of the database where it is made by an employee in the course of employment.

Importantly, Article 11 of the Database Directive imposes territorial qualifications on makers (or rightsholders) of databases. A maker or rightsholder must be a national of a Member State or else have their habitual residence in the Community. Where the maker or rightsholder is a company formed in accordance with the law of a Member State, their registered office, central administration, or principal place of business must be within the Community. What is the purpose of this territorial requirement and whom does it benefit?

---

[69] *Svenska*, para. 27; *OPAP*, para. 43; *Veikkaus*, para. 37.

[70] *Svenska*, para. 35; *OPAP*, para. 51; *Veikkaus*, para. 46.

[71] *Fixtures Marketing Ltd v Svenska Spel AB* C-338/02 Opinion of the Advocate General delivered on 8 Jun. 2004, para. 38.

[72] Ibid., para. 39.   [73] *Svenska*, para. 28.

Further, what is the position of those database makers that fail to meet the requirement? Article 11(3), read in conjunction with recital 56, is helpful on this latter point. The sui generis right can be extended by the European Council to databases made in countries that are not Member States where those countries provide 'comparable protection' to databases made by Community nationals or those habitually resident in the Community. In other words, the sui generis right, unlike copyright, is not subject to the principle of national treatment but instead is based on the principle of material reciprocity. Where a country such as the US protects its databases only by copyright law, what is the impact do you think of the territorial requirement plus material reciprocity rule?

What are the rights given to the database maker? According to Article 7(1) it is the right to prevent unauthorized extraction or reutilization of the whole or substantial part of the database contents. Article 7(2)(a) of the Database Directive defines 'extraction' to mean:

> the permanent or temporary transfer of all or a substantial part of the contents of a database to another medium by any means or in any form.

'Reutilization' is defined in the same provision to mean:

> Any form of making available to the public all or a substantial part of the contents of a database by the distribution of copies, by renting, by on-line or other forms of transmission. The first sale of a copy of a database within the Community by the rightholder or with this consent shall exhaust the right to control resale of that copy within the Community.

Questions regarding the scope of the above rights were referred to the ECJ in *British Horseracing*, so we turn once again to the ruling in that case.

British Horseracing Board Ltd v William Hill Organization Ltd Case C-203/02
[2004] ECR I-10415

For the facts, see p. 726 above.

Note that the Court of Appeal referred questions to the ECJ on whether extraction includes indirect transfer of the database contents and whether reutilization includes making available to the public the contents of the database indirectly from the database. These questions arose because the defendant had obtained the racing fixtures data indirectly via newspaper published the day before the race and via the raw-data feed from one of BHB's licensed distributors.

The Court of Appeal also referred questions about the meaning of 'substantial part, evaluated qualitatively and/or qualitatively, of the contents' of the database.

Judgment of the Court (Grand Chamber):

45. The terms extraction and re-utilisation must be interpreted in the light of the objective pursued by the *sui generis* right. It is intended to protect the maker of the database against 'acts by the user which go beyond [the] legitimate rights and thereby harm the investment' of the maker, as indicated in the 42nd recital of the preamble to the directive.

46. According to the 48th recital of the preamble to the directive, the *sui generis* right has an economic justification, which is to afford protection to the maker of the database and guarantee a return on his investment in the creation and maintenance of the database.

...

49. In Art. 7(2)(a) of the directive, extraction is defined as 'the permanent or temporary transfer of all or a substantial part of the contents of a database to another medium by any means or in any form', while in Art. 7(2)(b) , re-utilisation is defined as 'any form of making available to the public all or a substantial part of the contents of a database by the distribution of copies, by renting, by on-line or other forms of transmission'.

50. The reference to 'a substantial part' in the definition of the concepts of extraction and re-utilisation gives rise to confusion given that, according to Art. 7(5) of the directive, extraction or re-utilisation may also concern an insubstantial part of a database. As the Advocate General observes, in point AG90 of her Opinion, the reference, in Art. 7(2) of the Directive, to the substantial nature of the extracted or re-utilised part does not concern the definition of those concepts as such but must be understood to refer to one of the conditions for the application of the *sui generis* right laid down by Art. 7(1) of the directive.

51. The use of expressions such as 'by any means or in any form' and 'any form of making available to the public' indicates that the Community legislature intended to give the concepts of extraction and re-utilisation a wide definition. In the light of the objective pursued by the directive, those terms must therefore be interpreted as referring to any act of appropriating and making available to the public, without the consent of the maker of the database, the results of his investment, thus depriving him of revenue which should have enabled him to redeem the cost of the investment.

52. Against that background, and contrary to the argument put forward by William Hill and the Belgian and Portuguese Governments, the concepts of extraction and re-utilisation cannot be exhaustively defined as instances of extraction and re-utilisation directly from the original database at the risk of leaving the maker of the database without protection from unauthorised copying from a copy of the database. That interpretation is confirmed by Art. 7(2)(b) of the directive, according to which the first sale of a copy of a database within the Community by the rightholder or with his consent is to exhaust the right to control 'resale', but not the right to control extraction and re-utilisation of the contents, of that copy within the Community.

53. Since acts of unauthorised extraction and/or re-utilisation by a third party from a source other than the database concerned are liable, just as much as such acts carried out directly from that database are, to prejudice the investment of the maker of the database, it must be held that the concepts of extraction and re-utilisation do not imply direct access to the database concerned.

...

68. By its fourth, fifth and sixth questions, the referring court raises the question of the meaning of the terms 'substantial part' and 'insubstantial part' of the contents of a database as used in Art. 7 of the directive. By its first question it also seeks to know whether materials derived from a database do not constitute a part, substantial or otherwise, of that database, where their systematic or methodical arrangement and the conditions of their individual accessibility have been altered by the person carrying out the extraction and/or re-utilisation.

69. In that connection, it must be borne in mind that protection by the *sui generis* right covers databases whose creation required a substantial investment. Against that background, Art. 7(1) of the directive prohibits extraction and/or re-utilisation not only of the whole of a database protected by the *sui generis* right but also of a substantial part, evaluated qualitatively or quantitatively, of its contents. According to the 42nd recital of the preamble to the directive, that provision is intended to prevent a situation in which a user 'through his acts, causes significant detriment, evaluated qualitatively or quantitatively, to the investment'. It appears from that recital that the assessment, in qualitative terms, of whether the part at

issue is substantial, must, like the assessment in quantitative terms, refer to the investment in the creation of the database and the prejudice caused to that investment by the act of extracting or re-utilising that part.

70. The expression 'substantial part, evaluated quantitatively', of the contents of a data-base within the meaning of Art. 7(1) of the directive refers to the volume of data extracted from the database and/or re-utilised, and must be assessed in relation to the volume of the contents of the whole of that database. If a user extracts and/or re-utilises a quantitatively significant part of the contents of a database whose creation required the deployment of substantial resources, the investment in the extracted or re-utilised part is, proportionately, equally substantial.

71. The expression 'substantial part, evaluated qualitatively', of the contents of a database refers to the scale of the investment in the obtaining, verification or presentation of the contents of the subject of the act of extraction and/or re-utilisation, regardless of whether that subject represents a quantitatively substantial part of the general contents of the protected database. A quantitatively negligible part of the contents of a database may in fact represent, in terms of obtaining, verification or presentation, significant human, technical or financial investment.

72. It must be added that, as the existence of the *sui generis* right does not, according to the 46th recital of the preamble to the directive, give rise to the creation of a new right in the works, data or materials themselves, the intrinsic value of the materials affected by the act of extraction and/or re-utilisation does not constitute a relevant criterion for the assessment of whether the part at issue is substantial.

73. It must be held that any part which does not fulfil the definition of a substantial part, evaluated both quantitatively and qualitatively, falls within the definition of an insubstantial part of the contents of a database.

The ECJ indicated that the activities carried on by William Hill did amount to extraction and reutilization, but that they did not relate to a substantial part of the contents of the database. This was because extracting and reusing the names of the horses in the race, the details of the race, and the name of the racecourse, represented a very small proportion of the whole of the BHB database. Further, the resources used to establish this data represented an investment in the *creation* of data and thus had to be ignored. As such, the data extracted and reused could not represent a qualitatively substantial part of the BHB database (even though the data was incredibly useful to William Hill).

Is the ECJ's ruling that 'extraction' and 'reutilization' is not limited to direct access to the database a sensible one? In particular, is this interpretation consistent with the language and objective of the Database Directive? What about the ECJ's approach to determining 'substantial part', particularly in qualitative terms? Does it make sense to link the notion of substantial part with the notion of substantial investment, as opposed to looking at the intrinsic value of the materials that have been extracted or reutilized?

A more recent decision of the ECJ has further elaborated upon the scope of the 'extraction' right. In *Directmedia Publishing GmbH v Albert-Ludwigs-Universitat Freiburg*[74] a list of verse titles, known as the 'The 1,100 most important poems in German literature between 1730 and 1900', had been drawn up as part of the 'Vocabulary of the Classics' project directed by Professor Knoop of the University of Freiburg. DirectMedia marketed a CD-Rom, '1000 poems everyone should have' in which 856 of the poems included were also featured in the claimant's list. In selecting the poems for inclusion on its CD-Rom, DirectMedia had con-sulted the claimant's list of titles, but used additional selection criteria in deciding whether

[74] Case C-304/07 [2009] 1 CMLR 7.

to include a poem. The Bundesgerichtshof (German Federal Supreme Court) referred a question to the ECJ on the meaning of 'extraction', in particular whether it covered transfer of data following individual assessments resulting from consultation of the database or was limited to physical copying of data? The Court held that a broad construction of 'extraction' was supported by the objectives of introducing a sui generis right. Further, that it was immaterial whether the transfer of contents is based on a technical process of copying or simply a manual process, since the latter type of copying could be equally as harmful to the interests of the database maker. Where a person transferred data to another database only after a critical assessment of whether to include it did not prevent this from being 'extraction', but rather went to determining the eligibility of that other database for protection. Finally, the ECJ addressed the arguments that a broad construction of 'extraction' would limit the ability freely to access information and could lead to abusive monopolies on the part of database makers. It held that the sui generis right does not prevent third parties from consulting a database for information purposes only and that the rules of competition law would regulate any abusive monopolies. Thus, the ECJ ruled that 'extraction' did include transfer of material from a protected database to another database following an on-screen consultation of the first database and an individual assessment of the material contained in that first database.

Where the extraction or reutilization of database contents relates to an insubstantial part, logic would suggest that no infringement of the sui generis right occurs. This view is supported by Article 8(1), which provides that a maker of a database may not prevent a lawful user of the database from extracting or reutilizing insubstantial parts of its contents. However, Article 7(5) prohibits the repeated and systematic extraction and/or reutilization of insubstantial parts of the database contents where this conflicts with a normal exploitation of that database or unreasonably prejudices the legitimate interests of the maker of the database. How then to reconcile these two provisions? This issue was addressed by the ECJ in *British Horseracing*.

British Horseracing Board Ltd v William Hill Organization Ltd Case C-203/02 [2004] ECR I-10415

For the facts, see p. 726 above.

Judgment of the Court (Grand Chamber):

84. On that point, it appears from Art. 8(1) and from the 42nd recital of the preamble to the directive that, as a rule, the maker of a database cannot prevent a lawful user of that database from carrying out acts of extraction and re-utilisation of an insubstantial part of its contents. Article 7(5) of the directive, which authorises the maker of the database to prevent such acts under certain conditions, thus provides for an exception to that general rule.

85. Common Position No. 20/95 adopted by the Council on July 10, 1995 states, under point 14 of the Council's statement of reasons: 'to ensure that the lack of protection of the insubstantial parts does not lead to their being repeatedly and systematically extracted and/ or re-utilised, paragraph 5 of this article in the common position introduces a safeguard clause'.

86. It follows that the purpose of Art. 7(5) of the directive is to prevent circumvention of the prohibition in Art. 7(1) of the directive. Its objective is to prevent repeated and systematic extractions and/or re-utilisations of insubstantial parts of the contents of a database, the cumulative effect of which would be to seriously prejudice the investment made by the

maker of the database just as the extractions and/or re-utilisations referred to in Art. 7(1) of the directive would.

87. The provision therefore prohibits acts of extraction made by users of the database which, because of their repeated and systematic character, would lead to the reconstitution of the database as a whole or, at the very least, of a substantial part of it, without the authorisation of the maker of the database, whether those acts were carried out with a view to the creation of another database or in the exercise of an activity other than the creation of a database.

88. Similarly, Art. 7(5) of the directive prohibits third parties from circumventing the prohibition on re-utilisation laid down by Art. 7(1) of the directive by making insubstantial parts of the contents of the database available to the public in a systematic and repeated manner.

89. Under those circumstances, 'acts which conflict with a normal exploitation of [a] database or which unreasonably prejudice the legitimate interests of the maker of the database' refer to unauthorised actions for the purpose of reconstituting, through the cumulative effect of acts of extraction, the whole or a substantial part of the contents of a database protected by the *sui generis* right and/or of making available to the public, through the cumulative effect of acts of re-utilisation, the whole or a substantial part of the contents of such a database, which thus seriously prejudice the investment made by the maker of the database.

According to the ECJ an insubstantial part is whatever does not constitute a substantial part. Further, to infringe Article 7(5) there is the need for the *cumulative* effect of the acts of extraction and reutilization in relation to insubstantial parts of the database contents to *reconstitute* the database, either as a whole or in a substantial part. This seems to require looking at the insubstantial extractions or reutilizations in their totality, even if individually they are not still retained or are no longer being used.

The ECJ indicated that William Hill's acts of extraction and reutilization were repeated and systematic because they were carried out each time a race was held. However, these acts were not intended to circumvent Article 7(1) because their cumulative effect was not to reconstitute and make available to the public a substantial part of the contents of the BHB database. This was because the insubstantial parts that were taken and reused reflected investment in creation of data, as opposed to obtaining, verifying, or presenting its contents.

An important point of difference between the sui generis right for databases and copyright is the term of protection available. In the case of the sui generis right, Article 10 stipulates that the right lasts for 15 years. This is calculated from 1 January of the year following the date of completion of the database. Alternatively, where the database is not yet completed, it is calculated from 1 January of the year following the date when the database was first made available to the public. On the face of it, therefore, the sui generis right is much shorter than copyright protection, which will last for 70 years after the death of the author/s. However, the difference is not quite so great when Article 10(3) of the Database Directive is considered. This section provides:

Any substantial change, evaluated qualitatively or quantitatively, to the contents of a database, including any substantial change resulting from the accumulation of successive additions, deletions or alterations, which would result in the database being considered to be a substantial new investment, evaluated qualitatively or quantitatively, shall qualify the database resulting from that investment for its own term of protection.

Article 10(3) thus provides for a further 15-year term of protection if a substantial new investment is made to the database. This provision is meant to deal with the problem raised by dynamic databases, which require a steady stream of maintenance to ensure their currency, which in turn demands continuing investment. The provision may also benefit owners of reasonably static, but long-term, databases where what is required is continual verification of material.

There is, however, ambiguity over how Article 10(3) will operate: is the database 'resulting from that investment' referring to the entirety of the new (modified) database or only the new part of the database that is created with the later investment? The scope of Article 10(3) was raised in the *British Horseracing* case. The defendant argued that in updating and verifying the BHB database, new databases came into existence, each of which was protected for its own new term. As such, the defendant argued that it had not infringed the sui generis right because it had made insubstantial extractions or reutilizations from a series of related databases as opposed to from the one database. The Court of Appeal referred a question on Article 10(3) to the ECJ. However, in light of its rulings on Article 7(1) and (5) (that no infringement had occurred), the ECJ did not consider it necessary to reply to the question. This is a great shame since this is an important issue and, depending on how Article 10(3) is interpreted, leaves open the way for potentially perpetual protection of databases.

When it comes to balancing the interests of database makers and users, Article 9 permits Member States to introduce exceptions for lawful users of databases, to enable them to extract or reutilize a substantial part of the database contents in the following situations:

a. in the case of extraction for private purposes of the contents of a non-electronic database;

b. in the case of extraction for the purposes of illustration for teaching or scientific research, as long as the source is indicated and to the extent justified by the non-commercial purpose to be achieved;

c. in the case of extraction and/or re-utilisation for the purposes of public security or an administrative or judicial procedure.

Criticisms similar to those raised in respect of the exceptions available against infringement of copyright in databases are applicable here. When it comes to private purposes, the exception is limited to the extraction right and to hard copy databases. In respect of the exception for teaching or scientific research, this is also limited to extraction and is further narrowed by the requirement of non-commercial purpose. As such, the exceptions in Article 9 may be said to provide a weak counter-balance against the wide protection that is available to database makers under Article 7.[75]

The European Commission, in its first evaluation of the directive,[76] has considered the impact of the sui generis right on the European database industry's rate of growth. The Commission concludes that EU database production has recently fallen back to pre-directive levels and that, at present, the economic impact of the sui generis right on database

[75] C. D. Freedman, 'Should Canada enact a new sui generis database right?' (2002) 13 Fordham Intellectual Property Media & Entertainment LJ 35, 97; J. Lipton, 'Databases as intellectual property: New legal approaches' [2003] EIPR 139, 141–2.

[76] Commission of the European Communities, DG Internal Market and Services Working Paper, *First evaluation of Directive 96/9/EC on the legal protection of databases*, Brussels, 12 Dec. 2005 ('Evaluation Paper').

production is 'unproven'.[77] Further, it appears that the sui generis right has not significantly improved the competitiveness of the European database industry vis-à-vis the US.[78] Faced with an absence of empirical evidence about the success of the sui generis provisions, the Commission has suggested four possible options for the future, which are extracted below.

First evaluation of Directive 96/9/EC on the legal protection of databases
(12 December 2005)

6.1. Option 1: Repeal the whole Directive

Withdrawing the Directive in its entirety would allow Member States to revert to the situation that applied in national law prior to the adoption of the Directive. This would allow *droit d'auteur* Member States to keep their threshold of 'originality', to protect 'original' databases under copyright law and to choose other means e.g. unfair competition or the law of misappropriation, to protect 'non-original' compilations. Common law Member States, for their part, would be allowed to revert to the 'sweat of the brow' standard as a relevant copyright test.

But withdrawing the Directive in its entirety would give rise to a pre-directive scenario where Member States could protect 'original' databases under diverging levels of 'originality'. In particular, the UK and Ireland would be allowed to revert to the 'sweat of the brow' copyright test and Sweden, Denmark and Finland (and Norway and Iceland) would be allowed to revert to their 'catalogue rule'.

In this scenario, one could expect that the terms of use for collections of data or compilations would be dealt with only by contract law and right-holders would increasingly protect their databases (especially online databases) by means of access control systems. However, this option would have the disadvantage of doing away with the harmonised level of copyright protection for 'original' databases which has not caused major problems so far.

6.2. Option 2: Withdraw the 'sui generis' right

Another possibility would therefore be to withdraw the 'sui generis' right in isolation and thus maintain the harmonised level of copyright protection for 'original' databases.

Arguably, this partial withdrawal would still allow *droit d'auteur* Member States to keep their threshold of 'originality', to protect 'original' databases under copyright law and to choose other means e.g. unfair competition or the law of misappropriation to protect 'non-original' compilations. It would also allow common law Member States to revert to the 'sweat of the brow' standard as a relevant test to protect 'non-original' compilations.

The arguments for partial withdrawal would largely be based on a strict application of the 'better regulation' principles. These principles would probably suggest that the 'sui generis' right be withdrawn as it has revealed itself to be an instrument that is ineffective at encouraging growth in the European database industry and, due to its largely untested legal concepts, given rise to significant litigation in national and European courts. Empirical data underlying this evaluation show that its economic impact is unproven. In addition, no empirical data that proves that its introduction has stimulated significant growth in the production of EU databases could be submitted so far.

---

[77] Ibid., paras. 1.4 and 4.2.   [78] Ibid., para. 4.4.

Furthermore, withdrawal of the 'sui generis' right appears to be in line with an emerging trend in common law jurisdictions as the high standard of 'originality' introduced by the Directive would put them on a par with the US, thereby protecting fewer rather than more databases. It may thus well be that even the common law jurisdictions within the Community (UK and Ireland) would maintain the higher threshold for protection, thereby only protecting 'original' databases. The ruling in the *Feist* case and the economic evidence that points at the US as being a leader in database production could lead to significant reluctance in reintroducing 'sweat of the brow'.

Finally, withdrawing the 'sui generis' right would still leave companies with factual compilations that may not be fully protected under the standard of 'originality' as prescribed in copyright law, free to protect their works by other means such as contract law or use of technological protection measures or other forms of access control when the work is delivered on-line. It would also not exclude producers of compilations to claim protection by stating that their arrangements met the threshold of 'originality'. However, this paper acknowledges that European publishers and database producers would clearly prefer to retain the 'sui generis' protection.

6.3. Option 3: Amend the 'sui generis' provisions

Another option would be to amend and clarify the scope of protection awarded under the 'sui generis' provisions. Attempts could be made to reformulate the scope of the 'sui generis' right in order to also cover instances where the 'creation' of data takes place concurrently with the collection and screening of it. Amendments could also clarify the issue of what forms of 'official' and thereby single source lists would be protected under the 'sui generis' provisions.

Amendments could also be proposed to clarify the scope of protection and clarify whether the scope would only cover 'primary' producers of databases (i.e. those producers whose main business is to collect and assemble information they do not 'create' themselves) or would also include producers for whom production of a databases is a 'secondary' activity (in other words, a spin-off from their main activity). Amendments could, in addition, clarify the issue of what actually constitutes a substantial investment in either the obtaining, verification or presentation of the contents of a database. On the other hand, reformulating the scope of the 'sui generis' right entails a serious risk that yet another layer of untested legal notions would be introduced that will not withstand scrutiny before the ECJ.

6.4. Option 4: Maintaining the status quo

On the other hand, even if a piece of legislation has no proven positive effects on the growth of a particular industry, withdrawal is not always the best option. Removing the 'sui generis' right and thereby allowing Member States to revert to prior forms of legal protection for all forms of 'non-original' databases that do not meet the threshold of 'originality', might be more costly than keeping it in place. Arguably, the limitations imposed by the judgments of the ECJ mean that the right is now only available to 'primary' producers of databases and not those who for whom databases are a 'secondary' activity.

As matters stand, the fate of the sui generis right awaits further consultation between the Commission and relevant stakeholders on the above four options. In your view, which of the four options is preferable?

FURTHER READING

T. Aplin, 'The EU database right: Recent developments' [2005] 1 IPQ 52.

M. Davison and P. B. Hugenholtz, 'Football fixtures, horseraces and spin offs: The ECJ domesticates the database right' [2005] EIPR 113.

E. Derclaye, *The Legal Protection of Databases: A comparative analysis* (Edward Elgar, 2008).

E. Derclaye, 'The Court of Justice interprets the database sui generis right for the first time' [2005] European LR 420.

A. Kur et al., 'First evaluation of Directive 96/9/EC on the legal protection of databases: Comment by the Max Planck Institute for Intellectual Property, Competition and Tax Law, Munich' (2006) 37(5) IIC 551.

12.6 THE INTERNET

12.6.1 INTRODUCTION

The Internet is now such an established part of our daily lives that it is hard to imagine that it is a recent phenomenon. The origins of the Internet can be traced back to the ARPANET (Advanced Research Projects Agency Network) developed by the US Department of Defense in the 1970s, and the US NSFNet in the 1980s. Yet it was only in the early 1990s (with the development of the World Wide Web) that the Internet began to have public appeal and its usage grew rapidly. At present, it is estimated that there are approximately 1.596 billion Internet users.[79]

The importance of the Internet warrants a brief description of its technical nature. In simple terms, the Internet may be defined as a 'network of networks' that operates according to the Internet Protocol Suite referred to as TCP/IP (after its two main standards Transmission Control Protocol and Internet Protocol).[80] The Internet is a combination of numerous backbone networks (high capacity networks), their interconnections, and a huge number of internal networks within organizations that are connected to one of the backbone networks. This 'network of networks' is not controlled by a central computer or server, but is made possible by TCP/IP. TCP/IP may be described as a standard, or suite of protocols, that enables information to be communicated or exchanged across interconnected networks. TCP/IP operates at different network layers, which are typically broken down into seven levels. Frequently, however, TCP/IP is described in terms of only four: the data link, network, transport, and application layers.[81] TCP/IP is non-proprietary in nature, which is crucial to the openness of the Internet.

One of the most important features of TCP/IP is that it creates a packet-switched, as opposed to circuit-switched, network. A circuit-switched network functions by creating a dedicated connection (circuit) between two points (an example is a telephone system). Whereas, with a packet-switched network, data is transferred across a network by disassembling it into smaller pieces, called packets, and these packets may travel different routes

---

[79] <http://www.internetworldstats.com/stats.htm>.

[80] S. Biegel, *Beyond Our Control? Confronting the limits of our legal system in the age of cyberspace* (Cambridge, MA: MIT Press, 2003), pp. 189–90.

[81] Ibid., p. 191.

in order to arrive at their destination. This means the packets must be identified, delivered, and then reassembled and it is these tasks that are facilitated by TCP/IP.

The Internet may be used in a variety of ways. Two of the most common uses are e-mail (electronic mail) and the World Wide Web. Despite popular belief, the World Wide Web is not synonymous with the Internet; rather it is a vast set of documents, graphics, sounds, and other resources that are interlinked using hyperlinks and Uniform Resource Locators (URLs). A URL is a specific numeric address for the file or webpage that a user wants to access. Whereas hyperlinks are programmed links between items of information in different sections of a programme or in physically different locations within a network, which enable users easily to follow cross-references. Users generally access the World Wide Web via an Internet or web browser.

Another popular use of the Internet is file-sharing, a phenomenon that has been of particular concern to the music industry and is discussed below in s. 12.6.3. In more recent times, the Internet has been increasingly used for webcasting, i.e. the transmission of live or recorded broadcasts. For example, there are numerous existing radio and TV stations that simultaneously make their live broadcasts available via the Internet and also permit users to listen or view them at a later time (e.g. BBC Interactive). Voice telephony, known also as Voice over Internet Protocol (VoIP), is another growing use of the Internet and has become a viable, and much less expensive, alternative to traditional telephones. Finally, the Internet allows persons to connect to other computers and databases wherever they are situated (i.e. remote access). This, in turn, has facilitated more flexible work practices (such as working from home).

The various ways in which the Internet may be used has created enormous commercial opportunities. But these opportunities are accompanied by risks, including the unauthorized copying and distribution of creative content. This has raised challenges particularly for copyright law, which we turn now to discuss.

12.6.2 NEW MODE OF EXPLOITATION: NEW RIGHTS

The development of the Internet allowed creative content, such as music, graphics, video, and text, to reach audiences on a scale and in a manner previously unimaginable. While this was seen as positive, from the point of view of increasing accessibility to cultural and educational material, it was also seen as problematic in that it relied mainly on copyright material and copyright owners had often not granted permission for their works to be used in this way.

One of the early issues, therefore, to arise was whether copyright owners were entitled to prevent the dissemination of their works via the Internet. More specifically, did Internet transmissions fall within the exclusive rights granted to owners? This was a concern both from an international perspective (i.e. did the Berne Convention create obligations to protect against such exploitation?) and with regard to national laws (could existing rights be interpreted to cover this new mode of exploitation?).

12.6.2.1 WIPO Copyright Treaty

The WIPO Copyright Treaty ('WCT'), adopted at the Diplomatic Conference in December 1996, sought to provide a solution at the international level.[82] One suggestion was that the

---

[82] For a general discussion see 2.4.1.4.

exclusive right of reproduction, contained in Article 9(1) of the Berne Convention, should apply to Internet transmissions. This was because a copy was made when a file was uploaded to an Internet server, and transient copies were made as the file was transmitted between servers, in order to arrive at its destination. However, those present at the Conference disagreed about whether the reproduction right should be interpreted so broadly as to include any technical copy of a work. According to some, this would create a right of *access* and would be too far-reaching. A stalemate occurred on this issue and the most that was achieved was an agreed statement that:

> The reproduction right, as set out in Article 9 of the Berne Convention, and the exceptions permitted thereunder, fully apply in the digital environment, in particular to the use of works in digital form. It is understood that the storage of a protected work in digital form in an electronic medium constitutes a reproduction within the meaning of Article 9 of the Berne Convention.[83]

This statement achieved little apart from stating the obvious, namely that a reproduction could occur where it was in digital or electronic format. It did not answer the question of whether temporary or transient copies of a work would also constitute a 'reproduction' in legal terms.

Greater success came in the form of Article 8 of the WCT:

> Without prejudice to the provisions of Articles 11(1)(ii), 11*bis*(1)(i) and (ii), 11*ter*(1)(ii), 14(1)(ii) and 14*bis*(1) of the Berne Convention, authors of literary and artistic works shall enjoy the exclusive right of authorising any communication to the public of their works, by wire or wireless means, including the making available to the public of their works in such a way that members of the public may access these works from a place and at a time individually chosen by them.

The first part of this article supplements the existing communication to the public rights in the Berne Convention. The second part of the article, however, introduces a new right of making available to the public, as a subset of the right of communication to the public. In relation to performers and phonogram producers, the obligation to introduce a right of making available to the public by wire or wireless means is contained in Arts. 10 and 14 of the WPPT.

The solution provided by Article 8 came after much debate about the appropriate means to protect authors from unauthorized transmission of their works over digital networks. In the lead-up to the adoption of the final text of the WCT, various solutions had been proposed, such as treating digital dissemination as an act of distribution, an act of public display or rental, an act of communication to the public, or establishing a new specific digital transmission right. In the end, an 'umbrella' solution was adopted, namely, to create an obligation to grant an exclusive right to authorize on-demand transmission, but described in a neutral way so that the legal characterization of the right granted would be left to national law.

The right of making available to the public appears to cover offering works for access, along with the entire transmission to the user, if such a transmission takes place. The 'making available' has to be such that 'members of the public may access these works from a place

---

[83] There was an equivalent Agreed Statement for performers and phonogram producers in the WIPO Performances and Phonograms Treaty (WPPT) 1996, discussed at 2.4.1.5.

and at a time individually chosen by them'. This embraces on-demand situations, such as websites that offer MP3 files for download by Internet users. It also includes works distributed via electronic mailing lists or via peer-to-peer software. It excludes, however, broadcasting via traditional means or via digital networks where predetermined programmes are offered to the public at specified times; pay-per-view services; or services which repeatedly broadcast a series of works at regular intervals.[84]

In terms of what constitutes making available *to the public*, this is left to national law. Commentators have suggested that the concept of 'public' excludes the close family circle and closest social acquaintances, such that material stored on domestic intranets would not constitute making available to the public.[85] If this is correct then situations where material is placed on the Internet without being accessible to anyone but family and friends should also be excluded. The notion of 'public' would not necessarily exclude material made available via school or company intranets. Further, 'making available to the public' would clearly embrace placing a protected work on an Internet server, without restriction, along with an individual accessing that work.

The WCT is silent on where the act of making available occurs and how this is to be determined. This is an important issue because Internet transmissions by their very nature may be made to persons across the globe. According to which country's law will it be decided whether an infringing act has occurred? Assuming the applicable law is determined by the *lex loci delicti* (as opposed to *lex fori*), is the sole applicable law that of the country where the copyright material is uploaded? Or is it where the Internet server hosting the material is located? Or is the sole applicable law that of the countries in which the transmission is accessed or accessible? Unfortunately, these questions are, as yet, unanswered.

12.6.2.2 Information Society Directive (Directive 2001/29/EC)

The Information Society Directive sought to implement the international obligations contained in the WCT and WPPT and also to harmonize certain substantive aspects of copyright law to prevent distortion of the internal market.

Article 8 of the WCT and Articles 10 and 14 of the WPPT are implemented via Article 3 of the Information Society Directive. This provision ensures that all rightsholders have an exclusive right to make available to the public copyright works by way of interactive on-demand transmission, which are characterized by the fact that members of the public may access them from a place and at a time individually chosen by them. Authors of traditional works, however, will acquire this right as part of the right of communication to the public, which right is to be:

> understood in a broad sense covering all communication to the public not present at the place where the communication originates... [and] should cover any such transmission or retransmission of a work to the public by wire or wireless means, including broadcasting.

Article 3 of the Information Society Directive, like the WIPO Treaties whose obligations it seeks to implement, does not address *where* the act of making available takes place.

The UK implemented Article 3 of the Information Society Directive as s. 20 of the CDPA, i.e. the right of communication to the public. This right applies to all categories of works, with the exception of typographical arrangements, and includes—but is not restricted

---

[84] J. Reinbothe and S. von Lewinski, *The WIPO Treaties 1996*, p. 109.   [85] Ibid., p. 111.

to—broadcasting and making available to the public. 'Broadcasting', according to s. 6 of the CDPA, refers to wire or wireless transmission of visual images, sounds, or other information, excluding Internet transmissions, except of a limited kind akin to traditional broadcasting. 'Making available to the public' is thus relevant to on-demand and Internet transmissions and this has been confirmed in *Polydor Limited v. Brown*.[86] Like the WIPO Treaties and Directive, the CDPA is silent on where the act of making available takes place.

The Information Society Directive also harmonized the right of reproduction, Article 2 obligating Member States to provide:

> the exclusive right to authorise or prohibit direct or indirect, temporary or permanent reproduction by any means and in any form, in whole or in part.

This provision, read together with recital 2 of the Information Society Directive, clearly shows that the reproduction right is to be broadly construed in the Member States. In other words, it prima facie extends to the transient copies that are made in a user's computer whilst browsing the Internet or to the transient copies made during the transmission process. As we shall see below at 12.6.4, the harshness of this broad definition of 'reproduction' is mitigated somewhat by a mandatory exception for temporary copying contained in Article 5(1).

The UK did not have to amend the CDPA in order to implement Article 2 of the Information Society Directive since s. 17(6) defines 'copying' to include 'the making of copies which are transient or are incidental to some other use of the work'.

In conclusion, copyright law has been adapted to enable owners to authorize or prohibit the exploitation of their copyright works via the Internet. There are, however, lingering uncertainties about the scope of the right of making available to the public, in particular, determining where the act of making available takes place.

FURTHER READING

M. Ficsor, *The Law of Copyright and the Internet: The 1996 WIPO Treaties, their interpretation and implementation* (Oxford: Oxford University Press, 2002).

P. B. Hugenholtz, 'Adapting copyright to the information superhighway' in Hugenholtz (ed.), *The Future of Copyright in a Digital Environment* (The Hague: Kluwer, 1996), pp. 81–102.

M. Makeen, *Copyright in a Global Information Society: The scope of copyright protection under international, US, UK and French law* (London: Kluwer, 2000).

J. Reinbothe and S. von Lewinski, *The WIPO Treaties 1996* (London: Butterworths, 2002).

12.6.3 PEER-TO-PEER FILE-SHARING

Napster, Morpheus, KaZaa, Gnutella, BitTorrent, Fasttrack, eDonkey, and Freenet are all examples of peer-to-peer file-sharing software. What this software has in common is that it enables the direct transfer of files between individual users of the Internet, bypassing

---

[86] [2005] EWHC 3191.

central servers (or possible points of regulation). This type of software has struck fear in the hearts of many copyright owners, particularly those in the music industry, because many of the files that are 'shared' are copyright works and 'sharing' can occur on a massive scale that is difficult to control. To better understand the legal issues relating to peer-to-peer file-sharing, we turn briefly to a description of the technology.

12.6.3.1 Nature of the technology

The legalities of peer-to-peer file-sharing were first raised in the US and it is fair to say that the bulk of copyright litigation concerning this software has occurred in this jurisdiction. The following description of peer-to-peer file-sharing software comes from a US Court of Appeals decision in a leading case that will be examined later at 12.6.3.3.

Metro-Goldwyn-Mayer Studios Inc v Grokster Ltd 72 USPQ 2d 1244 (2004)

US Court of Appeals for the Second Circuit, Circuit Judges Boochever, Noonan and Thomas, at pp. 1246–7:

To analyze the legal issues properly, a rudimentary understanding of the peer-to-peer file-sharing software at issue is required—particularly because peer-to-peer file sharing differs from typical internet use. In a routine internet transaction, a user will connect via the internet with a website to obtain information or transact business. In computer terms, the personal computer used by the consumer is considered the 'client' and the computer that hosts the web page is the 'server.' The client is obtaining information from a centralized source, namely the server.

In a peer-to-peer distribution network, the information available for access does not reside on a central server. No one computer contains all of the information that is available to all of the users. Rather, each computer makes information available to every other computer in the peer-to-peer network. In other words, in a peer-to-peer network, each computer is both a server and a client.

Because the information is decentralized in a peer-to-peer network, the software must provide some method of cataloguing the available information so that users may access it. The software operates by connecting, via the internet, to other users of the same or similar software. At any given moment, the network consists of other users of similar or the same software online at that time. Thus, an index of files available for sharing is a critical component of peer-to-peer file-sharing networks.

At present, there are three different methods of indexing: (1) a centralized indexing system, maintaining a list of available files on one or more centralized servers; (2) a completely decentralized indexing system, in which each computer maintains a list of files available on that computer only; and (3) a 'supernode' system, in which a select number of computers act as indexing servers.

The first Napster system employed a proprietary centralized indexing software architecture in which a collective index of available files was maintained on servers it owned and operated. A user who was seeking to obtain a digital copy of a recording would transmit a search request to the Napster server, the software would conduct a text search of the centralized index for matching files, and the search results would be transmitted to the requesting user. If the results showed that another Napster user was logged on to the Napster server and offering to share the requested recording, the requesting user could then connect directly with the offering user and download the music file.

Under a decentralized index peer-to-peer file-sharing model, each user maintains an index of only those files that the user wishes to make available to other network users. Under this model, the software broadcasts a search request to all the computers on the network and a search of the individual index files is conducted, with the collective results routed back to the requesting computer. This model is employed by the Gnutella software system and is the type of architecture now used by defendant StreamCast. Gnutella is open-source software, meaning that the source code is either in the public domain or is copyrighted and distributed under an open-source license that allows modification of the software, subject to some restrictions.

The third type of peer-to-peer file-sharing network at present is the 'supernode' model, in which a number of select computers on the network are designated as indexing servers. The user initiating a file search connects with the most easily accessible supernode, which conducts the search of its index and supplies the user with the results. Any computer on the network could function as a supernode if it met the technical requirements, such as processing speed. The 'supernode' architecture was developed by KaZaa BV, a Dutch company, and licensed under the name of 'FastTrack' technology.

Both Grokster and StreamCast initially used the FastTrack technology. However, Stream-Cast had a licensing dispute with KaZaa, and now uses its own branded 'Morpheus' version of the open-source Gnutella code. StreamCast users connect to other users of Gnutella-based peer-to-peer file-sharing software. Both Grokster and StreamCast distribute their separate softwares free of charge. Once downloaded onto a user's computer, the software enables the user to participate in the respective peer-to-peer file-sharing networks over the internet.

Users of the software share digital audio, video, picture, and text files. Some of the files are copyrighted and shared without authorization, others are not copyrighted (such as public domain works), and still others are copyrighted, but the copyright owners have authorized software users in peer-to-peer file-sharing networks to distribute their work. The Copyright Owners assert, without serious contest by the Software Distributors, that the vast majority of the files are exchanged illegally in violation of copyright law.

As the above extract highlights, not all peer-to-peer file-sharing involves copyright works and, where it does, authorization may have been given for this type of distribution. There are serious concerns, however, that the bulk of peer-to-peer file-sharing is neither of these two types and is particularly harmful to the music industry.[87] The music industry has adopted a multifaceted approach to tackling what it sees as wide-scale piracy. The following sections explore one of the prongs of that approach, namely the legal regulation of peer-to-peer software.

12.6.3.2 Liability under UK copyright law

One of the ways to regulate peer-to-peer file-sharing is to establish its unlawfulness and to litigate against those who are infringing. Here the argument has been that both users of peer-to-peer software and the providers of this technology are liable under copyright law.

According to UK copyright law, it is straightforward that users of peer-to-peer file-sharing software, whether as 'uploaders' or 'downloaders' of files, are prima facie infringers. This is because they are engaged in the act of 'communication to the public', as was

---

[87] For example, the International Federation of the Phonographic Industry ('IFPI') claims that in 2005 approximately 20 billion songs were illegally downloaded.

confirmed in the case of *Polydor Limited v Brown*.[88] Further, it is highly unlikely that such users would be able to rely upon a copyright exception to excuse their actions. But is suing individual peer-to-peer file-sharers a sensible or effective course to take? It seems that this route tackles only a fraction of those infringing. Moreover, the damages against individual users are unlikely to be a large, or even recoverable. Finally, while there may be a 'deterrence' value attached to suing individual infringers, the singling out of individuals also risks creating bad publicity.

For these reasons, owners of copyright works have turned their attention to the providers of peer-to-peer file-sharing software. Although litigation has not yet been brought against such entities in the UK, it is nevertheless important to examine the likelihood of such an action succeeding. The most likely basis of liability for providers of peer-to-peer file-sharing is that they *authorize* the infringing activities carried out by users of the service, contrary to s. 16(2) of the CDPA. The concept of authorization liability was explored at 3.2.1.3. It will be recalled that the leading UK decision is *CBS Songs v Amstrad*,[89] a case concerning the liability of manufacturers of dual-tape cassette-deck machines. What does this case suggest, if anything, about the likelihood of peer-to-peer file-share providers being held liable for authorization?

In this context, it is interesting, and somewhat instructive, to refer to *Universal Music Australia Pty Ltd v Sharman License Holdings Ltd*.[90] This is an Australian decision in which under similar principles of 'authorization' a peer-to-peer file-sharing provider was held liable. The case concerned the KaZaa peer-to-peer file-sharing system, which was controlled by Sharman Networks and several other parties. The applicants were various record companies who owned copyright in sound recordings and who alleged, *inter alia*, that the respondents had authorized users of the KaZaa system to make available online, or electronically transmit, to the public MP3 or other digital music files constituting copies of the whole or a substantial part of the relevant sound recordings.

The central issue in the case was whether Sharman authorized the infringing acts of KaZaa users. Wilcox J in the Federal Court of Australia discussed the law relating to authorization, including s. 101(1A) of the Copyright Act 1968 (Cth). This provision states that the following matters are to be taken into account in deciding whether a person has authorized the doing of an exclusive act:

(a) the extent (if any) of the person's power to prevent the doing of the act concerned;

(b) the nature of any relationship existing between the person and the person who did the act concerned;

(c) whether the person took any other reasonable steps to prevent or avoid the doing of the act, including whether the person complied with any relevant industry codes of practice.

Wilcox J explained the above provision as follows:

the intention behind the addition of s 101(1A) to the Act was to elucidate, rather than to vary, the pre-existing law about authorisation. I further accept, as did Bennett J in *Metro*, the continuing applicability of the *Moorhouse* test. A claim of authorisation can be made good only where it is shown that the person has sanctioned, approved or countenanced the infringement. It is not essential there be direct evidence of the person's attitude; as Gibbs J said

---

[88] [2005] EWHC 3191.　　[89] [1988] AC 1013.　　[90] [2005] FCA 1242.

> in *Moorhouse*, inactivity or indifference, exhibited by acts of commission or omission, may reach such a degree as to support an inference of authorisation or permission.[91]

Wilcox J concluded that Sharman was liable for authorization of infringement. In reaching this conclusion, he took into account several factors. First, he found that it was in Sharman's financial interest for there to be ever-increasing file-sharing and that Sharman knew users were likely to share files that were copyright works.[92] Second, Sharman had engaged in positive acts that would have the effect of encouraging copyright infringement. This included Sharman's website promotion of KaZaa as a file-sharing facility, their exhortations to use this facility and share files, and their promoting the 'Join the Revolution' movement, which was based on file-sharing of music. Third, these acts took place in the context that Sharman knew the files shared by KaZaa users were largely copyright works.[93] Although the judge accepted that KaZaa could be used in a non-infringing way he found it unlikely that non-infringing uses would sustain the huge quantity of traffic using the software and that Sharman and others knew copyright infringement on a massive scale was involved.[94] Finally, the judge held that Sharman had not taken reasonable steps to prevent copyright infringement. Sharman pointed to the use of copyright notices, which stated that it did not condone activities and actions that infringed the rights of copyright owners and that the End User License Agreements (EULAs) included copyright prohibitions. Wilcox J was completely dismissive of these steps:

> It is difficult to believe those directing the affairs of Sharman, or any of the other respondents, ever thought these measures would be effective to prevent, or even substantially to curtail, copyright file-sharing. It would have been obvious to them that, were those measures to prove effective, they would greatly reduce KaZaa's attractiveness to users and, therefore, its advertising revenue potential. However, if any of those people did have such a view, it could not have survived receipt of the Syzgy Report. That report showed the notices and EULA had had no effect on the behaviour of the focus group participants. As the participants were selected on the basis that they were representative of KaZaa users as a whole, or at least of young KaZaa users, those directing the affairs of Sharman (and Altnet) could not have done otherwise than appreciate that, notwithstanding what was on the website, copyright infringement was rife. Despite this, Sharman took no steps to include a filtering mechanism in its software, even in software intended to be provided to new uers. There is no credible evidence that filtering was ever discussed.[95]

Thus, the judge concluded that the copyright notices and EULAs were ineffective in preventing widespread infringement and that Sharman ought to have included filtering mechanisms in its software. More specifically, it should have included a form of filtering that would prevent or restrict access to identified copyright works. Other measures, such as monitoring users' activities, implementing a termination policy, and operating a user-identification system, were held not to be reasonable steps, given the absence of a central server.[96]

What can be drawn from the *Sharman* decision is the importance of the peer-to-peer provider actively taking steps to prevent users' infringing activity. The extent to which this decision will be transferable to the UK depends on how differently one sees the principles of authorization as stated in *CBS Songs v Amstrad* from those stated in *Moorhouse*. Having

---

91 *Sharman*, para. 402.   92 Ibid., para. 404.   93 Ibid., paras. 405–6.
94 Ibid., para. 186.   95 Ibid., para. 407.   96 Ibid., paras. 242–53.

reread the extract from *CBS Songs v Amstrad* at 3.2.1.3 and comparing it with the extracts above from *Sharman* do you think that there is an important difference in approach to authorization between UK and Australian copyright law?

12.6.3.3 Liability under US law

As mentioned above, a significant amount of the copyright litigation relating to peer-to-peer file-sharing has taken place in the United States. Whereas under UK copyright law the key issue is one of authorization, that is primary infringement, US copyright law has dealt with the issue according to the notions of contributory liability and vicarious liability, that is secondary infringement.

In *MGM Studios Inc v Grokster*[97] the US Supreme Court held that it was possible to establish contributory liability where a person 'distributes a device with the object of promoting its use to infringe copyright, as shown by clear expression or other affirmative steps taken to foster infringement'.[98] This may be thought of as the 'inducement' basis of contributory liability. The Supreme Court found there was considerable evidence of intent to induce copyright infringement. The court was willing to accept that the vast majority of usage of the software was infringing. In addition, it pointed to three notable indicators of intent.[99] The first was that the defendants were clearly aiming to capture the market comprising former Napster users (who had been engaging in infringing activities). The second indicator was the defendants' failure to develop filtering tools or other mechanisms to diminish the infringing activity that could be carried out using their software. Finally, the defendants' business model, which depended on advertising revenue, needed a wide user base which in turn depended on unlimited access to copyright works.

Although the *Grokster* decision is of limited relevance to UK law, given that it rests on the principle of contributory liability rather than authorization, it is interesting to note that the US Supreme Court arrived at the same conclusion as the Australian Federal Court in *Sharman* and in doing so appeared to rely on similar factors.

12.6.3.4 The way forward

Establishing the copyright liability of peer-to-peer providers is undoubtedly an important part of the armoury of copyright holders against infringers. However, there are many who argue that this is not enough in itself to tackle the problem of peer-to-peer piracy. Various additional solutions have been suggested. These include educating the public about the importance of respecting copyright; making available copyright works for download through useable and affordable online means (e.g. iTunes); criminalizing large-scale piracy as a deterrent mechanism; and using technological protection measures to prevent unauthorized copies of copyright works being made. Most recently, the record industry has argued that Internet Service Providers (ISPs) should play a more active role in preventing copyright infringement, by suspending or terminating the accounts of repeat infringers. Which of these suggested solutions, if any, do you think could or should be adopted?

FURTHER READING

IFPI, *The Recording Industry 2006 Piracy Report: Protecting creativity in music*, available at: <http://www.ifpi.org/content/library/piracy-report2006.pdf>.

---

[97] 125 S Ct 2764 (2005) ('*Grokster*').   [98] Ibid., p. 2780.   [99] Ibid., pp. 2781–2.

C. Nasir, 'Taming the beast of file-sharing: Legal and technological solutions to the problem of copyright infringement over the Internet: Part 1' [2005] Ent LR 50.

C. Nasir, 'Taming the beast of file-sharing: Legal and technological solutions to the problem of copyright infringement over the Internet: Part 2' [2005] Ent LR 82.

R. C. Piasentin, 'Unlawful? Innovative? Unstoppable? A comparative analysis of the potential legal liability facing P2P end-users in the United States, United Kingdom and Canada' (2006) 14(2) IJL & IT 195.

12.6.4 EXCEPTIONS AND LIMITATIONS

12.6.4.1 International and EC position

We have seen that the WCT and WPPT introduced exclusive rights to cater for new forms of exploitation in an Internet and digital environment. However, it was important also that the interests of users were catered for. To that end, Article 10 of the WCT states that Contracting Parties may provide for exceptions or limitations in their national legislation in respect of the rights granted under the treaty. This is provided it complies with the so-called 'three-step' test, namely, in certain special cases that do not conflict with the normal exploitation of the work and do not unreasonably prejudice the legitimate interests of the author. The agreed statement to the WCT highlights the intention of Article 10 is to allow Contracting Parties 'to carry forward and appropriately extend into the digital environment limitations and exceptions in their national laws which have been considered acceptable under the Berne Convention'. A similar approach is taken in the WPPT in Article 16 and its corresponding agreed statement.

The Information Society Directive sought to implement the obligations contained in the WCT and WPPT, as well as harmonize certain aspects of copyright law. Article 5(1) sets out a mandatory exception for certain acts of temporary reproduction, which acts as an important counterbalance to the very broad right of reproduction in Article 2 and is particularly relevant to the Internet. Article 5(2)–(3) contains an optional, but exhaustive, list of exceptions and limitations, some of which are particularly applicable to the Internet or online context. In terms of the harmonization goal, this is somewhat thwarted by the optional nature of the list and the fact that there are 20 exceptions in total. This approach, however, does have the advantage of allowing different legal traditions in the Member States comfortably to coexist and the exhaustive nature of the list means that some headway is being made towards harmonization.

An issue that the Information Society Directive virtually ignores is the extent to which exceptions may be overridden by contract.[100] This is surprising, particularly given that it deals with the situations in which exceptions may be constrained or overridden by technological protection measures.[101] Also, there are other fields, namely computer programs and databases, where there has been a real and more explicit attempt to determine which

---

[100] Note that R. Burrell and A. Coleman, *Copyright Exceptions: The digital impact* (Cambridge: Cambridge University Press, 2005), pp. 67–70, are somewhat less concerned by this issue than other commentators. This is because it is not clear how often owners will seek to use contracting-out terms, and doubts remain about whether contractual terms seeking to exclude the operation of copyright exceptions would be deemed to be validly incorporated, are enforceable, and how they may be interpreted. Also, there is a growing list of exceptions (for software and databases) that cannot be contracted-out of.

[101] See discussion at 12.6.5.2 below.

exceptions are fundamental enough not to be overridden by contract.[102] Certainly this is a matter that ought to be given further consideration in the future.

In the following sections we focus on some of the exceptions covered by Article 5 of the Information Society Directive that are particularly pertinent to use of copyright works in digital and online environments.

12.6.4.2 Temporary reproduction

Article 5(1) of the Information Society Directive states:

> Temporary acts of reproduction referred to in Article 2, which are transient or incidental, which are an integral and essential part of a technological process whose sole purpose is to enable:
>
> (a) a transmission in a network between third parties by an intermediary, or
>
> (b) a lawful use
>
> of a work or other subject matter to be made, and which have no independent economic significance, shall be exempted from the right provided for in Article 2.

The transmission of material over the Internet, from an originating server to a user, is made possible by packets of data being routed via a series of ISPs. Each of these ISPs will make fleeting copies of the material during the process. Article 5(1) permits temporary, technical acts of reproduction that occur as part of a network transmission and thus excludes this type of copying from infringement.

Additionally, Article 5(1) exempts temporary acts of reproduction that occur whilst 'browsing'. To 'browse' online material via the World Wide Web, a user must be connected to the Internet through an ISP. To access a webpage or file the user enters a Uniform Resource Locator (URL), which is a specific numeric address for the webpage or file that the user wants to access. This request is then sent to the remote web server that stores the webpage or file, whereupon that web server transmits a copy of the relevant file back to the user's computer. When a file is transmitted from a remote web server, it is copied temporarily to the random access memory (RAM) of the user's computer.

Thus, 'browsing' is the final link in the transmission process—without it, the network transmission would not be complete. As such, 'browsing' falls within Article 5(1) because it involves incidental reproduction as part of a technological process whose sole purpose is to enable a network transmission. Alternatively, it could be argued that 'browsing' is a 'lawful use', that is a use which is 'authorised by the rightsholder or not restricted by law'[103] because of either an express or implied licence granted by the rightsholder. The case law establishes a number of bases upon which a licence to do an exclusive act may be implied. In a contractual context, a term will be implied if it is necessary to give business efficacy to the contract and it satisfies the 'officious bystander' test.[104] Where there is a particular, non-contractual arrangement between the parties, a licence may be implied to give business efficacy to that arrangement.[105] A licence may also be implied from conduct, in the absence of any contractual relations.[106]

---

102 For a discussion see Aplin, *Copyright Law in the Digital Society*, pp. 163–4, 166–9, 172–3, 176.
103 Recital 33, Information Society Directive.   104 *Robin Ray v Classic FM* [1998] FSR 622, 641.
105 *Fylde Microsystems Ltd v Key Radio Systems Ltd* [1998] FSR 449 and *Trumpet Software Pty Ltd v OzEmail Pty Ltd* (1996) 34 IPR 481.
106 *Redwood Music Ltd v Chappell & Co* [1982] RPC 109.

Access to a particular website may be possible only by entering into a 'click on' agreement with the website producer, although this does not appear to represent the norm of Internet access at present. Where there is a 'click on' agreement, it is likely that the express terms and conditions of such agreement will include viewing or 'browsing' the website contents. If there are no express terms to this effect, it would seem necessary to give effect to that agreement that the user be able to 'browse' the contents of the website and such a licence would likely be implied on the grounds of business efficacy. Where there is no 'click on' agreement between the parties, but a 'click on' subscription instead, where the user is able to access the website upon registering their personal details, thereby creating a bare licence, one could probably identify an express permission to browse the website. In the absence of express permission, such a term probably would be implied into the bare licence on the grounds of business efficacy.

In many cases of 'browsing' the Internet, however, there is neither a 'click on' agreement nor subscription and the contents of a website are made available to a user upon entering the relevant URL. Here there is neither a contractual nor other arrangement between the parties and one would have to rely on the conduct of the copyright owner in placing, or agreeing to place, those materials online to imply a licence to browse. This seems plausible on the basis that it would be nonsensical to place, or agree to place, materials online (without restrictions) if it was not intended that Internet users should view them.

Of course, the above arguments in favour of an implied licence to browse Internet material rest on the assumption that the copyright material has been placed online with the permission of the copyright owner. If the copyright owner has not consented to inclusion of their works in a website then the basis for any implied licence would be negated.

Article 5(1) would also appear to exempt acts of local and proxy caching. Local caching refers to the situation where the web-browser software of an Internet user stores recently accessed webpages. This allows a user to call up these webpages faster than if the computer had to fetch them from their source server on the Internet. Proxy caching occurs at the network level on proxy servers. Proxy servers act as intermediaries between local client servers and remote content servers. They store copies of the most frequently requested pages, so that these copies can be delivered to users, rather than having to search out the data from the original source. This process has all sorts of benefits; it makes user access faster, reduces bandwidth used by both users and server, and generally reduces the amount of congestion on the Internet. Unfortunately, however, caching impedes the ability of websites to calculate 'hits' and page impressions, which information is crucial to selling advertising. There is also the risk that Internet users will access 'stale' documents. While proxy servers may be configured so that their caches are regularly updated there is no fixed schedule whereby this is guaranteed.

Caching should be exempt according to Article 5(1) and this is emphasized by recital 33, which states:

> To the extent that they meet these conditions, this exception should include acts which enable browsing as well as acts of caching to take place, including those which enable transmission systems to function efficiently, provided that the intermediary does not modify the information and does not interfere with the lawful use of technology, widely recognised and used by industry, to obtain data on the use of information.

Local caching should be exempt as a temporary, technical act of reproduction whose sole purpose is to enable lawful use, namely that of 'browsing'. In the case of proxy caching, the temporary acts of reproduction may be considered as an integral and essential part of a technological process whose sole purpose is to enable network transmissions. There may be an issue, however, about whether proxy caching lacks independent economic significance. If proxy caching is viewed as ancillary to non-exploitative acts of network transmission this condition should be satisfied.

In the UK, Article 5(1) of the Information Society Directive has been implemented in s. 28A of the CDPA, using language that is virtually identical to Article 5(1). It is important to note, however, that computer programs and copyright databases are excluded from this exception. This exclusion appears to be consistent with EC law.[107]

12.6.4.3 Private use: format-shifting

Article 5(2)(b) states that Member States may provide for exceptions or limitations to the reproduction right in respect of 'reproduction on any medium made by a natural person for private use and for ends that are neither directly nor indirectly commercial'. The UK (unlike France) has never recognized a 'private use' exception and, in implementing the directive, did not decide to include one. However, following the Gowers Review,[108] the UK IPO has been consulting on proposed changes to copyright exceptions.[109] One of the proposals (recommendation 8) is to introduce a limited private use exception for format-shifting. The proposal is 'to create a new exception that would allow consumers to make a copy of a work they legally own, so that they can make the work accessible in another format for playback on a device in their lawful possession'.[110]

There are various rationales for introducing such an exception.[111] One is the widespread belief amongst consumers that this type of copying is reasonable and thus already permissible. Another is the difficulty of enforcement in relation to this type of copying. There is also the fact that many in the copyright industries have accepted this type of copying as reasonable and the sense of unfairness that prohibiting it engenders amongst consumers.

It is important to note that the proposed 'format-shifting' exception would be narrow in scope. It would be restricted to personal, private use and would not allow users to sell, loan, or give away the copy or distribute it more widely (such as through peer-to-peer file-sharing systems). Further, a user would not be able to retain the copy if he or she was no longer in possession of the original from which it was made. Copying to a different format would have to be carried out by the individual user and could not be done by a third party acting on their behalf. Finally, the only copying that would be permitted is for the purpose of format-shifting. Other types of private use would not fall within the scope of the exception.

The UK IPO is consulting on several key issues concerning the scope of this proposed exception, including whether it should apply to all types of works or only sound recordings and films? There is also the question of whether there should be a limit on the number of format-shifts that are made. Finally, should the exception apply to all works copied after the exception takes effect, or only to works published or purchased after such date?

An important issue is whether a format-shifting exception would require payment of fair compensation to copyright owners. According to Article 5(2)(b) fair compensation is

---

[107] Aplin, *Copyright Law in the Digital Society*, p. 106.

[108] *Gowers Review of Intellectual Property* in Dec. 2006.

[109] UK Intellectual Property Office (UK IPO), *Taking forward the Gowers Review of Intellectual Property: Proposed changes to copyright exceptions* ('Exceptions Consultation Paper') at: <http://www.ipo.gov.uk/c-policy-copyexceptions.htm>.

[110] Ibid., para. 85.   [111] Ibid., paras. 80–4.

a condition of any private-use exception for reproduction. This concept is elaborated upon in recital 35 of the Information Society Directive:

> In certain cases of exceptions or limitations, rightholders should receive fair compensation to compensate them adequately for the use made of their proected works or other subject matter. When determining the form, detailed arrangements and possible level of such fair compensation, account should be taken of the particular circumstances of each case. When evaluating these circumstances, a valuable criterion would be the possible harm to the rightholders resulting from the act in question. In cases where rightholders have already received payment in some other form, for instance as part of a licence fee, no specific or separate payment may be due. The level of fair compensation should take full account of the degree of use of technological protection measures referred to in the Directive. In certain situations where the prejudice to the rightholder would be minimal, no obligation for payment may arise.

The UK IPO takes the view that there is no obligation to remunerate copyright owners in the case of a limited format-shifting exception. This is for several reasons. The first is that fair compensation appears only to be payable where there is significant harm to the rightsholder and here the harm is likely to be minimal given that the proposed exception is very narrow in scope. Second, although various Member States, such as France and Germany, operate levy systems to ensure fair remuneration to rightsholders this is not a desirable option for the UK. This is because consumers would be forced to pay additional charges on certain devices and recording media, even though they may never be used to copy copyright works. Further, it would not be warranted for a narrow format-shifting exception, as compared with the far wider private copying exceptions that exist in other Member States. Finally, if rightsholders wish to be compensated for format-shifting activities they could incorporate an increase into the sale price of the original work.

Whether the government will introduce a format-shifting exception is yet to be seen. Having considered the current proposal and the questions posed by the UK IPO do you think this is a desirable step to take?

12.6.4.4 Educational purposes

Developments in information and communication technologies have created various new educational tools. These include Virtual Learning Environments (VLEs), in which material is made available online to students, to be accessed at a time and place convenient to them; where students and tutors can discuss issues via Discussion Boards or Chat facilities; where announcements can be posted electronically; and where assessments can be taken and marked.[112] The existing exceptions for educational establishments were crafted at a time when such tools were not available and when the Internet was in its infancy. It is therefore unsurprising that the Gowers Review remarked that ss. 35–6 of the CDPA do not cover interactive learning tools, such as VLEs, and suggested their amendment to take into account such technological developments.[113]

According to the UK IPO, ss. 35–6 of the CDPA and the proposed changes to them fall within Article 5(3)(a) of the Information Society Directive. This provision permits exceptions

---

[112] Blackboard Vista and Moodle are examples of two pieces of software used in Higher Education to create VLEs.

[113] *Gowers Review of Intellectual Property*, Nov. 2006 ('Gowers Review'), paras. 4.15–4.19.

and limitations, with respect to reproduction and communication to the public, for the sole purpose of illustration of teaching or scientific research, as long as there is sufficient acknowledgement and to the extent justified by the non-commercial purpose to be achieved.

Section 35 of the CDPA permits educational establishments to make recordings of broadcasts (or copy such recordings) for the educational purposes of that establishment, provided the educational purposes are non-commercial and there is a sufficient acknowledgement. This provision prevents there from being infringement of copyright in the broadcast or in any work included in it. Further, it permits such recordings or copies thereof to be communicated to the public 'by a person situated within the premises of an educational establishment provided that the communication cannot be received by any person situated outside the premises of that establishment'. The exception does not apply to the extent that a licensing scheme for this type of use exists.

In its Exceptions Consultation Paper, the UK IPO explains that s. 35 applies to recordings of broadcasts in the traditional sense and not interactive, on-demand broadcasts, such as those available via BBC iPlayer. Moreover, it is limited to communicating recordings of broadcasts (or copies thereof) to students *on the premises* of the educational establishment. The proposal is to widen the exception to include both traditional and on-demand broadcasts and to make these accessible via secure VLEs to 'teachers and pupils of an educational establishment and other persons directly connected with the activities of the establishment'.[114]

Section 36 of the CDPA creates an exception for reprographic copies of passages from published literary, dramatic, or musical works made by or on behalf of an educational establishment for the purposes of instruction that is non-commercial and provided there is sufficient acknowledgement (unless this would be impossible for practical reasons). Copyright in the literary, dramatic, and musical works, along with any typographical arrangement of the edition is not infringed. However, not more than 1 per cent of any work may be copied in any quarter of the year. This exception does not apply where there are licences available authorizing the copying in question.

The UK IPO suggests widening s. 36 to include the communication of such passages via secure VLEs and e-mail, provided there is sufficient security, to 'teachers and pupils of an educational establishment and other persons directly connected with the activities of the establishment'.[115] It raises for discussion the question of whether the exception should be extended to all types of works, as opposed to being limited to literary, dramatic, and musical works.[116]

Does it make sense to extend ss. 35–6 in the ways suggested above? Do they go far enough? Will such changes be highly beneficial to educational establishments, in particular distance-learning providers, and are the risks to copyright owners outweighed by these benefits?

12.6.4.5 Library privileges

Article 5(2)(c) of the Information Society Directive permits exceptions for:

> specific acts of reproduction made by publicly accessible libraries, educational establishments or museums, or by archives, which are not for direct or indirect economic or commercial advantage.

---

[114] Exceptions Consultation Paper, paras. 46–53.
[115] Ibid., paras. 63–6.   [116] Ibid., paras. 67–71.

Section 42 of the CDPA is consistent with Article 5(2)(c). It permits prescribed libraries and archives to make copies of any items in their permanent collections in order to preserve or replace them or to replace the item in the permanent collection of another prescribed library or to archive an item which has been lost, destroyed, or damaged. The exemption from infringement relates only to copyright in any literary, musical, or dramatic works, any illustrations accompanying such works, and the typographical arrangement of a published edition.

The Gowers Review commented that s. 42 of the CDPA is a fairly narrow exception, in so far as it does not apply to all classes of works, limits the number of copies that can be made and also limits the ability to format-shift.[117] The UK IPO is thus consulting on whether the exception should be widened to apply to sound recordings, films, and broadcasts and, further, whether format-shifting should be permitted, since this is an important way of dealing with unstable media and also obsolete formats. There is also the issue of whether to permit multiple copies since this will cater for digital preservation, where more than one copy is often necessary in order to protect against data loss or corruption. Finally, the UK IPO has asked for views on whether the exception should be extended to museums and galleries, in recognition of the role they play in preserving cultural heritage.[118]

Obviously there is a strong public interest in preserving copyright works, in order to maintain our cultural heritage. Are the suggested reforms to s. 42 in keeping with this goal, without being at the expense of rightsholders?

FURTHER READING

R. Burrell and A. Coleman, *Copyright Exceptions: The digital impact* (Cambridge: Cambridge University Press, 2005).

L. Guibault, *Copyright Limitations and Contracts* (The Hague: Kluwer, 2002).

12.6.5 ENFORCEMENT: TECHNOLOGICAL PROTECTION MEASURES

12.6.5.1 International position

Establishing that copyright owners have the exclusive right to make their works available via the Internet or other digital networks is one thing. Enforcing that right is another, given the scale of infringing activity and multitude of locations in which it can occur. Copyright owners, therefore, began to look at other, non-legal mechanisms for trying to protect against the unauthorized digital exploitation of their works. These took the form of technological protection measures ('TPMs') or, in more popular parlance, digital 'locks'. Various types of TPMs can be used, ranging from passwords, to encryption, to copy-protection software. What they have in common is the aim of controlling unauthorized copying and/or distribution of copyright works in digital form. TPMs, however, can and have been circumvented. Therefore, copyright owners looked to bolster the practical obstacle of digital 'locks' with a legal obstacle, namely the prohibition of circumvention and circumvention means. This was achieved via Article 11 of the WCT and Article 18 of the WPPT.

---

[117] Gowers Review, paras. 4.79–4.84. [118] Exceptions Consultation Paper, paras. 173–81.

Article 11 of the WCT provides:

> Contracting Parties shall provide adequate legal protection and effective legal remedies against the circumvention of effective technological measures that are used by authors in connection with the exercise of their rights under this Treaty or the Berne Convention and that restrict acts, in respect of their works, which are not authorized by the authors concerned or permitted by law.

Article 18 of the WPPT is in virtually identical terms, except that it refers to performers and their performances and phonogram producers and their phonograms. The language of Article 11 WCT and Article 18 WPPT is broad, thus permitting signatories a wide discretion as to how to implement their obligations. Certainly, there have been divergent approaches to implementing these provisions. We turn now to examine the EU position.

12.6.5.2 EU position

The Information Society Directive implements the above obligations in the WCT and WPPT via Article 6. Article 6(1)–(2) of the Information Society Directive obliges Member States to provide adequate legal protection against circumvention of any effective technological measure and 'trafficking' in circumvention devices or services.

A 'technological measure' is defined by Article 6(3) to mean:

> Any technology, device or component that, in the normal course of its operation, is designed to prevent or restrict acts, in respect of works or other subject-matter, which are not authorised by the rightholder of any copyright or any right related to copyright as provided for by law or the *sui generis* right provided for in Chapter III of Directive 96/9/EC.

Article 6(3) goes on to state that technological measures shall be deemed 'effective':

> where the use of a protected work or other subject-matter is controlled by the rightholders through application of an access control or protection process, such as encryption, scrambling or other transformation of the work or other subject-matter or a copy control mechanism, which achieves the protection objective.

Thus, a 'technological measure' appears to include access control and copy-protection technology. This is implicit in Article 6(3) which refers to 'any technology...designed to prevent or restrict acts'. Further, in defining 'effective', Article 6(3) explicitly refers to an access control process and copy control mechanism.

Where a technological measure is capable of circumvention it has been argued that it is 'ineffective' and outside Article 6. The problem with this interpretation is that it would render Article 6 redundant since most TPMs are, to some extent, fallible. Indeed, the objective of the provision is to protect effective technological measures against acts of circumvention, which assumes that such measures can and will be circumvented. Further, Article 6(3) states that a technological measure is to be assessed 'in the normal course of its operation'. Thus, the better view is that a technological measure is not ineffective simply because it can be circumvented.

Article 6(1) obligates Member States to 'provide adequate legal protection against the circumvention of any effective technological measures' in situations where the person carries out the circumvention with actual or constructive knowledge that she is pursuing that objective. It is clear that circumvention of both access control and copy control measures is prohibited.

Article 6(2) obligates Member States to prohibit the 'trafficking' in circumvention devices or services. Specifically, it states:

> Member States shall provide adequate legal protection against the manufacture, import, distribution, sale, rental, advertisement for sale or rental, or possession for commercial purposes of devices, products or components or the provision of services which:
>
> (a) are promoted, advertised or marketed for the purpose of circumvention of, or
>
> (b) have only a limited commercially significant purpose or use other than to circumvent, or
>
> (c) are primarily designed, produced, adapted or performed for the purpose of enabling or facilitating the circumvention of,
>
> any effective technological measures.

Unlike the prohibition against circumvention per se, the above prohibition against 'trafficking' in circumvention devices or services does not contain a knowledge requirement. Article 6(2) also targets those devices or services that have circumvention as their primary or commercial purpose (as opposed to sole intended purpose).

Importantly, Articles 6(1)–(2) applies to copyright works *other than computer programs and databases* protected by the sui generis right. This creates a disparity in regulation of TPMs as applied to computer programs and those applied to other works. This is because, as described above at 12.2.3.6, Article 7(1)(c) of the Software Directive does not prohibit circumvention per se and prohibits commercially dealing in circumvention devices or services whose *sole intended purpose* is to facilitate circumvention and where there is actual or constructive knowledge. Although this inconsistency has been criticized by commentators, the European Commission has no intention of amending of Article 7 of the Software Directive until more experience has been gained from application of Article 6 of the Information Society Directive.[119]

A major concern, and one that almost brought the adoption of the Information Society Directive to a halt, is the extent to which TPMs may override copyright exceptions. More specifically, should it be the case that circumvention of TPMs is unlawful, even where it is done for the purpose of carrying out an act that is excused by one of the exceptions? The solution to this clash of interests was to insert Article 6(4), which provides:

> 4. Notwithstanding the legal protection provided for in *paragraph 1, in the absence of voluntary measures taken by rightholders, including agreements* between rightholders and other parties concerned, Member States *shall take appropriate measures* to ensure that rightholders make available to the beneficiary of an exception or limitation provided for in national law in accordance with *Article 5(2)(a), (2)(c), (2)(d), (2)(e), (3)(a), (3)(b) or (3)(e) the means of benefiting from that exception or limitation*, to the extent necessary to benefit from that exception or limitation and *where that beneficiary has legal access to* the protected work or subject-matter concerned.

---

[119] *Commission Staff Working Paper on the review of the EC legal framework in the field of copyright and related rights*, Brussels, 19 Jul. 2004, SEC (2004) 995, para. 2.2.1.4.

A Member State *may* also take such measures in respect of a beneficiary of an exception or limitation provided for in accordance with *Article 5(2)(b)*, unless reproduction for private use has already been made possible by rightholders to the extent necessary to benefit from the exception or limitation concerned and in accordance with the provisions of Article 5(2)(b) and (5), without preventing rightholders from adopting adequate measures regarding the number of reproductions in accordance with these provisions.

The technological measures applied voluntarily by rightholders, including those applied in implementation of voluntary agreements, and technological measures applied in implementation of the measures taken by Member States, shall enjoy the legal protection provided for in paragraph 1.

The provisions of the first and second subparagraphs shall not apply to works or other subject-matter made available to the public on agreed contractual terms in such a way that members of the public may access them from a place and at a time individually chosen by them.

When this Article is applied in the context of Directives 92/100/EEC and 96/9/EC, this paragraph shall apply *mutatis mutandis*. [emphasis supplied]

Article 6(4) does not create exceptions that an alleged infringer can rely upon to exclude liability for circumvention of technological measures. Instead, it introduces 'a unique legislative mechanism which foresees an ultimate responsibility on the rightsholders to accommodate certain exceptions to copyright or related rights'.[120]

Sub-paragraph (1) of Article 6(4) imposes a mandatory obligation on Member States. However, this only applies in relation to persons seeking to circumvent technological measures and *not* in relation to persons 'trafficking' in circumvention devices or services. Further, the obligation arises only in the *absence of voluntary measures* taken by rightsholders. Article 6(4) and recital 51 of the Information Society Directive indicate that voluntary measures include 'agreements' between rightsholders and other parties concerned. Apart from agreements, however, it is unclear what else might constitute a 'voluntary measure'. Recital 51 also indicates that Member States do not have an obligation to adopt appropriate measures *unless* a rightsholder has failed to take voluntary measures within a 'reasonable period' of time. What constitutes a 'reasonable period' is also unclear.

The obligation on Member States imposed by sub-para. 1 of Article 6(4) only relates to *specific* exceptions listed in Article 5(2)–(3) (assuming they exist in the law of the respective Member State) and not to all exceptions. These exceptions are: reproductions on paper and any similar medium (Article 5(2)(a)); specific acts of reproduction by libraries, educational establishments, museums, or archives (Article 5(2)(b)); ephemeral recording by broadcasting organizations (Article 5(2)(c)); reproduction of broadcasts made by certain social institutions (Article 5(2)(e)); use for illustration for teaching or scientific research (Article 5(3)(a)); use for the benefit of people with disability (Article 5(3)(b)); and use for the purposes of public security or for administrative, parliamentary, or judicial proceedings (Article 5(3)(e)). The basis upon which these seven exceptions have been singled out as important matters of public policy has not been made clear, nor why the remaining exceptions listed under Article 5(2)–(3) have been omitted. This is particularly a concern since Member States are not under any obligation to ensure that beneficiaries of the remaining exceptions or limitations can benefit from them. Indeed, it is arguable that a natural reading of Article 6(4) is

---

[120] N. Braun, 'The interface between the protection of technological measures and the exercise of exceptions to copyright and related rights: Comparing the situation in the United States and the European Community' [2003] EIPR 496, 499.

that Member States would not be permitted to assist beneficiaries in respect of the exceptions omitted from sub-paras. (1) and (2).

Article 6(4), sub-para. (1) obligates Member States to *take appropriate measures* to ensure that rightsholders make available, to the beneficiary of the listed specific exception or limitation, the *means* of benefiting from it. The Information Society Directive is not particularly illuminating on what will constitute 'appropriate measures' and 'means', although recital 51 indicates that 'means' could include modifying an implemented technological measure.

Finally, sub-para. (1) of Article 6(4) emphasizes that the beneficiary of a specific exception or limitation must have *legal access* to the protected work or subject matter. This requirement indicates that the obligation on a Member State to take appropriate measures exists only in relation to *copy control* measures and not access control measures. This undoubtedly reduces the value of Article 6(4) to those where lack of access stands in the way of relying upon copyright exceptions.

The scheme described above is narrowed considerably by sub-para. (4) of Article 6(4). This is because it stipulates that the obligation under sub-para. (1) and the discretion under subpara. (2) shall not apply 'to works or other subject-matter made available to the public on *agreed contractual terms* in such a way that members of the public may access them from a place and at a time individually chosen by them' (emphasis supplied). Recital 53 indicates that the exclusion relates to where interactive on-demand services are governed by contractual arrangements. Thus, the assistance created by Article 6(4), sub-paras. (1)–(2) can be potentially overridden by the use of click-wrap and browse-through licences.

Article 6(4) represents one model of balancing the interests of owners who wish to utilize TPMs and users who wish to rely on copyright exceptions. Having considered its scope, would you agree that it is a desirable model? Alternative models are available. These include: (a) leaving the use of TPMs completely unregulated; (b) permitting the sale of circumvention devices or services, but punishing those persons who use such devices to infringe copyright; (c) prohibiting the manufacture and sale of circumvention devices, but allowing individual users to circumvent TPMs; or (d) regulating TPMs but creating a list of exceptions to circumvention or trafficking in circumvention devices (as in the US). What would be the advantages or disadvantages of these alternative models? Here, it is important to consider whether they would comply with the WCT and WPPT and also whether the correct balance between owner and user interests would be struck.

12.6.5.3 UK position

The Information Society Directive was implemented via the Copyright and Related Rights Regulations 2003, SI 2003/2498 and inserted new ss. 296ZA–F in the CPDA to implement Article 6.

Here it is interesting to note the way in which the UK has implemented Article 6(4) of the Information Society Directive. This has occurred via s. 296ZE and Sch. 5A of the CDPA. According to s. 296ZE, where the application of any effective technological measure to a copyright work prevents a person from carrying out a permitted act then that person, or a person representative of a class of persons prevented from carrying out a permitted act, may issue a notice of complaint to the Secretary of State. A 'permitted act' is an act which may be done in relation to copyright works by virtue of a provision in the CDPA listed in Part 1 of Sch. 5A. Upon receiving a notice of complaint, the Secretary of State may give relevant directions to the copyright owner, for the purpose of establishing whether any voluntary measure or agreement subsists in relation to the copyright work under complaint. Where it is established that there is no subsisting voluntary measure or agreement, the Secretary of

State may give relevant directions ensuring that the copyright owner or exclusive licensee makes available to the complainant the means of carrying out the permitted act to the extent necessary to so benefit from it. The Secretary of State may also give directions as to the form and manner in which the notice of complaint, or evidence of any voluntary measure, may be delivered to him, and generally as to the procedure to be followed in relation to a complaint made under s. 296ZE. Directions given by the Secretary of State under this provision must be in writing and may be varied or revoked by a subsequent direction under this provision.

Article 6(4) has been implemented differently in other Member States. As such, this provision has created rather a loose harmonization of the way in which copyright owners' and users' interests are balanced when TPMs are applied to copyright works and sui generis databases.

FURTHER READING

N. Braun, 'The interface between the protection of technological measures and the exercise of exceptions to copyright and related rights: Comparing the situation in the United States and the European Community' [2003] EIPR 496.

S. Dusollier, 'Exceptions and technological measures in the European Copyright Directive of 2001: An empty promise' (2003) 34 IIC 62.

12.7 DOMAIN NAMES: META-TAGS AND KEYWORDS

12.7.1 INTRODUCTION

There are various tools which enable information available via the Internet to be located and displayed to users, including domain names, meta-tags, keywords, and search engines. Because such tools may use trade marks or trade names, this has given rise to issues about liability for trade mark infringement and passing off. Since most of the disputes thus far have involved domain names, the bulk of this section will be devoted to examining this area. However, in recognition of the growing concerns surrounding meta-tags and keywords, these will be briefly considered as well.

12.7.2 DOMAIN NAMES

12.7.2.1 Nature of domain names

A domain name is a unique alphanumeric label for an Internet Protocol (IP) address. An IP address is a numerical identification assigned to devices operating within the Internet, however, these are much less memorable than domain names. For example, the domain name intellectualproperty.co.uk might have an IP address of 191.166.100.1. When an Internet user enters a domain name into an Internet browser program, the software sends the name to one of several Domain Name Server computers. The Domain Name Server computer then searches its database for the IP address that matches the domain name and returns the IP address to the requesting software. Once the IP address is received it can be used to communicate with the server to which the domain name refers. This is the reason why domain names must be unique; if they labelled more than one IP address, it would be uncertain which server was to be contacted.

Domain names exist at several levels, but perhaps the most important are generic Top Level Domains (gTLDs) (eg .com, .net, .org, .int, .edu., .gov, .mil) and country code top level domains (ccTLDs) (eg .au, .uk, .jp). The Internet Corporation for Assigned Names and Numbers (ICANN) has overall responsibility for managing the domain name system. It directly governs gTLDs and delegates ccTLDs to the particular country-level domain registries. For example, Nominet[121] regulates the .uk ccTLD. The allocation of domain names by the various registries is done according to a first come, first served registration process.

Trade mark disputes concerning the use of domain names have arisen partly because of the first come, first served nature of the registration process and partly because domain names must be absolutely unique, whereas trade marks are only relatively unique. To explain this latter point further, there can be only one holder of the domain name apple.com; however, multiple persons and organizations might have trade mark (or unregistered) rights in respect of the same name for different classes of goods and services.

Various conflicts have arisen between trade mark proprietors and domain-name holders. Broadly speaking, these may be divided into three categories. The first is where there is genuine use of a domain name, which happens to overlap with a registered or unregistered trade mark. Second, there is the situation where a person creates a domain name that parodies a registered or unregistered trade mark. Finally, there is the practice of cyber-squatting, which is where a person purchases a valuable domain name with a view to transferring it to the relevant trade mark proprietor for profit.

The following sections examine the way in which the law of passing off and trade marks has responded to these conflicts, and the dispute-resolution procedure that has been developed specifically to deal with them.

FURTHER READING

J. Phillips, *Trade Mark Law: A practical anatomy* (Oxford: Oxford University Press, 2003), Ch. 17.

A. Willoughby, 'United Kingdom' in T. Bettinger (ed.), *Domain Name Law & Practice: An international handbook* (Oxford: Oxford University Press, 2005).

12.7.2.2 Passing off liability

The problem of cyber-squatting is the one that has mainly occupied English courts. Enterprising individuals saw an opportunity to acquire domain names that were valuable to large and well-known companies before they had had a chance to do so themselves. Was this an unfortunate case of businesses failing to protect their intangible assets or of unlawful behaviour on the part of those registering domain names? In the Court of Appeal decision examined below, the court's sympathies lay with the trade mark owners, rather than the cyber-squatters.

BT v One in a Million [1999] 1 WLR 903

The defendants in this case traded in domain names, i.e. registering domain names comprising well-known names and trade marks for the purposes of sale to relevant companies. They registered, *inter alia*, the domain names marksandspencer.

---

[121] <http://www.nominet.org.uk/>.

com, marksandspencer.co.uk, bt.org, sainsburys.com, virgin.org, and ladbroke.com and offered them for sale to Marks and Spencer plc, British Telecommunications plc, J. Sainsburys plc, Virgin Enterprises Ltd, and Ladbroke Group Plc, respectively. For example, the defendants offered to sell bt.org to British Telecommunications for £4,700 plus VAT and burgerking.co.uk to BurgerKing for £25,000 plus VAT.

The claimants brought actions alleging that the defendants' acts amounted to actual or threatened passing off and to threats to infringe their registered trade marks. Summary judgment was granted in each action at first instance and injunctions granted to prevent the use of their names. The defendants appealed.

Aldous LJ (with whom **Swinton Thomas** and **Stuart-Smith LJJ** agreed) **dismissing the appeal, at pp. 914–15:**

It was not suggested by the plaintiffs that relief was appropriate on the basis that the defendants' actions rendered them joint tortfeasors with others who would or had passed off. However it was the plaintiffs' case that there was passing off or at least a threat to pass off. Further, despite the conclusion of the judge that the creation of an instrument of deception was not actionable without a threat actually to cause deception, the plaintiffs submitted that the law enables a plaintiff to prevent another trader equipping himself or others with a name, the use of which would be likely to give rise to a false representation that such trader is the plaintiff or is associated or connected with him. In short, the court will not stand by and allow, what can be graphically called, an 'instrument of fraud' to remain in the hands of a trader, if it is likely the name could result in passing off.

. . .

Mr Wilson, who appeared for the defendants, accepted that where a name was inherently deceptive, in the sense that use by a trader was bound to cause passing off unless special remedial measures were taken, injunctive relief was appropriate despite the fact that the name had not actually been used to pass off. Such a name was a true instrument of fraud and injunctive relief was appropriate to prevent threatened use and dissemination. But if the name could be used for a legitimate purpose, it was not a vehicle of fraud and injunctive relief would not be granted unless it was established that the defendant either threatened to pass off or was, with another, part of a common design to pass off. He submitted that the jurisdiction depended upon the plaintiff establishing that the name was of such a character that the trader would be a joint tortfeasor when carrying out the threatened use or that the trader would be identified as the person who had performed the passing off.

. . .

[at pp. 919–20]

Fletcher Challenge Ltd v Fletcher Challenge Pty Ltd [1982] FSR 1 was decided by Powell J in the Supreme Court of New South Wales. The plaintiffs were a company formed as a result of an amalgamation of three well known New Zealand companies. The defendants were formed in anticipation that they could be sold to the plaintiffs at a substantial profit. At the hearing, counsel for the defendants told the judge that the defendants had not traded and offered undertakings that they would not trade without making it clear that they were not associated with the plaintiffs. It followed that the defendants would not make a misrepresentation which was the basis of a passing off action.

The judge considered each of the characteristics of passing off set out in the *Warnink* case [1979] AC 731. He went on to hold that, if the defendants started trading, they would be associated with or treated as part of the plaintiffs and that could affect the plaintiffs' reputation. He granted injunctions preventing passing off and requiring the name to be changed. In so doing he must have concluded that the name of the company was an instrument of fraud as its use would mean that passing off would result.

Glaxo Plc v Glaxowellcome Ltd [1996] FSR 388 was a similar case. The second and third defendants formed the first defendant in anticipation of the merger of Glaxo and Wellcome. The idea was to require the plaintiffs to pay £100,000 for the name. Lightman J held that the defendants had acted dishonestly. It was, in his view, a dishonest scheme to appropriate the goodwill of the plaintiff and to extort a substantial sum as the price for not damaging the plaintiffs' goodwill. He said, at p. 391:

> The court will not countenance any such pre-emptive strike of registering companies with names where others have the goodwill in those names, and the registering party then demanding a price for changing the names. It is an abuse of the system of registration of companies' names. The right to choose the name with which a company is registered is not given for that purpose.

Direct Line Group Ltd v Direct Line Estate Agency Ltd [1997] FSR 374 was another case where a company was formed with a view either to selling the company to the plaintiffs or to a third party. Laddie J made it clear that the courts would not permit such a course of conduct and granted injunctive relief pending trial despite the fact that it seemed that the defendants had not traded.

The ability to restrain dissemination of an instrument of fraud was recognised by the Court of Appeal in *Norwich Pharmacal Co v Customs and Excise Commissioners* [1974] AC 133. That was an action in which the plaintiffs sought discovery of the names of patent infringers. The plaintiffs submitted, by analogy to trade mark and passing off cases, that the customs could be ordered to give discovery of the names. The most pertinent passage to the issue in this case is in the judgment of Buckley LJ, at pp. 145–146:

> If a man has in his possession or control goods the dissemination of which, whether in the way of trade or, possibly, merely by way of gifts (see *Upmann v Forester* (1883) 24 Ch D 231) will infringe another's patent or trade mark, he becomes, as soon as he is aware of this fact, subject to a duty, an equitable duty, not to allow those goods to pass out of his possession or control at any rate in circumstances in which the proprietor of the patent or mark might be injured by infringement ensuing. The man having the goods in his possession or control must not aid the infringement by letting the goods get into the hands of those who may use them or deal with them in a way which will invade the proprietor's rights. Even though by doing so he might not himself infringe the patent or trade mark, he would be in dereliction of his duty to the proprietor. This duty is one which will, if necessary, be enforced in equity by way of injunction: see *Upmann v Elkan* (1871) LR 12 Eq. 140; LR 7 Ch App 130. The man having possession or control may also be under a duty to give information in relation to the goods to the proprietor of the patent or mark: *Upmann v Elkan.*

In my view there can be discerned from the cases a jurisdiction to grant injunctive relief where a defendant is equipped with or is intending to equip another with an instrument of fraud. Whether any name is an instrument of fraud will depend upon all the circumstances. A name which will, by reason of its similarity to the name of another, inherently lead to passing off is such an instrument. If it would not inherently lead to passing off, it does not follow that it is not an instrument of fraud. The court should consider the similarity of the names, the intention of the defendant, the type of trade and all the surrounding circumstances. If it be the intention of the defendant to appropriate the goodwill of another or enable others to do so, I can see no reason why the court should not infer that it will happen, even if there is a possibility that such an appropriation would not take place. If, taking all the circumstances into account the court should conclude that the name was produced to enable passing off, is adapted to be used for passing off and, if used, is likely to be fraudulently used, an injunction will be appropriate.

It follows that a court will intervene by way of injunction in passing off cases in three types of case. First, where there is passing off established or it is threatened. Second, where the defendant is a joint tortfeasor with another in passing off either actual or threatened. Third, where the defendant has equipped himself with or intends to equip another with an instrument of fraud. This third type is probably a mere quia timet action.

...

[at pp. 924–5]

It is accepted that the name Marks & Spencer denotes Marks & Spencer Plc and nobody else. Thus anybody seeing or hearing the name realises that what is being referred to is the business of Marks & Spencer Plc. It follows that registration by the defendants of a domain name including the name Marks & Spencer makes a false representation that they are associated or connected with Marks & Spencer Plc. This can be demonstrated by considering the reaction of a person who taps into his computer the domain name marksandspencer.co.uk and presses a button to execute a 'Whois' search. He will be told that the registrant is One In A Million Ltd. A substantial number of persons will conclude that One In A Million Ltd must be connected or associated with Marks & Spencer Plc. That amounts to a false representation which constitutes passing off.

Mr Wilson submitted that mere registration did not amount to passing off. Further, Marks & Spencer Plc had not established any damage or likelihood of damage. I cannot accept those submissions. The placing on a register of a distinctive name such as 'marksandspencer' makes a representation to persons who consult the register that the registrant is connected or associated with the name registered and thus the owner of the goodwill in the name. Such persons would not know of One In A Million Ltd and would believe that they were connected or associated with the owner of the goodwill in the domain name they had registered. Further, registration of the domain name including the words 'Marks & Spencer' is an erosion of the exclusive goodwill in the name which damages or is likely to damage Marks & Spencer Plc.

Mr Wilson also submitted that it was not right to conclude that there was any threat by the defendants to use or dispose of any domain name including the words 'Marks & Spencer'. He submitted that the second and third defendants, Mr Conway and Mr Nicholson, were two rather silly young men who hoped to make money from the likes of the plaintiffs by selling domain names to them for as much as they could get. They may be silly, but their letters and activities make it clear that they intended to do more than just retain the names. Their purpose was to threaten use and disposal sometimes explicitly and on other occasions implicitly. The judge was right to grant quia timet relief to prevent the threat becoming reality.

I also believe that domain names comprising the name 'Marks & Spencer' are instruments of fraud. Any realistic use of them as domain names would result in passing off and there was ample evidence to justify the injunctive relief granted by the judge to prevent them being used for a fraudulent purpose and to prevent them being transferred to others.

The other cases are slightly different. Mr Wilson pointed to the fact that there are people called Sainsbury and Ladbroke and companies, other than Virgin Enterprises Ltd, who have as part of their name the word Virgin and also people or firms whose initials would be BT. He went on to submit that it followed that the domain names which the defendants had registered were not inherently deceptive. They were not instruments of fraud. Further there had been no passing off and none was threatened and a transfer to a third party would not result in the defendants becoming joint tortfeasors in any passing off carried out by the person to whom the registrations were transferred. Thus, he submitted, there was no foundation for the injunctive relief in the actions brought by four of the plaintiffs.

> I believe that, for the same reasons I have expressed in relation to the Marks & Spencer Plc action, passing off and threatened passing off has been demonstrated. The judge was right to conclude, at p. 273:
>
>> The history of the defendants' activities shows a deliberate practice followed over a substantial period of time of registering domain names which are chosen to resemble the names and marks of other people and are plainly intended to deceive. The threat of passing off and trade mark infringement, and the likelihood of confusion arising from the infringement of the mark are made out beyond argument in this case, even if it is possible to imagine other cases in which the issue would be more nicely balanced.
>
> I also believe that the names registered by the defendants were instruments of fraud and that injunctive relief was appropriate upon this basis as well. The trade names were well known 'household names' denoting in ordinary usage the respective plaintiff. The defendants registered them without any distinguishing word because of the goodwill attaching to those names. It was the value of that goodwill, not the fact that they could perhaps be used in some way by a third party without deception, which caused them to register the names. The motive of the defendants was to use that goodwill and threaten to sell it to another who might use it for passing off to obtain money from the plaintiffs. The value of the names lay in the threat that they would be used in a fraudulent way. The registrations were made with the purpose of appropriating the plaintiffs' property, their goodwill, and with an intention of threatening dishonest use by them or another. The registrations were instruments of fraud and injunctive relief was appropriate just as much as it was in those cases where persons registered company names for a similar purpose.

Do you agree with the finding that the defendants' registration of domain names, as opposed to actually using them in any way, such as to host a website, amounted to passing off? Does the mere registration of a domain name lead to a false representation that a person is associated with the company whose name is registered?[122] In terms of using domain names as 'instruments of fraud', Aldous LJ held that any realistic use of marksandspencer.co.uk and marksandspencer.com would result in passing off—do you agree? Further, Aldous LJ held that the defendants' registration of the other domain names were instruments of fraud because they intended to take advantage of the goodwill associated with those names. In what circumstances do you think registration of domain names that comprise well-known names will *not* amount to instruments of fraud?

BT v One in a Million is the leading case on when registration of domain names will amount to passing off and/or instruments of fraud and it has been followed and applied on numerous occasions. One example is *Global Projects Management Ltd v Citigroup Inc.*[123] Global Projects Management (GPM) had registered 'citigroup.co.uk' the day that a merger between Citicorp and Travelers Group (to form Citigroup) was announced. GPM also applied to register the domain name citigroup.com but failed because the name had already been registered. It never used the 'citigroup.co.uk' domain name or attempted to sell it. Proceedings were initiated by Citigroup under the Uniform Dispute Resolution Policy (see 12.7.4 below for more details of this policy), but were suspended when GPM brought an action for unjustified threats of infringement under s. 21 of the TMA. Citigroup claimed, by

---

[122] For scepticism that the mere fact of registration itself constitutes passing off see 'UK' in T. Bettinger (ed.), *Domain Name Law & Practice: An international handbook* (Oxford: Oxford University Press, 2005), para. 123.

[123] [2006] FSR 39.

way of counterclaim, passing off by GPM. Park J, following and applying *BT v One in a Million*, held that GPM's actions amounted to passing off. Although GPM did not have a cyber-squatting record, and had not offered to sell the domain name to Citigroup, the timing of the domain name registration showed that the object of it was to obtain a domain name that carried the potential threat of deception harmful to Citigroup.

Another example of where *BT v One in a Million* has been applied is *Phones4u Ltd v Phone4u.co.uk Internet Ltd*.[124] In this case the claimants adopted the trading name 'Phones4U' in May 1995 and registered the domain name 'phones4U.co.uk' in May 1997. By the end of 1999 the claimants had a Phones4U store in most major towns and cities in England and, in 1999 alone, sold 185,000 mobile phones. The defendants registered the domain name 'phone4U.co.uk' in August 1999 and established a website selling mobile phones using that domain name, which became operational in March 2000. The claimants sued, *inter alia*, for passing off. At first instance, Judge Richard Sheldon QC rejected the claim of passing off. However, the Court of Appeal allowed an appeal on this issue. Jacob LJ (Carnwarth and Tuckey LJJ in agreement) held that the judge had erred in finding that the claimants did not have goodwill in the expression 'phones4U'. The judge had incorrectly applied a test of distinctiveness that was appropriate to trade mark law, but not when it came to establishing goodwill for the purposes of passing off, and there was sufficient proved use of the name by the claimants to infer that it was known to a substantial section of the public.[125] Further, Jacob LJ held that registration of the domain name amounted to an instrument of fraud, since there could not be any realistic use of the domain name without causing deception.[126] There was evidence to show that the defendant had received numerous emails from customers who thought they were dealing with the claimant. Although there was no trade diversion from the claimant to the defendant, this was nevertheless damaging to the goodwill of the claimant because customers were emailing their complaints, which were being ignored.[127] Finally, Jacob LJ held that the trial judge was wrong to conclude that there was no confusion or deception because the claimants and defendants had been trading side-by-side for a long period of time without significant confusion. This was because there was no evidence of side-by-side use since the defendants' trade was exiguous.[128]

There have been cases, however, in which claims of passing off or use of domain names as instruments of fraud have been unsuccessful. *French Connection Ltd v Sutton*[129] is one such example. Unlike *BT v One in a Million*, this was not a case of blatant cyber-squatting. A Mr Sutton had registered the domain name 'fcuk.com' on 21 April 1997 and set up a website advertising his services as an Internet consultant the following year. In February 1997, French Connection had conceived the idea of using the word 'fcuk', which stands for French Connection UK, to advertise its casual clothing. French Connection's 'fcuk' advertising campaign was both high profile and successful and the company later applied for summary judgment for passing off arising from the registration and use of the 'fcuk.com' domain name. French Connection failed to satisfy Rattee J that, on the evidence, Mr Sutton had no arguable defence to the passing off claim. Rattee J distinguished *BT v One in a Million* on the basis that the domain name 'fcuk.com' was not an instrument of fraud because it was not registered with a view to passing off, but as a useful name for his Internet and email consultancy. It was not proved beyond argument that use of the domain name would inherently lead to passing off. The 'fcuk' name was not synonymous with the claimant. Further,

---

124 [2007] RPC 5.   125 Ibid., paras. 30–4.   126 Ibid., para. 35.
127 Ibid., para. 37.   128 Ibid., paras. 41–7.   129 [2000] ETMR 341.

anyone logging on to the defendant's website would not be misled into thinking that the claimant was in any way involved, given the very different nature of the claimant's and defendant's activities. Thus, French Connection had failed to establish any real likelihood of confusion and there was no evidence of actual or likely damage to it, and the summary judgment application was dismissed.

The claimant also failed to establish passing off in the case of *Radio Taxicabs (London) Ltd v Owner Drivers Radio Taxi Services Ltd*[130] where the defendant registered 'radiotaxis.com', which provided a direct link to the defendant's website. The claimant failed to show the necessary goodwill in the name 'radio taxis' but, even if it could have shown this, there was no proof that the defendant's website gave rise to any relevant likely confusion; the phrase had a genuinely descriptive meaning and the defendant did in fact operate a radio taxi service. There was no danger that a visitor accessing the defendant's site via the link from 'radiotaxis.com' would believe it to be a website of the claimant or even associate it with that of the claimant.

In conclusion, it seems that whether registration and/or use of a domain name will amount to passing off or constitute an instrument of fraud depends on several factors. These include: whether there is goodwill in the claimant's name and, if so, the strength of that goodwill; whether there is genuine use of the domain name by a defendant in relation to his goods or services; and whether that use creates a likelihood of confusion between the claimant's and defendant's activities.

As we shall see from the following section, the registration and use of domain names has also given rise to claims of trade mark infringement.

12.7.2.3 Trade mark liability

In *BT v One in a Million* the claimants also claimed that the defendants actions amounted to trade mark infringement under s. 10(3) of the Trade Marks Act 1994. This was accepted at first instance and the appeal against this decision was dismissed. Aldous LJ in the Court of Appeal held that the domain names indicated origin, were confusingly similar to the registered trade marks, and that their use would take unfair advantage of the distinctive character and reputation of the marks. He reached this conclusion with minimal reasoning.

Cyber-squatting, of a particularly novel kind, was held to infringe the claimant's trade marks in the case extracted below. Here we see a more detailed explanation of why the defendant's activities amounted to infringement.

Tesco Stores Ltd v Elogicom Ltd [2007] FSR 4

The claimant, who held registered trade marks for 'Tesco' and 'Tesco.com', had entered into an arrangement with a third party, whereby 'affiliates' would provide an advert or button which, when clicked, took the user to the Tesco website. Software tracked this activity and sales made as a result of a referral led to Tesco paying the affiliate a commission via the third party. The defendant registered their two main websites, 'Avon4me.co.uk' and 'Avonlady.co.uk' as affiliate websites to Tesco. However, they also registered several domain names with the word 'Tesco' and added these to the system, so that if an Internet user typed in these domain names he/she was taken directly to the Tesco website. If a user made a purchase on the Tesco website, Tesco would then be charged

---

130 [2004] RPC 19.

a commission on those sales. This resulted in a huge increase in commission payments to the defendant—some £26,688. On learning about the activities of the defendant, the claimant brought an action for trade mark infringement and passing off. The defendant denied liability and counterclaimed for payment of the £26,688 commission earned. Tesco applied for summary judgment on its claim and to dismiss the defendant's counterclaim.

Deputy Judge Mr Philip Sales:

33. In my judgment, the use of internet domain names is itself a service offered to the public, whereby the entry of such a name in the address bar of the computer of an individual browsing the internet will take them to a website. In my view, by registering and making its 'tesco' related domain names available as pathways on the internet to Tesco websites with a view to generating income for itself in the form of commission, Elogicom did use in the course of trade a series of signs (those domain names) which were each similar to the trade marks registered by Tesco and were each used in relation to services (the provision of internet access to Tesco websites) identical with or similar to those for which the trade marks were registered, and in circumstances where there existed a likelihood of confusion on the part of the public, including the likelihood of association of Elogicom's service (the provision of internet access to Tesco websites) with the trade marks. In the case of trade mark no. 2321013, the service provided by Elogicom was identical to the service for which the trade mark was registered, since class 35 in that trade mark expressly includes 'assistance relating to all of the aforementioned services [ie including viewing and purchasing goods from a general merchandise Internet website]', and I consider that the provision of domain names allowing speedy access to such a website is itself a service in the form of provision of 'assistance' relating to the viewing and purchasing of goods on such a website. Further, in relation to trade mark nos 2258927 and 2238995 (in which class 35 does not include express reference to 'assistance' of the kind referred to in trade mark no 2321013, but does include reference to 'assistance in the selection of goods brought together'), I also conclude that the provision of domain names allowing speedy access to Tesco's internet websites is itself a service in the form of provision of 'assistance in the selection of goods brought together'. In the case of all three trade marks, even if the service provided by Elogicom was not identical with services for which the trade marks were registered, the service provided by Elogicom would in my view be similar to those for which the trade marks were registered (namely, in broad terms, the provision of internet access to shopping services), within the meaning of s. 10(2)(b) of the Act.

34. Therefore, subject to the defences put forward by Elogicom to which I turn below, I consider that its use of 'tesco' related domain names infringed Tesco's three trade marks, contrary to s. 10(2) of the Act; and I also consider that Elogicom's use of those domain names infringed Tesco's three trade marks, contrary to s. 10(3) of the Act, in that Elogicom used the domain names in the course of its trade in relation to services, they were similar to Tesco's trade marks, Tesco's trade marks had a reputation in the United Kingdom and—subject to Elogicom's defences—its use of those domain names was 'without due cause' and took 'unfair advantage of' the distinctive character and the repute of Tesco's trade marks. In my view, Elogicom took unfair advantage of the Tesco brand, reflected in its trade marks, by using the word 'tesco' in its domain names specifically with the object of trading on and benefiting from Tesco's reputation with the general public, by capturing part of the traffic of persons browsing the internet and entering Tesco related names in the address bars on their computers in the hope of being taken to Tesco websites, and then obtaining payment of commission from Tesco via TradeDoubler in relation to that traffic. Moreover, on the authority of

the Court of Appeal's decision in *British Telecommunications Plc v One in a Million Ltd* [1999] FSR 1, it seems to me that the situation which Elogicom brought about would also fall to be regarded as detrimental to the distinctive character or the repute of Tesco's trade marks, within the meaning of s. 10(3), since the following observation of Aldous LJ at 25 would apply: 'The domain names were registered to take advantage of the distinctive character and reputation of the marks. That is unfair and detrimental.'

. . .

[The judge went on to consider the defences raised:]

36. First, it is said that the defendants' use of the 'tesco' related domain names was purely to direct the browsing public to Tesco's own websites and that Elogicom did not use any of Tesco's trade marks in any manner in its own business. I accept that Elogicom did not use the domain names to direct customers to its own websites. In my judgment, however, this is not a good defence to the claim. As set out above, I consider that Elogicom was offering a service to the public under the various domain names, and that in doing so it was in substance making use of and trading upon the Tesco brand as reflected in Tesco's registered trade marks.

. . .

38. Thirdly, the defendants sought to rely upon s. 10(6) of the Act. They maintain that their use of the 'tesco' related domain names merely enabled individuals to have direct access to Tesco's own websites, and that therefore they were used merely for the purposes of identifying goods and services available at those websites as those of Tesco itself. In my judgment, however, there are two reasons why this defence cannot succeed. First, as set out above, I consider that Elogicom used the 'tesco' related domain names as signs under which it offered and provided its own service to the public, in the form of providing a pathway through the internet to Tesco websites. That use simply does not fall within s. 10(6) at all. But in any event, in my judgment, the use by Elogicom of the 'tesco' related domain names was not in accordance with honest practices in commercial matters and (as set out in the context of s. 10(3) above) without due cause took unfair advantage of the distinctive character or repute of Tesco's trade marks. The notion of 'honest practices' in commercial matters is an objective one: compare *Reed Executive Plc v Reed Business Information Ltd* [2004] EWCA Civ 159; [2004] RPC 40, at paras [131]–[132] per Jacob LJ. I do not think that Elogicom's trading without Tesco's consent on Tesco's own goodwill and by reference to Tesco's own trade marks in order to generate business for itself, and commission payments to it from Tesco, could be described in objective terms as an honest practice. Therefore, although it appears to me that Mr Ray may well have honestly thought that Elogicom could do what it did, I consider that he could not satisfy the condition laid down in the last sentence of s. 10(6).

. . .

40. Fifthly, the defendants maintain that Tesco should have used available internet domain name dispute resolution procedures rather than issuing proceedings. However, Tesco and the defendants are not party to any agreement between themselves which would make use of such procedures mandatory in preference to court proceedings. In any event, the internet dispute resolution procedures to which the defendants make reference make it clear on their face that they are provided as a possible alternative to court proceedings, and not with a view to excluding recourse to the courts. Nor do I consider that there was anything unreasonable in Tesco deciding to have recourse to the courts to protect its rights in the circumstances of this case. Use of the internet dispute resolution procedures would not have provided Tesco with access to injunctive relief of the sort which it seeks in these proceedings, to protect its position for the future. Nor would they have provided Tesco with protection in respect of costs.

. . .

42. For all these reasons, I conclude that Elogicom did contravene Tesco's trade marks through its use of the 'tesco' related domain names. Further, in my judgment, Elogicom's refusal to transfer those domain names to Tesco and its determination to retain them as its own registered domain names gives sufficient indication of a risk of future or continuing violation of Tesco's trade mark rights to warrant injunctive relief of the kind sought by Tesco. This is on the basis of the judgment of the Court of Appeal in *British Telecommunications Plc v One in a Million Ltd* [1999] FSR 1.

Do you agree that use of a domain name is a service, insofar as it provides access to a website? Do you also agree that the defendant here took 'unfair advantage of' the distinctive character and repute of the claimant's trade marks? Finally, does it seem appropriate, as a remedy, to order the transfer of the domain name from the defendant to the claimant, as opposed to prohibiting the defendant from using the domain name in a way that would infringe the trade mark rights of the claimant?

Thus far we have examined the way in which the law of passing off and trade marks has regulated the activities of cyber-squatters. While the law has provided considerable assistance to owners of registered and unregistered trade marks, litigation is often an expensive and slow route to take, particularly where there are multiple complaints. In order to resolve conflicts caused by registration of domain names in a low-cost and effective manner, a dispute-resolution procedure was developed by ICANN. We turn now to examine this procedure.

12.7.2.4 Uniform Domain Name Dispute Resolution Policy

In 1999 ICANN adopted the Uniform Domain Name Dispute Resolution Policy (Policy) and also an accompanying set of procedural rules (Rules).[131] Together, the Policy and Rules create a legal framework for resolving disputes between domain name holders and third parties (aside from the registrar). The Policy applies to all gTLDs (e.g. .com, .net, .org, .biz, .info) and also to ccTLDs where the Policy has been adopted by the relevant ccTLD domain name registry.[132]

The Policy is incorporated into the Registration Agreement between the domain name holder and the relevant registry. In other words, this is a contractually agreed dispute resolution procedure. It requires domain-name holders to submit to a mandatory administrative proceeding in the case of applicable disputes and these proceedings are brought before one of the approved service providers. These are the WIPO Arbitration and Mediation Centre (WIPO Centre), the Asian Domain Name Dispute Resolution Centre (ADNDRC), the National Arbitration Forum (NAF), and (since January 2008) the Czech Arbitration Court.[133]

Applicable disputes are those where a complainant asserts that:

(i) the domain name is identical or confusingly similar to a trade mark or service mark in which the complainant has rights; and

---

[131] For a discussion of the history of the Policy and Rules see M. Geist, 'Fair.com?: An examination of the allegations of systematic unfairness in the ICANN UDRP' (2002) 27 Brook J Intl L 903, 913–18.

[132] For example, Nominet, which is responsible for registration of the .uk ccTLD, has adopted the Policy.

[133] See <http://www.icann.org/en/dndr/udrp/approved-providers.htm>.

(ii) the domain-name holder has no rights or legitimate interests in respect of the domain name; and

(iii) the domain name has been registered and is being used in bad faith.[134]

The Policy provides guidance as to evidence of rights and legitimate interests and evidence of registration and use in bad faith. In terms of the former, para. 4(c) states that the following shall constitute evidence of the domain name holder's rights or legitimate interests:

(i) before any notice of the dispute, there has been use or preparations to use the domain name in connection with bona fide offering of goods or services; or

(ii) the domain-name holder has been commonly known by the domain name; or

(iii) the domain-name holder is making legitimate non-commercial or fair use of the domain name, without intent for commercial gain to misleadingly divert consumers or to tarnish the trade mark or service mark at issue.

Paragraph 4(b) of the Policy states that the following shall be evidence of registration and use of the domain name in bad faith:

(i) circumstances indicating that the domain name has been registered or acquired primarily 'for the purpose of selling, renting or otherwise transferring the domain name registration to the complainant who is the owner of the trade mark or service mark or to a competitor of that complainant, for valuable consideration' in excess of out-of-pocket costs directly related to the domain name; or

(ii) registering the domain name in order to block the owner of the trade mark from doing so, provided this is a pattern of conduct; or

(iii) registering the domain name primarily for the purpose of disrupting the business of a competitor; or

(iv) using the domain name intentionally to attract, for commercial gain, users to a website or other online location website by creating a likelihood of confusion.

Any person or company can file a complaint according to the procedure with one of the approved service providers. The case is conducted wholly in writing, without in-person hearings and is heard by an Administrative Panel (of either one or three panellists). A decision can be made to cancel or transfer the domain name.[135] Commencing proceedings under the Policy does not, however, preclude resort to litigation in the courts.[136]

There are three main advantages to the administrative procedure created by the Policy and Rules. The first is that it offers a quicker and more cost-effective means for resolving disputes about domain names, as compared with litigation in the courts. The second advantage is that the procedure is significantly more informal than litigation. Finally, the procedure has an international scope insofar as it provides a single mechanism for resolving domain name disputes regardless of where the domain name holder or complainant are situated.

The success of the system in resolving domain name disputes is arguably illustrated by the number of complaints that have been handled by service providers. For example, since 1999 one of the main service providers, the WIPO Centre, has handled 13,729 complaints. In 8,777 cases the domain name was transferred; in 113 cases the domain name was

---

[134] Policy, para. 4(a).   [135] Ibid., paras. 3(c) and 4(i).   [136] Ibid., para. 4(k).

cancelled; there were 1,557 instances of the complaint being denied; and proceedings were terminated in 3,282 cases.[137]

Praise and support for the Policy has not, however, been unequivocal. Some commentators have suggested that complainants engage in forum shopping when it comes to choosing service providers and that decisions of one member Administrative Panels dramatically tend to favour complainants. This has led to a call for mandatory three-member Panels across the board.[138] Other commentators have criticized the narrow interests protected by the Policy, namely that of trade mark holders. The suggestion is that the Policy should be adapted to apply to instances of non-commercial cyber-squatting, along with disputes between persons that have legitimate claims to using the domain names and disputes involving celebrity, geographical, or culturally significant names.[139] Concerns have also been raised about inconsistencies between Panel decisions.

In your view do the Policy and Rules create a fair and effective alternative dispute resolution mechanism to that of litigation when it comes to domain name disputes? If so, is this a mechanism that could be used for other types of intellectual property conflicts?

12.7.3 META-TAGS

A meta-tag is a key word that is contained in the invisible 'header' of web pages and provides a means for search engines to identify relevant material in response to a search request from a user. It is up to the webpage provider to determine which meta-tags are inserted. As such, the webpage provider could include meta-tags that are their competitors' trade marks or trade name, or well-known trade marks, even if they have little or no relevance to their own activities.

The question of whether use of a trade mark as a meta-tag gives rise to trade mark infringement or passing off has been considered by the UK Court of Appeal in *Reed Executive Plc v Reed Business Information Ltd*.

Reed Executive Plc v Reed Business Information Ltd [2004] RPC 40

The claimants ran employment agencies, which they operated through physical offices as well as their website www.reed.co.uk. They were the registered proprietor of 'Reed' in respect of 'employment agency services, included in class 35'. The defendants were publishers who had long used the term 'Reed' in relation to their business. In 1999, the defendants started a UK based recruitment website, www.totaljobs.com, and used 'Reed', *inter alia*, as a meta-tag. At first instance, Pumfrey J held that the meta-tag use amounted to passing off and trade mark infringement. This was overturned on appeal.

Jacob LJ (with whom Auld and Rix LJJ agreed), at pp. 803–4:

145. Search engines have elaborate indexing systems which can take account not only of visible matter in a website but also matter which never appears visibly—so-called 'metatags'. The consequence is that whenever a user conducts a search which includes a word in

---

[137] See statistics available at <www.wipo.org> as at 15 Nov. 2008.

[138] Geist, 'Fair.com?', pp. 922–7 and pp. 930–3.

[139] J. Lipton, 'Beyond cybersquatting: Taking domain name disputes past trademark policy' (2005) 40 Wake Forest LR 1361.

a metatag, the search results will include that site along with all other sites which use that matter, either in visible or hidden form. That is why, when you conduct a search, some of the results appear to have nothing to do with your search term. Sometimes the metadata is translated into visible text in a search engine results page, for instance in a phrase 'totaljobs is the new recruitment service from Reed Business Information'.

147. [The trial judge]...held that RBI's metatag use was passing off and an infringement. The totaljobs site, in various versions, had the words 'Reed Business Information' as a metatag. Evidence was led as to what happened if a search under the phrase 'Reed jobs' was made. In all cases where totaljobs was listed, it came below the Reed Employment site in the search results (which, as is usual, included many other results, irrelevant to both sides). Obviously anyone looking for Reed Employment would find them rather than totaljobs. I am unable to see how there could be passing off. No one is likely to be misled—there is no misrepresentation. This is equally so whether the search engine itself rendered visible the metatag or not.

148. Nor can I see any scope for trade mark infringement under Art. 5.1(b). Assuming metatag use counts as use of a trade mark, there is simply no confusion here. I confess to not following the judge's reasoning on the point. He said that the 'ultimate purpose [of the metatag] is to use the sign to suggest a connection which does not exist'. But purpose is irrelevant to trade mark infringement and causing a site to appear in a search result, without more, does not suggest any connection with anyone else. The judge also said 'the sign in a metatag is being used to suggest that this site is to be treated in a manner appropriate to the way in which the trade mark owner's site should be treated'. Even if that be so (and I doubt it, no 'suggestions' are being made) it does not answer the 'global assessment' test laid down by the ECJ.

149. Again I would wish to reserve my opinion in relation to Art. 5.1(a). There are several difficult questions:

(a) First, does metatag use count as use of a trade mark at all? In this context it must be remembered that use is important not only for infringement but also for saving a mark from non-use. In the latter context it would at least be odd that a wholly invisible use could defeat a non-use attack. Mr Hobbs suggested that metatag use should be treated in the same way as uses of a trade mark which ultimately are read by people, such as uses on a DVD. But in those cases the ultimate function of a trade mark is achieved—an indication to someone of trade origin. Uses read only by computers may not count—they never convey a message to anyone.

(b) If metatag use does count as use, is there infringement if the marks and goods or services are identical? This is important: one way of competing with another is to use his trade mark in your metatag—so that a search for him will also produce you in the search results. Some might think this unfair—but others that this is good competition provided that no-one is misled.

(c) If metatag use can fall within the infringement provisions of Art. 5, can the defences under Art.6.1(a) apply, for instance the own name defence? The judge thought they could not because the use was invisible. That makes little sense— why should visibility be irrelevant to Art. 5.1 (both limbs) but relevant to Art. 6.1? Mr Hobbs felt unable to support the judge in this regard, accepting (again as a member of the realist school) all defences were in principle available to metatag use. However, as I say, I do not have to consider this further.

150. Accordingly I hold that there was no infringement by the use of the 'Reed Business Information' metatags.

Jacob LJ held that the use of the 'Reed' meta-tags did not amount to passing off or trade mark infringement because there was a lack of confusion. He also identified, but left open, some important questions regarding trade mark infringement, including whether the use of meta-tags can amount to trade mark use or use of one's own name. Taking into account the principles that you have considered at 6.2.2, do you consider that a meta-tag which replicated a trade mark would constitute use as a trade mark?

12.7.4 KEYWORDS

Given how essential search engines are to users of the Internet, it is unsurprising that search-engine operators, such as Google and Yahoo!, developed ways to increase their revenue from providing these services. One such way is through selling advertising keywords (or 'adwords'). These are individual keywords, which are purchased by businesses so that whenever a third party conducts a search that includes the keyword/s, the company's advertisement will appear next to the search results (known as a 'sponsored link').

Trade mark proprietors have contested whether search-engine operators are entitled to sell keywords that correspond to their registered trade marks. Several cases have come before the French courts on this issue and the Cour de Cassation has referred them to the ECJ for preliminary rulings.[140] One of the questions that has been referred is whether Article 5(1)(a)–(b) of the Trade Marks Directive should be interpreted as:

> meaning that a provider of a paid referencing service who makes available to advertisers keywords reproducing or imitating registered trade marks and arranges by the referencing agreement to create and favourably display, on the basis of those keywords, advertising links to sites offering goods identical or similar to those covered by the trade mark registration is using those trade marks in a manner which their proprietor is entitled to prevent?

The only UK decision to have considered whether search engine operators are liable for selling keywords corresponding to trade marks is *Wilson v Yahoo! UK Ltd*. We turn to consider this decision.

Wilson v Yahoo! UK Ltd [2008] ETMR 33

The claimant had operated since 1985 a mobile catering service, under the name 'Mr Spicy', selling Afro-Caribbean and Halal South Asian snacks. He had registered 'Mr Spicy' as a Community trade mark for class 29 (which refers to meat, fish, poultry, and game); class 30 (which refers to condiments and spices) and class 42 (providing food and drink, including restaurant and bar services). The first defendant (Yahoo! UK Ltd) makes available the search results from the sponsored search engine technology operated by the second defendant. The claimant alleged that the defendants had infringed his trade mark on the ground that when 'Mr Spicy' was typed into the defendants' search engines, it would direct them to sponsored links to the websites of Sainsbury's supermarket and Pricegrabber.com. The defendants sought summary

---

[140] See *Google France, Google Inc v Louis Vuitton Malletier* Case C-236/08 OJ C209/26 of 15 Aug. 2008; *Google France v Viaticum, Luteciel* Case C-237/08 OJ C209/27 of 15 Aug. 2008; *Google France v CNRRH, Pierre-Alexis Thonet, Bruno Raboin, Tiger* Case C-238/08 OJ C209/27 of 15 Aug. 2008.

judgment, or else an order for striking out the claimant's claim, on the basis that it was the search-engine user and not them who had used the 'Mr Spicy' mark, that there was no use in respect of the goods or services for which it is registered, and there had been no use as a trade mark. The judge accepted these arguments and granted summary judgment for the defendants.

Morgan J, at pp. 570–2:

58. At this point Mr Brandreth develops the further argument, which was foreshadowed in the defence, that if one ever gets to the stage of saying there has been a user by the defendants of 'spicy' or 'Mr Spicy' it is not use as a trade mark. Mr Brandreth referred to the decision of the European Court of Justice in *Arsenal Football Club Plc v Reed* (C-206/01) [2003] ETMR 19. The facts of that case are well known and it is not necessary to recite them in this judgment. That decision did not concern the Regulation with which I am concerned. It concerned Directive 89/104. But that Directive contained a recital, Recital 10, in the same terms as the recital I have earlier mentioned and Art. 5(1) of the Directive is in essentially the same terms as Art. 9(1) of the Regulation.

59. The decision is of help in the present context because, in [48] of the judgment of the court, the function of a trade mark is explained. It is to guarantee the identity of origin of the marked goods or services to the consumer or end user by enabling him, without any possibility of confusion, to distinguish the goods or services from others which have another origin. It is said that the purpose of the mark is to offer a guarantee that all the goods or services bearing it have been manufactured or supplied under the control of a single undertaking responsible for their quality.

60. In order to enforce, in a practical way, this guarantee of origin which is the essential function of a trade mark, the proprietor of the trade mark must be protected against competitors wishing to take unfair advantage of the status and reputation of the trade mark by selling goods illegally bearing it. However, the exercise must be reserved to cases in which a third party's use of the sign affects or is liable to affect the functions of the trade mark, in particular its essential function of guaranteeing to consumers the origin of the goods. In those passages I have been summarising, [48]–[51] of the judgment.

61. In [54] the matter is then put in the negative sense of what the proprietor is not entitled to do, and I will read a sentence from [54]:

> The proprietor may not prohibit the use of a sign identical to the trade mark for goods identical to those for which the mark is registered if that use cannot affect his own interests as proprietor of the mark having regard to its functions.

...

63. ...I find this is a proper case to give summary judgment for the defendants. I essentially accept Mr Brandreth's submissions, both as set out in the defence and as developed in oral argument in the course of this hearing.

64. I can put my conclusions really quite concisely, and in my own words, as follows: the trade mark in this case is not used by anyone other than the browser who enters the phrase 'Mr Spicy' as a search query in the defendants' search engine. In particular, the trade mark is not used by the defendants. The response of the defendants to the use of the trade mark by the browser is not use of the trade mark by the defendants. That is enough to decide the case in the defendants' favour. But the matter does not stop there. If, by some process of reasoning, one were to hold that the search engine's response to the words used by the browser was, itself, use by the defendants, in my judgment, it is not use of the mark 'Mr Spicy'. What, instead, is being used is the English word 'spicy' as it appears in that phrase.

65. Further, even if, contrary to what I have now held are two fatal answers to Mr Wilson's claim, I were to hold that the defendants were using his trade mark in doing what they did, then they are not using it as a trade mark as explained in the *Arsenal Football Club* case. In my judgment, this case, very comfortably and clearly, comes within [54] of the decision in that case; that is, Mr Wilson is not able to prohibit the use of the words 'Mr Spicy' even when they are being applied to goods identical to those for which the mark is registered if that use cannot affect his own interest as proprietor of the mark having regard to its functions. That is satisfied here.

66. I remind myself of what actually appears on the search results, or what did at the relevant time appear, if one typed in the words 'Mr Spicy'. There is a reference to Sainsbury's. It does not say that all the food sold at Sainsbury's has Mr Wilson's trade or business as an origin. It is not pretending that Sainsbury's food all comes from Mr Wilson's trade or business, MR SPICY. It does not even say that Sainsbury's, amongst the many brands they stock, stock Mr Wilson's foods under the brand name 'Mr Spicy' or under the trade mark MR SPICY. I do not begin to see how what is described in the search response with reference to Sainsbury's has any impact of an adverse character on Mr Wilson's rights as proprietor of the Community trade mark. The same comments apply to the reference to Pricegrabber.

67. By that process of reasoning and really for those various reasons in combination, any one of which on its own would be enough, I hold that the claim as pleaded at the present time does not disclose a cause of action and there should be summary judgment for the defendants against the claimant.

Wilson v Yahoo! suggests that the sale of adwords in the UK will not constitute trade mark infringement. Yet this may be too sanguine a view of the decision, given that it dealt with very particular facts. What if, for example, the facts differed and the trade mark involved was well known or the sponsored link was to an advertisement for counterfeit goods of the same kind?[141] One of the main search engine providers, Google, changed its adword policy in the UK and Ireland[142] as a result of *Wilson v Yahoo!*. It now allows companies to purchase another's trade mark as a keyword to trigger their own advertisements. Whether Google will be able to continue with this policy very much depends on the outcome of the three ECJ references made by the Cour de Cassation. Thus, we await with interest the rulings from the ECJ, which will have to address the issue of whether selling trade marks as adwords constitutes use as a trade mark. Based on your understanding of the ECJ decisions in *Arsenal v Reed*[143] and also *Adam Opel AG v Autec AG*[144] what you do think the outcome is likely to be?

FURTHER READING

S. Blakeney, 'Keyword advertising: Will the ECJ provide an answer?' [2008] CTLR 209.

N. Shemtov, 'Searching for the right balance: Google, keywords advertising and trade mark use' [2008] EIPR 470.

A. Vranaki, 'On-line sponsored links: *Wilson v Yahoo! UK Ltd & anor* [2008] EWHC 361 (Ch)' [2008] Communications Law 135.

---

[141] A. Vranaki, 'On-line sponsored links: *Wilson v Yahoo! UK Ltd & anor* [2008] EWHC 361 (Ch)' [2008] Communications Law 135, 136.

[142] Effective from 5 May 2008.   [143] Case C-206/01 [2002] ECR I-1027.

[144] Case C-48/05 [2007] ECR I-1017.

INTELLECTUAL PROPERTY

IN ACTION

13.1 INTRODUCTION

In this chapter we turn from the substantive law to look at the procedural law relating to intellectual property disputes, including the appropriate forum for bringing these disputes and the available remedies. We begin by identifying the international and regional agreements that govern UK law in this area. We then turn to examine intellectual property disputes and the civil courts. It is in these courts that a vast majority of intellectual property cases are heard. We finish by looking at IP disputes and criminal procedure. Although substantially fewer cases are brought in the criminal courts, nonetheless this is an increasingly important aspect of IP enforcement, as it addresses cases of piracy on a large or commercial scale.

13.2 INTERNATIONAL AND REGIONAL FRAMEWORKS

13.2.1 TRIPS AGREEMENT

The TRIPS Agreement differs from other major conventions, such as Berne[1] or Paris,[2] in that it has reasonably detailed obligations concerning the enforcement of intellectual property rights ('IPRs'). This was a deliberate inclusion at the behest of developed countries because they believed that substantive protection for IPRs would only be as good as the means for their enforcement in practice. Part III of TRIPS lays down minimum standards in the following areas:

Section 1: General Obligations (Article 41), regulating, in particular, the obligation to take effective action against infringements of the rights protected under the TRIPS

[1] Berne Convention for the Protection of Literary and Artistic Works 1886.
[2] Paris Convention for the Protection of Industrial Property 1883.

Agreement, to guarantee fair and equitable proceedings with respect to fundamental procedural rights, and to provide for judicial review of decisions on the merits of a case.

Section 2: Civil and Administrative Procedures and Remedies (Article 42–9), regulating procedures for the enforcement of all rights protected under the TRIPS Agreement (including rules on producing evidence), of claims to injunction orders, to damages, to information, and to destruction.

Section 3: Provisional Measures (Article 50), regulating the prevention of infringements and the preservation of relevant evidence.

Section 4: Special Requirements Related to Border Measures (Articles 51–60), regulating the requirements for and consequences of the suspension of the release of imported goods by the customs authorities.

Section 5: Criminal Procedures and penalties (Article 61), which must be provided at least in cases of willful trademark counterfeiting or copyright piracy undertaken on a commercial scale.

13.2.2 THE EU AND THE ENFORCEMENT OF IPRs

13.2.2.1 The EU Enforcement Directive

Member States have recently implemented the EU Enforcement Directive[3] and a Regulation intended to protect IPRs using border controls.[4] The latter sets out measures which enable rightsholders and customs authorities to collaborate in closing borders to pirated and counterfeit goods.

The impetus for the Enforcement Directive reflected the prevailing view amongst Member States that significant harmonization of the substantive law of intellectual property, for example by the Information Society Directive, had to be accompanied by a reasonably uniform approach to enforcement. Without such an approach there was a concern that disparities between Member States would interfere with the free movement of goods and services within the internal market and thus undermine competition, along with discouraging investment in innovation and creativity (see recitals 3–9). Thus, the object of the directive, according to recital 10, is to 'approximate legislative systems so as to ensure a high, equivalent and homogeneous level of protection in the Internal Market'. One major impetus for the directive, as pointed out by Kirstin Huniar, was the growth of and changes to the telecommunications sector.

K. Huniar, 'The Enforcement Directive: Its effects on UK law'
[2006] EIPR 92, 92–3

The latest directive, the Enforcement Directive, deals with problems related to the telecommunication sector of the economy. The telecommunication sector provides new methods of

---

[3] Directive 2004/48/EC of the European Parliament and of the Council of 29 Apr. 2004 on the enforcement of intellectual property rights OJ 2004 L195/16.
[4] Council Regulation (EC) 1383/2003 of 22 Jul. 2003 concerning customs action against goods suspected of infringing certain intellectual property rights and the rights and measures to be taken against goods to have infringed such rights OJ L196/7, 2 Aug. 2003.

exploiting intellectual property, such as through aiding the distribution of copyright-protected content over the internet. Copyright-protected materials, including infringing, pirated goods, are, as a consequence of advancing telecommunications technology, easily retrievable. The European Union considers national disparities in copyright law to be prejudicial to the Common Market. It has stated that in order to combat organised crime, which costs European businesses billions of euros per year, the effective enforcement of intellectual property rights is required. The latest Directive's objective is therefore to approximate the legislative systems and to assimilate disparities in civil procedure leading to the better enforcement of substantive rights.

The Enforcement Directive is the first directive to call for harmonisation across the spectrum of exclusive rights: a form of horizontal harmonisation. In contrast to earlier directives, the Enforcement Directive provides measures, procedures and remedies for all areas of intellectual property, regardless of whether registration is required (patents, designs, or trade marks) or not (copyright). Prior directives were of a vertical nature. They dealt with very specific areas of intellectual property, such as those harmonising various aspects of copyright law, where several directives were required to complete harmonisation in stages.

[Kuniar then goes on to look at the background to the Directive and its general contents:]

History of the Directive

On October 15, 1998, the Commission published a Green Paper on 'Combating Counterfeiting and Piracy in the Single Market'. On November 17, 2000, a follow-up to the Green Paper was released. Two years later, on January 30, 2003, the European Commission presented a 'Proposal for a Directive on Measures and Procedures to Ensure the Enforcement of Intellectual Property Rights'. Intense lobbying, as well as discussions between the European Parliament, the Commission and the Council, took place regarding the proposed directive. However, once the proposal was presented, it took only one-and-a-quarter years until the Directive was ratified.

The time invested in passing the Directive was unusually short. It has been argued that the enlargement of the European Union on May 1, 2004 and the subsequent elections for the European Parliament were reasons for the rapid enactment. As enacted, the Directive represents a compromise between the Member States of the European Union based on expediency; otherwise, the ratification of the Directive likely would have been delayed for some years, as has been the history of other directives in this field. On March 9, 2004, the European Parliament passed the amended Commission proposal in its first hearing. On March 11 of that year, the European Council discussed the Directive and indicated it would be passed, accepting the amended proposal on April 26. On April 29, 2004, the Directive was ratified by the President of the European Parliament and published in the Official Journal of the European Union.

Contents of the Directive

The Enforcement Directive aims to provide harmonisation in the area of civil legal procedures in order to protect intellectual property and to promote creativity, to develop employment and to improve competitiveness. It helps to enforce substantive rights without affecting them. Criminal sanctions were finally, after discussions and arguments with consumer groups, omitted. The Directive's recitals merely refer to the criminal aspects of infringements. Changes to, and the harmonisation of, the laws of the Member States regarding enforcement were considered necessary in the application of injunctions and provisional measures, in the right of information and recall, and in the calculation of damages. Outside the scope of the Directive, Member States remain free to apply other, appropriate sanctions. The Directive is based on existing best practices already used in Member States.

The directive looks at both pre-trial and post-trial remedies. Its particular provisions will be considered in this chapter in relation to both. However, it is generally accepted that in the case of the United Kingdom implementation of the directive has entailed minimal change to the existing law relating both to enforcement and to remedies.[5]

It is an interesting question why each successive directive that has addressed the protection of IPRs in the EU has inevitably increased that protection, as is clearly the case with the Enforcement Directive. Does there come a point when such increases stifle trade between Member States rather than give it the encouragement that this directive intended? Such questions may become even more urgent since the EU is now considering introducing a Criminal Enforcement Directive.[6]

FURTHER READING

E. Bonadio, 'Remedies and sanctions for the infringement of intellectual property rights under EC law' [2008] EIPR 320.

W. R. Cornish et al., 'Procedures and remedies for enforcing IPRs: The European Commission's Proposed Directive' [2003] EIPR 447.

T. Dreier, 'TRIPs and the enforcement of intellectual property rights' in F.-K. Beier and G. Schricker (eds.), *From GATT to TRIPS* (IIC Studies, vol 18, 1996), p. 248.

C. H. Massa and A. Strowel, 'The scope of the Proposed IP Enforcement Directive: Torn between the desire to harmonise remedies and the need to combat piracy' [2004] EIPR 244.

J. Smith, C. Wheeler, and S. Burke, 'The New intellectual property enforcement regulations' [2006] EIPR N125.

13.3 INTELLECTUAL PROPERTY LITIGATION

13.3.1 INTRODUCTION

Despite the recent moves to harmonize certain aspects of IPR enforcement across the EU, intellectual property disputes are almost exclusively a matter for domestic courts. Even in the case of EU IPRs (most notably CTMs and Community designs), certain UK courts have been designated Community Courts for the purposes of hearing infringement and invalidity proceedings in relation to these rights. As a result, the focus of the next section of this chapter will be on domestic intellectual property litigation. Almost all intellectual property litigation is carried on in the civil courts. It is to civil proceedings that this chapter now turns. Criminal sanctions for IPR infringement will be considered at 13.8 below.

---

[5] See The Intellectual Property (Enforcement, etc) Regulations 2006, SI 2006/1028 and The Civil Procedure (Amendment No 4) Rules 2005, SI 2005/3515.

[6] See, 13.8.4 below.

13.3.2 CIVIL PROCEEDINGS

Most disputes involving intellectual property begin with a letter before action from the rightsholder or his legal representatives to the alleged wrongdoer. The exceptions are disputes which are initiated by an ex parte order, such as a search order. The UK Intellectual Property Office seeks to encourage the use of Alternative Dispute Resolution (ADR) in IP cases and offers a Mediation Service. ADR can be a useful way of avoiding the costs of litigation. Nonetheless, the UK IPO itself admits that mediation is not appropriate where the injured party seeks a speedy resolution to a dispute and in particular an injunction to prevent further wrongdoing. Since the most frequent outcome of intellectual property disputes is a pre-trial settlement, it is the case that ADR has only a very limited role to play in intellectual property litigation. In the case of domain name disputes, ICANN oversees the 'uniform dispute resolution procedure' (UDRP). The purpose of the UDRP is to obviate the need to litigate domain disputes at all, since such litigation might be particularly costly and complex given the international nature of the internet. The UDRP is available at WIPO's Arbitration and Mediation Centre and other regional centres. For the most part, the UDRP has successfully fulfilled its brief.[7]

13.3.3 RELEVANT COURTS

Intellectual property disputes, involving most major IPRs, including registered trade marks and CTMs, unregistered design rights, moral rights, and database rights may be heard in the Chancery Division of the High Court and in any county court which has a Chancery District Registry.[8]

13.3.3.1 Patents, registered designs, and Community designs

Patent disputes may be heard either at the Patent Court, the Patents County Court, or before the Comptroller of Patents, as may UK registered design disputes. European Community design cases involving infringement and declarations of invalidity may be heard at the Patents Court and the Patents County Court, as the designated Community Design Courts. In the case of Community registered designs, the OHIM can consider issues of validity. The Patents Court is part of the Chancery Division of the High Court. The Patents County Court was established by the Copyright Designs and Patents Act 1988 ('CDPA') and opened in 1990. It was designed to offer a speedier and cheaper forum for deciding patent disputes than the Patents Court, although there is no upward limit on the amount of damages which might be awarded.[9] It is possible for patent agents as well as lawyers to represent clients at the Patents County Court. A judge in the Patents County Court may transfer a matter to the Patents Court if it involves an important point of law or is particularly complex. The Comptroller of Patents may also hear infringement actions and disputes over validity, if the parties agree. Appeals from the Comptroller's decisions are heard by the Patents Court. Finally, it is possible that a UK court may find itself hearing an infringement action concerning a European patent (UK) while that same patent is the subject of opposition proceedings at the EPO. Following the Court of Appeal decision in *Unilin Beheer BV v Berry*

---

[7] See 12.7.4.

[8] Practice Direction, supplementary CPR, Part 63, Section II, Allocation (r. 63.13) 2007.

[9] Registered trade mark actions may also be heard in the Patents County Court.

Floor NV,[10] if the holder of a European patent (UK) succeeds in an infringement action in the UK courts, the defendant may not challenge his entitlement to an account of profits (or damages) even if the patent is subsequently revoked by the EPO. Furthermore, it is within a judge's discretion whether he orders a stay in an action concerning the infringement of a European patent (UK) until revocation proceedings are heard by the EPO. He may certainly choose not to do so.

13.3.4 STANDING

In general, the rightsholder of any form of IPR will of course be able to initiate proceedings. But there are others who, depending upon the particular IPR, might also do so.

13.3.4.1 Patents

The registered proprietor of a patent will most likely be the claimant, but others who may sue include the equitable owner of a patent (who must perfect his title before judgement), an assignee, and an exclusive licensee.[11] In the latter case, the registered owner may either join as a co-claimant or be joined as a defendant. In the case of patents which have been compulsorily licensed or of a licence of right, the registered proprietor is given two months to initiate proceedings after which it is open to the licensee to do so, joining the owner as a defendant.

13.3.4.2 Designs

Actions relating to UK unregistered designs may be brought by the proprietor or by an exclusive licensee. In the case of a Community unregistered design the proprietor may sue, and so may the exclusive licensee, if the proprietor after notice fails to do so. In UK registered design actions, the registered proprietor may sue as may an assignee but only if his name has been entered on the Register. In the case of Community registered designs, the proprietor may sue. An exclusive licensee may bring an action relating to a UK unregistered design right[12] as may a non-exclusive licensee with the consent of the proprietor. By contrast, exclusive licensees of a UK registered design have no right to sue. With respect to Community registered and unregistered designs, the exclusive licensee may sue, as may the non-exclusive licensee with permission. Under certain circumstances, the equitable owners may also be able to sue.

13.3.4.3 Copyright

The claimant is most likely to be the owner of the copyright or an assignee. In the case of moral rights, the individual in whom the right is vested may sue. An equitable owner may also sue, but must join the legal owner as a party or have the copyright assigned. Exclusive licensees may also bring actions[13] except against the copyright holder. And so under certain circumstances may a non-exclusive licensee.[14] In such actions, the copyright owner may be joined as a claimant or a defendant.

---

[10] [2007] FSR 25; see also *Kimberley-Clark Worldwide v Procter & Gamble* [2000] FSR 235.
[11] Patents Act 1977 ('PA 77'), s. 67.   [12] Copyright Designs and Patents Act 1988 ('CDPA'), s. 234.
[13] Ibid., s. 101.   [14] Ibid., s. 101A.

13.3.4.4 Trade marks

The registered proprietor may sue as may an equitable owner provided he perfects his title before judgment. Actions may also be brought by the exclusive licensee.[15] The proprietor may join as a co-claimant or be joined as a defendant. However, an exclusive licensee cannot sue the proprietor.[16] A non-exclusive licensee may call upon the proprietor of a registered trade mark to take infringement proceedings in respect of any matter which affects his interests. If the proprietor fails to do so within two months, then the licensee may do so in his own name, although the proprietor must be joined as a co-claimant or a defendant.

13.3.4.5 Other IPRs

In a passing off action, it is the owner of the goodwill who will have the standing to bring an action. Generally, in actions for breach of confidence it is the confider of the information who will be the claimant and in actions for breach of privacy, the individual whose privacy has been invaded. The situation has been complicated following the House of Lords judgment in *Douglas v Hello!*, which appeared to hold that the assignees of confidential information might also bring an action for breach of confidence.[17]

13.3.5 THREATS

13.3.5.1 Introduction

The Patents Act 1977 ('PA 77') provides an action for groundless threats in relation to patent infringement.[18] Similar provisions have now been introduced in relation to trade marks.[19] They also apply to registered and unregistered designs.[20] There are no equivalent provisions against groundless threats either in relation to the law of copyright or passing off. An action against groundless threats, first introduced into the 1888 Patents and Designs Act, marks a recognition that a threat by one party to issue proceedings against another for the infringement of an IPR may have serious economic consequences for the latter. A shopkeeper who is threatened with legal proceedings for selling goods which carry an allegedly infringing trade mark may feel he has no choice but to withdraw the goods from sale even if the threats are groundless. It has been suggested that the threats provisions under the PA 77 are a model for those which relate to other IPRs.

13.3.5.2 Patents

Under the PA 77, if any person threatens another person with proceedings for patent infringement, the person aggrieved by the threats may bring proceedings against the person making the threats. The exceptions to this action are threats based on acts of primary infringement, such as making or importing a product for disposal or of using a process and, since 2004, the sale of that infringing product.[21] The person who threatens need not be the rightsholder, while the person who is aggrieved need not be the person to whom the threats

---

15 Trade Marks Act 1994 ('TMA'), s. 31.   16 *Northern & Shell v Conde Nast* [1995] RPC 117.
17 *Douglas v Hello! Ltd* [2008] 1 AC 1. See 8.4.3.   18 PA 77, s. 70.
19 TMA, s. 21.   20 Registered Designs Act 1949 ('RDA'), s. 26 and CDPA, s. 21 respectively.
21 PA 77 (as amended), s. 70(4); *Cavity Trays Ltd v RMC Panel Products Ltd* [1996] RPC 361.

are made.[22] He may for example be a trade rival who would be harmed if his products were taken off the shelves of the shopkeeper to whom the threats were directed. Furthermore, threats may be implicit or explicit. However, a mere notification of the existence of a patent does not constitute an actionable threat.[23] It is a defence to an action for groundless threats that the acts complained of were an infringement and that the patent is valid.[24] Remedies may include a declaration that the threat was unjustified, an injunction against further threats, and damages.[25]

13.3.5.3 Trade marks

As is the case with patents, an action for threats in relation to trade mark infringement is brought by the person aggrieved, who may not have been the direct recipient of the threats. Threats relating to primary infringement are not actionable,[26] which according to s. 21(1) of the Trade Marks Act 1994 ('TMA') includes the following acts:

(a) the application of marks to goods or their packaging,

(b) the importation of goods to which, or to the packaging of which, the mark has been applied, or

(c) the supply of services under the mark.

It is a defence to show that the threats relate to infringing actions,[27] but the claimant may yet succeed if he can show the mark is invalidly registered or is liable to be revoked.[28] It is not a threat to notify a third party that a trade mark is registered or that an application for registration has been made. This latter point is important since applications for damages in an infringement action may be backdated to the date of application for the trade mark and it is often a useful tool for this to be pointed out to an alleged infringer by the applicant. In *Prince plc v Prince Sports Groups Ltd Inc*,[29] Neuberger J held that the test for whether a communication constituted a threat was whether it would have been read by the ordinary reader, in the position of the claimant, as constituting a threat. This could include a general threat of litigation and not just a threat relating to a particular infringing act. Remedies under s. 21 of the TMA are the same as those under s. 70 of the PA 77.

13.3.5.4 Registered and unregistered designs

In relation to UK registered designs, the provisions against groundless threats are set out in s. 26 of the Registered Designs Act 1949 ('RDA') and to unregistered designs by s. 253 of the CDPA. As of 2005, these provisions also apply to Community registered and unregistered designs.[30] In the case of registered designs, it is a defence against groundless threats to show that there has been a primary infringement (i.e. the making or importing of anything).[31] A mere notification that a design is registered does not constitute a threat of proceedings.[32] The wording in relation to unregistered designs is practically identical. In the case of a design

---

[22] *Johnson v Edge* (1892) 9 RPC 142; *Brain v Ingledew Brown Benninson & Garrett (No 3)* [1997] FSR 511.
[23] PA 77, s. 70(5).   [24] Ibid., s. 70(2)(a)–(b).   [25] Ibid., s. 70(3)(a)–(c).
[26] TMA, s. 21(1)(a)–(c).   [27] Ibid., s. 21(2).   [28] Ibid., s. 21(3).
[29] [1998] FSR 21.   [30] Community Design Regulations 2005, SI 2005/2339 ('CDRs').
[31] RDA, s. 26(2A).   [32] Ibid., s. 26(3).

right, it is not a threat to notify a third party that a design is protected by design right.[33] Again, as with patents and trade marks, the aggrieved person need not be the person to whom the threats are made, nor need the defendant be the rights holder. Threats may be written or oral. It is a defence to show that the acts complained of by the defendant would constitute an infringement of a registered design[34] or of an unregistered design right.[35] Furthermore in the case of a registered design, the defence does not apply if the design is shown to be invalidly registered.[36] The available remedies in relation to both registered and unregistered designs are the same as those under the PA 77 and TMA, i.e. a declaration, an injunction, and damages.

13.4 PRE-TRIAL RELIEF

13.4.1 INTRODUCTION

Actions involving IPRs infrequently come to trial. This is because rightsholders are usually most interested in preventing the offending behaviour in a timely fashion, with remedies of only secondary concern. There are three key orders which may be obtained pre-trial. They are the search order (formally known as an Anton Piller order), the freezing order (also known as a Mareva injunction) and the Norwich Pharmacal Order. Although directed towards trial, if successfully implemented by the rightsholder, these orders may persuade the potential defendant that it is not worth fighting on. Indeed, in *Bank Mellat v Nikpour*, Donaldson LJ described the Anton Piller and the Mareva orders as 'the law's two nuclear weapons'.[37] In addition, a rightsholder may succeed in obtaining an interim injunction to prevent the allegedly infringing behaviour of the third party until trial. Once again, this may obviate the need for further proceedings. The following section will examine pre-trial orders and then go on to look at interim injunctions.

13.4.2 THE SEARCH ORDER

13.4.2.1 Definition of the search order

This order which is granted in the High Court and obtained ex parte is defined by the Civil Procedure Act 1997:[38]

> 7 Power of courts to make orders for preserving evidence, etc
>
>   (1) The court may make an order under this section for the purpose of securing, in the case of any existing or proposed proceedings in the court—
>   (a) the preservation of evidence which is or may be relevant, or
>   (b) the preservation of property which is or may be the subject-matter of the proceedings or as to which any question arises or may arise in the proceedings.
>   (2) A person who is, or appears to the court likely to be, a party to proceedings in the court may make an application for such an order.

---

[33] Ibid., s. 253(4).   [34] Ibid., s. 26(2).   [35] Ibid., s. 253(2).   [36] Ibid., s. 26(2).
[37] *Bank Mellat v Nikpour* [1985] FSR 87, 92.   [38] 1997 (c 12), s. 7.

(3) Such an order may direct any person to permit any person described in the order, or secure that any person so described is permitted—

(a) to enter premises in England and Wales, and

(b) while on the premises, to take in accordance with the terms of the order any of the following steps.

(4) Those steps are—

(a) to carry out a search for or inspection of anything described in the order, and

(b) to make or obtain a copy, photograph, sample or other record of anything so described.

(5) The order may also direct the person concerned—

(a) to provide any person described in the order, or secure that any person so described is provided, with any information or article described in the order, and

(b) to allow any person described in the order, or secure that any person so described is allowed, to retain for safe keeping anything described in the order.

(6) An order under this section is to have effect subject to such conditions as are specified in the order.

(7) This section does not affect any right of a person to refuse to do anything on the ground that to do so might tend to expose him or his spouse [or civil partner] to proceedings for an offence or for the recovery of a penalty.

(8) In this section—

'court' means the High Court, and

'premises' includes any vehicle.

13.4.2.2 The development of the search order

The search order was formerly known as an Anton Piller order, named after the case in which it was first described.

Anton Piller KG v Manufacturing Processes Ltd [1976] Ch 55

The claimants, Anton Piller KG ('Pillers'), designed and manufactured, *inter alia*, a frequency converter especially for the computers of International Business Machines. The claimants were a German company and Manufacturing Processes Ltd ('M.P.L.'), were their agents in the UK. M.P.L. was supplied with a good deal of confidential information concerning the product including working manuals and copyright drawings. Mr A. H. S. Baker and Mr B. P. Wallace were directors of the company. The claimants alleged that M.P.L had been in secret talks with other German, Canadian, and US companies about supplying them with the confidential material and other information. They were informed of these talks by two employees of the defendants. There were also supporting documents. The claimants sought to obtain an interim injunction from the High Court to restrain this infringement, but were concerned that the evidence would be destroyed. They therefore asked Brightman J in the High Court both for an interim injunction and also an order to permit them to enter and search the defendant's premises and remove evidence of infringement. Brightman J refused to grant the second order and the claimants appealed. The judgment was given by Lord Denning MR who differentiated the order sought by the claimants from a search warrant.

Lord Denning, pp. 60–70:

Let me say at once that no court in this land has any power to issue a search warrant to enter a man's house so as to see if there are papers or documents there which are of an incriminating nature, whether libels or infringements of copyright or anything else of the kind. No constable or bailiff can knock at the door and demand entry so as to inspect papers or documents. The householder can shut the door in his face and say 'Get out'. That was established in the leading case of *Entick v Carrington* (1765) 2 Wils KB 275. None of us would wish to whittle down that principle in the slightest. But the order sought in this case is not a search warrant. It does not authorise the plaintiffs' solicitors or anyone else to enter the defendants' premises against their will. It does not authorise the breaking down of any doors, nor the slipping in by a back door, nor getting in by an open door or window. It only authorises entry and inspection by the permission of the defendants. The plaintiffs must get the defendants' permission. But it does do this: It brings pressure on the defendants to give permission. It does more. It actually orders them to give permission—with, I suppose, the result that if they do not give permission, they are guilty of contempt of court.

...

It seems to me that such an order can be made by a judge ex parte, but it should only be made where it is essential that the plaintiff should have inspection so that justice can be done between the parties: and when, if the defendant were forewarned, there is a grave danger that vital evidence will be destroyed, that papers will be burnt or lost or hidden, or taken beyond the jurisdiction, and so the ends of justice be defeated: and when the inspection would do no real harm to the defendant or his case.

Nevertheless, in the enforcement of this order, the plaintiffs must act with due circumspection. On the service of it, the plaintiffs should be attended by their solicitor, who is an officer of the court. They should give the defendants an opportunity of considering it and of consulting their own solicitor. If the defendants wish to apply to discharge the order as having been improperly obtained, they must be allowed to do so. If the defendants refuse permission to enter or to inspect, the plaintiffs must not force their way in. They must accept the refusal, and bring it to the notice of the court afterwards, if need be on an application to commit.

You might think that with all these safeguards against abuse, it would be of little use to make such an order. But it can be effective in this way: It serves to tell the defendants that, on the evidence put before it, the court is of opinion that they ought to permit inspection— nay, it orders them to permit—and that they refuse at their peril. It puts them in peril not only of proceedings for contempt, but also of adverse inferences being drawn against them; so much so that their own solicitor may often advise them to comply. We are told that in two at least of the cases such an order has been effective. We are prepared, therefore, to sanction its continuance, but only in an extreme case where there is grave danger of property being smuggled away or of vital evidence being destroyed.

[In their judgments, **Ormrod LJ** and **Shaw LJ** also sought to underline the exceptional nature of the order:]

Ormrod LJ, p. 62:

There are three essential pre-conditions for the making of such an order, in my judgment. First, there must be an extremely strong prima facie case. Secondly, the damage, potential or actual, must be very serious for the applicant. Thirdly, there must be clear evidence that the defendants have in their possession incriminating documents or things, and that there is a real possibility that they may destroy such material before any application inter partes can be made.

Shaw LJ, p. 62:

The overriding consideration in the exercise of this salutary jurisdiction is that it is to be resorted to only in circumstances where the normal processes of the law would be rendered nugatory if some immediate and effective measure was not available. When such an order is made, the party who has procured the court to make it must act with prudence and caution in pursuance of it.

Lord Denning differentiates what came to be known as the 'Anton Piller Order' from a search warrant, because the former does not authorize anyone to enter the defendant's premises against his will. In fact, the defendant must give his 'permission' before the claimant's can gain entry. But failure to do so results in the defendant being found in contempt of court. Does this really describe a voluntary action by the defendant? Indeed, what if the defendant is not in a position to obtain informed legal advice or the order is served at a time and in a place, for example the defendant's home, when the defendant or his family might find service both intrusive and intimidating? Would not these facts further militate against the voluntary nature of the order? Inevitably, these questions came to be an issue for the courts.

Columbia Picture Industries Inc v Robinson [1987] Ch 38

The claimant, who made and distributed films, acted on behalf of all the other members of the Motion Picture Association of America Inc. The first defendant, Robinson, and the second defendant, a company wholly under his control, ran various businesses connected with video cassettes and video cassette recorders. The claimants sought and obtained Anton Piller and Mareva injunctions on the basis that the defendant was making illegal video copies of their films, which were hired out to the public. Under the Anton Piller order, searches were made of a number of premises including the home of the first defendant and a large number of allegedly infringing video tapes were discovered, which were removed together with other documentary evidence. At the trial the defendants accepted that there had been copyright infringement and passing off. On the return date specified in the ex parte order, the defendants gave undertakings in terms of the injunctions previously granted. The defendants also gave undertakings not to dispose of certain assets with the consequence that the Marvea injunction was discontinued. A year and a half later the defendants applied to discharge the Anton Piller order. The application was directed to be heard at the trial of the action but was listed to come on immediately before the trial. At the trial the claimants alleged infringement of copyright, trade mark infringement, and passing off. But the defendants also made a number of serious complaints about the obtaining, execution, and consequences of the Anton Piller order. They also alleged that the claimants had executed other Anton Piller orders in a similarly unsatisfactory manner. In particular, it was alleged that the claimants had given the impression that the defendants' business was secret, when it was not. Furthermore, evidence was taken that was not included in the order although the defendant had signed a consent to it being taken; the claimant's solicitors retained the evidence, including items that formed no part of the claimant's copyright claim. A number of these seized items were lost while in the custody of the claimant's solicitors. The defendants ceased trading, and it was alleged that this was the outcome the claimants had sought when they obtained the orders. In his judgment, Scott J emphasized the potentially oppressive nature of the Anton Piller order and the need for strict safeguards.

Scott J, at pp. 69–77:

The Anton Piller order

This is in many ways the most important part of this case. The damage done by the defendants to the plaintiffs' intellectual property rights are [sic], of course, very important to the plaintiffs and I hope I have dealt with them accordingly. But the defendants' complaints regarding the manner in which the Anton Piller order was obtained and executed raise questions of general importance concerning the administration of justice.

...

Now let the possible and, perhaps, probable effects of an Anton Piller order be considered. The order is served and executed. If the order is in the terms of the order in the present case and is executed as it was in the present case, there will be a wholesale removal of all business material, whether stock-in-trade, bank statements, cheque books or correspondence. The continuance of the business by the respondent to the order is thereby made impossible. How can a business be continued without records? How can it be continued without stock-in-trade? It will be recalled that, in the present case, the order authorised the removal of, inter alia, the video recorders at 8, Frederick Street. They were not, in the event, removed but, if they had been, the whole of Mr Robinson's copying business would for that reason alone have been closed down. It is customary, on account of the Mareva injunction accompanying Anton Piller orders, for a copy of the order to be served on the respondent's bankers. That was done in the present case. The almost certain effect of that being done will be that the bankers will decline to allow any further credit to the respondent. The order will throw such a question mark over the business of the respondent as to make any other course commercially imprudent and, therefore, unlikely. In the present case, Barclays Bank, upon service of the order, refused to allow the defendants any further credit.

The service and execution of an Anton Piller order is likely to have on a respondent a personal as well as a commercial effect. Anton Piller orders are often granted not simply in respect of business premises but in respect of the respondent's home. He is required, on pain of committal, to open the doors of his house to the plaintiffs' representatives and to permit a search of the contents thereof. The plaintiffs and their representatives are at liberty to search and rummage through the personal belongings of any occupant of the house and to remove the material they consider to be covered by the terms of the order. The traumatic effect and the sense of outrage likely to be produced by an invasion of home territory in the execution of an Anton Piller order is obvious.

When, in 1974 and shortly thereafter, Anton Piller orders became established weapons to combat, inter alia, copyright piracy, it was supposed that they would be relatively infrequently granted. They lay, it was said, at the very limit of the in personam jurisdiction proper to be exercised by the courts. But, since 1974, Hamlins [the claimant's solicitors] have obtained and executed, I was told, some 300 Anton Piller orders, 200 in audio piracy cases and about 100 in video piracy cases. Other firms of solicitors may perhaps be able to match those figures. Anton Piller orders are not rarities at all. They are regularly applied for and granted in all the divisions of the High Court. In no case previously, I was told, had the propriety of the obtaining and execution of an Anton Piller order been examined otherwise than in inter- locutory proceedings. I was told by one or other of the Hamlins witnesses—it matters not which—that this is the first case in the experience of that firm which has come to a full trial after the grant and execution of an Anton Piller order. This case provides, therefore, an oppor- tunity, after a full hearing and after oral evidence from all the relevant participants, for a long, careful look at Anton Piller procedure and at the manner in which it is operating. It justifies, in my judgment, very grave disquiet.

It has to be accepted that a common, perhaps the usual, effect of the service and execu- tion of an Anton Piller order is to close down the business which, on the applicants' evidence, is being carried on in violation of their rights. Mr Cumberland, Hamlins' experienced legal executive, accepted this.

. . .

The third comment is that respondents are safeguarded by the duties of full disclosure that the solicitors and counsel acting for the applicant owe to the court and that execution of Anton Piller orders is customarily required to be supervised by solicitors. This comment underlines, in my view, the unsatisfactory position in which the Anton Piller procedure places solicitors and, to a lesser extent, since they depend on solicitors for their instructions, coun- sel. The solicitors are retained by and owe a duty to their clients, the applicants. They satisfy themselves that their clients' interests require the protection of an Anton Piller order and are instructed by their clients to obtain one. They have a duty to see that full disclosure is made to the court of any relevant evidence. But relevance and irrelevance are not matters of white and black. There is usually a grey area of arguable relevance and arguable irrelevance. What is a solicitor's duty in respect of evidence falling into the grey area? It is to be borne in mind that the solicitor, when taking his decision as to what is relevant to be included in the affidavits in support of the Anton Piller application, will be likely already to have satisfied himself, as his clients will have been satisfied, that the respondent is a rogue against whom an Anton Piller order ought to be granted. The solicitor does not, and cannot be expected to present the avail- able evidence from the respondent's point of view.

Finally, it may be pointed out that an Anton Piller order always contains a liberty for the respondent to apply on short notice for the order to be set aside. But this cannot in practice be done until after the order has been executed. In order to obtain back his business records and place his business once more in a viable position, the respondent to the order has to make a successful application to the court. There are often very real financial difficulties which stand in his way. As happened in the present case, the respondent's bankers may, on learning of the order, have cut off his funds. The obtaining of legal aid may not be possible and, even if possible, may involve lengthy delays. and the will of a respondent to take on a powerful and determined opponent in expensive litigation may waver. The respondent, often with very good reason, may lack confidence in the successful outcome of the litigation.

These answers to the criticism of Anton Piller procedure do not, in my opinion, match the force of the criticism. There is and can be no adequate substitute for the right of a person against whom immediate mandatory judicial relief is sought to appear and be heard at the judicial hearing which deals with the matter. But this is not possible where Anton Piller pro- cedure is concerned.

I have made these general comments about Anton Piller orders not for the purpose of casting doubts on the jurisdiction of the court to make them nor for the purpose of casting doubt on the propriety, in appropriate cases, of Anton Piller orders being granted. But a deci- sion whether or not an Anton Piller order should be granted requires a balance to be struck between the plaintiff's need that the remedies allowed by the civil law for the breach of his rights should be attainable and the requirement of justice that a defendant should not be deprived of his property without being heard. What I have heard in the present case has disposed me to think that the practice of the court has allowed the balance to swing much too far in favour of plaintiffs and that Anton Piller orders have been too readily granted and with insufficient safeguards for respondents.

The Draconian and essentially unfair nature of Anton Piller orders from the point of view of respondents against whom they are made requires, in my view, that they be so drawn as to extend no further than the minimum extent necessary to achieve the purpose for which they are granted, namely, the preservation of documents or articles which might otherwise be destroyed or concealed. Anything beyond that is, in my judgment, impossible to justify. For example, I do not understand how an order can be justified that allows the plaintiffs' solicitors to take and retain all relevant documentary material and correspondence. Once the plaintiffs' solicitors have satisfied themselves what material exists and have had an opportunity to take copies thereof, the material ought, in my opinion, to be returned to its owner. The material need be retained no more than a relatively short period of time for that purpose.

Secondly, I would think it essential that a detailed record of the material taken should always be required to be made by the solicitors who execute the order before the material is removed from the respondent's premises. So far as possible, disputes as to what material was taken, the resolution of which depends on the oral testimony and credibility of the solicitors on the one hand and the respondent on the other hand, ought to be avoided. In the absence of any corroboration of a respondent's allegation that particular material, for instance, divorce papers, was taken, a solicitor's sworn and apparently credible denial is likely always to be preferred. This state of affairs is unfair to respondents. It ought to be avoided so far as it can be.

Thirdly, no material should, in my judgment, be taken from the respondent's premises by the executing solicitors unless it is clearly covered by the terms of the order. In particular, I find it wholly unacceptable that a practice should have grown up whereby the respondent to the order is procured by the executing solicitors to give consent to additional material being removed. In view of the circumstances in which Anton Piller orders are customarily executed (the execution is often aptly called 'a raid'), I would not, for my part, be prepared to accept that an apparent consent by a respondent had been freely and effectively given unless the respondent's solicitor had been present to confirm and ensure that the consent was a free and informed one.

Fourthly, I find it inappropriate that seized material the ownership of which is in dispute, such as allegedly pirate tapes, should be retained by the plaintiffs' solicitors pending the trial. Although officers of the court, the main role of solicitors for plaintiffs is to act for the plaintiffs. If the proper administration of justice requires that material taken under an Anton Piller order from defendants should, pending trial, be kept from the defendants, then those responsible for the administration of justice might reasonably be expected to provide a neutral officer of the court charged with the custody of the material. In lieu of any such officer, and there is none at present, the plaintiffs' solicitors ought, in my view, as soon as solicitors for the defendants are on the record, to be required to deliver the material to the defendants' solicitors on their undertaking for its safe custody and production, if required, in court.

Finally, the nature of Anton Piller orders requires that the affidavits in support of applications for them ought to err on the side of excessive disclosure. In the case of material falling into the grey area of possible relevance, the judge, not the plaintiffs' solicitors, should be the judge of relevance. Whitford J, whose experience in these matters probably exceeds that of any other first instance judge, has recently drawn attention to the particular importance of full disclosure on Anton Piller applications. In the *Jeffrey Rogers Knitwear* case [1985] FSR 184 Whitford J said, at p. 189:

> I wholly reject the suggestion…that when seeking an Anton Piller order there is no need to investigate the question whether or not in the absence of an order there is a real possibility that infringing material or evidence will be done away with. Any plaintiff seeking an Anton Piller order must place before the court all the information they have relating to the circumstances of the defendant which they can suggest points to the probability that in the absence of an Anton Piller order material which should be available will disappear.

In this case the respondent, Robinson, succeeded and was awarded damages. A Practice Direction[39] and a draft order prescribed by the court followed the judgment in *Columbia v Robinson*. The safeguards introduced by the Practice Direction include, *inter alia*, the requirements that: there be an independent supervising solicitor when an order is executed;[40] that orders should only be executed during business hours and on a weekday, so that the defendant might have access to a solicitor; that, if the order is to be executed at a premises where there is likely to be a lone woman, either the supervising solicitor must be a woman or be accompanied by one; and finally that the claimant's solicitors must undertake to return the originals of all documents obtained under the order within two working days. But it must still be an open question whether, despite these safeguards, the secret nature of the search order and the fact that it allows an unexpected intrusion into an individual's premises, including his or her home, can ever make it seem less than arbitrary and an encroachment on personal freedom.

13.4.2.3 Search orders and the privilege against self-incrimination

What if a claimant obtains a search order to search the premises of a defendant whom he suspects of breach of confidence? In the course of the search the defendant's computer is seized. Subsequently, the defendant agrees to a court order allowing an independent expert to examine the computer's files. The expert discovers indecent images of children. Can the defendant prevent these images being disclosed to the police on the basis of the privilege against self-incrimination? This was the question raised in the recent Court of Appeal case, *C plc v P*.[41] The danger that an Anton Piller order might lead to a defendant's incriminating himself by complying with the order was examined early in its history by the House of Lords in *Rank Film Distributors v Video Information Centre*. In this case, the House of Lords recognized the existence of such a threat.

Rank Film Distributors Ltd v Video Information Centre
(a firm) [1982] AC 380

The claimants were a motion picture company with copyright in certain films and the defendants made cassettes of those films for sale to the public in breach of copyright. An Anton Piller order was made which required the defendants, including Messrs Dawson, Lee, and Gomberg, to give discovery of certain documents and to answer interrogatories relating to the supply and sale of infringing copies. The order was summarized

---

[39] [1994] 1 WLR 1233.
[40] Following the decision in *Universal Thermosensors Ltd v Hibben* [1992] 1 WLR 840.
[41] [2007] EWCA Crim 1139.

by Lord Wilberforce as:

> (1) Requiring the respondents to supply information. (2) Requiring the respondents to allow access to premises for the purpose of looking for illicit copy films and to allow their being removed to safe custody. (3) Requiring the respondents to disclose and produce documents.

The defendants objected to complying with the order on the basis that it would be tanta-mount to self-incrimination in relation to a number of criminal offences. The House of Lords upheld the defendants' claim in relation to parts (1) and (3) of the order.

Lord Wilberforce, at pp. 438–9, 441:

My Lords, this appeal relates to two interlocutory orders made by Walton J on July 2 and 5, 1979. They are of a type which have come to be known as 'Anton Piller orders' so called after a tortious infringer of copyright whose case reached the Court of Appeal in 1976 (*Anton Piller KG v. Manufacturing Processes Ltd* [1976] Ch 55).

They are designed to deal with situations created by infringements of patents, trade marks and copyright or more correctly with acts of piracy which have become a large and profitable business in recent years. They are intended to provide a quick and efficient means of recovering infringing articles and of discovering the sources from which these articles have been supplied and the persons to whom they are distributed before those concerned have had time to destroy or conceal them. Their essence is surprise. Because they operate drastically and because they are made, necessarily, ex parte—i.e. before the persons affected have been heard, they are closely controlled by the court: see the judgment of Lord Denning MR in *Anton Piller* [1976] Ch 55, 61. They are only granted upon clear and compelling evidence, and a number of safeguards in the interest of preserving essential rights are introduced. They are an illustration of the adaptability of equitable remedies to new situations.

...

[at p. 441] The privilege against self-incrimination is invoked as regards (1) and (3). The essential question being whether the provision of the information or production of the documents may tend to incriminate the respondents, it is necessary to see what possible heads of criminal liability there may be. There are three: (1) Section 21 of the Copyright Act 1956 creates summary offences under a number of headings, some of which would have potential applicability to the respondents. For a first offence there is a maximum fine of £50 however many infringing articles are involved. (2) Conspiracy to commit a breach of section 21 of the Act. By virtue of the Criminal Law Act 1977 no greater punishment can be imposed for such a conspiracy than for the substantive offence under section 21. (3) Conspiracy to defraud—an offence at common law left unaffected by the Act of 1977.

...

However, it is only too clear (and I deliberately use the language of reluctance) that supply of the information and production of the documents sought would tend to expose the respondents to a charge of conspiracy to defraud. In the very nature of this activity, a number of persons are certain to be involved in it—in printing the master tapes, copying from the master tapes, seeking and accepting orders, and distributing the illicit copies. A charge of conspiracy to defraud, so far from being, as it sometimes is, a contrived addition to other charges, is here an appropriate and exact description of what is being done. So far from it being contrived, fanciful, or imagined, it is the charge on which Mr Dawson, who appears on the existing evidence to be closely connected with Mr Lee and Ms Gomberg, is to stand trial.

It cannot be said that charges under this head would be nothing but charges under section 21 of the Act of 1956 under another name. An essential ingredient in them is dishonesty, which may exist in cases brought under section 21, but which may not. The much heavier penalties also make it more likely that charges would be brought of conspiracy to defraud. Unless some escape can be devised from this conclusion, the privilege must inevitably attach.

The House of Lord's decision in *Rank* undoubtedly brought a much needed safeguard to the Anton Piller order, which many judges saw as potentially oppressive or indeed as Lord Wilberforce himself put it as 'drastic'. However, the decision in *Rank* also undermined the key rationale behind the Anton Piller, allowing a defendant to withhold the very evidence for which the search order had been granted. Parliament recognized this and shortly after the decision implemented s. 72, Supreme Court Act 1981.[42] This provision removed the right for a defendant to claim privilege against self-incrimination in cases involving infringement of IPRs. The relevant provisions read:

(1) In any proceedings to which this subsection applies a person shall not be excused, by reason that to do so would tend to expose that person, or his or her spouse or civil partner, to proceedings for a related offence or for the recovery of a related penalty—

    (a) from answering any question put to that person in the first-mentioned proceedings; or

    (b) from complying with any order made in those proceedings.

(2) Subsection (1) applies to the following civil proceedings in the High Court, namely—

    (a) proceedings for infringement of rights pertaining to any intellectual property or for passing off;

    (b) proceedings brought to obtain disclosure of information relating to any infringement of such rights or to any passing off; and

    (c) proceedings brought to prevent any apprehended infringement of such rights or any apprehended passing off.

(3) Subject to subsection (4), no statement or admission made by a person—

    (a) in answering a question put to him in any proceedings to which subsection (1) applies; or

    (b) in complying with any order made in any such proceedings,

shall, in proceedings for any related offence or for the recovery of any related penalty, be admissible in evidence against that person or (unless they married or became civil partners after the making of the statement or admission) against the spouse or civil partner of that person.

(4) Nothing in subsection (3) shall render any statement or admission made by a person as there mentioned inadmissible in evidence against that person in proceedings for perjury or contempt of court.

But what of the defendant in *C v P*? In this case, the majority in the Court of Appeal[43] held that, since this case concerned intellectual property the defendant had to comply with s. 72 of the SCA 1981 and allow his computer to be seized. The Court of Appeal then went on to differentiate between evidence, such as the images, which existed independently of

---

[42] As amended by s. 261(1) and Sch. 27, para. 69, Civil Partnership Act 2004.
[43] Collins LJ dissenting on the reasoning but not the result.

the search order and evidence that the defendant might be compelled to give as a result of the order. According to the Court of Appeal, privilege could not be invoked in relation to independent evidence (i.e. the images). The court cited, *inter alia*, in support a case which had been decided by the ECtHR, *Saunders v United Kingdom*[44] and which had held that evidence which existed 'independently of the will of the suspect' was not covered by privilege and was compatible with Article 8 of the ECHR. Controversially, the Court of Appeal distinguished the situation in *Rank* from that in the present case by observing that in the former, the defendants had had an obligation not only to disclose but also to verify the documents and that the latter might be protected by privilege. Interestingly, Collins LJ took a different view. He believed that the introduction of a principle that there was no privilege in independent or pre-existing evidence was best left to Parliament. His own view was that the evidence in this case was not, in any event, covered by privilege because it was simply evidence which had been collected under the terms of the order during the legitimate search. Obviously, the majority judgment in *C v P* supports the continuing efficacy of search orders in intellectual property cases. Can it therefore be that Collins LJ is being too cautious in arguing that what appears to be a change in the UK approach to the privilege against self-incrimination should be ratified by the legislature rather than introduced by the courts? In any event, is there a justifiable reason for making intellectual property actions an exception to the general rule against self-incrimination?

13.4.3 FREEZING ORDERS

13.4.3.1 Definition and development

These orders, otherwise known as Mareva injunctions, are intended to restrain a defendant from dissipating his assets before trial; in other words, his assets are frozen. The order does not attach to the defendant's assets as such, but rather to the defendant *in personam*. Although frequently deployed in intellectual property disputes, often in conjunction with a search order, the Mareva injunction has most commonly been used in shipping disputes not least because as a result of such an injunction assets may be frozen worldwide as well as in the UK.[45] Indeed, the case in which the order was first described was itself a shipping dispute.

Mareva Compania Naviera SA v International Bulkcarriers SA
[1975] 2 Lloyd's Rep 509

Lord Denning, at pp. 510–11:

In my opinion that principle applies to a creditor who has a right to be paid the debt owing to him, even before he has established his right by getting judgment for it. If it appears that the debt is due and owing—and there is a danger that the debtor may dispose of his assets so as to defeat it before judgment—the Court has jurisdiction in a proper case to grant an interlocutory judgment so as to prevent him disposing of those assets.

---

[44] [1996] 23 EHHR 313, 331. See also *Attorney-General's Reference No 7 of 2000* [2001] 1 WLR 1879.
[45] *Prince Abdul Rahman Bin Turki Al Sudairy v Abu-Taha* [1980] 3 All ER 409.

Following the *Mareva* decision, it was held that Mareva injunctions only applied at an interlocutory stage and that there must be substantive cause of action.[46] Indeed, it had to be shown that the claimant had a 'good arguable case'.[47] In *Third Chandris Shipping v Unimarine*, Lord Denning further elaborated on a series of guidelines which should be applied to Mareva injunctions.

Third Chandris Shipping Corporation v Unimarine SA; Aggelikai Ptera Compania Maritima SA v Same; Western Sealanes Corporation v Same [1979] QB 645

Lord Denning, at pp. 668–9:

The guidelines

Much as I am in favour of the *Mareva* injunction, it must not be stretched too far lest it be endangered. In endeavouring to set out some guidelines, I have had recourse to the practice of many other countries which have been put before us. They have been most helpful. These are the points which those who apply for it should bear in mind:

(i) The plaintiff should make full and frank disclosure of all matters in his knowledge which are material for the judge to know: see *Negocios Del Mar SA v Doric Shipping Corporation SA (The Assios)* [1979] 1 Lloyd's Rep 331 .

(ii) The plaintiff should give particulars of his claim against the defendant, stating the ground of his claim and the amount thereof, and fairly stating the points made against it by the defendant.

(iii) The plaintiff should give some grounds for believing that the defendant has assets here. I think that this requirement was put too high in *MBPXL Corporation v Intercontinental Banking Corporation Ltd* August 28, 1975; Court of Appeal (Civil Division) Transcript No. 411 of 1975. In most cases the plaintiff will not know the extent of the assets. He will only have indications of them. The existence of a bank account in England is enough, whether it is in overdraft or not.

(iv) The plaintiff should give some grounds for believing that there is a risk of the assets being removed before the judgment or award is satisfied. The mere fact that the defendant is abroad is not by itself sufficient. No one would wish any reputable foreign company to be plagued with a *Mareva* injunction simply because it has agreed to London arbitration. But there are some foreign companies whose structure invites comment. We often see in this court a corporation which is registered in a country where the company law is so loose that nothing is known about it—where it does no work and has no officers and no assets. Nothing can be found out about the membership, or its control, or its assets, or the charges on them. Judgment cannot be enforced against it. There is no reciprocal enforcement of judgments. It is nothing more than a name grasped from the air, as elusive as the Cheshire Cat. In such cases the very fact of incorporation there gives some ground for believing there is a risk that, if judgment or an award is obtained, it may go unsatisfied. Such registration of such companies may carry many advantages to the individuals who control them, but they may suffer the disadvantage of having a *Mareva* injunction granted against them.

---

[46] *Siskina v Distos Compania Naviera SA* [1979] AC 210.

[47] *Rasu Maritima SA v Perusahaan Pertambangan Minyak Dan Gas Bumi Negara (Government of the Republic of Indonesia intervening) (Pertamina)* [1978] 1 QB 644.

> The giving of security for a debt is a small price to pay for the convenience of such a registration. Security would certainly be required in New York. So also it may be in London. Other grounds may be shown for believing there is a risk. But some such should be shown.
>
> (v) The plaintiff must, of course, give an undertaking in damages—in case he fails in his claim or the injunction turns out to be unjustified. In a suitable case this should be supported by a bond or security: and the injunction only granted on it being given, or undertaken to be given.
>
> In setting out those guidelines, I hope we shall do nothing to reduce the efficacy of the present practice. In it speed is of the essence. Ex parte is of the essence. If there is delay, or if advance warning is given, the assets may well be removed before the injunction can bite. It is rather like the new injunction in Chancery, the *Anton Piller* injunction (*Anton Piller KG v Manufacturing Processes Ltd* [1976] Ch 55), which has proved equally beneficial. That must be done speedily ex parte before the incriminating material is removed. So here in *Mareva* injunctions before the assets are removed. The solicitors of the City of London can, I believe, continue their present practice so long as they do it with due regard to their responsibilities: and so long as the judges exercise a wise discretion so as to see that the procedure is not abused.

It is interesting that in this extract, Lord Denning refers to the Anton Piller order, since it is generally acknowledged that like the Anton Piller order, a Mareva injunction has the potential to be oppressive. Such oppression might arise, for example, if by freezing a defendant's assets he is no longer able to pursue his normal business activities. As a result, as with the Anton Piller order, a series of safeguards have been developed by the courts to offset the potentially damaging effects of a Mareva injunction. These include allowing the defendant sufficient funds to carry on his business and for living expenses. Furthermore, a freezing order has to be revoked within 31 calendar days after it has been executed if no proceedings have begun. Nonetheless, is a freezing order really balanced fairly between the claimant and the defendant, particularly when it is combined with a search order? As with the search order there is now a standard form for use by the courts.[48]

13.4.4 NORWICH PHARMACAL ORDERS

13.4.4.1 Definition and development

A Norwich Pharmacal order is designed to obtain information which is necessary to identify a wrongdoer. The order places an individual, who becomes involved in another's wrongdoing whether or not innocently, under a duty to disclose information which might identify the alleged wrongdoer to the person who is injured by the wrongful acts. The jurisdiction to make a Norwich Pharmacal order was first established in the eponymous case of *Norwich Pharmacal v Customs and Excise*: an action for patent infringement which eventually reached the House of Lords.

---

48 Practice Direction [1996] 1 WLR 1552 amending Practice Direction [1994] 1 WLR 1233.

Norwich Pharmacal Co v Customs and Excise Commissioners
[1974] AC 133

The appellants were proprietors of a patent for a chemical compound, furazolidone. They suspected that the chemical was being manufactured abroad and illegally imported into the United Kingdom. They sought the names and addresses of the importers from Customs and Excise. Originally, the claimants had brought an action against Customs and Excise for infringement of their patent and an order for discovery. By the time the case reached the House of Lords, the claimants were simply seeking an order for discovery against Customs and Excise and the Lords allowed their appeal.

Lord Reid, at p. 175:

My noble and learned friends, Lord Cross of Chelsea and Lord Kilbrandon, have dealt with the authorities. They are not very satisfactory, not always easy to reconcile and in the end inconclusive. On the whole I think they favour the appellants, and I am particularly impressed by the views expressed by Lord Romilly MR and Lord Hatherley LC in *Upmann v Elkan* (1871) LR 12 Eq 140; 7 Ch App 130. They seem to me to point to a very reasonable principle that if through no fault of his own a person gets mixed up in the tortious acts of others so as to facilitate their wrong-doing he may incur no personal liability but he comes under a duty to assist the person who has been wronged by giving him full information and disclosing the identity of the wrongdoers. I do not think that it matters whether he became so mixed up by voluntary action on his part or because it was his duty to do what he did. It may be that if this causes him expense the person seeking the information ought to reimburse him. But justice requires that he should co-operate in righting the wrong if he unwittingly facilitated its perpetration.

I am the more inclined to reach this result because it is clear that if the person mixed up in the affair has to any extent incurred any liability to the person wronged, he must make full disclosure even though the person wronged has no intention of proceeding against him. It would I think be quite illogical to make his obligation to disclose the identity of the real offenders depend on whether or not he has himself incurred some minor liability. I would therefore hold that the respondents must disclose the information now sought unless there is some consideration of public policy which prevents that.

The order was revisited by the Court of Appeal in *Totalise v The Motley Fool.*[49] Here, the court held that the Norwich Pharmacal order did not offend against s. 6 of the HRA. Thus, according to Aldous LJ, it does not 'unjustifiably' invade the right of an individual to respect for his private life, especially when that individual is in the nature of things not before the court. The court also held that was it not incompatible with the Data Protection Act 1998. More recently in *Mitsui & Co Limited v Nexen Petroleum UK Limited,*[50] Lightman J identified three conditions that should be satisfied in order for the court to grant a Norwich Pharmacal order. They are:

i) a wrong must have been carried out, or arguably carried out, by an ultimate wrongdoer;

ii) there must be the need for an order to enable action to be brought against the ultimate wrongdoer; and

---

[49] *Totalise PLC v The Motley Fool Ltd* [2002] FSR 50, paras. 24–5.
[50] [2005] 3 All ER 511.

iii) the person against whom the order is sought must: (a) be mixed up in so as to have facilitated the wrongdoing; and (b) be able or likely to be able to provide the information necessary to enable the ultimate wrongdoer to be sued.

13.4.4.2 Norwich Pharmacal orders and EU law

In the UK, the Norwich Pharmacal order has become a frequently employed tool wielded by rightsholders seeking to compel ISPs to supply the names and contact details of individuals illegally downloading music. Similar orders have been employed in other EU countries to the same effect. Recently, the ECJ looked at the question of whether the Norwich Pharmacal order and its European equivalents were a legitimate method for enforcing IPRs.

Productores de Música de España (Promusicae) v Telefónica de España SAU
Case C-275/06 [2008] ECR I-271

The Spanish organization, Promusicae, which represents music and film producers, sought a court order from an internet provider, Telefónica, for the disclosure of the names and contact details of individuals involved in illegal file-sharing using the KaZaa file sharing network. This request was granted by the Spanish Commercial Court. Telefónica appealed on the basis that under Spanish law the disclosure of such information should only be authorized in the course of criminal investigations or those concerned with national security. The court then asked the ECJ whether Community Law, and in particular Directives 2000/31/EC (the E-commerce Directive), 2001/29/EC (the Information Society Directive), and 2004/48/EC (the Enforcement Directive) must be interpreted as requiring Member States to lay down, in order to ensure effective protection of copyright, an obligation to communicate personal data in the context of civil proceedings. The ECJ held, *inter alia*, that these three directives did not impose a duty on Member States to compel such disclosure. But it also considered whether Member States were precluded from making such orders except in limited circumstances, which did not include intellectual property infringement, and found that they were not.

The three Directives mentioned by the national court

57. It should first be noted that, as pointed out in [43] above, the purpose of the Directives mentioned by the national court is that the Member States should ensure, especially in the information society, effective protection of industrial property, in particular copyright. However, it follows from Art. 1(5)(b) of Directive 2000/31, Art. 9 of Directive 2001/29 and Art. 8(3)(e) of Directive 2004/48 that such protection cannot affect the requirements of the protection of personal data.

58. Article 8(1) of Directive 2004/48 admittedly requires Member States to ensure that, in the context of proceedings concerning an infringement of an intellectual property right and in response to a justified and proportionate request of the claimant, the competent judicial authorities may order that information on the origin and distribution networks of the goods or services which infringe an intellectual property right be provided. However, it does not follow from those provisions, which must be read in conjunction with those of para. 3(e) of

that Article, that they require the Member States to lay down, in order to ensure effective protection of copyright, an obligation to communicate personal data in the context of civil proceedings.

59. Nor does the wording of Arts. 15(2) and 18 of Directive 2000/31 or that of Art. 8(1) and (2) of Directive 2001/29 require the Member States to lay down such an obligation.

60. As to Arts. 41, 42 and 47 of the TRIPs Agreement, relied on by Promusicae, in the light of which Community law must as far as possible be interpreted where—as in the case of the provisions relied on in the context of the present reference for a preliminary ruling—it regulates a field to which that agreement applies (see, to that effect, *Parfums Christian Dior SA v Tuk Consultancy BV* (C-300/98 & C-392/98) [2000] ECR I-11307 at [47], and *Merck Genericos Produtos Farmaceuticos Lda v Merck & Co Inc* (C-431/05) [2007] 3 CMLR 49 at [35]), while they require the effective protection of intellectual property rights and the institution of judicial remedies for their enforcement, they do not contain provisions which require those Directives to be interpreted as compelling the Member States to lay down an obligation to communicate personal data in the context of civil proceedings.

65. The present reference for a preliminary ruling thus raises the question of the need to reconcile the requirements of the protection of different fundamental rights, namely the right to respect for private life on the one hand and the rights to protection of property and to an effective remedy on the other.

66. The mechanisms allowing those different rights and interests to be balanced are contained, first, in Directive 2002/58 itself, in that it provides for rules which determine in what circumstances and to what extent the processing of personal data is lawful and what safeguards must be provided for, and in the three Directives mentioned by the national court, which reserve the cases in which the measures adopted to protect the rights they regulate affect the protection of personal data. Secondly, they result from the adoption by the Member States of national provisions transposing those Directives and their application by the national authorities (see, to that effect, with reference to Directive 95/46, *Lindqvist* at [82]).

67. As to those Directives, their provisions are relatively general, since they have to be applied to a large number of different situations which may arise in any of the Member States. They therefore logically include rules which leave the Member States with the necessary discretion to define transposition measures which may be adapted to the various situations possible (see, to that effect, *Lindqvist* at [84]).

68. That being so, the Member States must, when transposing the Directives mentioned above, take care to rely on an interpretation of the Directives which allows a fair balance to be struck between the various fundamental rights protected by the Community legal order. Further, when implementing the measures transposing those Directives, the authorities and courts of the Member States must not only interpret their national law in a manner consistent with those Directives but also make sure that they do not rely on an interpretation of them which would be in conflict with those fundamental rights or with the other general principles of Community law, such as the principle of proportionality (see, to that effect, *Lindqvist* at [87], and *Ordre des Barreaux Francophones et Germanophone v Conseil des Ministres* (C-305/05), unreported, June 9, 2006, at [28]).

. . .

70. In the light of all the foregoing, the answer to the national court's question must be that Directives 2000/31, 2001/29 , 2004/48 and 2002/58 do not require the Member States to lay down, in a situation such as that in the main proceedings, an obligation to communicate personal data in order to ensure effective protection of copyright in the context of civil proceedings. However, Community law requires that, when transposing those Directives, the Member States take care to rely on an interpretation of them which allows a fair balance to

be struck between the various fundamental rights protected by the Community legal order. Further, when implementing the measures transposing those Directives, the authorities and courts of the Member States must not only interpret their national law in a manner consistent with those Directives but also make sure that they do not rely on an interpretation of them which would be in conflict with those fundamental rights or with the other general principles of Community law, such as the principle of proportionality.

Some have criticized the *Promusicae* decision, suggesting that the ECJ did not go far enough in protecting the interests of rightsholders by interpreting the directives as compelling Member States to impose an obligation to provide personal data when copyright is being infringed. But is that fair? After all, the ECJ did leave it to the discretion of Member States to make the equivalent of Norwich Pharmacal orders provided they are 'fairly balanced' with other fundamental rights. Might we take the view that this decision leaves considerable scope for rightsholders to obtain information on infringers, without the need for the presumption of compulsion?

13.4.5 CONCLUSION

We have noted that the judiciary recognizes that both the search order and the freezing order are extreme remedies which should be used with considerable discretion. The same point may be made about the Norwich Pharmacal order. It is noteworthy then that when the EU sought to harmonize the enforcement mechanisms in Member States, through the EU Enforcement Directive, the result was a regime entirely compatible with these three orders which had been developed in the UK. This suggests that the directive was designed to strengthen the options open to rightsholders in intellectual property disputes, rather than merely to harmonize enforcement provisions in the interests of an integrated European market. The only caveat is that under the directive these orders will be made only in relation to infringements on a 'commercial scale'. Furthermore, under the directive, the Norwich Pharmacal order may not be sought before proceedings have been initiated and not just at the interlocutory stage as in the UK. Although, both the ECJ and domestic cases have found these orders compatible with fundamental human rights, is it not possible that they were predisposed to do so in any event, given the sometimes considerable value of intellectual property?

FURTHER READING

I. Davies and R. Helmer, 'Case comment: *Productores de Musica de España ('Promusicae')* v *Telefónica de España SAU ('Telefónica')* (C-275/06) [2008] EIPR 307.

C. Kuner, 'Data protection and rights protection on the Internet: the *Promusicae* judgment of the European Court of Justice' [2008] EIPR 199.

R. Moules, 'The scope of privilege against self-incrimination in civil proceedings' (2007) Archbold News 4.

H. Suen and S. O. Cheung, 'Mareva injunctions: Evolving principles and practices revisited' [2007] Const LJ 117.

13.5 INJUNCTIONS

An injunction is an equitable remedy. It is up to the court's discretion whether to grant an injunction. An interim injunction may be granted before trial to preserve the claimant's position until the outcome of the proceedings. A final or perpetual injunction may be granted to a successful claimant once the matter has been resolved. This section will look at both.

13.5.1 INTERIM INJUNCTIONS

The granting of an interim (previously known as an interlocutory) injunction is designed to ensure that a claimant will not be irrevocably harmed by the defendant's actions in the period between the issuing of proceedings and trial. In essence, it is intended to preserve the status quo until the matter can be determined at trial. The claimant must show both that the award of damages at trial will not be an adequate remedy given the actions of the defendant but also, should he be unsuccessful at trial, that he can recompense the defendant for damage caused as the result of the injunction. As with other forms of interim relief, it is inevitable that where a claimant obtains an interim injunction, this may bring an immediate end to the proceedings. Interim injunctions are often used in intellectual property disputes where it will be frequently the case that damages will not be an adequate remedy. In *Amercian Cyanamid v Ethicon*, the House of Lords set out the conditions for the granting of an interim injunction.

American Cyanamid Co v Ethicon Ltd [1975] AC 396

This was a patent infringement action. The claimants had a patent for absorbable surgical sutures. The defendants, who like the claimants were an American company, planned to launch a suture into the UK which the claimants alleged was infringing. In turn, the defendants claimed that the claimants' patent was invalid. The claimants' application for an interlocutory (interim) injunction was granted in the High Court but this decision was reversed by the Court of Appeal and the claimant appealed.

Lord Diplock, at pp. 406–9:

My Lords, when an application for an interlocutory injunction to restrain a defendant from doing acts alleged to be in violation of the plaintiff's legal right is made upon contested facts, the decision whether or not to grant an interlocutory injunction has to be taken at a time when ex hypothesi the existence of the right or the violation of it, or both, is uncertain and will remain uncertain until final judgment is given in the action. It was to mitigate the risk of injustice to the plaintiff during the period before that uncertainty could be resolved that the practice arose of granting him relief by way of interlocutory injunction; but since the middle of the 19th century this has been made subject to his undertaking to pay damages to the defendant for any loss sustained by reason of the injunction if it should be held at the trial that the plaintiff had not been entitled to restrain the defendant from doing what he was threatening to do. The object of the interlocutory injunction is to protect the plaintiff against injury by violation of his right for which he could not be adequately compensated in damages recoverable in the action if the uncertainty were resolved in his favour at the trial; but the plaintiff's need for such protection must be weighed against the corresponding need of the defendant to be protected against injury resulting from his having been prevented from exercising his own legal rights for which he could not be adequately compensated under the plaintiff's undertaking in damages if the uncertainty were resolved in the defendant's favour at the trial. The court must weigh one need against another and determine where 'the balance of convenience' lies.

In those cases where the legal rights of the parties depend upon facts that are in dispute between them, the evidence available to the court at the hearing of the application for an interlocutory injunction is incomplete. It is given on affidavit and has not been tested by oral cross-examination. The purpose sought to be achieved by giving to the court discretion to grant such injunctions would be stultified if the discretion were clogged by a technical rule forbidding its exercise if upon that incomplete untested evidence the court evaluated the chances of the plaintiff's ultimate success in the action at 50 per cent or less, but permitting its exercise if the court evaluated his chances at more than 50 per cent.

[Having stated that the granting of an interim injunction should be based upon a determination of where the balance of convenience lies between the parties, Lord Diplock went on to discuss and to reject the alternative view that the court should assess the strength of the case between the parties or whether the claimant had a 'strong' prima facie case:]

Your Lordships should in my view take this opportunity of declaring that there is no such rule. The use of such expressions as 'a probability,' 'a prima facie case', or 'a strong prima facie case' in the context of the exercise of a discretionary power to grant an interlocutory injunction leads to confusion as to the object sought to be achieved by this form of temporary relief. The court no doubt must be satisfied that the claim is not frivolous or vexatious, in other words, that there is a serious question to be tried.

It is no part of the court's function at this stage of the litigation to try to resolve conflicts of evidence on affidavit as to facts on which the claims of either party may ultimately depend nor to decide difficult questions of law which call for detailed argument and mature considerations. These are matters to be dealt with at the trial. One of the reasons for the introduction of the practice of requiring an undertaking as to damages upon the grant of an interlocutory injunction was that 'it aided the court in doing that which was its great object, viz. abstaining from expressing any opinion upon the merits of the case until the hearing': *Wakefield v Duke of Buccleugh* (1865) 12 LT 628, 629. So unless the material available to the court at the hearing of the application for an interlocutory injunction fails to disclose that the plaintiff has any real prospect of succeeding in his claim for a permanent injunction at the trial, the court should go on to consider whether the balance of convenience lies in favour of granting or refusing the interlocutory relief that is sought.

As to that, the governing principle is that the court should first consider whether, if the plaintiff were to succeed at the trial in establishing his right to a permanent injunction, he would be adequately compensated by an award of damages for the loss he would have sustained as a result of the defendant's continuing to do what was sought to be enjoined between the time of the application and the time of the trial. If damages in the measure recoverable at common law would be adequate remedy and the defendant would be in a financial position to pay them, no interlocutory injunction should normally be granted, however strong the plaintiff's claim appeared to be at that stage. If, on the other hand, damages would not provide an adequate remedy for the plaintiff in the event of his succeeding at the trial, the court should then consider whether, on the contrary hypothesis that the defendant were to succeed at the trial in establishing his right to do that which was sought to be enjoined, he would be adequately compensated under the plaintiff's undertaking as to damages for the loss he would have sustained by being prevented from doing so between the time of the application and the time of the trial. If damages in the measure recoverable under such an undertaking would be an adequate remedy and the plaintiff would be in a financial position to pay them, there would be no reason upon this ground to refuse an interlocutory injunction.

It is where there is doubt as to the adequacy of the respective remedies in damages available to either party or to both, that the question of balance of convenience arises. It would be unwise to attempt even to list all the various matters which may need to be taken into consideration in deciding where the balance lies, let alone to suggest the relative weight to be attached to them. These will vary from case to case.

Where other factors appear to be evenly balanced it is a counsel of prudence to take such measures as are calculated to preserve the status quo. If the defendant is enjoined temporarily from doing something that he has not done before, the only effect of the interlocutory injunction in the event of his succeeding at the trial is to postpone the date at which he is able to embark upon a course of action which he has not previously found it necessary to undertake; whereas to interrupt him in the conduct of an established enterprise would cause much greater inconvenience to him since he would have to start again to establish it in the event of his succeeding at the trial.

Save in the simplest cases, the decision to grant or to refuse an interlocutory injunction will cause to whichever party is unsuccessful on the application some disadvantages which his ultimate success at the trial may show he ought to have been spared and the disadvantages may be such that the recovery of damages to which he would then be entitled either in the action or under the plaintiff's undertaking would not be sufficient to compensate him fully for all of them. The extent to which the disadvantages to each party would be incapable of being compensated in damages in the event of his succeeding at the trial is always a significant factor in assessing where the balance of convenience lies, and if the extent of the uncompensatable disadvantage to each party would not differ widely, it may not be improper to take into account in tipping the balance the relative strength of each party's case as revealed by the affidavit evidence adduced on the hearing of the application. This, however, should be done only where it is apparent upon the facts disclosed by evidence as to which there is no credible dispute that the strength of one party's case is disproportionate to that of the other party. The court is not justified in embarking upon anything resembling a trial of the action upon conflicting affidavits in order to evaluate the strength of either party's case.

I would reiterate that, in addition to those to which I have referred, there may be many other special factors to be taken into consideration in the particular circumstances of individual cases. The instant appeal affords one example of this.

13.5.2 INTERIM INJUNCTIONS AFTER *AMERICAN CYANAMID*

The general principles to emerge from *American Cynamid* are the following:

1. That the claimant must establish there is a serious issue to be tried.

2. That damages would not be an adequate remedy at trial.

3. That were the defendant to succeed at trial, damages would be an adequate compensation.

4. But where it is not clear that damages will be adequate compensation either for the claimant or the defendant the court should look at the balance of convenience.

For the most part, these principles continue to be authoritative. There are, however, exceptions.

13.5.2.1 *Series 5 Software*

In *Series 5 Software Ltd v Clarke*[51] Laddie J held that while not deviating from the *American Cyanamid* principles, the court might also consider the relative strength of the parties' cases when determining whether to grant an interim injunction. However, it is submitted that such a view is not compatible with *American Cyanamid*; nor has the *Series 5* judgment been generally followed.

13.5.2.2 Section 12(3) of the HRA 1998

The *American Cyanamid* principles will not be followed in cases which involve the need to balance the right to confidentiality (or, indeed privacy) against the right to freedom of expression. In particular, s. 12(3) of the HRA 1998, imposes a threshold test to be satisfied before a court might grant an interim injunction in cases involving the right to freedom of expression. The House of Lords considered the application of s. 12(3) in the case of *Cream Holdings v Banerjee*.[52]

13.5.2.3 Special circumstances

In his judgment in *American Cyanamid*, Lord Diplock noted that, 'there may be many other special factors to be taken into consideration in the particular circumstances of individual cases'. Since his judgment, courts have taken into consideration a range of circumstances which have enabled them to deviate from strict adherence to the *American Cyanamid* principles. Indeed, it is perhaps this built-in flexibility of Lord Diplock's judgment which has given it its longevity. A key exception, and one which is often a factor in cases involving IPRs, arises where the granting of an interim injunction would settle the outcome of the case. In *NWL Ltd v Woods*, Lord Diplock himself identified this exception:[53]

> Where, however, the grant or refusal of the interlocutory injunction will have the practical effect of putting an end to the action because the harm that will have been already caused to the losing party by its grant or its refusal is complete and of a kind for which money cannot constitute any worthwhile recompense, the degree of likelihood that the plaintiff would have succeeded in establishing his right to an injunction if the action had gone to trial, is a factor to be brought into the balance by the judge in weighing the risks that injustice may result from his deciding the application one way rather than the other.

We might easily see, for example, in cases involving trade mark infringement or passing off, how an interim injunction might put an end to the proceedings. For example, a trader who has introduced a new product which allegedly carries an infringing trade mark may prefer to re-brand his product rather than withdraw it from the market until after trial, whether

---

[51] [1996] 1 All ER 853.

[52] [2005] 1 AC 253. This case and the relationship between breach of confidence and interim injunctions more generally is discussed at 8.6.3.

[53] *NWL Ltd v Woods* [1979] 1 WLR 1294, 1307.

or not he believes in the merits of the rightsholder's claims against him. Indeed, despite the caveat introduced by *NWL Ltd*, it remains the case that very often, indeed probably more often than not, the granting of pre-trial orders or interim injunctions will determine the outcome of a case in favour of the claimant. Yet failure to grant such orders might result in a claimant suffering long-term damage to its IPRs in the period before trial, for which there will be no adequate compensation once the trial is concluded. It is thus important to ask whether the courts have found the correct balance between the interests of the claimants and the defendants when granting these orders? Might it be the case that such orders, while a necessary tool in the protection of IPRs, will inevitably favour the rightsholder over the accused?

FURTHER READING

A. Keay, 'Whither *American Cyanamid*?: Interim injunctions in the 21st century' [2004] CJQ 132.

J. Phillips, 'Interlocutory injunctions and intellectual property: A review of *American Cyanamid v Ethicon* in the light of *Series 5 software*' [1997] JBL 486.

13.5.3 FINAL INJUNCTIONS

13.5.3.1 Introduction

Final injunctions, sometimes called perpetual injunctions, may be granted at the discretion of the court to a successful claimant at the conclusion of a trial. Final injunctions may also be imposed as a result of a settlement made between a claimant and a defendant in the course of litigation. This latter circumstance is undoubtedly the more common in intellectual property actions, since, as we have noted, such disputes rarely come to trial. However, the granting of a final injunction is not 'inevitable'. If no future threat exists the courts may decline to grant an injunction.[54]

13.5.3.2 When will an injunction be granted?

As was put by Aldous J (as he then was) in *Chiron v Organon Teknika*, it is a general rule 'that a defendant who interferes with a proprietory right of a plaintiff or threatens to continue to do so, will be injuncted'.[55] The court will tailor the injunction to match the wrong which has been committed and is threatened. Thus, in a patent action, the usual forms of relief would include an injunction to stop the defendant from infringing the patent. However, an injunction should not be imposed in such wide terms that it is not fair to the defendant.[56] In other words, an injunction should be proportionate. In *Sun Microsystems v Amtec*,[57] a trade mark infringement action, an injunction which had the effect of shutting down a defendant's legitimate business was held to be a disproportionate remedy. Furthermore, an injunction will be granted when other remedies would not do justice to the claimant's case even

---

[54] *Proctor v Bayley and Son* (1889) 6 RPC 5, cited in *Coflexip SA v Stolt Comex Seaway MS Ltd* [1999] FSR 473.

[55] *Chiron Corporation v Organon Teknika Limited (No 10); Chiron Corporation v Murex Diagnostics Limited (No 10)* [1995] FSR 325, 328.

[56] *Coflexip v Stolt*, paras. 3 and 6.   [57] [2006] FSR 35.

if, superficially at least they would appear to offer some compensation.[58] An apt illustration of this rule was offered by Aldous J in *Chiron v Organon*, which was itself a patent action (at p. 330):

> Many judges have stated, and I emphatically agree with them, that a person by committing a wrongful act (whether it be a public company for public purposes or a private individual) is not thereby entitled to ask the Court to sanction his doing so by purchasing his neighbour's rights, by assessing damages in that behalf, leaving his neighbour with the nuisance, or his lights dimmed, as the case may be.
>
> In such cases the well-known rule is not to accede to the application, but to grant the injunction sought, for the plaintiff's legal right has been invaded, and he is prima facie entitled to an injunction.

13.5.3.3 When will an injunction be refused?

There are some situations in which a court may be slow to grant an injunction. A claimant may disentitle himself to an injunction because of his behaviour and a court may instead award damages. More specifically, an injunction may not be granted if there is only minor injury to a claimant's rights, if money is an adequate remedy (especially if it is a small money payment), and where it might be oppressive to the defendant to grant an injunction.[59] The court may also take into account how third-party interests might be affected by the granting of an injunction, including the public interest.[60] Thus, in *Roussel-Uclaf v GD Searle*, it was suggested by Graham J that a court may decline to grant a final injunction where to do so might deprive the public of access to a life-saving drug.[61] More generally, in *Coflexip v Stolt*,[62] Laddie J pointed out in typically robust fashion the dangers of simply assuming that in the case of a proven infringement, the claimant should automatically be granted an injunction as protection against the defendant's presumed future wrongdoing:

> 33. But to go from that to the general proposition that all infringers of intellectual property rights are to be treated as devious and that plaintiffs need much wider orders in intellectual property cases to protect them against future ingenious, but yet unthought of, acts of infringement is unjustified. It comes close to asserting class guilt. Most losing defendants, even in passing off and copyright claims, are perfectly respectable and honest traders. Few businessmen are interested in knowingly infringing valid intellectual property rights...If I consider patents alone, in 30 years experience of litigation in this area, I have never come across a defendant who engaged in infringement knowing that what he was doing was wrong. They all thought that they either did not infringe or the patent was invalid or both. Most of those who lose think that they have been unlucky or worse. I never came across a defendant who, having lost, expressed any desire to take the risk of infringing again. The costs of patent litigation are too high...When the court is asked to grant an injunction in a patent action, it is not considering the actions of an anonymous member of a uniform class of infringers. It has to consider the facts of the particular case and the behaviour, both past and threatened, of the

---

[58] *Coflexip v Stolt*, para. 18.
[59] *Chiron v Organon*, p. 330; see also *Shelfer v City of London Electric Lighting Co* [1895] 1 Ch 287.
[60] *Miller v Jackson* [1977] 1 QB 966.
[61] *Roussel-Uclaf v GD Searle & Co Ltd* [1977] FSR 125, 131; see also *Chiron v Organon*.
[62] [1999] FSR 473.

particular defendant. As Cotton LJ said in *Proctor v Bayley*, it is necessary to consider all the circumstances of the case before deciding what is the correct injunction to grant. It cannot be right to simply treat all patent infringers as bad apples.

13.5.3.4 Final injunctions: a judicial summary

In the recent case of *Cantor Gaming v Gameaccount*, Daniel Alexander QC sitting as a Deputy High Court Judge provided a useful summary of the circumstances in which a final injunction will be granted in intellectual property disputes.

Cantor Gaming Ltd v GameAccount Global Ltd [2008] FSR 4

The claimant alleged that the defendant had infringed its copyright in two computer programs and also breached the terms of a licence between them for use of the programs. The program was a database for an online golf game and its users which the defendant allowed to be used by a third party in contravention of the licence term. The defendant had also infringed the claimant's copyright by incorporating some images from the claimant's game into a game of its own. The defendant admitted it had violated the terms of the licence and gave undertakings that it would no longer provide the database to the third party. In the event, after these undertakings were given, it was discovered that a demonstration copy of the infringing game remained on the defendant's website. One question for the court was whether under these circumstances it would be just to grant the claimant an injunction since to do so would only enforce the undertakings the defendant had already given. In the course of his judgment, Mr Alexander summarized the law relating to final injunctions in intellectual property cases.

Deputy High Court Judge Daniel Alexander:

General principles

100. The Court has a wide power to grant or withhold an injunction founded on s. 37(1) of the Supreme Court Act 1981. Although injunctions are granted almost automatically in certain kinds of case, the court is nonetheless required to have regard to all the circumstances. As Lord Bingham said in *South Bucks District Council v Porter* [2003] 2 WLR 1547 at 1562–1563:

Underpinning the court's jurisdiction to grant an injunction is section 37(1) of the Supreme Court Act 1981 conferring the power to do so 'in all cases in which it appears to the court to be just and convenient to do so'.

...

In all cases the court must decide whether in all the circumstances it is just to grant the relief sought against the particular defendant.

Intellectual property cases

101. It is normal for an injunction to be granted in a case involving infringement of intellectual property rights, once it has been established that there has been infringement and the infringement has not completely ceased at the time of trial. Part of the reason that an

injunction will normally be granted in such a case is that, at trial, there often remains a dispute as to whether the defendant is or is not entitled to undertake the acts of which complaint is made. The defendant is usually maintaining that it does have the right to do so and may expressly or implicitly be threatening to do so.

102. The approach in copyright cases was set out by the Master of the Rolls, Lord Woolf, giving the judgment of the Court of Appeal in *Phonographic Performance Ltd v Saibal Maitra* [1998] FSR 749 at 771:

> when a person establishes infringement of copyright and a threat to continue infringement, an injunction will in the ordinary case be granted without restriction... But the court, when granting an injunction, is still required to exercise a discretion and in so doing there could be circumstances where restriction or refusal of an injunction would be warranted.

103. A similar approach was taken by the Court of Appeal in the patent case, *Coflexip SA v Stolt Comex Seaway MS Ltd* [2001] RPC 9, where Aldous LJ said at [6] and [7]:

> whenever a court at the end of a trial grants permanent injunctive relief, the purpose should be to give effect to its judgment on liability... The injunction granted should protect the plaintiff from a continuation of the infringements of his rights by the threatened activities of the defendant. But the injunction must also be fair to the defendant.
>
> ... Normally, when a defendant has infringed, the court will assume it is not a one-off activity and will grant an injunction to stop repetition. This course is not inevitable. In a few cases courts have concluded that even though infringement has occurred, no future threat exists. In such cases, injunctive relief has been refused...

104. The same principles must surely apply where a person establishes that there has been a breach of contract which prohibits an act akin to infringement of an intellectual property right.

No threat to infringe

105. The court may, however, refuse to grant an injunction and, ordinarily, would refuse to do so, where no threat to infringe existed at the time that the order came to be considered. In *Landor & Hawa International Ltd v Azure Designs Ltd* [2007] FSR 9, Neuberger LJ said at [46]:

> It seems to me plainly inappropriate in principle to grant an injunction in favour of a claimant against a defendant who clearly and unequivocally agreed, before the action for the injunction was even started, to refrain from taking that very action which the injunction would have forbidden him from taking.

106. In that case, the defendant had initially offered an unequivocal undertaking before the action was commenced but the undertaking was withdrawn in terms which made it clear that the defendant was again threatening to infringe the claimant's rights. An injunction was held by a unanimous Court of Appeal to have been rightly granted at trial.

More complex cases

107. There are more complex cases in which, although the defendant may have clearly and unequivocally agreed before the trial not to undertake the actions which the injunction would forbid him from taking, it may nonetheless be appropriate to grant an injunction. Examples may be cases in which, for one reason or another, the court considers that it would be appropriate for the assurances given by the defendant to be backed by court sanction.

108. For example, there may be situations where a defendant has previously given contractual undertakings not to undertake certain acts but has acted in breach of those undertakings. Another example may be where there is a dispute over the scope of the under-takings given, with the claimant contending that the defendant is not free to undertake cer-tain acts and the defendant contending that he is. In such situations, I do not understand Neuberger LJ's statement of principle as deciding that the court is invariably bound to accept the defendant's agreement, clear and unequivocal as it may be, without regard to other cir-cumstances which may place that agreement in context.

109. In such a case, the court may conclude that adequate protection for the claimant and its rights requires that the contractual undertaking is backed by an injunction so that com-pliance is, so far as possible, guaranteed. This may be, in part, because of the impact of an injunction, as compared with a contractual undertaking on the steps that a defendant will have to take in order to avoid serious penalties in the event of a further breach. Because liabil-ity for breach of an injunction prohibiting infringement of copyright or breach of contract is, unless specifically qualified, strict, a corporate undertaking subject to such an injunction will be liable for contempt of court, even if the source of the breach is, for example, an employee acting contrary to specific instructions. The nature of any penalty for breach of an injunction may depend, among other things, on the seriousness of the breach and on the steps that have been taken by the undertaking to prevent any breach from happening. A person or undertaking subject to an injunction may take greater care in compliance than one subject only to contractual restriction. So, for example, an injunction may be of greater utility than contractual undertakings where it appears that the defendant's approach to ensuring compli-ance is more casual than necessary to guarantee protection of the claimant's rights.

110. An illustration of this approach comes from *British Telecommunications Plc v Nextcall Telecom Plc* [2000] FSR 679 where the defendant had given contractual undertakings which it did not fully honour. The claimant sought an injunction in unqualified form to enforce the contract. The defendant contended, in effect, that it was impossible to guarantee compliance with its obligations, because of the possibility that a rogue employee may continue to make the misrepresentations that its contractual undertakings were intended to prevent. Jacob J granted an injunction in unqualified form observing that he was *'only enforcing by injunction precisely what the defendants undertook not to do by contract'*. Jacob J also pointed out that it did not follow from the absence of qualification of the injunction that the claimant would sensibly bring proceedings for contempt of court for the slightest breach. He said:

> If [they] were nonetheless so to proceed, then if the defendants had truly taken all reasonable precautions to prevent a breach, it is most unlikely that they would be punished. There may well be no order as to costs . . . or even an order for costs against [the claimant] if the court thought the application pointless. All would depend on the circumstances.

Trivial breaches

111. On the other hand, the court may refuse to grant relief where the interference with a claimant's rights is trivial (see *Imperial Gas Light & Coke Co v Broadbent* (1859) 74 HL Cas 600). The court has refused an injunction where the dispute was one for 'the application of reason, common sense and ordinary forbearance, not for an injunction' (*Behrens v Richards* [1905] 2 Ch 614) or where 'the violation of the right is so slight, formal, and unsubstantial that the plaintiff can have no ground in conscience to complain of it . . .' (*Harrison v Good* (1871) LR 11 Eq 338, 352).

112. Mr Turner for Cantor refers to *Insurance Co v Lloyd's Syndicate* [1995] 1 Lloyds Rep 272 for the proposition that it is not necessary for a claimant to show that it is likely to suffer

actual damage in order for an injunction to be granted. While his submission is correct, it does not follow that the court has no power to withhold injunctive relief where the breach in question is a technical one or is unlikely to occur again, or, if it does, it is unlikely to cause any real damage. That power is reinforced by one of the authorities cited to Colman J in that case, *Sharp v Harrison* [1922] 1 Ch 502. An injunction was refused despite a finding of breach and a declaration was made that the defendant had breached the covenant. Nothing in the more recent approaches to the law, whether in the CPR or the EU Enforcement Directive (Directive 2004/48/EC) or regulations made thereunder, suggests that the power of the court to refuse relief in the case of technical breaches or trivial matters has been removed. To the contrary, the concept of proportionality has been given greater status in recent times, reinforcing the fact that the court should not encourage costly litigation over very little by granting relief even in trivial cases.

Summary of principles

113. I therefore summarise the applicable principles as follows. First, an injunction may be granted pursuant to s. 37(1) of the Supreme Court Act 1981 whenever it is just and convenient to do so. Secondly, the grant of an injunction involves the exercise of the court's discretion, and the court should, in so doing, take account of all of the circumstances, one factor of which is the importance or triviality of the breach. Thirdly, there are certain kinds of case, of which intellectual property cases are examples, in which an injunction will normally be granted if a claimant has established infringement of its rights and there is a threat to continue (or at least no clear and unequivocal undertaking not to continue). Fourthly, where there is no threat to continue acts which have been held to be unlawful, because the defendant has clearly and unequivocally agreed not to do them before the action was brought, it is not right in principle to grant an injunction. Fifthly, there may, however, be situations where, even though a defendant may have agreed not to undertake the acts in question, an injunction may be just and convenient, having regard to all the circumstances. This may be, for example, because of the greater incentive for respect of a claimant's rights that an injunction would provide, and which, in particular cases, it may appear just to grant. Sixthly, the court may, in appropriate cases, take proportionality into account in granting or refusing injunctive relief.

It was the opinion of the judge[63] that an injunction would have some 'probably marginal, utility' in enforcing the contractual undertakings which the defendant had given and it would encourage the defendant to be 'assiduous' in removing the offending software from its website. For that reason, and because the defendant had already given undertakings not to infringe in future, the granting of an injunction was held just and convenient, even though of 'questionable proportionality'. Furthermore, the judge held that even though the injunction would make only an 'incremental difference' and indeed was probably 'unnecessary', the fact that it was normal to grant an injunction in intellectual property cases predisposed him to grant an injunction in this case. The decision in *Cantor Gaming v GameAccount Global* appears to suggest that despite the myriad caveats which now surround the granting of a final injunction, there will be a strong bias towards granting final injunctions in intellectual property cases.[64]

---

[63] At paras. 123–5.
[64] Contrast the position taken by the US Supreme Court in *eBay Inc v MercExchange LLC* (2006) 547 US 388. For a discussion see S. Subramanian, 'eBay ruling and US obligation to the TRIPs Agreement' [2008] EIPR 444, 449–50.

13.5.3.5 Final injunctions and the EU Enforcement Directive

Article 11 of the EU Enforcement Directive provides that Member States must ensure that where there has been a finding of infringement of an IPR, the court may issue an injunction to prevent the continuation of the infringement. National law may also provide for a recurring penalty payment where there is non-compliance with an injunction. In addition, Member States should ensure that rightsholders may apply for injunctions against intermediaries whose services are used by a third party to infringe IPRs, although in this case certain safeguards may obtain such as a right to confidentiality. It is generally accepted that UK law in relation to injunctions will comply with the terms of the directive.

13.5.3.6 Conclusion

In the case of *Chiron v Organon*, Aldous J suggested that injunctions granted in intellectual property cases will inevitably have the effect of enforcing a monopoly. As a result, a final injunction will restrict competition and allow the rightsholder to charge a monopoly price for its products. Should we be concerned about this? After all, the purpose of IPRs is in effect to endow a monopoly, albeit with many limitations. And, as we have seen, through the case law, the courts have developed a number of caveats against the automatic granting of final injunctions or at least final injunctions which are broadly drafted. Nonetheless, in the real world, it is a fact that intellectual property actions, whether resolved at trial or by agreement between the parties, will almost inevitably result in the granting of an injunction against an unsuccessful defendant. Bearing in mind the somewhat draconian nature of the pre-trial orders we examined earlier, should we be concerned that in the area of remedies, at least the ones we have examined so far, the defendant might seem to be at a distinct disadvantage?

FURTHER READING

V. Denicolo, D. Geradin, A. Layne-Farrar, and A. J. Padilla, 'Revisiting injunctive relief: Interpreting eBay in high-tech industries with non-practicing patent holders' [2008] JCL & E 571.

J. Seymour, 'Injunctions enjoining non-parties: Distinction without difference?' [2007] CLJUK 605.

13.6 MONETARY REMEDIES

Persons who successfully bring actions for infringement of their IPRs will be keen to obtain, in addition to a final injunction, some sort of financial recompense for the wrong committed by the defendant. This following section examines the monetary remedies that are available to successful claimants.

13.6.1 DAMAGES

13.6.1.1 General principles

An award of damages seeks to compensate for the loss or injury caused by an infringement. In *General Tire*, the House of Lords laid down the key principles relevant to determining an assessment of damages when it comes to patent infringement.[65] These principles have subsequently been applied to infringements of other IPRs.[66]

General Tire and Rubber Co v Firestone Tyre and Rubber Co Ltd [1976] RPC 197

The respondents patented in the US, UK, and elsewhere an invention relating to synthetic rubber compounds suitable for tyre treads. This was an important and valuable invention that brought about substantial reductions in the manufacturing costs of tyres. The respondents sued the appellants for infringement of their UK patent. The award of damages granted at first instance was appealed. The appeal was dismissed by the Court of Appeal and subsequently allowed by the House of Lords.

> **Lord Wilberforce** (with whom the other law lords agreed), **at pp. 824–7:**
>
> As in the case of any other tort (leaving aside cases where exemplary damages can be given) the object of damages is to compensate for loss or injury. The general rule at any rate in relation to 'economic' torts is that the measure of damages is to be, so far as possible, that sum of money which will put the injured party in the same position as he would have been in if he had not sustained the wrong (*Livingstone v Rawyards Coal Co* (1880) 5 App Cas 25 *per* Lord Blackburn, at p. 39).
>
> In the case of infringement of a patent, an alternative remedy at the option of the plaintiff exists by way of an account of profits made by the infringer—see Patents Act 1949, section 60. The respondents did not elect to claim an account of profits: their claim was only for damages. There are two essential principles in valuing that claim: first, that the plaintiffs have the burden of proving their loss: second, that, the defendants being wrongdoers, damages should not be liberally assessed but that the object is to compensate the plaintiffs and not punish the defendants (*Pneumatic Tyre Co Ltd v Puncture Proof Pneumatic Tyre Co Ltd* (1899) 16 RPC 209, 215).
>
> . . .
>
> . . . it is useful to refer to some of the main groups of reported cases which exemplify the approaches of courts to typical situations.
>
> 1 Many patents of inventions belong to manufacturers, who exploit the invention to make articles or products which they sell at a profit. The benefit of the invention in such cases is realized through the sale of the article or product. In these cases, if the invention is infringed, the effect of the infringement will be to divert sales from the owner of the patent to the infringer. The measure of damages will then normally be the profit which would have been realized by the owner of the patent if the sales had been made by him.

---

[65] Note that damages are recoverable for patent infringement from the date of publication of the patent application, although no action can be brought until the patent is granted: s. 69(1) and (2)(a), PA 77.

[66] For example, for passing off via false endorsement (*Irvine v Talksport Ltd* [2003] FSR 35); for trade mark infringement (*Reed Executive Plc v Reed Business Information Ltd* [2002] EWHC 2772 (Ch)); and copyright infringement (*Blayney v Clogau St David's Gold Mines Ltd* [2003] FSR 19). For the approach in breach of confidence cases see 8.6.1. Laddie, Prescott, and Vitoria, *The Modern Law of Copyright & Designs* (3rd edn., London: Sweet & Maxwell, 2000), para. 13.43 suggest that damages for moral rights infringement (which is actionable as breach of statutory duty—see s. 103, CDPA) will be assessed 'on the basis of the damage to the goodwill and reputation enjoyed by the author . . . [and that] an author may also claim compensation for injured feelings'.

...

2 Other patents of inventions are exploited through the granting of licences for royalty payments. In these cases, if an infringer uses the invention without a licence, the measure of damages he must pay will be the sums which he would have paid by way of royalty if, instead of acting illegally, he had acted legally.

...

Before a 'going rate' of royalty can be taken as the basis on which an infringer should be held liable, it must be shown that the circumstances in which the going rate was paid are the same as or at least comparable with those in which the patentee and the infringer are assumed to strike their bargain.

...

3 In some cases it is not possible to prove either (as in 1) that there is a normal rate of profit, or (as in 2) that there is a normal, or established, licence royalty. Yet clearly damages must be assessed. In such cases it is for the plaintiff to adduce evidence which will guide the court. This evidence may consist of the practice as regards royalty, in the relevant trade or in analogous trades; perhaps of expert opinion expressed in publications or in the witness box; possibly of the profitability of the invention; and of any other factor on which the judge can decide the measure of loss. Since evidence of this kind is in its nature general and also probably hypothetical, it is unlikely to be of relevance, or if relevant of weight, in the face of the more concrete and direct type of evidence referred to under 2. But there is no rule of law which prevents the court, even when it has evidence of licensing practice, from taking these more general considerations into account. The ultimate process is one of judicial estimation of the available indications.

...

...the judge assessing damages [must]...take into account any licences actually granted and the rates of royalty fixed by them, to estimate their relevance and comparability, to apply them so far [as] he can to the bargain hypothetically to be made between the patentee and the infringer and to the extent to which they do not provide a figure on which the damage can be measured to consider any other evidence, according to its relevance and weight, upon which he can fix a rate of royalty which would have been agreed.

Lord Wilberforce went on to set aside the judge's finding of damages. He held that the trial judge and Court of Appeal had erred in their reasoning in two key ways: first, by focusing on what the infringer should fairly have paid, rather than the loss to the patentee; and second, in seeking to measure the loss by considering a bargain struck between an abstract licensor and abstract licensee rather than the actual licensor and actual licensee. There was little evidence to support the basis for awarding damages adopted by the trial judge and ample evidence of a royalty rate at which the respondents would have been willing to license use of the invention.

In *Blayney v Clogau St David's Gold Mines Ltd*[67] the issue before the Court of Appeal was whether a claimant in a copyright infringement action could claim damages computed both by reference to profits foregone in respect of lost sales and by way of royalty for other infringing sales. Morritt V-C (with whom Rix and Jonathan Parker LJJ agreed) observed that:

[67] [2003] FSR 19.

> there is nothing in the speech of Lord Wilberforce [in *General Tire*] to suggest that a claimant can recover damages on the basis of the first group in respect of sales he can show to have been lost and on the basis of the third group for those he cannot. But there was no reason for Lord Wilberforce to consider that point. As he said, all he was doing was referring to three groups of reported case which exemplified the approach of the courts to typical situations.[68]

The Vice-Chancellor concluded that given that this type of computation was available in patent cases, there was no reason not to apply it in cases of copyright infringement. He added that '[t]he fact that the claimant may not be able to prove the application of one measure of damages, namely lost sales, does not mean that he has suffered no damage at all, rather some other measure by which to assess the compensation for that interference must be sought'.[69]

The Intellectual Property Enforcement Regulations 2006, SI 2006/1028, implementing the Enforcement Directive, introduced regulation 3 concerning damages. This provision states:

> (1) Where in an action for infringement of an intellectual property right the defendant knew, or had reasonable grounds to know, that he engaged in infringing activity, the damages awarded to the claimant shall be appropriate to the actual prejudice he suffered as a result of the infringement.
>
> (2) When awarding such damages—
>
> (a) all appropriate aspects shall be taken into account, including in particular—
>
>   (i) the negative economic consequences, including any lost profits, which the claimant has suffered, and any unfair profits made by the defendant; and
>
>   (ii) elements other than economic factors, including the moral prejudice caused to the claimant by the infringement; or
>
> (b) where appropriate, they may be awarded on the basis of the royalties or fees which would have been due had the defendant obtained a licence.

Regulation 3 gives rise to some uncertainties. In particular, the phrase 'any unfair profits made by the defendant' in para. (2)(a) is at odds with the statement in para. (1) that the award of damages shall be appropriate to the actual prejudice suffered as a result of the infringement and the compensatory purpose of damages.[70] Further, it seems that assessing damages according to royalties or licence fees is an alternative to calculating them on the basis of lost profits. What impact does this have on a situation such as that in *Blayney* where damages were calculated using both bases? The view taken in Copinger is that these alternative measures of damages would not invalidate the approach taken in *Blayney,* where 'in effect the terms of regulation 3(2)(a) were applied to some parts of the loss while those of regulation 3(2)(b) were applied to the rest'.[71] Finally, it is not clear what is meant by 'moral prejudice caused to the claimant by the infringement'. It has been suggested that this phrase encompasses damage caused to the commercial image or good reputation of the IPR holder,

·

---

[68] Ibid., para. 12.　　[69] Ibid., para. 20.　　[70] See recital 26 of the Enforcement Directive.

[71] *Copinger and Skone Jones on Copyright,* 15th edn., Second Cumulative Supplement (S&M, 2007), para. 22–162.

as a result of infringers selling poor quality imitations.[72] Yet this would seem to be an economic, rather than moral, interest.

13.6.1.2 Consequential loss

What about the situation where the claimant suffers secondary or consequential losses flowing from the act of infringement? This question was considered in the case extracted below.

Gerber Garment Technology Inc v Lectra Systems Ltd [1997] RPC 443

The patents in suit related to machines for the automatic cutting of fabric. The claimant commonly sold with these machines computer-aided design (CAD) machines to produce cutting patterns. The sale of the CAD machines did not infringe any patent right, but the trial judged awarded lost profits in respect of the CAD machines that the claimant could have been expected to sell with the manufacturing machines. The defendants appealed to the Court of Appeal against the award of damages and argued, *inter alia*, that damages were limited to lost profits relating to activities that in themselves constituted patent infringement.

Staughton LJ (Hobhouse and Hutchinson LJJ agreeing), at pp. 451–6:

Mr Hobbs submits that the damages which a patentee can recover from an infringer by way of loss of profits are limited to the profits that would have been earned in activities for which the patent provides a monopoly. In other words, any activities of the infringer that do not in themselves constitute infringements cannot form part of a claim for lost profits. For the purpose of the present case, that submission would disqualify the claim in respect of the CAD systems. They could be sold by the infringers without infringing any right of the patentees; they are not within section 60(2) and (3); at most they are what are called convoyed goods (or 'fellow travellers' as I would say), because they are commonly sold together with the patented product. The argument also extends to spare parts, servicing, and the springboard damages which relate to goods sold after the patent has expired.

...

Infringement of a patent is a statutory tort; and in the ordinary way one would expect the damages recoverable to be governed by the same rules as with many or most other torts. We were referred to *Halsbury's Laws of England* (4th edn) vol. 12 para. 1128 and following, to establish the elementary rules (i) that the overriding principle is that the victim should be restored to the position he would have been in if no wrong had been done, and (2) that the victim can recover loss which was (i) foreseeable, (ii) caused by the wrong, and (iii) not excluded from recovery by public or social policy. The requirement of causation is sometimes confused with foreseeability, which is remoteness. The two are different—see *Halsbury* para. 1141:

1141. *Causation in tort*. Subject to foreseeability and the principles of public policy it is *prima facie* necessary and sufficient for a plaintiff to prove that a defendant's wrongdoing was a cause and not necessarily the sole or dominant cause of his injuries, as a matter of physical

---

[72] E. Bonadio, 'Remedies and sanctions for the infringement of intellectual property rights under EC law' [2008] EIPR 320, 325.

consequences or common sense, but subsidiary principles associating foreseeability and causation have been evolved in certain categories of concurrent or intervening causes.

It is not enough that the loss would not have occurred *but for* the tort; the tort must (for present purposes at any rate) be, as a matter of common sense, a cause of the loss.

There is no dispute about foreseeability or causation in the present case. It is conceded that both requirements (if there are two) are satisfied. What is said is that either the general rules in *Halsbury* do not apply to the Patents Act, or else there is now a fourth limitation which must be satisfied.

That fourth limit is to be derived from the speech of Lord Hoffmann in *South Australia Asset Management Corporation v York Montague Ltd* [1996] 3 WLR 87 (aka the *Banque Bruxelles* case) at pages 92–194:

> Much of the discussion, both in the judgment of the Court of Appeal and in argument at the Bar, has assumed that the case is about the correct measure of damages for the loss which the lender has suffered.
>
> I think that this was the wrong place to begin. Before one can consider the principle on which one should calculate the damages to which a plaintiff is entitled as compensation for loss, it is necessary to decide for what kind of loss he is entitled to compensation. A correct description of the loss for which the valuer is liable must precede any consideration of the measure of damages. For this purpose it is better to begin at the beginning and consider the lender's cause of action.
>
> In the present case, there is no dispute that the duty was owed to the lenders. The real question in this case is the kind of loss in respect of which the duty was owed.
>
> How is the scope of the duty determined? In the case of a statutory duty, the question is answered by deducing the purpose of the duty from the language and context of the statute: *Gorris v Scott* (1874) LR 9 Ex 125. In the case of tort, it will similarly depend upon the purpose of the rule imposing the duty.
>
> Rules which make the wrongdoer liable for all the consequences of his wrongful conduct are exceptional and need to be justified by some special policy. Normally the law limits liability to those consequences which are attributable to that which made the act wrongful. In the case of liability in negligence for providing inaccurate information, this would mean liability for the consequences of the information being inaccurate.

My answer would be, at first impression, that the Patents Act is aimed at protecting patentees from commercial loss resulting from the wrongful infringement of their rights. That is only a slight gloss upon the wording of the statute itself. In my judgment, again as a matter of first impression, it does not distinguish between profit on the sale of patented articles and profit on the sale of convoyed goods. So I must look to see whether any such distinction emerges from the case law.

...

Viewing the cases as a whole, I cannot find any rule of law which limits the damages for infringement in a patent case in such a way as to exclude the loss claimed by the patentees in the present case. In *General Tire & Rubber Co v Firestone Tyre & Rubber Co Ltd* [1976] RPC 197 at page 214 Lord Wilberforce approved a passage in the judgment of Fletcher Moulton LJ in the *Meters* case which concluded:

> But I am not going to say a word which will tie down future judges and prevent them from exercising their judgment, as best they can in all the circumstances of the case, so as to arrive at that which the plaintiff has lost by reasons of the defendant doing certain acts wrongfully instead of either abstaining from doing them, or getting permission to do them rightfully.

> Beyond that the assessment of damages for infringement of a patent is in my judgment a question of fact. There is no dispute as to causation or remoteness in the present case; nor can I see any ground of policy for restricting the patentees' right to recover. It does not follow that, if customers were in the habit of purchasing a patented article at the patentee's supermarket, for example, he could claim against an infringer in respect of loss of profits on all the other items which the customers would buy in the supermarket but no longer bought. The limit there would be one of causation, or remoteness, or both. But the present appeal, in so far as it seeks to restrict the scope of recovery, should be dismissed.

When it comes to damages recoverable for infringement of IPRs general tort principles will apply. In the above case, therefore, damages were available in respect of the lost sales of CAD machines sold alongside the patented machines because this was a foreseeable loss caused by the defendant's infringing activities and there were no policy grounds for restricting the patentees' right to recover.

A similar conclusion was not reached, however, in *Claydon Architectural Metalwork Ltd v DJ Higgins & Sons Ltd*.[73] In this case the claimant sought damages against the defendant for infringement of its copyright and/or design right in drawings and designs for metalwork. As well as the primary loss of profit resulting from the copyright infringement, the claimant sought damages for the expense of repairing damage done to its cash flow. The defendant sought to strike out the claimant's claim for this consequential loss. The application was dismissed, but an appeal to Deputy Judge Mann QC was allowed. The judge distinguished *Gerber Garment* on the basis that it was factually very different and because the consequential losses were foreseeable.[74] Further, he stated that the 'law does not allow recovery where the damage alleged is beyond the scope of the protection afforded by the tort'[75] and that the practical result of a policy of allowing damages of the type sought by the claimant 'would be the unwarranted extension of the statutory protection to the owner's general business interest'.[76]

13.6.1.3 Innocent infringement

In relation to copyright, the sui generis database right, UK unregistered design, UK registered design and patent infringements, innocent infringers will be exempt from paying damages subject to certain conditions being met. No such exemption is available for infringement of the Community design rights or for trade mark infringement or passing off.

Section 97(1) of the CDPA stipulates that if, at the time of infringement, the defendant 'did not know or have reason to believe that copyright subsisted in the work to which the action relates' the claimant is not entitled to damages against him.[77] Importantly, the defendant's knowledge or lack thereof must relate to copyright *subsistence* as opposed to whether his or her behaviour was infringing in nature. As such, this is a limited defence. This point was made by Pumfrey J in *Nottinghamshire Healthcare National Health Service Trust v News Group Newspapers Ltd*[78] when he stated:

---

[73] [1997] FSR 475. [74] Ibid., p. 482. [75] Ibid., p. 480. [76] Ibid., p. 482.
[77] It is important to note that this provision does not appear to apply to infringement of moral rights, the remedies for which are set out in s. 103, CDPA.
[78] [2002] RPC, para. 49.

> It goes only to the defendant's knowledge whether copyright subsisted in the work. It is only available if on the facts it is reasonable to suppose that copyright did not subsist in the work. As a practical matter, this can only be the case where the work is old, or is of such a nature that copyright is unlikely to subsist in it.[79]

In *Infabrics Ltd v Jaytex Ltd*,[80] Buckley LJ suggested how the presence or absence of knowledge that copyright subsists in a work could be shown:

> No doubt every case must depend upon its own particular facts, but if no adequate inquiries or investigations are made, it must, it seems to me, be difficult to suppose that the person proposing to use the work has no grounds for suspecting that it may be subject to copyright.[81]

In other words, a defendant would have to make relevant inquiries to ascertain whether or not the work is subject to copyright.

With regards to the sui generis database right, regulation 23 of the Copyright and Rights in Databases Regulations 1997[82] stipulates that ss. 96–8 of the CDPA will apply 'in relation to database right and databases in which that right subsists as they apply in relation to copyright and copyright works'. Thus, a similar sort of approach should be taken when it comes to innocent infringement of the database right.

With regards to the UK unregistered design right, s. 233(1) of the CPDA provides that where 'at the time of the infringement the defendant did not know, and had no reason to believe, that design right subsisted in the design to which the action relates, the plaintiff is not entitled to damages against him'. This defence is similar in terms to the one discussed above for copyright and probably also similarly limited in scope. In addition, s. 233(2) of the CDPA states that where a claim of secondary infringement is brought against a defendant, if the infringing article was innocently acquired by him, 'the only remedy available against him in respect of the infringement is damages not exceeding a reasonable royalty in respect of the act complained of'. According to s. 233(3) of the CDPA an article is innocently acquired if the person acquiring it did not know and had no reason to believe that it was an infringing article. This has been characterized as an objective test[83] and, according to Laddie, Prescott, and Vitoria, is available:

> in a wider variety of circumstances than the equivalent defence to the primary infringer. It comes into operation where, for example, the infringer or one of his predecessors in title did not know or believe that an article was an infringing article because he did not know design right subsisted, or did not know that the article was an infringing copy or, if he did, he had reason to believe it was licensed. Only the first of these provides a defence for the primary infringer.[84]

However, the defence for primary infringers of the UK unregistered design right will provide a complete bar against damages, whereas the defence for secondary infringers will still lead to a claim of damages amounting to a reasonable royalty.

---

79 Ibid., para. 52 (p. 986). 80 [1980] Ch 282. 81 Ibid., p. 295. 82 SI 1997/3032.
83 *Badge Sales v PMS International Group Ltd* [2006] FSR 1, para. 8.
84 Laddie, Prescott, and Vitoria, *The Modern Law of Copyright & Designs* (3rd edn., London: Sweet & Maxwell, 2000), para. 39.45.

For innocent infringers of UK registered designs an exemption from damages *and* an order of account of profits was recently inserted into the RDA.[85] According to s. 24B(1) of the RDA, a defendant 'who proves that at the date of the infringement he was not aware, and had no reasonable ground for supposing, that the design was registered' shall not have damages or an account of profits awarded against him. Guidance as to what constitutes relevant knowledge is provided in s. 24B(2) of the RDA, which states that marking a product with the word 'registered' or any abbreviation thereof or with words expressing or implying that the design applied to, or incorporated in, the product has been registered, will not be enough to establish actual or constructive knowledge, *unless* the number of the design accompanied the word or words in question. It has been commented that the defence of innocent infringement for UK registered designs may offer more scope than that available for UK unregistered designs 'since the infringer may have to have some positive reason to suppose that the design is registered, or at least be engaged in an activity where it is a matter of prudent business practice for him to search the register'.[86]

There is no similar innocent infringement defence for the Community design rights (both unregistered and registered), as was made clear by the following case.

J Choo (Jersey) Ltd v Towerstone Ltd [2008] FSR 19

As we have seen,[87] in this case the claimant held a Community registered design for its 'Ramona' handbag and an unregistered Community design in a design document for the same handbag. It sought summary judgment against the defendants who sold similar bags that it had purchased from a third party. Floyd J held that the defendants had infringed both the Community registered and unregistered design rights and went on to consider whether the claimant was entitled to damages, or an account of profits, against them.

Floyd J:

24. The first defendants say that they are innocent infringers and had no reason to believe when they purchased the bags in question that they were infringing copies. The claimant does not accept this, but Ms Reid did not seriously suggest that it was an issue I could decide by way of summary judgment, if it is one which properly arises in law. Where the parties are divided is as to whether innocent infringement is a defence to damages at all.

25. The starting point is Council Regulation 6/2002 (the 2002 Regulation) directly applicable here. It relates to both registered and unregistered Community designs. Article 89 of the 2002 Regulation provides:

Sanctions in actions for infringement
1. Where in an action for infringement or for threatened infringement a Community design court finds that the defendant has infringed or threatened to infringe a Community design, it shall, unless there are special reasons for not doing so, order the following measures:
   (a) an order prohibiting the defendant from proceeding with the acts which have infringed or would infringe the Community design;

---

[85] Intellectual Property Enforcement Regulations 2006, SI 2006/1028.
[86] *Russell-Clarke and Howe on Industrial Designs* (7th edn., London: Sweet & Maxwell, 2005), para. 6–54.
[87] At 11.2.3.5.

(b) an order to seize the infringing products;

(c) an order to seize materials and implements predominantly used in order to manufacture the infringing goods, if their owner knew the effect for which such use was intended or if such effect would have been obvious in the circumstances;

(d) any order imposing other sanctions appropriate under the circumstances which are provided by the law of the Member State in which the acts of infringement or threatened infringement are committed, including its private international law.

2. The Community design court shall take such measures in accordance with its national law as are aimed at ensuring that the orders referred to in paragraph 1 are complied with.

26. The 2002 Regulation, therefore, does not directly require the court to give a remedy in damages at all. It requires the court, unless there are special reasons, to 'make any order imposing sanctions appropriate under the circumstances which are provided under the law of the Member State'.

27. There followed the EC Directive 2004/48 on The Enforcement of Intellectual Property Rights (the 2004 Directive). The Directive required by Art. 13:

Damages

Member States shall ensure that the competent judicial authorities, on application of the injured party, order the infringer who knowingly, or with reasonable grounds to know, engaged in an infringing activity, to pay the rightholder damages appropriate to the actual prejudice suffered by him as a result of the infringement. When the judicial authorities set the damages:

(a) they shall take into account all appropriate aspects, such as the negative economic consequences, including lost profits, which the injured party has suffered, any unfair profits made by the infringer and, in appropriate cases, elements other than economic factors, such as the moral prejudice caused to the rightholder by the infringement;

or

(b) as an alternative to (a), they may, in appropriate cases, set the damages as a lump sum on the basis of elements such as at least the amount of royalties or fees which would have been due if the infringer had requested authorisation to use the intellectual property right in question.

2. Where the infringer did not knowingly, or with reasonable grounds to know, engage in infringing activity, Member States may lay down that the judicial authorities may order the recovery of profits or the payment of damages, which may be pre-established.

28. Paragraph 1 is mandatory. It requires damages to be recoverable where there is knowing infringement. Paragraph 2 is discretionary. Member States may also provide for damages to be available against innocent infringers.

29. Next comes the United Kingdom's own Community Design Regulations 2005 SI 2005/2339. As originally enacted these had no provisions about damages, but the Intellectual Property Enforcement Regulations 2006 SI 2006/1028 (the 2006 Regulations) inserted a para. 1A as follows:

Infringement Proceedings

(1) This regulation and regulations 1B to 1D are without prejudice to the duties of the Community design court under the provisions of Article 89(1)(a) to (c) of the Community Design Regulation.

(2) In an action for infringement of a Community design all such relief by way of damages, injunctions, accounts or otherwise is available to the holder of the Community design as is available in respect of the infringement of any other property right.

30. At the same time the 2006 Regulations made provisions for an amendment to our domestic Registered Designs Act by inserting a s. 24B:

...

31. Of course, in the Registered Designs Act, as so amended, the reference to a design is to a design registered under that Act, i.e. a UK-registered design. On the face of it, therefore, the 2006 Regulations, by the amendments which it effected, gave an innocent infringer a specific defence if he proves certain facts in the case of infringement of a UK-registered design. In contrast, this court can grant all such relief by way of damages for infringement of a Community design as is available for infringement of any other property right.

32. Mr Bartlett argues that Parliament cannot have intended such an odd result. Whilst it is entirely reasonable that the legislature could have decided to implement Art. 10 of the 2004 Directive by allowing damages against an innocent infringer, it is odd in the extreme that it should do so in respect of a Community registered design but not in respect of a UK registered design. He says that the only other options are that Parliament has made a mistake and enacted something which it cannot have intended—an unpalatable result—or that it thought, correctly, that the effect of the provisions it was enacting in the two cases would, in practice, be the same. He says, in these circumstances, that either s. 24B as inserted into The Registered Design Act 1949 applies directly, or, alternatively, there is no provision which deals with the question of innocent infringement. In those circumstances, he says one goes back to Art. 89(1)(d) and relies on the words 'appropriate under the circumstances' as giving the court power to refuse damages in a case comparable to a case under s. 24B.

33. I agree with Mr Bartlett that there is no possible policy reason for giving an innocent infringement defence to the infringer of the national right whilst denying it to the infringer of the Community right. But that, it seems to me, is precisely what the legislature has done. I cannot see any way in which one can apply s. 24B directly, nor can I accede to Mr Bartlett's ingenious, 'appropriate in the circumstances', argument. It is national law which must provide the sanction appropriate in the circumstances. The sanction ultimately provided is to provide for damages on the same basis as any other property right. It is that sanction that the court must apply unless there are special reasons, and none are provided here.

34. Moreover, when the 2004 Directive came to be translated into English law, the legislature knew that it had to make a clear choice between allowing damages generally and allowing them only for knowing infringement. It chose the former in the case of Community design right and the latter in the case of UK-registered design. I cannot accept that the legislature thought that it was introducing some kind of discretionary right to damages for infringement of Community design right.

35. The position is even clearer in respect of unregistered design right when Mr Bartlett accepts that a relevant comparison is the United Kingdom unregistered design right...

36. Thus, there is an innocence defence for primary infringers ('makers' under s. 233(1)) which requires the defendant to prove innocence that the design right subsisted and for secondary infringers under s. 233(2) where damages are restricted to a reasonable royalty if the defendant can show 'innocent acquisition'. It is impossible to suppose that the legislature thought this regime should apply to unregistered Community design right which is infringed under Art. 19 of the 2002 Regulation by making or dealing in the article, irrespective of the state of knowledge of the defendant.

37. It therefore seems to me that there is no defence of innocent infringement provided for in the legislation in respect of registered or unregistered Community design. It follows that the claimant is entitled to an enquiry as to damages or, at its option, an account of profits for infringement of both registered and non-registered design right.

The above case acknowledges a clear disparity between UK designs law and Community designs law when it comes to innocent infringement. Is this a desirable situation? If not, what should be done to create a uniform approach?

When it comes to patent infringement, s. 62(1) of the PA 77 provides that damages shall not be awarded and no order shall be made for an account of profits where the defendant proves that at the date of infringement he was not aware and had no reasonable grounds for supposing that the patent existed. Knowledge is not to be imputed by reason only of applying the word 'patent' or 'patented' to a product or any word or words expressing or implying that a patent has been obtained for the product, unless the number of the patent accompanies the word or words in question.

13.6.2 ADDITIONAL DAMAGES

For both copyright and the UK unregistered design right, the CDPA[88] provides that courts may award additional damages as the justice of the case may require. The court must have regard to all the circumstances and, in particular, the flagrancy of the infringement and any benefit accruing to the defendant by reason of the infringement.

The nature of additional damages, in particular whether they are compensatory or punitive, has been a controversial issue that has not been resolved by UK courts. There is some authority to suggest, however, that they are compensatory in nature.

Nottinghamshire Healthcare National Health Service Trust v News Group Newspapers Ltd [2002] RPC 49

The claimant owned copyright in a photograph of a patient at Rampton Hospital, which formed part of the patient's confidential medical records. A copy of the photograph had been leaked to a regional reporter for the defendant's newspaper, *The Sun*. It was subsequently published in the newspaper alongside a sensationalist article concerning a letter sent by the patient to an employee of McDonalds that he encountered when on an escorted rehabilitation visit. The claimant sued for infringement and claimed an injunction and damages. It also sought additional damages and claimed that these should include a substantial punitive element.

Pumfrey J:

42. The nature of the damages to be awarded under section 97(2) has been expressly left open by the House of Lords in *Redrow Homes Ltd v Bett Brothers plc* (above). Laddie J had expressed the view that it was sui generis in *Cala Homes* (above). Laddie J's conclusion in this regard was not discussed by the House of Lords in *Redrow Homes* although he was overruled on the principal point in the case, the question whether an account of profits and an award of damages under section 97(2) could be made simultaneously. Lord Jauncey declined to express a view on the question whether 'additional damages are by nature punitive or purely compensatory'. Lord Clyde, following the terminology of *Rookes v Barnard* left open the question whether 'the character of an award of damages under section 97(2) is defined as exemplary damages, or, more probably, aggravated damages'. There is no Court of Appeal authority on the point, although an award of additional damages has been upheld by the Court of Appeal in *MCA Records Inc v Charly Records Ltd* [2001] EWCA Civ 1441, [2002]

---

[88] s. 97(1), CDPA for copyright, and s. 229(3), CDPA for UK unregistered design right.

EMLR 1 at paragraphs 63ff. Neuberger J was confronted with this question in *O'Mara Books v Express Newspapers* [1999] FSR 49, but did not express a concluded view:

> It is an open question whether damages awarded pursuant to section 97(2) of the 1988 Act…are exemplary damages or aggravated damages or, as I am inclined to think, a separate category of damages which may have some features which are similar to those of exemplary or aggravated damages.

43. The correct characterisation of damages under section 97(2) was also left open by Hirst LJ in *ZYX Music GmbH v King* [1997] 2 All ER 129 at 147…

...

45. Finally, among the cases I should mention the decision of Ferris J in *Springsteen v Flute International* [1999] EMLR. 180. Ferris J found flagrant infringement, but that the infringement was not particularly beneficial to the defendant. He awarded additional damages, at a provisional rate of £1 per compact disc manufactured but not sold and £5 per compact disc sold. He is not explicit on the basis of the award. His judgment was not appealed on this point.

46. It is settled that aggravated damages are compensatory in their nature, but exemplary damages are not. No starting point is available for the computation of an exemplary award, other than the court's practice in respect of fines.

...

48. Section 97 identifies two factors in particular as matters to which (among all the circumstances of the case) the court must have attention in considering whether to award additional damages, the flagrancy of the infringement and the benefit to the defendant. I consider that if benefit to the defendant is to be a factor relevant to an award of such additional damages as 'the justice of the case may require', that is a strong suggestion that those damages may include a restitutionary element. It echoes Lord Devlin's second category of exemplary damages, whose purpose is to teach the defendant that 'tort does not pay'. The reference to the flagrancy of the infringement does not seem to me necessarily to suggest that an award of additional damages may include a punitive or exemplary element, since it seems to me to be primarily concerned with the question whether the infringement was deliberate. Flagrancy has been described by Brightman J in *Ravenscroft v Herbert* [1980] RPC 193 at 208 as implying 'scandalous conduct, deceit and suchlike; it includes deliberate and calculated infringement'.

49. It should also be noted that the CDPA provides its own criminal offences. Section 107 provides for offences which may be summarised as knowing infringement of copyright by sale or manufacture and knowing possession of articles for making infringements. Different penalties are provided for different offences, and the maximum is an unlimited fine and two years' imprisonment on conviction on indictment.

50. The textbooks differ in their views. Copinger and Skone James (14th Edn.) regards the point as arguable. Laddie, Prescott & Vitoria (3rd Edn.) suggests that the discretion under section 97(2) is a wide one, subject to the single qualification that an award of damages whose sole purpose is to punish the defendant is not permissible under the section.

51. In my view, there are good reasons to think that the approach of the editors of Laddie, Prescott & Vitoria is right. There is no reason why a purely punitive, or exemplary, element in an award of damages should be appropriate, given that there is a relevant statutory offence and that the infringer might in a case of concurrent copyrights (as in the case of a counterfeiter of compact discs, for example) be exposed to successive actions by the owners of the different, copyrights each seeking punishment in respect of their interest…the section is

drafted in the widest terms and, although it is not concerned with punitive damages, it permits, in my judgment, an aggravation at common law. In particular, it permits an element of restitution having regard to the benefit gained by the defendant, and I should envisage such an award being made where the normal compensation to the claimant leaves the defendant still enjoying the fruits of his infringement. Such an award overlaps with the alternative remedy of an enquiry as to damages to some extent, but it is not co-extensive with it. In particular, it permits benefit to the defendant which forms no part of the financial profits to be taken into account, as for example in a case where the defendant has established himself in the market and generated a goodwill by a flagrant infringement. Furthermore, the fact that the flagrancy of the infringement, with its overtones of dishonesty and intentional wrongdoing, is one of the factors specifically mentioned may well entitle the court to deal with the question of damages as it would in other cases of intentional wrong-doing:

...

52. I conclude that the provisions of section 97(2) are apt to provide for a measure of damages appropriate in cases of deliberate infringement. The section does not, in terms, provide that additional damages are to be awarded only in cases of deliberate infringement...carelessness sufficiently serious to amount to an attitude of 'couldn't care less' is in my judgment capable of aggravating infringement and of founding an award of damages under section 97(2). Recklessness can be equated to deliberation for this purpose.

Pumfrey J went on to award £450 in damages and £10,000 in additional damages. In arriving at the latter figure, Pumfrey J took into account the flagrancy of the infringement, the fact that the photograph was obviously stolen and would have appeared so to the reporter, the defendant's conduct in the case, the lack of apology for the photograph's use, and the degree of upset caused at the hospital.

Knowingly infringing the claimant's copyright will not necessarily lead to an award of additional damages, unless the infringement is cynical in nature. An example of cynical infringement could be where the defendant infringes, having calculated that paying compensatory damages for infringement is more cost-effective than obtaining a licence (particularly where the claimant has clearly refused a licence).[89] However, infringing activities in reliance on a well-based belief that a licence agreement will be reached has not been characterized as cynical infringement warranting an award of additional damages.[90]

When a claimant has successfully obtained summary judgement, an assessment of additional damages may not be possible unless the defendant has had an opportunity to put in evidence factors that might be relevant to this assessment.[91]

FURTHER READING

C. Michalos, 'Copyright and punishment: The nature of additional damages' [2000] EIPR 470.

Laddie, Prescott, and Vitoria, *The Modern Law of Copyright & Designs* (London: Sweet & Maxwell, 2000), para 39.42.

---

[89] *Ludlow Music Inc v Williams* [2002] FSR 57, para. 53.
[90] This was the case in *Ludlow Music Inc v Williams* [2002] FSR 57, paras. 57–9.
[91] *Michael O'Mara Books Ltd v Express Newspapers Plc* [1999] FSR 49.

13.6.3 EXEMPLARY DAMAGES

The predecessor to s. 97(1) of the CDPA, discussed in the previous section, was s. 17(3) of the Copyright Act 1956. It was believed by some that s. 17(3) introduced a statutory form of exemplary damages.[92] However, there was authority to suggest that it was in fact a statutory form of aggravated damages.[93] As we have seen in the previous section, there has been debate about whether s. 97(1) of the CDPA is compensatory or punitive in nature and the current view appears to be that it is the former. As such, it is unlikely that the provision will be seen as incorporating a statutory form of exemplary damages.[94] An award of exemplary damages may nonetheless be available as part of the court's inherent jurisdiction. According to the House of Lords decision in *Kuddus v Chief Constable of Leicestershire Constabulary*[95] a court may award exemplary damages where the defendant's behaviour amounts to oppressive, arbitrary, or unconstitutional action by the servants of the government; or where the defendant's conduct has been calculated by him to make a profit for himself which may well exceed the compensation payable to the claimant.[96] In the field of intellectual property infringements is it desirable for courts to be able to exercise this inherent jurisdiction?

13.6.4 ACCOUNT OF PROFITS

A claimant may seek, as an *alternative* to damages, an order for an account of profits.[97] This is an equitable remedy and thus it is within the court's discretion whether to order it or not. An account of profits differs from damages in that it calculates the gain made by the defendant as a result of the infringing behaviour, as opposed to the loss caused to the claimant. The different focus of an account of profits, as compared with an award of damages, was considered in the case below.

Celanese International Corp v BP Chemicals Ltd [1999] RPC 203

The patent in suit concerned a method for manufacturing a form of acetic acid that was free of iodide impurities. The patent had been found valid and infringed by the defendants and the claimants claimed an account of profits. A settlement having been reached with the second defendant, the account proceeded with respect to the first defendant. The claimants contended that if the court could not apportion profits relating to the infringement then all profits should be paid over by the defendant or, at least, 20 per cent

---

[92] Copyright Committee of 1952, Cmnd 8662, para. 294.

[93] *Rookes v Barnard* [1964] AC 1129, 1225, per Lord Devlin; *Williams v Settle* [1960] 2 All ER 806; *Beloff v Pressdram Ltd*, at 65.

[94] See also Laddie, Prescott, and Vitoria, *The Modern Law of Copyright & Designs* (3rd edn., London: Sweet & Maxwell, London, 2000), para. 39.43.

[95] [2002] 2 AC 122, 130, and 134, per Lord Slynn; 138 and 140, per Lord Mackay; 145, per Lord Nicholls; 150, per Lord Hutton.

[96] See *Rookes v Barnard* [1964] 1 AC 1129, 1225–6 per Lord Devlin, as followed in *Kuddus v Chief Constable of Leicestershire Constabulary* [2002] 2 AC 122, 130 and 135, per Lord Slynn; 140, per Lord Mackay; 150, per Lord Hutton.

[97] See s. 96(2), CDPA for copyright; s. 229(2), CDPA for UK unregistered design right; s. 24A(2), RDA for UK registered designs; reg. 1A, CDRs for Community registered and unregistered designs; s. 14(2), TMA 1994 for trade marks; s. 61(1)(d) and 61(2), PA 77 for patents; and at 8.6.2 above for confidence.

of all profits. The defendant argued for an incremental approach, based on the difference between the profits received by use of the patented process and the profits which would have been achieved without using the patented process. Laddie J dealt with the general principles applicable to an account of profits.

Laddie J:

35. A plaintiff who is successful in patent litigation has an entitlement to elect between damages and an account. The differences between them are considerable. Where the plaintiff seeks damages, the purpose of the inquiry is to determine what loss he has actually suffered. That loss may far exceed any gain made by the infringer through the infringing activity. Furthermore if the activity of the defendant infringes different rights held by different plaintiffs, he will have to compensate them all for the damage they have suffered. In this respect there is no upper limit on the compensation he may have to pay. The more damage he inflicts, the greater the financial burden imposed on him. In working out *quantum* the court has to determine what acts of infringement have been committed (an issue which may have been resolved on the trial as to liability) and what damage has been caused, in the legal sense, by them...

36. An account of profits is very different. Instead of looking to the harm inflicted on the plaintiff it considers the profit made by the infringer. The defendant is treated as if he conducted his business and made profits on behalf of the plaintiff. A number of consequences flow from this. One of them is that the maximum payment which can be ordered is the total profit made by the defendant. It may be that that figure far exceeds the damage suffered by the plaintiff as was pointed out in *Colburn v Simms* (1843) 2 Hare 543. The hope of obtaining more is the normal reason why plaintiffs elect an account in those comparatively rare cases in which they do so. Furthermore there is only one profits 'pot'. If different plaintiffs seek accounts in respect of different infringing activities of a defendant within a single business, the totality of the profits ordered to be paid should not exceed the total profits made by the defendant in that business...

37. Although an account may give rise to a very different figure to that on an inquiry as to damages, they both proceed on a common principle of legal causation. On an inquiry the court is trying to determine what damage has been caused, in a legal sense, by the defendant's wrongful acts. It has to decide whether the breach was the cause of the loss or merely the occasion of it (see for example *Galoo v Bright Grahame Murray* [1994] 1 WLR 1360). In an account the court is trying to determine what profits have been caused, in a legal sense, by those acts. This was stated expressly by the Canadian Federal Court of Appeal in *Imperial Oil v Lubrizol* [1996] 71 CPR (3d) 26 at 30: 'Just as in a reference on a claim for damages issues of fact relating to causality and remoteness may properly be explored, so may they be likewise on an accounting of profits...It may be possible for Imperial to show that some part of the profits made on the infringing sales are not profits "arising from" the infringement in that they are not caused by but made on the occasion of such infringement.'

38. One consequence of this is that where the defendant carries on multiple businesses or sells different products and only one infringes, he only has to compensate the plaintiff for the damage inflicted by the infringements or he only has to account for the profits made by the infringements...As Lord Watson said in *United Horse Shoe and Nail v Stewart* (1888) 5 RPC 260, it would be unreasonable to give the patentee profits which were not earned by use of his invention.

39. A further consequence of these common principles is that it should be no answer to an account that the defendant could have made the same profits by following an alternative, non-infringing course. The question to be answered is 'what profits were in fact made by

the defendant by the wrongful activity?'. It should not matter that similar profits could have been made in another, non-infringing way.

...

42. If this is right, it cuts both ways. Just as the defendant cannot reduce the profits by saying that he could have made all or most of them if he had taken a non-infringing course, so also the plaintiff must take the defendant as he finds him. He cannot increase the profits by saying that the defendant could and should have generated higher profits: see *Dart Industries v Décor Corp Pty Ltd* [1994] FSR 567 at 590.

43. Although the infringer cannot avoid paying over profits by relying on possible non-infringing alternatives, the patentee, as noted above, cannot recover profits which were not earned by use of his invention.

...

47. Sometimes the court may come to the conclusion that all the profits are attributable to the act of infringement. That is what Pennycuick J did in *Peter Pan*. There the whole of the defendant's brassieres were made by misuse of the plaintiff's confidential information. Without it brassieres to that design would not have existed. No apportionment was appropriate. Similarly, the court may come to the conclusion, as a matter of fact, that the invention was the essential ingredient in the creation of the defendant's whole product or process. If so, it may be appropriate not to apportion. See *Dart Industries v Décor Corp*.

48. However, once it is conceded or proved that an apportionment is appropriate, the course must do its best to split the profits between infringing and non-infringing parts. A particularly clear example of this is the architect's copyright case, *Potton v Yorkclose*. Although Millett J held that all the profits made as a result of constructing 14 infringing houses were to be paid to the plaintiff, he explained that this did not mean that all profits realised by the defendants through sale of them had to be handed over. He said at page 16 that it would be necessary, for example, to exclude any part of the profits which may be attributable to (i) the purchase, landscaping and sale of the land on which the houses were built; (ii) any increase in value of the houses themselves during the interval, if any, between the completion of the infringing building works and the sale; and (iii) the advertising, marketing and selling of the houses. In addition, the defendants claimed that they had done much work, such as installing kitchen equipment, which had nothing to do with the plaintiffs' drawings and did not reproduce them in any sense. Millett J decided at page 18 that if on taking the account these assertions were shown to be true and if such work could sensibly be distinguished from the admitted infringing acts of constructing the houses, then any part of the profits properly attributable to it ought to be excluded.

...

51. In deciding whether the defendant has to account for all or only a part of the profits made on a particular venture, I respectfully agree with the view expressed by the Canadian Federal Court of Appeal in *Imperial Oil v Lubrizol* that this is a matter of fact and that form must not be allowed to triumph over substance.

...

53. Even when an apportionment is required, it may be no easy matter to decide precisely what proportion of the profits should be attributed to the acts of infringement. This was considered in *Potton*:

It is said that in one case, faced with the impossible task of apportioning the profits of a book between those parts which infringed copyright and those which did not, the master cut out the offending passages with a pair of scissors and weighed them in the scales against the rest of the book. This method, I fancy, has nothing to commend it except literary precedent (see: Aristophanes *The Frogs* lines 1387 *et seq.*). Fortunately it would not be available in the present case. I do not think that I can do more than give some general guidance without intending to bind the master. Generally speaking, however, in a case like the present the profits ought not in my view to be apportioned by reference to evidence of or speculation about the motives of real or hypothetical purchasers or the relative attractions to such purchasers of different aspects of the work. A better guide is likely to be provided by ordinary accounting principles whereby, in the absence of some special reason to the contrary, the profits of a single project are attributed to different parts or aspects of the project in the same proportions as the costs and expenses are attributed to them. It should, however, also be borne in mind that, as Slade J said in *My Kinda Town Limited v Soll* at page 58, what is required on an inquiry of this kind is not mathematical exactness but a reasonable approximation. ([1990] FSR 11 at 18)

54. By this method the whole project 'cake', the size of which is determined by its costs and expenses, is divided into slices. It is only the profit icing on the infringing slice (the relative size of which is also measured by reference to its relevant costs and expenses) for which the defendant has to account.

Having read the above extract, what do you see as the advantages and disadvantages of opting for an account of profits, as opposed to an award of damages?

Importantly, a claimant may not seek both an award of damages *and* an order for an account of profits, but must choose between them. How that choice is to be made is considered in the following case.

Island Records Ltd v Tring International Plc [1996] 1 WLR 1256

The claimant was the owner of copyright in sound recordings that contained performances of the musical works of Cat Stevens. The claimant alleged that the defendant had infringed copyright in its sound recordings and sought an injunction restraining further infringement, an order for delivery up of infringing copies, an inquiry as to damages for infringement, and in the alternative an account of profits. The claimant brought a motion for judgement and it was common ground that the claimant was entitled to judgement. However, there was an issue as to when the claimant would have to elect between damages or an account of profits. The claimant contended that it should not be required to elect until it could make an informed choice, whereas the defendant argued that the election had to be made at the hearing of the motion.

Lightman J, at pp. 1258–60:

In proceedings in which the plaintiff claims in the alternative damages or an account of profits, the plaintiff may seek and obtain a trial at which will be determined all issues of liability, of the assessment of damages and of calculation of profits. In such a case full discovery will include all documents relevant to the assessment and calculation, and the plaintiff can make an informed election between damages and profits in the course of the trial in the light of the information revealed on discovery and in the evidence at the trial. With a view to the saving of costs, the practice has developed, in particular in intellectual property cases, when this is practicable, to have a 'split trial'. The action is divided into two stages. The first stage is the trial at which the issue is limited to that of liability, i.e. whether the plaintiff's rights have been infringed. The second stage, which is contingent upon liability being established at the first stage, is concerned with the question of assessment of damages and calculation of profits. In this way, the costs of exploring the issue of damages and profits are put off until it is clear that the defendant is liable and the issue really arises and requires determination. As a concomitant with this practice, there has likewise developed the practice of limiting discovery at the first stage to documents relevant to the issue of liability and excluding documents relevant only to the second stage. In this way the burden of discovery at the first stage is reduced, and the invasion of confidence necessarily involved in discovery is postponed and (if liability is not established) entirely obviated: see *Baldock v Addison* [1995] 1 WLR 158…The price at which this cost and time saving is achieved is that the plaintiff will not before judgment at the first stage on the issue of liability have the benefit by means of discovery or otherwise of the information otherwise available on which the plaintiff is able to make an informed election as to remedy between an assessment of damages and an account of profits. The question which arises is whether in this situation (as in the case of a motion for judgment where likewise the plaintiff is deprived of the opportunity to obtain such information before judgment) in the course or at the conclusion of the hearing the plaintiff must elect between the two remedies or is entitled first to sufficient information to make an informed election.

Four principles are clear. First, whilst a plaintiff can apply in proceedings in the alternative for damages and an account of profits, he cannot obtain judgment for both: he can only obtain judgment for one or the other: see *Neilson v Betts* (1871) LR 5 HL 1 and *De Vitre v Betts* (1873) LR 6 HK 319, 321. Second, once judgment has been entered either for damages or an account of profits, any right of election is lost: any claim to the remedy other than that for which judgment is entered is forever lost: see *United Australia Ltd v Barclays Bank Ltd* [1941] AC 1, 30. Third, a party should in general not be required to elect or be found to have elected between remedies unless and until he is able to make an informed choice. A right of election, if it is to be meaningful and not a mere gamble, must embrace the right to readily available information as to his likely entitlement in case of both the two alternative remedies. It is quite unreasonable to require the plaintiff to speculate totally in the dark as to whether or not the sum recoverable by way of damages will exceed that recoverable under an account of profits. In an analogous situation, it has been held unreasonable to require a plaintiff to speculate whether a payment into court is sufficient to satisfy his claim for damages for infringement of copyright before he has been afforded inspection of the records of sales in the defendant's books: see *Mate & Son v Samuel Stephen Ltd* [1928–1935] Mac CC 257, 261. Fourth, the exercise of the right of election should not be unreasonably delayed to the prejudice of the defendant.

The question raised is whether the court can adopt a procedure which reconciles the four principles and enables a plaintiff who has established the liability of the defendant and his right to elect between remedies to secure the wherewithal to make an informed election before thereafter with reasonable promptitude committing himself to either remedy. The need for such procedure is made the more acute by the desirability of supporting the practice of limited discovery in case of split trials and of encouraging a plaintiff who is so entitled to enter judgment at an early stage in the proceedings (thereby saving court time and costs). Whilst it is true that there is no English authority where such a procedure has been adopted or even hinted at, I think that it is open to the court to develop such a procedure and that it is just and convenient that it should do so.

…

In my view, the court can at the split trial or on any other application for judgment be invited to defer entry of judgment for damages or profits. At this stage the court may either make no order as to the remedy for infringement (as in the *Minnesota* case) or (as I would prefer) may grant a declaration that the plaintiff is entitled at his election to judgment for either. The court may at the same time or thereafter give directions which secure that such information as is available and is reasonably required to enable the plaintiff to make an informed election (and accordingly is necessary for fairly disposing of the cause or matter: see Ord. 24, rr. 8 and 13(1)) is made available to him and that the election is made within a reasonable time thereafter. To secure that the plaintiff has the required information, the court may direct discovery, but if the information may be made available by some other satisfactory means (e.g. in an affidavit by the defendant or by way of audited accounts or reports) the court may hold that the alternative means be adopted. The court should not be deterred from this course by the fact that the information required may likewise be required on the taking of an account or an assessment. There should be no over-lengthy or unnecessarily sophisticated exercise. The plaintiff is not entitled to know exactly the amount of any damages or profits to which he is entitled, but only to such information as the court considers to be a fair basis in the circumstances of the particular case for an election.

Lightman J resolved the dilemma of claimants making an informed choice about whether to opt for an account of profits or damages, without having had the benefit of full discovery, by holding that a court can order the defendant to make available to the claimant such information that is reasonably required to enable an informed choice to be made. Further, to order claimants to make their choice about whether to elect for an account of profits or damages within a reasonable time thereafter. Subsequent cases have considered how much information a defendant should have to provide in order for the claimant to make its election. In *Brugger v Medicaid*,[98] Jacob J (as he then was) sought to strike an appropriate balance between what the claimant needed to make a choice and the burden placed on the defendant. He concluded that:

it is sufficient for an informed election to be made that the defendants should supply an affidavit setting forth the numbers of infringing devices made and sold, the sums received or receivable and an approximate estimate of the costs incurred, that approximate estimate to include a statement as to how the estimate was made.[99]

13.7 DELIVERY UP AND DISPOSAL

13.7.1 DELIVERY UP

A statutory remedy exists for the delivery up of articles which infringe copyright,[100] UK unregistered design right,[101] UK registered design right,[102] the Community design rights,[103] patents,[104] or trade marks.[105]

In relation to trade marks, s. 16 of the TMA states that the registered trade mark proprietor may 'apply to the court for an order for delivery up to him, or such other person as the court may direct, of any infringing goods, material or articles, which a person has in his possession, custody or control in the course of business'. Similarly, s. 61(1)(b) of the PA 77 provides that the proprietor of a patent may apply for an order for an infringer to deliver up 'any patented product in relation to which the patent is infringed or any article in which that product is inextricably comprised'. Normally, the order requires the delivery up of these goods which are in the UK and within the defendant's possession, custody, power, or control

---

98 [1996] FSR 362.   99 Ibid., at p. 364.   100 CDPA, s. 99.   101 CDPA, s. 2301(1).
102 RDA, s. 24C.   103 CDRs, reg 1B.   104 PA 77, s. 61(1)(b).   105 TMA, s. 16.

on the day that the order is made, even where there is a delay between the granting of the order and the date of judgment.[106]

An order for delivery up is available in the case of copyright[107] where a person has an infringing copy of a work in his possession, custody, or control in the course of business[108] and, in the case of the various design rights, where a person 'has in his possession, custody or control for commercial purposes an infringing article'.[109] The circumstances giving rise to a delivery-up order are broader when it comes to copyright and the UK and Community unregistered and registered design rights. This is because the order is also available where a person has in his possession, custody, or control an article specifically designed or adapted for making copies of a particular copyright work, or anything specifically designed or adapted for making articles to a particular design, knowing or having reason to believe that it has been or is to be used to make infringing copies or infringing articles. This would seem to cover 'moulds, transfers or printing plates intended for making infringing articles, but would not cover general purpose machinery which could make infringing articles but which could make non-infringing articles as well'.[110] The delivery up will be to the owner of copyright or the relevant design right or to such other person as the court may direct.

13.7.2 DISPOSAL

The provisions on delivery up must be considered together with those dealing with the destruction, forfeiture, or other disposal of infringing goods or articles. Where infringing goods or articles have been delivered up pursuant to a delivery-up order, an application may be made to the court for an order that they be destroyed or otherwise dealt with as the court thinks fit or forfeited to the owner of the relevant intellectual property right (or in the case of trade marks, to such person as the court may think fit).[111] In the case of patents, however, an order for destruction may be sought as an alternative to an order for delivery up.[112] Relevant to the courts' discretion whether to order destruction or forfeiture of infringing goods or articles is whether other remedies are available in an action for infringement and whether these would be adequate to compensate the owner and protect his interests. Forfeiture, rather than destruction, may be sought where the infringing goods are genuine articles but are parallel imports in which certain rights have not been exhausted.[113]

In the case of copyright, where an infringing copy of a work is exposed or otherwise immediately available for sale or hire, and an owner would be entitled to an order for delivery up, the owner or his representative may seize and detain the infringing copy, according to s. 100 of the CDPA. This is subject to certain conditions being met. First, notice of the time and place of the proposed seizure must be given to a local police station. Second, the

---

[106] *Mayne Pharma v Pharmacia Italia* [2005] EWCA Civ 294.

[107] Note that it is also available in criminal proceedings—see s. 108, CDPA.   [108] CDPA, s. 99(1).

[109] s. 24C(1)(a), RDA; reg 1B, CDRs; s. 230(1), CDPA. 'Commercial purposes' is defined as acts being done with a view to the article in question being sold or hired in the course of business: s. 24C(7), RDA; reg 1B(7), CDRs.

[110] *Russell-Clarke and Howe on Industrial Designs* (7th edn., London: Sweet & Maxwell, 2005), para. 6–65.

[111] s. 19, TMA (trade marks); s. 231, CPDA (UK unregistered design right); s. 114, CDPA (copyright); s. 24D, RDA (UK registered designs); reg. 1C, CDRs (Community unregistered and registered designs).

[112] PA 77, s. 61(1)(b).

[113] J. Phillips, *Trade Mark Law: A practical anatomy* (Oxford: Oxford University Press, 2007), para. 14.100.

right may be exercised in relation to premises which are publicly accessible, and not private premises nor at a permanent or regular place of business. Third, force may not be used. Fourth, a notice in the prescribed form is left at the place where the seizure occurred. Finally, the goods must actually be infringing, as opposed to only suspected of being infringing.

13.8 CRIMINAL PENALTIES

Intellectual property infringements may in certain circumstances give rise to criminal penalties and it is possible for either the state to institute criminal proceedings or for an individual to instigate a private prosecution. The ability to bring criminal proceedings was introduced in the 19th century in fairly limited circumstances.[114] Since that time, criminal penalties have been expanded, frequently in response to pressure from rightsholders wishing to deter wide-scale piracy and counterfeiting.

We begin by considering the rationale for criminalizing infringements of certain IPRs (in particular copyright and trade mark) and then turn to consider the advantages and disadvantages of bringing criminal proceedings, the circumstances in which criminal penalties are available and the existing proposal to harmonize criminal enforcement of IPRs in the European Community.

13.8.1 RATIONALE

The criminal prosecution of infringements of IPRs may lead to severe consequences, such as fines and even imprisonment; therefore, it is important to explore the reasons for criminalizing such behaviour in the first place.

Geraldine Moohr has suggested that, 'a decision to criminalize conduct that was previously subject only to civil remedies depends on identifying some component of harmfulness or immorality'.[115] The notion of harm is linked to consequentialism, in that the justification for criminalizing conduct is that it may prevent future harmful conduct through its potential deterrence value,[116] whereas immorality is tied to retributivism, namely that it is 'appropriate to treat conduct as criminal when it is morally wrong'.[117] In relation to copyright, Moohr argues that harm may occur to the copyright holder where infringements are carried out by competitors or those acting for commercial gain.[118] There may also be harm to the copyright policy of providing incentives to create, although Moohr is sceptical about whether criminalization successfully tackles this type of harm given that lawful users are likely to be dissuaded from building upon existing copyright material for fear of being penalized.[119]

In terms of the immoral nature of acts of copyright infringement, Moohr notes that, '[i]nfringement is sometimes presented as immoral because it is like stealing: infringement is then per se immoral. The reasoning is that the material protected by copyright is

---

[114] In relation to trade marks, see Merchandise Marks Act 1862. In relation to music copyright, see the Musical (Summary Proceedings) Copyright Act 1902, as amended by the Musical Copyright Act 1906.

[115] G. S. Moohr, 'The crime of copyright infringement: An inquiry based on morality, harm and moral theory' (2003) 83 Boston Univ LR 731, 752.

[116] Ibid., pp. 749–51.   [117] Ibid., pp. 747–9.   [118] Ibid., p. 755.   [119] Ibid., pp. 758–61.

a kind of property.'[120] Although Moohr recognizes the rhetorical force of this argument, she rejects it for several reasons, including the fact that viewing copyright as property does not acknowledge the significant ways in which copyright is limited. Further, it does not explain why other intellectual property right infringements, especially patent ones, are not criminal. Finally, the property argument 'assumes what is at issue, which is whether the taking is immoral (or harmful) and therefore subject to criminal treatment'.[121] Moohr also argues that there is an absence of strong community norms that regard certain types of infringement—namely, personal, unauthorized use of copyrighted material—as sufficiently immoral to warrant criminal sanctions.[122]

Alternative justifications for enforcing IPRs via the criminal law, albeit in the context of harmonizing this type of enforcement in the European Community, are proffered in the Explanatory Memorandum to the Proposed Directive on criminal measures aimed at ensuring the enforcement of intellectual property rights:[123]

> Counterfeiting and piracy, and infringements of intellectual property in general, are a constantly growing phenomenon which nowadays have an international dimension, since they are a serious threat to national economies and governments. The disparities between the national systems of penalties, apart from hampering the proper functioning of the internal market, make it difficult to combat counterfeiting and piracy effectively. In addition to the economic and social consequences, counterfeiting and piracy also pose problems for consumer protection, particularly when health and safety are at stake. Increasing use of the Internet enables pirated products to be distributed instantly around the globe. Finally, this phenomenon appears to be increasingly linked to organised crime. Combating this phenomenon is therefore of vital importance for the Community. Counterfeiting and pirating have become lucrative activities in the same way as other large-scale criminal activities such as drug trafficking. There are high potential profits to be made without risk of serious legal penalties. Additional provisions to strengthen and improve the fight against counterfeiting and piracy are therefore necessary to supplement Directive 2004/48/EC of 29 April 2004 on the enforcement of intellectual property rights. In addition to the civil and administrative measures, procedures and remedies provided for in Directive 2004/48/EC, criminal penalties also constitute, in appropriate cases, a means of enforcing intellectual property rights.

In your view, which of the above, if any, are the most persuasive reasons for criminalizing IPR infringements? Are the reasons more compelling in the case of some IPRs than others?

13.8.2 ADVANTAGES AND DISADVANTAGES

In what circumstances would an IPR owner seek to bring a criminal prosecution, rather than pursue a civil action, in respect of infringing activities? In the extract below, Gwilym Harbottle considers the advantages and disadvantages of instigating criminal actions in the context of copyright or performers' rights infringement.

---

[120] Ibid., p. 765.   [121] Ibid., p. 766.
[122] Ibid., pp. 767–9.   [123] COM (2005) 0276 final, Brussels, 12 Jul. 2005.

G. Harbottle, 'Criminal remedies for copyright and performers' rights infringement under the Copyright Designs and Patents Act 1988'
[1994] Ent LR 12, 14–15

The Advantages and Disadvantages of Criminal Proceedings

The major advantage of criminal proceedings is their shock value. For many defendants, the receipt of a summons to appear in the Magistrates' Court will be much more alarming than the receipt of a writ. The shock value will be substantially increased when it becomes apparent to a company director or other officer that he or she may be prosecuted personally even though the offence was committed through the medium of a company.

Moreover, the sanction of imprisonment is clearly one which the courts are determined to impose.

...

In extreme cases, shock value can be obtained at the very start of proceedings by obtaining a warrant to secure the accused's attendance at court. In the normal course of events, proceedings under the Act are commenced by the laying of an information on the basis of which a summons will be posted by the court to the defendant's address. Only if the defendant fails to attend court on the date specified in the summons will a warrant be issued.

...

The issue of a warrant for arrest following the laying of an information is comparatively unusual. There is clear authority for the proposition that a warrant should not be issued when a summons will be equally effective. However, in serious cases of large-scale piracy, the issue of a warrant may well be appropriate. The same might be said of a case where infringing copies are being sold by a street trader whose address has proved impossible to ascertain.

...

The second major advantage of criminal proceedings concerns costs. While costs are, as in most civil proceedings, always in the discretion of the court, the following observations may be made: first, where a defendant is acquitted, the court may order that the defendant's costs be paid out of central (that is government) funds. Second, whether a defendant is convicted or acquitted, the court may order that the prosecution's costs be paid out of central funds. This rule applies only to prosecutors who are not publicly funded and is restricted to prosecutions for indictable offences (including those triable either way). Third, where a defendant is convicted, the court may order that he pay to the prosecutor such of the costs of the prosecution as the court considers 'just and reasonable'. Finally, by virtue of the Costs in Criminal Cases (General) Regulations 1986, witnesses called by private prosecutors *shall* be allowed their expenses out of central funds unless the court states to the contrary. The amount payable can include compensation for loss of earnings and travel expenses.

It will be seen that, for obvious public policy reasons, the costs regime in the criminal courts differs markedly from that in the civil courts. A private prosecution which is brought on reasonable grounds but nevertheless results in an acquittal may well not have the catastrophic costs consequences which can accompany defeat in civil proceedings.

The third major advantage of criminal over civil proceedings is the comparative speed with which an issue can be brought to trial. In summary proceedings, it is unusual for a case not to be resolved within a period of 12 months. A complex trial may well take longer to come to court, but the opportunities for delay on the part of the defence are less than in civil proceedings. Moreover, in view of the potentially serious consequences of a conviction, all criminal tribunals are anxious to prevent delay since this obviously diminishes the court's ability to conduct a fair trial.

Do the criminal courts' powers to permit searches of premises and to order seizure or delivery up compare well with those of the civil courts? ...

The criminal alternative to the Anton Piller order requires the assistance of the police. Under sections 109 (copyright) and 200 (performers' rights) of the 1988 Act, a police officer may obtain from the magistrates and execute a warrant to search premises. This power is complementary to the limited power given to the private citizen by section 100 of the 1988 Act to seize infringing copies which are exposed or otherwise immediately available for sale or hire. Clearly, the disadvantages of the section 109 and 200 powers is that their operation depends on the willingness of the local police station to co-operate with the prosecutor. The extent to which this is forthcoming will depend as much on local police policies as on the gravity of the offence alleged.

Sections 108 and 199 of the 1988 Act empower the criminal court to make orders for delivery up in proceedings for the infringement of copyright and performers' rights respectively. A conviction is not a prerequisite for obtaining an order for delivery up. What must be shown is that at the time of the defendant's arrest or charge (defined as including service of the summons), he had in his possession, custody or control in the course of a business an infringing copy, an article designed for making infringing copies, or an illicit recording. The problem for the private prosecutor is that the items in question, if not seized or voluntarily surrendered at the time of discovery of the offence, may well have 'disappeared' by the time the court comes to adjudicate on the question whether the requirements of the relevant section have been fulfilled (for example at the end of a trial). It will be apparent that the powers of the private prosecutor in the field of search, seizure and delivery up of infringing articles do not stand much comparison with those of the plaintiff in civil proceedings who has a strong *prima facie* case of infringement.

Difficulties of a similar magnitude will attend the private prosecutor who seeks compensation by way of damages in criminal proceedings. Section 35 of the Powers of Criminal Courts Act 1973 gives the court dealing with an offender for any offence the power to order him to pay compensation for any loss or damage resulting from the offence. In the Magistrates' Court, the maximum compensation which can be awarded is £5,000. In the Crown Court, there is no such limit. However, compensation orders are only appropriate when there is no doubt about the offender's liability and about the amount of such liability. This may well not be so in cases of copyright infringement where the law is relatively complex and is unlikely to be familiar to the court. Thus, a private prosecutor may well be forced to resort to additional civil proceedings in order to recover full compensation.

It remains to consider the evidential disadvantages of criminal as opposed to civil proceedings. The most obvious is the criminal standard of proof, that is, proof beyond reasonable doubt. In addition, while (as mentioned above) the requirement to prove actual knowledge has been 'relaxed', the presumptions about authorship, originality and first publication contained in sections 104 and 105 of the 1988 Act are disapplied in criminal proceedings by section 107(6). Thus, criminal proceedings should only be brought if the prosecutor is confident of being able to prove each and every element of the offence, including (in copyright cases) the subsistence of copyright (see below).

The second evidential disadvantage concerns the prosecutor's substantial duties of disclosure, which are not matched by any equivalent duties on the defence. Two such duties may be mentioned briefly here. The first is the duty to disclose 'advance information' of the prosecution case before the decision is taken as to mode of trial of an either-way offence. The prosecutor's obligation may be fulfilled either by the disclosure of 'a copy of those parts of every written statement which contains information as to the facts and matters of which the prosecutor proposes to adduce evidence in the proceedings' or merely by the provision of 'a summary of the facts and matters of which the prosecutor proposes to adduce evidence in the proceedings'. Documents referred to in the advance information must also be produced. There is an exception if the prosecutor believes that disclosure will result in intimidation. The second duty of disclosure is the duty to disclose 'unused material' helpful to the defence. This duty extends to the disclosure of written statements of witnesses who have been interviewed by the prosecutor and have made statements favourable to the defence. It thus extends considerably beyond any duties of disclosure in civil proceedings. By contrast, the defendant is under no duty to disclose his defence in advance (unless it is alibi or involves expert evidence), and no adverse inferences may be drawn from a defendant's refusal to answer questions. There is little point in bringing criminal proceedings unless the case is a strong one.

In the above extract, Gwilym Harbottle identifies three main advantages of bringing criminal proceedings for copyright and performers' rights infringements, namely the shock value accompanying such an action, the ability to recover costs regardless of whether the prosecution is successful, and the comparative speed with which prosecutions are heard. The disadvantages, however, are the limited armoury of remedies available to the private prosecutor, particularly in the field of search, seizure, and delivery up of infringing articles and with regards to compensation, as well as the evidential disadvantages of a higher standard of proof and the substantial duties of disclosure placed on the prosecution. Although Harbottle discusses the advantages and disadvantages in the context of copyright and performers' rights, it is fair to say that these are equally applicable when it comes to the criminal prosecution of other intellectual property right infringements. In your view, which types of IPR owners are most likely to pursue criminal prosecutions and against whom are they most likely to be used?

FURTHER READING

G. Harbottle, 'Private prosecutions in copyright cases: should they be stopped' [1998] EIPR 317.

13.8.3 CRIMINAL OFFENCES AND PENALTIES

Before turning to discuss the criminal offences for IPRs infringement that exist under UK law, brief mention should be made of the international obligations governing this area. Article 61 of the TRIPS Agreement stipulates that:

Members shall provide for criminal procedures and penalties to be applied at least in cases of willful trademark counterfeiting or copyright piracy on a commercial scale.

This article creates a fairly restricted obligation to criminalize certain trade mark and copyright infringements. That said, controversy surrounds the scope of this provision (in particular what constitutes piracy *on a commercial scale*), as evidenced by the dispute between China and the United States before the WTO.[124]

---

[124] See Panel Report on 'China—Measures affecting the protection and enforcement of intellectual property rights', DS 362, 26 Jan. 2009, paras. 7.516–7.669 at <http://www.wto.org/english/news_e/news09_e/362r_e.htm>.

Broadly speaking, under UK law there are commonalities between the offences that exist with regard to registered IPRs, namely patents, registered designs, and trade marks. As such, these will be discussed together while the offences concerning copyright will be considered separately.

13.8.3.1 Registered rights

It is an offence for a person to make or cause to be made a false entry in the register of patents, UK designs, or trade marks, or a writing falsely purporting to be a copy of an entry in any such register, knowing the entry or writing to be false. The offence is punishable, on a summary conviction by fine or imprisonment not exceeding six months or both (note only fine for patents) and on indictment, to imprisonment for a term not exceeding two years or a fine, or both.[125] Further, it is an offence falsely to represent that a mark or design is registered knowing or having reason to believe that the representation is false. A person guilty of this offence is liable on summary conviction to a fine.[126]

Falsely representing that anything is a patented product is an offence, punishable on summary conviction by a fine. However, it will not amount to an offence where the representation is made in respect of a product after the patent for that product or process in question has expired or been revoked and there has not been reasonably sufficient time for the accused to take steps to ensure that the representation is not made (or does not continue to be made).[127] It is also an offence falsely to represent that a patent has been applied for when no such application has been made or any such application has been refused or withdrawn. The offence is punishable on summary conviction by a fine.[128] In relation to both offences, it shall be a defence for the accused to prove that he used due diligence to prevent the commission of such an offence.

Section 92 of the TMA makes counterfeiting[129] activities of various kinds an offence punishable on summary conviction to a fine or a term of imprisonment not exceeding six months or both; and on indictment to a fine or imprisonment for a term not exceeding ten years or both.[130] More specifically, a person commits an offence who, with a view to gain for himself or another, or with intent to cause loss to another, and without the consent of the trade mark proprietor does any of the following acts:

- applies a sign identical to, or likely to be mistaken for, a registered trade mark to goods or their packaging;
- sells, hires, or offers to sell or hire goods which bear such a sign;
- has in his possession, custody, or control in the course of a business any such goods with a view to selling or hiring or offering to sell or hire such goods;
- applies a sign identical to, or likely to be mistaken for, a registered trade mark to material intended to be used for labelling or packaging goods, as a business paper in relation to goods or for advertising goods;
- uses in the course of business material bearing such a sign for labelling or packaging goods or has in his possession, custody, or control in the course of a business any such material with a view to using it in this way;

---

[125] s. 109, PA 77; s. 34, RDA; s. 94, TMA.   [126] s. 95, TMA; reg. 3, CDR; s. 35, RDA.
[127] PA 77, s. 110.   [128] Ibid., s. 111.
[129] In *R v Johnstone* [2003] UKHL 28, [2003] FSR 42 Lord Nicholls described counterfeit goods at p. 752 as 'cheap imitations of the authentic article, sold under the trade mark of the authentic article'.
[130] TMA, s. 92.

- makes an article specifically designed or adapted for making copies of a sign identical to, or likely to be mistaken for, a registered trade mark or has such an article in his possession, custody, or control in the course of a business, knowing or having reason to believe that it has been, or is to be, used to produce goods, or material for labelling or packaging goods, as a business paper in relation to goods, or for advertising goods.

In order to commit any of the above offences, the goods must be those in respect of which the trade mark is registered or else it must be the case that the trade mark has a reputation in the UK and the use of the sign takes or would take unfair advantage of, or is or would be detrimental to, the distinctive character or repute of the trade mark. There is a defence where a person shows that he believed on reasonable grounds that the use of the sign was not an infringement of a registered trade mark.

The scope of s. 92, in particular whether it is a defence to a criminal charge under this section that the defendant's acts do not amount to a civil infringement of the trade mark, was considered by the House of Lords in the following case.

R v Johnstone [2003] FSR 42[131]

The accused had produced several hundred bootleg recordings (i.e. unauthorized recordings of a live performance) relating to the band Bon Jovi. He was convicted under s. 92 for having in his possession, custody, or control in the course of a business a compact disc entitled 'The B Sides Collection—Volumes One and Two' bearing the trade mark 'Bon Jovi'. At trial the accused submitted that before the Crown could establish an offence under s. 92 it must prove a civil infringement of the registered trade mark in question. The accused wished to rely upon the defence in s. 11(2)(b) of the TMA that the use of the band's name was merely descriptive, as opposed to an indication of origin. These submissions were rejected by the trial judge who ruled that s. 92 was a 'stand alone' provision. Mr Johnstone then pleaded guilty to the offences with which he was charged and was subsequently sentenced to six months' imprisonment concurrent on each count. The Court of Appeal allowed Mr Johnstone's appeal, finding that the defences available to a claim for civil infringement were also available under s. 92. The Crown appealed to the House of Lords, which dismissed the appeal.

Lord Nicholls (delivering the leading speech), pp. 759–60:

25. The certified question on this appeal to your Lordships' House is whether it is a defence to a criminal charge under s. 92 of the 1994 Act that the defendant's acts do not amount to a civil infringement of the trade mark. On this, although he substantially modified his stance in the course of his reply, Mr Perry's opening submissions to the House were to the following effect. The 1994 Act provides for two separate regimes for the protection of trade marks and consumers. One regime is concerned with civil infringement, the other with criminal unauthorised use of trade marks in relation to goods. As a matter of construction s. 92 does not require proof of civil infringement. In keeping with other offence-creating provisions, the ingredients of the offences created by s. 92 appear on the face of the section. Parliament intended to create offences which would be simple for local weights and measures authorities to enforce and for magistrates and jurors to understand. Parliament did

---

[131] This case is also discussed at 6.2.2.2 in relation to trade mark use.

not intend to introduce questions of civil infringement into the criminal courts, save to the limited extent that an accused's belief he was not infringing a registered trade mark might amount to a defence.

26. I agree that the ingredients of the offences created by s. 92 are to be found within the section itself. Where I part company with Mr Perry's opening submissions is on the interpretation of s. 92. Section 92 is concerned to prohibit the wrongful exploitation of registered trade marks. It replaced s. 58A of the Trade Marks Act 1938. Section 58A made the fraudulent use of a trade mark an offence. Difficulties arose in practice in proving the necessary intent in cases where at point of sale the trader disclaimed the authenticity of his goods. The trader would describe his counterfeit products as 'brand copies' or 'genuine fakes'. Section 92 avoids this problem. In particular, intention to infringe a registered trade mark is not an ingredient of the offence. Instead, s. 92 focuses simply on unauthorised use of 'a sign identical to, or likely to be mistaken for, a registered trade mark': s. 92(1)(a), (2)(a) and (3)(a).

27. In my view it is implicit in these provisions that the offending use of the sign must be use as a trade mark. Take, as an illustration, s. 92(1)(a). This prohibits the application to goods of a sign identical to, or likely to be mistaken for, a registered trade mark. Apply this to a case where the registered trade mark consists of words capable of being used descriptively. Use of these words in their descriptive sense would be, in terms of trade mark law, unobjectionable. The registration of the word 'Alabaster' as a trade mark would not preclude others from lawfully stating that their product was 'made from alabaster'. Section 92 cannot have been intended to criminalise such conduct.

28. This is my starting point. Within the section there are two clear indications confirming this interpretation. First, a prescribed ingredient of each offence is that the conduct in question is done 'without the consent of the proprietor' of the registered trade mark. This assumes the proprietor could object to the acts in question. Without his consent the acts could not lawfully be done. The section is aimed at criminalising conduct of this character, namely, conduct to which the proprietor could object. This is as one would expect. Parliament cannot have intended to criminalise conduct which could lawfully be done without the proprietor's consent. Parliament cannot have intended to make it an offence to use a sign in a way which is innocuous because it does not infringe the proprietor's rights. That would be to extend, by means of a criminal sanction, the scope of the rights of the proprietor.

29. Secondly, s. 92(5) presupposes that the conduct of the person charged was an infringement of a registered trade mark. It would make no sense for reasonable belief in non-infringement to provide a defence if infringement was irrelevant so far as the criminal offences are concerned.

30. Further, and looking more widely, the 1994 Act as a whole must be interpreted so far as possible to give effect to the trade mark directive. This obligation applies to provisions such as s. 92, whose terms do not derive from the trade mark directive, as it does to provisions, such as s. 10, which derive directly from the directive. Articles 5 to 7 of the directive embody a 'complete harmonisation' of the rules relating to the rights conferred by a trade mark: see Case C-355/96 *Silhouette International Schmied GmbH & Co KG v Hartlauer Handelsgesellschaft mbH* [1998] ECR I-4779 [1998] FSR 729, 735, para. [25]. They define the rights of trade mark proprietors in the Community: see Joined Cases C-414/99-416/99 *Zino Davidoff SA v A&G Imports Ltd* [2001] ECR I-8691, para. [39]. If s. 92 were to be interpreted as applying in circumstances beyond those within ss. 9 to 11, there might well be inconsistency with the trade mark directive.

31. For these reasons s. 92 is to be interpreted as applying only when the offending sign is used as an indication of trade origin. This is one of the ingredients of each of the offences created by s. 92. It must therefore be proved by the prosecution. Whether a sign is so used

is a question of fact in each case. The test is how the use of the sign would be perceived by the average consumer of the type of goods in question: see Case C-251/95 *Sabel BV v Puma AG, Rudolf Dassler Sport* [1997] ECR I-6191, 6224, para. [23].

32. This should not give rise to practical difficulties for weights and measures authorities or for magistrates or jurors. Despite Mr Perry's submissions, I see no reason to doubt that all those concerned are well able to grasp and apply the notion of a sign being used as an indication of trade origin as distinct, for instance, from a sign comprising words being used descriptively. In the overwhelming majority of cases there should be little difficulty.

Lord Nicholls' conclusion that in order for an offence to be committed under s. 92 of the TMA this must also constitute a civil infringement seems correct. However, would you agree that it is straightforward for enforcement authorities and criminal courts to assess whether there has been trade mark use amounting to an infringement?

Importantly, Lord Nicholls went on to consider the defence of reasonable belief, holding that s. 92(5) applied equally to situations where the defendant is aware of the existence of the trade mark and to those situations where he is not.[132] Further, he held that the burden of proof for establishing this defence lies with the accused person, who must prove the relevant facts on the balance of probability.[133]

In the later case of *R v Boulter*[134] the Court of Appeal rejected the submission that an offence under s. 92 did not occur where a counterfeit was of such poor quality so as to avoid any risk of confusion. In the court's view, this failed to recognize the distinction between s. 10(1) and (2) of the TMA (where, under the former, use of an identical mark on identical goods does not require confusion) and because s. 92 was intended to combat the counterfeiter who sells his wares as 'genuine fakes'.[135]

13.8.3.2 Copyright

Turning to the criminal provisions under copyright law, s. 107 of the CDPA creates offences for making and dealing in infringing articles. Specifically, s. 107(1) makes it an offence, without the licence of the copyright owner, to make for sale or hire; import into the UK otherwise than for private and domestic use; possess in the course of business with a view to committing any act infringing copyright; or sell, hire, offer for sale or hire, exhibit or distribute in the course of business, or distribute otherwise in the course of business to such an extent as to affect prejudicially the owner of the copyright, an article which is, and which he knows or has reason to believe is, an infringing copy of a copyright work. Section 107(2) stipulates that an offence is committed where a person makes an article specifically designed or adapted for making copies of a particular copyright work or where he has such an article in his possession. This is provided the person has actual or constructive knowledge that the article is to be used to make infringing copies for sale or hire or for use in the course of business.

Offences also exist where a person infringes copyright in a work by communicating it to the public in the course of business or otherwise than in the course of business but to such an extent as to affect prejudicially the owner of the copyright.[136] This is provided he knows or has reason to believe that, by doing so, he is infringing copyright in that work.

---

[132] *R v Johnstone* [2003] FSR 42, para. 43.   [133] Ibid., para. 53.   [134] [2009] ETMR 6.
[135] Ibid., para. 9.   [136] CDPA, s. 107(2A).

Similarly, where a person causes an infringing public performance of a literary, dramatic, or musical work, or an infringing playing or showing in public of a sound recording or film, this will amount to an offence where he knew or had reason to believe that copyright would be infringed.[137]

The penalties for the above offences vary depending on the particular offence. For infringing communications to the public it is, on summary conviction, a term of imprisonment not exceeding three months or a fine, or both; and on indictment a term of imprisonment not exceeding two years or a fine, or both.[138] In relation to offences of making or selling, importing other than for private and domestic use, distributing in the course of business, or distributing otherwise than in the course of business to such an extent as to affect prejudicially the copyright owner the penalties are, on summary conviction, a term of imprisonment not exceeding six months or a fine or both; and on indictment a fine or term of imprisonment not exceeding ten years or both.[139] For all other offences under s. 107, the penalties are, on summary conviction, a term of imprisonment not exceeding six months or a fine or both.[140]

Criminal offences exist in relation to devices and services designed to circumvent effective technological measures that are applied to copyright works. According to s. 296ZB, it is an offence to make for sale or hire, or import otherwise than for private and domestic use, or commercially deal in the course of business, or distribute to such an extent as to affect prejudicially the copyright owner, any device, product, or component which is 'primarily designed, produced, or adapted for the purpose of enabling or facilitating the circumvention of effective technological measures'. It is also an offence to provide, promote, advertise, or market in the course of business, or to such an extent as to affect prejudicially the copyright owner, a service 'the purpose of which is to enable or facilitate the circumvention of effective technological measures'. However, anything done by or on behalf of law enforcement or intelligence services in the interests of national security for the purpose of prevention or detection of crime, or the investigation of an offence or the conduct of a prosecution is not unlawful. Further, the accused will have a defence if he can prove that he did not know and had no reasonable grounds for believing that the device, product, or component, or the service, enabled or facilitated the circumvention of effective technological measures. The penalty for summary conviction is imprisonment for up to three months or a fine not exceeding the statutory maximum or both. For conviction on indictment it is a fine or imprisonment for up to two years or both.

13.8.3.3 Liability of corporate officers

Where any of the above offences[141] has been committed by a body corporate and it is proved to have been committed with the consent or connivance of, or to be attributable to any neglect on the part of, a director, manager, secretary, or other similar officer of the body corporate, or any person who was purporting to act in any such capacity, he, as well as the body corporate, shall be guilty of that offence and shall be liable to be proceeded against and punished accordingly.[142]

---

[137] Ibid., s. 107(3).   [138] Ibid., s. 107(4A).   [139] Ibid., s. 107(4).   [140] Ibid., s. 107(5).
[141] In the case of copyright, it is only an offence under s. 107, CPDA.
[142] s. 101, TMA; s. 113, PA 77; s. 35A, RDA; s. 110, CDPA.

13.8.4 FUTURE DEVELOPMENTS: PROPOSED EC DIRECTIVE

As we have seen there is now a Proposed Directive on criminal measures aimed at ensuring the enforcement of intellectual property rights. The original proposal[143] has been amended[144] and has gone to a first reading by the European Parliament.[145] It has not, however, progressed any further.

According to the original Proposal,[146] Article 3 obliges Member States to ensure that 'all intentional infringements of an intellectual property right on a commercial scale, and attempting, aiding or abetting and inciting such infringements, are treated as criminal offences'. The range of penalties that must be provided by Member States is stipulated in Article 4 and includes: custodial sentences, fines, confiscation of infringing goods, destruction of infringing goods, total or partial closure of the establishment used primarily to commit the offence, a permanent or temporary ban on engaging in commercial activities, and placing under judicial supervision. The Amended Proposal[147] differs insofar as it prescribes the level of penalties that Member States must provide. According to Article 5, this includes custodial sentences for natural persons for a 'maximum sentence of at least four years' and fines 'to a maximum of at least EUR 100,000' for less serious cases and 'to a maximum of at least EUR 300,000' for serious ones, these latter being offences which are committed under the aegis of a criminal organization or which carry a health or safety risk.

The Proposed Directive, in its original and amended form, has been the subject of numerous criticisms, some of which are reflected in the following extract.

R. M. Hilty, A. Kur, and A. Peukert, 'Statement of the Max Planck Institute for Intellectual Property, Competition and Tax Law on the Proposal for a Directive of the European Parliament and of the Council on criminal measures aimed at ensuring the enforcement of intellectual property rights' (2006) IIC 970, 973–6

III. Issues Concerning Elements of Crime

10. In contrast to substantive IP law, European harmonisation in the field of criminal law is not far advanced. This entails considerable risks regarding the—possibly diverging—understanding of certain *notions* (e.g. 'intentional'; 'aiding, abetting or inciting') as well as the compatibility of the legal *concepts* underlying the proposal (e.g. criminal liability of legal entities) with the principles generally applying under criminal law.

11. Criminal penalties can have a far more severe impact compared to sanctions under civil law. In most legal systems, they are therefore regarded as a remedy of last resort (*ultima ratio*). Furthermore, they are subject to specific principles frequently anchored in constitutional law, like the elements of a crime having to be set out specifically in a legal text in order to be punishable (*nullum crimen sine lege*). It can be questioned already whether that principle is fully observed in pertinent national law concerning criminal prosecution of IP

---

[143] COM (2005) 0276 final, Brussels, 12 Jul. 2005. The original proposal has been commented upon by the Economic and Social Committee COM (2005) 276 final–2005/0127 (COD) 2007/C256/02.

[144] COM (2006) 168 final, Brussels, 26 Apr. 2006.

[145] COM (2006) 0168–C6–0233/2005–2005/0127 (COD).

[146] COM (2005) 0276 final, Brussels, 12 Jul. 2005. The original proposal has been commented upon by the Economic and Social Committee COM (2005) 276 final–2005/0127 (COD) 2007/C256/02.

[147] COM (2006) 168 final, Brussels, 26 Apr. 2006.

infringements. In any case, it must be avoided that the potential for legal conflicts that exists at present is enhanced by measures taken by the Community legislature.

12. While there is no doubt that combatting counterfeiting and piracy, also by means of criminal law, is an important and urgent task, it is more questionable whether the extension of criminal penalties and prosecution measures to all kinds of IP infringement can be viewed as an appropriate and useful tool to safeguard protection of IP rights. There is even a risk that, by enhancing the threatening potential this entails, the (desirable) freedom of market actors to engage in business is curtailed beyond proportion, which would produce results adverse to the aims of the common market.

13. It follows that harmonisation of criminal law in the field of IP, if admissible at all, must remain confined to cases of clear piracy and counterfeiting. In less straightforward cases—in particular when the conflict concerns the scope of protection granted vis-à-vis similar goods or achievements—sanctions under civil law can usually be regarded as sufficient from a Community perspective (notwithstanding rules of national law).

14. Restricting the application of the directive to infringements carried out 'on a commercial scale' fails to provide for an *appropriate and sufficiently precise definition* of the elements of a crime, all the more as it would practically only exclude acts undertaken in good faith by consumers. An example of a more precise definition of what constitutes counterfeiting and piracy can be found in Regulation 1383/2003.

15. Indeed, when proper account is taken of the proportionality principle (see above, 6), harmonisation of criminal penalties can only be justified in relation to acts fulfilling the following elements *cumulatively*:

- *Identity with the infringed object of protection* (the infringing item emulates the characteristic elements of a protected product or distinctive sign in an unmodified fashion [construction, assembly, etc.]).

- *Commercial activity with an intention to earn a profit.*

- *Intent or contingent intent (dolus eventualis)* with regard to the existence of the infringed right.

16. *Parallel importation* of genuine goods which have been marketed with the consent of the rightholder in a non-EU country and/or measures accessory to such imports cannot be considered as piracy or counterfeiting. In accordance with what was said above, harmonisation of IP penalties should not be contemplated for such cases.

17. Criminal law is primarily a tool for protecting the public interest, without excluding the use of that tool, in appropriate cases, also for the protection of private interests, like the protection of property. Nevertheless, in order to mark the priority given under criminal law to acts that are *particularly dangerous* from the viewpoint of the public interest, it would be recommendable to regulate specific forms of IP infringement falling into that category *separately* and impose qualified penalties for commitment of such acts. This concerns infringements that carry health or safety risks or severely jeopardise the economic interests of consumers; it would also concern infringements carried out in the form of organized crime. That those aspects shall be taken into account as qualifying elements for the fashioning of penalties based upon one single rule of criminal law, as envisaged (Arts. 5(1), 6(1)), is only the second-best solution.

18. Considering the proposal is motivated by the claim that it is necessary for the proper functioning of the internal market (see above, 3. 4.), it appears inconsistent that it only prescribes a minimum level for the maximal sanction to be imposed. If divergences regarding the penalties imposed would indeed result in distortions of the internal market, one would expect that not only the minimum, but also the maximum level of such sanctions must be

prescribed in order to arrive at more uniform conditions applying in that regard in the Member States.

19. Ambiguities must be avoided with regard to the question of *which* (national) *IP rights* are encompassed by the harmonisation of criminal penal ties. A catalogue, like the one contained in the statement of the Commission concerning Directive 2004/48, needs to be set out *in the directive* itself.

IV. Issues Regarding Misuse

20. The *potential of a rightholder to deter potential infringers* increases considerably if criminal penalties are threatened. Furthermore, *procedural misuses* are conceivable. A harmonisation of IP criminal sanctions, therefore, calls for *countermeasures*.

The European Parliament, in its first reading of the Amended Proposal,[148] has sought to tackle some of the criticisms identified in the above extract. First, it seeks to exclude from the scope of the Proposed Directive infringements relating to patent rights, utility models, and plant-variety rights, along with parallel imports of original goods from a third country which have been allowed by the rightsholder. Further, IPRs are defined to mean copyright, related rights, the database right, rights in topographies of semiconductor products, trade mark, design rights, geographical indications, and trade names, insofar as these are protected as exclusive property rights in the national law concerned. Second, there is an attempt to elucidate certain key phrases. Thus, 'infringements on a commercial scale' are defined to mean 'any infringement of an intellectual property right committed to obtain a commercial advantage', excluding acts carried out by private users for personal and not-for-profit purposes and 'intentional infringements of an intellectual property right' are defined as 'any deliberate and conscious infringement of the right concerned for the purpose of obtaining an economic advantage on a commercial scale'. Third, it is made clear that certain fair uses of a protected work, for purposes such as criticism, comment, news reporting, teaching, scholarship, or research, do not constitute a criminal offence. Finally, an obligation is imposed on Member States to ensure that threats of criminal sanctions are not misused and that the rights of defendants are duly protected and guaranteed.

Even with the European Parliament's amendments, we may query whether the circumstances in which infringements should be penalized, along with the level of penalties to be imposed, are defined with sufficient precision and ask whether the suggested measures are all too draconian.

FURTHER READING

E. Bonadio, 'Remedies and sanctions for the infringement of intellectual property rights under EC law' [2008] EIPR 320.

V. Lowe, 'The law of unintended consequences: A perspective on the draft Directive on criminal measures to enforce intellectual property rights' [2006] Criminal Lawyer 3.

---

[148] COM (2006) 0168–C6–0233/2005–2005/0127 (COD).

INDEX